A DIGEST

OF THE

EARLY CONNECTICUT

PROBATE RECORDS.

COMPILED BY

CHARLES WILLIAM MANWARING,

Member Connecticut Historical Society.

Vol. II.

HARTFORD DISTRICT,

1700—1729.

Volumes I and II were originally published
in 1904, Volume III in 1906.
Reprinted 1995 by Genealogical Publishing Co., Inc.
Baltimore, Maryland 21202
Library of Congress Catalogue Card Number 94-74584
International Standard Book Number, Volume II: 0-8063-1470-2
Set Number: 0-8063-1472-9
Made in the United States of America

PREFACE.

In presenting Volume II of this Digest to the public, it is necessary to say but little, and what is said must be principally by way of explanation.

First, the reader is to be reminded that the first thirty-two pages of Volume I contain a list showing the changes made in the different Probate Districts of Connecticut from the beginning, and also what towns were comprised by them at every change. This list is of great value to any one tracing their ancestry, as they are correctly guided from district to district and town to town in the backward path of genealogical research without extra expense or unnecessary loss of valuable time.

Abbreviations have been made use of as follows: Invt., Inventory; Adms., Administration and derivatives; Dist., Distribution and derivatives; Recog., Recognizance; W. R., Windsor Records; P. C., Private Controversies; Cert: for "Certified by." This latter contraction will appear in cases of guardianship. It was the law that a minor over 14 years of age could go before a justice of the peace and choose a guardian, of which act the justice of the peace *certified* to the Probate Court. Hence the abbreviated form: "Cert: *John Doe, J. P.*"

The law allowed a widow the use of one-third part of the real estate of her deceased husband during her life, and one-third of his personal estate forever; but the husband, by will, could devise to his wife the use of one-third of his real estate *while she remained his widow*. So, "I give to my wife her dower rights" was a shortened way of stating the case.

In Volume X of the original records (the last volume in this book) many inventories were found where the figures had not been carried out from the lines of items into columns to be footed, and others where the figures had been carried out into columns but not footed, and this continued in the succeeding volumes. Why the Court should have accepted, under oath, inventories offered in such an incomplete condition, is not clear. The compiler has himself footed a great many of these inventories, in order to give his work a better appearance; but to foot them *all* was too great an undertaking.

To make this same Volume X *more* incomplete (aside from its badly broken-up leaves), more than sixty wills which ought to have been recorded therein were laid over and recorded in Volume XII, which dates nearly ten years later. These will be found in their proper places in this Digest.

C. W. Manwaring.

PROBATE RECORDS.

VOLUME VII.

1700 to 1710.

MEMORANDUM:

That it hath been the Constant Custome and Practice of the Judge and Justices of the County Courts and Courts of Probates in this County of Hartford, when any Inventory of the Estate of a deceased person is Exhibited in Court,—To Administer an Oath to the Executor or Administrator of the person deceased, or Such person as produceth and Sheweth the Estate to the Apprisers, and doth exhibit the Inventory thereof in said Court,—in the manner and form following, or fully to this purpose—That is to Say:—

"You, A. B., do Swear that you have truly and fully presented all and every part of the Estate of C. D., deceased, that at present you know of to the apprisers thereof (which is Contained in the Inventory thereof made and now Exhibited in this Court) ; And that if hereafter any more of the Estate of the said C. D., deceased, Shall come into your hands or knowledge, you will present a true account thereof to this Court, that it may be added to the said Inventory."

Test: Caleb Stanly, Clerk.

PROBATE RECORDS.

VOLUME VII.

1700 to 1710.

Page 27-28.

Abby, John, Windham.   Died December, 1700.   Invt. £118-13-03, reported 4 September, 1701, by Joshua Ripley and Jonathan Crane.

Windham, the 10th of December, 1700.   The will of John Abbey was that his wife should enjoy the house and homested, and the meadows that are already laid out, with the moveables, during her life, and to dispose of it to her children as she shall see cause.   And the rest of the unlaid out land to be divided equally amongst his children, and not to be sold away from my family, not any of the lands; and the thirty acres adjoining to Goodman Bingham's and Goodman Larrabee's land to be at my wive's dispose, and to give deed and to make sale of, according to law.

Witness: *Robert Hebard, Sen.,*
John Reed, Senior, both of the same town.

Windham, 8 April, 1701.

The said Robert Hebard and John Reed gave oath that they were present when John Abbey, that is decd., did give this direction to make his will as is above written; and when it was read to him, he said just so he would have it.   *Before me, Joshua Ripley, Justice.*

Court Record, Page 17—4 September, 1701: Hannah, the widow of John Abby, exhibits will and inventory.

Page 19—11 November, 1701: Will now accepted, but as there was no executor appointed, Adms. to Hannah Abby, the relict, with the will annexed.   Bonds, £50.

Page 94.

Ackley, Thomas, Haddam.   Died 16 January, 1703-4.   Invt. £75-08-00.   Taken by Daniel Braynard and Thomas Robinson, Selectmen.

Court Record, Page 56—26 May, 1704: This Court grants Adms. to Hannah Ackley, the widow of Thomas Ackley, decd.

Page 68—14 August, 1705: Benjamin Trowbridge, in right of his wife Hannah, renders an account of Adms. on the 7th of November, 1705.

This Court order that the sd. Benjamin Trowbridge and Hannah his wife, Adms., may keep the lands belonging to the estate in their hands at present for their bringing up the small children, provided they keep the buildings and fences in repair. This Court appoint John and Nathaniel Ackley, of Haddam, guardians to Thomas, Job, Hannah and Ann, the four children of the sd. late Thomas Ackley. Dist. by John Fuller, Timothy Fuller and James Bates, of Haddam.

Page 71—7 November, 1705: Hannah Trowbridge, late Hannah Ackley, presented to this Court an account of her Adms., which this Court do allow and grant her a *Quietus Est.*

Page 17 (Vol. VIII) 3 July, 1710: Nathaniel Ackley, guardian to the four above mentioned children, having died, John Ackley assumes full guardianship.

Dist. File: 7 February, 1721-2: An agreement between the heirs for a dist. of the estate of Thomas Ackley, late of Haddam, decd., wherein Job Ackley made choice of his father-in-law, Benjamin Trowbridge, to be his guardian.

> BENJAMIN X TROWBRIDGE, LS.
> HANNAH X TROWBRIDGE, LS.
> ALEXANDER X SPENCER, LS.
> ANN X SPENCER,
> THOMAS X ACKLEY, LS.
> JOB ACKLEY, LS.
> JOHN X LORD, LS.
> HANNAH X LORD.

Page 138 (Vol. X) 6 December, 1726: An agreement made 7 February, 1721-2, for the dividing and settling of the estate of Thomas Ackley, late of Haddam, decd., was now exhibited by the heirs to sd. Estate, viz: Benjamin Trowbridge for himself and Ann his wife, relict to sd. decd.; Alexander Spencer for himself and Ann his wife; John Lord for himself and Hanna his wife, late decd.; Thomas Ackley and Job Ackley. And before this Court they acknowledged sd. agreement to be their free act and deed, which agreement is accepted by this Court to be a settlement of sd. Estate.

Page 5.

Adkins, Elizabeth, Middletown, Widow of Josiah. Invt. £111-19-00. Taken 5 November, 1700, by Nathaniel Stow, Alexander Rollo and Joseph Wetmore. Legatees: Solomon, age 22 years; Josiah 21, Benjamin 19, Ephraim 16, Sarah 26, Abigail 24, Elizabeth, 14 years of age.

Court Record, Page 3—13 November, 1700: Adms. to Solomon Adkins.

Page 10—8 April, 1701: Adms. account accepted. Nathaniel Stow, Thomas Ward and Israhiah Wetmore were appointed to dist. the estate. Benjamin Adkins and Ephraim Adkins, minor children of Elizabeth

Adkins, made choice of their brother Solomon Adkins to be their guardian. And this Court appoint Nathaniel Stow to be guardian to Elizabeth Adkins, daughter of sd. deceased.

Dist. File, 22 April, 1701: To Solomon, to Josiah, to Benjamin, to Ephraim, to Sarah, to Abigail and Elizabeth Adkins, by Nathaniel Stow, Thomas Ward and Israhiah Wetmore, dist.

Record on File.

Adkins, Thomas, Hartford. Invt. £12-14-06. Taken 28 October, 1709, by John Burnham and Samuel Burnham. Later was added to the inventory the following Items:

	£ s d
Credit due to him by ye Country,	8-12-06
Land to be added to the inventory,	12-00-00
A square to be added,	0-04-00

Taken by Samuel Burnham and John Burnham.

Court Record, Page 134—7 November, 1709: Adms. to Josiah Adkins of Simsbury (brother of sd. decd.), who gave bonds and exhibited invt.

Invt. in Vol. VIII, Page 12.

Alford, Jeremiah, Windsor. Died 6 June, 1709. Invt. £264-06-11. Taken 23 June, 1709, by Job Drake and Samuel Moore.

Court Record, Page 130—4 July, 1709: Jane Alford, of Windsor, widow, relict of Jeremiah Alford, exhibited in this Court an invt. of sd. estate, which the Court order recorded, and grant letters of Adms. to the sd. widow, and order that she render an account of her Adms. to this Court on or before the 1st Monday of July, 1711.

Page 55 (Vol VIII) 5 February, 1711-12: Jane Alvard, of Windsor, widow, Adms. on the estate of Jeremiah Alvard, exhibited an account of her Adms.:

	£ s d
Inventory, with the debts due to the same,	264-06-11
The real part,	176-00-00
The moveable part,	93-06-08
Debts and charges subtracted from the moveable part,	63-09-04
There remains of the moveable part to be dist.,	29-17-04

Account approved. Order distribution as followeth:

	£ s d
To the widow, of the moveable estate,	9-19-01
After the widow's part is taken out, there remains	195-18-03
To Benedict Alvard, eldest son,	55-19-09
And to Jeremiah, Job, Jane, Johanna and Elizabeth, to each,	27-19-09

And appoint Col. Matthew Allyn, Mr. John Moore and Sergt. Daniel Loomis distributors. And this Court now grant to the sd. Jane Alvard a *quietus est.*

Page 83—7 July, 1712: This Court appoint Jane Alverd to be guardian to her four children: Jane Alverd, 14 years; Joanna, 10; Elizabeth, 6; Job, 4; children of Jeremiah Alverd, late of Windsor, deceased.

Page 258—5 July, 1715: Jane Alverd, a minor, now 17 years of age, made choice of James Enno, of Windsor, to be her guardian. Recog. £50. Johanna Alverd, 14 years of age, chose Eleazer Hill to be her guardian. Recog. £50. Also this Court appoint Eleazer Hill to be guardian to Elizabeth Alverd, age 9 years. Recog. £50. And appoint Benedict Alverd to be guardian to his brother, Job Alverd, age 7 years, all children of Jeremiah Alverd, late decd.

Page 57 (Vol. IX) 1st April, 1718: Whereas, Colo. Matthew Allyn, Mr. John Moore and Serjt. Daniel Loomis, of Windsor, were formerly appointed by this Court to distribute the estate of Jeremiah Alverd, sometime of Windsor, deceased, which distribution by them was not fully finished, this Court do now appoint Daniel Loomis, Josiah Cooke and Timothy Loomis, of Windsor, to finish the distribution according to the order formerly given by this Court to distribute the sd. estate.

Page 64—6 May, 1718: There was now exhibited a return, under the hands of the distributors, that the estate of the sd. deceased so remaining being houseing and land, to divide the same would much wrong if not spoil the whole, whereupon the Court order the sd. distributors to set out the houseing and lands of the sd. deceased unto Benedict Alverd, eldest son, he paying unto the rest of the children their equal and proportional parts or share of the true value of the aforesd. houseing and lands (after a double part thereof unto the sd. eldest son is taken out).

Page 97—3 March, 1718-19: A report of the distributors allowed. This Court appoint Jeremiah Alverd, of Windsor, to be guardian unto Elizabeth Alverd, a minor, age 14 years, daughter of Jeremiah Alverd, late of Windsor, deceased. Recog. £50.

Page 128—7 June, 1720: Elizabeth Alverd, of Windsor, about 14 years of age, appeared before this Court and made choice of Mr. John Palmer, of Windsor, to be her guardian. Rec. £50.

Page 136—6 September, 1720: John Palmer, of Windsor, guardian to Elizabeth Alverd, exhibited accot. of what estate he had received of Jeremiah Alverd, her former guardian, amounting to £3-06-00, which accot. is accepted.

Page 160—5th day of September, 1721: Jeremiah Alverd, being cited to render accot. of his guardianship over Elizabeth Alverd, ordered continued.

Page 163—6 February, Anno Dom. 1721-2: John Palmer, guardian to Elizabeth Alverd, of Windsor, minor, summoned Jeremiah Alverd, of sd. Windsor, to this Court to render an accot. of his guardianship while he was guardian to sd. minor, who now appeared and rendered an accot. whereby it appears to this Court that the sd. Jeremiah Alverd hath the pewter plater in his custody, which he demanded for his trouble and charge amounting to the sum of £18-06-00 in the time of his guardianship, which by this Court is allowed, and the sd. Jeremiah Alverd is discharged of his account of guardianship except £11-03-07, which it is said he received as guardian to sd. minor of Benedict Alverd, his brother; and John Palmer is ordered to pay sd. Jerem. Alverd his cost, which is 5s.

Page 174—7 August, 1722: Whereas, the house and the homelott of Jeremiah Alverd, decd., was by order of this Court on the 16th of May, 1718, set out the whole of it to Benedict Alverd, eldest son, provided he pay the rest of the heirs their proportionable parts in sd. homestead, the sd. Benedict appeared in Court and produced receipts that he had fully paid to sd. heirs their parts, excepting Job Alverd, a minor, to whom the sd. Benedict is guardian.

Page 71 (Vol. X) 19 February, 1724-5: Job Alverd, a minor, about 16 years of age, son of Jeremiah Alverd, late decd., chose James Enno, of Windsor, to be his guardian. Recog., £50.

Page 124—5 April, 1726: This Court direct Thomas Moore and Nathaniel Drake to set out lands by meets and bounds to Job, Joanna and Elizabeth Alverd, all children of the deceased.

Page 199—3 September, 1727-8: A dist. according to order of the Court, 6 April, 1726, by meets and bounds, to three of the children of Jeremiah Alverd, late of Windsor, decd., vizt.: Job, Joanna and Elizabeth Alverd, under the hands of Thomas Moore, Nathaniel Drake and Timothy Loomis, dist.

Dist. File: 7 July, 1727: To Job, Joanna, and to Elizabeth's heirs, and to Joanna Alverd, alias Loomis, by Thomas Moore, Nathaniel Drake and Timothy Loomis.

Page 199-200-1-2-3-4.

Add. Invt. in Vol. XII, Page 231-2.

*Allin, Alexander, Windsor. Died 19 August, 1708. Invt. £2706-04-02. Taken 5 November, 1708, by Timothy Thrall and Daniel White, and was apprised by us at the value thereof in silver money reckoned at 15 pennyweight or 8 shillings the ounce. Additional invt. of £135-15-00, taken 14 March, 1726-7, by Major Wolcott and Capt. Samuel Mather, executors; also, 80 acres of land in Suffield, valued at £110, taken 2 March, 1722-3, by Daniel White and Samuel Strong. Will dated 7 August, 1708:

In the name of God, Amen. I, Alexander Allin, of Windsor, in the County of Connecticut, doe make and ordain this my last will and testament: I give to my wife Elizabeth the real estate she possessed at the time of my marriage with her; also, that which belongs to her (out of her father's estate) in reversion, £100 in Cash at 15 pennyweight, also

---

*The will written and signed by the testator, "*Allin.*" Caleb Stanly, the Clerk, wrote in and upon the records, "*Allyn.*"

the use and improvement of £150 during her natural life, to be paid to my son Fitz John if he survive his mother; if not, the £150 to be and remain to her and her heirs forever. Also, I give her the use and improvement of the homested, bounded south on Samuel Gibbs and Henry Wolcott, north on my father-in-law, John Cross, also land I bought of my sister-in-law, Abigail Grant, now wife of Doctor Mather. I give to my son Alexander, to be paid and delivered to him at 21 years of age, my now dwelling house, warehouse, shop and barn, with the upland and pasture land thereunto belonging, bounded west on a highway, south on Samuel Gibbs, Sen., and Mr. Henry Wolcott's land, north on land belonging to John Grant, decd., east on a highway. Also, I give to my sd. son Alexander, when he comes to be of age as abovesd., £400 in cash at 15 pennyweight, or other pay equivalent. I give to my son John, out of my estate in cash, at 15 pennyweight, or other pay equivalent, the sum of £500, to be paid him when he shall attain to the age of 21 years. I give to my daughter Mary, out of my estate, £450 cash, at 15 pennyweight, when she shall be 18 years of age. Also, I give to my sd. daughter Mary a sealskin trunk, with those things that are therein, which were her mother's apparrel. I give to my youngest son Fitz John, out of my estate, £400 in cash or other pay equivalent, to be paid him when he comes to the age of 21 years. And I declare it to be my will that my sd. wife Elizabeth shall have the use of the £400 I have given to my son Fitz John, towards the education and bringing up my sd. son till he comes to the age of 21 years. As a token of my love, I give to my two brothers, William Allin and Robert Allin, living in Scotland, £10 to each of them, in cash, to be laid out in Boston in that which may be most for their benefit, by my honoured and much respected friend, Mr. John Borland, of Boston, and by him sent to my sd. brothers, which I desire and impower Mr. Borland to do. I give towards the building of a school-house upon the meeting-house Green, on the west side of the Great River, in Windsor, £15 in cash, provided it be built within two years after the date hereof. I give to the Scots Boxx in Boston £5 in cash. I appoint my wife and Mr. John Borland, merchant, of Boston, Capt. Matthew Allyn, Mr. John Moore, Sen., Doctor Samuel Mather, Mr. Roger Wolcott and Mr. Thomas Fyler to be my executors.

Witness: *Zerubbabell Fyler, Sen.,*   ALEXANDER ALLIN, LS.
      Eleazer Gaylord, John Stoughton, Jr.

A codicil, dated 16 August, 1708: I give to Rev. Mr. Mather, our pastor, £5 in cash. I give to the Rev. Mr. Jonathan Marsh, our present minister, £5 in specie. I give to my mother-in-law, Mary Cross, £5 in specie. I give to Sarah Grant, daughter of Thomas Grant, which now lives with us, 20 shillings to buy her a Bible. I desire and impower my executors to be overseers to my three children, Alexander, John and Mary, and I leave my son Fitz John with my dear and loveing wife Elizabeth.

Witness: *Zerubbabell Fyler, Sen.,*   ALEXANDER ALLIN, LS.
      Atherton Mather, Bethesda Fyler.

Court Record, Page 117—13 September, 1708: Will proven. And whereas, the sd. Elizabeth Allyn, widow, Major Matthew Allyn, John Moore, Sen., Samuel Mather, Roger Wolcott and Thomas Fyler, all of Windsor aforesd., nominated and appointed executors of the sd. last will and testament of Alexander Allyn, decd. (with Mr. John Borland, merchant, of Boston), have declared before this Court that at the present they declined to accept that trust, but did not positively refuse it, and desire some time to consider of that matter, it is granted to them by this Court.

Page 119—6 December, 1708: Major Matthew Allyn and John Moore, Sen., positively refused to take upon them that work, but Elizabeth Allyn, widow, relict of sd. Allyn, and Samuel Mather, Roger Wolcott and Thomas Fyler, of sd. Windsor, appeared before this Court and declared their acceptance. Wherefore, this Court allow and approve the sd. Elizabeth Allyn, Samuel Mather, Roger Wolcott, Thomas Fyler and John Borland to be joynt executors, and grant them letters of Adms., with the will annexed.

Page 149 (Vol. X) 7 March, 1726-7: Major Roger Wolcott, Capt. Samuel Mather and Thomas Fyler, executors of the last will and testament of Mr. Alexander Allyn, late of Windsor, decd., appeared before this Court, Symon Chapman, Jr., in right of his wife, and the rest of the heirs of the sd. Allyn's estate, being notified to be present, the sd. executors proceeded in perfecting the inventory of sd. decd. by rendering an account of debts paid out of sd. estate, and at this time were accepted of debts paid out to the value of £189-11-11, for the greater part whereof they produced receipts, and the remainder the sd. executors made oath that they had truly paid the same as due from sd. estate, and also exhibited an addition to the inventory of the sd. deceased's estate amounting to the sum of £135-15-00, which account is by this Court accepted.

Page 178-9.

Allyn, John, Windsor. Invt. £320-13-06. Taken 27 August, 1707, by Benjamin Newbery and Samuel Moore. Will dated 25 May, 1697. The last will and testament of John Allyn, of Windsor, is as followeth: Imprimis: After the payment of all due debts and funeral charges, I dispose of my outward estate as followeth: All my land at Hartford swamp I give to my brother Benjamin, and to his heirs and assigns after him, never to be alienated from the name. If he have no male heir, then to be to my brother Thomas, or, next, to my brother Samuel. For the rest of my lands and moveable estate, I give to the children of my brothers and sisters; only to my sister Gilbert's child and to my sister Jane's child I give £5 more than to any of the rest. To my brother Matthew Allyn and his children I give nothing; only to his son Josias I give a set of silver buttons. I appoint my brother Thomas Allyn my executor, and with him my brother Benjamin Allyn when he shall be of age.

Witness: *Samuel Mather,*　　　　　　　　　JOHN ALLYN, LS.
　　John Moore, Senior.

Court Record, Page 99—20 October, 1707: Thomas Allyn and Benjamin Allyn, of Windsor, exhibited in this Court the last will and testament of their late Brother, John Allyn, decd., whereof they are appointed executors. Will proven. Capt. Matthew Allyn and Henry Wolcott, of Windsor, appealed from this determination of this Court, allowing the will of John Allyn, to the Court of Assistants to be holden at Hartford May next. Recog. £20.

Page 141 (Vol. VIII) 18 May, 1713: Whereas, Thomas and Benjamin Allyn, who were executors, are now decd., this Court grant Adms., with the will annexed, to Col. Matthew Allyn.

Page 188—5 April, 1714: This Court now grant Adms., with the will annexed, to Samuel Allyn, of Windsor, and Ebenezer Gilbert, of Farmington.

Page 214—6 September, 1714: Ebenezer Gilbert of Farmington, Adms. on the estate of John Allyn, late of Windsor, appeared in Court and declared that he justly suspected Capt. Timothy Thrall, Samuel Allyn and Joanna, the wife of Samuel Bancroft, and Anne Allyn, widow, all of Windsor, to have in custody or possession some considerable part of that estate. Citation was issued for these persons to appear at Court to be interrogated upon oath.

Page 14 (Vol. X) 2 April, 1723: Timothy Loomis, Jacob Drake and Israel Stoughton are appointed to divide the real estate according to the will of John Allyn, decd.

Page 9 (Vol. XIV) 3 August, 1742: Samuel Allyn, of Windsor, Adms. on the estate of John Allyn, was cited to appear and render an account of his Adms. as per writ on file. Sd. Adms. now produced in Court an account of his Adms. on sd. estate, which, being imperfect, is not allowed. He prays for time to perfect sd. account, which is allowed.

Page 13—26 November, 1742: Ann Allyn, alias Loomis, Adms. on the estate of Benjamin Allyn, which sd. Benjamin was an executor on the estate of John Allyn, of Windsor, decd., by her son Benjamin, her attorney, presented to this Court an account of sundry debts and charges against the estate of John Allyn, whereby it appears the sd. Benjamin Allyn, executor aforesd., decd., has paid in debts and charges £60-16-09; also an account of charges against the estate of £2-07-09, which was exhibited by Henry Wolcott, of Springfield, which account is accepted by the Court. Also, Benjamin Allyn, attorney, exhibited an account of credit received to the sd. estate of £5-17-02; accepted.

Note: Sd. Henry Wolcott appeared as atty. to Thomas Wolcott, of *Ancrom,* James Ward and Timothy Thrall, heirs to the estate of the sd. decd.

Dist. of lands on file: 7 January, 1751: To Henry Wolcott, to heirs of Joanna Stoughton, to heirs of Ebenezer Gilbert, to heirs of Samuel Allyn, to heirs of Thomas Wolcott, to heirs of Sarah Ward, to heirs of William Thrall, to heirs of Thomas Allyn; by Jonathan Hills, Samuel Wells and John Pitkin.

Page 15-16.

Allyn, Joshua, Sen., Windham. Died 27 December, 1699. Invt. £109-15-00. Taken 8 January, 1699-1700, by Joseph Hall and Samuel Storrs.

Court Record, Page 5-6—18 December, 1700: Adms. to John Allyn, eldest son, who gave bond with John Arnold, Sen., of the same town.

Page 45—26 July, 1703: Dist. to the widow, to John, to Gideon Allyn, and to the daughters; by Lt. Shubael Dimock, Lt. John Fitch and Jonathan Crane, distributors.

Page 52.

Allyn, Obadiah, Jr., Middletown. Died September, 1702. Invt. £94-01-00. Taken 23 February, 1702-3, by Thomas Alling and Nathaniel Bacon, Jr. The children: Obadiah, age 7 and 1-2 years, and Dorcas, 8 months old.

Court Record, Page 40—2 March, 1702-3: Invt. of the estate of Obadiah Allyn, Jr., was exhibited in Court by Dorcas, the relict. Adms. granted to the widow. John Cornwall, Sen., gave bond of £50 on behalf of Dorcas Allyn.

Page 10 (Vol. VIII) 1st May, 1710: Obadiah Allyn, a minor, 10 years of age, and Dorcas Allyn, 8 years old, desired Thomas Allyn to be their guardian, which this Court allow.

Page 11—1st May, 1710: Dorcas Wetmore, widow, Adms. on her husband's estate, now renders to this Court an account of her Adms:

	£ s d
Paid in debts and charges due from the estate,	4-01-06
And for bringing up the children,	10-00-00
Credit received,	8-09
There remains of moveable estate,	30-08-03
And of houseing and lands to be distributed,	50-00-00

To the widow, her thirds of moveable estate during life, and 1-3 part of the improvement of the lands. To Obadiah, his double share; and to Dorcas the daughter, her single part. And appoint Joseph Rockwell, Andrew Bacon and Nathaniel Stow, distributors. And order that Thomas Allyn, guardian to sd. children, do forthwith take into his care and charge their portions to be set out by the sd. dist. And this Court grant the Adms. a *Quietus Est.*

Andrews, Edward, Estate. Court Record, Page 101—5 January, 1707-8: David Forbes, who married Sarah Treat, daughter of Sarah Treat, alias Sarah Andrews, deceased, one of the children of Edward Andrews and Ann his wife, late of said Hartford, deceased, made complaint to this Court that there was never yet any distribution made of the estate of the said Edward Andrews, decd., and that there was no inventory ever yet made of the estate of the said Ann Andrews, decd., and that there is no Adms. ever yet appointed upon the estate of the sd. Ann, who was executrix of the last will of the said Edward Andrews, and that therefore the said David Forbes and Sarah his wife cannot obtain their portion thereof; and Solomon Andrews, William Warren and Mary his wife, and Matthias Treat, of Hartford, were notified to appear before this Court upon the said complaint that they would endeavor that then the said complaint might be heard and considered at this Court on the first Monday of February next. Wherefore this Court do order the said parties all to appear before this Court on that day accordingly.

Page 103—2 February, 1708-9: David Forbes, Solomon Andrews, William Warren and Matthias Treat, of Hartford, appeared now before this Court as they were ordered to do by this Court, 5 January last, and the said William Warren and Matthias Treat relinquished to the said Solomon Andrews all their right and claim whatsoever to the estate of Edward Andrews the elder and Ann Andrews (father and mother of the sd. Solomon) and Edward Andrews the younger (brother of the sd. Solomon), late of Hartford, deceased.

Inventory on File.

Andrews, Ann, Hartford. Invt. £15-12-02. Taken 25 February, 1707-8, by Cyprian Nichols, Roger Pitkin and Nathaniel Hooker.

Court Record, Page 103—2 February, 1708-9: This Court grant letters of Adms. on the estate of Ann Andrews, who was sole executrix of the last will of sd. Edward Andrews, joyntly unto Solomon Andrews and David Forbes.

Inventory on File.

Andrews, Edward, Jr., Hartford. Invt. £9-11-00. Taken 25 February, 1707-8, by Cyprian Nichols, Roger Pitkin and Nathaniel Hooker.

Court Record, Page 103—2 February, 1707-8: Adms. granted unto Solomon Andrews and David Forbes. Recog. £60.

Page 154.

Andrews, Joseph, Sen., Wethersfield. Invt. £413-07-04. Taken 23 May, 1706, by Nathaniel Stodder and John Curtis, Jr. Apprised as money. Will not dated.

The last will and testament of me, Joseph Andrews, Sen., of Wethersfield, in my own apprehension near unto death, is as followeth: Imprimis: My will is that my wife Rebeckah Andrews have 1-3 part of the profits of my lands; one end (vizt., the new end) of my dwelling house, and some pasture land; all these during her natural life. My will is that my eldest sonn Joseph have 16 acres of land where his house stands. Item. I give to my sonn Benjamin all that land which lyeth between the Mill Pond and my pasture, where his house standeth. Item. My will is that the rest of my lands not hereby disposed of be equally divided between my sonns; Joseph having a double portion thereof after his mother's decease. Item. It is my will that my daughters have their portions out of the moveables according as the Court shall think meet. Item. It is my will that all my lands before bequeathed to my sonns do remain with them, and that none of them dispose of my lands given to them except it be to one another.

Witness: *Thomas Buckingham,*   (Not signed.)
         Bartholomew Foster.

Court Record, Page 84—20 May, 1706: Rebeckah Andrews, of Wethersfield, widow, relict of Joseph Andrews, Sen., and Joseph Andrews, Benjamin Andrews and William Andrews, sons of the sd. late Joseph Andrews, decd., all appeared in this Court and exhibited the last will and testament of the sd. decd in writing, but not subscribed by the testator, and all declared that to their certain knowledge the same writing was and is the last will and testament of Joseph Andrews, late decd., and thereunto they did all consent and agree. Will proven and letters granted to Rebeckah the relict and Joseph the eldest son, with the will annexed.

Page 128—2 May, 1709: Rebeckah Andrews and Joseph Andrews, Adms., exhibited now an account of their Adms., whereby it appears that the whole of the inventory of moveable estate and of debts they have re-

	£	s	d
ceived amounts to	134-12-07		
Paid in debts and charges,	48-10-11		
There remains of moveable estate,	86-01-08		

Account allowed. And this Court order that Daniel Andrews, of Farmington, and Ephraim Whaples and Samuel Hunn, of Wethersfield, shall dist. and divide the remaining estate of the sd. Joseph Andrews, both real and personal, to and amongst the widow and children of the sd. deceased according to his last will.

Page 132—5 September, 1709: Rebeckah Andrews, 17 years of age, and Caleb, 15 years, and Ann, 13 years, children of Joseph Andrews, Sen., chose their mother, Rebeckah Andrews, to be their guardian.

Page 4 (Vol. VIII) 6 February, 1709-10: Caleb Andrews, age 15 years, and Ann Andrews, 13 years, now appeared before this Court and made choice of their brother Joseph Andrews to be their guardian (their mother, who was their guardian, being dead).

Dist. of the real estate on file: 18 February, 1709-10: To Joseph, to Benjamin, to William, to Ephraim, to Caleb; and the personal estate to be divided to Rebeckah and Anne Andrews.

Page 9—3 April, 1710: A report of the dist. of the estate of Joseph Andrews, Sen., made by Ephraim Whaples and Samuel Hunn, of Wethersfield, was now exhibited in Court and accepted.

Page 261—2 August, 1715: Joseph Andrews, guardian to his sister, Ann Andrews, exhibited in this Court a full and ample discharge, under the hand and seal of the sd. Ann Andrews, executed by her since she arrived to full age to act. Whereupon this Court do release the sd. Joseph Andrews from his trust of guardianship.

Page 120-1-2.

Ashley, Jonathan, Sen., Hartford. Invt. £1030-19-06. Taken 28 February, 1704-5, by Joseph Wadsworth, Ciprian Nichols and Joseph Talcott. Will dated 27 January, 1704-5.

The last will and testament of Jonathan Ashley, late of Hartford, is as followeth: I give to my son Jonathan the house, with all my land in the ox pasture, and the land that is mine over the river, which place is commonly called Bridgefield, and the frame of the new barne. I give to my son Joseph my now dwelling house and barn, and all my land adjoining with or belonging to it; also, the Soldiers' Field land belonging to me. Item. Eleven acres lying west of Samuel Olcott's land, which I bought of Mr. William Gibbins and Mr. Ebenezer Way; 3 acres in the North Meadow which I bought of John Kelsey; 18 acres of woodland which was formerly my Father Wadsworth's, adjoining with Thomas Dickinson's land; my right in the land purchased of Joshua Sachem, lying on the east side of the Great River, which land lyes in partnership. I give to my son Samuel 4 score acres of land lying in Plainfield, which I bought of Major James Fitch. I give to my wife 1-3 part of my whole estate during her natural life, and that she have the use of the south room, inner cellar, and the use of the ovens. I give to my daughters Sarah and Rebeckah £50 apiece. I appoint my son Joseph to be sole executor.

Witness: *Joseph Wadsworth,*   JONATHAN ASHLEY, LS.
       Joseph Talcott.

Codicil, dated 29 January, 1704-5: Further, I give to my son Samuel my cutlash and one of my gunns. I appoint my brother Joseph Wadsworth and Joseph Talcott to be overseers.

Witness: *Joseph Wadsworth,*   JONATHAN ASHLEY, LS.
       Joseph Talcott.

Court Record, Page 64—6 March, 1704-5: Will proven.

Page 146-7.

Ayrault, Nicholas, Wethersfield, Physician. Will dated 2 March, 1705-6:

I, Nicholas Ayrault, of Wethersfield, doe make this my last will and testament. Imprimis: I give unto my sonn Peeter Ayrault my gold buttons. And all the rest of my estate, goods, chattells and debts whatsoever, in France or elsewhere, not hereinbefore bequeathed, after my debts and funeral expenses be discharged, I doe give and bequeath to my dear and loveing wife Marian Ayrault, and make her my sole executrix. And all this estate before mentioned to be at the disposal of my wife Marian Ayrault so long as she continues a widow; but if she should marry again, then my will is that 2-3 of my estate shall be distributed among my children.

Witness: *Moses Crafts,*   NICHOLAS AYRAULT, LS.
     Stephen Hurlbutt, Philip Alcock.

Court Record, Page 78—8 March, 1705-6: Will approved.

Page 141.

Bacon, Nathaniel, Sen., Middletown. Invt. £221-01-10. Taken 8 February, 1705-6, by Alexander Rollo and Israhiah Wetmore. Will dated 24 February, 1697-8:

I, Nathaniel Bacon, Senior, do ordain this my last will and testament: Imprs. I give to my eldest sonn Thomas all that was mine in the ox-pasture as it is mentioned in a deed of guift made to him from myself, with three acres in the lower end of the south meadow; also, I give him my last division of land lying toward Farmingtown; all this I give him my sd. son Thomas and his heirs forever. 2nd. To my sonn John I give my now dwelling house and barn, with about 11 acres of land adjoyning it, being the east end of my homestead, as is expressed in his deed of guift from myself, with the one-half of my long meadow and swamp adjoyning, Hanna's part being first excepted, which lyeth on the north side of my lott as it is now bounded, by a highway between John Hall's and she, through the meadow and the swamp butting on John Hall's and the neck and Nathaniel Brown northward; also 20 rods in width the whole length of my lott on the north side; also a third part of my second division of land westward; all this I give to him and his heirs forever. 3d. To my son Andrew I give one-half of the remainder of my homestead up to the highway, and the whole half of that lott to the westward of the highway, with the building upon it; all this I give to him my son Andrew and his heirs forever. 4th. To my son Nathaniel I give the remainder of both my homestead lying on the east and west side of the upper highway, and all the rest of my land on the west side the Great River, Hannah's and John's part being first taken out. I give to Nathaniel and Andrew to be equally divided between them for his and their heirs forever. 5. To my sonn Beriah I give my first division of upland lying on the east side the Great River near to John Gill's, part of which lyeth between the pond and the Great River next to Deacon John Hall's, which part butts north and west upon the highway; also I give him one piece of meadow and swamp at Wongunk butting north and east upon John Wetmore and south upon

Robert Warner and Joseph Hubbard. All the rest of my land on the east side the Great River I give to John, Andrew, Nathaniel and Beriah, to be equally divided between them. 6th. I give to my daughter Hannah 2 acres of meadow lands and half my wood lott lying between Ensign William Ward and Robert Warner. Also my will is that after my decease all my household goods should be divided equally between my three daughters, that is, Mary, Abigail and Lydia. The remainder of my land at Hartford I give to my two sonns, John and Andrew, to be equally divided between them, they paying all my just debts. Further, my will is that my executors do pay to my much esteemed friends, Capt. Nathaniel White, Mr. Noadiah Russell and Mr. John Hamlin, and to the Church of Christ in Middletown: to the church, 20s; to Mr. Noadiah Russell 20s; to Capt. Nathaniel White, 10s; and to Mr. John Hamlin, 10s. I appoint my two sonns John Bacon and Andrew Bacon, to be executors, and I request Capt. Nathaniel White and Mr. John Hamlin to assist my executors.

Witness: *John Hamlin,*   NATHANIEL BACON, LS.
          Noadiah Russell.

Court Record, Page 76—13 February, 1705-6: Will proven.

Page 4 (Vol. XIII) 22 March, 1736-7: Nathaniel Bacon, one of the sons of Nathaniel Bacon, late of Middletown, showing by the will of Nathaniel Bacon, that there were certain lands given to his son Beriah Bacon, and that he gave all the rest of his lands to be equally divided between John and Andrew, Nathaniel and Beriah Bacon. And whereas, the executors of sd. will have neglected or refused to divide sd. land according to the will, the sd. Nathaniel moves in behalf of himself and the heirs of Andrew Bacon decd., and the heirs of the other two brothers, decd., that this Court would appoint freeholders to divide sd. lands to Nathaniel, to heirs of John, to heirs of Andrew, to heirs of Beriah Bacon: This Court appoint Joseph Frary, Jr., Benjamin Adkins and Solomon Adkins to set out sd. lands by meets and bounds according to sd. will.

Invt. in Vol. VIII, Page 35.

Baker, Timothy, Wethersfield. Invt. £21-08-08. Taken 15 December, 1709, by Moses Crafts and Hezekiah Deming.

Court Record, Page 136—5 December, 1709: This Court grant letters of Adms. on the estate of Timothy Baker, late of Wethersfield, unto Jonathan Deming, Jr.

Page 8 (Vol. VIII) 3 April, 1710: Jonathan Deming, Adms., exhibits an inventory of the estate of Timothy Baker.

Page 33—5 April, 1711: James Brown, of Norwalk, atty. for William Baker, now dwelling in the Province of New Jersey, brother of Timothy Baker, late of Wethersfield, decd., exhibited evidence that he is the only surviving brother of Timothy Baker, decd. Whereupon Jonathan Deming, Adms., passed over the estate to James Brown, atty. for William Baker.

Page 218-19.

Barber, Samuel, Sen., Windsor. Invt. £598-04-10. Taken 29 March, 1709, by John Moore, Sen., Job Drake, Sen., and Thomas Marshall. Will dated 21 February, 1708-9: I, Samuel Barber, Sen., of Windsor, doe make and ordain this my last will and testament. I give unto my wife Ruth 2 acres of meadow land in the Great Meadow, which I had with her, to be at her own dispose; also the use and improvement of my dwelling house and barn and outhouseing, with the lands adjoining thereunto, and with other lands adjoining which I bought of John Saxton, John Barber and Andrew Hilliyer, and 14 acres of Benjamin Gardner and John Gillett, until my son John come to the age of 21 years. Item. I give to my eldest son Samuel (besides the several parcels of lands made over to him, as by a deed of gift bearing date with these presents doth appear) £3. Item. I give to my grandson William Barber, son to my son William Barber, deceased, besides what I have already made over to him, 8 acres of swamp land bounded north on Samuel Clark's land, west by land of my sd. sonn William, east by sonn Samuel's land and south on Jonathan Brown's land; also 8 acres at the Mill Brook, bounded north on land of John Brown exchanged with the Town, south on land of my sonn Joseph, and east and west on the Commons, which land I make over to my grandson William upon the conditions hereafter mentioned, vizt: that whereas there was about 4 or 5 acres of land which I formerly made over to my son William which I sold for conveniency to Mr. Thomas Cook with other of my own land at Scotland, that in case my said grandson or his heirs or any other person claiming any right to my son William's estate, do any way molest or disturb Mr. Thomas Cook or any of his heirs in the quiet and peaceable possession of the land at Scotland which was made over to my son William, then it is my will that the land abovesaid shall be and remain to the sd. Mr. Thomas Cook and his heirs as a full recompense for the land sold him which was my son William's. Item. I give to my sonn David the land I purchased of Mr. Buckingham at Hebron; also 2 acres of land at Windsor, being 2 acres of the four I received in the legacy given to my wife. I give to my son Joseph, at Scotland, 20 rods in breadth, lying on the north side of the land given to my son Samuel; also 8 acres at the Mill Brook in Windsor; also the 6 acres of land I bought of Timothy Horsford, lying near the Mill Brook; also I give to my son Joseph 2 acres of land where he has built his house, to be 12 rods wide from the fence to the bottom of the hill; also 13 acres adjoyning, being the remainder of the lott known by the name of Branker's lott, which is about 12 acres, and one acre bought of John Enno, he paying to my wife 20s yearly in current pay during her life. Item. I give to my sonn Benjamin that lott that I bought of Samuel Cross; also, I give to my sonn Benjamin the remainder of my lott at the field called Wheat Field, the other part being given to my son Joseph; also, I give to my son Benjamin 3 acres in Palmer's Swamp, next to Joseph's land and running the same length. Item. I give to my sonn John, when he shall be 21 years of age, half my houseing and half the land given to my wife (excepting 2 1-2 acres of meadow), and the other half after my wive's decease; also I give to my sonn John, when he comes to be of age, about one acre of land which is called Fitch waters bottom. Item. I declare it to be my will that my three daughters, Elizabeth, Mindwell and Sarah, shall have £25 apiece paid to each of them when they shall be 18 years of age, to make them equal with their two sisters that are married. And I give to my five daughters (both those that are married and those that are not) the remainder of my estate which is yet undisposed of, both personal and real, to be equally divided between my five daughters, Mary, Ruth, Elizabeth, Mindwell and Sarah, to them and their heirs forever. I appoint my wife Ruth and my son-in-law William Phelps to be executors.

Witness: *John Moore, Sen.,*   SAMUEL BARBER, LS.
        Thomas Marshall.

Court Record, Page 125—4 April, 1709: Will proven.

Page 103-4.

Barber, William, Windsor. Invt. £136-03-03. Taken 17 August, 1704, by Timothy Loomis, Thomas Marshall and Thomas Moore.

Court Record, Page 58—7 September, 1704: Adms. to Easter Barber, the relict, with her father-in-law, Samuel Barber.

Page 14 (Vol. IX) 1st May, 1714: William Barber, a minor son of William Barber, late decd., chose John Bissell of Windsor to be his guardian. Recog. £200.

Invt. in Vol. VIII, Page 40.

Benjamin, Caleb, Hartford, formerly of Stonington. Invt. £9-06-00. Taken 10 April, 1710, by Jonathan Hill and John Goodwin.

Court Record, Page 135—15 November, 1709: Adms. granted to John Benjamin, of Hartford, brother of sd. decd.

Page 12 (Vol. VIII) 1st May, 1710: John Benjamin, Adms. on the estate of Caleb Benjamin, now exhibits an inventory.

Page 22—16 November, 1710: John Benjamin, Adms. on the estate of Caleb Benjamin, late of Hartford, decd., exhibits now an account of his Adms.:

£ s d   £ s d
Paid in debts and charges, 4-06-00 | There remains,   5-00-00

Which account is allowed. This Court now order that the sd. remaining estate be equally divided to and amongst the sd. John Benjamin and his four sisters, the next heirs of the sd. decd. And appoint Lt. Jonathan Hills and Joseph Keeny, of Hartford, distributors.

Page 89.

Benton, Andrew, Hartford. Died 5 February, 1703-4. Invt. £94-03-04. Taken by Benjamin Graham and James Ensign.

Court Record, Page 54—27 March, 1704: Samuel Benton presents an inventory of his deceased brother Andrew Benton's estate. Adms. is granted to Samuel Benton. Recog. £100.

Page 56—12 April, 1704: John Benton and Mary Benton, minor children of Andrew Benton, chose their uncle, Samuel Benton, to be their guardian.

Page 110—5 April, 1708: The estate is reported insolvent and Capt. Aaron Cooke and Caleb Stanly, Jr., are appointed commissioners.

Page 115—2 August, 1708: The commissioners report an average to creditors, and Samuel Benton asks for longer time to finish his Adms.

Page 133—5 September, 1709: Ebenezer Benton, a minor, now 13 years of age, chose Samuel Benton to be his guardian.

Page 22 (Vol. VIII) 6 November, 1710: Ebenezer Benton, 14 years of age, now made choice of Jonathan Bigelow, Sen., to be his guardian.

Page 28—5 March, 1710-11: This Court do allow Joseph Benton, of Hartford, to be guardian to Ebenezer Benton, his former guardian, Jonathan Bigelow, being decd.

Page 9-10-11 (Vol. VIII).

Bidwell, Sarah, Hartford. Invt. £462-16-08. Taken 7 March, 1708-9, by Samuel Kellogg and Nathaniel Hooker.

Court Record, Page 122—7 March, 1708-9: This Court grant letters of Adms. on both the estate of John Bidwell and Sarah Bidwell, the relict, joyntly to John Bidwell and Thomas Bidwell, sons of the sd. decd. James Bidwell, of Hartford, 17 years of age, one of the sons of John Bidwell, chose his brother Thomas Bidwell to be his guardian.

Page 126—4 April, 1709: John and Thomas Bidwell, Adms. on the estate of their late father and mother, John and Sarah Bidwell, now before this Court present an inventory.

Page 127—2 May, 1709: John and Thomas Bidwell, Adms., exhibited an inventory and informed the Court there is yet something to add thereunto. The Court order them to appear again before this Court and present the inventory with addition.

Page 129—6 June, 1709: The Adms. are allowed by this Court further time to finish their Adms.

Page 130—4 July, 1709: John and Thomas Bidwell, Adms., now in this Court exhibit an inventory of the sd. estate upon their oath, and this Court do also order that there shall be added to the inventory the sum of £10, money due to sd. Thomas from a person he had lent it to, and also the sum of £12 in money which sd. Thomas Bidwell paid to Basey Baker for land; and that both the sd. sums shall be reckoned to sd. Thomas Bidwell as part of his portion.

Page 17 (Vol. VIII) 3 July, 1710: This Court do order that the Clerk do issue forth a writ to require John Bidwell and Thomas Bidwell, of Hartford, Adms. on the estate of their late father and mother, John and Sarah Bidwell, to appear before this Court and render an account of their Adms. on the same, on the 2nd Monday of this instant month of July.

Page 22—6 November, 1710: John and Thomas Bidwell, Adms., are ordered by this Court to render an account of their Adms. on the 1st Monday of December next.

Page 23—4 December, 1710: This Court now order the sd Adms. to render their account of Adms. on the 1st Monday of January next, without any further delay.

Page 25—11 January, 1710-11: John and Thomas Bidwell, Adms., appeared now before this Court and presented an accompt of debts and charges that they have paid out:

	£ s d
Paid in debts and charges,	123-12-06
Debts due to the estate,	79-14-09
Further debts not received,	14-01-02

This Court, having examined the accounts, order to be kept on file and order dist:

	£ s d
To Jonathan,	26-02-06
To the heirs of Hannah Judd,	18-00-00
To Sarah Robbins,	24-00-00

The estate having been much bettered by the service of Thomas Bidwell and the above named persons after they came of age until their mother's decease, which was about 5 years, the Court do grant unto Thomas land, and unto the others the above named sums. The remaining part of the estate to be distributed as followeth:

	£ s d
To John Bidwell, eldest son,	246-16-07
To Thomas,	114-05-05
To Jonathan,	169-05-07
To David,	169-05-07
To James,	169-05-07
To heirs of Hannah Judd,	69-05-07
To Sarah Robbins,	91-09-06

And appoint Capt. Hezekiah Wyllys, Lt. James Steele and Samuel Kellogg, distributors. Thomas Bidwell, as well for himself as also guardian of the sd. James Bidwell, being unsatisfied with this order and decree of this Court, appealed from the same to the Court of Assistants. And Joseph Judd, of Farmington (who married the sd. Hannah), guardian to his son Joseph Judd, a minor, being unsatisfied with this order of Court for that in the same decree there is charged to the sd. Hannah, as formerly paid to her, the sum of £100, which the sd. Joseph Judd denies, and said she never received it, he also appeals to sd. Court of Assistants.

Invt. in Vol. VIII, Page 17.

Bissell, Hezekiah, Windsor. Died 17 October, 1709. Invt. £148-18-11. Taken 2 December, 1709, by Capt. Daniel Hayden, Benjamin Holcomb and Jonathan Elsworth.

Court Record, Page 136—5 December, 1709: This Court do now grant letters of Adms. on the estate of Hezekiah Bissell unto Daniel Bissell, a brother of the sd. decd.

Page 36 (Vol. VIII) 2 July, 1711: Daniel Bissell, Adms., exhibited in this Court an account of his Adms:

	£	s	d
Paid the debts and charges, the real part of the estate is	105-00-00		
The moveable part is	22-00-00		
There remains to be distributed,	127-00-00		

Order to dist. the estate to his four brothers and three sisters:

To Daniel, to Josiah, to Jeremiah and Samuel, his brothers, and Dorothy, Ann and Mary, his sisters, in equal parts or shares, to each of them the sum of £18-02-10. And appoint Mr. Atherton Mather, Capt. Timothy Thrall and Jonathan Elsworth, distributors.

Page 8-9-10-11.

Bissell, Samuel, Sen., Windsor. Died 3 December, 1700. Invt £495-03-07. Taken 9 December, 1700, by John Moore, Sen., Matthew Allyn and Benajah Holcomb. Will dated 2 August, 1697:

I, Samuel Bissell, Sen., of Windsor, doe make this my last will and testament. I give to my son Samuel £140 besides that land which I have already given him, on which his house standeth, which is about 6 acres. Item. I give to my two daughters, Abigaile and Mary, which are already marryed, £20 to each beside what they have already had. Item. I give to my three younger daughters, Elizabeth, Deborah and Hannah, £75 apiece. All wch legacies my will is that it shall be and remain to my children above named, to them and their heirs forever. Item. I give to my son Joshua all that meadow land at Simsbury, wch belongs to me, wch I bought of Mr. Stone and Jonathan Gillett (17 acres), excepting two acres which my son Jacob did improve in his life, which sd. two acres I give to my grandson Jacob Bissell, son of Jacob Bissell decd., if he live to the age of 21 years. In case he do not survive to that age, my son Joshua shall have it. Also, two acres of upland on ye north side of the brooke known by the name of Bissell's Brooke, at Simsbury, I give to my son Joshua. I give to my grandson John Bissell, son of John Bissell decd., £5; and £2-10 to my granddaughter Abigaile Bissell. I give to my grandson Jacob Bissell my dwelling house at Simsbury. I give to my wife Mary 20 shillings in silver money, and for security of the payment of the £5 per annum which I engaged to pay her while she remained my widow, I make over 10 acres of my meadow land at the south end known as the Great Meadow. I nominate my son Samuel to be executor, and desire John Moore, Lt. John Higley, Matthew Allyn and Michael Taintor to be my overseers.

Witness: *John Moore, Sen.,*   SAMUEL BISSELL, SEN., LS.
   John Higley, Sen.

The wise disposeing providence of God having made a breach in my family by bereaveing of the son of my hope, whom I had nominated executor, has given me occasion to add this my codicil: The estate that I had devised to my son Samuel (who is deceased) shall, after my decease, be equally divided amongst my five daughters. I appoint my sonn-in-law, James Enno, executor, and supervisors as above. 23 April, 1698.

Witness: *Daniel Clarke,*   SAMLL BISSELL, SENR., LS.
   Martha Clarke.

A codicil, dated 25 November, 1700: The testator nominates his son-in-law John Pettebone, Jr., joint executor with James Enno; and to issue any differences that may arise in the division of the estate, he appoints his brother Benajah Holcomb and John Moore, Sen.

Court Record, Page 4—16 December, 1700: James Enno, of Windsor, and John Pettebone exhibit the last will of their father-in-law, Samuel Bissell, of the same Windsor, deceased. Will proven by the witnesses.

Page 196-7.

Blackleach, Mrs. Elizabeth. Died 12 June, 1708.   Invt. £272-02-06. Taken August, 1708, by Joseph Wadsworth and Capt. Aaron Cooke.

The nuncupative and last will and testament of Elizabeth Blackleach, late of Wethersfield, widow, decd., contained and expressed sundry testimonies and evidences thereof, as is here recorded:

First, the testimony of John Stedman, of lawful age, is as followeth: That I being at the house of Mrs. Blackleach, 8th June, 1708, I then and there heard Mrs. Elizabeth Blackleach say unto me, "Cousin Stedman,

go unto Mr. Thomas Wickham's and get my will, for I will have none
out, for my daughter Mary shall have it and do what she will with it,
for Mary shall have all that I have, for I see what has become of what
Betty had, and I see how it is with Mrs. Jesse now; for Mary has not
carried herself so." And I did judge that she was in good understanding
and memory.

Sworn before the Court of Probates, 5th July, 1708.

Test: Caleb Stanly, Clerk.

Thomas Wickham, aged 57 years, testifieth as followeth: That
sometime in June last, Mrs. Blackleach sent to me to bring her will
over, which accordingly I did, and she desired me to read it over and
I read it to her; and when I read it to her, then, with her leave, I read
it to her daughter; and her daughter desired to have a perusall of it
for to read it and promised me to return it, and so I left it in her hands,
and this was the last will written of Mrs. Blackleach that ever I saw.
2 August, 1708. Being sworn before the Court of Probates.

Test: Caleb Stanly, Clerk.

The testimony of Sarah Benjamin, of lawful age, is as followeth:
That I, being at the house of Mrs. Elizabeth Blackleach in Wethersfield,
8th June, 1708, then and there I heard Mrs. Blackleach order her will
to be fetcht, which accordingly Mr. Thomas Wickham brought it unto
Mrs. Elizabeth Blackleach and the sd. Mrs. Blackleach desired Mr.
Wickham to read the sd. will, which accordingly he did, and then
Mrs. Blackleach bid her daughter Mary to take the will and keep it
and " do what you will with it, for I give you all I have to dispose of
as you see cause for my daughter in Boston has had her portion
already, about £500," and said her daughter Mary had not had her
portion, and so declared that this was her will, and said the last
will must stand. And further said she did not see cause her daughter
should stoop to her children, but let them wait upon her as she has
done upon me. Sarah Benjamin made oath on the 16th of June, 1708,
before me.

Robert Welles, Justice.

At a Court of Probates holden at Hartford, 2 August, 1708, the
within named Sarah Benjamin, being further examined upon her oath,
did affirm and declare that Mrs. Elizabeth Blackleach, decd., spake
those words within mentioned ("Take the will and keep it and do what
you will with it, for I give you all I have to dispose of as you see
cause") to her daughter Mary Olcott immediately upon Thomas Wickham his reading the sd. written will and delivering it to the sd. Mary.

Test: Caleb Stanly, Clerk.

Testimony of Hannah Northway and Susannah Dix, who also
appeared before the Court and testified to the above written statement.

Court Record, Page 115—2 August, 1708: John Olcott and Mary
Olcott his wife, one of the daughters of Mrs. Elizabeth Blackleach, late

of Wethersfield, decd., presented evidences which were accepted by this
Court as annulling all former wills and devising her whole estate to
her daughter Mary Olcott. Adms. to John and Mary Olcott.

Page 122—7 March, 1708-9: Invt. exhibited.

Page 24 (Vol. VIII) 1st January, 1710-11: This Court now grant
to John Olcott, of Hartford, and Mary his wife, Adms. on the estate of
Mrs. Elizabeth Blackleach, late of Wethersfield, decd., further time to
finish their Adms.

Page 43 (Vol. X) 3 March, 1723-4: This Court grant Adms. on
the estate of Mrs. Jo (hn) Blackleach, late of Wethersfield, decd.,
unto Mrs. Mary Wadsworth, daughter of sd. decd., provided bond be
given according to law.

Note: Page 201—Probate Side (Vol. III): *Bond of John Blackleach to support his father, Benj. Harbord, and his mother, Jane Harbord, in consideration of their making over estate to him; and also
see page* 211: *Mrs. Elizabeth Blackleach's appeal to the Court of Assistants relating to the will of Christian Harbert, wife of Benjamin Harbert, who was father to Mrs. Elizabeth Blackleach.*

Page 66-7-8.

Blackleach, John, Sen.,   Wethersfield. Died 7 September, 1703.
Invt. £1576-19-00. Taken October, 1703, by Benjamin Churchill and
Thomas Wickham, Sen. There are debts still due at Antigua that
cannot be put in the inventory. Will dated 3 September, 1703:

Whereas my wife, Elizabeth Blackleach, hath been for divers years
sometime past left in the management of my concerns in Hartford and
Wethersfield, and hath taken much pains and care and thereby has found
difficulty, and she knowing how my children have behaved towards
her, and also out of that care and respect that I bear towards her comfortable maintenance, I do in this my last will and testament give and
bequeath all my estate, both real and personal, unto my beloved wife
Elizabeth Blackleach, leaving the settlement thereof to her, hereby giving her full power to will and bequeath the said estate as she shall see
meet. And so hereby constitute and appoint my wife Elizabeth Blackleach to be my sole executor, desireing Mr. John Chester and Joshua
Robbins to be overseers. In case my wife die intestate, I say it to be
remembered that I have given my daughter Elizabeth Harris, in Boston,
a very considerable estate—I think it not short of £500.

Witness: *John Chester,*   JOHN BLACKLEACH, LS.
    Thomas Wickham, Sen.

Court Record, Page 48—24 September, 1703: Will approved.

Page 51—12 January, 1703-4: This Court, upon the prayer of Mrs.
Elizabeth Blackleach as executrix to the last will of her deceased husband, Mr. John Blackleach, do grant letters of administration on her

deceased husband's estate, provided she give sufficient bond. Ensign John Stedman becomes surety, in a bond of £500, to render a true accot by the first Tuesday of September, 1704.

Page 18.

Blackleach, John, Jr., Farmington. Invt. £165-03-09. Taken by Ciprian Nickols and Joseph Talcott:

	£	s	d
Some estate to be added to the estate of Mr. John Blackleach,	152-18-09		
To rents of house and homested at Wethersfield, of Wm. Butler,	2-00-00		
To rents for ditto, received of John Walker,	5-06		
To a debt received of John Wyott,	6-15-00		
To a debt received of Peter Blyn, Sen.,	3-04-06		

165-03-09

6 January, 1700-1: Mr. John Olcott, late Adms. on the estate
  of Mr. John Blackleach, late of Farmington, merchant,
  is Dr   165-03-09
Per Contra, the accomptant,   Total,   165-03-09

Court Record, Page 12 (Vol. VIII) 1st May, 1710: The General Assembly, 12 May, 1709, granted power to John Olcott, Adms. on the estate of John Blackleach, of Farmington, decd., to sell land in Hartford (2 acres) that did belong to Thomas Wells, and by him mortgaged to John Sadd. The Assembly now order the sale and payment to the executors of John Sadd's will, vizt., Mr. William Pitkin and Mr. Zachariah Sandford, of £30-17-09, and to improve the residue of such sale for the benefit of the relict and children of the said Thomas Welles, decd.

Page 20—6 November, 1710: John Olcott, Adms., now exhibits an account of his Adms. on the estate of John Jr. and his father, Mr. John Blackleach, Sen., by which it appears that all the moveable part of the estate is disposed of in payment of debts and charges. The Adms. account is allowed and is granted a *Quietus Est.* And this Court now order that all the houseing and lands of the sd. John Blackleach, Jr., be equally divided between Elizabeth Harris of Boston, widow, and Mary Olcott, wife of John Olcott, sisters and next of kin to the deceased.

Page 185-6.

Boarn (Bourn), John, Middletown. Invt. £99-18-01. Taken 27 October, 1707, by John Bacon and Andrew Bacon. There is also given to Hannah Boarn, widow of the said decd., by her Father Bacon, 2 acres of land in Longmeadow with some swamp adjoyning to it, for her to hold and enjoy during her life, which she will not yet have inventoried or distributed to her children. The children now living are John Boarn, eldest son, Joseph and Nathaniel Boarn, Ann Boarn, alias Foster, and Frances Boarn.

Court Record, Page 102—2 February, 1707-8: Hannah Bourn, of Middletown, exhibited in this Court evidences to prove that her husband, John Bourn, late of Middletown, is dead, and that in all probability he was lost at sea several years ago, which evidences this Court do conceive to be good and valid. The said Hannah Bourn also exhibited in Court an inventory of the estate of the said John Bourn, and this Court grant letters of administration on the estate to Hannah Bourn.

Page 109—5 April, 1708: Hannah Boarn, Adms., exhibited now an account of her Adms. Accepted. This Court order that the estate be distributed to the widow and children, and appoint Lt. Thomas Ward, Deacon Joseph Rockwell and John Bacon, distributors.

See File, 5 August, 1708: Dist. of the estate of John Boarn as followeth: To the widow, to Thomas, to Joseph, to Ann, to Frances. By Joseph Rockwell and John Bacon.

Page 49-50.

Booth, Symon, Hartford. Died 28 February, 1702-3. Invt. £57-04-00. Taken 9 March, 1702-3, by Joseph Wadsworth and Gerrard Spencer:

Whereas, wee whose names are underwritten were at Symon Booth's house to visit him in his last sickness, 23 February, 1702-3, he the said Booth desired us to bear witness how his will and pleasure was concerning the dispose of his estate after his decease, which was as followeth: That his wearing clothes should be divided between his two sonns, William and Zachariah Booth, and gave Zachariah Booth's sonn Robert his loom, and gave 30s in money to his daughter Pheebe. And desired his wife, if she see cause, to give his three daughters, Bridgett Allyn, Elizabeth Peese and Mary Spencer, six or tenn or twenty shillings to each of them, if shee was willing, in such things she could best spare; and when his debts were paid, he gave the remainder of his estate to his wife and child Sarah that he had by her. As witness our hands, 2 March, 1702-3.
Witness: *Joseph Colyer,*
Disbrow Spencer.

Court Record, Page 38—1st March, 1702-3: Adms. to Elizabeth, the relict, who gave bond with Disbrow Spencer.

Page 41—7 April, 1703: Will accepted. Adms. to Elizabeth Booth, with the will annexed.

Page 64—6 March, 1704-5: Adms. account rendered, and a *Quietus Est.* granted.

Page 168-9.

Bowman, Nathaniel, Wethersfield, Inn Holder. Invt. £13-08-06. Taken 14 January, 1706-7, by William Goodrich and Philip Alcock. Will dated 14 January, 1706-7.

The last will and testament of Mr. Nathaniel Bowman, late of Wethersfield: In the name of God, amen. The 14th day of January, Anno Dom. 1706-7, being of perfect memory, I doe make this my last will and testament. I give unto Samuel Buck all my estate, he paying my lawful debts and buryall. In witness whereof I have set my hand and seal the day and date above mentioned.

Witness: *Timothy Baker*   NATHANIEL X BOWMAN, LS.
Mabel Buck, Samuel Butler.

Part of Nathaniel Bowman's inventory, as followeth:

	£ s d
Imprs: Wearing apparrel, £3-14; plate, 21 shillings,	4-15-00
A bedsted, bed, bolster, pillows, blanketts, rugs and coverlids,	3-11-00
Linen, £3-6; books, bottles and odd things 12 shillings,	3-18-00
Old chest, a box and old chairs, £0-17-06; and odd things, £0-05,	1-02-06
One pair of spectacles with silver bows,	1-06
Total,	13-08-06

Court Record, Page 90—3 March, 1706-7: Will exhibited, and Adms. granted to Samuel Buck.

Page 21.

Brooks, John, Simsbury. An account of my administration on the estate of John Brooks, late of Simsbury, is as followeth:

	£ s d
In moveables, as is mentioned in the last inventory,	15-03-00
And for real estate I find none, tho I suppose there was a bargaine intended between Mr. Sanders and sd. Brooks. The other halfe I bought of G. G. for £80, so that I imagine he has in the farme,	90-00-00
	95-03-00
Out of which take for the son,	10-00-00
	85-03-00
Toe debts being paid,	55-03-09
There remains to be divided among five,	29-19-03
To Mary, Lydia, Marcy and Susannah, to each,	6-00-00

Also my owne share of Samuell's part,   6-00-00
Paid to the widow besides her £6 that was set out before,   9-00-00
Ouerpaid and due to me,   ,   9-00-00
March 11th, 1700.   As witness my hand,   JOHN HIGLEY.
  Note: See Vol. I (Digest), Page 277, John Brooks's estate.

Page 187-8.

Brounson, Jacob, Sen., Farmington. Invt. £166-01-02. Taken 25
March, 1708, by Thomas Porter and John Porter.   Will dated 13 March,
1707-8.
  The last will and testament of Jacob Brounson, Sen., of Farmington,
as followeth: I give to my wife Mary Brounson the use and improvement
of the room I dwell in, and the cellar under it, during her time of widowhood, and also 1-3 part of my personal estate, to be at her own dispose in
life and at death; and also the improvement of 1-3 part of my improved
lands during said term of her widdowhood.   I give to my son Samuel
Brounson all that part of my house lott that is southward of the brook
that runneth through the same, and to extend up to the brow of the hill
on the northward side of said brook so as to come up to the west corner
of Samuel's now dwelling house, and also so farr on the fore side of sd.
house northward as to the middle of the doorway, and up to the gate
by the highway.   Also I give to my son Samuel two acres of land in 80
acres at the east end of my lott there next to the Common fence.   I give
to my son Roger Brounson all the remainder of my homestead, with my
dwelling house and the orchard upon it, only allowing my wife her right
in said house as is above expressed.   Also, I give to my son Roger all
the remainder of my land in eighty acres, besides the two acres given to
my son Samuel. I give to my son Isaac Brounson all my land in Nod Meadow, and two and a half acres of upland at the barn place at said Nod.
All my divisions of outlands in Farmington that I have not disposed of already I give to my four sons, Samuel, Jacob, Roger and Isaac Brounson,
to be equally divided amongst them. I do give to my two daughters, Elizabeth Harris and Rebeckah Dickinson, £10 apiece out of my moveable estate. I nominate my two sons, Samuel and Roger Brounson, to be executors.
Witness: *Thomas Porter,*   JACOB X BROUNSON, SEN.
         John Hart, Sen.

    Court Record, Page 108—5 April, 1708.   Will proven.

Page 34-5.

Bulkeley, Peter, Wethersfield. Invt. £67-03-00. Taken 30 March,
1702, by Robert Wells, Samuel Wright and David Goodrich. Inventory

not complete, as there is money due at Delaware and parts of a broken sloop at Block Island.

Court Record, Page 25—9 March, 1701-2: This Court grant letters of Adms. on the estate of Mr. Peter Bulkeley, mariner, late of Wethersfield, decd., unto Rachel, his relict, who gave bond with Ebenezer Kilbourn of £100.

Page 27—12 March, 1701-2: An inventory of the sd. estate was now exhibited and accepted.

Page 29—3 September, 1702: There being no issue, the surviving children of Rev. Gershom Bulkeley, having an interest in the estate, quitclaim to the sd. estate, desireing that the entire estate might be distributed to the widow, reserving to the heirs of Mr. Charles Bulkeley, late of New London, decd., her part if she should ever demand it. For this security was given by Mrs. Rachel Bulkeley, widow.

Page 134.

Bull, John, Hartford. Invt. £237-19-06. Taken 24 July, 1705, by John Stanly and Samuel Lewis.

Court Record, Page 73—21 November, 1705: Adms. to the widow, Easter Bull, with Deacon Thomas Bull of Farmington.

Page 94—2 June, 1707: This Court appoint the said Thomas Bull and Easter Bull joint guardians of the three sons of the said John Bull deceased, viz., Thomas, Nehemiah and John, minors.

Page 113—7 June, 1708: Whereas, this Court did appoint Deacon Thomas Bull and Easter Bull to be guardians to Thomas, Nehemiah and John Bull, minors, and Deacon Thomas Bull is since deceased, this Court do now appoint Samuel Kellogg of Hartford and the said Easter Bull to be joint guardians of the said minors.

Page 112 (Vol. IX) 6 October, 1719: Esther Bull, Adms., exhibits an account of her Adms. Allowed:

	£ s d
Inventory,	237-19-06
Moveables,	102-19-06
Paid in debts and charges,	49-02-06
There remains to be distributed,	188-17-00
To the widow Esther Bull (dower) and	17-19-00
To Thomas Bull, eldest son,	85-09-00
To Nehemiah Bull and John Bull, the rest of the children, to each of them the sum of	42-14-06

And appoint Isaac Cowles and Josiah Hart, of Farmington, and Abram Merrells, of Hartford, distributors.

Page 37-8-40.

Bull, Major Jonathan. Died 17 August, 1702. Invt. £1344-05-02. Taken 4 September, 1702, by Thomas Bunce, Sen., Aaron Cooke and Samuel Howard. More added to the abovesd. inventory:

	£ s d
½ of the sloop named "The Two Brothers," apprised by James Ward and Joseph Rockwell in money,	60-00-00
½ of the sloop named "The Benneta," apprised by Capt. Jeremiah Tothill and John Rolland in N. Y. money,	75-00-00
100 acres of land at Cedar Swamp,	24-00-00
40 lbs. copporas at £0-13-04; an old brass kettle, £0-01,	14-04
4 lbs. old pewter, £0-04; an old musket, £0-30,	1-14-00

161--08-04

Court Record, Page 32—8 September, 1702: Adms. granted to Mrs. Sarah Bull, the relict, who gave bonds, with Mr. Samuel Howard and William Whiting, of £500.

Page 113—7 June, 1708: Mrs. Sarah Bull of Hartford, widow, relict of Major Jonathan Bull, Adms., now presented in this Court a further account of her Adms. on that estate, wherein the inventory amounted to

	£ s d
the whole sum of	3049-03-06
Paid in debts and charges,	1614-07-02
Hath sustained losses of	36-01-06
And spent upon the children for subsistence and clothing,	166-00-00
There remains to be distributed,	1232-17-10
In houseing, lands, stock and household goods,	708-07-04
And debts yet due,	524-10-06
Order dist. of the houseing, lands, stock and household goods,	708-07-04

To the widow 1-3 part, and to Jonathan, the eldest son, a double portion; and the rest of the children each a single portion. And this Court appoint Joseph Talcott, Joseph Bull, Sen., and Samuel Howard, distributors. This Court appoint Mrs. Sarah Bull to be guardian to her three sons, viz., Jonathan, Moses and Ebenezer, children of Major Jonathan Bull, late decd. Ruth Bull and Abigail Bull, minor children, also appeared before the Court and made choice of their uncle, Major William Whiting, to be their guardian.

Dist. File: 3 March, 1714-15: Estate dist. as followeth: To Jonathan, to Moses, to Ebenezer, to Susannah Porter, to Sarah, to Sybell, to Ruth, to Samuel Bull. By Joseph Talcott and Thomas Seymour.

Page 196 (Vol. VIII) 17 May, 1714: Moses Bull, 15 years of age, made choice of his mother, Mrs. Sarah Bull, to be his guardian.

Page 261—2 August, 1715: A dist., made on the estate of Majoi Jonathan Bull, late of Hartford, decd., by Major Joseph Talcott and Thomas Seymour, of Hartford, was now exhibited in Court by Mrs.

Sarah Bull, Adms. on that estate, which dist. this Court doth allow and confirm as a full settlement of that estate, and order that it be kept on file.

Page 193-4-5.

Bull, Thomas, Deacon, Farmington. Died 13 May, 1708. Invt. £745-12-01. Taken by John Stanly, Sen., Thomas Porter and Isaac Cowles. Will dated 7 May, 1708:

I, Thomas Bull, of Farmington, doe make this my last will and testament: I give to my wife Mary Bull the use and improvement of one-third part of my real estate during her life, she to have said third part out of my house, homestead and lands in the Common Field in Farmington. And my wife shall have the service and command of my negro man named Taylor during her abode in my said house. I further give and bequeath unto my said wife £30 of my personal estate, to be at her own dispose, and that shee shall have free liberty to choose the sd. £30 in what part of my personal estate she seeth cause. I give and bequeath unto my three grandchildren, Thomas Bull, Nehemiah Bull and John Bull, children of my eldest son John Bull, deceased, to each of them £10. I give to my daughter, Susannah Porter, £20. I give to my son Samuel Bull and his heirs my lott in Farmington in the division of land southward from the Town between the mountains. And it is my will that if he die without issue, then the said lott shall return unto my two sons, Jonathan and David Bull, and to their heirs in equal proportion. I give to my son Samuel Bull my negro man named Taylor, reserving to my wife her right in him. I give and bequeath unto my son Jonathan Bull all my lands in Hartford bounds, and my lott in Farmington that lyeth in a division of land against Hartford bounds, and my lott in Farmington bounds lying in a division of lands against Wethersfield bounds. I give to my daughter Sarah Bull £60. I give to my son David Bull my house and home lot and other buildings upon sd. lott in Farmington, and all my land within the Common Field in Farmington, still reserving a right therein to my wife. I give to my son David Bull my great swamp, and my lott in the division of land belonging to the great swamp, both said lotts in Farmington bounds. And my will is that what shall remain of my estate shall be equally divided among my now surviving children. And I constitute my two sons, Jonathan and David Bull, to be joint executors, and desire the Rev. Samuel Whitman and Mr. John Hooker, both of Farmington, to assist my executors by their advice and as overseers.

Witness: *Samuel Hooker,*   THOMAS BULL, LS.
      Thomas Wadsworth.

Court Record, Page 115—2 August, 1708: Will proven.
Page 13 (Vol. IX) 1st May, 1716: David Bull, executor, is now discharged from his bond.

See File.

Burd, James. An agreement, dated 5 November, 1708, witnesseth:
That we, the subscribers, being the heirs and proper inheritors of the estate
of our honoured father, James Bird, late of Farmington, decd., for a quiet
and peaceable settlement of the sd. estate, have universally and mutually
agreed upon the dist. of the sd. estate in manner and form following:—
First, it is agreed and concluded that Thomas Bird, his heirs and assigns,
shall have and enjoy all the lands that was the sd. James Bird's at the
time of his decease, in consideration whereof the sd. Thomas Burd doth
covenant and agree to discharge and pay all those debts that were due from
the sd. James Burd at the time of his decease, and also his funeral charges.
Secondly, it is agreed that Samuel Lamb of Springfield, son-in-law to the
sd. James Burd, in right of his wife Rebecca, Nathaniel Morgan of
Springfield, in right of his wife Hannah, Peletiah Morgan of Springfield,
in right of his wife Lydia, Mehetable Burd, the daughter of James Burd,
and Elizabeth Burd, daughter of James Burd, shall enjoy their portions
in personal estate. In witness whereof we have set to our hands and
seals:

Witness: *Thomas Orton,*   THOMAS BIRD, LS.
        John Clark.   SAMUEL LAMB, LS.
                            NATHANIEL MORGAN, LS.
                            PELETIAH MORGAN, LS.
                            JAMES BURD, LS.
                            MEHETABEL X BURD, LS.
                            ELIZABETH X BURD, LS.

Court Record, Page 119—6 December, 1708: Thomas Burd of Farmington, eldest son of James Burd, Sen., late of Farmington, decd., and
Adms. on his estate, now exhibited in this Court an agreement made in
writing under his hand and seal, and the hands and seals of his brethren
and sisters, heirs of the sd. estate, for the division of the same which
agreement was also acknowledged by all the sd. parties before John
Hooker, Esq., Justice of the Peace, and therein the sd. Thomas Burd hath
obliged himself to pay all the debts due from the sd. estate to the creditors thereof: This Court do allow and approve the sd. agreement to be
a full division and settlement of the estate of sd. James Burd, Sen., and
order that it be put on file.

Invt. in Vol. VIII, Page 19-20.

Burd, James, Farmington. Invt. £109-15-09. Taken 14 November,
1709, by Stephen Lee and Daniel Judd.
Court Record, Page 133—7 November, 1709: Adms. granted to
Thomas Burd, a brother of the deceased.
Page 136—5 December, 1709: Thomas Burd, Adms., exhibited an
invt. of the estate of his brother, James Burd. Accepted, ordered recorded
and kept on file.

Page 59 (Vol. VIII) 3 March, 1711-12: Thomas Burd, Adms. on his brother's estate, exhibited now an account of his Adms. on that estate. Accepted. And affirmed before the Court that he knows of no more debts from the sd. estate. Also, exhibited now in this Court an agreement subscribed by the sd. Thomas Bird:

NATHANIEL MORGAN, in right of his wife HANNAH,
SAMUEL LAMB, in right of his wife REBECCA,
EBENEZER ALVERD, in right of his wife ELIZABETH,
PELETIAH MORGAN, in right of his wife LYDIA, and
MEHETABELL BURD,

Who have rights in sd. estate in equal degree, which agreement respects the division and partition of the sd. estate. All signed and sealed, and bears date 5 January and 6 March, 1709-10. Allowed by the Court. And this Court grant the Adms. a *Quietus Est.*

Page 188.

Burd, Joseph, Farmington. Invt. £161-01-06. Taken 9 March, 1707-8. (No names of apprisers given.) Will dated 16 February, 1707-8:

I, Joseph Burd, doe make this my last will and testament: I give to my wife Mary Burd, to be at her own dispose, in life and in death, one-third part of my personal estate and the improvement and profit of half my house and half my homelott, and one-third part of all my lands during her natural life. I give unto my only son Joseph Burd all my house and homelott and all other of my lands that I have in possession or reversion, to him, his heirs and assigns forever, to be possessed by him at full age or day of marriage, which shall first happen. Only his mother to enjoy an interest in it as above expressed. I give to my daughter Mary Burd one-third part of my personal estate, to be delivered to her by my executrix at her marriage or at 18 years of age. I give to my daughter Ruth Burd, at her marriage or at 18 years of age, also 1-3 part of my personal estate. My will further is that my executrix shall have the improvement of all the estate I have here willed to my children, to enable her in the bringing up of my said children. I appoint my wife Mary Burd to be sole executrix, and I desire Thomas Burd and Joseph Judd to assist my wife as overseers.

Witness: *John Judd, Sen.,*   JOSEPH BURD, LS.
    Thomas Orton.

Court Record, Page 111—3 May, 1708: Will approved.
Page 46 (Vol. IX) 2 December, 1717: Upon the motion of the heirs of Joseph Bird that the dist. may be finished according to the will, this Court appoint Daniel Andrews, Sen., Daniel Judd and Joseph Hawley, of Farmington, to accomplish the dist.

Page 174 (Vol. X) 6 February, 1727-8: Upon motion of Joseph Hart, of Farmington, in right of his wife, formerly Mary Bird, daughter of sd. deceased, for a dist. of the estate of sd. deceased to and among the heirs, who were then cited to a hearing in this Court.

Page 208—18 December, 1728: Whereas, according to act of Court, 2 August, Samuel Bird, Adms. on sd. estate, with the will annexed, having exhibited an invt. of the estate, anew apprised in order to make an equable proportion to the heirs, several of the heirs now object against sd. inventory, this Court, after a hearing, order that Daniel Judd, John Porter and John Steele, Jr., agreed upon by the parties, do make another inventory of sd. estate, the moveable part thereof that any of the heirs have received to be apprised at double value of what they were in the former inventory, and the real estate at its present value.

Page 214—4 March, 1728-9: Joseph Hart, in right of his wife Mary, one of the heirs of Joseph Bird, formerly of Farmington, deceased, moved for an appeal from the judgment of the Court, 18 December, 1728, appointing Daniel Judd, John Porter and John Steele, Jr., to make another inventory of the sd. (estate) of Joseph Bird for distribution to and among the heirs of said deceased, to the Superior Court.

Page 7 (Vol. XI) 2 December, 1729: Upon the motion of Mary Burd, of Farmingtown, widow of Joseph Burd, decd., for a dist. on the estate, this Court appoint Capt. Joseph Hawley, Lt. Isaac Cowles and Sergt. Joseph Woodruff, distributors, to set out 1-3 part of the lands to Mary Burd, widow, and 1-3 part of the moveables for her own, the rest to be divided equally between the two daughters, Mary and Ruth Burd.

Page 14—3 March, 1730: Report of the distributors.

Page 78-79.

Burd, Nathaniel, Farmington. Invt. £139-14-00. Taken 23 January, 1703-4, by Thomas Burd and Joseph Burd. Will dated 11 December, 1703:

I, Nathaniel Burd, of Farmington, do make this my last will and testament: I give to my wife Sarah Burd, to her and her heirs and assigns forever, my dwelling house and homested, and land thereto belonging or adjoyning, that is in Farmington, and all my household stuff or things needfull or convenient for housekeeping, and one cow. Also, that she have the use and improvement of all other estate, both real and personal, during her life. I give to my two brethren, Joseph Burd and Thomas Burd, what remains of my lands after the decease of my wife. Should my brethren, or either of them, be taken away by death, leaving no male issue surviving, my will then is that my cousin, Samuel Burd, son of my brother Samuel Burd deceased, shall then enjoy it in whole or in part as his own forever.   NATHANIEL BURD, LS.

Witness: *John Hooker,*
  Ephraim Smith.

Court Record, Page 51—12 January, 1703-4. Will proven.

Page 171-2.

Burd, Thomas, Farmington. Invt. £66-08-01. Taken 28 February, 1706-7, by John Judd, Sen., Joseph Hawley and Joseph Bird.

The last will of Thomas Burd: the Sun of Joseph Bird desesed, was writen at ffarmingtown on the 25 daye of desember: the year 1706, and is declard In the Lins folowing: First, my will is that all my just debts shall be payd out of my estate; and then I giue and bequeue: to Samuell bird, my Brother Samuell's Sun; and to wiliam Smith, my sister Mary's Sun: and unto Joseph Bird, my Brother Joseph bird's Sun: and to ebenezer Smith, my sister mary Smith's second Sun: to each of them twentey shillings out of my estat. And ffor the rest of my estat that shall then remain, I giue and beqeue to my louing mother tow-thurds of it, and the other third part I giue to my sister, mindwell bird: Firther, my desier is that if my mother or Sister mindwell doe sell the land that I haue giuen them in the medow: that then my Brother Joseph Bird, or aney other next of kind, maye haue it, hee or thaye giuing as much for it as others will. Farther, my desier is that my louing mother shall be executor to my estat: That the a boue writen Is my Last will and testment, is witnest by my hand.

Witness to the a boue writen,   THO. X BIRD.
being present at the time of signing:
Thomas bird of iams,
Thomas Orton.

Court Record, Page 91—7 March, 1706-7. Will proven.

Page 146.

Burge, Joseph, Windsor. Invt. £8-05-03. Taken 11 January, 1705-6, by Samuel Wolcott, Job Drake, Sen., and Eleazer Gaylord.

Court Record, Page 78—8 March, 1705-6: Adms. granted to John Burge, he refusing to accept the letters of Adms.

Page 83—5 April, 1706: Adms. now granted to Daniel Bissell, he also refusing.

Inventory on File.

Cakebread, Isaac, Hartford, Invt. £   Taken 22 December, 1709, by Ebenezer Hopkins and Thomas Seamore.

Court Record, Page 137—5 December, 1709: Adms. granted unto Daniel Merrells (tanner) of Hartford, after letters had been offered to Edward Smith of Suffield, brother-in-law, and he refusing.

Page 13 (Vol. VIII) 5 June, 1710: Daniel Merrells, Adms., exhibited an invt. Accepted.

Page 122—1st February, 1712-13: The Adms. having rendered an account of his Adms., now moves for a dist: Whereupon the estate is ordered to be dist. to Margaret Cakebread and Hepzibah Smith (formerly Cakebread), the two sisters of the deceased. And appoint Samuel Howard, Nathaniel Stanly and Caleb Bull, distributors.

Page 169—4 January, 1713-14: Report of the distributors.

Page 83-4-5-6-7-8-9.

Case, John, Sen., Simsbury. Invt. £562-05-01. Taken 2 March, 1703-4, by John Slater, Sen., James Cornish and Andrew Robe. The legatees: Elizabeth the relict, John the eldest son, Samuel, William his children, Richard, Bartholomew, Joseph, Elizabeth, Mary, Sarah and Abigail Case. Will dated 21 November, 1700.

The last will and testament of John Case, Sen., late of Simsbury, decd.: I give to my wife Elizabeth Case £5 annually during life, which was engaged before marriage. I give to my son John Case land I bought of Mr. Samuel Stone in Simsbury, also £5. I give to my son William Case land I bought of Thomas Hart in Farmington, joining lands of the heirs of Capt. Marshall, and land in Weataug I bought of John Clark. I give to my son Samuel 5 acres of land given me by the inhabitants of Simsbury at Weataug, adjacent to Benajah Holcomb's houselott; also I give him my whole share in the two mills, viz., corn mill and saw mill, standing on Hop Brook in Simsbury; my share in the mill lott and the lott in Hazell Meadow I bought of John Humphries; also the land in Hazell Meadow I bought of Joseph Skinner. I give to my son Richard Case that allotment being situate in Weataug Meadow which I bought of Eliakim Marshall, and the houselott at Weataug which I bought of John Clark. I do give to my son Bartholomew Case my proper allotment given me in Hazell Meadow and at the Common Land lying on the west side of the river, and 12 acres adjacent to it, and 1-2 of the new barn, and 5 acres of land on the Plaine against Sergt. Wilcockson's houselott. I give unto my son Joseph Case, by deed of gift, in consideration of his living with me during my lifetime and managing my whole affairs and business of husbandry according to my ordering and discretion, my now dwelling house in Simsbury and the whole of my houselott, bounded east by the river, north by John Pettebone's houselott, west by the highway and south by Benajah Holcomb's lott, with the barn, fences, orchards, and all edifices directed and built thereon. I give to my daughter Elizabeth Tuller £10 more besides what she hath already received. To my daughter Mary £15, also 12 acres of land lying in Simsbury. To my daughter Sarah Case, alias Phelps, £20. To my daughter Abigail Case £30. And although William be dead, yet an equal share shall appertain to his estate to be distributed to his children. Moreover, if there be not estate enough left of the moveables at the time of my death to discharge the several legacies herein held and contained, after my other debts be paid, as these legacies (John £5, Elizabeth

£10, Mary £15, Sarah £20, Abigail £30, Joseph £2, total £82), then it is my will that my sons herein named, or their heirs, do make good to each legatee herein mentioned their several sums by an equal dist. of each person excepting Joseph, who shall pay double to the rest of his brethren, whose names are William, Samuel, Richard, Bartholomew and Joseph Case. I appoint my brother Samuel Spencer of Hartford and my son John Case of Simsbury to be Adms.

Witness: *John Slater, Clerk,*   JOHN x CASE, SEN., LS.
    William Gillett, Elias Slater.

An addition to the before going will, dated 12th February, 1703-4: On that certain day received at the will and pleasure of John Case, Senior, who thus explained himself in reference of that small estate which it pleased God to give him in his lifetime: Therefore do now explain myself as to my will and pleasure: That my homestead should be divided, and one half at my pleasure disposed to that son that shall live with me, with the messuages, and the other half to be disposed between my three sons, Samuel, Richard and Bartholomew; only that son that lives with me to have the half reserved, northward part; and that my wive's dowry, viz., five pounds annually during her life, shall be paid out of said homestead. And that my son Joseph Case, seeing he has declined his due respects and service from me in this time of distress and sickness contrary to my expectation and agreement, yet, notwithstanding, I do give him my Nodd meadow lott with the upland adjacent, granted me by the inhabitants of Simsbury, as appears upon record; as also I give unto him the half of the land on the plain, by Doctor Jacob Read's, given me by Simsbury inhabitants, half of that said lott from sd. Read's lott to my old lott or former grant. I give him said Joseph the one-half of this my last grant. This being in consideration of his whole proportion on all account and portion. As also I give unto my daughters my moveables after my debts are paid. As also I give to my son William Case's children that estate in land that I gave to my son William. And unto my son John Case, as the sole and full of his portion, that land he now stands possessed of, with the addition of pay as is expressed in my will. And be it further known, that whatsoever estate I have disposed of by former wills or by these presents, that none of these my children shall be put in possession or have right to till after my death, only reserving this liberty to myself to order and dispose of the one-half of my homested as in this case of my necessity I see occasion. There being one thing slipped memory, but we underwritten do testify that this is fully expressed by the sd. John Case, Sen., who did express that the sd. portion given out of my own estate to my daughter Mary shall be and appertain to her children. Witness my hand:

Witness, *John Slater, Sen.,*   JOHN X CASE, SEN.
    James Cornish.

Court Record, Page 53—9 March, 1703-4: Will exhibited by Mr. Samuel Spencer and John Case. Proven and ordered to be recorded.

Page 67 (Vol. IX) 4 June, 1718: Upon the motion of the heirs of John Case, Sen., of Simsbury, decd., for a dist. to be made of the remaining part of the estate, this Court appoint John Humphries, Samuel Pettebone and John Sexton, of Simsbury, to dist. that part of the estate of the sd. John Case, decd., not yet dist., according to the direction given in the last will and testament.

File: Now, whereas, the heirs of John Case of Simsbury, deceased, did, 9th June 1718, obtain an order from this Court of Probates for a distribution of the remaining part of the estate of sd. decd.: Therefore we, the subscribers hereunto, being appointed, have made this following distribution: Imprimis: Set out to John Case, Samuell Case, Marcy Hely and Abegall Westover, the marsh under the west mountains, they having agreed to take that for their parts of the sd. estate, and to be equally divided amongst them. 2ly. Set out to Richard Case, son to the deceased, one-third part of that lot that lies on Calve's Tongue Brook. 3ly. Set out to Barthelme Case, son to the deceased, one-third part of that lot that lies on Calve's Tonge Brook. 4th. Set out to Joseph Case and the heirs of Sarah Case that lot at the West River, up the river, on the northwesterly side of Majr. Talcott's land. 5ly. Set out to the heirs of Elizabeth Tuller the other lot at the West River. 6th. Set out to the heirs of William Case, who was son to sd. deceased, one-third part of that lot at Calve's Tongue Brook.

28 November, 1718.

> JOHN HUMPHRIES,
> SAMLL PETTEBONE,
> JOHN SAXTON.

4 May, 1719: Accepted in Court. *Test: Hez: Wyllys, Clerk.*

Page 24-5.

Case, William, Simsbury. Died 31 March, 1700. Invt. £276-09-08. Taken 29 May, 1700, by Samuel Humphrey, John Case, Jr., John Slater, Sen., and Thomas Holcomb. The children: William, born 22 March, 1690-1; James, 12 March, 1692-3; Joshua, 1st June, 1698; Elizabeth, September, 1689; Rachel, 10 December, 1694; Mary, 23 August, 1696; and Mindwell, 21 March, 1700,

Court Record, Page 11—8 April, 1701: Elizabeth, the relict, exhibited an invt., and this Court grant Adms. to the widow, with John Case, a brother of the decd.

Page 94 (Vol. VIII) 3 November, 1712: This Court appoints John Slater of Simsbury to be guardian to James Case, Richard Case, Mary Case and Joshua Case, children of William Case decd., they all being minors above 14 years of age.

Page 120—3 March, 1712-13: This Court allows John Slater, Jr., of Simsbury, to be guardian to Mindwell Case, a minor 13 years of age, daughter of William Case, late of Simsbury, decd. John Slater now appeared with a report, as well as the sd. Mindwell, as also James, Rachell, Mary and Joshua Case, all minors above 14 years of age. John Slater now exhibits an account of his Adms. in right of his wife Elizabeth, formerly Elizabeth Case, widow, relict of the sd. William Case, late decd. Order to dist. the estate:

	£ s d
Inventory,	280-06-05
The moveable part,	89-16-05
Paid in debts and charges,	34-14-05
There remains of moveable estate to be dist.,	55-02-00
To which add the real part,	247-02-00

Which accot. this Court allow and order dist. as followeth:

To the widow,	18-17-04
To William Case, eldest son,	57-03-08
To James, Joshua, Elizabeth, Rachel, Mary and Mindwell, to each,	28-11-10

And appoint Joseph Case, Jonas Westover and Nathaniel Holcomb, Jr., of Simsbury, distributors. And grant to John Slater and Elizabeth, his wife, Adms., a *Quietus Est.*

Page 134-5.

Cheeny, William, Middletown. Invt. £259-03-06. Taken 12 November, 1705, by John Collins, Joseph Rockwell and William Harris. Will dated 17 September, 1704.

I William Cheeny, of Middletown, do make this my last will and testament: I give to my kinsman, Benjamin Hand, of Middletown, 80 acres of land out of my lot in the second part of the first division of land in Middletown, to be laid out to him 20 rods in breadth the whole length of the said lot, the eastern side of which will then butt east on a highway betwixt that and the Lucas lot, and north on the Commons, west on the remainder of the lot, and south on the extremity of Middletown bounds, which land shall be the property of the said Benjamin Hand and his heirs forever. My will is that if Cheeny Clark (the son of John Clark decd., my son-in-law) shall live to be of the age of 21 years, he should have his choice, either to take that allotment of mine which lyeth betwixt Benjamin Hand's home lot and Samuel Cornwall's or else to take my wood lot (about 30 acres of land) abutting on Mr. John Hamlin's lot south, and on the highway or Common land east, west and north, being half a mile long. Also the said Cheeny Clark shall have the one-half of what remains of my second part of the first division lot after Benjamin Hand's part is laid out, and the one-half of my long lott on the east side of the Great River. The whole lot consists of about 327 acres. Those above expressed to be the property of the sd. Cheeny Clark forever. Also Ambrose Clark, son of sd.

John Clark decd., shall have the other half of the land or lots set out to Cheeny Clark, his brother. Item. It is my will that all my personal estate and moveables whatsoever, as money, goods, debts, merchandise, household goods, cattle, grain and utensils, or other estate whatsoever not herein disposed of, shall be equally shared amongst the three children of the sd. John Clark, decd., being the two sons above named and one daughter named Eunice, and each respective share to be carefully improved and secured for their benefit as my sd. after-named executors shall jointly find to be most feasible, until the sd. children be of age to choose guardians according to law. If all these three children die before they come of age, their portions to become the property of the Church of Middletown, to be improved and laid out upon sacrament utensils. I appoint my son-in-law John Williams and my daughter-in-law Abigail, his wife, to be joint executors, and request John Hamlin, Esq., and Joseph Rockwell to be overseers.

Witness: *Nathaniel Brown,*   WILLIAM CHEENY, LS.
Nathaniel Brown, Jr., Alexander Rollo.

Court Record, Page 73—6 Desember, 1705-6: Will proven.

Page 26 (Vol. IX) 5 February, 1716-17: John Williams, executor, exhibited now in this Court an account of debts, which account is accepted. Order the estate to be distributed to Cheeny Clark, to Ambrose Clark and to Eunice Clark, to each of them the sum of £17-19-08. And appoint Lt. Joseph Rockwell, Israhiah Wetmore and John Bacon, distributors.

Page 44—5 November, 1717: Cheeny Clark, a minor 19 years of age, son of John Clarke, late decd., chose Capt. Joseph Rockwell of Middletown to be his guardian.

Page 127-8.

Chester, Stephen, Wethersfield. Invt. £200-15-06. Taken May, 1705, by Thomas Wickham, Sen., and Samuel Butler.

Court Record, Page 70—6 September, 1705: Adms. granted to John Chester, a nephew.

Page 92—20 March, 1706-7: Major John Chester, Adms., exhibited now an account of his Adms. on the estate of the decd. This Court order that the remaining part of the estate of the sd. Stephen Chester, decd., consisting of some lands, a warehouse and some movables, shall be distributed and divided into three equal parts, whereof one part shall be for the children that are now living of Capt. John Chester, late of Wethersfield, who was brother of the said Stephen Chester, decd. And one other part to and for Mr. Samuel Whiting, of Billirica, and Dorcas, his wife, one of the sisters of the sd. Stephen Chester, deceased. And the residue or one other part to and for the children that are now living of Capt. Thomas Russell, late of Charlstown, decd., who married one of the sisters of the sd. Stephen Chester, decd. And this Court do order, appoint and impower John Curtis, Jr., Benjamin Gilbert and

Jonathan Belden, of Wethersfield aforesd., to dist. the same accordingly.

Page 93—24 May, 1707: This Court again considering the order made the 20th of March last past, for the dist. of the estate of Stephen Chester, decd., do now further order that the distributors then appointed do subdivide and distribute that third part of the sd. estate appointed for the children of Capt. John Chester, decd., as follows, viz: To Major John Chester, the eldest son, a double part or portion; and to the other children single portions of the same. And that also they do subdivide and distribute that third part of the sd. estate appointed for the children that are now living of Capt. Thomas Russell, decd., as follows, viz: To Thomas Russell, his son, a double portion; and to Prudence Russell, his daughter, a single portion thereof.

Clark, George, Milford. This will of George Clark was not discovered by me until too late for insertion in the proper place and under the proper date in Volume I of this Digest.   C. W. M.

Superior Court Records, Vol. No. 4, 1724 to 1728. In the custody of the Secretary of State.

The will of George Clark of Milford, dated 15 April, 1678, and 18 August, 1688: I, George Clark, one of ye Deacons of ye Church of Christ, at Milford, in the County of New Haven and Colony of Connecticut, planter, do make this to be my last will and testament:

I give unto my wife, Sarah Clark, my dwelling house and homestead, with all ye outhouses, buildings, edifices and appurtenances thereunto belonging, as allso ye one-half part or moiety of all my arable land and pasture and meadow in my present possession, for her own proper use, benefit and behoof, during her natural life.

I give unto my son George Clark ye reversion of ye sd. moiety of my sd. house and homestead, arable land, meadow and premises, after ye decease of my sd. wife, as also ye other moiety and half part of my sd. house, homestead, outhouses, buildings, edifices and appurtenances, lands, pasture, meadow and premises, to him and his heirs forever.

I give to my son Samuel Clark ye westward half part of my sd. pasture (excepted as above).

And my will and true meaning is that my son George Clark shall have ye eastward half part and moiety of my sd. pasture above mentioned, after my decease.

Whereas, I have already given portions in land and other estate unto my sons Thomas Clark and Samuel Clark, and also a portion unto my daughter Sarah Laws, yet out of my fatherly affection to my sd. children I give to each of them ten pounds. I give to my son George Clark ye like sum of ten pounds.

I give to my grandchild George Clark, ye son of my son Thomas Clark, all my two parcels of unfenced land known by the name of

Mowhawk Swamp, and ye other parcel lying right against my other land to ye Ferry Ward.

I give to my son Thomas Clark for ye use of his son George Clark, twenty pounds to buy books for him if he prove capable of learning and his father bring him up at the College, or to help to maintain him there.

As a token of my love I give to ye rest of my grandchildren, vizt., to Samuel, Thomas, John, Joseph and Sarah Clark, ye children of my son Thomas, five pounds apiece. To Mary, ye daughter of my son Samuel Clark, five pounds. And to Jonathan Laws, son of my daughter Sarah, five pounds.

I give to my son Thomas Clark ye long table in ye hall, after my wife's decease.

I give two of my negroes, a man and a woman, to my son George Clark, which he shall chuse; to my son Thomas Clark, one negro; and another negro to my daughter Sarah; that is, I give them as above (if living) after my wife's decease.

I give ye time I have in my apprentice, Samuel Phillips, to my son Samuel Clark, likewise after my wife's decease.

My mind and will is that my copper furnace, ye table in ye chamber over ye kitchen, and ye form and seats belonging to it, and ye bedstead, bed and furniture of it in ye parlour, shall be and remain as standards belonging to ye house, as also ye cupboard in ye hall, so to be and remain standards in ye house as above.

I do nominate, constitute and appoint my dear and loving wife, Sarah Clark, my sole and only executrix, and to request and desire my loving and honoured friends, Elder Buckingham and Deacon Richard Platt, to be my overseers.

The testator did request, desire and appoint ye Hon. Deputy Governor Major Treat to be one of his overseers.

Witness: *Wm. Jones, Senr.,*   GEORGE CLARK, LS.
          Wm. Jones, Junior.

Further, my will is that besides ye gift of a negro to my daughter Sarah Law, I do give unto my 2d. daughter Sarah Law my negro boy named Ishmail, desiring her to bring him up to reading, and to set him at liberty when he comes to the age of thirty-two years, or, if she please, a little sooner. And if her son Jonathan Law should marry and need him more than she, I do give her liberty to dispose of him to ye sd. Jonathan.

Witness: *Samuel Eells,*   GEORGE CLARK, LS.
          Timothy Baldwin.

18 August, 1688.

This will was recorded here, 27 December, 1737.

                              D. Edwards, Clerk.

Page 90-91.

Clarke, Thomas, Hartford (Tanner). Invt. £234-14-00. Taken 10 December, 1703. (Apprisers' names not given.)

Court Record, Page 54—27 April, 1704: Adms. to Elizabeth, the relict, with Jonathan Burr, Rec., £100.

Page 65—6 March, 1704-5: Adms. account rendered, accepted and order to dist.: To the widow, to the son, and to the daughter. And this Court appoint Thomas Burr, Sen., Ebenezer Hopkins and Daniel Clarke, joiner, of Hartford, distributors.

Page 120 (Vol. VIII) 3 March, 1712-13: This Court appoint Daniel Clark and Samuel Wells, Jr., to be guardians to Joseph Clark and Anne Clark, son and daughter of Thomas Clark, late of Hartford, tanner, decd.

Page 132—7 April, 1713: Daniel Clark and Samuel Wells, Jr., guardians to Joseph Clark and Anne Clark, children of Thomas Clark, decd., moved this Court to have the children's estate put into their hands. The Court refuse.

Inventory on File.

Clarke, William, Wethersfield. Invt. £28-05-05. Taken 27 November, 1708, by William Burnham and George Kilbourn.

Court Record, Page 116—13 September, 1708: Margaret Clark, widow of the deceased, not having taken letters of Adms. on sd. estate, this Court now grant letters unto Jonathan Colefax, of Wethersfield, one of the creditors of the estate.

Page 120—6 December, 1708: Jonathan Colefax, Adms., made complaint to this Court, before John Chester, Esq., Assistant, against Peter Blinn and Margaret Clarke, widow, that they have sundry goods in custody and refuse to deliver the same to the Adms.

Page 190-1.

Coale, Nathaniel, Sen., Hartford. He died 20 April, 1708. Invt. £572-09-08. Taken 3 June, 1708, by Cyprian Nickcolls, Sen., Hezekiah Willis and Thomas Hosmer. Will dated 17 April, 1708:

I, Nathaniel Coale, of Hartford, do make this my last will and testament: I give and bequeath to my wife Mary Coale one-third part of all my moveable estate forever (my sd. wife to let Ebenezer Benton have a bed out of it), and also one-third part of all my real estate to improve during her natural life (only my said wife is to pay one-third part of the purchase money for that land I bought of Ichabod Coale). Also, I give my said wife the improvement of the south end of my house, to live in, and one-third of the barn, during the time she shall remain a widow. Item. I give to my son Nathaniel Coale all the rest of my moveable estate not given to my wife, as also all my land (except the improvement of one-third part of them given as above to my said wife). Also, my will is that Ebenezer Benton should be maintained by my wife and my son jointly so long as my wife shall remain a widow; but if she should marry, that then my son Nathaniel Coale shall take care to maintain him during his natural life if my son Nathaniel should live to survive him; and that my said son shall have what estate was given to maintain the said Ebenezer Benton, not yet disposed of, for his maintainance. And I do make and constitute my son Nathaniel sole executor of this my last will and testament.

Witness: *Hezekiah Willis,*   NATHANIEL COALE, SEN, LS.
          Jonathan Webster.

Court Record, Page 112—7 June, 1708: Adms. to Nathaniel Coale, with will annexed. Will proven.

Page 114—5 July, 1708: Invt. exhibited.

Page 12 (Vol. VIII) 1st May, 1710: This Court order and appoint Lt. James Steele, Samuel Kellogg and Thomas Seamore, of Hartford, to dist. the houseing and lands late belonging to Nathaniel Coale, Sen., of Hartford, decd., between the relict and the son of the sd. decd., according to the intent of his last will, viz: To the relict (now wife of Jonathan Bigelow, Sen.), so much of the sd. lands (the homelott excepted) as is the full 1-3 part of the whole with the homelott, without any allowance for the houseing and buildings; and to Nathaniel Coale, son of the sd. decd., all the houseing, barn and other buildings, and the residue or other 2-3 of the sd. lands.

Page 19.

Cockshott, Elizabeth, Widow, Haddam. Died 20 March, 1699-1700. Invt. £9-01-05. Taken 29 March, 1700, by Timothy X Spencer, Josiah X Arnold and William Scovell.

Court Record, Page 7—8 March, 1700-1: Adms. to Edward Purple.

Page 198.

Cole, John, Jr., Farmington. Invt. £266-04-07. Taken 1st September, 1708, by Daniel Andrews, Sen., and Isaac Cowles.

Court Record, Page 111—7 September, 1708: This Court grant letters of Adms. on the estate of John Coale (son of John Coale, formerly of sd. Farmingtown, decd.) jointly to Mehetabell Coale, widow, relict of the decd., and John Lee of Farmington.

Page 95 (Vol. VIII) 3 November, 1712: Mehetabell Coale and John Lee, of Farmingtown, Adms., exhibited now in this Court an account of their Adms. on that estate. Accepted. This Court order the estate dist. as followeth:

	£ s d
To the Widow Mehetabell,	14-07-11
To John Coale, eldest son,	52-09-00

To Stephen, Matthew, Sarah, Mary, Ruth and Mehetabell Coale,
　　　　to each of them, the sum of　　　　　　　　　　26-06-06
　　And appoint Joseph Wadsworth, Daniel Andrews and Timothy
Porter, distributors.

Page 118-19.

Cooke, John, Middletown. Died 16 January, 1704-5. Invt. £331-
02-03. Taken 5 March, 1704-5, by Thomas Ward, William Ward and
Joseph Johnson. The children: John and Mary, both of age; Daniel,
age 14 years; Sarah, 12, and Ebenezer, 7 years old. Will dated 15
August, 1698.

I, John Cook, of Middletown, in the County of Hartford, do
make this my last will and testament: I give unto my son John 200 acres
of land, being part of my lott in Cockingchauge. I give unto my
daughter Mary a silver spoon as her portion. I give unto my son
Daniel my house and homestead where I now live, when he comes
to age. I give unto my daughter Sarah the choice and best of my
feather beds. And for as much in probability my wife is now with
child, wherefore I give and bestow upon that child, whether male
or female, 100 acres of land, being the remainder of my lott in Cockingchauge. Lastly, I do give unto my wife Hannah the use and improvement of the house and homelott, and all the appurtenances, till my
son Daniel come to age, and after, if she bears my name. I appoint
my wife to be my executrix.
Witness: *Daniel Harris,*　　　　　　　　　　JOHN COOKE, LS.
　　　Alexander Rollo.

Part of the inventory is as followeth:

	£ s d
His stock and cattle and 6 swine,	22-00-00
382 acres of wilderness land lying in the westernmost range of lots,	100-00-00
60 acres of land that his father Harris gave him out of his farm,	30-00-00
His dwelling house, homelot and barn,	80-00-00

Page 23-24.

Cook, Nathaniel, Windsor. He died 19 May, 1688. Invt. (real
estate) £111-05-00. Taken by Jeremiah Alford and Cornelius Gillett, Jr.

It is mutually and jointly agreed by and between Nathaniel Cook,
John Cook, Josiah Cook, Samuel Baker, in behalf of his wife Sarah
and Joseph Baker, all of Windsor, and Daniel Hoit of Deerfield, in
the County of Hampshire, in behalf of his wife Abigail, all of them
children and of the family of Nathaniel Cook, late of Windsor, decd.,

to promote an amicable accord in dividing the inheritance of said Nathaniel Cook, decd., that the three sons of the deceased, viz., Nathaniel, John and Josiah Cook, shall have, hold and enjoy all the lands of their deceased father, to themselves, their heirs and assigns, as they shall agree among themselves for the dividing of said lands, to each one his proportion. And that by them there shall be paid to the said Samuel Baker, David Hoite and Joseph Baker, to each of them £5 in current money of New England. In confirmation of this agreement the parties herein named have hereunto subscribed their names and affixed their seals, 2 December, 1700.

> DAVID HOIT, LS.
> NATHANIEL COOK, LS.
> JOHN X COOK, LS.
> JOSIAH COOK, LS.
> JOSEPH BAKER, LS.
> SAMUEL BAKER, LS.

Signed and sealed in the presence of us: *John Richards, Thomas French, Daniel Clark, Moses Clark, Samuel Grant, Jr., Joseph Skinner, Jr.*

(This agreement was appended to the inventory.)

The testimony of Cornelius Gillett, Senior, of Windsor, of lawful age, saith that some years ago Lydia, the relict of Nathaniel Cook, who died 14 June, 1698, late of Windsor, desired myself and my wife to be witnesses of her mind and will respecting her dispose of a piece of land that Richard Vore, father to said Lydia, bequeathed to her in his last will. Her expressed will was that after her death her son Josiah should have and enjoy said piece of land lying in Windsor, commonly called by the name of Vore's Point.

Priscilla, the wife of said Cornelius Gillett, testifieth to what is above written.

Cornelius Gillett and Priscilla, his wife, personally appeared this 14th of November, 1700, and gave their respective oaths to the testimony above written. Before me, *Daniel Clark, Justice.*

NATHANIEL COOK, this 14th December, 1700, declares his approbation of what is above testified respecting his mother's dispose of the land mentioned. As witness his hand.

JOHN COOK, January 14th, 1700-1, declares his approbation of his mother's will as above expressed. As witness his mark.

> NATHANIEL COOK,
> JOHN X COOK.
>   *Attest:*   *Daniel Clark, Justice.*

Nathaniel Cooke and Lydia Voar were married 29 June, 1649.

Daughter	Sarah	was born		28 June,	1650
	Lydia	"	"	9 February,	1652
	Hannah	"	"	21 September,	——
Son	Nathaniel	"	"	13 May,	1658
	Abigail	"	"	1 March,	1659-60

Son   John   was born   3 August,   1662
         Josiah   "   "   22 December,   1664
    Lydia Cooke, a daughter, died 23 May, 1676, in the 24 year of
her age.   (W. R.)

Page 192.

Cornwall, Jacob, Sen., Mariner, Middletown. Died 18 April, 1708.
Invt. £406-14-08. Taken 11 May, 1708, by John Bacon and Joseph
Rockwell. The children: Jacob, Nathaniel, Daniel, Isaac, Waite,
Timothy, Mary and Elizabeth.
    Court Record, Page 112—7 June, 1708: Letters of Adms. on the
estate of Jacob Cornwall, mariner, deceased, to Mary Cornwall, widow,
relict of the sd. decd.
    Page 114—5 July, 1708: Invt. exhibited.
    Page 118—6 December, 1708:   Order dist. of the estate, and
appoint John Hamlin, Nathaniel White and Mr. Alexander Rollo, dist.
Isaac and Waite Cornwall chose their mother to be their guardian, and
she was allowed to be guardian to Timothy and Elizabeth Cornwall.
    Dist. on File mentions all the above-named legatees as in the inven-
tory.

Page 182-3-4.

Cornwall, John, Sen.,   Middletown. Invt. £317-17-00. Taken 26
December, 1707, by Samuel Doolittle and Zacheus Cande. Will dated
17 September, 1707:
    I, John Cornwell, Sen., of Middletown, being infirm and weak, do
therefore make this my last will and testament: I will that my wife
Martha shall have the use, benefit and improvement of all my homelott
whereon my dwelling house stands (excepting what is in this will given
to my son William), together with the eastward end or rooms, both
higher and lower, of my dwelling house, with the barn and orchard and
all the clear meadow that lies in my lot at Goose's Delight, half the
breadth of my Boggy Meadow lot, called Ko-Lot, next the river. Also,
I leave unto her all the moveables, within doors and without; all which
land and moveables may be improved by her for her comfort and subsistence so long as she remains a widow. I give unto my eldest son
John Cornwall 1-3 part of my Proper Lott in the Boggy Meadow Quarter, reckoning that I have given 1-3 part thereof to my son-in-law Samuel
Doolittle, and part of the other third is given to Joseph. Also I give
unto my sd. son John half the breadth of my Ko-Lott next the upland,
and at his mother's death or marriage the whole Ko-Lott unto John;
also ½ of my lands or rights on the east side of the Great River, and
the other half to Joseph and Benjamin, my sons. I give to my son William Cornwall the west end or rooms, both higher and lower, of my

now dwelling house, with the yard that lies to the west and north, and what fruit trees are therein, and the garden plott. And the other half of my homelott, next my Brother Jacob's, I give to my daughters, Martha, Hannah and Thankfull, equally. I give unto my son Paul the westward end of that lott of land that lieth beyond my brother Samuel's houselott, where now Paul's house stands, unto the middle row of apple-trees in the orchard there. Also, I give unto Paul ½ of my lott in the westernmost range of lotts; the other half of that lott I give unto my daughters, Martha, Hannah and Thankful. It is my will that my son-in-law, Richard Hubbard, shall have one acre of it, to be laid out from the highway to his boggy meadow, on that side next Mr. Southmayd, and the remainder to be equally divided betwixt Paul, Joseph and Benjamin, so that their bredths be equal without respect to the length of either. It is my will that what moveables shall be extant of household goods shall be equally shared amongst my four daughters. My will is that my wife Martha shall be sole executrix. I desire Mr. John Hamlin and Mr. Noadiah Russell to be overseers.

Witness: *Thomas Stevens,*   JOHN CORNWALL, LS.
John Lane, Alexander Rollo.

Court Record, Page 101—5 January, 1707-8: Will approved.

Page 107—4 March, 1707-8: The widow Martha Cornwall, now deceased, this Court grant letters of Adms. to John Cornwall, son of John Cornwall, late of Middletown, deceased, with the will annexed.

Page 147.

Cornwall, Jonathan, Middletown. Invt. £121-09-06. Taken 14 February, 1705-6, by John Cornwall and Samuel Cornwall.

Court Record, Page 78—8 March, 1705-6: Invt. exhibited by Capt. John Hall, Adms. on the estate of Thomas Cornwall, "in place of Jonathan Cornwall, who was Adms. to his father's estate until his decease, then Capt. John Hall was appointed Adms., and presents an inventory of both estates together."

Page 52-147.

Cornwall, Thomas, Middletown. Died November, 1702. Invt. £185-13-06. Taken 22 December, 1702, by John Hall and John Cornwall.

Court Record, Page 39—2 March, 1702-3. Adms. to Jonathan Cornwall, eldest son, John Cornwall surety, and to be overseer to the estate and children.

Page 53—9 March, 1703-4: Jonathan Cornwall presented an account of his Adms. so far as he hath proceeded:

	£ s d
Paid in debts and charges,	58-10-05
Yet unpaid,	21-12-04
Sundry things abated out of the inventory,	10-07-00

And for as much as the personal estate will extend no further, the Court accept the account and order it to be filed.

Page 69—14 August, 1705: Whereas, Jonathan Cornwall, who was Adms. on the estate of his father, Thomas Cornwall, died intestate and none of his relations appear to take Adms., this Court do therefore order the Clerk to signify to the relations of sd. Jonathan, decd., that in case none of them shall appear before this Court in September next for that purpose, that then letters of Adms. shall be granted to the creditors, or one of them.

Page 72—21 November, 1705: This Court grant letters of Adms. on the estate of Thomas Cornwall unto Capt. John Hall of Middletown, the former Adms., Jonathan Cornwall, the son, being dead.

Page 73—21 November, 1705: This Court appoint John Hall, of Middletown, to be guardian unto David Cornwall, a minor son of Thomas Cornwall, late of Middletown, deceased.

Page 78—8 March, 1705-6: Capt. John Hall of Middletown, Adms. on the estate of Thomas Cornwall, decd., presented to this Court a new or second invt. of the sd. estate now remaining, and also of the estate of Jonathan Cornwall, son of the sd. Thomas and late Adms. on his estate, upon oath made thereunto by Abraham Cornwall, son of the sd. Thomas, which inventory this Court orders to be recorded and put upon file.

Page 129 (Vol. VIII) 3 December, 1713: Daniel Hall, of Middletown, executor of the last will of John Hall, Sen., exhibited now in this Court an account of his Adms. on the estate of Thomas Cornwall, which this Court allows and orders put upon file.

Page 247—4 April, 1715: David Cornwall, a minor, 16 years of age, made choice of Joseph Rockwell to be his guardian. Recog., £20.

Page 4 (Vol. X) 16 January, 1722-3: Daniel Hall, executor, exhibits now an account of his Adms. on the estate of Thomas and Jonathan Cornwall, John Hall, the former Adms., being deceased and not having finished his Adms. before his decease. Account allowed. Order to dist. to the children and heirs of sd. Thomas and to the brother and sisters of sd. Jonathan Cornwall, viz., to David Cornwall, Sarah Benton, Ann Penfield, Silence Cornwall, and to the heirs of Stephen Cornwall, decd. And appoint Daniel Hall, John Gains and Comfort Davis, distributors. This Court appoint Capt. Giles Hall of Middletown to be guardian to the children of Stephen Cornwall, formerly of Middletown, late decd. at Antigua. Also to take care of the estate at Middletown, which is to be distributed to them, and render an account thereof. Recog., £20.

Dist. per File, of the estate of Thomas and Jonathan Cornwall, 1727: To David Cornwall, to Sarah Benton, to Ann Penfield, to Silence Boardman, and to Stephen Cornwall.

Page 115.

Cornwall, William, Middletown. Died 25 December, 1704. Invt. £100-12-09. Taken 12 January, 1704-5, by Samuel Cornwall, William Ward and Daniel Harris. Two children: Jemima, about 5 years old, and Lois, about 3 years old.

Court Record, Page 63—6 March, 1704-5: Adms. to the relict, Mrs. Hester Cornwall. Rec., £100.

Page 173-4.

Inventory in Vol. IX, Page 355.

Crane, Israel, Wethersfield. Died 28 April, 1707. Invt. £287-12-00. Taken 29 May, 1707, by John Russell and Ebenezer Belden. Inventory £444-18-10. Taken 1719-20, by Joshua Robbins and Joseph Belding. The children: Lydia, age 5 years, 4 August, 1706; Hannah, 4—24 November, 1706; Elizabeth, 2—23 September, 1706; and Martha, 1 year, 18 March, 1706-7.

Court Record, Page 94—2 June, 1707: Adms. granted to Lydia Crane, the relict.

Page 114—5 July, 1708: This Court, pursuant to an order of the General Assembly of this Colony, made 13 May, 1708, direct and order Lydia Crane, Adms., to sell so much of the land as may produce the sum of £11, for payment of debts.

Page 137 (Vol. VIII) 4 May, 1713: This Court appoint Jonathan Belding of Wethersfield to be guardian to Lydia Crane, Hannah, Elizabeth and Martha Crane, children of sd. decd. Recog., £200.

Page 116 (Vol. IX) 5 January, 1719-20: Whereas, Adms. was formerly granted on the estate of Israel Crane, the sd. estate remains unsettled, no account of Adms. rendered. The administratrix being incapable to manage, this Court grant letters of Adms. unto Lt. Jonathan Belding of Wethersfield.

Page 119—9th February, 1719-20: Lydia Crane and Jonathan Belding, Adms., exhibit an account of their Adms.:

	£	s	d
Have paid in debts and charges,	7-00-00		
The inventory amounted to,	444-19-06		
The moveable part was	42-09-06		
Subtracting the sum of	7-00-00		
There remains for distribution,	437-19-06		

Order to distribute the estate as followeth:

To Lydia Crane, widow, her dower and 11-16-06
To Lydia, Hannah, Elizabeth and Martha Crane, daughters of
the sd. decd., to each of them the sum of 106-10-09

And appoint David Goodrich, Joshua Robbins, 2nd, and Thomas Wright, distributors.

Page 52 (Vol. XI) 17 August, 1731: Martha Crane, one of the daughters of Israel Crane, late of Wethersfield, showing to this Court that in the dist. of her father's estate returned into the Court of Probate in the year of 1719-20, there being only four daughters, each one having distributed to them £7-10-00 right in the dwelling house of her father, deceased, the widow having her third part in whole, yet the distributors did not declare nor ascertain in their return the parts of sd. house in severallty to sd. daughters, which remains still to be done, and the sd. Martha having her right not only through her own share, but also hath bought of her sister Elizabeth Crane her part or right in sd. house, and so hath just and good right to ½ of sd. house, and moved to this Court that some meet persons may be appointed to set out to her in severallty ½ part of sd. house for her use and improvement, including ½ of her mother's thirds: Whereupon this Court do appoint Nathaniel Burnham, Deacon Jonathan Belding and Ensign Joshua Robbins of Wethersfield to set out to sd. Martha Crane ½ part of the dwelling house of sd. Crane, decd., including the widow's thirds, and make return of their doing thereon unto sd. Court of Probates.

Page 179-180.

Crane, Joseph, Wethersfield. Invt. £223-00-06. Taken 22 December, 1707, by William Goodrich and Charles Deming.

Court Record, Page 100—5 January, 1707-8: Adms. granted to Sarah Crane, the widow.

Page 137—5 December, 1709: This Court direct Sarah Crane, widow, Adms., to sell so much of the lands of the sd. estate for the payment of his debts, unto the best bidders that shall appear to buy the same, as shall produce the sum of £40 in money.

Page 27 (Vol. VIII) 5 February, 1710-11: Adms. granted further time to finish her Adms.

Page 122—17 March, 1712-13: Whereas, Abraham Kilbourn of Wethersfield, who was appointed guardian to Benjamin Crane, a minor of 19 years, son of Joseph Crane, late of Wethersfield, decd., is now late deceased, the sd. Benjamin Crane makes choice of John Wright of Wethersfield to be his guardian. Recog., £100.

Page 191—16 April, 1714: Benjamin Crane, son of Joseph Crane, made choice of Abraham Morrison of Wethersfield to be his guardian. Recog., £100.

Page 202—7 June, 1714: Sarah Leonard, Adms. on the estate of Joseph Crane, exhibited an account of her Adms.:

	£	s	d
Inventory of the estate,	233	00	06
Moveable part,	68	17	06
Paid in debts and charges,	101	11	03

Which account the Court allows, and ordered to be kept on file. Order to dist. to widow and children. And appoint Benjamin Churchill, David Goodrich and Lt. Jonathan Belding, distributors.

Page 203—8 June, 1714: Whereas, the Adms. on the estate of Joseph Crane is married and removed out of this Government, this Court doth now grant letters of Adms. unto Joseph Kilbourn of Wethersfield, who gave bonds, and the former Adms. is granted a *Quietus Est.* This Court appoint Joseph Kilbourn of Wethersfield to be guardian to Isaac Crane, age 6 years, and Esther Crane, age 12 years, children of Joseph Crane, decd. Recog., £60.

Page 233—18 January, 1714-15: This Court grant letters of Adms. on the estate of Joseph Crane (that remains yet unadministered) unto Abraham Morriss(on?) of Wethersfield, who gave bonds and took the letters.

Page 23 (Vol. IX) 2 October, 1716: It is ordered that the Clerk cite Abraham Morrison, Adms. on the estate of Joseph Crane, that he appear before this Court on Monday next at 9 o'clock in the morning.

Page 48—29 December, 1717: Upon motion made to this Court for a dist. of the estate, this Court appoint Edward Bulkeley, Capt. Ephraim Goodrich and Jonathan Smith distributors to distribute the estate: To Sarah Crane, alias Leonard, relict of the decd., 1-3 part of the real estate for the term of her natural life, and 1-3 part of the personal forever. And the remainder of the estate to be dist: To sd. Benjamin Crane a double part, and to Sarah Poole, Hannah Purple, Esther Crane and Isaac Crane, younger children, to each a single portion.

Page 60—1st April, 1718: Dist. was exhibited in Court, accepted and ordered to be kept on file.

Dist. File: 3 January, 1719: Dist. of the estate of Joseph Crane, late of Wethersfield, decd.: To the widow, relict; to Benjamin Crane, eldest son; to Isaac Crane, youngest son; to Sarah Poole, eldest daughter; to Hannah Purple; to Esther Crane, youngest daughter. By Edward Bulkeley, Ephraim Goodrich and Jonathan Smith.

The dist. of the estate of Joseph Crane: The houseing and homested not having been set out by meets and bounds, this Court order that the same be done by the former dist., Edward Bulkeley, Ephraim Goodrich and Jonathan Smith, unto the heirs of the decd., according to their proportion set in the aforesd. dist.

Page 26 (Vol. XI) 4 August, 1730: Dist. exhibited by Hezekiah Graham.

Page 28—6 October, 1736: On the 7th of September, 1730, Hezekiah Graham of Wethersfield was summoned to appear to return the order of dist. which he had for setting out the widow's dower on Joseph Crane's estate, and show cause why the whole of Esther Butler's part of the lott at Tappin's Hill was set out to the widow, and why this dist. should not be set aside and a new one ordered. And Joseph and James Righley, persons interested in the estate of Joseph Crane, appeared and moved the dist. be set aside. Capt. Bulkeley and Capt. Goodrich decline having anything more to do in the affair. This Court appoint Deacon Jonathan Curtice, Lt. Samuel Wolcott and Ensign Jacob Williams to set out to the widow, Sarah Andrews, formerly widow of Joseph Crane, to take as just and equal portion as they can upon the right of each of the heirs.

Page 180.

Cross, Capt. Samuel, Windsor. Died 5 November, 1707. Invt. £467-18-06. Taken 14 November, 1707, by Nathaniel Gaylord, Sen., Jonathan Elsworth and Eleazer Gaylord. Will dated 31 July, 1707.

I, Samuel Cross, of Windsor, do make and ordain this my last will. Imprs. I give to my wife, Elizabeth Cross, the use of my houseing and homestead and 10 acres of land lying in the Great Meadow, during the time of her natural life. And after the decease of my wife, my will is that my son-in-law, Symon Chapman, shall have my houseing and homestead and the 10 acres of land, to be his and his heirs forever, except my brother John Cross should have a son that shall live to be twenty-one years of age, then it shall be his; otherwise I give to my brother John Cross £5. Also, I give to my brother Nathaniel Cross his daughter which he had by his first wife, £10; also I give to my cousin John Bates £3; also I give to my cousin Samuel Bates £3; also I give to my cousin Jonathan Bates £3; also I give to my cousin Sarah Kitchum £3; also I give to my cousin Jonathan Jaggers £3; also I give to my cousin Hannah Webb £3; also I give to my cousin James Pickett £3; also I give to my cousin Mary Hoit £3; also I give to my cousin Ephraim Phelps, to be paid when he comes of age, £5; also I give to my son-in-law Symon Chapman all my land lying at a place called the "swamp," near to Hoit's meadow; also 10 acres of land which I bought of Mr. John Eliot, lying on the west side of the Riverett, near to a place known by the name of Gravelly Hill; also I give to the aforesaid Simon Chapman my cart and wheels, with the boxes and bands and all belonging to it; also my plow and the irons belonging to it; also my collars and traces and whatever other tackling I have belonging to a team. And as for the rest of my estate, I put it into the hands of my son-in-law Symon Chapman, Thomas Fyler and Return Strong, Junior, for the payment of my just debts, whom I do hereby make executors of this my will and testament.

Witness: *Return Strong, Sen.,*   SAMUEL CROSS, LS.
   Samuel Moore.

Court Record, Page 100—5 January, 1707-8: Will now proven. The executors named in the will refused the trust, and letters of Adms. were granted to Symon Chapman with the will annexed.

Page 100 (Vol. IX) 3 April, 1719: Symon Chapman, Adms., exhibits an account of his Adms., and there being no assets in his hands, this Court do accept of the account and grant him a *Quietus Est.*

Page 148-169.

Curtiss, Samuel, Wethersfield. Invt. of personal estate, £40-01-03. Taken 30 January, 1688, by Nathaniel Bowman and John Welles. An apprisement of lands, including two parcels of land apprised as money £90-00-00. Taken 30 March, 1705-6, by Thomas Wickham, Sen., David Goodrich and Samuel Buck.

An agreement for settling the estate of Samuel Curtis deceased: That Samuel Curtis of Wethersfield, cordwainer, son and heir to Samuel Curtis late of Wethersfield deceased, the one party, and Ebenezer Hale of Wethersfield, weaver, in behalf of his wife Ruth Curtis (alias Hale), the other party, have deliberately considered and come to this loving agreement, that the sd. Samuel Curtis shall deliver to Ebenezer Hale half the home lot, the north side of that lott which was his Father Samuel Curtis's in Wethersfield, bounded on George Wolcott north, Tho. Wickham east, Samuel Curtis south, and the street highway west. Also certain moveables. The sd. Samuel Curtis to bear all Court charges and to clear the sd. Ebenezer Hale from paying any thirds to his Mother Curtis. In consideration the sd. Ebenezer Hale, with his wife Ruth Hale, promise and engage to give to Samuel Curtis a full remission, release and quitclaim of any of our father Samuel Curtis's estate, and also of my mother's thirds, that may be in reversion. For confirmation of the premises we bind ourselves this 22 November, 1706.

Witness: *Nathaniel Bowman,* Signed: SAMUEL CURTIS, LS.
  Philip Alcock.   EBENEZER HALE, LS.
           RUTH X HALE, LS.
           SARAH X CURTIS, LS.

Widow Sarah Curtis of Wethersfield doth consent to the above written agreement of her children, as witness her hand and seal, this 26th of February, 1706-7.

In presence of
David Goodrich,   *Test: Caleb Stanly, Clerk.*
Thomas Wickham.

Court Record, Page 81—2 April, 1706: Sarah Curtiss, widow of Samuel Curtiss, and Adms. on his estate, exhibited in this Court an invt. of his estate with an accompt of her Adms. thereon, which sd. Court allow and ordered to be recorded and put on file, and grant the widow a *Quietus Est.* This Court order that the estate be dist., and appoint Thomas Wickham, Sen., Lt. David Goodrich and Samuel Buck, of Wethersfield, distributors of the remaining part of the estate, to be distributed to the widow, to Samuel Curtis, son, and Ruth Curtiss, daughter.

Page 88—13 November, 1706: The distributors were now sworn before this Court to make division of the estate of Samuel Curtiss.

Page 91—3 March, 1706-7: Sarah Curtiss of Wethersfield, widow, and Samuel Curtiss and Ruth Curtiss, children of sd. decd., appeared before this Court and exhibited an agreement for the settlement of the estate, and acknowledged the same to be their act and deed. Allowed and ordered recorded and put on file.

Page 158.

Davis, Jemima, of Hartford. Invt. £10-15-08. Taken 23 July, 1706, by Ichabod Welles and Samuel Howard.

Page 132.

Deming, John, Sen., Wethersfield. (No inventory or apprisers mentioned.) Will dated 26 June, 1690:

I, John Deming, Senior, do declare this to be my last will and testament: I having already done well by my son John, I now give him my great Bible, Geneva print, and my feather bed and bolster, and my great kettle. I give to my son Jonathan my fifty-acre lot at the west side of the bounds, to be to him and his heirs forever. I give to my son Samuel my house and home lot, with all the buildings upon it, containing nine acres be it more or less, and bounded as in the record; as also my meadow adjoining, containing about 17 acres, and abutting on Mr. Willis south, Thomas Standidge his land east, the highway north, and my homelott west; and 12 acres in the West Swamp, at the rear of my son David's lott. Also I give unto him my flock of sheep, and my neat cattle, and all my horses and swine, and all my moveables, within doors and without (not otherwise disposed of by this my last will), and all my husbandry tools, he paying my just debts, funeral charges and such legacies as I do hereby appoint him to pay. I give to my son David all my materials and tools in my shop, and my book debts, he paying those debts I owe about my trade. I give to my son Ebenezer my best coat and my best hat. I give to my daughter Morgan, my daughter Beckly, my daughter Hurlbut and my daughter Wright, five pounds apiece, to be paid by my executor within five years after my decease. I give to my cousin Unis Standidge, and to my cousin Sarah Wyer, wife of John Wyer, twenty pounds apiece, to be paid within two years after my decease. I give to my daughter Moody 10s, having already given her a good portion. I give to my grandchild Ann Beckley £5. I appoint my son Samuel executor, and desire Capt. Samuel Talcott and my son Ebenezer Deming to be overseers.

Witness: *John Allyn,*   JOHN DEMING, SEN., LS.
    George Grave.

Codicil, dated 3d February, 1692: Whereas, I gave to my son John my great Bible, my feather bed and bolster, and my great kettle, I now withdraw that gift and give unto my son John all my materials and tools in my shop and my book debts, he paying those debts I owe about my trade. And whereas, in my will I gave my grandchild Ann Beckley £5, shee having miscarryed, I withdraw my gift from her, and that £5 I give to my son David.   JOHN DEMING, LS.

Witness: *John Allyn,*
    Zachariah Sandford.

Court Record, Page 72—21 November, 1705: Will exhibited by Samuel Deming. Proven by testimony of Zachary Sandford, the other witness being dead.

Invt. in Vol. VIII, Page 15.

Dibble, George, Windsor. Died 25 April, 1709. Invt. £8-16-07. Taken by Job Drake and Samuel Rockwell, Jr.

Court Record, Page 131—1st August, 1709: Benjamin Eglestone, Jr., of Windsor, exhibits an invt. of the estate of George Dibble. Also, Adms. refused by Benjamin Eglestone and Abraham Dibble, brethren of sd. decd.

Page 134—7 November, 1709: Adms. granted to Ammy Trumble, one of the creditors.

Page 27 (Vol. VIII) 5 February, 1710-11: Ammy Trumbull of Windsor, Adms., presented an account of the debts due to the creditors, whereby it appears that all the sd. estate is not sufficient to pay all the debts. This Court order the Adms. to pay out of the sd. estate to the creditors by proportion as the same will allow, saving thereof first to himself his own cost and charge of Adms.

Page 69—8 April, 1712: Mr. Ammy Trumbull, Adms. on the estate of George Dibble, exhibited in this Court an account of his disposition of the estate of the sd. decd. to and among the creditors, which account is approved and allowed and ordered to be kept on file. And the Adms. is granted a *Quietus Est.*

Page 6-7-8.

Dibble, Thomas, Sen., Windsor. Invt. £60-14-01. Taken 1st November, 1700, by Samuel Cross, Nathaniel Gaylord and Alexander Allen. Will dated 17 February, 1699-1700:

I, Thomas Dibble, Sen., of Windsor, doe make this my last will and testament: Imprimis: To my son Samuel and his wife I give the north half part of my orchard whereon he liveth, during his natural life, and the remainder to his son Samuel. To my son Thomas Dibble and his wife I give the other half of my orchard during life, and the remainder to his son Abram. Item. I give to my daughter Miriam Gillett that two acres of meadow she now possesseth. Item. To my said daughter Miriam I give, for the use of her son, my best broadcloth coat, hatt and breeches. All the rest of my apparrel to be divided, two parts to my sons Samuel and Thomas, the other part to be to my grandsons Josiah Dibble and Wakefield Dibble. I appoint Mr. John Elliot and son-in-law Samuel Gibbs to be executors.

Witness: *John Eliot,*   THOMAS X DIBBLE, SENIOR.
Alexander Allin.

A schedule, expressing the form and manner how I would have my household stuffe and other moveables disposed and divided, is as follows: To my daughter Miriam 2 pewter basons, 1 platter, 1 quart pot, two porringers, one saucer, one dram cup, a chafendish, a choping knife, 2 old skilletts, a settle, and the cest (chest) that use to stand by my bedside, five yards of tow cloth and 40 shillings in pay, to be paid by my son-in-law Samuel Gibbs out of that he oweth me. To my grand daughter, Eliza: Gibbs, the bedstead, feather bed, and all thereto appertaining, which is in the parlour, 1 iron pot and crooks, best table, and box with lock and key, 3 chairs, best brush, 1 square basket, one pressing iron, best shears, one bodkin, pair stillyards. To Experience Gibbs, 1 iron kettle, 2 chairs, an old chest, the trundle bedstead, bed and green rug, best and worst pillows, 1 little table and a gridiron. To Mirriam Gibbs, the worst of ye beds and bedstead, 1 blue rug, one of the best pillows, the bolster, 2 blankets, the worst table and a little basket. To Hepzibah Dickson, a brass candlestick. To Palidence Denslow, a half pint cup and a corn bowl. To Joanna Loomis, 2 smoothing irons and a pair of pot hooks. To the Rev. Mr. Samuel Mather, Senior, my gun and sword and my andirons, tongs and spit.

Witness: *John Eliott,*   THOMAS X DIBBLE, SENIOR.
         Alexander Allin.

Court Record, Page 3—13 November, 1700: Will proven.

Page 25.

Dickinson, Obadiah, Jr. An inventory of the estate of Obadiah Dickinson, Jr., late of Wethersfield, decd., taken by us whose names are underwritten:

	£	s	d
Imprimis: 9 acres of wilderness upland, 10s per acre	4	10	00
92 pieces of gold that came from Madagascar, 11s pr peice,	50	12	00
Total,	55	02	00

Taken (by the desire of Daniel and Eliphalet Dickinson) this 8th day of April, 1701, by John Stedman and Nathaniel Foote.

An account of some charges in recovering and getting the sd. gold is:

	£	s	d
One journey to New York, 40s; and expenses there on that accot., 43s; paid out of the same for its transportation from Madagascar, £4 more; for time and expenses about the same, 15s; all is	8	18	00

Court Record, Page 8—8 March, 1700: Adms. granted to Eliphalet and Daniel Dickinson, brothers of the sd. decd.

Page 12—8 April, 1701: Invt. exhibited.

Page 18—4 September, 1701: Daniel and Eliphalet Dickinson ask for longer time to finish their Adms.

Page 22—13 November, 1701: Adms. time continued until March next.

Inventory from File. Recorded on Page 210-11.

Duce, Abda, alias Ginnings, a mulatto, Hartford. Died 17 January, 1708-9. Invt. £14-13-00. Taken by Benjamin Graham and Thomas Richards. Lydia Duce, widow, made oath to the invt., that the same was a true presentment. Accepted by the Court.

Court Record, Page 121—7 February, 1708-9: Adms. granted unto Robert Shurley, who was also appointed guardian to Joseph Duce, a minor son of sd. Abda, sd. minor being about 7 years of age.

Page 24 (Vol. VIII) 1st January, 1710-11: Robert Shurley, Adms. on the estate of Abda Duce, alias Abda Ginnings, exhibited an account of his Adms., by which account it appears that the sd. Robert Shurley hath paid to the creditors of the sd. estate in debts due to them, and to Lydia, widow, for her part thereof, all the whole of the sd. estate and more than all the value thereof. Account accepted. And this Court grant the sd. Adms. a *Quietus Est.*

Page 222-3.

Dyxx, Sarah, Wethersfield. Died 27 March, 1709. Invt. £10-15-03. Taken by Joseph Belden, Moses Goffe and Samuel Walker. Will dated 20 March, 1705:

I, Sarah Dyxx, of Wethersfield, do make this my last will and testament: I give unto my daughter Elizabeth Vincent 1 shilling in pay. I give and bequeath to my son Samuel Dyx one bushel of Indian corn. And as for the cow which my husband gave me, I have disposed of all the increase already for my firewood. I give to my daughter Mercy Goff my cloke and a stuff coat. To my daughter Hannah Rennolds I give my cow, that is to say, a black cow with a white face. And the remainder of my estate I give to my son John Dyxx, and appoint him to be executor.

Witness: *Abraham Crane,*   SARAH X DYXX, LS.
        Samuel Walker.

Court Record, Page 126—4 April, 1709: Will proven.

Edwards, Richard. Court Record, Page 105—16 February, 1707-8: The Judges and Justices of this Court have constituted and appointed, and do now hereby constitute and appoint, Mr. Richard Edwards of Hartford to be their attorney, with full power to commence and prosecute all such actions of debts due to the said Judges and Justices from any person and persons whatsoever, by bond or obligation formerly given or hereafter to be given to this Court, according to the direction of the said Judges and Justices from time to time.

Page 44-5.

Eliot, Mrs. Elizabeth, Windsor. Will dated 25 April, 1700:

I, Elizabeth Eliot, do make and ordain this my last will and testament, for the disposal of that estate it hath pleased God to give unto me, and which I reserve in an indenture signed the 30th of August, 1699, by Mr. John Eliott and Capt. Thomas Stoughton and myself, which reserve is £1378—£100 to dispose of when I please, and £1278 to dispose of at my death: I give to John Stoughton my lott at the marsh and my orchard that was Thomas Eglestone's. I give to William Stoughton my house, barn, shop and warehouse and homested. I give to Elizabeth Stoughton £50. And these things I give to them and their heirs forever, sons and daughters of John Stoughton my brother. I give to Mary Stoughton £200, daughter of my brother Thomas Stoughton; and to Thomas Stoughton £100, son of Thomas. I give to Samuel Stoughton £100, son of my brother Samuel Stoughton; and to Dorothy £100, daughter of Samuel my brother. I give to Israel Stoughton £200, my brother. I give to William Mather, son of my sister Rebeckah Mather, £195 with lands besides, if I have no issue. But if I have any children of my own body begotten, whether son or daughter, or either, that then my whole estate, which is two thousand three hundred and seventy-eight pounds, shall be his or hers or theirs and their heirs forever; if they live to be 21 years of age if sons; or until 18 years of age if daughters. But if they die and have no issue, then I ordain it to be as above written, and this part of my estate, which is thirteen hundred and seventy-eight pounds, is to return to the heirs at my death; and the other thousand, which is to return at Mr. John Eliot's death, if it be not spent, by the providence of God shall be equally divided between my brothers' and sisters' children. I appoint my brothers John, Thomas and Israel Stoughton to be my sole executors.

Witness: *Samuel Mather, Jr.,*   ELIZABETH ELIOT, LS.
        Michael Taintor, Sen.

Court Record, Page 36—22 December, 1702: Will proven.

Page 157-8.

Elsworth, Josiah, Windsor. Died 4 May, 1706. Invt. £377-14-06. Taken 27 June, 1706, by Abraham Phelps, Sen., Benajah Holcomb and Nathaniel Loomis. The sons of sd. decd: Josiah, Samuel and Joseph Elsworth (W. R.) Will dated 19 April, 1706:

I, Josiah Elsworth, of the Town of Windsor, do make this my last will and testament: Imprimis: I give unto my wife the use and improvement of my whole estate during the time of her widowhood; and if she marry after my decease, the one-half during the time of her natural life.

2ndly. I give to my three sons all my housing and lands, with the appurtenances thereto belonging, to be equally divided between them, except necessity calleth for the sale of any of it.

3dly. I will that my wife pay out of my estate to my three daughters that are unmarried so much as to make them equal with my daughter Martha, when and as they shall want it.

4thly. My will is that my three sons each of them pay sixteen pounds in current pay to their four sisters: twelve pounds to Martha, twelve pounds to Elizabeth, twelve pounds to Mary, and twelve pounds to Abigail—in all, forty-eight pounds, the sons to pay their proportions of the abovesaid sums to their sisters within a year after they come to possess the above said housing and lands, which is to be the one-half at my wife's marriage, if she marry after my decease, the other half at her death.

5thly. I do nominate and appoint my well beloved brother Jonathan Elsworth to be executor, and my loveing wife to be executrix, to this my last will and testament. JOSIAH ELLSWORTH, LS.

Witness: *Henry Stiles, Sen.,*
Jonathan Stiles, Israel Stoughton.

Court Record, Page 86—5 August, 1706: Will exhibited by Martha Elsworth, the widow.

Page 284 (Probate Side, Vol. IX): An agreement, dated 5 August, 1718, for settling the estate of Josiah Elsworth, late decd.: This writing witnesseth that Josiah Elsworth and Samuel Elsworth, sons of Josiah Elsworth late of Windsor decd., and Jonathan Elsworth, executor to the last will of sd. decd., in behalf of the minor Joseph Elsworth, do agree to divide all the lands belonging to the sd. decd. (it being all given to sd. three sons by will).

Witness: *Samuel Mather, Jr.,*   Signed: JONATHAN ELSWORTH, LS.
　　　　 David Clark. 　　　　　　　　　 JOSIAH ELSWORTH, LS.
　　　　　　　　　　　　　　　　　　　　 SAMUEL ELSWORTH, LS.
　　　　　　　　　　　　　　　　　　　　 JOSEPH ELSWORTH.

This agreement was acknowledged before Samuel Mather, J. P.

Court Record, Page 133—8 July, 1720: Joseph Elsworth, a minor 17 years of age, son of Josiah Elsworth, chose Peletiah Allyn of Windsor to be his guardian.

Page 149—4 April, 1721: Jonathan Elsworth, upon the motion of Peletiah Allyn, being cited to this Court to take on an order of dist. of the estate of Josiah Elsworth, now appeared and declared that he had returned a dist. of sd. estate unto the Court, which was accepted.

Page 154—6 June, 1721: Whereas, there is a dist. of the estate of Josiah Elsworth upon record, but not to be found, that the Court accepted the same supposing the accepting thereof to have been omitted entering on record, this Court do now allow and accept the sd. dist. of sd. estate and order it to be kept on file.

Invt. in Vol. VIII, Page 33.

Filley, Mary, Widow, Windsor. Invt. £30-05-07. Taken 12 February, 1708-9, by John Moore, Sen., and James Enno, Jr.

Court Record, Page 122—15 February, 1708-9: This Court grant Adms. unto Benjamin Newbery.

Page 123—7 March, 1708-9: Samuel Filley, with his wife and Mary his daughter, were summoned into Court to disclose personal estate in their possession or custody.

Page 1 (Vol. VIII) 2 January, 1709-10: Whereas, Capt. Benjamin Newbery, late of Windsor, decd., was by this Court on the 15th of February last appointed Adms., he being now dead, this Court now grant letters of Adms. to Mrs. Hannah Newbery, widow and relict of sd. Capt. Benjamin Newbery, of sd. Windsor.

Page 8—3 April, 1710: Inventory exhibited. Ordered to pay debts and report.

Page 184-5.

Filley, William, Windsor. Invt. £202-09-06. Taken 4 October, 1707, by Job Drake and Jeremiah Alford. Will dated 11 August, 1707.

The last will and testament of William Filley, late of Windsor: I give to my now wife Elizabeth all my estate, both real and personal, provided that if she have issue begotten by me in marriage and it live (if male to the age of 21 years, or if female unto the age of 18 years), then my will is that the estate shall be equally divided betwixt mother and child. Otherwise, the whole estate to her as before expressed. I constitute my wife sole executrix, and desire Nathaniel Cooke to be supervisor.

Witness: *Daniel Clarke,*   WILLIAM FILLEY, LS.
   Nathaniel Cooke.

Court Record, Page 98—6 October, 1707: Elizabeth, the widow, with Samuel Filley, brother of the said deceased, appeared in Court, when Samuel Filley opposed the probate of the will.

Page 99—3 November, 1707: This Court order the parties to appear again on the third Tuesday of this November.

Page 101—9 January, 1707-8: Will and invt. exhibited and approved, Samuel Filley having nothing further to object.

Page 125-6.

Fitch, Thomas, Wethersfield. Died 18 October, 1704. Invt. £111-03-00. Taken 13 November, 1704, by John Curtis, Sen., John Goodrich, and Daniel Boardman. The children: Samuel Fitch, Abigail the wife of Abraham Kimberly, Sibbell the wife of Joseph Hurlbut, and Martha Fitch.

Court Record, Page 68—26 April, 1705: Sarah Fitch, widow, relict of Thomas Fitch, late of Wethersfield, decd., exhibits invt. Adms. granted to Mrs. Sarah Fitch, widow.

Page 156 (Vol. VIII) 7 September, 1713: Samuel Fitch, a minor son of Thomas Fitch, late of Wethersfield decd., made choice of William Whiting to be his guardian.

Page 216—4 October, 1714: Sarah Fitch of Wethersfield, Adms. on the estate of Mr. Thomas Fitch, late decd., exhibits now in this Court an account of her Adms. Paid in debts, subsistence of the family, and illness of the daughter for some years, £90-06-3½. And received of debts due to the estate, £28-11-06. Which account this Court allow and order to be kept on file.

Dist. File: 9 April, 1717: To Sarah Fitch, widow; to Samuel; to Abigail, wife of Abraham Kimberly; to Sibbel, the wife of Joseph Hurlbut; Joseph Kimberly of Newtown, Joseph Hurlbut his attorney, all sealed.

Inventory and Will in Vol. VIII, Page 5.

Fox, Richard, Glastonbury. Invt. £111-15-06. Taken 29 April, 1709, by Jonathan Smith, Joseph Smith and Samuel Smith. Will dated 10 July, 1708:

I, Richard Fox, of Glastonbury, husbandman, do make this my last will and testament: Imprs. I give and bequeath to Beriah, my beloved wife, the use of my dwelling house, cellar, orchard and improveable lands during the time of her natural life, and then to return to my sons hereafter named. It. I give to Beriah my wife all my moveables, both within doors and without, for her use and comfort so long as she doth live, and then to dispose of the abovesaid moveables, if any are left, to any or all of her children as she pleaseth. I give to my son Richard Fox 50 acres of land which the Town gave to me, lying in the Great Swamp, which appears by a deed which I gave to him. Ite. I give to my son Ebenezer Fox one-half of my upland joining to my house, namely, the north side of my lot, bounding north upon land belonging to Capt. Wells, east upon John House and west upon Salmon Brook, to him and his heirs forever. It. I give to my son John Fox 25 acres of my land in the Great Swamp which the Town gave to me. If my son John see cause to live on the land, I give it him and his heirs forever; but if he said John Fox will not

live upon the land, then the above said 25 acres of land I give to my son Ebenezer Fox and to my son Abraham Fox equally. It. I give to my son Abraham Fox 25 acres in the Great Swamp of land which the Town gave to me. It. I give to my son Joseph Fox the one-half of my land which my dwelling house now stands upon, with the dwelling house, which parcel of land is the south side of my upland and is bounded on the north on land given my son Ebenezer Fox above mentioned, and south upon Joseph Smith Senr his land, and east upon John House his land, and west upon Salmon Brook, which parcel of land and house I give to my son Joseph Fox and his heirs forever.   RICHARD X FOX.
Witness: *Benjamin Talcot,*
          Thomas Morly.

Court Record, Page 130—6 June, 1709: Beriah Fox of Glastonbury exhibits an invt. of the estate of her late husband Richard Fox.

Page 132—5 September, 1709: Will exhibited and proven. There being no executor appointed in the will, Adms. is granted to Beriah Fox, widow, with the will annexed.

Page 40 (Vol. VIII) 19 November, 1711: Beriah Fox now exhibits an account of her Adms. Approved, and this Court grant her a *Quietus Est.*

Page 4.

Gains, Samuel, Glastonbury. Invt. £6-07-00. Taken 5 June, 1700, by Samuel Hale, Sen., and Thomas Hale, Sen.

Court Record, Page 2—7 September, 1700: Hannah Gains, the relict, exhibits an inventory.

Page 124-5.

Gilbert, Josiah, Wethersfield. Died 2 February, 1704-5. Invt. £85-16-02. Taken 15 February, 1704-5, by Daniel Bordman and Jonathan Belden. Will dated 24 January, 1704-5:

I, Josiah Gilbert, of Wethersfield, being weak and low through sickness, do now make this my last will and testament. Imprimis: I give to my Brother Benjamin Gilbert 1-3 part of all my land, and he to have the first choice in taking his third part of my lands at Divident in Wethersfield. I give to my brother Moses Gilbert 1-3 part of my lands at Divident. I give to my sister Mary, the wife of Symon Willard, the remaining third part of my land at Divident. I give to my brother Caleb Gilbert 5 shillings. I give to my sister Elizabeth Deming 5 shillings. I give to my sister Lydia Riley 5 shillings. I give to my cousin Josiah Willard (the son of my brother Willard) all my cooper's tools. I give my new Bible to my cousin Mary Willard, daughter of my brother Willard. It is my will that, my just debts being first paid, my sister Amy Gilbert have all the remaining part of my estate which I have not given, viz., all my debts due to me and all other estate which I have not disposed of in this my last will, whatsoever it be. I appoint my brother Benjamin Gilbert executor.

Witness: *Peter Bulkeley,*   JOSIAH GILBERT, LS.
Mary Boardman.

Court Record, Page 66—5 April, 1705: Will and invt. exhibited, approved and ordered to be recorded and kept on file.

Page 144-5-6 (Vol. VI).

Gilbert, Mary, Widow. Died 3 July, 1700. Invt. £562-13-07. Taken 9 July, 1700, by Jonathan Bull and Samuel Spencer, Sen.

Will: In the name of God, amen. The three and twentieth day of May, in the year of our Lord 1700 *Annoqe R. R. Gulielmi Tertis Anglae and Duodecimo.* I, Mary Gilbert, of the Town of Hartford, in the County of Hartford, within the Colony of Connecticut in New England, in America, widow and innholder. I give to my son Thomas Gilbert 18 acres in the Long Meadow in Hartford, abutting east on a pathway, west on the Neck, north on land sometime belonging to Wm. Edwards, and south on land of John Day. I give to my son Samuel Gilbert a parcel of land usually called the Pine Field, in Hartford, 3 acres more or less, and to my son Ebenezer Gilbert land in the Long Meadow that I bought of Thomas Butler; to my grandson Thomas Dickinson £20, also all that is due to me from my son-in-law Charles Dickinson. I give and bequeath all the rest of my estate, real and personal, to be divided into 5 equal parts, and one part to each of my children: To Thomas Gilbert one part, to Ebenezer Gilbert one part, to my daughter Lydia Chapman one part, to my daughter Rachell Marshfield one part, and to the children of my late daughter Sarah Belcher one part, which is to be accounted as one instead of their deceased mother. One-seventh part of the legacy given to Lydia Chapman to be paid to the two sons of my late grandson Jonathan Richardson deceased, when they attain to 21 years of age, the children of my said daughter Lydia which she had by her husband Richardson deceased. And my mind and will is that the rest of the fifth-part legacy given to my daughter Lydia, not otherwise disposed of to the heirs of the late Jonathan Richardson decd., shall be equally divided amongst the children of my said daughter Lydia which she had by her husband Richardson decd., and paid to them, the daughter at 18 years and the sons at 21 years of age. I appoint Mr. Richard Edwards and my son Ebenezer Gilbert executors, and desire Caleb Standly, Esq., and Mr. John Haines to be overseers.

Witness: *Simon Booth,*   MARY X GILBERT, LS.
Samuel Parsons, Caleb Standly, Sen.

Court Record, Page 141-2—10 July, 1700: Invt. exhibited, and executors accept the trust. Samuel Gilbert and Capt. Chapman object. They are overruled by the Court, and appeal to the Superior Court.

Page 22 (Vol. VII) 14 November, 1701: Capt. Caleb Standly and Lydia his wife appearing in Court, made oath that they heard Mrs. Mary Gilbert, late of Hartford decd., declare before her death and some time after her will was finished, that her two daughters, viz., Lydia Chapman and Rachel Marshfield, should have all her wearing clothes divided between them, and that they should be well paid for their pains in tending of her in her last sickness. Ordered to be recorded.

Page 29 (Probate Side): The testimony of Caleb Stanly, Sen., and Lydia his wife is as followeth: That we being at divers times together with Mrs. Mary Gilbert in her last sickness, did hear her declare that it was her will that her two daughters that attended her in the time of her sickness, viz., Lydia Chapman and Rachel Marshfield, after her death should have all her wearing clothes divided between them, and that they should have them as they were apprised in the inventory, and be well paid for their attendance upon her. All which the sd. Mrs. Mary Gilbert declared to us. Unto what is above written we can give our oaths, if called, hereunto. December the 8th, 1701.
Caleb Stanly, Sen.,
Lydia Stanly.

Page 126 (Probate Side).

A dist. of part of the estate of Mrs. Mary Gilbert to her son Thomas Gilbert and the children of her daughter Sarah Belcher, deceased:

Know all men by these presents: That we, Richard Edwards and Ebenezer Gilbert, both of the Town of Hartford, executors of the last will and testament of Mary Gilbert, late of Hartford aforesd., widow, deceased, have this 17th day of July, 1705, made computation of the estate of the said Mary Gilbert to find the just value of what is remaining, after payment of debts, particular legacies and other charges, to be divided and distributed to and amongst her children (and their representatives) in five equal parts, according to her said will, and thereupon do find one-fifth part thereof to amount to the sum of £155-09-08. Now for the payment of the same: To Capt. Thomas Gilbert of Boston, who has interest and right to one-fifth part thereof, and also to the children of Andrew and Sarah Belcher, who have interest and right to one other fifth part. We the said Richard Edwards and Ebenezer Gilbert, executors aforesd., have set out, paid and delivered to them the several parcels of the estate of the said Mary Gilbert mentioned, contained and comprehended in the accompt respectively hereafter following. That is to say, 1705, July 17th.:

	£ s d
Capt. Thomas Gilbert,	155-09-08
The children of Sarah Belcher,	155-09-08

Witness our hands: *Richard Edwards,*
Ebenezer Gilbert.
Endorsed.

Memorandum: *That on the* 18*th day of July, Anno Dom.* 1705, *the within-named Richard Edwards and Ebenezer Gilbert did enter into and did take and had full and peaceable possession and seisin of and in the messuage or dwelling house, outhouses, homelott and appurtenances of the late Mary Gilbert, within named, deceased (sometime belonging to William Gibbon), situate, lying and being in Hartford; and after full and peaceable possession and seisin so had and taken, the said Richard Edwards and Ebenezer Gilbert did deliver full, quiet and peaceable possession and seisin of two fifth parts thereof to the within-named Thomas Gilbert, and of other two fifth parts thereof to Major William Whiting, attorney for the children of Andrew and Sarah Belcher within mentioned, according to the effect and true meaning of the within-written distribution.*

In the presence of us, witnesses:
Caleb Stanly, Jr., John Stedman.

Court Record, Page 69—14 August, 1705: Richard Edwards and Ebenezer Gilbert, executors of the last will of Mrs. Mary Gilbert, exhibited in this Court a dist. by them made of 2-5 parts of both the real and personal estate of the sd. late Mary Gilbert unto Capt. Thomas Gilbert and the children of Andrew Belcher, Esq., of Boston. This Court allow and proves sd. dist., and order it recorded and kept on file, which bears date 17 July, 1705; and this Court order that the letters of attorney relating to this affair granted to William Whiting of Hartford shall be put on file in the Clerk's office.

Page 148.

Gilbert, Thomas, Glazier, Hartford. Invt. £33-12-00. Taken 16 March, 1705-6, by Joseph Wadsworth and Joseph Talcott.

Court Record, Page 79—15 March, 1705-6: This Court grant letters of Adms. unto Joseph Gilbert of Hartford, brother of the sd. deceased.

Page 81—4 April, 1706: Invt. exhibited and accepted.

Page 101—5 January, 1707-8. This Court order the Clerk to signify to Joseph Gilbert, Adms., that he must render an account to this Court of his Adms. on the 1st Monday of February next.

Page 104—2 February, 1707-8: Josiah Marshfield, of Hartford, moved to this Court for an order to be made to cause a new apprisement of the estate of Thomas Gilbert, late decd., by jury, for that he the sd. Marshfield, being one of the creditors of the estate, is aggrieved with the apprisement thereof, and gave his reasons for the same. Upon consideration of all which, this Court do not see cause to order any new apprisement of sd. estate.

Page 120.

Grant, Rachell, Spinster, Hartford. Died 25 January, 1704-5. Invt. £18-00-00. Taken February, 1704-5, by Benjamin Graham and Thomas Richards Will dated 24 January, 1704-5:

I, Rachell Grant, of Hartford, having my reason through God's mercy, praised be His name, therefore it is my pleasure to give to my sister Sarah my cow for her own, to enjoy with quiet. Item: I give to my cousin Ann Wheeler my great kettle, and my best sute between Sarah Wheeler and Ann; and to my cousin Rachell Wheeler I give my trunck and my chest; and the rest of what I have I give to my brother and sister Wheeler, they paying my just expenses and debts to all persons which are due.   RACHELL X GRANT, LS.

Witness: *Henry Brace,*
         Ichabod Coale.

Court Record, Page 64—6 March, 1704-5: Will proven. Adms. to Samuel Wheeler, who gave a bond of £30—5 May, 1705.
Page 71—6 September, 1705: The Adms. granted a *Quietus Est.*

Page 35-36-37.

Grave, John, Hartford. Invt. £213-16-09. Taken 3 September, 1702, by James Steele, Jr., and Joshua Carter. Will dated 20 August, 1702:

I, John Grave, of Hartford, do make this my last will and testament: I give to my son John Grave my house and ten acres of land adjoining, out of my home lot; also a small gun, his grandmother's Bible, a small box, a brass candlestick, and a silver spoon. The remainder of my estate to be divided amongst my three daughters, Mehetabell, Elizabeth and Sarah, only that Elizabeth shall receive one-third part more than Mehetabell and Sarah upon consideration of what she hath done for me, as well that which is due to me from the estate of Mr. Robert Webster, decd., in right of my wife Susannah, as that which I have in possession. The income of my real estate to be disposed of for the bringing up of my youngest child until she recover her health. I constitute my beloved friends John Catlin and Thomas Richards executors.

Witness: *Richard Lord,*   JOHN GRAVE, LS.
         William Whiting.

Court Record, Page 32—8 September, 1702: Will and invt. exhibited. Thomas Richards and John Catlin reject this executorship. Will was proven, ordered recorded and kept on file. This Court considering that the executors refuse their trust, grant Adms. with the will annexed to James Hannison, son-in-law to the sd. decd.
Page 40—2 March, 1702-3: James Handerson, Adms., presented to this Court an account of debts, £76-05-11, and credits, £3-15-05. A further accot. of debts due from the estate is £7-01-10.
Page 82—5 April, 1706: James Handerson, Adms. on the estate of John Grave, exhibited an account of his Adms., which account this Court have examined and do find that the sd. Handerson having sold:

	£	s	d
13 acres of land of the sd. estate to Joseph Cook for		59-15-00	
And also hath in his hands all the moveables,		34-11-02	
He stands debtor in		94-06-02	
Paid out		81-13-05	
Court allow sd. Handerson for his trouble,		8-05-00	
Credits,		89-18-05	
There remains due from him,		4-07-09	

The Court order the sd. James Handerson to pay to the three daughters of John Grave, or their guardians, respectively: To Mehetabell, the wife of sd. Adms., 21 shillings and 11 1-4 pence; to Elizabeth, £0-43-10; and to Sarah, £0-21-11. Adms. ordered to bring receipts of the payment and take a *Quietus Est.* This Court appoint Thomas Richards, tailor, of Hartford, to be guardian to John Grave and Sarah Grave, children of John Grave decd.

Page 87—3 September, 1706: Whereas, James Handerson of Hartford was ordered to appear at this time and bring receipts and take out his *Quietus Est.,* he having not appeared, this Court do again so order.

Page 122—7 March, 1708-9: John Grave, a minor now 16 years of age, chose Thomas Richards, tailor, to be his guardian, his former guardian still to be guardian. Affirmed.

Page 153 (Vol. VIII) 17 August, 1713: Thomas Richards of Hartford, guardian, moved this Court that the estate of the sd. minor may be put into the hands of the sd. guardian for its better improvement for sd. minor. This Court therefore order the Clerk to notify Sarah Shurley of Hartford, widow (who has under her management some of the sd. estate), that she may appear at the Court of Probate to be holden at Hartford on the 1st Monday of September next, to show reason (if any she hath) why sd. estate should not be disposed of.

Page 26 (Vol. IX) 5 February, 1716-17: James Handerson, Adms., prays this Court for an order to sell some land pursuant to an Act of the General Assembly, 13 May, 1703. This Court cite John Grave, son of the decd., to appear at a hearing 1st Tuesday of March next.

Page 42—3 September, 1717: This Court having heard the pleas of John Grave, Jr., by his attorney, and also finding upon the records of the Court of Probate, 1706, a full settlement of sd. estate, do not see cause to give James Hannison any further direction in the premises.

Page 56.

Graves, Martha, Wethersfield, Widow. Died 1701. Invt. £22-16-11. Taken by Robert Welles and Jonathan Boreman.

Court Record, Page 35—11 November, 1702: Adms. on the estate of Martha Graves, relict of Nathaniel Graves, late of Wethersfield deceased, to Mr. John Russell and Mr. John Deming, Jr. John Russell gave bond of £100, and Richard Burnham became surety.

Page 43—7 April, 1703: Invt. exhibited and accepted.

Invt. on File. (Add Invt. in Vol. VIII, Page 261.)

Griffee, John, Haddam. Died 19 February, 1697-8. Invt. £118-16-06. Taken 22 March, 1697-8, by John Chapman, Samuel Spencer and John Booge. The surviving children are 3: John, Thomas and Mehetabell. Additional inventory of lands, apprised 19th day of March, 1713-14, by Thomas Hungerford and John Booge:

	£ s d
Imprimis: 40 acres of land, £27; 16½ acres, £8,	35-00-00
13 acres of land £3-10-00; £27-10, right belonging to the land,	31-00-00
Total,	66-00-00

See File.

Worshipfull and Respected Sir: Mr. Nathaniel Stanly: These few lines are to give your worship an account that the above inventory was taken by myself and the other two subscribers at a time when there was a difference in Haddam about the choice of their Townsmen, so that what was done was rather done as neighbors than as Selectmen; and for mine own part I thought no more about it, supposing the widow had, by her-selfe or some other, made presentment of the paper to ye Court of Probate long before this time, until within this little time some discourse was at my house concerning how she and her second husband did carry on together, for she hath marryed again. I was informed that most of the moveable estate was already disposed of, and she had not been at Court for letters of Adms. Fearing lest the estate might be quickly consumed, and the children wronged of that which their father wrought hard for, in a little time might be wholly ruined, wherefore I inquired of one of the neighbors with whom the above inventory was left for her, to be by her exhibited into the Courte, who informed me of the state of things so farr as was with him and brought me the paper, wherefore I thought it necessary to give your worship this account, that ye fatherless may be cared for. I also made inquiry for a suitable person that may, if ye Courte see meete, be trusted with power of Adms. to secure the estate, at least the land, for the sons. I have not spoken with ye woman, but have sent to her by her brother to inform her that I would take care to send the inventory to yourself that she might appear before yourself if she hath ought to say. The person that is, so farr as I know, most suitable to be trusted with this affair is John Willy, the woman's brother and own uncle to the fatherless children, a sober, discreet man, one that I believe will be faithful to his trust. There is, I am informed, since the taking of the inventory, a £40 right in the undivided land on the east side of the river in Haddam Township, and am also informed that she hath received £3, being part of her portion out of her father's estate, (since) her husband's estate, that is not in the above inventory. That I have given your worships a faithful account so farr as is with me, hoping you will take care of the matter at the next opportunity, that that which is right may be done, both to ye widow and the fatherless, I rest yours to command.   JOHN CHAPMAN. Haddam, 20th, 1700.

Court Record, Page 8—10 March, 1700-1: An inventory of the estate of John Griffe, of Haddam, was sent up to this Court by Capt. John Chapman, of sd. town, but no person appearing to make oath or to accept of Adms., the matter is deferred until the adjourned Court in April next, and that the widow be cited up to Court in order to the settlement thereof.

Page 161 (Vol. VIII) 2 November, 1713: This Court grant letters of Adms. on the estate of John Griffee, late of Haddam decd., unto John Griffee, eldest son.

Page 165—17 December, 1713: John Griffee, of Haddam, Adms., exhibited now in this Court an account of his Adms:

	£ s d
Paid in debts and charges,	2-10-00
There remains to be distributed,	36-00-00
Adding his right in the Commons or undivided lands,	27-10-00

To John a double portion; to Thomas and Mehetabell, to each of them, a single portion. And appoint Capt. Thomas Gates, John Booge and John Spencer, dist.

Page 179—1st March, 1713-14: Report of the dist., and this Court grant John Griffee a *Quietus Est.*

Page 108-9-10-11-12.

Griswold, George, Sen., Windsor. Died September, 1704. Invt. £362-08-00. Taken 2 October, 1704, by Timothy Phelps, Joseph Griswold and Benajah Holcomb.

An agreement made by the widow and children of George Griswold, Sen., late of Windsor, decd., for the division and settlement of his estate: Whereas, by the overruling providence of God our hond. father, George Griswold, Sen., of Windsor, hath departed this life and left a considerable part of his estate not made over unto his wife and children by will or otherwise, according to law, but left a draught drawn, unsubscribed or witnessed, wherein is expressed how he would have sd. estate distributed to his sd. wife and surviving posterity hereinafter nominated: We therefore whose names are subscribed, being heirs or legatees unto the estate fore mentioned, for the settlement of sd. estate and maintenance of peace and love one with another, have come to this agreement with and amongst ourselves, if it shall please the Hond. Court to grant us a confirmation: 1st. We agree in general that what our honoured father's will was, as expressed in the writing fore mentioned, excepting in some few particulars, shall stand. It is agreed that Daniel Griswold, eldest son, shall, after

our honoured mother's decease, have one parcel of marsh land in Simsbury, under the mountain; also one parcel lying in the bounds of New
London, and also ½ of the upland which was John Tinker's, which belonged to our father, and that which was our father's part at the Grist
Mill. We also agree that sd. Daniel shall have a peice of woodland in
Quarry Field. Whereas, it is said a parcel of land in New London
bounds, it seems, was a mistake, but it is our father's right to a parcel of
land made over to him by our grandfather Griswold as a grant from
the General Court in Killingworth Town. And that Thomas Griswold
shall have out of our father's estate ½ of the upland belonging to Tinker's
farm, 1 acre. We agree that George Griswold shall have a parcel of land
bounding south and east by Ensign Griswold, and from the highway 100
rods in length, and in breadth 5 rods, with the house which stands on it.
We further agree that John Griswold shall possess one parcel of land
bounded southerly by Andrew Moore, northerly by the way which leads
to Simsbury. Also agreed, that Benjamin Griswold, besides what land
he hath in possession, formerly given to sd. Benjamin by deed, shall have
also in reversion one parcel of land in the Third Meadow. Also agreed,
that Edward Griswold, son to Edward Griswold decd., shall have £20
paid to him, and the gr. daughter Abigail Griswold 40 Shillings, and to
have the south end of the house called Benjamin's house. Also, that the
two daughters, Mary Cooly and Deborah Moore, shall have their portion
out of the estate now divided. It is also further agreed, that our honoured
mother, Mary Griswold, shall have during her natural life the use and
improvement of the dwelling house, barn, and orchards and lands which
our father had in possession at his death, with the moveable estate and
household goods, cattle, sheep, swine and corn, and our father's part of
the Corne Mill, or what shall be meet for her comfortable subsistence,
while she liveth. Now, that this is our mutual agreement, wee signify
by our subscribing our Hands and fixing our Seals.

MARY GRISWOLD, LS.
DANIEL GRISWOLD, LS.
THOMAS GRISWOLD, LS.
GEORGE GRISWOLD, LS.

Attest: *Matthew Allyn, Justice,*   JOHN GRISWOLD, LS.
      William Whiting, Clerk.   BENJAMIN GRISWOLD, LS.

EDWARD GRISWOLD, LS.
ABIGAIL GRISWOLD, LS.
JOSEPH COOLY, LS.
THOMAS MOORE, LS.

And we do all agree to abide by the awarde of Joseph Wadsworth,
Matthew Allyn and Joseph Barnard. 9 November, 1704.
    Court Record, Page 61—10 November, 1704: This Court grant
Adms. unto Daniel and George Griswold. Recog. £300. Joseph Cooly
and Thomas Moore, who married two other of the daughters, all personally appeared before this Court and acknowledged the same to be their

free act and deed, and the widow acknowledged the same before Matthew Allyn, Esq., Justice of the Peace. Allowed, ratified and confirmed.

Page 79—7 March, 1705-6: Report of the Adms.

Page 36 (Vol. VIII) 2 July, 1711: The Court grant Daniel and George Griswold a *Quietus Est.*

Page 210.

Hail, John, Windsor. Invt. £56-01-01. Taken 25 January, 1708-9, by James Enno, Jr., and John Bissell.

Court Record, Page 120—24 January, 1708-9: This Court grant Adms. on the estate of John Hail, late of Windsor decd., carpenter, unto Samuel Barber, Sen.

Page 125—4 April, 1709: Samuel Barber being now deceased, this Court appoint Enoch Drake Adms.

Page 136—5 December, 1709: The Adms. is ordered to sell land to pay the debts.

Page 15 (Vol. VIII) 5 June, 1710: Whereas, this Court, 15th November, 1709, did order and direct Enoch Drake of Windsor, Adms. on the estate of John Hale, carpenter, decd., to sell all the lands belonging to that estate, for the payment of the debts, to the best bidder that should appear to buy and purchase the same, and whereas the sd. Enoch Drake hath given public notice that the land was so to be sold, and thereupon nobody hath yet appeared or offered to buy the sd. land, but the sd. Enoch Drake hath now offered to take the sd. lands himself and to pay for them the value thereon set in the inventory. Accepted by the Court.

Page 217 (Vol. X) 6 May, 1729: Whereas, it is represented that there is some estate belonging to John Haill, sometime of Windsor, that never yet has been brought into any inventory, and the Adms. on the estate, viz., Enock Drake, has omitted to cause the same to be done and has neglected to finish his accompt of Adms. on sd. estate, and the heirs moving to this Court by Thomas Remington, their attorney, that Adms. may be granted to him sd. Remington to make and bring to this Court an invt. of such estate of sd. John Haill that has not been yet inventoried, in order for a dist. to and amongst the heirs: This Court grant Adms. to Thomas Remington.

Page 30-1-2-3.

Harris, Capt. Daniel, Middletown. Invt. £501-09-00. Taken 19 December, 1701, by William Sumner, John Hamlin and Israhiah Wetmore. Will dated 13 March, 1698-9:

I, Daniel Harris, Sen., of Middletown, do make this my last will and testament. I give to my son Daniel all that lott he now dwells on, excepting only that part already disposed of to Comfort Starr. Also the remainder of that lott lying to the southward of the Town, about 12 acres ; also 1 parcel of land lying at Pecowsett; also ½ of my great lot abutting on Farmington and Wethersfield bounds, to be equally parted in the middle of the lott north and south, and my son Daniel to take his choice. Item. I give to my son Thomas Harris all that parcel of land which he now stands possessed of, as by deed of gift is specified. Item. I give unto my son William Harris all those parcels of land as by deed of gift are specified. Item. I give unto my son John Harris my now dwelling house, barn, barnyards, orchards, gardens and inclosures now belonging to my home. Also so much of my land not inclosed as reaches from my south fence to my son Thomas Harris and John Cook's north line, abutting on Kirby's land west and on Isaac Johnson's land east. Also 1 parcel of land in Hop Swamp, about 26½ acres. Also my negro Mengo, to be wholly at his dispose for and during the term of 20 years after the date hereof, provided that my sd. son John shall provide for myself and my wife all such comfortable and convenient maintenance, both for food and physic, rayment, lodging, firing and what else shall be comfortably and conveniently necessary for our comfortable being during our natural lives. And accordingly to take the estate I now stand possessed of into his care, custody and management, to improve the same to the best advantage for his and our comforts, and then at our decease to stand lawfully seized and possessed of each and every particular given to him in this my last will. I give to my daughter Mary Johnson one parcel of land in my farm, 65 acres. I give to my daughter Elizabeth the other half of my lott abutting on Wethersfield and Farmington bounds, after my son Daniel has taken his choice ; also to my daughter Elizabeth that 2 acres of land in Middletown which I bought of Joseph Bull of Hartford. I give to my daughter Hannah Cook all those two parcels of land which by a deed of gift are already certified. I give unto my grandchild Thankfull Bidwell one parcel of land lying in my farm, 133 acres, which is my last division in my farm. I give unto my grandchild Abiell one parcel of land in my farm, 43 acres. Also it is my will that if either or both of these my grandchildren shall decease before they come to the age of 18 years or the time of their marriage, that the lands given to them shall fall to their parents, that is, Abiell's to her mother (my daughter Elizabeth), and Thankfull Bidwell's to her father (my son-in-law), Samuel Bidwell. Also I commit the sd. Abiell unto the care and custody of my son John Harris until she attain the age of 18 years or the time of her marriage. I appoint my son John Harris and my son-in-law Samuel Bidwell joint executors, hereby giving, ratifying and confirming to my sd. son-in-law Samuel Bidwell what in reversion was to have been my daughter Sarah's.

Witness: *Daniel Johnson,*   .Daniel Harris, ls.
    Alexander Rollo.

    Court Record, Page 24—1st January, 1701-2: Will proven.
    Page 39 (Vol. VIII) 9 November, 1711: Mr. John Harris of Middletown, executor of the last will of Capt. Daniel Harris (his the said

John's father), late of Middletown decd., presented to this Court a distribution of some remaining part of the estate. Allowed, and to be kept on
file.

Page 40—19 November, 1711 : Isaac Johnson objects against the dist.
The Court order them to present reasons.

Page 69—8 April, 1712 : Whereas, Daniel Harris and Isaac Johnson
of Middletown did summon and cite John Harris and Samuel Bidwell of
said Middletown to appear before this Court of Probate, as executors to
the last will of Capt. Daniel Harris, late of sd. Middletown decd., to answer the complaint of sd. Daniel Harris and Isaac Johnson, wherefore the
said John Harris and Samuel Bidwell have not performed the trust committed to them, in neglecting to set out to them their legacies according
to the said will of the decd., upon consideration whereof this Court are of
opinion that this case is not cognizable before this Court, and therefore do
dismiss the same and do declare that this case is proper and cognizable
before the Inferior Court of Common Pleas, and therefore have considered
that the said John Harris and Samuel Bidwell shall recover their costs
of this Court, and cost allowed is fifteen shillings money, and this Court
do order that execution be issued forth upon this order.

Page 1.

Harris, Thomas. Died 24 August, 1700. Invt. £186-00-03. Taken
4 September, 1700, by John Hall and William Ward. One daughter,
Mary, 5 years of age.

Court Record, Page 1—5 September, 1700: Adms. to Mrs. Tabithy
Harris, the relict; Isaac Johnson, Sen., surety.

Page 53.

Hayes, Elizabeth,Farmington. Invt. £22-10-00. Taken 2 April, 1703,
by Samuel Hooker and Samuel Cowles.

Court Record, Page 41—7 April, 1703: Joseph Lancton of Farm-
ington exhibited invt. of the estate of Elizabeth Hayes, the daughter of
Deacon John Lancton, formerly of Farmington, decd., and moved this
Court for a distribution. Opposed by Luke Hayes and deferred.

Dist. File: 7 September, 1703: An agreement between Luke Hayes
and Joseph Lancton: It is agreed by and between Luke Hayes of Farmingtown, in the Colony of Connecticut, in New England, of the one part,
and Joseph Langton, of the sd. Farmington, for and in behalf of himself
and as attorney to the heirs of his brother Samuel Lancton decd., of the
other part, for a division and partition of the estate of the late wife of the
sd. Hayes, sister of the sd. Langton, as follows: That is to say, that the
sd. Luke Hayes, his heirs and assigns are forever to have and enjoy half an

acre of land where his (   ) house now stands, to be set out as they have agreed; and the said Joseph Langton, for himself and the heirs of his brother as aforesd., doth hereby relinquish and release to sd. Hayes all his and their right and title thereunto; and that the sd. Joseph Langton, his heirs and assigns, and the heirs of his sd. brother Samuel deceased, shall forever have and enjoy all the rest of the land belonging to the sd. Luke Hayes his wife deceased, and that ever did or ought to belong to her. And the sd. Luke Hayes doth by these presents relinquish and release all his right, title and interest thereunto unto the sd. Joseph Langton, his heirs and assigns, and unto the heirs of the sd. Samuel Langton aforesd.

Witness: *Thomas Sheldon,*   LUKE HAYES, LS.
         Caleb Stanly, Jr.   JOSEPH X LANGTON, LS.

Court Record, Page 46—8 September, 1703: Agreement presented in Court respecting the estate that did belong to Elizabeth Hayes, late wife of Luke Hayes, late of Farmington deceased. Accepted.

Page 136-7.

Haynes, Mrs. Sarah, Widow, Hartford. Will dated 17 February, 1697-8: I, Sarah Haynes, of Hartford, do dispose of my estate as followeth: I give to my grandchild Abigail Pierpont £50, 30 pounds of it to be paid out of that money which I paid to Mrs. Wilson for Mr. Pierpont, and £20 pounds in money by my executor. I give to my other two grand-children, Joseph and Sarah Haynes, £50 to each. I give to my daughter, Mabell Haynes, £10; to my daughter, Mary Haynes, £20. I give to my son John Haynes my lands at Hoccanum, reserving one-third of the profits of them to my daughter Mabell during life. Of the rest of my estate, I give 2-3 to my son John Haynes and 1-3 to my daughter Mabell, my son John Haynes to be sole executor.   SARAH HAYNES, LS.

Witness: *Samuel Willis,*
         Caleb Stanly, Sen.

Court Record, Page 74—19 December, 1705: John Haynes of Hartford exhibited will. Proven. Also informed this Court that there had never yet been a division made of the household goods of his father, Mr. Joseph Haynes, decd. Therefore he cannot make a perfect invt. of the estate of his late mother, deceased, she having some interest and share in them. This Court appoint Mr. Richard Lord, Hezekiah Willis and Samuel Spencer, Sen., to make a division and distribution according to the will of Mr. Joseph Haynes decd.

Page 177 (Vol. VIII) 8 February, 1713-14: Mr. John Read (atty. for Mr. James Pierpont and his daughter, Mrs. Abigail Pierpont, of New Haven) moved this Court that whereas Mr. Joseph Haynes and Mrs. Sarah Haynes, late of Hartford, decd. respectively, in their lives' time did make wills and dispose of their estate, and constituted executors for the due execution of their sd. wills, and the sd. executors are now since departed this life, not having finished their work as executors of the sd. wills, that letters of Adms. on the several estates of the sd. decd. might be granted *Cum Testamento annexo* unto some person or persons as this Court shall think meet: Decission deferred until 1st Monday of March next.

Page 191—16 April, 1714: Mrs. Mary Haynes, wife of John Haynes, is notified by this Court to appear at the next hearing, relating to granting letters of Adms. on the estate of Mr. Joseph Haynes, that she may have opportunity to object.

Records of Court of Assistants, Vol. II, Page 146-7, Secretary of State's Office.

Hemsted, Joshua, New London. Will dated 7 October, 1683: I, Joshua Hemsted, of New London, do make this my last will and testament: I give unto my wife Elizabeth one-third of my personal estate forever, and the use of one-third of my real estate during widowhood. I give to my son Joshua Hempsted my house, housing and home lott, excepting two acres, which I give to my four daughters, Elizabeth, Mary, Phebe and Hannah, to each one-half acre, out of my home lott, to be laid out to them equally, and to butt upon the street near William Chapman's which goes to the Meeting House, the eldest daughter to front next the street at the upper corner next the Meeting House, Mary to have the second portion fronting the street, Phebe to have the third half acre, and Hannah the youngest daughter, to be at the west corner. I give to my son Joshua that 200 acres of land which lyeth at Mystick, which Father Robert Hemsted gave me, 8 acres on the west side of Mystick River, 6½ acres of salt marsh land remaining at the head of Breame Cove, and 26 acres bought of Samuel Spencer. I give to my four daughters that 150 acres of land on the east side of Queenabaug River, 100 I bought of Capt. John Mason and 50 acres of Morgan Bowers. Also, land promised by Owaneco, 100 acres, to adjoin the 150 acres. If this promise be performed, this land I give to my four daughters. And if that farm be enjoyed which was given John and Daniel Stubbins by Uncas, joining unto Jeremiah Addams's farm, wherein myself, Charles Hill and Abell Moore were to be equal partners with them, then my son Joshua shall have a farm of 200 acres out of my proportion; and if there be a surplus, I will it be divided amongst my four daughters.

Witness: *Charles Hill,* JOSHUA HEMSTED.
     Robert Douglas.

Page 71—Joshua Hemsted, of New London, being aggrieved with the act of the Court of Probates holden at New London, 1st October, 1706, in their denial to allow a will which he presented to them to be the last will and testament of his deceased father, Joshua Hemsted, bearing date 7th October, 1683, with testimony of Charles Hill, Recorder of New London, who wrote the will from dictation of sd. Joshua Hemsted, the testator, and also the testimony of Robert Douglas, a witness to the will, this Court now approve the will and appoint Elizabeth, relict (now Elizabeth Edgecomb), of sd. testator, Adms. with will annexed. And order to pay the daughters born since the will was made their portions of the estate equal to the daughters born before the will was made.

Page 143—11 October, 1709: John Edgecomb, of New London, who had married the relict Elizabeth, appeared to oppose the probating of the will, which was before the Court of Assistants upon an appeal from an adverse decision by the Probate Court of New London. The Court of Assistants decree the will to be valid, revoke the power of Adms. which was granted Elizabeth Edgecomb, and do now grant letters of Adms. to Joshua Hemsted with the will annexed. And whereas, there were two daughters of the said Joshua Hemsted, deceased, viz., Patience and Lucy, born since the time of makeing the will, who had legal right to a portion of sd. estate, and to whom sd. Court of Assistants, held at Hartford 1st May, 1707, did order a part, the sd. Joshua Hemsted, their brother, having paid and satisfied them, this Court do allow and approve the same.

Page 186.

Higby, John, Middletown.   Invt. £107-09-03.   Taken 28 December, 1688, and 4 December, 1693, by John Hall, Francis Whitmore and Nathaniel Stow.

Court Record, Page 105—1 March, 1707-8: Adms. to Edward Higby, one of the sons of John Higby decd., his mother Rebeckah Higby, relict of the said decd. and late Adms. on the said estate, being dead. A former inventory was ordered recorded.

Page 105-6-7.

Hill, Thomas, Sen. (Joiner), Hartford.   Invt. £175-01-03.   Taken by John Merrells, Sen., and Thomas King.   Will dated 13 June, 1704.

I, Thomas Hill of Hartford, do make this my last will and testament: I give unto my wife Mary the one-half of all my estate, housing and lands, movable and unmovable, real and personal, to be at her own dispose during the term of her natural life. I give unto my son Thomas the other half of all my estate, and after my wife's decease I give unto my aforesaid son Thomas the other half of my estate, real and personal, which I have herein given to my wife during her natural life, my son Thomas paying such legacies as I shall appoint him. My will is that my son John be learned to read and write well, and also that he be put forth apprentice to some good trade. And when my son John shall attain to the age of 21 years, I order my son Thomas to pay unto him £10 in current country pay. Further, I order my son Thomas to pay unto his sister Mary Dudley 40 shillings, and unto his sister Elizabeth Dudley 40 shillings. I give to my daughter Sarah £5, to be paid her by my son Thomas when she shall attain the age of 22 years. I appoint my wife and my son Thomas sole executors.

Witness: *Ebenezer Hopkins,*   THOMAS HILL, LS.
        Edward Allyn.

Court Record, Page 59—7 September, 1704: Will proven.

Page 174.

Hill, Thomas, Jr., Hartford. Invt. £104-04-01. Taken 21 March, 1706-7, by Gerrard Spencer, Sen., and Daniel Merrells.

Court Record, Page 94—2 June, 1707: This Court grant Adms. on the sd. estate unto Ann Hill, the relict and widow, and James Steele.

Page 107 (Vol. VIII) 6 January, 1712-13: This Court order the Clerk to cite Ann Foster of Hartford, Adms. on the estate of Thomas Hill, Jr., late of Hartford, decd., that she appear before the Court of Probate to be holden at Hartford on the 1st Monday of February next ensueing and render an account of her Adms. on that estate.

Page 111—2 February, 1712-13: This Court grant letters of Adms. unto Edward Foster of Hartford, Adms. being formerly commited to the widow, who hath not finished her Adms. on sd. estate.

Page 253—2 May, 1715: Edward Foster, Adms., exhibits an account of debts due from the estate and reports that the personal property is not sufficient to pay the debts.

Page 33 (Vol. IX) 4 June, 1717: Edward Foster, Adms., now exhibits an account of his Adms., which is allowed.

Page 88—12 December, 1718: This Court appoint Edward Foster and Ann his wife guardians to Thomas and Susannah Hill, minor children of Thomas Hill, late of Hartford, decd., Recog. £50.

Page 116—5 January, 1719-20: Edward and Ann Foster are appointed by this Court to be guardians to Thomas Hill, 14 years of age, and Susannah Hill, age about 12 years; children of Thomas Hill, late decd. Recog., £100.

Page 117 (Vol. X) 1st February, 1725-6: Edward Foster, guardian unto Thomas Hills, late of Hartford, who died at Suffield, exhibited an account of guardianship whilst he (the sd. Thomas Hill) continued in his sickness, amounting to the sum of £31-06-04, which by this Court is allowed. And Susannah Hills, sister of sd. decd., appeared and claimed what estate is belonging to sd. decd., and offered to pay the sum above mentioned. And upon the sd. Susannah giving security for the payment of sd. £31-06-04 unto sd. Edward Foster, this Court do direct and advise Daniel Merrells and Obadiah Spencer to pass over and convey the estate in lands that they purchased of Mr. Ebenezer Devotion by order of General Court holden at Hartford, May, 1718, for the sd. Thomas and Susannah, unto the sd. Susannah to be to her, her heirs and assigns forever.

Susannah Hills before this Court declared that she had no demands to make upon Edward Foster, and the sd. Foster declared that he had no demands to make upon the sd. Susannah as his ward, and do discharge each other from all demands whatsoever under the capacities aforesd.

Invt. in Vol. VIII, Page 31.

Hollister, Lazarus, Wethersfield. Invt. £260-16-09. Taken 28 November, 1709 by James Steele and Thomas Chester.

Court Record, Page 135—15 November, 1709. This Court grant letters of Adms. on the estate of sd. Lazarus, decd., unto John Hollister, Jr., son of John Hollister of Glastonbury, and unto Jonathan Hollister of Wethersfield.

Page 82 (Vol. VIII) 2 June, 1712: John Hollister of Glastonbury and Jonathan Hollister of Wethersfield exhibit an account of their Adms. and move for a dist. The Court order the Clerk to issue notification to the relations to appear and be heard.

Page 85—7 July, 1712: Whereas, by the accompt of Adms. the

	£ s d
amount of Inventory is:	272-06-09
Paid in debts and charges,	69-00-07
There remains to be distributed,	203-06-06
To Mrs. Mary Welles of Strattford, a sister,	33-17-08 1-6
To the heirs of Mr. John Hollister,	33-17-08 1-6
To the heirs of Thomas Hollister,	33-17-08 1-6
To the heirs of Stephen Hollister,	33-17-08 1-6
To the heirs of Elizabeth Hollister (otherwise Wells),	33-17-08 1-6
To the heirs of Sarah Hollister, alias Baker, of Northampton,	33-17-08 1-6

And appoint Thomas Chester, Edward Bulkeley and James Patterson dist. This Court now grant John Hollister and Jonathan Hollister, Adms., a *Quietus Est.*

Page 89—1st September, 1712: John Hollister, joynt Adms. with Elizabeth Hollister, daughter of John Hollister, Sen., with will annexed, appealed from the decree of the Court of July last past, for a dist. of part of the estate of Lazarus Hollister. The reason assigned is that the sd. John Hollister's part of the sd. Lazarus Hollister's estate ought to be dist. to sd. Elizabeth, it being bequeathed to sd. Elizabeth by the sd. John Hollister in his last will and testament.

Page 94—3 November, 1712: This Court, for sundry reasons, do defer the consideration and determination hereupon until the 1st Monday of December next. And this Court order that no dist. be made of John Hollister's part until such determination be had.

Page 99—1st December, 1712: This Court do now resolve and order that the sd. John Hollister's part of sd. estate shall be dist. and set out to the sd. Elizabeth, anything in the sd. order of 7th July to the contrary notwithstanding.

Page 123—21 March, 1712-13: This Court do now order that the land and real estate of which Lazarus Hollister died seized or that does in any way belong to his estate shall be dist. and divided to and among the surviving brothers and sisters and their legal representatives according to an order or decree of this Court held here on the 7th of July last past, any other act or decree of the Court of Probate holden since the sd. 7th July to the contrary notwithstanding, and appoint George Stilman, David Goodrich and James Patterson distributors. And John Hollister appealed to the Superior Court.

Page 204—8 June, 1714: John Hollister of Glastonbury appearing now before this Court and moving that whereas the dist., who were appointed to dist. the estate of Lazarus Hollister, as appeared by the decree of this Court of the 21st March, 1712-13, did not go through with that work in setting out to the heirs of Lt. Thomas Hollister their part of the sd. estate in particular among them as called collatterall heirs, viz., Joseph Hollister, Abijah Hollister and Mary Harris, children of the sd. Thomas Hollister, their respective shares in severalty, do now order that the sd. dist. shall again proceed and set out to the sd. Joseph, Abijah and Mary their respective shares in severalty according to sd. former decree.

Page 34.

Hollister, Lt. Thomas, Wethersfield. Died 8 November, 1701. Invt. £369-12-06. Taken 19 December, 1701, by Benjamin Churchill, Isaac Boreman and Samuel Wright.

Court Record, Page 23—9th December, 1701: Adms. is granted to Elizabeth the relict and Thomas the eldest son. Walter Harris of Glastonbury and John Williams of Wethersfield, sureties for £150.

Page 25—9 March, 1701-2: Invt. exhibited by Elizabeth the relict, who made oath that she had truly presented the estate that her decd. husband died seized of in his own right and as Adms. on the estate of Amos Williams decd. John Hollister, a son of Lt. Thomas Hollister, decd., chose John Hollister, son of John Hollister of Glastonbury, to be his guardian; and Joseph Hollister, son of Lt. Thomas Hollister, decd., chose Walter Harris to be his guardian. This Court order a dist. of the estate and appoint Ensign Jonathan Boreman and Jonathan Ryly to dist. the estate accordingly.

Page 28—12 March, 1701-2: Adms. to Thomas Hollister revoked; Mrs. Elizabeth Hollister to be sole Adms. Recog., £150.

Dist. File, 1702-3: Estate of Lt. Thomas Hollister: to Thomas, to Jonathan, to John, to Walter Harris in right of his wife Mary, to John Williams in right of his wife Sarah, to John Hollister in right of his wife Abigail, and to the widow. By Jonathan Boreman, Jonathan Riley and Nathaniel Foote.

Holyoke, Thomas. Court Record, Page 54—9 March, 1703-4: Thomas Holyoke, whom Capt. Richards brought out of England, appeared in Court and made choice of Capt. Joseph Wadsworth for his guardian, which choice this Court approve and confirm.

Page 95.

Hopewell, Sarah, Wethersfield, Indian woman. Invt. £5-13-00. Taken 22 April, 1704, by James Treat and Benjamin Gilbert.

Court Record, Page 56—26 May, 1704: Adms. granted to Joseph Belden.

Page 59—7 September, 1704: Report of the Adms.

Page 73—6 December, 1705: Dist. to her relatives, to Robin Masshoot, to Sarah Onepenny and Munnumquask.

Page 74-5-6.

Hopkins, Stephen, Hartford. Died 11 October, 1703: Invt. £538-10-08. Taken 1st November, 1703, by John Shepherd, Edward Allyn and James Steele.

Court Record, Page 49—6 November, 1703: Adms. is granted to Mrs. Hannah Hopkins the relict, with Ebenezer Hopkins.

Page 60—8 November, 1704: Adms. account rendered and accepted.

Page 61—16 November, 1704: This Court appoint Hannah Hopkins, widow, to be guardian to Thomas Hopkins, her son; and Sarah Hopkins, one of the daughters of Stephen Hopkins, decd., chose Ebenezer Hopkins to be her guardian. Also Rachel, another daughter, and Joseph, a son, chose Ebenezer Hopkins to be their guardian. Approved.

Dist. File: 22 November, 1704: Dist. of the estate of Stephen Hopkins as followeth:

	£ s d		£ s d
To the Widow,	154-17-00	To Sarah,	73-09-05
To Thomas,	148-15-10	To Rachel,	73-09-05

And appoint Ciprian Nicols and Capt. Aaron Cooke to dist. the estate.

Page 165-6-7-8.

Hoskins, Anthony, Sen., Windsor. Died 4 January, 1706-7. Invt. £984-09-07. Taken 8 January, 1706-7, by John Moore, Sen., Matthew Allyn and Samuel Moore. Will dated 1st May, 1704:

I, Anthony Hoskins, Sen., of Windsor, being grown ancient, doe make this my last will and testament: I give to my now wife Mary the £40 that before marriage I obliged myself to give her, as also the improvement of the north end of the house I purchased of Tahan Grant, during her widowhood. I give unto my son John Hoskins a double portion of my estate, and in consideration that he hath lived with me and been very carefull of me and helpfull to me in my aged state, my will is that he should have £20 added to it. And if I live any considerable time after the ratification of this will, my mind is that he shall have further added £10. I give to him my dwelling house and barn and my homestead and orchard, about 10 acres; also in the Great Meadow 5 acres. And after my decease the rest of the sd. parcel of land, being about 10 acres, which I purchased of Samuel Farnsworth, also 17 acres of woodland on the north side of the Rivulet at Rocky Hill, bought of Samuel Gardner of Salem, I also give to my said son John Hoskins. I give to Robert Hoskins, my son, all my land at Simsbury, the homelott, 4 acres, and 16 acres of meadow that I had of John Owen; also 4 acres, a homelott, and 20 acres of meadow which I purchased of Capt Benjamin Newbery, and 10 acres of upland the Towne gave me; also my share in the Commons. I give to my son Thomas Hoskins the homelott and orchard I bought of Simon Mills, about 7 acres, and 10 acres of upland in the woods. I give him in the Great Meadow 3 acres bought of Alexander Allyn, merchant, and I give him all that he owes me. I give unto my son Anthony Hoskins all the land I have at Greenfield, 10 acres of which I bought of Josiah Clarke, and of Nathan Messenger I bought 10 acres more; and also the marsh at Wash Brooke which I purchased of Messenger; as also I give him the £12 cash I paid for him to Stedman as attorney for Mrs. Wilson of Hartford. I give to my son Joseph Hoskins the house and homestead I bought of Tahan Grant, excepting the north end of the house, which he is not to have during my wive's widowhood. Also, I give unto him my lott on the east side of the Great River which I had of John Witchfield, being 30 rods in breadth and holding the same breadth 3 miles. I give unto my daughter Grace Eglestone £60; also give her 15 acres of land near Miles Hole. I also give unto my daughter Jane Alford £60, to be paid her as to my other daughter, besides what I have already given her. I give to my deceased daughter Isabell Alford all that I have already given her and 2 shillings pay. My mind is that all should have the privilege of the Commons. I have yet undisposed of 12½ acres in the Great Meadow and also 8 acres at Podunk. Now my will is that this undisposed land and my stock and moveables should goe toward the payment of my wive's £40, and to my daughters' £120-02-00. I appoint my son John Hoskins and my son Jeremiah Alford executors. I desire William Phelps, son of Capt. Timothy Phelps, and Samuel Moore to be overseers.

Witness: *Henry Wolcott, Sen.,*　　　ANTHONY X HOSKINS SEN., LS.
　　　　　Samuel Wolcott.

Court Record, Page 89—3 February, 1706-7: Will and Invt. exhibited, but Anthony and John Hoskins, two of the sons of the decd., prayed the Court that the will be not proved.

Page 90—3 March, 1706-7: In Court, no further objections being offered, the will was proven.

Page 90.

House, William, Glastonbury. Invt. £119-13-04. Taken 22 February, 1703-4, by Joseph Smith and Thomas Hale, Sen. The children: John, age 30 years; Sarah Smith, 28; Mary Hale, 26; Anne House, 20; William House, 19; Joseph House, 16 years of age.

Page 316 (Vol. IX, Probate Side): An agreement for the division of the estate of William House, late decd.: We, Joseph Smith and Thomas Hale Jr., who married two of the daughters of the above sd. William House, have since the death of our father received £3 apeice, with which, besides what we received before his death, we acknowledge ourselves fully satisfied. Ann House has received out of the estate £20. William and Joseph House has assigned, set over and confirmed to them by the general consent and concurrence of their guardians, overseers and brethren and sisters, 66 acres of land at the east end of their father's land, some whereof is cleared and has been improved, and also the house their father dwelt in, which house and parcel of land is equally to be divided betwixt them. John House has, by general consent, 33 acres of land at the west end of his father's land, which sd. John is to improve the land belonging to the two youngest brethren till they come to the age of 21 years, he also to pay the debts due from his father's estate and to take the remainder of the moveables to his own proper use. We having agreed, received and had set over unto us out of our father's estate, then be it known that we and every of us do forever release, remise and quitclaim to any part or parcel of our honoured father's estate, deceased, besides what we have received, assigned and set over to us in the premises, mutually engaging that every of us shall hereafter possess his or her part according to the tenour of this writing without any quarrels, controversies or demands whatsoever. In witness whereof we have each of us set to our hands and seals, 8th March, 1703-4.

In presence ot

Jno. Bevins,
Gershom Smith,

JOHN X HOUSE, LS.
JOSEPH SMITH, LS.
THOMAS HALE, JR., LS.
ANN X HOUSE, LS.
WILLIAM X HOUSE, LS.
THOMAS X HALE, SEN., LS.
JOSEPH X HOUSE, LS.
MARY X HALE,
SARAH X SMITH,
JOSEPH SMITH.

Court Record, Page 54 (Vol. VII) 9 March, 1703-4: Adms. granted unto John House. Joseph House, a minor son of William House, late of Glastonbury decd., chose Joseph Smith of the same town for his guardian. William House, also son of William House, chose Thomas Hale, Sen., to be his guardian.

Will and Invt. recorded in Vol. VIII, Page 1.

Howard, Henry, Hartford. Invt. £649-01-00. Taken March, 1708-9, by Joseph Wadsworth and Aaron Cooke. Will dated 20 January, 1707-8.

I, Henry Howard of Hartford, doe now make my last will and testament: I give to my son John all my lands in the South Meadow in Hartford, excepting one peece at the hether end of sd. meadow, which I have already made over to my son Samuel. I give to my son John 1 parcel of land I bought of Joshua Sachem, lying on the east side of the Great River, on the east side of the mountain, containing 100 acres, as will appear by deed; also my stock of cattle and sheep which I do not otherwise dispose of, and horse or horses if any remain; also what may remain after my dices (decease), and my wive's, of pork, of money, malt or grain, with book debts; also in household stuff and tooles, £5. I give to my son Samuel, besides what I have already given him of my estate, the cupboard with drawers which stands in the hall chamber. My will is that that which remains of household stuffe shall be equally divided between my two daugters, Mary and Lydia. My will is that John Achett, my grandson (upon consideration of his relation to me and living with me and promising to live with me or my wife if we live two years from the date hereof following, and if we both decease sooner his service shall be at an end) shall have out of my estate the 40 acres of land, more or less, lying at 4-Mile Hill, by Farmington Path, and abutting upon Nathaniel Stanly his land on the north, with personal estate, if he live with me and my wife the term of 2 years, shall then have this estate set out and delivered to him for his own use and behoof. Also, I give to my grandson Samuel Achett 2 pewter platters of the bigger sort. Item. I give to my beloved wife the use of all my estate during her life for her comfortable maintenance. I make Sarah, my wife, my sole executrix, and desire Mr. Nathaniel Stanly, Sen., Capt. Joseph Wadsworth and Joseph Talcott to be overseers.

Witness: *Nathaniel Stanly, Sen.,*   HENRY HOWARD, LS.
Joseph Wadsworth, Joseph Talcott.

Codicil, dated 12 March, 1708-9: He disposes of £5, before set to his son John, now to be given to his two daughters, Mary and Lydia. Also gives to his son Joseph Barnard what he is indebted to me, and adds something to what he gave to his grandson John Achett.

Witness: *Nathaniel Stanly,*
Joseph Wadsworth, Joseph Talcott.

Court Record, Page 125—4 April, 1709: The last will and testament of Henry Howard, late of Hartford, maltster, decd., was now exhibited in this Court, whereby Sarah Howard of Hartford, widow, relict of the said deceased, is appointed sole executrix. And now two of the witnesses of the said will were sworn before this Court in manner accustomed, and the same will, with the codicil or addition underwritten on the same sheet of paper, was proved, and is by this Court approved and allowed to be recorded and kept upon file.

Page 130—6 June, 1709: Sarah Howard of Hartford, widow, relict of Henry Howard, late of Hartford, maltster, decd., and sole executrix of his will, exhibited now in this Court an inventory of the estate of the said deceased, upon oath in manner accustomed, which inventory this Court do order to be recorded and kept on file.

Page 25 (Vol. IX) 4 December, 1716: Whereas, Mrs. Sarah Howard, executrix to the last will of Henry Howard, decd., through infirmity of age is incapable of executing that trust, this Court grant letters *Cum Testimento annexo* unto John Howard of Wethersfield and Joseph Barnard of Hartford.

Page 114-115.

Hubbard, Daniel, Middletown. Died November, 1704. Invt. £214-18-03. Taken 5 December, 1704, by John Cornwall, Sen., and John Hall. Will dated 8 November, 1704.

I, Daniel Hubbard of Middletown, doe make this my last will and testament: I leave unto my loving wife Sarah the use and improvement of my dwelling house, barn and homelott, and 2 acres of my boggy meadow, for her comfortable subsistence during her natural life, and 1-3 part of all my personal estate, to be disposed of as she shall see meet. The rest of my lands and personal estate it is my will that it be equally shared amongst all my children. I appoint my wife to be executrix, and request Lt. Thomas Ward to be overseer.

Witness: *Samuel Hall,*   DANIEL X HUBBARD, LS.
 Richard Hubbard, John Hall.

Court Record, Page 63—6 March, 1704-5: Will proven.

Page 78—8 March, 1705-6: Sarah Hubbard, widow, executrix, exhibited now an account of her Adms., and this Court order dist. of the estate and appoint Capt. John Hall, Lt. Thomas Ward and Mr. Alexander Rollo distributors.

Record on File: To Daniel Hubbard of Haddam, son of the decd., to Margaret, to Sarah, to Mehetabell, and to Mary Hubbard; by John Hall, Thomas Ward and Alexander Rollo.

Page 117-118.

Johnson, Nathaniel, Middletown. Died 19 February, 1704-5. Invt. £121-12-03. Taken 5 March, 1704-5, by Thomas Ward, William Harris and John Harris. The children: Nathaniel, about 3 years of age, and Mary, 5 years of age.

Court Record, Page 64—6 March, 1704-5. Adms. to Mary Johnson, the widow, and Joseph Johnson, a brother of the decd. Recog., £60.

Page 70-1-2.

Judd, Rachel, Farmington. Invt. £101-10-08. Will dated 6 February, 1701-2.

I, Rachel Judd of Farmington, do make this my last will and testament: I give to my honoured mother the ½ of all my wearing clothes. I give to my brother Samuel my long table and £2 that is due to me from my brother Thomas Judd. I give to Sarah Strong, daughter of my sister Mary Janes, 1 pair of sheets. I give to Rachel Janes, daughter of my sister Mary Janes, 1 pair of sheets. I give to Rachel Judd of Waterbury, daughter of my brother Thomas Judd, 1 pair of sheets. I give to my brother John's William that scarf that my brother John has in keeping. I give to my brother Daniel Judd £6 out of that £20 of land that I have already received, and £6 out of that £20 that belongs to me after my mother's decease. And I give to my brother Daniel Judd all those debts that be due to me for my labour, all those that be within 7 years standing, excepting what my mother and brothers owe me. And I give to my brother John 20 shillings of that he owes me. And I give to my brother Samuel Judd £1 he owes me. I give to my sister Elizabeth Judd all the rest of my land and goods, chattells and debts, and all my estate not hereinbefore given or bequeathed, only she is not to trouble my mother for what she owes me during her life. I make my brother Daniel Judd sole executor.

Witness: *Daniel Woodruff,*   RACHEL X JUDD, LS.
        Joseph Judd.

Court Record, Page 48—1st November, 1703. Will proven.

Page 50-1.

Judd, Thomas, Lt., Waterbury. Invt. £407-00-00. Taken 30 January, 1702-3, by Thomas Judd and Stephen Upson.

Court Record, Page 39—2 March, 1702-3: Adms. granted to Thomas Judd and John Judd.

An agreement, made this 4th day of March, Annoqe Dominy 1702-3, for a distribution and settlement of the estate of Sergt. Thomas Judd, late of Waterbury, deceased, by Thomas Judd and John Judd of Waterbury, sons of the aforesd. Sergt. Thomas Judd deceased, and Stephen Hopkins of Hartford in behalf of his children and as heirs to the estate of the sd. Lt. Thomas Judd, that they should have 1-3 of the outlands in Farmington, laid out or not laid out, excepting 10 acres at Buck's Brook which Thomas Hopkins, son of Stephen, shall have wholly free.

Witness: *T. Woodbridge,*   (Signed)   THOMAS JUDD, LS.
   Hez: Wyllys.   JOHN JUDD, LS.
           STEPHEN HOPKINS, LS.

Page 145 (Vol. X) 7 February, 1726-7: Whereas, it is represented to this Court that Thomas Hopkins of Hartford, grandchild to Lt. Thomas Judd of Waterbury, and one of his heirs, that there is an estate in lands lying in Farmington that has not been inventoried, this Court order that the rest of the heirs of sd. deceased, by a copy hereof, be notified to appear before this Court on the 1st Tuesday of March next, if they or any of them shall see cause, to show wherefore Adms. should not be granted, that an invt. of sd. estate might be exhibited in order for a dist. thereof to and amongst the heirs of sd. decd.

(Invt. in Vol. VIII, Page 14.)

Kellogg, Samuel, Colchester. Invt. £270-12-00. Taken 21 September, 1708, by Joseph Wright and Nathaniel Loomis.

Court Record, Page 131—1st August, 1709: This Court grant Adms. unto Hannah Kellogg, widow, relict.

Page 252 (Vol. VIII) 2 May, 1715: Hannah Kellog, widow, Adms., exhibits an account of her Adms. Accepted. Order to dist. the estate as followeth:

	£ s d
To Hannah Kellog, widow,	24-12-08
To Samuel, eldest son,	93-02-00
To Joseph, Hannah and Eunice Kellogg, to each the sum of	46-11-00

And appoint Israel Wyatt, Samuel Loomis and Joseph Wright, of Colchester, distributors. Joseph Kellogg, a minor, 19 years of age, chose Nathaniel Kellogg to be his guardian. And this Court appoint Mrs. Hannah Kellogg to be guardian to Hannah, 16 years of age, and Eunice, 14 years. Recog., £100.

Page 111 (Vol. IX) 1 September, 1719: Upon motion of Nathaniel Clark of Lebanon and Hannah Clark, his wife, as the sd. Hannah is one of the daughters and co-heir of Samuel Kellogg, late of Colchester decd., representing that Adms. was granted August, 1709, unto Hannah Kellogg, widow, relict of sd. decd., and no account having yet been rendered or estate set out to the sd. Hannah Clark, Hannah Kellogg, being summoned into Court, affirmed that she made up her account of Adms. with the Court of Probate, 2 May, 1715, which account was allowed and accepted and which was found recorded, but was ordered to complete the dist. and report 1st Tuesday of October next.

Dist. per File: September, 1719: To Hannah Kellogg, widow, lands in Colchester, lands east of New London and in Hatfield, also lands east of Norwich; to Samuel, to Joseph, to Hannah Clark, to Eunice Kellogg; by Joseph Wright and Israel Wyott.

Page 112—8 September, 1719: A distribution of the estate of Samuel Kellogg, late of Colchester, under the hands of Joseph Wright and Israel Wyatt, was exhibited, allowed, and ordered on file.

Page 59-60-1-2.

Kilbourn, John, Sergt., Sen., Wethersfield. Died 9th April, 1703. Invt. £348-10-01. Taken by Jonathan Boreman and Jonathan Belding. Will dated 24 September, 1688.

I, John Kilbourn, Senior, of Wethersfield, yeoman, do appoint this my last will and testament: I give to my son John Kilbourn, besides what I have formerly given and settled on him and his heirs, my whole right and title to that tract of land sometime since purchased of the Indians on the east side of the Great River; also I give to my son John my great Bible and one great booke of Mr. Perkins his works. I give to my son Thomas Kilbourn and to his heirs forever the remainder of my land at Naubuck and £6 in current country pay. I give to my daughter Naomi Hale (besides what I have given her) my silver beaker and one pair of sheets. My will is that my wife Sarah Kilbourn shall enjoy and possess one-half of my housing and homelot abutting on the Broad Street east, and one-third part of all my lands lying on the west side of the Great River, during the time of her natural life. I give to my son Ebenezer Kilbourn and to his heirs one-half of my housing and homelot facing the Broad Street, to be to him and to his heirs at my decease; and the other half of the same to him and to his heirs forever at the decease of his mother, Sarah Kilbourn. I give to my daughter Sarah Crane, besides what I have already given her, the sum of £15 as country pay. I give to my son George Kilbourn my house and homelot facing against Bell Lane (with other lands). I also give my sd. son George one silver spoon marked "G. M. G. K.," provided he shall pay £10 to my daughter Mary Kilbourn in good country pay within four years after my decease, and 20s to his brother Thomas Kilbourn within the same time. I give to my daughter Mary Kilbourn £38 in country pay, whereof her brother George is to pay £10, and £28 to be paid by my executors within 2 years after my decease or after her marriage. I give to my son Joseph Kilbourn the one-half of my land at the whirlpools in the Great Meadow, and half my land at Mile Meadow, and half my land at Beaver Meadow, and one-fourth part of my long lot at the Town's End, that is to say, he, his heirs or assigns to enjoy two-thirds of those lands at the age of 21 years, and the rest at his mother's decease. He also shall pay 20s to his brother Thomas Kilbourn. I give to my son Abraham Kilbourn one-half of the land described as those given to Joseph Kilbourn. Lastly, I give all the rest of my moveable estate, chattel or chattels whatsoever, to my loveing wife Sarah Kilbourn, shee paying all my just debts and legacies. And I appoint my wife and son Ebenezer Kilbourn to be executors, to whom I give the power of dividing my lands to my sons respectively as above exprest.

Witness: *Samuel Boreman,*   JOHN KILBOURN, SENIOR, LS.
            Samuel Butler.

Court Record, Page 44—4 May, 1703: The will exhibited by the executors. One of the witnesses appeared in Court, viz., Samuel Boreman, the other (Samuel Butler) being dead. The children appearing in Court and manifesting their satisfaction with the will, it was proven and approved.

Page 211.

Kimberly, Eleazer, Glastonbury. Died February, 1708-9. Invt. £356-04-11. Taken 11 February, 1708-9, by John Kilbourn, Sen., and William Wickham. Will dated 30 January, 1708-9.

I, Eleazer Kimberly, being sick and weake, do make this my last will and testament: I give to my son Thomas Kimberly my housing and all my lands in Glastonbury, to be to him and his heirs forever, reserving to my two daughters, Elizabeth and Ruth, who now live with me, convenient and comfortable room in my dwelling house so long as they shall have need of it, they to have the benefit of the new room until my sd. son puts a new covering upon the roof of the old room and clap-boards the sides of it and mends the windows, and makes it comfortable for them; also 1-2 of the fruit in my orchard. I give them also 1-2 of my garden, sufficient quantity of grass land for the wintering of 3 cows, and also convenient pasture for the 3 cows. And what other estate I have in debts, goods or whatever, my will is that it be equally divided amongst my 4 daughters, consideration being had of what either of them have already received. My will is that my daughter Elizabeth shall have my lands at the lower end of Wethersfield Meadow, at the value of £30. I appoint my son Thomas and daughter Elizabeth executors. I desire my friends, Lt. Samuel Hale and John Curtis, Sen., to be overseers.

                                                    ELEAZER KIMBERLY.

Court Record, Page 121—15 February, 1708-9: Will proven. The signatures of the legatees, under their hands and seals, were endorsed upon the original will as presented to the Court in acceptance of the will of their father, Eleazer Kimberly, written by his own hand and signed by him, but not sealed or witnessed.

Signed: THOMAS KIMBERLY, LS.   RUTH KIMBERLY, LS.
         ELIZABETH KIMBERLY, LS.   MARY HUBBARD, LS.
         JOHN KILBOURN, LS.   JOHN HUBBARD, LS.
         SARAH KILBOURN, LS.

This Court grant letters of Adms. unto Thomas Kimberly, Elizabeth having refused to accept the trust of executorship.

Page 40.

King, Edward, Windsor. Invt. £74-00-00. Taken 13 July, 1702, by John Stoughton, Nathaniel Loomis and Henry Wolcott.

Court Record, Page 33—8 September, 1702: Mary Hillyard, daughter of Edward King, late of Windsor, deceased, exhibited in Court a writing signed by the sd. Edward King, which they call a will. Not accepted. Adms. to Zachary Sanford upon the desire of Mary Hillyard and Sarah Kady, daughters of the deceased, who dwell at Long Island. Lt. Sandford, rec., £20.

Page 147.

King, Sarah. Invt. £28-09-05. Taken 6 March, 1705-6, by Thomas King and Thomas Richards. Sarah King, late wife of Capt. John King of Northampton.

Court Record, Page 59—30 November, 1704: Adms. to Benjamin Graham and Joseph Mygatt of Hartford, who gave bond of £100.

Page 79—8 March, 1705- 6: Invt. exhibited.

Page 20.

Knight, George, Hartford. Invt. £257-07-00. Taken 15 June, 1699, by Aaron Cooke and Samuel Olcott.

Court Record, Page 20—13 November, 1701: Sarah, the relict, presents an account of her Adms. and is granted a *Quietus Est*. The Court distributes the estate as followeth: Debts being deducted, £30-04-09. To the widow, 1-3 part of the real estate during life, and 1-3 part of the moveables forever. To the rest of the children (they being all daughters) an equal share in the remaining estate. And appoint Capt. Cooke, Lt. Talcott and Samuel Olcott distributors.

Lefeavor, Philip, Windsor. Court Record, Page 71—6 September, 1705: Adms. to John Moore. He refused to give bond, and the papers and letters that he exhibited in this Court were returned to him again.

Page 159.

Lewis, Joseph, Simsbury. Invt. £24-00-00. Taken 13 May, 1706, by Samuel Wilcoxson, Sen., and Samuel Pettebone.

Court Record, Page 88—13 November, 1706: John Tuller and Elizabeth his wife, Adms. on the estate of Joseph Lewis, having finished their Adms., this Court do grant them a *Quietus Est*. The sd. John and

Elizabeth Tuller release right of dower unto the children of sd. Joseph Lewis, and lands in value £24 were then divided: To Joseph Lewis, John Lewis, and Elizabeth Smith, children of the sd. decd. Joseph Case, of Simsbury, attorney for these children. This Court appoint Samuel Humphries, Sergt. Samuel Wilcox and John Pettebone, Jr., distributors.

Page 105.

Loomis, Isaac, Windsor. Invt. £53-00-00. Taken 4 September, 1704, by Daniel Loomis and Timothy Loomis.

Court Record, Page 58—7 September, 1704: Adms. granted to Stephen Loomis of Windsor, a brother to Isaac Loomis, late of Windsor, deceased.

Page 179.

Loomis, Jonathan, Windsor (Blacksmith). Invt £98-10-00. Taken 28 November, 1707, by John Moore, Sen., William Burnham and Nathaniel Loomis.

Court Record, Page 100—1st December, 1707: Nathaniel and Sarah Loomis exhibit an inventory of their father's estate. Adms. to Nathaniel and David Loomis, brothers of the sd. deceased, who refused. This Court appoint Nathaniel Loomis guardian to Jonathan Loomis, 13 years of age, and Nathaniel Loomis, a minor, chose David Loomis to be his guardian.

Page 31 (Vol. VIII) 2 April, 1711: Whereas, this Court, 1st December, 1707, granted Adms. to Nathaniel Loomis and David Loomis, brothers of the sd. decd., they having refused, this Court grant letters to Joseph Newbery of Windsor, son-in-law of sd. deceased.

Page 32—2 April, 1711: Jonathan Loomis, 16 years of age, one of the sons of Jonathan Loomis of Windsor decd., chose his uncle, David Loomis, to be his guardian.

Page 49—4 February, 1711-12: Adms. on the estate of Jonathan Loomis, decd., to Nathaniel Loomis, son of sd. decd., with Joseph Newbery of Windsor.

Page 128—6 April, 1713: Nathaniel Loomis and Joseph Newbery, Adms., exhibit now an account of their administration as followeth:

	£ s d
Inventory.	123-04-04
Beside the reversion of land in the hand of Widow Case.	
Paid in debts and charges,	25-06-10
There remains to be distributed,	97-13-06
Account accepted. This Court order dist. as followeth:	
To Nathaniel Loomis, eldest son,	48-16-09
To Jonathan Loomis,	24-08-04½
To Sarah Newbery, formerly Sarah Loomis, only daughter,	24-08-04½

And appoint Daniel Loomis, Thomas Moore and James Enno, Jr., distributors.

Page 123.

Lucas, John, Middletown. Died November, 1704. Invt. £59-13-05. Taken 2 March, 1704-5, by Samuel Bidwell and Job Paine. The children: Easter, age 11 years; Mary 9, John 5, Thankful 3, Daniel, one year old.

Court Record, Page 65—6 March, 1704-5: Adms. granted to Mary Lucas, the widow and relict of the sd. decd.

See File.

Marshall, Benjamin, Hartford. Invt. £44-15-11, according to a dist., 1696; also £10 given him by his brother, Thomas Marshall, should he live to be 21 years of age.

Court Record, Page 28—12 March, 1701: This Court grant power of Adms. on the estate of Benjamin Marshall, late of Hartford, who died intestate, unto Elizabeth Marshall, his sister, provided she give bond as the law directs. Ensign John Stedman became surety in a £100 bond to exhibit an inventory and render an account by the 1st Thursday of September next.

Page 33—8 September, 1702: Whereas, Benjamin Marshall, son of Thomas Marshall, decd., died in his minority having estate belonging to him, this Court dist. the same unto the child of Nathaniel Stoddard by Mary Marshall, and to Elizabeth Marshall, alias Elizabeth Darrow, in equal proportions. And forasmuch as letters of Adms. was granted to Elizabeth Marshall, upon the estate of Benjamin, this Court do call in the sd. letters and discharge the Adms. from her bond.

Page 40—2 March, 1702-3: This Court appoint and impower John Catlin and Sergt. Caleb Standly and Jonathan Webster, or any two of them, to dist. the estate of Benjamin Marshall, decd., according to an order of Court made in September last, and order that they return an account of their doings thereon to the Court to be holden on the 1st Tuesday of April next.

Page 4-5.

Marshall, Thomas, Seaman. Will dated 15 February, 1696-7: Thomas Marshall of Hartford, in the Colony of Connecticut, in New England, seaman, now resident in Boston, being bound on a voyage to sea, do therefore make and ordain this my last will and testament: I give to my sister Elizabeth Marshall of Hartford aforesaid, spinster, £5 money; and to my brother Benjamin Marshall of Hartford, when he come of age, £10 money; and to my uncle John Catlin of Hartford, yeoman, 20 shillings. I do give, devise and bequeath my lands and farm at Hartford abovesaid, with the rights, members and appurtenances thereunto belonging, together with the rest and residue of all my real and personal estate whatsoever, unto my beloved friend Mary Chauntrell of Boston aforesaid, spinster, and to her heirs forever, and of this my last will and

testament do ordain and appoint the said Mary Chauntrell to be sole ex-
ecutrix.   THOMAS MARSHALL.
Witness: *Richard Wilkins,*
Ralph Pirkins, Eliezer Moody.
A (True) Copy.
Per Isaac Addington, Reg'r.

Court Record, Page 2—22 October, 1700: Mary the relict of
Thomas Marshall, late of Boston, formerly of Hartford, decd., exhibited
a copy of her late husband's will wherein she is appointed executrix, at-
tested by Hond. Wm. Stoughton, Esq., Judge of Probate, and Mr. Sec'y
Addington. Also presented some evidences of being married to sd.
Thomas Marshall. The will was proven and approved.

Page 11—8 April, 1701: Upon motion of Nathaniel Foote, attorney
for the widow of Thomas Marshall, this Court order Major Jonathan
Bull, Joseph Whiting and Ensign Thomas Bunce to make distribution of
the estate of Thomas Marshall deceased.

Page 13—16 June, 1701: Mary the relict of Thomas Marshall, late
of Boston, deceased, makes complaint to this Court of difficulties in obtaining her husband's right in the estate of his father Thomas Marshall,
Sen., deceased. Parties were cited to appear in Court. Bevil Waters and
John Catlin were ordered to distribute the estate according to the will of
the testator and according to the order of this Court bearing date 21
August, 1693.

Page 137-8-9.

Meakins, John, Sen., Hartford. Invt. £480-08-00. Taken 1st April,
1706, by Joseph Olmsted and Roger Pitkin. Will dated 22 November,
1702.

I, John Meakins, Sen., of Hartford, do make and ordain this my last
will and testament: I give to my wife 1-3 part of all my moveable estate, she to have her choice of the same, and 1-3 part of my housing
and lands during her natural life only. I give to my 2 sons, John and
Joseph Meakins, my homested, that is to say, that part of my houselot
where my dwelling house now standeth, John to have that house that
he built and Joseph to have my dwelling house. And my will is that
my barn, orchard, garden and all that part of my lot up to the country
highway east of my dwelling house shall be equally divided between
them. To my son Samuel Meakins I give the 1st of the 3 parcels of
land lying on the east side of the country highway. The rest of my upland
lot lying eastward of that given to my son Samuel, as well that that is
improved as that that is not improved, I give to my three sons, John,
Joseph and Samuel Meakins, to be equally divided betwixt them, as also
my interest in the undivided land. To my three sons, John, Joseph and
Samuel, I give that part of my lot that lyeth westward from my dwelling
house as it buts on my brother Daniel Bidwell north and land belonging

to the Olcotts west. To my son John Meakins I give my half of that meadow lot that was given me by my honoured father-in-law John Bidwell, as by his will may appear. Sd. land lyeth between the lands of William Goodwin on the north and lands sometime of Richard Case on the south. To my two sons, Joseph and Samuel, I give my meadow lot commonly known by the name of Disbrow's lott. To my son Samuel Meakins I give my three acres of land that I bought of Mr. Eleazer Way. To my daughter Mary Belden I give £20 besides what she hath already had. To my daughter Sarah Spencer I give £20 besides what she hath already received. To my two daughters, Rebeckah and Hannah Meakins, I give £40 to each of them. I make my wife Mary executrix, and my son John executor, and my brother-in-law Daniel Bidwell and my friend Roger Pitkin overseers.

Witness: *Daniel Bidwell, Sen.,*   JOHN X MEAKINS, LS.
       Roger Pitkin.

Court Record, Page 74—22 January, 1705-6: Will proven.

Page 144.

Miller, William, Glastonbury (Tanner). Invt. £348-01-06. Taken 7 November, 1705, by Jonathan Smith and Joseph Smith. The children: William, age 11 years; Mary, 8; Martha, 7; Sarah, 6; John, 4; Jonathan, 1 year old.

Court Record, Page 70—6 September, 1705: Adms. to Mary, the widow, and Joseph Smith of Glastonbury.

Page 91 (Vol. VIII) 6 October, 1712: This Court order the Adms. on the estate of William Miller to appear with an account of their Adms.

NOTE: Mr. Samuel Smith of Glastonbury, a bondsman for the sd. Adms., appeared now before this Court and declared that he would stand no longer in that case as surety.

Page 108—6 January, 1712-13: This Court order Joseph Smith of Glastonbury, and Joseph Butler and Mary his wife, also Adms. on the estate of William Miller, to appear to render an account of their Adms.

Page 134—7 April, 1713: Adms. ordered to appear without further delay.

Page 150—6 July, 1713: This Court order the Clerk to issue forth a writ to bring the Adms. on the estate of William Miller, late of Glastonbury, decd., before this Court on the 1st Monday of August next ensuing, to render a full account of their Adms. on that estate, *without fail.*

Page 153—3 August, 1713: This Court order Joseph Butler and his wife Mary, and Joseph Smith, to appear and render an account without further delay.

Page 154—17 August, 1713: Adms. not being prepared to render an account, this Court extend the time until September next.

Page 157—7 September, 1713: Samuel Smith and Joseph Smith

of Glastonbury now discharged from bonds of Adms. on the estate of William Miller, and this Court now grant letters of Adms. on the unadministered estate of the sd. decd. unto Joseph Butler of Wethersfield and Mary, his wife (who was widow and relict to the sd. decd.).

Page 173—5 January, 1713-14: Whereas, Joseph Butler and Mary his wife, Adms. on the abovesd. estate, neglected to render an account of their Adms., although often summoned, there did arise this charge: £0-20-06 money for records, citations and officers' fees in serving the writ. This Court now order the Clerk to issue forth execution directed to a sheriff of the County, or either of the constables of the Town of Wethersfield, to levy the aforesd. sum according to law.

Page 91 (Vol. IX) 6 January, 1718-19: Jonathan Miller of Middletown, a minor, age 14 years, chose his brother William Miller of Glastonbury to be his guardian.

Page 11 (Vol. X) 22 March, 1723: Joseph Butler of Wethersfield, in right of his wife Mary, as she is Adms. on the estate of William Miller, late of Glastonbury, decd., exhibited an account of their Adms. on sd. estate of debts paid out of that estate, with loss and spent in the family, and allowed for keeping the two youngest children, the whole amounting to more than what has been received due to the estate. Account accepted. Whereas, it is represented that it is needful to make a second invt. of the estate of William Miller, late of Glastonbury, decd., and another apprisement made in order that the sd. estate may be more regularly distributed to and amongst the heirs, this Court order that another invt. be taken of sd. estate and exhibited to this Court by the Adms. And appoint Thomas Kimberly, Thomas Wells and Gershom Smith apprisers.

Page 177-8 (Probate Side): An invt. of William Miller's estate in the hands of Martha, William, Mr. and Mrs. Butler and Mary Hubbard, amounting to the sum of £587-15-06, taken by Thomas Kimberly and Gershom Smith.

Court Record, Page 22—2 July, 1723: Invt. exhibited and accepted.

Page 33—26 November, 1723: It being moved that an order for distribution might be granted, this Court, having considered that the moveable estate of the sd. decd. shall be dist. according to a former invt. made thereof, on record, amounting to the sum of £107-11-06, and the real estate shall be dist. according to a late invt. made thereof, amounting to the sum of £535-00-00, this Court order the estate dist. in the following manner, viz.:

	£ s d
To Mary Butler, sometime widow of the decd.,	17-11-10
To William Miller, eldest son,	162-18-02
To John and Jonathan Miller, Mary Hubbard, Martha Hollister, and Sarah Miller, the rest of the children, to each,	81-09-01

And appoint Thomas Kimberly, Thomas Wells and Gershom Smith distributors.

Page 149-50-51.

Moore, Dorothy, Farmington (late wife of Deacon Isaac Moore). Invt. £367-10-06. Taken 27 April, 1706, by Samuel Sherman, Benjamin Coney and Robert Bassett. Will dated 21 May, 1700.

I, Dorothy Moore of Farmington, having some estate left by my first and second husbands which is properly my own to dispose of in life or at death, I do make this my last will and testament. Imprimis: My sons having all received their portions left them by their father, and some lands besides their portions, I give to my grandchild Joseph Blackman my dwelling house and homested, only with this provisall, that Mary Hall, the daughter of my husband Francis Hall* decd., shall have the use and improvement of the eastermost room of the house during her life, and the privilege of the whole house for her convenience for fire-room, baking and washing, and he to provide fire-wood for her; but if my grandchild Joseph do not return to possess the sd. house and home-sted, I give it to his two brothers, John and Samuel Blackman, on the same conditions of providing for Mary Hall as aforesd. Item. I give all my lands at Cla-board Hill, and all my meadow in Stratford, to be equally divided between my two sons, John and Ebenezer Blackman, and my grandson Joseph Blackman; but if Joseph do not return, his two brothers, John and Samuel, to have his part. I give my land at Hatfield to my son Ebenezer Blackman, and all the moveables which I had of my mother's legacy at Hadley I give to my grandchild Elizabeth Blackman. I give to my grandson Joseph Blackman a featherbed. I give all the rest of my moveable estate to be equally divided between my four grand-children, namely, Abigail and Rebeckah, daughters of my son Joseph, and Dorothy and Elizabeth, daughters of my son Ebenezer. Only my will is that Mary Hall shall have liberty to make use of what household goods of mine she hath occasion for during her life. I appoint my two sons, Ebenezer Blackman and John Blackman, to be joynt executors of this my will. I desire Mr. Joseph Curtice and Mr. Israel Chauncey to be overseers.

Witness: *John Booth,*   DOROTHY MOORE, LS.
   Jacob Walker.

Court Record, Page 83—17 April, 1706: Ebenezer Blackman of Stratford, executor to the will of his mother Dorothy Moore, exhibits will and inventory. Will proven and ordered to be recorded and kept on file.

Page 199.

Morton, Thomas, Windsor. Died 20 July, 1708. Invt. £72-06-04. Taken 8 September, 1708, by Samuel Burnham, John Strong and Samuel Rockwell, Jr.

---

*See will of Francis Hall, Vol. I, Page 457.

Court Record, Page 116—7 September, 1708: Adms. to Hannah Morton, widow.

Page 116 (Vol. VIII) 2 March, 1712-13: This Court appoint Hannah Morton, widow, to be guardian to Hannah Morton, minor, daughter of Thomas Morton, late decd. Recog., £100.

Page 117—2 March, 1712-13: Hannah Morton of Windsor, Adms. on the estate of her husband, exhibits an account of her Administration:

	£ s d
Inventory,	74-04-10
Paid in debts and charges,	13-16-04
Remains for distribution,	60-08-06
Account allowed, and order dist. of the estate:	
To the widow,	20-02-10
To Hannah Morton, only child,	40-05-08

And appoint Capt. Thomas Stoughton, Matthew Grant and Samuel Rockwell, of Windsor, dist. And this Court now grant the widow a *Quietus Est.*

Page 163-4-5.

North, Samuel, Farmington. Invt. £177-19-03. Taken 25 November, 1706, by John Norton, 2nd, John Wadsworth and Daniel Andrews. Will dated 11 November, 1706.

The last will and testament of Samuel North of Farmington, in the County of Hartford, in the Colony of Connecticut, in New England, husbandman, at present residing in Boston, being under bodily illness and infirmities, but through mercy of sound disposing mind and memory, do make this my last will and testament, in manner and form following: Imprimis: I give unto my nephew Josiah North, son of my brother John North, my house and barn with the one moiety or half-part of all the lands adjoining and appertaining thereunto, containing about 102 acres, situated in Farmington. I give unto my nephew Daniel North, son of my brother Thomas North, the other moiety or half-part of my lands aforesd. And it is my will that my aforenamed brothers have and enjoy the profits of my sd. lands given unto each of their sons respectively until they attain the age of 21 years. I give unto my brother Thomas North my 9 acres of land lying near Clatter Valley in Farmington, which I purchased of Thomas North; also my husbandry tools. I give unto my sister Hannah Northaway one cow and a yoke of oxen. I appoint my two brothers, John North and Thomas North, to be the executors of this my last will, and I do hereby revoke and disannul all wills by me heretofore made———In witness———annoqe R. R. annee Quinto———

As a codicil to my foregoing will, and to be accepted and taken as part and parcel thereof, I do give unto my brother Thomas North 3 acres

and 1-2 of land at a place called Nod, a parcel of land lying at the hop
garden, a tract of land in the southwest division, and 40 acres in the
north division near the Pinnacle, all which sd. lands are in Farmington.
Witness: *John Cutlar,*   SAMUEL NORTH, LS.
John Perkins, Ezekiel Lewis.

PROVINCE OF THE MASSACHUSETTS
BAY IN NEW ENGLAND.
[Seal]   BY HIS EXCELLENCY THE GOVERNOR.

Upon the 11th day of December, 1706, before me at Boston, within
the Province of the Massachusetts Bay, personally appeared John Cutlar
and Ezekiel Lewis, two of the witnesses, subscribers to the instrument
or will of Samuel North hereto annexed, and seuerally made oath that
they saw Samuel North, therein named, sign and seal, and heard him
declare and publish the sd. writing or will, with the codicil added thereunto, to be his last will and testament. And that at the time he so did he
was of sound disposing mind and memory, to their best understanding
and discerning. And that they, the deponents, set to their names as witnesses of the execution of the sd. will in the sd. testator's presence, and
that John Perkins was then also present and Subscribed his name as a
witness. Given under my hand and the publick seal of the said Province,
the day and year above written.   J: DUDLEY.
Court Record, Page 89—3 February, 1706-7: Will and invt. exhibited at Hartford and approved.

North, Thomas, son of Samuel North. Court Record, Page 106—
1st March, 1707-8: This Court appoint Thomas North to be guardian to
his son Daniel North, a minor, 6 years of age; also appointed guardian to
his son Josiah, age 2 years.

Page 91-2-3.

Olcott, Samuel, Hartford. Invt. £550-08-00. Taken 3 April, 1704,
by Aaron Cooke, Robert Sandford and John Pratt. Will dated 1st December, 1703.
I, Samuel Olcott, do make this my last will and testament: I give
unto my daughter Sarah Williams and to her children £20 in current
country pay or in the moveables of my estate. I give to her son John
Williams 1-2 of swamp or meadow land. I give to my daughter Mary
Bigelow's children, to be equally divided between them, the whole of
my land in the South Meadow, lying in two parcels, or £20 in good country pay, which my executors shall choose; and I allow them the space
of 10 years to determine their choice. I give to my daughter Elizabeth,
besides what she hath already received, £20 in current country pay or in
moveables. I give to her my woodlot lying in the pine field over Brick

Hill bridge, provided she shall pay £10 country pay to my grandchild Sarah Williams within four years after my decease. I give to my two sons Thomas and George all my housing and homelot, to be equally divided between them, saving that I give to my son George the shop with all the weaving furniture. Also, I give to my son George the choice of the two dwelling houses. I give to my son Thomas the east end of my Bluehill lot, the whole breadth and 20 rods of the length. I give to my son George the next part of the sd. lot, the whole breadth and 44 rods in length. I give to my son Thomas all the remainder of my sd. lot westward. I give to my son Thomas 1-2 of the remainder of my upper lot on the east side of the Great River, and unto my son George the other half. I give to my sons Thomas and George all my right in the Five-Mile Purchase, over the Great River, and also all my moveable estate whatsoever, to be equally divided between them, obliging them jointly and equally to pay all my aforementioned debts and legacies. I constitute my sons Thomas and George to be my sole executors, and desire Capt. Aaron Cook and Mr. Joseph Talcott to be overseers.

Witness: *Timothy Woodbridge,*   SAMUEL OLCOTT, LS.
       Richard Goodman.

Court Record, Page 55—12 April, 1704: Will proven.

Page 155-6.

Osbourne, Sergt. John, Windsor. Invt. £665-00-00. Taken 10 April, 1706, by John Moore, Sen., Daniel Heydon, Sen., and Daniel White. Will dated 9 March, 1705-6.

I, John Osbourne of Windsor, do make my last will and testament: I give to my wife the new house, barn, orchard and pasture adjoining during her widowhood. Furthermore, I give to my wife during her widowhood my lot called Burge's lot and my other lot called Drake's lot, and my other lot called Pryar's lot, and my lot next about the brook; all these I give to my wife during her widowhood towards the bring-up of my children. My will is that my two younger sons should have the land above specified after their mother. Willing also that my two younger sons should pay to their sister Mary £30. Furthermore, I give to my wife half the team and half what appertains thereto, and the other half to my son John. Furthermore, I give to my wife, to be hers forever, one brass kettle and one warming-pan. Nextly, I give to my son John all my lands from the stake now set northward, running from the river east 3 miles, and also the housing, barn, orchard and pasture, after my wife, to be his. Nextly, I give to my daughter Elizabeth my lower lot next to Scantick. Nextly, I give to my daughter Martha £30, to be paid her out of the stock; and to Elizabeth £16, to be paid out of the stock. My will is that my white horse shall belong to my wife. My will further is that my son John should pay to my two daughters, Abigail and Mindwell, £10 to each

of them. My will further is that my son John shall pay to my two daughters, Elizabeth and Martha, to each of them £5. And my will is that my son
John be executor.

Witness: *Samuel Osborne, Sen.*   JOHN X OSBOURN, SEN.
Samuel Mather, Jr., Jacob Gibbs, Jr.

Court Record, Page 84—24 May, 1706: John Osbourne exhibited the
last will of his late father, John Osbourn, Sen. Also exhibited an agreement between Martha Osbourn, widow, and her son John Osbourn.

Page 61 (Vol IX) 1st April, 1718: Whereas, Isaac Perse of Enfield,
Henry Gibbs and Isaac Bissell of Windsor, in right of their wives, children of John Osbourn, late decd., moved this Court for a dist. of about
107 acres of land described in a writ dated 24 March, 1718, on file in
this Court, affirming it to be intestate estate and not disposed of by the
last will of John Osbourn, decd., Mrs. Martha Osbourn, Isaac and Jacob
Osbourn being cited. And the Court having heard the pleas of the parties, are of the opinion that distribution ought not be granted on the sd.
estate.

Page 73—5 August, 1718: Upon motion of John Osbourn, executor
of the will of John Osbourn deceased. A citation to Mrs. Martha Osbourn, relict, and Thomas Elsworth and Jonathan Elsworth, to appear and
disclose if they have concealed any part of sd. estate. This Court find
that they have not concealed any part thereof.

Page 63.

Pampenum, Indian Woman. The last will and testament of Pampenum, an Indian woman, late of the Town of Haddam, decd., vizt.: I,
Pampenum, an Indian Squaw of or belonging to Haddam, alias Thirty-
Mile Island, in the County of Hartford, widow, having no issue or children of my own body, to prevent inconveniency and trouble which may
arise in the disposing of my estate, do make this my last will and testament: I give unto Wawquashat, my own natural brother, now residing
or dwelling in Hartford, 2-7 parts of my island, situate in (or surrounded
and invironed with) the Great River, near Haddam aforementioned, usually known by the name of Thirty-Mile Island, which 2-7 parts shall be
and remain for his son named Seemook (after the decease of the sd.
Wawquashat) and his heirs forever. I also give unto my 2 cosens, Maskpooh and Takamisk Nannicos, son and daughter, and unto Pauhakehun
Nannicoes, grandson, 3-7 parts of my sd. island, to be equally divided
amongst them. And unto Wampeawask, a woman, and her son Mahametups, I give the rest of my sd. island, being 2-7 parts thereof, equally
to be divided between them, every one of which parts or parcels of my sd.
island given to my sd. relations and friends as above mentioned shall be
by them respectively taken, entered on and possessed immediately after
my decease, and shall remain to them, their heirs or assigns, forever, as

their proper and real estate, and shall not be by them nor any of them alienated or sold to any person or persons at any time or times hereafter forever. For confirmation and establishment of all which I have to these presents subscribed and sealed at Hartford this 20th day of May, Anno Dom. 1697.

Witness: *Caleb Stanly, Junr.,*   PAMPENUM X LS.
       Joseph Easton, Junr.   *an Indian Woman.*

Pampenum, an Indian woman, belonging to Haddam, personally appeared in Hartford this 20th day of May, 1697, and acknowledged or owned that she fully understood the contents of what is above written, and that it was fully her will and minde and her last testament.

Before me,   *Samuel Mason, Assistant.*

Court Record, Page 54—9 March, 1703-4: Joseph Arnold presented the last will of Pampenum to this Court. And whereas, there was another will made by the sd. squaw formerly exhibited in Court by Caleb Standly, which was prior to this that is now presented, the consideration whereof the Court refer to their sessions to be holden on the 2nd Tuesday of April next.

Page 208-9.

Parsons, Samuel, late of Simsbury. Invt. £36-03-02. Taken September, 1708, by Joseph Hopkins, Samuel Peck, Samuel Hubbard, James Handerson and Josiah Clarke. The nuncupative last will and testament of Samuel Parsons, late of Simsbury, and lately residing at Hartford, deceased, as followeth: Sarah Bull and Mary Clark, both of sufficient age, testify and say that on the 11th day of August, 1708, they being both together with Samuel Parsons, late of Hartford, deceased, did ask him how he would have his estate disposed of after his death. And that thereupon the sd. Parsons (being then of sound mind and understanding, as these deponents observed) did say that he would have all his just debts paid out of the same, and that his brother at Cull should have his land, and his two sisters the rest of his estate equally between them.

Taken upon oath before the Court of Probates at Hartford, September 13th, 1708.

Test: *Caleb Stanly, Clerk.*

Court Record, Page 117—13 September, 1708: Will and invt. exhibited by Robert Westland and Ebenezer Williams, with testimony of the abovesd. witnesses. Proven. And this Court grant letters of Adms. unto Robert Westland and Ebenezer Williams with the will annexed.

Page 148.

Pettebone, Benjamin, Simsbury. Invt. £12-16-00. Taken 30 March, 1706, by Samuel Humphreys and James Cornish.

Court Record, Page 81—4 April, 1706: John Pettebone, Sen., exhibited the inventory of the estate of his son Benjamin Pettebone, decd., and was appointed Adms.

Page 65-81-2-3.

Pitkin, George, Hartford. He died 23 December, 1702. Invt. £169-06-10. Taken 28 August, 1703, by Joseph Olmsted, Sen., and John Maken, Jr.

Page 81—Division and partition of George Pitkin's estate:

This indenture *Septi partite,* made the 10th December, 1703, and in the second year of the reigne of our souereigne Lady Anne, by the grace of God Queen of England, Scotland, France and Ireland, defender of the faith: Between Roger Pitkin, of the Town of Hartford, in the County of Hartford, in the Colony of Connecticut, in New England, of the first part; William Pitkin, of the same Hartford aforesaid, of the second part; John Pitkin, of the same Hartford, of the third part; Nathaniel Pitkin, of said Hartford, of the fourth part; Ozias Pitkin, also of the same Hartford, of the fifth part; Timothy Cowles and Hannah Cowles, his wife, of Hartford aforesaid, of the sixth part; and John Marsh, Junr., of the said Town of Hartford, and Elizabeth Marsh, his wife, of the seventh part: Witnesseth, that it is covenanted, granted and agreed by and between the said partys for a partition between them to be had and made of the messuages, tenements, lands and estate lying and being in the Township of Hartford aforesaid, and of certain land in that tract called "Joshua's guift land," as is hereinafter mentioned and specified, late the estate and inheritance of George Pitkin of Hartford aforesaid, decd., as heirs of the said George Pitkin, they the said Roger Pitkin, Wm. Pitkin, John Pitkin, Nathaniel Pitkin, Ozias Pitkin, Timo. Cowles and Hannah his wife, John Marsh and Elizabeth his wife, of one assent and consent for them and their heirs, have made full and clear division of all the said messuages, lands and premises with their appurtenances, in form as follows: The same is already divided and parted between them, vizt., to each of them an equal part and share thereof. In witness whereof the said parties to these presents have hereunto set their hands and seals the day and year first above written.

Roger Pitkin, ls. William Pitkin, ls. John Pitkin, ls. Nathaniel Pitkin, ls. Ozias Pitkin, ls. Timothy Cowles, ls. Hannah Cowles, ls. John Marsh, Jr., ls. Elizabeth X Marsh, ls. Signed, sealed and delivered in the presence of us: *Robert Sandford, Nathaniel Marsh, Caleb Stanly Jr.*

Court Record, Page 43—7 April, 1703: Adms. to Roger Pitkin.

Page 52—7 March, 1703-4: A writing under the hands and seals of George Pitkin's heirs was now exhibited in Court. This Court grant Roger Pitkin a *Quietus Est.*

Page 140-1.

Pitkin, John, Hartford. Invt. £418-09-07. Taken 27 March, 1706, by Joseph Olmsted and John Meakins. Will dated 26 November, 1705.

I, John Pitkin, being weak of body but sound of mind and memory, do make this my last will and testament: I give to my honoured mother 20 shillings a year during her natural life, to be paid her by my brothers Roger, William, Nathaniel and Ozias. I give to Mr. Samuel Woodbridge £5 in current country pay if he shall be ordained and settled in the work of the ministry on the east side of the Great River in the Township of Hartford. I give to my brother William Pitkin one piece of meadow land which I bought of Richard Burnham, lying in Podunk Meadow, in the Township of Windsor, about 2 acres; also, one piece of upland near his dwelling house in the homelot which I had out of the estate of brother George, decd., it being in consideration of the many kindnesses I have received from him and upon the accompt of my entertainment; this, together with what I have paid him, to be in full satisfaction of the accompt above mentioned, if he please to accept it. I give to my sister Hannah Cowles (including her now husband) £20. I give to my sister Elizabeth Marsh (including her now husband) £20. I give unto my brothers, Roger Pitkin, William Pitkin, Nathaniel Pitkin and Ozias Pitkin, all the remainder of my estate, both real and personal, to be equally divided between them. And I appoint my brothers Roger Pitkin and William Pitkin to be executors.

Witness: *Daniel Bidwell,*   JOHN PITKIN, LS.
    Thomas Olcott.

Court Record, Page 74—22 January, 1705-6: Will proven.

Page 79-80.

Pratt, Daniel. Invt. £814-03-06. Taken 6 March, 1703-4, by Aaron Cooke and Timothy Phelps.

Court Record, Page 52—7 March, 1703-4: This Court grant letters of Adms. unto Elizabeth Pratt, widow. Recog., £300, with Richard Lord and Capt. Aaron Cooke.

Page 70—6 September, 1705: Elizabeth Pratt of Hartford, Adms. on the estate of Daniel Pratt, presented an account of her Adms.:

	£ s d
Paid in debts and charges,	120-09-08
Still due from the estate,	2-13-08
She has now received,	6-18-02
There is left in Thomas Gilbert's hands,	2-01-03

This Court accepts the above account and orders it to be kept on file.
Page 102 (Vol. VIII) 5 January, 1712-13: This Court, being moved to make an order and decree for the dist. of the estate of Daniel Pratt

to and among the relicts and children of the sd. decd. Account of the
Adms. as followeth:

	£ s d
Paid in debts and charges,	123-03-04
Inventoried estate with debts paid in,	823-02-01
From which subtracting,	123-03-04

| There remains to be distributed, | 699-18-09 |
| The real part thereof is | 594-00-00 |

Order to be distributed as followeth:
To Elizabeth Sheldon, late Elizabeth Pratt, widow of sd. decd.,

with the use of real estate,	35-06-03
The residue of the moveable estate,	70-12-06
And the real estate to be distributed,	664-12-06
To Elisha Pratt, the eldest and surviving son, double portion,	332-06-03
To Elizabeth Pratt and Rebeckah Pratt, daughters, to each,	166-03-01

And appoint Capt. Aaron Cooke, Mr. Robert Sandford and Mr. John
Skinner, distributors.

Page 103—5 January, 1712-13: This Court appoint Mr. John Sheldon, of Hartford, and his wife Elizabeth Sheldon, late Elizabeth Pratt, to
be guardians to the three children of Daniel Pratt, late of Hartford, decd.

Page 41-2.

Pratt, Esther, Hartford. Invt. £48-00-10. Taken 10 November,
1702, by John Marsh, Sen., and Caleb Stanly, Jr. Will dated 6 October,
1702.

I, Esther Pratt of Hartford, do make this my last will and testament:
I give to my brother John Skinner my great Bible and my best bed for
his care and kindness toward me in my sickness at his house. I give all
my wearing clothes, both linen and woolen, with all my household goods,
to my sisters, Hannah Clarke, Elizabeth Goodwin, Sarah Phelps, Rachel
Skinner, and the children of my sister Mary Sandford, decd. (the sd.
children to have their deceased mother's part), to be equally divided
amongst them. I give the remainder of my estate, be it what it will,
that is to say, what is due to me from my brother Daniel Pratt as part
of my legacy given to me by my deceased father's will, to my sisters,
Hannah Clarke, Elizabeth Goodwin, Sarah Phelps, Rachel Skinner, and
the children of my deceased sister Mary Sandford, and my brother Daniel Pratt, to be equally divided amongst them. I ordain my brother John
Skinner sole executor.

Witness: *John Haynes,*   ESTHER X PRATT, LS.
            Thomas Skinner.

Court Record, Page 34—11 November, 1702: Will proven.

Page 113.

Reynolds, Jonathan, Wethersfield. Died 21 October, 1704. Invt. £249-03-09. Taken 24 November, 1704, by John Curtis, John Goodrich and Daniel Boardman. Two children: Keziah and Anna Reynolds.

Court Record, Page 62—19 December, 1704: This Court grant letters of Adms. unto Elizabeth Reynolds, relict of the sd. decd., and to John Reynolds, who gave bond of £150.

Page 6 (Vol. VIII) 6 February, 1709-10: Elizabeth Hollister of Wethersfield, widow (late Elizabeth Reynolds, widow), Adms. on the estate of Jonathan Reynolds, late of Wethersfield, being summoned, appeared before this Court to render an account of her Adms. on that estate. This Court do now order the sd. Elizabeth Hollister to again appear before this Court to render her account on the 1st Monday of March next, to the end that Ebenezer Seymour of Farmington, joint Adms. with the sd. Elizabeth Hollister on the estate of Capt. Stephen Hollister, decd., may give his reason why an allowance should be made out of the Reynolds to the sd. Hollister's estate for keeping sd. Reynolds his children for some time.

Page 6—6 March, 1709-10: Elizabeth Hollister, Adms. on the estate of her late husband Jonathan Reynolds, exhibited now in this Court an account of her Adms. on that estate, which is by this Court approved and ordered to be kept on file. And whereas, it appears that of the moveable estate of the sd. Jonathan Reynolds there is now remaining in the hands of Elizabeth Hollister and Ebenezer Seymour, Adms. on the estate of Capt. Stephen Hollister, the sum of £42-16-06, whereof 1-3 part, or £14-05-06, belongs to the estate of Stephen Hollister, decd., by virtue of his marriage to the sd. Elizabeth Reynolds, the other 2-3 belongs to the heirs of Jonathan Reynolds. This Court order Elizabeth Hollister and Ebenezer Seymour to set out £28-11-00 for the use of the heirs of the sd. Jonathan Reynolds, and that the sd. Elizabeth Hollister do take, receive and keep the same until further order.

Page 117 (Vol. IX) 2 February, 1719-20: This Court appoint Elizabeth Hollister of Wethersfield to be guardian to Anne Reignolds, one of the children. Recog., £50.

Page 118—2 February, 1719-20: Upon the motion of Elizabeth Hollister, of Wethersfield, widow, that an order of distribution might be granted on the estate of Jonathan Reignolds, late of Wethersfield, deceased: It appearing that the real estate of the sd. deceased remains yet to be distributed, this Court appoint Joshua Robbins, 3d, William Warner and Philip Goff of Wethersfield to distribute the real estate, housing and lands as it is inventoried, amounting to the sum of £175, to the sd. Elizabeth Hollister, sometime widow of the sd. deceased, the 1-3 part of houseing and lands for her use during life. To Keziah Stoddard and Anne Reignolds, daughters of the sd. deceased, the sum of value of £87-10-00, which is their equal part or portions.

Page 125—5 April, 1720: Report of the distributors.

Page 46.

Richards, Obadiah, Waterbury. Invt. £136-18-00. Taken 24 November, 1702, by Thomas Judd, Sen., and Thomas Judd, Jr. Invt. of lands valued at £12, apprised by John Hart and Daniel Andrews. The children: John, Obadiah, Thomas, Benjamin, Mary, Hannah, Esther, Elizabeth, Sarah and Rachel.

Court Record, Page 38—2 March, 1702-3: Adms. granted to John Richards, son of the decd.

Page 50—5 November, 1703: John Richards, Adms., moves this Court for a dist. of the estate. This Court order that the estate be distributed to the widow and to each of the children above named. And appoint Lt. Timothy Standly, John Hopkins and Thomas Judd, distributors. Benjamin Richards, son of the decd., chose Thomas Judd, Jr., to be his guardian. And Thomas Richards, son of Obadiah Richards, of Waterbury, chose Deacon Thomas Judd to be his guardian.

Dist. File, 8 February, 1703-4: This Court order the estate dist. as followeth:

	£ s d		£ s d
To the widow.	37-21-04	To Mary,	9-07-00
To John,	8-00-00	To Hannah,	8-07-00
To Obadiah,	9-07-00	To Esther,	9-07-03
To Thomas,	3-08-04	To Elizabeth,	8-07-03
To Benjamin,	9-05-10	To Sarah,	9-07-01
		To Rachel,	10-10-00

By Timothy Stanly, John Hopkins and Thomas Judd. John Richards, Adms., presented to this Court a dist. of the estate of his father under the hands of Timothy Stanly, John Hopkins and Thomas Judd. Approved and ordered to be kept on file.

Vol. IX, Page 135—6 September, 1720: Mr. Peter Pratt of Hartford, attorney to Jabez and Sarah Waters of Lyme, Adms. on the estate of Obadiah Richards, late of Lyme, decd., one of the sons and co-heirs of Obadiah Richards, sometime of Waterbury, decd., moving this Court that the part of sd. Obadiah Richards, sometime of Lyme, deceased, in his father's homested, and his part in one lot at the upper end of Steele's Meadow, may be set out in severalty according to a former dist. of fiis sd. father's estate, it appears to this Court that by the sd. former dist. there was ordered to the sd. Obadiah of Lyme one-third part and 1-33 part of the homested of the sd. Obadiah of Waterbury, and 1-5 part of one lot of land at the upper end of Steele's Meadow in Waterbury. This Court appoint Lt. John Hopkins, Stephen Upson and Ensign Hickock of Waterbury to set out the lands by meets and bounds.

Invt. in Vol. VIII, Page 22.

Rollo, Alexander, Middletown. Died 22 July, 1709. Invt. £283-12-00. Taken 30 July, 1709, by Thomas Ward and Joseph Rockwell.

Also, lands lying in Haddam, prised 25 August, 1709, by Daniel Brainard, Joshua Brainard and William Spencer.

Court Record, Page 132—5 September, 1709: Hannah Rollo of Middletown, widow, and William Rollo of Haddam, son of sd. decd., exhibit an invt. Adms. to William Rollo, who gave bond.

Page 144-5.

Rowley, Moses, Sen., Haddam. Invt. £68-10-03. Taken 15 June, 1705, by William Spencer and Thomas X Crippen. Will dated 16 August, 1704.

I, Moses Rowley, do make this my last will and testament: My will is that, my just debts being paid, the remainder to be disposed of as followeth: As for the rest of my children, I have done what hath been with me, and now I have no expectation of being any more capable to help myself, wherefore I do give and bequeath my land unto my son Moses Rowly, that is to say, my half of the lot I now live upon. The other half I have given already to my son Matthew. To be equally divided between my sons Moses and Matthew. I also give unto my son Moses that £25 right that I formerly gave to Matthew, which my son Matthew hath lovingly resigned up again to me. I give to my daughter Mehetabell Fuller all my moveables, both stock and household stuff, whether without door or within. I give half of my young mare to my son Matthew. My will further is, and it is upon the account of not only what my sons Moses Rowley and John Fuller hath done for me and been kind to me, but especially their willingness to take the care of me and my wife during our natural lives, and I do expect that care and kindness of them that is meet and needful both to myself and my wife, and I therefore have done what I have done to oblige them what I can, and do repose my trust, next unto God, upon these my two sons Moses Rowley and John Fuller for what I shall and for what my wife shall stand in need of between this and the grave. I appoint my sons, Moses Rowley and John Fuller, executors.

Witness: *John Chapman,*   MOSES X ROWLEY, SEN., LS.
Matthew X *Rowley, Mary* X *Crippen.*

Court Record, Page 77—8 March, 1705-6: Will proven.

Page 193.

Rowley Thomas, Sen., Cordwainer, Windsor. Invt. £164-09-00. Taken 1st May, 1708, by Eleazer Hill, Daniel Loomis and Timothy Loomis.

Court Record, Page 114—5 July, 1708: This Court grant letters of Adms. unto Thomas Rowley and Mary Rowley, widow.

Page 114—2 August, 1708: Grace Rowley, 16 years of age, daughter of Thomas Rowley, decd., chose her brother Thomas Rowley of Windsor, currier, to be her guardian.

Page 16 (Vol. VIII) 3 July, 1710: Thomas and Mary Rowley, Adms., exhibit an account of their Adms. Order to dist. the estate:

	£ s d		£ s d
To Mary Rowley, widow,	4-08-03	To Martha,	20-16-03
To Thomas Rowley, son,	38-12-06	To Grace,	20-16-03
To Mary,	16-00-03	To Elizabeth,	5-06-03
To Deborah,	5-11-04	To Abigail,	18-03-07

And appoint Daniel Loomis, Thomas Marshall and Eleazer Hill, of Windsor, distributors.

Page 27 (Vol. XI) 1st September, 1730: Mary Rowell, Adms., exhibited a dist. in Court, which is accepted and ordered to be kept on file.

NOTE: *In the dist. on file, 1710, the name "Rowley" is written "Rowell" but recorded "Rowley."*

Page 69.

Russell, Daniel, Charlestown. Whereas, John Hubbard and Mabell Hubbard, his wife, of Jamaico, on Nassau Island, in the Province of New York, having received of Mr. Timothy Woodbridge of Hartford, in the Colony of Connecticut, executor in right of his wife Mabell, deceased, to the last will of Mr. Daniel Russell of Charlestown, in the Province of Massachusetts Bay, in New England, deceased, in full of the legacy, portion or part of estate that was given to the said Mabell Hubbard by her father, the said Mr. Daniel Russell deceased, by his last will, we, the said John and Mabell Hubbard, forever discharge and acquit the said Timothy Woodbridge from all dues and demands whatsoever. The legacy consisted of a farm lying in the Township of Newtown, in the Province of Massachusetts Bay, containing by common estimation 500 acres more or less, and is now in our possession, and also in some other parts of estate which we have received. For this we have remised and released all other estate.   JOHN HUBBARD, LS.

Witness: *Samuel Willis,*   MABELL HUBBARD. LS.
       Hezekiah Willis.

Page 158-9.

Ryley, Joseph, Wethersfield. Died 5 May, 1706. Invt. £69-17-00. Taken by William Warner, Sen., and Jonathan Belden.

Court Record, Page 86—5 August, 1706: Invt. exhibited by Jonathan Ryly, a brother, who, with Benjamin Gilbert, were appointed dist.

Page 103—2 February, 1707-8: Jonathan Ryly and Benjamin Gilbert of Wethersfield exhibited an account of their Adms. on the estate of

Joseph Ryly: Received debts due to the estate, £3-13-03. And have paid in debts £13-12-00. The difference, £9-18-09, which must be abated from the inventory account. Accepted, and this Court grant the Adms. a *Quietus Est.* And the Court order a dist. to his brother and sisters, viz., John Ryley, Jonathan Ryly, Isaac Ryly, Mary Gilbert, Grace Goodrich and Sarah Sears, to each of them 1-6 part. And appoint William Warner, Sen., and Jonathan Belding distributors.

Page 56-7-8.

Sage, David, Sen., Middletown. Invt. £753-02-07. Taken 5 June, 1703, by John Hamlin, Nathaniel White and John Clarke, Sen. Will dated 27 March, 1703.

I, David Sage, Sen., of Middletown, do make this my last will and testament: I give unto my eldest son David that lott whereon there is a frame of a house, commonly called David's lot, and that 1½ acres of boggy meadow which I bought of mother, and the 1-4 part of my boggy meadow in Goose Delight, and my great woodlot on the east side of the Great River. I give unto my son John that lot whereon he hath built and doth now inhabit, and my upper lott at Pistol Point which butts of Scovell's, and the ¼ part of my Goose Delight meadow; also my great woodlot next Wethersfield bounds. I give unto my two daughters, Bull and Johnson, £30 to each, to be paid at my wife's decease. I give to my daughter Mercy £50, £20 of it to be paid when she needs it and the other £30 at her mother's decease. The rest of my estate, personal and real, I leave it with my wife, to be managed by my sons Jonathan and Timothy so that she have a comfortable and creditable maintenance during her natural life, and at her decease to be shared betwixt sd. Jonathan and Timothy, debts and legacies paid. It is my will further, that my son John shall have my 2 lots in the Round Meadow.

Witness: *John Stow,*　　　　　　　　　　DAVID X SAGE, LS.
John Arnold, Alexander Rollo.

Court Record, Page 44—4 May, 1703: Will proven and invt. exhibited. This Court grant Adms. with the will annexed (as no executor was appointed) to Mary the widow, and Jonathan and Timothy Sage, sons of the decd..

Page 55—12 April, 1704: Jonathan Sage presented an account of his Adms. with his mother and brother on the estate of David Sage, late of Middletown, decd. Account of debts amounting to £25-01-07. Also what some of the children have received before the death of their father David Sage, late of Middletown, decd.

	£ s d		£ s d
David Sage,	126-01-00	Ezekiel Bull,	20-00-00
John Sage,	41-14-06	Samuel Johnson,	20-00-00

Which account this Court accept and order it to be filed.

Page 119 (Vol. VIII) 2 March, 1712-13: Timothy Sage of Middletown, son of David Sage, late of Middletown, decd., moved this Court to appoint some suitable persons to make a division of certain lands which was bequeathed by the sd. David Sage in and by his last will and testament jointly to the sd. Timothy Sage and to his brother Jonathan Sage, decd.; that the same lands are to be shared equally between the sd. Timothy Sage and the heirs or legal representatives of Jonathan Sage, decd. This Court appoint John Hamlin, Esq., Joseph Rockwell and John Clark, Sen., distributors.

Page 127—6 April, 1713: The Court appoints Sergt. Samuel Hall of Middletown to join with and assist such men as have been appointed to divide certain lands belonging to the estate of David Sage, late of Middletown, who shall attend that work pursuant to an order of this Court, 2nd May last past.

Page 135—4 May, 1713: A dist. of certain lands belonging to the estate of David Sage was now exhibited in this Court by Timothy Sage, which dist. this Court accepts and orders to be kept on file. The Court grants the sd. Timothy Sage a *Quietus Est.*

Page 112.

Sampson (Negro), Farmington. Invt. £40-17-04. Taken 15 December, 1704, by John Hart, Sen., and Daniel Andrews, Sen.

Court Record, Page 62—19 December, 1704: Thomas Bird exhibited in this Court the inventory of Sampson. Accepted. And this Court grant Adms. unto Joseph North, who gave bonds of £100.

Page 63—6 March, 1704-5: Joseph North of Farmington, Adms. on the estate of Sampson (Negro), sent to this Court an account whereby it appears that the inventory amounts to £41-07-04, and that there are debts due from the estate, £28-16-02. And there being set out to the widow £6-07-01, there remains £6-03-09. And that therefore some of the land must be sold for the payment of the sd. debts.

Page 124 (Vol. IX) 5 April, 1720: Whereas, complaint was made that Joseph North, formerly empowered Adms., had not rendered a full account of his Adms. on sd. estate, writ was issued to summons him to this Court. He now appeared and rendered an account, which this Court accepts; ordered recorded, and kept on file.

Page 130—5 July, 1720: This Court grant Joseph North, Adms., a *Quietus Est.*

Page 64-5.

Scofell, Edward, Haddam. Invt. £111-10-06. Taken 11 May, 1703, by John Ventrus, William Scofell and Timothy Shailor.

Court Record, Page 46—8 September, 1703: Adms. is granted to Hannah the relict. Recog., £50, with William Scofell.

Page 52—7 March, 1703-4: William Scofell, Adms. on the estate of Edward Scofell, having proceeded as far as the personal estate can extend, yet there remains debts due from the estate which cannot be discharged unless some land is sold. This account the Court accepts.

Page 77—6 March, 1705-6: Thomas Shaylor and William Scofell, of Haddam, are appointed by this Court to be guardians unto Susannah Scovell and Hannah Scofell, orphans, children of Edward Scovell, late of Haddam, decd.

Page 80—2 April, 1706: Hannah Scofell, relict of Edward Scofell, late decd., now wife of Benjamin Smith, Adms. on the estate of her late husband Edward Scofell, renders her account of Adms. and is granted a *Quietus Est.* This Court order and appoint James Wells, Josiah Arnold and Timothy Shaylor to distribute the estate to Hannah the relict and to Susannah and Hannah, children of the deceased.

Page 210.

Scott, Joseph, Farmington. Invt. £20-01-00. Taken November, 1708, by John Stanly and Nathaniel Wadsworth.

Court Record, Page 120—7 February, 1708-9: Adms. to Samuel Scott.

Page 42-3.

Seamore, Zachariah, Wethersfield. Invt. £200-04-03. Taken by Robert Welles and Jonathan Boreman, Selectmen. Will dated 14 April, 1702.

I, Zachariah Seamore of Wethersfield, do make this my last will and testament: As to my housing and land which I have in the Township of Wethersfield, and all other estate, I do bequeath to my wife 1-3 part, having the command of one room in my dwelling house as part of her third, which is to be at her command so long as she shall remain my widow, and then to receive a reasonable rent for her part of the house. I give to my four daughters the whole and sole right to all my estate, especially my houseing and lands, after the decease of my wife, and 2-3 of all my estate to them I give as they come of age, and I give to each alike. Further, I do choose my loving brethren John Seamore, Sen., of Hartford, and Richard Seamore, of Farmington, to be overseers with John Seamore, Jr., and Thomas Seamore, of Hartford. And they may put out my children at their discretion.

Witness: *John Seamore, Jr.,*   ZACHARIAH SEAMORE.
         Thomas Seamore.

Court Record, Page 34—11 November, 1702: Will proven. This Court grant letters of Adms., with the will annexed, unto the widow and John Seamore, who gave bond of £100.

Page 71—6 September, 1705: John Seamore, Jr., and Mary Seamore, widow, presented to this Court an account of their Adms.: Paid in debts and charges, £16-09-01. Which account this Court allow and order to be put on file.

Page 72—7 November, 1705: Adms. account accepted, and this Court grant them a *Quietus Est.*

Page 284 (Vol. VIII): Inventory of some land belonging to the estate of Zachariah Seamore, late of Wethersfield, decd., valued at £48-10-00. Taken 28 April, 1714, by John Hart, Sen., and John Stanly, Sen.

Court Record, Page 184—5 April, 1714: This Court grant letters of Adms., with the will annexed, to Henry Grimes of Wethersfield, son-in-law.

Page 187—5 April, 1714: Ruth Seamore, age 15 years, daughter of Zachariah Seamore, late of Wethersfield, chose Josiah Churchill of Wethersfield to be her guardian. Recog., £50.

Page 191—3 May, 1714: Henry Grimes of Wethersfield, Adms. on the estate of Zachariah Seamore of Wethersfield, exhibited additional inventory consisting of certain lands of the sd. deceased lying within the bounds of the Township of Farmington. The Court orders the same recorded and kept on file. Also this Court order that the lands shall be equally divided among the surviving daughters or their legal representatives, first setting out to the widow her thirds or dowry. And appoint Capt. Ephraim Goodrich, Mr. George Kilbourn and Philip Goff, Jr., to dist. the sd. estate.

Dist. File: 3 May, 1714: Estate of Zachariah Seamore: To the widow, to Mary the wife of Henry Grimes, to Elizabeth the wife of Henry Belding, to Abigail and to Ruth Seamore. By Ephraim Goodrich, George Kilbourn and Philip Goff, Jr.

Page 174-5-6.

Shepherd, Sergt. John, Hartford (Cooper). Died 12 June, 1707. Invt. £278-05-09. Taken by John Bunce, James Steele and Thomas Richard.

Court Record, Page 95—7 July 1707: John Shepherd, of Hartford, cooper, and Martha Shepherd of Hartford, widow, relict of Sergt. John Shepherd, late of Hartford, cooper, decd., exhibit invt. This Court grant letters of Adms. unto John and Thomas Shepherd, sons of sd. decd.

Page 126—4 April, 1709: John Shepherd and Thomas Shepherd, Adms. on the estate of Sergt. John Shepherd, presented now an account of debts which they have paid out of the estate:

		£	s	d
Paid in debts and charges,	.	98-08-03		
And more debts still due,		15-16-05		

	£ s d
In the whole,	114-04-08
Moveables,	98-17-11
Debts due from the estate,	15-06-09

Over and above what the moveables will reach to do. And this Court order and direct the Adms. to make their application to the General Assembly to obtain power to sell so much of the lands of the estate as will produce money to defray the sd. remaining debts, and also £8 more for the sd. Adms. charges; and likewise so much more as shall be necessary to supply the widow with bedding and other things needful for her subsistence.

Page 128—6 June, 1709: The General Assembly, holden 12 May, 1709, did grant authority to John and Thomas Shepherd, Adms. on the estate of John Shepherd, to sell so much of the land belonging to sd. estate as might be sufficient to pay all the debts remaining due, with the Adms. charges, and wherewith to furnish the widow to the value of £10 for her use.

Page 17 (Vol. VIII) 4 September, 1710: John and Thomas Shepherd having notified the children of the sd. decd., or their representatives, to bring into this Court an account of what they each of them have had and received towards their portions, the sd. children met together and made an agreement among themselves relating to what they each of them had formerly had, to be reckoned to them as part of their portion, and relating to the claim of the children of Rebeckah Bigelow, decd., which agreement is allowed and approved by the Court and ordered to be kept on file. And this Court now order that the remaining estate shall be dist.: 1-3 part of the housing and land to the relict during life, and the remainder of land and estate to be dist. and divided as followeth:

	£ s d
To John Shepherd, eldest son,	13-16-04
To Samuel Shepherd,	2-14-09
To Thomas Shepherd,	4-04-09
And to each of the 7 daughters of the sd. decd., to each	13-10-07

And appoint Deacon Joseph Easton, John Catlin and Lt. James Steele distributors. And this Court now grant John and Thomas Shepherd a *Quietus Est.*

Dist. File: To the widow Martha Shepherd, to John, to Thomas, to Samuel, to Elizabeth Goodwin, to Rebeckah Bigelow decd. or her legal representatives, to Sarah Stone, to Deborah White, to Abigail Butler, to Violet or her legal representative, to Hannah Ensign. By John Catlin, Lt. James Steele and Joseph Easton.

Page 2.

Slater, Thomas, Simsbury. Died 14 May, 1700, age 27 years. Invt. £15-10-09. Taken 17 May, 1700, by John Moses, Samuel Humphrey and John Case, Jr., Selectmen.

Court Record, Page 1—5 September, 1700: Adms. to John Slater, father of the deceased. Rec., £30.

Page 112.

Smead, Richard, Hartford. Died 27 November, 1704. Invt. £12-07-02. Taken 8 December, 1704, by Benjamin Graham and Samuel Richards.

Court Record, Page 62—19 December, 1704: Adms. to Thomas Richards. Rec., £50.

Page 177-8.

Smith, Samuel, Hartford. Died 28 August, 1707. Invt. £567-04-10. Taken 10 September, 1707, by Joseph Olmsted and Roger Pitkin.

Court Record, Page 98—6 October, 1707: Mary Smith, the widow, with George Stilman, are appointed Administrators.

Page 115—2 August, 1707-8: This Court direct Mary Smith, widow, and George Stilman, Adms., to sell so much of the lands as shall produce the sum of £80, towards the payment of debts.

Page 16 (Vol. VIII) 3 July, 1710: Mary Smith, widow, and George Stilman exhibit now an account of their Adms. on the sd. estate until this time, with the effects of 3 parcels of land sold, and what they have paid out of the sd. estate:

	£	s	d
In debts and charges and spent for the use of the family,	295-01-02		
Inventory, with some debts received,	341-07-01		
There remains of the moveable part of the estate,	46-05-11		

Account allowed and ordered to be kept on file.

Page 127—6 April, 1713: Mary Smith and George Stilman, Adms., having formerly rendered an account of their Adms., this Court order the estate to be dist. as followeth:

	£	s	d
To the widow, her part of the housing and lands during life,	15-09-00		
To Samuel Smith, eldest son,	64-05-10		
And to Benoni Smith,	32-02-11		
To Timothy,	32-02-11		
To Mary Smith, daughter,	32-02-11		
To Rebeckah Smith,	32-02-11		
To Mehetabell Smith,	32-02-11		
To Marcy Smith,	32-02-11		

And appoint Jonathan Hill, Hezekiah Porter and Timothy Cowles distributors.

Page 167—4 January, 1713-14: Report of the dist. to be recorded and kept on file.

Page 6 (Vol. X) 7 February, 1715-16: Samuel Smith, a minor son of Samuel Smith, late of Hartford, decd., chose Philip Smith to be his guardian.

Page 46-7-8-9.

Southmayd, William, Middletown (mariner). Died December, 1702. Invt. £1085-17-06. Taken 23 February, 1702-3, by John Hamlin, William Sumner and William Whiting.

Court Record, Page 38—2 March, 1702-3: This Court grant Adms. unto Margaret Southmayd, widow, who gave bonds, with Joseph Whiting and Capt. Aaron Cooke, of £500.

Page 47—8 September, 1703: Upon motion of Mrs. Margaret Southmayd this Court do proceed to dist. the sd. estate: To the widow, 1-3 part of personal estate, and 1-3 part of the real estate during her natural life, the remaining part to be distributed equally among the children of the sd. decd. And appoint Capt. John Hamlin, Capt. Nathaniel White and William Whiting to dist. the estate.

(See File.)

Southmayd, John, Waterbury. Know all men by these presents: That I, John Southmayd of Waterbury, in the County of Hartford, son to Mr. Wm. Southmayd, late of Middletown, deceased, doe hereby constitute and appoint my loving friend James Wadsworth of Farmington, in the aforesaid County, my true and lawful attorney in my name and behalf to apply himself to the Court of Probates now sitting in Hartford, and then in my name and behalf to move the honored Court for a distribution of the estate my honored father, Mr. Wm. Southmayd aforesd., was possessed of at the time of his decease, that I, the aforesaid John Southmayd, may rescue my portion according to law. And I, the aforesaid John Southmayd, do hereby authorize my aforesaid attorney to use all devices in the law for the obtaining of my proportion of the aforesaid estate, and to remove the case from Court to Court as there shall be occcasion. And whatsoever my aforesaid attorney shall lawfully do or cause to be done in the premises I doe here by confirm as if I was personally present. And in witness hereunto I have set to my hand and seal this seventh day of November in the year of our Lord one thousand seven hundred and five. In the presence of

Witness: *Samuel Hooker,*   JOHN SOUTHMAYD, Ls.
John Wadsworth.

Page 78—8 March, 1705—6: Whereas, John Southmaid of Waterbury, clerk, hath made his application to this Court to have an order made directing the distributors appointed to divide the estate of his late father, Wm. Southmaid of Middletown, decd., to set out to him, the said John

Southmaid, his double part or portion of his sd. father's estate. And the sd. distributors appointed have also made application to this Court for direction to be given to them how much to abate from the said John's double part or portion of the said estate for his having been brought up to school learning. This Court, upon consideration of the case, do order and appoint that the said distributors shall abate out of the said John Southmaid's double portion of his said father's estate the sum of £81 according to invt., for his having been kept at learning as aforesd., and then distribute and set out to him so much of the said estate as with that sum and what also he hath already received may make up his double portion thereof. The said Jno. Southmaid (by his attorney, James Wadsworth) appealed from this decree and judgment to the Court of Assistants to be holden at Hartford in May next ensuing. And the sd. James Wadsworth acknowledged himself to stand bound to the Treasury of this County in a recog. of £20 to prosecute the sd. appeal to effect and answer all damages in case he make not his plea good.

Page 184 (Vol. VIII) 5 April, 1714: This Court do appoint Capt. Aaron Cooke of Hartford and Deacon Joseph Rockwell of Middletown to join with Mr. Hamlin and Col. William Whiting, who were with Col. Nathaniel White, decd., who was formerly appointed to dist. the sd. estate. And this Court order the distributors to proceed with the distribution.

Page 230—3 January 1714-15: This Court doth appoint Margaret Southmayd of Midletown to be guardian unto Joseph Southmayd, William Southmayd and Millicent Southmayd, sons and daughter of William-Southmayd, late of Middletown, decd. Recog., with Capt. Aaron Cooke of Hartford, £200.

Dist. File, 21 January, 1714-15: To the widow, to John, to Giles, to Allyn, to Margaret, to Anne, to Joseph, to William, to Millicent Southmayd. By John Hamlin, William Whiting and Aaron Cooke.

Page 145-6.

Spencer, Samuel, Haddam. Invt. £50-10-10. Taken 7th February, 1705-6, by Capt. John Chapman and William Spencer, Jr.

An agreement, appended to the Inventory on file:

To all whom these presents concern, greeting: Know ye that we, John Spencer and Isaac Spencer, do by these presents jointly and severally promise and engage to our honoured mother-in-law, Miriam Spencer, to pay her twelve pounds in current country pay, to be paid at £3 per year, annually, at or before the first of September yearly. This engagement is for and in consideration of our mother's thirds in our honored father Samuel Spencer his estate deceased, and in case we and our honored mother do all of us survive the fifth year, we do, out of respect to her, further promise to pay her £3 the fifth year as above, in consideration of the above premises.

I, Miriam Spencer, do accept of the conditions as above specified, and do by these presents resign up all my right and title of dower or third part of the estate of my honored husband Samuel Spencer, deceased, unto his two sons, John and Isaac Spencer, as their own proper estate to their proper use and behoof.

As witness our hands this 5th of March, 1705-6.

Witness: *John Chapman,*   JOHN SPENCER,
   William Layns.   ISAAC SPENCER,
            MIRIAM SPENCER.

Court Record, Page 78—8 March, 1705-6: John Spencer of Hartford exhibited an inventory of his late father, Samuel Spencer of Haddam. Ordered recorded and put on file. And this Court grant letters of Adms. unto John Spencer. The sd. John Spencer also exhibited in this Court an agreement made between the widow and children of the sd. John Spencer.

Page 102-3.

Spencer, Timothy, Haddam. Invt. £240-00-05. Taken 6 May, 1704, by Thomas Brooks and James Wells. The children: Timothy, Sarah, Hannah and Deborah, all of age; Jonathan, age 12 years; Ruth 15 years.

Court Record, Page 57—4 August, 1704: Adms. to Timothy Spencer, son of the deceased.

Page 57—7 September, 1704: Account of Adms. exhibited and accepted. Ruth Spencer chose James Braynard of Haddam to be her guardian; allowed. And Jonathan Spencer chose his brother Timothy Spencer to be his guardian; allowed. This Court appoint Daniel Braynard, Sen., Ensign James Wells and Thomas Brooks to dist. the estate to the surviving heirs.

Dist. File: 1705: To Timothy Spencer, to Joseph Chapman and wife Sarah Spencer, to Azariah Dickinson and wife Hannah, to John Hungerford and wife Deborah Spencer. A further division to Timothy, to Ruth, to Jonathan, to Sarah (the wife of Joseph Chapman), to Hannah (the wife of Azariah Dickinson), and to Deborah (the wife of John Hungerford). By Daniel Braynard and Thomas Brooks.

Page 70—6 September, 1705: Report of the distributors.

Page 110—5 April, 1708: James Braynard, guardian to Ruth Spencer, exhibits in Court an acquittance or discharge, under the hand of sd. Ruth, now of age. Bond now cancelled.

Page 161-2.

Stanly, Capt. John, Farmington. Died 19 December, 1706. Invt. £360-07-01. Taken 13 January, 1706-7, by John Norton 2nd and Samuel Wadsworth. Will dated 24 April, 1705.

I, John Stanly, Sen., of Farmington, do make this my last will and testament: I give to my wife Sarah my 4-acre lot lying beyond the 2nd mountain in the southerly end of a larger piece of land that I have recorded to me and 10 acres of land southward from the field called 80 acres. These two parcels of land I give to my wife forever. I give to my son Isaac Stanly all my land in the Great Meadow at Crane Hall, and the farm which I have not given to my son Thomas Stanly by deed of guift, and my lot of about 5 acres lying by Isaac Cowles's homelot, reserving half the improvement of it for my wife during her natural life; and 4 acres of land of my lot eastward of the 2nd mountain, butting southerly on the land I have given to my wife, and my lot at the Great Swamp, containing 20 acres more or less. I do hereby appoint that my son Isaac Stanly shall have no power to dispose of any land or other estate I have given him in this will without the consent of my son John Stanly and my son-in-law John Hooker, anything in this will to the contrary notwithstanding. I give to my daughter Sarah Gaylord £5, to be paid by my sons, John Stanly, Thomas Stanly and Timothy Stanly. I give to my daughters Abigail Hooker and Elizabeth Wadsworth 5 shillings apiece. I give all the remainder of my estate, not formerly disposed of by deeds of guift, to my sons, John Stanly, Thomas Stanly and Timothy Stanly, to be by them equally divided. I appoint my wife sole executrix.

Witness: *Thomas Bull,*   JOHN STANLEY, SEN., LS.
        William Brounson.

Court Record, Page 89—3 February, 1706-7: Will proven.
Dist. File, 14 February, 1714: Estate of John Stanly: To the widow Sarah, to Isaac, to John, to Thomas, to Timothy, to Abigail Hooker, to Elizabeth Wadsworth and to Sarah Gaylord.

Witness: *Luke Hayes,*
        Ebenezer Steele.

Invt. in Vol. VIII, Page 38.

Stedman, Simmons, Wethersfield. Invt. £83-06-02. Taken 26 November, 1709, by Nathaniel Stoddar and Jonathan Deming.

Court Record, Page 134—7 November, 1709: Adms. granted to Thomas Stedman, a brother of sd. decd. residing in Wethersfield.

Page 137—5 December, 1709-10: Benjamin Judd was summoned to Court to answer to the charge of retaining goods and chattels belonging to the estate of Simmons Stedman, decd., and examined under oath. Benjamin Judd was ordered by this Court to deliver all the goods and estate of Simmons Stedman in his hands or custody, which sd. Simmons did not sell and deliver to him in his lifetime, unto Thomas Stedman of Wethersfield, Adms., and to adjudge the sd. Benjamin Judd to pay to sd. Thomas Stedman £17-08-00 for the cost of his prosecution in this case.

Page 14 (Vol. VIII) 5 June, 1710: Thomas Stedman, Adms., exhibits now an account of his Adms. And this Court order the estate to be dist. to the brothers and sisters as followeth: To John, Thomas and Samuel Stedman and Violet Rowell (the wife of Thomas Rowell of Windsor), the next of kin to the decd., in equal degree. And appoint George Kilbourn, John Curtis, Jr., and Michael Griswold distributors. Benjamin Judd and John Woodruff of Farmington appealed from this order of Court to the Court of Assistants to be holden at New Haven on the 1st Tuesday of October next, giving bond. John Woodruff withdrew his appeal 14th of June, 1710.

Page 28—5 March, 1710: Report of the dist.

Page 55 (Vol. X) 29 September, 1724: Ebenezer Gilbert, of Farmington, showing that a part of the estate in land of sd. decd. that was by order of Court, 5 June, 1710, distributed on the 26th of February, 1710-11, to John Stedman and Violet Rowell, his sister, was not set out by meets and bounds. And now the sd. Gilbert, having purchased sd. land, prays this Court to appoint distributors to set out sd. part by meets and bounds. Stephen Lee, Joseph Smith and Isaac Lee were appointed.

Page 76-7-8.

Stodder, John, Sen., Wethersfield. Died 4th December, 1703. Invt., £725-09-06. Taken 10th January, 1703-4, by Nathaniel Stodder and John Curtis, Jr. Will dated 30 November, 1703.

I, John Stodder, Sen., of Wethersfield, being visited with dangerous sickness and apprehending approaching death, I will that all my just debts be truly paid. I give to my beloved wife Elizabeth 1-3 part of my estate, both real and personal. I will to my eldest son Thomas Stodder all my lands lying in the west lots, adjoining to Farmington bounds, 75 acres. The remainder of my estate to be equally divided amongst the rest of my children when they come to lawful age. Their names are as follows: Jonathan, David, Samuel, Elizabeth and Mary. It is to be understood that I will to my eldest son a double portion. And I do constitute my loving wife executrix. And I do make my friends, John Curtis, Jr., and Nathaniel Stodder, my overseers.

Witness: *John Curtis, Jr.,* JOHN STODDER, LS.
Nathaniel Stodder.

Court Record, Page 51—12 January, 1703-4: Will and invt. exhibited by Elizabeth the relict. Proven.

Stoddar, Nathaniel. Court Record, Page 64—6 March, 1704-5: This Court appoint Nathaniel Stoddar guardian to his son Nathaniel. Rec., £20.

Stoughton, John. Court Record, Page 13—17 April, 1701: John and William Stoughton, sons of John, choose their father to be their guardian.

Page 116.

Stow, Sergt. Nathaniel, Middletown. Died February, 1704-5. Invt. £368-09-09. Taken 20 February, 1704-5, by John Hall, Seth Warner and Alexander Rollo.

Court Record, Page 63—6 March, 1704-5: Adms. to Thomas Stow, Sen., a brother of the deceased. Rec., £200.

Page 82—4 April, 1706: Thomas Stow of Middletown, Adms. on the estate of Nathaniel Stow, presented an account of his Adms.:

	£ s d
Has paid in debts and charges,	92-14-05
Inventory,	384-03-03
The real part,	231-00-00
Personal part,	153-03-03
Deducting 1-2 real part given Samuel Stow by deed,	115-10-00
There remains of the real estate,	115-10-00
And of personal estate there remains,	92-14-05
There remains to be distributed in equal parts,	57-08-10

To Thomas Stow, to Samuel Stow, to heirs of John Stow, to Mary Spalding, to Thankful Hill, and to heirs of Elizabeth Bidwell, decd.

This Court order a distribution of the estate, and appoint Lt. Thomas Ward, Alexander Rollo and Deacon Joseph Rockwell distributors.

To John Stow, to Thankful Hill, to Samuel Cotton (son of Mary Spalden alias Cotton), to Samuel Bidwell (husband of Elizabeth Bidwell, decd.), and to Thomas Stow (brother of Sergt. Nathaniel Stow). By Thomas Ward, Alexander Rollo and Joseph Rockwell.

Court Record, Page 95—7 July, 1707: Report of the dist. on file.

Page 95-6-7-8-9-100-1-2.

Stow, Rev. Samuel, Middletown. Invt. £303-08-04. Taken 20 June, 1704, by Nathaniel Stow, Ebenezer Hubbard and Noadiah Russell. Will dated 13 August, 1702.

I, Samuel Stow of Middletown, do make this my last will and testament: I give unto my son John Stow and to his son Samuel Stow the residue of that which we have called the middle pasture, all being about 3 acres more or less, butting upon my 5-acre home lot east, and on the heirs of my daughter Gilbert west. I give unto my son-in-law Israhiah Wetmore 3 1-2 acres of swamp and meadow on the west side of the Crook bridge, that we have made for carting, which sd. 3 1-2 acres are thus bounded: on the east on my son John's; on Mr. Collins south; on my Cousin Sergt. Nathaniel Stowe west; and on Cousen John Stow's heirs from a great stump to a bush between Obadiah Allyn, Senior, and my heirs. If the quantity reach so far, the north is the Lammas highway, and the line between it and my heir, Samuel Stow, to whom I do give the residue of swamp northward and meadow adjoining unto my son Ichabod's heir west, and butting upon the Rivulet north and east, the south on his uncle Israhiah. Item. I having given my son Sergt. Israhiah Wetmore and my daughter Rachel part of my houselot which was five acres, the residue being three, I give the value of the sd. land to my daughter Elizabeth Barns and to my daughter Margaret Wetmore, each of them half of the value he gave for his brother Benjamin's land. I give unto my daughters Elizabeth Barns and Margaret Wetmore all my propriety in that which is called the Round Meadow, my daughter Rachell's husband having by exchange set over his third part which their deed mentioned to his brother Beriah, the husband of my daughter Margaret. Item. Further, having given to my daughter Rachel, as their deed given doth mention, ten acres on the east side of the Great River in that lot of eight or nine and thirty acres more or less, I give to my daughter Elizabeth abovesd., and unto my daughter Margaret, each of them, 10 acres of land in sd. lot of 39 acres, the over-plus of the thirty being given to my daughter Thankful Trowbridge mentioned in the deed given to her husband William Trowbridge. The abuttments of these parcels to my four daughters in the whole is thus: On the highway east, on the land of Henry Coles west, and Andrew Warner south, and Mr. Giles Hamlin's heirs north, having a highway through it to Wongunk 8 rods wide. My sons Israhiah Wetmore and Maybee Barnes having, with my approbation, sold their wives' parts to Goodman Gill, the other two must take up theirs on the east end. As to a parcel of land in the westermost range of the Great Lott, containing 605 acres, I have given to six children, to each 1-6 part: the first lott to my son John Stow in behalf of his eldest daughter Hope Stow; the 2nd to Beriah Wetmore or his wife (my daughter Margaret); the 3rd to Maybee Barnes for his wife (my daughter Elizabeth); the 4th to William Trowbridge for his wife (my daughter Thankful); the 5th to my son Israhiah Wetmore as a trustee for the orphans of my daughter Gilbert; the 6th to myself, being 100 acres or more, upon an account of 100 acres I let my son Israhiah Wetmore have at the Fall Lott in lieu of his wife's 6th part in this parcel. Item. As to my interest in the division of the Half Mile, and as to the additional 3 miles belonging to it in case of a new plantation, I give to Ebenezer Gilbert, the posthumous son of my deceased daughter Dorothy; to Samuel Barnes, the son of my daughter Elizabeth; to Ichabod Wetmore, son of my daughter Rachel; and to Beriah Wetmore, the husband of my daughter Margaret. I give 5 acres to my daughter Hope Stow, the daughter of my son Ichabod Stow. I intreat my friends, Mr. John Hamlin, Rev. Mr. Noadiah Russell and my kinsman, Rev. Mr. James Pierpont of New Haven, to be overseers.

And my son John and my son-in-law Israhiah Wetmore to be my principal executors. It is further my will, as to my household stuff and moveables, it is my desire that what my wife did say before her decease (that such or such a daughter should have that as they shall agree) which I wish them to do among themselves that it be fullfilled, which I suppose done in a great part as to dammas, fine linen, cushions of needle work, velvet covers for stool and chairs. And as she wills, I will. And that my daughter Margaret shall have the high bed with the curtains and vallents broidered, with what necessary bedding and bolsters, besides the bed and bedsted, that hath been improved about me. Besides, I will Margaret the value of half the long table and carpet, and daughter Rachel the whole, paying the value of half of the whole to Margaret, Mr. Pierpont judging of it. The great carved chest I have willed to Margaret, as also the silver spoon which she possesseth, marked "S. S. M." And that marked "S. S. E." to my daughter Elizabeth. The spoon marked "S. S. D." let it be reserved for little Sarah Gilbert when of age. As to what more of silver, brass and iron in the house that was mine, I will it to my daughter Rachel because tender and careful of me in my old age.

SAMUEL STOW, LS.

Forasmuch as daughter-in-law Robinson hath not, according to my proffers, attended to comply with me in the establishing of this my last will to which I have set my hand and seal, I do will that land in controversy be sold for the just defraught of extraordinary debts and charges before there be any distribution of my estate, that all due debts be paid. If she doth comply, then what may be wanting out of my responsible estate may answer it. April 20th, 1704.

Witness: *John Cornwall, Sen.,*   SAMUEL STOW, LS.
John Collins, Samuel Warner.

Court Record, Page 57—4 July, 1704: Will proven.

Page 222.

Stow, Samuel, son of John Stow, flax dresser, Middletown. Invt. £163-15-06. Taken 24 March, 1708-9, by Israhiah Wetmore and Joseph Rockwell.

Court Record, Page 125—4 April, 1709: Adms. to George Phillips of Middletown, mariner (brother-in-law of said deceased).

Page 129—6 June, 1709: George Phillips of Middletown, mariner, Adms. on the estate of Samuel Stow, late of Middletown, deceased, exhibited an account of his Adms. and is granted a *Quietus Est.* And this Court do now order and decree that all the residue of the estate of the sd. Samuel Stow, decd., both real and personal, mentioned and contained in the inventory thereof, upon record in this Court, shall be and remain to the said George Phillips and Hope Phillips his wife, the only surviving sister and heir-in-law of the said Samuel Stow, deceased, and to their or her heirs and assigns forever.

Invt. in Vol. VIII, Page 34.

Stratton, William, Windsor.   Invt. £41-19-06.   Taken 31 March, 1709-10, by Benajah Holcomb, Josiah Owen and Nathaniel Pinney.

Court Record, Page 136—5 December, 1709: Adms. granted to Abigail Stratton, widow.

Page 8 (Vol. VIII) 3 April, 1710: Abigail Stratton, Adms., exhibited an inventory.

Page 88 (Vol. X) 7 June, 1725: This Court appoint Edward Griswold of Windsor to be guardian unto Serajah Stratton of Windsor, a minor, 18 years of age. Recog., £50.

Page 45.

Strickland, Joseph, Simsbury. Died 9th February, 1702-3. Invt. £111-15-00. Taken 27 February, 1702-3, by Thomas Barber, Peter Buell, Nathaniel Holcomb, Sen., and Samuel Beaman. The children: Elizabeth, age 17 years; Hannah 15, Joseph 13, Mary 11, Samuel 5, Edward one and a half years old.

Court Record, Page 37—2 March, 1702-3: Adms. to the widow, Elizabeth Strickland. Rec., £50, with Samuel Cross of Windsor.

Page 55—12 April, 1704: Adms. account rendered and accepted.

Page 198 (Vol. VIII) 7 June, 1714: Elizabeth Strickland exhibited now an account of her Adms. on the estate of her late husband, Joseph Strickland of Simsbury:

	£	s	d
Inventory, with debts paid,	124	02	11
Paid out,	47	02	10
There remains to be distributed,	77	00	01

Account accepted and ordered on file. Order for distribution: To the relict, to Samuel the eldest son, to Edward Strickland, to Elizabeth, Hannah and Mary Strickland. And appoint Nathaniel Holcomb, Sen., Peter Buell and James Cornish, distributors. This Court appoint Elizabeth Strickland to be guardian to her son Edward Strickland, a minor about 13 years of age. And Samuel made choice of his mother for his guardian. Recog., £10.

Page 210—2 August, 1714: Adms. granted a *Quietus Est.*

Page 209.

Strong, Return, Jr., Tanner, Windsor. Died 6 August, 1708. Invt. £334-06-00. Taken 4 November, 1708, by John Moore, Sen., and John Wolcott, Sen.

Court Record, Page 117—13 September, 1708: This Court grant letters of Adms. on the estate of Return Strong, Jr., tanner, late of Windsor, decd., jointly to Elizabeth Strong, widow, relict of the sd. decd., and Samuel Strong of Windsor, brother of the sd. decd.

Page 120—7 December, 1708: Samuel Strong refusing to accept the trust, this Court now grant letters of Adms. to Elizabeth Strong, widow, who gave bond of £200.

Page 9 (Vol. VIII) 3 April, 1710: Elizabeth Strong of Windsor, Adms., presented now to this Court an account of a parcel of tanned leather belonging to the estate, valued at £50-05-07, to be added to the invt.

Page 166—7 December, 1713: Elizabeth Strong, Adms., exhibited now an account of her Adms.:

	£ s d
Inventory, with debts paid,	419-13-09
The real part,	266-00-00
Accounts paid in debts, charges, etc.,	67-07-06
There remains of moveable estate,	84-06-03
Which, added to the real part to be distributed,	350-06-03

Account accepted and estate ordered to be distributed as follows:

To Elizabeth Strong, widow, with thirds of housing and lands,	28-02-01
To John Warham Strong, eldest son,	214-16-02
To Elizabeth Strong, only daughter,	107-08-00

And appoint John Eliot, Esq., Mr. John Moore and Eliakim Marshall of Windsor distributors. This Court appoint Elizabeth Strong to be guardian to John Warham Strong, age 7 years, and Elizabeth Strong, age 5 years, children of Return Strong, Jr. Recog., £100.

Page 65-6.

Sumner, William, Middletown. Died 20 July, 1703. Invt. £432-11-10. Taken 18 August, 1703, by Nathaniel Stow, Sen., Samuel Bidwell and William Ward, Sen. The children: Hezekiah, age 20 years; Daniel 15, Sarah 18.

Court Record, Page 47—8 September, 1703: This Court grant letters of Adms. unto Hannah, the widow, who gave bonds, with Capt. John Hamlin and Samuel Bidwell, of £150.

Page 58—7 September, 1704: Hannah Sumner, widow, Adms., exhibited an account of her Adms.: Received, £6-09-11; paid in debts, £26-15-00 money. Account accepted and order of dist. to the wife and children equally amongst themselves. And appoint John Hamlin, William Ward and Deacon Rockwell distributors.

Page 205 (Vol. VIII) 5 July, 1714: Mrs. Hannah Hall of Middletown, Adms. on the estate of Mr. William Sumner, late of Middletown, exhibited an account of her Adms. and also a distribution thereof made by John Hamlin, William Ward and Joseph Rockwell, pursuant to an order of this Court, 1704, which account the Court allow and confirm and order to be kept on file. And this Court grant the Adms. a *Quietus Est.*

Page 143 (Vol. IX) 3 January, 1720-1: Hezekiah Sumner now exhibited a settlement upon an award dated 17 June, 1720, of the remaining part of the estate of William Sumner, decd., not before distributed, and likewise of his brother Daniel Sumner, decd., under the hands and seals of James Wadsworth, Esq., and Hezekiah Brainard, which award is by this Court accepted for the full settlement of sd. estate, and ordered to be kept on file.

See File: 3 May, 1720: Hezekiah Sumner requests this Court, in the settlement of the estate of Daniel Sumner, who had died, to allow him to buy and pay Sarah for the homested.

Page 176-7.

Taylor, Stephen, Sen., Windsor. Died 3 August, 1707. Invt. £380-10-09. Taken 20 August, 1707, by Job Drake, Thomas Stoughton and Roger Wolcott.

Court Record, Page 96—1st September, 1707: This Court grant Adms. unto Joanna the widow, relict, and her son Stephen Taylor. William Taylor, one of the sons, 18 years of age, chose Roger Wolcott of Windsor to be his guardian. Said Roger refused.

Page 102—2 February, 1707-8: William Taylor of Windsor, one of the sons of Stephen Taylor, Sen., 18 years of age, chose William Wolcott of Windsor to be his guardian.

Page 106—1st March, 1707-8: Joanna Taylor, widow, and Stephen Taylor, her son, presented to this Court an account of her Adms. on the estate of Stephen Taylor, decd., which account is allowed: Have paid in debts £34-18-09, which sum being deducted from the total sum of the inventory, the surplusage thereof, both real and personal, this Court order distributed to the sd. widow and to Stephen Taylor, her son, and to the rest of the children. And appoint Capt. Thomas Stoughton, Deacon Job Drake and Roger Wolcott of Windsor, distributors. And grant Joanna and Stephen Taylor, Adms., a *Quietus Est.*

Dist. File: 31 March, 1708: The estate of Stephen Taylor was distributed as follows:

	£ s d
To Joanna Taylor, widow,	41-19-02
To Stephen Taylor, eldest son,	130-14-10
To William Taylor, 2nd son,	65-03-05
To Sary, eldest daughter,	65-07-05
To Joanna, 2nd daughter,	65-07-05

By Thomas Stoughton and Job Drake, Sen.

We whose names are underwritten, being children and heirs to the above sd. Stephen Taylor, decd., do hereby declare that we are well pleased and satisfied with the above sd. distribution.

Windsor, September 6th, 1708.

> JOANNA X TAYLOR,
> STEPHEN TAYLOR,
> SARAH X TAYLOR,
> EPHRAIM BISSELL,
> JOANNA BISSELL,
> WILLIAM TAYLOR.

Page 137.

Thompson, Thomas, Sen., Farmington. Invt. £456-13-05. Taken 18 January, 1705-6, by John Thompson, Sen., Samuel Woodruff, Sen., and Joseph Hawley.

Court Record, Page 74—22 January, 1705-6: Adms. granted unto Thomas Thompson, son of the deceased. This Court appoint John Thompson, Sen., to be guardian to Daniel Thompson, a minor son of Thomas Thompson, decd.

Page 78—8 March, 1705-6: This Court appoint Joseph Hawley to be guardian to Samuel Thompson, a minor son of Thomas Thompson, decd.

Page 80—2 April, 1706: This Court appoint Nathaniel Coale of Farmington to be guardian to Daniel Thompson, a minor son of Thomas Thompson, deceased.

Page 105—1st March, 1707-8: This Court appoint John Clark, Jr., to be guardian to Mercy Thompson, a minor 3 years of age, daughter of the sd. Thomas Thompson, deceased. Thomas Thompson, Adms., presented an account of his Adms., which is accepted. This Court appoint Mr. John Hooker, John Wadsworth and Samuel Newell to dist. the estate. And the Adms. is granted a *Quietus Est.*

See File: Distribution of the estate of Thomas Thompson, 1st April, 1708:

	£	s	d
To Thomas Thompson, eldest son,	123-06-08		
To Elizabeth and Mary Woodruff, children of Elizabeth Woodruff, deceased,	61-13-04		
To Samuel Thompson,	61-13-04		
To Anne, Daniel and Mary Thompson, to each,	61-13-04		

By John Hooker, Samuel Newell, Sen., and Jno. Wadsworth.

Page 148 (Vol. VIII) 6 July, 1713: Joseph Hawley, of Farmington, now discharged from his trust of guardianship to Samuel Thompson, son of Thomas Thompson, late of Farmington, decd.

Page 110 (Vol. X) 3 January, 1725-6: This Court grant an appeal to Daniel Thompson, son of sd. decd., from a decree of this Court accepting an inventory of sd. estate on the 22nd January, 1708 (accepted and allowing of a dist. of sd. estate) to the Superior Court in March next.

Page 72-3-4.

Thornton, Thomas, Hartford. Died 22 September, 1703. Invt. £498-12-03. Taken 15 October, 1703, by Thomas Bunce, Sen., Hezekiah Willis and Samuel Howard. Will dated 11 April, 1694.

I, Thomas Thornton of Hartford, do make this my last will and testament: I give to my wife Hannah Thornton the use of two rooms in my dwelling house, part of the cellar, part of the barn to lay hay to keep one cow, during her widowhood, with the use of all my estate till my son Samuel shall attain the age of 21 years. I give to my wife the use or rent of all my other lands, excepting my homelot in Hartford, during her natural life, only my son Samuel shall have liberty to improve it, he paying to his mother the rent of sd. lands. I give to my son Samuel, when he shall attain the age of 21 years, my now dwelling house and barns and out-houses, excepting what is above mentioned, as also my homelot with all the privileges thereon, only his mother shall have the use of part of the garden during her widowhood. I give to him my part of the warehouse at the Common Landing Place in Hartford. As for my other estate, my will is that it shall be equally divided between my wife and my son Samuel. I appoint my wife sole executrix till my son Samuel shall attain the age of 21 years; then he shall be joined an executor. I desire my brother Nathaniel Farren and John Wilson to be my overseers.

Witness: *Samuel Kellogg,*   THOMAS THORNTON, LS.
  John Wilson.

Court Record, Page 49—1st Tuesday, November, 1703: John Wilson being deceased, the executors named in the will appeared in Court and did declare that they are satisfied that it was the testator's will, and desire the probation thereof. Will approved.

Page 213-14-15-16.

Treat, James, Sen., Wethersfield. Died 12 February, 1708-9. Invt. £1235-14-02. Taken 3 March, 1708-9, by Jonathan Belden, Edward Bulkeley and John Lattimer. Will dated 9 January, 1708-9.

The last will and testament of James Treat, Sen., of Wethersfield: I give unto my eldest son James Treat a double share or portion of my land lying in Wethersfield. I give unto my 2nd son Samuel Treat the homelot with the house thereon standing, which lot of land I purchased of John Edwards and his mother according as sd. lott is bounded in the

Records. I give my sd. son 10 acres of land in the Plaine, bounded
upon Mr. Nathaniel Stanly's heirs, on land of John Chester, on sundry
homelots, and my own land in the Great Plaine; 4 acres of land in the
Great Swamp, next to Thomas Hollister, decd.; 2 acres of land in the
Great Plaine next to the land of James Steele. I give unto my son
Salmon Treat 200 acres of land which lyeth near the Great Pond near
the road leading towards Colchester, for which 200 acres of land I have
a Grant from the General Assembly; and also gave or paid the Native
Purchase, and the same was laid out to me by order of Court. I give unto
my son Salmon an equal share of my personal estate, which I leave in the
hands of my wife. I give to my son Richard Treat, moreover and above
what I have already given to him sd. Richard as by deed of guift sheweth,
I say I give unto him a single share of the estate I leave in the hands of
his mother. I give to my son Joseph Treat 1-2 of my lot lying on the
West Field Hill, containing 6 acres or more, which piece of land is to be
between my sons Richard and Joseph. And I leave the partition to be
made by my sd. sons as may best accommodate and suit each other. Also,
I give unto my sd. son Joseph Treat my now dwelling house and homelot,
with all the buildings thereon, after the decease of his mother. I give
unto my daughter Jerusha, the wife of Capt. Thomas Welles, to be to her
and her eldest son William Welles forever, 3 score acres of land lying on
Cow Plaine, to be on the north side of my lot, which Estate I give to be an
addition to my daughter to what I have already given her. I give unto
my daughter Rebeckah, the wife of Ebenezer Deming, to be to her and
her son Joseph Deming forever, the remainder of my lot on the Cow
Plaine, being about 54 acres on the south side. I give to my daughter
Mabel Treat £100 current country pay. I give, or my mind is that my
loving wife Rebeckah Treat shall have, the improvement of all my lands
that I have not given to any of my children in this my last will or by deed
of guift heretofore, that my wife have the use of sd. lands for her maintenance, subsistence and comfort during her natural life. I give unto my
four sons, James Treat, Samuel Treat, Richard Treat and Joseph Treat,
all those lands which I leave in the hands of my wife. I do appoint my
sons James Treat and Samuel Treat to be executors. I give my purchase
of 200 acres of land near the Stone House beyond the bounds of Glastonbury, and also a right I purchased in the lands at Oweantinuck, both
which I give to my executors, James and Samuel Treat and their heirs
forever.

Witness: *Samuel Boreman.*   JAMES TREAT SEN., LS.
        Ebenezer Kilbourn.

    Court Record, Page 122—7 March, 1708-9: Will proven. This
Court grant letters of Adms. to James Treat and Samuel Treat, executors,
with the will annexed.

    Page 34 (Vol. XII) 1st October, 1735: It appearing to this Court
that, in order to a dist. of the estate of James Treat according to his last
will, an invt. of the lands by deed of guift to his sons James Treat and

Richard Treat should be taken: Whereas, John Lattimer and Jonathan Belding, formerly appointed to take sd. invt., are deceased, this Court now appoint Jonathan Belding, Lt. Joshua Robbins and Capt. Edward Bulkeley to apprise sd. lands at the value when the former inventory was taken, 3rd March, 1708-9.

Page 35—4 November, 1735: James Treat, one of the heirs to the estate of James Treat, late decd., and one of the executors of the will, informs this Court that the heirs did not and would not agree among themselves to divide the land or real estate of the sd. deceased, and that Samuel Treat, one of the executors and son of the sd. deceased, being deceased, he, the sd. James Treat, executor, had not power alone to divide sd. real estate, therefore cited the heirs to appear before the Court to object if they see cause why freeholders to divide the estate should not be appointed at the hearing. This Court decides that there cannot be equal division unless there be a new apprisal, forasmuch as the deceased, in and by his will, left the real estate in the possession of his widow, and after her decease to be divided by their sons, and the sd. widow being lately deceased, and the dwelling house decayed, this Court order a new apprisal of sd. estate. James Treat, heir and executor, appealed from this decree to the Superior Court.

Page 19.

Trill, Thomas, Hartford. Invt. £24-03-00. Taken 19 November, 1700, by John Catlin and John Pitkin.

Court Record, Page 9—10 March, 1700-1: Invt. exhibited by Ann the widow, relict of sd. decd.

Page 90 (Vol. IX) 6 January, 1718-19: This Court grant letters of Adms. unto Thomas Trill, son of the decd.

Page 143-4.

Turner, Ephraim, Hartford. Invt. £62-01-10. Taken January, 1705-6, by Joseph Wadsworth and Hezekiah Willis.

Court Record, Page 74—19 December, 1705: Adms. to Capt. Ciprian Nichols, Mary Turner, the widow, having refused Adms.

Page 82—4 April, 1706: Proclamation to creditors to appear.

Page 28.

Ventrus, William, Haddam, about 78 years of age. Died 2 July, 1701. Invt. £237-16-00. Taken 10 July, 1701, by Daniel Brainard, Nathaniel Spencer and Joseph Arnold. Part of William Ventrus' inventory is as followeth:

	£	s	d
The house and homestead which he bought of Wiatt,	30-00-00
Two lots in the Cove meadow, which is at Moodus,	30-00-00
All the right which he bought of Wiat, one lot excluded,	25-00-00
All the right that he bought of Wiat which lyeth upon the plain over against 30-mile Island on the east side of the river,	03-00-00
A lot of 16 acres that he bought of Wiatt,	02-00-00
All the right of Wiat's beside what is above written, both divided and undivided, on the west side of the Great River.	08-00-00

Will dated 21st March, 1699-1700. I, William Ventrus of Haddam, being very aged and crazy of body, do make and constitute this my last will and testament: I do hereby ratify and confirm the deed of guift or sale formerly made to my son Moses Ventrus. I give and bequeath to my son John Ventrus, forever, that house and homelot which I purchased of John Wiat, and the upper and lower lot in Cove meadow, and a £100 right on the west side of Connecticut River, which I purchased of said Wiat. And in case John Ventrus hath no issue of his own body, or said issue decease before it comes to age, that it shall go and fall to Moses his child or children. I give unto my wife Elizabeth Ventrus 40 shillings per year in provision pay, to be paid her yearly during her widowhood by my son John Ventrus upon consideration of what I give him; and also I give my wife liberty to dispose of what estate she brought with her that is yet left. It is my will that my two sons John and Moses Ventrus pay unto their sister Susanna Brainwood, my daughter, each of them £5 in provision pay, two full years after my decease, as her portion from me, and this legacy of £10 to be all she shall expect. I do give and bequeath all my whole right and rights, lands and privileges on the east side of the Cove and Great River, on Machamoodus, to my two sons John and Moses, to them and their heirs forever. I appoint my son Moses Ventrus executor, and appoint Mr. William Eely and Mr. John Smith of Haddam to be the overseers.   WM. X VENTRUS.
Witness: *John Smith,*
    William Scovill.

Court Record, Page 18—6 September, 1701: Will proven.

Page 22-23.

Waldo, John, Windham. Died 14 April, 1700. Invt. £292-07-00. Taken 30 April, 1700, by John Fitch and Jonathan Crane. Will dated 14 April, 1700. I, John Waldo of Windham, do nominate, appoint and ordain my loving son John Waldo, my dear wife Rebeckah, and Thomas Huntington, to make my will or wills, to settle my estate, and make deed or deeds as they shall think meet according to the rules of equity and righteousness, as there shall be occasion, of all my estate, real and personal, that is to be found here and at Chensford or elsewhere. To the confirmation hereof I have hereunto set my hand and seal this 14th day of April, 1700.

Witness: *Shuball Dimmock,*   JOHN WALDO, LS.
    John Barnard.

Mr. John Waldo acknowledged this instrument to be his act and deed the day and year above written. Before me, *Joshua Ripley, Justice of the Peace.*

Court Record, Page 19—11 November, 1701: Will and invt. exhibited.

Page 36—2 March, 1702-3: Adms. granted to Rebecca Waldo, widow relict, and John Waldo, son of John Waldo, late of Windham, deceased. Record on file of distribution in 1709 to John, to Edward, to Katharine, to Rebeckah, to Ruth, to Sarah, and to Abigail Waldo; by John Fitch and Jonathan Crane, distributors.

Page 2-3.

Warner, John, Middletown. He died 24 June, 1700. Invt. £290-14-00. Taken September, 1700, by John Hall and David Sage.

Court Record, Page 2—7 September, 1700: Adms. to John Warner, eldest son. Rec., £200. Jonathan Warner and Robert Sandford, sureties.

Page 7—8 March, 1700-1: Order to distribute the estate, and appoint Mr. John Hamlin, Capt. Nathaniel White and Sergt. John Clark distributors.

Page 10—8 April, 1701: Report of dist. accepted. John North to be guardian to two children he had by Mary Warner, viz., Anna North and Mary North.

Record on file, 19 March, 1700: To John Warner, to Jonathan, to Hannah and Elizabeth Warner, to John North's children by his first wife, to Ebenezer Ranny in right of his wife.

Page 172-3.

Warner, John, Sen., Waterbury. Died at Farmington. Invt. £71-04-00. Taken March, 1706-7, by Thomas Bull, John Stanly, Sen., Thomas Warner and Thomas Judd, Jr. Will dated 27 December, 1706.

I, John Warner, Sen., late of Waterbury, but now residing in Farmington, do make this my last will and testament: I give unto my son Ephraim Warner my 8 acres of land in Waterbury lying in that called the Old Town Plat, and about 1-2 an acre in the north end of my houselot in Waterbury Town. This, with what I have formerly given him, shall be his whole portion. I give to my son John Warner my house and the remainder of my homested in sd. Waterbury, and the 1-2 of all my land, both meadow and outlands, within sd. township. I give to my other two sons, Robert and Ebenezer Warner, all the remainder of my lands in Waterbury, to be equally divided between them. I give to my daughter Lydia Brounson all my beds and bedding and furniture to them, and all my household stuff, both iron, brass, pewter, tin and wood, and all my sheep. Finally, I give all the rest of my estate to be equally divided between my son John Warner and my son-in-law Samuel Brounson, whom I appoint my executors.

Witness: *Thomas Porter,*   JOHN X WARNER, SEN.
       John Hart, Sen.

Court Record, Page 92—7 April, 1707: Will proven.

Page 30.

Way, Mrs. Mary, widow, Hartford. Invt. £54-13-00. Taken 3d September, 1701, by John Blackleach and Ciprian Nickols.

Page 151—20 October, 1703: This indenture between Ebenezer Way of Southold, on Long Island, of the first part; Ichabod Welles of Hartford and Sarah Welles, his wife, 2nd part; Elizabeth Welles of Hartford, widow, 3d part; and Lydia Way of Hartford, 4th part; witnesseth: That it is agreed for a division of several parcels of lands, goods, etc., being part of the inheritance and estate of Mr. Eleazer Way and Mrs. Mary Way, late of Hartford, deceased, as heirs and legatees of the said Eleazer and Mary Way.

Witness: *John Wadsworth,*   Signed: EBENEZER WAY, LS.
      John Lattimer.   ICHABOD WELLES, LS.
                         SARAH WELLES, LS.
                         ELIZABETH WELLES, LS.
                         LYDIA WAY, LS.

At a Prerogative Court held at Wethersfield, 26 October, 1703, John Chester, Esq., Judge; John Haynes, Esq., and James Treat, Esq., Justices. At this Court appeared Mr. Ebenezer Way, Mr. Ichabod Welles and Sarah his wife, Mrs. Elizabeth Welles and Mrs. Lydia Way, and each of them acknowledged the partition entered, signed and sealed by them, to be their voluntary act and deed, and this Court accepts and allows the same. And the Clerk of the Prerogative Court is hereby ordered to make record of said instrument.

Pr. Caleb Stanly, Clerk.

Page 207-208.

Webster, John, Hartford. Died 6 December, 1694. Invt. £409-08-00. Taken 3 January, 1694-5, by Joseph Mygatt, Samuel Benton and Thomas Seamore.

Court Record, Page 8 (Vol. V) 7 March, 1694-5: Adms. to Sarah Webster, widow of the sd. decd.

Page 106—1st March, 1707-8: This Court order the Clerk to cite Benjamin Graham and his wife to appear and give an account of their Adms. of the estate of John Webster. Ebenezer Webster, one of the sons of the decd., chose Major William Whiting to be his guardian. And Jacob and Daniel Webster, minor sons, chose their brother John Webster to be their guardian.

Page 117—13 September, 1708: Benjamin Graham presented to this Court an account of sundry disbursements, £99-08-07, subtracted from the invt. of moveable estate, which is £150-01-00. There remains £50-12-05 of the moveable estate to be distributed. Account accepted and ordered to be recorded.

Page 275 (Probate Side, Vol. XI): An agreement made for the settlement of the real and personal estate included in the invt. of the estate of John Webster to the relict and children of sd. decd in manner following: That Sarah Graham, alias Webster, relict of John Webster, shall have the sum of £12, to be paid her in equal parts by her four sons, viz., John, Ebenezer, Jacob and Daniel. To John Webster, the eldest son; to Ebenezer Webster, 2nd son; to the heirs of Jacob Webster, 3rd son, who is deceased; to Daniel Webster, the 4th son; to Sarah Talcott, widow; to Ann Olmsted, the wife of Thomas Olmsted, Jr.; to Abigail Merrells, widow, the three daughters of sd. John Webster decd., to each of them their respective share or portion of sd. estate. For confirmation whereof the parties hereunto have set their hands and seals the 7th day of August, Anno Dom. 1728.

	DANIEL WEBSTER, LS.
SARAH TALCOTT, LS.	SARAH GRAHAM, LS.
THOMAS OLMSTED, JR., LS.	JOHN WEBSTER, LS.
ABIGAIL MERRELLS, LS.	EBENEZER WEBSTER, LS.

CYPRIAN NICHOLS, Guardian to the Children and Heirs of JACOB WEBSTER, DECD., LS.

The foregoing agreement recorded by me,

Jos: Talcott, Jr., Clerk.

Page 128-9-30-31.

Webster, Mrs. Susannah, Widow of Robert Webster, of Hartford. Invt. £32-03-03. Taken 19 November, 1705, by John Marsh and John Marsh, Jr. Will dated 23 January, 1698.

I, Susannah Webster, of the Town of Hartford, widow (sole executrix to the last will and testament of my honoured husband Robert Webster, decd.), doe now make and ordain this to be my last will and testament: And touching the dist. of both that estate late of my deceased husband Robert Webster, and of those temporal goods and estate which God hath blessed me withal, my will is that the same be dist. and disposed of as followeth: I give to my five sons, Jonathan, Samuel, Robert, Joseph

and William Webster, and to the now surviving children of my eldest son
John Webster, decd. (to-wit: John, Ebenezer, Jacob, Daniel, Sarah, Ann
and Abigail) the full sum of £100 in current silver money of New England
(being so much as was given me by my good friend John Hull of Boston,
decd.), their several parts of which sum is and shall be reckoned as included in the lands hereinafter to them respectively assigned, which legacy
or devise I make to them especially in consideration of their prudence, industry and help in paying the debts of my husband Robert Webster, their
father above-named, and saving the estate. I give to my above-named
grandchildren, John, Ebenezer, Jacob, Daniel, Sarah, Ann and Abigail
Webster in right of their father, my deceased son John Webster, all that
capitol, messuage, tenement, barn, outhouses and 8 acres of land (being
part of the homelot of my deceased husband). I give to my son Jonathan
Webster 8 acres of my homelot with his dwelling house, barn, outhouses
and appurtenances. I give to Samuel Webster, my son, 8 acres of my
homelot with his dwelling house and outhouses and appurtenances thereto
belonging. I give to my son Robert Webster my lands situated below
Rocky Hill, about 40 acres, on which his dwelling house now standeth,
with his house, outhouses and all their appurtenances. I give to my son
Joseph Webster 15 acres of my lot or land called the Plaine. I give to my
son William Webster 15 acres of my lott or land called the Plaine. I
give to my daughter Sarah Mygatt (she having already received her portion of her father's estate) 12 pence. I give to my two granddaughters,
Mabel and Elizabeth Grave, daughters of my deceased daughter Susannah
Grave, late wife of John Grave, to make the full sum of £32. I give to my
daughter Mary King, the wife of Thomas King, with what she has already received, £32. I give to my daughter Elizabeth Seamore, the wife
of John Seamore, besides what I have already given her, £32. I appoint
my five sons to be joint executors.

Witness: *Caleb Stanly,*   Susannah X Webster, ls.
      Samuel Richards.

Court Record, Page 71—7 November, 1705: Will proven.

Page 128—2 May, 1709: An agreement by the heirs of Mrs. Susannah Webster confirming and approving the division and settlement of
the sd. deceased, made by the last will and testament of the sd. Susannah
Webster, which agreement was signed by

Sarah Webster, ls.
John Webster, ls.
Ann Webster, ls.
Abigail Webster, ls.
Jonathan Webster, ls.
Samuel Webster, ls.
Robert Webster, ls.
Joseph Webster, ls.
William Webster, ls.

Minors:
Daniel Webster, ls.
Jacob Webster, ls.
Ebenezer Webster, ls.

By their Guardians,

John Webster,
William Whiting.

Witness: *Benjamin Graham,*
      Jonathan Smith.

Page 216-17-18.

Westover, Jonah, Sen., Simsbury. Died January, 1708-9. Invt. £401-15-08. Taken 26 January, 1708-9, by John Higley, Sen., John Slater, Sen., and John Case. Will dated 20 September, 1702.

I, Jonah Westover, Sen., being very sick, do make this my last will and testament: I give to my wife £10 out of my personal estate; also the house and household goods that are necessary for her use during life; also 1-3 part of my land to her order during life. Also, all my land that I stand possessed of, I give to my two sons Jonah and Jonathan, to be equally divided between them; also my housing, after their mother's decease. I do will unto my daughters that each of their portions (with what they have received) shall be £15. What has been paid to my daughters already: to Margaret, £5; to Hannah, £3; to Jane £2-12-06; to Mary, £9-00-06. I appoint my son Jonah and my son-in-law Samuel Case to be executors. And as for my son Jonathan and my daughter Johanna, they shall be paid their portions as they come to lawful age.

Witness: *Dudley Woodbridge,*   JONAH WESTOVER, SEN., LS.
Nathaniel Holcomb, Sen.

Court Record, Page 123—7 March, 1708-9: Will proven. And this Court grant letters of Adms. unto Jonah Westover and Samuel Case, with the will annexed.

Page 241 (Vol. VIII) 7 March, 1714-15: Upon motion of Samuel Case, executor to the last will of Jonah Westover, Sen., this Court now order and appoint John Pettebone, Sen., and Joshua Holcomb to divide and distribute the lands of the decd. according to his last will.

Page 12-13-14-15.

Wetmore, ffrancis, Middletown. Died 9th September, 1700. Invt. £947-12-09. Taken 4 December, 1700, by Nathaniel White, John Hall, Sen., and William Sumner. The children: Francis, age 25 years; Hannah 23, Elizabeth 21, Abigail 19, Martha 17, Joseph 14, William 12, Edith 10, Isabell 6, John, 3 years of age.

Court Record, Page 4—16 December, 1700: Adms. to Hannah the widow, relict, and Francis, eldest son. Rec., £500, with Capt. John Hall of Middletown.

Page 30—4 September, 1702: Adms. account presented:

	£ s d
Have paid in debts and charges,	185-11-09
Debts yet unpaid,	15-00-00
Debts due to the estate,	38-08-06

Order to dist. the estate to the widow and children. And appoint Capt. John Hamlin, Capt. John Hall and Lt. Thomas Ward distributors. Joseph Wetmore, son of the decd., chose Capt. John Hamlin for his guardian. And the children under age are left under the care of their mother by order of the Court.

Dist. File: 1703-4: Dist. of Francis Whitmore's estate as followeth:

	£ s d
To the widow, 1-3 of the personal estate,	50-00-00
All the house and houselot during life,	270-00-00

To Francis, eldest son,	81-07-05	To Joseph,	40-19-06
To Hannah,	40-18-11	To William,	40-19-00
To Elizabeth,	41-16-00	To Edith,	40-19-06
To Abigail,	40-18-00	To Isabell,	40-10-00
To Martha,	40-19-06	To John,	40-19-06

By John Hamlin, Thomas Ward and John Hall.

Page 52 (Vol. IX) 4 March, 1717-18: John Whetmore, a minor 19 years of age, chose William Whitmore to be his guardian.

Invt. in Vol. VIII, Page 4.

Wetmore, Nathaniel, Middletown. Died 7 March, 1708-9. Invt. £159-12-04. Taken by Beriah Wetmore, Thomas Ward and Joseph Rockwell.

Court Record, Page 127—2 May, 1709: Adms. to Dorcas Wetmore, widow, and Beriah Wetmore, a brother of the decd.

Page 11 (Vol. VIII) 1st May, 1710: Dorcas and Beriah Wetmore exhibit now an account of their Adms. Accepted. Order to dist. the estate: To Dorcas Wetmore, widow, 1-3 part of the remaining moveable estate, and 1-3 part of the sd. lands for the term of her natural life. And all the rest of the sd. moveables and lands to Easter Wetmore, daughter and only child of sd. decd. And appoint Joseph Rockwell, Andrew Bacon and Nathaniel Stow distributors. This Court appoint Beriah Wetmore to be guardian to Esther Wetmore, a minor daughter of Nathaniel Wetmore, late decd.

Page 27—5 February, 1710-11: Report of the distributors.

See File: These may certifie whome it may concerne: That the sd. widow, now Dorcas Andrews, doth hereby fully and freely give an acquittance unto the sd. Beriah Wetmore as Adms., and the sd. Beriah Wetmore doth hereby also, as guardian, give an acquittance to the sd. Dorcas as Adms. In testimony whereof they have set to their hands and seals: 30th November, 1710.

> BERIAH WETMORE,
> BENJAMIN ANDREWS,
> DORCAS ANDREWS.

Page 25-6-53-4-5.

White, Jacob, Ensign. Invt. £652-02-02. Taken 29 May, 1701, by Jonathan Bull and Cyprian Nickols.

ARTICLES OF AGREEMENT

Betwixt Elizabeth, the widow and relict of Ensign Jacob White of Hartford, late decd., and Capt. Nathaniel White of Middletown, Lt. Daniel White of Hatfield, John White and John Graves (in his wive's right) of Hatfield, legal representatives to John White sometime of Hatfield decd., Sarah Hixson alias Hinsdell alias Taylor alias White of Hatfield by her lawful attorney Samuel Partrigg, all of whom are next of kin to the said Ens. Jacob White deceased, in order to a settlement of the estate of the said deceased:

That the said Elizabeth, relict as abovesaid, have the free use and improvement of all the real estate, vizt., houseing and lands of what kinds soever within the precincts of Hartford or elsewhere, with all the privileges, rents, profits and advantages as by her management thereof may accrue, belonging or in any wise appertaining to the said deceased, for the full term that she is in a widowhood condition, viz., the widow of the said deceased, she keeping and maintaining the housing and fences in like good repair as they are now in, except only the oxhouse and the old barn that are in a tottering condition and for which she is not liable, but to keep them up so long as they may be of use, and when they fall it shall not be in her wrong or liable to any repair of them; yet, nevertheless, after the widowhood condition (should she see cause to change her present condition by marriage), then and at such time she is from thenceforward to enjoy only one-third part of the aforesaid housing and lands with the profits thereof.

2d. That Capt. Nathaniel White aforesaid, brother to the said Ens. Jacob White deceased, after the widowhood of the said Elizabeth as aforesaid terminates, shall have one-fourth or quarter part of all the real estate, viz., housing and lands of what kinds soever (the widow Elizabeth's thirds, which are to her for the term of her life as aforesaid, excepted) that are of right, or may grow to be as a right, of the said deceased, both for quantity and quality, set out to him to be to him and his heirs forever; and the like proportion in the said widow's thirds in reversion, in quantity and quality as abovesaid, also to be to him and his heirs forever. And furthermore, that he now receive and enjoy, of the personal estate or moveable goods of the said deceased, one-eighth part by equal division and proportion, which at present amounts to the sum of £20-07-10, as also the like proportion of any moveable estate that shall or may appear by any additional inventory over and above what is contained in the original inventory.

3d. That Lieut. Daniel White aforesaid, brother to the said deceased Ens. Jacob White, after the widowhood of the said Elizabeth as aforesaid terminates, shall have one-fourth or quarter part of all the real estate, etc., etc., etc., including the £20-07-10.

4thly. That John White and John Graves (in his wive's right), and both as legal representatives to John White deceased, brother to said Jacob White deceased, after the widowhood of the said Elizabeth terminates, shall have one-fourth or quarter part of all the real estate, both housing and lands, of what kinds soever, etc. etc. The one-half part to said John White, and the other half part as aforesaid to John Graves in his wive's right; always provided, that if the said John White make full payment of the full value of his sister Graves her part in sufficient good pay, he is to enjoy the whole of her part in the housing and lands, and the like proportion including the 1-2 part of personal estate, which amounts to the sum of £10-03-11.

5. That Sarah Hixson alias Hinsdall alias Taylor alias White aforesaid, sister to the said Ens. Jacob White deceased, after the widowhood of the sd. Elizabeth as aforesaid terminates, shall have one-fourth or quarter part of all the real estate, viz., housing and lands of what kinds soever (including) £20-07-10, etc., etc., etc.

6. The abovesaid articles of agreement we the subscribers do mutually agree to, and do humbly present this our agreement to the Honoured Court of Probates within the County of Hartford in the Colony of Connecticut in New England, humbly desiring their approbation and confirmation thereof as a full settlement of the estate of Ens. Jacob White deceased, to which we subscribe and seal this 12th day of December, 1701, in the thirteenth year of the reign of William the Third of England, Scotland, France and Ireland, King, Defender of the Faith.

Signed, sealed and delivered
in the presence of
John Blackleach,   Elizabeth X White, ls.
Jonathan Bull,   Nathaniel White, ls.
Ciprian Nickolls.   Daniel White, ls.
          John White, ls.
          John Graves, ls.

Samll. Partridge as attorney to Sarah Hixson.
Test: Caleb Stanly, Clerk.

Court Record, Page 13—16 June, 1701: This Court grant letters of Adms. unto Elizabeth the widow.

Page 42—7 April, 1703: Elizabeth the widow presented an account of her Adms. There is due to the estate the sum of £13-05-05. Also presented an agreement, under the hands and seals of the persons interested in the estate, which the Court confirmed and ordered to be recorded and filed. And this Court grant the Adms. a *Quietus Est.*

Williams, Francis. Court Record, Page 67—5 April, 1705: This Court grant letters of Adms. on the estate of Francis Williams, late of Simsbury, decd., unto Thomas Bacon.

Page 107—4 March, 1707-8: This Court do advise and direct the sd. Thomas Bacon to sell either all or so much of the lands of Francis Williams to pay the debts, taking the advice of Col. Matthew Allyn of Windsor therein.

Williams, Dr. Richard. Court Record, Page 26—9 March, 1701-2: This Court grant Adms. on the estate of Dr. Richard Williams, formerly of this Colony, decd., unto William Whiting, and order him to present an inventory of any estate he finds within the Colony. (None found.)

Page 159-60.

Williams, Thomas, Sen., Wethersfield. Invt. £132-15-00. Taken 28 February, 1692-3, by Benjamin Gilbert and Daniel Boreman. Will dated 20 December, 1689.

I, Thomas Williams, Sen., of Wethersfield, do make this my last will and testament: I give to my wife all my housing and barn, orchard, pasture and homelott, all being about 8 acres; also, 5 acres on the west side of Beaver Brook; also, I give to my wife all my other lands during her natural life. I give to my son Thomas Williams 1 acre of my grass land on the west side of Beaver Brook. I give to my son John and my son Jacob Williams 5 Shillings apeice. I give to my son Abraham Williams 4 acres of my 5-acre lot on the west side of Beaver Brook. I give to my son Abraham that part of my west lot next to Farmington that I have not otherwise disposed of; also all that piece of land that lies by Hogg Brook and by the road to Mr. Bulkeley's Mill (that I have not otherwise disposed of). I give to my daughter Hannah the bed, bedding, and all the furniture thereto belonging, that my wife and I lie upon. All the rest of my estate of stock or moveables, after my wive's decease, shall be equally divided between all my four daughters, only my eldest daughter Rebeckah is to fall short £10 in the sd. division because she hath had £10 already. I have reserved £15 in the hands of my son Jacob Williams to be paid to whom I shall will the same. I will that he shall pay to my daughter Rebeckah £5, and £5 to my daughter Mary, and £5 to my daughter Ruth. I make my son Thomas Williams executor, and also I make my sd. son Thomas and Lt. William Warner my overseers.

Witness: *Samuel Talcott,*   THOMAS X WILLIAMS, SEN., LS.
   John Welles.

Court Record, Page 89—3 February, 1706-7: Will proven.

Willis, John. Court Record, Page 88—13 November, 1706: John and Henry Willis of Windsor, minors above 16 years of age, chose their father Lt. Joshua Willis for their guardian. Allowed. This Court also appoint Joshua Willis to be guardian to his son Jacob Willis, age 13 years.

Page 63-64.

Wilson, Nathaniel, Hartford. Invt. £608-16-00. Taken 12 June, 1703, by Zachariah Sandford and Nathaniel Hooker.

Court Record, Page 32—8 September, 1702: David Jesse appeared in Court with some evidence of the death of sd. Wilson.

Page 32—8 September, 1702: Whereas, Mr. David Jesse of Boston appeared in this Court and did exhibit some evidences to prove the death of Mr. Nathll. Wilson, late of Hartford, who is supposed to be dead (the sd. Jesse prays that the estate that did belong to the said Nathll. may be preserved), a writ was made out by order of this Court requiring Susannah, ye wife of the said Nathll., to appear before them to hear what was offered by the said Jesse, but the said Susannah was not to be found. The Court, upon consideration of the whole matter, do see cause to order that there shall be appointed some suitable persons as conservators of that estate until the Court to be held on the 2nd Tuesday of November next, who shall take care that the estate be not wasted. And the Court do appoint Samll. Benton and Thomas Whaples to be conservators as abovesd., and impower and order them to act in that capacity. And, further, the Court order that the abovesaid Susannah be cited to appear at the abovesd. Court in November next to give in such information of the death of her husband as shall come to her knowledge.

Page 35—11 November, 1702: Mrs. Susannah Wilson, wife of said Nathaniel, appeared in Court with reasons that her husband was not dead. John Stedman appeared in behalf of David Jesse. This Court appoint Mr. Ephraim Turner as conservator of the estate.

Page 41—2 March, 1702-3: This Court, being moved by Ensign John Stedman in behalf of David Jesse of Boston, came to believe Mr. Nathaniel Wilson dead.

Page 42—7 April, 1703: Susannah Wilson appears in Court upon citation to be appointed administratrix upon her husband's estate. She refuses, seeing no cause. Whereupon this Court appoint William Whiting. And she appealed the case to the next Court of Assistants.

Page 45—14 June, 1703: An inventory of the estate was exhibited in Court.

Page 94—4 June, 1707: Report of Major Whiting, Adms., Joseph Rowlandson and Mary Jesse being present. Reports debts all paid and some personal estate left for division.

Page 104—16 February, 1707-8: Nathaniel Wilson, supposed to be dead, now returned to Hartford, but in a discomposed and shattered condition. Then this Court ordered Major Whiting to turn in the estate to the Court, when he was granted a *Quietus Est.*

Page 109—5 April, 1708: Major William Whiting, Adms. on the estate of Nathaniel Wilson, in pursuance of an order of this Court of 16th February last past, appeared now before this Court and gave an account of the goods and moveables remaining of the sd. estate, and of the rents of lands belonging to the same which he had delivered and ordered to be delivered and paid to the Selectmen of Hartford, for the time being to be improved according to the sd. order, which account this Court order to be put on file. And whereas, upon the 4th of June last past, upon examination of the sd. Adms. account, did find that there was due from the sd. estate of the sd. Nathaniel Wilson (who was then supposed to be dead) to the sd. William Whiting, Adms., the sum of £36-00-09 money or so much that he hath paid out for the proper debts of the sd. Nathaniel Wilson and for his care about it; and whereas, Mary Jesse, widow, sister of the sd. Nathaniel, hath paid to Mr. Whiting the sd. sum of £36-00-09 money due to him as aforesd: This Court now order that there shall be paid to the sd. Mary Jesse by the sd. Nathaniel Wilson, or out of his estate, the sum of £36-00-09 money.

Page 131—1st August, 1709: Whereas, the General Assembly of this Colony, held at Hartford 12 May, 1709, did grant full power and authority to Capt. Aaron Cooke and Mr. Richard Edwards of Hartford to sell so much of the housing and lands belonging to Nathaniel Wilson of Hartford (an idiot or distracted person) as may and shall be sufficient to procure money for his support and maintenance from time to time, and also for the payment of all his just debts according to the advice and direction of this Court. And whereas, there is yet remaining due from the sd. Nathaniel Wilson to his sister Mary Jesse, widow, Adms. on the estate of David Jesse, late of Boston, goldsmith, decd., the sum of £36-00-09 money for so much which she hath paid to Col. William Whiting (who administered on the estate of the sd. Wilson while he was absent) for defraying his own proper debts, also there is the sum of £18-06-00 lawful money (viz., 17d. weight at 6 Shillings) due from the sd. Nathaniel Wilson to the sd. Mary Jesse, Adms. aforesd., by mortgage made and executed by the sd. Nathaniel Wilson to David Jesse, bearing date 5 September, 1701, both which sums making £54-06-09 money, this Court do therefore now order, advise and direct the sd. Capt. Aaron Cooke and Mr. Richard Edwards to sell so much of the lands of the sd. Nathaniel Wilson as may procure the sum of £54-06-09 money, and pay the same to the sd. Mary Jesse accordingly.

Page 9 (Vol. VIII) 21 March, 1709-10: Sundry accounts were presented to the Court by the Selectmen against the estate of Nathaniel Wilson, late of Hartford, deceased, in favor of Samuel Benton, Sen., and to Mrs. Elizabeth Wilson, and to Doctor Daniel Hooker; in whole £27-14-01, which ought to be paid. Order to sell land to pay the debts.

Page 86—4 August, 1712: Whereas, this Court, on the 24th day of May, Anno Dom. 1707, did grant letters of Adms. on the estate of Nathaniel Wilson of Hartford (who was then absent and supposed to be departed this life) to Mrs. Mary Jesse, widow, late of Boston, decd., and it appearing to this Court that the said Nathaniel Wilson is not dead, this Court now therefore discharge the sd. Mary Jesse from her bond of Adms., and she is hereby discharged.

Page 121—February, 1712-13: Samuel Benton now exhibits account of debt due for subsisting Nathaniel Wilson of Hartford, an idiot or distracted person; amount, £49-18-00. And pursuant to an act of the General Assembly of this Colony holden at Hartford 12 May, 1709, do order and advise Captain Aaron Cooke and Mr. Richard Edwards of Hartford to sell so much of the lands of the said Nathaniel Wilson as may produce the sum of £49-18-00 current money, and make payment of sd. debts as speedily as may be.

Page 131—6 April, 1713: Report of the dist.

Page 65 (Vol. IX) 6 May, 1718: A petition of Joseph King and Mary his wife, representing that the estate of Nathaniel Wilson, sometime of Hartford, was delivered to the Selectmen of Hartford by order of the County Court for the maintainance of a person supposed to be sd. Nathaniel Wilson, but by the petitioners suspected to be a pretender and impostor, and that they are able to prove the sd. pretended Nathaniel Wilson not to be the very Nathaniel Wilson, but in truth one John Clements, an utter stranger. The Court do not see cause for it to act, but advise Joseph and Mary King to apply to the General Assembly.

Page 68—Joseph King appears in Court, 21 June, 1718, and pursuant to an act of the General Assembly, 8 May, 1718, to enter a review.

Page 72—Court Record of 4 July, 1718: Joseph King and Mary King, his wife, a daughter of Phineas Wilson, late deceased, having obtained an act of the General Assembly granting liberty to enter a review or appeal from a decree of the Court, 16 February, 1707-8, determining and admitting a certain person supposed to be Nathaniel Wilson, who was concluded by a former determination of this Court to be dead, Joseph King entered a review and summoned the pretended Nathaniel Wilson and the Selectmen of Hartford into Court to prove that the pretended Nathaniel Wilson is verily Nathaniel Wilson son of Phineas Wilson deceased. The Court decided against the pretender and reversed its former decree.

Page 133—2 August, 1720: Samuel Benton of Hartford, before the Court, produced an account of his keeping Nathaniel Wilson alias John Clements, late deceased, and disbursements upon him from the time he had formerly received payment. It was found due to sd. Benton the sum of £62, to be paid him out of the estate of the sd. Nathaniel Wilson per act of the General Assembly.

Page 189-190.

Wilson, Stebbin, Hartford, Carpenter. Invt. £112-01-09. Taken 26 April, 1708, by John Skinner and William Goodwine.

Court Record, Page 111—3 May, 1708: Invt. exhibited by John Wilson, a brother to the deceased, who refused the Adms. This Court appoint Richard Seamore, blacksmith, Adms.

Page 126—4 April, 1709: John Wilson, Thomas Day and Hannah his wife, Richard Seamore and Mary his wife, heirs of sd. estate, exhibit in Court an agreement in writing for the settlement of the estate of Stebbin Wilson, late decd. Approved.

Dist. File, 4 April, 1709: Signed by
JOHN WILSON,
THOMAS DAY and HANNAH HIS WIFE,
RICHARD SEYMOUR and MARY HIS WIFE.

Wolcott, Henry. Court Record, Page 99—20 October, 1707: This Court appoint Henry Wolcott Jr., son of Simon Wolcott, late of Windsor, decd., to be guardian to his two sons, Henry and Thomas Wolcott, minors.

Woodruff, John. Court Record, Page 105—1st March, 1707-8: This Court appoint John Woodruff of Farmington to be guardian to his two children, Elizabeth and Mary Woodruff, minor children.

Invt. and Will in Vol. VIII, Page 7.

Wright, Jonas, Middletown. Invt. £222-14-00. Taken 10 May, 1709, by John Gill, Sen., Shamgar Barn, James Ward and William Ward. Will dated 8 May, 1709.

I, Jonas Wright, of Middletown, do make this my last will and testament: I give to Olive my wife all my moveable estate so far as she needeth, be it all or less as she stands in need, for her comfortable subsistence during life, the use and profits of my buildings and lands until my child is 18 years of age, and 1-3 part of the income of my lands during her life; and then I give all my land to my child Eunice. And whereas, my lands was given by my father between me and my brother Thomas, and we have not as yet divided or known which part each shall have, I appoint my brothers James and Daniel to divide sd. land and make a final issue.

Witness: *Daniel Wright,*   JONAS X WRIGHT, LS.
John Bevin.

Court Record, Page 130—6 June, 1709: Olive Wright, widow, exhibits will. Approved. And this Court grant Adms. unto Olive Wright and Thomas Wright, a brother of sd. decd.

Page 40 (Vol. VIII) 5 December, 1711: Thomas Wright and Olive Wright, Adms., exhibit an account of their Adms. Approved. Ordered to be kept on file. And this Court grant the Adms. a *Quietus Est.*

Page 93 (Vol. IX) 6 January, 1718-19: Eunice Wright, age 14 yrs, a daughter of Jonas Wright, late of Middletown, decd., chose Daniel Wright of Glastonbury to be her guardian.

PROBATE RECORDS.

VOLUME VIII.

1710 to 1715.

Page 31.

Ackley, Nathaniel, Haddam. Invt. £130-12-10. Taken 7 March, 1709-10, by Daniel Brainard, Joshua Brainard and James Parsivall.

I, Nathaniel Ackley of Haddam, do make my last will and testament: I give to Esther Hungerford £16 cash. The rest of my estate to be divided into nine equal parts, to be paid to my brothers' and sister's children: to my brother John Ackley's children a ninth part, to be divided equally between them; and so of the rest, to my brother Thomas Ackley (deceased) his children, and to my sister Elizabeth (deceased) her children. This to be secured in the hands of my brother Thomas Robinson, to be paid to said children when they come of age. The rest of the children's part to be put into the hands of the parents, to be paid to the children when they come of age. I appoint my brother James Ackley and my brother Thomas Robinson to be executors of this my will.

Witness: *Ebenezer Hills,*   NATHANIEL X ACKLEY, LS.
Hannah Rowley, William Spencer, Jr.

Court Record, Page 8—21 March, 1709-10: Adms. with the will annexed to James Ackley and Thomas Robinson.

Page 17—3 July, 1710: Whereas, this Court, the 14th of August, 1705, did appoint John Ackley and Nathaniel Ackley of Haddam to be guardians to Thomas, Job, Hannah and Anne, four children of Thomas Ackley, late of Haddam, decd, and the sd. Nathaniel Ackley being lately dead, the sd. John now appears and offers to take the guardianship upon himself.

Record on File: 14 May, 1711: We the undersigned have received into our hands both real and personal estate of Thomas Robinson and James Ackley, Adms. to sd. estate, that doth belong to our children.

WILLIAM SPENCER,
SAMUEL ACKLEY,
EDWARD X PURPLE,
THOMAS GIPSON,
JOHN ACKLEY.

Page 248-9.

Addams, Daniel, Simsbury. Invt. £432-14-01. Taken 23 November, 1713, by Samuel Humphrey, Joseph Case and John Slater. Will dated 29 July, 1713.

I, Daniel Addams of Simsbury, do make this my last will and testament: I give to my wife Mary the management of my whole estate, both personal and real, for her maintenance during her natural life. And if need so require, she shall have power to sell and dispose of the same, or any part thereof. Nevertheless, if my son shall provide comfortably for her such things as are necessary both in health and in sickness during her natural life, then the abovesd. shall be void and of non-effect. I give to my son Samuel half my meadowland on the west side of the river. I give the other half of my farm at Pease Marsh to my grand children, Daniel, Abraham and James Addams, children of my son Daniel Addams, decd. I give to my son Benjamin that parcel of land on the east side of the mountain. I give to my son Joseph the land where his now dwelling house stands, and half the north pasture and the land that belongs to it. I give to my son Thomas that parcel of land called the new field, 40 acres or upward, joining Richard Porter's land north, and south on land belonging to Willcockson. Also, that parcel of land called Matson's Field, bounded north on John Robbins, east on John Cooke, west and south on Mr. Woodbridge. I give to my son Ephraim my house and homested; also that peice of land called Joshua's Field. I give to each of my three daughters an equal part or share of all my moveable estate (except team, tackling and gun) after one-third part thereof is set out to my wife. I constitute my son Benjamin sole executor.

Witness: *John Slater,*　　　　　　　　DANIEL X ADDAMS, LS.
　　David Buttolph.

Court Record, Page 164—7 December, 1713: Will proven.

Page 241—7 March, 1713-14: This Court appoint Samuel Addams to be guardian to his brother Ephraim Addams, a minor 14 years of age, son of Daniel Addams, late decd.

Page 225-6.

Addams, Daniel, Jr., Simsbury. Invt. £182-13-06. Taken 4 February, 1712-13, by John Higley, Sen., John Case and Samuel Pettebone. Will dated 9th January, 1712-13.

I, Daniel Addams Jr. of Simsbury, do appoint this to be my last will and testament: I give to my wife Thanks Addams the 1-3 part of my whole estate, real and personal, during life, and £10 in money to her at her dispose. I give to my son Daniel £8 in pay above his equal share of the rest of my estate. I give unto my sons Daniel, Abraham and James all my land to be equally divided among them. I give unto my daughters Thanks and Hannah my moveable estate after their proportion of my debts are paid out of them. If the income of my estate is not sufficient to bring up the children, they shall be brought up on their several shares. I appoint my wife Thanks sole executrix.

Witness: *Timothy Woodbridge, Jr.,*　　　DANIEL ADDAMS, LS.
　　Jonah Westover.

Court Record, Page 136—4 May, 1713: Will proven.

Page 11 (Vol IX) 3 April, 1716: This Court doth appoint Joseph Case, John Pettebone and John Slater of Simsbury to divide and set out the lands of Daniel Addams, late of Simsbury, decd, in severalty according as directed in the last will of the said decd., among the heirs. And this Court appoint Samuel Pettebone of Simsbury to be guardian to Daniel Addams, age 10 years, and Hannah Addams, age 6 years, children of Daniel Addams Jr., decd. Rec., £30.

Page 12—3 April, 1716: Joseph Pettebone to be guardian to Abraham Addams, age 8 years, James Addams, age 4 years, and Thanks Addams, age 12 years, children of Daniel Addams. Rec., £50.

Page 73 (Vol X) 9 March, 1724-5: William Wilcox of Simsbury, in right of his wife Thanks, one of the daughters of sd. decd., moved this Court that he might have an appeal from the judgment of this Court, 14 May, 1713, allowing and approving the will and invt. of sd. Addams. Granted.

Page 150—4th April, 1727: Daniel Addams, the son of sd. deceased, now moved this Court for a dist. of sd. estate. A citation was issued to Joseph Pettebone and Thanks his wife, alias Addams, relict of sd. deceased, who was executrix, and who exhibits now an account of executorship. Accepted.

Page 193—6 June, 1728: Joseph Mills of Simsbury, in behalf of his wife Hannah Mills, formerly Hannah Addams, daughter of Daniel Addams Jr., decd., being now 18 years of age, desires liberty of an appeal from the judgment of this Court in approving the last will of sd. Daniel Addams to the Superior Court. Granted.

Page 51 (Vol. XI) 7 September, 1731: James Addams, a minor 19 years of age, together with Joseph Pettebone, his guardian, appeared in Court and joyntly applied for a discharge of sd. Pettebone, and the minor chose his brother Abraham Addams to be his guardian. Allowed. Recog., £50.

Page 138.

Adjett, John, Hartford, Invt. £94-00-00. Taken 3 November, 1712, by Thomas Hosmer, Samuel Thornton and Thomas Olcott.

Court Record, Page 91—6 October, 1712: This Court grants letters of Adms. on the estate of John Atchett, late of Hartford, decd., unto Samuel Howard of Hartford and John Howard of Wethersfield.

Page 165—17 December, 1713: Mr. Samuel Howard of Hartford exhibited now in this Court an account of his own and of his brother's Adms. on the estate of John Adjett, late decd.:

	£	s	d
Have paid in debts and charges,	29	05	06
And credit to that estate,	21	16	08

Which account this Court allowed and ordered filed. This Court do now order and decree that the rest of the sd. estate, both real and personal, shall be set out to John Adjett, sometime of Hartford, father of the sd. John Adjett decd., being next of kin. Samuel Howard being dissatisfied with this decree, alleging the sd. John Adjett the father not to be next of kin to the decd. in the instrument of the law to inherit the estate, but that there were others (viz., uncles on the side of the mother) who are now the next of kin as intended by the law, and therefore the sd. Samuel Howard appealed from this decree unto the Superior Court.

Page 138.

Adjett, Samuel, Hartford. Invt. £138-02-01. Taken 3 November, 1712, by Thomas Hosmer, Samuel Thornton and Thomas Olcott.

Court Record, Page 91—6 October, 1712: This Court grant letters of Adms. on the estate of Samuel Adjett unto Samuel and John Howard.

Page 107—6 January, 1712-13: John Adjett, formerly of Hartford (and late resident of Block Island, a transient person), father to John and Samuel Adjett, late of Hartford, decd., appeared now and moved the Court to reverse their former decree of committing Adms. on the estate of the sd. John and Samuel Adjett, decd., to John Howard of Wethersfield and Samuel Howard of Hartford, he the sd. John Adjett the father now claiming Adms. thereon, alleging the same to be his right by law as next of kin to the sd. decd. This Court having considered the sd. motion and the several pleas and objections that have been offered for and against the same, do not see cause to reverse their sd. former order.

Page 238.

Adkins, Josiah, Hartford. Died 25 June, 1713. Invt. £108-01-06. Taken by Timothy Cowles and William Williams.

Court Record, Page 152—3 August, 1713: Adms. to Joanna Adkins, the widow, relict of the decd.

Page 117 (Vol. IX) 2 day of February, 1719-20: Joanna Colt, late widow of and Adms. on the estate of Josiah Adkins, late of Hartford, decd., exhibited an accot. of debts amounting to the sum of £64-04-07. Allowed. It being represented to the Court that the moveable estate of the sd. decd. was consumed by fire and very little left to pay debts, this Court, in pursuance of an act of the General Assembly held at Hartford 13 May, 1714, do order and direct the sd. Joanna Colt to sell all the lands of the sd. Josiah Adkins for the payment of the aforesd. sum. John Elmor, Joseph Elmor, Robert Reeve and Jonas Williams appeal from the judgment of this Court to the Superior Court. Rec., £5.

Page 130—5 July, 1720: Benjaimn Colt of Windsor in right of his wife (and she was Adms. on the estate of Josiah Adkins, late of Hartford, decd.), having finished their accot. of Adms. on sd. estate, this Court grant them a *Quietus Est.*

Page 16.

Adkins, Thomas, Hartford. Invt. £33-10-06. Taken 28 October, 1709, by John Burnham and Samuel Burnham. No Court Record found.

Page 194.

Allyn, Benjamin, Windsor. Died 14 December, 1712. Invt. £654-05-00. Taken 2 February, 1712-13, by John Moore, Sen., and Timothy Thrall.

Court Record, Page 104—5 January, 1712-13: Adms. granted unto Anne Allyn, widow.

Page 142—1st June, 1713: This Court, pursuant to an act of the General Assembly of this Colony holden at Hartford, 14 May, 1713, do allow and direct Anne Allyn, Adms., to sell 3 acres of land situated in Windsor, at a place commonly called the Island.

Page 184 (Vol. X) 7 June, 1728: Benjamin Allen, a minor, age 16 years, chose Matthew Allyn Jr. of Windsor to be his guardian. Recog., £100.

Page 165.

Allyn, Obadiah, Middletown. Invt. £343-12-01. Taken 28 April, 1712, by Joseph Wetmore, Nathaniel Stowe and Joseph Rockwell.

Will dated 14 March, 1706-7: I, Obadiah Allyn of Middletown, do make this my last will and testament: I give unto my son Thomas Allin, and to his heirs forever, that whole settlement of land in the boggy meadow quarter upon which he now lives. Item. I give unto my grandson Obadiah Allin, son of Obadiah deceased, 100 acres of land, being part of my long lot on the east side of the Great River, to be laid out to him without damnifying the rest of the lot, I having formerly by deed of guift given to him and his mother other land besides this. I give to my two sons, Samuel and John, 100 acres more of that lott on the east side of the Great River, and my lotment in the 2nd part of the first division, and my lot in this west range of lots. Further, it is my will that my houses, homestead, and my lands on the West River, with what of my lands is within the Common Field, as also all my moveable estate (after my just debts are paid), shall be equally shared amongst my two sons Samuel and John and my two daughters Mary and Anna. Also I do except what is provided for my dear wife in the long meadow lot. And if any of my two sons Samll and John or daughters Mary and Anna should depart this life before marriage, then their shares or what may not be expended by them shall fall to their survivors equally. The consideration that moves me to this is because said sons Samuel and John and my two daughters have been very dutiful and helpful to their deceased mother and me in our many long and tedious sicknesses and are very probable to be still helpful to me in my old age. (A covenant in writing was made with his wife before marriage that she was to have paid to her £20.) Also I do further add that if my said dear wife shall have any child or children by me, that then she shall have the remainder of my long lot on the east side of the Great River, which I judge about 130 acres of land, to dispose of as she sees meet. I appoint my sons Thomas and Samuel to be executors. Where Dorcas lives, it is my will that the half of that new field lot within the fence shall be Samuel's and John's.

Witness: *Noadiah Russell,*   OBADIAH ALLYN, LS.
Joseph Rockwell, Alexander Rollo.

Court Record, Page 72—5 May, 1712: Will proven.

Page 4.

Allyn, Thomas, Windsor. Died April, 1709. Invt. £217-15-08. Taken by Samuel Moore and James Enno, Jr.

Court Record, Page 31—2 April, 1711: This Court appoint Benjamin Allyn of Windsor to be guardian to Joanna Allyn, a minor, age 8 years, daughter of Thomas Allyn, deceased.

Page 35—2 July, 1711: This Court grant further time unto Samuel Bancroft and Joannah his wife on the estate of Thomas Allyn, to finish their work of Adms.

Page 112—2 February, 1712-13: Lt. Samuel Bancroft, with his wife (late Johanna Allyn) exhibits an account of their Adms. Account accepted and allowed and order to dist. the estate as followeth:

	£ s d
Inventory,	258-10-08
Paid in debts and charges,	81-12-06
There remains to be distributed,	176-18-02

Account allowed and order to dist. as followeth:

To Johanna, the widow, of moveables, with dower in lands,	4-19-04
To Johannah, only child, of moveables,	9-18-08
And also the real estate,	162-00-00

And appoint Lt. Nathaniel Loomis, Deacon Job Drake and Mr. Henry Wolcott of Windsor dist.

Page 114—2 March, 1712-13: This Court appoint Col. Matthew Allyn of Windsor and Lt. Samuel Bancroft guardians to Joanna Allyn, minor child of Thomas Allyn, deceased. Recog., £100.

Invt. in Vol. IX, Page 46.

Alverd, Jane, Windsor. Invt. £50-09-00. Taken 6 September, 1715, by Thomas Moore, Josiah Cooke and James Enno.

Court Record, Page 256—7 June, 1715: This Court grant letters of Adms. on the estate of Jane Alverd, late of Windsor, decd., unto Benedict Alverd, eldest son.

Page 262—6 September, 1715: Benedict Alverd, Adms. on the estate of Jane Alverd, late of Windsor, exhibited an invt. of the estate. Ordered recorded and kept on file.

Page 54 (Vol. IX) 4 March, 1717-18: Benedict Alverd of Windsor, Adms. on the estate of Jane Alverd, late of Windsor, decd., exhibited now in this Court an account of his Adms:

	£ s d
Has paid in debts and charges,	29-07-01
The estate amounts to,	49-09-03
There remains,	19-19-02

Which accot. this Court allows. Order to dist. as followeth:

To Benedict Alverd, eldest son, his double portion,	5-14-00
To Jeremiah, Job, Jane, Joanna and Elizabeth Alverd, to each,	2-17-00

Which is their single portion of the sd. estate. And appoint Daniel Loomis, Josiah Cooke and Timothy Loomis distributors.

Page 57—1st April, 1718: Report of the distributors.

Page 100.

Andrews, Samuel, Hartford. Invt. £414-07-00. Taken 29 January, 1711-12, by Garrard Spencer, Sen., and Gershom Sexton. Will dated 1st January, 1711-12:

I, Samuel Andrews of Hartford, do make this my last will and testament: I give to my wife Elizabeth the whole use of my estate during her natural life for her subsistence. And when the oxen are put off or otherwise made use of, I do order that my wife Elizabeth shall have 1-3 part of them, or their price, or anything of the estate that is moveable. I give to my three eldest sons my lands that I bought of Mr. John Haynes, to be equally divided among them. I also give to my son Nathaniel Andrews my now dwelling house and his part of the land lying next to the aforementioned house. I give to my son John Andrews my barn standing near my son John's house, provided that that part of the above-named that I have already given by deed of guift to my son Thomas Andrews shall be part of his third part of the land already specified to be divided to him. I give to my son Samuel Andrews, my younger son, my lot that I bought of John Skinner, which was sometime Mr. Stone's land, abutting on Mr. Thomas Hooker's land west, on my own land east, on the Mill River south, and on Jonathan Ashley's land north. I order that my daughter Abigail Stedman and my daughter Elizabeth Andrews shall have my moveable household goods. Also, I give my daughter Abigail 1 cow and 6 sheep. Unto my daughter Elizabeth I give 2 cows and 6 sheep. I do further order that my son Samuel Andrews shall have £3 of money after my wife Elizabeth's decease. My will is that my son John Andrews shall have the use of my team in consideration of finding his mother (my wife) her fire-wood if she see cause. I appoint my wife Elizabeth executrix.

Witness: *Garrard Spencer,*   SAMUEL ANDREWS, LS.
    George Sexton.

Court Record, Page 52—5 February, 1711-12: Will proven.

Page 166-7.

Andrews, Solomon, Hartford. Invt. £981-04-10. Taken 26 April, 1712, by Joseph Wadsworth and Hezekiah Wyllys. Will dated 11 April, 1712.

I, Solomon Andrews of Hartford, do make this my last will and testament: I give to my loving wife 1-3 of all my lands during her life and 1-3 part of my moveable estate forever. I give to my daughter Mary Andrews all my lands and housing and other personal estate, after my wife's decease, excepting what of my estate I do hereafter give and bequeath. I give to my kinsman Matthias Treat 30 acres of woodland lying on the east side of the road, bounded south on David Forbes's land, north on land of Capt. Cyprian Niccols, east on my own land, and west on the aforesd. road, on the account of an agreement I made with him. I give to my loving sister Mary Warren £12 cash. I give to my brother William Warren my Culliver or English gun. I give to Matthias Treat my Indian gunn. And further I give unto Matthias Treat 20 shillings cash. I appoint my wife Elizabeth Andrews sole executrix.

Witness: *Joseph Wadsworth,*   SOLOMON X ANDREWS, LS.
    Hezekiah Wyllys.

Court Record, Page 72—5 May, 1712: Will proven.

Page 6 (Vol. IX) 7 February, 1715-16: Adms., with will annexed, granted to William Warren and David Forbes. (*The Executrix Elizabeth Andrews now deceased.*)

Page 189.

Arnold, Josiah, Haddam. Invt. £195-17-00. Taken 21 February, 1711-12, by Simon Smith, Benjamin Smith and William Brainard. Will dated 23 November, 1708.

I, Josiah Arnold, of the Town of Haddam, yeoman, being often by Divine Providence brought to the brink of the pit, do make and ordain this my last will and testament: I give to Mary my wife a new Bible and the sum of £55 out of my moveable estate, with the use of my now dwelling house and homestead during her widowhood. I give to my son David Arnold a young horse. I give to my daughter Mary Arnold, she arriving at the age of 18 years, £16. It is to be understood, and it is my real honest meaning therein, that my wife shall have the improvement of the whole of my estate until my children come of lawful age; and if she need, I do hereby allow her to expend £25 of the remainder of my estate towards the bringing up of our children. And all the remainder of my estate shall be equally divided between my three sons, David, Josiah and James. I appoint my wife to be executrix. And appoint my brethren James Wells and Joseph Arnold to be overseers.

Witness: *John Smith,*   JOSIAH X ARNOLD, LS.
Thomas Brooks, John Clarke.

In a codicil, dated 22 January, 1711-12, provision was made for another child born after the will was executed. Her name was Irene.

JOSIAH X ARNOLD, LS.

Court Record, Page 221—1st November, 1714: Adms., with the will annexed, is granted to James Wells of Haddam.

Page 227-8—6 December, 1714: Capt. James Wells of Haddam. Adms., exhibits an account of his Adms:

	£	s	d
Paid in debts and charges,	16	08	00
There yet remains a debt of,	16	00	

And also the 4 sheep contained in the invt. are lost. Capt. Wells, Adms., is appointed to be guardian to Josiah Arnold, age 16 years, and Irene, age 5 years. This Court appoint Joseph Arnold of Haddam to be guardian to David, age 20 years, and Mary, age 13 years. Recog., £50. Joseph Smith of Haddam to be guardian to James Arnold, 8 years of age. Recog., £30.

Baker, Samuel, Windham. Court Record, Page 256—7 June, 1715: This Court grant letters of Adms. on the estate of Samuel Baker, late of Windham, decd., unto Abigail Baker, widow, and John Huntington, son-in-law.

Page 35.

Baker, Timothy, Wethersfield. Invt. £21-08-08. He died 15 December, 1709. Invt. taken by Moses Crafts and Hezekiah Deming.

Court Record, Page 8—3 April, 1710: Jonathan Deming, Adms., exhibits inventory.

Page 33—4 April, 1711: Now exhibited in Court an account of the administration. The account is allowed, approved and ordered on file.

Page 191.

Will from File.

Barber, John, Simsbury. (See File: Died 1st March, 1711-12.) Invt. £161-19-10. Taken 2 April, 1712, by Andrew Robe, Thomas Holcomb and John Slater, Sen. (See File: The legatees of the deceased: Mary, his wife; Marcy, his eldest daughter, 9 years old; John, 7; William, in his 5th year; Mary, born 4 January, 1708-9; and Isaac, born 2 May, 1711.) Will dated 27 February, 1711-12.

I, John Barber of Simsbury, do make and ordain this my last will and testament: I give unto Mary, my wife, whom I make sole executrix, my whole estate, both real and moveables, to her sole dispose. Further, it is my will and desire that she take a wise and prudent care for to bring up these children to some lawful calling. Further, it is my will that this my well-beloved wife (to whom I give, by virtue of this writ, full power to make her will from henceforward to the day of her death) shall so act as may conduce to the best and most equitable disposing of this our estate, both real and personal, to those our children, of what then may be in her possession, desiring her to use her best discretion towards these our children. Further, it is my desire that she be wise and prudent, to see to it she do use prudence to maintain herself honourably out of the estate during her natural life or state of widowhood, after funeral charges and debts paid.

Witness: *Andrew Robe,*   JOHN X BARBER, LS.
   Jonathan Higley.

Court Record, Page 65—7 April, 1712: Mary Barber, relict of the deceased, exhibited the last will and testament of John Barber now in this Court. This Court do see cause to defer the matter until the 1st Monday in June.

See File.: *The pretended will of John Barber of Simsbury, deceased, was exhibited in Court and was disallowed and disapproved.*
     Test: Thomas Kimberly, Clerk.

Page 104 (Vol. IX) 12 May, 1719: This Court appoint Mary Buell of Simsbury, widow, to be guardian to Mercy Barber, about 16 years of age, William Barber 13, Mary 11, Isaac 8, all children of John Barber, late of Simsbury, decd.; also, Mindwell Buell, about 4 years, and Ephraim Buell, about one year, children of Ephraim Buell, late decd. The sd. Mary Buell and Samuel Buell jointly and severally bound in £300.

Inventory on File.

Barber, Mindwell. Invt. £61-11-00. Taken 16 February, 1712-13, by Thomas Marshall and Thomas Moore.

Court Record, Page 180—1st March, 1713-14: This Court grant letters of Adms. on the estate of Mindwell Barber, late of Windsor, single woman, decd., unto Joseph Barber, brother of sd. decd.

Page 193—3 May, 1714: Joseph Barber of Windsor, Adms., exhibited now in this Court an account of his Adms:

	£ s d
Paid in debts and charges,	8-05-10
Invt., with what was dist. to her of her father's estate,	61-11-00
Subtracting,	8-05-10
There remains to be distributed,	53-05-02

To Samuel, David, Joseph, Benjamin, John, William, Mary, Ruth, Elizabeth and Sarah Barber, brothers and sisters, to each, 5-06-06
And appoint John Moore, John Bissell and James Enno of Windsor distributors.

Page 220—1st November, 1714: Report of the dist. And this Court do grant the Adms. a *Quietus Est.*

Dist. File: 24 October, 1714: To the brothers and sisters of the decd. children of Samuel Barber: To Samuel, William, David, Joseph, Benjamin and John; to Daniel Loomis and his wife Elizabeth; to Peter Browne and his wife Mary; to William Phelps and his wife Ruth; to Sarah Barber, and to William Barber son of William Barber decd. By John Moore, John Bissell and James Enno.

Page 237-8.

Barber, Thomas, Sen., Simsbury. Invt. £488-18-03. Taken 21 May, 1713, by James Cornish, John Slater and Joseph Case.

Court Record, Page 142—1st June, 1713: This Court grant letters of Adms. on the estate of Thomas Barber unto Thomas Barber, son of sd. decd.

Page 149—6 July, 1713: Thomas Barber of Simsbury, Adms., exhibited an account of his Adms:

	£ s d
Paid in debts and charges,	3-19-02
There remains to be distributed,	484-19-01

Account allowed, and order to dist. as followeth:

To Mary, the relict,	51-06-01
To Thomas Barber, eldest son,	133-18-00

To John Barber's heirs, to Samuel Barber, Sarah Robe, Ann Higley and Joanna Adkins, daughters, to each, 61-19-00

And appoint Joseph Phelps, Joseph Case and John Slater distributors.

Page 214—6 September, 1714: Whereas, this Court heretofore granted letters of Adms. on the estate of Thomas Barber, Sen., late of Simsbury, decd., unto Thomas Barber, eldest son of sd. decd., who has since also departed this life not having finished his Adms. thereon, this Court doth now grant letters of Adms. on that estate unto Jonathan Higley of Simsbury, son-in-law.

Page 2 (Vol. IX) 1st November, 1715: This Court grant extension of time unto Jonathan Higley of Simsbury, Adms., until the 1st Tuesday of May next.

Page 124—5 April, 1720: Whereas, it appears to this Court that the Adms. on the estate of Thomas Barber, Sen., deceased, hath not fully administered on sd. estate before his decease, the Court do therefore grant letters of Adms. unto Joseph Case of Simsbury.

Inventory on File.

Barber, Thomas, Jr., Simsbury. Died 17 July, 1714. Invt. £339-04-07. Taken by James Cornish, Joseph Case and John Slater.

Court Record, Page 213—6 September, 1714: This Court grant letters of Adms. on the estate of Thomas Barber, Jr., late of Simsbury, decd., unto Abigail Barber of Simsbury, widow and relict of sd. decd.

Page 2 (Vol. IX) 1st November, 1715: Extension of time granted the Adms. to finish their Adms. on sd. estate.

Page 84.

Bartlett, Samuel, Hartford. Invt. £38-09-07. Taken 4 June, 1711, by Joseph Wadsworth and Ciprian Nichols.

Court Record, Page 36—2 July, 1711: Adms. to William Porter of Haddam, brother-in-law, who exhibited inventory.

Page 269.

Belding, John, Wethersfield. Invt. £891-00-03. Taken 17 February, 1713-14, by Jonathan Belding, Jacob Griswold and David Wright.

Court Record, Page 179—1st March, 1713-14: Adms. granted to Dorothy Belding, widow, and Josiah Belding, eldest son of sd. decd.

Page 185—5 April, 1714: Josiah Belding of Wethersfield, Adms., exhibited an account of his Adms. on that estate:

	£	s	d
Paid in debts and charges,		15-15-00	
Hath received,		11-00	

Account allowed. Order to distribute as followeth: To the widow, her dowry in housing and lands during life, and 1-3 of the personal estate forever. And appoint Jonathan Belding, Ebenezer Prout and Joshua Robbins the 2nd, dist.

Page 185—5 April, 1714: Stephen Belding and Ezra Belding of Wethersfield, minor children of John Belding, chose Josiah Belding of Wethersfield, their brother, to be their guardian. Recog., £200.

Dist. File: 5 April, 1714: To Widow Dorothy Belding, to Josiah, to John, to Benjamin, to Stephen, to Ezra, to Hannah, to Lydia Belding. By Jonathan Belding and Joshua Robbins. Report Page 194—19 April, 1714.

Page 233.

Benton, Edward, Glastonbury. Invt. £188-04-00. Taken 29 May, 1713, by Joseph Smith and Thomas Hale.

Court Record, Page 142—1st June, 1713: Adms. is granted to Mary Benton, the widow.

Page 203-4.

Bidwell, Jonathan, Hartford. Invt. £1434-13-01. Taken 17 December, 1712, by Joseph Mygatt, Thomas Bidwell and Edward Allyn. Will dated 4 November, 1712.

The last will and testament of Jonathan Bidwell of Hartford is as followeth: First, I desire to commit and commend my soul into the hands of God my Creator and Jesus Christ my Redeemer, and my body to a decent burial. And after my funeral charges are defrayed and my just and honest debts paid, I do dispose of what God hath graciously given or lent me as follows: vizt.: Item. I give and bequeath unto my dear and loving wife Martha all my estate I stand possessed of, to her and my child Martha, to them and their heirs forever; and do constitute my loving wife to be sole executrix to this my last will and testament. And further, I desire my loving brother Thomas Bidwell to assist and be helpful to my wife in her business.

Witness: *Joseph Mygatt,*   JONATH: BIDWELL.
        Edward Allyn.

Court Record, Page 105—15 December, 1712-13: Will proven.

Page 65-6-7-8.

Bigelow, Jonathan, Sen., Hartford. Invt. £549-04-04. Taken 29 January, 1710-11, by Benjamin Graham, John Skinner and Thomas Seamour. Will dated 8 January, 1710-11.

I, Jonathan Bigelow, Sen., of Hartford, do make this my last will and testament: I give to Mary my wife 1-3 part of all my moveable and personal estate during her widowhood, and also the profits and improvement of 1-3 part of my housing and lands during life. Of my house and orchard she shall have 1-2. My will is that my whole estate shall be equally divided amongst my children, to Jonathan, John, Mary, Sarah, Violet, Joseph, Abigail, Daniel and Samuel. I give all my houseing and lands in equal proportion between my three youngest sons, Joseph Bigelow, Daniel Bigelow and Samuel Bigelow. My will is that the portions belonging to my daughter Violet be by the executors of this my last will secured for her and her heirs and for no other whatsoever. I appoint my wife Mary Bigelow and my son Joseph Bigelow sole executors.

Witness: *Nathaniel Hooker,*   JONATHAN BIGELOW, LS.
          Samuel Benton.

Court Record, Page 26—5 February, 1710-11: Will proven.

Page 27—5 February, 1710-11: Daniel Bigelow, 18 years of age, and Samuel Bigelow, 16 years of age, sons of Jonathan Bigelow, Sen., late of Hartford, decd., chose their uncle Thomas Olcott to be their guardian.

Page 105—6 January, 1712-13: This Court appoint Samuel Benton to be guardian unto Daniel Bigelow, 20 years of age, son of Jonathan Bigelow.

Page 106—6 January, 1712-13: Samuel Bigelow of Hartford, a minor 18 years of age, son of Jonathan Bigelow, late of Hartford, decd., chose Samuel Shepherd to be his guardian. Recog., £50.

Birchard, Samuel. Court Record, Page 233—3 January, 1713: This Court order the Clerk to cite a writ to the widow of Samuel Birchard, late of Coventry, decd., that she appear before the Court of Probate to be held on the 1st Monday of February next, to take Adms. on the estate of the sd. decd. or declare her refusal of that trust.

Page 246.

Bissell, Joseph, Windsor. Invt. £64-01-04. Taken 17 August, 1713, by John Bissell and James Enno.

Court Record, Page 155—7 September, 1713: This Court grant letters of Adms. on the estate of Joseph Bissell, late decd., unto his brother Benoni Bissell.

Page 259—7 June, 1715: Benoni Bissell of Windsor, Adms., exhibited now in this Court an account of his Adms., which this Court allow, and order the remaining part of the estate to be set out to the sd. Benoni Bissell as next heir. And this Court grant him a *Quietus Est.*

Page 273.

(See also Page 100-1 for Will and Invt., in Vol. IX.)

Bissell, Nathaniel, Windsor. Invt. £657-00-02. Taken 24 March, 713-14, by Job Drake and John Elsworth. Will dated 23 September, 1713.

The last will and testament of Nathaniel Bissell is as followeth: I give to my wife her choice of any two rooms in my house, or to live with David; also furniture. Also, I give her £6 yearly to be paid by my sons

Jonathan and David equally. I give to my son Jonathan my housing and barns and ten roods on the north side of my lot to the trench at the foot of the hill, and the rest of my cow pasture, for which Jonathan is to pay £20. I give to my son David half the lower lot from the Great River to that which he has already, on the lower side of the lot. I give to my three eldest daughters £20 apeice, to wit, Mindwell, Abigail and Elizabeth ; and I give to my three youngest daughters £60 apiece, to wit, Dorothy, Anne and Mary. I give to my son Jonathan's son Jonathan, if he live to come to the age of 21 years, the Neck (of land). Further, I give to my daughter Hannah Bancroft's six children 20s apiece. I desire Mr. Roger Wolcott, Job Drake and Matthew Grant to be overseers to see this my will performed in Case any difference should arise between my executors, that any of them should determine it that so no law suits may be attained by either of them.

Witness : *Job Drake,*   NATHANIEL BISSELL, LS.
             Matthew Grant.

Court Record, Page 184—5 April, 1714 : Jonathan Bissell refuses the trust, David Bissell to be sole executor. Will proven.

Page 146.

Boreman, Lt. Jonathan, Wethersfield. Died 21 September, 1712. Invt. £693-19-05. Taken by Jonathan Smith and Joseph Grimes. Nuncupative will.

The minutes of the last will and testament of Lt. Jonathan Boreman of Wethersfield: First: He gave 1-2 of his estate to his wife during life. The other half he gave to his son Jonathan, to him forever, and the other half of his personal estate, Jonathan paying to each of his younger daughters as much as his daughter Mary Wright hath already received. 3rdly. The outlands, and all rights to any outland, he gives to his 3 daughters to be equally divided among them, that is, a lott of 10½ acres granted to Andrew Atwood, 29½ acres granted to himself by Wethersfield in the last division, a right in that land on the back side of Rocky Hill, rights at Glastonbury, and undivided lands in Wethersfield. The half of the moveable estate given to his wife at her decease to return to her son Jonathan (i. e., that part of it which is given to her beyond what the law allows). If his son Jonathan die without issue, then the real estate to return to his three daughters, only an equal part to be to his widow. The two negros are to be given to the testator's wife during her natural life. His wife and his son Jno. Wright to be executors.

Witness : *Stephen Mix,*   (Not signed.)
             Joseph Grimes.

Court Record, Page 96—3 November, 1712 : Invt. exhibited by Mercy Boreman, widow, and John Wright, and will proven.

Page 83 (Vol. IX) 18 September, 1718: Upon the motion of Mercy Wright, one of the heirs to the estate of Jonathan Boreman decd., this Court order that dist. or division of the outlands, and rights to the outlands, given by the sd. Jonathan Boreman in the third paragraph of his last will, be accordingly made. And whereas, one of the daughters mentioned in the sd. will being dead, her part is to be divided equally between the surviving children. This Court appoint Messrs. Joseph Graham, Thomas Wright and Abram Morriss of Wethersfield, or any two of them, distributors.

Page 140—6 December, 1720: A distribution of some part of the lands of Lt. Jonathan Boreman, late of Wethersfield, deceased, given by his last will to his three daughters in the 3d paragraph of the sd. will, under the hands of Messrs. Joseph Graham, Abraham Morriss and Thomas Wright, distributors.

Page 193.

Boreman, Nathaniel, Wethersfield. Invt. £433-15-00. Taken 22 January, 1712-13, by Jonathan Deming, William Warner Jr. and Daniel Boreman.

Will (nuncupative), 26 November, 1712: We whose names are hereunto subscribed heard Nathaniel Boreman of Wethersfield declare as his will that the movable estate that he hath be given to his wife to dispose of as she pleaseth, and all the rest of my estate during her natural life. But after her decease my mind is that my son shall have my lands if he attain to the age of twenty-one years, but if not, my lands to be equally divided between my brother's sons and my sister Sarah Fitch her son Samuel. Also, I do oblige my wife to bring up my son to good learning.
Witness: *Isaac Ryly,*   (Not signed.)
Benja. Deming, James Steele.

Court Record, Page 110—2 February, 1712-13: Will proven. And there being no executor expressly nominated, this Court grant Adms. unto Elizabeth Boreman, with the will annexed.

Inventory in Vol. IX, Page 7.

Boarne, Joseph, Middletown. Invt. £100-13-09½. Taken 23 March, 1714, by Francis Whitmore and Daniel Pryor.

Court Record, Page 193—3 May, 1714: This Court grant letters of Adms. on the estate of Joseph Boarne unto Elizabeth Bourne, widow of sd. decd.

Page 88 (Vol. X) 7 June, 1725: Joseph Driggs, in right of his wife Elizabeth decd., as she was Adms. on the estate of Joseph Boarne, late of Middletown, exhibited an account of Adms. on sd. estate amounting to the sum of £30-13-01 due to him from sd. estate more than the moveable part of sd. estate amounts to, which account is by this Court accepted.

Inventory on File.

Boarne, Nathaniel, Middletown. Invt. £19-11-02. Taken 30 January, 1712-13, by Samuel Hall and Solomon Adkins.

Court Record, Page 107—6 January, 1712-13: This Court grant letters of Adms. on the estate of Nathaniel Boarne, late of Middletown, decd., unto Joseph Boarne, brother of sd. decd.

Page 185.

Boarne, Thomas, Middletown. Invt. £17-07-04. Taken 27 February, 1711-12, by Samuel Hall and Francis Whitmore.

Court Record, Page 47—4 February, 1711-12: Adms. granted to David Foster, brother-in-law.

Page 69—7 April, 1712: Invt. exhibited and allowed.

Invt. and Agreement in Vol. IX, Page 37.

Brainard, Daniel, Haddam. Invt. £834-10-03. Taken 19 April, 1715, by Nathaniel Spencer, Gerrard Spencer and Joseph Arnold.

An agreement, dated the 2nd of May, 1715: A distribution of the estate by an agreement among the children, Daniel, James, Joshua, William, Caleb, Elijah and Hezekiah (sons), Thomas Gates and Hannah his wife (only daughter): Our father's will not being so full and clear as we could wish, we have thought best to agree upon a distribution of the estate of our hond. father. And having first come to a loving agreement with our hond. mother-in-law, Hannah Brainard, we have proceeded to make the following distribution: I, Thomas Gates, acting in behalf of my wife Hannah, and we, Daniel, James, Joshua, William, Caleb, Elijah and Hezekiah, have fully and freely made up our hond. father's Daniel Brainard his estate, and do hereby promise and engage, for ourselves and heirs, each to take up satisfied of lands heretofore set down to us and to make no more challenges or demands of any more lands or rights, neither by virtue or under color of any deed of gift received from our father in his lifetime or upon any other color or pretense whatsoever, and that we do receive sd. lands and every parcel of them as our sd. father held them the day of his death, each running the risk of the title our father had to them, and being obliged to defend the same for his own part if there (was) occasion. Moreover we the sd. Daniel, James, Joshua, William, Caleb, and Elijah, do hereby (declare) that we have received £8-01-00 apiece out of the personal estate. I, Thomas Gates, do acknowledge that I have received £33-01-00, and I, Hezekiah Brainard, have received £32-12-00. Moreover we do all and each of us for ourselves and heirs hereby covenant and promise that we shall make no more demands of estate, real or personal, that was our father's, and that we will in no wise disturb or annoy each other, but each of the eight aforementioned and their heirs may quietly enjoy his part aforementioned. Under the full ratification of all which premises we have all and each of us hereunto set our hand and affixed seal this 2nd May, 1715.

DANIEL BRAYNARD, LS.
JAMES BRAYNARD, LS.
JOSHUA BRAYNARD, LS.
WILLIAM BRAYNARD, LS.
CALEB BRAYNARD, LS.
ELIJAH BRAYNARD, LS.
HEZEKIAH BRAYNARD, LS.

To Thomas Gates, acting in behalf of his wife Hannah (only daughter to our hond. father) 50 acres of land bought of Mr. Blackleach, on the north side of Haddam bounds in Colchester bounds more, in personal or moveable estate. Total, £45-10-00.

Court Record, Page 253—14 April, 1715: Adms. granted to Daniel and Hezekiah Brainard jointly. They exhibited an invt. of sd. estate and also an agreement for a division of the estate, which was accepted by the Court.

Page 202.

Browne, Eleanor, Middletown. Invt. £42-02-08. Taken 28 March, 1713, by Israhiah Wetmore, John Collins and Joseph Rockwell. The inventory being her part of her late father Nathaniel Browne's estate. Will dated 11 January, 1712-13.

I, Eleanor Browne of Middletown, do leave this as my last will and testament: I give unto my sister Mary Browne, to be improved by her for her own and for my mother's comfort so long as my mother shall stand in need thereof, except about 10 shillings out of that which is my due from Mr. Russell, which I do bestow upon the Church of Christ in Middletown. I give unto my brother Nathaniel Browne's daughter Sarah either one of my Bibles, or else do order my sister Mary to procure her a new Bible with my money. I do give to my sister Mary all my just dues, either by bill or otherwise, and do order her to pay all my just debts and funeral charges. And as for the lands which I have right unto, I desire my sister Mary may order for the benefit of herself and my mother, so long as my mother shall continue in this world, to make use of the benefit thereof, and after my mother's death then to be divided equally between my sister Mary Browne and my brother Nathaniel Browne. I appoint my sister Mary Browne to be my sole executrix.

Witness: *John Collins,*   ELEANOR X BROWNE, LS.
Thomas Stow, Joseph Rockwell.

Court Record, Page 118—12 February, 1712-13: Will proven.

Page 186.

Browne, Nathaniel, Sen., Middletown. Invt. £437-07-01. Taken 30 May, 1712, by John Collins, Israhiah Wetmore and Joseph Rockwell.

Court Record, Page 78—2 June, 1712: Adms. granted to Martha Browne, widow, and Nathaniel Browne, only son of the decd.

Page 138—4 May, 1713: Nathaniel Browne, Adms., exhibited an account of his and his mother's Adms. Approved, and this Court order a dist. of the estate as follows:

	£ s d
To Martha Browne, the widow,	20-01-08
To Nathaniel Browne, eldest son,	199-08-02
To the heirs of Eleanor Browne, decd.,	99-14-01
To Mary Browne,	99-14-01

And appoint Capt. Thomas Ward, Israhiah Wetmore and Lt. Samuel Hall distributors. And this Court grant the Adms. a *Quietus Est.*

Page 42.

Brounson, Jacob, Farmington. Invt. £44-03-11. Taken 30th May, 1710, by John Hart, Sen., and Thomas Hart, son of Stephen.

Court Record, Page 13—5 June, 1710: This Court grant letters of Adms. on the estate of Jacob Brounson unto Ebenezer Kilbourn of Wethersfield.

Page 53—5 February, 1711-12: Whereas, this Court, held June 5th, 1710, did grant letters of Adms. on the estate of Jacob Brounson unto Ebenezer Kilbourn, late of Wethersfield, decd., and the sd. Ebenezer Kilbourn being now since dead, and not having finished his Adms. on that estate, this Court grant Adms. on the remaining and not administered estate unto Eliphalet Dickinson of Wethersfield, brother-in-law of the sd. decd.

Page 132—6 April, 1714: Eliphalet Dickinson of Wethersfield, Adms., exhibited now in this Court an account of his Adms.:

	£ s d
The whole of the estate, invt. and debts,	50-01-04
Paid in debts and charges,	32-01-10
There remains to be divided,	18-19-06

Order to dist. among the brother and sisters of the deceased. And appoint Capt. James Steele, Mr. Edward Bulkeley and Mr. George Kilbourn distributors. And this Court grant the Adms. a *Quietus Est.*

Dist. File: 9 April, 1713: Estate of Jacob Brounson: To Eliphalet Dickinson, to Samuel Brounson, to Roger Brounson, to William Harris, and to Isaac Brunson or his heirs. By Edward Bulkeley and George Kilbourn.

Page 187—5 April, 1714: Report of the distributors.

Brounson, Moses. Court Record, Page 68—7 April, 1712: This Court do grant the conservation of the estate of Moses Brounson, who hath been many years abroad, to his brother William Brounson, that no waste be made thereof.

Page 173.

Brounson, Sarah, Widow, Farmington. Invt. £37-00-01. Taken 25 January, 1711-12, by John Wadsworth and Daniel Andrews, Sen.

Court Record, Page 63—4 March, 1711-12: Adms. granted to John Brounson.

Page 67—7 April, 1712: John Brounson of Farmington, Adms. on the estate of his late mother, exhibits an account of his Adms.:

	£ s d
Inventory,	37-01-07
Paid in debts and charges, etc.,	5-13-00
There remains to be distributed,	31-08-07
To John Brounson, eldest son,	7-17-01
And to William Brounson, Ebenezer Brounson, Moses Brounson, Sarah Brounson, Dorothy Brounson and Grace Brounson, to each,	3-18-07

And appoint Sergt. John Wadsworth and Daniel Andrews of Farmington distributors. And the Court order John Brounson, Adms., to appear and take out his *Quietus Est.*

Dist. File: To John, William, Ebenezer and Moses Brounson, to Sarah Buck, to Dorothy Kelsey, and to Grace Brounson. By John Wadsworth and Daniel Andrews.

Page 217.

Buck, Ezekiel, Wethersfield. Invt. £308-15-09. Taken 17 March, 1712-13, by James Patterson and Joshua Robbins. Will dated 2 March, 1712-13.

I, Ezekiel Buck of Wethersfield, do make this my last will and testament: I give unto Rachell, my wife, my house and 1-3 of my estate in moveable and land as followeth: viz., 8 acres of land lying on the north side of my lands butting on a highway east, and west on land of Enock Buck, north butting on lands of Jonathan Buck, Sen., to have and to hold said lands during her natural life, and after her decease then to return to my grandchild Ezekiel Buck, my eldest son's son, to him, his heirs and assigns forever. Also, I give to my son Enock Buck 14 acres of land lying on the west end of my lands, butting on the Commons west, east on lands of my wife and lands given to my son Jonathan, north on Jonathan Buck, Sen., and south on lands belonging to Daniel Borman and Richard Borman. Also, I do give to my son Enock 4 acres of land to lie upon a triangle for a passingway to the sd. 14 acres. I do give to my son Jonathan Buck all that tract of land lying south on lands given to my wife, bounding on lands of Enock Buck south and west, and on a highway east. I give to my son Stephen Buck 13 acres of land lying in the west division, west on Farmington, east on his own land, south on land of Jonathan Buck, Jr., north on lands of Mrs. Jemima Chester. I do give to my beloved daughters, namely, Hannah, Abigail and Comfort, the rest of my movables, to be equally divided between them. I have given to my daughter Rachel Bronson, deceased, and to Sarah Welton and Mary Kelsy their whole portions already, and to my eldest son Ezekiel Buck his portion. I do make my son Enock Buck my executor.

Witness: *John Deming, Jr.,*   EZEKIEL BUCK, SENOR, LS.
      Josiah Belding.

Court Record, Page 125—6 April, 1713: Will proven.

Page 29.

Buck, Samuel. He died 12 April, 1709, in Wethersfield. Invt. £350-12-06. Taken 26 January, 1709-10, by Benjamin Churchill, James Butler and Josiah Churchill.

Court Record, Page 4—6 February, 1709-10: Adms. to Sarah Buck, the relict, and James Butler.

Page 51 (Vol. IX) 4 February, 1717-18: Sarah Buck and James Butler exhibit an accot. of their Adms. Allowed. Order to distribute the estate. Invt. amount, £350-12-06, moveables whereof is £116-02-06, and there is to be paid out of that estate to the sd. Sarah Buck for maintenance of a child and trouble of Adms., with charge of distribution, the sum of £12-10-00. There remains to be distributed the sum of £338-02-06. The Court order that the estate shall be divided in proportion following: To Sarah Buck, widow, with dower, the sum of £34-10-10; to Isaac Buck, eldest son, £75-17-11; and to Dorothy (Woodhouse), Peletiah, Sarah, Elizabeth, Samuel and Martha Buck, the rest of the children of the sd. decd., to each of them £37-18-11, which is their single share. And appoint Lt. Benjamin Churchill, Capt. David Goodrich and Josiah Churchill distributors.

Page 186.

Buckland, Elizabeth, Hartford. Invt. £26-01-05. Taken 11 May, 1712, by Daniel Bidwell and Timothy Cowles.

Court Record, Page 79—2 June, 1712: This Court grant letters of Adms. unto Charles Buckland of Hartford, son of the sd. deceased.

Page 156—7 September, 1713: Adms. exhibits accounts of his Adms. and is ordered to deliver accounts to his brother William Buckland, Adms.

Page 192—3 May, 1714: William Buckland, Adms., is ordered to pay credits in proportion, there not being funds to pay in full. And appoint Capt. Roger Pitkin, Mr. Joseph Olmsted and Timothy Cowles to distribute the estate to the creditors.

Dist. File, 15 May, 1714: To William Buckland, to Robert (   ), to Richard Edwards, to Samuel Haward, to Daniel Hooker, to Samuel Woodbridge. By Roger Pitkin and Timothy Cowles.

Page 279.

(Will copied from File.)

Bulkeley, Gershom, Wethersfield, alias Glassenbury, in ye County of Hartford, in her Matyes Colony of Connecticutt, in N. England, Practitioner in Physick.

Last Will, made on ye Twenty-sixth day of May, 1712: I, ye said Gershom Bulkeley, having much more than twenty years walked upon ye very mouth of ye grave, and under so great infirmity yt I can yt but wonder how I have all this while escaped falling into it, have not been wholly unmindfull of yt wch nature and comon prudence calls for in such cases. But in ye meantime sorrowful changes from ye right hand of ye most High have passed over me, and some yt I had hoped would have survived me have prevented me and left me behind them, whereby, with some Incident considerations I am moved to alter some things wch otherwise I should not have done. And therefore, remaining still, though very weak in body yet of sound mind and memory, I do now make this (I hope) my last will and testament, hereby revoking and annulling all former wills whatsoever made by me: In ye first place, casting myselfe upon ye riches of Sovereign Grace, my body I commit to ye dust as it was (to be as near to my late dear wife as conveniently may be) decently, but obscurely buryed, without much cost or ceremony. I neither deserve nor desire those things, yet desire a part in ye first and better resurection of ye just. I wish all my just debts to be paid. And as for these few poor children wch I shall leave behind me————As for ye little real estate wch I had, I have already by acts executed in my own lifetime disposed it: some to others, and ye rest of it among my sons, or to their use and behoof respectively, as occasion hath required. Some part also of my personal estate I have bestowed upon my Children already. Ye remnant of my personal estate I dispose of as follows: Imprimus. To my son Charles his daughter Hannah Goodrich I give £8. To my good daughters-in-law, Hannah Avery and Rachel Wolcott, I give to each of them a golden ducat (or 10s piece) if I happen to leave a couple. Item. To my son Edward's present wife Dorothe I give a golden guinea (or 20s piece) if I happen to leave one. Item. To my brother Peter's children (Gershom, Peter, Grace, Margaret and Dorothe) I give each of them 10 shillings in current money; and if any of them owe me not exceeding 10s, I will yt it be remitted to ye debtor. And in particular to ye said Grace I give my great red rugge wch was her mother's. To my son Edward I give and bequeath ye clock now standing in its case in his house, as also my seal ring, ye great gilt spoon, ye least of my two silver porringers, and all ye books and manuscripts yt I have touching matters of law, except ye notes wch I had sometime written out, as Coke's first, 2d, 3d and 4th Institutes, wch notes I formerly gave to my son John, and wch, though now in my hand, yet my will is that he shall have them again if they may be of use to him. I give my said son Edward also my whipsaw, tenon saw and timber chain, being of use for his mill. Item. To my son John I have already given ye greatest part of my books and my silver pocket watch (wch last I mention yt my executors may not be at a loss for it, but know what is become of it). I give and bequeath to him all ye rest of my books wch I now have, and also all my manuscripts (written by my grandfather, my father or others), I say all such my books and manuscripts as concern only Divinity or other learning, except ye law (wch books and manuscript I have given to Edward), and except also medicine and chemistry and some few books wch, wth those yt concern medicine and chemistry, I shall otherwise dispose of by and by. Item. To my grandson Richard Treat (ye son of Thomas and Dorothe Treat) I give and bequeath all my books and manuscripts wch any way concern medicine and chemistry, among which I include all Glauber's and Boyle's wch I have, whether in Latin or English, as also Georgius Agricola De Re Metallica and Lazarus Eacher Translated by sir John Pettus, called Fleta minor, also Littleton's Dictionary for ye Latin Tongue, and my Dutch Grama for ye Dutch Language, together wth all my vessels and instruments useful, whether of glass, brass or copper, iron, stone or earth. All these I give to him, Provided he hold and pursue his inclination to yt study. And to my daughter Catherine Treat, now deceased (I had given her portion to her only child and daughter Catherine Treat), I give and bequeath my lesser silver tankard, my lighter Silver Cucumbet (to be distinguished by its weight from that I have given to my daughter Dorothe. 'Tis not that which belongs to the Silver Retort, but is much taller and bigger than that). I give her also the silver Salt Seller and the small dram cup, all which I had intended for her mother had she survived me, which I doubt are worth £20 in money. Yet I reserve and give liberty to my daughter Dorothe to redeem any of thse Silver vessels aforsaid for ye full value thereof if she desire to do so. In case of the decease of Catharine Treat, to her father (my good son-in-law Richard Treat) if he be then living. To my daughter Dorothe I give all the rest of my personal estate (in particular to her I bequeath my negro maid Hannah) whether it be in my own hand or in the hands of others or due and owing from others to me. Except only yt if there shall be any poor widow or widows or other truly poor persons not able to pay their debts to me, my will is that my executor shall remit it and not trouble them for it, wch I must leave to his discretion, yet wth this advertisement, that by "poor" I mean such as are indeed poor—at least by Divine Providence and not by idleness, nor such as say they are poor and yet can find wherewith to drink, revel and swagger and make themselves poor and others too. I appoint my trusty son-in-law Thomas Treat executor.

Witness: *John Hollister,*   GERSHOM BULKELEY, LS.
Samuel Brooks, Daniel X *Andross.*

P. Script: Thomas Treat having died, my daughter Dorothe Treat to be sole executrix.

Witness: *Samuel Brooks,*   24 Nov., 1713. G. BULKELEY, LS.
Joseph Easton, Sarah X *Brooks.*

Proven 7 December, 1713.

An inventory of yt part of ye estate of Dr. Bulkeley which he gave to his son Edward in his last will and testament:

	£	s	d
A gold ring, 32 shillings; 1 silver cup and spoon, £1-08-08,	3	00	08
To a clock, £8; whip saw, 12s; tenant saw, 10s; timber chain, 15s,	1	17	00
To manuscripts and law books,	32	17	04

Taken by George Stilman and John Russell.

An inventory of Books of Divinity, not including those taken away by John Bulkeley, and of medical books. Apprised 7 April, 1714, by Timothy Stevens and Samuel Smith.

A further inventory of medicines and tinctures; also a Negro woman, valued at £25-00-00. Apprised 20 April, 1715, by Timothy Stevens and Ebenezer Prout.

Invt. in Vol. IX, Page 6.

Bull, Jonathan, Jr., Hartford. Invt. £298-02-00. Taken 4 October, 1714, by Samuel Newell, Sen., and John Wadsworth.

Court Record, Page 213—6 September, 1714-15: Adms. granted to Josiah Hart, a brother-in-law of sd. decd.

Page 7 (Vol. IX) 7 February, 1715-16: Josiah Hart, Adms., exhibits an account of his Adms. Allowed. Order to dist. the estate to the brothers and sisters: To the heirs of John Bull, decd., to Samuel Bull and David Bull, brothers, and Susannah and Sarah Bull, sisters of sd. Jonathan Bull, to each of them £33-07-07 1-5. And appoint John Wadsworth, Daniel Andrews and John Porter of Farmington, distributors.

Page 182-259.

Bull, Joseph, Hartford. Invt. £890-04-08 as money. Taken 18 April, 1712, by Ciprian Nichols, Hez. Wyllys and Daniel Merrells.

Court Record, Page 74—5 May, 1712: Adms. to Hannah, the relict, and Caleb the son. Distribution by agreement made the 9th November, 1713:

	£ s d
To Widow Hannah Bull,	161-06-08
To Joseph Bull, eldest son, a double portion,	161-06-08
To Caleb Bull his portion (and for the payment of debts),	197-08-06
His part,	80-13-04
To Mary Bull, her part,	80-13-04

Daniel Bull had received his by deed of gift.

Know all men by these presents: That we, the said Hannah Bull, Joseph Bull, Daniel Bull, Caleb Bull and Mary Bull, parties aforementioned, the relict and children of the said Joseph Bull, deceased, do for ourselves and each of us respectively, our and each of our heirs, executors and administrators, fully and absolutely agree to the aforesaid distribution, and that the same shall be and remain as a firm settlement of the estate aforesaid amongst us. In witness whereof we have hereunto set our hands and seals.

> HANNAH X BULL, LS.
> JOSEPH BULL, LS.
> DANIEL BULL, LS.
> CALEB BULL, LS.
> MARY BULL, LS.

Signed, sealed and delivered in presence of us: *Hez: Wyllys, Joseph Tillotson.*

Court Record, Page 162—20 November, 1713: This agreement approved.

Page 72 (Invt., 161).

Bunce, Thomas, Hartford. Invt. £1683-12-01. Taken 25 April, 1712 (as money), by William Whiting, Aaron Cooke and Samuel Thornton. Will dated 25 April, 1709.

I, Thomas Bunce, do ordain this to be my last will and testament: Imprimis: I give to my eldest son Thomas these following parcels of land, vizt: My homelot in Hartford on which I now dwell, with all the housing and outhousing thereon, with all the privileges and appurtenances thereto belonging. It. My whole lot on Rocky Hill lying between the lands of Mr. Joseph Bull and Mr. Samuel Howard. It. An upland lot lying in Wethersfield bounds, about fifteen acres, near unto Joseph Skinner's land. It. Half my lot lying in Willcock's lots. It. The free use of a drift highway to the said land, already laid out, between the land lately belonging to Mr. Bidwell and Samuel Benton. It. My mowing pasture commonly called Graves's lot, lying between Mr. Buckingham's land and Mr. Bull's. It. Those parcels of land on the east side of the Great River in Hartford, viz., the whole of my upland lot. It. Half my meadow lot, viz., that half on the north side, it being divided from the west to the east. It. My whole right in the five-mile purchase. It. Those several parcels of land lying in the south meadow in Hartford, viz., my lot I bought of Mr. Samuel Whiting. It. One acre and half lot lying in the swamp, given me by my father. It. A two-acre lot I bought of Goodman Cadwell. It. One acre and a half lying in the middle swamp, bought of Thomas Andrews. It. My propriety lot in the West Division uplands, with all my interest in the mills, I give to my son Joseph,* to him and his heirs forever. It. I give to my son Jonathan my home lot in Wethersfield with all the housing and out housing thereon. It. All my uplands and meadow land within the Township of Wethersfield (excepting only that lot lying by Joseph Skinner's lands, already given to my son Thomas), these I give to my son Jonathan and his heirs forever. It. I give to my son Joseph and his heirs forever the home lot in Hartford that was my father's and on which he now dwells, with all the housing and outhousing thereon. It. I give to him the southern half of my meadow lot on the east side of the Great River in Hartford. It. To my daughter Susannah, besides what I have already given her, I give her 10 shillings. It. To my daughter Sarah, £9. It. I give to my daughter Abigail £10. I do appoint my son Thomas sole executor.

Witness: *Timothy Woodbridge,*   THOMAS BUNCE, LS.
          John Bunce.

Court Record, Page 38—3 September, 1711: Will proven.

Page 57—7 February, 1711-12: Administration of the estate of Thomas Bunce, Sen., to his son Jonathan Bunce, with the will annexed. Thomas Bunce, Jr., the executor named in the will and since the probate of sd. will being deceased.

Page 179.

Bunce, Thomas, Jr., Hartford. Invt. £1185-10-03. Taken 26 March, 1712, by Joseph Wadsworth, Hez: Wyllys and James Steele.

Court Record, Page 57—7 February, 1711-12: And this Court grant letters of Adms. on the estate of Thomas Bunce, Jr., late of Hartford, decd., to Jonathan Bunce, brother of the said deceased, and to Elizabeth Bunce, widow of the said deceased.

Page 59-60—3 March, 1711-12: Mr. Richard Edwards, attorney for Mrs. Elizabeth Bunce, moved this Court to set aside their order of 7 February, 1711-12, appointing Jonathan Bunce with said Elizabeth as Adms., and to grant letters entirely to Mrs. Elizabeth Bunce. The Court refusing, an appeal was taken to the Superior Court, Jonathan Easton, her brother, giving bond.

---

*NOTE: See Page 276 (Vol. IX, Probate Side): "A correction of an error in his will, where it appears that legacies he had given to his son Thomas was after given to Joseph." A perfect mistake of the name Joseph instead of Thomas. It was truly given to *Thomas Bunce.*

Page 110—2 February, 1712-13: Elizabeth Bunce, Adms., exhibits invt.

Page 148 (Vol. X) 7 March, 1726-7: Caleb Bull, in right of Elizabeth his wife, Adms., being cited to appear with Adms. account, produced several sums paid, but no receipts. He was ordered to procure and produce receipts.

Page 150—4 April, 1727: Exhibits now account of Adms. Accepted. Estate now £1185-10-03. Order to dist: To Elizabeth Bull, relict of the decd., and to Susannah, the only child. By John Skinner, James Ensign and James Easton.

Page 151—Susannah Bunce, age 16 years, chose James Easton of Hartford to be her guardian. Rec., £400.

Page 187.

Butler, Charles, Wethersfield. Died 25 September, 1711. Invt. £163-18-00. Taken by Ephraim Goodrich and Jonathan Smith.

Court Record, Page 78—2 June, 1712: Adms. to Susannah Butler, widow of said deceased.

Page 124 (Vol. IX) 5 April, 1720: Susannah Butler, Adms., exhibits account of her Adms. Allowed. This Court appoint Susannah Butler of Middletown to be guardian to her daughter Bathsheba Butler, 10 years of age. Recog., £80.

Page 131—5 July, 1720: Mary Butler, 14 years of age, chose her mother, Susannah Butler, widow, to be her guardian. Recog., £100.

Page 132—5 July, 1720: Susannah Butler, Adms., exhibits an account:

	£ s d
Paid in debts and charges,	22-13-09
Hath received,	2-02-00
Inventory,	166-00-00
Movable part,	66-00-00
Subtracting,	22-13-09
There remains to be distributed,	143-06-03
Order to dist. to Susannah Butler, widow,	14-08-09
The rest of the sd. estate to Mary and Bathsheba Butler,	
daughters, to each of them the sum of	64-08-09

And appoint Jonathan Curtice, Abram Morriss and Samuel Williams, distributors.

Page 143—6 December, 1720: Report of the distributors.

Page 151.

Butler, Samuel, Hartford. Invt. £193-13-08. Taken 26 November, 1712, by Robert Sandford and Nathaniel Goodwin, Junior.

Court Record, Page 100—1st December, 1712: Adms. to Hannah, the widow, and Thomas Butler, a brother.

Page 65 (Vol. X) 5 January, 1724-5: Thomas Butler, Adms. on the estate of Samuel Butler, late of Hartford, exhibited an account of his Adms. on sd. estate amounting to the sum of £10-10-00. Accepted and ordered on file.

See File for dist. of the estate of Samuel Butler, late of Hartford, 1726, as followeth:

	£	s	d
To the widow,	12-09-11		
To Samuel Butler, son of the decd.,	70-00-00		
To Marcey Butler, eldest daughter,	35-00-00		
To Sarah Butler, another of the daughters,	35-00-00		

By John Sheldon, Nathaniel Marsh and Samuel Welles, distributors. Page 219—3 June, 1729: Report of the distributors.

Page 171-2.

Butler, Samuel, Wethersfield. Invt. £233-06-00. Taken 27 February, 1711-12, by James Patterson and Thomas Standish. Will (nuncupative) dated 24 December, 1711.

He gave to his wife one-third of his personal estate forever, and one-third of his lands during life. He gave to his son Samuel Butler his house and homested and all his lot at the upper end of the meadow on the south side of the highway and siding on the Great River, to him and his heirs forever. The rest of his estate he gave to his other children, to George, to Daniel, to Abraham, and to Elizabeth Butler, his only daughter. His wife to be sole executrix, and desired his brothers Abraham Kilbourn and James Butler to be his overseers.

Witnessed by us: *George Kilbourn,*
John Howard, Abraham Kilbourn,
and James Butler.

Court Record, Page 66—7 April, 1712: Mary, the relict, executrix, exhibited the last will of her late husband, Samuel Butler. Proven.

Invt. in Vol. IX, Page 16.

Butler, William, Wethersfield. Invt. £67-08-10. Taken 17 November, 1714, by James Patterson and George Kilbourn.

Court Record, Page 223—6 December, 1714: Adms. granted to Hannah Butler, the widow of sd. decd.

Page 70.

Camp, John, Sen., Hartford. Died 14 March, 1710-11. Invt. £158-14-06. Taken 27 March, 1710-11, by William Webster and Benjamin Graham. Will dated 8 February, 1710-11.

I, John Camp of Hartford, Sen., being of a long time sick and weak, do make this my last will and testament: I give to my wife Lydia my dwelling house and lands adjoining to it, for her to use for her benefit and comfort during the term of her life, and after her decease I give it to my two sons John Camp and Joseph Camp, that is to say, John Camp 2-3 and Joseph Camp 1-3, and I also appoint my two sons John and Joseph Camp my executors. Further, if my wife should want or stand in need, I do empower her by this my last will to dispose of my houseing and lands for her comfort. I give to my daughter Hannah, in addition to what she hath already received, 20 shillings. I give to my daughter Sarah 20 shillings. I give to my daughter Abigail 20 shillings. The rest of my moveables I give to my wife.

Witness: *Benjamin Graham,*   JOHN CAMP, SEN., LS.
      Grace Eglestone.

Court Record, Page 31—2 April, 1711: Will proven.

Page 136 (Vol. X) 4 October, 1726: An addition to the invt. of the estate of John Camp was now exhibited by John Camp, executor, amounting to the sum of £24-05-00.

Page 209.

Camp, Joseph, Wethersfield. Invt. £226-10-05. Taken 23 December, 1712-13, by Thomas Richards and William Webster.

Court Record, Page 105—15 December, 1713: Adms. granted to Abigail Camp, widow, and Samuel Benton, Sen., of Hartford. Also they exhibited an inventory.

Page 228—6 December, 1714: Samuel Benton and Abigail Camp, Adms., exhibited an account of their Administration:

	£ s d
Inventory,	226-10-05
Moveable part thereof,	59-00-05
Paid in debts and charges,	26-15-00
There remains to be distributed,	199-14-10
To Abigail Camp, widow,	10-15-00
To Hannah Camp, only child,	188-19-11

And appoint William Webster, Nathaniel Churchill and Hez: Deming, distributors.

Page 229—6 December, 1714: This Court appoint Abigail, widow, to be guardian to Hannah Camp, minor daughter. Recog., £100.

Carrington, Ebenezer. Court Record, Page 32—2 April, 1711: This Court grant letters of Adms. on the estate of Ebenezer Carrington, late of Waterbury, and lately residing in Hartford, unto William Parsons, a brother-in-law, the other relations of the sd. decd. having refused to administer.

Invt. in Vol. IX, Page 34.

Chapman, Henry, Windsor. Invt. £45-12-06. Taken 15 December, 1713, by Eleazer Gaylor, Jonathan Elsworth and Ebenezer Hurlbut.

Court Record, Page 190—14 April, 1714: Adms. granted to Hannah Chapman, widow, relict of sd. decd.

Page 87 (Vol. IX) 4 November, 1718: Symon Chapman and Jonathan Elsworth of Windsor moved the Court for care to be taken of the estate of Henry Chapman sometime of Windsor decd., his widow being now deceased that was Adms., and also that care be taken of the children. This Court grant Adms. to Symon Chapman and Jonathan Elsworth. This Court appoint Jonathan Elsworth to be guardian to the children of Henry Chapman, viz., to Sarah Chapman and Henry Chapman. Recog., £100.

Page 162.

Chapman, Capt. John, Haddam. An agreement, made among the heirs of Capt. John Chapman, late of Haddam, decd.: Know all men by these presents: That we, Joseph Chapman of Saybrook in the County of New London, and David Chapman of Haddam in the County of Hartford, and Samuel Chapman of the aforesd. Haddam, the only natural sons now surviving of Capt. John Chapman, late of Haddam, decd., and Stephen Chalker of Saybrook and Joseph Selden of Lyme, in the County of sd. New London, and Lemuel Richardson of Stoningtown in the County of New London, sons-in-law of the abovesd. Capt. John Chapman, decd. (by affinity with his three daughters, Elizabeth, Anne and Mehetabell Chapman), and Lydia Chapman of Haddam, do hereby declare that for as much as it hath pleased Almighty God in his holy providence to take from us our aged and honorable father, Capt. John Chapman, decd., and left behind him a considerable estate in lands, goods and chattels, to be disposed of, all his just and lawful debts being hereby secured to be paid, we whose names are above written being the true and lawful heirs to all and every part of sd. estate, both real and personal, do hereby, for ourselves, our heirs and successors, mutually and firmly agree to the dist. of or dividing the whole sd. inheritance. Moreover, it is hereby agreed upon that Jabez Chapman, with the approbation of the Honoured Court of Probate, is chosen to administer on sd. estate and to pay all the just and lawful debts due from the sd. estate out of his own part of the estate, the rest of the heirs to be freed from all entanglements whatsoever.

Signed: JOSEPH CHAPMAN, LS.
JABEZ CHAPMAN, LS.
SAMUEL CHAPMAN, LS.
STEPHEN X CHALKER, LS.
JOSEPH SELDEN, LS.
LEMUEL RICHARDSON, LS.
LYDIA CHAPMAN, LS.

Witnesses:
William Spencer and
Alexander Spencer.

Court Record, Page 68—8 April, 1712: An agreement of the children of Capt. John Chapman, late of Haddam, decd., for a division of the estate, was now exhibited in Court by Joseph Chapman, Jabez and Samuel Chapman, sons of the deceased, and Stephen Chalker and Lemuel Richardson, sons-in-law. These appeared in Court and acknowledged this to be their free act and deed.   z

---

Chauncey, Charles, Clerk, of Stratford. Court Record, Page 21—6 November, 1710: This Court appoint Charles Chauncey of Stratford to be guardian to his three children, viz., Robert, age 6 years, Ichabod Wolcott, 5 years, and Abiah, 8 years of age.

Page 249—14 April, 1715: Abiah Chauncey, a minor daughter of Rev. Charles Chauncey, late of Stratford, chose John Moore of Windsor to be her guardian. And this Court appoint John Moore guardian to Robert Chauncey, 12 years old, and Ichabod Wolcott Chauncey, age about 11 years.

Page 37 (Vol. IX) 2 July, 1717: Abiah Chauncey chose Daniel Bissell of Windsor to be her guardian. Recog., £100.

Page 104.

Chester, John, Esq., Wethersfield. Invt. £4277-07-11. Taken 26 January, 1711-12, by Jonathan Belding, Joshua Robbins, 2nd, and Samuel Wolcott. Will dated 5 December, 1711.

Imprimis. I give and bequeath to my eldest son John Chester, to him, his heirs, etc., as hereafter mentioned, vizt.: I give and grant to my said son all the lands which were given me by my father, Capt. John Chester, deceased, save only one homelot. That is, I give unto him my home lot where my father dwelt, with all the buildings thereon; also my land in the Great Plain and at the lower end of the meadow; and also Sele's lot and Clark's lot; also about seventy acres at the mill, and the mill; and one hundred and four acres at the West Division next Farmington bounds; also fifty acres on Cow Plain. All which lands I give and grant to my said son, to be an estate in fee tail generall, vizt., to him and the heir male or heir males of his body lawfully begotten. Further, I give to my son John Chester my lot on Cow Plain, divided to me by the Town, of eighty and two acres and one-half, and one hundred acres my father gave me which the General Court gave my father near Wallingford bounds, laid out by Mr. John Brocket and Mr. Thomas Yale. I give, I grant, I bequeath to my son Thomas Chester my home lot which I now dwell upon, with all the buildings, together with all my purchased lands, as the deeds and records thereof show, vizt., my land in Mile Meadow, purchased of Colo. Pynchon; my land at the Swamp, purchased of the heirs of Robt. Reve; my lands purchased of Elizur Talcot both in the meadow and at Hangdog Plain; my land purchased of Mr. Nathl. Foot, in the Great Meadow; my land purchased of Nathl. Butler, in said meadow; and my land purchased of Nicholas Morecock in the Great Plain; and my land purchased of Mr. Westwood Cook on the east side the Great River in Glastonbury; also my lands I purchased of Mr. Joshua Robbins, Mr. Samuel Whiting, Mr. Simon Wolcott and Mr. James Treat, Jr., all lying, vizt., the woodland in the West Division next Farmingtown line and mine own land, divided to me, coming from my uncle Stephen Chester, in the aforesaid tier or furlong; also the eighty and two acres and half on Cow Plain. This eighty and two acres and half I give to John, which I had of the Town by division. Also, my land purchased of John Hollister to be to my said son Thomas Chester, and to the heir or heirs male of his body lawfully begotten, in such tenure as I give to my son John Chester. And in want of heir males born to either of my sons, I give said lands in tenure as aforesaid to my daughters or those that legally represent them. I give to my son Thomas Chester one acre and a half and 20 rods of land at the Goodrich lot which I purchased of Captain Prentis. I have given to my son John Chester all my land on Cowe Plain because I account the outlands given to my son Thomas a more growing estate than lands near home. Item. I give unto my daughters Mahetabell, Mary, Penelope, Hannah, Prudence, Eunice and Sarah, the sum of £200 each, to be paid in money or bills of credit as it goes at this time, vizt., fifteen pennyweight at six shillings. I give to my wife Hannah Chester the use of all my improvable lands till my sons come to the age of 21 years, with use of one-third of my improveable lands, etc., after my sons come of age and also during her natural life; also £100 in household goods, to be at her own dispose. I do nominate and appoint my wife Hannah Chester to be executrix, and my sons John Chester and Thomas Chester executors when they shall come to years of discretion or be able to manage the trust herein committed to them. I do desire Lt. Jonathan Belding, Mr. Joshua Robbins, the 2nd, and Mr. Samuel Wolcott to be assisting to my wife and to oversee.

JOHN CHESTER, LS.

Codicil, dated 11 December, 1711: I give the half of the lot given me by the Town of Wethersfield at their last General Division of lands to my eldest son John Chester, vizt., the west end thereof; the other half of the same tract, the east of the same, to my son Thomas Chester. And the goods lying in bottom, which came from England, I will they should be distributed among my family for their common good as they need. I will also that, relating to my estate in England and the concerns thereof, that my executrix and my sons when capable should improve Mr. Noah Neal, Esq., of Stamford in the County of Lincoln, and his son and heir after him. JOHN CHESTER, LS.
Witness: *Stephen Mix,*
Robert Wells.

Court Record, Page 49—4 February, 1711-12: Will proven.
Page 136—4 May, 1713: Mrs. Hannah Chester to be guardian to John Chester, a minor about 10 years old, son of Mr. John Chester, late decd.
Page 155 (Vol. IX) 25 July, 1721: Adms. granted to Mary Chester, the widow.
Page 156—26 July, 1721: Upon information of Mrs. Mary Chester of Wethersfield, widow, Adms. on the estate of her husband John Chester, sometime of Wethersfield, deceased, that she vehemently suspected that John Lattimore, Bezaleel Lattimore, and Sybill the wife of Bezaleel, Mary, the wife of Thomas Baxter, and Elizabeth the daughter of sd. Thomas, have unfairly gotten a certain quantity (unknown) of ready silver money, parcel of the estate of sd. decd., and have concealed and do still conceal the same from the sd. Adms. contrary to law, they were summoned and now appeared and were respectively examined upon oath concerning the matters contained in the sd. information as on file. The Court having considered what had been answered upon oath by the respective persons summoned, above named, that nothing appears against them that they are guilty, therefore they are respectively discharged. And it is further considered by the Court that there was sufficient grounds of suspicion for the above complaint, and that the same arose from out of the family that the persons complained of belong to. Therefore no costs be allowed them.

Page 192.

Chester, Thomas, Wethersfield. Invt. £1648-09-01. Taken 23 January, 1712-13, by James Steele, James Treat and George Kilbourn.
Court Record, Page 109—2 February, 1712-13: Adms. to Mary Chester, widow of sd. deceased.
Page 224—6 December, 1714: Mrs. Mary Chester, Adms., exhibits an account of her Adms.:

	£	s	d
Inventory,	1657-13-07		
Paid in debts and charges,	12-09-00		
There remains,	1645-04-07		
Real part,	1189-00-00		
To the widow, Mary Chester,	152-01-07		
To Eunice Williams and Mary Chester, daughters, to each,	746-11-06		

And appoint George Kilbourn, Joshua Robbins and James Treat, distributors. This Court appoint Mrs. Mary Chester to be guardian unto Mary Chester, 9 years of age, daughter of Thomas Chester, late decd. Recog., £250.

Dist. File: To the Widow Jemima, to Eunice Williams (the wife of Elisha Williams), and to Mary, the other daughter of sd. decd. By George Kilbourn, Joshua Robbins and James Treat.

Page 52.

Clarke, Daniel, Capt., Windsor. Invt. £95-00-08. Taken 8 September, 1710, by Matthew Allyn and John Moore, Sen. Will dated 31 August, 1709.

The last will of Daniel Clarke, late of Windsor, deceased, is as followeth: I do will and dispose as followeth: In the first place, all my just debts and funeral charges to be paid. And whereas, I obliged to my now wife £40 to be paid her out of my estate in case she shall survive me, as will appear by an instrument to which I have signed and sealed, my will is that sd. sum be truly paid according to the tenor thereof in my engagement, in such estate as may conduce to her comfort, with £5 in provision as an addition to the sum aforementioned of £40. For the rest of my estate, my will is that my wearing apparel should be divided among my sons that shall be living to receive them. My will is that if the confirmation be obtained from Owaneco of the 100 acres he promised, which is laid out and bounded, and for which I have obtained the grant of the General Court, I do order that it be entirely sold, whereof 1-4 part of the product of it shall redound to my now wife* if she be living to receive. The other three parts shall be equally divided amongst my three daughters, Elizabeth, Mary and Sarah, or to their children if any of them do die before it be affected. I give to my son John the ox chain that he borrowed of me, and to my son Samuel my musket. I give to Johnny

---

*(Added): 2 March, 1743: Should be Martha (not Mary) Clarke. See original inventory among the files of the Court of Probate. "This lady was the sister of William Pitkin, one of the early settlers of Hartford. She married for her first husband Simon Woolcott, son of Henry Wolcott, one of the first settlers of Windsor, on the 17th of October, 1661, and survived him, he having died on the 11th September, 1687. She married for her second husband Capt. Daniel Clarke, whose inventory is here recorded."   NATHANIEL GOODWIN.

my best powder horn, and to my son Daniel I give my cutlass and my buff belt and buff coat. And I do hereby ratify and confirm those alienations that my sons have made of lands that I gave them. And to my wife, if she survive me, I order towards the sum aforementioned of £40 particularly the bed, bedsted and furniture that we used to lie on, and my best trunk with bars on the cover, and the lesser of the great kettles, with what she desires of pewter and other utensils in the house, to be valued according to the agreement. And to my son Jonas I give 10 shillings besides his proportion of my wearing apparrell. And I do constitute my son John Clarke and my son-in-law Roger Wolcott executors. And I desire my honored kinsman Col. Matthew Allyn (if God please to grant him a safe return) to be supervisor if need require.

Witness: *John Moore, Sen.,*   DANIEL CLARKE, LS.
    Thomas Moore.

Codicil, dated 10 July, 1710: On serious consideration I think meet to alter somewhat in my will, on the other side, in 2 particulars: First, respecting my daughter Elizabeth Drake, wife to Lt. Job Drake, my will is that she shall have a double portion out of my dividable estate, and the other two parts to be divided between my other two daughters, Mary and Sarah.

Witness: *John Moore, Sen.,*   DANIEL CLARKE, LS.
    Thomas Moore.

Court Record, Page 18—8 September, 1710: Will and invt. exhibited.

Page 17-18-19.

Clark, John, Jr., Farmington. Invt. £323-15-07. Taken 2 December, 1709, by John Wadsworth and Isaac Cowles.

Court Record, Page 71—7 April, 1712: Upon motion of Samuel Woodruff, Sen., of Farmington, who married with Rebecca Clark, one of the sisters of Sergt. John Clark, late of Farmington, decd., for an order of distribution to and among the brothers and sisters of the deceased: Order to distribute to Matthew Clark, to the heirs of Elizabeth Gridley, late wife of Thomas Gridley, Sen., of Farmington, sister to John Clark, decd., to Rebecca Woodruff, wife of aforesaid Samuel Woodruff, to Mary Huntington, wife of Samuel Huntington of Lebanon, to Sarah Root, the wife of Thomas Root of Lebanon, to Martha Clark, wife of Thomas Clark of Milford, to Abigail Pixley, wife of Joseph Pixley, to heirs of Hannah Woodruff, decd., late wife of Joseph Woodruff, to Rachel Jones, widow, relict of Caleb Jones, late of Hebron, to Mary Clark of Milford, sister of said John Clark, Jr., decd. And appoint John Wadsworth, Daniel Andrews and Thomas Stanly distributors.

Page 212.

Clark, John, Sen., Farmington. Invt. £167-08-05. Taken 19 January, 1712-13, by John Wadsworth and Daniel Andrews, Sen. Will dated 8 February, 1709-10.

I, John Clarke, Sen., of Farmington, do ordain and make this my last will and testament: Imprimis: I give to my son Matthew Clark all my estate remaining at my decease not legally conveyed by me in my lifetime, he paying the several legacies hereinafter mentioned to my daughters that survive me, to each £5, to be paid by my executor. I appoint my son Matthew Clark my only and sole executor. I desire Mr. John Hart, Sen., and Deacon Samuel Porter to be overseers.

Witness: *John Hart, Sen.,*   JOHN CLARK, SEN.
       John Hart, Jr.

Codicil, dated 21 November, 1712: And as an addition to this my will, I the sd. John Clark, Sen., do declare it to be my will that my youngest daughter Marcy Clark, not being disposed of in marriage and so not having had anything as her portion as the rest of my daughters have had, and also being by the providence of God under greater disadvantages than the rest of them, that she shall have after my decease all my movable estate of household goods forever. And I do further add that it is my will that my daughter Rebecca Woodruff, with whom I am, be well rewarded by my executor for all her labor, care and trouble about me in this time of my sickness, according to the judgment of my two friends, Deacon Samuel Porter and John Hart, Sen.

Witness: *John Hart, Sen.,*   JOHN CLARK, SEN.
       John Hart, Jr.

Court Record, Page 103—5 January, 1712-13: Will now exhibited by Matthew Clarke, executor, with request of approval. Opposed by Richard Edwards and some of the children. Will proven and ordered to be kept on file.

Page 193.

Clark, Josiah, Hartford. Invt. £56-03-09. Taken 17 December, 1712, by Thomas Hosmer, Nathaniel Goodwin and Isaac Hinsdale.

Court Record, Page 110—2 February, 1712-13: Adms. to Elizabeth Clark, the widow.

Page 168.

Clark, William, Sen., Wethersfield. Invt. £35-05-00. Taken 11 February, 1711-12, by George Kilbourn, James Patterson and Josiah Churchill. Will dated 15 January, 1710-11.

I, William Clark of Wethersfield, carpenter, do make this my last will and testament: I give to Susannah, my wife, the use and improvement of all my household goods during the time of her widowhood. I give to my son Thomas Clark, whom I make my only and sole executor, my great brass kettle and all carpenter tools and husbandry utensils. I give to my daughter Elizabeth Morie £5, to be paid out of my household goods. The remainder of my goods I give to my other daughters, to be equally divided among them.

Witness: *Josiah Churchill,*   WILLIAM X CLARKE, LS.
Hezekiah Deming, James Francis.

Court Record, Page 73—5 May, 1712: Will exhibited by Thomas Clark, who refused to be the executor. And this Court grant letters of Adms. to Susannah the widow, with the will annexed.

Page 206—15 July, 1715: Susannah Clarke, Adms., exhibited an account of her Adms: Paid in debts and charges, £37-03-02, which is more than the sum contained in the inventory account. Allowed, and grant the Adms. a *Quietus Est.*

Page 84-85.

Coale, Ichabod, Middletown. Invt. £143-18-02. Taken 23 April, 1711, by Beriah Wetmore, Thomas Allyn and Joseph Rockwell.

Court Record, Page 34—4 June, 1711: Adms. to Sarah Cole of Middletown, relict of sd. deceased, and Joseph Hopkins of Hartford.

Page 36—2 July, 1711: Exhibit of inventory.

Page 208 (Vol. X) 25 December, 1728: Nathaniel Peck of Wallingford, in right of his wife Sarah, administrator, exhibits now an account. Allowed. Order to distribute to Sarah Peck alias Cole, to Rachel Cole alias Doolittle (only child of sd. deceased). By Joseph Rockwell, Benjamin Adkins and Zacheus Candee.

Page 252.

Coal, Nathaniel, Hartford. Invt. £607-06-07. Taken October, 1713, by Cyprian Nichols, Ichabod Wells and Thomas Hosmer.

Court Record, Page 160—2 November, 1713: Adms. to Elizabeth Coal, widow, relict.

See File: We the subscribers do covenant and agree to dist. that part of our father, Nathaniel Cole deceased his estate as followeth: That is to say, the two daughters, Elizabeth and Lydia Cole, shall have equal with John Cole (reckoning them two together), and that they are to take their portions as follows: the moveables at inventory price, and 1 piece of land, one 40 acres and the other piece at the lower end of the South Meadow, at invt. price, and all the pasture land, which was prised at £67. I, the subscribing John Cole, agree to pay unto Eliz(abeth) and Lydia after the rate of £100 for the same, and if that shall not amount to their full parts of our sd. father's estate, that then I will make it up in money. As witness our hands and seals this 4th day of March, 1729.

JOHN COLE, LS.
ELIZABETH X COLE, LS.
LYDIA X COLE, LS.

Witness: *J. Gilbert, Jr.,*
   Jn. Whiting.

4th March, 1728-9: John Cole, Elizabeth and Lydia Cole appeared and acknowledged this within written agreement to be their free act and deed. And Jonathan Mason as guardian to the sd. Lydia, signed as consenting to the same.

Test: Hez: Wyllys, Clerk.

Page 125.

Colfax, Jonathan, Wethersfield. Invt. £170-12-10. Taken by Michael Griswold, Abraham Kilburn and Josiah Belding.

Court Record, Page 58—3 March, 1711-12: Adms. to Sarah Colfax, the relict. Invt. exhibited and allowed.

Page 61 (Vol. IX) 1st April, 1718: Sarah Colefax, alias Webster, Adms. on the estate of Jonathan Colefax, exhibited now an account of her Adms:

	£ s d
Paid in debts and charges,	90-14-07
With loss of,	20-08-10
Which, added, amounts to,	111-03-05
Inventory,	170-12-10
There remains to be distributed,	59-09-05

To Sarah Colefax, alias Webster; to John Colefax, the eldest son; to Jonathan, Sarah, Elizabeth and Mary Colefax, children, their single portions. And appoint James Butler, Samuel Curtis and James Belding distributors.

Page 116—5 January, 1719-20: This Court appoint Robert Webster and Sarah his wife to be guardian to John Colefax, age 18 years, Hannah 15, and Jonathan 12 years of age, children of Jonathan Colefax, decd.

Page 56 (Vol. X) 6 October, 1724: Report of the distributors.

Page 115.

Coleman, Noah, Colchester. Invt. £304-00-08. Taken 20 December, 1711, by Michael Taintor, Thomas Day and Samuel Loomis.

Court Record, Page 42—7 January, 1711-12: This Court grant Adms. unto Hannah Coleman, widow.

Page 90—6 October, 1712: Adms. granted longer time to finish her Adms.

Page 57—7 September, 1713: Adms. allowed further time.

Page 208—15 July, 1714: Hannah Coleman, Adms., exhibits now an account of her Adms.:

	£ s d
Inventory,	314-11-03
Real estate,	210-00-00
Paid in debts and charges,	69-05-03
There remains to be distributed,	245-06-00
To Hannah Coleman, widow,	11-15-04
To Noah Coleman, eldest son,	116-15-04
To Joseph Coleman and Hannah Coleman, to each of them,	58-07-08

And appoint Michael Taintor, Samuel Norton and Nathaniel Foote distributors. And grant Hannah Coleman a *Quietus Est*. This Court appoint Mrs. Hannah Coleman to be guardian to Noah Coleman, aged 11 years, Joseph 8, and Hannah, 13 years, children of Noah Coleman, decd. And the sd. Hannah Coleman recognizes with John Coleman of Wethersfield for £200.

Page 255—7 June, 1715: Report of the distributors.

Page 79.

Coult, Jonathan, Cordwainer, Windsor. Invt. £14-13-04. Taken 22 August, 1711, by Samuel Burnham and Joseph Fitch.

Court Record, Page 31—2 April, 1711: Adms. to Matthew Grant. Joseph Coult and the rest of the brothers having refused to administer.

Page 181.

Cooke, John, Windsor. Invt. £155-13-07. Taken 21 April, 1712, by Joseph Phelps, John Bissell and Josiah Cooke.

Court Record, Page 72—5 May, 1712: Adms. to Sarah Cook, widow.

Page 240—7 March, 1714-15: Sarah Cooke, Adms., exhibits an account of her Adms.:

	£ s d
Inventory,	158-06-03
Real part,	104-00-00
Paid in debts and charges,	32-12-06
There remains to be distributed,	125-13-09
To Sarah Cooke, widow,	7-04-09
To John Cooke, eldest son,	59-04-06
To Theophilus Cooke and the children of Sarah, daughter of the sd. decd., which she hath by Josiah Grant, to each,	29-12-03

And appoint John Moore, John Bissell and James Ennoe distributors.

Page 92 (Vol. IX) 6 January, 1718-19: Whereas, an order of distribution was granted by this Court, 7 March, 1714-15, there now appears a corrected distribution, wherein Sarah had already received £16-10-00, which, added to the former dist., makes their portions as followeth: Gives John, £67-09-06; and to Theophilus, £33-14-09; and to Sarah, £17-04-09; to which adding the £16-10-00 makes her portion £33-14-09.

Page 122—1st March, 1720: Report of the distributors.

Page 85.

Cornish, James, Wethersfield. Will dated 17 August, 1710. I, James Cornish of Wethersfield, do make this my last will and testament: I give to my sister Dammary Cornish all my lands within the bounds of the Township of Westfield, and my chest and clothes in the custody of my uncle George Wolcott of Wethersfield, during her life, and after her decease to her eldest son forever.

Witness: *Josiah Churchill,*   JAMES X CORNISH.
George Kilbourn, Joseph Kilbourn.

Court Record, Page 35—2 July, 1711: Adms., with the will annexed, to William Tuller of Simsbury.

Page 251.

Crane, Abraham, Wethersfield. Invt. £345-03-07. Taken 19 November, 1713, by John Coleman, Jonathan Pratt and Michael Griswold.

Court Record, Page 152—3 August, 1713: Adms. granted to Hannah Crane, widow, and Joseph Belding of Wethersfield.

Page 163—7 December, 1713: Exhibit of an inventory.

Page 59 (Vol. XI) 25 January, 1731-2: Hannah Crane, Adms., exhibited an account of her Adms., which account this Court accepts.

Page 16 (Vol. XIII) 4 October, 1737: Hannah Crane, the widow, moves this Court that her dower may be set out to her from the estate of Abraham Crane. This Court appoint Lt. Joshua Robbins, Joseph Boardman and Ebenezer Belding to set out the widow's thirds.

Page 53—7 August, 1739: Report of the distributors.

Page 56—6 November, 1739: Hannah Crane exhibits a further account of her Adms., and moves for a distribution to the heirs of the sd. decd., which this Court doth order:

	£ s d
To Hannah Crane, the relict,	9-08-10
To John Crane, eldest son,	5-07-10
To Benoni, Abraham, Mary, Hannah and Lucy Crane, to each,	2-13-11¼

And appoint Ebenezer Belding, Joseph Boardman and Noadiah Dickinson distributors.

Page 79 (Vol. XVI) 7 November, 1752: James Treat and Mary his wife, of Wethersfield, one of the daughters of Abraham Crane, deceased, notified the heirs to the estate of the deceased to appear before this Court and show cause why sd. estate should not be distributed according to law. The parties appeared and were heard and agreed to have a distribution as follows: To John Crane, eldest son, a double part of the estate, and to Benoni and Abraham Crane, Mary Treat, Hannah Crane and Lucy Forbes, to each of them their single shares. And appoint Mr. Hezekiah May, Jonathan Belding and Joseph Boardman, of Wethersfield, distributors.

Page 98—26 April, 1753: Report of the distributors. Accepted.

Page 145. Invt. on Page 205.

Crane, Isaac, Wethersfield. Invt. £225-13-10. Taken 5 February, 1712-13, by John Russell and David Tyron. Will nuncupative. The date is of 15 September, 1712.

The testimony of Joseph Grimes and of John Wright, both of lawful age: Being present with Isaac Crane when he made his will, we heard him make his will as followeth: In the first, he ordered that his debts should be paid, and that his four brothers by his mother should have all his estate, to be equally divided amongst them. But if that either of them were sickly or weakly, that he should have more than the rest of them. And that he further said that he counted that they were the nearest relations that he had.

Joseph Grimes and John Wright.
Sworn in Court, 6th October, 1712.

Test: *Thomas Kimberly, Clerk.*

Court Record, Page 89—6 October, 1712: Samuel Terry of Enfield, in the County of Hampshire, in the Province of Mass. Bay, exhibited in this Court the nuncupative will of Isaac Crane, decd., and Joseph Grimes and John Wright, the witnesses to the sd. will, were now sworn thereunto, and the sd. will was proved and approved. And there being no executor named in sd. will, this Court grant letters of Adms., with the will annexed, unto the sd. Terry.

Page 131—3 March, 1712-13: Samuel Terry of Enfield, Adms. on the estate of Isaac Crane, late of Wethersfield, decd., exhibited now in Court an invt. of sd. estate, and is granted further time to finish his Adms.

Page 102 (Vol. X) 4 October, 1725: Whereas, Isaac Crane, son of Joseph Crane, late of Wethersfield, decd., lately died, being under age, and in the dist. of the estate of Joseph Crane there being dist. to the sd. Isaac Crane 71 acres of land at Tappin's Hill at £22-08-00, and 25 shillings right in the homelot of sd. Joseph Crane (on the north side of sd. homelot, next to Joseph Hollister, Sen., in Wethersfield), Thomas Deming, as attorney to two other sisters of sd. Isaac Crane, moved that an order for the distribution of sd. estate in lands may be granted. This Court appoint Edward Bulkeley, Ephraim Goodrich and Samuel Belding distributors, to distribute sd. estate in lands, by meets and bounds, in equal parts, unto Sarah Tooley, Hannah Purple and Esther Crane, sisters of the sd. Isaac Crane.

Page 51.

Crippin, Thomas, Sen., Haddam. Invt. £47-03-00. Taken 24 January, 1709, by John Fuller, Thomas Robinson and Samuel Rowley. Will dated 10th May, 1705.

I, Thomas Crippin, Sen., of East Haddam, commonly called Machamoodus, in the County of Hartford, do make this my last will and testament: I give by deed to my son Thomas Crippin one-half my land at Machamoodus, and to my son Jabez Crippin the other half, reserving only the dwelling house and one-third part of above said land for the use of my wife Frances Crippin if she outlive me, and after her decease to be to my son Jabez Crippin and his heirs forever. After the decease of my wife Frances Crippin, all my movable estate left to be equally divided between my four daughters, viz., Katharine Rowley, Mary Corbee, Mercy and Experience Crippin.

Witness: *William Spencer,*   THOMAS X CRIPPIN.
        Samuel Arnold.

Court Record, Page 18—4 September, 1710: Adms., with will annexed, to Jabez Crippin.

Page 62—3 March, 1711-12: The Adms. exhibits account of sundry legacies paid and discharged by him, under the hands of the persons to whom the legacies were due, which account this Court accept *Consideratum Est.,* order on file, and grant a *Quietus Est.*

Invt. in Vol. IX, Page 6.

Crow, John, Hartford. Invt. £321-12-09. Taken 1st October, 1714, by Roger Pitkin and William Roberts.

Court Record, Page 214—6 September, 1714: Adms. granted to Hannah Crow, widow.

Page 217—6 October, 1714: Invt. exhibited, and John Kilbourn of Hartford is appointed guardian to Nathaniel Crow, 3 years of age, son of John Crow, late decd.

Page 1 (Vol. IX) 4 October, 1715: Hannah Crow of Hartford, widow, Adms. on the estate of John Crow, late of Hartford, deceased, exhibited an accompt, by which accot. and by the inventory of that estate it appears that the whole of the sd. estate as it is inventoried, with the profits of the land, amount to £328-11-03; the real part is £233; and that she hath paid out, £62-19-11. Which account this Court allow, and order distribution of the estate: To Hannah Crow (dower), and £10-17-02 to be her own forever; and lands to be distributed or set out to Nathaniel Crow, son and only child of sd. John Crow, deceased. And appoint Capt. Roger Pitkin, Lt. Jonathan Hill and Joseph Olmsted distributors.

Page 58—1st April, 1718: Report of distributors allowed. Hannah Crow, Adms. on the estate of John Crow, is granted a *Quietus Est.*

Page 99 (Vol. X) 7 September, 1725: Nathaniel Crow of Hartford, 14 years of age, chose Daniel Dickinson of sd. Hartford to be his guardian. Recog., £50.

Page 206-7.

Curtis, John, Jr., Wethersfield. Died 7 November, 1712. Invt. £1004-15-09. Taken by John Curtis, Jr., and Nathaniel Stoddard.

Will dated 7 November, 1712: My body I commit to the earth, and my soul unto the Lord in hope of a glorious resurrection. And my worldly goods which it hath pleased the Lord to bestow upon me I dispose of as followeth: Impr. I give Jacob, my negro servant, to my beloved wife; also all the crops that is now upon my land. Also, I give my wife the use of all my land until my sons come to lawful age, for the bringing up of my son John to learning, and also for the bringing up of the rest of my children. And when my son John cometh to lawful age, to have a double portion, and the rest of my estate to be disposed of to my wife and children according to law. But if that before named be not sufficient to the bringing up of the children, that what more is needful be deducted out of their portions. Also, I give my son Josiah 20 pounds more than to my daughters. Also, I constitute my well-beloved wife to be executrix.

Witness: *Joseph Camp,*   JOHN CURTIS, JR.
Joseph Andrews.

Court Record, Page 108—6 January, 1712-13: Will exhibited by Elizabeth Curtis, widow, and test: by Joseph Andrews (physician), Joseph Camp being deceased. Will proven with invt. Allowed.

Page 248—4 April, 1715: This Court appoint Thomas Wright of Wethersfield to be guardian to Josiah Curtis, 11 years of age, Elizabeth 8, and Hannah Curtis, 3 years of age, children of John Curtis, Jr., late decd.

Page 162 (Vol. IX) 6 February, 1721-2: Elizabeth Curtis, executrix, moved this Court that distribution be made of the estate. Order to distribute the estate according to the last will of John Curtis, Jr.: To Elizabeth Curtis, the widow, to John Curtis, only surviving son, to Martha Robbins, to Mary Welles, to Elizabeth Curtis and Hannah Curtis. And whereas, two of the children of the sd. John Curtis are deceased since the bequest of their father, this Court order that the estate that would have belonged to them had they been living be deducted out of the estate

of their father and distributed in equal parts and shares unto the co-heirs
of the sd. deceased children, vizt., the aforesd. John Curtis, Martha Robbins, Mary Welles, Elizabeth Curtis and Hannah Curtis. And whereas,
there is estate in houseing and lands to the value of £192-10-02 of the estate of John Curtis, Sen., decd., grandfather, to be distributed unto the
sd. co-heirs, this Court order that the same be also distributed unto the
aforesd. children.   And appoint Robert Welles, Thomas Wright and
James Butler, distributors.   Also, this Court appoint Mrs. Elizabeth
Curtis guardian to her children, Elizabeth Curtis, a minor 14 years of age,
and Hannah Curtis, 10 years. Recog., £100.

Page 169—5 June, 1722: Whereas, the homestead of John Curtis,
Jr., as it is distributed, 1-2 thereof unto three of the children, John, Elizabeth and Hannah Curtis, proves to be inconvenient and prejudicial to the
whole, it being moved to this Court by the sd. son John that the sd. 2
parts in the sd. half of the homestead belonging to the 2 daughters may
be set out to him, the Court order him to take the homestead and pay to
his sisters Elizabeth and Hannah Curtis their proportional parts according to the apprisal.

Will and Invt. in Vol. IX., Page 57.

Deming, Elizabeth, Wethersfield.   Invt. £37-00-07.   Taken by Samuel Williams and Philip Goff, Jr.   Will nuncupative, dated 4 September,
1714: Elizabeth Deming, widow, relict of Jonathan Deming, declared in
presence of the subscribing witnesses that she gave what estate she had
to her two daughters, Mary and Ann Deming, to be equally divided between them.
Witness: *Sarah Deming,*
           Abigail Deming.

Court Record, Page 217—4 October, 1714: Will proven and allowed, but there being no executor appointed in sd. will, Adms. is granted
to Jonathan Deming and John Edwards, with the will annexed.

Page 3 (Vol. X) 7 December, 1715: Jonathan Deming and John
Edwards, Adms., exhibit an account of their Adms., which this Court accept, order recorded and kept on file.

Page 43-4-5.

Deming, Ebenezer, Wethersfield.   Died 2 May, 1705.   An agreement
for the settlement of the estate of Ebenezer Deming:
We the subscribers, inhabitants in Wethersfield, widow and children
of Ebenezer Deming of Wethersfield, have agreed and do agree to the
following: That the Widow Sarah Deming shall have during her natural life 1-3 part of all the real estate that the sd. Ebenezer Deming her
husband died seized of, and shall have the whole of the personal estate

to be to her forever, as also one-third part of either of the dwelling houses
of the sd. Ebenezer Deming which she the sd. Sarah shall choose. And
the sd. Sarah shall pay all the just debts of the sd. Ebenezer, decd. That
Ebenezer Deming, eldest son, shall have all that tract of land which is
bordering or near the Town Plot, by estimation 40 acres, and a tract of
land in the West Swamp, of 18 acres. The remainder to be equally
divided between Ephraim Deming and Josiah Deming, two younger sons.
A tract of land of two parcels, one of which, containing 50 acres, being
granted to the sd. Ebenezer by the Town of Wethersfield, and another lott
of 50 acres which was granted by the Town in the last division of land,
numbered 116-17-18, said lotts to be divided to John, Ephraim and Josiah
Deming, to each a third part. The aforesd. Sarah Deming, widow of sd.
Ebenezer, decd., shall pay or caused to be paid to Joseph Talcott of Wethersfield and Thomas Wright, Jr., sons-in-law of sd. Sarah, so much of
the movable estate as may make what each of them have already received
as the portions of their wives, Sarah and Prudence (the latter of which is
deceased), £80 each. In testimony we, Sarah Deming, widow of abovesd.
Ebenezer Deming, decd., Ebenezer Deming, John Deming, Ephraim
Deming and Josiah Deming, Joseph Talcott and Thomas Wright, Jr.,
children of sd. Ebenezer, decd., have set to our hands and seals:

> WIDOW SARAH DEMING, LS.
> EBENEZER DEMING, LS.
> JOHN DEMING, LS.
> JOSIAH DEMING, LS.
> JOSEPH TALCOTT, LS.
> SARAH TALCOTT, LS.
> THOMAS WRIGHT, LS.,
> *(In behalf of his wife).*

Court Record, Page 13—5 June, 1710: This agreement accepted and
ordered to be recorded and kept on file.

Page 23.

Deming, Samuel, Wethersfield. Invt. £648-12-06. Taken by Moses
Crafts and James Patterson.

Court Record, Page 133 (Vol. VII) 5 September, 1709: This Court
grant Adms. unto Sarah Deming, the widow of sd. decd.

Page 8 (Vol. IX) 6 March, 1715-16: This Court orders the estate
to be distributed as followeth:

	£ s d
Inventory,	648-12-00
To Sarah Churchill, formerly Sarah Deming,	85-04-00
To John Deming, eldest son,	187-16-00
To David, Samuel, William and Honour Deming, to each,	93-18-00

And appoint Capt. David Goodrich, Lt. Joseph Talcott and Mr.
James Patterson of Wethersfield to distribute the estate accordingly.

Page 216 (Vol. X) 1st April, 1729: An agreement for a division of the estate of Samuel Deming, decd.: To the widow, now Sarah Churchill, to John, to David, to Samuel, to William, and to Honour Deming. By Samuel Talcott and Francis Hanmer. Accepted and ordered on file.

Page 191.

Dibble, Benjamin, Simsbury. Invt. £2-15-05. Taken 1st August, 1712, by Joseph Phelps, Thomas Holcomb and Andrew Robe.
Court Record, Page 86—4 August, 1712: This Court grant Adms. unto John Matson of Simsbury.

From File.

Dickinson, Thomas, Wethersfield. Died 17 January, 1712-13. Invt. £128-18-06. Taken by Joseph Barnard and Joseph Belding. Additional Invt. of £19-06-00. Taken 19 February, 1712-13, by James Steele and Joseph Belding. An addition of lands in Hadley belonging to Thomas Dickinson, late of Wethersfield, decd., is as followeth, viz:

	£ s d	
In ye meadow called Hockanum, 5 acres,	4-10-00	per acre
Also in ye Great Meadow Plaine, 2½ acres,	4-10-00	" "
Also in ye Skirts in ye Forte Meadow and acres not cleared,	2-00-00	" "
Alsoe in ye Commons,	40-00	" "

Prised all as money. Taken 1713-14, by Nathaniel Dickinson and Samuel Barnard.
A further addition to the inventory as followeth:

Two steers,	8-00-00
Two steers,	5-10-00
One cow,	2-15-00

Taken 18 March, 1714, by Samuel Welles and Leonard Dixx.
A further addition to the inventory as followeth:

One side upper leather, £3-10-00; one do., £3-10-00,	7-00-00
One do., £4-05-00; to 4 horse skins, £4-05-00,	12-10-00
Small dog skins, 6 Shillings,	06-00
Small side of upper leather,	3-00-00
18 lbs. of sole leather, at 9s. per lb.,	8-02-00
Cart rope,	1-10-00

Court Record, Page 130—7 April, 1713: This Court grant Adms. unto Hannah Dickinson, widow, and Thomas, the eldest son.
Page 116 (Vol. IX) 5 January, 1719-20: Thomas Dickinson, Adms., cited into Court by Elihu Dickinson to render an account of his Adms., that dist. may be made.

Page 120—9 February, 1719-20: Thomas Dickinson now exhibits an account of his Adms. This Court appoint Obadiah Spencer, Joseph Barnard of Hartford and Joseph Belding of Wethersfield to apprise the real estate.

Page 125—5 April, 1720: An invt. of an addition of the real estate was exhibited. Whereas, Thomas Dickinson declared himself aggrieved, this Court now appoint a jury of 12 men to apprise land lying in the cow pasture and in the neck in Hartford, given in the lifetime of the sd. decd. by deed of guift to his son, the sd. Thomas Dickinson, to apprise the land at the time it was given by the sd. deed.

Page 146—7 March, 1720: Hannah Dickinson and Thomas Dickinson, Adms. on the estate of Thomas Dickinson, late of Wethersfield, deceased, exhibited an account of their Adms., whereby it appears that they have paid out in debts and charges, with loss upon the estate, £26-07-02 more than they have received due to the estate, and that there was formerly paid to several of the children of sd. deceased towards their portions, £52-07-06 besides what Ebenezer Dickinson, one of the sons of sd. deceased, has received by deed of gift and in cattle to the value of £137-10-00. The sum remaining of sd. Estate is £140-06-04. Account allowed, and an order to distribute to Hannah Dickinson, widow, relict, £14-03-09 for her own, and one-third use of real estate during life; to the children (excepting Ebenezer Dickinson, who has received more than his proportion): to Thomas Dickinson, eldest son, £44-10-00 with what he has formerly received, his double portion; to Elihu Dickinson, £29-08-00; to Elizabeth Addams, £13-08-00; to Esther Porter, £12-14-06; to the heirs of Hannah Leffingwell, £26-02-00. This Court appoint Ephraim Goodrich and Jonathan Belding, of Wethersfield, and Thomas Seymour, of Hartford, distributors.

Report of the distributors on file 5 June, 1722: To the widow in personal estate, £28-07-07, and in lands, £97-00-00. To Thomas, £59-10-00; to Elihu, £29-15-00; to Elizabeth, £29-15-00; to Esther, £29-15-00; to Hannah's heirs, £29-15-00.

Will and Invt. in Vol. IX, Page 51-52.

Doolittle, Samuel, Middletown. Invt. £364-06-03. Taken 28 October, 1714, by Israhiah Wetmore, Samuel Gipson and John Warner.

Will (not dated): I, Samuel Doolittle of Middletown, being weak and low, brought by sickness and sore pain, do make this my last will and testament: I do will 1-3 part of the moveable estate to my dear wife, and this eastern room, with the back room, with free gress and progress in the lower room for washing and baking, and answerable cellar room, during her life or widowhood. Item. I give to my son Jonathan my home lot with the house and barn, to say, the east end of this lot beginning at the Boggy Meadow River and running up westward to the first brook below the orchard where the bridge stands; also I give to him 4 acres of boggy meadow which I bought of Ebenezer Hubbard, only my will is that after an apprizement of this estate above named with the rest of my whole estate, that Jonathan shall have his double portion with his brothers and sister, and what overplus there is after the prisall Jonathan shall pay to his sisters. Further, my will is that my wife shall have free liberty of passage in and out of her part in the house, also a garden spot; and that my daughter Mary shall have the loom and tackling belonging to it as part of her portion, and further to have liberty of that place in the house where the loom stands so long as she lives single. Further, my will is that all my children, Jonathan only excepted (being before mentioned), shall have an equal share of my whole estate, real and personal, both in this town and in Wallingford, only that my sons shall have liberty to keep all the lands if they can make payment to their sisters in some short convenient time after they come of age to receive their portion. My wife and son Jonathan to be executors. Further, that Thomas Allyn shall be overseer, to be helpful to my wife and Jonathan.

Witness: *Thomas Allen.*   SAMUEL DOOLITTLE, LS.
Isaac Lane, Benjamin Cornwall.

Court Record, Page 219—1 November, 1714: Will exhibited by Mary and Jonathan Doolittle, executors. Proven.

Page 225—6 December, 1714: This Court appoint Mary Doolittle to be guardian to Thankfull Doolittle, age 12 years, Joseph, 10 years, Nathaniel, 8 years, Esther, 6 years, children of Samuel Doolittle, late decd.

Page 14 (Vol. IX) 1st May, 1716: Upon the motion of Jonathan Doolittle, this Court appoint Israhiah Wetmore, Joseph Rockwell and Samuel Gipson to set out the estate to the legatees, according to the will.

Dist. per File: 4 June, 1717: To the widow, to Jonathan, Samuel, Abraham, Nathaniel and Joseph Doolittle, to Mary, the wife of Solomon Goffe, to Abigail, Martha, Hannah, Thankfull and Esther Doolittle. By Israhiah Wetmore, Joseph Rockwell and Samuel Gipson.

Page 34—4 June, 1717: Report of the distributors.

Page 102-222.

Drake, Job, Sen., Windsor. Invt. £541-05-03. Taken 19 December, 1711, by Thomas Griswold, Sen., and Timothy Thrall.

AN AGREEMENT FOR THE SETTLEMENT OF THE ESTATE OF JOB DRAKE: *Know all Christians to whome these presents shall come*: That we, Elizabeth Drake, the relict, and Jacob Drake, John Porter and Mary his wife, Roger Wolcott and Sarah his wife, being children and the only surviving heirs and successors unto Lt. Job Drake, late of the Town of Windsor, decd., have mutually and lovingly agreed to make a settlement, and do hereby make a final division and settlement, of the estate of our loving husband and honoured father, Lt. Job Drake.

Imprimis: Elizabeth Drake, the relict, to have the negro servant Diego, the great brass kettle, featherbed, bedsted, boulster, pillows, ruggs, two coverletts, curtains and valians during her natural life. In ratification and confirmation of this agreement and settlement of the estate of the aforesd. Lt. Job Drake, we have hereunto set our hands and seals this 27th day of October, 1712.

ELIZABETH DRAKE, LS.
JACOB DRAKE, LS.
JOHN PORTER, LS.
MARY PORTER, LS.
ROGER WOLCOTT, LS.
SAMUEL WOLCOTT, LS.
Recorded per me,   *Thomas Kimberly, Clerk.*

Court Record, Page 45—17 January, 1711-12: This Court grant Adms. to Elizabeth, the widow, and Job Drake, the son.
Page 93—6 November, 1712: Agreement accepted.

Page 144.

Drake, Job, Jr., Windsor. Will dated 14 October, 1712: I, Job Drake, Jr., son of Lt. Job Drake, decd., do make this my last will and testament: I give to my honoured mother Elizabeth Drake the use and improvement of the new dwelling house and lands belonging to it which was my grandfather's, Job Drake's, and set out to me in the division of my father Drake's estate, during her natural life, and after her decease my brother Jacob's son Jacob to have it. I also give to my nephew Jacob Drake, son of my brother Jacob Drake, 4 acres I bought of my Father Drake which was my grandfather Clarke's. I give to my brother the improvement of sd. 4 acres until my nephew shall come of age, also 2 acres which was my grandfather Clarke's, called the Rye Plot. I give to my brother Jacob half of the lot which is set out to me in the division of my Father Drake's estate in the Great Meadow, bounded north on Mr. Wolcott's land and south on John Moore's land, provided he pay to my sister Mary's daughter Mary £5 in money at the age of 18 years; if she die, to be paid to my sister Mary's daughter Katharine; and also £5 to my sister Sarah's daughter Elizabeth; in case she die before the age of 18 years, to be paid to my sister Mary's son Alexander, 24 years of age. I give to my mother's negro servant, Dick, 40 shillings. My personal estate to be for the payment of my debts. I appoint my honoured mother Elizabeth Drake and my brother Jacob Drake executors.
Witness: *John Moore, Sen.,*   JOB DRAKE, JR., LS.
Anthony X *Hoskins, Jane* X *Alvord.*

Court Record, Page 93—6 November, 1712: Will proven.

Page 176.

Drake, Symon, Windsor. Invt. £93-11-00. Taken 25 April, 1712, by Thomas Moore, Thomas Marshall and William Phelps.

Court Record, Page 47—4 February, 1711-12: Adms. to Hannah Drake, widow of sd. decd.

Page 96-97.

Dyxx, John, Wethersfield. Invt. £83-12-05. Taken 29 January, 1711-12, by Daniel Boardman, Joseph Belden and Abraham Crane.
Court Record, Page 50—4 February, 1711-12: Adms. to John and Leonard Dyxx, sons of the decd. Exhibit of inventory.

Page 133.

Easton, Joseph, Sen Hartford. Invt. £986-03-02. Taken 1st February, 1711-12, by John Catlin and John Shepherd.
Will signed and sealed 8 February, 1709-10.
I, Joseph Easton, Sen., of Hartford, do make this my last will and testament: I give to my son Joseph the house in which he now dwelleth, with the lot on which it stands, extending to the country highway on the east, with all the privileges and appurtenances thereto belonging. Item. Half my meadow lot lying on the east side of the Great River, known by the name of Phillips lot, to be divided by a line from east to west. Item. Half of my two meadow lots which I bought of Samuel Andrews. Item. Half my boggy meadow, all lying on the east side of the Great River. These I give to my son Joseph and his heirs forever, and, upon the division of said lots, he to have his first choice. Item. I give to my son James the house in which he now dwelleth, with the home lot on which it stand-eth, extending from the highway on the west eastward the whole breadth of my lot till ten acres be fully made up, with all the privileges and appur-tenances thereto belonging. Item. The other half of my meadow lot com-monly called Phillips lot, with the other half of the two lots I bought of Samuel Andrews, and the remaining half of my boggy meadow, all lying on the east side of the Great River, which I give to my son James and his heirs forever. Item. All the remainder of my upland lot on the east side of the Great River, with all its privileges, with all my other rights of land, these I give to my sons Joseph and James and their heirs forever, to be equally divided between them. Item. I give to my son Jonathan my house in which I now dwell, with the home lot on which it standeth. I give him those several parcels of land, vizt.: my pasture lot commonly called Skinner lot and my lot lying in the ox pasture adjoyning to Edward Cadwell's land; also my lot at the Blue Hills, with my lot at Four-Mile Hill, with all my meadow lying in the south meadow, as also my two pas-tures (the one I bought of Mr. Blackleach and the other given me by my father). Item. I give to him my two meadow lots lying over the Great River, the one called Stedman's lot and the other called Spencer's lot, which I bought of John Michell. Those several parcels of land I give to

my son Jonathan and to his heirs forever. Item. I give to my son Jonathan all my goods and chattells whatsoever. I give to my son Richard Miles, beside what I have already given him, ten pounds in current country pay. Item. I give to my two daughters, Elizabeth and Thankfull, £6 to each, in country pay. I appoint my son Jonathan to be sole executor to this my last will, and appoint him out of what of my estate I have given him to pay all my just debts and funeral charges, with the legacies I have given to my son-in-law Richard Miles and my daughters Elizabeth and Thankfull.

Witness: *Timothy Woodbridge, Sen.,*   JOSEPH EASTON, LS.
    Timothy Woodbridge, Jr.

Court Record, Page 59—3 March, 1711-12: Will proven.

Page 151.

Edwards, Thomas, Wethersfield. Invt. (part) £118-00-00. Taken 3 November, 1712, by John Hubbard, Sen., and Francis Smith.

Court Record, Page 64—4th March, 1711-12: Samuel and Mary Hale of Glastonbury, grandchildren, cited to appear and take Adms., which if they decline the same may be committed to some other person or persons as this Court shall think fit.

Page 92—6 October, 1712: The administration had been granted to his son-in-law, Samuel Hale, now decd., and the administration being unfinished, this Court now grant Adms. unto Thomas Kimberly in right of his wife Ruth Kimberly, a gr. daughter of sd. Thomas Edwards, deceased.

Page 134—7 April, 1713: Upon the motion of Thomas Kimberly of Glastonbury, this Court orders that the lands of Thomas Edwards shall be distributed and divided as follows: viz: To Samuel Hale, grandchild, a double portion; to Mary Hale and Ruth Kimberly, to each of them a single portion. And appoint Thomas Hale, Sen., Thomas Hale the 2nd and John Kilbourn distributors.

Page 157—7 September, 1713: Report of the distributors.

Page 122.

Elmore, John, Windsor. Invt. £71-13-09. Taken by Joseph Fitch and Thomas Stoughton.

Court Record, Page 48—4 February, 1711-12: Adms. granted unto John Elmore, son of the deceased.

Page 18 (Vol. X) 7 May, 1723: Whereas, John Elmore died and left an estate, real and personal, and Adms. being granted to his son John Elmore, who also died not having finished his Adms. or made any account of that Adms. to the Court, the Court now grant Adms. unto Joseph Elmor, son of sd. decd.

Page 49—5 May, 1724: Joseph Elmer allowed another year in which to finish his Adms.

Page 113—4 January, 1725-6: This Court grants letters of Adms. on the estate of John Elmore, sometime of Windsor, decd., unto William Elmore and Thomas Elmore, grandsons of sd. decd. Recog., £200.

Page 114—4 January, 1725-6: Whereas, it is represented that to make an equal dist. of the estate of John Elmore the 1st, sometime of Windsor, decd., it will be necessary that the real estate of sd. decd. be anew apprised, this Court order and appoint Joseph Rockwell and John Anderson to apprise the real estate of sd. decd., those lands that were cleared and improved at the time of the decease of the sd. John Elmore, according to their present value thereof, and those lands that were rough and unimproved at his decease to be apprised as such according to their present value.

Page 233.

Elmer, Mary, daughter of Edward Elmer. Invt. £6-14-06. Taken 26 February, 1712-13, by James Patterson and Moses Crafts.

Court Record, Page 119—12 February, 1712-13: The Court orders the Clerk to issue forth a writ to cite Edward Elmer to take Adms. on the estate of his late daughter, Mary Elmer.

Page 145—1st June, 1713: This Court grant Adms. unto Dr. Daniel Hooker of Wethersfield.

Will and Invt. in Vol. IX, Page 11-12.

Enno, James, Sen., Windsor. Invt. £642-17-06. Taken 5 August, 1714, by Cornelius Brown and John Palmer. Will dated 24 June, 1709.

I give unto my eldest son James Enno my right and title to that part of the house and homestead where sd. James now dwells, which pertained to me of my father Bissell's; also a lot of near four acres in great meadow which was formerly belonging to Nathaniel Phelps; also a piece of swamp and upland adjoining, all 20 acres more or less; also my part in the grist mill at Pohquanuck. I give to my son William Enno one-third part of all my lands within the bounds of Simsbury, and two parcels lying in Windsor limits (the one on Wash Brook which lyeth in partnership with Benajah Holcomb, Sen., and about seven acres called plumb tree swamp). These forementioned parcels of land as aforesaid one-third part on an equal division to William. He, in the marsh lot, is to take his part at the south end where his house and barn standeth. I give unto my son John one-third part of my lands in the limits of Simsbury and of my part in land at Wash Brook and plumb tree swamp above mentioned, on an equal division. Also, I give unto my son Samuel one-third part of the land above mentioned, to be divided between him and his two brothers, William and John. I give also to my youngest son

David my lot which I bought of Samuel Farnsworth, known by the name of Timm's lot, and also my land in second meadow, about four acres, and my lot on the Mill Brook. I give unto Abigail my wife a lot in the Great Meadow which was Father Bissell's, about 4 acres, to be at her dispose forever; and also all my homestead, housing and orchards, both that on which I dwell and the lot which I bought of Josiah Gillett, with the lands on the west side of the way, I give to my wife during her natural life. I give to my two daughters £20 a piece, my three sons to pay to their 4 sisters, Anne, Abigail, Mary and Susannah, £10 apeice. My wife Abigail and my son James sole executors.   JAMES ENNO, LS.
Witness: *John Moore, Sen.,*
          Job Drake, Sen.

Court Record, Page 213—6 September, 1714: Abigail Enno and James Enno, Jr., of Windsor, exhibited now in this Court the last will of James Enno, Sen., deceased. Mr. John Moore, one of the witnesses, now sworn (the other witness to the sd. will being departed this life). The will was proven and approved and allowed. Joseph Case and Samuel Humphrey, of Symsbury, and Samuel Phelps, of Windsor (sons-in-law of the sd. decd.), being dissatisfied with the decree of this Court in approving and allowing the sd. will, appealed therefrom unto the Superior Court.

Page 237—7 February, 1714-15: Samuel Enno, a minor about 19 years of age, chose Joseph Case to be his guardian.

Page 108 (Vol. IX) 7 July, 1719: David Enno, a minor 17 years of age, son of James Enno, made choice of Samuel Phelps to be his guardian.

Page 120.

Filley, Samuel, Windsor. Invt. £327-03-02. Taken 10 January, 1711-12, by John Bissell, James Enno and Joseph Phelps. Will dated 12 December, 1711.

I, Samuel Filley, of Windsor, do make this my last will and testament: I give to my son Jonathan Filley all my land that adjoins to his land on which his house now standeth, be it 3 acres more or less; also 1 full third part of my lot in the Great Meadow that I bought of Mr. Gardner. To my son Josiah Filley I give half my lott in the 1st Meadow; also 5 acres of land in Filley's swamp, that was brother William Filley's and fell to me by agreement; also, 20 acres of woodland that I bought of brother Josiah Gillett. I give to my son John Filley half my lot in the 1st meadow; also half my lot in the 2nd meadow; also my dwelling house, barn and homestead, with the land adjoining that I bought of Job Drake; and also one full half of my lot at Nowell Swamp, that was George Alexander's; and 1-3 part of my lot in the Great Meadow bought of Mr. Gardner. I give to my granddaughter, Sarah Skinner, £5. I give to my daughter, Abigail Loomis, 1-3 part of my lot in the Great Meadow; also half the lot at Horsford's meadow, that was brother William Filley's; and also half of all my personal estate. I give to my daughter Mary Barber half my lot at second meadow; also 1-2 of all my personal estate. I give to my grandson Samuel Filley, son of Josiah Filley, 1 full half of my lot at Nowell Swamp, that was George Alexander's. I give to Deborah Sackett, that now liveth with me, a cow when she comes to be of age. I appoint my two sons, Jonathan Filley and John Filley, executors.

Witness: *John Hoskins,*   SAMUEL FILLEY, LS.
Cornelius Browne, Matthew Allyn.

Court Record, Page 42—7 January, 1711-12: Jonathan Filley and John Filley, of Windsor, exhibited now in Court the last will. Proven and ordered to be kept on file.

Page 75—5 May, 1712: Jonathan Filley, of Windsor, prays for an order of dist. and division of the lands among the heirs of the sd. Samuel Filley. This Court order that the Clerk issue forth a citation to all persons concerned to appear at this Court.

Page 82—3 June, 1712: Whereas, it appears to this Court that there are 2 acres of land belonging to the estate of Samuel Filley which is left out and not disposed of in the last will of Samuel Filley to any of the children or heirs of the decd., this Court now order that the 2 acres of land be dist. and set out to the eldest son. And appoint Col. Matthew Allyn to dist. and set out the sd. estate.

Page 84—7 July, 1712: John Filley, one of the sons of Samuel Filley, moved for an appeal for the setting of the 2 acres of land to his brother Jonathan Filley. But no appeal should be granted.

Page 108 (Vol. X) 7 December, 1715: Samuel Filley, a minor about 19 years of age, chose Josiah Filley of Windsor to be his guardian. Recog., £50.

Page 246.

Fitch, Martha, Single Woman, Wethersfield. Invt. £8-12-08. Taken 3rd September, 1713, by Samuel Wright and Daniel Boardman.

Court Record, Page 155—7 September, 1713: Adms. granted to Sarah Fitch, mother of the decd.

Invt. in Vol. IX, Page 43.

Foote, Nathaniel, Wethersfield. Invt. £13-11-07. Taken 4 July, 1715, by Samuel Northam and Joseph Wright. A further invt. of sd. estate was apprised by George Stilman and Benjamin Belding.

Court Record, Page 249—7 March, 1714-15: Adms. granted to Margaret Foote of Colchester, widow of sd. decd.

Page 5 (Vol. IX) 3 January, 1715: Margaret Foote of Colchester, Adms., exhibited an account of her Adms. She had paid out more than the invt. of the estate. This Court do see cause to grant her a *Quietus Est.*

Page 196.

Forbes, John, Hartford. Invt. £231-14-00. Taken 30 April, 1713, by Roger Pitkin, Timothy Cowles and William Roberts.

Court Record, Page 136—4 May, 1713: Adms. to David Forbes and William Roberts, brothers of said deceased. John Forbes, a minor 14 years of age, son of sd. deceased, chose Timothy Cowles to be his guardian; William Roberts to be guardian to Mary Forbes, 14 years of age, and Lydia Forbes, under 14 years of age; and David Forbes of Hartford to be guardian to Joseph and Samuel Forbes, under 14 years of age, sons of John Forbes, decd.

Page 146—1st June, 1713: Adms. now granted to James Forbes, a brother of the deceased, and recall the Adms. from William Roberts.

Page 182-3—1st March, 1713-14: Adms. account allowed. Order to distribute the estate to the children of sd. deceased: To John, eldest son, £73-02-01; to Joseph, to Samuel, to Mary and to Lydia Forbes, to each of them the sum of £36-11-00. And appoint Mr. Joseph Olmsted, Daniel Bidwell and Nathaniel Pitkin distributors.

Page 187—5 April, 1714: Report of dist. not allowed, and David Forbes appeals to the Superior Court, supposing the law to have been duly observed. This Court now grants the Adms. a *Quietus Est.*

Page 28 (Vol. IX) 5 March, 1716-17: Joseph Forbes, age 14 years, son of John Forbes, made choice of his brother John Forbes to be his guardian. Recog., £50.

Page 60—1st April, 1718: Samuel Forbes, a minor 15 years of age, son of John Forbes, made choice of John Forbes to be his guardian.

Page 95.

Francis, John, Sen., Wethersfield. Invt. £687-07-00. Taken 31 January, 1711-12, by William Goodrich and John Curtis.

Court Record, Page 50—4 February, 1711-12: Adms. granted to Mary Francis, the widow.

Page 182—1st March, 1713-14: Mary Francis, Adms., exhibits now in this Court an account of her Adms:

	£ s d
Whole estate, real and personal,	713-07-00
Real part,	558-03-06
Paid in debts and charges,	20-00-00
There remains for distribution,	693-07-00
To Mary Francis, widow,	36-06-06
To John Francis, eldest son,	93-17-02

To James Francis, Thomas Francis, Robert Francis, Joseph
    Francis and Daniel Francis, younger sons, and to Syb-
    barance, Abigail, Hannah, Sarah, Prudence and Marcy,
    to each,   46-18-07

And to Mary Francis alias Griswold, wife to Samuel Gris-
    wold, daughter of sd. deceased, including the sum of
    £26 which the sd. Mary hath already had,   46-18-07

    And appoint Joseph Talcott, George Kilbourn and James Butler
distributors.

Francis, Robert, Wethersfield. Court Record, Page 64—4 March,
1711-12: John Stedman of Wethersfield, being by this Court, held here
5th February, 1711-12, made Adms. on the estate of Robert Francis, he
now appeared before this Court and positively refused that trust.

Page 56.

    Fyler, Samuel, Hebron. Invt. £129-06-04. Taken 25 September,
1710, by Return Strong, Samuel Strong, Nathaniel Phelps and Samuel
Palmer.
    Court Record, Page 20—6 November, 1710: Adms. granted to
Thomas Fyler of Windsor, a brother of sd. decd.
    Page 148—6 July, 1713: Adms. account exhibited and allowed.
Thomas Fyler now discharged because of remoteness of place, and letters granted to Timothy Phelps of Hebron, a brother-in-law of the deceased.
    Page 240—7 March, 1714-15: This Court grant Thomas Fyler a
Quietus Est.
    Page 108 (Vol. IX) 7 July, 1719: This Court appoint Sam-
uel Holcomb to be guardian to Abigail Fyler, a minor about 17 years of
age, daughter of Samuel Fyler, late decd. Recog., £50.
    Page 112—6 October, 1719: This Court also appoint William
Phelps of Windsor to be guardian to Samuel Fyler, a minor 10 years of
age, son of Samuel Fyler, late of Hebron decd.
    Page 124—5 April, 1720: Timothy Phelps of Hebron, Adms., exhi-
bits an account of his Adms:

	£ s d
Paid in debts and charges,	24-16-01
Inventory,	129-09-04
Deducting,	24-16-01
There remains to be distributed,	104-13-03
To Samuel Fyler, only son,	52-06-07
To Abigail and Ann Fyler, the rest of the children, to each,	26-03-04

    And appoint Benjamin Skinner, Morris Tillotson and Joseph Phelps
distributors.

Invt. and Agreement in Vol. IX, Pages 30 and 50.

Fyler, Zerubbabell, Windsor. Invt. £374-17-05. Taken 24 February, 1714-15, by Nathaniel Hosford and Jonathan Elsworth.

An agreement, made this 13th day of April, Anno Dom. 1716, for the settlement of the estate of sd. Zerubabell Fyler, late of Windsor, deceased, between the heirs of Zerubabell Fyler: For the peaceful settlement of the estate, we, the subscribers, heirs, do agree in manner and form following: First: We mutually agree that the widow of the sd. deceased, or the mother, shall have, besides her thirds of the movables to be at her disposal, which she hath received and is therewith content, 1-3 of the real estate of the sd. deceased, viz., 1-3 of the homestead, on the north side; also, 8 7-8 acres of land in the Great Meadow, on the north side, for her sole use during her natural life. Secondly: We agree that Wakefield Dibble and Jonathan Deming have, besides what they have received of the movables, with which they are content, the 54 acres of First Grant Lands and 30 acres of Second Division Lands in Suffield. Thirdly: We agree that Zerubabell Fyler have, besides the movables, the 30 acres of woodland up by the marsh. Fourthly: We agree that Experience Fyler have, besides the movables, 3 acres of the meadow land in Suffield; also 1 1-2 acre and 30 rods of the lot by Horsford. Fifthly: We agree that Elizabeth Fyler have, besides the movables, 3 acres of the meadow land in Suffield; also one acre, 1-2 and 30 rods in the lot by Horsford. Lastly: We mutually agree that Thomas Fyler and Stephen Fyler have, besides the movables, the remaining part of the lot by Horsford; also the remaining 2-3 of the homestead on the south side; also the remaining part of the meadow land in the Great Meadow, on the south side, in equal proportion, to the value of £3-15-00 each, and then the sd. Thomas to have 2-3 and the sd. Stephen 1-3 of all the remainder. In testimony and confirmation thereof we hereto set our hand and seals.

Signed and sealed
in presence of
John Eliot,
Mary Eliot,
Josiah Churchill and
Philip Goff, Jr.,
Witnesses to
Jonathan Deming.

EXPERIENCE FYLER, LS.
THOMAS FYLER, LS.
ZERUBABELL X FYLER, LS.
STEPHEN FYLER, LS.
WAKEFIELD DIBBLE, LS.
EXPERIENCE X FYLER, JR. LS.
ELIZABETH X FYLER, LS.
JONATHAN DEMING, LS.

Court Record, Page 239—7 March, 1714-15: Adms. granted jointly to Experience Fyler, the widow, and Thomas Fyler, son of sd. decd.

Page 15 (Vol. IX) 14 April, 1716: Agreement exhibited, allowed and confirmed. And upon the motion of Experience Fyler of Windsor (who was, with the son, Thomas Fyler, appointed Adms.), this Court doth now dismiss and discharge her from her trust of Adms. on sd. estate, and declare the sd. Thomas Fyler sole Administrator.

Page 278.

Gardner, Benjamin, Wethersfield. Invt. £175-04-02. Taken 27 February, 1713-14, by James Patterson and Benjamin Churchill.

Court Record, Page 173—5 January, 1713-14: Whereas, Benjamin Gardner, late belonging to Wethersfield, has been long absent abroad at sea and is supposed to be dead, Adms. is granted to Margaret Gardner, who was wife of sd. Benjamin Gardner.

Page 262—2 August, 1715: Adms. on the estate of Benjamin Gardner unto William Howard of Wethersfield, son-in-law.

Page 263—6 September, 1715: William Howard, Adms., exhibits now in Court an account of his Adms. on that estate:

	£ s d
Inventory,	175-04-02
Moveable part,	55-04-02
Paid in debts and charges, etc.,	1-15-06
There remains to be distributed,	173-08-08
To Margaret, the widow,	17-16-02
To Moses Gardner, eldest son,	51-17-06
To Peter, Sarah, Martha and Margaret Gardner, to each,	25-18-09

And appoint David Goodrich, George Kilbourn and Thomas Wright, distributors. This Court appoint Joseph Skinner of Hartford to be guardian to Peter, 12 years, and Margaret Gardner, 13 years of age, children of Benjamin Gardner of Wethersfield, decd. Josiah Churchill of Wethersfield to be conservator of such estate of Benjamin Gardner, decd., as was distributed and set out to Moses Gardner, 19 years of age, son of Benjamin Gardner, sd. Moses being now absent at sea. Recog., £30.

Page 4 (Vol. IX) 3 January, 1715-16: Report of the distributors. Richard Skinner, guardian to two of the children of the sd. decd., appeared now before this Court and recognized in the sum of £10.

Page 188.

Gates, Joseph, Haddam. Died 18 March, 1711-12. Invt. £332-14-00. Taken by Thomas Gates, Daniel Brainard and Daniel Cone.

Court Record, Page 78—2 June, 1712: Adms. granted to Elizabeth Gates, widow.

Page 35 (Vol. IX) 2 July, 1717: Elizabeth Gates, Adms., exhibited now an account of her Adms. Allowed. Order to distribute the estate: To Elizabeth Gates, widow, 1-3 part of the real estate; to Joseph Gates, eldest son, his double portion of sd. estate; to Elizabeth, John, Sarah, Jonathan, Susannah, Jacob, Samuel and Patience Gates, the rest of the children, to each of them their single portion of sd. estate. And appoint Capt. Thomas Gates, Mr. Daniel Brainard and Daniel Cone distributors. Also, this Court appoint Capt. Thomas Gates guardian to John Gates, 19 years of age, and Sarah Gates, 17 years of age, children of Joseph Gates decd.

And this Court appoint Elizabeth Gates of Hartford to be guardian unto Jonathan 14 years, Sarah 12, Jacob 9, Samuel 7, and Patience 5 years, all children of Joseph Gates. Recog., £70.

Invt. in Vol. IX, Page 47.

Gaylord, Eleazer, Windsor. Invt. £353-13-11. Taken by Jonathan Elsworth and Ebenezer Fitch.
Court Record, Page 229—3 January, 1714-15: Adms. granted to Martha Gaylord, widow.
Page 247—7 March, 1714-15: Invt. exhibited.
Page 13 (Vol. IX) 1st May, 1716: Martha Gaylord, Adms., exhibits an account of her Adms. as follows:

	£ s d
Inventory,	395-17-06
Moveable part,	186-17-06
Debts and charges paid,	142-09-00
There remains to be distributed,	153-08-06
Account allowed and order to distribute as follows:	
To Martha Gaylord, her dower, also	14-16-03
To Eleazer Gaylord, eldest son,	68-03-06
To Samuel, Martha, Elizabeth, Sarah and Hannah Gaylord, the rest of the children, to each of them,	34-01-09

And appoint Jonathan Elsworth and Ebenezer Fitch distributors.

Page 188.

Gibbs, Jacob, Windsor. Invt. £278-08-10. Taken 3 January, 1711-12, by Eleazer Gaylor, Samuel Forward and Samuel Strong.
Court Record, Page 62—3 March, 1711-12: Adms. to Abigail Gibbs, widow.
Page 1 (Vol. IX) 4 October, 1715: Abigail Gibbs, Adms., exhibits an account of debts.
Page 12—1st May, 1716: Abigail Gibbs, Adms., exhibits an account of her Adms., as follows:

	£ s d
Debts and charges,	95-01-07
Inventory,	278-08-10
Moveable part,	82-08-10
Remaining real estate to be distributed,	161-00-00

To Abigail Gibbs, to Jacob Gibbs, eldest son, to Ebenezer, John, Abigail, Elizabeth, Mary and Easter Gibbs, younger children. And appoint John Moore, Capt. Timothy Thrall and Mr. Israel Stoughton, distributors.
Page 117 (Vol. IX) 2 February, 1719-20: Ebenezer Gibbs, a minor

about 17 years of age, chose Nathaniel Hosford of Windsor to be his guardian.

Dist. File: 3 March, 1720-1: To Mrs. Abigail Gibbs, widow, to Jacob, to Ebenezer, to Abigail, to Esther, to Elizabeth, to John, and to Mary Gibbs. By Timothy Thrall and Israel Stoughton. Recorded in Windsor, 4th Book of Records, Fol: 297.

Page 23 (Vol. XI) 5 June, 1730: Report of the distributors.

Page 99.

Gilbert, Benjamin, Wethersfield. Invt. £288-15-06. Taken 29 January, 1711-12, by Edward Bulkeley, Jonathan Belding and Isaac Ryley.

Court Record, Page 50—4 February, 1713: Adms. is granted to Mary Gilbert, widow, and to Michael Griswold, Jr., son-in-law of sd. decd.

Page 109—7 February, 1712-13: Adms. allowed further time to finish their Adms.

Page 199 (Probate Side): A dist. and division of the estate of Benjamin Gilbert, late of Wethersfield, decd., among the heirs of the sd. deceased, and relict:

	£ s d
Imprimis. The inventory amounted to,	297-16-03
By debts paid out of the estate,	37-12-04

The remainder of sd. estate is divided as followeth:

	£ s d
To Mary Gilbert, the afore relict, in severable moveables,	23-05-06
To Michael Griswold, in right of Mary his wife,	25-08-04
To Hannah Gilbert, in several moveables,	24-08-01
To John Belding, Jr., in right of wife Kezia,	20-00-00

The real estate divided as followeth, allowing the widow the thirds of all the land's income:

	£ s d
To Michael Griswold, a piece of land in the Plain,	08-00-00
To four acres in Beaver Meadow,	16-00-00
To the right of lands willed our mother by her father, John Ryly,	10-00-00
To Hannah Gilbert, five acres of pasture land lying near to Ebenezer Dickinson,	25-00-00
To four acres in West Swamp,	10-00-00
To John Belding, two acres of land in Beaver Meadow,	08-00-00
The house and homestead, undivided,	75-00-00
And the lot in Beesett Plain, undivided,	12-00-00

These two last parcels, by agreement, belongs to Michael Griswold and Hannah Gilbert, to them and their heirs, equally to be divided between them when they see cause.

Lost of measure of the corn, being not so many bushels as accounted in the apprizement, and some spent,	06-02-00
	£297-16-03

NOTE: That before signing it is agreed that each party above named shall and may forever hereafter peaceably and quietly have, hold, occupy, possess and enjoy the several parcels of land, be the same more or less, as above, and their heirs and assigns after them. And John Belding doth by these presents quitclaim to all the estate left by Benjamin Gilbert above named other than what is set out to him by this division, being freed for all encumbrances as to paying any debts that hereafter may appear. And if any should appear, Michael Griswold, above named, and Hannah Gilbert, do agree to pay the same; and, if advisable, they mutually agree to give each other a quitclaim so as quietly to enjoy their rights as above.

In witness whereof they set to their hands the 1st of May, 1713.

> MARY GILBERT, LS.
> MICHAEL GRISWOLD, LS.
> HANNAH GILBERT, LS.
> JOHN BELDING, LS.

The foregoing is a true copy of the original. Examined and here recorded.   Pr. me,   *Thos. Kimberly, Clerk.*

Court Record, Page 137—4 May, 1713: Adms. exhibit now an account of their Adms., which this Court allow. Also, they exhibited, annexed to sd. account, an agreement made among themselves for a division of the estate. Allowed and proven.

Page 170.

Gill, John, Sen., Middletown. Invt. £285-03-00. Taken 19 May, 1712, by Samuel Hall, Nathaniel Savage and Ebenezer Smith. Also land within the bounds of Haverhill, in Massachusetts Province, valued at £70.

An agreement, signed 19 May, 1712: We whose names are underwritten do jointly and severally agree to the disposal made by our father John Gill of Middletown, decd., although not legally disposed, as followeth:

	£ s d
To Richard, the eldest son, a tract of land, 20 acres,	20-00-00
One piece of 4 acres,	3-06-08
To land in Haverhill, Mass.,	18-00-00
Personal estate,	6-15-00
To Joshua, second son, 20 acres valued at,	20-00-00
2 acres,	1-15-04
Land at Haverhill, Mass.,	18-00-00
Personal property,	2-08-00
To Ebenezer, 20 acres with buildings,	106-00-00
2 1-2 acres of land,	9-00-00
To John, land, 30 acres,	30-00-00
7 acres,	14-00-00
Personal estate,	2-00-00
To Judith the daughter, land at Haverhill,	30-00-00

In witness to this agreement we have set our hands.

RICHARD GILL, LS.
JOSHUA GILL, LS.
EBENEZER GILL, LS.
JOHN GILL, LS.
JUDITH GILL, LS.

Court Record, Page 80—2 June, 1712: Adms. granted to Ebenezer Gill his son, who, with his brother, Richard Gill, exhibit an inventory. Also they exhibit an agreement. Accepted and approved.

Page 232.

Gill, John, Jr., Middletown. Invt. £86-04-08. Taken 21st May, 1713, by Samuel Hall, Jr., Ebenezer Smith and John Gains. Will dated 25 April, 1713.

I, John Gill of Middletown, do make this my last will and testament: I give 1-4 part of my estate to my eldest brother Richard. I give to my 2 brothers, Joshua and Ebenezer, 1-4 part of the estate, equally to be divided between them. I give to my sister Judith 1-4 part of my estate. I give to my espoused friend Elizabeth Fox of Glastonbury 1-4 of my estate. It is my will that my brother Richard be sole executor.

Witness: *Samuel Hall, Jr.,*   JOHN GILL, LS.
Joseph Warner.

Court Record, Page 142—1st June, 1713: Will proven.

Page 184—5 April, 1714: Richard Gill, executor, now exhibited in Court an account of debts due from and paid out of the estate, which account this Court allow and order to be kept on file.

Page 81.

Gillett, Cornelius, Sen., Windsor. Invt. £44-07-06. Taken 27 July, 1711, by Samuel Moore and John Palmer. The children: Priscilla, Abigail, Cornelius, Mary, Hester, Sarah, Joanna and Daniel. (W. R.)

Will dated 2nd June, 1711: I, Cornelius Gillett, Sen., of Windsor, do make this my last will and testament: My will is that after my debts and funeral expenses be paid, all my personal or moveable estate shall be and remain to my wife Priscilla for her use and to her own dispose as she shall see cause, which I do give to her as her own. Whereas, I have made over my lands by deed of gift, excepting 4 acres at Wash Brook and 2 acres now in possession of John Grimes, my will is that whereas my son-in-law Joseph Phelps is become surety for my son Cornelius for a debt which he owes to Capt. Timothy Thrall, that the sd. 4 acres of marsh at Wash Brook shall be and remain to my son Joseph Phelps and to his heirs and assigns forever. And I do hereby give to him my sd. son Joseph Phelps, also, the 2 acres of land in John Grimes's possession. And I appoint my wife executrix.

Witness: *John Moore,*   CORNELIUS GILLETT, SEN.
    Sarah Enno.

Court Record, Page 37—3 September, 1711: Will proven.

Page 126.

Goffe, Aaron, Wethersfield. Invt. £101-08-06. Taken 1st March, 1711-12, by Jonathan Boardman and Joseph Grimes. Also, a piece of land near Pilgrim's Harbour, £30-00-00, prised by Samuel Peck and Samuel Hubbard. The children: Solomon, Aaron, Gershom and Samuel Goffe.

Court Record, Page 58—3 March, 1711-12: Adms. granted to Hannah Goffe, the widow.

Page 148.

Goffe, Moses, Wethersfield. Died 2 October, 1712. Invt. £335-12-06. Taken by Samuel Williams, Samuel Smith and Joseph Grimes. Will dated 30 September, 1712.

I, Moses Goffe of Wethersfield, do make this my last will and testament: I give to my son Jacob Goffe £10 over and above an equal share of my estate, real and personal, and to Benjamin, Ephraim and David, and my daughter Jerusha, my five above-named children, I give and bequeath unto them an equal proportion of my estate, real and personal, excepting the £10 first given. I make my son Jacob Goffe and my Cousin Philip Goffe executors.

Witness: *Gideon Belding,*   MOSES GOFFE, LS.
    Ebenezer Prout.

Court Record, Page 92—6 October, 1712: Will proven.

Page 137—4 May, 1713: Benjamin Goffe, a minor 17 years of age, son of Moses Goffe, chose John Rennolds of Wethersfield to be his guardian. Recog., £20.

Page 214—6 September, 1714: Ephraim Goffe, 15 years of age, son of Moses Goffe, chose his cousin Philip Goffe to be his guardian. Recog., £30.

Page 218—5 October, 1714: Jacob Goffe, executor, exhibits now an account of sundry debts due from the estate, and it appears that there is not sufficient moveable or personal estate to defray the just debts by the sum of £18, which account this Court allow.

Page 32 (Vol. IX) 7 May, 1717: David Goffe, a minor, appeared in Court and made choice of John Dyxx to be his guardian. Recog., £40.

Page 266.

Goodwin, Nathaniel, Sen., Hartford. Invt. £437-08-06. Taken 29
January, 1713-14, by John Skinner and John Marsh, Jr. Will dated 21
August, 1712.

I, Nathaniel Goodwine, Senior, of Hartford, do make and declare
this to be my last will: Imprimis. I have already given to my son Nathaniel, and I give him £7 more, current country pay, with the finest of
my weaving reeds. Item. Besides what I have given to my son John
already, I give to him and his heirs two acres of meadow lying on the
east side of the Great River, given to me by my father, with all my right
in the undivided lands on that same side of the Great River, appointing
him to pay to my son Nathaniel six pounds in current country pay. Item.
I give to the heirs of my son Samuel (besides what I have already given
to their father) and to their heirs, my lot lying in Brick Kiln Swamp, lying
between lands belonging to Joseph Gilbert and Samuel Church; and also
four acres of land at the Blue Hills, lying next to land I have given to my
son Nathanll. Item. I give to them all the charges I have been at and
money I have disbursed in building their father's house, provided they
make no demand of any debt of my executors upon the accompt of my
son Samuel's living and working some time with me after he was of the
age of twenty-one years. But provided the children of my son Samuel
(or any in their behalf) shall make any such demand as aforesaid of my
executor or executors, then my will is that my executors shall have the
aforesaid money I have disbursed in building my son Samuel's house to
the full, to answer any such demand, and the remainder of it to the forsaid
children. Item. I give to my loving wife Elizabeth the sum of fifty pounds
in current country pay, to be taken out of my movable estate at her choice;
and besides the lands given to her by her father, I give to her during her
natural life the use of one-half of my dwelling house, which part she shall
like best; also one-half of my orchard and one-third part of my barn with
one-third part of my land in the Neck or Souldiers' Field, the several
parts to be at her choice. Item. I give to my daughter Elizabeth the
sum of fifty pounds in current country pay, to be paid her within three
years after my decease. But if it shall happen that she shall marry before
the said three years be expired, then twenty-five pounds of the above-
mentioned fifty shall be paid her at her marriage. Item. I give to my
son Ozias my house and home lot, with all the outhousing thereon and
privileges belonging thereunto. Item. I give him all my land in the Neck
or Soldiers' Field. Item. I give him four acres of land lying at Blue
Hills, being part of the lot I bought of Goodman Cadwell. These severall
parcels of land, with the housing thereon, I give to my son Ozias and his
heirs forever, only reserving to his mother the use of that part of them I
have above given to her. Item. All the rest of my estate whatsoever I
give unto my son Ozias, appointing him to pay all the above-mentioned
legacies and all my just debts, excepting the £6 that my son John is to pay
to my son Nathaniel, and also except my second weaving reed, which I

give to my son John. Item. I do appoint my loving wife Elizabeth and my son Ozias to be executors.

Witness: *Timothy Woodbridge,*   NATHANIEL GOODWIN, LS.
    John Barnard.

Court Record, Page 175—1st February, 1713-14: Will proven.

Goodwin, Lois. Court Record, Page 64—4 March, 1711-12: This Court appoint Nathaniel Goodwin of Hartford, Jr., weaver, to be guardian to his daughter Lois Goodwin, a minor 16 years of age. And this Court also appoint Timothy Porter of Farmington guardian to Eunice Goodwin, 14 years of age, daughter of Nathaniel Goodwin, Jr.

Page 111.

Goodwin, Samuel, Hartord. Invt. £199-01-09. Taken 23 January, 1711-12, by Aaron Cooke and Robert Sandford.

Court Record, Page 52—5 February, 1711-12: Adms. to Mary Goodwin, widow, to Nathaniel Goodwin, a brother, and to Lt. James Steele.

Page 197 (Vol. X) 5 April, 1726: Samuel Goodwin, a minor son 15 years of age, chose Ozias Goodwin of Hartford to be his guardian.

Page 200—3 September, 1727: Nathaniel Goodwin, Adms., exhibited an account of his Adms., which is accepted by the Court and ordered to be kept on file.

Page 48.

Grant, Samuel, Carpenter, Windsor. Invt. £245-04-08. Taken 30 May, 1710, by Thomas Bissell, Sen., Job Drake, and Samuel Burnham.

Court Record, Page 13—5 June, 1710: Adms. granted to Grace Grant, widow, and Matthew Grant, a brother.

Page 116—12 February, 1712-13: Grace Grant and Matthew Grant, Adms., exhibit an account of their Adms:

	£ s d
Inventory,	294-19-00
Real part,	107-00-00
Paid in debts and charges,	87-16-00
There remains to be distributed,	150-03-00
Total,	257-03-00
To Grace Grant, widow,	50-01-00
To Samuel Grant, eldest son,	41-03-04
To Noah Grant, Ephraim, David and Ebenezer Grant, and Sarah Skinner, Hannah Morton, Abigail and Grace Grant, to each,	20-14-02

And appoint Capt. Thomas Stoughton and Samuel Rockwell distributors. And grant Grace and Matthew Grant a *Quietus Est.*

Page 266.

Graves, Thomas, Hartford. Invt. £51-10-11. Taken 29 January, 1713-14, by Samuel Sedgewick and William Taylor. Will dated 11 December, 1713.

I, Thomas Graves, of Hartford, do ordain this to be my last will and testament: I give and bequeath unto my wife all my estate, personal and real, actually possest by me, and whatsoever debts or legacies belong to me, under whatsoever consideration, I give and bequeath to her. Further, and notwithstanding what has been already exprest, tis my will that my only daughter, Deliverance, at 18 years of age (if she live to it), shall have two-thirds of my estate, and the whole if she survive her mother. I appoint my wife sole executrix.

Witness: *Benjamin Colton,*   THOMAS GRAVES, LS.
Samuel Sedgewick, Thomas X Morgan.

Court Record, Page 173—5 January, 1713-14: Inventory now exhibited by Sarah, the relict.

Page 78 (Vol. IX) 2 September, 1718: Whereas, letters of Adms. on the estate of Thomas Graves, late of Hartford, was granted unto Sarah Graves, widow, and sd. Sarah dying before she had made up and finished her account, this Court now grant letters of Adms. on sd. estate unto Thomas Morgan of Hartford, who is also appointed guardian to Deliverance Grave, his granddaughter, a minor.

Page 98—3 March, 1718-19: Thomas Morgan, guardian to Elizabeth Graves. Recog., £40.

Page 139.

Gridley, Samuel, Farmington. Invt. £823-15-02. Taken 30 May, 1712, by John Wadsworth, John Porter and Isaac Cowles.

Court Record, Page 72—5 May, 1712: Adms. granted to Mary Gridley, relict, and Joseph Gridley, a son.

Page 79—2 June, 1712: This Court appoint Samuel Porter, Isaac Cowles and Mary Gridley, widow, to be guardians unto the 4 youngest children of Samuel Gridley, late decd., viz., Nathaniel, Hezekiah, Daniel and Mary Gridley.

Page 95—3 November, 1712: Mary and Joseph Gridley of Farmington, Adms., exhibited an account of their Adms:

	£	s	d
Paid in debts and charges,	15	12	02
There remains of moveables,	389	09	00
To which add the real part,	418	14	00

	£ s d
There remains to be distributed,	808-02-00
To Mary Gridley, the widow,	129-16-03
To Samuel Gridley, eldest son,	148-10-04
To John, Joseph, James, Nathaniel, Hezekiah, Daniel and Esther Gridley alias Hart, to Sarah and Mary Gridley, to each,	79-03-02
By sd. account Thomas Gridley, 2nd son, hath already received of his father in his lifetime,	99-15-00

And appoint Mr. John Wadsworth, John Porter and Isaac Cowles distributors.

Page 30 (Vol. IX) 17 April, 1717: Mary Gridley alias Wadsworth, and Joseph Gridley of Farmington, Adms., exhibit account of their Adms., whereby it appears there is due from the estate:

	£ s d
To Mary Gridley alias Wadsworth,	3-13-05
To Joseph Gridley,	19-04
There remains in lands,	4-04-00
And in moveable estate not yet distributed,	42-04-06
Order dist. of remaining estate,	37-11-09
To Mary Gridley alias Wadsworth,	12-10-07
To Samuel Gridley, eldest son,	4-17-06
To John, Joseph, James, Nathaniel, Hezekiah, Daniel, Esther alias Hart, Sarah and Mary Gridley, to each	2-08-09

Thomas having already received his share of the estate. And appoint John Wadsworth, John Porter and Isaac Cowles distributors. And this Court grant the Adms. a *Quietus Est.*

Page 215 (Vol. X) 1st April, 1729: Whereas, it is represented to this Court that there is a parcel of land lying in the Parish of Southington belonging to Daniel Gridley, a minor, Capt. Wyllys, and the heirs of John Wadsworth, undivided: Upon motion in behalf of sd. minor to appoint some person to divide sd. land, this Court appoint John Porter of Farmington in behalf of sd. minor, with Mrs. Mary Wadsworth, his guardian, to divide sd. land accordingly.

Page 283.

Gridley, Samuel, Jr., Farmington. Invt. £199-08-11. Taken April, 1714, by John Wadsworth and Daniel Andrews, Sen.

Court Record, Page 193—3 May, 1714: Ruth Gridley of Farmington, widow, relict of Samuel Gridley of Farmington, Jr., decd., exhibited in this Court the last will and testament of the sd. decd., and moved to have the same approved and allowed. Thomas Gridley of Farmington, brother of the sd. decd., objected against the probate thereof, whereupon this Court deferred a further hearing and consideration thereof until the first Monday of June next. And the sd. Ruth Gridley exhibited an invt. of sd. estate, which invt. is ordered to be recorded and kept on file.

Page 197—7 June, 1714: Ruth Gridley of Farmington appeared now and prosecuted her former motion viz., for the probate of a writing (by her) pretended to be the last will of her last husband, Samuel Gridley, late of Farmington, Jr., decd. This Court having considered the several pleas for and against the sd. will, are of opinion that the same is illegal and don't contain the mind of the testator when of sound memory, and therefore do disallow and not approve the same. The sd. Ruth Gridley being disatisfied with this resolve, appealed therefrom unto the Superior Court to be holden at Hartford for the County of Hartford on the third Tuesday of September next, and the sd. Ruth Gridley acknowledged herself bound in a recog. of £10.

Page 230.

Griffin, Nathaniel, Simsbury. Invt. £58-01-02. Taken 12 March, 1712-13, by Jonathan Higley, Thomas Holcomb, Sen., and Thomas Griswold, Jr.

Court Record, Page 65—7 April, 1712: Citation to the brothers of Nathaniel Griffin to appear and take letters of administration, the relict having refused.

Page 74—5 May, 1712: Adms. to Thomas Griffin, a brother, and to Thomas Holcomb.

Page 27—4 October, 1714: May sell land by order of the General Assembly, £33-11-02 of value.

Invt. in Vol. IX, Page 44.

Griswold, Edward, Windsor. Invt. £427-08-02. Taken 5 March, 1715-16, by Thomas Griswold and Thomas Griswold, Jr.

Court Record, Page 261—2 August, 1715: Adms. granted to Joseph Barnard, brother-in-law to the deceased.

Page 7 (Vol. IX) 6 March, 1715-16: Joseph Barnard, Adms., exhibits an invt. of sd. estate.

Will and Invt. on File.

Hale, Mary, Glastonbury, Invt. £435-16-06. Taken 26 March, 1715, by Samuel Welles and Benjamin Talcott. Will dated 4 March, 1714:

I give to my son Jonathan the silver cup that was mine and a feather bed and furniture; I give also to Jonathan the land, orchard and plowland, with the appurtenances, that I bought of Joseph Hills, Sen., viz., upon this condition, that he keep and maintain my son Benjamin to school until such time as he shall be fit to go to a trade. To my son David

I give 4 score pounds and also the two-eared silver cup that was his father's, and one silver spoon, one dram cup, and the feather bed in the parlor and furniture to sd. bed. To my son Benjamin I give £100 and the silver tankard, one silver spoon, a silver dram cup, and the featherbed and furniture to sd. bed in the chamber over the parlor. To Samuel I give his father's cane and one of his father's coats, which he shall choose. To Mary I give my damask sute, and a great kettle that was her father's, and a great platter and a brass pan that was my mother's, and a pare of sheets and a silver spoon. To Ruth I give my silk crape sute, the bigest brass pan, and a pare of sheets. To my sister Steele I give my black russet sute, and it is my minde that she have the refusal of my share of my Uncle Lazarus' homelot. To Jonathan I give all the debts that are due to me upon condition that he, out of the same, pay all my just debts. I also give to Jonathan the use and benefit of what I give to Benjamin so long as he maintains sd. Benjamin to school. As for what shall remain of my estate after the above-mentioned have had what is particularly given to them, I do give it equally to be divided between my three sons, Jonathan, David and Benjamin.

That the above written is a true account of Mrs. Mary Hale giving and disposeing of her estate when she was, though weake of body, yet of sound minde, we whose names are underwritten do testify, this 15 February, 1714.   *Ruth Welles,*
                                        And Anne Steele.

This may inform whome it may concerne: that I do testifie and can witness to the whole of Mrs. Hale's manner of disposeing of her estate except that clause wherein yt is mentioned that Jonathan shall have the use of what his mother hath given to Benjamin so long as Jonathan doth maintain him at school.

Witness my hand: *Timothy Stevens.*

Court Record, Page 246—7 March, 1714-15: Jonathan Hale of Glastonbury now exhibits a writing said to be the last will and testament of Mrs. Mary Hale, his mother. Proven.

Page 251—2 May, 1715: This Court grant letters of Adms., with the will annexed, unto Benjamin Talcott and Samuel Hale of Glastonbury.

Page 21 (Vol. IX) 4 September, 1716: Mr. Benjamin Talcott and Samuel Hale, Adms., exhibited an account of their Adms,. which account contained a division and settlement of the estate among the legatees by them, made according to the will of the decd., which account is by this Court accepted. This Court grant the Adms. a *Quietus Est.*

Dist. per File, 4 September, 1716: The estate dist. as followeth:

	£ s d		£ s d
To Samuel Hale,	149-01-07	To Benjamin Hale,	162-17-06
To David Hale,	136-06-09		

Jonathan Hale hath already been paid more than his proportional part of sd. estate.

By Benjamin Talcott and Samuel Hale, distributors by agreement.

Page 189.

Hale, Phebe, Wethersfield. Invt. £02-10-06. Taken 5 June, 1712, by Benezer Hale and Thomas Couch.

Court Record, Page 82—7 July, 1712: Adms. to Thomas Dickinson of Glastonbury. Exhibit of inventory.

Page 139-40—7 May, 1713: Adms. account allowed. Order to distribute the estate to creditors.

Page 145—1st June, 1713: Adms. exhibits receipts from the creditors, and is granted a *Quietus Est.*

Page 88-101-159.

Hale, Samuel, Sen., Glastonbury. Invt. £1406-05-05. Taken 30 May, 1712, by Samuel Smith, Samuel Welles, Thomas Treat and Richard Smith, Sen. Will dated 23 February, 1708-9.

I, Samuel Hale, Sen., of Glastonbury, do make this my last will and testament: I give to my eldest son Samuel Hale land I bought of Josiah Wolcott, and all the messuages or tenements, with the outhouses, fruit trees and fences thereon, and all that my lot of land near a place called Nayog, containing 80 acres, and also my lot of land in the meadow in Wethersfield, containing 5 acres, which I bought of Stephen Hollister, reserving the use and improvement of the sd. 5 acres of meadow land unto and for my wife during all such terms as she shall remain my widow and no longer. I give unto his brother Jonathan, my son, all that my lot of land whereon I now live, being in Glastonbury, both meadow, swamp and upland, with the messuages, tenements, outhouses, fences, and all other the appurtenances thereof. Also, all that land lying in the Town of Wethersfield which I had, and have, and ought to have, for my wife's portion of the estate of her late father, Capt. Samuel Welles, decd., by division and distribution thereof, reserving the use for my wife during her natural life. I give to my son David Hale all that my lot of land lying in Glastonbury between the lots of Thomas Hale and Benjamin Talcott, about two acres more or less, which I bought of Joseph Welles. I give to Benjamin Hale, my son, all that my lot of land lying in Glastonbury which I bought of Mr. Bulkley; also, 2 1-2 acres in Wethersfield which I bought of Joseph Welles. I give to my daughter Mary Hale £15 in country pay and £5 lawful money. I give to my daughter Ruth Kimberly £15 country pay and £5 lawful money. I give to Eleazer Kimberly, my grandson. one good cow, and to Thomas and Samuel Kimberly, my grandsons, 2 good steers or heifers of 2 years old, one to each of them. I give to Mary Hale, my wife, the use of all my houseing and land reserved for her in this my will; also all the residue of my estate, that is to say, all my household goods, moneys, plate, stock of cattle and creatures, corn, clothing,

moveable estate, lands, goods, chattels, and all my estate whatsoever not
otherwise disposed of in this my last will and testament. I appoint my
wife executrix.

Witness: *Caleb Stanly, Jr.,*   SAMUEL HALE, SEN., LS.
          Thomas Bunce, Jr.

Codicil, dated 18 March, 1709-10, witnessed by Thomas Hooker and
Caleb Stanly.

Court Record, Page 41—19 December, 1711: Will proven.

Page 71—7 April, 1712: Mrs. Mary Hale, relict of Samuel Hale,
with her attorney, Mr. John Read, appeared before this Court and
moved that the sd. Mary Hale may have benefit of the law of the colony
as to title and dowries, and that she may be instated in one-third part of
the real estate. Mr. Thomas Kimberly objected, claiming a jointure was
a bar to the claim. Her attorney, John Read, admitted the paper, but
claimed it was not sufficient.

Page 85—4 August, 1712: Jonathan Hale, son of Samuel Hale,
decd., chose Capt. James Steele to be his guardian.

Page 88—1st September, 1712: Mrs. Mary Hale, widow, exhibited
now in this Court two receipts, which were signed, as she said, by Mr.
Samuel Hale and Mary Hale, son and daughter, which receipts did contain an account of some of the estate of sd. decd. delivered and paid to them,
and moved that the receipts be recorded and filed in the Records of the
Court, which this Court allow, provided the widow agree at the cost
thereof.

Page 149—16 July, 1713: Jonathan Hale, son of Samuel Hale, now
made choice of Benjamin Talcott to be his guardian. Recog., £50.

Page 248—7 March, 1714-15: David Hale, a minor son of Samuel
Hale, chose his brother Samuel Hale to be his guardian.

Page 21 (Vol. IX) 4 September, 1716: Benjamin Hale, a minor son
of Lt. Samuel Hale, decd., chose Samuel Hale to be his guardian. Recog.,
£200.

Page 135-188.

Hall, Elizabeth, Sen., Middletown. Invt. £18-09-00. Taken by Nathaniel Savage and Thomas Buck. Will dated 21 February, 1707-8:

I, Elizabeth Hall, of the Town of Middletown, do make this my last will
and testament: I give unto Samuel, my eldest son, a feather bed and
boulster and three pillows, a pewter platter, a couple of pewter pots containing a half a pint, a brass chafing dish, half of my books except my
Bible, and half of my silver cup, agreeing betwixt themselves vizt., Samuel and Thomas, who shall possess the cup, he that hath the cup paying
the other half of the value of the cup in money. I give to my son Samuel a silver dram cup. I give to Elizabeth, the daughter of my son John,
decd., £3 in money, obliging my son Thomas to pay the money; also a
pare of fine Holland sheets, and also a silver spoon. I give to Thomas,

my youngest son, a bed and a blanket and 3 pare of sheets, a great iron kettle and a little iron kettle, and an iron pot, also a small brass kettle, and a brass candlestick, also a cow, an equal share and part of my books with my son Samuel, in particular my Bible, also a silver spoon and a small bell-metal skillet. I make my son Samuel executor.

Witness: *David Deming,*   ELIZABETH HALL, LS.
     Margaret Sage.

Court Record, Page 52—4 February, 1711-12: Will exhibited by Samuel Hall.
Page 77—2 June, 1712: Will proven.

Page 112.

Hall, Capt. John, Middletown. Invt. £735-06-06. Taken 28 January, 1711-12, by Samuel Hall, Joseph Rockwell and Thomas Foster. Will dated 23 November, 1711.

I, John Hall, Sen., of Middletown, do make this my last will and testament: I give to my son Daniel, besides what I have already made sure to him by deed of gift, all my movable estate, both within doors and without. That is to say, all my stock of what name so ever, with all my bedding, pewter, brass, iron, tin, chairs, tables, and all other household goods excepting two young horses of mine in the woods that came of my son Jacob's breed, of which I give to my son Richard the eldest of them and to my son Giles the other. All these I give, with these exceptions, to my son Daniel: he to pay to my wife, his mother-in-law, £6 per annum in currant silver money, or provisions at money price, so long as she lives a widow; and to my son Jonathan's daughters £10 to each of them within one year after they shall be married; and also provide and give to my wife a mourning suit; as also 5s to each of my son John's two daughters as soon as I shall decease. Item. I give to my other two sons, Richard and Giles, all my lands on the east side of the Great River, in Middletown, to be equally divided between them, they paying all my just debts that are not above specified to be paid by my son Daniel. Item. I give to my grandson Samuel, son of my son Richard, all that land in Wallingford that of right doth belong to me. Also, my will is that my beloved wife shall have what room and cellaridge she shall desire in my dwelling house during her widowhood. And further, my will is that my three sons, Richard, Giles and Daniel, be joint executors.

Witness: *John Hamlin,*   JOHN HALL, LS.
William Russell, Noadiah Russell.

Court Record, Page 54—4 February, 1711-12: Will proven.

Page 135.

Hall, John, Jr., Mariner, son of Capt. John Hall of Middletown. Invt. £147-04-04. Taken 1st March, 1711-12, by John Collins, John Bacon and Giles Hamlin.

Court Record, Page 37—3 September, 1711: Adms. granted to William Ward and Frances his wife, late widow of sd. decd.

Page 54—5 February, 1712: This Court grant letters of Adms. to William Ward, guardian to a minor daughter of John Hall, decd., and Samuel Lewis of Durham, in the County of New Haven, in his wive's right, provided they the sd. William Ward and Samuel Lewis do give bond as the law requires.

Page 58—3 March, 1711-12: Exhibit of an inventory.

Page 101—1st December, 1712: The Adms. now appeared before this Court and exhibited an account of their Adms.

	£ s d
Paid in debts and charges,	6-02-08
There remains to be distributed, of moveable estate,	2-09-10
And of the real estate,	138-11-10
To Frances Ward of Middletown, formerly Frances Hall,	16-07-00
The remainder to be divided equally between Elizabeth Lewis	
and Mary Hall, two daughters of John Hall, mariner,	
to each of them the sum of,	70-02-07

And appoint John Hamlin, Esq., and Capt. Thomas Ward, of Middletown, distributors.

Invt. in Vol. IX, Pages 43 and 107.

Hand, Esther, Guilford. Invt. £162-02-06. Taken 2 April, 1715, by William Ward, Joseph Rockwell, and George Phillips.

An Agreemt for the Settlemt of the Estate of Esther Hand, Deceased:

Articles of agreement, made this 2nd day of April, 1716, between Janna Hand of Guilford, in the County of New Haven and Colony of Connecticut, in New England, and his sister Esther Hand of sd. Guilford, single woman, concerning the division of the lands which falls to them by descent from their mother (they being the only son and daughter of Joseph Hand of sd. Guilford, decd., by his wife Esther, who was daughter of John Willcock of Middletown, decd.):

Witnesseth: That the sd. Janna Hand and Esther Hand do hereby agree and conclude that the sd. Janna shall have a tract of land lying at Middletown, at a place commonly called the Northwest Quarter, containing about 133 acres more or less; and also one tract of land in sd. Middletown lying on the east side of the Great River, being a part of a lot commonly called The Half-Mile Lot, containing 7 1-2 acres; and also 180 acres upon the south side of the tract of land lying in sd. Middletown on the east side of the Great River, the whole lot containing about 600 acres.   And the sd. Esther shall have the remaining part of the sd. lot of 600 acres last mentioned, being 420 acres more or less, on the north side of sd. lot.

In witness of and for confirmation of the above sd. agreement, the said Janna Hand and Esther Hand have hereunto set their hands and seals this 2nd day of April, 1716.

Witness: *Joseph Belding,*   JANNA HAND, LS.
       Josiah Willard.   ESTHER HAND, LS.

Court Record, Page 246—4 April, 1715: Adms. granted to Janna Hand, eldest son of the decd.   He also exhibits an account of such part of the estate as lies in this County.

Page 10 (Vol. IX) 3 April, 1716: Janna and Esther Hand of Guilford, children of Esther Hand, late of Middletown, exhibited now in this Court an instrument in writing, under their hands and seals, for the division and settlement of the estate of sd. decd., which this Court doth confirm.

Page 98.

Will on File.

Handerson, Martha, Hartford.   Invt. £16-09-06.   Taken 30 February, 1711-12, by Edward Allyn and Joseph Hopkins.   Will dated 22 September, 1699.

I, Martha Handerson, of Hartford, do make this my last will and testament: I give to my son James Handerson my house and house lot where I now dwell, and my land in ye Neck, all my lands in Hartford that I now stand possessed of, to be to him ye sayd James Handerson and his heirs forever.   My will is that my son shall not sell nor alienate ye house or house lot herein given him until he attain the age of twenty-one years or more.   But ye land in ye meadow I desire he will sell as soon as possible hee can, to pay Mrs. Wilson a debt I owe her.   The looms and all the tackling to be to my son James Handerson.   In case my son James shall not live to attain the age of 21 years, then I give my sd. house and home lot to my three daughters, namely, Miriam Orvice, Mary Wright and Sarah Handerson, to be divided equally; always provided, my will is, that if my daughter Mary Wright does not come and dwell, makeing her settled abode within this Collony within the time abovesaid, then neither she nor her heirs to receive any partt in my house and land as expressed, but to be equally divided between my other two daughters, Miriam Orvice and Sarah Handerson, and their heirs forever.   I will that my son James Handerson pay each of his sisters, namely Elizabeth Hadlock, Miriam Orvice and Mary Wright, 5 shillings.   They have received considerable already.   I appoint my son James Handerson executor.

Witness: *Edward Allyn,*   MARTHA X HANDERSON.
      Rachel Allyn.

Court Record, Page 54—5 February, 1711-12: Sarah Handerson of Farmington cited to appear and take Adms., James Handerson having refused the executorship.

Page 64—4 March, 1711-12: Defer the probate of the last will and testament of Martha Handerson until the next Court.

Harris, Ephraim, Hartford. Court Record, Page 121—3 March, 1712-13: This Court grant letters of Adms. on the estate of Ephraim Harris, late of Hartford, decd., unto William Harris, a brother of sd. decd.

Page 140—7 May, 1713: This Court now grant Adms. unto Capt. Cyprian Nickolls and James Ensign of Hartford, William Harris neglecting to take out letters of Adms.

Page 211.

Harris, Mary, Single Woman, late of Middletown, daughter of Thomas. Invt. £142-05-09. Taken 28 January, 1712-13, by Thomas Ward and William Ward.

Court Record, Page 107—6 January, 1713-14: Adms. granted to Daniel Harris, uncle of the sd. decd.

Page 187—6 January, 1714: Daniel Harris, Adms., exhibits an account of his Adms: Paid in debts and charges, £10-15-06. Order the estate dist. to the heirs, and appoint Capt. Thomas Ward, Lt. Samuel Hall and Sergt. William Ward, distributors.

Dist. File: 5 April, 1714: To Samuel Harris, to William, to John Harris, to Samuel Cadwell, Jr., his daughter Thankfull Cadwell, to the heirs of Elizabeth Honeywell, to Hannah Savage. By Thomas Ward, William Ward and Samuel Hall.

Page 197—7 June, 1714: Report of the distributors.

Invt. in Vol. IX, Pages 30-1-2-3. Agreement on File.

Hart, Capt. John, Farmington. Invt. £1096-06-07. Taken 4 February, 1714-15, by John Wadsworth and Daniel Andrews.

Court Record, Page 223—6 December, 1714: Adms. granted to Mary Hart, widow, and John Hart, eldest son.

Page 234—18 January, 1714-15: This Court appoint Mrs. Mary Hart of Farmington to be guardian to Nathaniel, Matthew and Mary Hart, minor children of Capt. John Hart, decd.

See File: A dist. of the estate of Capt. John Hart, made by the widow and heirs, as followeth:

	£	s	d
To the widow (with 1-3 of lands during life),	74	02	12
To John Hart, eldest son,	262	03	02

	£ s d
To Isaac, Samuel, Nathaniel and Matthew Hart, to each,	107-16-00
To Sarah Hart, alias Steele,	101-12-06
To Mary Hart, youngest daughter,	65-14-04

Signed: MARY HART, LS.

Witness: *Samuel Gridley,*   JOHN HART, LS.
         Thomas Norton.   ISAAC HART, LS.
                        SAMUEL HART, LS.
                        NATHANIEL HART, LS.
                        MATTHEW HART, LS.
                        EBENEZER STEELE, LS.
                        MARY HART, LS.

Page 239—7 March, 1714-15: Mary Hart of Farmington, relict, John, Isaac, Samuel, Nathaniel and Matthew Hart, and Ebenezer Steele and Mary Hart, children of John Hart, exhibit now an agreement for a division of the estate. Mary Hart, as guardian to Nathaniel, Matthew and Mary Hart, all acknowledged the agreement to be their free act and deed.

Page 226.

Hayden, Daniel, Windsor. Invt. £134-16-02. Taken 30th April, 1713, by Nathaniel Gaylor, Daniel Bissell and Benajah Holcomb.

Court Record, Page 135—4 May, 1713: Adms. granted jointly to William and Samuel Hayden, sons of the sd. decd.

Page 165—17 November, 1713: Daniel Hayden, Samuel Hayden, Ebenezer Hayden and Miriam Hayden, widow, relict of William Hayden, exhibit an account of their Adms.:

	£ s d
Inventory,	154-01-10
Paid in debts and charges,	116-00-00
There remains to be distributed,	152-05-00
To Daniel Hayden,	11-00-07
Also to Daniel, 1-3 of the lands, which is,	16-03-04
To the heirs of William Hayden,	1-04-07
Also to them, 1-3 of the lands, which amounts to,	16-13-04
To Samuel Hayden, including lands,	28-08-00
To Ebenezer, including lands,	28-11-03
To Hannah Hayden,	50-00-00

Page 260.

Hayden, William, Windsor. Died 3 July, 1713. Invt. £326-03-08. Taken by Nathaniel Gaylord, Daniel Bissell and Israel Stoughton.

Court Record, Page 152—3 August, 1713: Adms. to Mrs. Miriam Hayden, relict of said deceased.

Page 167—4 January, 1713-14: Exhibit of inventory.

Page 73 (Vol. X): Miriam Bissell, alias Heydon, widow of sd. decd., Adms. on the estate of her 1st husband, exhibits account of Adms: Invt. was £325-15-08; of this £101-17-11 was of moveable estate, and by the marriage with her second husband Josiah Bissell, late decd., before distribution the moveables had been carried into sd. Bissell's estate. In order to distribute this Heyden estate, his children's part was to be sought for in the Bissell estate, that each child, viz., Miriam, Mary and Elizabeth Heyden, should each have £22-12-10 of moveable estate, and their mother, now Miriam Bissell, widow, should have £33-19-03 in moveables if so much could be found after the children's part was made up. Of the real estate, to each of the children, £72-08-08, including the widow's thirds after her decease. Dist. by Jonathan Elsworth, Daniel Bissell and Ebenezer Heydon. The Court appoint Daniel Bissell to be guardian to Miriam Heydon, age 17 years, and Mary Heydon, age 15 years. Also appoint Miriam Bissell to be guardian to her daughter, Elizabeth Heydon, age 13 years.

Page 103—5 October, 1725: Report of distributors.

Page 144. (Invt. on Page 15, Vol. IX.)

Hayes, Luke, Farmington. Invt. £19-17-00. Taken 7 July, 1713, by Joseph Root and John Porter. Will dated 20 October, 1712.

The last will and testament of Luke Hayes: I, Luke Hayes of Farmington, do make this my last will and testament: I give to my brother-in-law, Joseph Langton, all the remaining estate that I received of and by my former wife, sister to sd. Joseph Langton. I give all the rest of my estate, real and personal, to Lt. John Stanly and Lt. Samuel Wadsworth, to be to them and their heirs forever. And appoint Lt. John Stanly and Lt. Samuel Wadsworth to be my sole executors.

Witness: *Samuel Whitman,*   LUKE HAYES, LS.
John Wadsworth, Joseph Root.

Court Record, Page 94—3 September, 1712: Will now proven.

Page 105—5 February, 1712-13: Mrs. Maudlin Hayes, the widow, was bound by a recog. of fifty pounds by John Hooker, Esq., to appear in Court to answer interogations touching estate of her late husband, Luke Hayes, decd.

Page 154—17 August, 1713: Will now exhibited in Court by the executors, and praying this Court to approve, when John Hart, atty. for Mrs. Maudlin Hayes, widow, declared himself aggrieved, and that some of the articles in the inventory did not belong to the said estate, and appealed to the Superior Court.

Page 168—4 January, 1713-14: Capt. John Hart of Farmington, being bound over to this Court by the worshipfull John Hooker to answer to charges of concealing some part of the estate of Luke Hayes, decd., now appeared and was examined upon oath accordingly. These interrogations and answers were ordered to be kept upon file. Maudlin Hayes of Farmington, widow, being bound over to this Court to answer to some further interrogatories touching the estate of her late husband, Luke Hayes, and the said Maudlin Hayes being sick and not able to appear before this Court, it is therefore ordered, that the said Maudlin Hayes shall appear before the Worshipfull Thomas Hart and John Hooker of Farmington, Esqrs., Justices of the Peace and Quorum, on the second Monday of this instant January.

Page 261.

Haynes, John, Esq., Invt. £3330-13-08. Taken in Hartford, 12th January, 1713-14, by Joseph Talcott, Hezekiah Wyllys and John Skinner. Part of his Invt:

	£ s d
In apparrel, money, rings and silver seal,	58-06-00
Tankard, £16; salver, £5; new spoons, 28 shillings,	22-08-00
Spoons and dram cup, £6-12; wrought cup, £5; salt cellar, £4;	
silver tumbler, £3-10-00,	19-02-00

Court Record, Page 162—20 November, 1713: The Honourable Judge Haynes being departed this life and the General Justices being met, they made choice of the Honourable William Whiting to preside.

Page 177—8 February, 1713-14: Adms. granted to Mrs. Mary Haynes, widow, relict of sd. decd.

Page 95 (Vol. IX), 3 February, 1718-19: Mrs. Mary Haynes, widow, relict of John Haynes, late decd., is appointed to be guardian to Mary Haynes, 15 years of age, daughter of sd. decd.

Haynes, Miss Mabell. Court Record, Page 172—5 January, 1713-14: Rev. James Pierpont, of New Haven, moving this Court that Adms. upon the estate of Miss Mabell Haynes, late of Hartford, single woman, deceased, might be committed to some suitable person or persons as the law directs, this Court order that the Clerk forthwith shall issue forth notification to Mrs. Mary Haynes of Hartford, widow, relict of the Honll. John Haynes, late of Hartford, Esq., deceased, who was brother of the sd. Mabell Haynes, decd., that she appear before this Court on the first Monday of February next ensuing, and show reason (if any she hath), why Adms. should not be granted or committed.

Page 176—8 February, 1713-14: Rev. Mr. James Pierpont, by his attorney, Mr. John Read, now presented his former motion to this Court, whereupon Adms. is granted to Mrs. Abigail Pierpont of New Haven, single woman, who is niece to the said decd.

Page 55.

Hibbard, Robert, Sen., Windham. Invt. £264-07-08. Taken 24 May, 1710, by Joshua Ripley, Richard Hand, Jonathan Crane and Richard Hendee.

Court Record, Page 19—2 October, 1710: Adms. to Robert and Joseph Hibbard. Sarah Hibbard and Abigail Hibbard of Windham, daughters of Robert Hibbard, Sen., decd., have each of them made choice of Jonah Palmer of sd. Windham to be their guardian, which this Court allow and approve.

Page 20—6 November, 1710: Adms. account allowed and approved. Order to distribute the estate: To the Widow Mary Hibbard, £32-01-00 for her own, and her thirds use of real estate during life; to Robert Hibbard, £37-01-10; to Joseph and Nathaniel Hibbard, to each £14-00-01; to Ebenezer Hibbard, £11-00-11; and to Mary Crane, £17-14-11; to Martha Culver, £17-00-11; and to Hannah, Sarah and Abigail Hibbard, to each, £23-00-11. And this Court do appoint Mr. Joshua Ripley, Deacon Joseph Carey and Mr. Samuel Webb distributors.

Page 230—3 January, 1714-15: Jonah Palmer of Windham, guardian to Abigail and Sarah Hibbard of Windham, before this Court produced receipts proving that what estate of the sd. minors was put into the sd. guardian's hands he had delivered and paid unto the sd. minors, now of full age. The Court discharge Jonah Palmer from his trust of guardianship.

Record on file (Robert Hebard, Sen., estate): Widow, Mary X Hibbard: to Robert, to Joseph, to Nathaniel, to Ebenezer, to Jonathan Crane, Jr., and Mary his wife, to Ephraim Culver of Lebanon and Martha his wife, and to Hannah, Sarah and Abigail Hebbard. By Joseph Carey, Samuel Webb and Joshua Ripley.

Page 45.

Hide, Timothy, Hartford. Invt. £186-13-06. Taken 27 January, 1710, by Thomas Hosmer and Josiah Clark. Will dated 7 April, 1710.

I, Timothy Hide of Hartford, do make this my last will and testament: I give unto my uncle and aunt, Caleb Watson and Mrs. Mary Watson, six acres of meadow land in the south meadow in Hartford, which I bought of my uncle Thomas Olcott and Mr. John Olcott by deed of May 25, 1705, which I received from my said uncles, to be to them the sd. Caleb Watson and Mrs. Mary Watson and their heirs forever. Also, the use of 13½ acres of land bought of my uncles, Thomas Olcott and John Olcott, during their natural lives. Also, I give to my uncle Caleb Watson and my aunt Mary Watson my shop, looms and appurtenances, and all of my movable estate whatsoever. And after their decease I give to my uncles, Thomas Olcott and John Olcott, the 13½ acres of land to be divided equally between them the said Thomas Olcott and John Olcott, and to their heirs forever. I appoint my uncle and aunt, Caleb Watson and Mrs. Mary Watson, to be executors.

Witness: *John Harris,*   TIMOTHY HIDE, LS.
John Bunce.

Court Record, Page 14—5 June, 1710: Will proven.

Will and Invt. in Vol. IX, Page 41-42.

Higley, Capt. John, Simsbury. Invt. £605-00-07. Taken 30 September, 1714, by James Cornish and John Slater. Will dated 6 May, 1714.

Imprimis: I give unto my loving wife Sarah 1-3 part of my moveable goods and housing stuff and utensils thereto belonging, to be at her disposal as she sees cause to dispose of them to my children by her; also, I give her that third part of moveables of her former husband's (Joseph Bissell) estate which is yet undivided. I likewise give unto her the 1-3 part of this my real estate here in Simsbury, with the use of my now dwelling house, during the term of her natural life, or as long as she continueth my widow. And if she be married again, she shall be allowed by my executor £6 a year for the third of my real estate during life, to be disposed of among my children by her. Item. I give to my eldest son John Higley a double portion out of my whole estate; and to the rest of my sons, Jonathan, Brewster, Joseph, Samuel, Nathaniel, Josiah and Isaac, to each of them a single portion out of my whole estate. Item. I give unto my daughters, Katharine, Anna, Elizabeth, Mindwell, Sarah, Susannah and Abigail, to each of them half so much as each of my sons, excepting John, out of my estate. Item. My will further is, that my sons shall have all my lands, they paying to their sisters what is wanting of the moveables to make up their portions. Item. All the lands which I have at Windsor, which came by my first wife, I give to my five eldest sons which I had by her, an equal share, they paying to their eldest sisters twenty shillings to each. Item. I give my wearing apparel unto my youngest sons, Nathaniel, Josiah and Isaac. I appoint my sons John Higley and Samuel Higley executors.

Witness: *John Case,*   Signed: JOHN HIGLEY, LS.
Thomas Holcomb, Robert X Hoskins.

Court Record, Page 218—5 October, 1714: The will of John Higley exhibited. Proven.

Page 10 (Vol. IX) 3 April, 1716: Nathaniel Higley, a son of Capt. John Higley, late of Simsbury, about 16 years of age, chose his uncle Samuel Strong to be his guardian. This Court appoint Capt. Thomas Moore guardian to Isaac Higley, 8 years of age; and Sarah Higley appointed guardian to Abigail Higley, 12 years of age, son and daughter of Capt. John Higley.

Page 24—2 October, 1716: The executors are cited to appear in Court.

Page 70—21 June, 1718: This Court order that the real estate be dist. according to the will, and appoint (on motion of Thomas Moore and Samuel Strong, guardian to three of the children) Ebenezer Fitch and William Phelps of Windsor, and John Case of Simsbury, distributors.

Page 100—9 March, 1718-19: The executors now exhibit an account, which this Court accept.

Page 102—7 April, 1719: This Court now order distribution of the estate, first deducting £33-02-00 paid to the widow, and the sum of £101-14-11 due from the estate, the remainder to be distributed to children and heirs of sd. decd.

Page 142—6 December, 1720: Whereas, the distributors have not yet perfected their distribution to the satisfaction of the legatees, they move that other persons may be appointed to make distribution, whereupon the Court appoint Thomas Holcomb and Richard Case distributors.

Page 15 (Vol. X) 2 April, 1723: Samuel Higley, one of the executors of the last will of Capt. John Higley, late of Simsbury, decd., exhibited account that the estate of sd. decd. is yet further indebted the sum of £10-13-00; and whereas there is a parcel of land described in the distribution of sd. estate left to defray debts and charges, which this Court thinks needful to be done: This Court do direct sd. Samuel Higley, executor, to make sale of sd. parcel of lands, etc., for paying debts and charges due from sd. estate.

Page 43—3 March, 1723-4: Isaac Higley, 17 years of age, chose Sarah Higley, his mother, to be his guardian.

Page 48—5 May, 1724: Brewster Higley appeared before this Court and desired an appeal from an act of this Court, 2 April, 1723, directing the executors of the last will of Capt. John Higley to make sale of a parcel of land, part of the estate of sd. decd.

Page 82—4 May, 1725: Samuel Higley, one of the executors of the last will of Capt. John Higley, late of Simsbury, decd., exhibited a further accot. of charge arisen on sd. estate amounting to the sum of £5-03-10. Allowed by this Court and ordered to be added to the former charge, the whole being £18-02-05. And likewise the sd. executors exhibited an addition unto the estate of the sd. decd. that has not been distributed, prised at the sum of £23-06-03. Accepted and ordered to be kept upon file.

Will and Invt. in Vol. IX, Page 40.

Higley, Joseph, Simsbury. Invt. £11-17-10. Taken 31 August, 1715, by Samuel Griswold and Jonathan Westover. Will dated 21 December, 1714:

I, Joseph Higley of Simsbury, do dispose of my estate as followeth: I give and bequeath all my estate, both real and personal, of every kind, quality or specie whatsoever, and in all parts and places wheresoever the same shall be or may be coming or belonging to me from my father's estate by his last will and testament to me or my own proper estate, to my brothers John Higley and Brewster Higley, they to be executors.

Witness: *Timothy Stanly,*   JOSEPH HIGLEY, LS.
    Thomas Judd, John Southmayd.

Court Record, Page 263—2 August, 1715: John Higley and Brewster Higley, executors, exhibited now the will of Joseph Higley. Proven.

Inventory on File.

Hills, Benjamin, Jr., Tailor. Invt. £86-18-11. Taken 4 November, 1712, by Samuel Welles and Timothy Cowles.
Court Record, Page 97—21 November, 1712: Adms. granted to Joseph Keeney, Sen., of Hartford.
Page 100—1st December, 1712: Exhibit of an inventory.

Page 91.

Hills, Ebenezer, Doctor, Hartford. Invt. £108-03-07. Taken 21 December, 1711, by Samuel Welles, Thomas Kilbourn and Hezekiah Porter.
Will dated 4 December, 1711: I, Ebenezer Hills, now resident of Hartford, practicioner of physic, do make this my last will and testament: I give unto my Cousin Dorothy Hills, daughter to Lt. Jonathan Hills, now of sd. Hartford, my bed, bedsted, one pare of sheets, boulster and convenient blanketing, also the curtains and valiences. I give unto my relations (vizt., unto the heirs of Lt. Samuel Hale, late of Glastonbury, decd.; the heirs of John Hale, late of sd. town, decd.; the heirs of Nathaniel Hunn, late of Wethersfield, decd.; the heirs of Caleb Benjamin, late of sd. Town, decd.; to Thomas Hale, Sen., now of Glastonbury; Ebenezer Hale of Wethersfield, and the sd. Lt. Jonathan Hills) an equal share of the rest of my estate, either lands, goods or chattells whatsoever, my lawful debts being first paid. The remainder, being divided into 7 equal parts, I dispose of it to them as aforesd. I appoint my friend Thomas Kimberly of Glastonbury executor.

Witness: *Joseph Tryon,*   EBENEZER HILLS, LS.
    Joseph Hollister.

Court Record, Page 41—19 December, 1711: Will proven.

Page 257.

Hills, Joseph, Sen., Glastonbury. Died 8 November, 1713. Invt. £386-04-06. Taken by Samuel Welles, Richard Smith, Sen., and William Wickham.

Will dated 2 May, 1713: I, Joseph Hills of Glastonbury, do make this my last will and testament: I give unto Joseph Hills, my son, 100 rods in length of my upper lot which I bought of John Coleman. I give unto Benoni Hill part of that upper lot in Glastonbury. I give unto my daughter, Hannah Keeny, and to my daughter Susannah Kilbourn, to each 10 shillings money. I give unto my daughter Dorothy Hollister £6 money. With respect to the children I now have or hereafter may have by my present wife Elizabeth, my will is that they have, hold and enjoy that lot of land whereon I now dwell, with the buildings, fences and trees thereupon (which lot of land I made over to my sd. wife by way of jointure before my marriage with her, in that tenure that the remainder thereof should be to the children that I should happen to have by her). I give to my wife Elizabeth Hill the use and improvement of all my lands until the children come to age to receive them. I give unto my wife, whom I appoint sole executrix, the whole of my moveable estate in goods and chattells, etc. I give unto my son Henry Hill the remaining part of my upper lot joining to my son Joseph Hill.

Witness: *Thomas Welles,*   JOSEPH HILL SEN., LS.
   Thomas Kimberly.

Court Record, Page 163—7 December, 1713: Will proven. Joseph Hill, being dissatisfied, appealed to the Superior Court.

Page 283.

Hitchcock, Samuel, Waterbury. Died 22 October, 1713. Invt. £188-00-06. Taken by John Judd and Thomas Hitchcock.

Court Record, Page 188—5 April, 1714: Citation to Elizabeth Hitchcock, widow, relict of Samuel Hitchcock, decd., to appear and take Adms. on sd. estate if she please.

Page 197—7 June 1714: Adms. granted to Elizabeth Hitchcock, widow, who exhibited an inventory.

Page 12 (Vol. IX) 3 April, 1716: Elizabeth Hitchcock, Adms., exhibits in this Court an account of her Adms.:

	£ s d
Inventory,	188-00-06
Moveable part,	63-04-06
Paid in debts and charges,	53-03-06
There remains to be distributed,	135-17-00
To the widow,	3-13-08
Ebenezer Hitchcock,	31-04-00
To John, Gideon, Hannah, Elizabeth, Sarah and Silence Hitchcock, to each of them,	16-12-00

And appoint John Hopkins, William Hickcox and Joseph Lewis, of Waterbury, distributors.

Page 25—1st January, 1716: John Hitchcock, age 20 years, son of Samuel Hitchcock, late decd., chose Capt. Thomas Judd to be his guardian.

Page 123—5 April, 1720: Report of the distributors.

Invt. in Vol. IX, Page 13.

Hodge, James, Wethersfield. Invt. £36-15-03. Taken 30 January, 1712-13, by John Goodrich and James Patterson.

Court Record, Page 120—12 February, 1712-13: Adms. granted to Thomas Kircum of Wethersfield.

Page 215—6 September, 1714: Thomas Kircum, Adms., exhibits an account of his Adms., which this Court accepts.

Page 93.

Hollister, John, Sen., Glastonbury. Invt. £79-06-09. Taken 1st April, 1712, by Thomas Hale, Nathaniel Talcott and Samuel Hale. Will dated 22 November, 1711.

Know all men by these presents: That whereas, I, John Hollister, Sen., of Glastonbury, being sick, do make this my last will and testament: My will is that what I have already settled upon my sons, viz., John, Thomas, David and Ephraim Hollister, shall be the whole of what I shall give to each and every of them of my estate. What I have settled upon my daughter Sarah shall be the whole of her portion of my estate. What I have given my son Joseph Hollister and settled upon him, together with the seven acres of exchanged (lands), the which I do hereby give and bequeath to him, shall be the whole of what he shall have of my estate. I give to my daughter Elizabeth Hollister, single woman, all my moveable estate, a certain parcel of land and all that part of the estate of my late brother Lazarus Hollister that may fall to me by law, and also what belongs to me of my late brother Joseph Hollister's estate, all to be to her and to her heirs forever.

Witness: *Daniel Andrews,*   JOHN HOLLISTER, SEN., LS.
Thomas Kimberly.

(No executor.)

Court Record, Page 41—19 December, 1711: Joseph Hollister exhibits will and asks to have it proven. John Hollister, Jr., objects.

Page 44—7 January, 1711-12: Adms. to Joseph Hollister (there being no executors appointed). John Hollister, the eldest son, appealed to the Superior Court from the order of the Court with respect to the probate of the will.

Page 66—7 April, 1712: Invt. exhibited and allowed.

Page 88—1st September, 1712: This Court allow Elizabeth Hollister, daughter of the deceased, Adms. with Joseph Hollister, her brother, joyntly, with the will annexed.

Page 40.

Hollister, Stephen, Capt., Wethersfield. Invt. £133-17-05. Taken 30 March, 1710, by Thomas Welles, Sen., James Steele and Thomas Chester.

Court Record, Page 2—2 January 1709-10: Adms. granted joyntly to Elizabeth Hollister, the relict, and Ebenezer Seamour of Farmington, son-in-law of sd. decd.

Page 9—3 April, 1710: Nathaniel Hollister, 8 years of age, son of Stephen Hollister, late of Wethersfield, chose Capt. Thomas Wells to be his guardian.

Page 10—3 April, 1710: Samuel Hollister, 15 years of age, son of Stephen Hollister, chose John Curtis, Jr., of Wethersfield, to be his guardian.

Page 12—1st May, 1710: Adms. exhibit an inventory of the estate of Stephen Hollister.

Page 17—3 July, 1710: This Court now grant Adms. unto Elizabeth Hollister, widow, and Jonathan Hollister of Wethersfield. And this Court do order that Ebenezer Seamour, who was appointed Adms. on sd. estate with the sd. Elizabeth, do render and deliver to sd. Elizabeth and Jonathan Hollister all the money, goods, moveables, bills of credits, books and accompts and estate whatsoever belonging to the sd. decd. that he hath taken into his hands, for the speedy payment of the debts of the decd., and also that he do make a true and plain account of his transactions upon the sd. estate unto this time.

Page 23—6 November, 1710: This Court order and direct Elizabeth Hollister and Jonathan Hollister, Adms., to sell the dwelling house and homelot of the sd. decd., of about 25 acres, to Capt. Robert Welles or him that shall be the best bidder for the same, to produce effects wherewith to pay the debts due from sd. estate to the creditors thereof, according to an act or order of the General Assembly, 11th May, 1710.

Page 24—1st January, 1710-11: This Court order that the Clerk issue forth a writ to cite Elizabeth Hollister and Jonathan Hollister and Ebenezer Seamour, Adms., to appear before this Court on the 1st Monday of February next and render an account of their Adms. thereon, and how they have disposed of the sd. estate hitherto.

Page 27—5 February, 1710-11: Ebenezer Seamour of Farmington, late one of the Adms., being summoned, appeared before this Court and rendered an account of his Adms. thereon, whereby it appears that he hath received into his hands of the moveable part of the estate, £31-09-06. Paid in debts and charges, £16-09-00. And now paid to Jonathan Hollister, present, Adms., £1-07-06. There remains in his hands the sum of

£13-13-00. The Court order him to deliver the above-named sum to Jonathan and Elizabeth Hollister, Adms., and bring the receipt to this Court and take his *Quietus Est.*

Page 68—7 April, 1712: Ebenezer Seamour, late Adms., having made evidence to this Court that he ought to be allowed 20 shillings more in his Adms. account, this Court do now allow the same in the sd. account. This Court appoint Samuel Wolcott of Wethersfield to be guardian to Gershom Hollister, a minor son of Stephen Hollister, decd.

Page 75—5 May, 1712: Eunice Hollister, 17 years of age, daughter of Capt. Stephen Hollister, chose Ebenezer Deming to be her guardian.

Page 81—3 June, 1712: This Court order the Clerk to issue forth a writ to cite Elizabeth Hollister to appear before this Court 1st Monday of July next, to render an account of her transaction relating to that estate. This Court order and direct Elizabeth Hollister and Jonathan Hollister, Adms., to sell the 2 acres of land that yet remain not sold to Capt. Robert Welles.

Page 154—7 August, 1713: Elizabeth Hollister of Wethersfield, widow, exhibits an account of her Adms. and subscribed by the sd. Elizabeth, and also by Elizabeth Hollister, widow, relict of Jonathan Hollister, who was late Adms. with the sd. former Elizabeth, by which account it appears has paid to the creditors £118-16-10, which amounts to more than the inventory of the moveable estate with the produce of the land and houseing of the sd. estate sold. Account allowed. And now grant the sd. Adms. a *Quietus Est.*

Page 117 (Vol. IX) 2 February, 1719-20: This Court appoint Elizabeth Hollister to be guardian to Anne Reynolds, one of her children. Recog., £50.

Page 122—1st March, 1720: Daniel Hollister, age 19 years, son of Stephen Hollister, late of Wethersfield, chose Ebenezer Seamour to be his guardian. Recog., £50.

Page 58 (Vol. X) 3 November, 1724: Stephen Hollister, a minor 16 years of age, chose Samuel Goff of Wethersfield to be his guardian. Recog., £50.

Page 119—1st March, 1725-6: This Court appoint Mrs. Elizabeth Hollister to be guardian unto her son Stephen Hollister, a minor.

Page 79.

Hollister, John, Jr., Wethersfield. Invt. £30-15-00. Taken 2 July, 1711, by Thomas Treat and Thomas Kimberly. Will dated 13 September, 1710.

I, John Hollister, if I should not live to return home again, I give to my brother Thomas Hollister all that is mine; and if I live to return home again, he shall return it all to me again. (No executor.)

Witness: *Thomas Cole,*   JOHN HOLLISTER.
John Taylor.

Court Record, Page 35—2 July, 1711: Adms. to Thomas Hollister, with the will annexed.

Inventory on File.

Hollister, Jerusha, Wethersfield. Invt. £5-12-00. Taken by William Goodrich and John Francis.

Court Record, Page 21—6 November, 1710: This Court grant Adms. on the estate of Jerusha Hollister, daughter of Capt. Stephen Hollister, late of Wethersfield, decd., single woman, unto Capt. Thomas Welles.

Page 83—3 June, 1712: Thomas Welles of Wethersfield, Adms., exhibits now an invt. of Jerusha Hollister's estate, and this Court grant him a *Quietus Est.*

Invt from File. Recorded on Page 11, Vol. IX. Invt. of Lands, Vol. X, Page 242.

Hollister, Jonathan, Wethersfield. Lost at sea in the year 1712. Invt. £241-15-08. Taken 24 June, 1714, as money, by Philip Goff, Jr., and Joseph Grimes. The children: Jonathan, 15 years, Jacob 10, Stephen 6, Elizabeth 12, and Mary 2 years old. Lands of the decd. apprised as followeth:

	£ s d
To a dwelling house and 5 acres, with an orchard on it,	55-00-00
To 4 1-2 acres lying next to it, at £10 per acre,	45-00-00
To 3 1-2 acres lying over Hog Brook,	24-10-00
To 4 acres of meadow land,	80-00-00
To 49 acres and 33 rods,	42-00-00
To right of land lying on the east side of Rocky Hill,	00-10-00
To 1 1-2 acre of land taken out of Jacob Crane's lot adjoyning to the home lot, prised at £6,	06-00-00
Total,	£253-00-00

Taken by Samuel Williams and Joseph Grimes.

Court Record, Page 195—3 May, 1714: Elizabeth Hollister, widow, is appointed guardian to all of the children of the sd. Jonathan Hollister that are under 14 years of age.

Page 40 (Vol. X) 3 March, 1723-4: Whereas, it hath been represented to this Court that it is necessary that the lands of Jonathan Hollister should be anew apprised in order for an equal dist., the Court appoint Joseph Graham, Samuel Williams and Joshua Robbins apprisers. This Court appoint William Nott to be guardian unto Jacob Hollister, a minor 19 years of age. Recog., £50.

Page 44—27 March, 1724: Elizabeth Hollister, Adms., exhibits an account of her Adms., which was accepted. Order to dist. the estate:

	£ s d
To Elizabeth Hollister,	10-05-05
To Jonathan Hollister, eldest son,	91-03-06
To Jacob, Stephen, Elizabeth and Mary Hollister, to each,	45-11-09

And appoint Ephraim Goodrich, Joseph Graham and Jonathan Curtice, dist.

Page 52—4 August, 1724: Report of the distributors.

Page 50 (Vol. XVII) 7 January, 1755: Jonathan Lattimer, of Simsbury, showeth to this Court that he has land in Wethersfield, in right of his wife Mary, that lies in common or joynt tenancy with Elizabeth the wife of Samuel Goff, of sd. Wethersfield, and Jacob Hollister, a minor son of Jonathan Hollister, both deceased, and moves to this Court that freeholders may be appointed to assist in dividing sd. land so as that the sd. minor, by his guardian, and the other owners may improve their parts separate. Whereupon this Court appoint and impower Elisha Williams, Jr., Thomas Boardman and Timothy Wright of Wethersfield to divide sd. lands.

Page 113.

Holton, Mrs. Sarah, Widow, Hartford. Invt. £220-00-09. Taken 4 January, 1711-12, by Ciprian Nickols and John Bunce. Will dated 24 December, 1711.

I, Sarah Holton, of Hartford, do make this my last will and testament: I give to my granddaughter, Mary Strong, 3 parts; to Hannah Strong, 2 parts; and Esther Strong, 1 part of all my real and personal estate that is not otherwise disposed of, to them and to their heirs forever. I give to Mahumah Stebbin the 40-acre lot in Lebanon. I give to my brother, Josiah Marshfield, my husband's cloak. I give to Mr. Joseph Bradford, whom I appoint my executor, my husband's best hat.

Witness: *Edward Allyn,*   SARAH X HOLTON, LS.
         John Allyn.

Court Record, Page 44—7 January, 1711-12: Will now exhibited by Mr. Joseph Bradford of Lebanon. Proven.

Page 113.

Holton, William, Hartford. Will dated 16 December, 1711.

On the Sabbath Day of the 16th of November, 1711, Mr. William Holton sent for me and I went to him, and then he called me to his bedside and said he sent to me to desire me to be helpfull to him what I could in his sickness, and said to me: "I have had thoughts to settle my estate by a written will, but have neglected it; and it being Sabbath Day, I shall say as little as possible. But for fear I should be out in my head, as many

persons are, and so be not of a capacity to do it, I desire you and Sister
Sadd to take notice that I do make my will in short as follows: My dear
wife had been with me at the getting and keeping of what God hath given
me, and I do desire and my will is that she shall have all my estate, both
real and personal, for her own, and to be at her dispose as she shall see
good, as fully and well as if I had disposed more particularly myself of it.
I have sold my living at Lebanon for £360 and have taken a mortgage of
the farm for security, and so she will be sure of the money on the farm,
also what I have here in Hartford. And as for stock, I have put it off;
only my horse and 3 pounds worth in sheep I sold to Snow, but received
nothing for them. I say all my estate of what nature or kind soever I do
freely and fully give to my wife and her heirs forever. But in case my
wife shall die without a will, what she has not disposed of before she die
my will is that my granddaughter, Mary Strong, shall have 3 parts of all
my estate that is not disposed of to my wife, and my granddaughter Hannah Strong shall have two parts, and my granddaughter Esther shall
have one part, to be to them and their heirs forever."
Witness: *Edward Allyn,*
Mrs. Sadd, Mehumahne Stebbins.

Also, Mr. Holton said he had 40 acres of upland for which he was
proffered £40.
I, Hepzibah Sadd, testifie to the substance of the above-written will.
Hepzibah Sadd.
I, Mehumahne Stebbins, testifie with Mrs. Sadd.
Mehumahne Stebbins.

Court Record, Page 43—7 January, 1711-12: Mr. Joseph Bradford
of Lebanon exhibited the last nuncupative will of Mr. Holton, decd., and
Edward Allyn and Mehumahne Stebbins, two of the witnesses, testifie in
Court. And this Court grant Adms. unto Joseph Bradford, with the will
annexed.

Page 157.

Hooker, Nathaniel, Hartford. Invt. £2424-06-02. Taken 8 Febru-
ary, 1711-12, by Samuel Kellogg and Edward Allyn.
Court Record, Page 43—7 January, 1711-12: Adms. to Mary
Hooker, widow.
Page 65—7 April, 1712: Exhibit of inventory, which is allowed.
Page 172—5 January, 1713-14: Mrs. Mary Hooker having married
a stranger, Mr. Nathaniel Stanly (who was on her bond) was not willing
to continue bondsman, whereupon he was appointed Adms., but did not
give bond. Adms. was now granted joyntly to Mr. John Austin and
Mary, his wife, who was the widow, relict of the said deceased.
Page 25 (Vol. IX) 4 December, 1716: John Austin, Adms., moved
this Court that Abraham Morrison of Wethersfield, Adms. on the estate

of Joseph Crane, late of Wethersfield, be not discharged because of a pending suit at law.

Page 155 (Vol. X) 2 May, 1727: The Adms. on the estate of Nathaniel Hooker, late of Hartford, decd., now in this Court accounts of their Adms. by which accounts and the invt. of the estate it appears that the whole of the estate, real and personal, amounts to the sum of £2451-10-02, and that out of the moveable estate there is paid in debts and charges, etc., £630-00-09. There remains of moveable estate, £935-19-05. Adding the real part, the sum total to be distributed is £1821-09-05, which accounts the Court do allow and order dist. to Mary Austin alias Hooker, relict of the sd. decd., £311-19-09 out of the moveable estate, which is 1-3 part thereof, to be her own forever, and 1-3 part of the houseing and lands of sd. decd. for her improvement during life; and the rest and residue of the sd. estate to be dist. to Nathaniel Hooker, only son, £500-03-04, which is his double portion of sd. estate; to Alice Hooker alias Howard, Sarah Hooker and Abigail Hooker, the rest of the children of sd. decd., to each of them, £251-11-07, which is their single portion of sd. estate. And appoint John Hooker, Esq., of Farmingtown, Capt. Thomas Seymour and Deacon Daniel Merrells, both of Hartford, distributors.

Page 197—6 August, 1728: Report of distributors.

Invt. in Vol. IX, Page 33.

Hopson, John, Colchester. Invt. £441-08-08. Taken 28 March, 1714, by Nathaniel Dunham and Israel Wyatt.

Court Record, Page 190—14 April, 1714: Adms. granted to Elizabeth Hopson, the widow.

Page 215—4 September, 1714: This Court appoint Jonathan Northam, of Colchester, guardian to Mary Hopson, age 10 years, and John Hopson, age 7 years, children of John Hopson.

Page 230—3 January, 1714-15: Jonathan Northam, guardian to the abovesd. children, appeared with his father, Samuel Northam, and recog. in £100.

Page 238—7 March, 1714-15: Elizabeth Hopson, Adms., exhibited now an account of her Adms. Accepted. Order to dist. the estate among the surviving heirs, vizt.: To Elizabeth Hopson, widow, £40-13-08; to John Hopson, eldest son, £174-09-08; to Mary Hopson and Elizabeth Hopson, daughters, to each, £87-04-10. And appoint Thomas Skinner, Samuel Loomis and Israel Wyatt, distributors.

Page 257—7 June, 1715: This Court orders the worshipful Michael Taintor of Colchester to call before him Ebenezer Day and James Roberts of Colchester, to interrogate them of what they know relating to the estate of John Hopson, particularly of a parcel of Indian corn.

Page 260—5 July, 1715: Elizabeth Hopson, Adms., was cited to appear in Court upon the motion of Jonathan Northam, in order to a review of the accompt of her Adms. Joseph Root, her father Corning, and Joseph Chamberlin and lawyers abated their accounts, and the estate is credited for advance in the sale, £3-00-00.

Page 261—2 April, 1715: Elizabeth Hopson, Adms., now moved that whereas the Court did sometime order dist. be made, and pursuant thereunto she did deliver to Jonathan Northam, guardian to two of the children, considerable part of that estate (near £40) as part of sd. children's portion, that the sd. estate so delivered may by an order of this Court be returned into her hands, seeing this Court hath since reversed their sd. order by divers decrees. This Court order that Jonathan Northam forthwith, upon demand of Elizabeth Hopson, deliver sd. estate without fail.

Page 8 (Vol. IX) 6 March, 1715-16: Elizabeth Hopson, Adms., exhibits now a further account of debts and charges. This Court now order the remaining part of sd. estate to be dist: The real estate to be to the widow, to the eldest son a double portion, and to the rest of the children a single portion. And appoint Michael Taintor, Lt. John Skinner, of Colchester, and Samuel Palmer, of Hebron, distributors.

Page 68—10 June, 1718: This Court appoint Thomas Day of Colchester to be guardian unto Elizabeth Hopson, daughter of John Hopson, late decd.

Page 213 (Vol. X) 22 February, 1728-9: An addition of the estate of John Hopson was now exhibited in Court by John Hopson, it being a piece of boggy meadow of 5 acres, valued at £3 per acre, which addition this Court accepts.

Page 115.

Hopkins, Ebenezer, Hartford, Invt. £403-15-08. Taken 28 December, 1711, by Joseph Bull, Hez: Wyllys and Daniel Merrells.

Court Record, Page 42—19 December, 1711: Adms. to Mary, the widow, and Joseph Hopkins, brother of the deceased.

Page 149 (Vol. IX) 4 April, 1721: Mrs. Mary Hopkins, Adms., exhibits an account of her Adms.:

	£	s	d
Paid in debts and charges,	55-12-10		
Inventory,	433-15-08		
Subtracting,	55-12-10		
There remains to be distributed,	378-02-10		
To Mary Hopkins, widow,	18-10-08		
To Jonathan, eldest son,	89-18-00½		

To Ebenezer, Stephen, Hezekiah, Isaac, Mary and Sarah
Hopkins, to each of them,   44-19-00¼
And appoint Nathaniel Stanly, James Ensign and Jonathan Butler, distributors.

Page 150.

Hopkins, Joseph, Hartford. Died 3 November, 1712. Invt. £193-18-08. Taken 26 November, 1712, by Robert Sandford and Nathaniel Goodwin, Jr.

Court Record, Page 96—6 November, 1712: Adms. granted to Hannah Hopkins, the widow, and Samuel Sedgewick.

Page 221—6 December, 1714: Capt. Samuel Sedgewick and Hannah Porter, Adms., exhibit an account of their Adms:

	£ s d
Have paid in debts and charges,	123-05-10
Inventory,	350-09-09
There remains to be dist. of real estate,	246-00-00
To Hannah Porter, late Hannah Hopkins, widow (dowry in lands).	
To Joseph Hopkins, eldest son,	52-13-04
To Mary, Hannah, Dorcas and Ruth Hopkins, to each,	41-06-08

And appoint John Shepherd, Thomas Richards and James Ensign, distributors. This Court appoint John Porter of Hartford to be guardian to Mary Hopkins, 15 years of age, Hannah 12, Dorcas 10, Ruth 8, and Joseph 4 years, children of Joseph Hopkins, decd. John Porter and Samuel Sedgewick recog., £200.

Page 37 (Vol. X) 4 February, 1723-4: This Court appoint Thomas Hopkins of Hartford to be guardian to Dorcas Hopkins, a minor 18 years of age. Rec., £50.

Page 38—4 February, 1723-4: Thomas Hopkins, as guardian unto Dorcas Hopkins of Hartford, minor, moved to this Court that her former guardian John Porter of Hartford may be accountable for his guardianship to sd. minor. Order by this Court, that the sd. John Porter have liberty the 1st Tuesday of March next to make up his account of guardianship with sd. minor's guardian; but if he should neglect to do the same within sd. time, that then he appear at this Court on the sd. 1st Tuesday in March and render an account of his sd. guardianship, upon the forfeiture of his recognizance.

Court Record, Page 38—4 February, 1723-4: Whereas, Thomas Hopkins of Hartford, having purchased the right of Mary Harris and Anna Hopkins, two of the heirs of Joseph Hopkins, late of Hartford, decd., in and unto the houseing, barn and lands of the sd. decd. lying together in Hartford, bounding south on highway, west on the land of the sd. Thomas Hopkins, north on the land of John Bunce, and east on the land of James Handerson; and whereas, there hath never yet been any distribution of the sd. estate set out by meets and bounds so that the heirs may have their proper parts and portions, and the sd. Thomas Hopkins as a purchaser, and also as guardian to Dorcas Hopkins, daughter of the sd. decd., moved to this Court that the sd. houseing, barn and land may be laid out by meets and bounds, that the heirs may know their parts: This Court appoint Lt. Thomas Seymour, Sergt. James Ensign and Mr.

John Whiting of Hartford to distribute and divide, by meets and bounds, the sd. parcel of land and buildings thereon erected, to the relict of the sd. decd., her dowry therein for her improvement during life, and to the heirs according to former distribution made in value, vizt., to the sd. Thomas Hopkins in right of Mary Harris and Hannah Hopkins, both to the value of £50-06-08; to Dorcas Hopkins, to the value of £20; to Ruth Hopkins, to the value of £29-13-04.

Page 39—3 March, 1723-4: Report of the distributors.

Page 119.

House, John, Glastonbury. Invt. £135-03-06. Taken 23 January, 1711-12, by Joseph Smith, Joseph House and Abraham Fox.

Court Record, Page 47—4 February, 1711-12: Adms. to Eunice House, widow, and Joseph House, a brother of the deceased.

Page 99—1st December, 1712: Eunice House now exhibits an account of her Adms., which is accepted by the Court, and this Court grant her a *Quietus Est.* This Court appoint Eunice House to be guardian to her children: Eunice House, 8 years, Sarah 7, John 3, and Silence one year old. Recog. £100, with Richard Fox.

Page 132 (Vol. X) 5 July, 1726: Eunice House, alias Keeny, Adms., exhibited an account of the Adms.: Paid in debts and charges, £28-06-08; the invt., £133-07-06; subtracting £28-06-08, there remains, £105-00-10 to be distributed. Order to the sd. Eunice House, alias Keeney, relict of sd. decd., £11-07-07, with dower; John House, eldest son, £37-09-03, which is his double portion of sd. estate; to Eunice, Sarah and Silence House, the rest of the children of sd. decd., to each of them, £18-14-08, which is their single portion of sd. estate. And appoint Thomas Wells, Benjamin Talc————————nd Jonathan Hale, of Glastonbury, distributors.

Page 152—2 May, 1727: Report of distributors.

Inventory on File.

Howard, Benjamin, Windsor. Died 11 December, 1711: Invt. £28-04-00. Taken by Return Strong, Simon Chapman and James Enno.

Court Record, Page 42—19 December, 1711: Adms. granted to Mary Howard, sister of sd. decd. Exhibit of an inventory.

Inventory on File.

Hunnewell, Elizabeth, Middletown. Invt. £68-18-01. Taken 26 July, 1712, by William Harris and John Harris.

Court Record, Page 23—4 December, 1710: Adms. granted unto John Honeywell, son of sd. decd.

Page 84—7 July, 1712: Whereas, John Honneywell has gone out of this Colony and is absent at sea, and hath not finished his Adms. on sd. estate, this Court now grant Adms. unto Samuel Williams of Wethersfield, who married one of the daughters of sd. decd.

Page 87—4 August 1712: Exhibit of an inventory.

Page 145—1st June, 1713: Samuel Williams of Wethersfield, Adms., ordered to sell land to the highest bidder, to produce £11 current money for the payment of just debts.

Page 150—6 July, 1713: Samuel Williams exhibits now an account of his Adms:

	£ s d
Has paid in debts and charges,	17-17-05
Produce of the land sold,	52-00-00

Order to dist. to John Hunnewell, eldest son, a double portion, and to each of the two daughters a single portion. And appoint Joseph Rockwell, Sergt. William Ward and Mr. Joseph Starr, distributors. And this Court grant Samuel Williams a *Quietus Est.*

Dist. File: August, 1713: To John, only son; to Elizabeth Williams, a daughter of the sd. decd.; to Bridget Hunewell, youngest daughter. By John Rockwell, William Ward and Joseph Starr.

Page 216—4 October, 1714: Report of the distributors.

Page 86 (Vol. VII) 5 August, 1706: Bridget Hunewell of Middletown, 15 years of age, daughter of John Hunewell, late of Middletown, made choice of her uncle Isaac Johnson to be her guardian.

Inventory on File.

Humphries, Nathaniel, Hartford. Invt. £10-15-06. Taken 22 November, 1711, by Thomas Hosmer and Richard Saymore.

Court Record, Page 44—7 January, 1711-12: Adms. granted to Agnes Humphries, widow of sd. decd.

Page 100—1st December, 1712: Agnes Humphries, Adms., granted longer time to finish her Adms.

Invt. in Vol. IX, Page 34.

Humphrey, Thomas, Simsbury. Invt. £211-06-05. Taken 17 November, 1714, by Joseph Case and Samuel Pettebone.

Court Record, Page 246—4 April, 1715: Adms. granted to Hannah Humphrey, the widow.

Page 50 (Vol. IX) 4 February, 1717-18: Whereas, Adms. was granted to Hannah Humphrey, and she neglecting to take letters of Adms., this Court now grant letters of Adms. on sd. estate to James Cornish, present husband of the widow of sd. decd.

Page 50 (Vol. X): Thomas Humphrey of Simsbury, a minor 15 years of age, chose his uncle Samuel Humphrey to be his guardian. Recog., £50.

Page 123—14 March, 1726-7: The Adms. exhibited now an account of his Adms. Accepted. Order to dist. the estate:

	£ s d
To Hannah Cornish, alias Humphrey,	38-08-07
To Thomas Humphrey, only son,	59-18-06
To Damaris Pettibone, Hannah and Martha Humphrey, to each,	29-19-03

And appoint Joseph Case, Lt. Samuel Humphrey and Samuel Humphrey distributors.

Page 125—5 April, 1726: This Court having formerly appointed James Cornish of Simsbury to be guardian over Martha Humphrey, a minor, and no sufficient bond taken, the sd. James Cornish and James Hillier of Simsbury acknowledged themselves joyntly and severally in a recog. of £200.

Page 137—1st November, 1726: Report of the distributors.

Page 275.

Hungerford, Thomas, Haddam (East). Invt. £278-00-06. Taken 5 February, 1713-14, by John Willee, John Smith and Thomas Clarke.

Will dated 11 January, 1713-14: I, Thomas Hungerford, of Haddam, do dispose of my estate as followeth: I give to my wife Mary Hungerford all my buildings; also certain land joyning Abell Willee's land, during life. I give to my son Thomas Hungerford's eldest son Thomas one-half of my interest in lands in Stonington which descended to me from my father; also one-half-part of my fourth division on the east side of the Eight-Mile River. I give to my son John Hungerford and his male heirs my buildings and the whole of my 180-acre allotment, after my decease, excepting what I have given to my wife during her life. I give to my son Green Hungerford one-half part of my interest in lands in Stonington; also one-half part of my fourth division allotment east of 8-mile river; also all my right in Moodus Meadow upon the Falls River. I give unto my 5 daughters, viz., Elizabeth, Susannah, Sarah, Mary and Esther, the remainder of my personal estate. I give to my grandson John all my rights in Lyme and the undivided lands.

Witness: *Stephen Hosmer,*   THOMAS HUNGERFORD.
Daniel Brainard, Daniel Cone.

Court Record, Page 186—5 April, 1714: Will proven. Adms., with will annexed, to Thomas Hungerford, son of the deceased.

Page 209.

Hunn, George, Wethersfield. Invt. £19-18-06. Taken 1st January, 1712-13, by Josiah Churchill and Thomas Wright.

Court Record, Page 104—15 December, 1712: Adms. granted to Samuel Hunn, a brother.

Page 184—5 April, 1714: Adms. account now exhibited and allowed. This Court grant a *Quietus Est.*, and order the remaining estate to be put in to the widow's hands for the support of herself and her children.

Page 145 (Vol. X) 3 January, 1726-7: Joseph Hunn, a minor 17 years of age, appeared before this Court and desired to make choice of a guardian; and this Court being informed that sd. minor is apprentice unto Thomas Wyard of Wethersfield, do order that sd. Wyard be notified by a copy hereof to appear before this Court on the 1st Tuesday of February next, if he see cause, to show why the sd. minor may not have a guardian appointed to put him out to learn a trade.

On the 7th day of January, 1726-7, Joseph Hunn of Wethersfield, a minor 17 years of age, now appeared before this Court and made choice of Mr. Elizer Goodrich of sd. Wethersfield to be his guardian, which this Court do allow and approve of, and the sd. Elizer Goodrich acknowledged himself bound in a recog. of £50 to the Judge of this Court and his successors that he will faithfully discharge the trust of guardianship unto sd. minor according to law.

Page 220—3 June, 1729: This Court appoint David Forbes of Hartford to be guardian unto George Hunn, a minor 18 years of age. Recog., £50.

Page 1 (Vol. XI) 15 July, 1729: George Hunn, 18 years of age, now made choice of Samuel Hunn to be his guardian. Recog., £50.

Page 215.

Hunn, Nathaniel, Sen., Farmington. Invt. £75-15-10. Taken 7 December, 1712, by Hezekiah Deming, John Stoddar and John Root.

Will dated 4 December, 1712: I, Nathaniel Hunn, Sen., of Middletown, do ordain this to be my last will and testament: I give to my wife a third of my houseing and land during life, and then to return to my son Nathaniel. All the rest of my land I give to my son Nathaniel. All my moveable estate to be divided equally among my children, only my wife to have a third part of them. I make my wife executrix, and desire Stephen Lee and Thomas Curtis to be my overseers.

Witness: *Stephen Lee,*   NATHANIEL X HUNN, LS.
     Thomas Curtis.

Court Record, Page 118—2 March, 1712-13: Martha Hunn now exhibited the last will of her late husband, Nathaniel Hunn. Proven.

Page 183 (Vol. X) 30 May, 1727: Nathaniel H————, minor, of about 8 years, before this Court made choice of ————hn Root of Farmington to be his guardian.

Johnson, Mrs. Mary. Court Record, Page 91—6 October, 1712: Notification to Samuel Birchard of Coventry to appear at the next Court and take Adms. on the estate of Mary Johnson, widow, late of Coventry, decd.

Page 97—6 November, 1712: This Court appoint Nathaniel Rust and David Lee of Coventry to take account of the estate of Mary Johnson, widow, late of sd. Coventry, decd., and also to the estate of the children, and transmit to this Court. Mr. Richard Edwards allowed to be guardian unto Mary Douglas, alias Smith, a minor daughter of Mary Johnson.

Pages 59 and 143.

Johnson, William, Coventry. Invt. £53-03-08. Taken 4 November, 1710, by David Lee and Nathaniel Rust. Additional invt. of that part of the estate as came to the hands of John Stedman, Adms., £36-09-06. Taken 23 April, 1712, by Nathaniel Rust and Benj: Carpenter.

Court Record, Page 21—6 November, 1710: Adms. to Mary Johnson, widow of sd. decd.

Page 37—3 September, 1711: John Stedman of Wethersfield to be guardian to the only daughter of William Johnson, late of Coventry, decd.

Page 62—3 March, 1711: Adms. on the estate of William Johnson, late of Coventry, decd., to John Stedman of Wethersfield. (Mary Johnson, widow, relict, to whom Adms. was granted on sd. estate, is now departed this life, not having finished her Administration thereon.)

Page 81—2 June, 1712: John Stedman, Adms., exhibits an invt. This Court appoint Richard Edward to be guardian unto Mary Douglas, alias Smith, daughter of Mary Johnson, late of Coventry, decd., sd. minor being 9 years of age.

Page 98—1st December, 1712: John Stedman exhibits an account of his Adms. Allowed.

Page 134—7 April, 1713: John Stedman, Adms., is granted a *Quietus Est.*

Page 176.

Jones, Caleb, Hebron. Invt. £201-10-09. Taken 16 January, 1711-12, by Samuel Curtis and Stephen Post.

Court Record, Page 68—7 April, 1712: Adms. to Rachell Jones, widow relict. Exhibited inventory.

Page 207—15 July, 1714: Rachel Phelps of Enfield (formerly Rachel Jones of Hebron), Adms. on estate of Caleb Jones, late of Hebron, decd., now exhibits account of her administration. Allowed. Order to dist. the estate: To Rachel Phelps (who was) widow relict, to Caleb Jones, eldest son, to Sylvanus Jones, to Hezekiah, and to Mary Jones Lord of Saybrook, 38 ackers. (See file.) By John Elsworth, Matthew Grant and Job Elsworth.

Page 231—3 January, 1714-15: Report of distributors exhibited now by Israel Phelps of Enfield, and granted a *Quietus Est.*

Page 49.

Judd, John (son of William), Farmington. Invt. £381-02-02. Taken by Thomas Porter, Samuel Judd and Isaac Cowles.

Court Record, Page 13—5 June, 1710: Adms. to Rachell Judd, widow, and Daniel Judd, a brother of the deceased.

Page 47—4 February, 1711-12: Mrs. Rachel Judd, widow of John Judd, appointed guardian to her children, with the advice of John Wadsworth.

Page 185—5 April, 1714: Daniel and Rachel Judd, Adms., exhibited an account of their Adms. Accepted. And this Court grant the Adms. a *Quietus Est.*

Page 37 (Vol. IX) 2 July, 1717: Rachel Judd now being dead and not having finished her Adms., this Court grant Adms. unto Samuel Judd and direct him to finish the same. This Court appoint Capt. Thomas Judd of Waterbury to be guardian unto William Judd, a minor; and Samuel Judd appointed guardian unto Rhoda Judd of Farmington, children of John Judd. Recog., £100.

Page 40—23 July, 1717: Whereas, Samuel Judd, Adms., exhibited now an account of his Adms., and there being no debts due from the estate, this Court decree to distribute:

	£ s d
To Samuel Judd, as Adms. on Rachel Judd's estate,	39-10-09
To William Judd,	165-15-07
To Eunice Judd and Rhoda Judd, to each of them,	82-17-00

And appoint Deacon John Wadsworth, Capt. Ebenezer Steele and John Hart, Jr., of Farmington, distributors. This Court appoint Daniel Judd of Farmington to be guardian unto Eunice Judd, daughter. Recog., £40.

Page 101—7 April, 1719: Whereas, John Judd, son of William Judd, decd., being now dead and left three children, viz., William, Eunice and Rhoda, and in the agreement of the estate of William Judd there is part set out to the sd. children, Thomas Judd, Samuel Judd and Daniel Judd joyntly and severally gave bond to fulfill the above agreement.

Inventory on File.

Judd, Thomas. Invt. £56-10-00. Taken 6 December, 1714, by John Wadsworth and Stephen Upson.

Court Record, Page 205—5 July, 1714: Citation to Lt. John Judd to appear and answer to the motion of John Lee and Benjamin Loomis respecting the estate of Deac. Thomas Judd, late of Northampton, decd.

Page 210—15 July, 1714: Adms. to Lt. Thomas Judd of Waterbury and John Lee of Farmington.

Page 225—6 December, 1714: Thomas Judd and John Lee, Adms., exhibit an inventory.

Page 17 (Vol. IX) 3 July, 1716: Capt. Thomas Judd and John Lee, Adms., exhibit an account of sundry disbursements. Allowed. And this Court order the lands lying in Farmington to be dist. to and among the children of the sd. decd. or their legal representatives: To the heirs of William Judd, eldest son, to heirs of Thomas Judd, to John Judd, to Benjamin Judd, to Philip Judd, decd., to Samuel Judd, to Elizabeth Judd, to heirs of Mary Judd, to Ruth Judd. By John Wadsworth, Joseph Root and Joseph Hawley.

Page 135.

Keats, Richard, Hartford. Invt. £235-11-04 1-2. Taken 25 February, 1711-12, by Hezekiah Wyllys, Samuel Howard and Thomas Bidwell.

Court Record, Page 53—5 February, 1711-12: Intestate, and no legal representatives residing in this Government, an inventory is ordered, and Mr. John Eliot and Capt. Aaron Cooke appointed conservators. The estate was in several towns and in the hands of several persons. This Court grant letters of Adms. unto Mr. John Elliot of Windsor, Capt. Aaron Cooke and Jonathan Bunce of Hartford.

Page 56—5 February, 1711-12: Capt. Aaron Cooke, one of the Adms. on estate of Richard Keats, late residing at Hartford, decd., set forth before this Court that the said Richard Keats his estate lyeth in the hands of several persons and lyeth in several Towns in this Colony; that at the desire of the Adms. any Assistant or Justice of the Peace may call persons before him and interrogate them under oath touching the goods, chattells or estate of sd. Richard Keats, and proceed according to law in such cases where any of the goods, chattells or estate is or may be suspected to be in their custody, and as often as occasion may require. (So ordered by this Court.)

Page 92—6 October, 1712: Mr. Richard Thomas of London, merchant, moves this Court that Adms. be granted to him on the estate of Richard Keats, decd., as greatest creditor, in right of his now wife Sarah Thomas, formerly Sarah Hollybush. This Court grant the letters of Adms. and orders the conservators to turn over the estate accordingly.

Page 94—3 November, 1712: Upon further application of Mr. Richard Thomas, who as it appears to this Court is a principal creditor, in right of his wife Sarah Thomas, it also appears to this Court the sd. Keats was factor, this Court do now order the Adms. to deliver and pay to the sd. Richard Thomas such goods and estate as they have received into their hands, except so much as they have paid out in debts.

Page 64.

Kelsey, Stephen, Hartford. Invt. £516-01-10. Taken 20 December, 1710, by Aaron Cooke, Nathaniel Goodwin and Ebenezer Gilbert.

Court Record, Page 24—1st January, 1710-11: Adms. granted to Hannah, the relict, and William Kelsey.

Page 29—2 April, 1711: Hannah Kelsey and William Kelsey, son of sd. decd., exhibit an account of their Adms. Order to dist. the estate as followeth:

	£ s d
To the widow, Hannah Kelsey,	33-00-07
To Stephen Kelsey, eldest son,	95-13-02
To John Kelsey,	57-06-07
To Daniel Kelsey,	52-06-07
To William Kelsey,	57-07-06
To James and Charles Kelsey, to each,	57-07-06
To Hannah Kibbe,	34-19-10

And appoint Capt. Joseph Wadsworth and Ebenezer Gilbert, distributors.

Page 31—2 April, 1711: Charles Kelsey, a minor, 19 years of age, one of the sons of Stephen Kelsey, late decd., chose Capt. Aaron Cooke to be his guardian.

Invt. in Vol. IX, Page 45.

Kelsey, Thomas, Windsor. Invt. £231-18-02. Taken 4 July, 1715, by Thomas Moore and Job Loomis. Invt. of lands in Simsbury, taken by Nathaniel Holcomb and John Slater.

Court Record, Page 259—7 June, 1715: Adms. granted to Elizabeth Kelsey, widow, and Obadiah Spencer of Hartford.

Page 76 (Vol. IX) 5 August, 1718: Elizabeth Kelsey and Obadiah Spencer, Adms., exhibit an account of their Adms. Allowed. This Court appoint Elizabeth Kelsey, widow, to be guardian to her children, viz., to Ruth, age 14 years; Hannah 10, Rebecca 8, and Mabel, 6 years of age, children of Thomas Kelsey.

Page 80—5 August, 1718: Upon motion of Elizabeth Kelsey, Adms., for a distribution, this Court do appoint John Shelding, Joseph Barnard and James Enno, distributors.

Page 89—9 October, 1718: Elizabeth Kelsey and Obadiah Spencer, Adms., exhibited an account of their Adms. Accepted. Order to distribute the estate as followeth: To Elizabeth Kelsey, widow, 1-3 of personal estate and also £27-07-09; to Mark Kelsey, eldest son, his double portion of sd. estate; to Thomas, Elizabeth, Abigail, Rachel, Ruth, Hannah, Rebeckah and Mabel Kelsey, the rest of the children, their single shares. And direct John Sheldon, Joseph Barnard and James Enno to distribute accordingly.

Page 100—9 March, 1718-19: Thomas Kelsey, age 14 years, chose Obadiah Spencer to be his guardian.

Dist. File: February, 1718-19: To the widow, Elizabeth Kelsey, to Mark Kelsey, to Josiah Loomis, to Joseph Humphreys, to Thomas Elger, to Thomas Kelsey, to Ruth, Rebeckah, Hannah and Mabel Kelsey. By John Sheldon, Joseph Barnard and James Enno, distributors.

A later dist., per File, 14 April, 1726: To Mark Kelsey, to Thomas Kelsey, to Elizabeth Loomis, to Rachel Elger, to Abigail Humphrey, to Hannah Kelsey, Rebeckah and Mabel Kelsey. By Jacob Drake, Job Loomis and Timothy Loomis.

Page 39.

Kennard, John, Haddam. Invt. £124-10-01. Taken 14 November, 1709, by William Spencer, John Willee and John Hungerford.

Court Record, Page 10—1st May, 1710: Adms. granted to John Smith, brother-in-law of sd. decd.

Page 129.
(Vol. X, Page 252, for Add. Invt.)

Kirby, Joseph, Middletown. Invt. £53-07-02. Taken 28 February, 1711-12, by Thomas Stow, Samuel Wilcock and Daniel Stocking. Additional invt. of two tracts of land of Joseph Kerby not apprised with the rest of his estate, apprised by us the subscribers as followeth, being first sworn:

	£ s d
To 15¼ acres on the west side the Little River,	22-17-03
To 3 acres of land swamp butting on the upland east,	07-10-00

Taken in Middletown, 1st January, 1725, by John Warner and Samuel Gipson.

Will dated 27 November, 1711: I, Joseph Kirby, of Middletown, do make my last will and testament: I give to Mary, my wife, my house and home lot of about 4 acres to be at her own disposal, also all that she lately received or shall receive from her parents to be at her own disposal and not to be accounted as part of my estate. I give to my son John a parcel of land which buts upon land of his brother James Brown. My will is that all my sons that are or shall be born to me shall have a double portion to the rest of my children in the remaining part of my estate which I have not disposed of. And the rest of my children, which are daughters, shall have a single portion equally alike. I appoint my son John to be sole executor.

Witness: *John Warner, Jr.,* JOSEPH KERBY, LS.
John Ranny, David Hurlbut.

Court Record, Page 48—4 February, 1711-12: Will now exhibited by John Kirby, son of the deceased, and refusing to be the executor was thereupon appointed Adms. with will annexed.

Page 150—6 July, 1713: Adms. may sell land for the payment of debts.

Page 110 (Vol. X) 7 December, 1725: Upon complaint of Susannah Kerby, daughter of Joseph Kerby, by her attorney, John Rew, a writ was issued to cite John Kerby, Adms. on the estate of sd. decd., to answer for not rendering a true inventory of sd. estate. The Adms. now appeared, and the parties being heard, the Court having considered that the sd. Adms. have liberty till this Court in January next to make out sd. inventory.

Page 112—4 January, 1725-6: An invt. of the estate of Joseph Kerby was now exhibited by John Kerby, and accepted.

Page 225.

Kilbourn, Abraham, Wethersfield. Invt. £377-00-00. Taken 27 April, 1713, by William Goodrich, James Patterson and George Kilbourn.

Court Record, Page 129—6 April, 1713: Adms. granted to Sarah Kilbourn, widow.

Page 255—14 April, 1715: Sarah Kilbourn, Adms., exhibits an account of her Adms. Allowed. Order to dist. the estate:

	£	s	d
To Sarah Kilbourn,	23	12	00
To Samuel, eldest son,	151	17	00
To Abraham and to Sarah, to each of them,	75	18	06

And appoint David Goodrich, George Kilbourn and John Goodrich, Jr., distributors.

Page 256—7 June, 1715: This Court appoint Sarah Kilbourn, widow, to be guardian to Samuel Kilbourn, 14 years of age, Abraham Kilbourn, 8 years, and Sarah Kilbourn, 12 years, children of Abraham Kilbourn, late of Wethersfield, decd. Recog., £150.

Page 36 (Vol. X) 3 January, 1723-4: This Court appoint Jacob Goodrich to be guardian unto Abraham Kilbourn of Wethersfield, a minor 15 years of age. Recog., £50.

Page 244.

Kilbourn, David, Glastonbury. Invt. £44-10-09. Taken 14 August, 1713, by Ebenezer Kilbourn and Abraham Kilbourn.

Court Record, Page 128—6 April, 1713: Adms. granted to George Kilbourn of Wethersfield.

Page 147—11 June, 1713: Adms. now granted to John Kilbourn, George Kilbourn having refused.

Page 238—18 January, 1714-15: John Kilbourn now exhibits an account of his Adms. Accepted. Order to dist. the estate equally among the brethren, John, Ebenezer, Jonathan and Abraham, to each of them £7-19-09. And appoint Mr. John Hubbard and Thomas Hale, Sen., of Glastonbury, distributors.

Page 248—4 April, 1715: Report of the distributors. And this Court grant John Kilbourn a *Quietus Est.*

Page 101.

Kilbourn, Ebenezer, Wethersfield. Invt. £480-05-09. Taken 2 February, 1711-12, by James Steele, Jonathan Belding and John Lattimer.

Court Record, Page 49—4 February, 1711-12: Adms. granted to Grace Kilbourn, widow, and Abraham Kilbourn, a brother of sd. decd.

Page 128—6 April, 1713: Grace and Abraham Kilbourn exhibit an account of their Adms. Accepted.

Page 167—4 January, 1713-14: Ebenezer Kilbourn of Fairfield, a minor son of Ebenezer Kilbourn, late of Wethersfield, by a letter signified that he made choice of George Kilbourn to be his guardian. Recog., £40.

Page 168: This Court doth allow Michael Griswold of Wethersfield to be guardian to Ebenezer Kilbourn, a minor son of Ebenezer Kilbourn, late decd., he being now 18 years of age.

Page 169—4 January, 1713-14: This Court appoint Grace Kilbourn to be guardian to Josiah Kilbourn, age 12 years, Daniel 9, George 1 1-2 years, Margaret 7 years, and Sarah Kilbourn 4 years, all children of Ebenezer Kilbourn, and the sd. Grace Kilbourn recognizes with Michael Griswold in £200. Grace Kilbourn of Wethersfield, widow, exhibits now in this Court a further account of her Adms. Order to dist. the estate as followeth:

	£	s	d
To Grace Kilbourn, widow,	34	07	10
To Ebenezer Kilbourn, eldest son,	87	13	04
To Eleazer, Josiah, Daniel, George, Grace, Margaret and Sarah Kilbourn, to each of them,	43	16	08

And appoint Benjamin Churchill, Capt. David Goodrich and Jonathan Belding, distributors.

Page 104 (Vol. IX) 5 May, 1719: Upon the motion of Grace Kilbourn, widow of Ebenezer Kilbourn, late of Wethersfield, decd., that some persons may be appointed to finish the distribution by setting out lands by meets and bounds, this Court appoint David Goodrich, Joseph Belding and Nathaniel Burnham of Wethersfield.

Page 142—6 December, 1720: Ebenezer Kilbourn, son of the deceased, moves this Court to allow him to purchase that part of it (the homested) of the heirs, paying therefor in money, as a division would be very prejudicial to the estate.

Page 144—7 February, 1720-21: This Court order a new apprisal of the homested that it may be disposed of to the best advantage of the heirs. The Court now appoint Benjamin Churchill, Jonathan Belding and John Lattimore apprisers.

Page 146—7 February, 1720-21: Decree entered for a dist: The homested to be divided to Ebenezer and Eleazer: to Ebenezer in lands, and to Eleazer the housing with land.

Page 98 (Vol. X) 23 August, 1725: Upon the motion of Grace Kilbourn, widow of sd. decd., this Court appoint Jonathan Belding, Nathaniel Burnham and Jonathan Burnham of Wethersfield to set out by meets and bounds 1-3 part of the land of sd. decd. for her improvement during life.

Page 167—7 November: This Court appoint Eleazer Kilbourn of Wethersfield to be guardian unto his brother George Kilbourn, a minor 15 years of age. Recog., £50.

Page 204—7 October, 1728: George Kilbourn, a minor about 16 years of age, appeared before this Court and prayed for liberty to make choice of another guardian, his brother Eleazer being (appo)inted by this Court to be his guardian and omitting to bind him out to a trade that the sd. minor inclines to learn (which by this Court is granted), and the sd. minor made choice of Mr. Samuel Hunn of Wethersfield to be his guardian, which this Court allow. Recog., £100.

Page 43 (Vol. XI) 20 April, 1731: Daniel Kilbourn, 4th son of Ebenezer Kilbourn, late of Wethersfield, showing to this Court that by a dist. of his father's estate, 1st March, 1713-14, it was ordered in sd. dist. that Daniel Kilbourn his part £43-16-08 share in the east end of the long lot, and to Grace Kilbourn, eldest daughter, now wife of Benjamin Goodrich, her part £1-03-04 in the east end lot, and no proportion in sd. lands laid out by meets and bounds, so that he can't know how much or how his part of sd. lot shall be ascertained, and moves this Court to appoint some persons to set out his part by meets and bounds. And this Court appoint Samuel Wolcott, Capt. Samuel Curtiss and Mr. Jonathan Burnham, surveyor, to set out by meets and bounds. Whereas, it was ordered by the Court of Probates, 7 March, 1720, that Eleazer Kilbourn of Wethersfield, son of Ebenezer Kilbourn, should have the houseing and buildings on the homelot provided he paid a certain sum of money to the heirs, Eleazer Kilbourn now produced receipts under the hands of sd. heirs that he hath paid according to the order of Court.

Page 3 (Vol. XIII) 4 March, 1736-7: Grace Kilbourn, widow, not having her right of dower set out to her, moves this Court by her attorney, Ebenezer Kilbourn, that her right in the real estate of her late husband, Ebenezer Kilbourn, may be set out, this Court appoint Lt. Jonathan Belding, Noadiah Dickinson and Wait Welles of Wethersfield to set out 1-3 part of the real estate by meets and bounds.

Page 86-94.

Kilbourn, John, Glastonbury. Invt. £232-09-03. Taken by John Hubbard, Thomas Hale and Benjamin Talcott.

Will dated 5 December, 1710: I, John Kilbourn, Sen., of Glastonbury, do make this my last will and testament: Imprimis: I will that all
my just debts and funeral charges be well and truly paid and discharged.
Item. I give to my wife Elizabeth Kilbourn the sole benefit and improvement of my dwelling house and ¾ of my barn; also the use of ¾ of my
meadow and upland, with the use and benefit of my orchard, all being in
Glastonbury, and she to have the use of the same during her natural life.
I also give to my wife ½ of my moveable estate and also the estate that
was her own before I married her, to be hers forever. Item. I give unto
my son John Kilbourn all my land that is eastward of the land I gave my
son David, that is to say, the east end of my farm in Glastonbury, bounded
upon my sd. son David's land west and the undivided land east, land of
Thomas Kilbourn, Sen., south, and lands of Samuel Hill north, to him and
his heirs forever. Item. I give unto my son Ebenezer Kilbourn Mr. Taylor's book on "Titus," a share in the small books and a share in the moveables, to be at his own dispose, having regard to what moveable he hath already had. Item. I give unto my son Jonathan Kilbourn all my labour
which I laid out upon the land in Colchester which he now possesseth, the
clearing of 3 acres of land with all the posts and rails and a frame, to be to
him and his heirs forever; also Mr. Elton's "Sermon Book." Item. I give
unto my son Benjamin Kilbourn my pasture land adjoining my son
David's lot, and west upon my upland field, north upon Samuel Hale, and
south upon Joseph Hill, Sen., provided he return home to settle upon it;
and if he return not home and settle, then the same shall be equally divided
between my four sons, John, Ebenezer, David and Abraham, to them and
their heirs forever. I give to my son Abraham Kilbourn my dwelling
house, barn and orchard, with all my meadow land within the Town of
Glastonbury and my upland from the pasture aforesd. to the meadow, to
him and his heirs forever. I appoint my wife and my son Abraham Kilbourn executors.   JOHN KILBOURN, SEN., LS.
Witness: *Samuel Smith,*
Mary Smith, Philip Olcock.

Court Record, Page 41—19 December, 1711: Elizabeth and Abraham
Kilbourn of Glastonbury exhibited the last will of the sd. decd. Proven.

Page 150.

Kilbourn, Thomas, Hartford. Invt. £165-00-03. Taken 29 November, 1712, by Jonathan Hills and Samuel Welles.

Court Record, Page 101—1st December, 1712: Adms. granted to
John Kilbourn, son of sd. decd.

Page 219 (Vol. X) 3 June, 1729: Upon motion of Solomon Gilman,
in right of his wife, one of the daughters of Thomas Kilbourn, decd., that
John Kilbourn, Adms., may render an accompt of his Adms. on sd. estate,
the sd. Adms. being present at Court and being heard, etc., this Court
continues this matter until the 1st Tuesday of July next.

Page 220—3 June, 1729: Solomon Gilman made default of appearance, the Court dismiss the motion and order that sd. Gilman pay the costs.

Page 204.

Kilbourn, Thomas, Jr., Hartford. Invt. £331-16-00. Taken 8 October, 1712, by Jonathan Hill and Daniel Dickinson.

Court Record, Page 103—5 January, 1712-13: Adms. granted to Susannah Kilbourn, widow and relict of the sd. deceased.

Page 174—1st February, 1713-14: Susannah Kilbourn, Adms., presents an account of her Adms. Accepted. Order to dist. the estate:

	£ s d
To Susannah Kilbourn, widow,	13-12-00
To Thomas Kilbourn,	86-11-00
To Hannah, Susannah, Dorothy and Mabell, to each,	43-05-06

And appoint Jonathan Hill, Timothy Cowles and Hezekiah Porter, distributors. This Court appoint Susannah Kilbourn guardian unto Thomas Kilbourn, Hannah Kilbourn, Susannah Kilbourn, Dorothy Kilbourn and Mabel Kilbourn, minor children of Thomas Kilbourn. And Susannah Kilbourn recognized with Solomon Gilman in £250.

Page 97 (Vol. X) 3 August, 1725: Susannah Kilbourn, Adms. on the estate of Thomas Kilbourn, late of Hartford, decd., moving to the Court of Probate yt the order of the sd. Court, 1st February, 1713-14, for the distribution of sd. estate should be put in execution and completed, thereupon a citation was granted for David Smith and Hannah, his wife, William Miller and Susannah, his wife, heirs of sd. decd., to be heard concerning the same. The sd. Susannah Kilbourn, David Smith and William Miller now appeared and were heard concerning settlement of sd. estate, and upon the desire of the parties the same is referred to a further hearing on the 11th of this instant August.

Page 97—11 August, 1725: The widow, Susannah Kilbourn, David Smith and William Miller now appeared before this Court and was further heard as to the settlement of the estate of Thomas Kilbourn. It appears that two of the heirs have received in value more than their proportion of the moveable part of sd. estate of sd. Susannah Kilbourn, relict of sd. decd., and the real part of sd. estate being considerably advanced in value since the invt. was taken and order of dist. granted thereon (and not yet performed), which maketh it difficult to equalize and divide the sd. estate to and amongst the heirs, thereupon this Court order that the real estate of sd. decd. shall be anew apprised and a return thereof made to this Court, that another order of dist. of the whole estate may be granted, accounting what any of the heirs have already received as part or portions. This Court appoint Timothy Cowles, Joseph Olmstead, Jr., and William Pitkin, apprisers.

Page 112—4 January, 1725-6: A report of the new apprised inventory accepted.

Dist. File: Estate of Thomas Kilbourn, 26 June, 1726: David Smith and Hannah his wife of Hartford, William Miller and Susannah his wife of Glastonbury, John Cadwell and Dorothy Cadwell of Hartford, sell to Jonathan Hills and Susannah Kilbourn all claim or right which we have in and to the estate of our father, Thomas Kilbourn, Jr., deceased. Witness: *Isaac Cowles, Samuel Barnard, Ebenezer Williamson, Elizabeth X Haly.*
Signed and sealed, 26 June, 1726.

Page 123.

King, Thomas, Hartford. Invt. £95-02-11. Taken 28 January, 1711-12, by Benjamin Graham, Joseph Mygatt and Edward Allyn.
An acct. of what Abigail Sexton has recd. apprized as cash:

	£ s d
A table and a box, 1 s; 3 pewter platters, a bason, 3 platters, a spoon, a pint bason, a quart pot,	2-13-10
An old bason, a trammell and tongs, a slice, warming pan, iron pot and iron kettle,	2-04-02
6 new chairs, bedticking, coverlet, a bedstead, a bagg, 4 curtains, valance, old blanket,	2-06-00
A wainscot chest, frying pan, a heifer,	1-06-00
	£8-13-00

Court Record, Page 45—7 January, 1711-12: Adms. to Thomas King, son of the decd.
Page 58—Inventory exhibited.
Page 176—1st February, 1713-14: Citation to Thomas King to appear and render account of his administration.
Page 194—3 May, 1714: Thomas King now exhibits an account of his Adms. Accepted. Order to dist. the estate:

	£ s d
To Thomas King, eldest son,	25-03-09
To Robert, Abigail and Mary King, to each,	12-11-11

And appoint Benjamin Grimes, Thomas Seamore and Daniel Merrells, distributors.

Page 83.

Lane, Isaac, Sen., Middletown. Invt. £194-11-00. Taken 30 August, 1711, by John Hall, Thomas Ward and Giles Hamlin.
Court Record, Page 37—3 September, 1711: Adms. granted to John and Isaac Lane, sons of the sd. decd.

Page 129—6 April, 1713: John and Isaac Lane, Adms., exhibit now an account of their Adms. Order to dist. the estate: To John Lane, eldest son, to Isaac Lane, to Hannah Smith, to the heirs of Elizabeth Lane decd., to Eleanor Blakeley (wife of Samuel Blakeley), to Sarah Candee, to each their single portions. And appoint Capt. Thomas Ward, Joseph Rockwell and Ebenezer Smith, of Middletown, distributors.

Page 144—1st June, 1713: Upon the motion of Isaac Lane, this Court order the persons appointed by this Court, 6th April last, to distribute the estate of Isaac Lane, Sen., decd., to set a valuation upon such lands as he in his lifetime conveyed to his children by a deed or otherwise, and to have special regard thereunto in their work of distributing that estate.

Page 233—6 December, 1714: Sundry demands made against the estate by John Lane, Isaac Lane, Benjamin Smith (who married one of the daughters) and Zacheus Candee, a son-in-law, which this Court allow.

Page 5 (Vol. IX) 3 January, 1705: Report of the dist. And this Court grant the Adms. a *Quietus Est.*

Page 121.

Lattimer, Jonathan, Wethersfield. Invt. £446-02-04. Taken 2 February, 1711-12, by James Steele, Samuel Wright and Joseph Belden.

Court Record, Page 48—4 February, 1711-12: Adms. granted to Abigail Lattimer, widow, and Joseph Belding.

Page 195—3 May, 1714: The Adms. exhibit now an account of their Adms., which this Court doth accept.

Page 94 (Vol. IX) 3 February, 1718-19: Abigail Lattemore is appointed guardian to Charles Lattemore, age 13 years, David 12, Jonathan 9, and Ann Lattemore 7 years of age, children of the sd. decd. And Daniel Rose, with Abigail Lattemore, recog. in £200.

Page 3 (Vol. X) 1st January, 1722-3: Josiah Atwood and Bathshua, his wife, moved to this Court that guardians may be appointed for the children of Jonathan Lattemore, late of Wethersfield, decd., and that the estate may be dist. This Court order that the Clerk issue a citation for Abigail Lattemore, widow of sd. decd., to appear, if she see cause, at this Court in February next, to object against this motion.

Page 51—1st December, 1724: This Court do appoint John Rose of Wethersfield to be guardian unto Charles Lattemore, a minor 19 years of age, and a cripple, and Ann Lattemore, 13 years of age. Recog., £200.

Page 58—3 November, 1724: David Lattemore, 18 years of age, and Jonathan Lattemore, 15 years, made choice of Jonathan Welles to be their guardian. Recog., £500.

Page 59—1st December, 1724: Whereas, application being made to this Court for an order of dist., it being represented that the debts are all paid and that the estate remains as is inventoried to the full sum of £446-02-04 to be distributed: Order to Abigail Lattemore, widow, £46-

oo-09 with dower; to Charles Lattemore, eldest son of the decd., £160-
00-07, which is his double portion of sd. estate; to David, Jonathan and
Ann Lattemore, the rest of the children, to each of them, £80-00-04, which
is their single portion of sd. estate. And appoint Samuel Wright, Samuel
Robbins and Joseph Churchill.

Page 161—18 December, 1725: This Court grant Adms. on the estate of Jonathan Lattemore, late of Wethersfield, decd., unto John Rose
of sd. Wethersfield. The debts due from sd. estate being supposed to be
all paid and an order of dist. made out, the sd. John Rose is ordered to
deliver the estate aforesd. to the persons appointed to dist. sd. estate and
make return of dist. of the sd. estate to this Court. And whereas, of the
former Adms. one of them is decd. and the other gone it is not known
where, the creatures formerly inventoried and prised gone and others
raised in their room upon sd. estate: this Court do order that Samuel
Robbins, Samuel Wright and Joseph Churchill, appointed distributors,
be also apprisers, and that they take the appriser's oath and apprise what
stock shall be by John Rose, Adms., offered to them to distribute, and dist.
sd. stock to the heirs in part or portion according to the apprisement they
shall so make.

Invt. in Vol. IX, Page 15.

Lewis, John, Simsbury. Invt. £72-09-06. Taken 18 January, 1713-
14, by John Case and Andrew Robe.

Court Record, Page 175—1st February, 1713-14: Adms. granted to
Abigail Lewis, widow of sd. decd.

Page 215—4 October, 1714: Abigail Lewis, Adms., exhibits now in
Court an account of debts due, and the personal estate seems not sufficient
to pay them.

Page 258—7 June, 1715: Abigail Lewis, Adms., exhibits now an
account of Adms. Allowed. Order to sell real or personal estate to pay
the debts.

Page 90 (Vol. XI) 17 May, 1733: John Lewis, a minor, 12 years of
age, son of John Lewis, chose his aunt Bethia Bacon, now residing in
Hartford, to be his guardian. Recog., £50.

Page 110.

Long, Thomas, Sen., Windsor. Invt. £89-15-00. Taken (no date),
by Joseph Fitch, Sen., and Thomas Stoughton.

Court Record, Page 48—4 February, 1711-12: Adms. to Sarah
Long, widow, and Samuel Long, son of the deceased.

Page 18 (Vol. IX) 3 July, 1716: Sarah Long, Adms., exhibits now
in this Court an account of sundry debts due from the estate, whereby it
appears that there is not sufficient of the moveable part of the estate to discharge them. Account allowed.

Page 41—6 August, 1717: This Court allow the Adms. account and order the same to be put on file.

Page 30-177.

Loomis, Ebenezer, Windsor. Invt. £198-13-00. Taken 10 November, 1709, by. Nathaniel Loomis, Roger Wolcott and Samuel Tudor. Invt. of £122-00-09 of remaining estate of Ebenezer Loomis and his wife Jemima, both deceased. Taken 15 December, 1712, by Roger Wolcott and Samuel Tudor.

Court Record, Page 7—6 March, 1709-10: Adms. granted to Jemima Loomis, widow, relict of sd. decd. Nathaniel Loomis now exhibits the inventory of the estate of Ebenezer and Jemima Loomis, and this Court grant unto Nathaniel Loomis, brother of sd. decd., letters of Adms.

Page 112—2 February, 1712-13: Nathaniel Loomis, Adms., exhibits now an account of his Adms. Order to dist. the estate to the two surviving daughters, Abigail and Jemima Loomis. And appoint Henry Wolcott, Samuel Bancroft and William Wolcott, distributors. This Court appoint Nathaniel Loomis to be guardian to Jemima Loomis, 4 years of age, and Joseph Newbery to be guardian to Abigail Loomis, 6 years of age, daughters of Ebenezer Loomis.

Page 124—6 April, 1713: Report of the distributors.

Page 125.

(Add. Invt., Vol. IX, Page 46.)

Loomis, Stephen, Windsor. Invt. £175-10-00. Taken 30 November, 1711, by Daniel Loomis, John Bissell and Timothy Loomis. An invt. of £58-19-07 of the remaining estate of Stephen and Esther his wife, taken 2 April, 1715, by John Bissell and Daniel Loomis.

Court Record, Page 57—3 March, 1711-12: Adms. granted to Esther Loomis, widow and relict, on the estate of her deceased husband.

Page 230—6 December, 1714: Esther Loomis being now departed this life and her Adms. not finished, this Court grant Adms. unto Stephen Loomis, eldest son of sd. decd.

Page 231—3 January, 1714-15: This Court appoint James Loomis of Windsor to be guardian to Israel Loomis, age 9 years, Mary Loomis 6, and Sarah Loomis 3 years of age, children of Stephen Loomis. Recog., with Mr. John Bissell of Windsor, £150.

Page 249—4 April, 1715: Stephen Loomis of Windsor, Adms., exhibits an invt. of the moveable estate.

Page 58 (Vol. IX) 1st April, 1718: Stephen Loomis exhibits an account of his Adms. Allowed. Order to dist. the estate:

£ s d
To Stephen Loomis, eldest son, 30-05-10
To Israel, Amos, Hannah, Mary and Sarah Loomis, to each, 15-02-11

And appoint Daniel Loomis, John Bissell and Timothy Loomis, distributors.

Page 37 (Vol. X) 3 January, 1723-4: This Court appoint Jacob Drake of Windsor to be guardian to Israel Loomis of sd. Windsor, a minor 18 years of age.

Page 137—1st November, 1726: Sarah Loomis, a minor 15 years of age, daughter of Stephen Loomis, late of Windsor, deceased, chose Peter Mills, Jr., of Windsor, to be her guardian. Recog., £50.

Page 62.

Loomis, Timothy, Windsor. Invt. £462-08-08. Taken 29 November, 1710, by John Moore, Daniel Loomis and Thomas Moore.

Court Record, Page 15—3 July, 1710: Adms. granted to Rebeckah, the widow.

Page 72—5 May, 1712: This Court appoint Thomas Moore to be guardian unto Ichabod Loomis, a minor 19 years of age, son of Timothy Loomis, and Rebeckah Loomis to be guardian to the rest of her children.

Page 75—5 May, 1712. Rebeckah Loomis, Adms., exhibits now an account of her Adms. Accepted. Order to dist. the estate as followeth:

£ s d
To Rebeckah Loomis, widow, 55-18-06
To Timothy Loomis, eldest son, 117-02-06
To Ichabod, Uriah, Odiah, Anne and Rebeckah, to each, 58-11-03

And appoint Thomas Moore, James Enno and John Bissell, distributors. And grant the Adms. a *Quietus Est.*

Page 79—2 June, 1712: Report of the distributors.

Page 106.

Lord, Richard, Hartford. Invt. £6369-18-11. (The real estate part, £2956-15-09.) Taken 6 February, 1711-12, by William Whiting, Ciprian Nicholls and Aaron Cooke. The value of negro servants was: Andrew, £45; Robin, £40; Diego, £30; Sibbelle, £35; Hanna and Cuffe, £20; Hager, £15; Leazer, £12.

Court Record, Page 51—4 February, 1711-12: Adms. to Abigail Lord, widow, relict of the deceased. Exhibit of inventory. Accepted.

Page 204—8 June: Adms. account allowed: Paid, £190-01-11; remains for distribution, £6179-17-00. This Court order distribution of the estate: To the widow, the use of 1-2 the real estate during life, and

£1074-07-05 of personal estate forever; to Elisha Lord, eldest son, a double share, £1276-07-05; to Richard, to Epaphras, to Ichabod Lord, younger sons, and to Jerusha, Mary and Elizabeth Lord, daughters of the deceased, to each of them the sum or value of £638-03-08, which is to each a single share. By Capt. Cyprian Nicholls, Capt. Aaron Cook and Mr. Nathaniel Stanly of Hartford, or any two of them, to distribute and divide the said estate accordingly.

Page 4 (Probate Side, Vol. IX): We, John Whiting and Jerusha Whiting, wife of the sd. John Whiting, of Hartford, have received from Mr. Timothy Woodbridge of Hartford, as he is in right of his wife Mrs. Abigail Woodbridge Adms. on estate of Richard Lord, Esq., late of Hartford, deceased, the sum of £638-03-08, which is in full of all the part and portion distributed out of the estate of said Richard Lord, deceased, to her the said Jerusha Whiting, alias Lord, daughter of the said Richard Lord, as our full portion, and that the same is in full of all demands of our part out of the estate of the said Richard Lord, deceased. March, 1716.

Witness: *Robert Sandford,*   JOHN WHITING, LS.
         Richard Burnham.   JERUSHA WHITING, LS.
Recorded 3 May, 1716.   *Thomas Kimberly, Clerk.*

Page 97 (Vol. X) 3 August, 1725: Mrs. Abigail Woodbridge, Adms. on the estate of Richard Lord, Esq., late of Hartford, decd., exhibited an account of debts due to sd. estate carried into the inventory and dist. of sd. estate and are lost, amounting to £23-15-08; and also an account of what she had paid in debts due from sd. estate since dist., amounting t6 £36-12-00; and also an account of what she had received due to the sd. estate, amounting to £23-07-01; which account is accepted and ordered to be kept upon file. And likewise exhibited an average of abatement upon the respective portions of the relict and heirs of sd. decd. in the dist. of the sd. estate, which average is accepted and ordered to be accounted in the sd. dist. to the relict and heirs accordingly, and be kept on file.

Page 102—4 October, 1725: This Court do appoint the Rev. Timothy Woodbridge and Abigail his wife, of Hartford, to be guardians unto Richard Lord, 20 years of age, with Epaphras Lord, 16 years of age, and Ichabod Lord, 14 years of age. Rec., £500.

Page 122—14 March, 1726-7: Whereas, Mrs. Abigail Woodbridge, alias Lord, Adms. on the estate of Mr. Richard Lord, late of Hartford, decd., exhibited an addition of a parcel of land at Wethersfield containing 4 acres, lying between the land of Jonathan Colfax, decd., and Thomas Hurlbut, valued at £12, and also of loss on sd. estate of a parcel of land containing 10 acres of upland in the invt. and dist. to Richard Lord, son of sd. decd., valued at £30, which cannot be found: Whereupon this Court order that the loss aforesd. be made unto the sd. Richard Lord, the son, by distributing to him the aforesd. 4 acres, and what is wanting of the sd. £30 shall be proportionably borne and paid by the heirs of the sd. decd.

Page 210.

Macky, John, Wethersfield. Died 13 November, 1712. Invt. £112-15-02. Taken by Philip Goff, Jr., Joshua Robbins, Jr., and Jacob Goff.

Court Record, Page 104—15 December, 1712: Adms. granted to Mary Macky, widow.

Page 151—3 August, 1713: John Macky, a minor son, 19 years of age, son of John Macky, chose Bezaleel Lattimer to be his guardian.

Page 234—7 February, 1714-15: Mary Macky, widow, exhibits now an account of her Adms. Account allowed. Order to dist. the estate:

	£ s d
To Mary Macky, widow,	5-02-07
To John, eldest son,	27-15-08
To Daniel, Samuel, Mary, Elizabeth and Anna, to each,	13-17-10

And appoint William Warner, Philip Goff Jr. and Joshua Robbins the 2nd, distributors. Daniel Macky, a minor, 19 years of age, chose Mr. Robbins of Wethersfield to be his guardian. Recog., £20. This Court appoint Mary Macky of Wethersfield to be guardian to Anna Macky, 12 years of age, and Samuel, 7 years of age. Recog., £40.

Page 246—4 April, 1715: Report of the dist., and Mary Macky now granted a *Quietus Est.*

Page 114 (Vol. IX) 3 December, 1719: Daniel Macky, 14 years of age, chose Joseph Graham of Wethersfield to be his guardian. Recog., £20.

Page 167—1st May, 1722: Samuel Macky, a minor, 15 years of age, son of John Macky of Wethersfield, chose Lt. Samuel Royce of Wallingford to be his guardian. Recog., £50.

Page 180.

Manure, Philip, Windsor. Invt. £26-06-11. Taken 13 December, 1711, by Thomas Marshall, Joseph Phelps and Thomas Moore.

Court Record, Page 51—4 February, 1711-12: Adms. to William Tuller of Simsbury, it being supposed that Philip Manure left no apparent heir or legal representative alive surviving. This Court constitute William Tuller conservator upon the estate.

Page 107—6 January, 1712-13: Citation to William Tuller to render an account of his Adms.

Page 111—2 February, 1712-13: William Tuller now exhibits an invt.

Page 148—6 July, 1713: William Tuller, Adms., exhibits an account of his Adms., which this Court accepts, and grant him a *Quietus Est.*

Page 155.

Markham, Deacon Daniel, Middletown. Invt. £384-15-09. Taken 18 February, 1711-12, by John Hamlin, Joseph Rockwell and John Bacon.

Will dated 23 November, 1708: I, Daniel Markham, Sen., of Middletown, in the County of Hartford, do ordain this my last will and testament: I give and bequeath unto Patience my wife, whom I ordain my only and sole executrix, so much of my estate as she may choose to improve during life and £20; also my negro Sampson during her life, and then to be free, if she live fourteen years after the date hereof. I give to my daughters Martha and Edith £20. My sons Daniel and James Markham to have the refusal of my lands, they paying their sisters' portion. Also to my son Daniel and James Markham, to each of them, £50 in lands. I give to my daughter Elizabeth Bates, £38-15-00. l further give her feathers enough to fill a bed. To my daughter Martha Center, £44-10-08, to whom I further give 4 or 5 rods of ground where Jonathan Center's house standeth. I give unto my grandson Daniel Markham my gun and sword. I request Mr. Russell, Samuel Bidwell and Joseph Rockwell to be overseers.

Witness: *John Hamlin,*   DANIEL MARKHAM, LS.
Noadiah Russell, Samuel Kendall.

Court Record, Page 66—7 April, 1712: The last will of Daniel Markham was now exhibited by Patience Markham, widow, executrix. Daniel Markham the son appealed to the Superior Court.

Page 203—8 June, 1714: Upon motion of Daniel Markham, son of Deacon Daniel Markham decd., a citation issued to Patience Markham, widow, executrix of sd. decd., to appear and choose the £20 given her by the will during life, and give bond that at her death or marriage all those goods that remain except the £20, and all except what shall be needful for the payment of debts, shall be returned to the children in as good order as when taken, or the value thereof, and that the buildings and fences be kept in good repair.

Page 205—15 July, 1714: Patience Markham now appeared in Court, per order 8 June last. She being dissatisfied with the resolve of this Court, appealed to the Superior Court.

Page 66 (Vol. IX) 3 June, 1718: Patience Markham being summoned to answer the demands of James and Daniel Markham, sons of sd. decd., as set forth in the writ of April, 1718, this Court do not see cause to grant what is prayed for.

Page 75—5 August, 1718: James Markham appealed to the Superior Court from a decision of this Court in favor of Patience Markham.

Page 83.

Mason, Ann, Wethersfield. Invt. £32-02-08. Taken 29 March, 1711, by Joseph Talcott and John Curtis, Jr.

Will dated 6 February, 1707-8: I, Ann Mason, of Wethersfield, do make this my last will and testament: It is my will that my daughter Mary Hall shall have all my wearing apparrel after my decease. I give to

my son Jonathan Mason all the rest of my estate after my lawful debts
are paid and funeral charges. And I appoint and constitute Mr. Thomas
Welles of Wethersfield to be sole executor.
Witness: *Samuel Walker,*   ANN X MASON, LS.
    James Poisson.

Court Record, Page 34—4 June, 1711: Will exhibited by Thomas
Welles, Jr., executor.

Will on File.

Mercer, Mary. Nuncupative will, dated 17th day of November, 1712.
The deposition of Mary Jesse and Rachel Skinner, both of Hartford, is:
That we, the sd. deponents, being at the house of Mr. Thomas Hooker
in Hartford, 17 November, 1710, did then hear Mary Mercer (who was
sick at sd. house, but, as we apprehended, was at that time of sound mind
and memory) say that she gave her estate to her mother, and desired it
should be sent to her. And further saith not.

Mrs. Mary Jesse and Rachel Skinner, the deponents, made oath to
the abovesd. deposition, 6th September, 1711, at Hartford.

Test: *John Haynes, Assist.*

Court Record, Page 23—4 December, 1710: Adms. granted to John
Skinner, locksmith, on the estate of Mary Mercer, a single woman, formerly of Boston, who died in Hartford.

Page 67—7 April, 1712: John Skinner, Adms., now exhibits an account of his Adms: Invt. £36-04-00; after paying debts there remains £28-
00-05. And produced in Court an instrument or writing under the hands
and seals of Anna Moore, Lydia Barker, Sarah Jones and Rebeckah
Walker, of Charlestown, and Hopestill Sergeant of Boston, sisters of the
sd. Mary Mercer, decd., whereby they do convey their interest in sd. estate unto their mother, Anna Walker, of Charlestown aforesd., widow,
which instrument is now on file. This Court orders John Skinner to pay
to the Widow Walker the aforesd. sum of £28-00-05, and take a *Quietus
Est.*

Page 142-143.

Merrells, John, Sen., Hartford. Invt. £511-08-08. Taken 6 July
(1712), by John Shephard, John Skinner and Thomas Hosmer.

An agreement, made among the heirs of John Merrells, late of Hartford, decd., 1 December, 1712: Under divers considerations, and in consideration of our father not making a will at his decease and settling his
estate to each child, as is common in wills, we do now all agree for ourselves respectively and our heirs: Imprimis: That our father's estate
shall be all brought into the inventory, and that each child shall have
an equal part of said estate, only our eldest brother Nathaniel shall have

a double part. 2ndly. We do also agree that Jacob Merrells shall have and enjoy that which is given him by deed of guift as his part and share of the said estate, and no more, to be free (excepting our mother her thirds) from all incumbrances. 3dly. We do also agree that our mother, Sarah Merrells, shall have the thirds of the rest of the whole estate during her natural life. 4thly. We do agree that those of the brethren that have deeds of guift shall have liberty to have and to hold that part of sd. estate so given them as part of their portion. 5ly. We further agree that the double part or portion of the estate that shall be distributed or set out to our brother Nathaniel, if he shall live to spend it or come to the right use of his reason, to dispose of it at his decease. But if not, that then his part of sd. estate so agreed on shall be divided equally amongst the brethren and sisters. In witness whereof we have hereunto set our hands and seals the day and year above written.

Witness: *Hez: Wyllys,*
　　　　　 John Hinks.

SARAH X MERRELLS, LS.
JOHN SHEPHERD, LS., in behalf of
NATHANIEL MERRELLS, LS.
SAMUEL KELLOGG, LS.
JOHN MERRELLS, LS.
ABRAHAM MERRELLS, LS.
DANIEL MERRELLS, LS.
WILTERTON MERRELLS, LS.
JOHN TURNER, LS.
ABELL MERRELLS, LS.
ISAAC MERRELLS, LS.
JACOB MERRELLS.

Court Record, Page 94—13 November, 1712: This Court defers a resolution relating to the probate of the last will and testament of Mr. John Merrells until the 1st Monday of December next.

Page 100—1st December, 1712: This Court appoint Deacon John Shepherd of Hartford to act in behalf of Nathaniel Merrells of Hartford (who is *non compos mentis*) in settling the estate of his late father, Mr. John Merrels. Sarah Merrells, widow, relict of John Merrels, was appointed executrix. She refuseing to act, this Court grant Adms. to Mrs. Sarah Merrels and the son Daniel Merrells. Exhibit of an agreement. Approved and allowed.

Page 101—1st December, 1712: This Court appoint John Merrells and Samuel Kellogg to be guardians to Nathaniel Merrells of Hartford, eldest son of Deacon John Merrells, and the sd. John Merrells and Samuel Kellogg recog. £100.

Page 9-10 (Vol. IX) Probate Side: Dist. of the estate of Mr. John Merrels, who deceased 18 July, 1712:

To our honoured mother, Sarah Merrells, to half the dwelling house and barn with the homelot adjoining, to be her own to dispose to her

	£ s d
heirs and assigns forever,	50-00-00
To moveable estate,	29-12-04
To be paid her annually during life for her third of lands,	8-07-00
To Nathaniel Merrells,	104-07-00
To John Merrells,	52-06-06
To Abraham Merrells,	52-06-06
To Daniel Merrells,	52-06-06
To Wilterton Merrells,	52-06-06
To Isaac Merrells,	52-06-06
To Abell Merrells,	52-06-06
To Samuel Kellogg,	52-06-06
To John Turner,	52-06-06

Whereof we have hereunto set to our hands and seals the 7th day of June, in the thirteenth year of Her Majesties reign, Annoq. Dom. 1714.

Witness: *Daniel Foote,*   SARAH MERRELLS for herself,
        John Cole.   SAMUEL KELLOGG and
                     JOHN MERRELLS, Guardians to
                     NATHANIEL MERRELLS,
                     JOHN MERRELLS,
                     ABRAHAM MERRELLS,
                     DANIEL MERRELLS,
                     WILTERTON MERRELLS,
                     ABELL MERRELLS,
                     ISAAC MERRELLS,
                     SAMUEL KELLOGG in right of his wife,
                     JOHN TURNER in right of his wife.

Mills, Peter, Sen., Tailor, late of Windsor, decd. Court Record, Page 16—3 July, 1710: Adms. granted to Peter Mills, son of sd. decd.

Invt. in Vol. IX, Page 14.

Moore, Joseph, Windsor. Invt. £162-02-00. Taken 5 July, 1714, by Nathaniel Loomis and Daniel Loomis.

Court Record, Page 213—6 September, 1714: Adms. granted to Sarah Moore, widow, relict of sd. deceased.

Page 187 (Vol. X) 2 April, 1728: Sarah Moore, Adms., exhibited an account of her Adms. Accepted. Order to dist: To Sarah Moore, widow, her dower; to Joseph Moore, only son, his double share; and to Sarah Eglestone, to Phebe and Lydia Moore, the rest of the children, their single portions. And appoint Job Loomis, Josiah Moore and Timothy Loomis, distributors.

Page 216—5 April, 1729: Report of the distributors.
See dist. as per File: 12 April, 1728: To Joseph Moore, eldest son, to Lydia Moore, to Phebe Moore, to Sarah Eglestone, to Deborah and to Sarah Moore, widow. By Josiah Moore, Job Loomis and Timothy Loomis, distributors.

Page 118.

Morley, Thomas, Sen., Glastonbury. Invt. £191-02-08. Taken 30 January, 1711-12, by Samuel Smith, Thomas Hale, Sen., and Thomas Morley, Jr.

Will dated 23 January, 1711-12: I, Thomas Morley, Sen., husbandman, of Glastonbury, do make this my last will and testament: I give unto my wife Martha my entire estate with full power to make a will and to dispose of what estate is left at her decease to all the children equally, except Mary, to whom I have given her portion, and I do but give her one shilling more. Also, it is my will that my son Abell shall have ten pounds more than any of the rest of my children. I appoint my wife sole executrix.   (Not signed.)

Witness: *Samuel Smith, Sen.,*
Thomas Morley, Jr., Abel X Morley.

Court Record, Page 46—4 February, 1711-12: Will approved. Thomas Morley, son, and Thomas Wickham, son-in-law, appealed to the Superior Court.

Page 116.

Morton, William, Sen., Windsor. Invt. £297-10-10. Taken by Joseph Olmsted, Roger Pitkin and Samuel Burnham.

Court Record, Page 43—7 January, 1711-12: Adms. granted to John Morton, son of sd. decd.

Page 114—2 March, 1712-13: John Morton, Adms., exhibits now an account of his Adms. Order to dist. the estate:

	£ s d
To Mary Morton, widow,	63-12-00
To John Morton,	72-01-02
To Ann Drake, wife of Joseph Drake,	36-00-07
To Mary Colt, wife of Jabez Colt,	36-00-07
To the heirs of Thomas Morton,	36-00-07
To Samuel Morton,	36-00-07
To Sarah Morton,	36-00-07

And appoint Roger Wolcott, Jr., Deacon Joseph Olmsted and Nathaniel Pitkin, of Hartford, distributors. John Morton, Adms., is granted a *Quietus Est.*

Page 231—3 January, 1714-15: Report of the distributors.

Page 117.

Morton, William, Jr. Invt. £51-10-00. Taken by Samuel Burnham and John Burnham.

Court Record, Page 43—7 January, 1711-12: Adms. of estate of William Morton, late of Windsor, deceased, now granted to John Morton, brother of the decd.

Page 115—2 March, 1712-13: John Morton, Adms., exhibits now an account of his Adms. Order to dist. the estate to the surviving brothers and sisters or their legal representatives:

	£ s d
To John Morton, brother, who also	7-16-06
Recd. from Anne Drake and Mary Colt, by purchase,	15-13-00
To the heirs of Thomas Morton,	7-16-07
To Samuel and Sarah Morton, to each of them,	7-16-06

And appoint Roger Wolcott, Joseph Olmsted and Nathaniel Pitkin, distributors. John Morton granted a *Quietus Est.*

Page 160 (Vol. X) 4 July, 1727: It is represented to this Court by Noah Loomis that the estate of sd. decd. had not been distributed according to an order of Court, 2 March, 1712-13, and that William Morton died seized of real estate that hath not been inventoried. This Court order that John Morton, Adms. on sd. estate, exhibit an inventory of sd. real estate in this Court within one month.

Page 162—(Date not readable): John Morton, Adms., now exhibited invt. per order of this Court, 4 July last, and pleaded that the real estate ought not to be inventoried; that two parcels of land were bought by his father and himself joyntly and never divided; that upon the death of his father the whole of the two parcels of land is vested in him by "Wright" of survivourship. Upon what Noah Loomis, who married a sister of sd. deceased, and sd. Morton has offered, this Court decides the land ought to be inventoried. John Morton appealed to the Superior Court.

Page 179—5 March, 1727: John Morton neglected to present his appeal to the Superior Court, and Adms. was granted to Noah Loomis.

Page 232 (Probate Side, Vol. XII): An addition to the invt. of 2 parcels of land valued at £59-00-00, taken 1st April, 1728, by Richard Gilsman and Jno. Wood.

Invt. and Will in Vol. IX, Page 28.

Moses, John, Simsbury. Invt. £387-08-11. Taken 20 June, 1715, by Samuel Humphrey, Sen., Samuel Pettebone and Samuel Humphrey.

Will dated 1st August, 1714: I, John Moses, of Simsbury, do make this my last will and testament: I give to my wife Deborah a third part of all my improveable lands during her natural life, and the thirds of my moveable estate forever. I give unto my son John 5 shillings, seeing I have given him already £50. I give unto my son William the half of my land lying upon the West River in the West Mountain, seeing he has already received £40. To my son Thomas I give him a hollow lying next the river upon the right hand of Farmington Road, south of Thomas Humphrey, he having already received £40. I give my youngest son Caleb a double portion of the remainder of my estate. I give unto my son Joshua an equal portion with my three daughters, Deborah, Mary and Martha, that is to be understood my undivided estate. I appoint James Cornish, Sen., and my wife Deborah executors.

Witness: *Andrew Robe,*   JOHN MOSES, LS.
Mary X Humphrey, James Poisson.

Court Record, Page 219—1st November, 1714: Will exhibited by James Cornish and Deborah Moses, executors. Will approved. John Moses, a son of sd. decd., appeals unto the Superior Court.

Page 257—7 June, 1715: Adms. granted to John Moses, with the will annexed, the executrix appointed by the testator being now deceased.

Page 258—5 July, 1715: Caleb Moses, age 16 years, a son of John Moses, chose his brother Joshua Moses to be his guardian. Mary Moses, age 13 years, chose her brother William Moses to be her guardian. And this Court appoint Joshua Moses to be guardian to Martha Moses, age 10 years. Recog., £50 to each.

Page 62 (Vol. IX) 28 March, 1718: John Moses of Simsbury, Adms., exhibits an account of his Adms. Allowed. Order the estate dist.: To Caleb Moses a double portion; to Joshua, Deborah, Mary and Martha Moses, equal shares. William, John and Thomas Moses appealed to the Superior Court.

Page 108—7 July, 1719: Whereas, there is 1-3 part of the houseing and lands of John Moses (in and by his last will disposed of to his widow for her improvement during life, who being lately decd.) remains to be dist. to the children according to the will: This Court appoint Lt. Samuel Humphries, Joseph Case and John Humphries to dist. the sd. 1-3 part unto Joshua Moses, Caleb Moses, Deborah Roberts, Mary Moses and Martha Moses, children of sd. decd., according to his last will.

Page 115—5 January, 1719-20: Report of the dist.

Page 58 (Vol. XI) 17 December, 1731: This Court grant John Moses, Adms., a *Quietus Est.*

Page 24.

(Add. Invt. Vol. IX, Page 78.)

Newbery, Capt. Benjamin, Windsor. Invt. £1006-08-06. Taken 31 March, 1710, by John Moore, Sen., Matthew Allyn and Return Strong. Additional invt. of £279-03-00, taken 17 May, 1720, by Daniel Loomis, James Enno and Timothy Loomis.

Will dated 14 June, 1709: Whereas I, Benjamin Newbery of Windsor, am going forth in His Majestie's service, and do therefore leave this as my last will: I give to my wife Hannah £100 to be at her own disposal forever; also the use and improvement of my whole estate until my children arrive at age, my sons to 21 years and my daughters to 18 years. I give to my son Benjamin £200, to my son Roger £150, to my two daughters, Hannah £100 and Abigail £100. I appoint my wife Hannah to be sole executrix, and desire Mr. John Eliot, Esq., John Moore, Sen., Roger Wolcott and Thomas Moore to be overseers.

Witness: *John Moore, Sen.,*   BENJAMIN NEWBERY.

Court Record, Page 1—2 January, 1709-10: Will proven.

Page 99 (Vol. IX) 6 March, 1718-19: Hannah Newbery, alias Merriman, executrix of the last will of Capt. Benjamin Newbery, decd., exhibits now an account of her Adms. Accepted. And this Court order the estate dist. according to the last will of the sd. decd.:

	£ s d
To Hannah Newbery, alias Merriman, relict,	100-00-00
To the heir of Benjamin Newbery, decd., eldest son,	261-01-07
Also to him his portion in his own right of Abigail Newbery's part in sd. estate, who died before the eldest son.	
To Roger Newbery, 2nd son,	258-01-05
Including his portion of his sisters Hannah and Abigail Newbery, both deceased.	
To Mary Newbery, daughter of sd. decd.,	117-16-11

And appoint Col. Matthew Allyn, Roger Wolcott and Capt. Thomas Moore dist. This Court appoint Mrs. Hannah Newbery, alias Merriman, to be guardian to her children, viz., Roger Newbery, age 13 years, and Mary Newbery, 9 years, children of Benjamin Newbery, decd. Recog., £200.

Page 15 (Vol. X) 3 April, 1723: Upon the motion of Hannah Merriman, alias Newbery, relict of Capt. Benjamin Newbery, that her dower or third part of the real estate of sd. decd. may be ordered set out to her, a writ was issued to notify James Porter and Ruth Newbery, guardians to Benjamin Newbery, grandson to the sd. decd. The sd. James Porter and Hannah Merriman now appeared and were heard upon sd. motion, and the sd. Hannah Merriman declared that she renounced the bequest in the last will of the sd. decd. of £4-10-00 to be paid her during life, supposed to be given her in right of her dower, whereupon this Court have considered that 1-3 part of the houseing and lands of the sd. decd. shall be set out unto the sd. Hannah Merriman for her improvement during life. The sd. James Porter appealed from the judgement of this Court to the Superior Court to be held at Hartford in September next. Rec., £10.

Page 16.

Newbery, Benjamin, Windsor. Died 24 September, 1709. Invt. £234-18-00. Taken 7 November, 1709, by Roger Wolcott and Joseph Skinner, Jr.

Benjamin Newbery, being of sound understanding and memory, being about to undertake a journey toward Canada, not knowing how Providence may dispose of him, hath left this as his last will and testament: I give to my loving brother Joseph Newbery all my land, both meadow and upland, with the crop that now stands upon it, to be his and his heirs forever; and I give him also my horse now in the woods and my saddle and bridle and other horse furniture, and all my wearing clothes, both woolen and linen, provided that he pay my debts and other legacies. I give to my sister Hannah Wolcott £40. I give to my little Cosin Hannah Woolcot £20, to be paid by my executor to her when she shall arrive at the age of 18 years. I constitute my brother Joseph Newbery executor.

Witness: *William Woolcott,*　　　　　BENJAMIN X NEWBERY.
Abiah Woolcott.

Page 40.

North, John, Farmington. Died 2 February, 1709-10. Invt. £39-12-07. Taken by Samuel Newell, Sen., and Joseph North.

Court Record, Page 1—2 January, 1709-10: Adms. granted joyntly to Jane North, widow, and Thomas North, brother of sd. decd.

Page 126—6 April, 1713: Thomas North, Adms., exhibits now an account of his Adms. Order to dist. the estate:

	£	s	d
To Jane North, widow relict,		9-12-03	
To Thomas, eldest son,	(Broken page.)		
To Nathaniel, Joseph, Ebenezer, Hannah, Mary, Rebeckah, Lydia and Sarah North, to each of them,		2-02-08	

And appoint John Stanly, Samuel Newell and Joseph North, of Farmington, dist.

Page 11 (Vol. VII) 8 April, 1701: John North is appointed guardian to his two daughters which he had by Mary Warner.

Page 126—6 April, 1713: This Court appointed Hannah North of Farmington to be guardian to her two daughters Lydia and Sarah, both minors above 14 years, and also allow the sd. Hannah North to be guardian to her son Ebenezer North, 14 years of age. Joseph North, a minor, chose Thomas North to be his guardian. Recog., £100.

Page 216—4 October, 1714: Report of the distributors.

Page 261.

North, Thomas, Farmington. Invt. £233-13-10. Taken 19 December, 1712, by Samuel Newell, Joseph North and Thomas Burd.

Court Record, Page 99—1st December, 1712: Adms. to Hannah North, widow, and Thomas North, a son of the deceased.

Page 164—17 November, 1713: Adms. account allowed. Order to distribute the estate to Hannah North, widow, to Thomas, to Nathaniel, to Joseph, to Ebenezer, to Hannah, to Mary, to Rebecca, to Lydia, to Sarah North. By John Stanly, Samuel Newell and Joseph North.

Page 47.

Nott, John, Sen., Wethersfield. Invt. £624-01-09. Taken 27 June, 1710, by James Patterson, David Buck and Samuel Smith.

Court Record, Page 15—3 July, 1710: Adms. to Patience Nott, widow, and John Nott, a son.

Page 63—4 March, 1711-12: This Court appoint Patience Nott of Wethersfield to be guardian to her 3 children, minors, viz., Abraham, Thankfull and Anne.

Page 64—4 March, 1711-12: Adms. exhibits now an account of their Adms. Allowed. Order to dist. the estate:

	£ s d
To Patience Nott, widow,	40-02-04
To John, eldest son,	125-19-09
To Jonathan, William, Nathaniel, Gershom, Abraham, Thankfull and Anne Nott, to each,	62-19-10½

And appoint Capt. Robert Welles, John Curtis, Jr., and Benjamin Churchill distributors. And grant Patience and John Nott a *Quietus Est.*

Page 198 (Vol. X) 21 August, 1728: Ann Nott informs this Court that her father, John Nott the 2nd, died intestate about 18 or 19 years ago, and an invt. exhibited in Court, debts paid, and an order to distribute. The distributors set out to each child so many pounds in value, but did not set out each child's part by meets and bounds as they ought to have done. The children have by consent given the widow Patience Nott liberty to improve the whole of sd. lot ever since the sd. dist. Now the sd. Patience Nott, being willing to improve her part separately, moves this Court that sd. lot of land be set out to her and the rest by meets and bounds, to the end that she may know which is her particular part to improve. This Court appoint Benjamin Churchill, Jonathan Burnham and Capt. Robert Welles to set out by meets and bounds according to a former dist., allowing the widow to improve a third part of each child's portion.

Page 202—1st October, 1728: John Nott moves this Court that the home lot of his late father, John Nott, might be set out to him, he paying the rest of the heirs their portions according to just value.

Page 85 (Vol. XI) 13 March, 1732-3: Thomas Harris and William Blynn, in right of their wives Thankfull and Ann, heirs to the estate of John Nott of Wethersfield, moves this Court to set out the home lot of the decd. by meets and bounds to the respective heirs, according to an

order of the Court, 4 March, 1711-12. And it appears to this Court, by
the sd. distribution, that the sd. home lott was not divided to the heirs by
meets and bounds, and now appoint Jonathan Belding, Jacob Goodrich
and Jonathan Burnham to set out, etc. John Nott, the eldest son, appeals
to the Superior Court.

Page 8 (Vol. XIII) 31 May, 1737: Patience Nott, widow, showing
that her husband had been many years dead, yet there had not been set out
to her any right of dower in the real estate, this Court now appoint Nathaniel Burnham, Gideon Wells and Elizer Goodrich to set out to her 1-3
part of the land by meets and bounds.

Page 68.

Olcott, George, Hartford. Invt. £261-03-00. Taken 2 March, 1710-
11, by Joseph Barnard and James Steele.

Court Record, Page 27—5 February, 1710-11: Adms. to Sarah Olcott, widow, John Bunce and Thomas Olcott.

Page 177.

Olcott, John, Hartford. Invt. £560-19-09. Taken 2 May, 1712, by
Cyprian Nickolls, John Pratt and Thomas Olcott.

Court Record, Page 65—7 April, 1712: Adms. granted to Mrs. Mary
Olcott, relict and widow of sd. decd.

See File: We whose names are underwritten, being appointed to divide the estate of John Olcott, late of Hartford, deceased, and being under
oath thereunto, we dist. to the widow or relict of the sd. John Olcott one-
third part of the house and garden and 1-3 part of the land at Samuel
Cadwell's during life. And to Joseph Farnsworth and Marah his wife,
½ of the homelott with the house thereon, or 2-3 thereof, the other third
at the death of the widow. To Rachel Olcott, ½ of the homelott with the
little house thereon, valued at £100. To Abigail Olcott, the land lying
between land formerly Tymothy Phelps's and Samuel Cadwell, valued at
£50. The land in the south medow formally belonging to Timothy Hide,
now in the possession of Mr. Watson, and the reversion of which belongeth unto the heirs of the sd. John Olcott, we dist. to each of the sd. heirs
an equal part thereof when the reversion thereof returneth to them, the
widow then to have 1-3 thereof.

This we give in as our distribution, this 25th of June, 1722.
Test: Hez: Wyllys, Clerk.　　　　　　　　　　AARON COOKE,
　　　　　　　　　　　　　　　　　　　　　　JOHN PRATT.

We whose names are underwritten have agreed, divided and received
our parts of the moveable estate of John Olcott, late of Hartford, de-

ceased, the full proportion of our part thereof according to the order of the Court of Probate. As witness our hands and seals.

Witness: *Aaron Cooke,*   JOSEPH WADSWORTH, LS.
    John Pratt.   MARY WADSWORTH, LS.
                            JOS. FFARNSWORTH, LS.
                            MARY FARNSWORTH, LS.
                            RACHEL OLLCOT, LS.
                            ABIGAIL OLCOT, LS.

Page 102 (Vol. IX): At a Court of Probate held at Hartford, 26 May, 1722, Joseph Talcott, Judge, and Hez: Wyllys, Clerk:

Mrs. Mary Wadsworth, alias Olcott, Adms. on the estate of Mr. John Olcott, late of Hartford, decd., now exhibited an account of her Adms., in which it appears that she has paid in loss of estate and spent in the family, and also abated out of the inventory estate not belonging to the said John Olcott, amounting to the sum of £198-08-08, which accot. this Court accept and order it be kept on file. And whereas, it appears upon record that the inventory of sd. estate amounts to the value of £560-19-09, from which, substracting the sum of £198-08-08, there will then remain the sum of £362-11-01 to be dist. as followeth: viz., To Elizabeth Wadsworth, alias Olcott, relict of the decd., out of ye moveable estate the sum or value of £49-07-01, which is 1-3 part thereof, to be her own forever; and 1-3 part of the houseing and lands of the sd. decd. for her improvement during life. And the residue of sd. estate, including the relict's thirds after her decease, in houseing and lands, to be dist. as followeth: To Mary ffarnsworth, Rachel Olcott, and to Abigail Olcott, daughters of the deceased, the sum or value of £104-08-00, which is their equal part or portions of sd. estate. And this Court do appoint Capt. Aaron Cooke, Mr. Nathaniel Stanly and John Pratt of Hartford, or any two of them, to dist. and set out the sd. estate accordingly.

Page 170—25 June, 1722: Report of the dist. Also an agreement for dividing the moveable estate was now exhibited in Court under the hands and seals of Capt. Joseph Wadsworth, Mrs. Mary Wadsworth, Joseph Farnsworth and Mary Farnsworth, Rachel Olcott, and Abigail Olcott, which agreement is accepted by the Court, ordered recorded and kept on file.

Page 216.

Olcott, Thomas, Jr., Hartford. Invt. £128-05-06. Taken 30 January, 1712-13, by Aaron Cooke and Thomas Wadsworth.

Will dated 1st December, 1712: I, Thomas Olcott, being in expectation that my change is very near, do make this my last will and testament: I give to my wife Hannah 1-2 of my estate during her life, and the other half I give to my three sons, an equal share of, and my daughter half so much as one of my sons. I make my wife sole executrix.

Witness: *Joseph Talcott,*   THOMAS OLCOTT, LS.
    Hez: Wyllys.

Court Record, Page 102—15 December, 1712: Will exhibited and proven. The executrix refuses, and is appointed Adms. on the estate of Thomas Olcott, Jr., with the will annexed.

Page 212—2 August, 1714: This Court doth allow to Hannah Olcott, relict of Thomas Olcott, late of Hartford, decd., out of the estate for what she hath paid, £60-01-03; and for what the treasurer hath received, £59-10-00; remaining, £8-14-03.

Page 74 (Vol. IX) 5 August, 1718: Upon motion of Hannah Olcott, Adms., this Court order the administrators of the late Treasurer Whiting, decd., shall deliver the book of accounts in their hands late belonging to the sd. Thomas Olcott, decd., unto the sd. Hannah Olcott.

Page 50 (Vol. XI) 10 August, 1731: Hannah Olcott, the widow, moves this Court that her dower or third part of the lands of the decd. be set out to her. This Court appoint Capt. John Sheldon, Ensign Nathaniel Goodwin and Obadiah Spencer to set out sd. lands.

Page 85—22 March, 1732-3: Jonathan Olcott, son to Thomas Olcott and grandson to Samuel Olcott, both deceased, moves this Court to give judgement on such parts of the will of the sd. Samuel Olcott, decd., wherein he hath given or did give to Thomas Olcott, his son, and the heirs of his body, several parcels of land, that the Court will say in what proportion sd. lands shall be divided amongst the sons of sd. Thomas Olcott, decd., being the only surviving children of sd. decd. Decree: The land shall be equally divided in quantity and quality to and among the sd. heirs, Jonathan Olcott, Thomas Olcott and Joseph Olcott. And the sd. Jonathan Olcott appealed from this decree to the Superior Court.

Onepenny, Sarah. (Indian Woman.)   Court Record, Page 141—19 May, 1713: The nuncupative will of Sarah Onepenny, an Indian woman, who gave her land (3 or 4 acres in the South Meadow near the Wigwams, in Hartford) to Scipio, her grandson, was now exhibited in Court and testimony made thereto by her sister Hannah, an Indian woman, and Mrs. Mary Whiting, single woman, of Hartford, which testimony is confirmed by the Court. And Col. William Whiting was dedesired to oversee the sd. Scipio.

Page 191—19 April, 1714: This Court appoint Mr. Thomas Hosmore and Mr. Thomas Seamore of Hartford to set out or measure the land in the South Meadow given by Sarah Onepenny, an Indian woman, to her grandson Scipio, servant to Col. William Whiting.

Page 284—Probate Side: Pursuant to an order of the Court of Probate bearing date the 19th of April, 1714, land was set out or dist. to Scipio, an Indian: We, the undersigned, have laid out a piece of land in the South Meadow containing 4 acres and 55 rods beside the highway, and land on which the Indians dwell, and is thus butted and bounded: south on the land of Joseph Catlin 33 rods, west on the land of Capt. Wyllys 53 rods, and northeasterly upon the Great River 61 rods, which sd.

piece of land is and has been reputed to belong to the Indians for a great many years. We left Col. Whiting upon the sd. land, who is to improve it for the benefit of Scipio, an Indian boy, who dwells with him, as is mentioned in the order abovesd.

28 April, 1714.   *Thomas Hosmer,*
                                  Thomas Seamore.

Page 230.

Owen, Daniel, Windsor. Invt. £28-05-00. Taken 27 February, 1712-13, by Daniel Hayden and Josiah Bissell.

Court Record, Page 31—2 April, 1711: Whereas, Daniel Owen, son of Daniel Owen deceased, hath now for several years last past been absent abroad upon the seas, and his estate being in a suffering and wasting condition, this Court appoint Daniel Bissell of Windsor, uncle to Daniel Owen, and Joseph Burge, his brother, to take care of the estate.

Page 105—5 January, 1712-13: This Court order the Clerk to cite Daniel Bissell and Joseph Burge of Windsor, who were appointed conservators, to appear and render an account of management of the sd. estate.

Page 136—4 May, 1713: Invt. exhibited.

Owen, Isaac. Court Record, Page 7—6 March, 1709-10: This Court grants Adms. on the estate of Isaac Owen unto John Owen, a brother of sd. decd.

Page 246.

Palmer, Timothy, Windsor. Invt. £65-10-01. Taken 2 October, 1713, by Thomas Marshall and John Bissell.

Court Record, Page 158—5 October, 1713: Adms. to John Palmer, son of the deceased.

Page 200.

Pantry, John, Jr., Hartford. Invt. £72-02-04. Taken 21 April, 1713, by Nathaniel Goodwin and John Skinner.

Court Record, Page 127—6 April, 1713: Adms. to Mary Pantry, widow.

Page 185—5 April, 1714: Mary Pantry of Farmington, Adms., exhibits now in this Court an account of her Adms. This Court order the remaining estate to be left in the Adms. hands for subsisting the young child.

Page 220 (Vol. X) 3 June, 1729: This Court appoints Solomon Boltwood of Hadley, in the County of Hampshire, in the Province of Massachusetts Bay, in New England, to be guardian to Abigail Pantry, daughter of John Pantry, Jr., formerly of Hartford, decd., and the sd. Boltwood and Capt. Thomas Seymour of Hartford acknowledge themselves bound in a recog. of £100.

Page 238.

Pettebone, John, Sen., Simsbury. Died 15 July, 1713: Invt. £417-10-10. Taken 22 July, 1713, by Joseph Phelps, Joseph Case and John Slater.

Will dated 2 December, 1707: I, John Pettebone, Sen., do make this my last will and testament: I give to my wife Sarah, I will and give to her, my household goods that belongs to the house within doors, to be for her comfort while she lives, and at her disposal when she dies. I give to my eldest son John Pettebone, besides what I have formerly given him, all that land joining to Samuel Wilcockson, Jr. I give him my land at Brickiln Swamp. I give to my son Stephen Pettebone, besides what I have already given him, the 1-2 of my 40-acre lott; also my land which I have at Barn Door Hills. I give to my son Samuel Pettebone, besides what I have already given him, the other half of my lot at the West River with his brother Stephen, and my lot in Hazel Meadow, and the half part of my lotment of land at Second Brook. I give to my son Henry Pettebone the 1-2 part of my house and homested, with the lands that are mine adjacent thereunto; also 1-2 of my lot in Nodd Meadow. I give to my son Joseph Pettebone the other half of my house and homested and the land adjacent, the other half of my Nod Meadow lot, and the other moiety of my lot upon Second Brook. I give to my daughters, besides what they have already received: to Sarah, £20; to Rebeckah, £3; to Anne, £20; also to my grandchild Sarah Mills, that lives with me, £5; and in case of her decease this £5 to go to the other grandchildren by the name of Mills. I appoint my sons John Pettebone and Samuel Pettebone executors.

Witness: *Dudley Woodbridge,*   JOHN X PETTEBONE, LS.
John Higley, Sen., Samuel Wilcockson.

A codicil added to the will, bearing date 1st November, 1711.
Witness: *Samuel Wilcockson,*   JOHN X PETTEBONE, LS.
    Timothy Woodbridge, Jr.

Court Record, Page 151—3 August, 1713: Will proven.

Page 174.

Phelps, Timothy, Hartford. Invt. £486-11-11. Taken 29 April, 1712, by Aaron Cooke, John Pratt and Thomas Olcott.

Will dated 28 March, 1712: I, Timothy Phelps, do make this my last will and testament: I give to my wife Sarah 1-3 part of all my real and personal estate during her natural life. I give to each of my daughters severally £30 as money, to be paid in lands or goods at the discretion of my executrix. And with respect to my eldest daughter, now married, my will is that what she hath already received of me be part of her £30. All the rest of my estate not disposed of as before I give to my son Timothy and to his heirs forever. I give to my wife the use and improvement of all my estate for the bringing up of my children till the time of the payment of the several legacies above specified. I appoint my wife Sarah sole executrix.

Witness: *John Pratt,*   TIMOTHY X PHELPS, LS.
         John Skinner.

Court Record, Page 75—5 May, 1712: Will proven.

Page 21 (Vol. X) 4 June, 1723: This Court appoint Elisha Lord, Lt. Nathaniel Marsh and Joseph Pitkin to set out 1-3 part of sd. estate to Sarah Phelps, widow; also, legacies to be paid to the daughters of sd. decd., and to Timothy Phelps, only son.

Page 123.

Phelps, William, Windsor. Invt. £288-15-00. Taken 31 January, 1711-12, by Benajah Holcomb, Thomas Griswold and William Phelps.

Court Record, Page 51—4 February, 1711-12: Adms. granted to Hannah Phelps, widow, and Samuel Hayden.

Page 136 (Vol. IX) 6 September, 1720: Hannah Phelps and Samuel Hayden, Adms., exhibit an account of their Adms. Order to dist. the estate as followeth:

	£	s	d
To Hannah Phelps, widow,	19-07-03		
To William Phelps, eldest son,	57-03-07		
To Daniel, John, Charles, Hannah, Phebe and Elizabeth Phelps, the rest of the children, to each of them,	28-11-09		

And appoint Nathaniel Pinney, Timothy Loomis and William Phelps, distributors.

Page 13 (Vol. X) 2 April, 1723: Report of the distributors.

Page 20.

Pinney, Isaac, Windsor. Invt. £500-01-00. Taken 10 December, 1709, by Abraham Phelps, Sen., and Job Drake, Sen.

Court Record, Page 4—6 February, 1709-10: Adms. granted to Sarah Pinney, widow, and Isaac Pinney, son of sd. decd.

Page 190—14 April, 1714: Isaac Pinney declared he had not intermeddled with the estate and declined the trust. He was discharged, and Sarah Pinney to be sole Adms.

Page 13 (Vol. IX) 1st May, 1716: Sarah Pinney, Adms., exhibits an account of debts due from the estate, whereby it appears that there is not sufficient of the moveable part of that estate to discharge the sd. debts, which account is allowed.

Page 165—7 April, 1722: Sarah Pinney, Adms., exhibits now an account of her Adms. Accepted. Order to dist. the estate: To Sarah Pinney 1-3 part of the real estate for her improvement during life; to Isaac Pinney, eldest son; Jonathan Humphrey, Daniel, Noah, Sarah and Hannah Pinney and Mary Gridley, children of the sd. decd., to each a single part of sd. estate. And appoint Israel Stoughton, Ebenezer Fitch and Abraham Phelps, Jr., distributors. Noah Pinney, 18 years of age, chose Israel Stoughton of Windsor to be his guardian.

Page 48 (Vol. X) 5 May, 1724: Report of the dist. Accepted and ordered filed.

Page 41.

Porter, Nathaniel, Lebanon, late residing in Hartford. Invt. £305-01-04. Taken at Lebanon by William Clark, John Calkin and John Smith; at Hartford by Joseph Olmsted and Roger Pitkin.

Court Record, Page 13—5 June, 1710: Adms. to Hezekiah Porter of Hartford.

Page 87—4 August, 1712: Upon request of Samuel Buell of Killingworth, it is ordered that an order be made out to call Hezekiah Porter of Hartford, Adms. on the estate of Nathaniel Porter of Lebanon, before this Court to render account of his administration.

5 August, 1712: Hezekiah Porter was granted some more time, but ordered to report upon such a day, and further ordered to pay to Mr. Buell, now appointed guardian to Nathaniel Porter, son and heir (a minor, about 8 years of age), all monies, bills, credits, etc. And the sd. Samuel Buell recog. £120.

Page 91—6 October, 1712: Hezekiah Porter of Hartford, Adms. on the estate of his late brother, Nathaniel Porter, late of Lebanon, rendered account (to account further).

Page 144—1st June, 1713: Hezekiah Porter, Adms., now renders a supplementary report. Account allowed.

Page 80.

Porter, Deacon Thomas, Farmington. Died 28 March, 1711. Invt. £179-17-00. Taken 12 May, 1711, by John Hart, Sen., Daniel Andrews, Sen., and Isaac Cowles.

Will dated 28 March, 1711: I, Thomas Porter, being not like to continue long in this world, I desire to dispose of my estate as followeth: I give to my son Timothy Porter all my lands. I leave my wife Lois Por-

ter to the loveing care and keeping of my son Timothy Porter by reason
that she is not able to manage things so as may be for her own comfort alone. And my will is that my wife shall have the improvement of
all my household goods during the time of her natural life, and the whole
dispose of one cow in life and in death. My will is that after my wife's
decease my grandchild Eunice Goodwin shall have all that is left and remains of my household goods, now left with my wife. [At this point
Deacon Porter fainted and ceased to live.]
Attest: *John Hart, Sen.,*
       Samuel Porter, Sen.

This agreement endorsed on the back side of the will on file:
Whereas, by the prouidence of god Decon Thomas porter off ffar-
mington dyed before hee had ffinshed his Last Will & Testament respecting Some thing he intended to giue his Grandchild Lois goodwin of
Hartford, itt is this day ffully agreed Betweene his onely son & Heyer,
Timothy porter, & Nathaniell Goodwin in Behalfe off his daughter Lois
goodwin, that the sayd Timothy Porter shall giue unto the sayd Nathaniel Goodwin ffor his daughter Lois goodwin the ffull & just sum off
£15 att Inuentory price out of his ffather's Estate that is prised att mony
price, and that this Condition Being performed the aboue mentioned Will
& Testament off Decon porter shall stand in ffull power & vertue of as is
written on the other side of this paper respecting all other persons Concerned. As witness our Hands this 7th off June, 1711.
Witness: *Caleb Stanly, Senior,*   Timothy Porter,
      Daniel Smith.   Nathaniell Goodwin.

Court Record, Page 34—4 June, 1711: The last will of Thomas Porter was exhibited by Timothy Porter, only son, which was not wholly
finished and signed before his death, together with an agreement endorsed
on sd. will, made by the said Timothy Porter, only son, and Nathaniel
Goodwin, Jr., of Hartford, weaver, who married the only daughter of the
said deceased, for allowing said will. Adms., with the will annexed, to
Timothy Porter.

Invt. Page 40 (Vol. IX).

Porter, William, Haddam. Invt. £138-02-08. Taken 1st January,
1713-14, by Elijah Braynard and Hezekiah Braynard.
Court Record, Page 200—7 June, 1714: Adms. granted unto Sarah
Porter, widow. William Porter, 14 years of age, chose his mother, Sarah
Porter, to be his guardian. Recog., £100.
Page 254—12 May, 1715: Sarah Porter of Haddam, 14 years of age,
chose Hezekiah Brainard of Haddam to be her guardian.
Page 256—7 June, 1715: Sarah Porter, Adms., exhibits now an
account of her Adms. Also she prayes this Court for an allowance of
40 shillings for Adms. and £10 for subsisting the youngest child, Abiall

Porter, daughter of sd. deceased, the same being a year and 4 months old, which was allowed out of the estate before the dist. Order to dist. the estate:

	£	s	d
To the widow, Sarah Porter,	31-00-00		
To William, eldest son,	41-09-04		
To Amos, Sarah, Mary, Martha and Abial Porter, to each,	20-14-08		

And appoint Simon Smith, Elijah Brainard and Hezekiah Brainard, distributors.

Page 119 (Vol. IX) 9 February, 1719-20: This Court appoint Joseph Arnold of Haddam to be guardian to Amos Porter, age 15 years, and Mary Porter, age 13 years. Recog., £100.

Page 143—6 December, 1720: This Court appoint Elijah Brainard of Haddam to be guardian unto Martha and Abial Porter, minor children of William Porter, decd. Recog., £100.

Dist. File: 15 March, 1719-20: To the widow, Sarah Porter, now Sarah Ventrus, to Abial, to William, to Amos, to Mary, to Martha, to Sarah Porter. By Simon Smith, Elijah Brainard and Hezekiah Brainard.

Page 162—6 February, 1721-2: Report of the distributors.

Powell, Thomas. Court Record, Page 134—9 April, 1713: John Stedman, of Wethersfield, appointed guardian to Thomas Powell of Wethersfield, age 11 years, son of William Powell of Wethersfield, supposed departed this life.

Page 257.

Ranny, Hannah, Single Woman, Middletown. Invt. £38-05-05. Taken 24 November, 1713, by John Warner and Samuel Frary.

Court Record, Page 160—2 November, 1713: Adms. granted unto Joseph Ranny, a brother of sd. decd.

Page 163—7 December, 1713: Joseph Ranny exhibits an account of his Adms. Accepted. Order to dist. the estate to the surviving brothers and sisters. And appoint John Sage, Samuel Frary and John Warner, distributors.

Dist. File: 25 December, 1713: Dist of the estate to the surviving brothers and sisters: To Thomas, to John, to Joseph, to Ebenezer, to Mary the wife of Capt. John Savage, to Elizabeth the wife of Jonathan Warner, to Esther the wife of Nathaniel Savage, to Margaret and Abigail Ranny. By John Warner and Samuel Frary.

Page 167—4 January, 1713-14: Report of the distributors.

Page 253.

Ranny, Thomas, Middletown. Invt. £758-19-10. Taken 27 July, 1713, by John Sage, Samuel Frary and John Warner. Will dated 6 March, 1711.

I, Thomas Ranney of Middletown, do make this my last will and testament: I give to my wife Mary, during her natural life, the use of half of my dwelling house wherein she now lives, half of my homelot, half of my old barn, with the whole of my upper lot in Long Meadow, also that land that her Father Hubbard gave her. And I appoint my son Thomas to take care of his mother. I give to my son Thomas the lot on which his house stands, and 1 1-2 acres of my land in Wongonk Meadow, and the whole of the upper Long Meadow lot, after his mother's decease. That lot near Wongunk or Indian Hill, the east part, I reserve for myself; the west part thereof I will that it be divided unto my four sons equally betwixt them, viz., Thomas, John, Joseph and Ebenezer. I give to my son John that lot whereon his house stands, with one acre of land. I give to my son Joseph the lot whereon his house stands, with one acre of land. I give unto my son Ebenezer half of my dwelling house, homested and old barn, and the other half after his mother's decease, provided he do pay to Mary Savage, Elizabeth Warner and Easter Savage £5 apiece; also that he should give to his sisters, vizt., to Hannah, Margaret and Abigail, so much of his part of Cold Spring lot as shall amount to £15 in pay. I give to my son and daughter John and Mary Savage land in the lower meadow. I give unto my son and daughter Jonathan and Elizabeth Warner, in addition to what they have already had, £5. I give to my son and daughter Nathaniel and Easter Savage £5 in addition to what they have already had. I give unto my grandson Willett Ranney about 8 acres of a Timber Hill lot. I give unto my grandson Thomas Savage my lott in the Dead Swamp. Lastly, I now appoint my sons Thomas, John and Joseph to be executors, and desire Mr. David Deming and my son John Savage overseers.

Witness: *Nathaniel White,*   THOMAS X RANNEY, LS.
Samuel Frary, Timothy Sage.

Court Record, Page 147—6 July, 1713: Will proven.

Read, Arthur, late of Hartford (but lately residing in Hatfield).

Court Record, Page 30—2 April, 1711: Adms. granted to Col. Samuel Partridge of Hatfield, in the County of Hampshire and Province of Massachusetts Bay.

Page 29.

Read, Jacob, Simsbury. Died 3 December, 1709. Invt. £211-18-02. Taken December last, 1709, by John Higley, Sen., Samuel Wilcockson, Sen., and John Slaughter, Sen.

Court Record, Page 6—6 March, 1709-10: Adms. granted to Elizabeth Read, widow, and John Tuller.

Page 35—2 July, 1711: John Tuller, Adms., of Simsbury, complains against William Moses and Elizabeth his wife, Adms., and they were cited to appear and give account.

Page 39—19 November, 1711: This Court appoint Sergt. Wilcox to be guardian to Jacob Read, son of Jacob Read, and Richard Case to be guardian unto Lydia Read, daughter of sd. decd.

Page 61—3 March, 1711-12: Upon the petition of Elizabeth Moses of Simsbury, widow of Dr. Jacob Read, this Court grants the sole and entire Adms. unto John Tuller.

Page 84—7 July, 1712: Jacob Read and Lydia Read chose Sergt. Wilcox to be their guardian.

Page 101—1st December, 1712: This Court allows of Mr. Samuel Law of Concord to be guardian to Jacob Read and Lydia Read of Simsbury, children of Dr. Jacob Read, late of sd. Simsbury, decd., provided he give bonds.

Page 109—7 January, 1712-13: John Tuller, Adms., now exhibits an account of payments made by him of £90-07-11. Accepted. The Court order to deliver and pay out of the estate £22 to William Moses of Simsbury, who married with the widow, there being so much due to the sd. William Moses.

Page 119—2 March, 1712-13: William Moses of Simsbury, with his wife Elizabeth, complained to this Court against John Tuller, Adms., that the sd. John Tuller did sometime since take away from them a bed, bedding and sundry other things necessary for their comfortable subsistance. John Tuller was cited to answer the complaint.

Page 11 (Vol. IX) 3 April, 1716: Lydia Read, age 13 years, now appeared and made choice of Joseph Case to be her guardian. Recog., £40.

Page 58—1st April, 1718: John Tuller complains that Elizabeth Moses, the wife of William Moses, being sometime Adms., has in custody in value of £46-12-09 of sd. estate, and she was cited to appear and answer.

Page 121—22 February, 1719-20: John Tuller, Adms., now renders an account of his Adms., and is ordered to complete an inventory.

Page 151—8 May, 1721: John Tuller now exhibits an account of his Adms. Accepted.

Page 169—5 June, 1722: This Court appoint Joseph Phelps, Samuel Humphrey, Jr., and John Pettebone to set out to Elizabeth Read, alias Moses, 1-3 part of the houseing and lands of Jacob Read, late decd., for her improvement during life.

Page 49 (Vol. X) 5 May, 1724: John Tuller, Adms., exhibits a return of the sale of land of the sd. decd. for the payment of debts according to an act of the General Assembly held at Hartford 11 May, 1721, which is by this Court accepted and ordered to be kept on file.

Invt. in Vol. IX, Page 43.

Richards, Benjamin, Waterbury. Invt. £57-14-00. Taken 23 August, 1714, by Timothy Stanly and John Judd.

Court Record, Page 210—2 August, 1714: Adms. granted to Thomas Richards of Waterbury.

Page 7 (Vol. IX) 6 March, 1715-16: Thomas Richards, Adms., exhibits an account of his Adms. Allowed. Order to dist. the estate to the brethren in equal proportions: To John Richards (the heir of Obadiah Richards) and Thomas Richards, brothers, to Mary, Hannah, Easter, Elizabeth, Sarah and Rachel, sisters of sd. decd., to each of them, £4-09-06. And appoint Thomas Judd, John Hopkins and Joseph Lewis, distributors.

Inventory on File.

Richardson, Hannah. Invt. £2-03-06. Taken 1713, by Israel Brunson and Benjamin Barnes. Hannah Richardson, relict of Israel Richardson, late of Waterbury, decd.

Court Record, Page 210—2 August, 1714: Adms. granted unto Lt. Thomas Judd on the estate of Hannah Richards (Richardson), late of Waterbury, decd.

Inventory on File.

Richardson, Israel, Waterbury. Invt. £39-01-08. Taken 30 December, 1712, by John Hopkins and John Brunson.

The children: Joseph, 4 years of age; Israel, 1 year; Mary, 13 years, and Hannah, 7 years.

Court Record, Page 108—7 January, 1712-13: Adms. granted to John Hopkins of Waterbury.

Page 130—19 May, 1713: Samuel Woodruff is appointed guardian to Joseph and Hannah Richardson, children of Israel Richardson, decd.

Page 189—5 April, 1714: This Court appoints Thomas Judd of Waterbury, guardian to Israel Richardson, son of Israel Richardson, decd. Recog., £5.

Page 196—John Hopkins, Adms., exhibited an account of his Adms. Accepted. And this Court grant him a *Quietus Est.*

Page 2 (Vol. IX) 7 December, 1715: This Court appoint Capt. Thomas Judd of Waterbury to be guardian to Israel Richardson, age about 4 years, son of Israel Richardson, late decd. Recog., £10.

Page 277.

(See also Vol. IX, Page 48, for Invt.)

Richardson, John, Waterbury. Died 17th October, 1712. Invt. £95-15-02. Taken by John Scovell and Joseph Lewis.

Court Record, Page 109—7 January, 1712-13: Elizabeth, the widow, cited to take Adms. on her husband's estate.

Page 112—2 February, 1712-13: Adms. granted to Elizabeth, the widow.

Page 2 (Vol. IX) 7 December, 1715: Elizabeth Richardson, Adms., exhibits now an account of her Adms. Accepted.

Page 37—2 July, 1717: Elizabeth Richardson granted liberty to sell land.

Page 141—6 December, 1720: Adms. accounts now settled and this Court order dist. of the estate:

To Elizabeth, the widow, her dowry in houseing and lands.

	£	s	d
To John Richardson,	13	12	06
To Ruth, Elizabeth, Mary and Sarah Richardson, to each,	6	16	03

And appoint Ephraim Warner, John Scovell and Jeremiah Peck of Waterbury, distributors.

Page 232 (Probate Side, Vol. XII): An addition to the inventory, which was taken 1712, of £187-07-00. Taken by Ephraim Warner and William Judd. Also some land was inventoried belonging to his father, Thomas Richardson.

Court Record, Page 199 (Vol. X) 3 September, 1727-8: An addition to the invt. of £187-07-00 was now exhibited in Court, ordered recorded and kept on file.

Page 247.

Richardson, Lemuel, East Haddam. Died 24 May, 1713. Invt. £332-10-08. Taken by Joseph Selden and John Warner at Haddam, James Noyes and Stephen Richardson at Stonington. Will dated 2 May, 1713.

I, Lemuel Richardson, do see cause to dispose of my lands, etc., as followeth: I give unto my wife all my moveable estate during widowhood, and half of it forever. And I give her full power, after my decease, to give a full and lawfull title to John Noyes of Stonington for ninety acres of upland, agreed upon but not fully completed; and the money due for said land I will that my wife should dispose of according to her best judgement for her own comfort, paying of my debts and the bringing up of my children. Also the debts due to me to be at her dispose. And I appoint her sole administratrix of my estate. I give to mv two sons, Samuel and Lemuel, all my lands and buildings, to be divided between them, Samuel to have £20 more than Lemuel. I give to my daughter Mehetabell £40.

Witness: *Jabez Chapman,*   LEMUEL X RICHARDSON, LS.
Lydia Chapman, Sarah X Spencer.

Court Record, Page 159—5 October, 1713: Adms. to Mehetabell Richardson, widow, with the will annexed. Will proven.

Invt. in Vol. IX, Page 102.

Richardson, Nathaniel, Waterbury. Invt. £21-13-06. Taken 23 December, 1712, by John Hopkins and John Brunson.

Court Record, Page 211—2 August, 1714: Adms. granted to Ebenezer Richardson of Waterbury.

Page 18 (Vol. IX) 3 July, 1716: Ebenezer Richardson to be cited to appear and give account of his Adms.

Page 58—1st April, 1718: Ebenezer Richardson, Adms., exhibits now an account of his Adms. Order to dist. the estate to the brothers and sisters of sd. decd., the sum remaining being only £1-19-07, to be distributed equally among them: To John, Israel, Thomas, Ebenezer, Sarah, Rebeckah, Ruth and Joanna Richardson, to each of them £0-04-11 and 2 1-2 farthings. And appoint Thomas Judd, John Scovell and William Hickcox, of Waterbury, distributors.

Page 260.

Richardson, Thomas, Waterbury. Invt. £112-00-05. Taken 23 December, 1712, by John Hopkins and John Bronson, in Waterbury, and 6 April, 1713, by John Stanly and Samuel Wadsworth in Farmington.

Court Record, Page 108—7 January, 1712-13: Adms. to Thomas Richardson, eldest son.

Page 209—15 July, 1714: Adms. account allowed. Order to dist. the estate: To the eldest son a double part, and to each of the others a single part. And appoint Thomas Judd, Jeremy Peck and Benjamin Barnes, distributors.

Dist. File: 15 December, 1714: Dist. of the estate of Thomas Richardson, late of Waterbury, decd., as followeth:

	£ s d
To Thomas Richardson, eldest son,	15-15-00
To John Richardson,	7-17-06
To Israel Richardson's heirs,	7-17-06
To Sarah Williams, Rebeckah Warner, Ruth Richardson and Joanna Warner, widow, to each of them the sum of	7-17-00
By Benjamin Barnes and Thomas Judd.	

Page 232—3 January, 1714-15: Report of the dist. on the estate of Sergt. Thomas Richardson was now accepted, ordered recorded and filed.

Page 149.

Page 18, Vol. IX, Agreement.

Robbins, John, Wethersfield. Died 6 October, 1712. Invt. £391-14-04. Taken by Edward Bulkeley, Jonathan Belding and James Steele.

An agreement, dated 3 January, 1714, at Wethersfield, by and between Joshua Robbins, Samuel Robbins and Richard Robbins, heirs of the estate of our brother, John Robbins, decd., giving to each other quit-claims to all save that set out to one or another.

Court Record, Page 93—3 November, 1712: Adms. granted to Joshua Robbins, a brother of sd. decd.

Page 232—3 January, 1714-15: Exhibit of an agreement for the division of the estate of their brother, John Robbins, which this Court confirm.

Page 233—18 January, 1714-15: Joshua Robbins exhibits now an account of his Adms., which this Court accept.

Page 76-7.

Rockwell, Samuel, Windsor. Invt. £331-18-10. Taken 26 September, 1711, by Joshua Willes, Sen., John Strong and John Stoughton, Sen. Will dated 8 August, 1711.

I, Samuel Rockwell, Sen., of Windsor, do make and ordain this to be my last will and testament: I give to Mary my wife the third part of my dwelling house, barn, and all my upland and meadow, during her natural life, and also £12 in current pay out of my personal estate, to be at her own dispose. I give to my son Samuel Rockwell a certain tract of upland in the woods, in length 2 1-4 miles and in breadth 5 1-2 rods, and also £8 in current pay. I give to my son Joseph Rockwell land adjoining my son Samuel. I give to my son John Rockwell land adjoining to Joseph's land. I give to my son Josiah Rockwell my dwelling house, barn, orchards on the upland and pastures. I give to my daughter Mary Loomis, besides what she hath received, £6. I give to my daughter Abigail Smith, besides what she hath received, £14. I make my son Josiah Rockwell sole executor.

Witness: *Job Drake,*   SAMUEL ROCKWELL, LS.
    John Stoughton, Sen.

A codicil, dated 9 August, 1711: Upon further consideration, and by good advice, I do hereby declare it to be my will and pleasure that Mary my wife shall have the use and improvement of all my estate, both real and personal, that I am now in possession of, during her natural life.

Witness: *Job Drake,*   SAMUEL ROCKWELL, LS.
    Matthew Grant.

Court Record, Page 38—1st October, 1711: Will exhibited by Josiah Rockwell, and inventory approved.

Page 178.

Root, Caleb, Farmingtown. Invt. £340-14-06. Taken 12 August, 1712, by John Hart, Sen., and John Wadsworth.

Court Record, Page 87—4 August, 1712: This Court grant letters of Adms. to Elizabeth Root, widow of sd. decd.

Page 97 (Vol. IX) 3 March, 1718-19: Elizabeth Root, of Farmington, exhibited now an account of her Adms. Account allowed and order to distribute:

	£ s d
To Elizabeth Root, widow,	33-01-06
To Caleb Root, eldest son,	97-09-10
To Mary, Thomas, Elizabeth and Samuel Root, to each,	48-14-11

And appoint Joseph Root, John Hart and Isaac Cowles, distributors. This Court appoint Elizabeth Root to be guardian to Thomas Root, 17 years, Elizabeth, 12 years, and Samuel Root, 6 years of age. Recog., £100.

Page 124 (Vol. X) 14 March, 1726-7: Thomas Root, a minor, 14 years of age, chose Thomas Root of Farmington to be his guardian. Recog., £50.

Page 69.

Root, John, Farmington. Invt. £227-03-00. Taken by Jonathan Smith, Sen., John Woodruff and Joseph Woodruff.

Court Record, Page 7—6 March, 1709-10: A Court summons Nathaniel Winchell of Farmington and his wife, late wife of John Root, decd., to take letters of Adms.

Page 11—1st May, 1710: Adms. granted to Joseph Woodruff, brother-in-law of sd. decd., Nathaniel Winchell and his wife having refused to administer.

Page 19—8 September, 1710: Adms. now granted to John Root, son of the decd.

Page 73—5 May, 1712: This Court appoint Ebenezer Steele guardian to Mary Root, age 13 years, daughter of John Root; and also Samuel Woodruff, cordwainer, appointed guardian to Thankfull Root, 10 years of age.

Page 123—6 April, 1713: This Court doth appoint Samuel Woodruff to be guardian to Thankfull Root, 11 years of age, and allow Joseph Woodruff to be guardian to Samuel Root, 17 years of age, children of John Root, decd.

Page 158—5 October, 1713: John Root, Adms., exhibits an account of his Adms. Accepted. Order to dist. the estate:

	£ s d
To John Root, eldest son,	44-14-11
To Joseph Root, Samuel, Mary and Thankfull Root, to each,	22-07-05

And appoint Jonathan Smith, Sen., John Woodruff and Joseph Woodruff, distributors.

Page 268.

Root, Timothy, Farmington. Died 1713. Invt. £110-02-10. Taken by William Wadsworth and Isaac Cowles.

Court Record, Page 155—17 August, 1713: Adms. to Margaret Root, widow.

Page 80 (Vol. IX) 2 September, 1718: This Court appoint Zachariah Seamore of Hartford to be guardian to Jonathan Root, age 11 years, Stephen 7, and Timothy Root 5 years, all children of Timothy Root late decd.

Page 88—4 November, 1718: John Rew of Farmington, in right of his wife Margaret Rew, alias Root, Adms., exhibits now an account of Adms. Order to dist. the estate:

	£ s d
To Margaret Rew, alias Root,	22-04-05
To Jonathan Root,	23-14-05
To Stephen and Timothy Root, to each of them,	11-17-03

And appoint Ebenezer Steele, Isaac Cowles and Joseph Hawley distributors.

Invt. in Vol. IX, Page 33.

Rowley, Shubael, Colchester. Invt. £286-19-06. Taken 2 June, 1714, by Joseph Chamberlain and Andrew Carrier.

Court Record, Page 206—5 July, 1714: Adms. to Isaac Rowley, eldest son.

Page 244—7 March, 1714-15: Isaac Rowley, Adms., exhibits an account of his Adms. Allowed, and this Court order the estate dist. as followeth:

	£ s d
To Katharine Rowley, widow,	10-16-04
To Isaac Rowley, eldest son,	53-13-10
To Shubael, Thomas, Matthew, Elnathan, Jabez, Elizabeth, and to Mary Rowley, to each of them,	26-16-11

And appoint Moses Rowley, Thomas Crippin of Haddam and James Treadway of Colchester, distributors.

Page 103 (Vol. IX) 30 April, 1719: Report of the distributors. This Court appoint Isaac Rowley of Colchester guardian to Jabez Rowley, 17 years of age. Recog., £30.

Rowlandson, Joseph. Court Record, Page 113—17 February, 1712-13: This Court appoints Capt. James Steele of Wethersfield to be guardian to Wilson Rowlandson, 10 years of age, son of Mr. Joseph Rowlandson, late of Wethersfield deceased.

Page 20 (Vol. IX) 7 August, 1716: This Court now appoint Anne Steele to be guardian unto Wilson Rowlandson, 13 years of age. Recog., £50.

Page 172.

Rudd, Jonathan, Windham. Invt. £121-02-03. Taken 29 April, 1712, by Joseph Cary and Abell Bingham.

Know all men by these presents: That we, Nathaniel Rudd, Mary Leffingwell and Abigail Rudd, of Windham, in the County of Hartford, being all the heirs of Jonathan Rudd, of sd. Windham, decd., being met together at Hartford, 5 May, 1712, have by agreement mutually consented to make a settlement of sd. Jonathan Rudd his estate as followeth: Imprimis: Nathaniel Rudd and Abigail Rudd aforesd. to receive and have in partnership all the land belonging formerly to Jonathan Rudd decd., as well that he held in partnership with the abovesd. Nathaniel Rudd, with all other lands to him belonging, to have and to hofd to them, their heirs, successors or assigns forever. This to be their full part of sd. Jonathan Rudd's estate. Item. Mary Leffingwell is to have £35 in the personal estate of the sd. Jonathan Rudd as it was inventoried, to be the full of her part of sd. Jonathan Rudd's estate. In confirmation of the above agreement, and that every party is well satisfied therewith, we have hereunto set our hands and seals on the day of the date aforesd.

NATHANIEL RUDD, LS.
MARY LEFFINGWELL, LS.
ABIGAIL RUDD, LS.

Attest: Thomas Kimberly, Clerk.

See File: This agreement, made and concluded upon the 16th day of April, Anno Domoni 1712, with respect unto the division of the estate of our loving brother Jonathan Rudd, late of Windham deceased, as with respect to his lands being within the town of Windham and inventoried at £77: We have divided sd. land equally between Nathaniel and Abigail Rudd, each of the parts being just £35-16-05 after the necessary charges taken out of the inventory. We have also divided to Mary Leffingwell her whole share or part of the sd. estate in bills of credit and moveables, which is £35-16-05.

NATHANIEL RUDD, LS.
MARY LEFFINGWELL, LS.
ABIGAIL RUDD, LS.

Acknowledged 5 May, 1712.
Test: Thos. Kimberly, Clerk.

Court Record, Page 134 (Vol. VII) 7 November, 1709: Adms. granted to Nathaniel Rudd of Windham, a brother of sd. decd.

Page 73 (Vol. VIII) 5 May, 1712: Exhibit of an agreement touching the division of sd. estate.

Invt. in Vol. IX, Page 23-4.

Russell, Noadiah, Rev., Middletown. Invt. £845-05-06. Taken 1714, by Israhiah Wetmore and John Bacon.

Court Record, Page 193—3 May, 1713: Adms. granted to Mrs. Mary Russell, widow.

Page 137 (Vol. IX) 10 October, 1720: Mrs. Mary Russell, Adms., exhibits an account of her Adms. by her son William Russell. Accepted. Order to dist. the estate as follows:

	£ s d
To Mary Russell, widow,	97-12-06
To William Russell, eldest son,	167-11-03
To Noadiah, Mary, John, Daniel, Mabell and Hannah Russell, to each of them the sum of,	83-15-07

And appoint John Hamlin, Esq., Israhiah Wetmore and Capt. Joseph Rockwell, dist. This Court appoint William Russell guardian to his brother, Daniel Russell, a minor, 19 years of age, he desiring the same. Recog., £100.

Page 97.

Ryley, Sergt. Jonathan, Sen., Wethersfield. Invt. £467-12-10. Taken 29 January, 1711-12, by Jonathan Boardman, Joshua Robbins and James Steele. (Apprisers' names and date found only on file, not recorded.)

Court Record, Page 50—4 February, 1711-12: Adms. granted to Sarah Ryly, widow.

Page 125—6 April, 1713: Sarah Ryly, Adms., exhibits now an account of her Adms. Accepted. Order to dist. the estate:

	£ s d
To Sarah Ryly, the relict,	27-12-00
To Jonathan Ryly, eldest son,	102-13-06
To Jacob, Joseph, Stephen, David, Mehetabell, and to Joseph Cole in right of his wife Abigail, eldest daughter of Jonathan Ryley, Sen., decd. (see file for last item) to each of them the sum or value of	51-06-09

And appoint James Steele, Jonathan Deming and Isaac Ryley, distributors.

Page 148—6 July, 1713: Report of the distributors.

Page 201 (Vol. X) 1st October, 1728: Upon motion of Sarah Riley, widow, relict of sd. decd., this Court appoint Edward Bulkeley, John Curtis and John Riley to set out of the real estate of the decd. her dowry by meets and bounds.

Page 216—1st April, 1729: Whereas, it is represented to this Court that the dist. ordered 6 April, 1713, vizt., that part of sd. estate included in the homested, are not set out and distributed by meets and bounds, this Court now appoint Joseph Graham, Jonathan Curtis and John Riley to divide and dist. the homested and all the lands adjoyning thereto to the widow and heirs.

Page 64 (Vol. XIII) 22 April, 1740: It was represented to this Court of Probate, 1st Tuesday in April, 1729, that the dist. of the estate of Jonathan Riley, late of Wethersfield, decd., made upon an order of this Court, 6 April, 1713, viz., that part of sd. estate as included in the homested, and all the lands adjoining to sd. homested, belonging to the estate of the sd. decd., is not distributed, as appears in the dist. of sd. estate, so as the heirs can know their parts separately, the persons appointed by this Court in April, 1729, being deceased and not finished sd. dist. according to sd. order: whereupon this Court appoint Jonathan Burnham, Lt. Jonathan Belding and Stephen Williams to set out to each by meets and bounds.

Dist. File: We began 14 May, 1740: To Jacob, to David, to Jonathan, to Stephen Riley. By Jonathan Belding and Stephen Williams.

Page 2 (Vol. XIV) 6 April, 1742: Dist. of part of the real estate of Jonathan Ryley was now returned in Court and ordered to be kept on file.

Page 128.

Sadd, Hepzibah, Hartford, Widow. Invt. £71-09-06. Taken 28 January, 1711-12, by James Steele and John Shepherd. Will dated 27 December, 1711.

The last will and testament of Hepzibah Sadd, widow, is as followeth: I do give to my son Jonathan Pratt my farm in Wethersfield, containing 100 acres be it more or less, with the privileges thereunto belonging. I give to my son Thomas Sadd 2 acres of meadow land lying by the 40 acres which I bought of John Graves. I give to my son Thomas 1-2 of that lot which I bought of Martin Moore, adjoining to the tan yards formerly belonging to my late husband Sadd. I give to my son Thomas one brass kettle, one chest of drawers. I give to him also 2 cowes, 4 swine. I give to my daughter Susannah Merrells my wearing clothes, both woolen and lining. I give to my granddaughter Susannah Merrells one warming pan, 2 pewter platters and one knott bowle. I do give to my kinswoman Mary Graves £10. And my desire is that sd. Mary do continue with my son Thomas during the time of her single estate, and that he be very kind to her for her help and kindness to me in my lonely condition. I give to Lydia Graves £5. I constitute my son Thomas Sadd sole executor, and do leave to him all my moveable estate to pay my just debts.

Witness: *Joseph Bull,*   HEPZIBAH X SADD, LS.
       Hannah Hopkins, widow.

Court Record, Page 54—5 February, 1711-12: Will proven.

Page 214.

Sage, David, Jr., Middletown. Invt. £138-12-06. Taken 26 February, 1712-13, by John Warner and Samuel Gipson. 250 acres of land on the east side of the Great River, valued at £100, was apprised by Peter Blinn, Samuel Dyxx and Jonathan Smith. The children: Mary and Elizabeth.

Court Record, Page 118—2 March, 1712-13: Adms. granted to John Sage, brother of the sd. decd.

Page 188—5 April, 1714: John Sage cited to appear and render an account of his Adms.

Page 192—3 May, 1714: John Sage, who was appointed Adms., now appeared and declared before this Court that he hath not intermedled with that estate or acted thereon as Adms., but declined that trust; whereupon this Court doth grant letters of Adms. to Thomas Stedman of Wethersfield, son-in-law of sd. deceased.

Page 250—2 May, 1715: Thomas Stedman, Adms., exhibits now an account of his Adms. Accepted. Ordered to dist. the estate: To Mary Sage, widow, £9-00-02 and to the two daughters, Mary and Elizabeth, to each of them the sum of £50-09-02. And this Court appoint William Cornwall, Sergt. Samuel Hall and John Gains, distributors.

Page 260—5 July, 1715: Report of the distributors.

Page 227.

Sage, Jonathan, Middletown. Invt. £324-04-08. Taken 27 April, 1713, by Samuel Willcock, Sen., William Savage and John Warner, Jr.

Court Record, Page 111—2 February, 1712-13: Adms. joyntly to Amy Sage, the widow, and Timothy Sage, a brother.

Page 127.

Sage, Marcy, Middletown. Invt. £56-07-07. Taken by Samuel Willcock, Sen., and John Warner.

Court Record, Page 54—5 February, 1711-12: Adms. to John, Jonathan and Timothy Sage, brothers of the deceased.

Page 76—5 May, 1712: The Adms. exhibit now an account of their Adms. Accepted. Order to dist. the estate: To John, Jonathan and Timothy Sage, brothers, and to the heirs of David Sage, brother, to Elizabeth Bull of Rhode Island (the wife of Ezekiel Bull), and Mary Johnson, the wife of Samuel Johnson, the two sisters of sd. decd., to each of them £10-14-01. And appoint Joseph Rockwell, Thomas Miller and Samuel Hall, of Middletown, distributors.

Page 263.

Sandford, Zachariah, Lt., Hartford. Invt. £596-09-10. Taken 26 February, 1713-14, by John Marsh, Jr., and John Skinner. Will dated 2nd March, 1710-11.

In the name of God, amen. The second day of March, Anno Dom. 1710-11, I, Zachariah Sandford, of Hartford, in the County of Hartford, in the Colony of Connecticut, in New England, innholder, being of sound mind, understanding and memory, do make and ordain this my last will and testament, and I do hereby revoak and renounce all former wills whatsoever by me made by word, writing or otherwise: First, I commend my soull into the hands of Almighty God that gave it, and my body to a comly Christian burial. And as for my wordly goods and estate here, I do give and dispose the same in manner as hereinafter is expressed, that is to say:

I give and bequeath unto my sonn Jonathan Bunce and my daughter Sarah, his wife, all those household goods and all other moveable estate whatsoever which they have heretofore had and received of me, and also one more good feather bedd with all convenient furniture for the same, to be to them and their heirs forever.

Item. I give and bequeath unto my sonn Joseph Bunce all those household goods, and other moveable estate whatsoever, which he hath heretofore had and received of me, to be to him and his heirs forever.

Item. I give and bequeath unto my daughter, Abigail Sandford, two feather bedds and one other bedd, with convenient furniture for them, and all my pewter and brass, and my chest in the jury chamber with what is contained therein; also one pair of andirons, one pair of iron dogs, one pair of tongs, one fire slice, two iron trammells, and my mare, to be to her and her heirs forever. Also, I give unto my said daughter Abigail three (3) cows, to be delivered to her within one month after my decease by my son Jonathan Bunce, for and in lieu of those three cows of mine that are now in his hands.

Item. My will and mind is that my copper and my three longest tables be apprized by two or three indifferent men after my decease, and that my son Jonathan Bunce shall have and enjoy the said copper and tables, he paying half the value thereof to my said daughter Abigail.

Item. I give and bequeath to my said daughter Abigail the sum of six pounds mony when she shall arrive at the age of eighteen years, or day of marriage, which shall first happen.

Item. I give and bequeath to my three granddaughters, Susannah, Sarah and Abigail (the children of my son Jonathan Bunce), the sum of six pounds money, or forty shillings to each of them, as a token of my love, to be paid to them respectively, when they attain the age of eighteen years, by my executors hereinafter named. And in case either of them decease before she attain that age, the said six pounds to be paid to the survivours or survivour of them.

Item. I give and bequeath to my said son Jonathan Bunce and his heirs all the time and service that is due to me by and from my servants or apprentices, James Jarrell and Drusus (Indian man), provided the said Jonathan shall accept of them and fulfill my part of obligation in their indentures.

Item. I give unto my son Jonathan Bunce the full and free use and improvement of all my lands and other estate whatsoever, for and during the term of my natural life, he maintaining me comfortably whilst I live, and my daughter Abigail until she arrive at the age of eighteen years, or day of marriage, which shall first happen.

Item. I do give, grant, devise and bequeath unto my said sonn Jonathan Bunce and my daughter Sarah, his wife, and to their heirs forever, all my homelott, dwelling house, barn and other outhouses thereon being, with the yards, gardens, orchards, fences and appurtenances thereof; and also my lott of land lying at Poke Hill in Hartford, containing about nineteen acres, now in the improvement of my said son Jonathan Bunce.

Item. I do give, grant, devise and bequeath unto my grandson Abijah Bunce (son of my aforenamed sonn Joseph Bunce), and to his heirs forever, all my lott of land lying at Rocky Hill in Hartford, containing about twenty-two acres, with all and singular the appurtenances thereof. I give to my daughter Abigail Sandford that parcell of land in the South Meadow in Hartford, containing about 18 acres. I give unto my grandson Zachariah Bunce (son of my son Jonathan Bunce) 20 acres of my land in the West Division in Hartford. In case the said Zachariah Bunce or Abijah Bunce shall not attain the age of 21 years, then the said land shall be equally divided between my two daughters, Sarah and Abigail, or their heirs.

I do give and bequeath all my other lands lying in Hartford or elsewhere, with the rights, members and appurtenances, not otherwise disposed of, unto my son Jonathan Bunce and my daughter Abigail Sandford and their heirs, to be equally divided between them.

I do give and bequeath to my son Jonathan Bunce and his heirs all the residue of my whole estate vizt., monys, goods, chattells, rents, debts and other things whatsoever not herein otherwise disposed of.

I do hereby grant full power and authority to my executors hereafter named to sell part or all of my lands at Hoccanum, in Hartford, to procure mony to pay my debts and the legacies given in this my will, if they shall see meet. I appoint my son Jonathan Bunce and my daughter Sarah, his wife, and my daughter Abigail Sandford, executors.

Witness: *Caleb Stanly, Jr.,*   ZACHARIAH SANDFORD, LS.
        Abigail Stanly.

Court Record, Page 181—1 March, 1713-14: Will proven.

Page 61 (Vol. IX) 1st April, 1718: This Court appoint Joseph Bunce to be guardian to his son Abijah Bunce, to take care of his estate descending from his grandfather Zachariah Sandford, late of Hartford, decd.

Page 183.

Scovell, James, Middletown. Invt. £182-00-00. Taken 28 February, 1711-12, by Samuel Gipson and William Savage. Will dated 7 December, 1711.

I, James Scovell, of Middletown, do make this my last will and testament: I give to Hannah, my wife, all my moveable estate during her widowhood. I give to Hannah, whome I make my executrix, all and singular the use of my lands during her widowhood. I give my son James Scovell all my lands, both divided and undivided, after his mother's decease. To my daughters, all my moveable estate after my wife's decease. I desire Thomas Stow and John Warner to be overseers.

Witness: *Walter Harris, Jr.,*   JAMES X SCOVELL, LS.
Thomas Ranny, Francis Willcock.

Court Record, Page 77—2 June, 1712: Will exhibited and proven.

Page 215.

Scovell, John, Middletown. Invt. £176-08-02. Taken 26 February, 1712-13, by John Sage, John Warner and Samuel Gipson.

Court Record, Page 116—2 March, 1712-13: Adms. granted to Mary Scovell, widow.

Page 220.

Scovell, William, Haddam. Invt. £168-05-08. Taken 8 December, 1712, by Benjamin Smith, Thomas Shaylor and Joseph Arnold.

Court Record, Page 124—6 April, 1713: Adms. granted to Martha Scovell, widow.

Page 250—2 May, 1715: Martha Scovell, Adms., exhibits now an account of her Adms. Accepted. Order to dist. the estate:

	£ s d
To Martha Scovell, widow,	12-17-04
William Scovell, eldest son,	96-09-08
To John Scovell,	48-04-10

And appoint Capt. James Welles, Joseph Arnold and Timothy Shalor, distributors.

Page 251—2 May, 1715: This Court appoint Martha Scovell to be guardian to William Scovell and John Scovell, minor children of William Scovell, decd. Recog., £100.

Page 241.

Seamore, John, Sen., Hartford. Invt. £1158-14-01. Taken by James Ensign and Thomas Richards. Will dated 10 December, 1712.

I, John Seamore, Sen., of Hartford, do make this my last will and testament: Imprs. I give and bequeath unto my beloved wife Mary Seamore one-third part of my moveable estate to be at her dispose forever, and the rest of my moveable estate I give her the improvement of, with my dwelling house, barn, orchard, with three acres of land at home, and also the incomes or rents of one-half part of the rest of my lands, to be paid to her by my sons according to the quantity of land I shall give to them, during her natural life. It. I give and bequeath unto my son John Seamore twelve acres of land (with the dwelling house thereon) lying south of Robert Webster's land; also my land on the north side of my lot on the east side of Farmington Road. Also I give unto him that my lot of land lying on this side Four-Mile Hill, called the 17-acre lot. Also I give unto him one-third part of my two fifty-acre lots lying together in Wethersfield next Hartford bounds, after that ten acres shall be measured off the northeast corner of my said lots. It. I give and bequeath to my son Thomas Seamore all that land lying on the west side of Farmington Road, being south of that land given to my son John Seamore, with the dwelling house and barn that are thereon. Also I give him ten acres of land lying on the northeast corner of my two fifty-acre lots in Wethersfield. Also I give him one-third part of the remainder of my said two fifty-acre lots. It. I give to my son Richard Seamore the land where he now dwelleth, with the buildings that are thereon. Also I give unto him five acres of land lying at the east end of my lot on the east side of Farmington Road. Also I give unto him £20 in mony, to be paid in equal proportion by my three sons, John, Thomas and Zachariah Seamore. It. I give to my son Zachariah Seamore three acres of land on the south side of my lot lying on the east side of Farmington road, to extend east to the land given to my son Richard, and to be in weadth next the highway one rod north of the barn, with my dwelling house, barn and other buildings that are thereon, after my wife's decease. Also I give him all that my lot of land called the Mountain lot, lying in Wethersfield. Also I give him one-third part of my two fifty-acre lots lying together in Wethersfield when ten acres shall be measured off at the northeast corner of said lot, which parcels of land I give to my said son Zachariah Seamore. And it is my will that my son Zachariah Seamore shall pay to my two daughters £20 apiece, and that he quit my estate of charge for what he hath done to my barn. I give to my daughter Mary North £30, £20 to be paid by my son Zachariah, the remainder to be paid out of my moveable estate, after my wife's decease, by my executors. I give to my daughter Margaret Root £30. I appoint my wife Mary Seamore and my friends Mr. Ichabod Welles and Mr. Thomas Hosmer to be executors of this my last will.

Witness: *Hez: Wyllys,*   JOHN SEAMORE, LS.
Mary Macky, Sarah X Harris.

Court Record, Page 153—3 August, 1713: Will proven.

Page 193.

Seamore, Hannah, Farmington, late wife of Richard Seamore.

Know all men by these presents: That we whose names are underwritten do agree that for the third of our mother's state, decd., that the two sisters are to have all the moveables, and the three brothers are to have all the lands. Signed, 7 November, 1712.

Witness: *Ebenezer Gilbert,*   SAMUEL SEAMORE, LS.
     Gershom Hollister.   RICHARD SEAMORE, LS.
                       JONATHAN SEAMORE, LS.
                       JOSEPH POMEROY, LS.
                       GEORGE HUBBARD, LS.

Court Record, Page 110—2 February, 1712-13: Exhibit of an agreement, which this Court accepted and order to be recorded and kept on file.

Page 61.

Seamore, Richard, Farmington. Invt. £416-13-03. Taken 29 November, 1710, by Thomas Seamore, Thomas Hart and Thomas Curtis.

Court Record, Page 23—4 December, 1710: Adms. granted to Hannah Seamore, widow, and Samuel Seamore, son of sd. decd.

See File.

An agreement by the children and widow of Richard Seamore for a dist. of ye sd. estate, vizt:

To the widow, her thirds in the moveable estate and in lands; also a share in the lot called Bacholders, valued at £1-13-07.

To Samuel Seamore, half of the homested with ye house on it, valued at £60; also his part in the land that lies on the west of Mr. Gilbert, being 12 acres, and valued at £35-03-00.

To Ebenezer Gilbert, land on the east side of Mr. Gilbert, valued at £41; and part of the Bacholders lot, worth £3-16-08.

To Jonathan Seamore, his share in the land on the west side of Mr. Gilbert, valued at £18-01-03.

To Hannah Seamore, out of the moveable estate, which is £32-10.

To Mercy Seamore, her part in the dist. out of the moveable estate, which is £32-10.

                      HANNAH X SEAMORE, LS.
                      SAMUEL SEAMOUR, LS.
                      JONATHAN SEAMORE, LS.
                      EBENEZER SEAMORE, LS.
                      JOSEPH POMEROY, LS.
                      MERCY X SEAMORE, LS.

Page 24—1st January, 1710-11: Hannah Seamore of Farmington, widow, and Samuel Seamore, Jonathan Seamore and Ebenezer Seamore, sons of the sd. deceased, and Mercy Seamore and Jonathan Pomeroy in behalf of Hannah his wife, daughters of sd. decd., appeared before this Court and exhibited a writing under their hands and seals, made for the dist. or division of the greatest part of the estate of the sd. decd. amongst themselves. And each acknowledged the sd. writing or agreement to be their act and deed. Wherefore this Court allow and approve the sd. writing.

See File: Paper attached to agreement: November the 7th, 1712: Then reckoned with and received of Samuel Seymour ye whole of ye legacy yt was due to my wife from Father Seymour's estate. I say received in full.

Pr. JOSEPH PUMRY.

Inventory on File.

Saxton, Richard, Simsbury. Invt. £65-15-08. Taken 27 March, 1714, by John Case, Sen., John Roberts, Sen., and Jonathan Westover. The children: Hannah, Mary and Lucy.

Court Record, Page 198—7 June, 1714: Adms. granted to Hannah Saxton, widow, relict of sd. decd.

Page 27 (Vol. X) 3 September, 1723: Hannah Sexton, 16 years of age, and Mary Sexton, 14 1-2 years, chose their mother Hannah Sexton of Simsbury to be their guardian. Recog., £50.

Page 28—3 September, 1723: This Court do appoint Hannah Sexton to be guardian unto her daughter Lucy Sexton, 11 years of age. Recog., £30.

Page 150—4 April, 1727: Hannah Sexton, Adms. on her husband's estate, he having died in the year of 1714, now exhibits an account of her Adms. amounting to the sum of £42-00-05, which account is accepted. Order to dist. the estate after the sd. sum is deducted: 1-3 part of the moveable estate, with dower, to the widow, and the residue of the estate to be equally divided between Mary and Lucy Sexton, the two daughters of sd. decd. And appoint Thomas Holcomb, John Higley and Jonathan Higley, distributors.

Page 17-18, Vol. IX, for Invt. and Agreement.

Shaler, Thomas, Haddam. Invt. £117-15-00. Taken 22 December, 1714, by James Wells, Moses Ventrus, Joseph Arnold and Benjamin Smith.

An agreement, dated 22 December, 1714: Know all men by these presents: That we, the subscribers, viz., Thomas Shaler, Abell Shaler and Timothy Shaler, brethren, and sons of Thomas Shaler, late of Haddam, as we suppose deceased: And for what lands, rights in lands, or commonage, or buildings, that was our hond. father's, wee the aforsaid three Shalers, brethren, do for ourselves, our heirs and assigns, agree and determine that (notwithstanding the liberty given by law to the eldest son) they shall be thus divided, viz: To Thomas Shaler, eldest son, that house and lot that was Samuel Gains his original house lot, and a small lot in the Cove Meadow, and £53 right on the neck or plain on the east side of the Great River, and 18 acres of land that was James Hadlock's, and 24 acres of land at Cow Swamp, and one-third part of all rights in undivided lands and commonage on the west side of the Great River. And to Abell Shaler, a house lot that was William Corby's containing eight acres, and that tract of land called Shaler Farm, and one-third part of all the rights in all undivided lands and commonage on the west side of the Great River in said Haddam. And to Timothy Shaler, that house and homelot that was bought of Thomas Spencer of Saybrook, and one-third part of all the rights of undivided lands and commonage on the west side of the Great River in said Haddam bounds. To the above-written or division of the lands and rights in undivided lands and commonage that was our hond. deceased father's, as is above exprest, shall be and remain to be forever, and that we the said Thomas, Abell and Timothy Shaler, for ourselves, our heirs and assigns, are fully satisfied in the above premises, and do hereby oblige ourselves and foresaid heirs and assigns forever hereafter to abide by and rest satisfied. In testimony whereof, and in full confirmation of the above-written, we have put to our hands and seals the date above written.

Witness: *James Wells,*
    Joseph Arnold.

THOMAS SHALER, LS.
ABELL SHALER, LS.
TIMOTHY SHALER, LS.

Court Record, Page 227—6 December, 1714: Adms. granted joyntly to Thomas Shaylor and Timothy Shalor, sons of sd. decd.

Page 230—3 January, 1714-15: Thomas, Abell and Timothy Shalor exhibit now an agreement, which this Court confirm and order it to be recorded.

Page 174-224.

Shepherd, Edward, Middletown. Invt. £372-18-00. Taken 20 February, 1711-12, by John Savage, Joseph Rockwell and William Savage.

An agreement for the division and settlement of the estate, dated 1 May, 1713, giving to the heirs as followeth:

	£ s d
To the widow, £90-13-04 during life, £26-06-00 forever,	£116-19-04
To John,	119-11-10
To Edward,	106-00-00
To Samuel, youngest son,	79-03-04

We, the above-named, having agreed with the help and advice of our friends, and with the consent and assent of our honoured mother, for her comfortable subsistence and honourable maintenance, and to free her from care and trouble which otherwise she would be exposed unto, we do therefore acknowledge the within mentioned agreement to be our voluntary act and deed, and have hereunto set our hands and seals.

Witness: *Jacob White,*   JOHN SHEPHERD, LS.
     Samuel Stowe.   EDWARD SHEPHERD, LS.
     SAMUEL SHEPHERD.

Court Record, Page 39—1st October, 1711: Adms. granted to John Shepherd, eldest son, on the estate of Edward Shepherd, cooper, decd.

Page 138—4 May, 1713: Agreement accepted and confirmed by the Court. Ordered to be recorded and kept on file.

Page 134-170.

Sherman, Theophalus, Wethersfield. Invt. £265-01-03. Taken 27 February, 1711-12, by Jonathan Boreman, Joshua Robbins, Jr., and Philip Goff, Jr. Will dated 13 April, 1711.

I, Theophalus Sherman, of Wethersfield, do make this my last will and testament: I give unto my son Theophalus Sherman all my land situate in the bounds of the Township of Wethersfield, that is to say, I give to my sd. son my dwelling house, with all the land it standeth on or belongeth unto it, at the place where I now dwell, as also all uplands, meadows, pastures, woodlands, etc., according to the bounds and buttments of my purchases and records. I give unto my daughter Mary, now the wife of Elijah Crane, 5 acres of land near the bounds of Stratford or Stratfield, which I value at £10. I give my daughter Mary £10 in country pay. I give to my daughter Comfort, the wife of Richard Niccols, 10 acres of land in or near the bounds of Stratford or Stratfield, which 10 acres I value at £20. I give to my wife Mary Sherman the use of 1-3 part of my lands during her natural life, vizt., my lands lying in the Town of Wethersfield, also the sum of £8 in country pay. I appoint my son Theophalus Sherman sole executor.

Witness: *Eliphalet Dickinson,*   THEOPHALUS SHERMAN, LS.
     Philip Goff, Jr.

Court Record, Page 63—4 March, 1711-12: Will proven.

Page 73.

Shirley, Robert, Hartford. Invt. £315-15-01. Taken 6 September, 1711, by Cyprian Nichols, Hez: Wyllys and Thomas Hosmer. Will dated 10 August, 1711.

I, Robert Shirley of Hartford, doe make this my last will and testament: I give to my wife Sarah Shirley 2-3 of all my estate, real and personal, during her natural life, and after her decease I give the sd. 2-3 to my kinsman Richard Skinner. In case he should die before my wife's decease, I give that 2-3 of my real and personal estate equally to be dist. to the rest of the heirs of my brother John Skinner, decd. I give to Richard Skinner 1-3 part of my estate, real and personal, desireing and requesting him to take special care and charge of my wife and carefully manage her estate for her comfortable subsistence. I appoint my wife and Richard Skinner executors.

Witness: *Hez: Wyllys,*   ROBERT X SHURLEY, LS.
         Sarah X *Adkins.*

Court Record, Page 38—1st October, 1711: Will exhibited and proven.

Inventory in Vol. IX, Page 20.

Silsbe, Jonathan, Windham. Invt. £200-13-08. Taken 3 December, 1714, by Jonathan Crane and Joseph Cary.

Court Record, Page 229—3 January, 1714-15: Adms. granted unto Jonathan Silsby of Windham, son of the deceased.

Page 235-6-7.

Slater, John, Sen., Simsbury. Invt. £128-15-00. Taken 13 May, 1713, by Peter Buel and Andrew Robe. Will dated 15 August, 1712. I, John Slater, of the Town of Simsbury, in the County of Hartford, do for the love I bear unto Abiah, my wife, give unto her all my moveable estate, to be at her disposal. I do confirm unto my son John Slater the 15 acres of land where his new house now standeth, and also that lot at Hasell Meadow which formerly belonged to me. I do give to my son Samuel Slater half that lot that lyes on Salmon Brook, and that land all of it that lyes near Muntauk. I give to my son Elias all the house and houselot and all the meadow lot adjacent, and 6 acres on the Plaine, and 16 or 18 over Hop Brook, and 10 acres on the south branch of Hop Brook, and 4 acres over Hop Brook near Miller's lot. I give to my daughter Elizabeth Slater 1-2 of that lot that lyes on Salmon Brook and 5 acres on the hill near Raven Swamp. And I appoint my son Elias Slater to be my sole executor.

Witness: *Mary* X *Hoskins,*   JOHN X SLATER, LS.
         Timothy Woodbridge.

Court Record, Page 148—6 July, 1713: Will proven.

Page 174-210.

Smith, Arthur, Hartford. Invt. £272-15-04. Taken 3rd February, 1712-13, by John Stanly, Thomas Richards and Stephen Brace. Will dated 26 December, 1712.

I, Arthur Smith of Hartford, doe make this my last will and testament: I give to my daughter Sarah Smith my house and frame barn and shop, and 10 acres of land on the front of my lot, only I reserve a way 3 rods wide on the west side of the lot for the benefit of my other two daughters for to come at their land, which way is not to be taken out of Sarah's 10 acres. I give to my daughter Sarah 1-3 part of my land lying in the South Meadow, and 1-3 part of all my personal estate. I give to my other two daughters, Hannah and Phebe, the rest of my lands and my homelot, to be equally divided between them, and also the remaining 2-3 of my land in the South Meadow, to be equally divided between them, and also the remaining 2-3 of the moveable estate. I appoint my daughter Sarah Smith my sole executrix.

Witness: *John Stanly, Sen.,*   ARTHUR SMITH, LS.
         Thomas Richards.

Court Record, Page 110—2 February, 1712-13: Will exhibited by William Baker. Proven.

Page 120—2 March, 1712-13: Sarah Baker, formerly Sarah Smith, daughter of Arthur Smith, executrix, appeared before this Court and accepted the trust.

Page 181—1st March, 1713-14: This Court appoint William Baker of Hartford to be guardian unto Phebe Smith, a minor, 13 years of age.

Invt. in Vol. IX, Page 56.

Smith, Elisha, Windham. Invt. £207-09-09. Taken 22 July, 1714, by Samuel Webb and William Allen.

Court Record, Page 209—2 August, 1714: Adms. granted to Elizabeth Smith, widow of sd. decd.

Page 210—2 August, 1714: This Court appoint Jonathan Bingham of Windham to be guardian to Esther Smith, about 12 years of age, daughter of Elisha Smith, decd. Recog., £70.

Page 211—2 August, 1714: This Court appoint Ralph Wellock of Windham to be guardian to Seth Smith, 12 years of age, son of Elisha Smith, decd. Recog., £70.

Page 14 (Vol. IX) 1st May, 1716: Elizabeth Smith, Adms., by her attorney, Samuel Webb, exhibits account of her Adms. Allowed. Order to dist. the estate:

	£ s d
To Elizabeth Smith, widow, land, with	3-06-04
To Seth Smith, only son,	58-12-08
To Easter, Martha and Mary Smith, to each of them,	29-06-04

And appoint Capt. John Fitch, Jonathan Crane and Joseph Cary, of Windham, distributors.

Page 142.

Smith, John, Haddam. Invt. £415-09-11. Taken 2nd August, 1712, by Simon Smith, Thomas Brooks and James Wells.

Court Record, Page 86—4 August, 1712: Adms. to Lydia, the widow relict, and Joseph Smith, son of sd. deceased.

Page 156—7 September, 1713: Adms. account allowed. William Tully of Saybrook to be guardian to Lucy Smith, a minor, 4 years of age, daughter of John Smith, late of Haddam, decd.

Page 160—2nd November, 1713: This Court confirms Major John Clark of Saybrook to be guardian to Elizabeth Smith, a minor daughter of John Smith, late of Haddam, mariner, decd.

Page 161—2 November, 1713: Joseph Arnold of Haddam to be guardian to Thankfull Smith, age 18 years, and to Sarah Smith, age 16 years, children of John Smith, mariner, decd. This Court appoint Joseph Smith of Haddam to be guardian to Thankfull Smith, age 10 years, daughter of John Smith, late of Haddam, deceased. Joseph Smith of Haddam exhibited now in this Court a further accompt of his and his mother's administration account. Approved and order dist: To Lydia Smith, widow relict, her dower in the real estate, with £31-16-07 to be her own forever; to Joseph Smith, £55-16-09; to William, to Nathaniel, to Sarah, to Elizabeth, to Thankfull, and to Lucy Smith, to each the sum of £27-18-04 1-2, their single portions. And appoint James Wells, Thomas Brooks and Hezekiah Brainard, distributors.

Page 183.

Smith, Joseph, Hartford. Invt. £46-17-00. Taken 2 April, 1712, by Samuel Kellogg and Samuel Sedgewick.

Court Record, Page 60—3 March, 1711-12: This Court grants letters of Adms. on the estate of Joseph Smith, late of Hartford, decd. (vizt., that part of the sd. estate that hath not been administered upon by the widow relict in her lifetime, she being now deceased) to Simon Smith, son of sd. decd. (See Vol. I, Page 507, Digest.)

Page 183

Smith, Lydia, Widow, Hartford. Invt. £4-15-06. Taken 2 April, 1712, by Samuel Kellogg and Samuel Sedgewick.

Court Record, Page 60—3 March, 1711-12: Adms. granted to Simon Smith, son of the decd., on the estate of his mother, Lydia Smith, relict of Joseph Smith, late of Hartford, decd.

Page 116.

Smith, Nathaniel, Hartford. Invt. £88-00-04. Taken 2 January, 1711-12, by Ciprian Nicholls, Thomas Seamore and Henry Brace.

Court Record, Page 43—7 January, 1711-12: Adms. granted to Esther Smith, widow, and Thomas Dickinson.

Page 133—7 April, 1713: Adms. granted entirely to Easter Smith, widow, her brother Thomas Dickinson haveing neglected or refuseing to give bonds.

Page 157 (Vol. IX) 7 November, 1721: Esther Smith, alias Porter, Adms., exhibits now an account of her Adms. Order to dist. the estate among the surviving heirs as followeth: To Esther Porter, alias Smith, widow of the decd., to Nathaniel, eldest son, to Gideon, to Joseph, Susannah, Jerusha and Abigail Smith, children of the decd. And appoint Thomas Hosmer, Daniel Merrells and Thomas Warren distributors. This Court appoint Hezekiah Porter to be guardian to Abigail, Gideon and Joseph Smith, children of Nathaniel Smith, decd. Hezekiah Porter, attorney to Nathaniel Smith, eldest son of Nathaniel Smith, moved that the homelot of sd. Nathaniel decd. be set out to the sd. Nathaniel Smith, eldest son, provided bond be given to pay to the rest of the heirs their proportionable parts. This Court, being therewith satisfied, do so order.

Page 205.

Smith, Philip, Jr., Hartford. Died 17 October, 1712. Invt. £26-00-05. Taken by Timothy Cowles and John Goodwin. (Apprisers' names on file.)

Court Record, Page 103—5 January, 1712: Adms. granted to David Smith, a brother of sd. decd.

Page 95 (Vol. IX) 3 February, 1718-19: David Smith, Adms., exhibits now an account of his Adms. Accepted. There remains no estate to be dist., and this Court grants the Adms. a *Quietus Est.*

Page 39.

Smith, Thomas, Haddam. Invt. £38-12-04. Taken 25 November, 1709, by John Booge and William Spencer.

Court Record, Page 10—1st May, 1710: Adms. granted to Matthew Smith, a brother of sd. decd.

Page 46.

Sparks, John, Windsor. Invt. £54-14-00. Taken 20 May, 1710, by John Williams, Samuel Burnham and Benjamin Coult.

Court Record, Page 15—3 July, 1710: Adms. granted to Dorothy Sparks, widow.

Page 93—3 November, 1712: Adms. now granted to Jabez Coult of Windsor.

Page 137—4 May, 1713: Martha Sparks, a minor, 16 years of age, chose her father-in-law John Parsons to be her guardian. Esther Sparks,

18 years of age, chose Mr. Samuel Welles to be her guardian. And this Court appoints John Parsons of Hartford to be guardian to Ruth, John, Anne, Dorothy and Thomas Sparks, all minor children of John Sparks, late of Windsor, decd.

Page 200—7 June, 1714: John Parsons, sometime of Hartford, and formerly Adms. (in right of his wife Dorothy, decd.) on the estate of John Sparks, exhibited now in this Court an account of sundry disbursements necessarily made on that estate, which this Court accept.

Page 53 (Vol. X) 1st September, 1724: Jabez Coult, Adms., exhibits now an account of his Adms. Allowed. Noah Sparks offered to the satisfaction of this Court that the house and lands of John Sparks could not be divided without spoiling the whole, and prays that the house and lands may be set out to him the sd. Noah Sparks's eldest son, he giving bond for the payment to the rest of the heirs the worth thereof. Allowed. This Court appoint Noah Sparks to be guardian unto Thomas Sparks, a minor, 16 years of age, son of John Sparks, late decd.

Page 164.

Spencer, Jared, Sen., Hartford. Invt. £220-07-04. Taken 4 April, 1712, by Richard Edwards and John Pratt. Will dated 15 March, 1711-12:

I, Jared Spencer of Hartford, doe make this my last will and testament: I give to my 4 daughters, Hannah, Sarah, Elizabeth and Mary, to each of them, £10 over and besides what my daughter Hannah formerly received of me. The rest of my estate, both real and personal, I give unto my son Jared Spencer and to his heirs and assigns forever, whome I make my sole executor. My will further is, that my daughter Mary Spencer shall have one room in my house to dwell in so long as she shall continue unmarried.

Witness: *Richard Edwards,*   JARED SPENCER, LS.
      Nathaniel Goodwin.

Court Record, Page 66—7 April, 1712: Will proven.

Inventory on File.

(Page 31-47, Vol. IX, Agreement.)

Spencer, Jonathan, Haddam. Died 13 December, 1714. Invt. £88-08-06. Taken 10 January, 1714-15, by Daniel Brainard and Gerrard Cone.

An agreement, made for the settlement of the estate of Jonathan Spencer, late of Haddam, decd.: The brethren, Timothy Spencer, John Hungerford, Henry Williams and Joseph Chapman, do engage before witnesses to stand to this agreement, setting our hands to it 10 November,

1715: All us brethren have agreed to have a quarter part, each one, of the 40-acre lot that lyes between Moses Rowley's and John Fuller's. And of the other out lots we have agreed, by casting of lots, that Timothy Spencer should have the 24-acre lot by Green Hungerford's, and that John Hungerford should have the 20-acre lot by Sam Andross, and that Henry Williams should have the upper 20-acre lot by Thomas Gates, and that Joseph Chapman should have the 20-acre lot by John Smith. Also, we agree to take an equal share of £80-00-00 right that lyes on the east side of Salmon River, on Matchamodes side. And all we brethren have received now this day each one an equal share of the moveable estate that was Jonathan Spencer's, decd., to our full satisfaction.

> TIMOTHY SPENCER, LS.
> HENRY WILLIAMS, LS.
> JOHN HUNGERFORD, LS.
> JOSEPH CHAPMAN, LS.

Court Record, Page 238—7 February, 1714-15: Adms. granted to Timothy Spencer, a brother of sd. decd.

Page 2 (Vol. IX) 17 December, 1715: Joseph Chapman, John Hungerford, Timothy Spencer and Henry Williams, all of Haddam save Joseph Chapman, who is of Saybrook, exhibited now in this Court an agreement for the division and settlement of the estate of their late brother, Jonathan Spencer, which agreement they severally acknowledge before this Court to be their voluntary act and deed. And they were granted a *Quietus Est.*

Invt. in Vol. IX, Page 29.

Spencer, Joseph, Haddam. Invt. £66-15-08. Taken 14 January, 1714-15, by Daniel Braynard and Samuel Olmsted.

Court Record, Page 240—7 March, 1714-15: Adms. granted to Hannah Spencer, widow.

Page 131-2-3.

Spencer, Obadiah, Sen., Hartford. Invt. £98-12-09. Taken 26 May, 1712, by Thomas Meekins and Joseph Barnard. Will dated 22 June, 1709.

I, Obadiah Spencer, Sen., of Hartford, husbandman, do make and ordain this my present last will: I give to my son Obadiah Spencer all that homelot with the messuage or tenement, outhouses and appurtenances where he now dwells and which I have formerly given him in a deed of conveyance; also the south half of my lot of land commonly called the Brickhill lot. I give to Thomas Spencer, my son, all that my lot of land in the meadow upon the east side of the Great River in Hartford, excepting 2 acres given to my son John, my son Thomas paying £6 to my son Disbrow Spencer. I give to my son Samuel Spencer all that messuage where he now dwells, standing on the north side of the homelot whereon I now dwell, in the division of land usually called the Neck in Hartford, and the north half part of my homelot of land adjoining to the meadow on the east, he paying the £6 lawful money to my son Disbrow Spencer. I give to Ebenezer Spencer, my son, all that lot of land in the Long Meadow in Hartford, at a place called Hobs Hole, for which I have formerly given him a deed of conveyance. I give to my son John Spencer all that my messuage or tenement wherein I now dwell, and my barn and outhouses with the appurtenances, also all the residue or south half part of my home-lot and barn, yards and fruit trees not hereinbefore given to my son Samuel; also 2 acres of Meadow Lott land on the east side of the Great River. I give to Disbrow Spencer, my son, £12 lawful money to be paid by my sons Thomas and Samuel Spencer. I give to my daughter Mary King, besides what she hath already had, one good cow and all my bedding and household stuffe or implements of household use within doors, excepting one paire of andirons, one warming pan and one cupbard given to John. I appoint my son John Spencer to be sole executor, and Mr. Joseph Talcott and Mr. Caleb Stanly, Jr., to be overseers.

Witness: *Caleb Stanly, Jr.,*   OBADIAH X SPENCER, SEN., LS.
    Abigail Stanly.

A codicil, dated 2 May, 1712: Whereas, in my will I gave to my daughter Mary King some things therein expressed, my will is now (that since God in his sovereign pleasure hath taken her out of this world by death) that my son John shall have all that I gave her.

Witness: *Joseph Gilbert.*   OBADIAH X SPENCER, LS.
    John Church.

Court Record, Page 80—2 June, 1712: Will proven. The legatees appeal to the Superior Court.

Page 213.

Spencer, William, East Haddam. Invt. £112-13-06. Taken 16 February, 1712-13, by Daniel Brainard, James Ackley and Jabez Chapman.

Court Record, Page 119—2 March, 1712-13: Jonathan Dunham now presented for probate a writing purported to be the will of the sd. decd. Rejected. Adms. granted to Sarah Spencer, widow.

Page 223—6 December, 1714: Sarah Spencer, Adms., exhibits an account of her Adms. Accepted. Order to dist. the estate:

	£	s	d
To Sarah Spencer, widow,	6-00-00		
To Alexander Spencer, eldest son,	30-06-08		
To William Spencer, Mary Dunham, Sarah Spencer and Hannah Chapman (wife of Samuel Chapman, see File), to each,	15-03-04		

And appoint Capt. Thomas Gates, Capt. Daniel Brainard and Thomas Robertson to dist. the estate.

Page 1 (Vol. IX) 1st November, 1715: Report of the dist., and Sarah Spencer granted a *Quietus Est.*

Inventory on File. Agreement on Page 195.

Stanclift, James, Middletown. Died 3 October, 1712. Invt. £191-03-10. Taken 15 October, 1712, by Samuel Hall, William Russell and Ebenezer Smith.

An agreement, dated 4 April, 1713, between William Stanclift of the one part and James Stanclift of the other part, both of the Town of Middletown: The sd. James Stanclift, for a consideration hereafter mentioned, doth covenant with the sd. William Stanclift, Adms. on the estate of their father, James Stanclift, late of Middletown, decd., and to and with the heirs and assigns of the sd. Wm. Stanclift and every of them, firmly abide these presents: That upon the receipt of £31 current money of this Colony, well and truly paid by the sd. William Stanclift unto him the sd. James Stanclift upon the receipt of the firm and legal deed of sales or feoffment of all the sd. James Stanclift's part of the estate of their father, James Stanclift aforesd., which is by agreement to be 9 acres of upland in the Township of Middletown, on the east side of the Great River, lying between lands of Mr. John Hamlin, Esq., and lands of Ebenezer Hurlbut, and also the 1-2 or 2nd part of a piece of meadow land at the upper end of Bushy Pond, which their father bought of Ned Durin, containing about 7 acres, and also the 1-2 of the quarry containing in the whole half one acre, upon the receipt of the aforesd. £30 or upon the receipt of a firm and legal deed of sale or feoffment of the abovesd. parcels of land unto the sd. James Stanclift, doth by these presents firmly covenant and promise the sd. William Stanclift to acknowledge himself fully satisfied and paid for all his right, title and interest in and to all the estate of his father, James Stanclift, decd.

Witness: *Thomas Wright,*   JAMES STANCLIFT, LS.
    John Bevin.

Court Record, Page 92—3 October, 1712: Adms. granted to Mary Stanclift, the widow, and William Stanclift, the son of sd. decd.

Page 193—3 May, 1714: William Stanclift, Adms., exhibits an account of his Adms. Account accepted and ordered recorded.

Page 201.

Stanly, Caleb, Jr., Hartford. Invt. £774-09-05. Taken 24 March, 1712, by John Marsh, Jr., and John Skinner.

Court Record, Page 42—7 January, 1711-12: Mr. Caleb Stanly, heretofore Clerk of the County Court and Court of Probate, being dead, this Court made choice of Mr. Thomas Kimberly to be Clerk of this Court of Probate within and for the County of Hartford, and he is sworn to that office.

Page 48—4 February, 1711-12: Adms. granted to Abigail Stanly, widow, and William Pitkin, Esq.

Page 19 (Vol. X) 7 May, 1723: William Pitkin appointed guardian unto Timothy Stanly, who is now 17 years of age. Recog., £100. And this Court also appoint Joseph Pitkin guardian to Caleb Stanly, 15 years of age. Recog., £100. And Mr. William and Joseph Pitkin to be guardians to Jonathan, 13 years, and William Stanly, about 12 years. Recog., £200.

Page 124—14 March, 1725-6: This Court having considered that, in order to have an equal dist. of the estate, there ought to be a new invt. and apprisement of the personal as well as the real estate of the decd., thereupon do appoint John Skinner and Aaron Cooke apprisers.

Page 139—6 December, 1726: The former Adms. being deceased, Adms. is granted to William Pitkin in order to render estate for dist. And as it is necessary to make a new apprisement, this Court appoint Thomas Root, Nathaniel Rust and Benjamin Palmer, of Coventry, to apprise lands at Coventry, Bolton and Tolland, and John Skinner, Aaron Cooke and ————— Goodwin to apprise the real estate at Hartford.

Page 93 (Vol. XII, Probate Side): An invt. of the lands of Caleb Stanly, Jr., in Coventry, Bolton and Tolland, valued at £877-00-00, taken 6 December, 1726, by special order of the Court of Probates, by Thomas Root and Nathaniel Rust. An invt. of real estate in Hartford, valued at £724-00-00, and of personal estate, £170-04-11, taken by John Skinner and Aaron Cooke.

Dist. File: 21 March, 1726-7: To Timothy, to Caleb, to Jonathan, to William. By Timothy Cowles and Joseph Cowles.

Page 160—4 July, 1727: Report of the distributors.

Page 152.

Stanly, Nathaniel, Hartford. Invt. £1618-19-00. Taken 17 December, 1712, by Joseph Talcott, William Whiting and Aaron Cooke. Will dated 11 November, 1712.

I, Nathaniel Stanly of Hartford, do make this my last will and testament: I give to my wife Sarah Stanly one moiety or 1-2 part of all my estate, both real and personal, during her natural life. And further, my mind is that my sd. wife shall have the use of that part of my mansion house which she shall make choice of. I give to my sd. wife £100 out of my moveable estate to be at her disposal. I give to my son Nathaniel Stanly the other moiety of my estate, both real and personal; and further my mind is that after the decease of his mother that moiety of my estate which I bequeathed to her during her natural life shall be to my sd. son and his heirs forever. I give to my daughter Mary Hooker, besides what I have formerly given to her, by deed of guift, 20 shillings. I constitute my wife and my son Nathaniel executors.

Witness: *John Haynes,*　　　　　　　NATHANIEL STANLY, LS.
　　　　Nathaniel Goodwin.

Court Record, Page 107—6 January, 1712-13: Nathaniel Stanly, who was executor, exhibits the last will. Proven.

Page 234.

Stanly, Thomas, Farmington. Invt. £342-18-11. Taken 1713, by Daniel Andrews, Sen., Isaac Cowles and Nathaniel Stanly.

Court Record, Page 147—6 July, 1713: Adms. granted to Anna Stanly, widow.

Page 210—2 August, 1714: This Court appoint Anne Stanly to be guardian to her children, Thomas Stanly, 18 years, and Anne Stanly, 15 years, children of Thomas Stanly. Recog., with Isaac Cowles of Farmington, £100.

Page 74 (Vol. IX) 5 August, 1718: The Adms. of sd. estate being now deceased, this Court grant letters of Adms. on the estate of Thomas and Anna Stanly his wife unto Thomas Stanly, son of the decd.

Page 355 (Probate Side): We, Thomas Stanly and Ann Stanly of Farmington, only son and daughter of Thomas Stanly, late of sd. Farmington, decd., do hereby signify and declare that we have each of us received our respective parts, share and portion of the estate of our honoured father, Thomas Stanly, decd., and of the estate of our mother, Ann Stanly, to our full satisfaction, this 2nd February, 1719-20.

Witness: *Isaac Cowles,*   THOMAS X STANLY, LS.
      Hezekiah Wyllys.   ANNA X STANLY, LS.

Court Record, Page 118—2 February, 1719-20: An agreement exhibited for the division and settlement of the estate of Thomas Stanly, late of Farmington, made by Thomas Stanly and Ann Stanly, children and heirs of the sd. deceased, was before this Court acknowledged to be their free act and deed. Accepted and ordered recorded.

Page 207-8-9.

Steele, Lt. James, Hartford. Invt. £878-09-10. Taken 25 November, 1712, by Thomas Hosmer and Edward Allyn.

I, James Steele, Sen., of Hartford, do make this my last will and testament: I give unto my eldest son James Steele my house and barn, malt house, and all my land at home, with all the trees and wells, and also six acres of land at the lower end of the south meadow; also in 40 acres ten acres more of land, and 7 acres of land at Nod, and my lot called the Gate Lot, being about 7 1-2 acres, and Rocky Hill lot, being about 24 acres; also the mountain lot called the 28 acres. I give also all my moveable estate to him, he paying all my just debts and legacies hereafter given to my daughters. All these lands and estate to my son James and his heirs forever. I give to my son Jonathan Steele all my land at Durham. I give to my son Stephen Steele my land at 4-Mile Hill. I give to my three daughters, Sarah, Mary and Elizabeth, £6 to each. I give to my wife Sarah the use and improvement and income of all my lands in Hartford, and stock and houseing, given to my son James, during her widowhood, and appoint her and my son James sole executors.

Witness: *Edward Allyn,*   JAMES STEELE, SEN.
   Samuel Shepherd.

Court Record, Page 104—5 January, 1712: Will proven.

Page 96 (Vol. IX) 3 February, 1718-19: Upon application of John Watson in right of his wife Sarah, and Cyprian Watson in right of his wife Elizabeth, co-heirs with several others unto the estate of James Steele, late of Hartford, deceased, showing that sd. James Steele died intestate and without issue, and that at the time of his death he had an estate in fee simple unto several parcels of land in the Township of Hartford as appears by will of James Steele, late of Hartford, father of the sd. James Steele deceased, and that the sd. intestate hath two brothers, Jonathan Steele and Stephen Steele, and three sisters, Sarah Watson, Elizabeth Watson and Mary Ashley, to whom the sd. lands belong, saving the mother Sarah Steele's use during her widowhood: Sarah Steele, executrix to the last will of James Steele the father, late of Hartford, decd., Stephen Steel and Jonathan Steele, sons, Joseph Ashley and Mary his wife, all cited to appear in Court and show cause, if any, why distribution should not be made.

Page 98—3 March, 1718-19: This Court decide that the lands belong to the brothers and no part to the sisters, according to the will of their father, Capt. James Steele. John Watson appeals.

Page 244.

Steele, Capt. James, Wethersfield. Invt. £812-11-06. Taken 23 July, 1713, by George Stilman, Samuel Wright and Michael Griswold.

Court Record, Page 152—3 August, 1713: Adms. granted to Anne Steele, widow, and Samuel Steele, eldest son.

Page 81 (Vol. IX): This Court appoint Anne Steele to be guardian to her children, Ann Steele, 16 years of age, and David, 13 years. Recog., £200.

Page 82—9 September, 1718: Anna Steele and Samuel Steele, of Wethersfield, exhibited now in this Court an account of their Adms. on the estate of Capt. James Steele, by which accot. the inventory amounts to £824-02-03, the real part whereof is £449-10-00; and that out of the moveable part there has been paid in debts and charges, £200-13-03; there remains of the moveable estate £173-19-00, to which add the real part and the sum to be distributed and divided is £623-09-00. Account allowed and order distribution: To Anna Steele, widow relict (dower) and £57-19-00, to be her own forever; to Samuel Steele, eldest son, £161-11-03; to Joseph Steele, David Steele, Prudence Steele, Hannah Steele and Anne Steele, sons and daughters of the deceased, to each and every one of them,

£80-15-07 1-2. And appoint George Stilman, Jonathan Belding and Michael Griswold distributors.

Page 83—7 October, 1718: Report of the dist.

Page 14 (Vol. X) 2 April, 1723: David Steele, a minor, 18 years of age, son of Capt. James Steele, made choice of Samuel Judd to be his guardian, his mother who was his guardian consenting. Recog., £200.

Page 35.

Steele, Samuel, Sen., Hartford. Invt. £926-07-00. Taken 21 February, 1709-10, by James Steele and Thomas Hosmer.

Court Record, Page 1—2 January, 1709-10: Adms. granted to Thomas Steele and William Steele, sons of sd. decd.

Page 39—1st October, 1711: Mrs. Marcy Steele, widow, of Hartford, is appointed guardian to her son Eliphalet Steele, 11 years of age. Daniel Steele, a minor, 14 1-2 years of age, one of the sons of Samuel Steele, Sen., late of Hartford decd., made choice of his mother Marcy Steele, widow, to be his guardian. Allowed by the Court.

Page 55—5 February, 1711-12: Thomas and William Steele, Adms., exhibit an account of their Adms. Accepted. Order to dist. the estate:

	£ s d
To Mary Steele, widow,	47-15-02
To Thomas Steele, eldest son,	234-00-01
To William, Daniel, Eliphalet and Abiall Steele, to each,	117-00-00½

And appoint Capt. Hezekiah Wyllys, Lt. James Steele and Thomas Hosmer, of Hartford, distributors. The Court grant the Adms. a *Quietus Est.*

Page 38.

Steele, Samuel, Jr., Hartford, Blacksmith. Invt. £105-00-00. Taken 22 February, 1709-10, by James Steele and Thomas Hosmer.

Court Record, Page 2—2 January, 1709-10: Adms. to Thomas and William Steele, brothers of the deceased.

Page 22.

Steele, William, Hartford. Invt. £105-14-04. Taken 30 March, 1713, by Samuel Sedgwick and Thomas Ensign.

Court Record, Page 111—2 February, 1712-13: Adms. to Thomas Steele, a brother of the deceased.

Will and Invt. in Vol. IX, Page 14-15.

Stephens, Thomas, Middletown.   Invt. £78-18-03.   Taken 5 September, 1714, by John Collins, John Bacon and Joseph Rockwell.   Will dated 30th August, 1714.

I, Thomas Stephens of Middletown, do make my last will and testament: I give to my son Thomas Stevens, whom I ordain sole executor, all and singular my lands, messuages and tenements, by him freely to be possessed and enjoyed, by him and his heirs forever.   I give unto my wife Jane the use of my now dwelling house with a convenient garden spot and a choice of one cow, to use and improve during the whole time of her widowhood.   And the whole of that estate that she brought to me with her, I freely resign up to her again.   Item.   I give to my two daughters, Hannah and Sarah, with my son Thomas abovesaid, the whole of my moveable estate and debts, after my just debts and funeral charges are paid, which I do order to be paid out of that £34 bill which is in the hands of John Hamlin, Esq., of Middletown.   I do request Mr. William Russell and Joseph Rockwell to be overseers.

Witness: *Benjamin Adkins,*   THOMAS STEVENS, LS.
Thomas Allen, Joseph Rockwell.

Court Record, Page 216—4 October, 1714: Will proven.

Page 192.

Stiles, Samuel, Windsor.   Invt. £58-15-00.   Taken 30 January, 1712-13, by Nathaniel Gaylord, Sen., Israel Stoughton and Jonathan Elsworth.

Court Record, Page 110—2 February, 1712-13: Martha Stiles, widow, exhibited an invt. of the estate of her late husband.   Accepted.

Page 270.

Stocking, George, Middletown.   Invt. £359-09-00.   Taken 16 March, 1713-14, by Samuel Hall, Nathaniel Savage and William Cornwall.

Court Record, Page 183—5 April, 1714: Adms. granted to Elizabeth Stocking, widow, and Daniel Stocking, brother of sd. decd.

Page 138 (Vol. IX) 4 November, 1720: Elizabeth and Daniel Stocking, Adms., exhibit an account of their Adms.   Order to dist. the estate:

	£	s	d
To the widow, Elizabeth Stocking,	32-07-04		
To Stephen Stocking, eldest son,	90-17-04		
To Elizabeth, Samuel, Bethiah, George and Nathaniel Stocking, to each of them, the sum of	45-08-08		

And appoint Samuel Hall, William Cornwall, Sen., and John Gains distributors. This Court appoint Daniel Stocking to be guardian to George Stocking, age 15 years, and Nathaniel Stocking, age 14 years, children of George Stocking, late decd. Recog., £100.

Stocking, John. Court Record, Page 143—1st June, 1713: Per act of the General Assembly, this Court do order and direct George Stocking and Daniel Stocking of Middletown to sell so much of the lands of their brother John Stocking of Middletown (an idiot) as may produce the sum of £40 to be improved for his comfortable subsistenance for the payment of just debts. And they are to sell such lands of the sd. John Stocking as lie in the Township of Hartford.

Page 147.

Stoughton, John, Windsor. Invt. £271-02-09. Taken 24 May, 1712, by Job Drake, Sen., Thomas Stoughton and Samuel Burnham.

Court Record, Page 138—4 May, 1713: Sarah Stoughton, Adms., now exhibits an account of her Adms. Allowed by the Court. Order to dist. the estate to the surviving heirs as followeth: To Sarah Stoughton, widow, of the moveable estate the sum of £23-11-02; to Nathaniel Stoughton, 2nd son, Elizabeth, Sarah, Rebeckah, Anne, Hannah, Mary and Rachel Stoughton, to each of them, £27-02-09 1-2. William Stoughton hath already received his full double portion. And appoint Capt. Thomas Stoughton, Deacon Job Drake and Samuel Rockwell, distributors.

Page 147—6 July, 1713: This Court appoint Sarah Stoughton, relict of John Stoughton, late of Windsor, to be guardian to all the children of the sd. decd. that are under age. Recog., with Joseph Drake, in £150.

Page 156—7 September, 1713: By reason of some misrepresentation in the order of this Court for dist. of the estate of John Stoughton, late of Windsor, decd., the 2nd son (viz., William) was mistaken for the eldest son (vizt., John), who was intended thereby, though entirely by that means left out.

See File: 3 January, 1713-14: John, William and Sarah Stoughton and Joseph and Elizabeth Mather gave receipts for their several portions.

Page 144 (Vol. IX) 7 February, 1720-21: This Court appoint John Stoughton of Windsor to be guardian to his brother Nathaniel Stoughton, age 18 years. Recog., £50.

Page 44 (Vol. XI) 4 May, 1731: Sarah Stoughton, now Drake, formerly widow of John Stoughton, showing that she had not as yet had set out her dower or thirds of the lands of her sd. late husband, although there was long time an order of Court therefor, moves to this Court that some suitable persons may be appointed to set out one-third part of the lands of the sd. John Stoughton for her improvement during her natural life: Whereupon this Court appoint Thomas Stoughton, Joseph Rockwell and Deacon Joseph Skinner, of Windsor, distributors.

Page 47—28 June, 1731: William Stoughton of Windsor, son of John Stoughton, objects to the setting out, and is granted a review of the case at the Superior Court.

Page 122.

Stoughton, Samuel, Windsor. Invt. £272-17-03. Taken by Israel Stoughton, Daniel Bissell and Jonathan Elsworth.
Court Record, Page 49—4 February, 1711-12: Adms. granted to Dorothy Stoughton, widow.

Page 118.

Strickland, John, Jr., Glastonbury. Invt. £69-16-08. Taken 23 January, 1711-12, by Gershom Smith and Jonathan Judd. The children of the decd. are: Elizabeth, b. 12 December, 1705; John, b. 4 April, 1709; and William, 27 August, 1711.
Court Record, Page 47—4 February, 1711-12: Adms. granted to Elizabeth Strickland, widow, and Jonathan Judd.
Page 201—7 June, 1714: Elizabeth Strickland and Jonathan Judd, Adms., exhibit an account of their Adms. Accepted. The estate is to remain in the hands of the widow, who was appointed by the Court guardian to her children by John Strickland, deceased.

Invt. in Vol. IX, Page 17.

Strickland, Joseph, Simsbury. Invt. £27-01-06. Taken 18 May, 1714, by James Cornish and John Pettibone.
Court Record, Page 197—7 June, 1714: Adms. granted to Elizabeth Strickland, widow, and Samuel Strickland, mother and brother of sd. decd.

Page 38.

Taphannah, Richard (Indian man), Glastonbury. Invt. £10-13-09. Taken 2 February, 1709-10, by Samuel Smith and Thomas Dickinson.
Court Record, Page 2—2 January, 1709-10: Adms. to Samuel Loveland of Glastonbury.

Page 169.

Tappin, James, Sen., Middletown. Invt. £315-15-05. Taken 27 August, 1712, by Israhiah Wetmore, Joseph Rockwell and William Ward. Will dated 11 June, 1712.

I, James Tappin, Sen., of Middletown, do make this my last will and testament: My will is that my wife Anne Tappin have the whole possession and improvement of all the estate that I stand possessed of, deeds of gift excepted, during her natural life. It. I give to my son James Tappin, after my own and his mother Anna Tappin's decease, all my houseing and lands lying in the Township of Middletown; also to my son James Tappin I give all my tooles and materials for my trade as a felt maker and all my tools and utensils for husbandry. I give to my daughter Anna, after her mother's decease, the one-half of my household goods, that is to say, brass, pewter and beding, only it is to be considered, and my will is, that my daughter Mary have my best feather bed, ruggs and boulster. It. My will is that my daughter Mary Barnes have, at mine own and my wife's decease, the other half of my household goods equal with her sister Anna. The rest of my remaining living stock shall be equally divided between my three children, namely, James Tappin, Anna Ward and Mary Barnes. I appoint my wife Anne Tappin and my son James Tappin joynt executors.

Witness: *Thomas Foster,*   JAMES X TAPPIN, LS.
Richard Turner, Joseph Rockwell.

Court Record, Page 88—1st September, 1712: Will proven.

Page 130.

Taylor, Samuel, Wethersfield. Invt. £177-14-04. Taken 5 February, 1711-12, by Jonathan Hollister and William Nott.

The last will and testament of Samuel Taylor is as followeth: In my will I doe give unto my wife this house and land, and one cow, and my black mare, during her naturall life. Item. I give to my son John my homestead and my team and team tackling, one yoak of oxen, and two horses. Item. I give to my grandson Samuel Taylor the farm in the woods, that which is called Coles farme. I give to my 3 daughters eighteen acres of woodland and the rest of my moveable estate, to be divided amongst them. And I give unto my daughter Sarah the sum of £5, to her and her heirs forever.

Witness: *Samuel Smith,*   SAMUEL X TAYLOR.
William Nott.

Court Record, Page 45—7 January, 1711-12: Will proven. Adms. granted to Sarah Taylor, the widow, and John Taylor, son of the decd., with the will annexed.

Page 101—1st December, 1712: John Taylor, Adms., exhibits an account of his Adms. Approved.

Page 38.

(Agreement on File.)

Taylor, Stephen, Jr., Windsor. Invt. £189-03-00. Taken 21 October, 1709, by Roger Wolcott and Job Drake.

An agreement, dated 3 April, 1710, made between William Taylor of the one part, and Ephraim Bissell (who married Joanna Taylor 24 December, 1702, W. R., sister of sd. decd.) and Joseph Stedman on the other part, respecting an estate formerly belonging to Stephen Taylor, late of Windsor decd., is as followeth:

1st. That after the debts due from the estate are paid, that then the remainder of sd. estate shall be divided, to each of them an equal share and part.

But if the lands should amount in value to more than 1-3 part of the sd. estate, it is agreed that the sd. William Taylor shall have all the lands, he paying to the sd. Ephraim Bissell and Joseph Stedman so much money as shall make the sd. Ephraim Bissell and Joseph Stedman full 2-3 parts of sd. estate.

In witness whereof the parties to these presents have hereunto set their hands and seals the day and year above written.

Witness: *Hezekiah Wyllys,*   WILLIAM TAYLOR,
    Elizabeth Wyllys.   EPHRAIM BISSELL,
                                  JOSEPH STEDMAN.

Court Record, Page 8—3 April, 1710: Adms. granted to William Taylor, a brother of sd. decd.

Page 27—5 February, 1710-11: Agreement now exhibited in this Court. Allowed and approved. And order the sd. agreement to be kept on file.

Page 181—1st March, 1713-14: William Taylor, Adms., exhibits now an account of his Adms., which this Court allow, and he is granted a *Quietus Est.*

Page 124.

Thompson, John, Farmington. Invt. £174-01-02. Taken 3 March, 1711-12, by Joseph Hawley and Ebenezer Steele.

Court Record, Page 46—4 February, 1711-12: Adms. granted to John Thompson, son of sd. decd., and Thomas Hart, Jr., son-in-law.

Record of distribution on file, 27 January, 1742-3:

	£ s d		£ s d
To the widow Thompson,	32-04-08	To Hezekiah Thompson,	32-04-08
To Nathaniel Thompson,	32-04-08	To Margaret Beach,	32-04-08
To James Thompson,	32-04-08	To Hannah Bird,	32-04-08
To Ezekiel Thompson,	32-04-08	To Eunice Judd,	32-04-08
To Solomon Thompson,	32-04-08		

Date of report, 8 February, 1742-3.   By *Isaac Cowles,*
                                           John Hart,
                                           Thomas Wadsworth.

Invt. in Vol. IX, Page 21.

Thornton, Samuel, Hartford. Invt. £95-06-04. Taken 1st April, 1714, by Nathaniel Stanly and Thomas Hosmer.

Court Record, Page 178—19 February, 1713-14: Adms. granted joyntly to Capt. Joseph Whiting and Susannah Thornton, widow of sd. decd.

Page 3 (Vol. IX) 7 December, 1715: Capt. Joseph Whiting and Susannah Thornton, Adms., exhibit now an account of their Adms. Allowed. The estate is supposed to be insolvent. This Court therefore allow to the widow £20 for her subsistence.

Page 21.

Thrall, Samuel, Windsor. Invt. £145-05-00. Taken 29 December, 1709, by Jacob Gibbs, Jonathan Elsworth and John Thrall.

Court Record, Page 1—2 January, 1709-10: Adms. granted to Elizabeth Thrall, widow.

Page 41-2 (Vol. X) 3rd March, 1723-4: Samuel Pettebone, and Elizabeth his wife, formerly Elizabeth Thrall, the only child of Samuel Thrall, late of Windsor deceased, appeared before this Court for himself and in behalf of his wife and acknowledged that Elizabeth Case, sometime widow of Samuel Thrall and Adms. on his estate, hath delivered into their possession all that part of their father's moveable estate that belonged to them. Also, Samuel Case, husband to the aforesaid Adms., formerly widow to the said Samuel Thrall, acknowledged the receipt of her one-third part of the moveable estate. This Court now order a dist. of the real estate, one-third to the widow, now Elizabeth Case, and two-thirds to Samuel Pettebone and his wife, Elizabeth, only daughter of Samuel Thrall deceased. This Court appoint Thomas Griswold, John Griswold and John Barnard distributors. And grant to Samuel Case and Elizabeth his wife a *Quietus Est.*

Page 154.

Towsey, Thomas, Wethersfield. Invt. £387-19-00. Taken 3 December, 1712, by John Curtis, Nathaniel Stodder and David Goodrich. Will dated 12 November, 1712.

The last will and testament of Thomas Towsey is as followeth: My body I comit to the earth, and my soule to the Lord, in hopes of a glorius resurection. And that little of my worldly goods that it hath pleased God to bestow upon me, after my just debts are paid, I dispose of as followeth: Imprimis: I give to my son Thomas my dwelling house, and my shop and barn, and all my land, with all the appurtenances of the same. I give to George Northway 40 shillings as money. I give to my apprentice, John Welles, one weaver's loome and gears to weave durgget, sarge and kersey. And all the rest of my estate I give to my daughter Elizabeth Churchill, the wife of Josiah Churchill. And I constitute my daughter Elizabeth Churchill executrix.

Witness: *Robert Wells,*   THOMAS TOWSEY, LS.
John Curtis, Sen.

Court Record, Page 103—5 January, 1712-13: Will proven.

Page 230.

Treat, Richard, Wethersfield. Died 7 May, 1713. Invt. £636-02-06. Taken 1st July, 1713, by Jonathan Belding, Edward Bulkeley and Joshua Robbins. Will dated 2 May, 1713.

I, Richard Treat of Wethersfield, doe make this my last will and testament: I will that my just debts be paid by my executor. I will and bequeath all my lands, both in possession and reversion (that is to say, after the decease of my hond. mother Rebecca Treat), to come to me from my hond. father, Mr. James Treat, late of Wethersfield, decd., by his last will bearing date 29 January, 1708-9, together with all my goods, rights, debts and commodities whatsoever, with the profits and issues thereof, to my beloved daughter and only child Katharine Treat, and to her heirs and assigns forever. In case of her death before marriage or 18 years of age, then to my mother Rebecca Treat, if she be then living, and to my sisters, Jemima Chester and Mabel Treat, all my personal or household goods. And in case my daughter Katharine Treat die as aforesaid, then I bequeath my lands to my brethren, Salmon Treat of Boston and Joseph Treat of Wethersfield, to be equally divided between them. I appoint Salmon Treat and Joseph Treat executors.

Witness: *David Wright,*   RICHARD TREAT, LS.
Thomas Hurlbut.

Court Record, Page 141—19 May, 1713: Joseph Treat only accepts the trust. Will proven.

Page 177 (Vol. IX) 9 October, 1722: Joseph Treat of Wethersfield to be guardian to Katharine Treat, a minor, 17 years of age, daughter of Richard Treat, decd. Recog., £50.

Page 228.

(Invt. in Vol. IX, Page 29.)

Treat, Thomas, Glastonbury. Invt. £770-06-00. Taken 3 April, 1713, by Samuel Smith and Jonathan Smith. Invt. of lands taken 5 March, 1714. Will dated 13 June, 1709.

I, Thomas Treat of Glastonbury, being called forthwith to go upon Her Majestie's service against Canada, do therefore briefly make this my last will: I give all my estate, real and personal, to my sons (already born or to be born), to be divided among them in the proportion following: To Richard, my eldest first-born son, a share double to any one of his brethren; to all the rest an equal share, they to pay to each of their sisters, at 18 years of age, £100, Richard to pay double to any of his brothers. But if my son Richard shall recover of his malady so that he be brought up to learning at the College or otherwise, then he shall receive only an equal share with the others. I appoint my wife Dorothy executrix. To my wife Dorothy, besides her dower of the third part of my real estate given her by common law and by our law (Title Dower), I give her the use and improvement of, and profits of, the estate, real and personal, for the education of my children.

Witness: *Thomas Goodrich,*   THOMAS TREAT.
Daniel X *Andrews, Richard Goodrich.*

Court Record, Page 118—12 March, 1712-13: Will proven.

Copied from Original Paper on File:

Pursuant to the last will and testament of our hond. father, Thomas Treat of Glassenbury deceast, bearing date 13 June, Anno Domini 1709, we the subscribers, being heirs to ye estate of ye sd. deceased, have made a distribution of ye lands by his last sd. will given and bequeathed to us his sd. heirs, and are fully satisfied and contented with this our sd. distribution and settlement thereof, which is in manner following, viz.:

1. To Richard Treat, eldest son and heir of ye sd. deceased, within the fence, beginning on the north side, butting partly on land belonging to [. . . . .] and partly belonging to John Hollister, one piece containing forty acres an half and twenty four rods; also nine acres in a place called the lower meadow.

2. To Charles Treat, second son and heir of ye deceased, within the meadow fence, one piece butting northwardly upon land belonging to Richard Treat now mentioned, twenty-one acres and thirty-eight rods; also five acres in a place called the lower meadow.

3. To Thomas Treat, third son and heir of ye deceased, within the meadow fence, one piece butting northwardly upon land belonging to and set out by said distributors to Charles Treat now mentioned, twenty-seven acres and thirty-eight rods.

4. To Isaac Treat, fourth son and heir of the deceased, within the meadow fence, one piece butting northwardly upon the aforesaid piece of land distributed to ye aforesd Thomas Treat, containing thirty acres.

5. To Dorotheus Treat, fifth son and heir of ye deceased, one piece within the meadow fence butting northwardly upon the aforesd land distributed to the aforesd. Isaac Treat, and southwardly upon Richard Goodrich his land, containing twenty-eight acres an half and two rods.

Further, lands without the meadow fence eastwardly of the land before specified:

1. To Richard Treat, one piece of land butting south upon Nathaniel Bidwell his land, north upon land distributed to Charles Treat, west upon Dorotheus Treat his land, east upon commonage land, being fifty-six

rods, nine links in breadth, containing two hundred and nineteen acres.

2. To Charles Treat, one piece of land butting south upon the lot distributed to Richard Treat, west upon the heirs of John Hollister deceased, and east upon the commons, containing one hundred and fifty acres.

3. To Thomas Treat, the dwelling house of the deceased and land thereto belonging, containing sixteen acres and three-quarters.

4. To Isaac Treat, one parcel of land butting north upon Nathaniel Bidwell's land, south upon Richard Goodrich's land, east upon the commons, containing one hundred and five acres.

5. To Dorotheus Treat, land butting north upon land of heirs of John Hollister deceased, south upon Nathaniel Bidwell's land, west upon land of Thomas Treat, and east upon land of Richard Treat, ten acres and three-quarters; another piece containing sixty-seven acres.

To Isaac Treat, ten acres adjoining Nathaniel Bidwell and Samuel Brooks. And the aforesd. Richard Treat and Charles Treat do by virtue hereof acquit their right and title to a certain fourscore-acre lot in the southward bounds of said Glassenbury to Isaac and Dorotheus Treat, which lands so distributed as aforesd. are lying within the Township of Glassenbury at a place called Nayogg. As also that the sd. parties have made allowances for our hond. mother Dorothy Treat according to ye sd. will and testament of our aforesd. hond. father deceased.

And that we the subscribers are fully satisfied and contented with this our aforesd. distribution, and amicably agree thereunto, we do this day, in witness and in testimony thereof, set our hands and seals, this 17 July, Anno Dom. 1735.

Witness: *Benjamin Ross,*   RICHARD TREAT, LS.
          Elizabeth X *Andros.*   CHARLES TREAT, LS.
                                     THOMAS TREAT, LS.
                                     ISAAC TREAT, LS.
                                     DOROTHEUS TREAT, LS.

Tho: and Isaac Treat appeared before the
Court of Probate, January 23, 1753 and acknowl-
edged this agreement to be their free act and deed.
Test: Joseph Talcott, Clerk.

Page 111.

Tryon, William, Wethersfield. Invt. £309-08-08. Taken by Joshua Robbins, Sen., Joseph Belden and Thomas Welles.

Court Record, Page 45—7 January, 1711-12: By choice of the children of William Tryon, this Court appoint Capt. James Steele to administer on sd. estate. Joseph and David Tryon exhibited an inventory.

Page 87—4 August, 1712: Abiall Tryon, age 17 years, chose Abraham Kilbourn to be his guardian. Recog., £50.

Page 133—6 April, 1713: Capt. James Steele exhibits now an account of his Adms. Accepted. Order to dist. the estate:

	£	s	d
To Joseph Tryon, eldest son,	37-17-10		
To David, Thomas, Abell, Zybah and Abiall Tryon, sons, to each,	18-18-11		
To Sarah Gillett, eldest daughter, Elizabeth Hill, and to Mabell Tryon, to each,	18-18-11		

And appoint Benjamin Churchill, Capt. David Goodrich and Jonathan Belding, distributors.

Page 153—3 August, 1713: Report of the distributors.

Vibbard, John. Court Record, Page 233—3 January, 1714-15: This Court appoint Mary Vibbard of Hartford to be guardian to John Vibbard, age 8 years, and James Vibbard, age 6 years, children of John Vibbard, late of Hartford, decd.

Page 71.

Wait, William. An inventory of the estate of William Wait, Indian man, late of Hartford, deceased, is as follows: vizt.:

	£	s	d
To his wages due from the Colony for his service on the expedition against Canada, in the year 1709, besides what he had received and taken up there of himself as money,	06-04-05		

Hartford, April 2nd, 1711: This is a true inventory of all the estate of the sd. William Wait that I can hear of or come at.

Test: Nathaniel Hooker, Administrator.

Court Record, Page 37—3 September, 1711: Nathaniel Hooker, Adms., exhibits an account of his Adms. Accepted. And this Court grant him a *Quietus Est.*

Page 117.

Ward, Lt. James, Middletown. Invt. £161-02-07. Taken 1st February, 1711-12, by Seth Warner, Joseph Rockwell and Samuel Warner.

Court Record, Page 46—4 February, 1711-12: Adms. granted to Elizabeth Ward, widow.

Invt. in Vol. IX, Page 17.

Warner, Daniel, Waterbury. Invt. £150-04-05. Taken 6 November, 1713, by Thomas Judd and John Judd.

Court Record, Page 162—17 November, 1713: Adms. granted to Johanna Warner, the widow, and Joseph Lewis of Waterbury.

Page 190—14 April, 1714: Samuel Warner, a minor son of Daniel Warner, chose William Hickcock of Waterbury to be his guardian. Recog., £40.

Page 226—6 December, 1714: Joseph Lewis, Adms., exhibits an account of his Adms. Allowed. Order to dist. the estate:

	£ s d
To Johanna, widow relict,	9-06-04
To Samuel Warner, eldest son,	28-06-04
To Ebenezer, Abraham, Sarah, Abigail and Mary Warner, to each,	14-03-02

And appoint John Judd, Ephraim Warner and Thomas Hickcock, distributors.

Page 227—6 December, 1714: This Court appoint Thomas Judd of Waterbury guardian to Abraham Warner, 6 years of age. Recog., £30. And Joseph Lewis of Waterbury to be guardian to Ebenezer Warner, 8 years of age. Recog., £30. Joanna Warner, widow, to be guardian to Abigail Warner, 4 years, and to Mary Warner, 2 1-2 years of age; who, with Thomas Judd of Waterbury, recog. £50.

Page 277.

Warner, Hannah, Wethersfield. Nuncupative will, dated 2 March, 1713-14:

Our honoured mother, Hannah Warner, being very sick and near her death, declared her will relating to her estate in several particulars, which was taken from her mouth and immediately committed to writing, viz., on the 2nd and 3rd days of March, 1713-14, which here follows:

I give to my grandchild Mary Warner the best bed and curtains and best boulster, with two pillars and two coverletts, one of the best coverletts, and 1 blankett, 3 paire of sheets, and 1 of the best platters that stands upon the high shelf, and 1 of the least upon the high shelf, and 2 of the best that stand upon the middle shelf, and 2 plates, 2 porringers and 1 beaker that was her great grandfather's, and the plain chest, and my blue damask petticoat. To my daughter Abigail I give the great kettle when her mother hath done with it, and I give her my scarf, and £10 as pay, as my husband did desire me. I give to Sarah Warner my silk stuffed gowne (the oldest). I give to Ruth Warner the small chest. I give to my 2 daughters all the rest of my clothes.

A question was asked whether this was all she intended to give to her daughters, and she answered, "No, I give these as a free gift and not as any of their parts."

Witness: *Thomas Welles,*
            Joshua Robbins, 2nd.

Court Record, Page 187—5 April, 1714: William, Daniel and John Warner exhibited the last will and testament of their mother, Hannah Warner, late wife of William Warner. Proven, ordered recorded and kept on file.

Page 181.

Warner, John, son of Robert Warner, Middletown. Invt. £27-10-00. Taken 3d May, 1712, by John Collins, Joseph Rockwell and John Bacon.

John Warner aforesd. is indebted to Seth Warner for his keeping, etc., about 20 years, more than £100.

Court Record, Page 66—7 April, 1712: Adms. to Seth Warner, a brother of the deceased.

Invt. in Vol. IX, Page 16.

Warner, John, Wethersfield. Invt. £913-18-11. Taken 24 November, 1714, by Joshua Robbins, Edward Bulkeley and Daniel Boreman.

Court Record, Page 223—6 December, 1714: Adms. granted to Elizabeth Warner, widow, and Daniel Warner of Wethersfield, a brother of sd. decd.

Page 62 (Vol. XI) 7 March, 1731-2: Daniel Warner, who was appointed guardian to Ruth Warner, a minor daughter of John Warner, late of Wethersfield, was summoned to appear before this Court as per writ bearing date 29 February, 1731-2, to render an account of guardianship to sd. minor at this Court, who accordingly appeared and rendered an account, and is fully discharged from any further demands from sd. minor.

Invt. in Vol. IX, Page 23.

Warner, Seth, Middletown. Invt. £321-09-09. Taken 29 January, 1713-14, by John Bacon, John Warner and Joseph Rockwell.

Court Record, Page 168—4 January, 1713-14: Adms. granted to Mary Warner, widow, and Robert Warner, eldest son.

Page 235—7 February, 1714-15: Robert Warner, Adms., exhibits an account of his Adms. Account allowed. Order to dist.:

	£	s	d
To Mary Warner, the widow,	26	12	08
To Robert Warner, eldest son,	103	16	08
To Samuel, Seth and Mary Warner, to each of them,	51	18	04

And appoint John Collins, John Bacon and John Warner, Jr., distributors.

Page 237—7 February, 1714-15: Samuel Warner, 19 years of age, son of Seth Warner, late of Middletown, chose Joseph Rockwell of Middletown to be his guardian. Recog., with Robert Warner, in £100. This Court appoint Mary Warner to be guardian to Seth Warner, 10 years of age, son of Seth Warner. Recog., with Robert Warner, in £100.

Invt. and Agreement in Vol. IX, Page 25-41.

Warner, Thomas, Waterbury. Died 24 November, 1714. Inventory, £70-16-09. Taken 4 December, 1714, by Ephraim Warner and John Judd. An agreement of legatees, made 4 January, 1715, by and between Benjamin Warner of New Haven on the one part, and Samuel Chatterton, Thomas Warner, John Andrews, Ebenezer Richardson and Samuel Warner, the heirs of Thomas Warner deceased, wherein Mr. Benjamin Warner agrees to take the whole care of and provide for my mother, the widow of the said deceased Thomas Warner, with a comfortable maintenance during her natural life, in sickness and in health, and be at all charges. In consideration, we, the said Samuel Chatterton, Thomas Warner, John Andrews, Ebenezer Richardson and Samuel Warner, for ourselves, our heirs, executors and assigns, do hereby surrender all our right, title and interest unto the estate of our father, Thomas Warner of Waterbury deceased, unto our brother Benjamin Warner aforesaid.

Witness: *Abraham Bradley, J. P.,*   BENJAMIN WARNER, LS.
Thomas Judd, Thomas Richards.   SAMUEL CHATTERTON, LS.
                                    JOHN X ANDREWS, LS.
                                    THOMAS X WARNER, LS.
                                    EBENEZ: RICHARDSON, LS.
                                    SAMUEL X WARNER, LS.
                                    ELIZA X CHATTERTON, LS.
                                    MARTHA X ANDREWS, LS.
                                    MARGARET X RICHARDSON, LS.

Court Record, Page 232—3 January, 1714-15: Adms. granted to Benjamin Warner of New Haven, eldest son of sd. decd.

Page 246—4 April, 1715: Benjamin Warner, Adms., exhibits now sundry disbursements and reports not sufficient personal estate to pay the debts.

Page 255—7 June, 1715: This Court, pursuant to an order of the General Assembly of 12th May last past, do order and direct Benjamin Warner of New Haven, Adms., to sell the house, homested and 5 acres of land belonging to that estate to the highest bidder.

Page 7 (Vol. IX) 6 March, 1715-16: Benjamin Warner, Adms., exhibits now an agreement. Accepted, ordered recorded, and kept on file. Exhibited also an account of his Adms.

Page 270.

Warner, William, Wethersfield. Invt. £1321-04-04. Taken 1st April, 1714, by Edward Bulkeley and John Lattimere. Will dated 22 January, 1711-12.

I, William Warner of Wethersfield, do make this my last will and testament: I give to my wife Hannah Warner one-third of all my land during her natural life. Also, I give to her all my household goods and all that provision, as meat, meal, malt and the like, which is laid in for the good of my family, and half of all my grain, that is to say, half that remains when my debts are paid, and £20 in money and £10 worth of my cattle, which she shall choose, and a chamber, a lower room, and necessary cellarage, in either the house I now dwell in or that my son John at present dwells in, which of them she pleases. I give and bequeath to my son William Warner all my houseing and land, with the orchard thereon, which I bought of John Brounson, lying in the South Field; also, eight acres of my pasture land, lying in the South Field, which I bought of John and Luke Hitchcock, to be laid out to him in the south side of the said pasture land; also, the whole of the remainder of my two-and-twenty-acre lot in Fearful Swamp (called in Robert Welles's will, Fairfield Swamp), after the twenty acres, exact measure, formerly given by me to my brethren, John and Joshua Robbins, is measured off; also, one acre of the five acres and an half in the Great Meadow, which I bought of Mr. Josiah Woolcott; also, one-third part of the lot granted by the Town of Wethersfield to me in the last division of land; also, three acres of my land at Hangdog Plain; also, my right in Indian Purchase, on the east side of the Connecticut River, in the bounds of Glastonbury. Item. To my son John Warner I give the homelot which I purchased of the Graves's, and the buildings thereon (with other parcels of land). Item. I give to my son Daniel Warner my houseing and homelot which I now live upon; also, 6 acres of land in the South Field, which I purchased of my brother-in-law Eleazer Kimberly; also, 13 1-2 acres of land at Hangdog Plain; 1-3 part of that tract of land given me by the Town of Wethersfield; 1-3 part of the land I bought of Capt. Cyprian Nicholls of Hartford, which land lyeth partly in Mile Meadow and partly in Beaver Meadow; also, one acre in Mile Meadow, which I bought of Mr. Josiah Wolcott. Item. I give to my daughter Hannah Wells of my moveable estate to make up £140. Item. To my daughter Abigail Robbins of my moveable estate to make up £120. I do hereby constitute my sons, William Warner, John Warner and Daniel Warner, executors.

Witness: *Joshua Robbins,*   WILLIAM WARNER, SEN., LS.
    Joshua Robbins, 2nd.

Court Record, Page 187—5 April, 1714: Will proven.

Page 11 (Vol. IX) 3 April, 1716: This Court doth order Jonathan Belding, John Russell and Ebenezer Belding, of Wethersfield, to divide and dist. such lands belonging to the estate of Lt. William Warner, late decd., as the sd. deceased in and by his last will did give to his sons in general not ascertaining the division thereof; and also to make division and partition (in behalf of the heirs of John Warner, late of Wethersfield, decd., with Daniel Warner, brother of sd. John Warner, decd.) of such lands as were joyntly purchased by the sd. John and Daniel Warner in the lifetime of the sd. John Warner and yet remain undivided.

Page 126.

Watson, Samuel, Windsor. Invt. £194-02-01. Taken 23 November, 1711, by Abraham Phelps, Sen., Nathaniel Gaylord, Sen., and Samuel Moore.

Court Record, Page 40—25 November, 1711: Adms. granted to Ebenezer and Jedediah Watson, brothers of the sd. decd.

Page 70—9 April, 1712: Ebenezer and Jedediah Watson, Adms., exhibited an account of their Adms. It being objected to by persons interested, a notification was issued for a hearing.

Page 76—5 May, 1712: The Adms. now exhibit an account of their Adms. Accepted. Order to dist. the estate to the brothers and sisters of sd. deceased: To John, Ebenezer, Jedediah, to the heirs of Nathaniel Watson decd., to Mary Drake, widow of John Drake, late of Windsor, to the heirs of Hannah Bird deceased, sisters, to each of them, £29-19-05 1-2. And appoint Lt. Daniel Heydon, Jr., Thomas Moore and Lt. Joshua Willes, of Windsor, distributors.

Page 260 (Probate Side, Vol. IX): We whose names are hereunto subscribed, being appointed to dist. the estate of Samuel Watson, late of Windsor, decd., and having dist. to John Watson £16-00 out of the homelot, and not determined where it should lye, either on the north or on the south side, which homelot was prised at £44-00-00, and John Watson was to have £16 out of the £44, we therefore being now called to declare on which side it should lye, we have concluded that John Watson shall have 9 rods on the south side of the sd. Samuel Watson's houselot for his £16 which was dist. to him by Lt. Heydon, Lt. Joshua Wills and Thomas Moore. And that this is our determination, we have hereunto set our hands this 24 March, 1717-18.

JOSHUA WILLES, SEN.,
THOMAS MOORE.

Court Record, Page 60—1st April, 1718: Upon the motion of Jedediah Watson of Windsor, that the determination of Joshua Wills, Sen., and Thomas Moore, who are distributors of the estate of John Watson (Samuel Watson), late of sd. Windsor, deceased, may be recorded, this Court order the Clerk to record the sd. determination or conclusion according to his sd. Watson's desire.

Webb, Orange. Court Record, Page 180—1st March, 1713-14: Orange Webb, 18 years of age, son of Henry Webb, late of Wethersfield, decd. chose Consider Hopkins of Hartford to be his guardian.

Page 136.

Welles, Noah, Colchester. Invt. £411-04-00. Taken by Nathaniel Loomis and Samuel Loomis.

Court Record, Page 201—7 June, 1714: Noah Welles, Adms., exhibited an account of his Adms. on sd. estate. Allowed. Order to dist:

	£ s d
To Mary Welles, widow,	27-04-00
To Noah Welles, eldest son,	89-17-00
To John, Jonathan and Samuel Welles, to Mary Lester, to Sarah Foote and Hannah Welles, to each of them,	44-18-06

And appoint Capt. Samuel Gilbert, Samuel Loomis and Ephraim Welles, of Colchester, distributors.

Page 236—7 February, 1714-15: Jonathan Welles and Hannah Welles, minors, chose their brother, Noah Welles, to be their guardian. And this Court appoint Mrs. Mary Welles to be guardian to Samuel, age 10 years, children of Noah Welles, decd.

Will and Invt. in Vol. IX, Page 25-26-27.

Welles, Capt. Robert, Wethersfield. Invt. £3667-11-03. Taken 20 July, 1714, by Joshua Robbins, Edward Bulkeley and Ephraim Goodrich. Will dated 4 January, 1711-12.

I, Robert Welles of Wethersfield, do make my will as followeth: I give to my wife Mary the remaining part of that household goods which I had with her; also, a sixth part of all my silver, bills and plate which I dye seized of, together with two cows, all which is to be at her own dispose forever; and further, during the time that she remains my widow, eight pounds yearly to be paid by my four sons in equal parts, and the improvement of two or three acres of mowing land in that parcel of land which I bought of my brother John Hollister; and that Gideon my son pasture the two cows abovesaid for his mother. I also give her the improvement of my parlour and parlour chamber, half my garden, and liberty of my back room to wash, bake and brew in, with part of the cellar; only the punch bowl, given afterward to my grandson Robert, is excepted from my wife and children. I give unto my son Thomas, in addition to what I have given by deed of gift, several parcels of land, a third part of the three 50-acre lots which lye together, also half the island I bought of Mr. Nathaniel Foot, and a third part of my last division lot; also, land in Fairfield Swamp. I give to my son Joseph Welles the Westfield lot bought of Mr. John Hollister, together with house and barn, orchard, and all thereto belonging; and the land I had by exchange of Isaac Boreman and Jacob Griswold, Jr., and two acres of my upper lot in the meadow, and four acres in Fairfield Swamp which I bought of John Deming, Jr., and a third of my three fifty-acre lotts, and a third of my division lot. I give to my son Robert Welles the house and lands I bought of Ensign John Wyatt, as also 6 acres of my lower plowing lot in the meadow, and four acres in the upper meadow, and the rest of Fairfield Swamp not given to Thomas and reserved for Gideon as above, and the lot lying in the west swamp, bought of old Mr. Stephen Chester, and one 50-acre lot lying by Jabez Whittlesey, and the third part of the division lot, and half the island bought of Nathaniel Foot. And also I give to my son Robert Welles my negro Phebe, and he to take good care of her. I give to my son Gideon Welles the house, barn and lot I live upon, 3 acres, and 4 acres of my upper meadow lot, and 3 acres of the north side of Fairfield Swamp, and 4 acres in Beaver Meadow, and the lot lying upon the west swamp hill, bought of Joseph Churchill, Thomas Wright, John Nott and Isaac Curtis. Also, I give him a piece of land bought of George Wolcott and John Durrant, with a highway leading through Henry Buck's lot; also the third of the three fifty-acre lotts. I give to my grandson Robert Welles the house and land bought of Serjeant Jonathan Hollister, being formerly Capt. Stephen Hollister's deceased, and 10 acres bought of my Cousin Stephen Chester adjoyning thereto; also, I give to my said grandson my silver punch bowl. I give to my son Gideon Wells, to him and his heirs forever, of my moveable estate, one yoke of oxen, two cows 3 years old, two horses, a mare and colt, ten sheep, and all my swine, all my tackling as carts, plows, chains, plow irons, harrows, saddles, bridle, all mowing and reaping instruments, hods, hammers, nails, gun, sword, shingles and clapboards, and also a half of all my grain growing or gathered in; also, one bedstead with a bed (and a great table) and furniture to said bed, two chairs and two books, and to take his choice; also, one silver tankard, a large looking-glass and an iron back. I appoint my sons, Thomas, Joseph, Robert and Gideon, executors. My will is that my wife live with some of my children, and they to take care of her.

Witness: *Thomas Chester,*   ROBERT WELLES, LS.
David Goodrich, John Coleman.

Court Record, Page 206—5 July, 1714: Joseph, Thomas and Robert Welles exhibited now in this Court the last will and testament of Capt. Robert Welles, decd., whereof they are appointed executors; and John Coleman of Wethersfield, one of the witnesses subscribed to the said will, having now sworn thereunto before this Court (one other of the witnesses of the sd. will being departed from this life), the sd. will is thereupon proven by this Court, approved and allowed.

Page 173.

Welles, Thomas, Haddam. Invt. £130-00-01. Taken 19 January, 1711-12, by Thomas Gates, Daniel Brainard and William Spencer.

Court Record, Page 74—5 May, 1712: Adms. granted to Elizabeth Welles, the widow.

Page 171—5 January, 1713-14: Elizabeth Welles, Adms., exhibits now an account of her Adms. Accepted. Order to dist. the estate:

	£	s	d
To Elizabeth Welles, the widow, of moveable estate,	00	08	06
To Elizabeth, Mary and Martha Welles, daughters, to each,	28	15	07½

And appoint Capt. Thomas Gates, Daniel Brainard and Thomas Robinson, of Haddam, distributors.

Page 184—5 April, 1714: This Court appoint Mrs. Elizabeth Welles to be guardian to her 3 daughters above named.

Page 97.

Welles, Capt. Thomas, Wethersfield. Invt. £785-03-02. Taken 23 January, 1711-12, by William Goodrich, Ebenezer Deming and Samuel Treat.

Court Record, Page 50—4 February, 1711-12: Adms. granted to Jerusha Welles, the widow.

Page 70—8 April, 1712: This Court appoint Samuel Treat of Wethersfield to be guardian to Thomas Welles, a minor son of Capt. Thomas Welles, late of Wethersfield, decd. And sd. Samuel Treat gave bond.

Page 176—8 February, 1713-14: Samuel Treat, guardian to Thomas Welles, a minor son of Capt. Thomas Welles, was discharged, and Thomas the minor chose his uncle Thomas Sheldon of Northampton to be his guardian. Recog., £100.

Page 189—13 April, 1714: Whereas, the persons who were appointed by this Court on the 5th of this recent April to set out to Thomas Welles, a minor son, the sd. minor's part of his sd. father's estate, now meet with difficulty so that they cannot well proceed: 1st. For that they find that there is a piece of land valued in the inventory at £90, formerly devised by Mr. James Treat to another of the sons of the sd. Thomas Welles in and by his last Will. 2ndly. Because there is not rendered to this Court any account of the debts due from or paid out to that estate.

Page 189—14 April, 1714: Thomas Sheldon now appears with complaint that the distributors appointed to set out the estate to the sd. minor, vizt., George Stilman, George Kilbourn and Josiah Churchill, do refuse to go forward with setting out the estate to the sd. minor according to sd. order given them 13 April. This Court now appoint Mr. Thomas Wickham, John Howard, Josiah Churchill and Lt. Jonathan Belding, or any two of them, to dist. the estate.

Page 191—19 April, 1714: This Court accepts of the dist. presented by Deacon Thomas Sheldon of Northampton, guardian to Thomas Welles, eldest son of Thomas Welles.

Page 148 (Vol. X) 7 March, 1726-7: This Court do appoint Capt. Thomas Welles, James Treat and Ebenezer Deming, of Wethersfield, to dist. and divide the real estate of Capt. Thomas Welles, late of Wethersfield, decd., unto the relict of the sd. decd., giving her 1-3 part thereof, the residue to be dist. to William Welles, Wait Welles, John Welles and Ichabod Welles, the four sons of the decd.

Page 54 (Vol. XI) 5 October, 1731: Report of the dist. Likewise, the sd. Adms., Jerusha Goodrich, formerly Jerusha Welles, the relict, exhibited an account of her Adms., which was allowed. And this Court grant to Ephraim Goodrich, her now husband, a *Quietus Est.*

Page 233.

Welton, Stephen, Waterbury. Invt. £92-15-00. Taken 27 April, 1713, by George Scott, John Richards and Daniel Porter, Jr. The children of the deceased are Abigail and Mary Welton.

Court Record, Page 143—1st June, 1713: Adms. granted to Thomas Welton, brother of sd. decd.

Page 13 (Vol. IX) 1st May, 1716: Abigail Welton, a minor daughter of Stephen Welton, late of Waterbury, decd., chose John Richards to be her guardian.

Page 79—2 September, 1718: Adms. granted to Richard Welton.

Page 130—5 July, 1720: Thomas Welton is directed to sell lands to pay the debts. This Court order the estate distributed as followeth, Adms. account being accepted: To Joanna Welton, the widow, 1-3 part of the houseing and lands during life; to Abigail, Mary and Eunice Welton, daughters of the sd. decd., to each of them, £8-14-00, which is their equal portions of sd. estate. And appoint John Hopkins, Thomas Clarke and William Hickcocks, distributors.

Page 25 (Vol. X) 6 August, 1723: This Court do appoint George Welton of Waterbury to be guardian unto Eunice Welton, a minor, 7 years of age, daughter of Stephen Welton, late decd. Recog., £50.

Page 31—1st October, 1723: Whereas, this Court, 5th July, 1720, ordered a dist. of the estate of Stephen Welton, late of Waterbury, decd., it now appears due from sd. estate £25-05-10 more than the moveable part of the estate amounts to, and in pursuance of an act of the General Assembly, the former Adms. Thomas Welton and the present Adms. Richard Welton have sold so much of the lands of the sd. decd. as to answer the above sum, this Court now order that the real estate remaining shall be dist. to the widow and children: To Joanna Welton, widow, 1-3 part of the houseing and lands during life; to Abigail, Mary, and Eunice Welton, daughters of the sd. decd., to each of them equal parts. And appoint John Hopkins, William Clark and William Hickcox, of Waterbury, distributors.

Page 282.

Westover, Hannah, Symsbury, Widow. Invt. £17-12-03. Taken 6 May, 1714, by Richard Case and Jonathan Westover. Will dated 1st August, 1713.

In the name of God, amen. I, Hannah Westover of Symsbury, in the County of Hartford and Colony of Connecticut, relict to Jonah Westover of Town, County and Colony aforesd. decd., being weak and sick in body, yet of sound mind and judgement and of perfect memory, do dispose of what I have: First of all and principally, I give and bequeath my soul to God that gave it, and my body to Christian burial. And touching my worldly goods, I give in manner following: First, I give and bequeath to my six daughters 40 shillings to each daughter, and the remainder, if any be, to be equally divided to my daughter Hannah Alverd and my daughters Mary Case, Jane Byington and Johannah. 2. To Jonah, my stack of rye. 3. I give also to my daughter Johannah my biggest pig, and the smaller pig I give to my son Jonathan. August the first, 1713. This being my will and testament, I set to my hand this first day of August, 1713.

Witness: *John Slater,*   HANNAH X WESTOVER.
    Samuel Addams.

Court Record, Page 198—7 June, 1714: Will proven. There being no executor appointed, this Court grant letters of Adms., with the will annexed, unto Samuel Case and Jonathan Westover.

Invt. in Vol. IX, Page 29.

Westover, Jonah, Symsbury. Invt. £253-19-01. Taken 28 June, 1714, by John Case, Samuel Case and Jonathan Westover.

Court Record, Page 210—2 August, 1714: This Court grant letters of Adms. unto Abigail Westover of Simsbury, the widow of sd. decd.

Page 68 (Vol. X) 2 February, 1724-5: Mrs. Abigail Westover, Adms., exhibits an account of her Adms., which this Court accepts. Order to dist. the estate:

	£	s	d
To Abigail Westover, widow,	10-11-00		
To Nathaniel Westover, eldest son,	87-16-10		
To Jonah, John and Abigail Westover, to each,	43-18-05		

And appoint Thomas Holcomb, Joseph Case and Nathaniel Holcomb, distributors. This Court appoint Abigail Westover of Simsbury to be guardian unto her sons: Jonah, about 16 years of age (he desiring the same), and John, about 13 years. Recog., £150.

Page 119.

Wetmore, Thomas, Middletown. Invt. £135-17-03. Taken 29 February, 1711-12, by John Collins, Israhiah Wetmore and John Bacon. Also his part of his father Thomas Wetmore's estate, £87-03-07.

Court Record, Page 58—3 March, 1711-12: Adms. granted to Ephraim Adkins, brother-in-law by his wive's right.

Page 117—2 March, 1712-13: Ephraim Adkins, Adms., exhibits an account of his Adms. Accepted.

Page 218.

Whaples, Ephraim, Wethersfield. Invt. £235-17-01. Taken 31 March, 1713, by Thomas Richards and William Webster. Will dated 26 January, 1712-13.

I, Ephraim Whaples of Wethersfield, in consideration of the great love that I bear to my wife, Mindwell Whaples, do give all my estate to her until my boy comes of age, and 1-3 part of my estate so long as she remains a widow. I give to my son Ephraim Whaples all my real estate when he comes of age, he to pay to my 3 daughters £10 apiece.
Witness: *Eliphalet Whittlesey,*   EPHRAIM WHAPLES.
Joseph Hurlbut.

The sd. Ephraim Whaples doth put in Jabez Whittlesey overseer of the above written instrument, with my wife Mindwell Whaples.
Court Record, Page 124—6 April, 1713: Adms., with the will annexed, granted to Mindwell Whaples, widow. Will proven.
Page 243—7 March, 1714-15: Mindwell Whaples, Adms., exhibits now an account of her Adms. Accepted. And this Court order that the estate shall be dist. according to the will of the sd. decd. And appoint Jabez Whittlesey, John Deming and Richard Boreman, distributors.
Page 245—7 March, 1714-15: This Court appoint Mindwell Whaples to be guardian to Hannah Whaples, 11 years, and Mindwell Whaples, 8 years of age, children of Ephraim Whaples, decd.
Page 32 (Vol. IX) 7 May, 1717: A report of the dist. of a smaller amount than shown before the decree, but accepted by the Court.

Page 220.

Whaples, Thomas, Sen., Hartford. Invt. £203-01-01. Taken 3 April, 1713, by Samuel Benton, Sen., William Webster and John Camp. Will dated 10 February, 1712-13.
I, Thomas Whaples, Sen., of Hartford, do make this my last will and testament: I give to my son Nathan Whaples that piece of land lying in a place called the North Nook, given me by the Town and partly bought of my brother Ephraim Whaples, with the frame erected upon the sd. land, and also all the bricks, boards, nails provided for it, he paying such a legacy as I shall appoint him. I give to my son Joseph my house and homelot and a mare which I had of Samuel Howard. I give to my daughters all my moveable estate not given away to my sons, to be equally divided among them all. I order my son Nathan to pay to his sisters as followeth: To his sister Abigail, £14 cash; to his sister Rebeckah, £4 cash; to his sister Mary, £10 cash; and to his sister Elizabeth, £4 cash. And if Elizabeth do not learn the trade of a tailor, then she shall with Mary in the legacy above named be equal. My will is that my son Joseph shall pay to his sisters 20 shillings to each. I desire John White, Joseph Skinner and Joshua Carter to be executors.
Witness: *John White,*   THOMAS WHAPLES, SEN., LS.
Joseph Skinner, Joshua Carter.

Court Record, Page 130—6 April, 1713: Will proven.

Page 191.

Wheeler, Samuel, Hartford. Died 29 June, 1712. Invt. £102-00-06. Taken by Cyprian Nickolls, John Bunce and Jonathan Bunce. The children: Samuel, of full age; John 19 years, Isaac 17 years, Moses 9 years, Rachel 14 years, Mary 11 years, and Elizabeth Wheeler 7 years of age.

Court Record, Page 84—7 July, 1712: Adms. granted to Samuel Wheeler, son of sd. decd. This Court appoint Cyprian Nickolls to be guardian unto Rachel Wheeler, 14 years of age, and Elizabeth Wheeler, 7 years of age; and Thomas Hosmer is appointed guardian to Isaac Wheeler, age 17 years, and Moses Wheeler, 9 years; children of Samuel Wheeler, late decd.

Page 87—4 August, 1712: This Court appoint Thomas Buck of Middletown to be guardian to Elizabeth Wheeler, 7 years of age.

Page 96—6 November, 1712: Rachel Wheeler now appeared before the Court and made choice of Samuel Kellogg to be her guardian, she being 14 years of age.

Page 88 (Vol. IX) 4 November, 1718: Samuel Wheeler, Adms., exhibits an account of his Adms. Allowed. Order to dist. the Estate:

	£ s d
To Samuel Wheeler, eldest son,	22-04-02
To John, Isaac, Rachel, Mary and Elizabeth Wheeler, the rest of the children, to each of them,	11-02-01

And appoint Thomas Hosmer, Joseph Cooke and Richard Seymour, distributors.

White, Daniel. Court Record, Page 32—2 April, 1711: Daniel White of Windsor to be guardian to his 3 sons, Joel, Elisha and Simeon White, all under 14 years of age.

Page 74-110.

White, Capt. Nathaniel, Middletown. Invt. £927-11-05. Taken by Thomas Stow and John Warner. Lands inventoried in Hartford apprised by Joseph Wadsworth and Cyprian Nickolls. Will dated 16 August, 1711.

I, Nathaniel White of Middletown, in the County of Hartford, do make this my last will and testament: I give to my wife Martha the use of the household goods, and for her comfortable maintenance during widowhood £6 a year also, her firewood to be provided by my sons Daniel and Joseph. I also give her £10 in money to dispose of as she pleases. I give to my son Nathaniel all my houseing and lands in Hadley, he paying £10 to the legatees of his grandfather. I give to my son John, besides his deed of gift, all the right that I have in reversion unto the estate that was my brother Jacob's in Hartford, he paying £20 unto my daughters Elizabeth and Mary and representatives of my daughter Sarah, to be paid after the decease of the widow of my sd. brother. All this I give to my son John and his heirs forever. I give to my son Daniel the house, barn and other buildings he now lives in and is possessed of in Middletown, with 6 acres of upland adjoyning; also, one-third of my meadow and swamp at Wongunk, and also one-third part of my neck and wet meadow; all this besides what I have formerly given him by deed. I give to my son Jacob the house and lot I bought of Joseph Kirby; also, 2 acres of land next to his brother Daniel; also, 3 acres of meadow and swamp, and also one-third of my meadow and swamp at Wongunk. I give to my son Joseph my dwelling house, barn and home lot, and the garden plot, and the remaining part of my meadow and swamp at Wongunk, and one-third part of my neck and wet meadow. I give to my daughter Elizabeth the lot of upland that her son Nathaniel lives on, and 100 acres of my Plain lot northward of the Town. I give to my daughter Mary 100 acres of my Plain lot. I give to my daughter Sarah's children 200 acres out of my lot on the east side of the Great River; also 1-3 part of my moveables that was in being when my former wife died. My lot westward of the town, adjoining to Farmington, to be equally divided between my sons Daniel, Jacob and Joseph, they paying to my three daughters, Elizabeth, Mary and Sarah, or their representatives £12 in money apiece, and £4 money to the Rev. Mr. Noadiah Russell. A one-fourth part of my right in undivided lands to be and remain for the use of a public school already agreed upon. I intend what my now wife hath gained by her industry, and what she brought with her to me, should be at her own dispose. My two sons, Daniel and Joseph, to be executors.

Witness: *John Hamlin,*   NATH. WHITE, LS.
Thomas Stow, Daniel Stocking.

Court Record, Page 38—1st October, 1711: Will proven.

Invt. in Vol. IX, Page 44.

Whiting, John, Hartford. Invt. £201-15-10. Taken 27 May, 1715, by Benjamin Graham and Thomas Seamore.

Court Record, Page 254—28 May, 1715: Adms. granted to Joseph Whiting of New Haven.

Page 154 (Vol. IX) 6 June, 1721: Capt. Joseph Whiting of New Haven, Adms., exhibits now an account of his Adms., he having paid in debts and charges the sum of £333-18-08. This Court do accept of the account and grant him a *Quietus Est.*

Page 219.

Willcocks, Ephraim, Middletown. Invt. £212-11-00. Taken 23 January, 1712-13, by Samuel Willcocks, Sen., Samuel Hall and George Phillips.

Court Record, Page 124—6 April, 1713: Adms. to Silence Willcocks, widow of the deceased.

Page 197.

Willcoxson, Samuel, Simsbury. An agreement between the heirs of Samuel Wilcoxson. To all Christian people to whom these presents shall come, greeting: Know ye that we each of us, Samuel Willcoxson, William Willcoxson, Joseph Willcoxson and Margaret Willcoxson, children of our honoured father, Samuel Willcoxson of the Town of Simsbury, late deceased intestate, do by these presents mutually agree to appoint, constitute and ordain Thomas Holcomb, Samuel Case, John Pettebone, Samuel Pettebone and Joseph Case to make distribution of our honoured father's estate and appoint to each of us our respective portions of sd. estate in lands and where it shall be, all to be judged and finally issued according to the rules of equity and conscience, to which judgement, issue and determination we bind ourselves, our heirs, executors and administrators in a bond of £100 to agree and abide by, stand by, and sit down satisfied with the judgement of the above-said distributors. To the true performance of the above-written premises we set to our names and affix our seals this 31 day of March, 1712-13.

Witness:	SAMUEL WILLCOXSON, LS.
Joseph Pettebone,	WILLIAM WILLCOXSON, LS.
Samuel Tullar,	JOSEPH WILLCOXSON, LS.
Joseph Strickland.	MARGARET X WILLCOXSON, LS.

Court Record, Page 124—6 April, 1713: Adms. to Samuel, William and Joseph Willcoxson. Also exhibit an agreement, which this Court confirm.

Page 174 (Vol. X, Probate Side): On the 18th day of December, 1722, we, the subscribers hereunto, being desired by Joseph Case of Simsbury to go and view a certain house which was formerly the estate belonging to Sergt. Samuel Wilcoxson decd., since dist. to Margaret Wilcoxson, daughter of the sd. decd., and we having taken a view of sd. house, that is to say, part of the house, being the easterly end of sd. house, one room, we do value the same at £2-00-00 as money.

JAMES CORNISH,
JOHN HUMPHRIES.

Page 251.

Willcoxson, Samuel, Jr. Invt. £327-01-07. Taken 30 October, 1713, by Samuel Humphrey, Joseph Case and John Slater.

Court Record, Page 160—2 November, 1713: Adms. granted to Mindwell Willcoxson, widow.

Page 101 (Vol. IX) 7 April, 1719: Mrs. Mindwell Willcoxson, widow, is appointed by this Court to be guardian to Joseph Willcoxson,

18 years, Mindwell, 15 years, and Ephram, 12 years of age, they desiring the same.

Page 102—7 April, 1719: Mindwell Willcoxson, Adms., exhibits now an account of her Adms. Accepted. Order to dist. the estate:

	£ s d
To Mindwell Willcoxson, widow,	11-12-01
To Samuel Willcoxson, eldest son,	92-09-08
To John, Joseph, Ephraim and Mindwell Willcoxson, to each,	46-04-10

And appoint Joseph Case, Jonathan Holcomb and John Humphries, distributors.

Page 187.

Williams, Abraham, Wethersfield. Invt. £130-14-06. Taken 17 January, 1711-12, by Jonathan Boreman and Joseph Cole.

Court Record, Page 82—7 July, 1712: Adms. granted to Eunice Williams, widow, and Jacob Williams, brother of sd. decd.

Page 129—6 April, 1713: Eunice Williams, Adms., exhibits an account of some debts due from the estate, whereby it appears the moveable estate is not sufficient to pay the debts.

Page 143—1st June, 1713: Pursuant to an act of the General Assembly, this Court do order Eunice Williams, Adms., to sell so much of the land to the highest bidder as may produce the sum of £31-13-00, taking the advice of Thomas Kimberly of Glastonbury in the sale.

Page 44 (Vol. X) 27 March, 1724: Eunice Williams, Adms., exhibits an account of her Adms. Accepted. Order to dist. the estate: To Eunice Williams, the widow, 1-3 part of the houseing and lands, and to the five daughters, Eunice, Rebeckah, Abigail, Abiah and Silence Williams, the residue of the real estate. And appoint Ephraim Goodrich, Edward Bulkeley and Benjamin Wright, distributors.

Page 45—27 March, 1724: This Court appoint Jacob Williams of Wethersfield to be guardian to Silence Williams, age 12 years, and Abigail Williams, 16 years of age, children of Abraham Williams decd. Also, this Court appoint Samuel Frarey of Middletown to be guardian to Abiah Williams, age 14 years. Recog., £50.

Page 47—7 April, 1724: Report of the distributors.

Page 149.

Williams, Jacob, Wethersfield. Invt. £396-03-04. Taken 28 October, 1712, by Jonathan Smith and Joseph Grimes.

Court Record, Page 93—3 November, 1712: Adms. to Jacob Williams, son of the deceased, and Capt. James Steele.

Page 170—4 January, 1713-14: The Adms. exhibit now an account of their Adms. Accepted. Order to dist. the estate:

£ s d
To Jacob Williams, eldest son,   83-04-00
To Ephraim, Stephen, Daniel, David, Anne, Sarah and Mary
  Williams, to each of them,   41-12-00

And appoint Joseph Grimes, Samuel Williams and John Wright, distributors.

Page 178—2 March, 1713-14: Sarah Williams, a daughter, 17 years of age, chose Jonathan Deming to be her guardian. Daniel Williams, 18 years of age, chose his brother Ephraim Williams to be his guardian. And David Williams, age 14 years, and Mary, 12 years, chose their brother Jacob guardian. Also, report of the dist. accepted by the Court, and the Adms. are granted a *Quietus Est.*

Page 137.

Williams, John, Windsor. Invt. £222-08-02. Taken 14 May, 1712, by Benajah Holcomb, Thomas Griswold and Nathaniel Horsford. Will dated 10 February, 1707-8.

I, John Williams of Windsor, being aged, do make this my last will and testament: I give to Esther Williams, my dearly beloved wife, the use and improvement of that lot which I lately bought of Jacob Gibbs, Jr., being in quantity about 4 acres, bounded north on the lands of me, sd. John Williams, east on the highway, south on the land of Samuel Beamon, Nathll. Horsford and Samuel Dibble, and west on the land of John Phelps, Sen., during her widowhood, that is, so long as she shall remain my widow, and also 20s a year in country pay. Item. I give to my 4 daughters, vist., Rebecca Warriner, Anna Bancroft, Mary Gunn and Abiall Phelps, to each of them a cow. It. I give to my grandson Edward Griswold and to my granddaughter Abigall Barnard 20s to each of them. It. I give to my grandson John Williams my dwelling house and barn, together with all and singular my lands, messuages and tenements which to me appertain or in any wise belong, within the Township of Windsor, by him freely to be possessed and enjoyed when he shall attain to the age of 21 years. Item. I give to the rest of my son Nathaniel Williams's children all my household goods, to be equally divided among them. Lastly, I give to my son Nathaniel Williams, whom I likewise constitute, make and ordain my sole executor, the use, benefit and improvement of all that I have given to my grandson John Williams, always reserving what I have given to my wife during her widowhood, until he shall attain to the full age of 21 years. I give to my sd. son Nathaniel Williams all the residue of my estate undisposed.
Witness: *Nathaniel Gillett, Sen.,*   JOHN X WILLIAMS, LS.
Timothy Horsford, Matthew Allyn.

Court Record, Page 78—2 June, 1712: Nathaniel Williams of Westfield, Province of Massachusetts Bay, executor, now exhibited the will of his late grandfather John Williams of Windsor, and moved this Court that it be proven and allowed. Mr. Richard Edwards of Hartford, in behalf of sundry persons in interest, objected for the reason there was no executor appointed, and sd. John Williams, a person 96 years of age, had become childish and infirm in his intellectuals. The Court did approve and allow the will, whereupon Nathaniel Bancroft and John Gunn of Westfield appealed to the Superior Court.

Page 90—6 October, 1712: Adms., with the will annexed, to Edward Griswold of Windsor and Nathaniel Williams of Westfield, grandchildren of the deceased.

Page 96—6 November, 1712: Notification to the claimants of estate of John Williams to appear and show cause why Esther Williams, widow, should not now have her part of sd. estate set out to her.

Page 106—6 January, 1712-13: John Bissell, atty. for Esther Williams, moves that she the sd. Esther be put into the use of 1-3 part of the estate of her late husband John Williams. This Court decree that she may be instated into 1-3 part of the houseing and lands of the decd., provided she disclaims all her right to any legacy given her in the will of sd. John Williams decd. And appoint Capt. Timothy Thrall, John Palmer and Nathaniel Horsford to set out the widow's thirds. Nathaniel Williams and Jedediah Dewey of Westfield appealed and gave bond, with Williams Worthington of Hartford.

Page 122—3 March, 1712-13: Richard Edwards, atty. for Nathaniel Bancroft and Samuel Phelps of Westfield, moved this Court that Adms. on such estate of John Williams as is not devised by will might be committed to the sd. Nathaniel Bancroft and Samuel Phelps or such persons as have right therein by law. Deferred.

Page 146—1st June, 1713: Capt. Timothy Thrall and John Palmer of Windsor, having set out dower to Esther Williams, widow, from the estate of her late husband John Williams, the same is now allowed.

Page 205—5 July, 1714: Richard Edwards repeats his motion requesting that Adms. might be committed to Nathaniel Bancroft and Samuel Phelps. Deferred.

Page 48 (Vol. IX) 7 January, 1717-18: Whereas, this Court did on the 6th of October, 1712, grant letters of Adms. unto Edward Griswold, with the will annexed, and Nathaniel Williams of Westfield, grand children of the decd., and order that they should render an account of Adms. on sd. estate to this Court on or before the 1st Monday of October, 1713; and whereas, no account has yet been rendered to this Court, and the sd. Edward Griswold being dead, and the sd. Nathaniel Williams neglecting to give to this Court an account of his Adms. on sd. estate, this Court now grant letters on sd. estate, with will annexed, unto Joseph Barnard of Windsor, to finish the account of Adms. and render the same to this Court on or before the 1st Tuesday of January, Anno Dom. 1718-19.

Page 214.

Williams, John, Sen., Hartford. Invt. £326-06-06. Taken 16 February, 1712-13, by Nathaniel Pitkin and Timothy Cowles.

Court Record, Page 113—2 March, 1712-13: Adms. granted to John Williams, son of the decd.

Page 212—2 August, 1714: Jacob Williams, a minor, 15 years of age, chose his brother John Williams to be his guardian, who was also appointed guardian to Joseph Williams, age 13 years. This Court also appoint John Morton of Hartford guardian to Elizabeth Williams, 9 years of age. All children of John Williams, late of Hartford, decd.

Page 218—4 October, 1714: John Williams, Adms., exhibits an account of his Adms. Accepted. This Court order the estate distributed as follows:

	£	s	d
To John, eldest son,	95	13	04
To Jacob, Joseph, Jane and Elizabeth Williams, to each,	47	06	08

And appoint Joseph Olmsted, Nathaniel Pitkin and John Meekins, distributors.

Court Record, Page 23—7 March, 1737-8: Jabez Burnham of Hartford begs leave to lay before this Court, that in a former distribution of the estate of John Williams, late of Hartford deceased, there was one certain piece of his land (beginning at ye east end of John's eight acres and to run east to the end of sd. lot), which lot of land was divided into five parts: To John Williams one-fifth part, and to Jacob Williams, Joseph Williams, Jane Morton and Elizabeth Yeomans, children of the deceased, each a fifth part, and yet not subdivided to each one his particular part, and one of the heirs to sd. land (Abraham Williams, son of John Williams decd.) having a right to one-fifth part of sd. land, and being in his minority so not capable of acting with the rest of the heirs in making a subdivision, etc., and your memorialist having bought the fifth part thereof of John Morton's right which his wife Jane had in sd. lands, doth move to this Court that as the case is circumstanced as above expressed, I and the rest, etc., are hindered in our improvement for want of power to divide sd. land, pray that this Court would, as the law directs in such case, appoint freeholders, together with the guardian of sd. minor, to divide and make severance of sd. rights to the heirs, that we may improve.

This Court doth appoint Messers. William Cowles and Caleb Pitkin, with Jacob Williams, guardian to sd. minor Abraham Williams, and do order the rest of the surviving heirs forthwith to make partition of sd. land according to the intent of the former distribution as above expressed.

Inventory on File.

Recorded Page 30, Vol. IX.

Williams. Jonas, Hartford. Invt. £226-18-04. Taken 31 May, 1714, by William Williams and Samuel Burnham.

Court Record, Page 199—7 June, 1714: Adms. granted to Mary Williams, widow, and Jonas Williams, eldest son.

Page 241—7 March, 1714-15: Mary Williams and Jonah Williams, Adms., exhibit an account of their Adms. Accepted. Order to dist. the estate as follows:

	£ s d
To Mary Williams, widow,	16-19-10
To Jonah Williams, eldest son,	69-01-08
To Timothy, Eunice, Anne and Lydia Williams, to each,	34-10-10

And appoint Mr. Thomas Richards, William Williams and Samuel Burnham, distributors.

Page 247—4 April, 1715: Report of the dist. Anne Williams, a minor, 16 years of age, daughter of Jonah Williams, chose her mother, Mary Williams, to be her guardian. Recog., £60. This Court appoint Mary Williams to be guardian to Timothy Williams, age 14 years, and Lydia Williams, age 9 years, children of Jonah Williams, late decd. Recog., £60.

Williams, John. Court Record, Page 149—6 July, 1713: John Williams, a minor son of Nathaniel Williams, late of Windsor decd., chose Nathaniel Hosford of Windsor to be his guardian. Recog., £50.

Page 180.

Wilson, John, Hartford. Invt. £312-04-02. Taken 30 April, 1712, by Richard Edwards, Samuel Thornton and Jonathan Webster.

Court Record, Page 74—5 May, 1712: Adms. to Thomas Day and Richard Seamore of Hartford.

Page 133—7 April, 1713: Thomas Day and Richard Seamore exhibit account. Allowed, and are ordered to deliver the entire estate to John Haynes of Hartford, who is guardian to John Wilson, only child of the deceased.

Invt. and Agreement in Vol. IX, Page 34-36.

Wolcott, Abigail, Wethersfield. Died 9 November, 1714. Invt. £157-03-06. Taken 1714, by William Burnham and Samuel Wolcott.

Whereas, Abigail Wolcott of Wethersfield, daughter of Mr. Samuel Wolcott of Wethersfield, who died on the 9th day of November, 1714, intestate saving that by word of mouth she signified something of her mind concerning the disposal of her estate in the time of her sickness, we the subscribers, vizt., Judith Wolcott of sd. Wethersfield, mother of sd. Abigail Wolcott, Samuel Wolcott of Wethersfield and Abigail his wife, William Burnham of Farmington and Hannah his wife, Robert Welles and Sarah his wife, Samuel Robbins and Lucy his wife, Elizabeth Wolcott and Mary Wolcott, all of Wethersfield, the brethren and sisters of sd. Abigail Wolcott, being all the parties interested in the estate of sd. Abigail Wolcott, and all of lawful age to act for themselves, being desirous that what the sd. Abigail Wolcott declared to be her mind in the time of her late sickness concerning the disposal of sd. estate should in all parts be performed, we do hereby agree that Judith Wolcott, mother, shall have one acre and 1-2 of land in Wethersfield, and all the remainder of the estate, real and personal, to be equally divided among the brothers and sisters.

Witness: *Ebenezer Hale,*
         John Smith.

JUDITH WOLCOTT, LS.
WILLIAM BURNHAM, LS.
SAMUEL WOLCOTT, LS.
ROBERT WELLES, LS.
SAMUEL ROBBINS, LS.
HANNAH BURNHAM, LS.
ABIGAIL WOLCOTT, LS.
SARAH WELLES, LS.
LUCY ROBBINS, LS.
ELIZABETH WOLCOTT, LS.
MARY WOLCOTT, LS.

Court Record, Page 242—7 March, 1714-15: Adms. granted to Samuel Wolcott, brother of the decd.

Page 243—7 March, 1714-15: Agreement exhibited but not then allowed on account of illness of two of the parties, who could not attend.

Page 252—2 May, 1715: Agreement approved.

Page 59.

Wolcott, Henry, Windsor. Invt. £993-15-08. Taken 8 February, 1709-10, by John Moore, Sen., Return Strong and Eleazer Gaylord.

Court Record, Page 9—3 April, 1710: Adms. joyntly to Abiah Wolcott, widow, and Matthew Allyn, son-in-law of sd. decd.

Page 106—6 January, 1712-13: Abiah Wolcott and Matthew Allyn, Adms., exhibit now an account of their Adms. Allowed. Order to dist. the estate as followeth: To Mrs. Abiah Wolcott, widow, 1-3 part of the houseing and lands. The rest of the sd. houseing and lands shall be divided: 1-2 thereof, £325-00-00, to Elizabeth Allyn, wife of sd. Matthew Allyn and daughter of sd. decd., and the other half, £325, to the heirs of Sarah, late wife of the Rev. Charles Chauncey, of the village of Stratfield, in the County of Fairfield, daughter to sd. Henry Wolcott. And appoint John Moore, Sen., Lt. Return Strong and Mr. Eleazer Gaylord, distributors.

Page 242—7 March, 1714-15: This Court doth now appoint Capt. Thomas Moore, Lt. Return Strong and Mr. Daniel Loomis, of Windsor, to distribute and divide the houseing and lands of Henry Wolcott, late of Windsor decd., per order of Court, 6 January, 1712-13, excepting 3 1-2 acres of land contained in the inventory of that estate, that lies at the lower end of the Great Meadow, the same 3 1-2 acres of land being by the deceased set out in his lifetime to Col. Matthew Allyn as part of his wive's portion.

NOTE: The persons formerly appointed to do that work have neglected the same, and now one of them is deceased and another is guardian to a child that has an interest in that estate.

Page 248—4 April, 1714-15: Mr. Justice Moore of Windsor to administer the oath to the persons appt. to dist. estate of Henry Wolcott, late of Windsor, decd.

Page 261—2 August, 1715: Report of dist.

Page 38 (Vol. IX) 11 July, 1717: Col. Matthew Allvn, Adms., exhibits now an account of his Adms. Accepted. Order to dist. the moveable part of the estate as followeth: 1-3 part to be set out as estate belonging to Mrs. Abiah Wolcott decd., lately the widow of Henry Wolcott, to her legal representatives. And 1-3 part thereof to Col. Matthew Allyn in right of his wife. And 1-3 and last part thereof unto Robert Chauncey, Ichabod Wolcott Chauncey and Abiah Chauncey, children of the sd. Mrs. Sarah Chauncey, or their legal representatives. And appoint Capt. Thomas Moore, Samuel Strong and Daniel Loomis, distributors.

Page 139—28 November, 1720: A former order to dist. was modified, and instead of £101-15-01 being paid to Col. Matthew Allyn, he is to be paid but £45-03-07. The rest is to be sub-divided and dist. to the heirs of Sarah Chauncey decd.: to Robert Chauncey, to Ichabod Wolcott Chauncey, and to Abiah Chauncey.

Inventory on File.

Wolcott, John, Sen., Windsor. Invt. £910-03-05. Taken by Return Strong, Nathaniel Loomis and Daniel Loomis.

Court Record, Page 52—5 February, 1711-12: Adms. granted to Mrs. Hannah Wolcott, widow relict, and John Eliot, Esq., and John Wolcott, son of sd. decd.

Page 85—4 August, 1712: Mrs. Hannah Wolcott, widow, John Eliot, Esq., and John Wolcott, Adms., exhibit an account of their Adms. Allowed. Order to dist. the estate as followeth:

	£ s d
To Hannah Wolcott, widow,	150-16-08
To John Wolcott, eldest son,	445-01-04
To Charles Wolcott,	222-10-08
To Benjamin Wolcott,	222-10-08
To John Eliot, Esq., in right of his wife Mary,	222-10-08

And appoint Capt. Aaron Cooke, Deacon John Sheldon of Hartford and Lt. Daniel Heydon of Windsor, distributors.

Page 119—2 March, 1712-13: Mrs. Hannah Wolcott, widow, and John Wolcott, two of the Adms., exhibit now in this Court a writing said to be a will of sd. John Wolcott, and moved the Court to approve the same, which for sundry reasons was deferred.

Page 130—6 April, 1713: John and Charles Wolcott appear in Court to plead for the acceptance of an alleged will of their late father John Wolcott decd. Not allowed. An appeal to the Superior Court was then taken by John Wolcott, Charles Wolcott and Widow Hannah Wolcott. They gave bond of £10.

Page 103 (Vol. IX) 30 April, 1719: Whereas, this Court, holden 20 October, 1712, did appoint Col. William Whiting one of the distributors, and information being now made that the estate is not yet distributed, and that the rest of the distributors appointed cannot have the assistance of Col. Whiting, he being absent, in distributing sd. estate, it is moved that some other person may be appointed in his stead. This Court appoint Sergt. James Enno of Windsor to supply his place and join with Capt. Aaron Cooke and Deacon John Sheldon, formerly appointed.

Page 131 (Vol. X) 3 June, 1726: Hannah Porter, formerly widow of sd. decd., moves this Court that the estate may be distributed. The Court had appointed Aaron Cooke, John Sheldon and Sergt. James Enno to distribute it, and they are now directed to perfect the same and make return thereof.

Page 132—5 July, 1726: Capt. Aaron Cooke being now deceased, Col. Matthew Allyn is appointed distributor in his place.

Page 206.

Wolcott, Josiah, Wethersfield. Died 28 October, 1712. Invt. £620-03-03. (Apprisers' names not mentioned.) Nuncupative will.

Samuel Wolcott, of lawful age, testifyeth and saith that upon October 22nd, 1712, my brother Josiah Wolcott, now deceased, sent to call me and my sisters, and did declare to us that his will was that our honoured mother Judith Wolcott should have the improvement of all his estate, both real and personal, during her natural life, and at her decease his land to be equally divided between his brother and sisters, and the moveable estate to remain and be at the disposal of our hond. mother, she to dispose of it according to her pleasure. Lucy Wolcott testifyeth to the above written, 5 January, 1712-13. Sworn in Court.

Court Record, Page 104—5 January, 1712-13: Will exhibited by Judith Wolcott, appointed Adms. with the will annexed.

Page 210.

Wolcott, Capt. Samuel, Windsor. Invt. £83-09-02. Taken 12 November, 1712, by Return Strong and Timothy Thrall.

Court Record, Page 106—6 January, 1712-13: Adms. granted to Mr. Charles Chauncey of the Village of Stratfield and Col. Matthew Allyn of Windsor.

Page 262—2 August, 1715: Col. Matthew Allyn, Adms., exhibits an account of his Adms. Accepted. Order to dist. 1-2 of the estate of sd. decd., £32-00-10, to Elizabeth, now wife of sd. Matthew Allyn, sister of sd. decd., and the other half, £32-00-10, to the children of Sarah Chauncey decd., formerly Sarah Wolcott, sister of sd. Samuel Wolcott, viz., Robert Chauncey, Ichabod Wolcott Chauncey and Abiah Chauncey. And appoint William Wolcott, Roger Wolcott and Israel Stoughton, distributors.

Page 184.

Wood, Obadiah, Hartford. Invt. £199-07-11. Taken 12 May, 1712, by Jonathan Bigelow, Thomas Olcott and Timothy Cowles.

I, Obadiah Wood of Hartford, do make this my last will and testament: I give to my son John Wood all that part of my estate that was formerly my father King's, which lyeth in the bounds of Windsor, and 1-5 part of that estate that may fall to me in Old England. And to my four daughters, Mary, Martha, Abigail and Margaret, I give the remainder of that estate in England, to be equally divided between them. I give to my son Samuel £5 out of my moveable estate. I give my wife 1-3 part of my personal estate and real estate not above willed, the personal to be hers forever, and the real during her natural life. I give to my son Obadiah all that lot of land where my dwelling house stands, with my dwelling house, barn and orchard, and also my interest in the Five Miles, and all the rest of my moveable estate not willed, to be to him and his heirs forever. I appoint my wife sole executrix, and desire Daniel and Roger Pitkin to be overseers.

Witness: *Roger Pitkin,*   OBADIAH X WOOD, LS.
          John Goodwin.

See File:

Know all men by these presents: That I, John Shaw, Junr., of East Hampton, in the County of Suffolk, in the Province of New York, weaver, do make, constitute and appoint my loving friend Mr. Timothy Cowles of Hartford, in the County of Hartford and in the Colony of Connecticut, in New England, to be my lawful aturny to act and do in my behalf, or to empower and improve any other aturny or atorness he shall se cause, in all my concerns and business whatsoever, but more especially concerning what estate of right doth belong to me of the estate of Obadiah Wood, Gent., of Hartford, deceased, in right of my wife Mary, daughter to said Obadiah Wood deceased, that is, to demand, sue for, recover and receve all that which of right doth belong to me, the said John Shaw, of the estate of Obadiah Wood deceased abovesaid. Also, to contest will or wills as said Colle or any atorne or atorness improved by said Colle shall see cause, and to act and do for me in all the abovesaid premises as if I the said John Shaw were personally present here. As witness my hand and seal this 13th day of May, Anno Domini 1712.

Witness: *John* ——————,   JOHN SHAW, LS.
    Thomas Olcott.

13 May, 1712.
John Shaw personally appeared before me, subscriber, and acknowledged the abovesaid instrument to be his act and deed.

Nath: Stanly, Assistant.

Court Record, Page 83—7 July, 1712: Will exhibited by Martha Wood, widow. Proven. Timothy Cole, atty. for John Shaw of East Hampton, in the Province of New York, weaver, son-in-law of sd. Obadiah Wood, appealed to the Superior Court.

Page 57.

Woodbridge, Dudley, Rev., Simsbury. Invt. £470-14-09. Taken 1st September, 1710, by Nathaniel Holcomb, Sen., Peter Buell, Sen., and John Slater, Sen.

Court Record, Page 21—6 November, 1710: Adms. to Dorothy Woodbridge, widow. Exhibit of inventory.

Page 91—6 October, 1712: Timothy Woodbridge, who married the widow of the Rev. Dudley Woodbridge, in Court declared his dissatisfaction with the apprisal made by Nathaniel Holcomb, Sen., Peter Buel, Sen., and John Slater, Sen. This Court order a new apprisal.

Page 14 (Vol. IX) 1st May, 1716: This Court appoint Timothy Woodbridge of Simsbury to be guardian to Dudley Woodbridge, 8 years of age, son of Dudley Woodbridge, late decd. Recog., £200.

Invt. in Vol. IX, Page 56.

Woodbridge, Rev. John, Wethersfield. Died 13 November, 1696. Invt. £399-01-00. Taken 6 August, 1700, by Benjamin Churchill and John Stedman.

Court Record, Page 259—5 July, 1715: Adms. granted to Rev. John Woodbridge of Springfield.

Page 263—6 September, 1715: Mr. John Woodbridge of Springfield, Adms., appeared now before this Court and moved that whereas his late mother, widow relict of sd. decd., who had right by law to 1-3 part of the moveable or personal estate of the decd., is now departed this life before an orderly dist. of that estate or before her third part was set out to her, he prays that this Court will therefore notwithstanding make out an order for setting out the sd. thirds and that the same be put into the hands of the sd. Adms. that he may be enabled to pay and discharge the just debts of the sd. widow, contracted in her lifetime. A consideration and resolve hereupon is deferred until the 1st Tuesday of October next.

Page 2 (Vol. IX) 1st November, 1715: John Woodbridge of Springfield appeared now before this Court and pursued his former motion of the 6th of September last. The motion was again deferred.

Page 3—7 December, 1715: Rev. Mr. John Woodbridge of Springfield, Adms. on the estate of John Woodbridge, late of Wethersfield, did move this Court, upon the 6th day of September last past, that whereas his late mother, Mrs. Abigail Woodbridge, late of Simsbury, decd., widow relict of said John Woodbridge decd., had right by law to one-third part of the moveable or personal estate of the said John Woodbridge decd., and the said Abigail being now departed this life before an orderly distribution of that estate as the law directs, she having contracted debts to over £200 which remain unpaid, that therefore her said third part may be ascertained and put into the hands of said John Woodbridge the son, to be by him improved for the payment of debts. This Court so order.

Page 4—3 January, 1715-16: John Woodbridge, Adms., exhibits an account of his Adms. Accepted. And this Court order to dist. the estate: To John Woodbridge, eldest son, £133-17-10; to the heirs of Dudley Woodbridge decd., to Ephraim Woodbridge, to the heirs of Mercy, younger children of the decd., to each the sum or value of £66-18-00. And appoint Benjamin Churchill, David Goodrich and Jonathan Deming, distributors.

Page 9—8 February, 1715-16: Report of the dist. Accepted.

Page 3 (Vol. X) 4 September, 1729: Dudley Woodbridge of Simsbury, son and heir of Dudley Woodbridge, being now 21 years of age, desires an appeal from the decree of the Court of Probate, 2 August, 1715, accepting the invt. of Rev. John Woodbridge, late of Wethersfield, decd.

Page 57.

Woodford, Joseph, Sen., Farmington. Invt. £218-10-06. Taken 25 October, 1710, by John Stanly, Sen., and Samuel Newell, Sen. Will dated 10 December, 1701.

The last will and testament of Joseph Woodford, Sen., of Farmington, is as followeth: I, the aforesd. Joseph Woodford, Sen., being grown aged and infirm in my limbs, do make this my last will and testament: I give unto my daughter Mary Burd £16 in current pay. I give to my daughter Rebekah Porter £15-10-00. I give to my daughter Esther Burd £20. I give to my daughter Sarah Burd £20. I give to my daughter Hannah North £20. I give to my daughter Elizabeth Woodford £30. I give to my daughter Susannah Woodford £30. I give to my daughter Abigail Woodford £30. Lastly, I give to Joseph Woodford, my son, the rest of all my estate, whom I appoint my sole executor. And I desire my brother Samuel Newell and my friend Ensign John Hart to be overseers.

Witness: *John Hart, Sen.,*   Joseph X Woodford, Sen., ls.
          Samuel Newell.

Court Record, Page 21—6 November, 1710: Will proven.

Woodruff, Joseph. Court Record, Page 100—1st December, 1712: This Court appoint Joseph Woodruff of Farmington to be guardian to his two children, Hannah Woodruff, age 8 years, and Josiah Woodruff, age 6 years. Recog., £50.

Invt. in Vol. IX, Page 42.

Woodruff, Jonathan, Farmington. Invt. £28-03-00. Taken 1st November, 1715, by Joseph Root and Ebenezer Steele.

Court Record, Page 80—2 June, 1712: Adms. granted to Sarah Woodruff, widow of sd. decd., who recog. with her father-in-law, Samuel Woodruff.

Page 83—7 July, 1712: Adms. to Samuel Woodruff, father of sd. decd., with Sarah Woodruff, widow.

Page 262—6 September, 1715: Whereas this Court sometime since granted Adms. unto Sarah, the relict, and Samuel Woodruff, father of sd. deceased, and the sd. Sarah neglecting to pursue her part in the affair and signifying her desire to be dismissed therefrom, this Court now grant letters of Adms. on the estate entirely to sd. Samuel Woodruff.

Page 2 (Vol. IX) 1 November, 1715: Samuel Woodruff, Adms., exhibits an inventory.

Page 278.

Wright, John, Wethersfield. Died 8 March, 1713-14. Invt. £227-03-03. Taken by Joseph Grimes, Thomas Wright and Benjamin Wright.

Court Record, Page 199—7 June, 1714: Adms. granted to Marcy Wright, widow, and Thomas Wright, brother of sd. decd.

Page 76 (Vol. IX) 5 August, 1718: Mercy Wright and Thomas Wright, Adms., exhibit now an account of their Adms. Allowed.

Page 77—2 September, 1718: Mercy Wright exhibited a further account of Adms. Allowed, and order to dist. the estate:

	£ s d
To Mercy Wright, widow, in moveable estate,	18-17-08
To John Wright, son of the decd.,	83-15-07
To Mercy Wright, daughter of sd. decd.,	41-07-10

And appoint Joseph Graham, Thomas Wright and Abram Morris, distributors.

Page 79—2 September, 1718: This Court appoint Mercy Wright, widow, to be guardian to her children, viz., Mercy Wright, 11 years of age, and John Wright, 9 years, children of John Wright, late decd. Recog., £100.

Page 140—6 December, 1720: Report of the distributors.

Page 115 (Vol. X) 1st February, 1725-6: Mercy Heacox, guardian unto Mercy Wright, was cited before this Court to account with her ward for a cow and her increase. It appearing to this Court that there was an agreement between the sd. Mercy Heacox and the sd. Mercy Wright respecting the sd. cow with her increase, we do find that the sd. Mercy Heacox is not obliged to render any account concerning sd. cow.

Will and Invt. in Vol. IX, Page 21-22.

Wright, Joseph, Wethersfield. Invt. £499-18-09. Taken 5 February, 1714-15, by William Burnham, Thomas Standish and Samuel Wright. Will dated 14 February, 1711-12.

I, Joseph Wright of Wethersfield, do make and ordain this to be my last will and testament: I give unto my wife Mercy £20 in country pay of this Colony, to her and to her heirs forever, and the use of what part of my dwelling house she shall think needful for her, and that during her widowhood. I give to Joseph Wright, now of Colchester, my eldest son, to him and his heirs forever, 2 acres in Wethersfield Great Meadow which I purchased of Mr. Blackleach; also, 5 acres of land on the Great Island in Connecticut Great River, within the Township of Wethersfield, bounded east and west on the said Great River, on land of David Goodrich of Wethersfield north, and on land of Jonathan Smith of Glastonbury south. To my son Thomas Wright I give 2 1-4 acres of land in Wethersfield Great Meadow, bounded east on the Great River, west on a highway, north on my son Joseph's land, and south on land of John Deming, Sen., of Wethersfield; 3 acres in the Dry Swamp, bounded (in part) on land of Deacon Warner and Nathaniel Churchill; also half my pasture, bounded (in part) on land of John Curtis, Jr., Samuel Butler, and my son John Wright's land which sometime since I gave him—to him the said Thomas Wright and his heirs forever. I have given my son John Wright, by deed of gift formerly, the whole which I designed as his portion. I give to my son Jonathan Wright 50 acres of land in the Township of Wethersfield, butting on the Township of Farmington west, on a highway east, north on land of Robert Welles, Jr., and south on land of Major John Chester. To my two sons, Benjamin Wright and Nathaniel Wright, I give that tract of land which fell to me in the last general division of lands in Wethersfield, to be equally divided between them. To Benjamin Wright I give 3 acres in the Great Swamp in Wethersfield, bounded (in part) on land of my son Thomas Wright and (in part) on land belonging to heirs of Stephen Chester, Jr., decd.; also five and a half acres in the said swamp, bounded (in part) on land of Deacon William Warner, on my own land, and upon land of heirs of Stephen Chester. I give to my youngest son Nathaniel Wright 3 1-2 acres of land bounded (in part) on land of heirs of Stephen Chester, on land of my son Benjamin Wright, and on land of Nathaniel Boreman; also 3 acres bounded (in part) on land of Jacob Williams of Wethersfield, on land of Thomas Bunce of Hartford, and on land of Jonathan Smith of Wethersfield. I give the whole of what shall remain of my movable estate to my eldest daughter Mary Griswold, to my second daughter Elizabeth Curtis, and to the children of my youngest daughter Sarah Hand of East Guilford deceased—one-third part to each: to Mary Griswold, to Elizabeth Curtis, and to the children of Sarah Hand decd. I appoint my two eldest sons, Joseph Wright and Thomas Wright, executors.

JOSEPH WRIGHT, LS.

Witness: *John Nott,*
John Goodrich, Jr.

A codicil, dated 9 December, 1714.

JOSEPH WRIGHT, LS.

Witness: *George Kilbourn,*
John Goodrich, Jr.

Court Record, Page 234—7 February, 1714-15: Joseph Wright of Colchester and Thomas Wright of Wethersfield exhibit the will of their late father Joseph Wright of Wethersfield deceased. The will and codicil approved.

Page 85.

Wright, Thomas, Wethersfield. Invt. £300-16-00. Taken 1 May, 1711, by Joseph Wright and William Burnham.

NUNCUPATIVE WILL: SEE FILE.

Thomas Wright of Wethersfield, deceased, the night before his death, gave his estate to be distributed to several of his relations according to the minutes following, in the presence of us the subscribers:

1: To his sister Mary Belding, his house and homelot.

2: To his sister Lydia Crane, his great Bible, his corn and mault which were in his house, and one of his swine.

3: To the children of his brother David Goodrich, he gave as followeth: (1) To his son Josiah Goodrich, his horse and a piece of land in Wethersfield lying in a place ordinarily called the Wolf Swamp. (2) To Elizer Goodrich, his lot in that part of Wethersfield Meadow called the Great Swamp. (3) To David Goodrich, six acres in Wethersfield, in the Great Island lying in Connecticut River, the said six acres lying next to his said David Goodrich's father's land. (4) To Elizabeth Goodrich, an heifer, an iron pot, and forty shillings in money. (5) To Abigail Goodrich, a fire slice and a pair of tongs, a trammell, gridiron, and forty shillings in money.

4: To Silas the son of his brother Jonathan Belding, his gun.

5: To his abovesaid sisters, Mary Belding and Lydia Crane, the whole remaining part of his land lying in the abovesaid island, equally to them (David Goodrich's six acres only, as above given, excepted); also, the remainder of his personal estate to his said sisters, Mary the wife of his brother Jonathan Belding, and his sister Lydia Crane.

Mary Churchell,
Prudence Goodrich.

AGREEMENT:

To the Hond. Court of Probate now sitting in Hartford:

The nuncupative will and testament of Thomas Wright, Sen., late of Wethersfield, deceased, we the subscribers, his near relations, do for ourselves and our heirs acquiesce in and fully consent to, praying this honoured Court to pass their sanction thereon and grant administration according to the same.

JONATHAN BELDING, LS.	ELIZER GOODRICH, LS.
LYDIA CRANE, HER MARK, LS.	DAVID GOODRICH, LS.
JOSIAH GOODRICH, LS.	The mark A of
ALLEN GOODRICH, LS.	ABIGAIL GOODRICH, LS.

A true copy of the original.

Test: *Caleb Stanly, Clerk.*

COPY OF THE LETTER OF ADMINISTRATION ON THE ESTATE OF THOMAS WRIGHT, SEN., DECD., 1711.

From the Record on File.

Robert Wells, John Higley and Nathaniel Hooker, Esqrs., Judges of the Court for Probate of Wills and Granting Letters of Administration on the Estates of Persons Decd., having goods, chattels, rights or credits in the County of Hartford, within the Colony of Connecticut, in New England.

TO ALL UNTO WHOM THESE PRESENTS SHALL COME, GREETING:

Know ye that on the fourth day of June, in the year of our Lord 1711, before us at Hartford, in the County aforesaid, the will of Thomas Wright, Sen., late of Wethersfield, deceased, to these presents annexed, was proved, approved and allowed. Who, having while he lived, and at the time of his death, goods, chattels, rights or credits in the county aforesaid; and the probate of the said will, and power of committing administration of all and singular the goods, chattels, rights and credits of the said deceased, and also the hearing, examining and allowing the accounts of the same by virtue thereof, of right appertaining unto us: The administration of all and singular the goods, chattels, rights and credits of the said deceased, and his will in any manner concerning, lying and being in the County aforesaid or elsewhere, is hereby committed unto Capt. David Goodrich and Mr. Jonathan Belding of Wethersfield aforesaid, well and faithfully to administer the same, and to dispose thereof according to the said will of the said decd., and to make a true and perfect inventory of all and singular his goods, chattels, rights and credits, and to exhibit the same into the Registry of the said Court of Probate, at or before the first Monday of July next. Also, to render a plain and true account of his said administration on or before the first Monday of April, 1713. In testimony whereof, we have caused the Clerk of the said Court of Probate to sign these presents the day and year first above written.

Caleb Stanly, Clerk.

Court Record, Page 33—4 June, 1711: Will exhibited by Capt. David Goodrich and Lt. Jonathan Belding, brothers-in-law. The relations signed an agreement to accept the will. This Court accepts and allows, and appoints David Goodrich and Jonathan Belding Adms. with the will annexed. Capt. David Goodrich was appointed guardian to 3 of his children, viz., Eleazer, David and Abigail Goodrich.

PROBATE RECORDS.

VOLUME IX.

1715 to 1723.

Addams, John, Wethersfield. Court Record, Page 161—3 January, 1721 : Adms. granted to Elizabeth Addams, sister of sd. decd., and Joseph Churchill of Wethersfield.

Page 365.

Alderman, William, Simsbury. Invt. £47-09-00. Taken by Samuel Case and Samuel Pettebone.

Court Record, Page 32—7 May, 1717 : Upon motion of William Alderman, of Simsbury, desireing that Adms. be granted on the estate of his father, William Alderman, late decd., this Court issue a writ to cite Mary Hillier to appear.

Page 41—6 August, 1717 : This Court grant Adms. on the estate of sd. William Alderman, sometime of Simsbury, unto his son William Alderman of sd. Simsbury.

Page 126—3 May, 1720 : William Alderman, Adms., exhibits an account of his Adms. This Court order him to sell some lands to pay the debts.

Page 52 (Vol. X) 4 August, 1724 : Thomas Alderman of Simsbury, a minor, 18 years of age, chose William Alderman of Symsbury to be his guardian. Recog., £50.

Page 150—4 April, 1727 : In pursuance of an act of the General Assembly holden at Hartford 27 May, 1720, impowering William Alderman, Adms., to sell so much of the lands of the decd. as may be sufficient to pay the debts due from sd. estate with the direction of this Court, the sd. Adms. is directed by this Court to sell one parcell of land lying in Simsbury on the east side of Simsbury East Mountains, containing 10 acres, lying on the north side of John Roberts's farm.

Page 250.

Allyn, Samuel, Coventry. Invt. £38-10-00. Taken 30 September, 1717, by Thomas Root and Ebenezer Alexander.

Court Record, Page 41—3 September, 1717 : Citation to Mercy Allyn, widow, to take letters of Adms.

Page 43—1st October, 1717 : Adms. granted to Mercy Allyn, widow.

See File : Paper with invt., dated 5 November, 1717 : Mercy Allyn, widow of Samuel Allyn, late of Coventry, and Adms. on Samuel Allyn's estate, made application to the Court of Probates of the County of Hartford, 5 November, 1717, and declareth that the estate of sd. Allyn is insolvent, and prays this Court would set out to her the sd. Mercy Allyn what the law about intestate estates doth allow to be set out to the widow. And this Court doth accordingly set out to the sd. widow the household goods. And appoint Thomas Root, Ebenezer Alexander and Samuel Parker, commissioners.

Page 119.

Alverd, Josias, Simsbury. He died 10 May, 1722. Invt. £124-18-04. Taken by Joshua Holcomb, Benjamin Addams and Andrew Robe.

Court Record, Page 168—5 June, 1722: Adms. to Hannah Alverd, widow, and Josias Alverd, son of the deceased. This Court appoint Hannah Alverd guardian to her daughter Dorothy Alverd, age about 12 years.

Page 2 (Vol. X) 1st January, 1722-3: The Adms. exhibit an account of their Adms., which this Court accept. Order to distribute as follows:

	£ s d
To Hannah Alvord, widow,	11-01-06
To Josiah Alvord, eldest son,	34-14-04
To Hannah Welton, Nathaniel Alvord, Elizabeth and Dorothy Alvord, to each,	17-17-02

And appoint Andrew Robe, Benjamin Addams and Jonathan Westover, distributors.

Page 339.

Andrews, Benjamin, Wethersfield. Died 1719. Invt. £369-03-11. Taken by Jabez Whittlesey and Joseph Andrews.

Court Record, Page 112—6 October, 1719: Adms. granted to Elizabeth Andrews, widow.

Page 149—1st April, 1721: Elizabeth Andrews, Adms., exhibits an account of her Adms. Allowed. Order to dist. the estate:

	£ s d
To Elizabeth Andrews, widow,	17-19-06
To Joseph, eldest son,	103-06-04
To Phineas, Timothy, Jemima and Rebekah Andrews, to each,	51-13-02

And appoint James Patterson, Jabez Whittlesey and John Camp, distributors.

Page 169—5 June, 1722: This Court do appoint John Camp and Samuel Woodruff, of Farmington, to represent the heirs of Benjamin Andrews, late of Wethersfield, and assist in their behalf to divide a parcell of land in Farmington, lying in common between the said heirs, Joseph Clark, Thomas Cadwell, and the said Samuel Woodruff.

Page 57-249.

Andrews, Elizabeth, Widow, relict of Solomon Andrews decd. Invt.
£39-10-00. Taken 19 March, 1716-17, by Cyprian Nichols and Ichabod
Welles. Will nuncupative.

Anna Gains and Ruth Welles, both of lawfull age, testifie and say:
They being wth Wido Eliza Andrews in the time of her last sickness,
some little while before her death, heard the said Eliza declare that she
gave the feather bed whereon Ephraim Tucker then lay, or had frequently
layen on, with the furniture thereto belonging, unto the said Ephraim
Tucker. Moreover, sd. Anna Gains doth further add that at the same time
the said Elizabeth took hold of a cloak that lay on her bed and said, "I give
Ephraim Tucker this cloak." And further these deponents say not.

Court Record, Page 6—7 February, 1715-16: Adms. to John Brace.

Page 8—6 March, 1715-16: Ephraim Tucker of Hartford exhibited
now in this Court a writing in the nature of a nuncupative will of Elizabeth Andrews, late of Hartford, widow, deceased, whereby the said Elizabeth in her last sickness did devise and bequeath to the said Ephraim a bed
and furniture. And Anna Gains and Ruth Welles, witnesses thereof, before this Court now make solemn oath thereunto. This Court do now
thereupon prove, approve and allow the will so far as it relates to the devise aforesaid. David Forbes of Hartford, declareing himself dissatisfied
with the above order, appealed therefrom unto the Superior Court. Rec.,
£10.

Page 48.

Andrews, Solomon and Elizabeth his wife, late of Hartford, decd.
Invt. £175-12-04. Taken by Roger Pitkin and Timothy Cowles. (A
parcel of land not yet inventoried.)

Court Record, Page 29—5 March, 1716-17: William Warren and
David Forbes, upon the suit of John Bracy, being summoned to be interrogated of all and whatsoever they know relating to the estate of Elizabeth Andrews, late of Hartford, decd., appeared and were accordingly
interrogated. This Court order William Warren and David Forbes to
deliver the "weomen's" apparrell which is yet in their custody and
(which) they have put into Solomon Andrews's inventory, unto John
Bracy, Adms. on the estate of Elizabeth Andrews, late of Hartford, deceased.

Page 44—5 November, 1717: Whereas, William Warren and David
Forbes, Adms. on the estate of Solomon Andrews, moved to this Court for
advice respecting some estate of sd. Solomon Andrews which had been
contested (as estate of Elizabeth Andrews deceased, sometime the wife
of sd. Solomon Andrews) in the law by John Bracy, Adms. on the estate
of the sd. Elizabeth Andrews, with the above-mentioned William Warren
as Adms. aforesd., and the sd. John Bracy recovered a judgement of
County Court in June last for his delivery of the estate particularly mentioned in the writt, or £50 in lieu thereof: This Court, upon consideration

of the matter, do advise the sd. William Warren and David Forbes to deliver the estate inventoried as aforesd. and particularly sued for in the writt aforesd., or the sum of £50, according to the judgement of Court aforesd., unto the sd. John Bracy, and also advised the parties to let fall the action depending between them about the sd. estate.

Page 50—4 February, 1717-18: William Warren and David Forbes, Adms. on the estate of Solomon Andrews, exhibited account and wer~ granted a *Quietus Est.*

Page 120.

Andrews, William, Wethersfield.   Invt. £112-04-00. Taken 4 August, 1722, by Samuel Hunn, John Deming and John Camp.

Court Record, Page 171—3 July, 1722: Whereas, William Andrews, late of Wethersfield, being gone off to sea and having been absent about fourteen years and not heard of that he is alive, and a motion being made that Adms. should be granted on said estate, Adms. was granted to Joseph Andrews, a brother of the deceased.

Dist. File: 1723: To Joseph Andrus, to heirs of Benjamin Andrews, to Rebeckah Gillett, to Ephraim Andrews, to Caleb Andrews, to Ann Camp.   By John Camp and Samuel Hunn.   Signed:

> BENJAMIN GILLETT,
> AMOS CAMP,
> JOSEPH ANDREWS,
> CALEB ANDREWS.

Page 22 (Vol. X) 2 July, 1723: Report of the distributors.

Page 332.

Arnold, Jonathan, Hartford.   Invt. £624-18-07.   Taken 17 June, 1719, by Nathaniel Stanly and John Austin.

Court Record, Page 106—10 June, 1719: Adms. to Sarah Arnold, widow, and Peter Pratt.

Page 109—4 August, 1719: Philip Smith to be guardian to Jonathan Arnold, a minor about 9 years of age, son of Jonathan Arnold decd. Recog., £50.   The widow, Sarah Arnold, petitions for dower.   Granted.

Page 127—10 May, 1720: Adms. account approved.

Page 133—2 August, 1720: Permission to sell land for the payment of debts.

Page 175—2 September, 1722: Peter Pratt exhibits an account and reports the estate insolvent.

Page 20 (Vol. X) 4 June, 1723: Sarah Parker, alias Arnold, one of the Adms., exhibited an account of her Adms.   Accepted.

Page 87—1st June, 1725: Jonathan Arnold, a minor 14 years of age, chose Ebenezer Smith of Farmington to be his guardian.

Page 107—2 November, 1725: This Court appoint Sarah Bird of Farmington to be guardian to Jonathan Arnold, now 15 years of age. Recog., £50.

Page 15.

Arnold, Mary, Haddam. Invt. £30-18-05. Taken 4 December, 1714, by Simon Smith, Ebenezer Frisbie and Joseph Arnold. Will nuncupative, dated 2 July, 1714.

The widow, Mary Arnold, late wife to Josiah Arnold deceased, sometime before her death, and then at that time in her right mind and understanding, did declare to us, James Wells and Rebeckah Wells, in these words: "That what estate is mine I give and will it to my two dafters." Mr. James Wells and Rebeckah Wells his wife, above named, being neither of them able to attend Court at this time, appeared in Haddam and made oath that the above-named widow, now deceased, called them to her (and sayd as above) that what estate was hers she willed to her two daughters, and desired them to see that this was performed, and that the said words were spak to them ye same day she departed.

Before me: John Hamlin, Assistant.

Atwood, Edward. Court Record, Page 48—7 January, 1717-18: This Court grant letters of Adms. on the estate of Edward Atwood, sometime of Middletown, decd., unto Thomas Atwood, who made it appear, to the satisfaction of this Court, that he is nephew unto the sd. Edward Atwood of the City of Bristoll in Great Britain, provided bond be given as the law directs. The sd. Thomas Atwood gave bond.

Page 49.

Barnes, William, East Haddam. Died 18 February, 1715-16. Invt. £218-02-07. Taken by Daniel Cone and Daniel Braynard.

Court Record, Page 7—6 March, 1715-16: Adms. to James Smith and Mary Barnes joyntly.

Page 61-2—1 April, 1718: The Court appoint Joshua Braynard of Haddam guardian to William Barnes, age 19 years, and to Samuel Barnes, age 8 years, sons of William Barnes decd. Also appoint Samuel Evans of Haddam guardian to Thomas Barnes, age 12 years, and appoint James Smith of Coventry guardian to Abigail Barnes, age 13 years, and Eunice Barnes, age 9 years, all minor children of William Barnes, decd.

Page 67—3 June, 1718: James Smith, of Coventry, Adms., exhibits an account of his Adms. Accepted and allowed. Order to dist. the estate amongst the children as follows:

£　s　d

To William Barnes, eldest son,　　　　　　　　　　61-14-05
To Thomas, Samuel, Mary, Abigail and Eunice Barnes, to each, 30-17-03

And appoint Thomas Gates, Daniel Braynard and Daniel Cone, of Haddam, distributors.

Page 94—9 January, 1718-19: Distributors' report.

Page 303.

Bate, James, Haddam. Died 13th March, 1718. Invt. £569-05-10. Taken 6th and 7th May, 1718, by Samuel Parsons and Joseph Coe.

NOTE: (Included in this inventory his house and barn, £80; 1st division of land adjoyning to the house, containing about 50 acres, £224; seven-acre lott bought of Mr. Spencer, £10-10-00; land bought of Richard Beech, £8-00-00; 2d division lotts, about 40 acres, £40-00-00; 10 acres of meadow in the Great Swamp, bought of John Gaylord, valued at £40; and 200 pds. right in the undivided lands, £25; total, £427-05-10.

Court Record, Page 88—9 December, 1718: This Court grant letters of Adms. unto Hannah Bates, widow and relict of sd. decd.

Page 312-313-14.

Bates, John, Haddam. Died 15 January, 1718-19. Invt. £286-12-00. Taken 28 January, 1718-19, by James Braynard, Samuel Ingram and Joseph Arnold.

An agreement of heirs either of his body or by marriage: That our hond. mother Elizabeth Bate shall have the use and improvement of halfe the dwelling-house, half the barn and half the orchard in the home lott, and half said home lott, and half the land in the little meadow above the land of Mr. Symon Smith, and all the household goods proper for a woman's use, and a cow, and a mare, which she shall choose, and the sheep. These, being part of our hond father's estate, shall be intirely to the use of the forenamed Elizabeth during her natural life or widowhood.

Also, at our said mother's decease, Elizabeth Bailey or her heirs shall have one-third part of the personal or moveable estate. We agree that Jonathan Bate be put in Adms., and that he pay the lawful debts out of the personal estate, and also that he execute a deed for a small lott on the Plain in the second division upon the right of John Webb, to Nathaniel Spencer, Jr., it being sold to him before our sd. father's death. We the subscribers do each and every one of us, both for ourselves and our heirs, covenant and engage that we will forever remain satisfyed and contented with the foresd. distribution. Signed and sealed this 23 day of February, 1718-19.

Witness: *Joseph Arnold,*   John X. Bate, ls.
       Samuel Ingram,   Solomon X Bate, ls.
       Hez. Brainard.   Joseph X Graves, ls.
                       Jonathan X Bate, ls.
                       James Ray, Jr., ls.
                       Elizabeth X Bailey, ls.

I, Elizabeth Bate, relict or widow of the deceased John Bate above-named, am fully satisfied with the distribution that my children have now agreed upon, as is above expressed.

                               Elizabeth X Bate, ls.

Court Record, Page 96—3 March, 1718-19: Adms. granted to Jonathan Bates, son of the decd.

P^g^ 111—1st September, 1719: Agreement exhibited, which the Court accepts.

Page 232.

Beckwith, Nathaniel, Haddam. Invt. £245-18-02. Taken 3d April, 1717, by Isaac Spencer and John X Willey.

Court Record, Page 31—7 May, 1717: Adms. to Sarah Beckwith, widow.

Page 86—5 November, 1718: Sarah Beckwith, Adms., exhibits an account of her Adms. Allowed. Order to distribute as follows:

	£ s d
To Sarah Beckwith, widow,	19-04-08
To Job Beckwith, eldest son,	57-04-00
To Nathaniel, Jerusha, Sarah, Joseph and Patience Beckwith, to each of them the sum of,	28-12-00

And appoint John Bogue, John Holmes and Isaac Spencer, of Haddam, distributors. This Court appoint Nathaniel Beckwith of Lyme to be guardian to Job, Nathaniel, Jerusha, Sarah, Joseph and Patience Beckwith, minor children of Nathaniel Beckwith late deceased. Recog., £200.

Page 283.

Berry, Nathaniel, Mansfield. Invt. £165-18-06. Taken 16 August, 1718, by Thomas Huntington and John Arnold.

Court Record, Page 78—2 September, 1718: Adms. granted to Elizabeth Berry, widow.

Page 107—7 July, 1719: This Court appoint Elizabeth Berry to be guardian to her children: Sarah, age 14 years; Abigail, 11 years. Recog., £100. Also, the widow exhibits an account of her Adms. Allowed. Order to distribute the estate as followeth:

	£	s	d
To Elizabeth Berry, widow,	25-13-01		
To Nathaniel Berry, son,	20-07-00		
To Rachel Fulshom, Ann Fenton, Bethiah Gove, Elizabeth Berry, Sarah Berry and Abigail Berry, to each,	10-03-06		

And appoint Thomas Huntington, John Arnold and Thomas Storrs, of Mansfield, distributors.

Page 348-9-69.

Bidwell, Daniel, Deacon. Died 29 November, 1719. Invt. £581-17-07. Taken 30 December, 1719, by Joseph Olmsted, Ozias Pitkin and Timothy Cowles. Will dated August, 1719.

I, Daniel Bidwell, doe make this my last will and testament: I give to my loving wife the improvement of 1-3 part of my improved lands during her life, 1-3 part of my stock, and likewise the improvement of my son William's part of my estate until he comes to age, he to have his maintenance out of it, bestowing his labor and industry thereon. I give to my wife all the household stuffe, the remaining part of my real and personal estate to be equally distributed between my children, my son Daniel, my son William, my daughter Mary, my daughter Hannah, and my daughter Lydia, provided that my son Daniel's house or anything that I have done towards the building of it be not reckoned of the estate above mentioned, and also 4 acres of land adjoining thereunto. And also I give him the £10 that I have paid for him towards the meadow land that he hath bought. As for my son William, whome I choose should enjoy my dwelling house and barn, which are old buildings, these to be enjoyed by him besides that estate above-mentioned. To my daughter Hannah, my will is, what she has already received be reckoned as part of her share and portion. My wife and son Daniel to be executors.

DANIEL BIDWELL, LS.

Witness: *Samuel Woodbridge,*
Mary Williams.

A Codicil, dated 9 November, 1719.

DANIEL BIDWELL.

Witness: *Samuel Woodbridge,*
Joseph Benton.

Court Record, Page 115—5 January, 1719-20: Dorothy Bidwell, widow of the decd., exhibits the last will. Proven.

Page 134—4 September, 1720: This Court appoint Capt. Roger Pitkin, Ozias Pitkin and Timothy Cowles of Hartford to divide the estate of Deacon Daniel Bidwell according to his last will. And appoint Dorothy

Bidwell of Hartford, widow, to be guardian to her children, William Bidwell, 17 years, and Lydia Bidwell, 14 years of age. Recog., £100.

See File, 4 September, 1720: The estate was dist. to the following persons according to Daniel Bidwell's will, vizt: to the widow Dorothy Bidwell, to Daniel, to Mary Bidwell, to Daniel Biggelow and his wife Hannah Bidwell, to Lydia Bidwell, to William and to John Bidwell. By Roger Pitkin, Ozias Pitkin and Timothy Cowles.

Page 273.

Bidwell, James, Hartford. Invt. £343-12-00. Taken 16 June, 1718, by John Marsh and **Nathaniel Stanly.**

Court Record, Page 66—3 June, 1718: Adms. to Ruth Bidwell, widow.

Page 95—3 February, 1718-19: This Court appoint Ruth Bidwell to be guardian unto James Bidwell, age 2 years, son of the decd. Recog., £150.

Page 35-36.

Bidwell, Samuel, Sen., Middletown. Invt. £977-05-06. Taken 25 April, 1715, by John Hamlin, Joseph Rockwell and William Harris. Will dated 23 March, 1715.

I, Samuel Bidwell of Midletown, doe make this my last will and testament: I give to my son Samuel Bidwell a parcell of land in Wongonk, 75 acres more or less, butting on Pond land west, upon Thomas Ranny's land, upon Isaac Johnson and upon part of John Willcock's lands east, and north upon Nathaniel Bidwell's land, and south upon undivided swamp. I appoint, for the convenience of both my sons, Samuel and Nathaniel Bidwell, a lamas way between them, extending so far as the highland where that common passage now is, and then to extend northward so far as Joseph Butler's land, and then west to the highway. I also give to my son Samuel, from the stakes I set down on the west side, fourty rods in breadth through eastward to the lamas highway, and also five acres of my land on the Plain, and one-half of my swamp land I have for makeing fourty rods of fence, to my son Samuel Bidwell and to his heirs forever. I give to my son Nathaniel Bidwell, and to his heirs forever, a parcell of land adjoyning to the lands of my son Samuel Bidwell. I give to my daughter Sarah Braynard and her heirs one-half of my right in the great lott at the Streights Hills, which I bought of my brother-in-law Thomas Stow and also by gift in will by my father Stow. I give to my daughter Elizabeth Brainard and her heirs all the other half of my right in said great lot. I give to my daughter Abigail Sumner and her heirs my half-mile lott on the east side of the Great River, which was my father Stow's. I give to my daughter Mary Bidwell a hundred acres of land lying in my great lot in the southwest quarter of the Town bounds and sideing on Durham bounds. I give to my daughter Hannah Bidwell a hundred acres in the abovesaid lot. I give to my wife Abigail Bidwell and to my son Moses Bidwell my dwelling house, barn, orchard, all my enclosures belonging to my homestead, with my part of the sawmill, and stock and moveables, within doors and without, and about 32 1-2 acres of land I bought of David Hurlbutt; also about 35 acres I bought of John Conner; also the remainder of my great lott in the southwest quarter of the Township. And do here order that my three daughters, Mary, Hannah and Thankfull Bidwell, shall have each of them paid out of this estate ordered unto my wife and son, fifteen pounds apiece. My two sons shall have all that money which is due to me from Jonathan Warner, equally divided between them. I appoint my wife Abigail Bidwell sole executrix.

SAMUEL BIDWELL, LS.

Witness: *Daniel Harris, Sen.,*
  Samuel Miller.

Court Record, Page 31 (Vol. X) 1 October, 1723: Abigail Bidwell, executrix of the last will of Samuel Bidwell, exhibited an addition to the inventory of sd. estate amounting to the sum of £1-01-06, which is by the Court accepted, ordered recorded, and kept on file.

Page 109-10.

Bidwell, Thomas, Hartford. Invt. £940-00-00. Taken 15 January, 1716-17, by William Whiting, Richard Edwards and John Austin.

Court Record, Page 22—17 September, 1716: Adms. granted to Prudence Bidwell, widow.

Page 27—6 February, 1716-17: Richard Seamore is appointed to be joynt Adms. with Prudence Bidwell. Prudence Bidwell exhibited an invt. whereby it appears that the estate is insolvent. This Court appoint Col. William Whiting, Richard Edwards and John Austin to examine the claims.

Page 41—6 August, 1717: Prudence Bidwell makes application to this Court for her right of dower in her late husband's estate, and this Court appoint Benjamin Graham, Thomas Hosmer and Joseph Skinner of Hartford to set out of the real estate so much as is her right of dowery.

Page 119—2 February, 1719-20: Report of the commissioners. Also, they exhibit a list of claimants. Accepted by the Court, and they are ordered paid to the commissioners.

Page 113.

Bigelow, John, Hartford. Invt. £54-07-01. Taken 27 December, 1721, by Nathaniel Stanly and Thomas Hosmer.

Court Record, Page 159—5 December, 1721: Adms. granted to Rebeckah, the widow.

Page 167—1st May, 1722: Jonathan Butler moves this Court that an instrument in writing under the hand and seal of John Bigelow, late of Hartford deceased, dated 5 October, 1716, might be allowed and accepted as the last will of the sd. decd. This Court have considered that although the sd. writing be in form a deed of gift, and no person named executor in sd. writing, yet the Court considering that the sd. Jonathan Butler, to whome the estate was given, being appointed and obliged by the conditions of the sd. writing to do the office and duty of an executor, to pay all the debts that shall become due from or ought to be paid out of said Bigelow's estate to any person or persons whatsoever, this Court does therefore approve of sd. writing to be as the last will of the sd. John Bigelow deceased, and ordered to be recorded and kept upon file. Joseph Bigelow appealed from the judgement of this Court to the Superior Court. Rec., £10.

Page 303.

Bissell, Deliverance, Windsor (Widow of Nathaniel Bissell). Invt. £24-07-06. Taken 6 October, 1718, by John Collins and Israhiah Wetmore.

Court Record, Page 75—5 August, 1718: Adms. to Capt. Joseph Rockwell of Middletown, son of the decd.

Page 258.

Bissell, Ephraim, Tolland. Invt. £90-18-08. Taken 28 January, 1718, by Joseph Benton and Joshua Willes.

Court Record, Page 53—4 March, 1718: Adms. granted to Isaac Bissell of Windsor and to Nathaniel Taylor of Tolland.

Page 59—1st April, 1718: This Court appoint Thomas Bissell, Jr., guardian to Ephraim Bissell, a minor 14 years of age, and Benjamin Bissell, 3 years, children of Ephraim Bissell, late of Tolland. Recog., £50. Joseph Stedman of Windsor is appointed guardian to Abell Bissell and Stephen, sons of Ephraim Bissell, late of Windsor decd.

Page 131 (Vol. X) 3 June, 1726: Ephraim Bissell of Tolland moves this Court that the Adms. on the estate of his father be discharged from their Adms. and a dist. ordered, but there appears estate of the deceased that has never been inventoried, and prays that Adms. may be granted to him on sd. estate. Granted.

Page 135—5 September, 1726: Nathaniel Taylor and Isaac Bissell, Adms., exhibit now an account of their Adms. Accepted. Order to distribute:

	£	s	d
To Ephraim Bissell, eldest son,	89-00-09		
To Abell, Benjamin and Stephen Bissell, to each,	44-10-05		

And appoint Francis West, Jonathan Delano and Joseph Peck, of Tolland, distributors.

Page 74 (Probate Side, Vol. XII) : An invt. of the lands belonging to the estate of Ephraim Bissell, valued at £222-12-00, was taken 31 August, 1726, by Francis West and Jonathan Delano.

Court Record, Page 142 (Vol. XI) 6 December, 1726: Report of the distributors. And this Court grant the Adms. a *Quietus Est.*

Page 282.

Bissell, Mary, Simsbury. Died 24 June, 1718. Invt. £17-13-08. Taken 4 August, 1718, by Deacon Cornish, John Humphreys and Jane Hillier. Will dated 9 April, 1718.

I, Mary Bissell of Simsbury, doe make this my last will and testament: I give unto my eldest daughter Mary, the wife of Samuel Humphreys, my pillion; and to sd. Mary and my daughters Hannah and Elizabeth, all my wearing clothes, to be equally divided among them three. I give to the heirs of John Mills 5 shillings, and to the heirs of Sarah Elsworth 5 shillings. I do give unto my son Simon Mills the remainder of my estate, both personal and real. And appoint my son Simon Mills sole executor.

Witness: *James Hillier, Sen.,*   MARY BISSELL, LS.
       Joseph Phelps.

Court Record, Page 74—5 August, 1718: Will proven.

Page 71.

Bissell, Samuel, Windsor. Invt. £297-06-07. Taken 30 November, 1720, by Samuel Rockwell, Job Elsworth and David Bissell.

Court Record, Page 140—6 December, 1720: Adms. granted to Jeremiah Bissell of Windsor.

Page 46 (Vol. X) 7 April, 1724: Jeremiah Bissell, Adms., exhibits an account of his Adms. Accepted. Order to dist. the estate to the brothers and sisters of the sd. decd.:

	£ s d
To Daniel, Josiah and Jeremiah Bissell, to each,	42-18-01
To the heirs of Ann White,	42-18-01
To the heirs of Mary Birge,	42-18-01

And appoint Samuel Rockwell, Ebenezer Fitch and David Bissell distributors.

Page 341.

Boardman, Isaac, Sen.,Wethersfield. He died 12 May, 1719. Invt. £14-18-04. Taken 19 September, 1719, by Benjamin Churchill and William Burnham.

Court Record, Page 113—3 November, 1719: Adms. unto Abiah Boardman, daughter of sd. deceased.

Page 131—5 July, 1720: Abiah Boardman, Adms., exhibits account, which is allowed. Order to distribute: To Abiah Boardman, widow relict (her dower), £3-02-11; Isaac Boardman, eldest son, £1-16-00; Samuel Boardman, Thomas Boardman, Sarah Frary, Abiah Boardman and Eunice Williams, the rest of the children of sd. deceased, to each of them, 18 shillings, which is their single part of the sd. estate. Edward Bulkeley, William Burnham and Samuel Boardman are appointed distributors.

Page 74.

Boardman, Samuel, Wethersfield. Died 23 December, 1720. Invt. £1085-18-10. Taken 26 January, 1720-1, by Edward Bulkeley, Joseph Treat and Isaac Ryley. Will dated 20 December, 1720.

I, Samuel Boardman of Wethersfield, do make and ordain this my last will and testament: I give unto my dearly and well-beloved wife Sarah the sum of £70 to her forever, and the use of one-half of my dwelling house so long as she shall continue my widow. I give to my eldest son David Boardman my dwelling house, barn and homelott, containing two acres and a half, butted southeast on the Broad Street, northwest on Cole Lane, northeast on a highway, and southwest on land of the heirs of Ebenezer Kilbourn deceased; also, two acres in the Plain (joins) lands of Isaac Ryley; also, part of my 3 1-2 acre lott in the meadow, north on land of heirs of John Robbins deceased; also, 1 1-2 acres in the meadow, south on land of the heirs of Jonathan Ryley deceased; also, one acre, north on lands of the heirs of Richard Lord deceased; also, 2 acres in the great swamp, south on land of Jonathan Curtis; also, 2 acres in the wet swamp, south on Joseph Belding; also, 15 acres in the West Field lotts by Joseph Kilbourn's, south half of sd. lott, east on Jonathan Goodrich, west on the Commons, south on the heirs of old Leonard Dyxx; also, 5 acres at Rocky Hill, east on the highway leading to Middletown, west on the Commons, south on heirs of Lt. Jonathan Boardman deceased; also, one-half of my west division lott given to me by the Town of Wethersfield according to the list of my estate in the year 1693, on the west side of sd. lott, bounded west on land granted to John Durrant, butted on Middletown line south. The lands herein given to my son David shall be an estate in ffee simple to him and his heirs forever hereby willing, commanding and requireing him to pay to his mother, my widow, £3 annually during her life, and also provide meat summer and winter for one cow, and to provide the one-half of her firewood so long as she shall remain my widow; and also to assist his brother Joseph in finishing a new house which I shall herein give him until it be as good as this house I live in, at inventory price, which is herein given to my son David. I give to my son Joseph Boardman two acres of land I bought of my son-in-law Daniel Warner, and the house thereon standing, and what my son David is to do in finishing said house; also several parcels of land with mention of these adjoyning proprietors: William Goodrich, heirs of John Belding deceased, heirs of John Francis deceased, heirs of Samuel Buck deceased, William Knott, James Butler, Capt. Joshua Robbins, John Rose, John Reignolds—all given to Joseph with the same conditions as to David, i. e., in fee simple and the requirements to pay £3 annually to his mother, also to provide for her. I give to my daughter Mary Warner £20 as money additional to £94-14-00 paid her at the time of her marirage, which £20 makes the sum of £114-14-00. I give to my cozen Jemima Graves £15 besides what I have already given her. I do appoint my two sons, David and Joseph Boardman, executors.

Witness: *Josiah Deming,*   SAMUEL BOARDMAN, LS.
    John Bulkeley, John Andruss.

Court Record, Page 143—7 February, 1720-21 : Will proven.

Page 254. Additional Invt., 310.

Bowen, Josiah, Wethersfield. Invt. £40-00-00. Taken 3 December, 1717, by Moses Craffts and John Howard. A piece of land in Wethersfield six rods and three foots in length, and three rodds wanting three foots in breadth, abutting on a highway or street east, and land of William Clark west, the sides on land of Benjamin Addams north, and William Clark south, according to his deed of sale, with a dwelling house on said land, wee prize at fourty pounds in or as money. An addition to the inventory of an old poor bed and bedsted, 8s; five small pewter dishes, old cup and old porringer, 14s-06; old warming pan and old skillett, 6s; small iron pot, little iron kettle, 10s; two small earthern dishes, one broken one, 10d; old green rugg, 18s; two old Turkey work cushions, 7d; large good chest, 7s; one small trammell, an old frying pan, 6s-06; total, £3-17-10. Apprised by Moses Crafts and Thomas Wickham.

Court Record, Page 43—1st October, 1717: Upon motion of Joseph King of Hartford, that Adms. be granted on the estate of Josiah Bowen, sometime of Wethersfield, decd., this Court order a citation to Susannah Curtice, sometime the wife of said Bowen, to appear and show cause why Adms. should not be granted.

Page 44—5 November, 1717: Samuel Curtice, the present husband of the sd. Susannah, now appeared and took Adms. He was required to pay a charge due from the estate to Joseph King of £0-09-03.

Page 46—1 October, 1717: An inventory of the estate of Josiah Bowen, sometime of Wethersfield, deceased, was exhibited by Samuel Curtice of sd. Wethersfield, administrator. Accepted and ordered on file.

Page 93.

Brooks, Susannah, Wethersfield. Nuncupative will, dated 10 September, 1721 :

The testimony of Abigail and Lucy Robbins is as followeth: That Susannah Brooks, being very sicke and near her end, being asked what she intended to do with those worldly things, answered as followeth: That she would give to Thomas Robbins her chest in the chamber; and also that she would give to Lydia Brooks, the daughter of Samuel Brooks of Glastonbury, £6 in money; and also the money that was due to her in the hands of Samuel Robbins she gave to Samuel Robbins his children, to each of them 20 shillings, and the remainder of it that she would give to Joshua Robbins and Richard Robbins.

Witness: *Abigail Robbins,*
   Lucy Robbins.

Court Record, Page 159—5 December, 1721: Will accepted and proven, except the disposeing of 50 shillings to Joshua Robbins. Adms. granted unto Samuel Brooks of Glastonbury, brother of sd. decd.

Page 160—3 January, 1721-2: Samuel Brooks, Adms., exhibits an account of his Adms. Allowed. Order to dist. the estate: To Samuel Brooks, to Elizabeth Smith, to Mercy Brooks, and to Lydia Cook, brother and sisters of sd. decd., to each of them £5-19-08 1-2. And appoint Jonathan Belding, Joshua Robbins 2nd and Nathaniel Burnham, distributors.

Page 65.

Brown, John, Middletown. Invt. £135-06-03. Taken 23 November, 1719, by Joseph Rockwell, John Bacon and Robert Warner.

Will Copied from File:

I, John Brown of Middletown, do ordain and declare this to be my last will and testament: I give unto my wife Ann the one-third part of my moveable estate; also, the one-half of my now dwelling house, the north end, and half the benefit of the cellar, dureing her widowhood; and also the improvement and yearly rent of the north half of my farm whereon I now dwell; also, I give unto my wife the improvement of a third part of my team, horse and oxen, and team eutensels, dureing her widowhood. I give unto my son John Brown the one equell half of my farm whereon I now dwell, the south half, and also the south half of my now dwelling house, and half the cellar and barn, and two-thirds of my team, horse and oxen, and team eutensels, and also all my husbandry eutensels and team tackling of what name soever, after my wife's decease or marriage. And also the whole of my farme and buildings thereon, after my wife's decease, excepting the yearly rent of the northernmost half of my farm land under improvement, which is for my wife's support during her natural life. And my son John to pay to my daughter Abigail Brown ten pounds as after expressed. I give unto my daughter Abigail Brown all my household effects [ ] name soever, excepting her mother's thirds; and also one cowe and ten pounds in or as current money, to be paid to her by her brother John Brown, whome I do appoint executor of this my last will and testament. And I do appoint my well-respected friends, Mr. William Russell and Joseph Rockwell, to be overseers of this my last will.

Agreement:

Know all men by these presents: That we, Ann Brown, John Brown and Abigail Brown, the relict, son and daughter of John Brown, late of Middletown, in the Colony of Connecticutt, do declare and signify our consent and allowance of what is written on the other side as the last will of the sd. John Brown. And do agree for ourselves respectively that the same shall be a full settlement of the estate of the sd. deceased amongst us forever.

In witness whereof wee have hereunto set our hands and seals, 5 July, 1720.   ANN BROWN, X LS.
                                                JOHN BROWN, X LS.
                                                ABIGAIL BROWN, X LS.
Acknowledged in Court.

Test: Hez. Wyllys, Clerk.

Court Record, Page 129—5 July, 1720: Adms. granted to Ann Brown, widow, and John Brown, son of the decd.

Page 115-16-17.

Brown, Peter, Windsor. Invt. £296-18-08. Taken by William Phelps, John Palmer and Samuel Phelps. Will dated 2 February, 1721-2.

I, Peter Brown of Windsor, doe make this my last will and testament: I give unto my son Peter all my lands lying in a place called Scotland; also, I ratify and confirm to him what I have already given to him by deed of guift. I give to my son Samuel my dwelling house and land adjoining; also, I give my barn and the land adjoining, about 3 acres be it more or less, unto my son Samuel. I give to my son Samuel my lott which was formerly Nathaniel Gillett's, that I bought of Enock Drake. I give unto my two daughters, Dinah and Mary, the use and improvement of my lott that was formerly Jonathan Gillett's, that I bought of Enock Drake, in equal proportion, for the space of 10 years, and at the end of the terme of 10 years my will and pleasure is that my son Peter shall have that land to be his and his heirs forever. I give unto my daughter Dinah one piece of land, about one acre, which was my father Barbour's. I give unto my three daughters, Dinah, Mary and Mindwell, my woodlott, being about 8 acres. I give them, to be divided equally between them, 1-4 part of a 12-acre lott which I had out of my father Barbour's estate. I give them my land on the Mill Brook, to be to them and their heirs forever. I appoint my loving brothers, John Brown and Cornelius Brown, to be my executors, and my executors shall be overseers and guardians over my children.
Witness: *Jonathan Brown,*   PETER BROWN, LS.
    Abigail X *Enno, Esther Barber.*

The last will and testament of Peter Brown was exhibited in Court 15 March, 1722, and proven. This Court appoint Samuel Phelps of Windsor to be guardian to Samuel Brown, son of Peter Brown. Recog., £80. And Jonathan Brown appointed guardian to Mary Brown, 13 years of age. Recog., £40.

Page 235-6.

Brown, Thomas, Colchester. Invt. £182-15-08. Taken 2 May, 1717, by Joseph Chamberlain and Nathaniel Foote. Will dated 27 November, 1716.

I, Thomas Brown of Colchester, husbandman, do make this my last will and testament: I give and bequeath unto Hannah, my dearly beloved wife, the use and improvement of my dwelling house and home place so long as she shall remain my widow, together with all my pewter, one bed and covering convenient to the same, and one iron pot, one iron kettle, 2 chests at her own choice, and one box, one trammell, fire-slice, tongs, 2 chaires, with other wooden ware suitable and convenient for housekeeping, 2 cows, 6 sheep; the moveable estate above mentioned to be her own forever. I give my son Thomas Brown 10 shillings, haveing already advanced him by deeds of gift and other estate. Item. I give and bequeath unto my daughter Hannah Brown £30. I give unto my daughter Mary Brown £30. I give unto my daughter Sarah Brown £30. I give to my daughter Kezia Brown £30. I give to my grandson Daniel Brown, my son Samuel Brown his eldest son, my fourth division of land in Colchester, containing fifty acres, together with £50 right in the Commons or undivided land, with all priviledges to the same belonging. And further my will is, that except my son Samuel Brown do bring up his eldest son to learning so as (to) qualify him for an orthodox minister of the Gospel, then I give and bequeath unto him my sd. grandson Daniel Brown £12 out of my estate, to be paid to him when he shall come of lawfull age. I give unto my son Samuel Brown, whom I likewise constitute and ordain my sole executor, all and singular the remainder of my houseing and land, messuages and tenements in Colchester, together with all my debts and moveable estate.

Witness: *James Treadway,*   THOMAS BROWN, SEN., LS.
Jonathan Kellogg, Charles Loomis.

Court Record, Page 33—4 June, 1717: Will proven.

Page 52—4 March, 1717-18: This Court appoint Samuel Brown to be guardian unto Keziah Brown, a minor, age 11 years, daughter of Thomas Brown, late of Colchester, decd.

Page 321.

Buell, Ephraim, Simsbury. Died 16 January, 1719. Invt. £263-05-00. Taken by Nathaniel Holcomb, Sen., Thomas Holcomb and Joshua Holcomb.

Court Record, Page 103—5 May, 1719: Adms. granted to Mary Buell, widow.

Page 255-6.

Bunce, Jonathan, Hartford. Invt. £385-19-02. Taken 6 January, 1718, by Nathaniel Stanly and John Austin. Invt. of lands in Wethersfield, prised at £426-03-00, taken 1st January, 1718, by Benjamin' Churchill and Josiah Churchill.

Court Record, Page 47—11 December, 1717: Adms. granted to Sarah Bunce, the widow, relict of sd. decd., and Robert Sandford.

Page 50—25 January, 1717-18: Zachariah Bunce, a minor, age 15 years, chose his mother Sarah Bunce to be his guardian. She was also appointed guardian to the rest of her children, viz., Susannah, age 13 years, Sarah 11, Abigail 9, and Jonathan Bunce about 8 years, all children of Jonathan Bunce decd. Recog., £200.

Page 85—7 October, 1718: Per act of the General Assembly in May last, this Court direct Robert Sandford and Sarah Bunce, Adms., to sell land lying in Wethersfield to procure the sum of £100 for the payment of debts.

Page 9 (Vol. X) 5 March, 1722-3: In pursuance of an act of the General Assembly, May, 1718, impowering the Adms. to sell so much of the lands of the sd. decd. that may be sufficient for the payment of debts due from sd. estate, with the allowance of this Court, Lt. Robert Sandford and Sarah Bunce, Adms., are hereby directed and allowed to sell a parcell of land lying at the west division of lotts in Hartford to pay debts yet due from sd. estate.

Page 43—27 March, 1724: The Adms. may now sell land lying on the east side of the Connecticut River in Hartford, containing 5 acres more or less.

Page 302.

Burge, John, Windsor. Died June, 1718. Invt. £148-09-00. Taken 9th October, 1718, by Samuel Rockwell and John Elsworth.

Court Record, Page 87—4 November, 1718: Adms. to Abigail Burge, widow.

Page 80-1-4.

Burnham, John, Hartford. Invt. £487-18-07. Taken 15 May, 1721, by Samuel Burnham and Jabez Colt. Will dated 12th April, 1721.

I, John Burnham, do make and ordain this my last will and testament: I give to my loving wife 1-3 part of all my houseing and land; also 1-3 part of all personal estate to be at her own dispose. I give my son John Burnham 10 acres of meadow land, being part of my lower lott, he to have it on the south side of sd. lott as is abutted southerly on land of Samuel Burnham and Richard Gilman, the east end to be at the upland, the west end at Podunk River, the north side to be a straight line from the upland to Podunk River. Also, I give to my son John 17 acres of upland on the east side of the country road which lies westward of sd. son's now dwelling house. I give unto my three sons, Jonathan Burnham, Jabez Burnham and Caleb Burnham, all the rest of my meadow land and swamp land in Podunk Meadow (not given to my son John) to be equally divided between them. As to the number of acres, my sons Jonathan and Jabez to have my upper lott, my son Caleb to have his part next to and abutting upon the 10 acres of meadow given my son John. The remainder of my lower lott to be equally divided between my sd. sons Jonathan and Jabez. Also, I give to son Jonathan 1-2 of my piece of land lying westward of the lane or way that runs westward of my dwelling house to John Morton's house, my sd. son to have the north half of sd. piece of land; and also I give sd. Jonathan 1-4 part of all my land which lyeth eastward of the 17 acres of upland given to my son John. Also, I give to my son Jabez 1-2 of my dwelling house. I give unto my son Caleb 1-2 of my piece of land lying westward of the beforementioned lane or way to John Morton's house; also the easterly part of my orchard. Also I give my son Caleb the other half of my dwelling house and the land it standeth on, for and during the term of 10 years after he come to the age of 21 years, and at the end of that time the sd. half of my house to belong to my son Jabez. I give unto my daughter Mary Webster £10. I give unto my 4 daughters, Rachell, Amy, Sarah and Elizabeth, all the rest of my moveables or personal estate not before in this my will disposed of, to be equally divided between them. But my will is that if the sd. estate given to my 4 daughters shall or do not amount to the value of £35 as money at the inventory price for each of my sd. 4 daughters, that then my 4 sons, John, Jonathan, Jabez and Caleb, shall pay unto each of my sd. 4 daughters so much as will make up each of their portions to the sum of £35 as money, to be recovered of them or either of them my sd. sons as shall neglect or refuse to pay his part of the same to my sd. daughters or either of them within one year after their portions become due to them. I make my wife Mary executrix, and my son John Burnham executor.

Witness: *William Pitkin,*   JOHN BURNHAM, LS.
        Samuel Burnham, John Morton.

Court Record, Page 150—2 May, 1721: Will proven.

Page 242.

Buttolph, David, Simsbury. Died 5 April, 1717. Invt. £205-00-08. Taken 2 May, 1717, by Benjamin Addams, Joshua Holcomb, Sen., and William Case.

Court Record, Page 40—6 August, 1717: Adms. granted to Mary Buttolph, widow, and Jonathan Buttolph, son of the decd.

Page 114—1st December, 1719: Joseph Case, of Simsbury, appointed guardian to Mary Buttolph, about 13 years of age, daughter of sd. deceased.

Page 23 (Vol. X) 2 July, 1723: David Buttolph, a minor, 15 years of age, chose Daniel Case of Simsbury to be his guardian.

Page 30—1 October, 1723: Mary and Jonathan Buttolph, Adms., exhibit now an account of their Adms. Accepted. Order to dist. the estate:

	£ s d
To Mary Buttolph, widow,	10-02-04
To Jonathan Buttolph, eldest son,	29-02-01
To Martha Addams,	2-05-00
To David Buttolph, Penelope Case, Silence Mather, Mehetabell Holcomb, Mary Buttolph, Hannah and Temperance Buttolph, to each,	14-11-00

And appoint Joseph Case, Benjamin Addams and Daniel Porter distributors. This Court appoint Mary Buttolph to be guardian to her children, Hannah, age 11 years, and Temperance, 9 years, children of David Buttolph, late of Simsbury decd.

Page 329-30.

Cadwell, Edward, Hartford. Invt. £826-10-10. Taken by John Shepherd, James Ensign and George Sexton. Will dated 2 January, 1716-17.

I, Edward Cadwell, Sen., of Hartford, do now make this my last will and testament: I give to my wife Elizabeth the use and improvement of 1-3 part of all my houseing and land during the term of her natural life, and 1-3 part of my moveable estate to be at her own dispose forever. I also give her my negro or malatto boy Diego during the time my sd. wife shall continue my widow, and when that time shall terminate my will is my son William shall have sd. Diego, to be to him forever. I give my son Edward Cadwell 1 piece of upland near the north part of the Township of Hartford and within the sd. Township, containing about 5 or 6 acres, bounded upon land of the heirs of Richard Lord, Esqr., deceased, and upon the West River west; also two acres of land, little more or less, in the south meadow, bounded east upon Col. Partridge's land, west upon Capt. Joseph Whiting, south upon John Catlin, north upon John Shepherd, or land improved by them; also one piece of land in the sd. meadow, about two acres, abbuted upon a highway east, land of Nathaniel Stanly's south, upon land of the heirs of Thomas Bunce north; and also one piece in the long meadow, containing about one acre, abbutted upon the Great River easterly, land sometime since improved by Thomas Olcott deceased north, and Mr. Nathaniel Stanly's south, Capt. Joseph Wadsworth west. All which parcells of land I give to my sd. son Edward forever. Also 15 acres, more or less, lying in a greater parcell half whereof I have given

him by deed, butts on Deacon Easton's heirs east, on West River west, etc., in the same tenure. Item. All the rest of my lands, whatsoever and wheresoever situate, I give unto my two sons, the sd. Edwaid Cadwell and my son William Cadwell, to be equally divided between them. Item. I give unto my two daughters, Elizabeth and Rachel, to each of them, the sum of £50 reckoned in money. And further my will is, that after my decease John Cadwell, who now dwells and is bound to me, if I happen to die before his time is out, shall go to my sonn William according to the indentures, and that my sd. sonn William shall pay the £20 due by the sd. indenture unto the sd. John when his time is out. My will also further is, that if the sd. Diego happen to live so that by force of this my will he come to serve my sonn William, my sd. sonn William shall, in consideration thereof, pay to each of my two daughters or their heirs the sum of £5 current money. I appoint my two sons executors. In witness whereof I have hereunto sett my hand and seal this second day of January, *Anno RiRs Georgij Mage: Brite., &c., Tertio, Anno Dom.* 1716-17.
Witness: *Daniel Smith,*   EDWARD CADWELL, LS.
       Tho. Kimberly.

Court Record, Page 108—7 July, 1719: Will proven.

Page 9 (Vol. X) 5 March, 1722-3: An agreement for the settlement of the real estate of Edward Cadwell was now exhibited by Edward Cadwell and William Cadwell, sons, and they acknowledged the same to be their free act and deed, which this Court accepts, orders recorded and kept on file.

Page 334.

Cadwell, Matthew, Hartford. Invt. £830-10-11. Taken 30 June, 1719, by John Marsh, Jr., Nathaniel Stanly and Joseph Gilbert.

Court Record, Page 106—10 June, 1719: Adms. to Abigail Cadwell, widow, and Matthew Cadwell, son of sd. decd. Rec., £300, with Jonathan Easton.

Page 151—20 May, 1721: Abigail Cadwell, alias Leet, and Matthew Cadwell, Adms. on the estate of Matthew Cadwell decd., exhibit account of Adms. Accepted. Order dist. of the sd. estate as followeth, viz: To the sd. Abigail Leete, late widow of the deceased, 1-3 part of the moveable estate, and 1-3 part of the houseing and lands for her improvement during life. And the residue of sd. estate, including the widow's thirds in houseing and lands after her decease, is to be dist. to the children, viz:, To Matthew Cadwell, eldest son, a double portion; to the rest of the children, to Ann, John, Abell, Daniel, Abigail and Elias Cadwell, to each of them their single portions. And this Court appoint Nathaniel Stanly, Nathaniel Goodwin, weaver, and Joseph Gilbert, of Hartford, distributors. This Court also appoint Mr. Caleb Leete of Guilford guardian unto Abigail Cadwell, a minor, 9 years of age, and Elias Cadwell, 8 years, children of the deceased. Recog., £100. Matthew Cadwell is appointed guardian to his brother Daniel Cadwell. Recog., £50.

Page 160—3 January, 1721-2: This Court now appoint Matthew Cadwell guardian to his brother Abell Cadwell, a minor, 17 years of age. Recog., £50. Dist. as per file, 1721:

	£ s d		£ s d
To Matthew,	181-16-06	To Elias,	89-08-03
To John,	89-08-03	To Anne,	89-08-03
To Abell,	89-08-03	To Abigail,	90-12-02
To Daniel,	89-08-03		

By Nathaniel Stanly, Nathaniel Goodwin and Joseph Gilbert.

Another dist. of sd. Cadwell's estate distributed to the Widow Abigail Leete, allowing her £100-03-02, appears on file. (No date given.)

Page 47 (Vol. X) 7 April, 1724: Daniel Cadwell, a minor son, about 15 years of age, chose John Cadwell of Hartford to be his guardian.

Page 55—1st September, 1724: John Cadwell, a son of Matthew Cadwell, late decd., moves this Court that whereas the persons formerly appointed to dist. sd. estate did not set out the houseing and land by meets and bounds, this Court appoint Nathaniel Goodwin, John Skinner and Joseph Gilbert, Jr., to set out the houseing and lands unto the relict by meets and bounds.

Page 315.

Chapman, Hannah, Windsor. Invt. £22-07-00. Taken 2 December, 1718, by Ebenezer Fitch and Samuel Strong. Invt. exhibited by Jonathan Humphrey and Simon Chapman, Adms.

Page 307.

Church, Samuel, Hartford. Invt. £261-17-16. Taken 17 December, 1718, by Nathaniel Goodwin and George Sexton.

Court Record, Page 91—6 January, 1718-19: Adms. granted to Elizabeth Church, widow of sd. decd., and George Sexton.

Page 133 (Vol. X) 5 July, 1726: This Court add and appoint Ensign James Church of Hartford to be Adms. with the widow Elizabeth Church and George Sexton. And the sd. James Church and Joseph Barnard before this Court acknowledged themselves joyntly and severally bound to the Judge of this Court that the sd. James Church shall faithfully administer on sd. estate.

Page 145—7 February, 1726-7: The Adms. on the estate of Samuel Church exhibit an account: Paid in debts and charges, more than what had been received due to sd. estate, the sum of £54-04-06; inventory, £261-16-07; subtracting £54-04-06, there remains £107-12-01 to be distributed. Order to Elizabeth Church, widow relict, £11-04-01, with dower; to Samuel Church, eldest son, £65-09-04, his double portion; to Ebenezer, Esther, Sarah and Elizabeth Church, the rest of the children of sd. decd., to each of them £32-14-08, which is their single portion. And appoint Nathaniel Goodwin, Edward Cadwell and Charles Kelsey, distributors.

Page 52.

Churchill, Nathaniel, Wethersfield. Invt. £371-05-06. Taken 28 February, 1715-16, by Benjamin Churchill, Jabez Whittlesey and Josiah Churchill.

Court Record, Page 18—3 July, 1716: Adms. granted to Mary Churchill, widow and relict of sd. decd.

Page 96 (Vol. X) 3 August, 1725: Marcy Churchill, Adms., exhibits account: Paid in debts and charges, £18-08-08; the inventory, £371-05-00; subtracting £18-08-08, there remains £352-16-04 to be dist. Order to Mary Churchill, widow, £37-07-01, with dower; to Nathaniel Churchill, eldest son, £130-03-09, which is his double portion; to John, Daniel and Josiah Churchill, the rest of the children, to each of them £65-01-10, which is their single portion. And appoint Benjamin Churchill, Jabez Whittlesey and Josiah Churchill to be distributors.

Page 305.

Clark, Joseph, Windsor. Died 7 July, 1718. Invt. £17-02-00. Taken by Thomas Griswold, Jr., and Matthew Griswold.

Court Record, Page 90—6 January, 1718-19: Adms. to Samuel Clark of Simsbury.

Page 43.

Clarke, John, Windsor. Invt. £41-13-01. Taken 1715, by Daniel Loomis and Eleazer Hill.

Court Record, Page 3—3 January, 1715: Adms. granted to Mary Clarke, the widow.

Page 148—5th Tuesday in April, 1721: Mary Randall, alias Clark, Adms., exhibits an account of her Adms. Accepted. Order to dist. the estate as followeth:

	£	s	d
To Mary Randall, alias Clarke, her thirds in houseing and lands.			
To Solomon Clarke, eldest son,	16-18-08		
To Daniel, Benoni and Elizabeth Clarke, to each,	8-09-04		
To Jemima Cooley,	2-09-01		
To Mary Cooley,	7-11-04		
To the heirs children of Hannah Gillett,	5-13-10		
To Martha Eglestone,	4-18-10		

And appoint Daniel Loomis and Timothy Loomis distributors.

Page 167—1st May, 1722: This Court grant Mary Randall, alias Clarke, a *Quietus Est.*

Page 284.

Cole, Samuel, Farmington. Invt. £309-13-08. Taken 30 July, 1718, by Isaac Cowles and John Hart.

Court Record, Page 79—2 September, 1718: Adms. to Mary Cole, widow and relict.

Page 79 (Vol. X) 6 April, 1725: This Court appoint Samuel Lewis, Jr., of Farmington, to be guardian unto Samuel Cowles, age 16 years, Ann Cowles, 13 years, and Susannah, 9 years of age. Recog., £200.

Page 130—5 May, 1726: Samuel Newell asks this Court for a partition of land now in right of himself and Samuel Cole, a minor, sd. land lying south of the reserved lands between the mountains. This Court appoint Capt. William Wadsworth, John Hart and Samuel Lewis to be guardians to the sd. minors, to make a division and allottment of land in proportion according to the right of each therein.

Page 125 (Vol. XII, Probate Side): Whereas, Samuel Newell, Jr., and Samuel Cole, a minor, both of Farmington, having a right to land lying in partnership in the 26th lott in number as the lotts were drawn and laid out in the south division of land between the mountains and in the County of Farmington and undivided, we whose names are hereafter subscribed, being appointed by the Court of Probate, 12th May, 1726, to assist Samuel Lewis, guardian to sd. Samuel Cole, minor, in dividing sd. lott of land according to the trust committed unto us, having in company with sd. Samuel Newell, Jr., and Samuel Lewis, guardian, and Samuel Cole, minor, carefully run by the needle of a compass and viewed sd. lott of land from end to end, and find in our judgements the south side of sd. lott to be as good land as the north side, therefore have divided sd. lott as follows: Set out to sd. Samuel Newell, Jr., his part of sd. lott according to his purchased right on the north side of sd. lott; also set out to Samuel Cole, minor, his part of sd. lott according to the number of acres as appears by dist. of his father, Samuel Cole deceased, estate on the south part of sd. lott.

WILLIAM WADSWORTH,
JOHN HART.

Court Record, Page 136 (Vol. X) 4 October, 1726: A return of the setting out of the lands was exhibited in Court and accepted.

Page 263.

Cole, Samuel, Wethersfield. An agreement: Know all men by these presents: That we whose hands and seals are hereunto affixed, being children of Samuel Cole, late of Wethersfield decd., and heirs to his estate together with our mother (the widow or relict of the deceased), have agreed to divide and distribute sd. estate amongst ourselves as followeth: 1st. To Lydia Cole, the widow or relict of the deceased, 1-3 part of the whole estate during her natural life, to be taken out of each and every part as it is set out to each child respectively, as she shall choose, and also the now dwelling house for her to live in, and after her decease to be equally divided among us.

	£	s	d
2ndly, to Joseph Cole,	61	13	00
3rdly, to Thomas Cole,	63	13	00
4thly, to Lydia Cole,	25	06	08

And that this is our agreement relating to the premises, we hereunto set our hand and affix our seals this 1st day of April, in the fourth year of his Majestie's reign, Annoq Dom. 1718.

LYDIA X COLE, LS.
JOSEPH COLE, LS.
THOMAS COLE, LS.
LYDIA X COLE, LS., DAUGHTER.

The within-named Lydia Cole, Joseph Cole, Thomas Cole and Lydia Cole, the daughter, appeared before the Court of Probates held at Hartford first day of April, Anno. Dom. 1718, and acknowledged the within written instrument to be their free and voluntary act and deed.

Test: Hez: Wyllys, Clerk of Probates.

Page 280.

Colt, Abraham, Glastonbury. Died 31 August, 1717. Invt. £126-06-06. Taken by Thomas Hale and William Wickham.

Court Record, Page 74—5 August, 1718: Adms. granted to Susannah Colt, widow.

Page 24 (Vol. XI) 7 July, 1730: Isaac Colt, a minor, 14 years of age, chose Jonathan Hills to be his guardian.

Page 40—2 March, 1730-1: Abraham Colt, a minor, 16 years of age, chose David Hills to be his guardian. Recog., £100.

Page 44—4 May, 1731: Jonathan Hill, guardian to Isaac Coult, a minor, showing to this Court that Abraham Coult, Sen., of the Town of Glastonbury, did sell and convey unto Abraham Coult, Jr., father to sd. Isaac Coult, half his sd. Abraham Coult, Sen., his lands, viz., half his orchard and half his dwelling house in Glastonbury, to be equally divided between the sd. Abraham Coult, Sen., and sd. Abraham Coult, Jr., his heir, in quality and quantity, and the sd. Abraham Coult, Jr., being deceased, sd. Hill, being guardian to Isaac, one of his children, desired a division to sd. Abraham Colt, the donor also desireing the same: This Court appoint Capt. Thomas Welles, Ensign Jonathan Hale and Gershom Smith of Glastonbury, with Jonathan Hills, guardian to Isaac Colt, and David Hills, guardian to Abraham Colt, to make division and set out to Abraham Colt, Sen., one moiety or half-part, and the other moiety or half-part to the aforesd. minors, Isaac Colt, Abraham Colt and Mary Colt.

Page 16 (Vol. XII) 13 December, 1734: Abraham Colt, a minor, age 20 years, with David Hills, his guardian, mutually desires a release and discharge of the guardian, which was granted by the Court, when the sd. minor chose his grandfather, Abraham Colt, to be his guardian. Recog., £20.

Page 81.

Colt, Joseph, Windsor. Invt. £83-03-04. Taken 17 March, 1720-21, by Henry Wolcott and Samuel Elmer.

Court Record, Page 149—4 April, 1721: Adms. to Ruth Colt, widow.

Page 153—6 June, 1721: The moveable estate of Joseph Colt, amount £29-03-04, this Court allow Ruth Colt, widow, to have that for her subsistence.

Page 270-1.

Cone, Jared, Haddam. Died 11 April, 1718. Invt. £496-05-03. Taken by Joshua Braynard, Timothy Fuller and Daniel Cone.

Court Record, Page 66—3 June, 1718: Adms. granted to Stephen Cone, son of the sd. decd.

Page 91—6 January, 1718-19: Stephen Cone, Adms., exhibits an account of his Adms. Accepted. Order to distribute:

	£ s d
Addition to the inventory,	37-04-02
There remains to be dist. the sum of,	494-04-00
To Stephen Cone, eldest son,	164-14-08
To Thomas, Elizabeth, Ruth and Hannah Cone, to each,	82-07-09

And appoint Thomas Gates, Daniel Braynard and Daniel Cone, of Haddam, distributors.

Page 92—6 January, 1718-19: This Court appoint Capt. Daniel Braynard of Haddam to be guardian unto Elizabeth Cone, and Daniel Cone to be guardian unto Ruth Cone, and Ebenezer Cone of sd. Haddam to be guardian to Hannah Cone. And Daniel Braynard, Daniel Cone and Ebenezer Cone each of them acknowledged themselves joyntly and severally bound in a recog. of £50.

Page 91 (Probate Side): Whereas, our loving uncle, Daniel Cone, Sen., has in the quality of a guardian taken and had the oversight and care of that part of our father's estate, viz., Garred Cone deceased, ordered by the Court of Probate, and sett out to us by the dist. of sd. estate, wee do thankfully acknowledge our abovesd. uncle's care and faithfullness in the discharge of that trust, and do by these (presents) discharge him of all future care and trouble about the abovesd. part of our father's estate bestowed on us, acknowledging ourselves to have received the whole belonging to us and comitted to him, and that wee are sattisfied with his doings relating to every part of his trust on our behalf. And in testimony of his discharge and our sattisfaction, wee have hereunto sett our hands this 14 September, 1727.

Signed in Haddam East Side:

SAMUEL EMMONS, Jr.,
RUTH X CONE, *alias* EMMONS.

Page 64.

Cooke, Aaron, Hartford, son of Noah Cooke. Invt. £255-05-04. Taken by Thomas Richards and Daniel Merrells. Will dated 11 May, 1720.

I, Aaron Cooke, son of Noah Cooke, of Hartford, do make this my last will and testament: Item. I give and bequeath to my hond. mother, Sarah, all my real estate, the profits and incomes thereof, during her widowhood. And also I give my mother all my moveable estate of what nature and kind soever, to be at her own dispose forever. Item. I give and bequeath all my real estate and my land in North Hampton and my houseing and land in Hartford, at or after my sd. mother's marriage or decease, unto all my brothers and sisters, to be equally divided between them and their heirs forever, namely, Joseph Cooke, Noah Cooke, Eliakim Cooke, and Sarah Merrells, Elizabeth Clark, Miriam Webster and Esther Wright. I make my honoured mother to be sole executrix.

Witness: *Thomas Richards,*　　　AARON COOKE, LS.
Samuel Webster, John Seymour.

Court Record, Page 128—7 June, 1720: Will proven.

Page 308.

Crane, Jacob, Wethersfield. Invt. £77-02-04. Taken 2 January, 1718-19, by Edward Bulkeley and Richard Robbins.

Court Record, Page 82—16 September, 1718: Adms. granted to Jonathan Crane of Windham and William Warner of Wethersfield.

Page 105—2 June, 1719: William Warner, Adms., exhibited an account of debts. Accepted and ordered to be kept on file.

Page 114—1st December, 1719: Pursuant to an act of the General Assembly of May last, that the lands of Jacob Crane may be sold for the payment of his debts, this Court order William Warner to post the sd. lands for sale 15 days to the highest bidder.

Page 93.

Cross, John, Windsor. Invt. £235-01-09. Taken 17 August, 1721, by Jonathan Elsworth, Ebenezer Fitch and Samuel Strong.

Court Record, Page 156—1st August, 1721: Adms. to Symon Chapman of Windsor.

Page 160—5th December, 1721: Adms. to Joshua Hoyte of Stamford, with Symon Chapman.

Page 163—20 December, 1721: Adms. account allowed. Paid in debts and charges, £41-11-00; the inventory was £245-16-07; £41-11-00 subtracted, there remains £204-05-07 to be distributed. Order to dist. to the widow and co-heirs: To Mary Cross, widow relict (dower) and £26-12-09 forever; to the heirs of Nathaniel Cross deceased, £44-08-02; to the heirs of Sarah Bates deceased, £44-08-02; to the heirs of Mary Pickett decd., £44-08-02; to the heirs of Hannah Jagger deceased, £44-08-02; the brother and sisters of the said deceased. And this Court appoint Ebenezer Fitch, Samuel Allyn and James Enno, distributors.

Page 123.

Crowfoot, Joseph, Wethersfield. Invt. £37-14-06. Taken 1st October, 1722, by Ephraim Goodrich and Jonathan Curtice.

Court Record, Page 176—2 October, 1722: Adms. granted unto Margaret Crowfoot, widow.

Page 59.

Curtis, John, Wethersfield. Invt. £1127-18-07. Taken 18 March, 1714-15, by Benjamin Churchill and William Burnham.

Court Record, Page 5—7 February, 1715-16: Thomas Curtis, Adms., exhibits an account of his Adms. Order to dist. the estate as followeth:

	£ s d
To Lydia Curtice, the widow,	52-17-05
To the heirs of John Curtice, Jr., decd.,	266-10-02
To Thomas, William and Jonathan Curtice, to Dorothy Bridgman, to Elizabeth Woodruff, and to Abigail Lewis, to each,	133-05-01

And appoint Benjamin Churchill, James Patterson of Wethersfield, and Joseph Hawley of Farmington, distributors.

Page 20—7 August, 1716: Mrs. Lydia Curtis, widow, objects to the dist.

Page 22—4 September, 1716: This Court direct the dist., in setting out the dowry to Mrs. Lydia Curtis, to take into account what had been given to the children during the lifetime of their father John Curtis, so that she be not thereby abridged of her thirds therein.

Page 92.

Day, Jonathan, Windsor. Invt. £281-05-07. Taken 14 September, 1721, by Samuel Rockwell and David Bissell.

Court Record, Page 158—5 December, 1721: Adms. granted to Thomas Day of Colchester.

Page 19 (Vol. X) 7 May, 1723: Thomas Day of Colchester, Adms., exhibits an account of his Adms. on sd. estate, amounting to the sum of £82-03-01, which this Court doth accept.

Page 87.

Denison, Mary, Wethersfield. Died 18 May, 1721. Invt. £376-05-04. Taken 23 June, 1721, by Edward Bulkeley, Jonathan Deming and Ebenezer Belding.

Court Record, Page 155—4 July, 1721: Adms. granted to Joshua Robbins, son of sd. decd.

Page 161—3 January, 1721-2: Joshua Robbins, Adms., exhibits now an account of his Adms. Allowed. Order to dist. the estate:

	£ s d
To Joshua Robbins, eldest son,	177-12-06
To Samuel and Richard Robbins, to each of them,	88-16-03

And appoint Jonathan Belding, Nathaniel Burnham and Ebenezer Belding distributors.

Page 178—6 November, 1722: Joshua Robbins, Samuel Robbins and Richard Robbins exhibit an agreement of the settlement of the estate, approved under their hands and seals. Accepted.

Page 240.

Dewey, Daniel, Farmington. Invt. £192-01-04. Taken May, 1717, by Nathaniel Winchell and Thomas Curtice.

Court Record, Page 34—4 June, 1717: This Court grant letters of Adms. unto Katharine Dewey, widow and relict of the deceased.

Page 62.

De Wholph, Joseph, Middletown. Invt. £69-15-06. Taken 18 May, 1720, by Joseph Rockwell and John Collins.

Court Record, Page 127—10 May, 1720: Adms. granted to Elizabeth De Wholph, the widow.

Page 137—10 October, 1720: Capt. Joseph Rockwell exhibits an account of debts due from the estate for the subsistence of the widow, £26-04-10.

Page 69 (Vol. X) 2 February, 1724-5: Elizabeth De Wholph, Adms., exhibited an account of her Adms. Accepted. Order to dist: to the widow, 1-3 part of the houseing and lands, and to Azuba De Wholph and Elizabeth De Wholph, the two daughters of the decd., an equal share of the real estate of the decd. And appoint Joseph Rockwell, John Bacon and John Collins, distributors.

Page 144—3 January, 1726-7: Elizabeth De Wholph, Adms., exhibited a further account of her Adms. Accepted. Order to dist. the estate: To the sd. Elizabeth De Wholph, widow, alias Lewis, 1-3 part of the moveable estate during her life, and the remainder to be equally divided to Elizabeth De Wholph and Azuba De Wholph, the daughters. And the Court appoint Joseph Rockwell, John Collins and John Bacon, distributors.

Page 254.

Dickinson, Thomas, Glastonbury. Invt. £440-16-09. Taken 28 September, 1717, by Thomas Hale and William Wickham.

Court Record, Page 43—1st October, 1717: Adms. granted to Mary Dickinson, the widow, and Joseph Dickinson, son of the decd.

Page 154—21 June, 1721: Mary and Joseph Dickinson, Adms., exhibit an account of their Adms. Accepted. Order to dist. the estate:
To Mary Dickinson, the widow, her dowry and the use of 1-3
  part of the houseing and lands during her natural life.

	£ s d
To Joseph Dickinson, eldest son,	61-09-10
To Charity Waddams,	24-05-00
To Phebe, Mary, David and Deborah Dickinson, to each,	30-14-11

And appoint Thomas Kimberly, Thomas Hale and Samuel Hale, distributors.

Page 168—9 May, 1722: This Court appoint John Bigelow of Colchester to be guardian to Deborah Dickinson, 15 years of age, daughter of Thomas Dickinson decd.

Page 42 (Vol. X) 3 March, 1723-4: This Court do now appoint Thomas Kimberly as formerly, and Thomas Hollister and Gershom Smith instead of Thomas and Samuel Hale, to dist. the estate of Thomas Dickinson, deceased. David Dickinson, a minor, 18 years of age, chose his brother Joseph Dickinson to be his guardian.

Page 56—29 September, 1724: Report of the distributors.

Page 61.

Diggins, Thomas, Windsor. Invt. £55-10-08. Taken 2 April, 1720, by William Wolcott and Samuel Elmor.

Court Record, Page 126—3 May, 1720: Adms. granted to Jeremiah Diggins, Jr., brother of sd. decd.

Page 276.

Dimock, Timothy, Ashford. Invt. £56-07-00. Taken 26 May, 1718, by Daniel Fuller and Joshua Kendall.

Court Record, Page 72—8 July, 1718: Adms. granted to Abigail Dimock, widow.

Page 100.

Drake, Jonathan, Windsor. Invt. £153-16-02. Taken 2 July, 1716, by Samuel Rockwell, Samuel Moore and William Wolcott.

Court Record, Page 21—4 September, 1716: Adms. to Esther Drake, widow.

Page 45—2 December, 1717: Esther Drake, widow, exhibits an account of her Adms. Accepted. Order to dist. the estate: To Esther Drake, widow, for bringing up the children, £33-00-00; to Benjamin Drake, only son, a double portion of the estate; to Esther and Eunice Drake, daughters, their single portions. And appoint Samuel Rockwell, William Wolcott and Samuel Moore, distributors. This Court appoint Job Drake to be guardian to Benjamin Drake, son of sd. decd., and Mrs. Esther Drake to be guardian to her two daughters, Esther and Eunice Drake.

Page 260.

Dunham, Thomas, Mansfield, Yeoman. Died 30 January, 1717-18. Invt. £285-17-06. Taken by Shubael Dimock, Thomas Huntington and Thomas Storrs.

Court Record, Page 53—4 March, 1717-18: Adms. to John Dunham.

Page 164—23 March, 1721-22: John Dunham, Adms., exhibited an account of his Adms., which was accepted by the Court.

See File for Agreement:

This wrightin, made Jeneurie ye 17th, 1721-22, witnesseth an agreement made between the co-heirs of the estate of Thomas Dunham, late of Mansfield, decest, (viz.) : That whereas, our brother John Dunham hath returned his account of Adms. to ye Court of Probate, in the County of Hartford, to ye acceptance of the Court and to our acceptance, and it appeareth that there remaineth lands in the Town of Mansfield of our Brother Thomas Dunham aforesd., we the co-heirs, viz., John Dunham, Elisha Dunham, Benjamin Dunham, Desiah Studson and Marshy Dunham, having before the insealing of this agreement received full satisfaction from oure brother Ebenezer Dunham for all and every one of our parts of the estate that did belong to our brother Thomas Dunham deceased, we do therefore agree that our brother Ebenezer Dunham shall have all the lands and houseing yt is within the Township of Mansfield aforesd., or within the County of Hartford, that ever did or here after might any ways belong to our brother Thomas Dunham decest. And we, John Dunham, Elisha Dunham, Benjamin Dunham, Samuel Studson, Dessiah Studson and Marcy Dunham, do by these presents, for ourselves and heirs, quit all our and their claim, right and title in and to all the

forementioned premises unto our brother Ebenezer Dunham of Mansfield, in ye County of Hartford, and to his heirs, executors and administrators forever, so that nither we, John Dunham, Elisha Dunham, Benjamin Dunham, Samuel and Desia Studson and Mary Dunham, nor any of our heirs, shall have any right, title, interest or claim to ye forementioned premises or any part thereof, but shall hereby be utterly debared and excluded forever. As witness our hands and seals this 17th day of January, Anno Dominy.
Signed and sealed:

JOHN DUNHAM, LS.
ELISHA DUNHAM, LS.
BENJAMIN DUNHAM, LS.
SAMUEL STETSON, LS.
for DESIAH STUDSON, LS.
MARCY X DUNHAM, LS.
EBENEZER DUNHAM, LS.

Court Record, Page 171—17 January, 1721-22: At a Court of Probate held at Mansfield, in and for the County of Hartford: Present, Joseph Talcott, Esqr., Judge: An agreement for the settlement of the estate of Thomas Dunham, late of Mansfield decd., under the hands and seals of the heirs to sd. estate, was now exhibited in Court, and John Dunham, Elisha Dunham, Benjamin Dunham, Samuel Stetson, Desire Stetson, Marcy Dunham and Ebenezer Dunham, heirs to the sd. estate, before sd. Court appeared and acknowledged sd. agreement to be their free act and deed, which is ordered to be recorded.

Invt. in Vol. X, Page 2.   Will on File.

Dyxx, John, Hartford.   Invt. £107-06-04. Taken 30 August, 1722, by Charles Buckland and Philip Smith.   Will dated 28 May, 1722.

I, John Dike, Sen., of Hartford, being under some weakness of body but of sound and competent mind and memory, etc., do make and ordain my last will and testament: I give to my loveing wife Sarah Dike the 1-2 of my homelott, half the dwelling house, and half the profit of the orchard, at her own dispose, only what she dyes seased of shall bee and I hereby give it to my dafters now at home with me, viz., Rachell and Jemimah, free and clear forever. I give to my son Isaac Dike the one-half of my home lott, dwelling house, and half the orchard, and one piece of woodland lying northerly from my house, which I purchased of Philip Smith. I give to my son John Dike, to my dafters Margaret, wife of John Hills, Elizabeth Barnes, Susannah, wife of Jonathan Mason, Rachell Dike, Deborah Dike and Abigaill Dike, to each and every of them 5 shillings money or money's worth, to be paid one-half by Sarah my wife, the other half by my son Isaac Dike. I appoint my wife Sarah and son Isaac Dike to bee exetrix and executor. 28 May, 1722.
Witness: *Elizabeth Pitkin,*   JOHN DIKE.
Eliza: Pitkin, Jr., William Pitkin, Jr.

Back of the will of John Dike:

Hartford, October 2d, 1722.

Mrs. Elizabeth Pitkin, Elizabeth Pitkin, Jr., and William Pitkin, Jr., appeared and made oath that they see John Dike, Sen., sign, seal, and heard him declare the wrightin on the other side of this paper to be his last will and testament, on the day of the date thereof, and that he was then of disposeing mind and memory. Before me.

Hartford, Oct. 2, 1722: My wife and children say John Dix was very forgetfull at the time of making the within will, so I dought of giving them the above oath.

Wm. Pitkin, Attest.

Court Record, Page 176—7 October, 1722: An instrument was exhibited in Court to be the last will and testament of the sd. decd. Not proven. And this Court grant letters of Adms. unto John Hill, son-in-law.

Page 180—4 December, 1722: John Hill, Adms., exhibited an account of his Adms. Accepted. Order to dist. the estate:

	£ s d
To Sarah Dyxx, the widow and relict,	7-02-08
To John Dyxx, eldest son,	15-10-10
To Sarah Hunn, Margaret Hill, Elizabeth Barnes, Susannah Mason, Abraham, Isaac, Rachell, Deborah, Abigail and Jemima Dyxx, to each of them,	7-15-05

And appoint Timothy Cowles, Philip Smith and Charles Buckland, of Hartford, distributors.

Page 56 (Vol. X) 6 October, 1724: This Court appoint Stephen Bracy of Hartford to be guardian unto Jemima Dyxx, a minor, 15 years of age. Recog., £50.

Page 108-109.

Easton, John, Sen., Hartford. Invt. £756-10-11. Taken 28 December, 1718, by Daniel Merrells and Joseph Mygatt.

This 3d day of December, 1712, I, John Easton, Sen., of Hartford, in the County of Hartford and Colony of Connecticutt, in New England, being at the present in reasonable health but aged, and being now of sound mind and memory, do by these presents make and ordain this to be my last will and testament, in manner and form as followeth, vizt.: First, I desire to committ my soul into the hands of God my Creator and Jesus Christ my Redeemer, and my body to the grave to a decent buriall, there to rest in hope until the glorious resurection. I also do dispose of that part or portion of worldly goods which God has graciously given me, as follows: After my funeral charges are defrayed and all my just debts paid: Item. I give and bequeath unto my loveing son John Easton of Hartford, in the County and Colony aforesd., to him and his heirs forever, my dwelling house and barn and all the buildings, trees, fences and land thereunto belonging, namely, all my land at home and also all my land in Hartford, my two lotts at Rocky Hill, and all my land in the south meadow in Hartford, and also all my land lying on the east side of the Great River, and all my land at the West Division in Hartford. I do hereby give him my son John Easton all my lands in Hartford and elsewhere that I now stand possessed of, or may of lawfull right ever hereafter have right unto, with all the profits, priviledges and appurtenances that do or may at any time hereafter belong to them or any part of them. The butts and bounds of all my land herein given may and will fully appear on record. Further, I give unto my son John and his heirs forever, all my moveable estate, both without doors and within the house, of whatsoever nature or kind, in particular all my arms and amunition, and also my great Bible, and divinity books of Mr. Thomas Goodwin's works. I say all my estate, both real and personal, I give to my said son John and his heirs forever, he paying all the legacies hereafter by me appointed and named in this my last will. Item. I do hereby give and bequeath unto my four daughters, Sarah Goodwin, Mary Butler, Mehetabell Merrold and Abigail Easton, to them, that is to each of them, ye heirs, &c., the full sum of £40 in or as current money of the Colony, which said sums or legacies I do hereby appoint my son John Easton to pay or see paid and completed. And it is always hereby to be understood, and I do appoint, that whatsoever any of my daughters have already received shall be excepted and accounted as part of their portion, and John to make it up to them to £40 herein given to them and each of them. Further, I do, as a token of my love to my daughters, give to each of them, besides their portion above named, the sum of £4 as money, and do appoint my son John to pay the same unto each of them within the space of two years after my decease. Further, I do hereby constitute and appoint my loveing son John Easton to be the sole executor of this my last will and testament. The whole of all written I do declare to be my last will and testament. And in confirmation of all and every part of the premises, I have hereunto set my hand and seal this 3d day of December, in the year of our Lord one thousand seven hundred and eleven, and in the eleventh year of the reign of our sovereign Lady Queen Anne, Queen of Great Brittain, &c.

Signed and sealed in   JOHN EASTON, SEN., LS.
presence of us: *Caleb Bull,*
              Edw. Alleyn.
    Court Record, Page 26—1st January, 1716-17: Will now exhibited with inventory. Approved and allowed.

Page 53.

Edwards, John, Wethersfield. Died 25 March, 1716. Invt. £598-04-09. Taken by Philip Goff and Samuel Williams.
    Court Record, Page 17—3 July, 1716: Adms. granted to Lucy Edwards, widow.

Page 211 (Vol. X) 4 February, 1728-9: Lucy Edwards, Adms., exhibits an account of her Adms. Accepted, and ordered to be recorded and kept on file.

Page 266-287-8.

Edwards, Richard, Hartford. Invt. £1125-12-11. Taken 2 May, 1718, by John Austin, Thomas Meakins and Jonathan Arnold. Will dated 14 April, 1718.

I, Richard Edwards of Hartford, do make this my last will and testament: I give to my son Timothy £60. I give to my four eldest daughters £10 to each, viz., to Elizabeth, to Abigail, to Ann, and to Mabell. I give to my daughter Hannah £140; to my son Daniel, £50. I give to my son Samuel all my land in the long meadow in Hartford, also my new pasture lying by the road leading to Windsor, and also all my land in Colchester, lying in two pieces, containing 250 acres. I give him £20, to be payd when he is 21 years of age. I give unto my son John Edwards all other of my estate lying in cattle or kine, horses or swine, as also all sorts of corn or grain, cloth, woolen or linen, utensils of my house, timber, tools, houseing, lands, and whatsoever bills, bonds, debts, chattells and credits, and whatsoever appertains to me, either within doors or without, not given expressly before in this my last will, and do hereby oblige my son John to take due care and provide for his mother, my loving wife Mary, during her life, my son John to be sole executor. I desire brother Joseph Talcott and Sergt. John Skinner to be overseers.

Witness: *Jonathan Arnold,*   RICHARD EDWARDS, LS.
    Jonathan Bull.

A codicil was added, 15 April, 1718, witnessed by Jonathan Bull and Ichabod Wadsworth.

A 2nd codicil was added, dated 17 April, 1718, wherein he gave to Mary, the daughter and eldest child of my first wife, two shillings upon her demand.

Witness: *Jonathan Arnold,*   RICHARD EDWARDS, LS.
    Eunice Talcott.

Court Record, Page 65—6 May, 1718: Will proven.

Page 321.

Eliot, John, Esq., Windsor. Invt. £2045-01-04. Taken 9 April, to 1st July, 1719, by Daniel Bissell, Symon Chapman and Alexander Allyn; and lands at Colchester, valued at £140, apprised by Samuel Northam and Joseph Chamberlain.

Court Record, Page 100—3 April, 1719: The last will of Mr. John Eliot, late of Windsor deceased, dated 7 September, 1718, now exhibited in Court, wherein Mr. Jonathan Marsh, Mr. Ebenezer Fitch and Ensign

Jonathan Elsworth were named and appointed executors. Ebenezer Fitch and Jonathan Elsworth appeared in Court and declared that they accepted that trust. (Will not found.)

Page 104—12 May, 1719: Mrs. Mary Eliot made application to this Court that her right of dower in real estate might be set out to her. Roger Wolcott, Samuel Mather and Daniel Bissell were appointed to set out in severalty one-third part of the houseing and lands of the sd. decd.

Page 17 (Vol. XII) 6 January, 1734-5: Upon complaint of John Elsworth, executor of Mr. John Eliot decd., Mrs. Mary Eliot and Ann Eliot were summoned to Court to answer for concealing or withholding from sd. executor some estate. Mrs. Mary Eliot made default of appearance. Ann Eliot appeared and William Thrall, at the desire and in behalf of sd. Ann Eliot, pleads that the writ and process might abate in that the law of this Colony saith that the Adms. may make complaint to an Assistant and the Assistant may award warrants to apprehend the offender and bring him or her before sd. Assistant, who may bind the offender over to the Court of Probates to be examined, and no rule in the law does oblige such persons as conceal docts. of persons' estates to answer before the Court of Probates on oath except such persons be bound over as aforesd. Whereupon this Court considers the writ and process of examination shall abate.

Page 17—7 January, 1734-5: Mrs. Mary and Ann Eliot were heard before Joseph Talcott, Judge of Probate, when Mrs. Eliot declared they received of sd. Elsworth all the utensils in the house and warehouse, inventoried as mentioned.

Page 19—22 January, 1734-5: Roger Wolcott, atty. for Mrs. Eliot. The decree of the Court was adverse, and Mrs. Eliot appealed to the Superior Court.

Page 121.

Elmer, John, Windsor. Invt. £229-16-03. Taken 6 July, 1722, by Joseph Rockwell and John Anderson. .

Court Record, Page 170—27 June, 1722: Adms. to William and Thomas Elmer, sons of the deceased.

Page 123.

Elmore, John, Jr., Windsor. Invt. £25-13-02. Taken 6 July, 1722, by Joseph Rockwell, Jr., and John Anderson.

Court Record, Page 170—27 June, 1722: Adms. granted to William and Thomas Elmer, brothers of the sd. decd.

Page 70-71.

Elsworth, John, Lt., Windsor. Invt. £1778-04-06. Taken 18 November, 1720, by Nathaniel Loomis, Samuel Rockwell and David Bissell.

Court Record, Page 140—6 December, 1720: Adms. granted to Esther Elsworth, the widow, and John Elsworth, son of sd. decd.

Page 1 (Vol. X) 1st January, 1722-3: This Court appoint Esther Elsworth and John Elsworth to be guardians unto Anna Elsworth, age 17 years; and Esther and Daniel Elsworth are appointed guardians to Martha Elsworth, age 15 years; children of Lieut. John Elsworth, late of Windsor, decd. This Court also appoint the sd. Esther Elsworth to be guardian unto her daughter Ann Elsworth, a minor, 10 years of age.

Page 7—5 February, 1722-3: Esther and John Elsworth, Adms., exhibit an account of their Adms. Accepted. This Court order dist. of the estate, viz.:

	£ s d
To Esther Elsworth, widow,	52-05-00
To John Elsworth, eldest son,	429-14-06
To Daniel Elsworth, Esther Welles, Martha and Ann Elsworth, to each of them the sum of	214-17-03

And appoint Daniel White, Jonathan Elsworth and David Bissell, distributors.

Page 13—2 April, 1723: Upon motion made to this Court that the distribution of 2 farms among all the children would prove a great disadvantage, praying that the sd. farms may be set out to the two sons of the sd. Lt. John Elsworth decd., they paying to the daughters their proportional parts, there being no objection, this Court so order.

Page 284.

Elsworth, Josiah, Windsor. An agreement for settling the estate: This writing witnesseth, that Josiah Elsworth and Samuel Elsworth, sons of Josiah Elsworth deceased, and Jonathan Elsworth, executor to the last will of sd. Josiah Elsworth deceased, in behalf of the minor, Joseph Elsworth, do agree to divide all the land of sd. deceased (it being all given to sd. three sons by will). [Here follows the detail of bounds, with measurements in rods, feet and inches.]

Witness: *Samuel Mather, Jun.,*   JONATHAN ELSWORTH, LS.
   David Clark.   JOSIAH ELSWORTH, LS.
        SAMUEL ELSWORTH, LS.

Acknowledged 5 August, 1718.

       Samuel Mather, Just. Pac.

Elsworth, Martha. Court Record, Page 149—22 April, 1721: This Court grant letters of Adms. on the estate of Martha Elsworth unto Jonathan Elsworth of Windsor, Samuel Elsworth having refused.

Page 261.

Field, John, Coventry. Will not dated: I, John Field of Coventry, do dispose of my estate in manner and form following: I give to my wife Mary my house and homestead, with the first division of my land, during the time she remains my widow, with all the moveables. And if she marry again, she is to have only her thirds during her life; and after her decease they are to return to my children. Moreover, I constitute her the sole executrix of my estate. Further, it is my will that all my outlands, except what was before mentioned, shall be equally divided among my children, only my son John shall have ten acres more than any of the rest. It is my will that my homestead and first division shall equally be divided among my children after my wife's decease, or that she ceases to be my widow.

Witness: *Joseph Meacham,*   JOHN FIELD, LS.
     Samuel Parker.

    See File: At a Court of Probates holden in Coventry, for the County of Hartford, March the 6th, 1717-18, present Joseph Talcott, Judge: Mr. Joseph Meacham and Samull Parker personally appeared and made solemn oath that they saw John Field, ye testator, signe and seall the above wrighting, and heard him declare it to be his last will.

           Joseph Talcott, Judge of Probate.

    Mary Field, ye executrix named in the above will, appeared before this Court and accepted the trust of executorship.

Court Record, Page 73—8 July, 1718: Will proven.

Page 102.

Flowers, Lamrock, Hartford. (Died 19 June, 1716. See File.) Invt. £242-09-08. Taken 4 July, 1716, by Samuel Sedgewick and Thomas Steele. Will dated 21 October, 1715.

    I, Lamrock Flowers of Hartford, do make this my last will and testament: My will is that my honest and just debts be paid, and that such a parcell of land at the west end of my lott as will make the mony be sold and the mony be raised and paid without delay. And then the party who buyeth this land, if a stranger, will want a way to it. My will is that a driftway of ten foot wide, on the north side next Cadwell, from the highway to it, be reserved, the buyer and my children or successors to maintain the fence of this driftway equally according to their number of acres, so many rods as may fall out to one another when calculated by the number of acres. I give to my son Lamrock all that hath been due me or mine towards the building of his house, and the acre lot it standeth on, (he) maintaining the fence against our land. What land is left, to be divided equally among my 4 sons after my wife's marriage or decease; but whilst my wife remaineth my widow it shall be at her dispose, to let and sett as seemeth her good, to bring up those children who are yet under age. That whatsoever the moveables amounteth to when apprised, whosoever taketh them shall pay to my daughters the value thereof what in all can be made, the 2 younger (Mary and Ann) to have two-thirds, the other two older (Lydia and Elizabeth) to have one-third part, but not until their mother's marriage or decease; the other to Mary and Ann at my wife's discretion. I make my wife sole executrix.

Witness: *Benjamin Colton,*   LAMROCK FLOWER, LS.
         Joseph Butler.

Court Record, Page 19—7 August, 1716: Lydia Flowers, the widow, exhibited the last will of Lamrock Flowers. Not proven.

Page 21—4 September, 1716: Will proven.

Page 87—4 November, 1718: This Court appoint John Janes of Hartford to be guardian to Francis Flowers and Anne Flowers, minor children of Lamrock Flowers. Recog., £100. Lydia Flowers of Hartford, executrix, made return of her doings therein, and this Court doth allow her £5 for her trouble.

Page 88—4 November, 1718: This Court order that dist. be made of sd. estate according to the testator's last will, and appoint Capt. Joseph Wadsworth, Capt. Samuel Sedgewick and Sergt. Thomas Steele distributors.

Page 133—2 August, 1720: Joseph Flowers, 14 years of age, son of Lamrock Flowers, chose Lamrock Flowers to be his guardian. Recog., £50.

Page 96.

Foster, Ann, Windsor. Invt. £8-03-04. Taken 29 November, 1721, by Nathaniel Cooke and John Porter.

Court Record, Page 160—5 December, 1721: Adms. to Mrs. Elizabeth Drake of Windsor, widow.

Page 141, 241.

Fuller, Samuel, Mansfield. Died 29 September, 1716. Invt. £312-15-02. Taken 24 October, 1716, by Thomas Thatcher and Hezekiah King. Will dated 23 September, 1716.

I, Samuel Fuller of Mansfield, in the County of Hartford, do make this my last will and testament: I give all my land and all other my moveable estate unto Elizabeth my wife, whome I constitute sole executrix of this my last will.

Witness: *Thomas Root,*   SAMUEL FULLER, LS.
         Hannah Rust.

Page 263-4, 301.

Fuller, Thomas, Windham. Invt. £238-14-06. Taken by Robert Moulton and Thomas Durke. Will dated 27 November, 1716.

I, Thomas Fuller, plowright, of Windham, being aged, do make and ordain this my last will and testament: Imprimatur: I do will and bequeath, after my funeral charges and all other my debts and dues in right or conscious are paid, I do will and bequeath unto Martha Fuller, my wife, during the time of her widowhood, 1-3 part of the income of my lands situate in the Township of Windham aforesd., with convenient room for her residence in my now dwelling house. I bequeath unto Martha Fuller, my wife, 2-3 of all my moveable estate, to be at her dispose. I will and bequeath unto my 5 sons which dwell at Salem Village, each of them 5 shillings, viz., Thomas Fuller, Jonathan Fuller, John Fuller, Joseph Fuller and William Fuller, to be paid by my executor at the end of one full year after my decease. And the reason of my giving no more to these my sons is because I have already given them their portion of my estate. I bequeath unto my loving cozen Sarah Durke, daughter to John Durke, £10, to be paid at her marriage, provided she continue to live with my wife or widow until she be married, or provided she do not marry it shall be paid her at 21 years of age. I do bequeath unto my son Stephen Fuller all that tract of land which I purchased of Deacon Thomas Bingham of Windham aforesd., which land is situate in Windham. Also, I do give unto my son Stephen Fuller 1-3 part of my moveable estate. The land beforementioned, with the buildings thereon, I give to my son Stephen Fuller, his heirs and assigns forever. I do appoint Martha Fuller and Stephen Fuller executors.

Witness: *George Allyn,*   THOMAS FULLER, LS.
Jonathan Abbey, Benjamin Chaplin.

Court Record, Page 63—6 May, 1718: Will proven. Thomas Durke to be guardian to Stephen Fuller, a minor 16 years of age, son of Thomas Fuller deceased.

Page 125.

Gaylord, John, Windsor. Invt. £726-05-06. Taken 22 October, 1722, by Samuel Rockwell, Thomas Sadd and David Bissell.

Court Record, Page 178—6 November, 1722: Adms. granted to Hannah Gaylord, widow.

Page 161 (Vol. X) 1st August, 1726: Hannah Gaylord of Windsor to be guardian to her children: John, about 14 years of age; Alexander, 12 years of age; Ann Gaylord, 9 years of age; and Charles Gaylord, 7 years; provided bond be given.

Page 292 (Probate Side, Vol. XII): An agreement, dated 6 March, 1734-5: A Greement upon the astat of John Gaylord, lat of windsor dessed, by us the subscribers, for the division and settlement of sd. estate: First, we agree yt John Gaylord shall haue the homeloot. And our agreement forder is that the sd. John Gaylord shall pay to his two brothers, viz., Alexander and Charles, £70 to each. Our agreement forder is yt Charles Gaylord shall haue a lotment of land yt is now in the posseshon of Jaddadih watson by his wife, yt after her belongs to the estate of this same John

Gaylor decd. Our agreement forder is yt Ann Gaylord, dafter to the decd., shall haue a sarten tract of land yt is layed out in the mile and half-mile diuishen of the Town Commons, yt wors drawn by the estat of the sd. decd.

Signed: HANNAH X GAYLORD, LS.   CHARLES GAYLORD, LS.
JOHN GAYLORD, LS.   ANN GAYLORD, LS.
ALEXANDER GAYLORD, LS.

Page 62, 117.

Gaylord, Nathaniel, Windsor. Invt. £587-10-03. Taken 30 May, 1720, by Israel Stoughton, Jonathan Elsworth and Daniel Bissell.

An agreement and covenant made, executed and ratified, confirmed forever and everlastingly established, 3d April, 1722, between the heirs and claimers of the estate of Lt. Nathaniel Gaylord of Windsor, that is to say, Abigail Gaylord, relict of sd. deceased, Hezekiah Gaylord, Nathaniel Gaylord, Josiah Gaylord and Joseph Gaylord, sons of the sd. decd., Abigail Griswold, Elizabeth Griswold, Rachell Barbour, Ruth Gaylord and Esther Gaylord, daughters of the sd. decd., in a final and lasting settlement of the whole estate (to the sons all in lands) : to Abigail, £53; Elizabeth, £53; Rachell, £53; Ruth, £54; Esther, £54; Hezekiah to be paid £50. Doth therefore ratify and confirm these presents to all intents, constructions and purposes in the law. Now, for a full, final and lasting confirmation of the premises, the parties, that is to say, Abigail Gaylord, Hezekiah Gaylord, Nathaniel Gaylord, Josiah Gaylord, Joseph Gaylord, Abigail Griswold, Elizabeth Griswold, Rachell Barbour, Ruth Gaylord and Esther Gaylord, as also John Griswold, husband to sd. Abigail, Samuel Griswold, husband of sd. Elizabeth, and Jonathan Barbour, husband of Rachell, in testimony of our allowing hereof, consenting to and confirming these presents, together with the above-named natural children of the sd. deceased, do hereto mutually sett our hands and seals this day and date before expressed. And all appeared before the Court of Probate, held in Hartford on the 1st day of May, Anno. Dom. 1722, and acknowledged the within-written instrument to be their free and voluntary act and deed.

Court Record, Page 127—7 June, 1720: Adms. to Abigail Gaylord, widow, and Nathaniel and Josiah Gaylord, sons of the decd.

Page 166—1st May, 1722: The Adms. account, also agreement of heirs for the settlement of the estate, accepted.

Page 361-362.

Gibbs, Samuel, Windsor. (Died 8 February, 1719-20. See File.) Invt. £111-03-09. Taken 24 February, 1719-20, by Israel Stoughton, Jonathan Elsworth and Nathaniel Horsford. Will dated 1st October, 1718.

I, Samuel Gibbs, Sen., of Windsor, do make this my last will and testament: I give to my eldest son Samuel my gun, one-half my wearing apparell, besides what I have given him already by deed of gift. And as to the woodlott lying near Two-Mile Tree by Thomas Thrall, which was my father Dibble's, my son Benjamin hath it by deed, having paid Samuel for 1-2 of it. I give to my son Benjamin, besides what I have already given him, my cutless. I give to my son Benjamin all my lands which I have not already disposed of, viz., 4 acres in Hoit's Meadow, 3 acres in the Great Meadow, and 4 1-2 acres by Benjamin's home lott, provided he pay the full value of the sd. 3 pieces of land to my daughters hereafter named, viz., to the heirs of my deceased daughter Hepsibah Dickinson, to Patience Denslow, to Elizabeth Hayden, to Joannah Loomis, to Experience Huxley, and to Miriam Bissell, to all in equall proportions. Item. I give to my daughter Patience my great wainscot chest. Item. To my daughter Elizabeth, my great Bible. Item. To my daughter Joannah, a young mare. Item. I give to my daughter Experience a young mare and colt. Item. To my daughter Miriam, my featherbed and bedding belonging to it, with the bedstead; also, my bell-metal skillett. I hereby constitute my sons, Benjamin Gibbs, Josiah Bissell and Moses Loomis, to be executors. I also desire my trusty friends, Mr. John Eliot, Dr. Samuel Mather and Mr. Ebenezer Fitch, to be overseers.

Witness: *Samuel Strong,*   SAMUEL X GIBBS, LS.
John Allyn, Bridget Fitch.

Court Record, Page 121—1st March, 1719-20: Will proven.

Page 257.

Gilbert, George, Middletown. Invt. £105-07-10. Taken by John Williams and Giles Hall.

Court Record, Page 52—6 February, 1717-18: Adms. to Abigail Gilbert, widow of the decd.

Page 320.

Gillett, William, Simsbury. Died 27 January, 1718-19. Invt. £280-02-04. Taken by Nathaniel Holcomb and Andrew Robe.

Court Record, Page 101—7 April, 1719: Adms. granted to Mary Gillett, widow.

Page 29 (Vol. XI) 3 November, 1730: Mary Holcomb, Adms., and Jonathan Holcomb, husband of the sd. Mary Holcomb, were summoned before this Court to render an account of their Adms., and ordered to perfect the inventory.

Page 32—1 December, 1730: According to the continuance of the case between Mary and Jonathan Holcomb of the one party, Adms., and Daniel Gains on the other, did not appear.

Page 42—6 April, 1731: The Adms. exhibit an account, which this' Court accept, order recorded and kept on file.

Page 44-119. (See also File.)

Goring, William, Simsbury. Invt. £57-09-01. Taken December, 1715, by John Slater and Andrew Robe. A further invt. was taken 3 January, 1715-16, by Eleazer Hill and Elias Slater. Will dated 20 January, 1709-10.

Whereas, I, William Goring, am designed a voyage to England if God will, and not knowing how the providence of God may dispose of mee, doe therefore hereby declare it to be my will, and I doe hereby give to my loving wife, Sarah, all that small portion of worldly goods that it hath pleased God to bestow on mee, both of personal and real, to be and remain to her and to be at her own dispose as she see cause. And I doe hereby nominate and appoint my said wife Sarah to be my sole executrix to this my will.   WILLIAM X GORING, LS.

Witness: *John Moore, Sen.,*
         Mary Moore.

Court Record, Page 7—6 March, 1715-16: This Court grants letters of administration on the estate of William Goron, late of Symsbury deceased, unto Sarah Goron, widow, relict of sd. decd. She gave bond, took letters and exhibited inventory, and was ordered by the Court to render an account of her Adms. on or before the first Tuesday of April, 1717.

Page 169—5 June, 1722: The last will and testament of William Goring was now exhibited and proved by the oath of one of the witnesses to sd. will (the other being deceased), which by this Court is approved and ordered to be recorded and kept on file. The executrix named in sd. will being now wife to Elias Slater of Simsbury, declines that trust, whereupon this Court grant letters of administration on the estate of the sd. deceased, with the will annexed, unto the sd. Elias Slater, provided bond be given according to law, and order that he render an account of his administration on sd. estate on or before the first Tuesday of June, 1723, who accordingly gave bond and took out letters of administration this day. The following is written upon the will on file: At a Court holden at Hartford, June ye 5th, 1722, the above will was exhibited in Court, and ye question being asked why ye will lay so long dormon, and the answer was because that ye widow herd yt sd. Goring had made another will in England, but waiting until this time and none appearing, therefore now bring sd. will yt it may be aproved. Whereas, John Moore, one of the witnesses, being dead, Mary Moore, the other witness, now appeared in Court and made oath, etc. The will was approved, yet ye exetrix is obliged to pay all just debts due from William Goring. And Elias Slater, now husband to ye said exetrix, appeared in Court and refused to allow of his wife Sarah excepting ye trust of executrix, and he was appointed Adms. with will annexed.

Page 301.

Grant, Samuel, Windsor. Died 10th September, 1718. Invt. £202-15-00. Taken by Samuel Rockwell and John Elsworth.

Court Record, Page 84—7 October, 1718: Adms. to Matthew Grant and Samuel Grant, sons of the deceased.

Page 118—2 February, 1719-20: Adms. now exhibit account of debts due from the estate amounting to the sum of £222-10-00. Accepted.

Page 337-342.

Griffin, Ruth, Simsbury. Died 7 September, 1719. Invt. £106-09-08. Taken 16 October, 1719, by John Pettebone and Benjamin Addams.

The last will and testament of Ruth Griffin of Simsbury: Imprimis: I give and bequeath to Ann Higley, widow of Jonathan Higley decd., and her daughter Mary, £6 between them out of my estate. Thus much she said, and added she had not strength and breath to declare further, but desiring that she might lye and sleep a while, but dyed before any further opportunity. Which was in the presence and hearing of us, this 27th of August, 1719, at night.

Witness: *Mary* X *Griffin,* wife of *John Griffin,*
Elizabeth X *Griffin,* wife of *Thomas Griffin,*
Samuel Higley.

Will was exhibited in Court, 1719, by Samuel Higley.

Court Record, Page 113—3 November, 1719: Adms. granted to Samuel Wilson of Windsor.

Page 151—8 May, 1721: Samuel Wilson, Adms., exhibits an account of his Adms., which this Court accepts.

Page 155—4 July, 1721: Pursuant to an act of the General Assembly, Samuel Wilson, Adms., was allowed to sell land to pay the sum of £26-09-06 debts.

Page 343. (Moveable Estate Invt. in Vol. X, Page 3.)

Griffin, Thomas, Simsbury. Died 7 October, 1719. Invt. £367-07-10. Taken 16 October, 1719, by John Pettebone, Sen., John Humphries and Benjamin Addams. Invt. of the moveable estate, £68-13-02. Taken at the decease of Elizabeth Griffin, widow, by Samuel Bemond, Samuel Griswold and Samuel Higley.

Court Record, Page 113—3 November, 1719: Adms. granted to Elizabeth Griffin, widow.

Page 178—6 November, 1722: Joshua Holcomb, Jr., informs this Court that his mother-in-law, Elizabeth Griffin, Adms., is now deceased and had not finished her Adms. This Court do therefore appoint Joshua Holcomb, Jr., Adms.

Page 179—4 December, 1722: This Court appoint Thomas Holcomb guardian to John Griffin, 19 years of age, Stephen Griffin, 13 years, and

Benoni, 8 years of age, children of Thomas Griffin. Recog., £150. This Court also appoint Joshua Holcomb, Jr., to be guardian unto Nathaniel Griffin, 16 years of age. Recog., £50. John Richards of Waterbury to be guardian to Eunice Griffin, 10 years of age, daughter of Thomas Griffin. Recog., £50.

Page 57 (Vol. X) 6 October, 1724: Joseph (Joshua) Holcomb, Adms., exhibits an account of his Adms.:

	£ s d
Paid out more than he has received, the sum of	45-18-06
By a late invt. taken of moveable estate, to be added	73-16-01
Account accepted. Order to dist. the estate:	
To John Griffin, eldest son,	75-01-10
To Nathaniel, Stephen, Benoni and Eunice Griffin and Mary Holcomb, the rest of the children, to each,	37-07-11

And appoint Thomas Holcomb, Joseph Case and Samuel Griswold, distributors.

Page 87 (Vol. XI) 3 April, 1733: Benoni Griffin, age 17 years, son of Thomas Griffin, chose his brother Thomas Griffin to be his guardian. Recog., £100.

Page 106.

Griswold, Joseph, Windsor. Invt. £508-12-08. Taken 29 November, 1716, by Daniel Griswold, Sen., Thomas Griswold and Joseph Barnard. Will dated 6 September, 1716.

The last will and testament of Joseph Griswold is as followeth: I give to my wife Mary £40 out of my moveable estate, prised as money, and 1-3 part of my lands during her natural life. I give to my son Joseph Griswold and my son Francis Griswold all my lands which lyeth southeastwardly of my son Matthew Griswold's land, bounding northwest by Matthew Griswold and southeast by the Wilson's land, they to divide it equally by the acre. I give to my three sons, Joseph, Francis and Matthew, equally betwixt them, all my lands at Salisbury Plain which I bought of Mr. Mather. Also, I give to my three sons all my land in the Quarry Field. Also, I give to my son Francis one acre of meadow land near the south end of the fourth meadow. I give to my son Joseph all the remainder of my lott. Also, I give to my two sons, Joseph and Francis, all my land on the neck on the east side of the river. Also, I give to my son Francis 20 foots square of land which the Town gave me, a little below Windsor Ferry. Also, I give to my son Matthew my part of my land which was my father Gaylord's, lying near Rocky Hill near the upper end of the Town. I give to my son Joseph the small parcell of land by Naughtsock, bounding southeastwardly by his own land and northwest wardly by Matthew Griswold's land. Also, I give to my son Matthew Griswold all my lands which my house stands on, all my houseing and barn and meadow adjoyning, as it bounds southwestwardly by the highway, all the upland and meadow down to the fence near to Naughtsock, and the land bounding southeastwardly by his own land and northwestwardly by George Griswold's land. Also, I give to my son Francis 1-3 part of the apples in my new orchard, from my house to the foot of the first hill, for the first five years after the date hereof. Also, I give to my two daughters, Mary the wife of Joseph Gillett and Abigail the wife of Josiah Phelps, £25 apiece out of my moveables, to be prised as money. I give to my grandchild, Sarah Gillett, £5 out of my moveables. And the debts due to me which are likely to be recovered are to be reckoned as moveables.

Note: That what my daughters has formerly had is not to be reckoned in the above said legacies. If there be any overplus of moveables than pays what is above written, it is to be divided thus: My wife to have 1-3 of them, and the remainder to be divided equally among all my children.

I appoint my son Joseph Griswold and my son Francis to be executors of this my will, with my wife.

Witness: *Joseph Barnard,*   JOSEPH GRISWOLD.
Samuel Holcomb, Pellatiah Griswold.

Court Record, Page 24—4 December, 1716: Will proven.

Page 55.

Gross, Isaac, Windham. Invt. £57-09-04. Taken 30 April, 1716, by Joseph Cary and Richard Abby.

Court Record, Page 16—3 July, 1716: Invt. exhibited by Nathaniel Bassett of Mansfield, the widow having made oath to it before Justice Ripley at Windham. Allowed.

Page 61.

Hall, Hannah, Middletown. Invt. £35-07-11. Taken 4 March, 1719-20, by James Tappan, Joseph Rockwell and Robert Hubbard.

Court Record, Page 121—29 February, 1719-20: Adms. granted to Hezekiah Sumner, son of sd. decd.

See File: 14 June, 1720: The estate of Mrs. Hannah Hall, arbitration; the estate of William Sumner: Hezekiah Sumner versus Nathaniel Stow and Sarah his wife, who was daughter of William Sumner, Hezekiah and Sarah, brother and sister, co-heirs in the estate of Daniel Sumner decd., their brother, their mother Mrs. Hannah Hall also deceased.

Witness: *William Warde,*   *James Wadsworth,*
Daniel Hall.   *Hezekiah Brainard.*
                                   Arbitrators.

Court Record, Page 143—3 January, 1720-1: Hezekiah Sumner, Adms., exhibits an account of the settlement of Hannah Hall's estate, which account is accepted, ordered recorded and kept on file.

Page 60.

Hall, Joseph, Deacon, Mansfield. Invt. £355-15-05. Taken 27 June, 1716, by Shubael Dimock, Joseph Cary and Samuel Stetson.

Court Record, Page 16—3 July, 1716: Adms. granted joyntly to Mary Hall, widow, and John Hall of Mansfield.

Page 42—3 September, 1717: William Hall, Adms., exhibits an account of his Adms. Accepted. Order to dist: To Mary Hall, widow, 1-3 part of the real estate and 1-2 of the personal estate, the remainder of the moveable and real estate to be divided into 6 equal parts, 1-6 part to be set out to the legal representatives of John Hall decd., eldest brother of Joseph Hall decd., to Nathaniel Hall, to Gershom Hall, to William Hall, to Benjamin Hall, and to Elisha Hall, to each 1-6 part, all brothers of the decd. And appoint Capt. Thomas Huntington, Deacon Shubael Dimmock and Mr. Samuel Stetson, of Mansfield, distributors.

Page 293.

Hamlin, John, Jr., Middletown. Invt. £790-19-07. Taken April, 1718, by John Collins, Joseph Rockwell and John Bacon.

Court Record, Page 84—7 October, 1718: Adms. granted to Elizabeth Hamlin, widow of sd. decd.

Page 86 (Vol. XI) 22 March, 1732-3: Giles Hamlin, age 17 years, a minor son of John Hamlin decd., chose Return Megs of Middletown to be his guardian. Recog., £200.

Page 5, 42.

Hampton, William, New York. Invt. £200-00-06. Taken 4 October, 1715, by John Austin, Adms. (in Connecticut). Will dated 4 April, 1715.

I, William Hampton, late of the City of New York, but now residing in the Island of Barbadoes, merchant, being very sick and weak, do make and ordain this my last will and testament: I give, devise and bequeath (my estate): First, my desire is that my just debts here in this Island and funeral expenses be fully paid and satisfied, and that all my goods and effects whatsoever which now are or hereafter may be in this Island, and the produce thereof, may be by my sd. executor here remitted to such person or persons as they shall appear of right to belong to, either in Great Britain or elsewhere, by consignment to such person or persons in sugars, and what remains after such remittances made to remit by bills of exchange to my beloved sister Anne Hampton, living in Essex Street in the City of London. Item. As to all my other goods and effects which now are or hereafter shall be in New York or other parts of North America, and the produce thereof, may be by my executor hereafter named, who now resides in the City of New York, remitted to such person or persons as they shall appear of right to belong to, either in Great Britain or elsewhere, by

bills of exchange, and after such remittances made then to remit the residue of all my estate of what nature or kind soever to my sd. loving sister Anne Hampton, to whom I do hereby give all the rest and residue of my estate both real and personal (saving £6 which I do hereby give to my nurse Ruth for her care of me in my sickness, to be paid her immediately after my decease). And my desire further is that my doctors and bearers may have rings, scarfs and gloves at my funeral. And I do hereby nominate and appoint, make and ordain my trusty and well-beloved friends, Mr. Steven Thomas of the Island of Barbadoes, merchant, and Mr. Joshua Wroe of the City of New York, merchant, to be my executor and executors of this my last will and testament. In witness whereof I, the sd. William Hampton, have hereunto sett my hand and seal this 4th day of April, 1715.
In presence of:
H. Courtney,   Signed: W. HAMPTON, LS.
Will Ker, Antho: White.

Barbadoes,————— *By the Honourable, the President of His Majestie's Council and Commander-in-Chief, &c.,*
Mr. William Ker, one of the witnesses to the above-written will, personally appeared before me and made oath on the Holy Evangelists of Almighty God that he was present and saw the above-named William Hampton (now decd.) sign, seal, publish and declare the same as and for his last will and testament, and that at the time of his so doing he was of a sound and disposeing mind and memory, to the best of his (deponent's) judgement and belief.—————Given at Pilgrim, this 6th day of April, 1715.   Signed: WM. SHARPE.

Barbados, ————— *By the Honourable William Sharpe, Esq., President of his Majestie's Council and Commander-in-Chief of this and other His Majestie's Carribbee Islands to Windward of Guardaloope, &c.:*
To all to whom these presents shall come, greeting: Know ye that on the day of the date hereof before me personally came and appeared Alexander Skene, Esq., His Majestie's Secretary of this Island, and upon his solemn oath, taken on the Holy Evangelists of Almighty God, did testifie and declare that the copy hereunto annexed of the last will and testament of William Hampton decd., bearing date the 4th instant, with the probate thereof, is a true and exact copy, and was by this deponent carefully compared and examined with the record thereof remaining in the Secretary's office of this Island. In testimony whereof I have hereunto sett my hand and caused His Majestie's Great Seal, appointed for this and other His Majestie's said Carribbee Islands, to be hereunto appended. Given at Pilgrim the 16th of April, 1715, and in the first year of His Majestie's reign.

Signed: WILLIAM SHARPE.

By His Honour's command.
Alexa. Skene.
Entered April 6th, 1715.

The foregoing is a true copy, examined, compared and here recorded, 7th August, Anno Dom. 1716. Per me,

                                        Thomas Kimberly, Clerk.

Court Record, Page 264 (Vol. VIII) 16 September, 1715: This
Court grant letters of Adms. unto Mr. John Austin provided he give
bond as the law requires.

Page 20 (Vol. IX) 7 August, 1716: Will proven.

Page 94.

Hancox, William, Farmington, (Kensington, see File.)   Invt. £147-
08-03.   Taken by John Ashmun and Thomas Hancox.

Court Record, Page 159—5 December, 1721: Adms. granted to
Daniel Hancox, a brother of sd. decd.

Page 20 (Vol. X) 7 May, 1723: Daniel Hancox, Adms., exhibits an
account of his Adms. Accepted.

Page 28—3 September, 1723: This Court direct the Adms. to sell
some land to pay the debts, per act of the General Assembly.

Page 99—7 September, 1725: Report of the sale of land.

Page 100—7 September, 1725: Daniel Hancox, Adms., exhibits now
a full account of his Adms. Accepted. Order to dist. the estate: To John
Hancox, eldest son, to Daniel and Rachel Hancox, to Mabel Barnes,
brothers and sisters of sd. deceased, to each of them, £18-18-09. And appoint Thomas Hart, Thomas Curtice and John Root, distributors.

Page 43.

Harris, Walter, Wethersfield.   Invt. £38-15-11.   Taken 5 March,
1715-16, by John Lattemore and James Treat.

Court Record, Page 7—6 March, 1715-16: Mary Harris, Adms., exhibits an invt. of the sd. estate. Accepted.

Page 341.

Harris, William, Middletown. Inventory of lands, taken 7 November, 1719, by Israhiah Wetmore, William Savage and William Ward,
apprisers, under oath:

	£ s d
Item. Land in the northwest quarter, 442 acres,	442-00-00
Item. Land lying westward from the Town, 624 acres,	374-08-00
Item. Land, five and half acres of boggy meadow,	027-10-00
Item. Land in the round meadow, 12 acres,	12-00-00
Item. To two and half acres of land in the round meadow swamp,	003-02-00

Item. To two and half acres east side the Great River,   012-00-00
Item. To 34 acres of upland east side the Great River,   051-00-00
Item. To 40 acres, a half-mile lot east side the Great River,   027-00-00
Item. To 10 acres that was Bowe's, east side the Great River,   003-00-00
Item. To 150 acres of land east of Wangog, called Bowe's lot,   037-00-00
Item. To six and quarter acres at Pacowsett,   031-00-00

Court Record, Page 195 (Vol. VIII) 17 May, 1714: Solomon Coit of New London, grandson of William Harris, late of Middletown decd., moved this Court to grant Adms. to some suitable person. Mary Gilbert, Hannah Whitmore and Patience Markham of Middletown, children of sd. William Harris, appeared in opposition. Adms. not granted. Solomon Coit then appealed to the Superior Court.

Page 110 (Vol. X) 7 August, 1719: Upon motion of Solomon Coit, for himself and as attorney for John and Joseph Coit, heirs to Mrs. Martha Coit, late of New London deceased, daughter and one of the co-heirs of William Harris, sometime of Middletown deceased, that power of Adms. be granted on the estate of William Harris according to an act of the General Assembly at Hartford, 14 May, 1719: It appearing to this Court that the covenant of agreement, dated 17 September, 1717, signed by fourteen of the heirs of sd. estate, is not perfected according to the proviso made in said act concerning such agreement, this Court grant letters of Adms. to Capt. Joseph Rockwell, Francis Wetmore and Solomon Coit, heirs unto sd. estate. The Court also appointed Capt. William Savage, Sergt. Israhiah Wetmore and Sergt. William Ward to apprise sd. estate.

Page 113—3 November, 1719: Inventory exhibited.

Page 136—6 September, 1720: The Adms. now exhibit an invt. of several parcels of land passed by deed of gift by the sd. William Harris, deceased, in his lifetime, dated 12th December, 1678, and conveyed by deed of mortgage dated 7 March, 1687-8, to Francis Wetmore, late of Middletown deceased; also, several parcels of land recorded to John Ward, Daniel Markham and Edward Foster. Solomon Coit appealed from a decision of the Court to the Superior Court at Hartford March next.

Page 152—5 June, 1721: Upon consideration of the motion of Solomon Coit, Joseph Rockwell and Francis Wetmore, heirs-in-law to the estate of Mr. William Harris, sometime of Middletown deceased, respecting the opinion of the Superior Court, viz., that the estate given in the lifetime of the father cannot be joyned to the inventory of the estate of the deceased, but such estate shall be discounted in the distribuion of the decd. estate at the value of which it was at the time of the gift made, this Court having searched the law and not finding any law before 14 October, 1708, that obliged deeds of gift at large to be recorded, and finding in this case the records of the gifts of William Harris to his children were in 1668-1671 and 1674, and the heirs of sd. Harris have stood seized of them by sd. records and most of them by actual improvement, and do find Mr. Harris himself and most of the persons having land recorded to them in the Book of Records at Middletown are generally in those elder times after the same manner that these are, and having nothing more to show for their conveyance, this Court do therefore judge all the land given by deed, as also the lands anciently recorded to the heirs of the sd. Harris, were given in the lifetime of the deceased and shall not come unto the inventory, but be discounted in the distribution of the estate at the value of which it was at the time of the gift made.

Page 172—3 August, 1722: This Court order that the estate be dist. to the five daughters or their legal representatives: To Mary Gilbert decd., £230-04-05; to the heirs of Martha Coit decd., £244-14-05; to the heirs of Elizabeth Foster decd., £232-09-04; to Hannah Whetmore, £221-14-05; to Patience Markham, £219-00-00; which is their equal parts. And appoint Israhiah Wetmore, William Savage and William Ward, distributors.

Page 173—4 August, 1722: Dist. exhibited and accepted. Solomon Coit appealed from the judgement of this Court to the Superior Court.

Page 10 (Vol. X) 22 March, 1723: This Court direct the Adms. to sell some more land for the payment of debts.

Haynes, Joseph. Court Record, Page 27—16 February, 1716-17: Adms. granted to Mrs. Mary Haynes, of Hartford, on the estate of her son Joseph Haynes, late decd.

Page 54-55.

Higley, Jonathan, Simsbury. Invt. £223-08-08. Taken 21 May, 1716, by John Case, Thomas Holcomb and John Slater. Will dated 9 April, 1716.

I, Jonathan Higley of Simsbury, in the County of Hartford, do make this my last will and testament: Imprimis. I give to Ann, my well-beloved wife, 1-3 part of my personal estate, to her and her heirs forever. Item. I give her that lott at the northeast corner, that was her Father Barber's, to her and her heirs forever. I give her the improvement of all my lands in Simsbury until my daughter Mercy cometh to the age of 18 years or is married, and after that she shall have the improvement of the 1-3 part of my lands during her natural life. Item. I give unto my only daughter, Mercy Higley, all my lands excepting that lott which was her Grandfather Barber's, which I gave to my wife Ann. Item. I give her the two-thirds of my moveable or personal estate to her only disposal; but in case her daughter die before she comes to age or is married, then my will is that my wife Anne shall have the improvement of all my lands in Simsbury during her life, and the 1-3 part of them forever, with all the moveables or personal estate, to her own disposal forever. And that my cousin, David Higley, shall have my field out under the west mountains, to him and his heirs forever. All the remainder of my lands in Simsbury I give to my six brothers, John, Brewster, Samuel, Nathaniel, Josiah and Isaac, to be equally divided among them. All my lands at Windsor I give to my three eldest, brothers, John, Brewster and Samuel, forever, they paying what by my father's will I was obliged to pay to my sisters. I appoint my loveing wife Ann sole executrix.

Witness: *Nathaniel Holcomb,*   JONATHAN HIGLEY, LS.
Jonathan Holcomb, Abigail X Hayes.

Court Record, Page 17—3 July, 1716: Will proven.

Page 179—4 December, 1722: This Court grant Adms. on the estate of Jonathan Higley, late of Simsbury deceased, unto John Higley, a brother of the deceased. Adms. was formerly granted to the widow of the decd., who lately died not having finished her administration on sd. estate.

Page 65-81.

Higginson, William, Farmington. Invt. £159-16-09. Taken 1st July, 1720, by John Porter, John Hart and Hezekiah Hooker.

Court Record, Page 128—7 June, 1720: Adms. granted to Edward Neal of Farmington.

See File: An agreement between the heirs for a settlement of the moveable part of the estate of William Higginson, signed and sealed by each of them: Edward Neal in right of his wife Margaret alias Higginson, Samuel Warner in right of his wife Elizabeth alias Higginson, Clark Carrington in right of his wife Sarah alias Higginson, Abner Gillett in right of his wife Mary alias Higginson.

Page 142—6 December, 1720: An agreement was exhibited in Court for the division of the estate of William Higginson by Edward Neal, Samuel Warner, Abner Gillett and Clarke Carrington, who married the daughters of sd. decd., acknowledged by them to be their free act and deed, and each became bound for the payment of debts.

Page 58 (Vol. X) 1st December, 1724: Edward Neal, Adms., exhibited an account of his Adms., which this Court accepts.

Page 68.

Agreement on File.

Hillier, James, Simsbury. Died 29 July, 1720. Invt. £46-18-03. Taken by James Cornish, John Humphrey and John Moses.

To the honoured Court of Probate of the County of Hartford: These are to inform your honours that we, Marey Hillier, widow and relict of James Hillier, late of Simsbury, and James Hillier, Jr., and Daniel Palmer and Elizabeth Palmer his wife, being the subscribers hereunto, have this 8th day of August, 1720, agreed to deuid amongst ourselves the moueabel' part of the estate of James Hillier, Sen., and would humbley craue of the honoured Court, if thay think it conuenant, to confirm the estate on each of us as we haue deuided it: Imprimis: Deuided and set out to the widow her share in personal estate; to Daniel Palmer and Elizabeth his wife, all the moveable estate; to James Hillier, all the houseing and lands. For confirmation of which articles to each respectively and to their heirs and assigns forever, for a settlement of sd. estate, we have hereunto set our hands and seals the 9th day of August, 1720.

MARY X HILLIER,
JAMES HILLIER,
DANIEL PALMER.

Court Record, Page 134—10 August, 1720: Adms. granted to James Hillier, son of sd. decd. An agreement for the settlement of James Hillier's estate was now exhibited by the widow and children of sd. decd. Accepted, ordered recorded and kept on file.

Page 98. Will on File.

Hobart, Rev. Jeremiah, Haddam. Invt. £155-08-00. Taken 22 November, 1715, by Simon Smith, Joseph Arnold and James Brainard. Will dated 25 April, 1712.

I, Jeremiah Hobart, doe make this my last will and testament: I give to Elizabeth my wife my whole estate, both real and personal, whatsoever, after my decease, during the terme of her life, and I do hereby fully impower my wife to dispose of the whole of sd. estate, that shall be left after her decease, to my children as she thinks best. I constitute my wife Elizabeth sole executrix.

Witness: *Benjamin Smith,*   JEREMIAH HOBART, LS.
       James Welles.

Court Record, Page 21—4 September, 1716: Capt. James Welles, of Haddam, now exhibited the last will of Rev. Jeremiah *Hubburd,* late of Haddam decd. James Welles, a witness to sd. will, was now sworn. The other witness not being present, the probate was delayed.

Page 25—4 December, 1716: This Court doth now prove, approve and allow and confirm the will of Rev. Jeremiah Hobart. Accepted, ordered recorded and kept on file.

NOTE: *The Recorder entered and wrote the name Jeremiah "Hubburd," and in the index, "Hubbard." .The signature to the will was written by the testator himself, "Hobart."*

Page 237.

Add. Invt. in Vol. X, Page 3-4-5-6.

Holcomb, Benajah, Jr., Windsor. Died 30 October, 1716. Invt. £412-15-00. Taken by Thomas Griswold, Jr., and Samuel Holcomb. An inventory of £447-09-00. Taken after the decease of Benajah Holcomb's wife, on the 2nd day of November, 1722, by Nathaniel Pinney and Joseph Barnard.

Court Record, Page 33—4 June, 1717: Adms. to Martha Holcomb, widow. Exhibit of inventory.

Page 179—4 December, 1722: This Court grant letters of Adms. to Joseph Holcomb, a brother of the sd. deceased. Invt. exhibited and allowed. This Court appoint Joseph Holcomb to be guardian to Parnell Holcomb, 14 years of age, and Benajah Holcomb, age 12 years; also appoint Samuel Haydon to be guardian to Martha Holcomb, age 16 years, and Ann Holcomb, 6 years of age; all children of Benajah Holcomb deceased.

Page 34 (Vol. X) 2 December, 1723: Joseph Holcomb, Adms. on the abovesd. estate, exhibited accot. of his Adms. on sd. estate, whereby it appears that he has paid out of that estate in debts and charges, with some loss upon sd. estate, amounting to the sum of £28-10-10, which account the Court accepts and order it to be kept upon file. And whereas, the inventory of sd. estate, with additions upon record, amounts to the sum of £455-19-05, from which subtracted the sum of £28-10-10 there will then remain the sum of £427-08-07 to be distributed, this Court order that the estate of the sd. decd. so remaining shall be distributed to the children of the sd. decd. in the following manner, vizt.: To Benajah Holcomb, only son of sd. decd., the sum or value of £170-19-06, which is his double portion of sd. estate; to Martha Holcomb, Pernall Holcomb and Ann Holcomb, the rest of the children of the sd. decd., to each of them the sum or value of £85-09-08, which is their single portion of sd. estate. And this Court do appoint and impower Messrs. Timothy Loomis, Nathaniel Pinney and Joseph Barnard, of Windsor, or any two of them, to distribute and divide the sd. estate accordingly.

Page 42—3 March, 1723-4: Joseph Holcomb, Adms. on the estate of Benajah Holcomb, late of Windsor decd., exhibited a dist. of the estate, which dist. is by this Court accepted and ordered to be kept upon file.

Page 51—7 July, 1724: Joseph Holcomb, Adms., is granted a *Quietus Est.*

Page 53—1 September, 1724: This Court appoint Obadiah Owen of Windsor to be guardian unto Parnell Holcomb, a minor, 16 years of age, she desireing the same. Recog., £50.

Page 67—2 February, 1724-5: This Court appoint Nathaniel Pinney, Jr., to be guardian to Benajah Holcomb, a minor, about 14 years of age. Recog., £50.

Page 120.

Holcomb, Samuel, Windsor. Invt. £445-13-10. Taken by Thomas Griswold, Joseph Barnard and William Phelps.

Court Record, Page 175-6—2 October, 1722: Adms. to Martha Holcomb, widow, relict of the deceased. Exhibit of inventory.

Will and Invt. in Vol. X, Page 6-7-10-11.

Hollister, Jacob. Invt. £1691-03-03. Taken 8 November, 1722, by Giles Hall and George Phillips. Sloop Elizabeth (John Hames, master), value £328-00-00.

17 December, 1722: Then received of Mr. John Tyler and Mr. Thomas Collett, the estate mentioned in the foregoing inventory as it was taken according to books and invoices (excepting 4hhd. of rum and fifty pds. of prunes, improved for payment of debts due from sd. estate). Recd. pr. Robt. Cooke and Richard Sanger, Adms.

A further invt. of personal estate, valued at £1459-13-02, was taken 10 December, 1722, by Thomas Foster and Giles Southmaid under the apprisers' oath.

Court Record, Page 3 (Vol. X) 1st January, 1722-3: Whereas, this Court did grant Adms. on the estate of Jacob Hollister of Bristol, England, mariner, late decd. at Middletown, County of Hartford, on the 5 November last, to John Tyley and Thomas Collet of Hartford, they now exhibit invt., as also account of Adms. Allowed. Now Richard Sanger and Robert Cook appeared and paid sd. Tyley and Collet the sum of £155-14-08, which account was allowed. Also produced letters of Adms. on the estate from the Court of Probate in the City of New York, granted by His Excellency Col. Burnett, Judge, and in said letters of Adms. signified that Jacob Hollister deceased did in his lifetime, under his hand and seal, will and desire that if his life be taken, that then Jacob Read, Richard Sanger and Robert Cook should take his estate into their hands and dispose of it as in sd. writing expressed, vizt.:

New York, 30 July, 1722: I being now bound on a voyage to Rhode Island, in case of my death I constitute and appoint Mr. John Read, merchant, Mr. Robert Cook, both of New York, and Mr. Richard Sanger of Bristol, merchant, my true and lawful attorneys and trustees in mine and friends' affaires. My desire and order is that (my estate) be remitted to my well-beloved wife Elizabeth Hollister, in Bristol.
Witness: *Nathaniel Walker,*   JACOB HOLLISTER.
Thomas Roberts, Obadiah Hunt.

This Court grant Adms. to Robert Cook and Richard Sanger.

Page 48—5 May, 1724: Robert Cook, Adms., produced in Court a power of atty. to one Mr. James Gordon, from the widow and two of the creditors, to receive the estate from the Adms., and also produced receipts from said Gordon for the sloop and tackling and other estate sent to Great Britain for the widow and creditors. Account allowed.

Page 366.

Hooker, Thomas, Dr., Hartford. Will dated 12 October, 1719.

I, Thomas Hooker of Hartford, doe make this my last will and testament: I give to my brother Daniel Hooker my farm in West Division of

Hartford; also that tract of land at Bedford that I had of Atherton Mather; also one-half of my moveable estate. I give to my nephew Thomas Hooker, son of my brother Samuel Hooker, my house, homested, and all my meadow and upland in Hartford; also the other halfe of my moveable estate. I appoint my brother Daniel Hooker and my nephew Thomas Hooker executors.

Witness: *Edward Bulkeley,*   THOMAS HOOKER, LS.
Thomas Wickham, Joseph Churchill.

Court Record, Page 123—5 April, 1720: Will proven.

Page 135—6 September, 1720: Mr. John Hooker, Mr. John Austin as attorney for James Hooker, Stephen Buckingham and Sarah his wife, Mrs. Mary Pierpont, Mary Hooker and Alice Hooker, legal representatives of Dr. Thomas Hooker deceased, moved an appeal from an allowance of the will.

Page 147—4 April, 1721: John Austin, before the Court, agrees that when an action is brought by the executors he will produce in Court for the jury, if desired, all the papers late belonging to Dr. Thomas Hooker in his custody.

Page 169—5 June, 1722: Matters deferred until July next.

Court Record, Page 171—3 July, 1722: Mr. John Austin being summoned to this Court in June last to answer interrogatories tending to disclose the estate of Doct. Thomas Hooker deceased, upon pleas then made the matter was continued to this time. This Court consider upon the first plea made by sd. Austin that examination of parties supposed to have concealed estate of deceased persons is not limited to one or two times, but may upon occasion be often called. He, said Austin, has been sued in *detinue* of two tankards, and has finally recovered at the Superior Court upon his plea of justification upon an accord. And from thence a presumption lyeth that there is no demand in law for the executor of said deceased against said Austin for anything belonging to the deceased that came to his hands before 4th January, when the thing belonged to the deceased. This Court are of opinion that there may be in the hands or knowledge of said Austin sundry writings, bills, bonds, accounts, deeds, etc., that are not or cannot be supposed to be intended or included in said accord, and such really as are no estate to said Austin, nor any estate to said executor, nor was ever to the deceased, but only evidence what the estate is and whom it does belong to and where it lyeth, and therefore ought to be produced that the executor and legatees that have a just right to the estate may have the benefit of them. Therefore this Court have considered that said Austin shall answer to such interrogatories touching such writings as are or hath been in his custody or knowledge, as this Court shall think fitt to ask him concerning the premises, that was formerly belonging to Doctor Thomas Hooker.

Page 174—7 August, 1722: John Austin, on oath, stated that he had lately delivered to Mr. Thomas Hooker sundry bills and bonds, and now before the Court delivered to him sundry deeds and conveyances of land, and declared that he had delivered up all the writings that were in his custody, or ever knew of, that might disclose the estate of the deceased.

File Distribution: 18 March, 1758: Estate of Thomas Hooker ye elder, physition, formerly of Hartford. At this Court John Hooker appointed administrator, who now exhibits an inventory of such of ye real estate of sd. deceased as had been by his last will given to his nephew Thomas Hooker and his wife Hannah during life. Ye sd. nephew is also deceased. Order to dist. among the heirs of Thomas Hooker ye elder: To Mrs. Sarah Buckingham of Norwalk, only surviving sister of Thomas Hooker ye elder, a one-seventh part, and 1-7 part to John, Joseph and Roger Hooker, Abigail Hart, wife of Nathaniel Hart, Sarah Strong, wife of Newell Strong, and Widow Ruth Strong, late wife of Asahel Strong decd., all of Farmington, and Mary Hart, widow relict of Samuel Hart, late of Middletown, decd., these the only surviving children of John Hooker, late of Farmington decd., who was one of the brothers of ye sd. Thomas Hooker the elder. Also, one other seventh part to heirs of Samuel Hooker, viz., Samuel Giles and William Hooker, Esther, wife of Isaac Stiles of New Haven, and Mehetabell, wife of Daniel Coit of New London, which are ye only children and legal representatives of Samuel Hooker of Farmington decd., who was a brother of Thomas Hooker ye elder. Also, one other seventh part to Sarah Bartlett, widow of John Bartlett, late of Guilford decd., and to Mehetabell Smith, wife of John Smith of Rye, in the Province of New York, and Hannah, wife of Mr. ———— Smith of Orange County, Province of New York, which sd. Sarah, Mehetabell and Hannah are ye only children and legal representatives of Mr. James Hooker, late of Guilford decd., one other brother of Thomas Hooker ye elder. Also, one other seventh part to Nathaniel, Mary and Abigail Hooker and Sarah Edwards, wife of Daniel Edwards, all of Hartford, the only surviving children of Mr. Nathaniel Hooker, late of Hartford deceased, who was a brother to Thomas Hooker ye elder. And also one other seventh part to Mr. James Pierpont of New Haven, and to Sarah Edwards of Stockbridge, in the Province of Massachusetts Bay, the wife of Jonathan Edwards, only surviving children and legal representatives of Mrs. Mary Pierpont, who was one other sister of ye sd. Thomas Hooker ye elder. And one other seventh part thereof to Daniel Hooker of Hartford and to Susannah, the wife of ———— Bayley, living at Nine Partners, in the Province of New York, and to Sarah Chamberlain, widow of Benjamin Chamberlain, late of Middletown, and Mary Peck, wife of Elijah Peck of sd. Middletown, and Hannah, the wife of Reuben Norton of Guilford, the only surviving children and legal representatives of Doctor Daniel Hooker, late of Hartford deceased.

Page 114.

Howard, John, Wethersfield. Died 15 February, 1720-1. Invt. £630-09-06. Taken by Benjamin Churchill and John Rose.

Court Record, Page 165—5 April, 1722: Margaret Howard, Adms. on the estate of John Howard, late of Wethersfield deceased, exhibited an account of her Adms., which is accepted by the Court. And this Court order that the estate be dist. to the heirs, viz.:

	£ s d
To Margaret Howard, the widow,	33-05-04
To William Howard, eldest son,	132-09-04
To John, Jonathan, Mary, Sarah and Lydia Howard, to each,	74-19-08
And to Elizabeth Francis,	45-03-00

And appoint Joseph Talcott, Thomas Wright and John Rose, distributors. This Court appoint Margaret Howard to be guardian to her children, viz., Sarah Howard, age 16 years, Lydia 13, and Jonathan Howard, 8 years of age. Recog., £100.

Howard, John, Boston. Court Record, Page 32-33—8 May, 1717: Whereas, Mrs. Elizabeth Wilson, of Hartford, being indisposed in body and not able to go from home, desireing that a Court of Probate might be opened at her house, which being granted:

Present:

Joseph Talcott, Esqr., Judge; Hez: Wyllys, Clerk.

The said Elizabeth Wilson, as executrix to the last will of Mr. John Howard of Boston, Pub. Notary, late deceased, exhibited to this Court an account of lands at Dunstable sold for the sum of £100, and also an account made by virtue of her executorship amounting to the sum of £68-13-00, and made oath that all the articles of said account are just and true according to the best of her knowledge, and that she has not received any more of the estate of the deceased since the addition made to the inventory of the estate of the deceased, on the 27th of September, Anno. Dom. 1692, than what is contained in her sd. account.

Page 104.

Howard, Samuel, Hartford. Invt. £2205-17-07. Taken 30 May, 1716, by Joseph Wadsworth, Joseph Barnard and Thomas Hosmer. Will dated 25 February, 1716.

I, Samuel Howard, of the Town of Hartford, give and bequeath unto my loving and well beloved wife Susannah a third of my estate, personal and real (after my just debts are paid), to be by her enjoyed during her natural life. After her decease my will is that her thirds of personal estate to be disposed of according to her discretion, and that her thirds of real estate shall then revert to my son Samuel. Item. I give and bequeath unto my well-beloved son Samuel all my houseing and lands in Hartford and all my real estate lying or being any where else. Item. I give unto each and every of my three loving daughters, namely, Susannah, Abigail and Ruth, £100 in or as money, when they arrive at the age of 20 years, then to be paid; but if they marry before, then to be paid, meaning their portions.

Item. I constitute and appoint my wife Susannah and my son Samuel executors of this my last will and testament.
Witness: *Joseph Wadsworth,*   SAMUEL HOWARD, LS.
Daniel Hooker.

Court Record, Page 20—7 August, 1716: The will of Samuel Howard, shop-keeper, exhibited. Proven and allowed.

Page 73.

Hubbard, Jonathan, "Hanover." Invt. £173-14-00. Taken by Abel Shaylor and John Bissell of Bolton.
Court Record, Page 134—4 September, 1720: This Court grant Adms. on the estate of Jonathan Hubbard, late of Bolton decd., unto Hannah Hubbard, widow, and John Hubbard, Jr., of Glastonbury.
Page 205 (Vol. X) 12 November, 1728: John Hubbart and Hannah Euit, formerly Hannah Hubbart, Adms., exhibited an account of their Adms., which this Court allow. This Court appoint Jeams Euit of Guilford to be guardian to the children of Jonathan Hubbard, viz., to Hannah Hubbard, 10 years of age, and Rachel Hubbard, 9 years. Recog., £100.
Page 47 (Vol. XII) 17 June, 1736: A further account of Adms. was exhibited by the Adms. Paid in debts and charges, £66-12-08; invt. on file, £63-08-00; there remains yet to be paid the sum of £3-12-00, which the Adms., John Hubbard and Hannah Euerts, alias Hannah Hubbard, relict, acknowledged in Court that they freely give their proportionable part of the sd. £3-12-00, as land might not be sold. And James Euerts, guardian to one of the children, viz., Rachel Hubbard, a minor, moved that freeholders might be appointed to assist him as guardian in dividing the real estate. The Court appoint Timothy Olcott, Thomas Pitkin and Lt. John Talcott, of Bolton, distributors.

Jennings, Joseph, a Mulatto. Court Record, Page 95—3 February, 1718-19: Joseph Jennings, age 16 years, chose Thomas Stanly of Farmington to be his guardian.
Page 138—4 November, 1720: Joseph Jennings, age 18 years, chose Samuel Judd of Farmington to be his guardian. Recog., £50.

Page 358-362.

Johnson, Isaac, Middletown. Invt. £915-09-06. Taken by William Ward, Thomas Foster and Joseph Rockwell. Will dated 13 January, 1719-20.
I, Isaac Johnson, Sen., of Middletown, doe make this my last will and testament: I give to my wife Mary 1-2 of my household stuff, all my

stock and tools, and 15 acres of land which came by her brother Thomas, to be hers forever. I give to my son Isaac Johnson, besides what I have already given him, 120 acres of land lying out towards the Great Swamp. I give unto my son Nathaniel's heirs 55 acres of land in Haddam bounds, sd. land to be divided between the two sons, Nathaniel to have a double part and Jonathan a single share. And my will is that Nathaniel, my son's eldest son, should have a double portion of the estate I give to that family. Item. To my sons Daniel and Joseph, and Nathaniel's heirs, I give all my lands on the east side of the Great River. I give to my daughter Elizabeth my house, barn and all my homested, and 1-4 part of my household stuffe. I give to my daughter Mary the west end of my lott towards the Great Swamp, all the remainder which I have not already disposed of; also 1-4 part of my household stuffe. And I do appoint my three sons, Isaac, Daniel and Joseph, to be executors.

Witness: *William Russell,*   ISAAC X JOHNSON, SEN., LS.
William Harris, John Harris.

Court Record, Page 125—5th April, 1720: Will proven.

Page 273.

Judd, John, Waterbury. Invt. £305-18-00. Taken 3 January, 1717-18, by Thomas Hickox, William Hickox and William Judd. The children of the decd. are as followeth: John, 19 years of age, Samuel 16, Thomas 11, Benjamin 8, and Ebenezer 4 years.

Court Record, Page 69—1st July, 1718: This Court grant Adms. unto Hannah Judd, widow, and John Judd, the eldest son.

Page 141—6 December, 1720: John Judd, Adms., exhibits an account of his Adms. Allowed. Order to dist. the estate:

	£ s d
To Hannah Judd, the widow,	12-01-07
To John Judd, eldest son,	99-01-00
To Samuel, Thomas, Benjamin and Ebenezer Judd, to each,	49-10-06

And appoint Thomas Judd, William Hickcocks and Thomas Hickcocks, distributors. This Court appoint Capt. Thomas Judd to be guardian unto Samuel Judd, about 17 years, Thomas Judd 13, Benjamin Judd 10, and Ebenezer Judd about 6 years. Recog., £100.

Page 252.

Judd, Rachel, Farmington. Invt. £104-18-06. Taken 4 November, 1717, by Thomas Burd and Isaac Cowles.

Court Record, Page 40—6 August, 1717: Adms. granted to Daniel Judd.

Page 59—1st April, 1718: Daniel Judd, Adms., exhibits an account of his Adms. Accepted. Order to dist. the estate as followeth:

£   s   d
To William Judd, only son,   51-11-10
To Eunice Judd and Rhoda Judd, daughters of sd. decd., to
    each,   25-15-11

And appoint John Wadsworth, Isaac Cowles and John Hart, Jr., of
Farmington, distributors.
Page 74—5 August, 1718: Report of the distributors.

Page 307-8.

Kellogg, Abram, Hartford. Invt. £275-07-02. Taken 22 December,
1718, by Daniel Merrells, Thomas Hosmer and Joseph Cook. Will dated
15 August, 1718.
The last will and testament of Abram Kellogg is as followeth: Imprimis: I give to my mother Kellogg my part of the new cart. If my
wife have a child by me, I will all my real estate to her during life and
after her decease to my heir. But if my wife have no child by me, then I
will all my real estate after the death of my wife to return to my brethren
and their heirs. Further, I give my broad ax and drawing knife to my
brother Benjamin. To my brother Joseph I give my old hand saw and
inch augur. To my brother Daniel I give my little augur and little gouge
and compasses. Additional to my will: that Sarah, daughter of my
brother Samuel decd., be not comprehended among my brethren or their
heirs in inheriting part of my estate, but design she shall be wholly excluded.
Witness: *Benjamin Colton,*
         John Merrells.

Court Record, Page 92—6 January, 1718-19: Will proven. Adms.
granted to Miriam Kellogg, widow, and John Kellogg, a brother of the
decd., with will annexed.
Page 145—24 February, 1720: The Adms. exhibited an account of
their Adms. Allowed. Order to dist. the estate:
£   s   d
To Miriam Kellogg, alias Webster,   45-19-04
To John, Isaac, Jacob, Benjamin, Joseph and Daniel Kellogg,
    brothers, and Margaret Catlin, sister, to each of them,   2-00-07½
And appoint Thomas Judd, John Merrells and Abraham Merrells,
distributors.
Page 145—24 February, 1720: An agreement for the settlement of
the estate of Abraham Kellogg was exhibited by John Kellogg, Isaac Kellogg, and Daniel Webster in behalf of himself and his wife, late widow of
sd. deceased, under their hands and seals, acknowledged before the Court.
                    See Agreement as per File:
    I Miriam Kellogg, widow of sd. deceased, do agree with my broth-

ers John and Isaac Kellogg that I, Miriam Kellogg, shall my lifetime have the house that was my husband's and fifteen acres of land adjoyning to said house; and £45-19-04 in moveables which are to be ye said Miriam's forever. And for the same (do) to discharge the estate of the aforesaid Abraham Kellogg from any further dowry, resigning and surrendering all her right in personal and real estate, except as above mentioned, to John, Isaac, Jacob, Benjamin, Joseph and Daniel, my deceased husband's brothers.

Witness: *Thomas Judd,*   Signed: JOHN KELLOGG, LS.
          Aaron Cooke.   ISAAC KELLOGG, LS.
                                           MIRIAM X KELLOGG, LS.

Dist. per File, 4 November, 1719: To Miriam Kellogg, wife of Daniel Webster, to John, Isaac, Benjamin, Jacob, Joseph and Daniel Kellogg, and to Margaret the wife of Benjamin Catlin. By Thomas Judd, John Merrells and Abraham Merrells, distributors.

Page 233.

Kellogg, Deacon Samuel, Hartford. Invt. £895-01-00. Taken March, 1717, by John Seymour, Abraham Merrells and Daniel Merrells.

Court Record, Page 31—7 May, 1717: Adms. granted to Sarah Kellogg, widow, and Abraham Kellogg, son of the decd.

Page 49—23 January, 1717-18: The Adms. exhibited now an account of their Adms. Accepted. Order to dist. the estate as followeth: To the widow, Sarah Kellogg, 1-3 part of the personal estate to be her own forever, and 1-3 part of the real estate during her natural life; and to the eldest son his double share of sd. estate; and to the rest of the children their single shares. And appoint Thomas Judd, John Merrells and Abraham Merrells, distributors. This Court appoint Sarah Kellogg, widow, to be guardian unto Jacob Kellogg, 19 years of age, Benjamin 16, Joseph 14, and Daniel 11 years, sons of Samuel Kellogg decd.

Page 50—23 January, 1717-18: This Court appoint Joseph Root and Hannah his wife to be guardians to Sarah Kellogg, about 5 years of age, daughter of Samuel Kellogg, Jr., late of Hartford decd.

Page 93—9 January, 1718-19: This Court appoint John Kellogg to be guardian to Jacob Kellogg, age 20 years; to Benjamin, 18 years; and Isaac Kellogg is appointed guardian to Joseph Kellogg, age 15 years; and Benjamin Catlin appointed guardian to Daniel Kellogg, age 12 years; sons of Deacon Samuel Kellogg deceased.

Dist. as per File: To the widow, Sarah; to Sarah the daughter of Samuel Kellogg, Jr., decd.; to Daniel, Abraham, John, Isaac, Jacob, Joseph and Benjamin Kellogg, and to Margaret the wife of Benjamin Catlin. By Thomas Judd and John Merrells.

Page 309.

Kellogg, Sarah, Hartford. Invt. £167-12-09. Taken 1st January, 1718-19, by John Merrells, Samuel Richards and Abram Merrells.

Court Record, Page 93—9 January, 1718-19: Adms. granted to John Kellogg, son of the decd.

Page 113—3 November, 1719: John Kellog, Adms., exhibits an account of his Adms. Allowed. Order to dist. the estate:

	£	s	d
To Sarah Kellogg, daughter of Samuel Kellogg, late decd., who was the eldest son of Sarah Kellogg decd., the sum of	41	19	01
To John, Isaac, Jacob, Joseph, Benjamin and Daniel Kellog and Margaret Catlin, the rest of the children, to each,	20	19	06

And appoint Thomas Judd, John Merrells and Abram Merrells, distributors.

Page 111.

Lane, John, Middletown. Invt. £338-19-06. Taken by Israhiah Wetmore, Joseph Rockwell and Solomon Adkins.

Court Record, Page 24—4 December, 1716: Adms. granted to Anne Lane, widow, and Isaac Lane.

Page 144—15 February, 1720: The Adms. exhibit now an account of their Adms. Accepted. Order to dist. the estate: To Anne Lane, widow, £13-04-09; and to John Lane, only child, £293-09-05. And appoint Joseph Rockwell, Israhiah Wetmore and Solomon Adkins, distributors.

Page 9 (Vol. X) 5 March, 1722-3: An order to dist. the sd. estate was granted February, 1720. It now appearing to this Court that 1-2 of the lands and moveables of sd. estate was disposed of by deed of ffeoffees in trust in the lifetime of sd. John Lane, this Court consider that 1-2 of the estate shall be dist., viz., to Ann Lane (alias Bacon) her thirds, and to John Lane, only child.

Page 19—7 May, 1723: This Court appoint Nathaniel Bacon with his wife to be guardians to John Lane, her son, a minor about 7 years of age.

Page 76—6 April, 1725: Report of the distributors.

Page 6 (Vol. XI) 2 December, 1729: John Lane, a minor, 14 years of age, chose Deacon Thomas Allyn to be his guardian, his father and mother, who were his former guardians, consenting thereto. Recog., £50.

Page 63—17 January, 1731-2: Thomas Allyn, now guardian to John Lane, gives a receipt to Nathaniel Bacon, who was guardian for the estate, with the income thereof as received by me, Thomas Allyn.

Page 1 (Vol. XII) 28 March, 1734: John Lane now made choice of his father-in-law Nathaniel Bacon to be his guardian.

Page 96-7.

Marshall, Joel, Hartford. Invt. £125-02-10. Taken 1st January, 1721-22, by Thomas Richards and Jonathan Steele. Will dated 11 December, 1721.

I, Joel Marshall of Hartford, do make this my last will and testament: I give to my beloved son Samuel Marshall all my houseing and lands, my gunn, and all my utensils for husbandry, to him and his heirs forever. Item. I give to my daughter Sarah Marshall my bed and bolster with all the furniture thereto belonging, with my great Bible and a cow. Further, I give to my daughter Sarah Marshall the use and improvement of aple trees the fruit of them for three years, a russitin, bellybound and a pippin, of such as she shall choose, with 1-3 part of the remaining moveable estate. I give to my daughter Elizabeth 1-3 part, I give to my daughter Mary 1-3 part, to be equally divided amongst them. Further, I constitute my loveing kinsman, Benjamin Catlin, my sole executor.

Witness: *Samuel Catlin,*   JOEL X MARSHALL, LS.
William Baker, Sarah X Baker.

Court Record, Page 161—3 January, 1721: Will proven and allowed.

Page 67.

Mentor, Robert, Colchester. Invt. £67-09-08. Taken 20 July, 1720, by Richard Tozar and John Pendall.

Court Record, Page 133—10 August, 1720: Adms. granted to Ebenezer Coleman of Colchester.

Page 259.

Miller, Joseph, Middletown. Invt. £253-03-04. Taken 3 March, 1717-18, by Samuel Hall, William Harris and Joseph Rockwell.

Court Record, Page 57—1st April, 1718: Adms. granted to Rebeckah Miller, widow.

Page 168 (Vol. X) 7 November, 1727: Rebeckah Miller, Adms., exhibits an account of her Adms. Accepted.

Page 176—4 March, 1727-8: Nathaniel Miller is appointed guardian to Jared Miller, a minor, 13 years of age, son of Joseph Miller.

Dist. File: 14 March, 1727-8: To the widow Rebeckah Miller, to Joseph, to Nathaniel, to Elijah, to Jarred, to Tabitha, all of lawful age except Jarred. And appoint Joseph Rockwell, William Harris and Samuel Hall, distributors.

Page 196—6 August, 1728: Report of the distributors.

Page 66-7-8-9.

Mills, Dorcas, Windsor. Invt. £38-14-08. Taken by Thomas Fyler and Benjamin Gibbs. Will dated 22 November, 1714.

I, Dorcas Mills, do dispose of my estate in form and manner following: I give to John Mather of Windsor all my lands lying in Windsor.
To my cousin Dorcas Eglestone my chest and box and one suit of clothes,
I mean woolen, and which to be as she shall choose after my decease. I
give to my sister Esther Eaglestone all the rest of my clothes, both linen
and woolen, willing that my sister Esther Eaglestone shall give out of my
apparrel something to my sister Mary Soper. I give to John Mather all
my other goods or estate if any shall be in possession or reversion. And
I appoint John Mather to be my executor.
Witness: *Azariah Mather,*   DORCAS X MILLS, LS.
          John Maltbie.

Court Record, Page 132—8 July, 1720: Will approved.

Page 345-359-360.   Also, Invt. in Vol. X, Page 141.

Modsley, Capt. Joseph, Glastonbury.   Invt. £1701-14-03.   Taken December, 1719, by Benjamin Talcott and Thomas Welles. A new invt. ordered by the Court, viz., the lands and buildings, valued at £1465-00-00,
by Thomas Welles and Benjamin Talcott. Will dated the 12th of August,
1719.
    I, Joseph Modsley of Glosomberry, in the County of Hartford, and in
his Majestie's Colony of Connecticut in New England, husbandman, being very sick, do make and ordain this my last will and testament: Imprimis: I give and bequeath unto Abigail, my dearly beloved wife, ye sum
of £100. Item. I give unto my eldest daughter, Abigail Liman, £100,
reckoning what she hath already had. Item. I give and bequeath unto
my daughters, that is to say, Sarah, Mary, Hannah and Rachell, £100
apiece. Item. I give unto my four sons, Abner, David, Isaac and Job, an
equal division in all my estate reserved for them, saving only to my eldest son Abner an £100 more in the division than they the sd. other sons.
I appoint my wife and eldest son Abner sole executors.
Witness: *Jonathan Hale,*   JOSEPH X MODSLEY.
          Thankful X Modsley.

Court Record, Page 113—3 November, 1719: Will approved.
    Page 178—6 November, 1722: The executors now move this Court
to dist. the estate: Whereupon they order and appoint John Root, Consider
Moseley and Thomas Ingersoll, of Westfield, to distribute according to
the will.
    Page 180—4 December, 1722: It being found that the lands of Mr.
Joseph Moseley lying in Glastonbury had been apprised the whole together, this Court appoint Benjamin Talcott, Thomas Welles and Abram
Kilbourn to appraise anew the said lands into parts and parcells as may be
best for the heirs.
    Page 25 (Vol. X) 6 August, 1723: Invt. now exhibited, also a report
of the dist. Accepted.

Page 27—6 August, 1723: This Court appoint Mrs. Abigail Modsley to be guardian to her son Isaac Maudsley, 11 years of age, son of Joseph Maudsley late decd.

Page 352.

Moore, Andrew. Died 29 November, 1719.   Invt. £268-08-03. Taken by Nathaniel Pinney and Josiah Phelps.

Court Record, Page 116—5 January, 1719-20: Adms. to Sarah Moore, widow of the decd.

Page 124—5 April, 1720: Sarah Moore, Adms., exhibits now an account of her Adms. Accepted. Order to dist. the estate to the widow and children of the decd., vizt.:

	£ s d
To Sarah Moore, widow,	41-13-08
To Andrew Moore, eldest son,	62-01-06
To Jonathan Moore,	31-09-00
To William Moore,	31-00-09
To Benjamin,	25-00-00
To Sarah Winchell,	23-06-02
To Amos Moore,	31-00-09
To Deborah Forward,	26-01-07
To Abigail Stratton,	26-10-10
To Rachel Phelps,	27-14-04

And appoint Nathaniel Pinney, William Phelps and Timothy Loomis, distributors.

Page 150—2 May, 1721: Report of the distributors.

Page 275-278.

Moore, John, Sen., Windsor. Invt. £188-01-07. Taken 8 July, 1718, by Matthew Allyn, Roger Wolcott and Timothy Loomis. Will dated 18 January, 1717-18.

I, John Moore, Sen., of Windsor, do make this my last will and testament: Imprimis. I give to my wife Mary the £40 I promised to give her before our marriage. Also, I give her the side-sadle and pillion which she brought. And whereas, by a deed of gift dated 30 September, 1715, I gave her 1-2 of the house and land from the devicing fence between the pasture and orchard to the street, my will is that she shall have which half of the house she shall choose and elect. It. I give unto my son Samuel £40 in or as money, besides £10 I have already given him. It. I give unto my son Nathaniel £5, to be paid to him within four years after my decease. It. I give unto my daughter Martha £100 in money, to be paid to her when she shall arrive to 18 years of age or marriage, which shall first happen. Also, I give her the twenty shilling piece of gold.

Also, my will is that my wife shall have the interest of sd. £100 given to Martha, to be paid her yearly from the time of my decease till Martha shall arrive at the age of 18 or marriage as above sd. And the remainder of my personal estate my will is 1-4 part shall be given my daughter Martha besides what I have given her, and 1-4 part to the daughters of my son Joseph deceased, and the other half to my sons, viz., John, Thomas, Samuel, Edward and Josiah. My real estate I have already disposed of by deeds of gift to my sons. Finally, I do nominate and appoint my two sons John and Thomas to be executors.

Witness: *John Bissell,*   JOHN MOORE, SEN., LS.
Nathaniel Drake.

Court Record, Page 74—5 August, 1718: Will proven.

Page 113—6th October, 1719: Joseph Farnsworth, guardian to Martha Moore, moves this Court for a distribution of estate to Martha Moore. Not ordered.

Page 29 (Vol. XI) 6 October, 1730: Capt. Thomas Moore and John Moore, executors, accot. not accepted.

Page 67—15 May, 1732: This Court grant an appeal unto Job Drake, of Windsor, from one decree of this Court holden at Hartford on the third Tuesday of November, 1730, allowing an account of debts unto Thomas Moore and John Moore, executors of the last will of John Moore, Esq., late of Windsor deceased, unto the sd. Job Drake, of Windsor, unto the Superior Court to be holden by adjournment at Hartford on the last Tuesday of May instant. Capt. Thomas Moore and John Moore, executors to the last will of John Moore, Esq., being summoned to appear before this Court as per writ bearing date May 9th, 1732, to perfect the invt. of the estate and to render an account sufficient in the law to satisfy the legatees, viz., Job Drake of Windsor and Martha his wife, the parties appeared and the case is continued until 1st Tuesday in June next.

Page 70—6 June, 1732: According to the continuance of the case between Job Drake and Martha his wife of the one part, and John Moore and Thomas Moore, executors to the last will of John Moore of Windsor decd., the defendant pleaded that the plaintiff's writ ought to abate, for it cannot be known how the sd. Job Drake and Martha his wife became entitled to estate of John Moore, and hereof prays judgement, and judgement for his cost. And the Court are of opinion that sd. Job Drake is not sufficiently set forth how they became entitled to the action. The plaintiffs desire liberty to mend his writ, paying cost as the law directs, and the cost was paid by Job Drake. The writ was altered by the Court, and it is allowed by the defendant that sd. Job Drake was married to Martha Moore, daughter to John Moore, Esq., of Windsor, decd., and hereby Job Drake and Martha his wife becomes entitled to their action, and accordingly proceeded. And the sd. Thomas Moore, executor and plaintiff, produced in Court an evidence that he was not holden to render any further account of his executorship to the plaintiffs by one certain discharge from the plaintiffs in the following words:

Know all men by these presents: That we, Job Drake the 2nd and his wife Martha Drake, alias Martha Moore, both of Windsor, in the County of Hartford and Colony of Connecticut, have received of Capt. Thomas Moore of Windsor, executor in the last will and testament of John Moore, Esq., late of sd. Windsor deceased, full satisfaction for and on the account of a certain bequest or legacy given by the sd. John Moore, Esq., in his last will and testament, unto the above-named Martha with the respect to personal estate. And we do hereby acknowledge that we have received full satisfaction on the account of sd. legacy, and therefore do hereby discharge sd. executor or executors to sd. will of and from the same and every part thereof. And in witness whereof we have hereunto set our hand and seal this 2nd day of February, Anno. Dom. 1730-31.

JOB DRAKE 2ND, LS.
MARTHA DRAKE, LS.

Signed, sealed and delivered in presence of: *Nathaniel Drake,*
                   Henry Allyn.

A true copy, recorded by me. *Joseph Talcott.*
Whereupon this Court is of opinion that Thomas Moore is not obliged to render any further account as demanded of the plaintiff in sd. writ. Whereupon this Court orders the plaintiff to pay costs of prosecution, which is allowed to be 5 shillings.

Page 356.

Morton, Mary, Windsor. Invt. £52-06-00. Taken 30 January, 1719-20, by William Williams and Gabriel Williams. Will dated 18 January, 1719-20.

I, Mary Morton of Windsor, widow, do make this my last will and testament: I devise and give unto my two sons, John Morton and Samuel Morton, all my lands which do or ought of right belong unto me as my part or share of the lands belonging to my honoured father, Thomas Burnham deceased. Also, I give unto my sd. sons John and Samuel my plow irons, one timber chain, draft chain, all the irons belonging unto my cart, two stubbing hoes, one spade, one cart rope, one hamer, two collers, one hatchet, one wheat ridle, two sickles; all these to be equally divided between my sons as their own. I give to my sd. son John one paire of money scales and one pewter tankard. I give unto my son Samuel one paire of cobb irons, one paire of tongs, one tramel, one paire of brass scales with the weights belonging to them, one great Bible, one pewter platter called Old East or Old One, one frying pann, warming pann, one old chest wherein I keep my linen, one bedd with all the furniture belonging thereunto, one table, 1-2 of my earthern ware and 1-2 of my wooden ware, one hogshead, one meal trough, one looking-glass, four glass bottles, two bags, one brass skillett, one table cloth. I give and bequeath unto my granddaughter Esther Coult one bed, which I usually lye on, with all the furniture belonging thereunto, one trunk, 11 napkins, one Holland shift, all my wearing apparrell and other clothes, two boxes, one pewter basin and three of my biggest pewter platters and one table cloth, two little wheels, one great wheel; all these I bequeath to my sd. granddaughter to be her own. I give to my granddaughter Hannah Morton, the daughter of my son Thomas Morton, 1s; to each of the children of my daughter Ann Drake, 1s. I give and bequeath unto my daughter Sarah Loomis one new bed ticking and one bolster, one powdering tub, one blankett, all which particulars my sd. daughter hath already in her hands. All my other moveable estate of what kind soever I give and bequeath unto my daughter Mary Coult. I appoint my son John Morton executor.

Witness: *William Williams,*   MARY X MORTON, LS.
Gabriel Williams, William Williams, Jr.

Court Record, Page 122—1st March, 1720: Will proven.

Page 310-11.

Add. Invt. in Vol. X, Page 13.

Newbery, Benjamin, Windsor. Invt. £123-05-07. Taken 13 February, 1718-19, by Henry Wolcott and Samuel Bancroft.

Court Record, Page 94—3 February, 1718-19: Adms. granted to Ruth Newbery, widow, and James Porter, of Windsor.

Page 6 (Vol. X) 5 February, 1722-3: James Porter, one of the Adms. on the estate of Benjamin Newbery, exhibited an addition to the inventory. Accepted.

Page 281.

Olmsted, Nicholas, Hartford (son of Joseph). Died 29 November, 1717. Invt. £240-14-09. Taken by Ozias Pitkin and Timothy Cowles.

Court Record, Page 49—7 January, 1717-18: Adms. granted to Mrs. Mary Olmsted, widow.

Page 148 (Vol. X) 7 March, 1726-7: This Court appoint Mary Olmsted of Hartford to be guardian to her children, viz., to Stephen, age 18 years, Isaac 16, Nathaniel 12, Mary 10, and Abigail 8 years of age, children of Nicholas Olmsted decd.

Page 28 (Vol. XI) 1 September, 1730: Upon motion of Stephen, son and one of the heirs of Nicholas Olmsted, late of Hartford decd., to this Court that the lands given by the last will of Deacon Joseph Olmsted to the heirs of Nicholas Olmsted might be apprised in order to a just distribution among the heirs of Nicholas Olmsted decd.: This Court appoint Deacon Timothy Cowles, Deacon Joseph Olmsted and Mr. Joseph Pitkin, distributors.

Page 32—1st December, 1732: An apprisement of the estate given by the last will of Deacon Joseph Olmsted to the heirs of Nicholas Olmsted, according to an order of Court September, 1730, now exhibited by Stephen Olmsted and accepted. This Court order distribution as followeth: To the widow and relict of Nicholas Olmsted, the use of 1-3 part of the lands during life; to Stephen Olmsted, £10; the rest to be equally divided to Stephen, Isaac, Nathaniel, Mary and Abigail Olmsted, children of the sd. Nicholas Olmsted. This Court appoint Capt. William Pitkin, Deacon Timothy Cowles and Nehemiah Olmsted, distributors.

Page 56—19 November, 1731: Report of the distributors.

Page 122.

Owen, Josiah, Windsor. Invt. £199-03-00. Taken 21 September, 1722, by Thomas Griswold, John Griswold and Joseph Barnard. Will nuncupative.

We, the subscribers, being present with Josiah Owen of Windsor, now decd., at his dwelling house at Windsor, on the 11th day of September, he to our observations being apprehensive of approaching death, did *viva voce* earnestly declare the following disposition of his estate to be his last will and testament: Imprimis: That his wife Sarah should have half of his dwelling house and half of the barn and orchard during her widowhood. Item. That his daughter Elizabeth should have 5 shillings out of his estate, and the rest of his estate to be equally divided amongst his children.

Witness: *Thomas* X *Phelps,*
        Obadiah Owen, David Phelps.

On the 17th day of September, 1722, Thomas Phelps, Obadiah Owen and David Phelps appeared before the Court of Probate and made oath that they heard the above-named Josiah Owen declare as is above written, and that they put the above will into writing on the 14th day of September, 1722.

Court Record, Page 176—2 October, 1722: Adms. granted to Josiah Owen, eldest son, and Lt. Jonathan Elsworth.

Page 57 (Vol. X) 6 October, 1724: This Court appoint Thomas Griswold, Samuel Hayden of Windsor and Joseph Phelps of Simsbury to apprise 3 parcels of land that Josiah Owen of Hebron and John Owen of Windsor formerly received from their father Josiah Owen decd., so that an equal dist. may be made.

Page 74—22 March, 1724-5: Josiah Owen and Jonathan Elsworth, Adms., exhibit an account of their Adms. Accepted. Order to dist. the estate:

	£ s d
To Josiah Owen, eldest son,	34-09-04
To John Owen,	9-11-06
To Mary Phelps,	19-07-06
To Elizabeth Case,	23-03-07
To Rachel Phelps,	18-06-03

And appoint Timothy Loomis, John Griswold and Joseph Barnard, distributors. Josiah Owen now exhibited the apprisement of 3 parcels of land. Accepted.

Page 72-3-93.

Palmer, Stephen, Windsor. Invt. £181-03-01. Taken 29 November, 1720, by Thomas Moore and Nathaniel Drake.

Court Record, Page 141—6 December, 1720: Adms. to Sarah Palmer, widow, and John Palmer, son of the decd.

Page 168—9 May, 1722: John Palmer, Adms., reports amount of debts (£50-10-09) to be more than the value of the moveables.

Page 104 (Vol. XI) 28 December, 1732: Stephen Palmer, son of Stephen Palmer, chose John Palmer of Windsor to be his guardian.

Page 54 (Vol. XII) 1st February, 1736-7: Timothy Palmer, age 16 years, son of Stephen Palmer, chose his uncle John Barbour of Windsor to be his guardian. Recog., £100.

Page 99.

Phelps, Joseph, Windsor. Invt. £341-16-11. Taken 26 September, 1716, by James Enno, Timothy Loomis and John Palmer. Will dated 23 August, 1716.

I, Joseph Phelps, Sen., do make this my last will and testament: After my just debts be paid, I give unto my wife Sarah the use and improvement of 1-3 part of my estate, both personal and real, during her natural life; also, I give to my wife a new Bible. It is my will that my estate shall be divided equally amongst my ten children: Joseph, Daniel, Edward, John, Abell, Ichabod, Jonathan, Mary, Sarah and Abigail. I appoint my son Daniel and my wife Sarah to be executors.

Witness: *Jonathan Brown,*   JOSEPH PHELPS, LS.
       William Phelps.

Court Record, Page 23—2 October, 1716: Edward Phelps, 18 years of age, John 16, Mary 13, children of Joseph Phelps, chose Samuel Phelps to be their guardian. This Court appoint William Phelps to be guardian to Abell, age 11 years, Ichabod, 9 years. Will exhibited by Sarah and Daniel Phelps.

Page 25—1st April, 1716-17: Sarah Phelps, widow, accepts the trust of executrix.

Page 60—1st April, 1718: The executors exhibit an account. Accepted. Order to dist. the remaining part of the estate to Sarah Phelps, widow, to Joseph, Daniel, Edward, John, Abell, Ichabod, Jonathan, Mary and Abigail Phelps. And appoint Thomas Moore, James Enno and John Bissell, distributors.

See File: Dist. of the estate, 1st April, 1718: To the widow, to Joseph, to Daniel, to Edward, to John, to Abell, to Ichabod, to Jonathan, to Matthew Griswold in right of his wife Mary Phelps, and to Sarah and Abigail Phelps. By Thomas Moore and John Bissell.

Page 69 (Vol. X) 2 February, 1724-5: Report of the distributors.

Page 220—3 June, 1729: This Court appoint Cornelius Phelps of Windsor to be guardian to Jonathan Phelps, a minor, age 17 years. Recog., £50.

Page 338-350-51.

Phelps, Capt. Timothy, Windsor. Invt. £344-19-06. Taken by John Palmer and James Enno. Will dated 2nd March, 1716-17.

I, Timothy Phelps of Windsor, being very aged yet retaining a good measure of understanding and memory, do make this my last will and testament: Imprimis. I give, devise and bequeath all my estate whatsoever, both real and personal, to my three sons, William, Cornelius and Samuel, to have, hold and improve the same in trust for the use of my wife during her natural life, and after her decease my will is, and I hereby do give and devise all my houseing and lands with the appurtenances to my sons Timothy Phelps, William Phelps, Cornelius Phelps, Samuel Phelps, Nathaniel Phelps, and heirs of Joseph Phelps in the room of their father, to be equally divided into six equal parts, provided always, and it is my will, that they pay and make up to their sisters, Sarah, Hannah, Ann and Martha, my daughters, or to their heirs, and to the heirs of my daughter Abigail deceased, £48 as money apiece; and my will is that what they have already recd. as entered upon my book shall be reckoned as part of sd. summs, and yt my sd. sons and the heirs of my son Joseph shall pay their sisters and their heirs above mentioned in equal proportion, except that the heirs of Joseph shall pay £4 more than an equal proportion, and my son Cornelius £4 less than an equal proportion. And my will further is, that my wife shall have the free disposal of all her wearing apparell at her decease, and that my grandson Samuel Fyler shall have half of that bequeathed to the heirs of my daughter Abigail if he liveth with me so long as I live, or till he comes to the age of 18 years. I appoint my wife Mary and my three sons, William, Cornelius and Samuel, to be executors.

Witness: *John Mansfield,*   TIMOTHY X PHELPS, LS.
            Thomas Moore.

And whereas, I being aged and my wife soe, and not knowing how long it may please God to continue my life, and not knowing what debts and charge may arise before I leave this world, my will is that my sons and my daughters and their heirs shall pay their equal parts and shares of my debts and charges after my decease. And my daughters, Sarah, Hannah, Ann and Martha, and the heirs of Abigail, shall have £46 apiece with what they have already had, to be paid as money out of my estate after my decease. By the charge as above mentioned I intend that if there be any extraordinary charge, so that the improvement of my estate will

not maintain me. This addition of my will was made and published the 2nd day of March, 1716.
Witness: *John Mansfield,*   TIMOTHY X PHELPS, LS.
     Thomas Moore.

These witnesses appeared 28 September, 1719, and made oath that they saw Timothy Phelps sign and seal the will with the addition, before
                                        Matthew Allyn, Assistant.

Court Record, Page 112—6 October, 1719: Will exhibited and proven. William Phelps to be guardian to Samuel Fyler, son of Samuel Fyler, late of Hebron deceased, a minor about 10 years of age.

Page 118—19 January, 1719-20: Order to dist. the estate according to the will, by Ebenezer Fitch, John Palmer and Abram Phelps.

Page 5 (Vol. XII) 13 May, 1734: Jonathan Phelps of Northampton, Mass., heir by will to Capt. Timothy Phelps of Windsor, moves this Court that a division of the lands be made to the heirs. This Court appoint Capt. Henry Allyn, Lt. Roger Newbery and Lt. John Cook to set out by meets and bounds according to the will of sd. deceased.

Page 251-2.

Pinney, Isaac, Jr., Windsor. Died 11 August, 1717. Invt. £140-00-00. Taken 11 October, 1717, by Samuel Rockwell and John Elsworth.

Court Record, Page 44—5 November, 1717: Adms. granted to Abigail Pinney, widow.

Page 64—6 May, 1718: This Court appoint Abigail Pinney to be guardian to Prudence Pinney, age 7 years, and Ann Pinney, 5 years, children of Isaac Pinney, Jr., decd. Also appoint Joseph Skinner, Jr., of Windsor, to be guardian to Oliver Pinney, age 3 years, and Isaac Pinney, 2 years.

Page 105—2 June, 1719: Abigail Pinney, Adms., exhibits an account of her Adms. Accepted. Order to dist. the estate:

	£	s	d
To Abigail Pinney, widow,	16	19	10
To Oliver Pinney, eldest son,	31	11	10
To Isaac, Prudence and Ann Pinney, to each,	15	15	11

And appoint John Elsworth, Samuel Rockwell and Jonathan Bissell, distributors.

See Dist. File: 1719: To the widow Abigail, now the wife of Nathaniel Phelps; to Oliver, to Isaac, to Prudence, and to Ann Pinney. By John Elsworth, Samuel Rockwell and Jonathan Bissell.

Page 2 (Vol. XII) 18 April, 1734: Isaac Davise, having right in common with heirs of Isaac Pinney of Windsor to 1-2 of a parcel of land lying in the Town of Windsor on the east side of the Great River, viz., 1-2 of the 100 acres of land formerly laid out to Matthew Grant, moves this Court to appoint freeholders to joyn with the guardians of the Pinney

heirs to divide sd. land. This Court appoint Capt. Joseph Phelps of Hebron, William Wolcott and Deacon Joseph Skinner guardian to the or-
phan children of Isaac Pinney, to divide the land.

Page 3—29 April, 1734: Report of distribution of land to Isaac Davise, to Oliver Pinney, and to Isaac Pinney decd. By William Wolcott,
Joseph Skinner and Joseph Phelps.

Page 50-1.

Pinney, Sarah, Windsor. Invt. £28-19-05. Taken 26 December,
1715, by Benajah Holcomb and Joseph Phelps. Will dated 13 June, 1711.

I, Sarah Pinney of Windsor, widow, being aged and weak, doe make
this my last will and testament: I give to my four daughters, Sarah
Moore, Mary Addams, Abigail Winchell and Sarah Grant, the wife of
Thomas Grant, the whole of my estate, to be equally divided between
them. I make my brother Ensign Joseph Griswold and Sergt. Benajah
Holcomb executors.

Witness: *Nathaniel Griswold,*   SARAH X PINNEY, LS.
   Matthew Allyn.

Court Record, Page 6—7 February, 1715-16: Will proven. The executors decline the trust. Adms. is granted to Benjamin Addams of
Simsbury.

Page 124.

Porter, Nehemiah, Farmington. Invt. £408-08-11. Taken 5 November, 1722, by Thomas Hart and Samuel Smith. Will dated 23 May, 1722.

I, Nehemiah Porter of Farmington, do make this my last will and
testament: I give of my land equally to all my children. To my sons John
Porter and Jonathan Porter I have given something already by deeds of
gift, both their shares to be made equal to the rest of my children in the
distribution of my real estate. And concerning my personal or moveable
estate, I give unto my grandson John Porter £3 as money. I give unto my
granddaughters Ann and Abigail Porter the sum of thirty shillings to
each of them. Item. Unto my grandson, the son of my daughter Hannah, I give the young mare I bought of Sergt. Isaac Hart. Item. I give
unto my well-beloved son Jonathan the black mare bought of John North
and a sorrell mare about 3 years old. Item. I give unto my son Samuel
a dark brown mare colt about one year old. And when my debts and
necessary charges are paid, my will is that the rest of my estate in moveables be equally divided amongst all my children. And moreover, my will
is that the household stuff that my daughters Martha and Hannah have
gotten with their own labor shall not be brought into the inventory of my
estate. I appoint my sons Thomas Porter and Jonathan Porter executors.

Witness: *William Burnham,*   NEHEMIAH X PORTER, LS.
Hezekiah Hart, Isaac Hart.

Court Record, Page 176—2 October, 1722: Will proven.

Page 9 (Vol. X) 5 March, 1722-3: Thomas and Jonathan Porter, executors, exhibited an account. Accepted. Order to dist. the estate according to the last will and testament of the decd., viz. (see file) : To Martha, to Thomas, Jonathan, Samuel, Rachel and John Porter. By Isaac Newton, Thomas Hart and Isaac Hart.

Page 36 (Vol. XIII) 8 November, 1738: Nathaniel Winchell of Farmington informed this Court that he purchased 1-3 part of a lott of land in sd. Farmington of the heirs of Nehemiah Porter of Farmington, which lies in common with Daniel Woodruff and Doctor Samuel Porter's heirs, of which one is a minor, viz., Samuel Porter. Sd. lott of land was laid out on the right of Doctor Daniel Porter of sd. Farmington deceased, and lieth in a division commonly known by the name of Shuttle Meadow Mountain, and bounds south on a highway, north on land of the heirs of the Rev. John Hart of Guilford deceased, and the land lies in common or joynt tenancy as is above mentioned and with Mr. George Wilton of sd. Farmington. Nathaniel Winchell prays this Court for a division. This Court appoint Thomas Hart, Lt. Samuel Cowles and Mr. Samuel Hooker of Farmington, with Mr. Ezekiel Porter, guardian to Samuel Porter, a minor and one of the heirs of sd. estate, to divide sd. estate by meets and bounds.

Page 37—7 November, 1738: Report of the division to the several claimants.

Page 306-310.

Porter, Thomas, Farmington. Died 28 January, 1718-19. Invt. £421-10-01. Taken by Timothy Porter and Isaac Cowles. Will dated 18 December, 1718.

The last will and testament of Thomas Porter is as followeth: I give and bequeath to Abigail, my well-beloved wife, 1-3 part of my dwelling house, or two rooms and cellarage needful, and 1-3 part of my homelott which my house stands upon, and the 1-3 part of all my land which is hereafter given to my two younger sons Robert and Benjamin, all which above-mentioned particulars I give the use and improvement during her natural life. Further, I do give to my wife 2 cowes and 10 sheep and all the swine for the use of the family ; 1-3 part of my household stuff to be at her own dispose, to give to my own children. Further, I do give unto my beloved children as followeth: To my son William, 1 1-2 acres of land next to Samuel Smith's land and Nathaniel's land ; I give further two sheep. Item. I do give to Nathaniel land as followeth: Beginning at the north end and soe five rod wide, and soe to run north and south the length of my land, and so to take in that Deacon Porter did improve, and one acre of land in Paquabuck, and the two lotts that lie upon the west side of the river at Nodd, and four sheep. Item. I do give to Robert and Benjamin all the remainder of my land, after my wife's decease, to be equally divided betwixt them. Also, I give to the above-named Robert and Benjamin two yoke of oxen and the horses and the husbandry tackling and tools, they paying all my debts that are lawful. I do give unto my daughter Abigail £24, one cow and one yearling hefer, and to my daughter Elizabeth £22 and one young hefer. I make my well-beloved wife and my son Robert Porter sole executors.

Witness: *Samuel Cowles, Sen.,*   THOMAS PORTER, LS.
Nathaniel Cowles.

Court Record, Page 90—6th January, 1718-19: Will proven.

Page 94—3 February, 1718-19: This Court appoint Abigail Porter, widow, to be guardian to Elizabeth Porter, 16 years of age, and Benjamin Porter, 18 years, children of Thomas Porter. Recog., with Isaac Cowles of Farmington, £100.

Page 331.

Prior, Humphrey, Windsor. Invt. £03-05-06. Taken 6 July, 1719, by Eliakim Marshall and Samuel Strong.

Court Record, Page 103—9 April, 1719: Adms. to John Fyler, a creditor of the estate.

Page 109—4 August, 1719: John Fyler, Adms., exhibits accot. of his Adms. Accepted. There remains £0-02-01 to be paid to the widow.

Page 364.

Purple, Edward, Haddam. Invt. £85-15-06. Taken by James Brainard, John Arnold and Joseph Arnold. Will dated 19 December, 1718.

I, Edward Purple of Haddam, do make this my last will and testament: I give unto my wife Hannah all my household goods, and it is my will that my sons John and Edward afford her comfortable maintenance while she remains my widow. I give to my son John my orchard with all the land appertaining thereto, as it lyes, bounded north and east on land of John Bate, south on the highway; also, my dwelling house and all my land which it stands upon, from the white oak tree marked "I. P." and a line running from the said tree so as to make a right angle att the highway, across unto land belonging to Solomon Bate. I give unto him the whole of said land excepting only one acre of meadow from said line downwards toward the river. I give to my son Edward that tract of land upon which his dwelling house now stands, as it is bounded west on the highway, north on land of Deacon Joseph Arnold, east on Connecticut River, and south on a highway. I give to my son Richard one acre of my meadow land and the northwest end of the lott that my house stands upon. It is my will that in consideration of what I have given to my sons that they make payment of all my debts equally. I appoint Deacon Joseph Arnold executor.

Witness: *Samuel Ingram,*   EDWARD X PURPLE, LS.
Joseph Lewis, Phineas Fisk.

Court Record, Page 119—9 February, 1719-20: Will proven.

Page 2 (Vol. XI) 2 August, 1729: Edward Purple, Jr., 16 years of age, of Haddam, chose his uncle Samuel Ackley to be his guardian. Recog., £50.

Page 64.

Reignolds, Samuel, Coventry. Invt. £252-01-06. Taken 1st May, 1720, by Nathaniel Rust and Thomas Porter.

Court Record, Page 128—18 June, 1720: Adms. to Susannah Reignolds, widow.

Page 205 (Vol. X) 12 November, 1728: Susannah Rennolds, alias Richards, now exhibit account of Adms. with some additional invt. in land at Presson in partnership with Jonathan Rennolds as per deed bearing date 18 August, 1718, under the hand of John Rennolds. Ordered to be recorded. This Court orders and impowers Thomas Richards and his wife Susannah to be guardians to the child of Samuel Rennolds, late of Coventry decd., viz., Samuel Rennolds, age 8 years. Rec., £90. Dist. as per order of Court: 1-3 part of the personal estate to Susannah, the widow, now wife of Thomas Richards, and 2-3 to Samuel Rennolds, only child. And appoint Capt. Thomas Judd, John Scovell and William Judd distributors.

Richards, Thomas, Boston. Copy of will found on file in the Hartford Probate Records. Proven in Boston, and the granting of letters of administration.

In the name of God, amen. I, Thomas Richards of Boston, in the County of Suffolk, in the Provence of the Massachusetts Bay in New England, gentleman, do make and ordain this my last will and testament, being at this present time of sound disposing mind and memory, praise be given to God for the same: ffirst and principally, I resign my precious and immortal soul unto the hands of Almighty God my Creator and gracious benefactor, hopeing through the glorius mediation and prevailing intercession of Jesus Christ, my only Lord and Saviour, to receive the forgiveness of all my sins and justification unto eternal life. My body I committ unto the earth as it was, to be decently interred at the discretion of my executrix hereafter named. And as for that worldly estate which God of his great good hath graciously given to me, I give, devise and bequeath the same in manner and form as in this my will is expressed:

Imprimis: I will that all my just debts and funerall expenses, with all such legacies as I shall give and bequeath in this my said will, be well and truly paid and discharged by my executrix in convenient time after my decease.

Item. I give unto my dearly beloved wife and faithful companion, Joanna Richards, one-third part of the yearly incomes and profits of my real estate during her natural life.

Item. I give unto my said wife the free and full improvement, livings or annual incomes of the house wherein I now dwell, with all the land, shipyard and appurtenances thereunto belonging, situate in Boston aforesaid, during the term of her natural life.

Item. I give unto my said wife five hundred pounds in bills of credit on the Province aforesaid, to be at her own dispose as she shall think fitt.

Item. I give unto my loving kinswoman and niece, the wife of the Rev. Mr. Sampson Stoddard of Chelmsford, fifty pounds money as aforesaid, in token of my love to her.

Item. I give and bequeath a like sum of fifty pounds to Daniel Alford, son to my loveing nephew Benjamin Alford of Boston, merchant.

Item. I give to my brother-in-law, Edward Dodd, of Hartford, in the Colony of Connecticut, ten pounds.

Item. I give to the Revd. Doctor Increase Mather and Cotton Mather ten pounds apiece.

Item. I give to the Revd. Mr. Thomas Buckingham, of Hartford aforesd., five pounds.

Item. I give to Harvard College, in Cambridge, thirty pounds.

Item. I give to John Arcoss, who was formerly my servant, ten pounds.

Item. I give twenty pounds to the poor of the Town of Boston.

Item. I give to my loveing sister, Mary Alvord, ten pounds; and to her daughter Sarah, five pounds.

Item. All the rest and residue of my estate, both real and personal, as well that in Great Britain as what I have in Boston, Hartford or any other parts of New England, or whatsoever or wheresoever the same is or may be found, I give, devise and bequeath the same unto my loveing children and daughters, Joanna and Mary Richards, their heirs and assigns forever, part and part alike. And in case either of them should dye before she come of age or be married, then the survivor to have and inherit the whole; and in case both of them should dye before they come of age or be married (which God forbid), then and in that case I give, devise and bequeath all such estate of mine, both real and personal, as shall be to them left, unto my said beloved wife during her natural life, and one-third part thereof to her heirs and assigns forever. The other two-thirds, after the death of my said wife, I give and devise unto my loveing nephew William Davis, my loveing nieces his sisters, namely, Sarah Bill and Elizabeth Stoddard before named, and my loveing nephew Benjamin Alford, to be divided between them, viz., one-third part thereof to the said Benjamin Alford, and the remaining two-thirds unto the said William Davis and his sisters Bill and Stoddard, to be equally divided between them, upon condition, nevertheless, that they pay the several sums next following: to my brother-in-law Edward Dodd before named, fifty pounds; to the children of my niece Vryling, fifty pounds, equally to be divided among them; to my niece Joanna Alford, twenty pounds; and to the children of my sister Saltonstall deceased, twenty pounds apiece.

Item. I make and constitue my said beloved wife whole and sole executrix of this my last will and testament, and do hereby impower my said executrix, with the consent of my trustees hereafter named or the survivors of them, to mortgage or make sale of any part of my real estate for the payment and satisfaction of my just debts and the prospective or absolute legacies I have herein before given and bequeathed.

Item. I do hereby appoint, desire and impower my worthy and loveing friends, Paul Dudley, Esq., and Samuel Greenwood, merchant, both of Boston aforesaid, to be the trustees of this my last will, to assist my said executrix in the execution thereof; and unto each of them, as a token of my love, I give five pounds. Finally, I do hereby revoke and disanull all former or latter wills or testaments by me at any time heretofore made, declareing this to be my only last will and testament. In testimony whereof I have hereunto set my hand and seal the twenty-third day of November, Anno. Domini, 1714.

Signed, sealed, published and declared by the said Thomas Richards to be his last will and testament, before us who set our names as witnesses thereof in his presence.

THOMAS RICHARDS, LS.
Concordat Cum Originali.
Paul Dudley, Register.

Samuel Clark,
Samuel Tyley, Jr.,
Samuel Greenwood, Jr.

ISAAC ADDINGTON, ESQ., commissioned by His Excellency Joseph Dudley, Esq., Captain-General and Governor-in-Chief in and over His Majestie's Provence of the Massachusetts Bay in New England, by and with the advice and consent of the Council, to be Judge of the Probate of Wills and for granting Letters of Administration on the Estates of Persons Deceased having Goods, Chattels, Rights or Credits in the County of Suffolk, within the Province aforesaid:

To all unto whom these presents shall come, greeting:

Know yee that upon the day of the date hereof, before me at Boston, in the County aforesaid, the will of Thomas Richards, late of Boston, in the County of Suffolk, in New England, gentm., deceased, to these presents annexed, was proved, approved and allowed; who, having while he lived and at the time of his death, goods and chattels, rights and credits in the County aforesaid, and the probate of the said will and power comitting administration of all and singular the goods, chattels, rights and credits of the said deceased by virtue thereof appertaining unto me: The administration of all and singular the goods, chattels, rights and credits of the said deceased, and his will in any manner concerning, is hereby committed unto his relict and widow, Joanna Richards, sole executrix in the same will named, well and faithfully to execute the said will and to administer the estate of the said deceased according thereunto, and to make a true and perfect inventory of all and singular the goods, chattels, rights and credits of the said deceased, and to exhibit the same unto the Registry of the Court of Probate for the County aforesaid at or before the sixteenth day of March next ensueing, and also to render a plain and true account of her said administration upon oath.

In testimony whereof I have hereunto set my hand and the seal of the said Court of Probates.

Dated at Boston aforesd., the sixteenth day of December, Anno Domini 1714. Entered Nov. 15, 1716.

A

ISA ADDINGTON.

C

Page 91.

Roberts, John, Middletown. Invt. £139-14-01. Taken 24 July, 1721, by William Harris, John Harris and Joseph Johnson.

Court Record, Page 157—7 November, 1721: Adms. granted to Sarah Roberts, widow of sd. decd.

Page 180—4 December, 1722: This Court appoint William Whitmore of Middletown guardian to David Roberts, a minor about 20 years of age; also appoint John Blake to be guardian to Mary Roberts, age 17 years, Jonathan Roberts 15, Nathaniel 11, and Daniel Roberts 8 years of age, children of John Roberts late decd.

Page 5 (Vol. X) 5 February, 1722-3: Sarah Roberts, Adms., exhibits an account of her Adms. Allowed. Order to dist the estate:

	£ s d
To Sarah Roberts, widow,	8-14-09
To William, eldest son,	15-11-08
To John,	3-06-10
To Ebenezer, David, Mary, Jonathan, Nathaniel and Daniel Roberts, to each of them the sum of	13-06-10

And appoint Thomas Ward, William Harris and John Harris, distributors.

Page 79-347.

Robinson, John, Hartford. Invt. £15-14-07. Taken 5 October, 1719, by Thomas Spencer and Daniel Dickinson.

I, John Robinson, being in perfect mind and memory and in my right sences, do make this my last will and testament: Item. I give my soul to God that gave it, and my body to the earth decently to be buried. Item. I will that all my lawful debts may be payed, makeing my brother Philip Smith, living in Hartford on the east side of the Great River, my executor. Item. I give to my cousen Jonathan Arnold that tract of land being the 64 part of a towne betwixt Simsbury and Westfield. Item. I give to Philip Smith, whom I made my exr., 5 sheep. Item. I give to my cousen Eunice Turner five sheep. Item. I give to my executor my apparell and arms.

Witness: *Nathll. Mather,*   JOHN X ROBINSON.
Henry Merrow, Jonathan Tuthill.

Mr. Henry Merrow of Lyme, in the County of New London and Colony of Connecticut, seafareing man, personally appeared before me and made oath that he did see John Robinson signe the above written will.

Lyme, 28 December, 1719.   Pr. *Moses Noyes, Justice Peace.*

Court Record, Page 115—5 January, 1719-20: Will proven. Philip Smith, appointed executor, declined and was granted Adms. with the will annexed.

Page 148—4 April, 1721 : Invt. exhibited and accepted.

Page 230-31.

Root, Stephen, Sen., Farmington. Invt. £339-13-02. Taken 2 March, 1716-17, by John Wadsworth and Isaac Cowles. Will dated 16 October, 1716.

The last will and testament of Stephen Root is as followeth: Imprimis: I give to my wife Sarah Root that half of the house, barn and homestead that I now stand possessed of, and also that half of the meadow land that I now stand seized of in Paquabuck, during her natural life, and after her decease to be equally divided between my three grandsons, Jonathan, Stephen and Timothy Root. In case of the decease of my wife before these boyes come of age, then it shall remain in the hands of my two daughters, Sarah and Hannah Root, to be equally improved by them and delivered to the sd. boyes when they come of age. All my land lying on the back side of Paquabuck meadow I do give the improvement of to my wife during her natural life, then to return to my three grandsons, to be equally divided between them. And my land at the White Oak Plain and at the Long Swamp I do give unto my two daughters, Sarah and Hannah, to be equally divided between them. Also, I do give unto my son John Root a yoke of brown steers. Also, I give unto my wife and son John Root all my husbandry tools, to be divided equally between them. Also, I give unto my son John Root all my wearing clothes. Also, I give unto my daughter Mary Judd one cow. Also, I give unto my grandson Stephen Root all my land at Crane Hall. Also, I give and bequeath unto my wife and my two daughters Sarah and Hannah all my household goods and the remainder of my stock, horses, neat cattle, sheep and swine, to be equally divided between them, and all my grain and corne, Indian and English, they first paying my just debts, and the remainder to be equally divided between them. My wife and son John Root executors.

Witness: *Joseph Root,*   STEPHEN ROOT, SEN., LS.
    John Hart.

Court Record, Page 29—25 April, 1717: Will proven.

Page 345.

Rowley, Thomas, Colchester. Invt. £69-01-02. Taken by Thomas Robinson and Ebenezer Dibble.

Court Record, Page 114—1st December, 1719: Adms. granted to Mary Rowley, widow of the decd.

Page 144—7 February, 1720: Mary Rowley, Adms., exhibits an account of her Adms., which this Court accepts, orders recorded and kept on file. And this Court doth grant Mary Rowley a *Quietus Est.*

Page 249.

Rue, John, Hartford. Invt. £22-02-07. Taken 26 September, 1717, by Thomas Ensign and Jonathan Easton.

Court Record, Page 43—1st October, 1717: Adms. granted to John and Hezekiah Rue, sons of the sd. decd.

Page 79—2 September, 1718: The Adms. exhibited an account of their Adms., which was accepted, and this Court do grant them a *Quietus Est.*

Ruggles, Abigail. Court Record, Page 17—3 July, 1716: Abigail Ruggles of Farmington, a minor, having (before Mr. Justice Humphrey of Simsbury, as he hath certified this Court) made choice of Jonathan Humphrey of Simsbury to be her guardian, this Court approve and confirm the sd. Jonathan Humphrey to be guardian. Rec., £100. Samuel Hooker of Farmington, Jr., being dissatisfied with the Court's now approving and confirming the sd. Jonathan Humphrey to be guardian to the sd. minor, appealed therefrom to the Superior Court. Rec., £5.

Page 318-19.

Sexton, John, Simsbury. Died 4 December, 1718. Invt. £295-17-08. Taken 5 January, 1718-19, by John Case, Benjamin Addams and Andrew Robe. The legatees: Richard, eldest son, with 3 orphans; John, 2nd son; Mary, wife of Wm. Gillett. Will dated 19th March, 1716.

I, John Sexton of Simsbury, doe make this my last will and testament: I give unto my only son John Sexton all my land at the Plain, excepting 1-4 of an acre around the house that was my son Richard's; also I except that land which was my daughter Hannah's, improved 3 acres grass and 4 plow land, which I gave to her to improve so long as she keepeth her children with her, obliging my sd. son to pay unto my son Richard's three daughters £10 to each when they come to age. Also, I give him half of my land in and about Bissell's Marsh. Also, I give him the 1-3 part of my land in Salmon Brook lower meadow. Item. I give to my daughter Hannah, my son Richard's wife, the improvement of 3 acres of grass and 4 of plow land as above sd. in the land at the Plain, with 1-4 of an acre around her house; and also I give her the improvement of 5 acres of land in Bissell's Marsh as long as she keeps her children with her; and also I give her the improvement of 1 1-2 acres of plow land in

Salmon Brook lower meadows the time abovesd. Item. I give unto my son-in-law William Gillett 6 acres of land in Bissell's Marsh. Item. My will further is that my son John Sexton shall have the 1-3 part of all my outlands not yet disposed of, and the other 2-3 I give to be equally divided between my son William Gillett and my son Richard's three daughters. I appoint my son John Sexton sole executor.

Witness: *John Roberts,*   JOHN X SEXTON, L.S.
          Samuel Higley.

Court Record, Page 101—7 April, 1719: Will proven.
Page 151 (Vol. X) 4 April, 1727: Azariah Wilcoxson moves this Court he hath right to the estate of John Sexton by marriage with one of his granddaughters; that dist. may be ordered on the real estate of the sd. decd., according to his last will. The executor, John Sexton, appeared in Court, when the parties were heard upon a point in the construction of the will, vizt.: "Item. My son John Sexton shall have 1-3 part of all my outlands, and the other 2-3 I give to be equally divided between my son William Gillet and my son Richard's three daughters." This Court are of the opinion that the 2-3 of the undivided lands of the testator given as aforesd. is given in equal parts to the 4 persons abovenamed, to them or their heirs. David Enno, who married one of the daughters of William Gillet, appealed from this judgement to the Superior Court.

Page 82.

Shepherd, Edward, Middletown. Invt. £250-07-04. Taken 8 May, 1721, by William Savage and John Warner, Jr.
Court Record, Page 152—5 June, 1721: Adms. granted to John and Samuel Shepherd, brothers of sd. decd.
Page 168—5 June, 1722: John and Samuel Shepherd, Adms., exhibit an account of their Adms. Accepted. And this Court grant them a *Quietus Est.*

Page 265.

Shippason, Nathaniel, Hebron. Invt. £128-17-00. Taken 25 April, 1718, by Nathaniel Dunham, Samuel Waters and Benjamin Skinner.
Court Record, Page 63-4—6 May, 1718: Adms. to Mary Shippason, widow relict of the sd. decd.
Page 129—5 July, 1720: Mary Shippason of Hebron, Adms. on the estate of Nathaniel Shippason decd., exhibits an account of her Adms. Accepted. Order to dist. the estate to the widow and children: To Mary Shippason, relict, £14-16-03; to Jonathan Shippason, eldest son, £17-08-00; to Nathaniel, to John, to Elizabeth, to Mary, to Mercy, to Joanna Shippason, children of the sd. decd., to each, £8-14-01, which is their single portions. And this Court appoint Benjamin Skinner, Nathaniel Phelps and Ebenezer Mudge, of Hebron, distributors.

Page 130—5 July, 1720: This Court do appoint Mary Shippason of Hebron, widow, to be guardian to her children, Jonathan, Nathaniel, John, Elizabeth, Mary, Mercy and Joanna Shippason. Rec., £100.

Page 136—6 September, 1720: Report of the distributors.

Page 108.

Skinner, Richard, Hartford. Invt. £181-14-00. Taken 30 March, 1716, by Thomas Hosmer and John Sheldon.

Court Record, Page 11—3 April, 1716: Adms. granted to John Skinner, brother of sd. decd.

Page 27—5 February, 1716-17: John Skinner, administrator, exhibited now an inventory, which was ordered recorded and to be kept on file.

Page 244-247.

Slater, Deacon John, Symsbury. Died 2 May, 1717. Invt. £271-01-06. Taken 2 June, 1717, by John Pettebone, Sen., John Humphrey and Benjamin Addams. Will dated 26 April, 1717.

I, John Slater of Symsbury, do make this my last will and testament: I give and bequeath unto my wife Elizabeth, after my debts are paid, the improvement of ten acres of land before my door in the common field during her natural life, and the improvement of the whole of my house and well until my heirs shall come of age, and the one-half thereof during her natural life, and 1-3 part of my moveables to her forever. To my son Reuben I give the one-half of all my lands in Simsbury, to him and his heirs forever. To my son John I give the other half of my lands in Simsbury forever. To my daughters, Marah and Rebekah, I bequeath each of them 1-3 part of my moveable estate, with each of them £20 in money, to be paid as follows: £15 in money by my sonn Reuben, and £25 by my sonn John, to them the said Marah and Rebekah. I appoint Elizabeth my wife sole executrix.

Witness: *Timo. Woodbridge, Jun.,*   JOHN X SLATER, LS.
    John Pettebone, Sen.

Court Record, Page 41—6 August, 1717: Will proven.

Page 82-3-89.

Smith, Jonathan, Sen., Farmington. Invt. £493-00-08. Taken 14 June, 1721, by Isaac Cowles and John Hart. Will dated 25 June, 1720.

I, Jonathan Smith of Farmington, doe make this my last will and testament: I give unto Sarah my wife (besides her dowry) all that particular estate that was hers at the time I married her, also six pounds yearly; or if she marry, then but £3 during her life. I give to my eldest son Samuel Smith, besides what I have given him already, 20 acres of land lying in Farmington, it being part of a lott of land in the division southward frcm the Town between the mountains. I give unto my son Jonathan Smith, besides what I have given him, several parcells of land: one parcell, about 30 acres, in the division against the bounds of Wethersfield, joins land of Joseph Smith. I give to John North and Samuel Brunson, my sons-in-law, to each of them 10 acres of land, more or less, lying southward from the Town between the mountains. I give to my 6 grandsons, viz., Noah Smith, Daniel Smith, Jonathan Smith, John North, Elijah Brunson and Samuel Cole, to each of them a lott of land lying in Farmington and within the three 1st divisions of land lying west from the Town Plat. I also give to my son Jonathan one lott of land in the three aforesd. divisions of land lying west from the Town Plat. And further, it is my will that, provided and upon conditions that my said son Jonathan Smith shall at any time in his lifetime remove his settled abode and build and dwell upon land in that division of land against Wethersfield bounds, and shall have a mind to joyne with his brethren, William and Ebenezer Smith, in building of a mill or mills upon a stream included in lands that I shall give unto my sons William and Ebenezer Smith, and shall actually joyn with them in so building, that then he the said Jonathan Smith shall have an equal right with either of them in said stream for that use during the time they shall so joyn and maintain a mill or mills there. I give to my daughter Elizabeth North, in addition, 40s; to my daughter Mary Cole, besides what I have given her, 40s. I give to my daughter Sarah Smith, besides what I have already given her, £30. I give to my daughter Abigail Smith £30. And the sd. Sarah and Abigail Smith to have what is due from the estate of their grandfather Bird, now in the improvement of their grandmother Bird, and that to be part of what I have willed to them. I give unto my sons Samuel and Jonathan Smith, and my two daughters, Elizabeth North and Mary Cole, in equal proportion between them, the £20 given unto their own natural mother by their Grandfather Steele in his last will. I give unto my granddaughter, Mercy Brunson, 30s; unto my two sons, William Smith and Ebenezer Smith, now living with me, I give all the residue and remainder of my estate, both real and personal, in equal proportions, only my will further is that they nor neither of them shall have power for the space of thirty years next after my decease to sell or alienate the real estate, or any part thereof, which I have hereby willed unto them, that lyeth in the division of land against Wethersfield bounds, and southward from the lott of land there that was formerly Mr. Wyllys's. I make my two sons, William Smith and Ebenezer Smith, executors.

Witness: *John Hooker, Sen.,*   JONATHAN SMITH, SEN., LS.
Samuel Smith, Thomas Bird.

Court Record, Page 153—6 June, 1721: Will proven.

Page 8 (Vol. X) 5 March, 1722-3: Ebenezer Smith, a minor, 20 years of age, made choice of Jonathan Smith of Farmington to be his guardian. Recog., £100.

To all people whom it may concern: Know ye that whereas, our honoured father Jonathan Smith, Sen., of Farmington, deceased, in his last will, dated 25 June, 1720, gave unto his son Jonathan Smith and to his six grandsons then liveing, to each of them a lot of land apiece lying in the three first divisions of land lying west from the reserved lands in sd. Farmington, as may be seen in the will: Persuant thereto, we, William Smith and Ebenezer Smith, the subscribers, executors to the will above mentioned, have set out unto each of them the lots hereafter mentioned, lying in sd. divisions, viz.: Unto our brother Jonathan Smith, that lot that was drawn on the right of our grandmother Smith, in ye first of sd. divisions west. And unto Jonathan Smith, Jun., one of the grandsons, that lot that was drawn on the right of our uncle Jobanah Smith deceased, in the first division, both lying in the tenth allotment. And unto Noah Smith, that lot which was drawn on the right of our grandmother (the Widow Smith, so called), lying in the fourteenth allotment in the second division of land, lying west of the reserved lands. And unto Daniel Smith, that lot that was drawn on the right of our uncle Jobanah Smith, lying in the 2d division and in the sixteenth allotment. And unto Samuel Cole, that lot that was drawn on the right of our father in ye third division. And unto Elijah Brownson, or to his heirs, that lot that was drawn on our father's right in the 2d division, lying west of the reserved land. And as to that lot drawn on the right of our uncle Jobanah Smith, in the third division, west of the reserved land, being the eleventh number, we would have set to John North, the other grandson, if he were living, but he deceased 16 January, 1732-3, and so if any person or persons appear to have a right to any part thereof, we are free to divide with them, supposeing we ourselves to have a right to some part thereof, if not the whole.

12 February, 1753. 　　　　　　　　　　　WILLIAM SMITH,
　　　　　　　　　　　　　　　　　　　　EBENEZER SMITH.

At a Probate Court held at Hartford, 7 January, 1755, the above distribution was exhibited, approved and ordered to be kept on file.
　　　　　　　　　　　　　　　　　Test: *Joseph Talcott, Clerk.*

Farmington, 4 December, 1754: I, Samuel Cole, hereby declare that I accept ye lot set out to me by ye executors of my hond. grandfather's will herein mentioned, as my part of what was therein given to me.
　　　　　　　　　　　　　　　　　SAMUEL COLE, *Grandson.*

Page 292.

Smith, Joseph, Sen., Farmington. Invt. £309-09-09. Taken 18 September, 1718, by Thomas Bird and Daniel Judd.

Court Record, Page 79—2 September, 1718: Adms. unto Joanna Smith, widow of the decd., and Isaac Cowles of Farmington.

Page 98—3 March, 1718-19: Adms. account exhibited, allowed and accepted. Order to distribute the estate: To Joanna Smith, widow, dower for life and £31-07-08; to Joseph Smith, eldest son, £41-16-08; to Jobanna Smith, £10-18-04; to Lydia Woodford, to Mary Porter, to Joanna Porter, to Elizabeth Cowles, to Ruth Smith, to Susannah Smith, to Thankfull Smith, to Mercy Smith, to Esther Smith, and to Experience Smith, to each of them the sum or value of £21-18-04, which is their single parts of sd. estate. And this Court do appoint Thomas Bird, Joseph Hawley and Daniel Judd, of Farmington, distributors.

Page 291.

Smith, William, Farmington. Invt. £242-10-08. Taken 13 September, 1718, by Isaac Cowles and John Hart.

Court Record, Page 84—7 October, 1718: Adms. granted to Rebeckah Smith, widow of the decd.

Page 16 (Vol. XI) 7 April, 1730: Rebeckah Smith, a minor, 14 years of age, daughter of William Smith, chose Nathaniel Stanly to be her guardian. Recog., £50. Helena Smith, age 13 years, chose Timothy Stanly to be her guardian.

Page 21—2 June, 1730: Thomas North, of Farmingtown, showeth to this Court that he, having right in a lott of land called the First Lott, in the division butting upon Wethersfield bounds east, which lott lyeth in common with Rebeckah and Helena Smith, heirs of William Smith, late of Farmingtown deceased, minors, moving to this Court that the Court would appoint some suitable persons to assist the guardians of sd. minors, Rebeckah and Helena Smith, in making a division of sd. land, whereupon this Court doth appoint Capt. William Wadsworth and Joseph Judd to assist the guardians in making a division of sd. land.

Page 61—1st February, 1731-2: According to an order of this Court to divide a certain lott of land belonging to Thomas North of Farmingtown and the heirs of William Smith decd., sd. dist. was now exhibited by William Wadsworth and Joseph Judd, distributors, and under the hands of Nathaniel Stanly and Timothy Stanly, guardians to Rebeckah and Helena Smith, minor children of the sd. decd., which dist. this Court accepts and ordered upon file.

Soper, Mary. Court Record, Page 146—7 March, 1720: This Court appoint Mary Soper to be guardian to Peletiah, age 19 years, Sarah 16, John 13, Abigail 12, Dorcas 7, and Return 4 years of age, children of the sd. Mary Soper. Recog., £140.

Page 285-7.

Stanly, Caleb, Hartford. Died 5 May, 1718. Invt. £402-08-03. Taken 13 June, 1718, by John Marsh, Jr., and Nathaniel Stanly. Will dated 7 March, 1715-16.

I, Caleb Stanly of Hartford, do make and ordain this my last will and testament: I give to my wife Lydia Stanly, besides what I have given her in way of dowry before marriage, one cow, 40 shillings in household stuff, one swine, and lend her one feather bed and furniture during her natural life, and after her decease to be returned to my children. I confirm unto my daughter Abigail Stanly and her heirs forever my land on the east side of the Great River, after my decease, I to have the last crop growing upon it, my son Caleb having paid for it before his death, to be free of all common fence. I give my son Roger Pitkin five shillings as a token of my love besides what I have given to his wife. I give to my daughter, Wido. Abigail Stanly, five shillings as a token of my love besides the portion I gave her husband before his death, being above £300, set down in my book of accot., Ledger G, Page 138. I give to my four grandchildren, Timothy, Caleb, Jonathan and William Stanly, all my right in the last five miles of land on the east side of the Great River, purchased of Mr. Thomas Buckingham and Major ffitch. I give to my daughter Elizabeth Pitkin five shillings as a token of my love besides the portion I have already given her. I give the remainder of my estate, both personal and real, to my daughters, Ann and Abigail Stanly, forever, to be equally divided between them, excepting what is hereafter provided, that is to say, if it does not arise to more between them than what I have given already to my daughter Ruth; but if it does amount to more, then my daughter Ruth to have equally with them in the said estate, with what she hath already received. I make my son William Pitkin executor. I give him my gold ring partly as gift and partly to encourage him to be my executor, and give him power to sell any part of my land to pay my debts. I make my loveing friends, Ensign John Marsh and Sergt. John Skinner, my overseers.

Witness: *Hez: Wyllys,*   CALEB STANLY, LS.
    Edward Cadwell.

Court Record, Page 67—3 June, 1718: Will proven.

Page 255.

Starr, Jehoshaphat, late of Newport, in Rhode Island. Invt. £60-08-02. Taken in Middletown, 20 July, 1717, by Samuel Cornwall and Samuel Green.

Court Record, Page 38—2nd July, 1717: Whereas, Jehosaphat Starr, sometime of Newport, on Rhode Island, dyed at sea, and it appearing to this Court that there is estate of the deceast within the County of Hartford, and likewise informed by Joseph Starr of Middletown that he has in his hands considerable of the estate of the deceased: This Court do therefore grant letters of administration on sd. estate unto sd. Joseph Starr, who gave bond.

Page 45—29 November, 1717: Adms. exhibits invt. and an account of his administration: Debts and charges, £2-00-06; amount of inventory,

£60-09-02; for distribution, £58-08-08. Order to dist. the estate: To Capt. Thomas Ward in right of his wife Elizabeth, one of the sisters of sd. decd., £29-04-04; and to Hannah Greenfield of Newport, the other sister of the said decd., £29-04-04. And this Court do appoint Samuel Cornwall, Samuel Green and John White, of Middletown, distributors.

Page 91. (Vol. X, Page 238.)

Stedman, Robert, Windsor. Invt. £15-13-05. Taken 13 June, 1721, by William Wolcott and Samuel Rockwell.

Court Record, Page 153—6 June, 1721: Adms. granted to David Bissell of Windsor.

Page 48 (Vol. X) 5 May, 1724: David Bissell, Adms., reports that the estate is insolvent.

Page 126-127.

Steele, Ebenezer, Farmington. Invt. £1406-11-07. Taken 27 November, 1722, by Joseph Hawley, John Thompson and Samuel Judd. Will dated 20 September, 1722.

I, Ebenezer Steele, do make this my last will and testament: Item. Unto Sarah, my wife, I give the one-third part of all my personal estate, with free liberty of choice therein, to be her own forever. Also, I give to my wife, for her use and profit during her natural life, 1-2 of all my lott I now live upon, and 1-2 of all the buildings thereon standing. I give my wife the use and profit of my pasture at a place called Dirty Hole; also the use and profit of all my land in a place called the Great Meadow, that at More's Corner and in the Indian Neck only excepted. Item. Unto my daughter Mary Steele, and to her heirs forever, I give the 1-3 part of all my personal estate; also the whole lott I now live upon and all buildings standing upon the same; also all my land in the Great Meadow, that at More's Corner and that in the Indian Neck only excepted; half the home lott and buildings; also the pasture at Dirty Hole and the land in the Great Meadow, by her not to be possessed until after her mother's decease; also, I give and bequeath unto her 1-3 part of all my land at Moore's Corner. Item. I give and bequeath unto my daughter Sarah Steele, and to her heirs forever, all the rest of my estate, both real and personal, not before in this instrument given and disposed of, excepting lands in the several divisions of outlands lotted out or that may hereafter be lotted out. This legacy to my daughter Sarah is with this proviso, viz.: Provided and in case she my said daughter Sarah shall at any time match and marry with Gershom Lewis, now living in Farmington, which she full well knows is a thing very cross and contrary to my mind and will; that my will in that case is that the bequest and legacy I have here given her shall be utterly null and void; and then my will further in that case is that my foresd. daughter Mary, her heirs and assigns forever, shall have and injoy that part of my estate herein bequeathed to my daughter Sarah; and then I will and bequeath to my sd. daughter Sarah the sum of £5 personal estate, and no more. Item. I give and bequeath unto my sister Hannah Hart, as a token of my love and a reward for her charity and service to me in my sickness, one of my horses, which she shall choose. Item. I give and bequeath unto my nephew David Steele, son of my brother James Steele, and to his heirs and assigns forever, all my lands lying in the several divisions of outlands in Farmington already lotted out or that may be lotted out and not yet disposed of; always provided, and this my legacy to my nephew is upon considerations, that he my said nephew live with and serve me if I should live; or if I die, that he then live with and serve my wife in her widowhood until he arrive at the age of 21 years; which if he shall not do, then this my legacy to be void and of non-effect; and then I will the said outlands unto my aforesaid two daughters in equal proportion, except my said daughter Sarah shall marry with Gershom Lewis, which if at any time she shall, then I will and bequeath all of the sd. outlands unto my aforesaid daughter Mary Steele. I appoint my wife Sarah Steele and my loveing brother-in-law Lt. John Hart to be executors, and I desire the Rev. Mr. Samuel Whitman and Mr. John Hooker to oversee and be advisors unto my two children whilst in their young and youthful days.

Witness: *John Hooker,*　　　　　　　　　　Ebenezer Steele, ls.
Samuel Porter, Thomas Thompson.

Court Record, Page 178—6 November, 1722: Will proven.

Page 194—4 December, 1722: Invt. exhibited of the estate of Capt. Ebenezer Steele by the executrix to the last will. This Court do appoint Mrs. Sarah Steele, widow, to be guardian unto her daughter Sarah Steele, a minor aged 14 years. Rec., £200. And do appoint Deacon John Hart of Farmington to be guardian to Mary Steel, daughter of Capt. Ebenezer Steele. Recog., £200.

Page 16 (Vol. X) 23 April, 1723: Upon complaint of Samuel Judd, guardian to David Steele, a minor, that whereas Capt. Ebenezer Steele did in his will give certain lands to David Steele on condition that sd. David shall live with him if he should live, and in case he should die that then he should live with and serve his wife in her widowhood until the sd. David attain to the age of 21 years; and although the sd. David, being minded to fullfill the condition, did live with his uncle while he lived and since his uncle's death he hath lived with and served his aunt, widow to the sd. decd., for the space of 4 or 5 months, and is willing still to serve her according to the intent and terms in sd. will, but more lately she the sd. widow will not suffer him the sd. David to be in her service and keeps him out of the house by shutting the doors and turning the key upon him, also denys him sustinance: whereupon a writ was issued to cite the sd. widow to appear before this Court, the partys now appearing were heard upon sd. complaint, and it appears to the satisfaction of this Court that the sd. widow hath refused and doth refuse to improve the sd. David in her service or to take the care of him, do therefore order that Samuel

Judd, his guardian, take sd. David Steele into his immediate care to the intent that he may not spend his time negligently and unprofitably so long as until the sd. widow desires him to return to her service again, and at all times when she don't see cause to improve him that the sd. guardian improve him either in his own service or for some other person to the best advantage he can.

Page 66.

Steele, Mercy, Hartford. Invt. £81-10-09. Taken 24 May, 1720, by Samuel Sedgewick and Caleb Bull.

Court Record, Page 125—5 April, 1720: Adms. granted to Thomas Steele of Hartford.

Dist. File: October, 1724: An agreement for the distribution and settlement of the estate of our honoured mother, Mercy Steele, and of our brother, William Steele, to and amongst the heirs of sd. decd.

THOMAS STEELE, DANIEL STEELE,
JOHN WEBSTER *in right of his wife* ABIALL (Abiah?).
ELIPHALET STEELE.

Page 60 (Vol. X) 1st December, 1724: Agreement accepted.

Stoddard, Nathaniel. Court Record, Page 29—17 April, 1717: Thomas Stoddard, a minor son of Nathaniel Stoddard, late of Wethersfield decd., chose James Butler to be his guardian. And this Court appoint Thomas Wright guardian to Joshua Stoddard, age 13 years.

Page 128—18 June, 1720: Joshua Stoddard, now 17 years of age, chose John Frances to be his guardian. Recog., £100.

Page 327.

Storrs, Samuel, Sen., Mansfield. Invt. £73-07-07. Taken 2 July, 1719, by Shubael Dimmock and Thomas Huntington. Will dated 22 May, 1717.

I, Samuel Storrs, Sen., of Mansfield, in the County of Hartford and Colony of Connecticut, in New England, yeoman, being crazy and weake in body but of perfect mind and memory, do make this my last will and testament: I give and bequeath to Esther my wife the sum of £10 of current money of New England a year if she stand in need of it, and the use of two cowes and half of the orchard, and a fire-room in the dwelling house, and her firewood so long as she continues my widow. These particulars are to be fullfilled by my beloved son Thomas Storrs. Item. I give to my son Samuel Storrs my gunn, sword, hoan and razor, and I have given him a whole alottment of land, which I account his portion. Item. I give to my five daughters, Sarah, Anna, Elizabeth, Lydia and

Esther, at my decease, 100 acres of land that lyes at Coney Rock, and 10 acres that lyes there, and 50 acres that I purpose to lay there in the other divisions, equally among them; and after my decease and (my) wife's, all the moveables and household stuff within doors, and cattle if there be any, equally among them, only Lydia is to have my feather bed that I lye on, with the furniture thereof, over and above the rest. Item. I have given to my son Cordial, by deed of gift, 150 acres of land and 6 acres of meadow, which is his portion. Item. I have given to my son Thomas Storrs, whom I likewise constitute my sole executor, my homelott, pasture lott, horse barn and small divisions in a deed of gift, which I account his portion.

Witness: *Eleazer Williams,*   SAMUEL STORRS, LS.
Mary Williams, Mehetabell X Gary.

Court Record, Page 107—7 July, 1719: Will proven.

Page 86.

Styles, Robert, Hebron. Invt. £233-10-10. Taken 8 April, 1721, by Nathaniel Phelps and Moriss Tillotson.

Court Record, Page 155—4 July, 1721: Adms. granted to Ruth Styles, widow.

Page 92 (Vol. X) 6 July, 1725: Joseph Strong, of Coventry, in right of his wife, Adms. on sd. estate, exhibits account of Adms. Allowed. Order to dist. the estate:

	£ s d
To Ruth Strong, alias Styles, relict of the decd.,	17-01-00
To Nathaniel Styles, eldest son,	61-07-02
To Amos Styles, Job Styles, Jemima Strong and Hepzibah Styles, to each of them,	30-13-07

And appoint Jacob Root, Samuel Curtice and Moriss Tillotson, distributors. This Court appoint Joseph Phelps of Hebron guardian to Amos Styles, 19 years of age, and Hepzibah Styles, 16 years of age. Recog., £200. Nathaniel Styles appointed guardian to his brother Job Styles, 11 years of age. Recog., £100.

Page 1 (Vol. XII) 28 March, 1734: Report of the dist. Accepted.

Page 118.

Stow, John, Jr., Middletown. Invt. £228-15-02. Taken 28 March, 1722, by John Bacon, John Collins and Nathaniel Stow.

Court Record, Page 169—5 June, 1722: This Court appoint John Stow of Middletown to be guardian to Solomon Stow, a minor, about 15 years of age. This Court now grant Adms. on sd. estate unto John Stow, son of sd. decd. Bathsheba Stow, widow, is appointed guardian to two of her children, viz., Martha Stow, 10 years, and Ebenezer Stow, 8 years of age. Recog., £50.

This Court appoint Nathaniel Stow of Middletown to be guardian to Jeremiah Stow, a minor, 18 years of age. Recog., £50.

Page 38 (Vol. X) 3 March, 1723: John Stow, Adms., exhibits now an account of his Adms. Accepted.

	£ s d
Inventory,	227-16-02
Subtracting	42-01-00
There remains to be dist. of the real and personal estate,	185-15-02
To Bathsheba Stow, alias Hubbard, relict of the decd.,	4-16-09
To John Stow, eldest son,	51-13-07
To Elizabeth Hubbard, Jeremiah, Solomon, Martha and Ebenezer Stow, the rest of the children, to each,	25-16-11

And appoint John Collins, Nathaniel Stow and John Bacon, distributors.

Page 19 (Vol. XI) 5 May, 1730: Ebenezer Stow, 16 years of age, son of John Stow, made choise of his brother John Stow to be his guardian. Recog., £100.

Page 1 (Vol. XII) 28 March, 1734: Report of the distributors.

Page 336.

Taylor, Stephen, Colchester. Invt. £181-11-07. Taken 7 February, 1718-19, by Samuel Gilbert and William Worthington.

Court Record, Page 110—1st September, 1719: Adms. to Patience Taylor, widow, relict of sd. deceased. Rec., £100, with Ebenezer Coleman. This Court appoint Patience Taylor of Colchester, widow, guardian unto her two children, Stephen Taylor, age 11 years, and Mercy Taylor, age 8 years. Rec., £50, with Ebenezer Coleman of Colchester.

Page 247.

Tudor, Owen, Windsor. Invt. £161-11-04. Taken 31 July, 1717, by Daniel Loomis and John Bissell.

Court Record, Page 40—6 August, 1717: Adms. to Samuel Tudor.

Page 123—5 April, 1720: Adms. account accepted and allowed. Order to distribute the estate, £146-16-04, vizt.: To the said Samuel Tudor, brother to the said deceased, £36-14-01; to Sarah Porter, sister to the sd. deceased, £36-14-01; to the heirs of Jane Smith decd., another sister of the sd. deceased, £36-14-01; and to Mary Judson, another sister of the decd., £36-14-01; which is their equal portions. And this Court appoint Simon Wolcott, Henry Wolcott and Nathaniel Loomis, of Windsor, distributors.

Page 127—7 June, 1720: Report of the dist., and this Court grant the Adms. a *Quietus Est.*

Page 354.

Tuller, Samuel, Simsbury. Invt. £92-04-00. Taken 13 January, 1719-20, by John Pettebone, John Humphries and Joseph Case.

Court Record, Page 117—2 February, 1719-20: Adms. to Sarah Tuller, widow of the deceased.

Page 60 (Vol. XI) 1st February, 1731-2: Samuel Tuller, age 17 years, and Joseph Tuller, age 14 years, chose their mother, Sarah Garret, to be their guardian. Recog., £100.

Page 9 (Vol. XIII) 7 June, 1737: Isaac Tuller, age 17 years, son of Samuel Tuller of Simsbury, chose Samuel Pettebone to be his guardian. Recog., £100.

Page 239.   Invt. in Vol. X, Page 15.

Turner, Edward, Middletown. Invt., in lands of 137 acres, £68-10-00. Taken 28 February, 1722-3, by Thomas Stow, Zacheus Candee and Thomas Ward. Will dated 17 January, 1716-17.

I, Edward Turner of Middletown, doe make and ordain this to be my last will and testament: Imprimis: I give unto my son Richard Turner, whom I constitute my sole executor, all and singular my lands, messuages and tenements, freely to be possessed and enjoyed by him, his heirs and assigns forever, that is to say, all my lands and buildings already conveyed by deed, and also all my right, title and interest in all undivided lands and commonages within the bounds of the Township of Middletown, and also every part and particular of my moveable estate that I am the rightfull owner of, to be and remain the lawfull propriety and possession and at the sole dispose of my said son Richard Turner, and to his heirs and assigns forever. And it is my will that my son Richard above-named shall pay the several legacies or sums to the persons after named, within one year after my decease if demanded by the particular persons afternamed, to whom I do give the same in this my last will as followeth: I give and order my son Richard Turner to pay to my son John Turner twenty shillings in pay, or two-thirds so much in current money; to my son Stephen Turner 5 shillings; and to my grandson Stephen Turner I give 5 acres of land; and to Abigail, sister to the sd. Stephen, I give to her fourty shillings in pay, or two-thirds so much in money, these two (Stephen and Abigail) being the children of my son Edward Turner deceased. I give unto Mary, now the wife of Ebenezer Eglestone, daughter and only heir of my daughter Mercy deceased, 5 shillings in pay; and to Thomas and Abigail Miller, the children and only heirs of my daughter Elizabeth deceased, I give to them 5 shillings to each in pay, an equal part; and to Mary, my daughter, now the wife of Samuel Bow, I give 5 shillings in pay; and to my daughter Hannah, now the wife of John Ranny, I give five shillings in pay, to each, or two-thirds so much in money. It is my will that each and every of the above particular sums be paid at or before one twelve months be expired after my decease, if demanded to be paid, by my son Richard Turner or his heirs, executors or administrators.

Witness: *James Tappin,*   EDWARD X TURNER, LS.
Hezekiah Sumner, Joseph Rockwell.

Court Record, Page 34—4 June, 1717: Will proven.

Page 6 (Vol. X) 5 February, 1722-3: Jeremiah Leaming, who married Abigail Turner, and John Turner, heirs of Edward Turner, informing this Court that the sd. Edward Turner made a will which was proven 4 January, 1717, and disposed of part of his estate and died partly intestate, particularly of one piece of land (about 137 acres) lying in Middletown, this Court do therefore grant letters of Adms. unto Jeremiah Leaming *Cum Testimento annexo*. Also, he exhibits invt. of intestate estate.

Page 311.

Tyler, Isaac, Haddam. Died 22 January, 1718-19. Invt. £130-05-00. Taken 16 February, 1718-19, by Joseph Arnold, Benjamin Smith and Jonathan Arnold.

Court Record, Page 96—3 March, 1718-19: Adms. granted to Abigail Tyler, widow, relict of the decd., and Moses Pond of Haddam.

Page 122—1st March, 1720: Moses Pond, Adms., exhibited now an account of his Adms. Accepted and allowed. Order to distribute: To Abigail Tyler, widow, £11-03-11; to Abram Tyler, eldest son, £24-16-11; to Abigail, to Isaac, to Ann, to Watchfull, to Israel, to Hannah Tyler, to each of them, £12-08-05½, which is their single shares or portions. And this Court appoint Joseph Arnold, Benjamin Smith and Jonathan Arnold, distributors. Abigail Tyler, widow to be guardian to Abraham, age 13 years, Abigail 14 years, Isaac 11 years, Ann 9 years, Watchfull 8 years, and Hannah 4 years of age, her children, minors. Recog., £100.

Page 123—1st March, 1720: This Court appoint Moses Pond of Haddam to be guardian to Israel Tyler, age 6 years, a son of Isaac Tyler, late deceased. Rec., £40.

Page 143—6 December, 1720: Report of dist. accepted.

Page 328.

Ventrus, Mary, Farmington. Invt. £31-00-09. Taken 4 March, 1718-19, by Timothy Porter and Isaac Cowles.

Court Record, Page 97—3 March, 1718-19: Adms. granted to Jacob Barnes.

Page 108—7 July, 1719: Jacob Barnes, Adms., exhibits an account of his Adms., which this Court accepts, orders recorded and kept on file.

Page 95.

Ventrus, Moses, Farmington. Invt. £113-05-06. Taken 13 November, 1721, by John Hart and Jonathan Smith. Will dated 10 August, 1721.

I, Moses Ventrus of Farmington, doe make this my last will and testament: I give to my cousin John Brunson, of Farmington, my lott at the ox pasture in Paquabuck meadow, and my three lotts in the 3 divisions furthest west from the Town, and also my gunn and my lott on the east side of the river, against Nodd. I give to my cousin Mehetabell Ventrus my land at the Fort Hill. It is further my will that in case Jacob Barnes do give a good maintenance unto the sd. Mehetabell Ventrus until her decease, then at her decease he the sd. Barnes is to have and hold all that by this instrument was given to her; otherwise to be the aforesd. John Brunson's, provided he the sd. Brunson doth maintain the sd. Mehetabell. I give unto my cousin Moses Brunson, the son of William, all my right in the land at the Blue Hills that is not laid out. I make my cousin John Brunson sole executor.

Witness: *Jonathan Smith,*   MOSES VENTRUS, LS.
Thomas Cowles, Timothy Porter, Jr.

Court Record, Page 158—7 November, 1721: Will proven.

Page 159—5 December, 1721: Whereas, Moses Ventrus, late of Farmington, died intestate of estate to the value of £13-03-06, as appears by the will and invt., out of which has been paid debts due from sd. estate £2-14-02, there remains £10-09-04 to be dist. This Court order dist. to the heirs of Sarah Brunson decd., £3-09-09; also to the heirs of Grace Blackley decd., £3-09-09; and to the heir of Mary Ventrus, viz., Mehetabell Ventrus, £3-09-09. And appoint John Hart, Jonathan Smith and John Brunson, distributors.

Page 13 (Vol. X) 2 April, 1723: Report of the distributors.

Page 2 (Vol. XII) 1st April, 1733-4: Samuel Ventrus, a minor, son of Moses Ventrus, chose his uncle Daniel Brainard to be his guardian.

Page 277.

Waddams, John, Wethersfield. Died 30 June, 1718. Invt. £167-13-00½. Taken 22 July, 1718, by Edward Bulkeley, Jonathan Belding and John Russell.

Court Record, Page 73—5 August, 1718: Adms. granted to John Waddams, son of the decd.

Page 75—5 August, 1718: John Waddams informing this Court that his brother Daniel Waddams is so far an idiot that he is not capable of takeing care of himself, this Court order John Waddams shall be guardian until the Court order otherwise. Recog., £60.

Page 132—5 July, 1720: John Waddams, Adms., summoned to Court on complaint of Abigail Waddams, widow, to appear and render account of his Adms. This Court grant him further time.

See File: Know all men by these presents: That we, Abigail Waddams, widdow, relique of John Waddams, late of Wethersfield, in ye County of Hartford, in the Colony of Connecticut, in New England, decd., and John Waddams, eldest son of ye decd., for himselfe and as guardian to Danll. Waddams, second son of ye decd., an idiot, and in behalf of David Tryon in right of Hannah his wife, eldest daughter of ye decd., and order under sd. David Tryon his hand to do in his behalf, and Noah Waddams for himselfe and in behalf of Ebenezer Dickinson in right of his wife Susanah, second daughter of ye decd., who have, for a valuable sum of mony paid to ym by said Noah Waddams, given to him a quitt claime under their hands and seals bearing date June 15, Anno. Dom. 1720, of all their right in and to that estate of ye decd., and in behalf of John Dyxx in right of his wife Sarah, third daughter of ye decd., who have, for ye sum of ten pounds current mony of ye Colony paid to us by sd. Noah Waddams, quitt claimed to him under theire hands and seals bearing date June 15th, Anno. Dom. 1720, all the right in and to ye estate of ye decd., and also in behalf of ye Jonathan Blin in right of his wife Mary, youngest daughter of ye decd., who have given unto sd. Noah Waddams under their hands and seals a quitt claime bearing date 24 May, Anno. Dom. 1720.

ABIGAIL X WADDAMS, LS.
JOHN WADDAMS, LS.
DANILL WADDAMS,
DAUID TRYON,
NOAH WADDAMS, LS.
JOHN DIX,
EBENEZER DICKINSON,
JONATHAN BLIN.

The foregoing agreement was exhibited in Court, 3 August, 1720, and ordered to be kept upon file.

Page 288-365.

Wadsworth, Deacon John, Farmington. Invt. £885-05-09. Taken 1718, by John Porter, Timothy Porter and Isaac Cowles. Will dated 20 August, 1718.

I, John Wadsworth, do make this my last will and testament: I give to Mary my wife, to be for her use and improvement during the term of her natural life, viz., the one-half of the house I live in and the one-half of the lott that it stands upon, with one-half of all other buildings and appurtenances upon or belonging to said lott; also the one-third part of all the land which is mine within the common field in sd. Farmington. Also I do give and bequeath unto my said wife, to be to her own dispose forever, 1-3 part of all that personal estate which shall be left after my just debts are paid, only in case my said wife shall not be candid in exposeing all the estate that is mine or that was hers at the time of my marriage with her, that she knows of, to be inventoried as my estate, but shall endeavor to conceal part thereof, that then my will is that she shall be cut short of the third part of my personal estate given her as aforesaid and three times the value of the estate so endeavored to be concealed by her. Item. I give unto John Wadsworth, my eldest son, my house I live in and the lott it stands upon, with all other buildings and appurtenances standing upon or belonging unto the sd. lott, the one-half thereof in present possession, the other half at the decease of my said wife. Also I give and bequeath unto my sd. son the full and just half of all my other lands whatsoever, these to be to him, his heirs and assigns forever. Further, it is my will that my sd. son do, within two years after he arriveth to full age, pay unto his sister Sarah Cowles the sum of £5 equivalent unto money. Item. I give unto my son Daniel Wadsworth, and to his heirs, all the rest of my lands whatsoever not before in this instrument disposed of. Further, it is my will that my son Daniel do, within two years after he shall arrive at full age, pay unto his sister Elizabeth Wadsworth the sum of £5 equivalent to money. Item. I give unto my four daughters, viz., Sarah Cowles, Elizabeth Wadsworth, Lydia Wadsworth and Ruth Wadsworth, to be equally divided between them, all the rest of my personal estate not before disposed of, and what either of them have received from me already to be reckoned as part, and the rest divided accordingly, makeing each of them equal. As to a piece of land called the White Oak Plain, purchased by sd. wife before my marriage with her, as it was intended and agreed that one of her sons should have the said land, and to be accounted to him as part of his portion from his father Gridley's estate, viz., so much as the said land is worth, my will is therefore that it should be so. It is my desire that my brother William Wadsworth may be guardian unto my son John Wadsworth, and that my brother Hezekiah Wadsworth may be guardian to my son Daniel Wadsworth, and that my brother James Wadsworth may be guardian unto my daughter Lydia Wadsworth, and that my brother Thomas Wadsworth may be guardian unto my daughter Ruth Wadsworth, during the minority of sd. children. I make my brother, Capt. William Wadsworth, and my son John Wadsworth, when his age will allow him to act, executors.

Witness: *Samuel Hooker, Sen.,*   JOHN WADSWORTH, LS.
   John Porter.

Court Record, Page 80—2 September, 1718: Will proven.

Page 81—2 September, 1718: This Court appoint Capt. William Wadsworth of Farmington to be guardian unto John Wadsworth, age 16 years.

Page 89—17 December, 1718: This Court appoint James Wadsworth of Durham to be guardian to Lydia Wadsworth, daughter of John Wadsworth, and Thomas Wadsworth appointed guardian to Ruth Wadsworth, another daughter of sd. decd.

Page 304.

Wadsworth, Sarah, Farmington. Will dated 17 March, 1713-14: I, Sarah Wadsworth, doe make this my last will and testament: I give and bequeath all my Old England money, whether silver or gold, unto my 8 children, viz., to Samuel, to John, to William, to Nathaniel, to James, to Thomas, to Hezekiah, and to Sarah Root, to be equally divided between them my sd. 8 children. My will is, my just debts being paid, that my two youngest sons, Thomas and Hezekiah, have their portions made up to them according to my deceased husband's last will. For the remaining part of my estate my will is it be divided into two equal parts, the one of which, that is to say, the one-half of my remaining estate when the said money is divided as aforesd., my just debts paid and my two younger sons have had their portions made up to them as abovesd., I give unto my two youngest sons, Thomas Wadsworth and Hezekiah Wadsworth, which I give to them as a recompense to them for their care of me in my old age, and as for the other equal part of my estate, I give it unto my sons, Samuel Wadsworth, John Wadsworth, William Wadsworth, Nathaniel Wadsworth, James Wadsworth, and to my daughter Sarah Root, to be equally divided between them. My will is that my said daughter Sarah Root shall have all my wearing cloths, both woolen and linnen, over and beside what is abovementioned, not to be accounted as part of the abovesd. gift. I dc make my son Samuel Wadsworth sole executor.

Witness: *Samuel Hooker, Sen.,*   SARAH X WADSWORTH, LS.
      Joseph X *Lancton.*

Court Record, Page 89—17 December, 1718: Will proven.

Wadsworth, Thomas, Jr., late of Hartford. Court Record, Page 35—4 June, 1717: Adms. to Sarah Wadsworth, widow of the deceased.

Page 39.

(Add. Invt. in Vol. X, Page 98.)

Ward, Samuel, Middletown. Invt. £336-19-04. Taken 26 July, 1715, by William Harris, Robert Hubbard and Joseph Rockwell. Invt. of lands in Middletown, valued at £54-07-00. Taken 15 March, 1724-5, by John Collins and John Bacon. Invt. of lands in Brandford, £778-10-00. Taken 2 April, 1725, by John Russell and John Howd, and offered for apprisement by John Warner, Joseph Whitmore and Robert Warner, Adms.

Court Record, Page 70 (Vol. X) 19 February, 1724-5: Whereas, information being made to this Court by some of the heirs of Samuel Ward, late of Middletown, that the estate has not been inventoried nor settled, praying that power of Adms. may be granted: This Court grant letters of Adms. unto John Warner, Robert Warner and Joseph Whitmore, of Middletown.

Page 75—6 April, 1725: Invt. exhibited by the Adms.

Page 106—5 October, 1725: Whereas, the estate of Samuel Ward, late of Middletown, an invt. whereof has been exhibited, lying in the County of Hartford, that part of the estate £54-07-00, this Court order to dist. to the following persons:

	£	s	d
To the heirs of James Ward decd., eldest son of the decd.,	21-14-08		

To Mary Warner, Abigail Ward and Ann Warner, the rest of
the children of sd. decd., to each of them,   10-17-04

And appoint John Collins, John Bacon and Joseph Rockwell, distributors.

Page 108—9 November, 1725: Report of the distributors.

Invt. in Vol. X, Page 160.

Warren, John, Hartford. Died 31 July, 1722. Invt. £249-10-00, of house, barn and lands. Taken 29 March, 1723, by Ozias Pitkin, Timothy Cowles and Charles Buckland.

Court Record, Page 175—1st Tuesday in September, 1722: Adms. granted to Thomas Warren, brother of the decd.

Page 14 (Vol. X) 2 April, 1723: Thomas Warren, Adms., moved this Court for direction what may be reasonable for him to pay to Mary Warren, one of the daughters of the decd., for serving her father about 5 years after she came of age, and that, as he saith, she did with great care, labour and faithfullness. This Court advise and direct the Adms. to pay her, besides her victuals and clothes, 40 shillings per year for the time her father was in his right mind, and £3 per year for the time she took care of him in the time of his distraction. This Court appoint Thomas Welles of Glastonbury to be guardian unto Hannah Warren, age 14 years, daughter of John Warren decd.

Page 21—4 June, 1723: Ozias Pitkin is appointed guardian to John Warren, age 17 years, son of the decd.

Page 24—2 July, 1723: Thomas Warren, Adms., exhibits an account of his Adms. Accepted, and order to dist:

	£	s	d
To John Warren, only son of the decd.,	147-12-01		
To Elizabeth Hills,	46-15-11		
To Mary Corbett,	72-07-05		
To Sarah Graham,	51-19-06		
To Hannah Warren,	73-16-05		

And appoint Deacon Cole, Joseph Pitkin and Charles Buckland, distributors.

Page 29—3 September, 1723: Report of the dist., under the hands of Timothy Cowles and Joseph Pitkin. Accepted.

Page 346-357.

Waters, Joseph, Middletown. Died in Wethersfield, 3 November, 1719. Invt. £24-11-00. Taken 26 December, 1719, by Joseph Rockwell and John Collens. Invt. £6-00-08, of goods found in the custody of Josiah

Churchill and Widow Patience Nott, delivered to Samuel Waters of Colchester. Taken by David Buck and Josiah Churchill, 2 December, 1719.

Page 315.

Waters, Thomas, Hartford. Invt. £207-04-00. Taken 5 March, 1718-19, by Joseph Wadsworth and Samuel Webster.

Court Record, Page 100—6 March, 1718-19: Adms. granted to Joseph Waters, son of the decd.

Page 207 (Vol. X) 3 December, 1728: Upon the motion of Samuel Waters, son of Thomas Waters, this Court order the Clerk to issue a citation that Joseph Waters, Adms., appear before the Court to render an account of his Adms. in order for distribution thereof.

Page 41 (Vol. XI) 22 March, 1731: Joseph Waters, Adms., appeared in Court and exhibited an account of his Adms., and some of the heirs appeared and objected against his account, he not having produced receipts, with other reasonable objections. Case continued until 1st Tuesday of April next.

Page 120.

Webster, William, Hartford. Invt. £566-05-05. Taken 13 June, 1722, by James Ensign and Samuel Catlin.

Court Record, Page 23 (Vol. X) 2 July, 1723: Sarah Webster, Adms., exhibited an account of her Adms. Accepted. Order to dist. the estate: To Sarah Webster, besides her dowry, 1-3 part of the moveable estate forever, and the improvement of 1-3 part of the lands during life; to Cyprian Webster, his double part of sd. estate; and to William, Moses, Samuel, Susannah and Sarah Webster, to each of them their single portions. And appoint James Ensign, Thomas Richards and Samuel Catlin, of Hartford, distributors.

Page 28—4 September, 1723: Mrs. Sarah Webster to be guardian to William, age 20 years, Moses 17, Susannah 13, Sarah 11, and Samuel 9 years of age, children of the decd.

Page 242.

Welton, Thomas, Waterbury. Invt. £109-10-03. Taken 26 April, 1717, by Richard Porter and John Scovell.

Court Record, Page 36—2 July, 1717: Adms. granted to Richard Welton of Waterbury.

Page 81—2 September, 1718: Richard Welton exhibits now an account of his Adms. amounting to the sum of £50-10-03, which this Court accepts.

Page 130—5 July, 1720: Richard Welton now exhibits a further account of his Adms. Accepted. Order to dist. the estate: To Hannah Welton, widow, 1-3 part of the houseing and lands for her improvement during life, and to Josiah, the only child, the whole estate (including the widow's thirds after her decease) in houseing and lands. And appoint John Richards, William Judd and George Welton, distributors.

Page 238.

Wetmore, Joseph, Middletown. Invt. £254-04-09. Taken 31 May, 1717, by Joseph Rockwell, Thomas Allyn and Solomon Adkins.

Court Record, Page 34—4 June, 1717: Adms. granted to Lydia Wetmore, widow of sd. decd.

Page 114—1st December, 1719: Lydia Wetmore, widow, Adms., exhibits an account of her Adms. Accepted. And this Court appoint Lydia Wetmore to be guardian to her children, viz., Joseph, 13 years old, Lydia 11, Ann 7, and Nathaniel 4 years of age, children of Joseph Wetmore.

Page 240.

Whaples, Joseph, Hartford. Invt. £85-05-00. Taken 3 June, 1717, by Joseph Skinner and Thomas Hosmer.

Court Record, Page 35—4 June, 1717: Adms. granted to Joseph Skinner and Thomas Hosmer. Invt. was exhibited by Jonathan Barrett.

Dist. File: 27 June, 1718: Dist. of the estate of Joseph Whaples decd., viz., to Nathan Whaples, £10-16-00; to Jonath: Barrit, £27-17-00; and to Abigail, Mary and Elizabeth Whaples, to each, £10-10-09. By Thomas Hosmer and Joseph Spencer.

Page 147—7 March, 1720: Report of the dist. accepted, provided Jonathan Barrett be refunded the sum of £27-17-00 by the rest of the heirs to sd. estate for what he has paid in debts due from sd. estate.

Page 104.

White, Elizabeth, widow, Hartford. Invt. £87-05-04. Taken 20 July, 1716, by Cyprian Nichols and Thomas Hosmer.

Court Record, Page 19—3 July, 1716: Adms. joyntly to John Bunce, Jonathan Bunce and Thomas Meekins.

Page 26—5 February, 1716-17: Isaac Hynsdale, of Hartford, cited into Court to answer upon oath several interrogatories touching the estate of Elizabeth White, the answers to be kept on file.

Page 38—2 July, 1717: An extension of time to the Adms.

Page 53—4 March, 1717-18: John Bunce and Thomas Meakins report account of Adms. Allowed, and order to dist. the estate: To the heirs of Thomas Bunce decd., brother of the said Elizabeth White decd.,

£15-07-08¼ (to be sub divided: to Susannah Howard, £3-01-06½; to Joseph Bunce, the sum of £3-01-06½; to Sarah Wadsworth, £3-01-06½; to Jonathan Bunce his heirs, £3-01-06½; to Abigail Stanly, £3-01-06½; children and grandchildren of the sd. Thomas Bunce decd., which is their part and portion of sd. estate). Also to John Bunce, brother of the sd. Elizabeth White decd., £15-07-08¼, which is his part or portion. To the heirs of Mary White, sister of the sd. Elizabeth White decd., £15-07-08¼ (to be subdivided: to John White, £3-16-11; to Sarah White, £3-16-11; to Elizabeth Morton, £3-16-11; to William Worthington, £3-16-11; children of Sarah White decd., which is their portion. To the heirs of Mary Meakins, sister of the sd. Elizabeth White decd., £15-07-08¼ (to be subdivided: to John Meakins, £2-11-03¼; to Thomas Meakins, £2-11-03¼; to Sarah Jones, £2-11-03¼; to Mary Lewis, £2-11-03¼; to Mehetabell Dickinson, £2-11-03¼; to Jonathan Downing, £2-11-03¼; children of the sd. Mary Meakins, which is their part or portion of sd. estate). And this Court appoint Nathaniel Stanly, Thomas Hosmer and William Goodwin, of Hartford, distributors.

Page 57—1st April, 1718: Report of the distributors. Accepted, and grant a *Quietus Est.*

Page 295.

Whiting, Joseph, Hartford. Invt. £1849-06-08. Taken 26 February, 1717-18, by William Whiting, Aaron Cooke and Thomas Hosmer.

Court Record, Page 47—5 December, 1717: Adms. granted to Mrs. Anne Whiting, widow of sd. decd.

Page 84—7 October, 1718: Invt. exhibited by Mrs. Anne Whiting and John Whiting.

Page 151—8 May, 1721: Mrs. Anne Whiting, Adms., exhibits an additional invt. of £696-18-09. Accepted.

Page 101 (Vol X) 23 September, 1725: Anna Whiting and John Whiting, Adms., exhibit an account of their Adms. And the Court order that £38-15-11 be set out for the widow's necessary support.

Page 336 (Vol. X, Probate Side): This writing witnesseth an agreement made and concluded this day (24 January, 1738-9) by us the subscribers relating to the estate of our honoured father, Joseph Whiting, Esq., deceased, and our honoured mother, Mrs. Anna Whiting, as followeth: First. We have fully agreed and settled both of sd. moveable estates. 2nd. That all the lands are divided and made even, Nathaniel Stanly's part in the house and homested that his hond. father dwelt in having been paid to Jonathan Marsh for his part thereof. And Mr. Thomas Warren's part is ye sd. house and homested that was formerly belonging to his predecessor, Mr. Thornton, he having paid his brother Marsh for his part of sd. house and homested. The rest of the land belonging to the aforesd. estate is all belonging and appertaining to John Whiting, and divided and set out to him by our agreement as his part of the aforesd. estate, except what is under mentioned, which remains and belongs to us all in proportion as thereafter mentioned, sd. Whiting having paid Thomas Warren for his fifth part. First, a right of land in the northwest township named Hartland, which descended to us by our father being a £75 list in the patent, belongs three-fifths parts to John Whiting and one-fifth part to Nathaniel Stanly, and one-fifth part to Jonathan Marsh, yet lying in that maner in common between us. Also a right of land at Salmon Brook, about 10 acres, 2-5 to John Whiting and 1-5 a piece to Nathaniel Stanly, Jonathan Marsh and Thomas Warren. A right of land descended to us by our mother in the five miles on the east side of the Great River, and another in the three-mile lots, which descended to our mother by Col. Allyn, 2-5 of these lots belong to John Whiting and 1-5 apiece to Nathaniel Stanly, Jonathan Marsh and Thomas Warren. A right at Keney's Point, about 7 acres and 1-2, the same proportions. Another right of land in the neck at Hartford, descended to us by our mother from Col. Allyn, 2-5 belong to John Whiting, and 1-5 apiece to Nathaniel Stanly, Jonathan Marsh and Thomas Warren. A right in the house Moses Cook lives in, descended to us by our mother from Col. Allyn, 2-5 belongs to John Whiting, and 1-5 apiece to Nathaniel Stanly, Jonathan Marsh and Thomas Warren.

Signed: NATH: STANLY, JONATHAN MARSH,
THOMAS WARREN, JOHN WHITING.

Witness: *Elnathan Whitman,*
John Austin.

Page 7-8.

Wilcox, Samuel, Middletown. Invt. £601-08-01. Taken 8 April, 1714, by Thomas Stow, William Savage and John Warner.

An agreement, dated 30 April, 1714, between Samuel Wilcock and Francis Wilcock, both of Middletown, respecting the estate of their father Samuel Wilcock late decd., who died intestate. They being the only surviving heirs of sd. estate, have agreed for an equal division of sd. estate among themselves. In testimony whereof we have hereunto set our hands and seals the day and date above written.

SAMUEL WILCOCK, LS.
FRANCIS WILCOCK.

Witness: *William Savage,*
John Warner.

Page 45.

Willcoxson, Margaret, Simsbury. Invt. £78-12-02. Taken 21 December, 1714, by John Case, Samuel Pettebone and Andrew Robe.

Court Record, Page 9—6 March, 1715-16: Joseph Willcoxson, Adms., exhibited account. Allowed. Joseph Willcoxson moved this Court for a distribution of the estate to the brothers and sisters of the deceased, there being no lawful issue.

Page 11—8 February, 1715-16: This Court decided it as their opinion that in this case the said estate doth rightfully descend to the child of the deceased, though an illigitimate issue. Joseph Willcoxson appealed from this decree to the Superior Court, 3 September next.

Page 111-12.

Willes, Joshua, Windsor. Invt. £267-03-04. Taken 6 February, 1721-2, by Job Drake, Thomas Stoughton and Samuel Rockwell.

Whereas, our honoured father, Joshua Willes, late of the Town of Windsor, was at his death possessed of lands, goods and chattells to the value of £275-08-10, as the same is apprised, and we, Joshua Willes, Henry Willes, Jacob Willes, Abigail Willes, Hannah Willes and Susannah Willes, relict and children of the sd. decd., being all desirous to make a peaceable and friendly settlement of the sd. estate, do hereby severally, each one for themselves, mutually agreed to and with each other to make a final settlement of sd. estate. In testimony whereof we have hereunto set our hands this 10 March, 1721-2.

> ABIGAIL WILLES, LS.
> JOSHUA WILLES, LS.
> HENRY WILLES, LS.
> JACOB WILLES, LS.
> HANNAH WILLES, LS.
> SUSANNAH X WILLES, LS.

Agreement acknowledged in Court 14 March, 1721-3. Lampson (File: *Samuel*) Wills, a minor, 16 years of age, chose his uncle Henry Wills to be his guardian. Recog., £40.

Williams, Elias. Court Record, Page 34—4 June, 1717: Elias Williams, a minor, appeared in Court and made choice of Roger Wolcott to be his guardian.

Page 68-9.

Williams, Esther, Windsor. Invt. £7-00-06. Taken by Thomas Moore and Nathaniel Drake. Will dated 17 January, 1692-3.

I, Esther Williams, being now by reason of my age something weak of body but of perfect memory, do dispose of my estate as followeth: I do give unto my son Isaac my house and the land that I had of James Enno, which I value at £35, only reserveing the use and benefit of one of the lower rooms of sd. house to myself during my natural life if I need it for my own proper use. Also, that my son Isaac pay to my daughter Deborah £10 in 3 years after my decease, only if my son John desire to have the abovesd. house and land, I give it to him provided he pay to my son Isaac £35 in wheat and pork within one year after my decease. But if my son John is willing to renounce his right in the abovesd. house and homested, then my will is that my son John shall have my woodlott that I bought of James Enno. I appoint my sons John and Isaac executors.

Witness: *Job Drake,* ESTHER WILLIAMS, LS.
Elizabeth Drake.

Williamson, Alexander. Court Record, Page 24—26 November, 1716: This Court grants letters of administration on the estate of Dr. Alexander Williamson, late resident at Hartford, practitioner in physick, deceased, vizt., on that part of the estate of the said deceased as lycth within this Colony, unto Mr. John Read of Lovetown, in the County of Fairfield, provided he gives bond as the law requires in such case. And' the said John Read gave bond and took out letters of administration accordingly.

Page 245-6.

Wolcott, Mrs. Abiah, Windsor, relict of Mr. Henry Wolcott, late of Windsor decd. She died 15 June, 1717. Invt. £60-19-01. Taken by Thomas Moore, Daniel Loomis and Samuel Strong. Will dated 23 December, 1715.

I, Abiah Wolcott of Windsor, do make this my last will and testament: I give to my daughter, Elizabeth Allyn, my piece of gold which my father Wolcott gave me. I give to my gr. son Henry Allyn the gold ring, marked "S. W." I give to my gr. daughter Abiah Chauncey my 4 gold rings, also 2 paire of sheets, 4 pillow beeres and 5 napkins which I have made in my widowhood. And the remainder of my estate which belongs to me, viz., the third of my late husband's (Mr. Henry Wolcott's) estate, I give to my fatherless and motherless gr. children, Robert Chauncey, Ichabod Wolcott Chauncey and Abiah Chauncey, that is to say, 1-2 of all the same to Abiah Chauncey, and the other half to Robert Chauncey and Ichabod Wolcott Chauncey in equal proportions. I appoint Doctor Samuel Mather, Ebenezer Fitch and Abiah Chauncey to be sole executors.

Witness: *Daniel Bissell, Sen.,* ABIAH WOLCOTT, LS.
Thomas Fyler,
Samuel Strong.

Court Record, Page 38—11 July, 1717: Will proven.

Page 25 (Vol. X) 8 July, 1723: Will now exhibited by Mr. Ebenezer Fitch and Mrs. Abiah Chauncey, executors, who render an account of debts. This Court appoint Samuel Strong, Daniel Bissell and Thomas Fyler to dist. the estate according to the will of sd. decd.

Dist. File: 8 July, 1723: 1-2 of the estate to be dist. to Mrs. Abiah Wolcott Chauncey, and the other half to Robert Chauncey, to Ichabod Wolcott Chauncy, and to Abiah Chauncy. By Daniel Bissell, Thomas Fyler and Samuel Strong.

Page 142—6 December, 1726: Report of the distributors.

Page 56.

Woodbridge, Mrs. Abigail, Simsbury. Invt. £68-04-04. Taken by Caleb Williamson and Daniel Messenger.

Court Record, Page 3—7 December, 1715: Adms. granted to Rev. Mr. John Woodbridge of Springfield, son of the decd., who gave bond.

Page 4—3 January, 1715: Mr. John Woodbridge of Springfield, Adms., exhibits an invt., which was accepted, ordered recorded and kept on file.

Page 85.

Woodbridge, Rev. John, Springfield. Will dated 26th May, 1718. Gentlemen: It is my will and pleasure that my farme which lyeth at the place called the West Farmes, in the Town of Wethersfield, be divided amongst my four sons, John, Joseph, Timothy and Benjamin, as the law directs, and to the eldest a double portion, and the rest to have each his equal share in said lands, which land is to be and remain to my said children and to them only, respectively, and their heirs, forever. And I do by these presents confirm unto and set to and establish upon all and each of my sons respectively the sd. estate forever, unalterable, to be injoyed by them and their heirs as abovesaid and not to be conveyed, sold or alienated to any other persons whomsoever upon any manner of occasion or pretence whatsoever, forbidding and prohibiting all bargains, sales, leases or exchanges whatsoever, that may any wayes tend to make void, alter or defeat said entailment, confirmation or settlement of said lands. And ffurther, that none of my children shall at any time divide, or cause to be divided, into small parcells or quantities on pretence of distributing the same among their children, but the said estate shall descend wholely and intirely so divided to some one of their children according to their choice, and to such child they shall think meet, and that none of my children under any pretence whatsoever shall use or practice any method or device in the law to break, alter or defeat this my settlement and donation of my estate, under penalty of forfeiting his right, share and interest in the sd. lands and estate. And this bond and prohibition respecting the dividing, settleing and entailing my said estate shall take place as on my children so upon their children's children forever, in order that said estate may not be sold, mortgaged, leased or exchanged, but remain free and clear for the use of my children. I give unto my two daughters, Abigail and Jemima, £100 apiece, to be paid out of my moveable estate; if not sufficient, the rest to be paid by my sons to them; the moveables to be apprised upon delivery. and no estate to be imposed on my daughters that is not proper for housekeeping. My will and pleasure is that my wife shall have sole command and use of my estate, both lands and moveables, so long as she remains my widow. And in case my said wife Jemima shall see cause to alter her condition by a second marriage, that then she shall have liberty to have her thirds, both of real and personal estate, provided that sufficient bond be given that the same may be responded and returned, the whole of it, at her decease, to my heirs. Further, in case neither of the two foregoing propositions shall prove to my wife's contentment and sattisfaction, then she shall renounce all her right and interest in my estate by me before prescribed, and have the benefit of the provision made by the law for widows in that case. I appoint my wife Jemima sole executrix, except in case of marriage, and then to be left with the Court of Probates to order and appoint others.

Witness: *Jonathan Bull,*   JOHN WOODBRIDGE, LS.
Joseph Bodwitha, Samuel Ely.
        Will proven in Springfield Probate Court. 28 May, 1718.
                                                          Samuel Partridge,
                                  Test: *John Pynchon, Registr.*

Concordat Cum Originali.

Court Record, Page 36 (Vol. X) 3 January, 1723-4: Adms. granted to Lt. Thomas Seymour and John Woodbridge, son of the decd., with the will annexed, upon the estate that lyes in Hartford.

Page 195—3 July, 1728: This Court appoint Joseph Skinner of Hartford and Joseph Curtice and Thomas Stedman of Wethersfield to set out to Mrs. Jemima Wheeler, alias Woodbridge, relict of the Rev. John Woodbridge, in severalty 1-3 part of the farm late belonging to the sd. John Woodbridge in the bounds of Wethersfield for her improvement as dower.

Page 196—6 July, 1728: Adms., with will annexed, now granted to Joseph Woodbridge, son of sd. decd., in conjunction with Mr. John Woodbridge, son of sd. decd., and Capt. Thomas Seymour.

Page 32 (Vol. XII) 6 October, 1735: Joseph Woodbridge exhibited now in this Court an account of Adms., which is accepted.

Page 36—21 November, 1735: Per act of the General Assembly, 9th October, 1735, this Court do allow the Adms. to sell land in value to £376-11-00. The Court of Probate directed the Adms. to sell a farm in Newington Parish.

Page 38—6 January, 1735-6: Return of the sale of land to the Court on the 15 October, 1735. There were 4 parcels of land sold at vandue to the highest bidder, who was Samuel Hunn. Total, £380-00-00.

Wyer, Abigail. Court Record, Page 68—18 June, 1718: Adms. granted to William Pitkin, Esq., on the estate of Abigail Wyer, late of Hartford decd.

PROBATE RECORDS.

VOLUME X.

1723 to 1729.

Invt. in Vol. XII, Page 203.

Addams, Benjamin, Wethersfield. Invt. £ . Taken 3 December, 1725, by Joseph Talcott and Joseph Skinner.

Court Record, Page 100—7 September, 1725: Adms. granted to Abigail Addams, daughter of sd. decd.

Page 99—23 August, 1725: This Court appoint Ebenezer Dickinson of Wethersfield to be guardian unto Amasa Addams, a minor, 17 years of age. Recog., £20.

Page 244-5.

Adkins, Josiah, Middletown. Invt. £462-07-06. Taken 26 November, 1724, by Israhiah Wetmore, Solomon Adkins and Joseph Rockwell.

Court Record, Page 60—1st December, 1724: Adms. to Mary Adkins, widow,.who with Solomon Adkins gave joynt bond.

Page 120—1st March, 1725-6: Adms. account accepted.

Page 187—2 April, 1728: Solomon Adkins to be guardian to Joseph, Mary, Elizabeth and Abigail Adkins, minors, all about 14 years of age, they desireing the same.

Page 188—2 April, 1728: This Court appoint John Stedman of Middletown to be guardian to Josiah, age 13 years, and John, age 11 years, children of the decd.

See File: 27 April, 1727: An account of Adms. was exhibited by the Adms. Accepted, and this Court doth now order them to dist. the estate:

	£	s	d
To Mary Stedman, alias Adkins, the relict,	41	19	03
To Joseph Adkins, eldest son,	99	08	04
To Josiah Adkins,	49	14	02
To John, Mary, Elizabeth and Abigail Adkins, to each,	49	14	02

And appoint Joseph Rockwell, Nathaniel Bacon and Benjamin Adkins, distributors.

Page 204—5 November, 1728: Report of the distributors.

Page 6 (Vol. XI) 26 November, 1729: Josiah Adkins, a minor, 14 years of age, now appeared before the Court and made choice of Edward Higbee to be his guardian. Recog., £100.

Page 47—4 June, 1731: John Stedman, guardian to John Adkins, a minor son of Josiah Adkins, being removed out of the Colony, the sd. minor made choice of his brother Joseph to be his guardian. Recog., £100. Signified to this Court by John Hamlin, and approved.

Invt. in Vol. XII, Page 85.

Alford, Elizabeth, Windsor. Invt. £55-02-05. Taken 5 July, 1727, by Benedict Alford and Benjamin Loomis.

Court Record, Page 157—6 June, 1727: Adms. granted to Benedict Alford and Benjamin Loomis, a brother of the decd.

Page 202—1st October, 1728: The Adms. exhibited an account of their Adms. Allowed. Order to dist. the estate to the brothers and sisters: To Benedict Alverd, to Job Alverd, Jane Barbour and Joanna Loomis, to each of them the sum of £11-12-11; and to Jeremiah Alvord the sum of £0-09-04 besides what he hath already had. And appoint Thomas Moore, Nathaniel Drake and Timothy Loomis, distributors.

Page 46 (Probate Side, Vol. XI): Know all men by these presents: That we, the undersigned, have mutually agreed with each other that the estate of our sister Elizabeth Alverd, late of Windsor decd., shall be dist. And we hereby bind ourselves to stand and abide by this agreement. Signed and sealed:

BENEDICT ALVERD, LS.
JOB ALVERD, LS.
JANE BARBOUR, LS.
JOANNA LOOMIS, LS.
JEREMIAH ALVERD, LS.
JOHN BARBOUR, LS.
BENJAMIN LOOMIS, LS.

Witness: *Henry Allyn,*
Ann Allyn.

Page 63-4.

Allyn, John, Middletown. Died 22 November, 1724. Inventory taken 14 January, 1724-5, by Benajah Wetmore, Thomas Allen and Nathaniel Bacon.

Court Record, Page 66—2 February, 1724-5: Adms. granted to Mary Allyn, widow, and Thomas Allyn.

Page 95 (Vol. XI) 7 August, 1733: John Allyn, a minor, eldest son of John Allyn, late of Middletown decd., chose his uncle, Deacon Thomas Allyn, to be his guardian. Recog., £100.

Inventory on File.

Alsopp, Thomas, Simsbury, sometime of Suffield. Invt. £ .
Taken 8 March, 1724-5, by William Mather and William Alderman.
Court Record, Page 72—2 March, 1724-5: Adms. to Timothy Wood-
bridge and Samuel Humphrey, of Simsbury, and Daniel Merrells and
Moses Merrells, of Hartford.
Page 83—4 May, 1725: Invt. exhibited.
Page 105—5 October, 1725: Estate represented insolvent. This
Court appoint Timothy Woodbridge and Joseph Phelps, of Simsbury, and
Daniel Merrells, of Hartford, commissioners.
Page 143—3 January, 1725-6: Report nothing for the creditors.

Recorded in Vol. XII, Page 3-4. Invt. on Page 75.

Andrus, Benjamin, Farmingtown (Society of Southington). Invt.
£316-18-04. Taken 28 February, 1727-8, by Isaac Cowles and Samuel
Andrews. Will dated 7 December, 1727.
I, Benjamin Andrus of Southington, in the County of Hartford, in ye
Colony of Connecticut, do make this my last will and testament: Item.
Unto my wife Elizabeth Andrus I give 1-2 of my moveable estate to her
own dispose forever, and the improvement of all my lands, with ye house
and barn, during the time of her widowhood. Item. Unto my daughter
Joannah Andrus I give ye sum of £20 to be paid when she comes to be of
age. Item. Unto my two sons Jonathan and Gideon Andrus I give all
my lands and the remainder of my estate whatsoever, real or personal;
and what of my real estate I have given to my abovesd. wife for her use
and improvement for a time as abovesd., after ye time is expired it shall
return unto my two sons Jonathan Andrus and Gideon Andrus, to their
heirs and assigns forever. And I do constitute, ordain and appoint my
wife Elizabeth Andrus to be my sole executrix.

(Loco)
Witness: *John Andrus,*   BENJAMIN ANDRUS (SIGIL.)
Daniel Andrus, Samuel Andrus.

Court Record, Page 177—5 March, 1727-8: The last will and testament of Benjamin Andrews, late of Farmingtown, in the Parish of Southington, is now exhibited by Elizabeth Andrews, executrix named in the
sd. will, who accepted that trust in Court. The sd. will being proved, the
same is approved by the Court. And the sd. executrix exhibited an inventory.

Recorded in Vol. XII, Page 18-19-20-21.

Andrus, Benjamin, Sen., late of Farmington. Invt. £508-14-03.
Taken 23 October, 1727, by Isaac Cowles, Daniel Judd and Josiah Hart.
Will dated 15 April, 1725.

I, Benjamin Andrus, Sen., of the Town of Farmingtown, do make this my last will and testament: Item. Unto my wife Sarah Andrus I give and bequeath, to be at her own dispose forever, all that personal estate that ever was hers and I reced. with her upon marriage; also, for her support and comfort during her natural life, I give unto her the use, improvement and profit of 1-3 part of all improveable lands, both in the common field and in particular enclosures, this during her natural life. And further, I give unto my sd. wife, during the time of her widowhood and bearing my name, the 1-3 part of my now dwelling house, also so much of the cellar under it and well by it as she have need for her own use, with free ingress, egress and regress to, in and from the same; and this is upon conditions that she shall personally inhabit in the sd. house, that is, so long as she shall personally inhabit there bearing my name, which I reserved for the same purpose in a deed of gift made to my son James of the house and home lott, the sd. deed bearing date the 31st day of January, Anno. Dom. 1723-4. Item. Unto my five sons, viz., Benjamin Andrus, John Andrus, Stephen Andrus, Daniel Andrus and Samuel Andrus, besides what I have formerly given them and done for them in their settlement, I give to each of them 3 shillings, to be paid out of my estate by my executor; and unto each of the eldest sons of my sd. sons, and unto the eldest son of my daughter Mary Cowles, I say unto each of ym I give and bequeath 5 shillings to be paid out of my estate. Item. Unto my daughter Mary Cowles, besides what I have already given her, I give 20 shillings. Item. Unto my son James Andrus, now living with me, I give unto him, his heirs and assigns forever, all ye remainder of my estate, both real and personal, whatsoever and wheresoever it is, with the reversion of my real estate after the decease of my wife. I appoint my son James Andrus my sole executor.

Loco
Witness: *Thomas Hooker, Sen.,*   BENJAMIN ANDRUS, SEN., SIGIL.
Samuel Whitman, Daniel Andrus.

Court Record, Page 167—7 November, 1727: The last will and testament of Benjamin Andrus, late of Farmingtown deceased, was now exhibited in this Court by James Andrews, named executor in the will, who accepted the trust, which will is by this Court proved, approved and ordered to be recorded.

Page 308-309.

Arnold, Henry, Hartford. I, Henry Arnold, arrived at a great age whereby I am weak in body, do make this my last will and testament: Imprimis. I give to my loveing wife Elizabeth all my household stuff, and one of my cows (which she sees cause to make choice of), to be for her use and at her free and absolute disposal; and also one room in the lower house. And my will is that my two sons Henry and John Arnold maintain her with suitable apparrell and victuals during her natural life. But if they refuse or neglect so to do, my will is that she shall have the improvement of the land which I had of Mr. Wadsworth where the lower house stands, being about 8 acres, for her maintenance. Item. I give to my sons Henry and John Arnold all my lands, to be equally divided between them as to quantity and quality, yet is so to be understood that if my son Henry refuses to give to my son John a deed of one-half of the meadowland which they joyntly bought of Mr. Wyllys and the upland bought of Benjamin Hills, my will is that then my son John shall have the whole of my land to him and his heirs forever. But if he give him a deed of one-half of the meadow and upland above mentioned, that then my son Henry shall injoy the 1-2 of my land as above expressed. Item. My will is that my stock (the cow given to my wife excepted) be equally divided between my sons Benjamin and John, my just debts being first paid out of it. Also, that my sons above mentioned have an equal priviledge in my barn. Item. I give to my daughters, Sarah, Mary and Elizabeth, besides what they have already had, five shillings each. I ordain my wife Elizabeth and my son Henry to be executors.

The will as presented in Court: The signing, ensealing and witnessing thereunto is cut off or taken off from sd. will, and is not to be found. The widow and heirs signed an agreement, 3 August, 1724, for a settlement of the estate according to the will, allowing it to be good.

Signed: ELIZABETH ARNOLD, LS.   MARY RISLEY, LS.
EBENEZER FOX, LS.   JOHN ARNOLD, LS.
SARAH CASE, LS.   ELIZABETH FOX, LS.
JOHN RISLEY, LS.

Court Record, Page 93—6 July, 1725: John Arnold, son of sd. deceased, exhibited now a writing sd. to be the will of sd. deceased, with sworn evidences thereof. At present deferred, and for the time grant Adms. to John Arnold, the son, on the estate of Henry Arnold deceased.

Page 95—3 August, 1725: An agreement for the settlement of estate according to the last will, under the hands and seals of the widow and heirs of sd. deceased. Acknowledged and approved.

Arnold, Henry, Jr., Court Record, Page 93—6 July, 1725: Henry Arnold, Jr., late of Hartford, deceased, Adms. unto John Arnold, brother of sd. Henry Arnold, Jr., deceased.

See File: Articles of agreement made by the heirs on the estate of Henry Arnold, Jr., late of Hartford: That John Arnold, brother of sd. deceased, shall have all the real and personal estate; that John Arnold shall pay £20 to his sister Sarah Case; also to pay £20 to John Risley and Mary his wife; also pay £20 to Ebenezer Fox and Elizabeth his wife, another of the sisters of the deceased. Also, it is agreed that John Arnold shall pay all the just debts. In confirmation of the above-written articles, we have hereunto set our hands and seals this 3 August, 1725.

JOHN ARNOLD, LS.
SARAH X CASE, LS.
JOHN RISLEY, LS.
MARY X RISLEY, LS.
EBENEZER FOX, LS.
ELIZA X ffox, LS.

Court Record, Page 95—3 August, 1725: An agreement for the settlement of the estate of Henry Arnold, Jr. deceased, was exhibited in Court, John Arnold, brother of sd. deceased, to give security to the other heirs for the payment of money as mentioned. Done in Court.

Recorded in Vol. XII, Page 162-3-4.

Arnold, Jonathan, Haddam. Invt. £551-03-00. Taken 22 January, 1728-9, by Joseph Arnold, Caleb Cone and Josiah Arnold. Will dated 24 December, 1728.

I, Jonathan Arnold of Haddam, cordwainer, do make this my last will and testament: I give to Elizabeth my wife all my household goods, all except the two least featherbeds and their bedding, a chest of drawers, a table, four chairs, two plain chests, and a box; and also I give her two cows and my black pacing mare, to be at her own use and dispose forever, and the use of one-half of my dwelling house so long as she shall remain my widow. I give to my son Jonathan Arnold 2 acres of land of the south end of my four-acre lott, which, with the expense of his education, I count a large double portion. Item. To my well-beloved son Samuel Arnold I give my dwelling house and homestead, two small lotts in the meadow, the remainder of my four-acre lott, all my lands on Long Hill (both on the east and west side), and all my rights in the undivided land; and also I give him my barn, a yoke of oxen, a cow, a bay mare, and all my husbandry tackling and implements; all which I give him on condition that he provides suitably for his mother's subsistence while she shall be my widow. Item. To William Brainard, my well-beloved son-in-law, I give £5 and the charges of settleing my estate. Item. The remainder of my household goods, chattells, personal estate and debts (after my debts are paid and the charges of my funeral are discharged) I give to my five daughters, Elizabeth, Esther, Abigail, Mary and Huldah, to be equally divided between them. And I hereby impower and authorize my executor to make sale of all the remainder of my lands not above disposed of, and my will is that the produce be divided in equal proportion to my five daughters above sd., excepting to Esther, who shall be accountable for £40 I have already given her. I ordain my son-in-law William Brainard sole executor.

Witness: *Phineas Fiske,*   JONATHAN ARNOLD, LS.
Joh: Fiske, Benjamin Smith, Jr.

Court Record, Page 37 (Vol. XI) 2 February, 1730-1: William Brainard, executor, exhibits an account, which this Court accepts, orders recorded and kept on file.

Page 188-9-190-1-2.

Bacon, Andrew, Middletown. Invt. taken 26 July, 1723, by Israhiah Wetmore, Joseph Rockwell and John Collins.

Court Record, Page 26—6 August, 1723: Adms. to Mehetabell Bacon, widow, and this Court appoint her guardian to her daughters, Esther, age 13 years, and Abigail, age 11 years; and Israhiah Wetmore to be guardian to Joseph Bacon, age 17 years, children of Andrew Bacon deceased.

Page 30—5 October, 1723: John Bacon, a minor, about 15 years of age, son of Andrew Bacon decd., chose Nathaniel Bacon to be his guardian.

Page 133—5 August, 1726: Adms. account now exhibited. Allowed. Order to distribute: To Mehetabell Bacon, widow of the decd.; to Andrew Bacon, eldest son, to Nathaniel, to Josiah, to Daniel, to Joseph, to John, to Ann, to Mehetabel, to Esther, to Abigail Bacon. By Israhiah Wetmore, Joseph Rockwell and John Collins.

Page 63 (Vol. XI) 4 April, 1732: Nathaniel Bacon exhibited now in this Court a receipt under the hand of John Bacon, bearing date 31 January, 1731-2, by which it appears that John Bacon had received of Nathaniel Bacon, his guardian, all his estate due from sd. guardian, and also discharge him sd. guardian of any further demands from him.

Page 209-10.

Baker, Bazey, Middletown. Invt. £1042-06-07 (for dist.). Taken 4 October, 1723, by John Collins, Joseph Rockwell and Joseph Cornwell, Middletown. Land in Hartford by William Baker and David Ensign, 212 acres, £212. This in Farmington:

2 1-2 acres in the South Meadow, in ye Indian Ground,	£47-10-00
6 acres near Hog River, at £4-10-00 per acre,	27-00-00

Court Record, Page 29—5 October, 1723: Adms. granted to Hannah Baker and Nathaniel Baker, son of sd. deceased.

Page 37—3 January, 1723-4: This Court appoint Hannah Baker to be guardian to her children, viz., Timothy Baker, age 17 years, Thankfull 14 years, Jeremiah 11, Hannah 8, and Susannah 5 years of age. Recog., £500.

Page 59—1 December, 1724: Hannah and Nathaniel Baker, Adms., exhibited an account of their Adms. Accepted. This Court order the estate dist. to the heirs, viz.: To Hannah Baker, widow, £48-12-02; to Nathaniel Baker, eldest son, £397-09-08; to Timothy, Hannah and Susannah Baker, to each of them, £198-14-11, which is their single portion of sd. estate. And appoint Joseph Rockwell, Joseph Cornwall and Benjamin Cornwall, of Middletown, distributors.

Page 171—5 December, 1727: Joseph Webster of Hartford, now husband to Hannah Webster, formerly Hannah Baker (widow relict of Basey Baker, late of Middletown deceased), representing that the Court of Probates holden at Hartford 3 November, 1724, ordered a dist. of sd. estate and appointed Messrs. Joseph Rockwell, Joseph Cornwall and Benjamin Cornwall, of Middletown, distributors, and sd. men so appointed to

distribute sd. estate have hitherto neglected sd. service, or have not perfected and sent sd. distribution to sd. Court, and desires this Court to now
appoint James Ensign, William Baker and David Ensign, Jr., of Hartford, to make dist. of sd. estate: This Court do now appoint James Ensign, William Baker and David Ensign, Jr., of Hartford, to distribute sd.
estate.

Page 172—2 January, 1727-28: This Court appoint Nathaniel Baker
to be guardian (instead of his mother, Hannah Baker, alias Webster) to
his sister Hannah Baker, 12 years of age, and Susannah Baker, 9 years
of age. Recog., £500.

Page 31 (Vol. XIII) 4 July, 1738: Joseph Webster, husband to
Hannah Webster, alias Hannah Baker, showing this Court that in the
dist. of the estate of sd. decd. in a lott in Farmington her part was not set
out by meets and bounds, this Court appoint David Ensign, William
Baker and Jonathan Sedgewick to set out to sd. Hannah her right of
dower in sd. lott.

Invt. in Vol. XII, Page 226.

Barber, Abigail, Simsbury. Invt. £   . Taken 3 November,
1727, by Joseph Case, John Humphries and James Hillyer.

Court Record, Page 203— 7 October, 1728: This Court grant Adms.
unto Abigail Barbour, daughter of the decd. Thomas Barbour and Abigail Barbour, children of Thomas Barbour and Abigail Barbour his wife,
both decd., exhibited an agreement under their hands and seals for the
settlement of the estates of sd. Thomas and Abigail, and before this Court
acknowledged the same to be their free act and deed, which agreements
are by this Court accepted for the full settlement of the sd. estates.

Page 15.

Barber, Samuel,Windsor. Invt. not dated. Taken by Thomas Marshall, William Phelps and John Palmer.

Court Record, Page 8—5 March, 1722-3: Adms. on the estate of
Samuel Barber, late of Windsor, decd., unto Martha Barber, widow,
and Joseph Barber, brother of the sd. deceased.

Page 119—1st March, 1725-6: Joseph Barber and Martha Barber,
Adms. on the estate of Samuel Barber, late of Windsor, decd., exhibited
account of Adms., which account is accepted.

Page 79 (Vol. XI) 21 December, 1732: Samuel Barber, a minor, 15
years of age, son of Samuel Barber of Windsor, chose his uncle Joseph
Barber to be his guardian. Recog., £50.

Page 33 (Vol. XII) 6 October, 1735: Martha Barber, widow, desired that her brother Joseph Barber of Windsor should be guardian to
her son Ezekiel Barber, a minor under 14 years of age. He was appointed guardian.

Recorded in Vol. XII, Page 183.

Barbour, Samuel, Simsbury. Died 18 December, 1725. Invt. £306-06-07. Taken by John Case and Jonathan Westover. Will dated 7 December, 1725.

I, Samuel Barbour of Simsbury, do make this my last will and testament: Imprimis. I give unto my well-beloved wife Sarah 1-3 of all my improveable lands during life; 1-3 of my moveable estate, with £10 more to be levied out of my moveable estate, forever. I give unto my son Samuel 50 acres of land on the West Rider commonly called Cherrile's land, with £30 of my undivided land, to him and his heirs forever. Item. I give to my son Thomas 1-2 of my last division, with 1-2 of my lott called Rowley lott, to him and his heirs forever. Item. I give unto my son Jonathan 1-2 of my last division, with 1-2 of my lott called Rowley lott, to him and his heirs forever. Item. I give unto my two daughters, Sarah and Mercy, £40 to each of them, and that to be paid by my four sons at an equal proportion, Samuel, Thomas, Jonathan and John, at the day of marriage or at the age of 18 years (through forgetfulness for not entering this before the last paragraph). Item. I give unto my son John the house, homelott and meadow lott lying in Hop Meadow, to him and his heirs forever. I constitute my wife Sarah and my brother Benjamin Holcomb sole executors.

Witness: *Timothy Woodbridge, Jr.,*   SAMUEL X BARBOUR, LS.
Andrew Robe, Sen., Nathaniel North.

Court Record, Page 115—1st February, 1725-26: The last will and testament of Samuel Barbour, late of Simsbury, deceased, was now exhibited by Sarah Barbour, with Benjamin Holcomb, named executors in the will, who accepted the trust. The sd. will being proved, and by this Court approved and allowed, the executors exhibited an invt., which was accepted.

Page 42 (Vol. XIII) 23 February, 1738-9: John Barbour, a minor, age 19 years, son of Samuel Barbour of Simsbury, chose Benjamin Hooker to be his guardian. Recog., £300.

Page 26-7-36-7.

Barnard, Thomas, Simsbury. Invt. taken 16 December, 1724, by Joseph Phelps, Joseph Case and Joseph Gilbert for Simsbury. For Hartford, 2 January, 1724-5, by Joseph Gilbert, John Spencer and Jonah Gross. Will dated 2 September, 1724.

I, Thomas Barnard of Hartford, alias Simsbury, in the County of Hartford, do make this my last will and testament: Item. I give, demise and bequeath ye whole of my sd. estate, goods, chattells, housen, lands, moveables, and whatsoever else shall be mine at my decease, unto Jemima Smith, ye wife of Benjamin Smith, of Hartford, and to her heirs and assigns forever. I appoint ye sd. Jemima sole executor.

Witness: *Joshua Moses,*   THO. BARNARD, LS.
Joseph Gilbert, Jr., John Kirkum.

Court Record, Page 62—1 December, 1724: Will now exhibited by Jemima Smith, executrix named in sd. will. Proven.

Inventory on File.

Bartlett, John, Windsor. Invt. £220-00-00. Taken 4 March, 1728-9, by David Bissell, Robert Bartlett and Thomas Grant.

Page 305.

Belding, John, Wethersfield. Invt. £851-13-09. Taken 24 June, 1725, by Jonathan Belding, Isaac Ryley and Jonathan Belding, Jr.

Court Record, Page 91—6 July, 1725: Adms. to Sarah Belding, widow, Jacob Griswold and Josiah Belding. Exhibit of inventory.

Page 140—6 December, 1726: Jacob Griswold and Sarah Belding, Adms., exhibited an account of debts and charges paid, with loss. The account was accepted: The invt., £888-17-03; subtracting £27-07-09, there remains £861-18-00 to be distributed. The Court order to be distributed: To Sarah Belding, widow and relict, £93-13-02 out of the moveable estate, with dower; to John Belding, eldest son, £311-02-06, which is his double portion of the estate, and likewise more the sum of £51-17-01, which is his equal part of a child's portion that dyed since the decease of his father; to Ebenezer Belding and Timothy Belding, the rest of the surviving children, to each of them, £155-11-03, which is their single portion of sd. estate, and likewise more to each of them £51-17-01, which is their equal parts of a child's portion that dyed since their father. And appoint Samuel Wolcott, James Butler and Nathaniel Stilman, of Wethersfield, distributors. This Court do appoint Sarah Belding of Wethersfield to be guardian to her children, viz., Ebenezer Belding, about 7 years, and Timothy Belding, about 3 years of age. Rec., £100.

Page 73-4-5-6-7-8.

Belding, Joseph, Wethersfield, who died 7 December, 1724. Inventory taken 11 February, 1724-5, by Jonathan Belding and Joshua Robbins.

Page 73—2 March, 1724-5: Adms. to Mary Belding, widow, and Joseph Belding, son of sd. deceased. Exhibit of inventory.

Page 83—4 May, 1725: Mary Belding and Joseph Belding, Adms. on the estate of Joseph Belding, late of Wethersfield, deceased, exhibited an account: Paid out £29-09-01 in debts and charges; the inventory, £1805-01-01, real and personal; the moveable part, £706-06-01; subtracting £29-09-01, there remains £1775-12-00 to be distributed. Order to dist.: To Marah Belding, widow of the decd., £225-12-04 of moveables, with dower; to Joseph Belding, eldest son, £442-17-00, which is his double portion of sd. estate; to Thomas, Amos, Sarah, Mary and Esther Belding, the rest of the children, to each of them, £221-08-06, which is their single portion of sd. estate. And appoint Jonathan Belding, Lt. Robbins, 1st, and Silas Belding, of Wethersfield, distributors.

Page 84—4 May, 1725: This Court appoint Mary Belding to be guardian to her son Amos Belding, 18 years of age. Recog., £100. And Joseph Belding appointed guardian to his sister Esther Belding, 15 years of age. Recog., £100.

Page 202—1st October, 1728: Esther Belding appeared before this Court and declared that she had received of her guardian, Joseph Belding, the full of her portion in his hands to her satisfaction, and thereupon does discharge him of guardianship.

Page 219—3 June, 1729: Whereas, Mary Belding of Wethersfield, widow, was appointed guardian to her son Amos Belding during his minority, and the sd. Amos now being arrived at full age, appeared before this Court and declared that he had received his part of the estate of his father that was in his guardian's hands.

Inventory on File.

Bidwell, Samuel, Middletown. Invt. £335-04-01. Taken 1st May, 1727, by Nathaniel Savage, Ebenezer Smith and Joseph White.

Court Record, Page 83—2 May, 1727: At the request of Mary Bidwell, widow of sd. deceased, that Moses Boardman may have administration granted to him on the estate of her deceased husband, this Court grant Adms. unto Moses Boardman, who, with the widow, acknowledged themselves joyntly and severally bound in a recog. of £100.

Page 175—27 February, 1727-8: Moses Boardman of Middletown, Adms., exhibits an account of his Adms. Accepted, and likewise an addition to the estate of £1-19-00. [Here follows a blank space on the page for record of dist.]

Dist. per File: 15 March, 1727-8: To the widow, Mary Bidwell, to Samuel, to Daniel, to Sarah, and to Ann Bidwell; under the hands of Ebenezer Smith and Richard Goodrich, distributors.

Page 178—5 March, 1727-8: This Court appoint Mary Bidwell of Middletown to be guardian unto her children, viz., Daniel, 11 years of age, and Sarah, 8 years. Recog., £100.

Page 187—2 April, 1728: Report of the distributors.

Page 90 (Vol. XI) 17 May, 1733: Daniel Bidwell, age 15 years, son of Samuel Bidwell, late of Middletown, decd., chose his uncle, Lt. Hezekiah Sumner, to be his guardian. Recog., £150.

Page 282-3.

Bird, Thomas, Farmington. Invt. £550-05-01. Taken 5 June, 1725, by Isaac Cowles and Daniel Judd. Will dated 29 April, 1725.

I, Thomas Bird, of the Town of Farmington, being visited with a distemper which of late has proved mortal to many, do make this my last will and testament: Item. I give unto my wife Sarah Bird, whom I have lately married, to be at her own dispose forever, all that personal estate that was hers at the time when I married her; also my smallest brass kettle and a churn and one paile; and also, during her natural life, I do give her the use, improvement and profit of 1-3 part of all my real estate, houseing and lands. Item. I give unto my three sons, viz., John Bird, Joseph Bird and Jonathan Bird, all my wearing clothes of all sorts, to be equally divided amongst them, my boots only excepted, which I give solely to Jonathan Bird. Item. Unto my two sons John Bird and Joseph Bird (besides what I have already given them), the 1-2 part of my land at a place called Green Swamp; also the lotts that were firstly my father James Bird's, lying in three of the divisions west from the reserved lands, to be equally divided between them (they not to have that lott which lyeth in the sixth and furthest division west, which I design for Jonathan, but the other three lotts, all lying in Farmington bounds). Item. Unto my three daughters, viz., Mary Bird, Rebeckah Bird and Lydia Bird, I give unto each of them £35, to be paid to them out of my personal estate, and they each of them to have liberty of pastering a cow at my pasture at Woolfpit Path while they are unmarried. Item. Unto my grandson James Bird, son of Joseph Bird, I give and bequeath all the right which did formerly belong unto my father James Bird and that tract of land not yet lotted out, lying west of that division of land in Farmington bounds called Panthorn Division, between the mountains; also, unto my sd. grandson I give my raper and belt formerly my brother James Bird's. Item. Unto my son Jonathan Bird, now living with me, I give and bequeath all the residue and remainder of my estate, both real and personal, wheresoever and whatsoever it is, not before in this will disposed of, he to have and enjoy 2-3 part of the sd. real estate immediately after my decease, the other third part at the decease of my above sd. wife. I appoint my son Jonathan Bird sole executor.

Witness: *John Hooker, Sen.,*   THOMAS BIRD, LS.
Benjamin Andrews, Samuel Whitman.

Court Record, Page 88—7 June, 1725: Will proven.

Page 189—2 April, 1728: Thomas and James Burd now being both decd., this Court grant Adms. unto Samuel Burd and Mindwell Burd, both of Farmington.

Page 155.

Bissell, Josias, Windsor. Died 18 December, 1724. Invt. in land, £665-10-00. Taken March, 1725, by Daniel Bissell, Jonathan Elsworth and Ebenezer Hayden.

Court Record, Page 67—2 February, 1724-5: Adms. to Miriam Bissell, widow.

Page 103—5 October, 1725: Invt. exhibited by Miriam Bissell, Adms.

Page 130—5 May, 1726: Adms. account now exhibited and allowed.

Page 131—3 June, 1726: Per act of the General Assembly of May last, Miriam Bissell and Daniel Bissell may sell land to the amount of £93-04-09 in payment of debts.

Page 24-25.

Blake, John, Middletown. Died 8 December, 1724. Inventory taken 19 January, 1724-5, by Jonathan Blake, Stephen Blake and William Whittemore.

Court Record, Page 66—2 February, 1724-5: Adms. to Elizabeth Blake, widow of sd. decd.

Page 10 (Vol. XI) 8 January, 1729-30: Joseph Blake, a minor, 16 years of age, chose Capt. Daniel Hall to be his guardian. Recog., £50.

Page 45 (Vol. XII) 4 May, 1736: Freelove Blake, a minor, 17 years of age, son of John Blake, chose his uncle Stephen Blake of Middletown to be his guardian. Recog., £100.

Page 263-4-281.

Blinn, Peter, Wethersfield. Invt. £79-00-01. Taken 18 March, 1724-5, by David Goodrich, William Warner and Richard Montague. Will dated 2 March, 1724-5.

I, Peter Blinn of Wethersfield, having arrived at the age of 84 years, do make this my last will and testament: Item. I give to my beloved wife 1-3 part of all my moveable estate, except my wearing apparrell, my silver-headed cane and joyner tooles. Item. I give to my beloved son Peter all my wearing apparrell and all my joyners tooles, besides £18 he hath already received of me, as may appear in the 71st page of my Book of Accompt. Item. I give to my son James Blin 5 shillings. I give to my son William Blinn 1 shilling. I give to my daughter Mary Hurlbut 5 shillings. I give to Daniel Blinn, my grandson, son to my son Daniel Blinn, 5 shillings. I give to my son Jonathan Blinn 1 shilling. I give to my son Deliverance Blinn 1 shilling. Item. I give to my daughter Margaret Belding, after all my just debts are paid and the severall legacies before mentioned, 2-3 of my moveable estate, except my silver-headed cane, which I give to my grandson George Blinn, son of Deliverance Blinn. And I make my son Deliverance Blinn sole executor.

Witness: *David Goodrich,*   PETER BLINN, LS.
David Williams, Christopher Graham.

Court Record, Page 82—4 May, 1725: Will now exhibited and proven.

Page 88-89—6 July, 1725: Mary Blynn, widow, her 1-3 part set out by Joshua Robbins, John Russell and Richard Montague (per order of Court).

Page 124-5-134.

Boardman, Daniel, Wethersfield. Died 20 February, 1725. Inventory taken 26 March, 1725; in Litchfield, 8 April, 1725, by Joseph Kilbourn, Jacob Griswold and John Buell; taken 12 April, 1725, in New Milford, by John Bostwick and Zachariah Ferriss. Will dated 13 February, 1725.

I, Daniel Boardman of Wethersfield, do make and ordain this my last will and testament: Imprimis. I give unto Hannah, my beloved wife, 1-3 part of my land lying in Wethersfield, with half my dwelling house, to be to her use during her life, and all my stock, as horse, cattle and sheep, to be to her use together, with all houshold stuff, beds and lining, and all my moveables, to be at her dispose as she shall please. Item. I give to my son Richard Boardman the 1-2 of my barn near his dwelling house in Newington. I give to my son Daniel Boardman one gunn, in his own possession. Item. I give to my son Israel Boardman, in money, 3 shillings. Item. I give to my son Timothy Boardman my present dwelling house and barn and 13 acres of land, with all ye appurtenances belonging thereto, to be to him and his heirs forever. I give to my son Timothy half my land in Newington, one acre of land in Great Meadow more or less, and ten acres of land in Fearful Swamp, to be each parcell to him and his heirs forever, ordering that he should pay such sums to ye daughters or others as shall be hereafter herein expressed. Item. I give to my son Joshua Boardman my house and half my land at Litchfield and half my land at New Milford, to be to him and his heirs forever. Item. I give to my son Benjamin Boardman the other half of my land at Litchfield and ye half my land at New Milford, and £20, to be paid by my son Timothy Boardman in current money unto sd. son Benjamin Boardman. Item. I give unto my son Charles Boardman the other half of my homelott (the west end of it), 3 1-2 acres in ye south field, and 10 acres in Newington, all and every parcell to be to him and his heirs forever, after my decease, ordering that he shall pay such sums as shall be hereafter named herein. Item. I give to my daughter Mabel Nickolss £10, to be paid by Charles Boardman out of his estate. Item. I give my daughter Hannah Abbey £7, to be paid by my son Timothy Boardman out of his estate. Item. I give to my daughter Martha Churchill £20, to be paid by my son Timothy Boardman out of his estate. I appoint my wife and son Timothy to be sole executors.

Witness: *David Wright,*   DANIEL BOARDMAN, LS.
　　　　Jonathan Pratt.

Court Record, Page 80—12 April, 1725: Will proven. An agreement to settle the estate by the surviving heirs, Charles having died: £10 of his estate set out to Mabel Nichols, the rest to be divided to the brothers and sisters with the father's estate, according to this agreement, in equal parts, by Lt. Joshua Robbins, Jonathan Pratt and Samuel Benton, by meets and bounds. Mrs. Martha Boardman to be guardian to Benjamin Boardman, age 20 years.

Page 216.

Boardman, Isaac, Jr., Wethersfield. Died 9th May, 1719. Inventory taken 7 March, 1721-2, by Joseph Belding, Samuel Benton and Samuel Robbins.

Wethersfield, 27 December, 1723: We, ye subscribers, being desired by Isaac Boardman to apprise severall pieces of land which was given by deed of gift by Isaac Boardman, Sen., late of Wethersfield, decd., to his grandchildren, as may more fully appear by ye deed bearing date 20 May, 1719, is as followeth:

	£ s d
To 7 acres and about 20 rods, homelott,	71-05-00
To 3 acres, Gooseburry Swamp,	20-00-00
To 2 1-2 acres in ye Swamp,	25-00-00
To 1 acre in ye meadow,	15-00-00
To 3 acres in the Weat Swamp,	03-00-00
Total,	134-05-00

Joseph Belding,
Samuel Benton,
Samuel Robbins.

Court Record, Page 40—3 March, 1723-4: Adms. granted to Isaac Boardman, son of the decd. Isaac Boardman, Adms., exhibits account of his Adms. Accepted. Order to dist. the estate:

	£ s d
To Rebeckah Boardman, widow,	24-19-11
To Isaac Boardman, eldest son,	20-00-00
To Edward, Josiah and Ephraim Boardman, to each,	10-00-00

And appoint Joseph Belding, Samuel Robbins and John Rose, of Middletown, distributors.

Page 50—7 July, 1724: This Court appoint Isaac Boardman to be guardian to Ephraim Boardman, son of Isaac Boardman. Recog., £50.

Page 322-3.

Boardman, Israel. Died 24 April (1725). Invt. £1121-00-00. Taken 6 September, 1725, by Jacob Griswold and Josiah Belding.

Court Record, Page 105—5 October, 1725: Adms. to Elizabeth Boardman, widow.

Page 136—4 October, 1726: Elizabeth Boardman, Adms. on the estate of Israel Boardman, late deceased at Wethersfield, exhibited an account of debts paid and addition to sd. estate as on file, to lodge till some receipts are brought.

Page 36 (Vol. XI) 15 January, 1730-1: This Court appoint Jacob Gibbs of Windsor to be guardian to Olive Boardman, age 12 years, and Elisha Boardman, age 9 years, children of Israel Boardman, late decd. Recog., £100.

Invt. in Vol. XII, Page 193.

Bow, Edward, Middletown. Invt. £148-15-02. Taken 13 December, 1725, by Francis Whitmore and Benony Horton.

Court Record, Page 114—4 January, 1725-6: Adms. granted unto Anne Bow, widow of the decd.

Page 26 (Vol. XI) 1st September, 1730: Edward Bow, a minor, 10 years of age, and Martha Bow, 13 years, appeared in Court, and Anna Bow, the mother, made choice of Ensign John Fisk to be their guardian. Recog., £100.

Page 25 (Vol. XIII) 7 March, 1737-8: Edward Bow, son of Edward Bow, late of Middletown, made choice of Captain John Fisk of Haddam to be his guardian. Recog., £50. Cert: *James Welles, J. P.*

Page 31—24 July, 1738: Mary Bow, a daughter of Edward Bow, age 14 years, chose Enos Curtiss of Wallingford to be her guardian. Recog., £50.

Bowers, Ebenezer. Court Record, Page 128—5 May, 1726: Ebenezer Bowers, a minor, 19 years of age, chose Matthew Grant of Windsor to be his guardian. Recog., £50.

Page 27.

Brace, Elizabeth, Mrs., Hartford. Inventory taken 5 October, 1724, by Joseph Butler and Thomas Steele.

Court Record, Page 52—4 August, 1724: Adms. granted to Henry Brace, son of the decd.

Invt. in Vol. XII, Page 143-4. Add. Invt. in Vol. XI, Page 53.

Brainard, Daniel, Sergt., Haddam. Died 8 September, 1728. Invt. £1027-00-01. Taken 14 November, 1728, by Ebenezer Cone, Samuel X Ackley and Jabez Chapman. They also apprised the apparell of 3 children who deceased before their father, Daniel Brainard. Additional invt. of £33-12-07. Taken 10 March, 1729, by Samuel Ackley, Jabez Chapman and Ebenezer Cone.

Court Record, Page 206—3 December, 1728: Adms. granted to Hannah Brainard, widow, and Capt. Daniel Brainard, father of the deceased.

Page 18 (Vol. XI) 5 May, 1730: Add. invt. of £33-12-07 was exhibited in Court and accepted.

Page 31—1st December, 1730: An account of Adms. on the estate of Daniel Brainard, Jr., was now exhibited in Court, by which account it appears the Adms. have paid in debts and charges the sum of £19-08-05. Account accepted and ordered to be kept on file.

Page 1 (Vol. XIII) 1736-7: Daniel Brainard, a son of Daniel Brainard, chose his grandfather, Capt. Daniel Brainard, to be his guardian. Cert. *Samuel Olmsted, J. P.*

Page 74—6 November, 1740: Daniel and Hannah Brainard, Adms., exhibited a further account of Adms. This Court order that the estate be dist., viz.:

	£	s	d
To Hannah Brainard, alias Chapman,	86	17	11
To Daniel Brainard, eldest son,	86	07	11
To Susannah and Hannah Brainard, daughters, to each,	43	03	11

And appoint Jabez Chapman, Samuel Ackley and Ensign Daniel Cone distributors. Susannah Brainard, a minor, age 15 years, chose Noadiah Brainard to be her guardian. Cert: *Samuel Olmsted, J. P.*

Page 6 (Vol. XIV) 4 May, 1742: An additional account of Adms. was exhibited in Court by Jonathan Chapman, Adms. in right of his wife the relict of sd. decd., by which account it appears he has paid in debts and charges, £38-00-06. Account allowed.

Recorded in Vol. XII, Page 52-3.

Brainard, Hezekiah, Haddam. Died 24 May, 1727. Invt. £2442-03-03. Taken 24 June, 1727, by Joseph Arnold, Jared Spencer and Caleb Brainard. Will dated 23 May, 1727.

I, Hezekiah Brainard of Haddam, do make this my last will and testament: I give to my eldest son a double portion of all my estate, to be injoyed by him when he comes to the age of 21 years or day of marriage, which shall first happen, excepting those lands I hereafter appoint to be sold. Item. To the rest of my children I give an equal proportion of my estate. Item. I give to my wife Dorothy 1-3 part of my moveable estate forever, and 1-3 part of my houseing and lands during her natural life, and she to have her first choice. Item. I do appoint that my son Nehemiah be bred up to learning and be fitted to be serviceable thereby. I do appoint my loveing wife Dorothy to be sole executrix to this my last will, and I do desire her out of my whole estate to pay all my just debts. And also I do hereby fully impower her, for the bringing up of my son Nehemiah to learning or other necessary uses, to sell the following parcells of land, viz., yt which I bought of Samuel Smith, and also that parcell of land I bought of William Spencer, and also that parcell of land that I have in partnership with my brother Caleb Brainard.

Witness: *Timothy Woodbridge,*   HEZ: BRAINARD.
Richard Lord, Elizabeth Wyllys.

Court Record, Page 160—4 July, 1727: Will proven.

Page 68 (Vol. XI) 22 May, 1732: Dorothy Brainard, executrix of the last will and testament of Hezekiah Brainard, late of Haddam, not having fully perfected her account of executorship, and being decd., this Court do therefore grant letters of Adms. on sd. estate unto Hezekiah Brainard, son of the decd., with the will annexed. And the sd. Hezekiah Brainard became bound in the sum of £400.

Page 89—28 April, 1733: Hezekiah Brainard, eldest son of Hezekiah Brainard, moved to this Court that there may be a distribution according to the will; and this Court appoint Caleb Brainard, Elijah Brainard and Jared Spencer, of Haddam, to distribute the estate. Daniel Brainard, a minor, 15 years of age, and Martha Brainard, 17 years, chose their brother Hezekiah Brainard to be their guardian. And this Court appoint the sd. Hezekiah Brainard to be guardian to 3 of the children, viz., John, age 13 years, Elizabeth 10, and Israel 8 years of age. Recog., £300.

See Dist. per File: 17 May, 1733: Order to distribute to Hezekiah, to Nehemiah, to Dorothy Smith, to Jerusha Spencer, to Martha Brainard, to David, to John, to Elizabeth, and to Israel Brainard. By Caleb Brainard and Elijah Brainard.

Page 42 (Vol. XII) 31 March, 1736: It appears to this Court that there was 300 acres of land granted by the General Assembly of the Colony of Connecticut to James Wadsworth, John Hall and Hezekiah Brainard, Esq., bounded south by the Litchfield line and every way else by common land, lying neare the west line of the place called Torrington. Sd. Wadsworth hath sold his third part as undivided to Ebenezer Hill, Jr., Luke Hill and Isaac Hill, and sd. Hall's part now belongs to his eidest son John Hall of Wallingford, and in the dist. of sd. Brainard's estate according to his last will his third part of sd. land fell to his son Israel Brainard, who is yet under age, who, together with the other owners of sd. land viz., John Hall and the sd. Ebenezer, Luke and Isaac Hill, moves this Court that James Wadsworth, Esq., and James Wadsworth, Jr., of Durham, might assist Hezekiah Brainard, guardian to sd. minor, to divide the sd. 300 acres of land by meets and bounds, that each owner may know their part thereof.

Recorded in Vol. XII, Page 166-7-8.

Brown, John, Sen., Windsor. Invt. £375-05-00. Taken 26 February, 1728-9, by Cornet Joseph Phelps, Joseph Barbour and John Palmer, Jr. Will dated 19 July, 1728:

I, John Brown, Sen., of Windsor, do make and ordain this my last will and testament: Imprimis. I give and bequeath unto my son John the dwelling house and homested where he now liveth, being about 15 acres, being a parcell of land purchased of Lt. Barbour, provided that he shall yield and pay such a part and portion of my just debts (and funeral expenses) as may be due at the time of my decease, as I shall hereafter will and declare it to be my mind that he should. Further, I give unto my son John as aforesd. a piece of land I purchased of my brother Peter Brown decd., lying near the Mill Brook, containing about 2 1-2 acres, and also about 1 acre more bounding northerly on the same and extending southerly to the Mill Brook, being part of the parcell of land I purchased of

Capt. Phelps. Item. I give unto my son Isaac the south half of my home lott and also the fruit that may grow on half of the orchard, standing on the north half of the homested, for the space of three years next after my decease, with the priviledge of going and fetching of the same as occasion may be. Also, I give him as aforesd. all the land, both for quantity and quality, that I have lying on or near the Mill Brook not yet disposed of, the whole to be divided equally to him and his brother Daniel. And sd. Isaac is to have the above provided he shall pay so many of my debts or so much on that account as I shall hereafter declare to be my mind and will. Item. I give unto my son Daniel my dwelling house and the north half of my homelott, only Isaac to have half the fruit as aforesd.; and he is to have the same on this condition, that he shall pay so much toward the clearing of my just debts and satisfying my funeral expenses as I shall hereafter declare to be my mind and will; and I also give him' the half of my land at the Mill Brook as aforesd. Item. I give unto my three sons, John, Isaac and Daniel, all my right and share in Windsor Proprietors' Commons, and all my right and share in the western lands, or New Banton as is sometimes called, and all my share in the land lying northeasterly of Windsor, called the equivalent land, and also my barn to them. Said right in lands and sd. barn which standeth near my dwelling house I give to my sd. sons in equal shares. Item. I give unto my daughter Ann of my moveable estate so much as to make her even with my daughter Mary, which will appear by an account thereof on my Book of Accounts. I give unto my daughter Sarah out of my moveable estate in the same manner and in equal degree I give to my daughter Ann. Item. I give all the remainder of my moveable estate unto my three daughters, viz., Mary, Ann and Sarah, to be equally divided among them. I appoint my three sons, John, Isaac and Daniel, to be executors.

Witness: *Matthew Allyn, Jr.,*　　　　　　JOHN BROWN, LS.
Benoni Bissell, Henry Allyn.

Court Record, Page 214—4 March, 1728-9: The last will and testament of John Brown, late of Windsor, decd., exhibited and proven.

Page 86.

Brown, Peter, Windsor. Inventory taken by William Phelps, Cornelius Phelps and Joseph Barbor.

Court Record, Page 72—2 March, 1724-5: Adms. unto Rachel Brown, widow and relict. She gave bond with Robert Scott of Windsor. Rec., £100.

Page 111—4 January, 1725-6: Rachel Brown, Adms. on the estate of Peter Brown, exhibited an account: Debts, £170-03-09; set out for the family support, £3-12-08; so that there remains more than moveables due to answer the debt, the sum of £88-17-10, which this Court, pursuant to an act of the General Assembly in October last, do direct the sd. Adms. to make sale of so much of the real estate as may be sufficient to pay the sum of £88-17-10.

Page 15 (Vol. XIII) 14 September, 1737: Peter Brown, age 15 years, son of Peter Brown, chose John Barbour of Windsor to be his guardian. Recog., £100. Certified by *Henry Allyn, J. P.*

Page 82-3-4-5-6.

Brunson, Samuel. An inventory of the estate of Samuel Brunson, (son of Isaac Brunson who belonged in Kensington) of Farmington, deceased 20th February 1724-5. Taken by Thomas Curtis and Jonathan Lee. An invt. of his estate in Waterbury, apprised by John Scovell, Sen., and William Judd, 5 March, 1724-5.

Court Record, Page 73—9 March, 1724-5: This Court grant Adms. unto Isaac Brunson of Waterbury, brother of the decd.

Page 75—22 March, 1724-5: Elijah Brunson, a minor, 15 years of age, chose Isaac Brunson of Waterbury to be his guardian. Recog., £50. Mercy Brunson, daughter of sd. decd., made choice of Thomas Brunson of Waterbury to be her guardian. Recog., £50.

Page 108—7 December, 1725: Isaac Brunson, Adms., exhibits an account of his Adms.:

	£ s d
Paid in debts and charges,	32-14-02
Inventory of the estate,	575-04-00
Subtracting,	32-14-02
There remains to be distributed,	542-09-02
To Ruth Brunson, widow, of moveable estate,	46-01-04
To Elijah Brunson, only son,	330-19-00
To Mercy Brunson, her single portion,	165-09-06

And appoint Anthony Judd, Thomas Curtis and Jonathan Lee, distributors.

Page 147.

Buck, Daniel, Wethersfield. Inventory taken 11 April, 1726, by Martin Kellogg and Martin Smith.

Court Record, Page 129—5 May, 1726: Adms. granted to Elizabeth Buck, widow. Recog., £100, with John Sage of Middletown.

Page 53 (Vol. XIII) 7 August, 1739: Elizabeth Buck, age 17 years, and Hannah Buck, age 14 years, children of Daniel Buck, chose their father-in-law, John Deming, to be their guardian. Recog., £500.

Invt. in Vol. XII, Page 104.

Buck, David, Jr. Died 5 March, 1725-6. Invt. £632-03-09. Taken by Jabez Whittlesey and Richard Boardman.

Court Record, Page 189—2 April, 1728: David Buck and Eunice Buck, who were appointed Adms., exhibited now an account of their Adms.:

	£	s	d
Paid in debts and charges,	37-01-01		
Inventory,	362-03-09		
Subtracting,	37-01-01		
There remains to be distributed,	595-02-08		
To Eunice Buck, widow relict, with dower,	27-00-00		
To ( ) Buck, only son,	567-00-00		

And appoint (   ) Willard, Richard Boardman and Jabez Whittlesey, distributors. This Court appoint Jonathan Ryley and Eunice Ryley, of Wethersfield, guardians to David Buck, a minor, age 3 years, son of David Buck deceased. Recog., £200.

Dist. File: 2 April, 1728: To the relict and to David Buck, only son of the deceased.

Page 216—1st April, 1729: Report of the distributors.

Page 61 (Vol. XI) 19 February, 1731-2: This Court appoint Josiah Buck to be guardian unto David Buck, a minor, now 7 years of age. Recog., £300.

Page 41 (Vol. XIII) 6 February, 1738-9: David Buck, a minor, now made choice of Josiah Buck to be his guardian, Jonathan Riley, his former guardian, having made no objection. Recog., £200.

Will and Invt. in Vol. XII, Page 171-2.

Buckland, Nicholas, Windsor. Invt. £438-12-07. Taken 1st November, 1728, by John Thrall, James Enno and Timothy Loomis. Will dated 7 June, 1728.

I, Nicholas Buckland of Windsor, being far advanced in years, doe make and ordain this my last will and testament: I give unto my 4 daughters, Martha Strong, Elizabeth Hopkins, Hannah Mather and Mindwell Phelps, all my real estate, houseing and lands, to be equally divided between them. My will is that my sons-in-law, Daniel Strong and Daniel Phelps of Windsor, be my executors.

Witness: *Remembrance Sheldon,*   NICHOLAS BUCKLAND, LS.
John Allyn, Jacob Gibbs.

Court Record, Page 204—7 October, 1728: Will proven.

Dist. File: 7 February, 1728-9: To Samuel Strong and Martha his wife, to Robert Hopkins and Elizabeth his wife, to Samuel Mather and Hannah his wife, to Daniel Phelps and Mindwell his wife. By Remembrance Shelding and John Allyn.

Page 39, 59.

Buckland, William, Hartford. Died 12 December, 1724. Inventory taken by Timothy Cowles and Charles Buckland. Will dated 9 December, 1724.

I, William Buckland of Hartford, do make this my last will and testament: I give to Elizabeth Buckland, my wife, 1-3 part of my estate during her life. I give to my son William Buckland 3 acres of upland butted west on John Forbes's heirs and Obadiah Wood's heirs, north and east on ye country road, and south on sd.Forbes; and also half my homelott between ye country road and ye Pine Swamp or ye Indian Fort, that is to say, ye east end of sd. lott; and also a equal part of ye sd. lotts eastward, with ye rest of his brethren. Item. I give to my sons John Buckland and Jonathan Buckland my dwelling house and barn and half my homelott, that is, the west end of my abovesd. lott; and my sons John and Jonathan shall have the choice of 3 acres of meadow land and also that small upland lott butting on ye meadow bank west, and also all the loe land to the west side of ye pond; and the rest of my meadow land equally divided to my three sons. Item. I give to my daughter Mehetabell Cole £35 in money, of which she has already received the sum of £26-01-00. Item. I give to my daughter Prudence Easton the sum of £35, of which she hath received £35 already. Item. I give to my daughter Elizabeth ye sum of £35, to be paid to her at her arrival at ye age of 18 years. Item. I give to my daughter Ann £35 at 18 years of age. And my will is that my wife and my son William be executors.

Witness: *Samuel Woodbridge,*   WILLIAM X BUCKLAND, LS.
Charles Buckland, Joseph Case.

Court Record, Page 62—5 January, 1724-5: Will exhibited by Elizabeth Buckland and William Buckland, executors. Proven.

Page 72—2 March, 1724-5: John Buckland, 19 years of age, chose his mother, Elizabeth Buckland, to be his guardian. Recog., £100. And this Court appoint Elizabeth Buckland guardian unto her children, Elizabeth, age 15 years, Ann 12 years, and Jonathan, age 9 years. Recog., £300.

Recorded Vol. XII, Page 115-116.

Buel, Peter, Simsbury. Died 8 January, 1728-9: Inventory taken ye 30 May, 1729, by Nathaniel Holcomb, Sen., and Andrew Robe, Sen. Will dated 7 June, 1728.

I, Peter Buell of Simsbury, do make and ordain this my last will and testament: Imprimis. I give unto my wife Mary the use of all my moveable estate that is not yet disposed of, that is to say, after my sickbed and funeral charges with all my other lawfull debts are fully paid. Item. I give unto my son Samuel, and the heirs of Ephraim, 1-2 of my undivided land and 20 acres over, to be equally divided between Samuel and Ephraim's heirs, that is to say, 1-2 to Samuel and the other half to Ephraim's heirs, and that shall be their portions and no more, only I give unto Samuel my old musket. Item. I give unto my two younger sons, viz., William and Jonathan, five shillings to each of them and no more, because I have considered them already in giving of them lands by deeds of gift. Item. I give unto the heirs of my daughter Abigail 20 shillings and no more. Item. I give unto my other six daughters, namely, Martha, the heirs of Mary, and to Sarah, Hannah, Miriam and Esther, all the rest of my undivided lands not yet disposed of, to be equally divided between them, all six, to them and their heirs and assigns forever. Also, at the decease of my wife, then what remains of my moveable estate to be equally divided amongst my six daughters, namely, Martha, the heirs of Mary, and to Sarah, Hannah, Miriam and Esther, only I give unto Esther more than the rest a bed with bedding and fourty shillings. And further my will is my wife shall have at her own dispose at the day of her death her wearing apparrell and my linen, with 2 small chests. And furthermore I make my son William Buell to be sole executor.

Witness: *Andrew Robe,*   PETER X BUELL.
Benjamin X *Case, Mary Barber.*

Recorded in Vol. XII, Page 139.

Burnham, Samuel, Sen., Hartford. Died 19 April, 1728. Invt. £735-04-11. Taken 6 May, 1728, by Gabriel Williams and John Wood. Will dated 20 November, 1727.

I give to my wife Mary Burnham all the household stuff, goods and estate whatsoever yt she brought with her at the time of her marriage with me, and also one pide cow, to be at her own dispose forever. I give to my son Samuel Burnham the house in which he dwells and the land on which it stands, bounded west on a highway, south on land of John Burnham, north on land of John Wood's, the bredth of my lott (excepting two rods on the north side extending eastward within 8 rods of the house, hereafter given to my son Joseph Burnham). I give to my son Joseph Burnham his house and 14 acres of land. I give to my son William Burnham the house in which he dwells, with land bounded west on land of heirs of Thomas Burnham, Jr., decd., south on Jonah Williams, north on Charles Burnham. I give to my sons Daniel and Timothy Burnham, equally to be divided between them, my dwelling house, barn and homelott. I give to my daughter Hannah Drake, to my daughter Ann Trumble, and to her eldest son ———— Trumble, to my daughter Mary Church, and to my daughter Rebeckah Burnham. I appoint my sons Samuel Burnham and Joseph Burnham to be executors.

Witness: *Jonathan Burnham,*   SAMUEL BURNHAM, LS.
Jabez Burnham, William Pitkin.

Court Record, Page 193—May, 1728: Will proven.

Recorded in Vol. XII, Page 2-3. Invt. on Pages 228-9.

Burnham, Thomas, Sen., Hartford. Died 9 November, 1726. Inventory taken 31 March, 1726, by Samuel Burnham and John Wood. Will dated 15 March, 1726.

I, Thomas Burnham, Sen., of the Town of Hartford and Colony of Connecticut in New England, doe make this my last will and testament: Imprimis: I give to my wife Naomy Burnham my red cow and also ye 1-2 of all my moveable estate that is not hereafter given to my children. Item. I give to my son Thomas Burnham the sum of 5 shillings. Item. I give to my two other sons, John and Josiah Burnham, the sum of 5 shillings apiece. Item. I give to my son Charles Burnham all my shop tools and also all my carts, plows, and all other team tackling, and a certain parcell of shingles, and also all my horse kind, and my black cowe, and a 2-years-old heifer. Item. I give to my three daughters, Elizabeth Gilman, Sarey Molford and Naomey Gailer, ye sum of 5 shillings apiece. I give to my daughter Mary Anderson a red heifer of two years old. Item. I give to my daughter Abigail Williams my pide heifer about 3 years old, and also ye sum of 50 shillings as money. I also give to my son Charles ye 1-2 of all the rest of all my moveable estate, to be equally divided between him and my wife as above mentioned. I appoint my son Charles Burnham executor.

Witness: *Ozias Pitkin,*   THOMAS BURNHAM, SEN., LS.
Samuel Burnham, John Morton.

Court Record, Page 125—5 April, 1726: Will proven.

Page 136—1st November, 1726: Before this Court the last will of Thomas Burnham, late of Hartford decd., was allowed to stand good, the widow being present and not objecting against it.

Recorded in Vol. XII, Page 37.

Burnham, Thomas, Jr., Hartford. Invt. £324-15-00. Taken 20 May, 1726, by Matthew Grant and David Bissell. Will dated 11 February, 1725-6.

I, Thomas Burnham, Jr., of the Town of Hartford in the Colony of Connecticut, do ordain this my last will and testament: Item. I give to my son Thomas Burnham my dwelling house and barn and homelott on which they stand, lying and being within the Township of Hartford, as it butts on the east on land of Thomas and Samuel Burnham, south on land of Jonah Williams, west on land of Thomas Burnham, and north on the highway yt leads into the meadow and in part on lands of Thomas Burnham; and one piece of meadow land lying and being in the Township of Windsor, as it abutts west on land of Jno. Burnham and Jno. Anderson, south on land of Samuel Burnham, and north on Thomas Burnham his land; and also all my woodland or other lands whatsoever or wheresoever. Item. I give to my two daughters, Elizabeth and Esther Burnham, £25 apiece, and they to have all my moveable estate toward the payment of the same at inventory price after just debts are paid, the moveables to be equally divided between them; and my will is that what my moveable estate fall short of the sd. sum of £25 apiece my son Thomas Burnham shall pay to them in or as money when they attain to the age of 20 years. And I appoint my hond. father-in-law, Mr. Jno. Strong, of the Town of Windsor, to be my executor.

Witness: *Ozias Pitkin,*   THOMAS BURNHAM, LS.
Samuel Burnham, Charles Burnham.

Burrell, Charles. Court Record, Page 202—1st October, 1728: Charles Burrell, a minor, about 7 years of age, and Jonathan Burrell, about 5 years of age, chose Jonathan Westover to be their guardian. Rec., £200.

Page 332.

Butler, Thomas, Hartford. Invt. £625-14-00. Taken 12 November, 1725, by Capt. John Sheldon, Ensign Nathaniel Goodwin and Samuel Welles. Will dated 23 August, 1725.

I, Thomas Butler, do give unto my well-beloved wife Abigail 1-3 part of all my personal estate forever, and the improvement of 1-3 part of my real estate during life. I give unto my son Isaac, whom I brought up to learning, besides what I have already given him, 20 shillings. I give to my son Daniel Butler 1-2 of the lott called Brick Hill lott, containing about 7 acres. I give him 1-2 of my lott called Goodman's lott. I give to my son Daniel and his heirs forever. Item. I give to my son Thomas Butler 1-2 of my lott called Brick Hill lott. Also I give my son Thomas 1-2 of my land called Goodman's lott. Item. I give to my son Elisha my home lott and all the buildings thereupon and appurtenances thereto belonging. Also I give to him a piece of land at the Blew Hills called Spring Brook, about 15 acres. I also give to Elisha the land adjoyning to my home lott which I bought of Tixwell Endsworth, about 4 acres. The forementioned parcels of land I give to my son Elisha and his heirs forever, and my will is that my wife shall have the improvement of Elisha's lands, houseing and what shall be given him for to bring him up until he come of age, if he live so long, and also to help bring up my daughter Elizabeth. Item. My will (is) that what my daughters, (viz.), Abigail, Deborah, Sibel and Vilot, have got by their industry shall not be inventoried as any part of my estate. Item. My will is that Daniel shall have, and I do give to him, one yoke of oxen and my youngest mare of 3 years old past. I appoint my wife Abigail and my son Daniel to be executors.

Witness: *Joseph Talcott,*   Thomas Butler, ls.
Hannah Cadwell, Deborah X *Butler.*

Court Record, Page 109—7 December, 1725: Will now exhibited by Abigail Butler, the widow, and Daniel Butler, son of sd. decd., executors named in the will. Proven. Invt. exhibited and allowed.

Page 126—5 April, 1726: The executors exhibited now an account of their executorship, which this Court accepts. Order to dist. the estate according to the will: To the widow and children. And appoint John Shelding, Robert Sandford and Jonathan Butler distributors. And this Court appoint Daniel Butler guardian to Thomas Butler, a minor, 15 years of age. Recog., £100.

Page 143—3 January, 1726-7: Report of the distributors. And this Court appoint Abigail Butler, widow, to be guardian unto her children, viz., Elisha, 10 years, and Elizabeth, also 10 years, children of the decd.

Page 236.

Cadwell, Matthew, Hartford. Died 27 December, 1723. Invt. £281-07-03. Taken by Ozias Pitkin, John Pratt and John Skinner.

Court Record, Page 40—3 March, 1723-4: Adms. to Esther Cadwell, widow.

Page 66 (Vol. XIII) 6 March, 1739-40: An account of Adms. was exhibited in Court by Ozias Pitkin instead of his wife Esther, the relict of sd. deceased. Accepted.

Page 100-1-2.

Cadwell, Samuel, Hartford. Invt. £711-00-00 in lands. Taken by John Shelding, Robert Sandford and Nathaniel Goodwin.

Will dated 22 December, 1724.

I, Samuel Cadwell, Sen., of Hartford, husbandman, do make this my last will and testament: Item. I give unto my beloved wife Mary (her dower rights). Item. I give to my son Samuel Cadwell my house-ing and all my land and all my rights and priviledges at ye place called West Division. Item. I give unto my son Joseph Cadwell my housen and all my lands with all my rights and priviledges in ye Town. Item. I give unto my daughter Mary Cadwell ye sum of £50 in money. Item. I give to my daughter Elizabeth ye sum of £50 in money. I appoint my wife Mary and my son Samuel Cadwell executors.

Witness: *Edward Cadwell,*   SAMUEL X CADWELL, LS.
William Cadwell, Samuel Welles.

Court Record, Page 76—6 April, 1725: Will exhibited by Mary Cadwell, executrix. Proven.

Page 42 (Vol. XII) 6 April, 1736: Joseph Cadwell, age 18 years, son of Samuel Cadwell, chose Moses Nash of Hartford to be his guardian. Recog., £50.

Recorded in Vol. XII, Page 86.

Camp, Mary, Hartford. Invt. £39-08-06. Taken 28 February, 1726-7, by Zachariah Seamore and Jonathan Welles. Will dated 9 July, 1726.

In the name of God, amen. I, Mary Camp, being in perfect memory, do ordain this to be my last will and testament: I give to my son John Camp the rest of my land, he paying my lawfull debts. I give to my daughter Abigail Wadsworth my great kettle and porridge pot, and my skillett, and my feather bed and furniture to it, a paire of tongs and fire slice, trammell, stilyards, frying pan, bellows, lamp, trunk, chest, seive, kettle, a paile, and a heifer two years old past, and a heifer one year old and advantage, a box, iron and heters, and sheats, linen, a looking glass, a puter plate and platters. I give to my granddaughter Hannah Camp a puter platter. Item: To Sarah Stodder an iron kettle, and to Lydia Lee that which William Whiting oweth to me. And all the remainder of my goods to be divided to my two daughter's children, that is to say, Sarah Stodder and to Mary Lee's children, my wearing close to Abigail Wadsworth, and my cowe to be divided to Sarah and Mary Lee's children and Abigail Wadsworth equally between them. And I do appoint my son John Camp my executor.

Witness: *Robert Sandford,*   MARY CAMP, LS.
——————— *Spencer, Obadiah Spencer, Jr.*

Court Record, Page 157—6 June, 1727: Will proven, but the executor named in the will haveing declined, Adms. granted to John Camp, with will annexed, who gave bonds with Josiah Belding of Wethersfield Rec., £500.

Page 207—3 December, 1728: Adms. account exhibited and accepted.

On File.

Carpenter, David, Hartford. At a Courte of Probate for the County of Hartford, holden at New London, 2nd April, 1722, present Joseph Talcott, Judge of sd. Courte: This Court appoint Isaac Coules and Christopher Darrow to assist Daniel Lester, guardian to the children of John Lester, of New London, to make a distribution on the estate of David Carpenter of New London deceased, sometime formerly of Farmingtown, who made distribution or partition accordingly, and now returned to this Court and was accepted and allowed. Ordered to be recorded and kept on file. A dist. of several divisions of land in Farmington: 3-4 parts to Samuel Gridley, and 1-4 part to the heirs of John Lester of New London deceased.

ISAAC COWLES,
CHRISTOPHER DARROW.

Invt. on File.

Case, Bartholomew. Died 25 October, 1725. Invt. £674-12-09. Taken 18 November, 1725, by John Humphries, Joseph Case and James Hillier.

Court Record, Page 109—7 December, 1725: This Court grant 'Adms. on the estate of Bartholomew Case of Simsbury decd. unto Mary Case, widow, and Thomas Case, son of sd. decd.

Page 132—5 July, 1726: A bond of £400 was given with Thomas Case, son of the decd.

Page 150—4 April, 1727: John Humphrey is appointed guardian to Abigail Case, a daughter, 6 years of age.

Page 181—5 March, 1727-8: This Court appoints Mary Case, widow, to be guardian to Amos Case, age 14 years, and Isaac Case, 10 years, Abraham Case 7, and Sarah 12 years of age, children of the decd. And the sd. Sarah (Mary) acknowledged herself bound in a recognizance of £100 money to the Judge of this Court or his successors that she will faithfully discharge the trust of guardian to sd. minors during their minority according to law. Mary Case and Thomas Case, Adms., exhibit an account of their Adms., which this Court accepts. See File: Adms. account as followeth:

	£ s d
Paid in debts and charges,	1-11-08
Inventory,	696-05-09
Subtracting the sum of,	1-11-08
There remains to be distributed,	694-14-01
To the widow,	71-19-00
To Thomas, eldest son,	155-13-10
To Amos, Isaac, Abram, Elizabeth, Abigail, and Sarah Case, to each,	77-16-10

And appoint Joseph Case, Jno. Humphries and James Hillier, distributors.

Page 117.

Case, John, Hartford. Died 24 February, 1724-5. Inventory taken by Timothy Cowles, Charles Buckland and John Maken.

Court Record, Page 76—6 April, 1725: Adms. granted to Sarah Case, widow.

Page 153—2 May, 1727: Isaac Case, 17 years of age, and Mary Case, 16 years of age, chose Mr. John Bidwell to be their guardian. Recog., £100. And this Court appoint Sarah Case to be guardian to John Case, age 14 years, Lucy, age 11 years, Thomas 9 years, Abigail 7 years, Timothy and Sarah 4 years, and Phineas 3 years of age, children of John Case, deceased. Recog., £300.

Page 154: Sarah Case, Adms. on the estate of John Case, late of Hartford, decd., exhibited an account of her Adms.: Paid in debts and charges, £68-03-07. Whereas, it appears that there is paid out of that estate the sum of £68-03-07 more than has been received; and whereas, the inventory of sd. estate amounts to the sum of £361-02-02; subtracting £68-03-07, there remains £292-17-07 to be distributed. Order to Sarah Case, widow relict, £27-16-02, with dower; to Isaac Case, eldest son, £53-00-06, which is his double portion of sd. estate; to John, Thomas, Timothy Orpheus (Alpheus), Mary, Abigail and Sarah Case, the rest of the children, to each of them £26-10-03. And appoint Timothy Cowles, Joseph Pitkin and John Meakins, distributors.

Page 157—6 June, 1727: Report of distributors.

Page 62 (Vol. XI) 7 March, 1731-2: Thomas Case, a minor, 14 years of age, son of John Case, late of Hartford, made choice of Joseph Cowles of Hartford to be his guardian. Recog., £100.

Page 12 (Vol. XIII) 21 July, 1737: Sarah Case, now 16 years of age, daughter of John Case, late of Hartford, chose Joseph Cowles to be her guardian. Recog., £100.

Page 65—6 May, 1740: Timothy Case, 18 years of age, son of John Case, chose Samuel Smith of Hartford to be his guardian. Recog., £200.

Page 45 (Vol. XIV) 3 July, 1744: Alpheus Case, a minor, now 20 years of age, son of John Case, chose Ensign James Church of Hartford to be his guardian. Recog., £500.

Page 57—21 April, 1745: Disbrow Spencer of Hartford, in right of his wife Sarah, who was the widow and relict of John Case, late of Hartford, decd., now moves to this Court that the undivided lands of the sd. decd. may be set out to her for her improvement during life: Whereupon this Court appoint Col. Joseph Pitkin, Capt. Jonathan Hills and Lt. Samuel Welles of Hartford to set out to the sd. widow 1-3 part of sd. outlands by bounds and monuments, and make return thereof to this Court.

Page 106-7-8, 251.

Case, Richard, Hartford. Inventory taken by Timothy Cowles, John Meekin and Charles Buckland. Will (nuncupative) of Richard Case, who died Saturday, 22 February, 1724-5, (19) with the Inventory.

Sarah Case, widow, relict of Richard Case, testifieth: That before noon, being the day my husband died, when my son Joseph was going to call Capt. Roger Pitkin to wright his will, my sd. husband Richard Case said that he did not know but that his tongue might be clipt before anybody came to write his will, so that he should not be able to speak. Lieut. John Meakings, Jonathan Pitkin and Joseph Easton, Jun., being present, he called Lieut. Meakins and Joseph Easton by name and said: "I desire you to take notice or beare witness that I give my son Joseph all my lands and all my estate, and that he shall pay the girls, which I understand to be my two daughters, £35 apiece, legacies in money. And I give Carter one acre of land at the upper end next to William Bidwell, 16 rods long. I believe Carter has had about £20 already. I also give my wife a good maintenance out of my estate." When asked if he did not give Carter 2 acres of land as he used to tell of, in his next division, he replied "Aye." (26 March, 1724-5.)

Signed: ELIZABETH CASE.

Signed when under oath:
John Meakin, Joseph Easton, Jr.,
Jonathan Pitkin.

2nd March, 1724-5.

Before the Court of Probates.

Attest: J: Talcott, Judge.

Page 221-2-3.

Case, Samuel, Symsbury. He died 30th July, 1725: Invt. £447-03-08. Taken 10 August, 1725, by Joseph Case, Andrew Robe, Sen., and John Humphries. Will dated 28 July, 1725.

I, Samuel Case, Sener, being visited with sudden sickness, do make this my last will and testament: I give to Elizabeth my wife the use and improvement of my dwelling house and homestead, with half the orchard thereon, during her natural life. Item. I give to my son Samuel Case the land lying on Walnut Hill which was quitclaimed to me from the Town, to be reckoned to him at inventory price, and £10 more than the rest of the brethren and sisters; also a piece of swamp land bounded southerly on Cadwell's land and easterly on land that goes to Hartford, he paying the money that he has promised (about £8) to Nathaniel Goodwin, and what it amounts to at inventory price to be reckoned to him in part of his portion, not exceeding £8 more. Item. I give to the rest of my children the rest of my estate to be equally divided amongst them, only my son Nathaniel Case to have 5 acres of land joyning on his brother Samuel Case's swamp before mentioned, which he hath made some improvement on already, and also excepting my daughter Irenia. I give her an equall share excepting £15 which I have already given her. I appoint my sons, Samuel Case, Nathaniel Case and Jonah Case, my executors.

Witness: *Samuel Humphries,*   SAMUEL CASE, SEN., LS.
John Moses, Timothy Moses.

Court Record, Page 107—2 November, 1725-6: Caleb Case, a minor, 14 years of age, chose his brother Samuel Case of Simsbury to be his guardian. Recog., £50. Arriam Case, a minor, 17 years of age, and Benjamin Case, 15 years of age, chose their brother Samuel Case to be their guardian. Recog., £100.

Page 193—3 May, 1728: Peletiah Case, a son of sd. decd., and Josiah Alverd, who married one of the daughters, complain to this Court that the executors refuse or neglect to dist. the estate according to the will. This Court appoint Jonathan Westover, Joseph Case and Joseph Phelps to dist. the real estate according to sd. will.

Dist. File: 6 January, 1729-30: To Samuel Case, to Nathaniel, to Jonah, to Abigail, to Peletiah, to Azariacom, to Caleb, to Eunice, to Marcey, to Irena, to Mary, and to Hannah Case. By Jonathan Westover and James Case, distributors.

Inventory on File. Add. Invt. in Vol. XII, Page 389.

Chapman, Edward, Windsor. Invt. £8-08-01. Taken 3 September, 1724, by John Stoughton and Nathaniel Gillett, 2nd. Invt. of a certain piece of land, Draught No. 84, apprised September, 1736, by John Warham and Samuel Strong, Jr., valued at £6-10-00.

Court Record, Page 184—12 May, 1727: John Allyn and John Grant, brothers to Edward Chapman, late of Windsor, decd., signify to this Court that they refuse takeing Adms. on sd. estate, and desire that Adms. may be granted to Jacob Gibbs, this Court therefore grant Adms. unto Jacob Gibbs of Windsor. And the sd. Jacob Gibbs and Benjamin Denslow, of Windsor, recog. in £20 current money.

Chubb, Stephen. Court Record, Page 56—6 October, 1724: This Court do appoint John Palmer, Jr., of Windsor, guardian unto Stephen Chubb of Hebron, a minor, 4 years of age. Recog., £40.

Page 132-3-4-5.

Clark, Daniel, Middletown. Inventory taken by William Savage, Samuel Gipson and Joseph Whitmore. Will dated 3 March, 1724-5.

For as much as my time is uncertain and I know not ye time of my death, I account it my duty to make my last will and testament, which is as followeth: I give to my loveing wife Elizabeth Clark the 1-2 of my dwelling house and 1-2 of my barn and ye whole of the homestead, excepting 1-3 part of ye orchard, and so much of my moveable estate and of my stock of cattle as she shall think she shall stand in need of. The above-mentioned I will to her during her widowhood. And if she marrys, then ye half of it during the term of her natural life. I give to my son Daniel Clark the whole of my part of land at ye ledges which I bought of ye Adms. of my grandfather Harris estate; and also I give him the 1-2 of my other alottment of land at ye Ledges which I bought of my uncle Joseph White, and he shall have his choice of ye half of that lott; and I give him the old white mare, and ye use of the gray mare for one year. I give to my son Francis Clark the whole of my house and barn and homestead after his mother's decease, and the 1-2 of it when he comes to age; and also I give him three acres of land in the Hither Neck, and 1 acre of land in ye Boggy Meadow which I bought of John Ranney; and I also will to him 1-2 of my land upon the Plain, and also ye 1-2 of what land my father shall will to my heirs upon the east side of ye river. I give to my son Elisha Clark all my lands at ye Short Hills, which is about 34 acres, and ye 1-2 of that alottment of land at ye Ledges which I bought of my uncle Joseph White, and all ye remainder of my land in ye Boggy Meadow which I have not before disposed of. I give to my son Joseph Clark that alottment of land on ye east side of ye Great River, by William Cornwall, containing 150 acres, and also all my land on ye Island, and also ye 1-2 of what land my father shall give to my heirs. Also, I give to my four daughters, Hannah Sumner, Abigail Clark, Elizabeth Clark and Martha Clark, £30 apiece; and my will is that my daughters shall have ye 1-2 of my land upon the Plain as part of their £30 apiece. My will is that my right in ye last division on ye east side of ye Great River shall be sold to pay my debts; and also my land I bought of Joseph Kirby, on ye east end of ye lot that John Kirby now lives on, shall be sold also to pay my debts.

Witness: *Joseph Smith,*   DANIEL X CLARK, LS.
Timothy Sage, William Whitmore.

Court Record, Page 80—12 April, 1725: Will now exhibited and proven. As no executor was named in the will, Adms. to Elizabeth Clark, widow, with the will annexed.

Page 12 (Vol. XIII) 5 July, 1737: Joseph Clark, a minor son of Daniel Clark, chose his brother Francis Clark to be his guardian. Recog., £200. Cert: *Joseph White, J. P.*

Page 66—6 May, 1740: Elizabeth Williams, alias Clark, Adms. on the estate of her husband Daniel Clark, exhibited now an account of her Adms.: Paid in debts and charges, £67-16-11; credit received to sd. estate, £2-14-00. Which account is accepted in Court and ordered on file.

Page 70.

Clark, Daniel, Hartford. Inventory taken 25 January, 1724-5, by Ensign Nathaniel Goodwin, Joseph Collyer and Samuel Welles.

Court Record, Page 67—2 February, 1724-5: Adms. to Mary Clark, widow.

Page 120—1st March, 1725-6: Mary Clark, Adms. on the estate of Daniel Clark, exhibited account: Paid out, £54-17-01. Account accepted. Inventory, £698-06-03; subtracting £54-17-01, there remains £643-09-02 to be distributed. Order to Mary Clark, widow, £42-10-00, with dower; to Joseph Clark, eldest son, £117-12-00, having formerly received estate to the value of £80, which is his double portion to the rest of the children; to Daniel, Isaac and Aaron Clark, to each of them, £98-16-00; to Hannah Clarke, £92-07-00, she having formerly received to the value of £6-15-05; to Mary Clarke, £94-18-07, she having received £3-17-05; which is their single portion. And appoint John Skinner, Nathaniel Marsh and John Edwards, distributors. Isaac Clark, a minor, 16 years of age, chose Capt. John Shelding to be his guardian. Recog., £100. Daniel Clarke, 19 years of age, made choice of his mother, Mary Clarke, to be his guardian. Recog., £100.

Page 121—1st March, 1725-6: Aaron Clarke also chose his mother for his guardian.

Page 90 (Vol. XI) 1st May, 1732: Aaron Clarke, now 16 years of age, appeared in Court and made choice of me, the subscriber, to be his guardian, which this Court allows. And I, the subscriber, acknowledge myself bound to the Judge of this Court in a recog. of £100.

Signed: *Jos: Talcott, Jr., Clerk.*

Page 314-15.

Cone, Daniel, Deacon, East Haddam. Died 16 June, 1725. Invt. £858-17-10. Taken 16 July, 1725, by Daniel Brainard, John Bate and Thomas Robbinson.

Court Record, Page 99—7 September, 1725: Adms. to Mary Cone, widow of the sd. deceased. Exhibit of inventory.

Page 119—1st March, 1725-6: Adms. account exhibited: Paid in debts and charges, £42-07-11; invt. £1101-14-08; subtracting £42-07-11, there remains £1059-06-09 to be distributed. Order to Mary Cone, widow, £90-05-07, with dower; to Daniel Cone, eldest son, £211-19-04, he having received £9-11-06, which is his double portion of sd. estate; to the rest of the children, to George, Joseph and Jared Cone, to each of them, £110-15-05; to Sarah Gates, £89-16-03, she having received £20-19-02; to Mehetabell Williams, £82-03-03, she having received £28-12-02; to Mary Fuller, £79-09-01, she having received £31-06-09; to Dorothy Gates, £89-09-11, she having received £21-05-06; to Abigail Rowley, £83-17-00, she having received £26-18-09. And appoint Joshua Brainard, John Bates and Isaac Spencer, of Haddam, distributors.

Page 128—5 May, 1726: This Court do appoint Mrs. Mary Cone to be guardian to George, 17 years, Joseph 14 years, and Jared 12 years of age. Recog., £300.

Ante Page 1. Invt. Page 155 to 160.

Cooke, Aaron, Capt., Hartford. Invt., real estate in Hartford, £885-plus. Taken 2 December, 1725, by Robert Sandford and John Whiting. Invt. at Durham, £297-10-00. Taken 7 December, 1725, by Joseph Coe and Daniel Merwin.

To all Christian people to whom these presents shall come: Know ye that I, Aaron Cooke of Hartford, in the County of Hartford, in the Colony of Connecticut, in New England, being of sound mind and memory, and knowing it is my duty to settle my estate what God hath given me, I make and ordain this my last will and testament: First: After my just debts are paid, I give unto my beloved wife Martha 1-3 of my moveable estate for her own dispose, and 1-3 of my land during her life. Item. I give unto Aaron, my eldest son, a double portion of all my estate, reckoning all my children together. I also give unto my son John and son Moses a double portion of the remainder of my estate, or two times as much as any of my daughters. And the remainder of my estate I give to be equally divided between my three daughters, Martha, Mary and Annah. All the aforesd. legatees I give them and their heirs forever. And it is now the intent and meaning of this my will that in case this part of my estate set to my three daughters should surmount each of them above £120 as money, then my three daughters to have no more than £120 each of them; and the over-plus, if any be on the abovesd. division I give equally to my three sons aforesd. Also, what any of my children shall have received before this my will shall take place, and I have made them debtor for, shall be reckoned for part of their portion. I constitute my sons Aaron, John and Moses my executors to this my will. This I publish as my last will and testament, for the confirmation of which I have set to my hand and seal.

In the presence of   AARON COOKE, LS.
Jonathan Butler, John Barnard,
        John Talcott.

Court Record, Page 116—February, 1725-6: Will now exhibited by Aaron, John and Moses Cooke, executors named in sd. will. Proven. Invt. exhibited. Anna Cooke, a minor, age 17 years, chose John Whiting to be her guardian.

Page 183—12 May, (1727) 1728: Then Anna Cooke, age 18 years and 3 months, discharged Mr. John Whiting, Jr., from all demands on account of his guardianship.

Page 15 (Vol. XI) 3 March, 1729-30: Aaron Cooke, a minor, 14 years of age, chose John Cooke, Jr., of Windsor, to be his guardian. Recog., £50.

Cooke, Benjamin. Court Record, Page 180—5 March, 1727-8: Benjamin Cooke, a minor, 17 years of age, chose Job Loomis of Windsor to be his guardian. Rec., £50.

Page 264.

Cooke, Nathaniel, late of Windsor, decd. Invt. £207-16-08. Taken 2 April, 1725, by Daniel Loomis, James Enno and Timothy Loomis.

Court Record, Page 79—12 April, 1725: Adms. to Lydia Cooke, widow, and Richard Cooke, son of sd. deceased.

Page 158—6 June, 1727: Lydia Cooke and Richard Cooke, Adms., exhibit account of Adms. Report debts due from sd. estate, £105-11-05; and set out to the widow for her support, £22-05-10; in the whole, £127-16-03; moveable estate amounting to £98-16-00; there remains the sum of £29-01-03 more than moveables, for which the real estate must be sold to discharge sd. debts.

Page 66-7-8.

Cook, Thomas, Windsor. Will dated 27 February, 1718-19:

I, Thomas Cook of Windsor, do make and ordain this my last will and testament: I give to my grandchildren, that is to say, ye present children of Samuel Allyn, all my housen and lands which I have in sd. Town of Windsor, to be equally divided between them. I give to my sd. grandchildren what is due to me on 3 bonds: one of them for £20 in silver, due from Jacob Drake; one for £10 (half silver, 1-2 paper), the other for £6 in paper, the two last due from Jacob Drake also to me. I give to my son John Cook all ye rest of my estate, whether real or personal. I make and constitute my sd. son John Cook to be my executor.

THOMAS COOK, LS.

A codicil: Before signing and sealing I give also to my sd. grandchildren 1 bond due from Thomas Hoskins to me for £12 silver, with interest on ye same; and 1 bond from Isaac Bissell to me for about £6. I will

that my son-in-law Samuel Allyn have the oversight and use of what I give herein to his children until they come of age, and that it be delivered to him for that end by my executor within six months after my decease.
Witness: *James Ennoe,*   THOMAS COOK, LS.
William Mitchelson, Eb: Fitch.

Another codicil: I, Thomas Cook, do by these presents annull and make void part of ye foregoing will, vizt., that part relateing to my housen of buildings and lands lying or being in the Town of Windsor aforesd. And now by these presents I will, give and bequeath all my buildings and land in Windsor aforesd. to my son John Cook, to be to his use during his natural life and to his lawful heirs forever. In default of heirs or heir, I give and bequeath sd. buildings and land to my grandchildren, ye children of Samuel Allyn by his former wife (my daughter), to be divided between them after my sd. son John's decease. John Cook to be executor.
Witness: *James Ward,*   THOMAS COOK, LS.
Richard Holmes, Samuel Ward.

Before signing I give to my grandchildren abovesd. £100. to be equally divided among them.
Dated 27 day of April, Anno Domini 1724.
Court Record, Page 70—19 February, 1724-5: Will proven.

Page 312.

Cornwall, David, Middletown. Died 10 June, 1725. Invt. £79-03-06. Taken 2 August, 1725, by Samuel Hall and Ebenezer Smith.

Court Record, Page 95—3 August, 1725: Adms. to John Penfield, the widow of sd. deceased being deaf and dumb and thereby incapable of takeing Adms. Invt. exhibited.

Page 163—22 August, 1727: John Penfield, Adms., now exhibits receipts from Mary Cornwall, widow, where for the sum of £13-15-00, she discharges the estate from any further demands. And John Penfield exhibited account of his Adms. Some debts remain unsatisfied, for which some land must be sold.

Page 192—3 May, 1728: John Penfield now reports sale of land. Order to dist. the real estate remaining: To the children of Stephen Cornwall a 1-4 part; to Sarah Burton a 1-4 part; to Ann Penfield a 1-4 part; to Silence Boardman a 1-4 part. By Joseph Tracy, John Gains and Ebenezer Smith.

Page 39 (Vol. XI) 1st March, 1730-1: John Penfield, Adms. on the estate of David Cornwall, late of Middletown, decd., being summoned, appeared before this Court to answer the complaint of Samuel Burton for sd. Penfield not attending the order of the Court of Probates in the sale of part of the lands formerly belonging to David Cornwall, decd., to pay the debts due from the estate as per complaint lying in the files of this Court. Sd. Burton and Capt. Giles Hall, guardian to two of the children of the decd., appeared, and they all being heard on the case, this Court are of opinion that the order of the Court hath not been directly attended in the sale of sd. land, to the prejudice of the heirs, and do therefore declare sd. sale void, and now order that the Adms. shall set up an advertisement for the sale of so much of sd. land as shall be sufficient to procure the sum of £23-18-10. The sum allowed by the General Assembly holden at New Haven in October, 1727, being £35-08-10, and a house being sold for £11-10-00, there still remains the sum of £23-18-10. And that in sd. advertisement he describe the place where the land lyeth, 20 days before the sale, where the place of sale shall be, the quality with the bounds of sd. land, also at what hour of the day the sale shall be, and at beat of drum to the highest bidder, and to return his doings therein to this Court. John Penfield appealed from this judgement to the Superior Court to be holden at Hartford, in and for the County of Hartford, on the 2nd Tuesday of instant March, and sd. Penfield acknowledged himself bound to the Treasurer of the County of Hartford in a recog. of £10.

Page 6 (Vol. XIII) 20 April, 1737: A dist. of all the lands of David Cornwall, exclusive of what was sold according to law to pay the debts due from sd. estate, was now exhibited in Court under the hands of John Gains and Joseph Frary, distributors, which dist. is accepted and ordered upon file. This Court grant John Penfield a *Quietus Est.*

Recorded in Vol. XII, Page 160-1.

Cornwall, Samuel, Sen., Middletown. Invt. £25-01-02. Taken 24 January, 1728-9, by Joseph Starr, William Whitmore and Joseph Rockwell. Will dated 3 July, 1722: I give to my wife Rebeckah the use of all my moveable estate during life, and 1-3 part forever; the use of the south end of my dwelling house, and 1-3 part of all my cleared lands. To my son Samuel I give what I have made over to him by deed of gift. To my son Ebenezer what I have made over to him by deed of gift. To my daughter Rebeckah I give all my lands in Wongog Meadow. I give to my daughter Elizabeth 14 acres near 3-Mile-Hill, 60 1-4 acres at the west end after Elizabeth hath her eighty acres at the east end. I give to my granddaughters, Jemima and Lois Cornwall, £35 apiece, partly paid already (daughters of my son William Cornwall deceased). To my grandson Samuel Cornwall, who bears my name, I give a good Bible, and order my executors to procure it for him. I appoint my sons Samuel and Ebenezer to be executors.

Witness: *William Russell,*   Samuel X Cornwall, ls.
Jonathan Blake, Cheney Clark.

Court Record, Page 210—2 January, 1728-9: Will now exhibited by Samuel and Ebenezer Cornwall, executors named in sd. will. Proven.

Page 211—4 February, 1728-9: Exhibit of inventory.

Cornwell, Sergt. William, Middletown. This article relates to the will of Sergt. William Cornwell, Sen., whose will (Vol. I, Page 294-5) has the "X" mark in the signature, which is an error. The original on file has his own signature, *"William Cornwell."* Also, the Court Record is here given because of errors and obscurity on account of the loss of part of the record on the broken page. The lost words will here be supplied so far as later knowledge of the subject will warrant.—C. W. M.

Page 142—6 December, 1726: Whereas, Wm. Cornwell, sometime of Middletown deceased, in and by his last will and testament, on record, did give and bequeath unto his son William one-third part of his (   ) on the east side of the river, to be divided by the list in 1674, the other two-thirds (of the) aforesd. land to his sons Samuel and Thomas, equally to be divided (between) them: And it being represented to this Court by J(ohn) Penfield, legatee to sd. Land by his marriage to A(nn) Cornwell, daughter in (right of) Thomas Cornwell, now deceasd.: t(hat) the said lands have not been yet divided, and praying that it may be done according to the last will of the sd. Wm. Cornwell deceased: This Court do appoint and impower Messrs. Joseph Frary, Comfort (Davis) and James Johnson, of Middletown, or any two of them, to distribute and divide the aforementioned lands unto the sons of the sd. Wm. Cornwell, decd., or their legall representatives, according to the last will of the sd. William Cornwell, decd.

Page 162—First August, 1727: A distribution of part of the estate of William Cornwell, late of Middletown deceased, under the hands of Comfort Davis and Joseph Frary, appointed distributors, was now exhibited, accepted and ordered to be kept on file.

Here Copied from the Original Filed Paper:

We whose names are hereunto subscribed, being appointed by the Court of Probate held at Hartford December 22d, 1726, to distribute part of the estate of Will:m Cornwell, late of Middletown, deceased, to his sons, Will:m, Sam:ll and Thomas, that is to say, his land on the east sid the Great River, we haveing been sworn before John Hamlin, Esq:r, March 31st, and haveing been called to sd. work, we have distributed the long lot as followeth, to say, the east and west, the north divition, we have layed to William Cornwell, being eight chains and eighty-five links wid, bounded at each corner with a stake and stones about it. We allowed teen acres more to this divition than the other, be caus the land was not so good. The middle divition we layed to Sam:ll Cornweell, and the south to Thomas Cornwell, each being eight chains and thirty links wid, bounded as the other. And the lot in the eastermost divition we have divided into thre equall parts, each divitian being eighteen rods and three-quarters wide. The northermost divition we have layed to Will:m, the middle to Sam:ll, and the south to Thomas. As wittnes our hands:

aperill 5:th, 1727.   *Comfort Davis,*
                                            Joseph Frary.

Invt. in Vol. XII, Page 223.

Cowles, Caleb, Kensington.   Invt. £529-17-01.   Taken by Isaac Cowles, Thomas Hart and John Norton.

Court Record, Page 111—4 January, 1725-6: This Court grant Adms. unto Abigail Cowles, widow. The sd. Abigail Cowles and Samuel Cowles recog. in £400.

See File: 30 January, 1734-5: Dist. of the estate to the four daughters, viz., Abigail, Hester, Hannah and Mary, which was made and counted to them by the eldest son Hezekiah Cowles and the rest of the children that are of age, the eldest son haveing given deeds to the two youngest sons on condition that they do not molest the widows nor daughters in the injoyment of the moveable estate, and desire the dist. may be lodged in this Court.

Page 20 (Vol. XII) 4 February, 1734-5: Agreement exhibited and approved by the Court.

Page 41.

Cowles, Nathaniel, Jr. Inventory taken 26 December, 1724, by Thomas Thompson, Isaac Cowles and James Gridley.

Court Record, Page 64—6 January, 1724-5: Adms. to Sarah Cowles, widow.

Page 117—1st March, 1725-6: Isaac Cowles, who was appointed Adms., exhibits an account of his Adms. Accepted. Order to dist. as followeth:

	£ s d
To Sarah Cowles, widow,	35-04-04
To Nathaniel,	203-12-06
To Sarah Cowles, daughter,	101-16-03

And appoint Isaac Cowles, James Gridley and Timothy Porter, distributors.

Page 170—5 December, 1727: This Court appoint John Cowles of Farmington to be guardian to Nathaniel Cowles, a minor, 2 years of age. Recog., £50.

Page 87 (Vol. XIII) 7 April, 1741: Nathaniel Cowles, 16 years of age, chose Deacon John Hart to be his guardian. Recog., £300. Cert: *William Wadsworth, J. P.*

Page 114-15-16.

Day, Thomas, Hartford.   Invt. £319-08-06.   Taken 23 January, 1724-5, by Nathaniel Goodwin, Aaron Cooke and James Church.

Court Record, Page 65—20 January, 1724-5: Adms. granted to Hannah Day, widow.

Page 165—3 October, 1727: Hannah Day exhibited an account of her Adms., which this Court accepts, orders recorded and filed.

See File: To all people to whome these presents shall come: Nathaniel Dickinson of Hatfield, John Day of Hartford, and Thomas Barnes of Farmington, in their several and respective rights send greeting: Whereas, the estate of Thomas Day and Thomas Day, Jr., both late of Hartford decd., doth of right descend and belong to the following persons, viz., to sd. Nathaniel Dickinson in right of his wife Hannah Dickinson (late relict of the aforesd. Thomas Day the elder), her right of dower or thirds, and also the sum of £21-00-07, a debt due to her the sd. Hannah Dickinson on the estate aforesd.; and to John Day did of right belong a double portion and the sum of £16; and to Thomas Barnes and Hannah his wife, in right of the sd. Hannah, did belong one single share now due £72-19-10; and unto Mehetabell Day doth belong one whole single share, being £44-05-00; and unto Nathaniel Day, a minor, doth of right belong the whole single share also, the sum of £44-00-05. Know ye therefore that for the full and final settlement of sd. estate, they have each and every of them agreed for themselves, or those whome they represent, that the aforesd. estate shall be and are hereby divided, set out and apportioned in manner aforesd. In witness whereof the parties to these presents have hereunto set their hands and seals this 28th day of February, 1732-3.

NATHANIEL DICKINSON, LS.
HANNAH X DICKINSON, LS.
JOHN DAY, LS.
THOMAS BARNES.

Page 84 (Vol. XI) 28 February, 1732-3: Agreement exhibited and accepted by the Court.

Invt. in Vol. XII, Page 212.

Day, Thomas, Colchester. Invt. £288-06-10. Taken 14 February, 1728-9, by Nathaniel Kellogg and Nathaniel Foot.

Court Record, Page 215—1st April, 1729: This Court grant Adms. unto Thomas Day, son of the decd.

Recorded in Vol. XII, Page 128-29.

Dart, Mary. Will dated 15 June, 1726: I, Mary Dart, widow and relict of Richard Dart, late of New London decd., now living at Haddam, being aged and weake in body but of perfect mind and memory, do make and ordain this my last will and testament: Imprimis. I give to my daughter Elizabeth Remington, of Suffield, the half part of my wearing apparell and linen which I shall leave at my decease, and the half part of the household goods which I had in New London since the death of my husband, Richard Dart of New London aforesd. I give to my son and daughter, Joshua and Mehetabell Brainard of sd. Haddam, the other half of my wearing apparell and linen, and the half of the goods I had from New

London, as also whatsoever sum or sums of money shall be due to me at my decease, either by bill, bond or otherwise, from my son-in-law Roger Dart, of sd. New London, or from my own sons, Joseph Dudley or Daniel Dudley, or from my grandson William Dudley, or from my daughter-in-law Elizabeth Dudley alias Spencer, all of Saybrook, or whatsoever sum or sums of money, goods or estate of any kind which I may receive of them or either of them at any time during my natural life and which shall not be otherwise disposed of before my death. And the reason of my thus disposeing of my estate is because I think my eldest children have heretofore received their portions, and I have for divers years in my reduced age lived with my sd. loveing son and daughter Joshua Brainard and Mehetabell Brainard, to whom some part at least of what I have is due as a recompense of their care of me. And in testimony that this is my last will and testament, revokeing all others, I have hereunto set my hand and seal the day and year first above written. Also, I do hereby make and constitute my loveing son Joshua Brainard executor of this my last will and testament. Signed, sealed, published and declared to be the last will and testament of Mary Dart.

In presence of   MARY X DART, LS.
Jacob X Rook (or Roote), Hez: Brainard.

Whereas, our hond. mother, Mrs. Mary Dart, late of Haddam decd., did in and by her last will and testament, dated the 15 day of June, A. Dom. 1726, give and bequeath unto her daughter Elizabeth Remington, wife of Joseph Remington of Suffield, in the County of Hampshire and Province of the Massachusetts Bay, and Joshua Brainard of Haddam, in the County of Hartford and Colony of Connecticut, and Mehetabell Brainard his wife, all her estate, goods, chattells, debts, &c., as appears by the sd. will: Know all men by these presents: That we, the sd. Joseph Remington in behalf of himself and his wife Elizabeth aforesd., and Joshua Brainard in behalf of himself and Mehetabell his wife aforesd., have fully and absolutely agreed relateing to the sd. will of our sd. mother, and have distributed the estate, &c., therein to us bequeathed, between us according to the sd. will. And we do hereby covenant and agree that such our agreement and distribution shall be a full and final settlement of the sd. estate and premises, and shall be binding to each of us, our heirs, executors and administrators. In testimony whereof we have hereunto set our hand and seal, 7th May, Anno Regni Regis Georgie 2d Primo, Annoqe Domini 1728.

Signed and sealed in presence of   JOS. REMINGTON, LS.
Simon Chapmon, J. Gilbert, Jr.   JOSHUA BRAINARD, LS.

Court Record, Page 191—7 May, 1728: An agreement for the settlement of the estate of Mary Dart was now exhibited by Joseph Remington and Joshua Brainard in behalf of themselves and their respective wives, two of the daughters of the sd. decd., and acknowledged the sd. agreement to be their free act and deed. Accepted.

Invt. in Vol. XII, Page 43-4. Add. Invt. in Vol. XI, Page 167.

Deming, Jonathan, Wethersfield. Died 22 June, 1727. Invt. £1246-14-04. Taken 31 July, 1727, by Joseph Grimes, Thomas Deming and Jonathan Burnham. An amount of £4-06-04 was added to the inventory.

Court Record, Page 160—August, 1727: Adms. granted to Abigail Deming, widow, who, with Thomas Deming, recog. in £400.

Page 172—2 January, 1727-8: Upon motion of Benjamin Deming, a citation was issued for Abigail Deming, widow, to show reason why Adms. should not be granted on a parcel of land, about 15 acres, formerly granted by the Town of Wethersfield to Jonathan Deming, father of the sd. Benjamin Deming and Jonathan, late decd., the parties now appeared and were heard concerning the same: Whereupon this Court do grant Adms. on sd. parcel of land unto (   ) and Benjamin Deming.

Page 31 (Vol. XI) 3 November, 1730: Abigail Deming, Adms., exhibits an account of her Adms., which this Court accepts. And this Court appoint Abigail Deming to be guardian unto her son Charles Deming, a minor, 16 years of age.

Page 31-58.

Deming, Lemuell. Inventory taken 7 January, 1724-5, by John Cook and James Church.

The last will and testament of Lemuel Deming is as follows: First, I give to my wife and child £100. 2ndly, I give to my mother £10. 3rdly: I give to Timothy Phelps £6.

These articles were written within the space of 24 hours after they were delivered by word of mouth by ye aforesd. Lemuell Deming.

In witness whereof we, the subscribers, who being present both at the time of their being expressed by word of mouth and at their being written, do set our hands the 11th day of December, Anno Dom. 1724.
Witness: *John Butler,*
Daniel Smith, Francis Flower.

Items in the Inventory of Lemuell Deming:

	£ s d	
By 202 Rackoon skins,	15-05-06	By a bond by Caleb Bull.
By 31 gallons of rum,	6-04-00	By a bond by Timothy Phelps.
By 57 pounds of wool,	3-12-00	By Birchard and Tracy.
By 27 hat blocks,	12-00	By Noah Loomis.
By 2 beaver hats, part		By two notes by Joseph Easton.
made,	3-00-00	By a note by John Cadwell.
By 2 raccoon hats, part		By a note by John Knight.
made,	1-10	By a note by David Hurlbut.
By 9 3-4 of beaver,	3-18-00	By a note by Benjamin Cleveland.
		By a note by Joseph Talcot.
		By bills of publick credit.

Court Record, Page 63—5 January, 1724-5: Will now exhibited and proven. Adms. granted to Susannah Deming, the widow, and Samuel Edwards, with the nuncupative will annexed.

Deverieux, Jonathan. Court Record, Page 147—2 March, 1726-7: This Court appoint Sarah Smith of Hartford to be guardian to her son Jonathan Deverieux, 10 years of age. And sd. Mary Smith recog., £40.

Page 220-1. Invt. in Vol. XI, Page 151.

Dickinson, Thomas, Hartford. Invt. £492-18-08. Taken 27 January, 1723, by John Sheldon and Thomas Seymour.

Will dated 9th April, 1723: I, Thomas Dickinson, do make this my last will and testament: I give to my two sons, Thomas and Moses, all my houseing and lands in Hartford, to be equally divided between them. I give to my two sons, Thomas and Moses, all my wearing aparell and all my team tackling, my cart and wheels and plow and chain and plow iron, and whatsoever belonging to them; and all ye rest of my moveable estate I give to my wife and daughters, that is to say, 1-3 part of ye whole I give to my wife, and all ye rest to be equally divided amongst my daughters. It is to be understood that my will is that Elizabeth, my eldest daughter, shall have but an equall share with the rest of my daughters with what she hath already received, which is £14. Also, my daughter Esther hath received £4 towards her equall share with ye rest. I give also to my wife the use of half my lands in Hartford so long as she shall remain my widow or unmarried. I also give her the use of ye whole till my two sons come to lawfull age, and then half of it to return to them. Further, my will is that my two sons shall pay to my daughters £16, that is to say, my son Thomas £8, and my son Moses £8, which shall equally be divided amongst them all. I also give to my daughters that outland that is at Hadley, which I bought of my brother Elihu Dickinson, to be equally divided among them all.

Witness: *Nathaniel Marsh,*   THOMAS DICKINSON, LS.
Samuel Welles, John Church, Jr.

Court Record, Page 44—27 March, 1724: The last will of Thomas Dickinson, late of Hartford, decd., was now exhibited by Mehetabell Dickinson, the widow of said deceased. The will was proved, approved, and allowed, and by this Court ordered to be recorded and kept on file.

Vol. XI, Page 57—14 December, 1731: An inventory was now exhibited by Mehetabell Dickinson, widow, Adms. with the will annexed. Likewise exhibited an account of administration, which account this Court accepts, and order a distribution of the estate according to the will. And appoint Capt. Thomas Seymour, Capt. John Sheldon and Sergt. John Cook, distributors.

Page 58—4 January, 1731-2: Jemima Dickinson, age 14 years, a daughter of Thomas Dickinson, chose William Wadsworth to be her guardian. Recog., £50.

Dist. File: 6 March, 1732: To the widow Mehetabell Dickinson, to Mehetabell, to Lois, to Sarah, to Susannah, to Hannah, and to Jemima Dickinson. By John Sheldon, Thomas Seamore and John Cooke.

Page 6 (Vol. XIV) 4 May, 1742: Widow Mehetabel Dickinson, relict of Thomas Dickinson, moved to this Court that the lands given her for her improvement during life by the will of the sd. deceased may be set out to her by freeholders. Whereupon this Court appoint Lt. John Cooke, Caleb Church and Caleb Spencer, of Hartford, to set out the sd. real estate by bounds according to sd. will, and make return thereof to this Court.

Inventory in Vol. XII, Page 129-30.

Dodd, Edward, Hartford. Invt. £167-19-06. Of this £141-01-00 was the homested. Taken 2 August, 1728, by Jonathan Butler and Joseph Gilbert. Invt. of real estate in Farmington, £289-00-00. Taken by John Hart, Jr., John Hart, Sen., and Thomas Lee.

Court Record, Page 195—3 July, 1728: Adms. granted to Lydia, the widow.

Page 9 (Vol. XI) 6 January, 1729-30: Edward Dodd, a minor, age 16 years, chose his mother Lydia Dodd to be his guardian. Recog., £50.

Page 93-4-5.

Drake, John, Simsbury. Died 8 February, 1724-5. Inventory taken 24 February, 1724-5, by Samuel Pettebone, Joseph Case and Andrew Robe.

Court Record, Page 72—2 March, 1724-5: Adms. granted to Mary Drake, widow. And this Court appoint Mary Drake to be guardian to Mary Drake, a minor, 3 years of age, only child of sd. decd.

Invt. in Vol. XII, Page 209.

Easton, John, Hartford. Invt. £535-00-00. Taken 15 April, 1726, by Robert Sandford and Daniel Merrells. Invt. of lands on the east side of the river, apprised by Samuel Webster, Daniel Dickinson and John Hasseltine.

Court Record, Page 129—5 May, 1726: Adms. granted to Sarah Easton, widow of sd. decd., Nathaniel Goodwin and Jonathan Butler of Hartford. The sd. Sarah Easton, Nathaniel Goodwin, Jonathan Butler and Joseph Ashley, of Hartford, acknowledge themselves joyntly and severally bound in a recog. of £100, and exhibited an inventory.

Page 135—5 September, 1726: Jonathan Butler and Sarah Easton, two of the Adms. on the estate of John Easton, late of Hartford decd., informed that according to the direction of this Court in June last they have made sale of 10 acres of meadow land belonging to sd. deceased, to the highest bidder, viz., to Nathaniel Goodwin, one of the Adms. on the estate of sd. deceased, for the sum of £160-10-00 toward the payment of debts, which this Court accept of and direct the sd. Jonathan Butler and Sarah Easton to execute deeds of conveyance.

Page 138—1st November, 1726: This Court order that the widow's dowry be set out to her by Robert Sandford and Joseph Skinner.

Page 165—3 October, 1727: More debts appear, and more land must be sold to pay the debts.

Page 194—2 August (1727) 1728: By order of the General Assembly, 12 May, 1726, the Adms. may by direction of the Court of Probate sell the real estate of John Easton, a home lot with buildings in Hartford on the west side of the river, at vandue. The Adms. upon several times endeavored to sell, but could never get one-half of what is now offered by Samuel Edwards, viz., £150. The Court order to sell at that price. (The estate was in debt £360 above the value of the personal property.)

Page 198—6 July, 1728: Order to sell the reversionary interest in houseing and home lott. Debt, £69-09-06.

Page 200—3 September, 1728: Court order Nathaniel Goodwin and Jonathan Butler to sell an interest in the Five Miles.

Page 202—1st October, 1728: Adms. account now exhibited. Accepted.

Page 62 (Vol. XIII) 1st April, 1740: Nathaniel Goodwin and Jonathan Butler, Adms., exhibited receipts under the hands of the creditors to sd. estate, whereby it appears they have paid in debts and charges the sum of £496-13-08, which is £17 more than the average made on the estate. The Court accepts the account and orders it to be kept on file.

Page 24 (Vol. XV) 5 September, 1746: Sarah Easton, widow and relict of John Easton, moved to this Court that her right of dowry on the estate of the sd. deceased may be set out to her, particularly 2-3 of the farm lately in possession of Jacob Mygatt, in the Five Miles on the east side of the Great River: Whereupon this Court appoint Nathaniel Olcott and Josiah Olcott of Hartford to set out to the sd. widow 1-3 part of the sd. farm for her improvement during life, and make return thereof to this Court.

Page 28-29-30.

Easton, Jonathan, Hartford. Died 16 December, 1724. Inventory taken 7 January, 1724-5, by John Sheldon James Ensign and John Skinner.

Court Record, Page 65—5 January, 1724-5: Adms. to Elizabeth Easton, widow.

Page 85—11 May, 1725: The Adms. now exhibit account of debts amounting to £797-18-09, which appear to be more than the moveable estate. The Court order set out £62-04-06 for the widow's necessary support and subsistence,

Page 92—6 July, 1725: Per act of the General Assembly in May last, this Court do advise and direct Elizabeth Easton, Adms. on the estate of Jonathan Easton, to make sale of a parcel of meadow land and a lot of land lying at Rocky Hill, belonging to the estate, to the highest bidder, at 20 days' notice of sale, for the payment of debts.

Page 145—7 February, 1726-7: Upon motion of Elizabeth Easton, Adms. on the estate of Jonathan Easton, now decd., who was one of the sureties for the Adms. on the estate of Thomas Bunce, Jr., deceased: This Court order the Adms. on the estate of Thomas Bunce to render account of their Adms., and order a distribution of sd. Bunce estate.

Page 31 (Vol. XI) 1st December, 1730: Jonathan Easton, a minor, age 19 years, chose Jonathan Butler to be his guardian. Recog., £50.

Page 56 (Vol. XIII) 6 November, 1739: Thomas Easton, age 19 years, son of Jonathan Easton, chose his father-in-law Jonathan Butler to be his guardian.

Dist. File: 22 February, 1757: Pursuant to an order from the Court of Probates for the District of Hartford to dist. and set out to the heirs of Jonathan Easton, deceased, viz., to Jonathan Easton, Edward Cadwell, Eleazer Goodwin and John Spencer and Thomas Easton, the distributors set out the lands in manner and form following, viz.:

	£ s d
To Jonathan Easton, 1 piece of meadow land in Clark's lot adjoining Edward Cadwell's and Samuel Easton's; 1 piece woodland east of Lemuel Easton's, adjoining Caleb Pitkin, Lemuel Easton and Edward Cadwell,	24-11-10
To Edward Cadwell, 1 piece meadow land adjoining Phillips's lott, Eleazer Goodwin and Jonathan Easton; also 1 piece of woodland adjoining Lemuel and Jonathan Easton and Caleb Pitkin,	23-17-03
To Eleazer Goodwin, 1 piece of meadow land adjoining Phillips's and Edward Cadwell's land; and 1 piece of woodland,	23-11-03
To Thomas Easton, 1 piece of meadow land and woodland,	23-11-03
To John and Thankful Spencer, 1 piece of meadow and woodland,	23-11-03

By Joseph Cowles and William Pitkin, Jr., distributors.

See also File: We, the subscribers, being heirs to the estate of our honoured father, Jonathan Easton, late of Hartford decd., and also of the estate of our brother, Thomas Easton, late of New Hartford, decd., agree to dist. as followeth:

	£ s d
To Eleazer Goodwin and Hannah his wife, a lott of land, 60 acres, adjoining William Cadwell and Nathaniel Merrells,	44-02-06
To John Spencer and Thankfull his wife, 108 acres of land,	54-00-00

To the heirs of Thomas Easton, 76 acres of land adjoining
    Theodore Gilbert and John Spencer,   46-00-00
To Jonathan Easton, 16 acres of land,   8-00-00
To Ruth Cadwell, widow of Edward Cadwell, 16 acres of land
    adjoining John Spencer and Jonathan Easton,   8-00-00

New Hartford, March the 2nd, 1764: Then the within agreement
was signed and sealed by us, the subscribers, in presence of

Witness: *Isaac Kellogg,*   ELEAZER GOODWIN, LS.
Wm. Seymour, Jno. Butler,   HANNAH GOODWIN, LS.
Jasper Giddings.   JONATHAN EASTON, LS.
                    RUTH X CADWELL, LS.
                    THANKFULL X SPENCER, LS.

Inventory on File.

Edwards, Joseph, Wethersfield. Invt. £117-03-03. Taken 23 April,
1725, by Jonathan Pratt, Ephraim Williams and Daniel Stoughton. Upon
request of Samuel Churchill this Court appoint Samuel Copley, Caleb Allyn and John Pengilly, Jr., to apprise certain lands in Suffield this 31st
day of January, 1725-6.

Court Record, Page 123—14 March, 1725-6: We, the subscribers,
being present at the dwelling house of Jonathan Pratt, in Wethersfield,
when Joseph Edwards lay sick, and in our presence declared his will:
That his lame brother, Nathaniel Edwards, whom he supposed was not
able to maintain himself, to him he gave 1-2 of his estate, and that the
other half he gave was to be equally divided amongst all of his brothers
and sisters. And at the time was in his right mind and of sound disposing
memory and understanding, to the best of our judgements, 5 February,
1724-5. And he dyed on the 7th day of February, or about two days after
he made his will as aforesaid.

                  Signed: JONATHAN PRATT,
                  SAMUEL CHURCHILL, CHURCHILL EDWARDS.

Who made oath to the same. Adms. to Samuel Churchill and
Churchill Edwards.

Dist. File: 10 March, 1725: To Josias Churchill, to Jonathan, to David, to Nathaniel, to Edward, to Matthew Barnes, and to Mary Edwards.
By Jabez Whittlesey, Richard Boardman and John Deming.

Edwards, David, Wethersfield. Court Record, Page 42—3 March,
1723-4: David Edwards, a minor, 17 years of age, chose James Francis
of Wethersfield to be his guardian. Recog., £50.

Page 209-10, Vol. XII.

Elmore, Edward,Windsor.   Invt. £610-18-06.   Taken 26 November, 1725, by Richard Smith and Joseph Rockwell.

Court Record, Page 109—7 December, 1725 : Adms. granted to Caleb Elmore and Edward Elmore, sons of sd. decd.

Page 151—4 April, 1727 : Adms. account now exhibited and debts paid.

Page 155—2 May, 1727 : Whereas, the Adms. on the estate of Edward Elmore, late of Windsor decd., exhibited an accompt of debts due from sd. estate, which appears to be more than the moveable estate, and informeth that there are some debts yet to be brought in, so that land must be sold to discharge the debts due more than the moveable estate amounts to : This Court order that the real estate of sd. decd. (excepting six acres of meadow lying next to the Great River, bounded north on Mr. Timothy Edwards, south upon Major Roger Woolcott) be reserved to discharge the sd. debts, the residue thereof to be distributed as followeth, viz., to Hezekiah Elmore, eldest son of the sd. decd., a double portion of sd. real estate ; to Caleb Elmore, Amos Elmore, Edward Elmore, Rebeckah Elmore and Ann Elmore, the rest of the children of the sd. decd., to each of them a single part or portion of sd. real estate.

Page 162—1 August, 1727 : A distribution of the estate of Edward Elmore, deceased, under the hands of Mr. Henry Wolcot, Joseph Loomis and Richard Smith, was now exhibited, and by this Court accepted and ordered to be kept on file.

Page 165—3 October, 1727 : Edward Elmore and Caleb Elmore, administrators, exhibited a further account of their administration, which was accepted.

Will on File.   Invt. in Vol. XII, Page 164.

Enno, Abigail, late of Windsor, 19 April, 1728.   Invt. £33-07-07. Taken at Windsor, 1st October, 1728, by Thomas More, John Palmer and Jonathan Gillett.   £15-06-00 taken at Simsbury by James Hilyer, James Pettebone and Samuel Humphry, Jr.

Will : The testimony of Mary Pettibone, the wife of Lieut. John Pettibone, and Sarah Humphreys, the wife of Deacon John Humphreys, and Deborah Pettibone, the wife of Stephen Pettibone, all of lawfull age, is as foloeth : that we being att the now dwelling house of Joseph Cornish in Simsbury to se the widdow Abigail Enno, the wife of James Enno, late of Windsor decest, in the time of her sickness, and she supposed her sickness to be dangrus, she called us all three to bare witness that she did give to her fouer daughters all my weareing apparrell equally to be diuided amongst them. And I do give to my dafter Suzanna my silver bodkin. Also, give to my fouer dauters my to fether bedes with all the furnituer belonging to them, only reserveing to Samuell Enno the use of one fether bed and bolster, one couerlid, one blanket and one pair of sheets for the space of one year in case he doth not marrey, and then to be deliuered up unto the dafters; and in case he doth marray within one year, then to de-liuer it up to the dafters. Furthermore, I giue to my fouer daughters all my in dowers mooueables, to be equaly deuided amangst them. Further-more, I giue all my out dore mooue ables, stock and lands unto all my children, sons and daugters, to be equaly deuided amongst them after my just debts and funaral debts are paid. And we do further testifie that all the time she made this disposal of hur estate in this manner as aboue said, she was well, to our judgements, both in mind and memory. As witness our hands this 20th day of April, 1728.

Witness: *Mary Pettibone,*
Sarah X *Humphrey, Deborah* X *Pettibone.*

And further the deponents do testifie and say that the foregoing words in wrighting and verball will was fully declared by the sd. Abigail Enno, and without any urgency of any person as we know of. And about eight or nine days after keeping the sd. discourse perfectly in our minds, we comitted it to wrighting by James Hillior, who was the subscriber thereof.

Court Record, Page 190—2 April, 1728: Adms. granted to Joseph Case.

Page 195—3 July, 1728: A nuncupative will of Abigail Enno was ex-hibited in Court and ordered by this Court to lye on file.

Page 201—1st October, 1728: Invt. exhibited by Joseph Case, Adms. Ordered recorded and kept on file.

Invt. in Vol. XI, Page 68-345.

Ensign, David, Hartford. Invt. £288-16-00. Taken 1728-9 by Cip-rian Watson and Isaac Kellogg. Additional inventory of land valued at £14-10-00, lying in New Hartford, taken 6 November, 1734, by Cyprian Watson and Isaac Kellogg.

Court Record, Page 190—2 April, 1728: Adms. granted to David Ensign, son of the decd.

Page 108 (Vol. XI) 22 February, 1733-4: On the 7th day of July, 1730, Isaac Kellogg and Joseph Webster exhibited a wrighting in Court, signed by David Ensign, as followeth:

I, David Ensign of Hartford, Senr., purposeing to continue my abode with my son David during my natural life, he having obliged himself to provide temporals for the subsistence and comfort of my outward man, do by these presents covenant and promise that he shall be full, truly and sufficiently rewarded for the same out of my estate. For witness whereof I have hereunto set my hand this 7th day of April, Anno. Dom. 1721.

Witness: *Joseph Webster,*   DAVID ENSIGN.
    Isaac Kellogg.

Acknowledged in Court, 7 July, 1730, by Joseph Webster and Isaac Kellogg.

Page 10 (Vol. XII) 19 September, 1734: David Ensign, Adms., exhibited now an account of his Adms., and Thomas Ensign, one of the sons of the sd. decd., objected against the last article in sd. account as not appearing by evidence that his father did want maintenance all the time as is set down in sd. account. Whereupon the determination thereof is continued by consent of the parties until the 20th of this inst. at two of the clock, afternoon. The parties accordingly appeared and produced their evidences as per writ were cited respecting the premises. Also, Jeames Ensign, one of the heirs to sd. estate, was present. This Court, having heard the pleas of the parties, do order that the sd. David Ensign, Adms., shall be allowed out of the estate, for the supporting of the sd. decd., in sickness and in health, from the 7th of April, 1721, until December 13th, 1727, 7 shillings and sixpence pr week (excepting one month, when it is evident he was supported by others of his children), which amounts to the sum of £128-12-06. The whole of the sd. Adms. account amounts to £139-06-05, which account is accepted.

Page 15—4 December, 1734: David Ensign, Adms., is ordered to sell land amounting to the sum of £124-00-10 and charges of sale, at 20 days notice, at beat of drum, place, day and houre. Thomas Ensign appeals against this sale of land; also appeals from the acceptance of the account.

Page 22—25 February, 1734-5: Thomas Ensign granted an appeal to the Superior Court to be holden at Hartford, in and for Hartford County, on the fourth Tuesday of March next.

Page 243-4.

Ensign, Jonathan, Hartford. Invt. £236-19-06. Taken 17 August, 1724, by Thomas Richards and Samuel Catlin.

Court Record, Page 54—1st September, 1724: Adms. to Phebe Ensign, widow of the sd. decd. This Court appoint Sergt. James Ensign to be guardian to his grandson Jonathan Ensign. Recog., £100.

Page 172—January, 1727-8: Phebe Ensign to be guardian to her son James Ensign, 3 years of age. Recog., £50.

Page 173—2 January, 1727-8: Phebe Ensign, Adms., exhibits an account of her Adms. Allowed. Order to dist. the estate as followeth:

	£ s d
To Phebe Ensign, widow,	16-05-05
To Jonathan Ensign, eldest son,	128-11-04
To James Ensign, youngest son,	64-05-08

And appoint John Webster, Thomas Steele and Daniel Webster, distributors.

Page 196—6 July, 1728: Report of the distributors.

Page 46-7.

Fitch, Ebenezer, Windsor. Inventory taken 29 December, 1724, by Isaac DeMedina, Alexander Allin and Daniel Bissell, Jr.

Court Record, Page 62—18 December, 1724: Adms. granted to Bridget Fitch, widow, and Samuel Strong of Windsor.

Page 8 (Vol. XI) 25 December, 1729: Upon the motion of Mr. John Perrie, husband to Bridget Perrie, formerly Bridget Fitch, Adms., for longer time to make up her account, which this Court grants.

Page 26—5 September, 1730: Alice Fitch, a minor, made choice of her uncle, Deliverance Brown, to be her guardian. Recog., £100.

Page 45—18 May, 1731: This Court appoint Daniel Bissell, of Windsor, guardian unto James Fitch, 15 years of age. Recog., £100. John Fitch, Jr., of Windham, appointed guardian to several of the children, viz., Elijah, 13 years, Eleazer 11 years, Medinah 9 years, and Ebenezer Fitch 6 years of age, children of the decd. Recog., £300.

Page 101—15 December, 1733: Daniel Bissell, of Windsor, guardian to James Fitch, Jun., son of Mr. Ebenezer Fitch, late of Windsor, deceased, desireing to be released from his said guardianship, the said Fitch also desired the same; the said Daniel Bissell is accordingly released. James Fitch, who is 18 years of age, now chose Lieut. John Fitch, Jun., of Windham, to be his guardian. Recog., £200.

Page 13 (Vol. XII) 13 November, 1734: Mr. John Austin, of Hartford, and Mr. John Fitch, guardians to the minors and heirs of Mr. Ebenezer Fitch, late of Windsor deceased, showing to this Court that there is a certain tract of land, containing 532 acres (being part of 3800 acres called Fairweather and his Associates' Purchase; the whole tract is in length from west to east, 6 miles and 1-2; in breadth from north to south, 300 rods; being bounded south on land called New Milford, the North Purchase, bounded west on Ousatonack River, east and north on lands formerly called County lands); and the sd. 532 acres the bounds thereof begins at a white oak tree, marked and stones laid about it, standing in the north line of New Milford North Purchase and south from the west pond, and is the southeast corner of the aforesaid 3800 acres; and from thence runs west one mile to a maple post markd. "W. W. E. I. J. A.," standing in the north end of a swamp by the east side of the West Pond "Cobble;" then north 300 rods to a white oak post markd. "W. W. E. J. J. A.;" then east one mile, which ends in the West Pond and south line, to the white oak tree first above mentioned; within which lines and boundaries is contained 532 acres of land, beside a part of the pond, and lies in joynt tenantcy between said John Austin and ye heirs of the said Ebenezer Fitch. This Court appoint Capt. Stephen Nobles, David Nobles, John Bostwick, Paul Welch and Ensign Gaylord of New Milford, and Mr. Edmund Lewis of Fairfield, County Surveyor, if need be, to make a division.

Page 27 (Vol. XIII) 13 April, 1738: An account of Adms. was now exhibited by Samuel Strong, John Perry and Bridget Perry alias Bridget Fitch, Adms. John Fitch, of Windham, in right of his wife and guardian to Elijah, Medinah and Ebenezer Fitch, heirs to the sd. estate, and James Fitch, eldest son of sd. deceased, being present at the Court, consented and allowed the foregoing account.

Page 55—2 October, 1739: An application by John Austin of Hartford and John Fitch of Windham in behalf of his wife Alice Fitch and the minor children of Ebenezer Fitch, for a division of land adjoining to New Milford, 532 acres, being part of 3800 acres called the Fairweather and his Associates' Purchase. The whole tract is in length, in the west division, 6 1-2 miles; and in breadth from north to south, 300 rods; being bounded south on the land above called New Milford North Purchase, west on Ousatonack River, east and north on land formerly called Country land (bounds ommited). And whereas, the sd. land lyes in common or joynt tenancy between Mr. John Austin of Hartford and the heirs of the estate of Mr. Ebenezer Fitch of Windsor deceased, and the sd. John Austin, and the sd. John Fitch of Windham in behalf of his wife Alice Fitch, guardian as aforesd., with James Fitch and Elijah Fitch, moved to this Court, pursuant to a law of this Colony entitled "An Act to Enable Guardians to Divide Lands," would appoint some suitable persons to divide said land between John Austin and John Fitch, guardian to three of the children of the sd. deceased, and James Fitch and Elijah Fitch, heirs as aforesd. Whereupon this Court do appoint Capt. Stephen Nobles, Messrs. David Nobles, John Bostick, Paul Welch and Ensign Gaylord, of New Milford, and Edmund Lewis, Esq., of Stratford, in Fairfield County (Surveyor), if need be, to make a division of sd. land between sd. parties according to direction above given, and make return thereof to this Court.

Page 56—2 October, 1739: John Perry and Samuel Strong, Adms., move this Court to appoint persons to apprise the real estate of the deceased, in order to make a division of the land that belongs to the estate to and amongst the heirs. And whereas, the lands lie within the bounds of several townships in Hartford County, or otherwise, this Court gives liberty to the Adms. to choose such persons as they think proper in such towns wherein any of the said lands are, to apprise said lands for the end aforesaid.

Page 75—6 November, 1740: We, the subscribers, being appointed by the Honourable Judge of Probates for the County of Hartford, at a Court holden at Hartford on the 2nd day of October, Anno. 1739, to make division and partition of a certain tract of land which lyes in common and joynt tenancy between the heirs of Mr. Ebenezer Fitch, late of Windsor deceased, and Mr. John Austin of Hartford, into two equal parts, both for quantity and quality, containing five hundred and thirty-two acres, and is part or parcel of a certain large tract of land containing in the whole 3800 acres, commonly known by the name of Mr. Fairweather and his Associates' Purchase, and lies next adjoyning to New Milford North Purchase, and the aforesd. 532 acres is butted and bounded as follows: Beginning at a white oak tree, marked and several stones laid about it, standing in the north line of New Milford North Purchase, and south from the West Pond, and is the southeast corner of the above-named 3800 acres; and from thence it runs west one mile to a maple pole marked

"W. W. I. F. & J. A.," standing in the north end of a swamp by the east side of the West Pond Cobble; then north 300 rods to a white oak pole marked "W. W. E. F. I. A.;" then east 1 mile, which ends in sd. pond, then a south line to the white oak tree first above mentioned, within which lines and bounds is contained 532 acres, besides a part of said pond. And being appointed as aforesd., and at the request of Mr. John Fitch of Windham in behalf of his wife Alice Fitch, one of the heirs to the sd. Ebenezer Fitch, and as he is guardian to the minor heirs aforesd., viz., Eleazer, Medina and Ebenezer Fitch; and at the request and desire of Mr. James Fitch and Elijah Fitch in their own behalf as heirs aforesd.; as also at the request of Mr. John Austin of Hartford; being by him sd. Austin, and all parties concerned, fully authorised and impowered thereto, have proceeded according to the best of our judgements and abilitys to make division and partition of the aforesd. 532 acres of land into two equal parts, both for quantity and quality, in manner and form as followeth, vizt: First, we set out and divide to the heirs of Mr. Ebenezer Fitch the east part, beginning at the southeast corner of sd. land, which is a white oak tree with many letters set on it and stones at the root, then running west 205 rods to 2 small white oak poles with a large heap of stones at the roots and with the letters "J. A. & J. F." on 1 of the sd. poles, then running north about 1 mile to a black oak tree with a large heap of stones at the root and "I. A. I. F. S. N. & P. W." set on sd. tree, then running east to sd. corner in the West Pond, then south to sd. white oak tree, where we began the aforesd. parcell of land described within the bounds aforesd., being 1 equal half part of the 532 acres, both for quantity and quality. The other half part we set out and divide to Mr. John Austin beforesd., beginning at the aforesd. white oak poles, then running west 115 rods to a maple pole marked and several letters on it, then running north 1 mile to a white oak pole marked and stones at the root, with many letters on it, then east 115 rods to the black oak tree aforesd., then south to where we began the aforesd. parcel of land described within the bounds aforesd., being the other equal half part of the 532 acres, both for quantity and quality, the work and service being performed and finished by us as aforesd. on the 5th day of July, 1740. Signed pr us:

STEPHEN NOBLE,
PAUL WELCH.

The foregoing division or partition of land lying in common or joynt tenancy between Mr. John Austin of Hartford and the heirs of Mr. Ebenezer Fitch of Windsor deceased, as in sd. partition fully described, was exhibited in Court July the 1st, 1740, and ordered to be recorded.

Attest: Jos: Talcott, Junr., Clerk.

Page 1 (Vol. XIV) 7 April, 1742: James Fitch signified to this Court that John Fitch of Windham resigned his trust of guardianship to Ebenezer Fitch, a minor son of Ebenezer Fitch of Windsor, and the sd. minor made choice of James Fitch of Durham to be his guardian, and the sd. James Fitch recog. £600.

Page 56 (Vol. XII) 29 May, 1746: Court of Probate, present Joseph Buckingham, Judge; Jos: Talcott, Clerk. Windham, 14 March, 1745-6: Received of Bridget Perry of Ashford, widow and Adms. on Ebenezer Fitch his estate, the sum of £40 in old tenor bills, it being jn full of what is due from the sd. Adms. and as she is Adms. to the estate of Capt. Joseph Perry of Ashford decd., to all heirs of the aforesd. Ebenezer Fitch decd., to JOHN and ALICE FITCH, JAMES FITCH, ELIJAH FITCH, ELEAZER FITCH, MEDINAH FITCH, and EBENEZER FITCH, to say, received by us. Test: *Alice Fitch, Jedediah Huntington and John Fitch as Guardians.*

Page 12 (Vol. XV) 13 May, 1746: Mrs. Bridget Perry, formerly the widow and relict of Mr. Ebenezer Fitch of Windsor and sole Adms. on sd. estate, having fully administered and rendered her account of Adms., and also produced a receipt under the hands of all the heirs and guardians that they have received their full part and portion, this Court do now grant her a *Quietus Est.*

Invt. in Vol. XII, Page 87.

Fitch, Capt. Joseph, Windsor. Invt. £24-00-00, which was a parcel of land, taken 5 December, 1727, by Samuel Bancroft and Samuel Elmore.

Court Record, Page 165—3 October, 1727: Upon motion of Benjamin Loomis, that sd. Joseph Fitch was in sd. Loomis his debt, and that he hath a right to sd. estate by marriage to one of sd. Capt. Fitch's daughters, and that no Adms. hath been granted on sd. estate, he desireing that Adms. might be granted, the heirs were notified to appear and show cause, if any, why Adms. should not be granted. The Court grant Adms. to Peter Mills, Jr.

Fowdrie, James. Court Record, Page 151—4 April, 1727: James Fowdrie, of Horseneck, personally before this Court made choice of Mr. Edward Cadwell of Hartford to be his guardian, which this Court allow. Rec., £20.

Inventory on File.

Fox, Beriah, Glastonbury. Invt. £13-12-06. Taken 31 July, 1727, by William Wickham and Gershom Smith.

Court Record, Page 161—August, 1727: Adms. granted unto Ebenezer Fox, son of the deceased.

Page 165—3 October, 1727: Ebenezer Fox, Adms., exhibited an account of his Adms. Accepted.

Invt. in Vol. XII, Page 202.

Frank (a free Negro), Farmington. Died 3 January, 1725. Invt. £4-15-06. Taken by Isaac Cowles and Samuel Judd.

Court Record, Page 112—4 January, 1725-6: This Court grant Adms. unto Daniel Judd, one of the Selectmen of sd. Town. Recog., £10.

Recorded in Vol. XII, Page 127-8.

Fuller, John. Will, 28 February, 1725-6: I, John Fuller, Sen., of the Township of Haddam, on the east side of the river, in the County of Hartford, in the Colony of Connecticut, in New England, being crazy and infirm in body, do by this my last will and testament dispose of wt temporal estate God hath graciously given me: Imprimis. I give to my wife one cowe, such as she shall choose, 8 sheep, £4 in money, the bed she lies on, 1 room in my dwelling house, and so much interest in the plow land and grass land of my home lott as may be necessary for her comfortable support during her widowhood. And I do appoint my son Thomas to the care of her creatures from year to year, and I do appoint my sons Joseph and Benjamin each to give her a day's mowing in a year yearly, and my sons Shubael and John to do her weaving some proportion between them yearly. I give to my son Thomas, besides what I have already given him by deed of gift, £20 of my right or interest in the Common or undivided land, and all my interest in the iron ware belonging to the field, but not what is in or for the house. I give to my son Samuel, besides what I have already confirmed to him by deed of gift, £20 of my right or interest in the Common or undivided land, and 1-2 of my meadow lott called by the name of the Little Pine Swamp Meadow, together with sundry other valuable things which he has already had of me. I give to my son Shubael, besides what I have given him by deed of gift, £20 of my right or interest in the Common or undivided land, besides sundry other valuable things which he has had already. I give to my son Edward, besides what has been confirmed to him by deed of gift, £6 in money, that is to say, in case he never finds his lost money, yet ye demands upon him from me upon the account of the fat cattle he bought of me of late shall be abatted to the value of £6; also I give him sundry valuable things he has already had of me. I give to my son John, besides deed of gift, 1-2 of my first division meadow lot. I give to my son Joseph, besides deed of gift, £20 of my right or interest in the Common or undivided lands, and 1-2 of my meadow lott commonly called the Little Pine Swamp Meadow. I give to my son Benjamin, besides deed of gift, £20 of my right in the Common or undivided land, and 1-2 of my first division meadow lott. I give to my daughter Thankfull what she has already received, as brass, pewter, and sundry other valuable things which she has had of me. I give to my daughter Elizabeth sundry valuable things which she has already had of me. I give to my daughter Mehetable sundry valuable things which she has already had of me, and also a coverlid, an iron pott which she has not as yet received, as also the bedd I lie upon after mine and my wife's decease, not before. Also, my will is that my wife should have my mare, and that my son Thomas should have a steer coming two years old,

which things were forgotten to be mentioned in their proper place. My
two sons Thomas and John Fuller shall be executors.
Witness: *Samuel Olmstead,*   JOHN FULLER, SEN., LS.
Samuel Emmons, Jonathan Emmons.

Court Record, Page 185—21 April, 1726: Will proven and invt. exhibited.

Page 195-6-7-8-9.

Fyler, John, Windsor.   Inventory as presented by Thomas Fyler,
Adms., taken 21 November, 1723, by Ebenezer Fitch, Jonathan Elsworth
and Samuel Strong.
Court Record, Page 33—6 November, 1723: Eliakim Marshall, of
Windsor, exhibited in this Court the last will of Mr. John Fyler, late of
sd. Windsor decd., and desired it might be proved and allowed. Stephen
Fyler, Elizabeth Fyler and Wakefield Dibble appeared to contest the probate of sd. will, and this Court having considered the will with the evidences and pleas on both sides produced, and also the general capacity of
the testator, upon the whole do not allow nor approve sd. will for probation, and grant Adms. unto Thomas Fyler of sd. Windsor, son of Zerubbable Fyler deceased.
See File: An agreement concluded between all ye heirs of Mr. John
Fyler, deceased, for ye peaceable settlement of ye estate of sd. John Fyler.
Wee, the subscribers, heirs abovsd., do mutually agree. In witness
whereof we have set to our hands and seals this 23 April, 1726.

THOMAS FILER, LS.	ELIZABETH X WILLARD, LS.
STEPHEN FILER, LS.	EXPERIENCE X FYLER, LS.
ZERUBBABLE X FYLER, LS.	ABIGAIL DEMING, LS.
WAKEFILD DIBEL, LS.	NATHANIEL HIGLEY, LS.
JOSIAH WILLARD, LS.	JONATHAN SACKET, LS.

A special covenant for the division of lands, made between the heirs
or legatees of Mr. John Fyler, late of Windsor decd., viz., to Thomas
Fyler, to Stephen Fyler, to Zerubbabell Fyler, to Wakefield Dibble's wife
Jane, to Abigail the wife of Jonathan Deming, to Experience Fyler, Elizabeth the wife of Josiah Willard, and to the heirs of Samuel Fyler decd.
And in confirmation whereof we the subscribers have hereunto set to our
hands and seals this 5th day of April, 1726.

THOMAS FILER, LS.	JOSIAH WILLARD, LS.
ZERUBBABELL X FILLER, LS.	WAKEFILD DIBOL, LS.
STEPHEN FILER, LS.	JONATHAN SACKET, LS.
ABIGAIL DEMING, LS.	EXPERIENCE X FILER, LS.

Witness: *Joseph Backus, Jr.,*
            Eben: Williamson.

Whereas, there is made and confirmed articles of agreement among
and between the heirs of John Fyler, late of Windsor decd., upon the 5th
day of April, 1726, concerning the settlement of all his real and personall

estate, we the subscribers, being heirs of said estate, and pursuant to said agreement, haue and do ratifie and confirm the same in the dividing and settleing of all the lands laid out or that shall hereafter be laid out to the heirs of sd. John Fyler, lying in the Township of Torringtown, viz., the heirs of Thomas Fyler to haue 2-9 of all the lands as to quanity and quality, and Stephen Fyler to haue 1-7 and 1-2 part. And the remainder to be equally divided between Zerubbable Fyler and the heirs of Jane Debill decd., and the heirs of Abigail Deming decd., and Elizabeth Willard, and the heirs of Experience Chiles decd., and the heirs of Samuel Fyler decd. And we do further agree that Thomas Marshall, Benjamin Bissill, Noah Wilson, Abill Beach and Epaphras Shelding, all of Torinton, shall be the persons to dist. sd. lands. In confirmation whereof we have hereunto set our hands.

Whereas, Silas Fyler doth represent (by purchase) Thomas Fyler, Stephen Fyler and Zerubbable Fyler. Dated in Windsor, this 21 September, 1759.

SILAS FYLER,	CHARLES DEMING,
JONATHAN HOIT, JR.,	ELIZABETH WILLARD,
SAMUEL FILER,	JONATHAN DEMING,
JONATHAN SACKETT,	ABIGAIL DEMING,
NATHANIEL HIGLEY,	EBENEZER GOODRICH.

Page 44-45.

Gates, George, East Haddam. He died 12 November, 1724. Inventory taken by John Booge, Sen., and Isaac Spencer.

Court Record, Page 62—5 January, 1724-5: Adms. to Capt. Thomas Gates, son of the decd. Exhibit of inventory.

Page 63—And whereas, several of the heirs haveing already received some portions of sd. estate by deeds of gift, this Court order such portions to be appraised at the value when given, and bring account to this Court, in order to have distribution made as the law directs. John Booge, Isaac Spencer and James Bates, of Haddam, appointed appraisers.

Page 75—22 March, 1724-5: The Court here reverse the former order to appraise gift lands at the value when given, to an order to appraise at the present value and at the same time with other estate.

Page 86—1st June, 1725: Adms. account exhibited: Paid in debts and charges, £55-06-06. The heirs had formerly received £986-17-02. Whereas, the inventory of the estate on record is £529-00-05, from which deduct £55-06-06, there remains £407-15-11 to be distributed, to which adding the sum of £986-14-02, will make the whole sum £1460-08-01 to be distributed, includeing what has already been given by deeds of gift. To the heirs of Thomas Gates, eldest son, deceased, £324-10-08; to Samuel Gates, to Thomas Gates, to Daniel Gates, to George Gates, to Sarah Shaylor, to Mary Cone, to each of them, £162-05-04. And appoint John Bogue, John Bates and Isaac Spencer, distributors.

Page 110—7 December, 1725: Adms. is granted a *Quietus Est.*

Invt. in Vol. XII, Page 217.

Gaylord, Samuel, Middletown. Invt. £487-12-08. Taken by John Collins, Joseph Rockwell and Solomon Adkins.

Court Record, Page 220—3 June, 1729: Adms. granted to Margaret Gaylord, widow.

Page 35 (Vol. XI) 12 January, 1730-1: Whereas, Margaret Gaylord, who was appointed Adms. on her husband's estate, she being deceased and not having finished Adms. on sd. estate, this Court appoint Mr. Eleazer Gaylord, of Middletown, to take Adms. on sd. estate.

Page 36—12 January, 1730-1: This Court appoint Joseph Southmayd to be guardian unto Millicent Gaylord, a minor, 10 years of age, and Samuel Gaylord, 7 years of age, children of Samuel Gaylord. Recog., £100. This Court appoint Eleazer Gaylord to be guardian unto Eleazer Gaylord, a minor, 4 years of age. Recog., £50.

Page 48 (Vol. XII) 6 July, 1736: Millicent Gaylord, now 16 years of age, chose her uncle William Southmayd to be her guardian.

Page 44 (Vol. XIII) 13 March, 1738-9: Elizabeth Gaylord, formerly guardian to Eleazer Gaylord, now 11 years of age, son of Samuel Gaylord, his former guardian being dead, this Court appoint Seth Wetmore to be his guardian. Recog., £200.

Page 48—19 April, 1739: An account of Adms. was now exhibited in Court by Seth Wetmore, the former Adms. being deceased. Accepted. This Court order that the estate be dist., viz.:

	£	s	d
To Seth Wetmore in right of his wife Margaret, *relict of sd. deceased* (was she not a daughter?), 1-3 part of the moveables, amounting to the sum of	36-04-08		
To Samuel Gaylord, eldest son,	36-04-08		
To Eleazer Gaylord, the 2nd son,	18-02-04		
To Millicent Gaylord, daughter,	18-02-04		

And appoint Solomon Adkins, Ephraim Adkins and William Rockwell, distributors.

Gilbert, Eleazer. Court Record, Page 209—2nd January, 1728-9: Eleazer Gilbert, a minor, 18 years of age, chose Nathaniel Gilbert of Middletown to be his guardian. Recog., £100.

Invt. in Vol. XII, Page 94-5.

Gilbert, John, Middletown. Invt. £369-10-01. Taken 29 December, 1727, by Daniel Hall, Solomon Adkins and Jonathan Yeomans.

Court Record, Page 172—2 January, 1727: Adms. granted to Nathaniel Gilbert, brother of the decd., the widow desiring it.

Invt. in Vol. XI, Page 4.

Gilbert, Mary, Middletown. Invt. £12-09-06. Taken 30 August, 1729, by Joseph Rockwell and John Collins. (See File: Mary, widow of Andrew Ward.)

Court Record, Page 213—4 March, 1728-9: Adms. granted unto William Ward, son of the decd.

Page 1 (Vol. XI) 5 July, 1729: Esther Cornwall of Middletown and Mary Parsivell of Haddam were sworn at this Court that they would answer to all interogatories that should be asked them by this Court that may tend to disclose the estate of Mrs. Mary Gilbert, late of Middletown decd. Mary Cornwall declareth that she had of the estate several small articles that her mother gave her long before her death, and she can get no further account of sd. estate. Mary Parsivell under oath declareth that her mother, Mary Gilbert, gave her the looking-glass and the candle box in her lifetime, and she had them in actual possession long before her mother deceased; yet she saith that she having tendered her mother in her last sickness whereof she died, and some years before, which she supposeth worth £10, and for that service she had of clothes of her sd. mother's to the value of £4, which she saith her brother William Ward gave his consent to, and this is all she can remember that ever she had of what was her mother's that she died seized of, and as for anything more she cannot tell where it is.

Page 192-3-4.

Goff, Jacob, Wethersfield. He died 23 March, 1723. Inventory taken by Joseph Grimes and Philip Goffe.

Court Record, Page 27—2 July, 1723: Adms. to Ephraim Goff, a brother of sd. decd.

Goff, Philip, Middletown. Court Record, Page 158—4 July, 1727. Adms. to Philip Goff, son of the sd. deceased. Bond with Joseph Farnsworth.

Page 161—August, 1727: Invt. exhibited.

Invt. in Vol. XII, Page 131.

Goodrich, Ephraim, Wethersfield. Invt. £486-02-00. Taken 3 April, 1728, by Nathaniel Stilman, Hezekiah May and John Curtis.

Court Record, Page 188—2 April, 1728: Adms. granted to Susannah Goodrich, widow, and William Goodrich of Litchfield.

Page 48 (Vol. XIII) 20 March, 1738-9: This Court appoint Joseph Goodrich guardian to Ephraim Goodrich, son of Ephraim Goodrich. And the sd. Joseph Goodrich, guardian, moves to this Court that William Goodrich, Adms. on the estate of the sd. deceased, may be brought to render an account of his Adms.

Page 109—16 January, 1741-2: Ephraim Goodrich, now 14 years of age, chose Joseph Goodrich to be his guardian. Recog., £600. Cert: *David Goodrich, J. P.*

Page 241.

Goslin, Henry, Glastonbury. Invt. £201-16-11. Taken 22 May, 1724, by Thomas Welles and Joseph Fox.

Court Record, Page 52—4 August, 1724: Adms. granted to Mary Goslin, widow, and Thomas Goslin, son of the decd.

Dist. on File: 3 July, 1726: Mary Goslin, Adms., exhibited an account of her Adms. Accepted. Order the estate to be dist. as followeth:

	£ s d
To Mary Goslin, widow, of moveable estate,	11-04-06
To Henry Goslin, eldest son,	50-10-06
And to Timothy, Mary, Bethiah and Elizabeth Goslin, to each,	25-05-03
And to the heirs of Beriah Brewer, wife of Hezekiah,	18-17-00

And appoint Thomas Welles, Benjamin Talcott and Gershom Smith, of Glastonbury, distributors.

Page 73 (Vol. XI) 2 September, 1732: Henry Goslin, a minor, 19 years of age, son of Henry Goslin, chose his uncle Joseph Fox to be his guardian. Recog., £50.

Page 74—2 September, 1732: Henry Goslin now made choice of his uncle William Goslin to be his guardian.

Page 96—29 June, 1733: Timothy Goslin, age 15 years, chose Joseph Brewer of Glastonbury to be his guardian.

Page 30 (Vol. XIII) 27 June, 1738: Joseph Brewer desiring to be discharged of his guardianship over Timothy Goslin, son of Henry Goslin, the sd. Brewer was discharged from sd. trust, and the sd. Timothy Goslin made choice of Henry Goslin, his brother, to be his guardian. Recog., £200.

Page 80-1-2-112.

Graham, Benjamin. Inventory taken 15 February, 1724-5, by John Bunce, Jr., and Jno. Gilbert.

Will dated 4 February, 1724-5: I, Benjamin Graham of Hartford, do make this my last will and testament: Imprimis: I give and bequeath to my wife Sarah Graham 20 shillings. I give to my granddaughter Mary Graham, after my just debts are paid, 1-7 of my real and personal estate, that is to say, ye full value thereof in money as my estate shall be apprised or inventoried, besides what her father and mother and she has already received, to be paid her at ye age of 18 years or day of marriage. Item. I give to my son Benjamin Graham 1-3 part of ye full value of my real and personal estate after ye above legacies and my just debts are paid. I give one other third part of my estate, after my just debts and legacies are paid, to my son Samuel Graham, only it is my will that ye house and about 12 rods of land I have formerly given him by deed of gift shall be part of his third part. I give to my son Isaac Graham, after my just debts and legacies are paid, one other third part of my real and personal estate, and it is my will that my son Isaac shall have my dwelling house, barn and garden, and to make a line from ye south side of my garden to ye south side of ye gristmill, and that all my lands northward of sd. line, and my share of ye fulling mill, to be all included within his third part as apprised or inventoried. It is my will that my son Samuel shall have my share of ye sawmill included in his third part, only that my son Isaac shall have ye use of sd. mill until January next ensueing, he paying ye rent to my son Samuel as has been agreed on with me. I appoint my two sons, Samuel and Isaac Graham, executors.

Witness: *Thomas Andrus,*   BENJAMIN GRAHAM, LS.
Lydia Messinger, John Austin.

Codicil: It is to be further understood, in the explanation of my will, that my gristmill shall revert 1-2 to my son Samuel and his heirs, to be counted in his thirds as apprised, and the other half to my son Isaac, to be accounted to him and his thirds as apprised, to be to him and his heirs and assigns forever.

Witness: *Thomas Andrus,*   BENJAMIN GRAHAM, LS.
Lydia Messinger, John Austin.

Court Record, Page 102 (Vol. XI) 28 December, 1733: Hartford, the 2nd day of June, 1732: Then received of Isaac Graham 20 shillings money in full satisfaction for all demands that I have upon the estate of my father, Benjamin Graham, late decd., by will, or on Samuel and Isaac Graham, executors to the last will of the decd. I say received as aforesd.

Witness: *Jonathan Steele,*   Per me: BENJAMIN GRAHAM.
Joseph Farnsworth.

Page 9.

Graham, John, Jr., Hartford. Died 28 July, 1720: Inventory taken 5 August, 1720, by William Gaylord and William Kelsey.

Court Record, Page 4—1st January, 1722-3: Adms. to Benjamin Graham and Hannah Graham, widow.

Page 113—4 January, 1725-6: Account of Adms. Order to dist. the estate to the widow, Hannah Graham, and her child. Jared Spencer, Nathaniel Andrews and Wilterton Merrells, distributors. Mrs. Hannah Graham to be guardian to her child, name Mary, 5 years of age. Rec., £50.

Page 122—1 March, 1725-6: Hannah Graham, alias Tillottson, now granted a *Quietus Est.*

Invt. in Vol. XI, Page 144.

Grant, Noah, Tolland. Invt. £1418-09-05. Taken by Josiah Goodrich, Samuel Benton and Jonathan Delano.

Court Record, Page 167—7 November, 1727: Adms. granted to Martha Grant, widow.

Page 58 (Vol. XI) 4 January, 1731-2: Invt. exhibited.

Page 80—25 December, 1732: Noah Grant, a minor, age 14 years, son of Noah Grant, chose his uncle Ephraim Grant to be his guardian. Recog., £100.

Page 35 (Vol. XII) 11 November, 1735: Adoniram Grant chose his uncle Ephraim Grant of Tolland to be his guardian. Also appointed guardian to Solomon Grant, age 12 years, and Martha Grant, age 9 1-2 years, children of Noah Grant, late decd.

See agreement per File: To the worshipful Corte of Probates in the County of Hartford: Whereas, Noah Grant, late of Tolland, decd., died intestate, leaving Martha his widow with four children, all minors, viz., Noah, Adoniram, Solomon and Martha Grant, and the sd. widow being made sole Adms. upon sd. estate, and since sd. widow marrying to Peter Buell of Coventry, in Windham County, the sd. Buell by sd. marriage becoming Adms. upon sd. estate, and Ephraim Grant of sd. Tolland being appointed guardian for all of sd. minors; and whereas, Noah Grant and Adoniram Grant abovesd. are now of full age to act for themselves, and all parties concerned being disposed to an agreement in settling sd. intestate estate, have agreed as followeth: The sd. Peter Buell, as administrator with his wife Martha, Noah Grant and Adoniram Grant as legatees, Ephraim Grant as guardian to Soloman Grant and Martha Grant with the desire of Soloman and Martha, we find upon computation, after the debts are paid, there remains of the estate to be divided to the legatees £1832-05-00 in freehold and £62 in moveable estate.

To the widow, her thirds of real estate for life.

	£ s d
To Noah Grant, a double portion,	757-14-00 old tenor.
To Adoniram Grant,	378-17-00
To Solomon Grant,	378-17-00
To Martha Grant,	378-17-00

To this agreement we have set to our hands and seals this sixth day of February, A. D. 1743-4.

PETER BUELL, LS.
MARTHA BUELL, LS.
NOAH GRANT, LS.
ADONIRAM GRANT, LS.
EPHRAIM GRANT, GUARDIAN, LS.
SOLOMON GRANT, LS.
MARTHA GRANT, LS.

Witness: *Thomas Root,*
Solomon Root.

Page 38 (Vol. XVI) 13 February, 1743-4: An agreement for the settlement of the estate of Noah Grant, late of Tolland decd., was now exhibited by the heirs and acknowledged. Accepted and ordered to be placed on file.

Invt. in Vol. XII, Page 99-100.

Grant, Thomas, Windsor. Invt. £166-12-04. Taken 2 July, 1726, by Jonathan Stiles, Alexander Allen and John Allyn.

Court Record, Page 133—2 August, 1726: Adms. granted to Jehiel Grant, son of the decd.

Page 331-2.

Griffin, Ephraim, Simsbury. Died 27 September, 1725. Invt. £224-16-07. Taken by Samuel Griswold and Joshua Holcomb.

Court Record, Page 109—7 December, 1725: Adms. granted to Elizabeth Griffin, widow, and Samuel Griswold of Simsbury.

Page 139—6 December, 1726: Samuel Griswold and Elizabeth Griffin, Adms., exhibit an account of their Adms. Accepted. Order to dist. the estate as followeth:

	£	s	d
To Elizabeth Griffin, alias Holcomb, relict of sd. decd.,	7-17-03		
To Ephraim Griffin, eldest son,	62-05-02		
To Elizabeth, Anne, Silence and Sheba Griffin, the rest of the children, to each of them their single portions,	31-02-06		

And appoint Thomas Holcomb, John Case and James Case, of Simsbury, distributors. This Court appoint Elizabeth Griffin to be guardian unto her children, viz., Silence, 10 years, Sheba, age 4 years. Recog., £100. Elizabeth Griffin, a minor, 17 years of age, and Anna Griffin, 15 years, chose Mr. Samuel Griswold to be their guardian. Recog., £100.

Page 84 (Vol. XI) 6 March, 1731-2: Ephraim Griffin, age 14 years, son of Ephraim Griffin, chose Michael Humphrey of Simsbury to be his guardian. Recog., £100.

Giffie, Caleb. Court Record, Page 80—12 April, 1725: Caleb Giffie, a minor, 12 years of age, chose Thomas Giffie, of Haddam, to be his guardian. Recog., £50.

Griffin, Mindwell. Court Record, Page 102—4 October, 1725: This Court do appoint Samuel Pettebone of Simsbury to be guardian unto Mindwell Griffin, a minor daughter of Alyce Griffin. Recog., £50.

Page 260-1-2-3.

Griswold, Joseph, Windsor. Invt. £782-09-03. Taken 6 April, 1725, by William Phelps, Nathaniel Pinney and Joseph Barnard.

Court Record, Page 75—6 April, 1725: This Court grants Adms. to Lois Griswold, widow. Exhibit of inventory.

Page 125—5 April, 1726: Lois Griswold and Shubael Griswold exhibit account: Paid out in debts and charges, more than has been received due to sd. estate, £103-09-08. Accepted. Invt. £782-09-02; subtracting £103-09-08, there remains £ -19-07 to be distributed. Order to Lois Griswold, widow of sd. decd., £47-13-02, with dower; to Shubael Griswold, eldest son of sd. decd., £139-16-11, which is his double portion of sd. estate; to George, Jonah, Roger, Abell, Joseph, Lois and Deborah Griswold, the rest of the children, to each of them, £69-18-06, which is their single portions of sd. estate. And appoint Nathaniel Pinney, Joseph Barnard and William Phelps, distributors. George Griswold, 16 years of age, chose Shubael Griswold of Windsor to be his guardian. Recog., £150.

Page 53 (Vol. XI) 14 September, 1731: Abell Griswold, a minor, 17 years of age, chose Mr. Matthew Griswold to be his guardian. Recog., £100.

Page 86—22 March, 1732-3: Lois Griswold, Adms., is appointed guardian to Joseph, age 18 years, Lois 11 years, and Deborah 10 years of age. Recog., £50. And this Court grant the widow a *Quietus Est*.

Page 202.

Hale, Thomas, Sen., Glastonbury. Inventory taken 15 January, 1723-4, by John Hubbard and Nathaniel Talcott. An addition of £13-03-00.

In the name and fear of God, amen. The 3 day of June, Anno. Dom. 1723 Annoq. R. R. Georgij. Maga. Britta., &c., Nono: I, Thomas Hale, Sen., of Glastonbury, in ye County of Hartford, in ye Colony of Connecticut, in New England, make this my last will and testament: Imprimis: I will that my just debts and funeral expenses be paid by my executors hereinafter named out of my moveable or personal estate. I give to Thomas Hale, my eldest son, 8 1-2 rods wide of that my lot of land whereon I now dwell, both of meadow, swamp and pasture, bounded on ye Great River west, and from that running 8 1-2 rods wide eastward to ye west end of my orchard near my house, vizt., to ye ditch at ye end of my sd. orchard, and from ye east end of my sd. pasture hereby given to be 4 rods in wedth north and south, and to lye on ye north side of my sd. lott .... Also, all that land layd out to me by ye Town next to ye 3-mile lotts near Hartford bounds, and all ye rest of ye land granted to me not yet layd out to me, save 30 acres. And also I give to him a yoke of oxen, and also ye sum of £20. Item. All the rest of my lands, wheresoever and howsoever butted and bounded, with the buildings, fences, fruit trees, &c., thereon being, I give unto my son Timothy Hale and to his heirs forever, saving and reserving only to my sd. son Thomas Hale and to his heirs forever ye full use and liberty of ye causey from ye sd. highway into ye meadow to go with his team backwards and forwards as he shall have occasion. Also, I give my sd. son Timothy 1 yoke of good oxen, my cart, plows, harrows, collars, chain, and all my team tackling. Item. I devise and bequeath to my dearly beloved wife Naomi the use and improvement of 1-3 part of all my houseing and lands and of all my personal estate, goods and chattells, during her natural life, and ye remainder or reversion whereof, after my wife's decease, I give as followeth, vizt., to be equally divided amongst my four daughters, Naomi, Mary, Ruth and Eunice, or such as shall legally represent them. And I constitute my sons Thomas and Timothy executors. I give to Samuel Hale, who lately served his time with me, £5 of my estate, and to Elizabeth Kilbourn a mare or £5 more than I am bound to pay her, vizt., more than ye cowe I have promised her.

Witness: *Gershom Smith,*   THOMAS X HALE, LS.
William Wickham, Jr., Thomas Kimberly.

Court Record, Page 43—27 March, 1724: Will exhibited and proven.

Page 92 (Probate Side) 29 April, 1724: Then received of my father's estate, that is to say, 1 yoke of oxen prised at £8, and a mare and colt prised at £6, and a grey colt prised at £3-06, and a cane prised at £00-10, and square and hand-saw prised at 10 shillings, and a west coat prised at £1-08, and a hatt prised at 7 shillings. The above-mentioned things were received by me, the subscriber, on the account of the £20 which was willed to me by my father. I say received by me.

THOMAS HALE.

Know all men by these presents: That I, Thomas Hale of Glastonbury, in the County of Hartford, in the Colony of Connecticut, in New England, have this day received from my brother Timothy Hale, of the same Glastonbury, the sum of £10 money, the same being a legacy given by my hond. father Thomas Hale, late of Glastonbury aforesd., decd., in and by his last will and testament, for which I do hereby acquitt and discharge him my sd. brother Timothy Hale, his executors and administrators. In witness whereof I have hereunto set my hand the 3d of February, Anno. R. R. Georgij. Maga. Britta., &c., Undecimo Annoqe. Dom. 1724-5.

Witness: *Thomas Kimberly,*   THOMAS HALE.
     Samuel Kimberly.

Hall, Daniel. Court Record, Page 37—3 January, 1723-4: Daniel Hall, a minor, about 15 years of age, of Windsor, chose Thomas Elgar of Windsor to be his guardian. Rec., £30.

Page 42—3 March, 1723-4: Thomas Elgar, guardian to Daniel Hall of Windsor, a minor, about 14 years of age, appeared before this Court and desired to be discharged from his guardianship to sd. minor, which was accordingly granted. And Daniel Hall made choice of Stephen Loomis to be his guardian. Rec., £50.

Harris, Daniel. Court Record, Page 48—5 May, 1724: Daniel Harris, a minor, 19 years of age, chose his brother Thomas Harris of Wethersfield to be his guardian.

Page 143—3 January, 1726-7: Abraham Harris, a minor, 17 years of age, also chose his brother Thomas Harris of Wethersfield to be his guardian. Recog., £50.

Hart, John. Court Record, Page 59—1st December, 1724: This Court do appoint Jonathan Bull of Hartford to be guardian unto John Hart, only son of his sister, Mrs. Sarah Bull, alias Hart, decd., provided bond be given. Recog., £50.

Page 52 (Vol. XI) 11 May, 1731: John Hart, a minor, age 13 years, and Dr. Jonathan Bull, his uncle, guardian, together with Samuel Stanly, show this Court that there was in the Town of Bolton a tract of land belonging to sd. Stanly, sd. minor and others, held in joynt tenantcy or copartnership, and moved this Court might appoint Jonathan Burnham of Wethersfield, with Capt. John Bissell of Bolton, to assist in the division between the minor John Hart, Moses Bull's right sold to Samuel Stanly, and Jonathan Welles in right of his wife, and make return of their doings to this Court therein. Moses Bull's right in sd. land is 3-5 of the whole, to sd. Stanly; to John Hart, the minor, 1-5; and to Jonathan Welles, in right of his wife, 1-5.

Recorded in Vol. XII, Page 79-81.

Hart, Thomas, Sen., Farmington. Invt. in lands, £295-00-00. Taken 7 September, 1726, by Isaac Cowles and John Hart.

Will dated 24 July, 1721: To all Christian people to whom these presents shall come, greeting: Know ye that I, Thomas Hart, Sen., of the Town of Farmingtown, now in the 76th or 77th year of my age, do make this my last will and testament: I give to my beloved wife Ruth Hart the free use, benefit and improvement of all the rooms in my dwelling house and cellar that we now are in possession of, during the time of her natural life; also ye use of the garden that we have and as we now possess them, and 1-3 of the use and benefit of ye orchard and fruit therein, during the time of her natural life; also I give unto my wife 1-4 part of all my household goods, and to dispose of it as she shall see cause among her children, as by a writing given her will show; also I give to my wife a cow; also I give her £6 as money yearly, to be paid unto her by my executor out of my estate for her comfort and support during the time of her widowhood. I give unto my son Howkins Hart, besides what I have given him and his eldest son in deeds of gifts already, all my reed-making tools, great table and joynt stools which he has already in his hands. I give my two sons Thomas Hart and Hezekiah Hart all my right in lands that have fallen unto me within the limits of ye Great Swamp Society and that should or shall accrue by virtue of the same. Also I give unto them my own proper original lott or division of land against Wethersfield, only reserveing out of ye lott against Wethersfield 10 acres, which 10 acres of land I give unto my grandson Ebenezer Hart, and 11 acres that I bought of Nathaniel Wadsworth, which I give unto my grandson Hezekiah's eldest son, which lands to be possessed by these my grandsons when they shall attain unto lawful age. The remainder of sd. lands to be equally divided between them or as they shall agree. I give to my son John Hart, besides what I have already given him, all the right, title, claim or interest in property that I have, might, should or ought to have in the 300 acres of land granted by the General Assembly unto Mr. Anthony Howkins, being laid out within the Township of Middletown, as may be seen by their Book of Records. I give unto my grandson William Hart the remainder of my lott in the Middle Tier of the South Division. I give unto my son Josiah Hart the Corn Mill at ye lower end of my home lott with all its appurtenances, and the remaining part of my homelott that I have not given by deed of gift heretofore; all my rights in land at the Farm and the Great Meadow and in the Indian Neck, excepting 10 acres of land at the Farm, for quality with the rest, which I give unto his son Thomas Hart. I give to my son Josiah 11 acres of land at the Third Meadow and my 10-acre pasture beyond the Round Swamp; also I give him my lott on the east side of the river against Town, and my part of my Father Howkins's, and my six-acre grant at the north end of the Dead Swamp; also all my right in that lott of my hond. Father Howkins against Wethersfield bounds, and ye lott that I bought of Thomas Porter, tailor, against Wethersfield bounds; also the 1-2 of the lott of my hond. Father Hart's on the west side of the river against Nodd, and my long table and 2 joynt stools, and my trunk in which I kept my righting, allowing unto my beloved wife the use of them during life (excepting the trunk) ; also I give him my right or part of Richard (negro servant) on these conditions, that he my son Josiah Hart maintain for my beloved wife, so long as she bears my name, a cow and necessary firewood; also 2 joynt stools and small table in the chamber, and all my land at the Bass River. I give unto my two daughters, Mary Newell and Margaret Strong, £5 apiece each of them, as money. And I give unto their two eldest sons, my two grandsons, Samuel Newell and Israel Strong, my own proper original lott in the North Division of land on the west side of the river against Nod. I give to my five sons, Howkins Hart, Thomas Hart, John Hart, Hezekiah Hart and Josiah Hart, all the remaining part of my estate, to be equally divided among them, excepting 15 acres of land at the west end of my lott in the West Division and westermost range or tier of lotts, it being in the 6th tier of lotts, which I give unto Richard (negro) our servant, to be his own free and clear after he has finished his service according to the wrighting my son gave him, excepting my sons shall see cause to lay out unto him 15 acres in some other division of land, which 15 acres of land is for his encouragement if he tarry in the Town and improve it; but if he shall, after his time is out according unto his agreement with my son Josiah Hart, leave the Town, then to return to my sons. I appoint my two sons, Thomas Hart and Josiah Hart, sole executors.

Witness: *John Hart, Jr.,*   THOMAS HART, SEN., LS.
Timothy Porter, Sen., David Bull.

Court Record, Page 136—4 October, 1726: Will proven.

Recorded in Vol. XII, Page 153-4-5-6.

Hart, Thomas, Sergt., Farmington. Invt. £707-01-01. Taken 2 May, 1728, by John Hart, Sen., Joseph Judd and Isaac Cowles. Will dated 28 December, 1727.

I, Sergt. Thomas Hart, of the Town of Farmingtown, being infirm, impotent and weak in body, do make this my last will and testament: Item. Unto Elizabeth Hart, my beloved wife, I give during her natural life the use of 1-2 of my now dwelling house and 1-3 part of my barn, and 1-3 of every piece or parcell of my land hereafter in this instrument given to my sons; also I give her, to be at her own dispose forever, 1-3 part of all my personal estate. Unto my son Stephen Hart I give 1-5 part of all my right which I have in common in the reserved land; also I give unto him of my personal estate 5 shillings. Item. Unto my son Thomas Hart, besides what I have already given him, 5 shillings. Unto my son Joseph Hart, besides what I have already given him, I give to him and his heirs forever 1-5 part of all my right which I have in common within the reserved land. I also give unto him 5 shillings. To my two sons, Samuel Hart and Jeams Hart, to them I give and bequeath 2-3 parts for quantity and quality of that tract of land within the common fence by my house and northerly from it, which 2-3 parts is to be the northerly part of sd. tract of land, to be equally divided between them. Also I give unto them 2-3 parts of that tract of pasture land which I have on the east side of the common fence at Ware Swamp. I give unto them 2-3 parts of all my land at a place called The Old Farm. Also I give unto them, to be equally divided between them, my lott lately brought under improvement lying in that division of land in the north of the reserved lands on the east side of the river. Also I give unto each of them 1-5 of all my right which I have in common within the reserved land. Also I give unto them, in equal proportion between them, all the residue of my land or rights to lands, wheresoever and whatsoever it be, that shall not otherwise be found mentioned in this my will. Item. Unto my son William Hart I give my now dwelling house and barn; 1-2 part of the house in present possession and the other half in reversion; 2-3 parts of the barn in present possession and 1-3 part in reversion; also that lott in which sd. barn stands; also that southerly third part for quantity and quality of that tract of pasture land which I have on the east side of the common fence at Ware Swamp. Also I give unto him 1-3 part of all my land in the common field at a place called The Old Farm, and also 1-5 part of all my right which I have in common within the reserved land. I expect of my son William that he be careful of and kind to his mother. Item. Unto my daughter Elizabeth Hart I give and bequeath all the residue and remainder of my personal estate not before disposed of in this my will, whatsoever and wheresoever it be. And in case that this remainder of my estate do not prove to make up to her the value of £60, then my will is that my three youngest sons, vizt., Samuel, Jeams and William, shall pay to her in equal proportion so much as to make her part £60. I appoint my wife Elizabeth Hart and my son Samuel Hart executors.

Witness: *John Hooker, Sen.,*   THOMAS X HART, LS.
John Hart, Sen., Timothy Stanly.

Court Record, Page 191—7 May, 1728: Will exhibited by Elizabeth Hart and Samuel Hart, executors. Proven. This Court appoint Mrs. Elizabeth Hart to be guardian to her son William Hart, 18 years of age. Recog., £100.

Page 59 (Vol. XVII) 1st April, 1755: Hezekiah Winchell, of Farmington, showing to this Court that he has a right in lands that lie in common or joynt tenancy with the heirs of Thomas Hart, late of Farmington, deceased, and the rest of the surviving partners and tenants in common in sd. Farmington, and desires freeholders may be appointed to assist in dividing sd. land: Whereupon this Court appoint Samuel Thompson, Samuel Lankton and Joseph Porter, of Farmington, to assist in dividing sd. land lying in common as aforesd.

Inventory in Vol. XII, Page 233.

Hawley, Jehial, Middletown. Invt. £156-18-06. Taken 2 January, 1727-8, by Joseph Rockwell, Robert Warner, Benjamin Hawley and Thomas Stevens.

Court Record, Page 165—5 September, 1727: Adms. granted to Hope Hawley, widow of sd. decd., who gave bond with Noadiah Diggeson.

Page 17 (Vol. XI) 13 April, 1730: Hope Hawley is appointed guardian to three of her children, viz., Samuel Stow Hawley, age 7 years, Hope Hawley, age 10 years, and Hannah Hawley, age 4 years. Recog., £100. Hope Hawley, widow, Adms. on her husband's estate, exhibits an account of her Adms. Accepted, and this Court grant her a *Quietus Est.*

Page 317-18-19-20.

Hayes, George, Sen., Salmon Brook, Simsbury. (Age about 70 years.) Invt. £259-04-07. Taken by John Higley, Samuel Griswold and Jonathan Westover. Will dated 30 April, 1725.

I, George Hayes, Sen., of Simsbury, doe make this my last will and testament: I give my wife Abigail Hayes my homested and so much household furniture as may be necessary to her during her widowhood. I give unto my son Daniel the sum of £10 more than any other of my children (except it be my daughter Abigail) in money or equivalent thereunto out of my estate when the same may fall to them to be divided. I give unto my daughter Abigail £5 more than to any child or daughter I have, by reason of her lameness. I give to my son Benjamin, besides what I gave him already by deed, my 10-acre piece of marsh commonly called the Bener Marsh, and also my whole part or share in our sawmill at Salmon Brook, with this condition or promise, that he the sd. Benjamin shall dwell and live with me and support me in all my wants and necessities, and carefully carry on the business required and usual to be done and performed in my husbandry on my farm, and to behave himself toward me as a dutiful child ought to do towards a dutiful parent, during my natural life. And my will and desire also is that if I should happen to decease in such a time of the year so soon or soon after my sd. son has gotten in my crops of grain and hay, etc., or such other products of my sd. farm, that the same be not put nor entered in an inventory, but that the same be wholly for the use and benefit of my now present family, namely, my wife, my daughter Abigail and son Benjamin. I give unto my four sons, Daniel, George, William and Samuel, 2-3 parts of my remaining estate, to be equally divided between them. And the other third part of my sd. estate I give unto my daughters, Abigail, Sarah, Mary, Johanna, Thankfull and Doritha, to be equally divided between them. I make my wife and my son Daniel my executors.

Witness: *Joseph East,*   GEORGE HAYES, LS.
Lydia X *Hixley, Elizabeth* X *Bartlett.*

Court Record, Page 105—5 October, 1725: Will now exhibited by Abigail Hayes, widow, and Daniel Hayes, named executors in sd will. Approved. James Hillyer, of Symsbury, in right of his wife (one of the daughters of George Hayes decd.), desired an appeal from the judgement of this Court approveing the will. Granted.

Invt. in Vol. XII, Page 98.

Haynes, Mrs. Mary, Hartford. Invt. £544-07-06. Taken 23 January, 1726-7, by Nathaniel Stanly, Joseph Gilbert and John Skinner.

Court Record, Page 144—3 January, 1726-7: John Haynes and Mrs. Mary Haynes, his wife, being both deceased and she not having finished Adms. on her husband's estate, this Court grants Adms. on the estates of John and Mary Haynes his wife unto Mrs. Mary Lord, only child surviving, who gave bond with Hezekiah Wyllys of £600. Also exhibits an invt. of the estate of Mrs. Mary Haynes. Mrs. Mary Lord to be guardian to her son, John Haynes Lord, a minor, about 2 years of age. Recog., £500.

Page 18-19.

Henning, Andrew, Symsbury. He died 13 January, 1724-5. Invt. £45-00-00. Taken 29 January, 1724-5, by John Case, John Higley and Joshua Holcomb. Will dated 30 December, 1724.

The mind and will of Andrew Henning: My will and pleasure is that my hond. aunt, Katharine Veit, should have the use and improvement of my house and homelott during ye time of her life. And after her decease my will and pleasure is that her four children should have my house and homelott to be equally divided among them. Furthermore, my pleasure is that my cousin Thomas Holcomb should have my other lands, 77 acres.

Witness: *Thomas Holcomb,*   ANDREW HENNING.
Samuel Griswold.

Court Record, Page 69—2 February, 1724-5: A writing under his hand now exhibited, wherein there is a gift made to his aunt, Katharine Viett of sd. Symsbury, which this Court allow. Adms. granted to Thomas Holcomb, Jr.

Page 11-12.

Higley, Jonathan, Simsbury. Inventory taken 28 November, 1722, by Thomas Holcomb and Samuel Griswold.

Court Record, Page 1—1st January, 1722-3: This Court grant letters of Adms. on the estate of Jonathan Higley and Ann Higley his wife, late of Simsbury, unto John Higley, brother of sd. decd.

Page 46—7 April, 1724: John Higley, Adms. on the estate of Jonathan Higley, exhibited an account of his Adms.: Paid £38-05-02 more than he has received due to sd. estate. The Court order dist. unto Mercy Higley, only child of the sd. decd., and the same delivered unto her guardian for her use. And this Court do appoint Jonathan Westover, Samuel Griswold and John Sexton, of Simsbury, distributors.

Page 121-2-3-4.

Hill, Eleazer, Windsor. Inventory taken 5 April, Anno. Dom. 1725, by Daniel Loomis, James Enno and Timothy Loomis. Will dated 17 August, 1717.

I, Eleazer Hill of Windsor, doe make this my last will and testament: Imprimis. I give to my well-beloved son Eleazer all my houseing and lands together with all my real and personal estate (to be) to him and his heirs and assigns forever, with this provisal, that in case my wife survive me he shall honourably and comfortably provide for her during her widowhood and pay to his two sisters, vizt., Elizabeth and Sarah, £7 apiece as money after his mother's decease. I appoint my son Eleazer Hill executor.

Witness: *Daniel Loomis,* ELEAZER HILL, LS.
James Enno, Timothy Loomis.

Court Record, Page 79—12 April, 1725: Will now exhibited by Eleazer Hill, son of sd. decd., named executor in sd. will. Exhibit of inventory.

Page 248-9.

Invt. in Vol. XII, Page 139.

Hilyer, Mary, Widow, Symsbury. Died 12 August, 1725. Invt. £23-11-07. Taken 9 November, 1725, by Richard Case and James Hilyer. Will dated 17 August, 1725.

I, Mary Hilyer, widow, of Symsbury, do make this my last will and testament: I give to my three sons, William Alderman, John Alderman and Joseph Alderman, my lands, to wit: Two pieces or parcells lying and being in Simsbury aforesd. The first is a piece of pine plain lying on the west side of the river, containing 12 acres, known by the name of Case's Hollow, which was given to me by my father John Case decd. The other is 5 acres of marsh land lying under the West Mountain which fell to me by dist. of my father's estate. To be equally divided amongst them. And all my moveable estate excepting my wearing apparell. All of them I give to my daughter Elizabeth. And I appoint my well-beloved son John Alderman my executor.

Witness: *Samuel Pettebone,*   MARY HILYER, LS.
Jonathan Humphrey, Samuel Humphrey.

Page 184, Vol. XII.

Hills, Benjamin, Hartford. Invt. £208-14-00. Taken by Daniel Dickinson and Timothy Williams. Will dated 4 February, 1726.

I, Benjamin Hills, being weak in body and in expectation of my last change, and being willing to dispose of those worldly goods which God hath given me, and set my house in order before I die, do make and ordain this my last will and testament: My will is that my son Benjamin have and do enjoy that part of my estate which I have already given him in a deed. And further, I give him 5 shillings out of my estate, and that to be his whole share. 2ndly. I give to my two daughters, Susannah and Abigail, besides what they have already received, 5 shillings to each, to be paid out of my estate. 3rdly. I give to my son Samuel the remaining part of my estate, both real and personal, after the sons above mentioned are paid. And my will is that my son Samuel be the executor of this my last will.

Witness: *Jonathan Hills, Jr.,*   BENJAMIN X HILLS, LS.
John Hazeltine, Nathaniel Risley.

Court Record, Page 189—2 April, 1728: Will now exhibited by Samuel Hills, executor. Accepted.

Recorded in Vol. XII, Page 4-5-6-7-8-9.

Hill, Lieut. Jonathan, Hartford. Invt. £1817-19-03. Taken 30 December, 1727, by Ozias Pitkin and Timothy Cowles. Will dated 5 February, Anno Domini 1725-6.

I, Jonathan Hills, Sen., of the Town of Hartford, in the County of Hartford, Colony of Connecticut, in New England, though I am at present in health, am grown into years and know not how soon the times may alter with me nor how soon I must shake hands with all my worldly enjoyment, do make this my last will and testament: I give unto Dorothy, my well-beloved wife, the use and improvement of my dwelling house and the orchard and the inclosure adjoyning to the southward thereof, together with the use and improvement of 1-3 part of all my meadow and upland for and during the term of her natural life. Also I give unto her 1-3 part of all my moveable or personal estate, of what kind or nature soever, to be her own forever and to dispose of the same as she pleases. I give unto my daughter Dorothy, the wife of Caleb Pitkin, £75 over and above what I have already given to him, to be her own forever. I give unto my three granddaughters, Dorothy, Mary and Thankfull, children of my sd. daughter Dorothy, to each a good cow, at the age of 18 years. I give to my daughter Mary Forbes £150 money to be hers forever. I give unto my daughter Thankfull £150 to be her own forever. I give my grandson David, son of my son David Hills, at the age of 21 years, the sum of £5. I give all the rest in residue of my estate, real and personal, whatsoever and wheresoever, to my two sons Jonathan Hills and David Hills, to be equally divided between them, to them and their heirs forever. I make, ordain and appoint my sd. two sons, Jonathan and David Hills, executors.

Witness: *John Kilbourn,*   JONATHAN HILLS, LS.
Nathaniel Wrisly, Thomas Kimberly.

Court Record, Page 170—5 December, 1727: Will now exhibited by Jonathan and David Hills, executors. Proven.

Page 24 (Vol. XI) 7 July, 1730: Jonathan Hills, executor, exhibited an addition to the inventory of £84-08-02.

Hills, Samuel. Court Record, Page 170—5 December, 1727: This Court grant letters of Adms. on the estate of Samuel Hills, late of Glastonbury decd., unto Joseph Hills, brother, provided bond be given. The sd. Joseph Hills, with sufficient security, gave bond accordingly.

Page 287-8-9. Will in Vol. XII, Page 126-7.

Hinsdale, Barnabas, Hartford. Invt. £483-00-00. Taken 17 March, 1725, by John Skinner, Thomas Seymour and Samuel Catlin. Will dated 25 January, 1724-5:

I, Barnabas Hinsdale of Hartford, do make this my last will and testament: I give and bequeath to Martha, my beloved wife, the improvement of 1-2 of my house during the time she remains my widow; 1-3 part of all my moveable estate to be her own forever, and 1-3 part of all my real estate in housing and lands for her improvement during life. I give to my eldest son Barnabas Hinsdale £20 out of my estate (besides what I have given him in and by a deed of gift), to be to him, his heirs and assigns forever. I give all the rest of my estate, both real and personal, unto my children, Jacob, John, Daniel, Amos, Martha, Sarah, Elizabeth and Mary Hinsdale, to be equally divided among them, only Sarah to have £10 and John £15 less in their portions than the other children for the trades they have learned. Upon that account I think it reasonable so much of their portion should be abated. To be to them and their heirs and assigns forever. BARNABAS HINSDALE.

We, the subscribers, the widow and heirs of Barnabas Hinsdale, late of Hartford aforesd. decd., are well satisfied yt what is written on this sheat of paper was the mind and will of ye sd. Barnabas Hinsdale concerning the disposeing of his estate before his decease, and do acquiess in the same to be a settlement of sd. estate as though it had been executed his last will, and do request the Court of Probate to accept of the same for a final settlement of the sd. estate and give order for a dist. thereof to and amongst us according thereunto. In witness whereof we have hereunto set our hands and seals the 9th day of May, Anno. Dom. 1726.

BARNABAS HINSDALE, LS.
JOHN HINSDALE, LS.
AMOS HINSDALE, LS.
MARTHA X HINSDALE, LS.
SARAH X WHITE, LS.
MARY X HINSDALE, LS.
MARTHA X HINSDALE, LS., WIDOW.
JACOB HINSDALE, LS.
DANIEL HINSDALE, LS.
NATHANIEL WHITE, LS.
ELIZABETH X HINSDALE, LS.

Court Record, Page 71—2 March, 1724-5: Adms. to Mrs. Martha Hinsdale, widow, and Jacob Hinsdale, son of sd. deceased.

Page 128—5 May, 1726: An agreement to settle estate according to a drawn will, signed and sealed, now exhibited in Court and accepted. This Court appoint John Skinner, Thomas Seymour and Samuel Catlin to dist. according to the will.

Page 132—5 July, 1726: This Court appoint Martha Hinsdale to be guardian unto her children, John, age 20 years, Daniel 18, and Amos 16 years, they desiring the same. Bond given, £300.

Page 4 (Vol. XI) 7 October, 1729: Jacob Hinsdale, Adms., exhibits an account of his Adms., which this Court accepts, orders recorded and kept on file.

Dist. on File: 4 April, 1738: To the widow Martha Hinsdale, to Martha, to Jacob, to John, to Sarah, to Elizabeth, to Mary, to Daniel, and to Amos Hinsdale. By Samuel Catlin and John Skinner.

Page 27 (Vol. XII) 4 April, 1738: Report of the distributors.

Recorded in Vol. XII, Page 133-4-5.

Holcomb, Joshua, Ensign. Inventory taken 1st of March, 1728, by Joseph Case, James Case and Jeams Hilyer. Will dated 30 March, 1727.

I, Joshua Holcomb, Sen., of Simsbury, do make this my last will and testament: I give to my wife Mary 1-3 part of all my moveable estate for-ever, and the use of the third part of my improveable land, and also use of 3 acres of land joyning to my now dwelling house, and the east end of my house with 1-2 of my cellar, to enjoy during the time of her widow-hood. I give to my son Caleb a piece of land lying under the West Moun-tain called by the name of Caleb's Jerseys, and also 30 acres in the West Mountains north of John Barbour's lott, which sd. land is to him, his heirs and assigns forever. I give to my son Joshua 34 1-2 acres of land lying on the east side of the East Mountains in Farmingtown bounds, lying south of John Burr's farm, to him and his heirs forever. I give to my son Matthew 27 acres of land lying in Farmingtown bounds on the west side of the river at a place commonly called Nodd, and also 12 acres on the east side of the river and on the west side of the East Mountains, south of Jo-seph Woodruff's, in Farmingtown bounds. I give to my son David 1-2 of my land between my house and Jonathan Buttolph's, and his share is to be on the west end of sd. lott. I give unto my son David my house and barn with a third part of the lott which lyeth on the hill against Bissell's meadow, and also half the lott which lyeth on a mountain which is com-monly called Phelps's Mountain. I give unto my son Joell half of my lott which lyeth between my house and John Buttolph's, and his share is to be on the east end of sd. lott, which is next to sd. Buttolph's. Also I give him a third part of that lott which lyeth upon the hill against Bissell's meadow; also I give him half that lott which lyeth on Phelps's Mountain. I give to my son Phineas 14 acres of my land lying north of Terry's land on the mountain towards the falls. I also give him 8 acres of land which lyeth north of Samuel Griswold's. I also give him 9 acres of land north of Alford's lott within the meadow fence. I give unto my four daughters which I had by my first wife, vizt., Thankfull, Experience, Hannah and Elener, 20 shillings to each of them. I give to my daughter Mary £15. I also give unto my daughter Mercy £12. I give unto my daughter Miriam £12. Further, my will is that all my undivided land that is not here mentioned shall be divided amongst my 6 sons, vizt., Caleb, Joshua, Matthew, David, Joell and Phineas. I make my beloved wife Mary Hol-comb and my brother Joseph Hoskins sole executors.

Witness: *Andrew Robee,*   JOSHUA HOLCOMB, SEN., LS.
Josiah Alford, Edward Strickland.

Court Record, Page 187—2 April, 1728: Whereas, Mary Holcomb, widow of Joshua Holcomb, late of Simsbury decd., appeared in Court and declared that she desires the last will and testament of sd. decd. might not be broken, although the testator had disposed of 1-3 part of the real estate for the use and improvement of his wife during her widowhood, praying this Court would order that 1-3 part of sd. real estate be for her improve-ment during life, which by this Court is granted.

Page 58 (Vol. XIII) 1st January, 1739-40: Joel Holcomb, age 16 years, son of Joshua Holcomb, chose his mother Mary Holcomb to be his guardian. Recog., £200.

Holiberd, Joseph. Court Record, Page 130—5 May, 1726: Joseph Holliberd, a minor, 15 years of age, chose James Rogers of New London to be his guardian. Recog., £50.

Page 242. (See Vol. IX.) No date.

Hollister, Jonathan, Wethersfield. Invt of estate in lands:

	£	s	d
To a dwelling with 5 acres and an orchard,	55-00-00		
To four and a half acres at £10 per acre,	45-00-00		
To three and a half acres lying over Hog Brook,	24-00-00		
To four acres of meadow land,	80-00-00		
To forty-nine acres, at	42-00-00		
To a right of land lying on the east side of Rocky Hill,	00-10-00		
To an acre and a half of land taken out of Jacob Crane's lot,	06-00-00		

253-00-00

Taken by Samuel Williams and Joseph Grimes.

Recorded in Vol. XII, Page 175-6-7.

Holman, Samuel. Invt. £219-03-10. Taken 27 February, 1728-9, by Samuel Strong, Jonathan Stiles and John Strong. Will dated 1st January, 1728.

I, Samuel Holman of Windsor, do make this my last will and testament: I give unto my wife Katharine Holman her right and dowry according to law. Also, my will and pleasure is yt my executors shall have free liberty to dispose of my houseing and lands if they think it most advantagious, and do use and improve the money or effects that the houseing and lands produced for the best use and benefit of my two sons, vizt., Samuel and Ebenezer Holman, until they arrive at the age of 21 years, then to be equally divided between them. And in case the sd. executors do not dispose of sd. houseing and lands, then my will and pleasure is yt my two sons aforesd. shall have my houseing and lands to be equally divided between them when they shall arrive to the age of 21 years. Also my will and pleasure is yt my son Samuel Holman shall have a certain cane which was his Grandfather Holman's when he shall arrive at ye age aforesd. I give unto my daughter Abigail Holman, at 18 years of age, all my moveable estate. And in case there be not enough to make equall with my two sons, my will and pleasure is that my two sons pay proportionally so much until she be equal with ym. Further, my will also is that Samuel Haydon of Windsor and my wife Katharine Holman shall be executors and overseers, and guardians to my children.

Witness: *Nathan Gillett, 2nd,*   SAMUEL HOLMAN, LS.
John Allin, Hannah Shelding.

Court Record, Page 213—4 March, 1728-9: Will proven.

Page 67 (Vol. XIII) 3 June, 1740: Samuel Holman, a minor, 19 years of age, chose his uncle Benjamin Roberts to be his guardian. Recog., £200. And this Court appoint Benjamin Roberts of Hartford to be guardian to Ebenezer Holman, a minor, 13 years of age. Recog., £200.

Holmes, John. Court Record, Page 35—3 January, 1723-4: This Court appoint John Janes of Hartford to be guardian unto John Holmes, now residing at Hartford, a minor, 16 years of age, he desireing the same. Recog., £40.

Invt. in Vol. XII, Page 92.

Hopkins, Consider. Invt. £624-01-00. Taken 21 February, 1726-7, by Thomas Shepherd, William Gaylord and Ebenezer Wells.

Court Record, Page 147—7 March, 1726-7: Adms. granted to Elizabeth Hopkins, widow of sd. decd. The sd. Elizabeth Hopkins, Capt. Samuel Sedgewick and William Gaylord, all of Hartford, acknowledged themselves joyntly and severally bound in a recog. of £700.

Page 84 (Vol. XI) 6 March, 1732-3: John Hopkins, a minor, 18 years, and Elizabeth 17 years, chose their mother Elizabeth Hopkins to be their guardian. And this Court appoint Elizabeth Hopkins, widow, to be guardian unto Asa Hopkins 13 years, Consider 10, and Elias 7 years, all children of Consider Hopkins, late decd. Recog., £200.

Page 173 (Vol. XIV, Probate Side) : We, the subscribers, being the widow, children and heirs to the estate of Mr. Consider Hopkins, late of Hartford decd., have mutually agreed to divide the estate of the sd. decd. to us the sd. widow and heirs in the following manner :

	£ s d
To the widow, Elizabeth Hopkins, a brass kettle,	7-00-00
A warming pan and skillett, £2; a iron pott, £1-10; a box iron and heaters, 10 shillings,	4-00-00
A paire of stilyards, 7s; 16 3-4 pounds of pewter at 6s per lb, £4-19-00,	5-06-00
Two wheels, a churn, 10 shillings; a little table, 5 shillings; 2 pails, 8 shillings; 2 trammells, £1-05,	2-18-00
A meshing tub, 12s; a mare, £36; 4 cows, £51; 15 sheep and 8 lambs, £12-00-00,	106-12-00
1 swine, £12; low case of drawers, 25s; plain chest, 7s; great table, 14s,	6-06-00
Bedd and bedding,	13-12-07
1-3 part of the lands on the north side, with 1-3 part of the buildings,	
To John Hopkins, the eldest son of the sd. decd., land in the West Division, from the commons to the west end, excluding the 20 acres with the buildings,	588-00-00

	£	s	d
A swine, set of cart boxes and brands, £7; a shave and narrow axe and four yerlings,		15-02-00	
To Elizabeth: Received,		129-06-09	
Pewter, bedding and hetchell, £19-15-00; 2 heifers and paid by Elias, £16-08-00,		36-03-00	
To Asa: Received, £161-00-00; a yoke of steers, £16,		177-00-00	
1-3 part of the land in New Hartford,		106-13-04	
Right in the west end of the West Division lott,		22-06-08	
To Consider: a horse and yoke of steers,		65-00-00	
A sword and belt, 35s; 1-3 part of the lands in New Hartford, £106-13-04,		108-08-04	
1-2 of the land in Waterbury is		60-00-00	
Right in the west end of the West division lott,		72-11-08	
To Elias: a yoke of cattle,		34-00-00	
1-3 part of the land in New Hartford,		106-13-04	
1-2 of the land in Waterbury, £60,			
£105-06-08 rights in the west end of the West Division lott,		105-06-08	

To which agreements we, the sd. widow, children and heirs, have hereunto set our hands and seals, and acknowledged the same before the Court of Probate in Hartford, in the County of Hartford, on the 2nd day of April, 1745.

> ELIZABETH X HOPKINS, LS.   JOHN HOPKINS, LS.
> NEHEMIAH MESSENGER, and ELIZABETH HIS WIFE.
> CONSIDER HOPKINS, LS.   ELIZABETH X HOPKINS, LS.
> GUARDIAN TO ELIAS HOPKINS.

Invt. in Vol. XII, Page 214.

Hossington, John. Invt. £179-14-08. Taken 15 December, 1728, by Isaac Hart and Hezekiah Hooker.

Court Record, Page 209—2 January, 1728-9: Adms. granted to Elizabeth Hossington, widow, and Isaac Hart. This Court do appoint Elizabeth Hossington to be guardian unto her children, viz., Elizabeth, 11 years of age, and Elisha 8 years. Recog., £100.

Page 16 (Vol. XI) 7 April, 1730: Isaac Hart of Farmington, Adms., prays for longer time to make up his Adms. on sd. estate. Granted.

Page 93—3 July, 1733: Isaac Hart, Adms., now exhibits an account of his Adms. amounting to the sum of £80, which account is accepted, ordered recorded and filed.

Hubbard, John, Middletown. Court Record, Page 147—7 March, 1726-7: Adms. granted to Mary Hubbard, widow of sd. decd. And the sd. Mary Hubbard and George Hubbard recog. £500.

Page 328.

Add. Invt. in Vol. XI, Page 143.

Humphrey, Capt. Samuel. Died 20 September, 1725. Inventory taken 5 November, 1725, by Joseph Case, Lt. Samuel Pettebone and James Hilyer.

Court Record, Page 107—9 November, 1725: Adms. granted unto Mary Humphrey, widow.

Page 143—3 January, 1726-7: This Court grant further time unto Joseph Cornish, Adms., to make up his account.

Page 54 (Vol. XI) 5 October, 1731: The Adms. exhibits an account of his Adms. Accepted and ordered to be kept on file.

Page 55—5 October, 1731: Mary Humphrey, age 15 years, daughter of Capt. Samuel Humphrey, made choice of her father-in-law Joseph Cornish to be her guardian. Recog., £100. Also the sd. Joseph Cornish to be guardian unto Hezekiah Humphrey, age 12 years and 8 months. Recog., £100. Joseph Case of Simsbury appointed guardian unto Hepzibah Humphrey, daughter of sd. decd. Recog., £100.

Page 55 (Vol. XIII) 13 September, 1739: Bathsheba Humphrey, age 14 years, daughter of Capt. Samuel Humphrey, late of Simsbury, her guardian John Humphrey desires a discharge, and the sd. minor chose James Hilyer to be her guardian.

See the Page before the Index in Vol. XIV for the following receipts:

Then received of Joseph Cornish of Simsbury, Adms. of the estate of Capt. Samuel Humphrey of Simsbury decd., the sum of £44-00-00 money in full of all demands I have for moveable estate and for use of house and lands, and all other demands I have or can make, except one certain note of £44, bearing date with this discharge. I say received of me.
Witness: *Michael Humphrey,*   "HEKIAH" HUMPHREY,
      Ephraim Griffin.

March the 5th, 1739-40.
Then received of Joseph Cornish, Adms. upon the estate of our honoured father Samuel Humphrey decd., the sum of £16-00-00 in full of all our demands upon the moveable estate. As witness our hands in the presence of

                                   JAMES HILLYER,
                                   MARY HILLYER.
Witness: *Joseph Smith,*
      Isaac Pettibone.

March 5, 1739-40.
Then received of Joseph Cornish, Adms. upon the estate of our honoured father, the sum of £22-00-00 in full of our demands of our part of the moveable estate. As witness our hands:
In presence of   ISAAC PETTIBONE,
James Hillyer, Jr.,   HEPSIBAH PETTIBONE.
Joseph Smith.

March 5, 1739-40.
Then received of Joseph Cornish, Adms. upon the estate of our honoured father Samuel Humphrey decd., the sum of £22-00-00 in full of our
demands of our parts of the moveable estate. As witness our hands:

LUCY SMITH,
JOSEPH SMITH.

Simsbury, March ye 5: 1739-40: Then received of Joseph Cornish,
Adms. upon the estate of our honoured father Capt. Samuel Humphrey
decd., the sum of £22-00-00 in full of all demands of the moveable estate,
as I am guardian for Bathsheba Humphrey. As witness my hand.

In presence of *Isaac Pettibone,*   JAMES HILLYER, JR.
                 Jerusha Smith.

Invt. in Vol. XII, Page 191. Add. Invt. in Vol. XI, Page 85-6.

Hunt, Joseph, Stafford. Died 21 December, 1728. Invt. £82-15-11.
Taken by John Yeomans and John Dunham. An inventory of the real
estate, valued at £192-00-11. Apprised 31 October, 1729, by us, John
Dunham and Amos Richardson.

Court Record, Page 213—22 February, 1728-9: This Court grant
¹etters of Adms. unto Anne Hunt, widow, and Nathaniel Hunt, brother of
ₜd. decd.

Page 34 (Vol. IX) 9 December, 1730: Nathaniel Hunt and Anna
Hunt, Adms., exhibited an account of their Adms., which this Court accepted, and orders it to be kept on file.

Page 323.

Judd, Jonathan, Middletown, east side the river. Died 28 August, 1725. Inventory taken by Samuel Hall and Ebenezer Hurlbut.

Court Record, Page 105—5 October, 1725: This Court grant letters
of Adms. on the estate of Jonathan Judd unto Hannah Judd, widow, and
Francis Smith, of sd. Middletown, provided bond be given as the law
directs.

Invt. in Vol. XII, Page 224.

Judd, Samuel, Farmington. Invt. £861-07-09. Taken 21 February,
1727-8, by Thomas Judd, Isaac Cowles and William Judd.

Court Record, Page 177—5 March, 1727-8: Adms. granted to Daniel
Judd and Abigail Judd, widow of sd. decd.

Page 192—7 May, 1728: This Court appoint Daniel Judd of Farmington to be guardian to Anne Judd, a minor, 16 years of age. Recog., £100.

Page 14 (Vol. XI) 3 March, 1730: Daniel Judd, Adms., exhibits an account of his Adms. Accepted. Order to distribute: To the widow, £27-16-05, with her right of dowry; and the rest of the estate to be dist. to Sarah and Anna Judd, children, to each of them the sum of £360-06-09. And appoint Capt. Thomas Judd, Isaac Cowles and William Judd distributors.

Page 26-232-3-4.

Add. Invt. in Vol. XII, Page 85.

Judd, Thomas, Farmington. Invt. £447-00-00. Taken 1st February, 1724-5, by Samuel Woodruff, Isaac Merrells and Jacob Merrells. Inventory of sd. estate as followeth:
Land in the North Division against Simsbury, 85 acres.

	£ s d
Land in the 5th Division, 85 acres,	8-10-00
Land in the 4th Division, 85 acres,	8-10-00
Land in the 3rd Division, 85 acres,	8-10-00

Additional inventory of £30-00-00. Taken 27 November, 1727, by Thomas Smith and Joseph Wadsworth. Will dated 24 April, 1724.

The last will and testament of Thomas Judd of Hartford is as followeth: I give to my eldest son Thomas Judd, where his house stands, land that bounds from the highway south next to heirs of John Judd decd. 17 rods; then a straight line to the corner of the lott that was Skinner's, next Lt. Seamore's; then east from that into Hartford bounds 24 rods; so a straight line from sd. 17 rods to a stake 24 rods into Hartford bounds, next the highway; and the acre and the half given out of Farmington highway, the sd. land butting north on sd. highway is in Farmington bounds and Hartford bounds. I give to my son Joseph, next the highway (on the south side of the highway), 14 acres, to butt east on the little highway, west on that given to Thomas, so runs south till he has sd. 14 1-2 acres; the rest of sd. lott on the south side the highway from that given to Thomas and Joseph, I give to Joseph and Ebenezer, to be equally divided between them. Further, I give to Joseph and Ebenezer, in Farmington bounds, my right in fifth lott in that called the West Division. I give to my son Ebenezer the lott on the north side of the highway, and my house on sd. lott, on these conditions, he allowing his brother Joseph (if he needs it) the 1-2 of sd. house till he can provide one for himself, and give him 30 days work in building. Further, it is my will that my daughters, while they live single, shall have liberty of makeing my house their home, to be allowed fireroom, a lodging room and cellar room for their necessary use without paying for it, they providing other comforts for themselves. Also, they are to have a garden allowed them. I give to my daughter Sarah, besides what I formerly gave her, 8 acres of land in Farmington bounds, in the lott I bought of Deacon Daniel Porter, to be laid to her husband's 12 acres in sd. lott, the rest of sd. lott being assigned. More, 30 acres I give to my daughters Elizabeth and Joanna, to be equally divided between them. I give to my daughter Mary my lott in the North Division in Farmington, next Simsbury. I give to my daughter Rachel in Farmington my lott called the third lott in the West Division. I give to my daughter Abigail my lott called the fourth in the West Division. I give to Thomas, Joseph and Ebenezer the arms called theirs, and to Thomas a third right in the timber chain, in the collar, the horse hames called his, and to Joseph and Ebenezer the plow irons and cart irons, yoke and horse gears. I give to Thomas, Elizabeth and Joanna my right in a tract of land in Farmington bounds not laid out, being at the southwest corner, next to Waterbury bounds. I give the remainder of the boggy meadow in Farmington bounds, south of Thomas, to Joseph and Ebenezer. I give all my moveables not here given away, excepting the old oxen and my horse, I say all the rest, as neat cattle, sheep or swine, and all moveables within doors, to my daughters, Elizabeth, Joanna, Mary, Rachel and Abigail, to be equally divided amongst them all, except Mary, who is to have a half part or half so much of the moveables because she has it elsewhere. Further, my will is that my part in the Copper Mines shall belong in equal share amongst all my sons and daughters. I appoint my sons Thomas, Joseph and Ebenezer to be executors.

Witness: *Isaac Merrells,*   THOMAS JUDD, LS.
Joanna Richards, Noah Merrells.

Court Record, Page 55—29 September, 1724: Will proven. This Court do appoint Joseph Judd of Hartford to be guardian unto his sister Abigail Judd, 12 years of age. Recog., £50.

Page 68—2 February, 1724-5: This Court do appoint Ebenezer Judd of Hartford to be guardian unto Rachel Judd, 17 years of age. Recog., £50.

Page 69—2 February, 1724-5: Report of the distribution made by Ebenezer and Joseph Judd, executors, according to the last will of the decd.

Page 320-1-2-3-4.

Kellogg, John, Hartford. Invt. £1121-00-00. Taken 28 September, 1725, by Jacob Griswold and Josiah Belding.
Court Record, Page 104—5 October, 1725: This Court grant Adms. unto Sarah Kellogg, widow of sd. decd.

Kelsey, Elizabeth. Court Record, Page 118—1 March, 1725-6: This Court grant letters of Adms. on the estate of Elizabeth Kelsey, late of Windsor decd., unto Thomas Kelsey of Windsor and Josiah Loomis of Simsbury. Recog., £200.

Page 242.

Kilbourn, Sarah, Farmingtown. 14 July, 1724: An inventory of the estate of Sarah Kilbourn decd., late of Wethersfield, a part of which now is in Farmingtown. And being desired to apprise the same by Mr. George Kilbourn, Adms. to the sd. pt of estate, we whose names are under-written, being sworn all under oath as the law directs, to apprise the forementioned part of the foresd. Kilbourn's estate, it being in outlands, is apprised as followeth:

	£ s d
To 1-2 of a lott in a division south of the Town between the mountains, called 92 acres,	74-00-00
To 9 acres north of the Town east of the river,	02-00-00
To a lott west of the Town, 87 acres so-called,	09-15-00
Total is, errors excepted,	85-15-00

Thomas Bird, Isaac Cowles, Sen., William Judd.

Court Record, Page 45—7 April, 1724: Adms. to George Kilbourn, son of sd. decd.

Page 51—14 July, 1724: George Kilbourn, Adms., exhibits an account of his Adms., which this Court accepts. Order to distribute:

	£ s d
To the heirs of Ebenezer Kilbourn, eldest son of sd decd.,	27-00-08
To George Kilbourn,	19-01-04
To Joseph Kilbourn,	19-01-04
To the heirs of Abraham Kilbourn,	17-10-04

And whereas, Sarah Andrews and Mary Butler, the two daughters of sd. deceased, having formerly received more than their proportion of the estate of sd. decd., therefore cannot be allowed any part in this dist. And this Court do appoint Thomas Bird, Isaac Cowles and William Judd, of Farmington, to dist. the estate accordingly.

Page 8.

Lattimer, Luther, Wethersfield. Inventory taken 18 December, 1722, by William Goodrich, George Kilbourn and Isaac Riley.

Court Record, Page 1—1st January, 1722-3: Adms. to Mrs. Elizabeth Lattimore.

Page 197—6 August, 1728: Elizabeth Carter alias Lattimore, relict of Luther Lattimore, late of Wethersfield decd., and Adms. on sd. estate, exhibited an accompt of Adms. on sd. estate amounting to the sum of £36-13-02, which account this Court accepts and orders to be kept on file.

Page 37 (Vol. XII) 10 December, 1735: Wickham Lattimer, age 15 years, son of Luther Lattimer, chose his father-in-law Jonathan Carter to be his guardian.

Invt. in Vol. XII, Page 88.

Lawrence, Capt. John, of Boston, who went to sea nine years ago and never was heard of since his departure. Invt. £67-00-08. Taken by James Poyson and Peter Landue.

Court Record, Page 173—2 January, 1727-8: Adms. granted to Mary Ann Lawrence, widow of sd. decd.

Page 193—3 May, 1728: Mary Ann Lawrence, Adms., exhibited an account of her Adms. and reported £67-00-05 debts due from the estate. This Court order so much of sd. estate be set out to the sd. Mary Lawrence, widow, as may be necessary for her support.

Page 165-6-185-6-7-8.

Lee, John, Farmington. Inventory taken 27 June, 1723, by John Hart, Sen., Samuel Judd and Josiah Hart.

I, John Lee, of ye Town of Farmingtown, do make this my last will and testament: I give to my wife Elizabeth Lee her rights of dower. Unto my son Jonathan Lee, besides what I have already given him, 3 shillings. Unto my son Samuel Lee, besides what I have given him and done for him in his settlement, I give and bequeath unto him and to his heirs and assigns forever, 1 parcell of land of about 7 acres which I have near to a place called the Pond River; also all the right, title and interest belonging unto me from my father's estate in ye mountany lands lying southerly of ye reserved land and east of ye division of lands between ye mountains; also all my right, title and interest to and in all ye lotts drawn in my father's right in ye divisions of land lying west of the reserved land and that lye southward of ye road commonly used in going from Farmingtown to Litchfield, and my right is 1-2 part of sd. lotts; also I give to my sd. son Samuel my tract of land of about 6 acres lying northward of Gilbert's River, which I purchased of Thomas Wadsworth; all which parcells of land lye within ye Township of Farmingtown. Unto each of my daughters, vizt., Mary Newell, Elizabeth Langton and Ruth Lee, I give and bequeath so much, to be paid out of my estate by my executor within four years after my decease, as to make up to each of them for their portion, with what they have already received from me, ye sum of £40; and my sd. daughter Elizabeth Langton shall have my great brass kettle towards her part. Unto my grandson Nathan Newell I give and bequeath one of my cut-lashes, to be delivered to his father to be kept for him. Unto my son Hezekiah Lee, now living with me, whom I do constitute and ordain sole executor, to him and his heirs I do give all the remainder of my estate, both real and personal, whatsoever and wheresoever it is; and what of my real estate I have given to my aforesd. wife for her use and improvement during her natural life, after her decease it shall revert unto, be and belong to him ye aforesd. Hezekiah Lee, his heirs and assigns forever.

Witness: *Samuel Whitman,*   JOHN LEE, LS.
John Hooker, Sen., Daniel Andrews, Sen.

Court Record, Page 20—4 June, 1723: Will now exhibited, with inventory, and proven.

Invt. in Vol. XII, Page 213-14.

Lewis, Sergt. Samuel. Invt. £894-09-00. Taken by Isaac Cowles, Daniel Judd and Isaac Lewis.

Court Record, Page 114—1st February, 1725-6: Adms. granted to Mary Lewis, widow, and Samuel Lewis, eldest son.

Page 144—3 January, 1726-7: Mary Lewis and Samuel Lewis, Adms., exhibited an account of their Adms. Paid in debts and charges, £85-05-11. Accepted. Invt. with additions, £924-05-07; subtracting £85-05-11, there remains £838-19-00 to be distributed. Order to Mary Lewis, relict, widow, £44-18-10 with dower; to Samuel Lewis, eldest son, £235-19-00, which is his double portion of sd. estate; to John, Nehemiah, Nathan and Josiah Lewis, to each of them, £117-19-06; and to Hannah Gridley, £86-06-00, she having formerly received £31-12-00; the rest of the children of sd. decd., which is their single portion of sd. estate. And appoint Isaac Cowles, Daniel Judd and John Porter, of Farmington, distributors. This Court do appoint Mary Lewis of Farmington, widow, to be guardian unto her children, vizt., Nathan Lewis, 20 years, and Josiah Lewis, 17 years of age. Rec., £200.

Page 147—7 March, 1726-7: Report of dist. Adms. granted a *Quietus Est.*

Page 184—12 June (1726), 1728: Samuel Lewis of Farmington moves this Court that he be allowed, for serving his father, Samuel Lewis, decd., 7 years after he was 21 years of age, to the value of £140 out of the estate. Resisted by the mother, Mary Lewis.

Page 186—May, 1728: This Court decides the case not cognizable in this Court and dissmist the case, with costs to Samuel Lewis, who appealed to the Superior Court.

Page 174-228.

Long, Jerusha, Hartford. Died 11 January, 1722-3. Inventory taken 29 January, 1722-3, in Coventry by Samuel Parker and William Davenport; 5 April, 1723, in Hartford by John Webster and John Kellogg.

Court Record, Page 17—2 May, 1723: Joseph Long of Hartford and William Long of Coventry exhibit will, and though no executor was appointed as such, yet persons are desired in sd. will to pay her just debts and make dist. of the surplusage of her estate according to the will. Allowed to be proven. Adms. on sd. estate was granted to William Long and David Ensign, brethren to sd. deceased, *Cum Testamento Annexo.*

Page 20—7 May, 1723: Inventory now exhibited.

Page 43—3 March, 1723-4: William Long and David Ensign, Adms., exhibit account of Adms. Allowed. Decree to dist. to brethren and sisters of sd. decd.: To heirs of Mary Bushnell decd., to Joseph Long, to

William Long, to David Ensign, Jr., to Sarah Culver, and to Hannah Moore. By Samuel Parker, William Davenport and Ens............tor of Coventry.

Page 119—1st March, 1725-6: Report of dist. exhibited and ordered on file.

Loomis, Benjamin. Court Record, Page 185—21st April, 1726: Adms. account on the estate of Benjamin Loomis, late of Windsor decd., was now exhibited in Court by Ann Loomis, Adms. on sd. estate, amounting to the sum of .... which account is allowed in Court and ordered to be kept on file.

Page 145-6-292-3-4-5.

Lord, Elisha, Hartford. Invt. £2855-13-06. Moveables, £883-15-03. Taken 30 June, 1725, by Robert Sandford, John Skinner and Joseph Gilbert. Will dated 13 April, 1725.

I, Elisha Lord, being now of sound mind and memory, yet not knowing how soon God may put an end to my transitory life, I do hereby dispose of that estate God hath graciously given me. For that end I do make this and declare it to be my last will and testament, hereby making void all former wills by me made and declared: Imprimis: I give my soul to God, of whom I have my choice, and who hath redeemed it in and by the death of his beloved Son, with whom I have hope to reign forever. Item. I give to my beloved wife Mary Lord 1-3 part of all my real estate during the term of her natural life. Item. I give unto her 1-3 part of my personal estate forever. Item. The remainder of all my estate, real and personal, my just debts and funeral charges being paid, I give as followeth: To my son John Haynes Lord and to his heirs forever, I give and bequeath all ye remainder of my estate, real and personal, ye following legacies by me hereafter given being deducted. And in case my sd. son shall dye before he shall come of age, and without lawfull issue, then I bequeath to my loving wife the whole of my moveable estate forever, with the improvement of ye whole of my real estate during her natural life, and at her decease ye same to descend to my three brothers, Richard Lord, Epaphrus Lord and Ichabod Lord, and to their heirs forever, in equal proportion, to be divided according to inventory. Item. In case of this descent, I do hereby ordain and appoint my sd. three brothers, in equall proportion, to pay to my three sisters, Jerusha Whiting, Mary Pitkin and Elizabeth Lord, or to those that may represent them, £50 to each of them. But in case either of them dye before ye sd. legacies shall become due, ye survivor or survivors of them shall receive the whole. Item. In case of ye forementioned descent, I will and ordain my forenamed three brothers, in equal part, to pay to my brother Theodore Woodbridge the sum of £50; but in case he shall dye before this my will shall take place, not leaving lawfull issue, I appoint ye sd. legacies to remain in my three brothers' hands. Item. I do appoint, in case ye forementioned descent take place, that my aforenamed three brothers shall pay the aforenamed legacies within a year after this my will shall take place. Item. I do hereby appoint and constitute my beloved wife to be the sole executrix of this my last will and testament. Lastly, I desire my executrix to buy and give a silver cup to the First Church in Hartford for their use in their Communion. In confirmation of all and every the above mentioned premises, I have hereunto set my hand and seal this 13 day of April, in the year of 1725.

Signed and sealed and delivered
in presence of *Timothy Woodbridge,*   ELISHA LORD, LS.
Abigail Woodbridge, Elizabeth X Fox.

Court Record, Page 83—4 May, 1725: Will now exhibited by Mrs. Mary Lord.

Page 93—6 July, 1725: Invt. exhibited and proven.

Page 144—3 January, 1726-7: This Court appoint Mrs. Mary Lord to be guardian to her son John Haynes Lord, a minor, about 2 years of age. Recog., £500.

Loveman Children. Court Record, Page 100—7 September, 1725: Elisha Loveman, 16 years of age, chose Capt. Thomas Wells to be his guardian. And this Court appoint David Hollister of Glastonbury to be guardian to Mary Loveman 11 years, Benjamin 9 years, and Elizabeth 2 years of age, children of Thomas Loveman, Jr. This Court appoint Thomas Loveman, son of Thomas Loveman decd., to be guardian to his brother Joseph, 13 years of age, and his sister Sarah Loveman, 4 years of age. Recog., £50.

Page 127—28 April, 1726: This Court appoint Thomas Wells to be guardian unto Elisha Loveman, 17 years of age.

Recorded in Vol. XII, Page 103-4.

Mansfield, John and Sarah, of Windsor. No inventory. Will dated 1st February, 1726-7.

In the name of God, amen. I, John Mansfield and Sarah Mansfield of Windsor, in the County of Hartford, Colony of Connecticut, in New England, both being very aged and yet through the mercy of God maintaining a good measure of that understanding and memory that he hath been pleased to bestow upon us, do make and ordain this to be our last will and testament: First, we comit our souls to God in Jesus Christ our Saviour, and our body to the earth to be decently entered. As for my estate, real and personal, my just debts and funeral expenses being paid by our exacer., we will, devise and bequeath as followeth: And first, we give to our daughter Mary Searles, wife of James Searles, of North Hampton, £25 besides what she has already received. And next, we give son Cornelius Phelps and his wife Sarah all our moveable estate. The sd. James Searles and his wife is to receive their £25 within two years after our decease. And our son and daughter, Cornelius Phelps and his wife, they are to have the improvement of our effects from this time, only we to have the use of them as long as we live. And I do hereby nominate and appoint our son Cornelius Phelps to be our executor. In witness whereof that this is our last will and testament, we the sd. John Mansfield and Sarah Mansfield have hereunto put our hands and seals.

JOHN MANSFIELD, LS.
SARAH MANSFIELD.

Signed, sealed and delivered this as their last will and testament in the presence of us: *Hezekiah Persons,*
Robert Barrett.

Court Record, Page 170—5 December, 1727: Will exhibited by Cornelius Phelps, executor. Proven.

Agreement on File.

Mark, William, Middletown. Whereas, William Mark, late of Middletown decd., having estate in his lifetime not disposed of, both real and personal, the widow, Mary Mark, William, Joseph and Jonathan Mark, sons, and Mary and Sarah, daughters of the sd. decd., being all of lawfull age and desirous that the estate of the deceased may be settled in peace and love, have agreed as followeth:

To a small house claboarded and shingled, two loos floars, and 3-4 of an acre of land the house stands upon; to one acre and 3-4 of poor boggy meadow, and to the household goods and husbandry utensils and shoemaker tools and apparrell, one cow and 3 swine, 1 cowhide and calfskin.

We, the above named widow and children, have agreed as follows: To the widow, a third part of the house and lands during her lifetime; the other two parts to the two daughters, Mary and Sarah Marks; the widow and daughters paying the debts and receiving the dues, viz., each one to pay their equal part of debts and also receive their equal part of dues; and to have the cow and swine. The apparrell divided among the three sons as they have agreed to; the household goods divided between the widow and two daughters as they have agreed. To William Mark, hors, traces, color and hames, a pair of iron fetters and a broad hoe. The remainder of the husbandry utensils and shoemakers' tools to the widow and 2 daughters as they all have agreed.

To about 700 acres of land at Dunstable, in Boston Government, with all the lawfull rights belonging to itt, which we the above-named have agreed to divide equally (excepting William Mark, eldest son, having a double part). And in confirmation of the above-written agreement we have this 3 day of August, 1728, set to our hands and affixed our seals.

MARY MARK, LS.	JONATHAN MARK, LS.
WILLIAM MARK, LS.	MARY MARK, LS.
JOSEPH MARK, LS.	SARAH MARK, LS.

Witness: *Joseph Rockwell,*
Jonathan Smith, Jr.

Court Record, Page 196—6 August, 1728: An agreement exhibited in Court for the settlement of William Mark's estate. Accepted.

Recorded in Vol. XII, Page 27-8.

Marsh, John. Invt. £209-10-00. Taken 1st August, 1727, by John Skinner and Hezekiah Goodwin. Will dated 1726.

The last will and testament of John Marsh, Sen., of Hartford, in the County of Hartford and Colony of Connecticut, in New England:

As God hath given the earth to the children of man, divideing it to every one severally as He will, and doth induldge to them ye liberty of disposeing their worldly estate in a testimentary way to such as are to succeed them in the injoyment thereof, and their doing this seasonably and in a just and prudent manner being a likely means to prevent after trouble and contention about it, therefore I, who am old and now languishing under these delays of nature which forbode a speedy desolution of it, do, with submission to the will of God, make the following disposition of that part of the earth which through His goodness is continued in my possession:

Imp. My will is yt all my just debts and funeral expenses be first paid without fraud or delay.

Item. I give to each of my daughters now living, besides what they have already received, £10, to be paid within a year after my decease, either out of my lands at inventory price, or in current pay, at the election of my executors. Yet with this proviso, that they bear their several proportions of the debts and charges before mentioned.

Item. I give to the children of my daughter lately deceased £10 over and above what she hath received in her lifetime, to be divided equally among them and paid as the abovesd. sum and upon the same condition.

Item. I give to my son-in-law, Joseph Pratt, 5 shillings.

Item. I give the rest of my sd. estate, that is to say, all my lands not otherwise disposed of, whether divided or undivided, to my sons, to be equally divided between them, excepting that I give 40 shillings more to my eldest son than to either of his brothers.

Lastly, I do appoint and constitute my sons executors.

Witness: *Samuel Green,*   JOHN X MARSH, LS.
Hezekiah Goodwin, John Day.

Court Record, Page 162—27 August, 1727: Will proven, ordered recorded and kept on file.

Page 174—8 January, 1727-8: Capt. John Marsh, Lt. Nathaniel Marsh, Capt. Joseph Marsh and Jonathan Marsh, sons, heirs and executors of the last will and testament of John Marsh, late of Hartford decd., now exhibited an agreement under their hands and seals for a settlement of sd. estate to and amongst the sd. heirs, and before this Court acknowledged the same to be their free act and deed, which agreement is by this Court accepted and ordered to be recorded and kept on file. Signed and sealed.

Dist. File (no date) : Estate of John Marsh late of Lebanon, Nathaniel and Jonathan Marsh of Hartford, are held and firmly bound to pay unto Joseph Talcott, Judge of the Court of Probate, £80-10-00, the conditions being: As John Marsh decd. bequeathed to his four daughters, to Sarah £10, to Hannah £10, to Ann £10, to the children of Hepzibah decd. £10, and to his son-in-law John Pratt 5 shillings, if these legacies are truly paid, then this obligation to be void.

Witness: *Hezekiah Wyllys,*
  Samuel Talcott.

NOTE: *It is probable that the broken page record related to this case.*

Invt. in Vol. XII, Page 230.

Mather, Rev. Samuel, Windsor. Invt. £106-00-00. Taken 11 April, 1728, by John Allin and Jonathan Stiles.

Agreement on File: This writing witnesseth an agreement of the heirs of the Rev. Samuel Mather, late of Windsor decd., that hath not already received their full portions of the sd. estate. Joseph Mather, one of the sons (being deceased), had received in his lifetime his portion of sd. estate, and also Samuel Mather hath already received his part of the estate, and quitclaims to the rest of the heirs. And it is agreed by the rest of sd. heirs, viz., Asrahiah Mather, Nathaniel Mather and John Mather, for the settlement of sd. estate.

    AZ: MATHER, LS. JOHN MATHER, LS.
    NATH: MATHER, LS. SAMUEL MATHER, LS.

Court Record, Page 196—6 August, 1728: An agreement for the settlement of the estate of Rev. Samuel Mather was now exhibited, accepted, and ordered to be kept on file.

Mather, William. Court Record, Page 157—6 June, 1726: This Court do appoint Abigail Taylor of Wethersfield to be guardian unto her son William Mather, a minor, 5 years of age in August last. Recog., £50.

Page 249-50.

Invt. in Vol. XII, Page 150.

Matson, John, Simsbury. Died 11 May, 1728. Invt. £382-18-04. Taken by John Higley and Samuel Griswold. Will dated 28 May, 1725.

I, John Matson, Sen., yeoman, do on this 28 day of May, 1725, make, ordain and appoint this my last will and testament: I give to my eldest son, John Matson, Jr., the lott or parcell of land which I bought by way of exchange of my brother George Haies, being half of his whole lott commonly called the upper meadow lott, to him and his heirs forever.

And whereas I have given him before, by several deeds, severall tracts of land, now this is to cut him off from coming in for any more double portion, and it shall be in full of his portion together with the money he stands now indebted to me, and daily supplies and helps from and by me. I give unto my other two sons, Joshua and Edward Matson, my tract or a parcell of land containing 200 acres given to me by the Town, called the division land, in sd. Simsbury, in equal shares, to them and their heirs forever. I give unto my wife Mary Matson 1-2 of all the remaining part of my estate, both real and personal, as houses, barn, cattle, sheep and swine, and household furniture, and lands and meadows, that is to say, the houses, barn, orchard, land and the meadows, to possess and injoy during her natural life; and the cattle, sheep, swine and household furniture to do as she see good and at her own disposal at her will and pleasure. I give unto my daughter Elizabeth and my sd. two sons, Joshua and Edward Matson, the other half part of my sd. remaining estate, both real and personal, as houses, barn, orchard, cattle, sheep, swine and household furniture, to be equally divided between them, they paying out of the same the sum of £60 in current money or bills of credit of sd. Colony, that is to say, £20 unto my daughter Mary, now the wife of Ebenezer Lamson, and £20 unto my daughter Jane, now the wife of George Hayes, Junior, and £20 unto my daughter Esther, now single woman or maiden, the payment to be well and truly made within or at the expiration of three years after my decease. I give also unto my sd. daughter and sons, Elizabeth, Joshua and Edward, after the decease of their mother, my now dear and loving wife, all the abovesd. half of my real estate which I have left for her to injoy during her life, to them and each of them an equal share. I appoint my well-beloved wife Mary Matson and my trusty friends John Case, Sen., and Jonathan Westover, both of sd. Simsbury, my executors.
Witness: *Samuel Hays,*   JOHN MATSON, SEN., LS.
Jonathan Holcomb, Abraham Dibel.

Court Record, Page 194—3 July, 1728: Capt. Jonathan Westover and Mary Matson now appeared and accepted the executorship.
Page 20 (Vol. XI) 28 May, 1730: Edward Matson, a minor, chose Daniel House to be his guardian. Recog., £50.

Page 109-10-11.

Meakins, Joseph, Hartford. Died 29 January, 1724-5. Inventory taken by Timothy Cowles, Charles Buckland and Daniel Dickinson.
Court Record, Page 77—6 April, 1725: Adms. granted to John and Samuel Meakins, brothers of sd. decd.
Page 126—5 April, 1726: John and Samuel Meakins exhibited an account of their Adms. Accepted. And this Court appoints John Meakins to be guardian to Joseph Meakins, age 7 years, to Sarah 11, to Abigail 4 years of age. And Samuel Meakins is appointed guardian to Mary Meakins, age 12 years, Hannah 8, and Rebeckah 2 years.

Page 93 (Vol. XI) 3 July, 1733: Hannah Meakins, 16 years of age, chose William Pitkin to be her guardian. Recog., £100.

Page 94—3 July, 1733: Abigail Meakins, age 12 years, chose her uncle Thomas Spencer to be her guardian. Recog., £100. And John Meakins, a brother of the decd., to be guardian to Rebeckah Meakins, age 12 years. Recog., £100.

Page 20 (Vol. XIII) 7 December, 1737-8: Rebeckah Meakins, a minor, age 14 years, daughter of Joseph Meakins, late of Hartford: Lt. John Meakins, sometime her guardian, now resigns the trust, and the sd. Rebeckah chose Thomas Hurlbut of Wethersfield to be her guardian. Recog., £200.

Page 167-8.

Meakins, Thomas, Hartford. Inventory taken 5 June, 1723, by Nathaniel Goodwin and John Edwards.

Court Record, Page 21—June 25, 1723: Sarah Meakins, widow, Adms., exhibited inventory. Estate insolvent. And £12-00-00 was set out to the widow for her subsistence.

Merrells, Jacob, Hartford. Court Record, Page 85—4 May, 1725: Adms. to Mrs. Abigail Merrells, widow.

Page 324.

Merrells, Nathaniel, Hartford. Invt. £190-19-00. Taken 15 May, 1725, by Samuel Sedgewick and Joseph Gillett, Jr.

Court Record, Page 84—4 May, 1725: Adms. to Jacob Merrells, brother to the sd. deceased.

Page 104—5 October, 1725: Invt. now exhibited.

Page 149—7 March, 1726-7: This Court appoint Thomas Seymour, Richard Seymour and Thomas Welles to dist. the estate: To John Merrells, to Abram, to Daniel, to Wilterton, to Isaac, to Abell Merrells, to Susannah Turner, to the children of Sarah Kellogg deceased, to the children of Jacob Merrells decd., brothers and sisters of the sd. deceased.

Recorded in Vol. XII, Page 146-7-8.

Miller, Thomas, Haddam East Society. Invt. in land, £762-10-00. Taken 17 October, 1728, by John Spencer, John Church and Jabez Chapman. Will dated 26 July, 1728.

I, Thomas Miller of Haddam, do make this my last will and testament: I give unto Rebeckah Miller, my wife, 1-3 part of the use or income

of all my land, houseing, barn or orchards and wells, which she shall quietly and peaceably possess and improve as she shall judge most to her advantage during her widowhood. I give her 1-3 part of all my moveable estate as her own, excepting my husbandry tools. I give to my son Thomas Miller 1-2 of the lott on which I now dwell, 1-2 of another lott that lyes between the lands of Brother Joseph Dutton and the lott on which I now dwell. I give to him £40 right in the undivided land in the Society. I give to my son Matthew Miller the other half of the lott on which I now dwell. I give to him the other half of the aforesd. lott that lyes between me and brother Dutton, all which lands, houseing, barn and orchards I give to him forever. Also I give to him the half of the right that remains after Thomas hath his £40. Also I give to him all my husbandry tools, excepting what I shall hereafter dispose of in this my last will and testament. I give to my son John Miller 3 lotts of land in this Society, one in the sixth division and the other two in the eighth division, butted and bounded as will appear by the surveys on record. I also give to him the other half of my right in the undivided land in this Society, excepting what I have given to my son Thomas. Also I give to him 1 chain, 1 axx, 1 sythe and 1 plowshare, all which lands, rights and goods I give to him forever. I give to my loving daughter Rebeckah Miller 3 score and £5 to be paid to her in the following time and manner, that is to say, my son Thomas Miller shall pay to her £10 immediately after the execution of this my last will and testament; and he shall pay yearly, after the first payment, £10 a year until he hath paid up £30, which is the whole of what I require him to pay to her. My son Matthew shall likewise pay to her £10, and £10 yearly to the sum of £30, which, with what my son Thomas shall pay, will amount to £60. It is my will that my son John Miller shall pay to my daughter Rebeckah, six years after he shall come of age, £1-13-04 a year for the space of three years, which will amount to £5, which, with what the abovesd. Thomas and Matthew Miller are required as above to pay to her, will make up the aforesd. sum of £65, which is the whole of her portion. I give to my daughter Elizabeth the sum of 3 score and £5 to be paid to her at the same several times by ye abovesd. Thomas, Matthew and John Miller. I give to my daughter Hannah £65, to be paid by Thomas, Matthew and John Miller. I do hereby authorize Ensign John Church and Jabez Chapman to make as equal and equitable division of the lands that I have given to my two sons, Thomas and Matthew, as they can, according to the best of their judgement. I appoint my wife Rebeckah and my son Thomas Miller executors.
Witness: *John X Spencer,*   THOMAS MILLER, LS.
Isaac Wylley, Jr., Samuel Dutton.

Note: 30 November, 1728: A report of the divisions of the lands between Thomas and Matthew Miller, to which they unanimously agree.
Signed: JOHN CHURCH,
JABEZ CHAPMAN.

Court Record, Page 206—3 November, 1728: The last will and testament of Thomas Miller, late of Haddam, decd., was now exhibited by

Rebeckah Miller, widow, and Thomas Miller, son of sd. decd., executors named in sd. will, who accepted that trust in Court. Sd. will is proved, approved and accepted in Court, and ordered to be recorded and kept on file. And the sd. executor exhibited an inventory.

Page 216—1st April, 1729: This Court appoint Rebeckah Miller, widow, to be guardian to her children, viz., Matthew, age 19 years, and John Miller, age 16 years. Recog., £100.

Page 207—3 December, 1728: Rebeckah Miller to be guardian to her daughter Hannah Miller, age 13 years. Recog., £50.

Miller, Thomas, Middletown. Court Record, Page 172—2 January, 1727-8: Adms. granted to Mary Miller, widow, and Stephen Miller, son of the decd.

Page 177.

Miller, William, Glastonbury. Invt. in lands, £537-00-00. Taken (no date) by Thomas Kimberley and Gershom Smith.

Court Record, Page 11—22 March, 1723: Joseph Butler, of Wethersfield, in right of his wife Mary as she is Adms. on the estate of William Miller, late deceased, exhibited an account of administration of debts paid, loss, and allowed for keeping the two youngest children, which is more than has been received. The account accepted and ordered on file.

Whereas, it is represented that it is needfull to make a second inventory of the estate of William Miller in order that the estate may be more regularly distributed: This Court order that another inventory be taken of said estate and exhibited to this Court. Messrs. Thomas Kimberly, Thomas Wells and Gershom Smith to be apprisers.

Recorded in Vol. XII, Page 177-8-9-80-1-2. Add. Invt. in Vol. XI, Page 259.

Mitchell, William, Windsor. Inventory taken June, 1725, by Jonathan Elsworth, John Stoughton and Alexander Allyn. Additional inventory of £50, taken 4 March, 1728-9, by John Stoughton and Eleazer Hills. Will dated 11 December, Anno RiRs. Georgy Magte. Brittn. &c., Undecimo Anno. que Dom. 1724.

I, William Mitchell of Windsor, do make this my last will and testament: I give unto Experience Fyler of Windsor, single woman, £30 as a token of my love, to be to her and her heirs forever. I give unto William Perry of Hartford £10 as a token of my love, to him and his heirs forever. I give unto John Andrews, now resideing at Hartford, £20 as a token of my love, to him and his heirs forever. I will and bequeath all the rest of the residue of my estate of what kind or nature soever and wheresoever, not in this my last will otherwise disposed of, unto my well-beloved sisters, Genett Montgomery and Elizabeth Wollis, of the Parrish of Eaglesome, near Glasgow, in the Kingdom of Great Britain, to be equally divided between them or such as legally represent them, to be to them and their heirs forever. I give unto Katherine Holman, of Windsor aforesd., wife of Samuel Holman, my nurse and tender, the sum of £5 as a token of my regard, to be at her own dispose. I give unto Mr. Thomas Steele, of Boston, in New England, £30 to him and his heirs forever. I appoint the sd. Thomas Steele, with Thomas Kimberly, of Glastonbury, in the County of Hartford aforesd., and Samuel Strong, of Windsor aforesd., cordwainer, to be executors. I do hereby give and grant full power with lawfull authority to sell and convey away all or any of my houseing and lands lying in the limits of the Township of Windsor, or elsewhere within the sd. Colony, and with full power to make, seal and deliver good, authentick and ample deed thereof, to any person or persons that shall appear by the same, which deed or deeds so executed shall convey a good estate in fee simple to the purchaser or purchasers thereof, anything in this my above will to the contrary hereof in any wise notwithstanding. And the money procured by such sales of such my sd. land, after my just debts are discharged, to be delivered to the sd. Thomas Steele and by him to be remitted to my sd. sisters or their legal representatives.

Witness: *Simon Chapman,*   WILLIAM MITCHELL.
John Stoughton, Stephen Fyler.

Court Record, Page 87—2 June, 1725: Will now exhibited by Thomas Kimberly and Daniel Strong, two of the executors named in the will.

Page 212—5 February, 1728-9: Thomas Kimberly and Samuel Strong, executors, exhibit now an account: Bonds to the amount of £151-13-03, and debts due to the estate to the sum of £308-02-08. Account accepted.

Page 7 (Vol. XI) 8 December, 1729: Thomas Kimberly and Samuel Strong, executors, were summoned to Court as per writ dated 2 December, 1729, to perfect the invt. as set forth in sd. writ, or to answer to John Austin, attorney for the residuary legatees. Their accounts not being satisfactory, they were ordered to report to this Court 8 January, 1729-30.

Page 10—8 January, 1729-30: John Austin, attorney for Capt. John Steele of Boston, and of the residuary legatees of Thomas Mitchell, demanding Mr. Thomas Kimberly and Samuel Strong, executors, they now appeared, but did not answer the demands, rendering only an account of money received to be added to the invt.

Page 22—6 October, 1730: Exhibit of an addition to the inventory of £30.

Page 295-6-7-8.

Moore, Edward, Windsor. Invt. £651-05-07. Taken by Nathaniel Drake, Jeams Enno and Timothy Loomis.

Court Record, Page 91—6 July, 1725: Adms. granted to Mary More.

Page 173-4.

Morgan, Benjamin, Middletown. Invt. £5-15-06. Taken 26 March, 1724, by David Cornwall and John Powell.

Court Record, Page 32—6 November, 1723: Whereas, this Court are informed by Joseph Morgan of Middletown that his brother Benjamin Morgan dyed at Barbadoes, this Court grant letters of Adms. to the sd. Joseph Morgan.

Page 57-58—Invt. now exhibited by Joseph Morgan, Adms.

Page 276-8-9-80.

Morgan, Thomas, Hartford. Invt. £751-14-05. Taken 17 May, 1725, by Joseph Gillett and John Webster. Will dated 25 March, 1725.

I, Thomas Morgan, do make this my last will and testament: I give to my wife the use and improvement of all my corn mill and bolting mill, and the east end of my dwelling house, and half of my barn and cow house, and all my land on the north side of the river, and the third part of my land on the south side of the river, and the third part of my moveable estate, and the interest of £90 in money which is in the hands of Jobanna Smith, and £23-06-08 that is now in the hands of Jobanna Smith. Nevertheless it is to be understood that if my wife shall see cause to marry again, that then the abovesd. legacies shall return to my surviving children, all but what she has allowed her for her dowry. I give unto my daughter Leah about 30 acres of my whole right in a lott bought of Capt. Cook in and lying in the West Division of Hartford. And if her son Morgan shall live to be 21 years of age, then he shall have the abovesd. part to him and his heirs forever. I give also to my grandson Morgan Cadwell my cane and sword. I also give unto my daughter Leah £10-05-00 now in the hands of Jobanna Smith, also a two-year-old steer, also £6 in money, to be paid by my daughter Hannah Goodwin 40 shillings, and my daughter Rachel 40 shillings, and Deliverance Graves 40 shillings, all to be paid within a year after Jobanna Smith's bond is out for the payment of £90. I give to my daughter Hannah Goodwin my part of the sawmill and the east end of my dwelling house, and half my barn and half my cow house, and half my cow yard and half my garden, and after my wifes decease, the west end of my dwelling house, half of my barn, all my land on the south side of the river and £10-04-00 in money that is now in the hands of Jobanna Smith. I give to my daughter Rachel, after my wife's decease, the west end of my dwelling house, half of my barn, cow house and cow yard; half my land on the north side of the river to be equally divided between my grandchildren, Deliverance Graves and her. I give unto my daughter Rachel 10 shillings, and £30-04-00 which is in the hands of Jobanna Smith, and half of my corn mill after my wife's decease. I give unto my grandchild, Deliverance Graves, £10-04-00 in money which is in the hands of Jobanna Smith. I also give to my grandchild Deliverance two hefers. I give to John Legcome a loome and tackling belonging to it, and a new gunn which I bought of Mr. Goodrich, and £5 to be paid by my wife when he shall come to the age of 21 years. If he shall not faithfully serve out his time, then it shall be at the discretion of my loving wife to give him what she shall see cause. I do give to my two grandchildren, Sarah and Mehetabell Goodwin, two horse colts. I appoint my wife and my son Isaac Goodwin executors.

Witness: *Samuel Sedgwick,*   THOMAS X MORGAN, LS.
Jobanna Smith, Joseph Cornish.

Court Record, Page 86—1st June, 1725: Will proven.

Page 88 (Vol. XIII) 5 May, 1741: Abell Colyer of Hartford in right of his wife Rachell, one of the daughters and co-heirs to the estate of Thomas Morgan, late of Hartford, moves this Court that what was given her in the will of her father be set out to her, viz., the west end of the dwelling house, half the barn, 1-2 the cow house, 1-2 the yard, and half the land on the north side of the river. This Court appoint Lt. Isaac Kellogg, Sergt. David Ensign and William Bacor, of Hartford, to set out the above-named premises.

Morton, Thomas, Simsbury. Court Record, Page 115—1st February, 1725-6: Adms. granted to Hannah Morton, widow, who exhibited an invt. Capt. Thomas Holcomb, surety in £200.

Page 146—7 February, 1726-7: Hannah Morton is appointed guardian to her children, viz., Rachel, 9 years of age, Hannah, 7 years and William, 5 years of age, children of Thomas Morton deceased. Recog., £100.

Page 103.

The Will in Vol. XII, Page 38-9.

Mudge, Micah, Hebron. Inventory taken 14 September, 1724, by Ebenezer Willcox and David Porter. Will dated 17 March, 1720-1.

I, Micah Mudge of Hebron, being aged, do make this my last will and testament: Imprimis: To my wife Mary, during her natural life, to her use ye house I now dwell in and all the land from a straight line from ye well to ye bound mark called Lattemore's bound mark, and then yt is from sd. well 500 rods to the same line south-westerly to Ebener. Mudge's land or corner, or that lyes between ye meadow lotts and sd. Ebener. Also all ye stock and moveable estate to her use during her natural life, and after her decease to be disposed of as is hereafter ordered: Item. I will all ye abovesd. house and land to my daughter Thankfull Nicholls, to be to her use only during the time and untill the year 1740, if she survive her mother and live till that time, and after her decease or ye expiration of sd. term to be as hereafter ordered. I will and bequeath all the abovesd. house and land to my grandson Micah Mudge, son of the abovesd. Ebener., after ye abovesd. term is expired, to him and his heirs and assigns forever. Item. I give to my son Ebener. the remaining part of the 5 acres I bought of Lattemore, what remains of it after the above bequests are had, which his house now stands on, and to his heirs forever. I give and bequeath to my son Moses Mudge 30 acres out of my farm on the north side, provided he settles and dwells on it, and all ye remainder of sd. farm if he pays for it as it shall be inventoried to such as I herein order. I give to my grandsons and daughters, Elizabeth Allin £5, Noah Allin 20 shillings, grandson Rust 20 shillings, granddaughter Ruth 40 shillings, and to Isaac Tilden 20 shillings, to my daughter Susannah's daughter 20 shillings, to my daughter Sarah Palmer £5, and to Thankfull £5, and to Susannah £1. All the above legacies to be paid to my sd. grandsons, granddaughter and daughters within one year after my decease by my son Moses for ye remainder of the farm as is above expressed. But if he neglect to pay sd. legacies one year after my decease, then the legacies to be paid out of sd. remainder of sd. farm in land at inventory price according to each legacy. My will is yt all ye remainder of my whole estate, real and personal whatsoever, be equally divided by and between all my sons and daughters now living, and to those deceased to their heirs. I appoint Mr. Stephen Post and Nathaniel Phelps, of Hebron, to be executors.

Witness: *Ebener. Fitch,*   MICAH MUDGE, LS.
Samuel Wilson, Bridget Fitch.

Court Record, Page 67—2 February, 1724-5: This Court grants letters of Adms. on the estate of Micah Mudge, late of Hebron decd., with will annexed, unto Mary Mudge, widow of sd. decd., and John Palmer of Windsor.

Page 180—5 March, 1727-8: Whereas, Micah Mudge decd., in and by his last will ordered that his wife be supported out of his estate during life, and she being late decd. and left debts to be paid and no estate to answer sd. debts: This Court order that John Palmer, Adms. on the estate of the sd. Micah Mudge, with his will annexed, pay out of his estate and discharge the aforesd. debts, rendering an account thereof to this Court in his account of Adms.

Page 16-17.

Mygatt, Joseph, Hartford. Died 27 December, 1724. Invt. (in part), £510-00-00. Includes homelotts and buildings thereon, £300; 15 acres of land at Hog River, £90; corn mill, saw mill and utensils belonging thereto, £120-00-00. Taken by Daniel Messenger and Jonathan Hopkins.

Court Record, Page 64—5 January, 1724-5: Adms. to Elizabeth Mygatt.

Page 70—2 February, 1724-5: Invt. exhibited.

Page 119—1st March, 1725-6: Mrs. Elizabeth Mygatt to be guardian to her children, to Jacob, age 19 years, to Sarah, 12 years of age. Recog., £100.

Page 121—Mrs. Elizabeth Mygatt, Adms., desires to be released from her trust, which this Court allow, and appoint Zebulon Mygatt Adms. Recog., £200 with Jonathan Seymor.

Dist. per Record on File: An agreement, dated 23 March, 1726-7: That Benjamin Stephens of Danbury, in right of his wife Elizabeth Stephens alias Mygatt, the relict of Joseph Mygatt, late of Hartford decd., who is guardian to Jacob and Sarah Mygatt, and Zebulon Mygatt, who is guardian to Joseph and Mary Mygatt, children of the deceased, have agreed to distribute or divide the estate to Elizabeth Stephens alias Mygatt, to Jacob, to Joseph, to Mary and to Sarah Mygatt.

Page 212-13.

Newell, Thomas. Inventory taken 1st January, 1723-4, by Samuel Newell and Nathaniel Stanly.

Court Record, Page 34—2 December, 1723: This Court grant letters of Adms. on the estate of Thomas Newell, late of Farmington decd., unto Elizabeth Newell, widow, and Thomas Newell, son of the deceased.

Agreement on File: A dist. of the estate of Thomas Newell deceased, made by us the subscribers, is as followeth, in yt year 1724, noumber ye 10 days:

	£ s d
To Thomas Newell,	65-08-00
To Simeon Newell,	22-13-00
To Joseph Newell,	22-13-00
To Elizabeth Newell, widow,	29-17-09
To Elizabeth Lewis,	35-16-09
To Sarah Newell,	31-13-08
To Esther Newell,	31-13-08

Court Record, Page 76—6 April, 1725: An agreement for the settlement of the estate of Thomas Newell, late of Farmington deceased, under the hands and seals of Thomas, Simeon and Joseph Newell, Widow Elizabeth Newell, Elizabeth Lewis, Sarah Newell and Esther Newell, heirs to the estate, was now exhibited, and they appeared before this Court and acknowledged the sd. agreement to be their voluntary act and deed, which agreement is by this Court accepted and ordered to be kept on file.

Page 258-9-60.

North, Thomas, Kensington. He died 2 March, 1724-5. Invt. £1335-02-05. Taken by Thomas Curtice and Allen Goodrich.

Court Record, Page 76—6 April, 1725: Adms. to Martha North and Isaac North. Invt. exhibited.

Page 115—1 February, 1725-6: Isaac North, Adms. on the estate of Thomas North, late of Farmington decd., exhibited account of Adms. Paid in debts and charges, £168-03-02. Which account is accepted. The invt., with additions, £1350-19-05; the real part, £1090-00-00; subtracting £168-03-02, there will remain of real and personal estate, £1182-16-03, to be distributed. Order to Martha North, widow and relict, £30-18-09, with her dower; to Isaac North, £298-19-06, which is his double portion of sd. estate; to Martha Beckley, one of the daughters, £105-09-08, having formerly received £44; to Thomas, James, Joseph, Sarah and Hannah North, the rest of the children of sd. decd., to each of them, £149-09-06, which is their single part or share. And appoint Thomas Curtice, Allyn Goodrich and Joseph Smith distributors. James North, a minor, 17 years of age, chose Samuel Seymour to be his guardian. And this Court appoint Isaac North to be guardian unto Joseph North, 5 years of age. Recog., £40. Martha North appointed guardian to Sarah North, a minor, 14 years of age. Recog., £40.

Page 325-6-7.

Norton, John, Farmington. Invt. £344-14-01. Taken 1725, by Isaac Cowles and Daniel Judd.

Court Record, Page 88—7 June, 1725: This Court grant letters of Adms. on the estate of John Norton, late of Farmington decd., unto Ruth Norton, widow, and Thomas Norton, son of sd. decd.

Page 107—2 November, 1725: Invt. now exhibited by Ruth Norton, Adms.

Distribution of the estate on file, 9 November, 1725:

	£	s	d
To the widow, Ruth Norton,	87	01	01
To heirs of Ruth Seymour,	28	17	08
To heirs of Elizabeth Catlin,	28	15	07
To Mary Boltwood,	28	15	07
To Sarah Hewitt,	28	15	10
To Hannah Pratt,	28	14	06
To Dorcas Bird,	28	15	03

By John Hart and Daniel Judd.

Recorded in Vol. XII, Page 186-7-8.

Norton, Thomas, Sen., Farmingtown. Invt. £1033-05-10. Taken 26 May, 1729, by Isaac Cowles, Matthew Clark and Nathaniel Lewis.

Will dated 21 July, 1728: I, Thomas Norton, Sen., of the Town of Farmingtown, being crazy and infirm of body, do make this my last will and testament: To my wife, Hannah Norton, I give 1-2 part of all my personal estate, to be at her own dispose forever, with 1-3 part of all my real estate during her natural life. I give to my eldest son, John Norton, one piece or parcell of land in Farmingtown, in the great meadow, five acres more or less, it being 1-2 of a tract of land called the Ten-Acre Piece; also 4 acres of land commonly called my further pasture, bounded westerly and southerly with land of Matthew Woodruff; also 1 1-2 acre of land by a place called Dirty Hole, which I lately purchased of Nathaniel Woodruff; also 1-2 of my lott lying in the Little Plain, by a road to

Waterbury, containing 60 acres; all which lands are lying in Farmington. I give to my son Samuel Norton my homelott in sd. Farmingtown where I now live, with all the buildings thereon and all other appurtenances thereto, containing 12 acres more or less, bounded southerly with the Town Street. I give unto Elizabeth Norton, daughter of my son John Norton, £20 at the age of 18 years or day of marriage. which shall first happen. Item. Unto my cousin Ebenezer Dickinson, now living with me, provided he live with my wife or either of my sons (which he shall choose) and faithfully serve until he attain the age of 21 years, then to him I give the other half of my tract of land on the Little Plain in Farmingtown by the road to Waterbury. My will further is that whosoever ye sd. Dickinson shall live with and serve shall cause him to be well instructed in the art, trade or mistery of weaving. Unto my two sons, John Norton and Samuel Norton, to be equally divided between them, I give all the remainder of my estate, both real and personal, not before in this instrument disposed of. And I appoint my two sons, John Norton and Samuel Norton, to be executors.

Witness: *John Hooker, Sen.,*   THOMAS NORTON, LS.
William Porter, Joseph Hooker.

Court Record, Page 219—3 June, 1729: Will now exhibited by John Norton and Samuel Norton, executors named in the will. Proven.

Page 72 (Vol. XI) 4 July, 1732: John Norton, one of the executors, moved a distribution. This Court appoint Daniel Judd, John Rue and John Norton, distributors.

Page 192.

Norton, Thomas, Simsbury. Died 1st December, 1725. Invt. £90-09-09. Taken 24 January, 1725-6, by Thomas Holcomb, Nathaniel Holcomb and Jonathan Westover.

Recorded in Vol. XII, Page 81-2-3.

Olmsted, Joseph, Sen., Hartford. Died 1st day of October, 1726. Inventory in lands and money, £1132-05-00. Taken by Ozias Pitkin and Timothy Cowles. Will dated 29 May, 1722.

I, Joseph Olmsted, Sen., of Hartford, do make this my last will and testament: I give to my wife 1-3 part of all my moveable estate, she to have her choice, to be at her own disposal; and the use of 1-3 part of all my lands during her natural life, also as much of my houseing and barn and cellar as she shall judge she shall have need of for her use, always provided that it amount not to above 1-2 of the buildings. I give to my son Joseph Olmsted as followeth: I confirm to him all the houseing and lands given him by deed of gift, also 1-2 of the bogg meadow or wet land belonging to the lott where his dwelling house standeth. I give to my son Joseph Olmsted 10 acres of upland, which 10 acres is a part of a lott on which my dwelling house standeth, and is to begin after 10 acres is measured off from the land given to the Rev. Mr. Samuel Woodbridge east. I give to my son James Olmsted all that estate in houseing and lands given him by deed of gift, and I give to my son James Olmsted and his heirs 2-3 of the west land lying west from my dwelling house, to begin at ye dreign or ditch and to go west so far as my lot extends. Whereas, the providence of God took away my son Nicholas Olmsted by death before I alotted any estate upon him, I do therefore devise and give unto my son Nicholas's children in manner following: All that piece or parcell of land where the dwelling house of my son Nicholas decd. now stands, from the highway east as far as it was by my sd. son cleared and fenced in his lifetime, together with all my interest in the buildings; also 10 acres of upland and a part of the lott on which my dwelling house standeth, and abutts west upon lands of Mr. Samuel Woodbridge and east upon lands given to my son Joseph Olmsted. I give to my son Richard Olmsted, I confirm unto my sd. son all that estate in lands given him by deed of gift. I also give to my sd. son and his heirs all that piece of upland that lyeth east of his dwelling house not given by deed, to extend east to an old ditch formerly made cross the lott beyond the hill, at a place commonly called or known by the Plain. I give to my son Nehemiah Olmsted and his heirs forever, I confirm it unto my sd. son, all that estate given him by deed and also a piece of upland, being a part of that lott on which my dwelling house standeth. And I devise and give all the rest of my lands, both uplands and meadows, to be equally divided between my sons, Joseph, Jeams, Richard and Nehemiah, also to my son Nicholas's children so far as they represent their parent, that is, also my son Nicholas's children shall have but 1-5 part of the lands given to be divided. My will is that all the estate given to my son Nicholas's children shall be equally divided amongst them, except the eldest son, who shall have out of ye land given £10 more than any of the rest of his brother or sisters. And my will is that my daughter Mary Olmsted, sometime the wife of my sd. son Nicholas decd., shall have the use of the estate given to her children to bring them up to lawfull age, and the sd. widow shall have 1-3 part of the land given, that is, the use of it during her natural life. The estate given to my son Nicholas's children shall be to them and their heirs forever. I give to my daughter Elizabeth, the wife of Joseph Skinner, £23 in money, and that, with what she hath already had, shall be the whole of her portion from me. I give to my daughter Hannah, the wife of Zachariah Seymour, £22 in money. I give to my daughter Rebeckah, the wife of Jonathan Hills, £30. I make and appoint my two sons, Joseph and James Olmsted, executors.

Witness: *Roger Pitkin.*   JOSEPH OLMSTED, L.S.
Ozias Pitkin, William Pitkin, Jr.

Court Record, Page 138—6 December, 1726: Will now exhibited by Joseph and James Olmsted, executors named in the will exhibited.

Agreement on File: This agreement, made in 1726-7, witnesseth: That whereas our honoured father, Deacon Joseph Olmsted, by his last will and testament did give several pieces or parcels of land to be equally divided to Joseph Olmsted, James Olmsted, Richard Olmsted and Nehemiah Olmsted, and the children and heirs of Nicholas Olmsted decd.: To this agreement we have set to our hands and seals.

Witness: *Israhiah Wetmore, Jr.,*   Joseph Olmsted, LS.
    Edward Cadwell.   James Olmsted, LS.
                      Richard Olmsted, LS.
                      Nehemiah Olmsted, LS.
                      Mary X Olmsted, LS.
                      Mary Olmsted Grant, LS.

Mary Olmsted, last signing to this agreement, is one of the heirs of Nicholas Olmsted decd., and is of full age.

Page 148—7 March, 1726-7: An agreement for the settlement of the estate of Deacon Joseph Olmsted, signed and sealed by the heirs, was now exhibited and accepted by the Court.

Page 150.

Olmsted, Samuel, East Haddam. Died 13 January, 1726. Inventory taken by Joshua Brainard, Isaac Spencer and Samuel Emmons.

Court Record, Page 129—5 May, 1726: Adms. to Mary Olmsted, widow, and John Olmsted, son of sd. decd. Recog., £300, with Samuel Olmsted.

Page 131—3 June, 1726: John Olmsted, Adms. on the estate of Samuel Olmsted, late of Haddam decd., exhibited an account of Adms. of the estate: Paid in debts and charges, £16-08-09; the inventory, with addition, £580-13-04; subtracting £16-08-09, there remains £564-04-07 to be dist. Order: To Mary Olmsted, widow, £78-05-02 with dower; to Samuel Olmsted, eldest son, £2-18-00 with what he has received of his father's estate (£452-11-03), which is his double portion; to John, 2nd son, £79-15-00, he having formerly received £148; to Sarah Cone, eldest daughter, £202-14-11, she having formerly received £25-01-00. To Elizabeth Church, another daughter, £200-10-09, she having formerly received £27-04-03; which, with what they have respectively received, is their single portion of sd. estate. And appoint Joshua Brainard, Isaac Spencer and Thomas Cone, of Haddam, distributors.

Page 122—14 March, 1726-7: John Olmsted, and also the distributors, vizt., Joshua Brainard, Isaac Spencer and Thomas Cone, inform this Court that in sd. dist. therein ordered out of the homested of the decd. (to Sarah Cone £44-02-07 and to Elizabeth Church £4-10-07) will much damnify it, and desire that the sd. John may pay the sd. daughters in money and save the homested entire. Allowed.

Recorded in Vol. XII, Page 126.

Onepenny, Sarah(Indian Woman), Hartford. Will dated 27 May, 1727:

In the name of God, amen. I, Sarah Onepenny, Indian squaw, do hereby give and grant unto my well-beloved nephew, Scipio Two Shoes, his heirs and assigns forever, all the estate, both real and personal, of what kind or nature soever, that I am now possessed off or have in reversion whatsoever, hereby declaring this to be my last will and testament, and hereby also disannulling and making void all other wills or testaments by me heretofore made, being now of a disposeing mind and memory. And I especially hereby give the sd. Scipio all my lands at a place called Wongogn, near Middletown. In witness whereof I have hereunto set my hand and seal in Hartford ye 27th day of May, Anno Dom. 1727. Signed, sealed, pronounced and declared to be the last will and testament of the sd. Sarah Onepenny by her.

In the presence of us:

Thomas Clapp, Joseph Bigelow,   SARAH X ONEPENNY, LS.
     Jacob Hinsdall.

Court Record, Page 197—6 August, 1728: The last will and testament of Sarah Onepenny, an Indian woman, was exhibited, the sd. will being proven by the oath of the evidences thereto, and sd. will is by this Court approved and ordered to be recorded and kept on file.

Owen, Obadiah, Windsor. Court Record, Page 208—2 January, 1728-9: Adms. granted to Samuel Owen, brother of the deceased.

Page 21 (Vol. XIII) 7 February, 1737-8: Upon motion of Jedediah Owen, one of the heirs of the estate of Obadiah Owen, late of Windsor deceased, Samuel Owen, Adms., was summoned to appear before this Court and render an account of his Adms. Then Jedediah Owen appeared and acknowledged receipt of his full portion, and the Adms. account was accepted.

Agreement on File.

Peck, Paul, Hartford. Court Record, Page 70—2 February, 1724-5: Adms. granted unto John and Paul Peck, sons of the sd. decd.

AGREEMENT AS FOLLOWETH:

Whereas, our honoured father, Paul Peck decd., leaving some estate not disposed of by will, we agree that the moveable estate shall pay the debts as far as will pay, and we will set over to our brother Paul Peck one acre and 1-2 of land commonly called Peck's Island. And if the 1 1-2 acres of land will not pay all the debts, then we, the heirs of this estate, do oblige ourselves to pay to the abovesd. Paul Peck every one of us an equal part of what debts shall be remaining. And we agree that our brother Paul Peck shall have a double part of the estate, and the rest shall be equally divided amongst the rest of us. And make choice of Jonathan Butler and Thomas Hosmer, with the above-named Paul Peck, to make an equal division of the remainder of the abovesd. land as soon as the water will allow of measuring the land. In confirmation of the above agreement we have set to our hands and seals this 6th day of February, 1724-5.

PAUL PECK, LS.	RUTH X SEDGWICK, LS.
JOHN PECK, LS.	MARTHA X HUBBARD, LS.
ELIZABETH X BEECHER, LS.	JOHN PORTER, LS.
SAMUEL PECK, LS.	HANNAH X PORTER, LS.
SAMUEL HUBBARD, LS.	

Paul Peck, John Peck, Samuel Peck, Samuel Hubbard, Ruth Peck, Elizabeth Beecher, Ruth Sedgwick, Martha Hubbard and John Porter acknowledged the above agreement to be their free act and deed this 6th of February, 1724-5.

Page 70—19 February, 1724-5: Agreement exhibited and accepted by the Court.

Page 286-7.

Person, John, Farmington. Invt. £57-12-07. Taken 5 June, 1725, by Isaac Cowles and Daniel Judd. Will dated 9 May, 1725.

I, John Person, formerly of Great Britain, now of Farmington, I give to Mindwell Bird the sum of £12; to the Widow Esther Bird and her son Samuel, between them, £10; to John Stedman and William Persons, Sen., and William Persons, Jr., and Roger Orvis and John Andrews, son to Benjamin Andrews, I give and bequeath to each of them what they are now indebted to me. I give to my three brothers in Great Britain, in equal proportions, all the residue of my estate that shall be left when the foregoing dispositions are answered. I appoint my friend Samuel Bird to be sole executor.

Witness: *John Hooker, Sen.,*   JOHN PERSON, LS.
Nathaniel Lewis, Sen., Isaac Lewis.

Court Record, Page 88—7 June, 1725: Will now exhibited and proven.

Recorded in Vol. XII, Page 130-1.

Persivall, James, Haddam. Died 4 November, 1728. Invt. £802-16-06. Taken 29 November, 1728, by Timothy Fuller, Daniel Gates and Jeremiah Gates. Will dated 1st August, 1728.

I, James Persivall, Sen., do make this my last will and testament: I give to my wife Mary Persivall all the moveables that she brought with her, to be wholly at her own dispose; and so long as she continue my widow she shall have one room in my house (which she likes best), also a jade and a cow, which my son John shall take care to provide meat for, both summer and winter yearly; also she shall have yearly the use of corn land enough to raise her bread and corn; and in case she continues my widow and should stand in need, my son John shall yearly allow her what is necessary for her comfortable subsistence. Also I do appoint my wife sole executrix, or, if there be occasion, my son James shall assist her in the execution of this my last will and testament. I give to my eldest son Joseph Persivall all my lands lying at the place commonly called Fall Brook, except 10 acres; as also the lott which is yet to be laid out in the eighth division, and half my right in all the undivided land. I give to my son John Persivall my house, barn, orchard, shop and homelott, with the conveniences that belong thereto, as also 37 acres of land in Middletown bounds and 10 acres of land at the north end of my land at Fall Brook, and the other half of my right in all the undivided lands, as also all my chattells and moveables, unless what is otherwise expressly disposed of in this my will. I give to my daughter Mary, personally, the bed and bedding that is called hers; also £50 either in moveables or in money. If she chooses money, my son John shall take the moveables and pay her the £50. Now, to confirme and ratifye this my last will and testament to all intents and purposes, I have, in Haddam, on the east side of the river, this first day of August, in the year of our Lord one thousand seven hundred and twenty-eight, set my hand and seal.

In the presence of:
Daniel Brainard,   JEAMS X PERSIVALL, SEN.
Daniel Cone.

Court Record, Page 207—3 December, 1728: Adms. to John Persivall, son of sd. decd. Exhibit of inventory.

Invt. in Vol. XII, Page 219-20-21.

Phelps, Capt. Abraham. Invt. £858-06-02. Taken 21 March, 1728, by Israel Stoughton, Jonathan Stiles and Peletiah Allyn.

Court Record, Page 191—7 May, 1728: Adms. granted to Abraham Phelps, son of the decd.

Recorded in Vol. XII, Page 61-2-3.

Pinney, Josiah. Invt. £385-04-09. Taken 21st September, 1726, by Daniel Bissell, Jonathan Stiles and Pelatiah Allyn. Will dated 2 September, 1726.

I, Josiah Pinney of Windsor, do make my last will and testament: I give my cousin Samuel Pinney, son of my brother Samuel Pinney, of the aforesd. Windsor, my house, land and barn, orchard, garden, and all my homelott with all my land adjoining to it, and also my lott at the Marsh, and my Town Commons, all my land to him and his disposal, and all ye remainder of my estate whatsoever, with these provisos: it is to be for his part and portion of his father's estate; that he pay all my just debts and funeral charges; that he pay to my sister Mary Strong, wife of Jno. Strong of Windsor, the sum of 4 score pounds in the space of two years after my decease; that he pay to my cousin Humphrey Pinney, of sd.

Windsor, £15 within a space of two years after my decease. I appoint my brother Samuel Pinney sole executor.

Witness: *Israel Stoughton,*   JOSIAH PINNEY, LS.
John Gaylord, Pellatiah Allyn.

Court Record, Page 135—4 October, 1728: Will now exhibited by Samuel Pinney, executor named in the will. Proven. Invt. exhibited.

Page 168-9-70-1.

Pitkin, William, Sen. Will dated 15 October, 1722: I, William Pitkin, Sen., of Hartford, being of sound mind and memory and willing to set my house in order, doe make and ordain this my last will and testament: I give unto my wife the use of 1-3 part of my real estate during her natural life, and £100 as money out of the moveable estate, she to have her choice of my goods to that sum, which £100 I give to my wife to be at her own dispose; also she is to have the use of 1-2 of my dwelling house during her widowhood if she need it for her comfort and for the comfort of my children. I give to my son William Pitkin land bounding north on my brother Nathaniel Pitkin's, east on the street, south on Joseph Olmsted, and west on the meadow lott; also a piece of land near the ferry which my honoured father Capt. Caleb Stanly gave me; also one piece I had of William Morton; also all my land in Stafford; also 1-2 of my land in Coventry which I bought of Deacon Fuller, excepting one piece of 70 acres; also 10 acres on the Plaine, bounding west on Timothy Cowles, south on John Case, east on my brother Ozias Pitkin, and north on Deacon Olmsted. I give to my son Joseph land near William Warren's house. I give to my two sons William and Joseph my fulling mills (with right of stream to next fall below). I give to my son Thomas Pitkin all my land within the Town of Bolton; also 70 acres in Coventry; also 6 acres at Podunck. I give to my son John Pitkin my dwelling house, barn and other buildings (except my clothier's shop, which I give to my son William). To my son John my lot on which the corn mill and saw mill stand, except what is given to William and Joseph; to John all my parts of ye corne and saw mill; also I give to my son John all that my 210 acres of land which I bought of Capt. William Clark and Deacon Josiah Dewey in Lebanon, in ye new parish commonly called ye Crank. To my daughter Elizabeth Pitkin, to Martha Welles, to Sarah Porter, to Jerusha Pitkin. I appoint my wife Elizabeth and my sons William and Joseph executors.

Witness: *Nathaniel Pitkin,*   WILLIAM PITKIN, LS.
Ozias Pitkin, Timothy Cowles.

Court Record, Page 23—2 July, 1723: Will now exhibited by Mrs. Elizabeth Pitkin and sons William and Joseph, executors. Proven. Invt. exhibited and allowed.

Porter, Daniel. Court Record, Page 50—7 July, 1724: This Court appoint Timothy Loomis of Windsor to be guardian unto Daniel Porter of Windsor, a minor, 12 years of age. Recog., £50.

Invt. in Vol. XII, Page 96-7.

Porter, James, Windsor. Invt. £715-05-01. Taken 29 November, 1727, by Hezekiah Porter and William Talcott.

Court Record, Page 169—5 December, 1727: Adms. granted to Ruth Newbery, daughter of sd. decd.

Page 239-40.

Porter, John, Windsor. Invt. £308-14-11. Taken 5 May, 1724, by Samuel Loomis, Nathaniel Cook and Timothy Loomis.

Court Record, Page 50—5 May, 1724: The widow declining Adms., this Court grant letters unto Samuel Pettebone, son of John Pettebone.

Page 136—4 October, 1726: Samuel Pettebone, Adms., exhibits an account of his dist. Accepted. This Court appoint Jacob Drake to be guardian unto Lydia Porter, a minor, 15 years of age. Recog., £50.

Dist. File: 7 October, 1726: To Sarah Porter the widow, to Mary Pettebone, to Catharine Porter, to Lydia Porter, and to Ann Porter. By Thomas Moore, John Palmer and Henry Allyn.

Porter, Thomas, Farmington. Court Record, Page 152—2 May, 1727: Adms. to Timothy Porter, father of the sd. decd., who gave bond with James Church of Hartford. Rec., £100.

Page 237-8.

Quittafield, Clement, Colchester. Invt. £536-09-04. Taken 7 and 8 January, 1724, by Joseph Wright and Nathaniel Foote.

Court Record, Page 44—7 April, 1724: Adms. to Priscilla Quittafield, widow of sd. decd. Exhibit of inventory.

Page 152—2 May, 1727: Priscilla Quittafield, Adms. on the estate of Clement Quittafield, late of Colchester decd., exhibited an account of Adms.: Paid in debts and charges, £37-09-00; received in addition to the invt. £60-12-00; the estate with additions, £536-09-10; subtracting £37-09-00, there remains £470-00-07 to be distributed. Order: To Priscilla Quittafield, widow, £29-03-00 with dower; to Benjamin Quittafield, eldest son, £188-00-02, which is his double portion of sd. estate; to Richard Quittafield, John and Elizabeth Quittafield, younger children of sd. decd., to each of them, £94-00-01, which is their single portion. And appoint Lt. John Skinner, Capt. Joseph Wright and Nathaniel Foote, distributors.

Page 298-9.

Ranney, George, Middletown. Died 28 March, 1725. Inventory taken 29th June, 1725, by William Cornwell, Nathaniel Sauidg and Joseph White.

Court Record, Page 90—6 July, 1725: Adms. granted to Mary Ranney, widow, and Thomas Hall.

Will and Invt. in Vol. XII, Page 47-8-9-50-1-2.

Ranney, Thomas, Middletown.   Invt. £1284-00-00. Taken 1st March, 1727, by Joseph Ranney and Samuel Gipson.   Will dated 31 January, 1726-7.

I, Thomas Ranney of Middletown, in the County of Hartford, husbandman, doe make this my last will and testament: Imprimis: I give to Rebeckah, my wife, 1-2 of my now dwelling house, 1-2 of my land at home, 1-2 of my orchard and 1-2 of my land in the long meadow. This I give her during her natural life, excepting only my wearing apparell, which I give to my three sons, Thomas, Willet and Nathaniel. And what money that is lent out I give to my wife to be at her own disposal. I give to my son Thomas yt lottment of land whereon his house stands; also I give him my land lying on the Plain, north of lands belonging to my brother Joseph Ranney and south of land belonging to Lt. Frary, and butts on ye road from Middletown to Wethersfield west; also I give him 1-3 of my other land lying on the Plain easterly of land that belongeth to my brother Joseph Ranney and westerly on land belonging to my brother Ebenezer Ranney; also I give him half of my long meadow land after my wife's decease; also I give him the 1-2 of my land in Wangunk meadow; also I give him the 1-2 of my Burch Swamp Pasture; also I give him my meadow at Goose Delight, and all my Neck land that lyeth near sd. Goose Delight Meadow. I give to my son Willet all my land at Timber Hill; also my lower lott in Boggy Meadow; also I give him the remainder of my land at Passonchoague after my grandson George hath had 2 acres more than what I have given him and his sister by deed of gift, and 2 acres to lye next to that which I have given him and his sister as above, and then all the remainder of my land there or thereabout to be to my son Willet; also I give him 1-3 part of my lottment of land on the Plain that lyeth easterly of land that belongeth to my brother Joseph Ranney and westerly of land belonging to my brother Ebenezer Ranney. I give to the heirs of my son George in this my will what I have given them by deed of gift. Also I give to my grandson George Ranney, the son of my son George Ranney decd., two acres of land adjoining to that which I have given to him and his sister by deed of gift, which is the two acres above specified. I give to my son Nathaniel the 1-2 of my now dwelling house and half of my barn, 1-2 of my land at home, 1-2 of my orchard at my decease and the other half at my wife's decease. I give to my three daughters, Rebeca, Margaret and Anne, 2-3 of my moveable estate at my decease. Also, I give to my three daughters all my lands that are already laid out in the last division on the east side of the Great River. Also, I give them all my land in the Round Meadow. Also, I give them all my land lyeing on the Heither Neck, so called. Also, I give to my three sons all my propriety right in lands that are yet to be divided in Middletown. And whereas it is sayed in that part of my will that my son Willet shall have all my land at Timber Hill, it is thus to be understood that Willet is to accomodate his mother with pasturing for a cow or two if she needs it. I appoint my three sons, Thomas, Willet and Nathaniel, executors.

Witness: *Joseph Ranney,*   THOMAS X RANNEY.
Roger Gipson, John Warner.

Be it known to all men by these presents: That whereas I, Thomas Ranney of the Town of Middletown, have made my last will and testament in writeing bearing date 31st January, 1726-7, I, the sd. Thomas Ranney, by this present codicil, do ratify and confirm my sd. last will and testament, and do will and bequeath to my three daughters, Rebeckah, Anne and Margaret, the sum of £20 in money or bills of credit of this Colony or the neighboring provinces, to be paid unto them by my son Willet on consideration of his having all my land at Timber Hill, the sd. £20 to be paid after my wife's decease.

Witness: *Joseph Ranney,*   THOMAS X RANNEY.
Roger Gipson, John Warner.

Court Record, Page 146—7 March, 1726-7: Will now exhibited by Thomas, Nathaniel and Willet Ranney, executors named in the will. Proven. Exhibit of inventory.

Page 235.

Roberts, John, Jun., Simsbury. Invt. £163-16-11. Taken 8 April, 1724. by Benjamin Addams and Josiah Loomis.

Court Record, Page 47—7 April, 1724: Adms. granted to Frances Roberts, widow of the decd.

Page 32-91.

Roberts, Samuel, Jr., Middletown. Died 17 December, 1724. Inventory taken by Israhiah Wetmore, William Ward and Joseph Rockwell.

Court Record, Page 64—5 January, 1724-5: Adms. granted to Eunice Roberts, widow of sd. decd., and John Williams of Middletown.

Page 95—3 August, 1725: The Adms. exhibit an account of debts, and move that part of the moveable estate be set out to the widow Eunice Roberts. This Court order that moveable estate valued at the sum of £33-05-09 be set out to the widow.

Page 118—1st March, 1725-6: Per act of the General Assembly, 14 October, 1725, granting liberty to Eunice Roberts and John Williams of Middletown to sell real estate of sd. decd., with the approbation of this Court, to the value of £16-15-00, at 20 days notice, to the highest bidder.

Page 31 (Vol. XII) 5 August, 1735: Samuel Roberts, age 11 years, a son of Samuel Roberts of Middletown, chose Abijah Moore of Middletown to be his guardian. Recog., £100.

Invt. in Vol. XII, Page 88.

Roberts, William, Jun., Hartford. Invt. £12-01-06. Taken 30 December, 1726, by Nathaniel Marsh and Joseph Wadsworth.

Court Record, Page 143—3 January, 1726-7: Adms. granted to Samuel Spencer, who, with Abram Morriss, of Wethersfield, recog. £20.

Page 165—5 September, 1727: This Court appoint William Roberts of Hartford to be guardian to his grandson William Roberts, son of sd. decd., 6 years of age. Recog., £50.

Page 28 (Vol. XII) 3 June, 1735: William Roberts, son of William Roberts, late of Hartford decd., being now 14 years of age, appeared before the Court and made choice of his uncle Joseph Roberts to be his guardian. Recog., £100.

Invt. in Vol. XII, Page 97-8.

Robinson, Ensign Thomas, Haddam. Died 20 October, 1725. **Invt.** £707-09-01. Taken 20 November, 1725, by Daniel Brainard, Timothy Fuller and Thomas Cone.

Court Record, Page 124—5 April, 1726: Adms. granted to Charles Williams, son-in-law, by request of Lydia Robinson, the relict of sd. decd.

Page 185—21 April, 1726: Charles Williams, Adms., exhibited an account of his Adms. Accepted. Order to dist. the estate: To Lydia Robinson, the widow, the sum of £48-14-06 1-2 out of the moveable estate, which is 1-3 part thereof, to be her own forever, and 1-3 part of the real estate for her improvement during life. And this Court appoint Daniel Brainard, Robert Chapman and Thomas Cone, distributors.

See Dist. on File: 6 May, 1726: To Lydia Robinson, the widow, land that was formerly Nathaniel Ackley's; to Mary Robinson, only daughter, now wife of Charles Williams. By Daniel Brainard, Robert Chapman and Thomas Cone, distributors.

Rockwell, Matthew, Windsor. Court Record, Page 90—6 July, 1725: This Court appoint Joseph Rockwell, of Windsor, to be guardian unto Matthew Rockwell, of Windsor, 18 years of age. Recog., £100.

Page 302-3-4.

Rockwell, Samuel, Windsor. Died 13 May, 1725. Invt. £1100-05-03. Taken 12 May, 1725, by Job Drake, Job Elsworth and Daniel Bissell. Court Record, Page 89—6 July, 1725: Adms. granted to Elizabeth Rockwell, widow, and Thomas Grant, son-in-law.

Rockwell, Samuel, Jr., Windsor. Court Record, Page 89—6 June, 1725: Adms. granted to Elizabeth Rockwell, mother, and to Thomas Grant, brother-in-law of sd. deceased.

Invt. in Vol. XII, Page 208-9.

Russell, Mrs. Mary, Middletown. Invt. £114-12-00. Taken 28 February, 1725, by William Hamlin, John Collins and Giles Hall.

Court Record, Page 118—1st March, 1725-6: This Court grant Adms. unto Mr. William Russell, brother of sd. decd. The sd. William Russell and John Stedman recog. in £120.

Distribution of the estate from file:

	£	s	d
To Mr. William Russell,	15	07	05
To the heirs of Mr. Noadiah Russell,	15	07	05
To Mr. John Russell,	15	07	05
To Mr. Daniel Russell,	15	07	05
To Mrs. Mehetabell Russell,	15	07	05
To Mrs. Hannah Russell,	15	07	05
	92	04	09

Middletown, 18 July, 1727. By John Collins, William Hamlin and Giles Hall.

Invt. in Vol. XII, Page 207.

Russell, Noadiah, Rev., Middletown. Invt. £464-15-10. Taken 16 December, 1725, by John Collins, Samuel Hall and Joseph Rockwell.

Court Record, Page 110—4 January, 1725-6: This Court grant Adms. unto Desire Russell, widow of sd. decd. And the sd. Desire Russell and Thomas Cooper of Middletown joyntly and severally recog. in £300.

Page 100 (Vol. XIII) 30 September, 1741: Noadiah Russell, 18 years of age, son of Noadiah Russell, chose his uncle Rev. William Russell to be his guardian. Recog., £200.

Page 102—1st December, 1741: An account of Adms. was exhibited in Court by Desire Russell alias Cooper, relict of sd. deceased and Adms. on his estate, which account is accepted. Rev. William Russell, guardian to Noadiah Russell, moves this Court for a dist. This Court order 1-3 of £65-14-08 to the widow, Desire Russell, alias Cooper aforesd., and the other 2-3 parts thereof unto Noadiah Russell, minor. And appoint Major Jabez Hamlin, John Russell and William Rockwell, distributors. Also, this Court appoint the sd. dist. to set out the widow's dower of the real estate.

Page 106—5 January, 1741-2: Report of the distributors.

Page 141.

Sage, Timothy, Middletown. Inventory taken 23 April, 1725, by John Warner, Jr., Israhiah Wetmore and John Sage.

Court Record, Page 81—4 May, 1725: Adms. granted to Margaret Sage, widow, and John Sage, a brother of sd. decd.

Page 129—5 May, 1726: Margaret and John Sage, Adms., exhibited an account of their Adms. Accepted.

Page 143—3 January, 1726-7: Per act of General Assembly of October 12, 1726, Mrs. Margaret Sage and Capt. William Savage may sell land in payment of debts to the value of £39-06-04.

Page 183—30 May, 1727: Per order of General Assembly, 11 May, 1727, the widow Margaret Sage and Hugh White may sell land to the value of £39-06-04 to pay debts. Recorded 30th May, 1727.

Page 5 (Vol. XIII) 12 April, 1737: David Sage, age 19 years, Solomon, 17 years, and Amos, 15 years, sons of Timothy Sage, chose John Gipson of Middletown to be their guardian. Recog., £400.

Recorded in Vol. XII, Page 169-70.

Sandford, Robert, Hartford. Invt. £1680-02-10. Taken 2 January, 1728-9, by John Sheldon and Nathaniel Goodwin. Will dated 25 May, 1726.

I, Robert Sandford of Hartford, do make this my last will and testament: I give to my son Thomas Sandford all my houseing and lands wheresoever it is situate or lye, except one piece at the lower end of the long meadow in Hartford, containing about 2 1-2 acres, and one other piece lying in the place called Soldier's Field, containing 2 1-2 acres. Also I give to my sd. son Thomas all my moveable estate whatsoever, he paying the legacies hereafter meritioned. I give and bequeath to my daughter Hannah Pratt, to her and the heirs of her body lawfully begotten, the above-mentioned 2 parcells of land. Also, I give unto my sd. daughter Hannah £100 in or as money, to be paid her by my son Thomas in the space of one year after my decease besides what she has already received. I appoint my son Thomas sole executor.

Witness: *John Austin,*   ROBERT SANDFORD, LS.
Thomas Hooker, Mary Hooker.

Court Record, Page 197—6 July, 1728: Will now exhibited by Thomas Sandford, executor named in the will. Proven.

Recorded in Vol. XII, Page 57-8-9-60-1.

Savage, Capt. John, Middletown. Invt. £757-10-00. Taken by William Savage, Samuel Gipson and John Warner. Will dated 11 April, 1724:

I, John Savage of Middletown, do make this my last will and testament: I give unto my wife my now dwelling house and barn and the land adjoining, with pasture; also give her 4 1-2 acres of land lying on the near Neck, on the west side of sd. Neck; also I give to my wife 1-3 part of my moveable estate within doors, she taking that that suits her best; also I give her two cows, six sheep and four swine; this I give her during her natural life. I give unto my son Thomas the house he now lives in, to be his at my decease, and my now dwelling house and barn and the land adjoining to them (after his mother's decease), so far as the southermost fence and west of the fence that divides the pasture from the upland and orchard; also I give him a one-half of my pasture at home, his half to lye on the north side of sd. pasture next the highway, he allowing his brother William a passway to go through his part of sd. lott to cart or drive creatures, if need be; also I give him the 1-2 of my long meadow and half of my long meadow swamp and half of my upland on the east side of the Neck, so called, at my decease; and the other half of my land on the west side of the Neck, yt I gave his mother during her natural life, he is to have it after his mother's decease; also I give him the 1-2 of my lott at Sider Hill, to be equally divided between him and his brother William after my decease; also I give to my son Thomas 1-2 of my land in the Boggy Meadow and Further Neck and Round Meadow, half of each parcell; also I give him the 1-2 of my land in the northwest quarter, to be equally divided between him and his brother William after my decease; all this I give to my son Thomas and his heirs, he paying to his sisters the sum or sums after specified in this will. I give to my son William the homelott where his house now stands; also I give him the 1-2 of my pasture at home, south part of it; also give him the other half of the several parcells of land described as given to Thomas. And further, I give to my two sons Thomas and William all my carpenter tools and all my tool tackling and husbandry tools. I give to my five daughters, Mary, Elizabeth, Sarah, Rachel and Marcey, all my household goods, 2-3 of sd. goods at my decease and the other third after my wife's decease; and also all my cattle, sheep and swine, excepting only those that I have given to my wife. And what the household goods and stock doth fall short of £60 for each daughter, my will is that my two sons Thomas and William shall make up to their five sisters above named the sum of £60 to each sister with what they have already received, in consideration of their having all my land. And further, my will is that my two sons Thomas and William shall have all my lands that are not particularly disposed of in this will, both divided and undivided, to be equally divided between them. And further, my will is that my two sons Thomas and William pay to their five sisters £25 a year after my decease, until they have paid them in full of what I have given my daughters in this my will. I appoint my two sons Thomas and William executors.

Witness: *Jacob White,*   JOHN SAVAGE, LS.
Samuel Stowe, John Warner.

Court Record, Page 139—6 December, 1726: Will now exhibited by Thomas Savage and William Savage, sons of the decd. and executors named in the will.

Recorded in Vol. XII, Page 89-90-1.

Savage, Capt. William, Middletown. Invt. £906-18-09. Taken 15 February, 1726-7. Will dated 23 January, 1726-7.

I, William Savage of Middletown, do make my last will and testament: I give to Elizabeth my wife £22, to be paid out of my estate or the effects of it, £10 to be paid to her this present year and ye other £12 the next year, on the date hereof, and I do resign all up to her that she brought with her to my family after I married her. I give to my son William all my lott in the Nooks whereon he now dwells. I give him 40 acres of land lying in my land in the Northwest Quarter. Also I give 1-2 my long meadow lott to be divided between him and his brother Joseph, William to have the north side of sd. lott. I give to my son Joseph my now dwelling house and barn and homelott and all the land that is mine adjoining to it. Also I give him my pasture at Burch Swamp, so called. Also I give half my long meadow lott to be equally divided between him and his brother William. Also I give him my lott lying east of ye land that my brother John Savage gave to his sons Thomas and William in his last will, and west of land belonging to the heirs of Daniel Clark decd., and north of land that I have given to my son William. Also I give him 40 acres of my lott in the Northwest Quarter. All this I give him and his heirs. Also my will is that my son William shall have the profit of what I have given to my son Joseph for 3 years next coming, he paying the £22 I have given to Elizabeth my wife. And after the sd. 3 years, the profit of Joseph's part shall be equally divided amongst all my children until Joseph come to be of the age of 21 years. I give to my daughters, Martha, Christian, Hannah and Sarah, all my moveable estate excepting my husbandry tools and wearing apparell, which apparell and husbandry tools I give to my two sons William and Joseph. And the rest of my moveable estate I give to my four daughters above mentioned, my daughter Martha to have £10 more than the other three sisters. And what my daughter Sarah hath received already shall be accounted as part of her part of my moveable estate. Also I give to my 4 daughters all my land on the east side of the Great River that is already laid out. Also I give to my 4 daughters above mentioned what shall fall to them out of their grandfather Hugh Mold's estate at New London. I give unto my 4 daughters 40 acres of land lying in my lott in ye Northwest Quarter, or the value of it, which I esteemed to be worth 25 shillings per acre; but if William my son shall pay to his 4 sisters 25 shillings per acre for sd. land in the Northwest Quarter, that is, for 1-2 of it, he shall have the land, he paying sd. 25 shillings per acre within 12 months after my decease. The land shall be his and his heirs, that is to say, the one-half of it. Also I give to my son Joseph liberty, after he comes of age, to purchase of his 4 sisters the other half of sd. land I have given his 4 sisters conditionally, at the same value as his brother William is to have the other half upon. I make my son William executor.

Witness: *Joseph Smith,*   WILLIAM SAVAGE, LS.
Samuel Stowe, John Warner.

Court Record, Page 124—14 March, 1726-7: Will now exhibited by William Savage, son of the decd., named executor in the will. Proven. Exhibit of inventory. This Court appoint Samuel Hall, Joseph Ranney and John Collins to set out the widow's dower by meets and bounds, by her request, by the title dower.

Page 8 (Vol. XI) 6 January, 1729-30: Joseph Savage, a minor, 18 years of age, chose William Savage to be his guardian. Recog., £50.

Invt. in Vol. XII, Page 132.

Seymour, Jonathan, Farmington. Invt. £249-05-04. Taken by Isaac Northam and Isaac Hart.

Court Record, Page 104—5 October, 1725: This Court grant Adms. unto Eunice Seamore, widow, and Mr. Ebenezer Gilbert. And this Court do appoint Eunice Seamore, widow, to be guardian unto her children, Eliakim, 4 months old, Eunice, 10 years, Martha, 5 years, Jerusha, 5, and Lois, 1 year and 7 months.

Page 116—February, 1725-6: Whereas, Eunice Seamore, the widow, who was formerly appointed guardian over the children of the sd. decd., is now married to one Wm. Chitester, a poor shiftless man, and the children are in a suffering condition, not likely to be provided for, the brother and sisters of sd. decd. moveing this Court that some other persons may be appointed guardians, this Court discharge sd. Eunice of her guardianship and appoint Robert Booth of Farmington to be guardian to Eunice, Jerusha and Lois Seamore, children of the sd. deceased. George Hubbard of Middletown to be guardian to Martha and Eliakim Seamore, also children of sd. deceased.

Page 117—Upon motion of Eunice Chitester, alias Seamore, late widow of Jonathan Seamore, deceased, this Court set out of the moveable estate £6-09-00 for her necessary support.

Page 88-89.

Sedgwick, Samuel, Jr., Hartford. He died 25 December, 1724. Inventory taken by Simon Smith and Abram Merrells.

Court Record, Page 63—5 January, 1724-5: Adms. to Ruth Sedgwick, widow, and Capt. Samuel Sedgwick, father of sd. decd.

Page 71—2 March, 1724-5: Exhibited inventory.

Page 147—7 March, 1726-7: Ruth Sedgwick to be guardian to her children, viz., Ruth, age 16 years, Mary and Jerusha (twins), age 13, Daniel 8, and Thankful 5 years of age. Recog., £200.

Page 170—5 December, 1727: Dist. now exhibited and accepted. Adms. granted a *Quietus Est.*

Page 103 (Vol. XI) 5 February, 1733-4: Daniel Sedgwick, son of Samuel Sedgwick, chose his grandfather Samuel Sedgwick to be his guardian. Recog., £100.

Recorded in Vol. XII, Page 118-119-20.

Selden, Joseph. Invt. £1965-01-07. Taken 20 May, 1729, by John Booge, John Holmes and Abram Willey. Will dated 31st day of March, 1729.

I, Joseph Selden of Haddam East Society, in the County of Hartford and Colony of Connecticut, make this my last will and testament: I give to my wife Anne Selden the half of all my moveable estate excepting my husbandry tools, and the whole of my estate, that is, household goods, to be disposed of by her among my children when and in what proportion she shall think meet, she reserving to herself so much as she shall think needful and convenient. Moreover I give unto her the use of my house and barn that is on my farm at Lyme, during her natural life if she shall choose to live there. I give her the choice of which room (and the chambers over it) that pleaseth her best in my now dwelling house. Moreover I give her the use of the third part of my lands during her natural life, unless she and my children, as they come of age, otherwise agree. Moreover I give her a disposal of the land I received of her by my honoured father Chapman. But if she shall not dispose of it in her lifetime, I give it to my loving son Joseph. I give unto my loving son Joseph Selden all my lands, rights of lands, houseing, barn, orchards, with all the privileges and appurtenances belonging thereunto, which I have in this above sd. Haddam East Society. Moreover I give to him my son Joseph Selden the other half of my moveable estate and all my husbandry tools, to him and his heirs. I give to my 5 daughters, Hepsibah, Rebeckah, Anne, Elizabeth and Hannah Selden, all my rights of land, houseing, barn, with all the priviledges and appurtenances thereunto belonging, in the Township of Lyme, in the County of New London and Colony aforesd. I appoint my wife and my son Joseph Selden executors.

Witness: *Stephen Hosmer,*   JOSEPH SELDEN, LS.
John Holmes, John Church.

Court Record, Page 218—3d June, 1729: Will now exhibited by Ann Selden and Joseph Selden, son of sd. decd., executors named in sd. will. Proven.

Page 77 (Vol. XI) 28 November, 1732: Joseph Selden, of East Haddam, in his last will, gave his five daughters land, houseing and barn in the Town of Lyme. The eldest now being of age, moves this Court for dist. of the same. This Court therefore appoint John Holmes, John Church and Abell Wylley of Haddam to divide and dist. sd. lands.

Record on File.

Record of Distribution of Estate in Land, Houseing and Barn in Lyme:

Pursueant to ye order of his Honour ye Governor and Judge of ye Court of Probate in and for the County of Hartford, we the subscribers have made division of and distributed to the widow and five daughters of Joseph Selden, late of East Haddam deceased, of all his houseing and lands in ye Township of Lyme, in ye County of New London, according to his will, as followeth:

£ s d

To Anne Selden, widow, her thirds in lands, etc.
To Hepzibah Selden, eldest daughter,   171-00-00
To Rebeckah Selden, second daughter,   171-00-00
To Ann Selden, third daughter,   171-00-00
To Elizabeth Selden, fourth daughter,   171-00-00
To Hannah Selden, fifth daughter,   171-00-00
6th January, 1738. By *Abel Willey,* } *Distributors.*
John Church, }

Recorded in Vol. XII, Page 41-2.

Shaylor, Sergt. Timothy. Died 11 April, 1727. Invt. £275-07-06.
Taken 4 May, 1727, by Simon Smith, Thomas Shaylor and Joseph
Arnold.

Court Record, Page 158—13 June, 1727: Adms. granted to Martha
Shayler, widow relict, and Timothy Shayler, son of sd. decd., who recog.
in £100, with Samuel Ingram, of Haddam.

Page 180—5 March, 1727-8: Martha and Timothy Shayler, Adms.,
exhibited an account of their Adms., which this Court accepts. Order to
dist. the estate:

£ s d

To Martha Shayler, widow,   19-01-11
To Timothy Shayler, eldest son,   80-01-04
To Joshua Shayler,   40-14-00
To Elizabeth Bartlett,   25-01-00
To Jerusha Turner,   33-01-00
To Sarah Shayler,   40-14-00

And appoint Simon Smith, Joseph Shaylor and Thomas Shaylor,
distributors.

Page 331.

Shipman, William, Hebron. Invt. £36-02-04. Taken 24 December,
1725, by Nathaniel Phelps and Joseph Phelps.

Court Record, Page 125—5 April, 1725: Adms. granted to Samuel
Shipman, son of sd. deceased.

Page 43 (Vol. XIII) 8 March, 1738-9: An account of Adms. was
exhibited in Court by Samuel Shipman, Adms. Accepted.

Page 229-30.

Skinner, Joseph, Deacon, Windsor. Invt. of real estate, £181-02-05.
Taken 30 June, 1724, by Matthew Allyn, Thomas Marshall and Henry
Allyn. Will dated 13 January, 1715-16.

I, Joseph Skinner of Windsor, doe make this my last will and testament: I give unto Mary my wife the use and improvement of all my estate, both real and personal, for her subsistence during her natural life. I give to my eldest son Joseph, his heirs and assigns forever, besides what I have already given him, half of my meadow on the east side of the Great River in Windsor. Item. I give unto my son Richard the other half of my sd. meadow on the east side of the Great River besides what I have already given him. I give unto my son Isaac my dwelling house and barn in Windsor, with the homelott on which it standeth, being about 2 acres; also about 4 acres of land given to me and my wife by our father William Philley; also about 4 acres of land at a place called Swamp Field; also a paire of looms and tacklin which I have already given him to carry on his trade. It is to be understood that the abovesd. lands as they are given are to be injoyed by each of them from and after the death of my sd. wife now, and not before. And further, my will is that all my personal or moveable estate that remains after the death of my sd. wife, my just debts and funeral expenses being paid, shall be divided as followeth: To my grandson John Grant, son of my daughter Elizabeth decd., 20 shillings as money; the rest to be equally divided among my now surviving children or their legal representatives, viz., Joseph, John and Richard, and Isaac Skinner, Mary Hammond and Ann Rockwell. Finally, I do make, constitute and ordain my son Joseph Skinner sole executor.

Witness: *Matthew Allyn,*   JOSEPH SKINNER, LS.
        Josiah Allyn.

Court Record, Page 52—4 August, 1724: Will now exhibited by Joseph Skinner. Proven.

Slate, Daniel. Court Record, Page 121—1st day of March, 1725-6: This Court appoint Mr. Thomas Welles of Hartford to be guardian unto Daniel Slate of Windsor, a minor, 18 years of age, and Samuel Slate of Hartford, a minor, 15 years of age. Recog., £100.

Invt. in Vol. XII, Page 74.

Slater, Henry, Wethersfield. Died 24 February, 1727-8. Invt. £33-11-00. Taken 29 February, 1728, by Samuel Curtice, Joseph Woodhouse and Jonathan Dunham.

Court Record, Page 177—5 March, 1727-8: This Court grant Adms. unto Elizabeth Slater, widow of sd. deceased, and Samuel Curtice.

Page 5 (Vol. XIII) 5 April, 1737: Samuel Slater, age 16 years, son of Henry Slater, late of Wethersfield, chose Samuel Butler to be his guardian. Recog., £100.

Invt. in Vol. XII, Page 182.

Smith, Esther, Farmington. Died 18 May, 1725. Invt. £25-04-07. Taken 1st November, 1725, by Joseph Judd and Thomas Gridley.

Court Record, Page 106—2 November, 1725: This Court grant Adms. unto Nathaniel Porter.

Page 311-12.

Smith, George, Hebron. Invt. £593-10-03. Taken 1st July, 1725, by Jacob Root, Joseph Youngs and William Rollo. Will dated 12 June, 1725.

I, George Smith, late of Concord, in the Province of Massachusetts Bay, and now of Hebron, in the Colony of Connecticut, do make and ordain this my last will and testament: I give unto my mother Mary Smith £50 lawful money. I give unto my sister Margaret £20 of lawful money. I give to my sister Mary £30. I give unto my sister Elizabeth £100, to be raised out of my estate. It is my will that my clothing and the rest of my estate be equally divided between my well-beloved brothers William and James Smith. I constitute and ordain my trusty friends John Bliss and Hezekiah Taylor, both of Hebron, to be executors.

Witness: *Jeames Gillum,*   GEORGE SMITH, LS
Mary Gaylord, Mary Post.

Court Record, Page 98—23 August, 1725: The last will of George Smith was now exhibited in Court, and there being legacies given in sd. will of considerable sums of money to be levied out of his estate and no direction for disposing of lands (the estate of the deceased being principally in lands) to answer said sums of money, therefore the executors named in said will declared that they did decline the trust. And William Smith, brother of sd. deceased and as attorney for Mary Smith, mother, and also of the sisters of sd. deceased, appeared and declared that he refused, upon the reasons aforesaid, to take administration on sd. estate *Cum Testamento annexo.* Whereupon this Court do disallow said will, and grant Adms. unto William Smith, of West Town, in the County of Middlesex, in the Province of Massachusetts Bay.

Invt. in Vol. XII, Page 140.

Smith, Sergt. Jonathan, Wethersfield. Invt. £1091-11-03. Taken 1st January, 1728-9, by Jonathan Curtice, Benjamin Wright and Jacob Williams.

Court Record, Page 208—2 January, 1728-9: Adms. granted to Hannah Smith, widow, and Nathaniel Smith, son of sd. decd.

Vol. XI, Page 9—6 January, 1729-30: This Court grant an extension of time, on the estate of Jonathan Smith, to the Adms., Hannah and Nathaniel Smith, until 6 January, 1730-31.

Vol. XII, Page 4—2 May, 1734: Hannah Smith, Adms., now exhibited in Court an account of her administration: Paid in debts and charges, £108-06-05; and received, £5-01-00. The account allowed and ordered on file.

Page 224-5.

Smith, Joseph, Glastonbury. Invt. in lands, £1810-00-00. Taken by Benjamin Talcott and Samuel Gains. Will dated 14 September, 1725.

I, Joseph Smith, of Glastonbury, do make this my last will and testament: I give unto my brother Samuel Smith a certain lott or parcell of land in Glastonbury abutting on Connecticut River on the west, and from thence running three miles east and abutting upon the land of Daniel Wright on the south, and land of Capt. Samuel Welles on the north, excepting there out 1 acre of land which I formerly gave to the Rev. Mr. Timothy Stevens. I give unto Richard, Jeduthan and Manoah Smith, sons of my brother Benjamin Smith, to be equally divided amongst them, a certain piece of land in Glastonbury abutting west on Connecticut River, south on land belonging to Capt. Samuel Welles, north on lands formerly belonging to Thomas Bunce and now belonging to my brother Benjamin and myself, and east on a place where the meadow fence formerly stood, and in the division of the sd. last given land Manoah is to have the first choice and Jeduthan is to have the second choice, excepting always 5 acres there out which I formerly gave to the parsonage of Glastonbury. I give unto the sd. Richard, Jeduthan and Manoah Smith, equally to be divided amongst them, and to their respective heirs and assigns forever, a certain piece of upland formerly bought by my father Richard Smith of one Thomas Bunce in Glastonbury. Sd. upland begins at the brow of the hill not far from Connecticut River on the west, and runs the whole bredth of the lott which formerly belonged to the sd. Bunce east as far as where the meadow fence formerly stood. I give to my brother Samuel Smith 25 rods in bredth of land abutting on the River Connecticut west, and from thence running east 3 miles, south on Capt. Welles's land, and north partly on the parsonage land of Glastonbury and on land belonging to my brother Benjamin and myself, excepting out of his bequest 6 acres belonging to Richard Fox. I give unto the sd. Jeduthan Smith my horse, as also my small gun or carbine. I give unto the sd. Richard Smith my fowling piece. I give my brass kettle and all my pewter and bedding to my cousins Dorothy and Dinah Smith, daughters of my brother Benjamin Smith, to be divided between them. And as for all the rest of my goods and chattells, or other estate whatsoever, not herein before given, I give the same unto my brother Benjamin Smith, his heirs and assigns forever. My brother Samuel Smith to be executor.

Witness: *Sarah Neuill,*   JOSEPH SMITH, LS.
Samuel Gains, John Lynn.

Court Record, Page 114—1st February, 1725-6: Will now exhibited and proven. Ebenezer Fox appealed from this decree to the Superior Court.

Page 136—1st November, 1726: Invt. now exhibited and accepted.

Page 245.

Smith, Philip, Hartford. Invt. £770-16-02. Taken by Timothy Cowles, John Meakins and Daniel Dickeson (Diggeson).

Court Record, Page 67—2 February, 1724-5: Adms. to David and Samuel Smith, sons of sd. decd.

Page 72—2 March, 1724-5: This Court do appoint Samuel Smith, of Hartford, guardian to his brother Ebenezer Smith, age 19 years. Recog., £100. This Court appoint Mary Smith to be guardian to her children, Nehemiah 16, and Hannah 14 years of age. Recog., £200.

Page 73: This Court order that one-third part of the housing and lands and £20 in value of the moveable estate shall be set out to Mary Smith, widow and relict of said deceased, for her support and subsistence. And the widow shall have delivered to her £4 of the money due from the Town of Hartford to her late husband for procureing clothing for herself. The said £4 not to be accounted as part of her thirds of said estate.

Page 231 (Probate Side, Vol. XII): Whereas, Samuel Smith, son of Philip Smith, was granted by this Court, 15 July, 1725, the sum of £20 out of his father's estate for service since he was 21 years of age: Now, upon consideration that the above sd. Samuel Smith will release and give up his right to the sd. £20 so granted him unto us, we do hereby give up all the right and title we or our heirs, etc., have, or in time to come should have, unto a certain new house erected by the sd. Samuel Smith on his sd. father's land, which house was apprised at £32. In witness whereof we have hereunto set our hands and seals this 4 January, 1725-6.

SAMUEL SMITH, LS.	WIDOW MARY SMITH, LS.
DAVID SMITH, LS.	JOHN BENJAMIN, LS.
REBECKAH X SMITH, LS.	THOMAS WIARD, LS.

Court Record, Page 112 (Vol. X) 4 January, 1725-6: An allowance to Samuel Smith of £20 for his labour, to have it in a certain house, an agreement signed by the widow and heirs, exhibited and accepted.

Page 118-119—1st March, 1725-6: David Smith and Samuel Smith, Adms. on the estate of Philip Smith, late decd., exhibit an account: Paid in debts and charges (more than what has been received) £76-10-08; inventory with additions, £770-16-08; out of which deducting the sum of £31 for a horse in the invt. (agreed by the heirs of sd. decd. for Samuel Smith, one of the sons) and also the sum of £76-10-08, there will then remain of real and moveable estate £663-06-00 to be distributed. Order: To Mary Smith, widow, £30-18-04 with dower; to David Smith, eldest son, £115-04-09, he having formerly received £20 not inventoried, which is his double portion of sd. estate; to Martha Wyard, £59-08-05, she having received £8-04; to Mary Benjamin, £51-19-05, she having received £15-13-00; to Aaron (David) Smith, Samuel, Ebenezer, Nehemiah, Rebeckah and Hannah Smith, the rest of the children of sd. decd., to each of them, £67-12-05. And appoint Timothy Cowles, John Meakins and Joseph Pitkin, distributors.

Dist. File: 25 January, 1725-6: To the Widow Mary Smith, to David, to Ebenezer, to Nehemiah Smith, to Martha Wyard, to Mary Benjamin (wife of John Benjamin), to Rebeckah and Hannah Smith. By Timothy, Cowles and John Meakins.

Page 227-324.

Smith, Rebeckah, Wethersfield. Died 25 March, 1725. Invt. £59-03-00. Taken by Josiah Churchill and Nathaniel Stilman. £9 given to the abovesaid decd. by her uncle Joseph Church, in the hands of Joseph Church. Will dated 20 March, 1724.

I, Rebeckah Smith of Wethersfield, make this my last will and testament: I give unto my brother Benoni Smith all my meadow land on the east side of the Great River, bounded west on sd. river, east on land of Thomas Wadsworth, north and south unknown to me, but be it according to the records of sd. land. I give to my brother Benoni and to my brother Timothy Smith all my other land, to be divided between them by themselves. I give to Martha, the daughter of Deliverance Blynn, my pewter salt sellar and pan; and to Mollie, the daughter of sd. Blynn, a pewter plate; and to Rebeckah Blynn my Bible. As to my other personal or moveable estate, I give and bequeath to my honoured mother Mary Smith, my sisters, Mary Smith, Mehetable Smith and Mercy Smith, and my sd. brothers, Benoni Smith and Timothy Smith, to be divided to them in that proportion as shall seem suitable and convenient to my kinsman Deliverance Blynn of sd. Wethersfield, whom I constitute my sole executor.

Witness: *Daniel Stocking,*   REBECKAH SMITH, LS.
Christopher Graham, Nathaniel Burnham.

Court Record, Page 104—5 October, 1725: Will now exhibited, proven and accepted.

Page 19-20-21.

Smith, Samuel, Farmington. Inventory taken by Timothy Porter and Isaac Cowles. Will dated 8 December, 1724.

I, Samuel Smith of Farmingtown, do make this my last will and testament: To my wife Ruth Smith I give the use of ye whole of my house and lott where I now live, and all my land in ye Common Field, also my pasture called Dirty Hole, also my wheat lott over ye mountain, until my son Steven shall come to ye age of 21 years, and after that, during her natural life, the use of 1-2 of sd. house and lott, and ye 1-3 part of my sd. land. I give to my wife 1-3 part of all my personal estate and £10 more, to be at her dispose forever, only she to pay my son William Smith's two daughters, when they come of age, to each of them 20 shillings. Also, I give to my wife, and to her heirs forever, all my land lying in ye division of land west from ye reserved lands in sd. Farmingtown. Unto my son Thomas Smith I give my house, barn and house lott which I lately bought of Samuel Woodruff, lying in sd. Farmingtown, on ye east side of ye Town Street, against Samuel Judd's house. Unto my son John Smith I give my land in sd. Farmingtown of about 15 acres that lyeth joining to ye lott where my son William deceased built his house, and 21 acres more adjoining, also £20 to be paid him by my executor out of my personal estate. To my son James Smith I give a tract of land in Farmington lying near a place called Milford Pond, it being a half a lott containing about 52 acres; also 1 tract of land containing about 14 acres, it being half a lott lying in the middle tier of lotts in a division of land lying between the mountains; also £20 in money which is due to me from Samuel Bird for him the sd. James's last year's service with him; also £10 more out of my personal estate. Unto my son Stephen Smith I give my house and lott I now live upon, and also my land in the Common Field, and my pasture at a place called Dirty Hole, and my wheat lott of about 7 acres on the east side of the mountain, all in the Township of Farming-town, and 1-2 of my sd. house and lott by him to be possessed when he comes to the age of 21 years, and 2-3 parts of the other lands given to him by this instrument at sd. age, and the remainder of the whole at the decease of his mother. Also I give unto him the sd. Stephen all the re-mainder of my sd. estate not by this will disposed of, both real and per-sonal, he paying all the legacies by this instrument given to his sister and the £20 given to his brother John, also the £10 given to James. Unto my daughter Sarah Stanly, besides what I have formerly given her, I give her £5. Unto my daughter Martha Stanly, besides what I have formerly given her, I give her £5. Unto my two granddaughters, children of my son William decd., I give unto each of them 20 shillings at 18 years of age. I appoint my wife Ruth Smith and son Stephen Smith executors.

Witness: *John Hooker, Sen.,*   SAMUEL SMITH, LS.
Isaac Cowles, Sen., Joseph Woodruff.

Court Record, Page 66—2 February, 1724-5: Will now exhibited by Ruth Smith and Stephen Smith, the executors, and proven.

Invt. in Vol. XII, Page 145.

Southmayd, Giles, Middletown. Invt. £71-06-05. Taken 26 June, 1728, by John Collins, William Ward and Joseph Rockwell.

Court Record, Page 195—3 July, 1728: Adms. granted to Joseph Starr, son-in-law of sd. decd.

Page 1-2.

Steele, Elizabeth. Invt. £56-15-10. Taken 26 September, 1723, by James Ensign and Samuel Catling.

Court Record, Page 31—1 October, 1723: Adms. to Jonathan Steele. Exhibit of invt.

Page 49—5 May, 1724: Adms. account exhibited and allowed. Order to dist. to Jonathan Steele, to Stephen, and to Ebenezer Steele, to Mary Watson, to Sarah Ashley, and to Rachel Allyn, they being children of the brothers and sisters of sd. decd. By John Shepherd, James Ensign and Samuel Catlin.

Recorded in Vol. XII, Page 105-115 Inclusive.

Stevens, Rev. Timothy, Glastonbury. Invt. £1986-19-08. Taken 18 April, 1726, by Samuel Smith, Jr., and Deacon Nathaniel Talcott.

I, Timothy Stevens, do make my last will and testament: Item. I give my two-handled silver cup to the Church in Glastonbury for the use of the Sacrament after my wife's decease. I give my son Timothy my silver watch, my child's silk suit and lined silk blanket, my best silk gown and petticoats, 2 silver spoons, 2 gold rings, great seal skin trunk and my best gunn. I give to my son Joseph my silver box marked "E. S." at the bottom, a red broadcloth blanket, the next best silk gown and petty coat, 3 silver spoons, 1 of them to be a small child's or babe spoon as it is called, two gold rings, my great black leather trunk, 1 gunn and a silver chain for a pair of sisers. I give to my son Benjamin my silver dram cup and the other silk gown and petticoat, 1 red broadcloth blankett, 3 gold rings, 3 silver spoons, 1 of them to be a child's spoon, 1 pair of large silver clasps with stone or cristal or glass sett in the midst, 1 pair of pistols and 2 of the next best trunks. All the rest of my estate I give to my 3 sons, Timothy, Joseph and Benjamin, to be equally divided amongst them, only Timothy shall have the first choice of a place to dwell at upon any of my lands. As for my lands in Glastonbury and Middletown, I do give the same to them and their heirs forever. The rest of my lands in other towns I do give unto my sons, and it is my will that none of that land that is not in Middletown or Glastonbury be sold or exchanged, at least within the space of 25 years after my death. And all the rest of my estate I give also unto my sons. And as for my English books, vist., divinity, physick and history, I give to them and their heirs. In case my sons should all die without heirs, I give my dwelling' house and barn with the 2 acres of land that it stands upon, vist., the 2 acres I had of Mr. Benjamin Alford, to the Town of Glastonbury for a parsonage forever, only on this condition, that they shall within a space of 1 year after my decease pay to each of my executors £3. In case my sons all die without heirs, all the rest of my estate to be equally divided between my two brothers, Joseph and Samuel Stevens. I do give to my beloved wife all the estate she had a good right to before our marriage together, that is to say, that I give to her all the right that I have or may seem to have to what land she purchased at Hebron before I married unto her. I give to her that 120 acres that is there laid out together on ye 16 day of April, Anno. Domini 1724, according to the record of the survey of sd. land, notwithstanding that the land was laid out after our marriage together and so my name is mentioned in the record with hers. I do make choice of Deacon Benjamin Talcott, Capt. Thomas Welles and Mr. Jonathan Hale executors.

Witness: *Samuel Smith,*   TIMOTHY STEVENS, LS.
William Miller, Abner Maudsley.

Court Record, Page 127—27 April, 1726: Will exhibited by Benjamin Talcott, Thomas Welles and Jonathan Hale, executors. Proven. And this Court appoint Mr. Benjamin Talcott to be guardian unto Benjamin Stevens, a minor, 12 years of age. Recog., £100. Jonathan Hale appointed guardian unto Joseph Stevens, age 15 years. Recog., £100. And Timothy Stevens, age 17 years, made choice of Capt. Thomas Welles to be his guardian. Recog., £100.

Page 58 (Vol. XIV) 7 May, 1745: Report of the distributors. Accepted.

Recorded in Vol. XII, Page 185.

Stiles, John, Windsor. Died 12 November, 1728. Invt. £355. Taken 31 January, 1728-9, by Daniel Bissell, Israel Stoughton and Peletiah Allyn. Will dated 11 November, 1728.

I, John Stiles of Windsor, do make this my last will and testament: I give to my wife Elizabeth Stiles all my personal and moveable estate, to be at her own dispose forever. Also, it is my will and pleasure that in case the child which my wife now carrieth in and with her shall live to be born and to the age of 21 years if it be a son, and if a daughter to the age of eighteen years or on her marriage if sooner, then I say my will and pleasure is that the same child (whether it be son or daughter) shall be heir to all my real estate, and I give and bequeath all my real estate to him or her and to his or her heirs forever. And in case the child above mentioned, if any such shall hereafter be, should die before he or she shall arrive to the age above expressed, then I give and bequeath unto my loving wife Elizabeth my dwelling house and ye lott or piece of land it standeth on, which is about 2 acres and 1-2 be it more or less, to her and to her heirs forever, to be at her own dispose. I give to my kinsman Samuel Stiles of Windsor all the remainder of my lands and real estate wheresoever and whatsoever, to him and his heirs forever, in case the child should die as above said before it be of age. Item. I give unto my sister-in-law, Abigail Taylor of Windsor, £10 money, to be paid to her the sd. Abigail out of my estate by my executor hereafter named, within the space of 1 year after my decease. Also my will is that in case my aforenamed kinsman Samuel Stiles shall come to have and receive the legacy before expressed and given to him, then the sd. Samuel Stiles shall pay out of the sd. legacy £10 money unto my aforesd. sister-in-law Abigail Taylor in 6 months after receiving the legacy. My pleasure is that Lt. Jonathan Elsworth, of Windsor, and my wife Elizabeth Stiles shall be executors.

Witness: *Robert Barnett,*   JOHN X STILES, LS.
Daniel Bissell, Ruth X Crow.

Court Record, Page 211—4 February, 1728-9: Will now exhibited by Elizabeth, widow of the decd., one of the executors named in the will. Approved.

Page 92 (Vol. XI) 5 June, 1733: This Court appoint Jonathan Stiles, formerly of Stratford and lately of Hanover, in West Jersey, and Elizabeth his wife to be guardian unto John Stiles of Windsor, a minor, about 4 years of age, son to the sd. Elizabeth Stiles. Recog., £100.

Recorded in Vol. XII, Page 188-9-90-1.

Stilman, George, Wethersfield. Invt. £3622-04-07. Taken 14 January, 1728-9, by David Goodrich, Benjamin Smith and Martin Smith.

I, George Stilman of Wethersfield, do make this my last will and testament: I give my wife Rebeckah £100 current money to be her own forever. Also I give her the full remainder of my whole moveable estate to use and improve during her natural life (if she remain a widow to me, but, if she marry again, to be divided amongst all my children). I give to my son George Stilman £100 in money (besides what he has already received of me), to be paid him out of my estate. I give my son Nathaniel Stilman, as in addition to what I have already given him, a lott of land in Wethersfield which I bought of Nathaniel Nott, containing about 13 acres; also 1-2 of my swamp lott in Wethersfield meadow which I purchased of Joseph Wright; also the half of the lott of land I bought of John Hollister, Walter Harris and John Williams, being all in 1 piece about 5 acres in Wethersfield meadow; also 1-2 of the lott bought of John Brownson, being in Wethersfield, about 26 acres; also 1 more lott of land in Wethersfield meadow which I bought of George Kilbourn, about 4 acres and 1-2; all which pieces or parcells of land I give to my sd. son Nathaniel forever. I give to my grandson Nathaniel Stilman, son to Nathaniel, 1-2 a lott of land lying in Middletown which I bought of William Hamlin and was his father's, situated on the east side of the Great River, about 40 acres, which land I give to my sd. grandson forever. Item. I give to my son John Stilman, as an addition to what I have already given him, a lot of land in Wethersfield bott of Joseph and Thomas Tryon, about 7 acres; also a lot of land in Wethersfield, about 14 acres, bott of Joseph Crofoot; also the other half of my swamp lott in Wethersfield meadow, bott of Joseph Wright; also the other half of my lott bott of John Hollister, Walter Harris and John Williams, being in Wethersfield meadow; also the other half of that lott in Wethersfield which I bought of John Brownson; all which pieces or parcells of land I give to my sd. son John forever. I give to my son Benjamin Stilman, as an addition to what he has already had of me, my dwelling house and home lott, with all the buildings and appurtances thereon or thereunto belonging, the 1-2 thereof at my decease and the other half to my loving wife Rebeckah during to her widowhood, to revert to my son Benjamin. I give to my son Benjamin land in Wethersfield, 4 1-2 acres, bought of Joseph Hills and John Gilbert, 1-2 at my decease, the other half to revert to my son Benjamin; also 1 lott of land at Wethersfield, about 4 acres, bott of John Russell; also a lott of land in Glastonbury at a place called the Great Swamp, about 16 acres, bott of Benjamin Strickland; all which pieces of land I give to my son Benjamin, with a building thereon, forever. I give to my grandson John Stilman, son to John, a lot of land in Middletown on the east side of the Great River, bott of Jonathan Gilbert, about 40 acres, forever. I give to each of my daughters, Mary Blynn, Sarah Willard, Anne May, Elizabeth Blynn and Hannah Caldwell, I say to each of my sd. daters, £300 in money, including what they have each already received of me in my lifetime. Lest any difficulty should arise to know what is right about the interest I had in a house at Hartford formerly Benjamin Smith's, which I acquitted to my son-in-law John Caldwell and have charged to my daughter Hannah in my book, I say the amount of ye value of my interest in sd. house acquitted as aforesd. and charged in my books, is to be a part with ye other charges in my books of my daughter Hannah's. I give to my daughter Lydia £300 in money, clear and free of all charges, to be paid her forthwith out of my estate. I give my grandson George, son to Mary Blynn, 2 lotts of land bought of Jonas Holmes, about 50 acres, which was Ranney's and Attkison's, forever. I give to my grandson Samuel, son to Sarah Willard, a lott of land in Middletown on the east side the Great River, about 40 acres, being the 111th lott in number, forever. I give to my grandson Samuel, son of Anne May, the other half of that lott I bought of William Hamlin, to him and his heirs forever. I give to my grandson William, son to my dater Elizabeth Blynn, a lot of land on the east side of the Great River in Middletown, bott of Mr. Starr, which was James Brown's draught. I give to my grandson James, son to Hannah Caldwell, 2 lotts of land in Middletown on ye east side the Great River, about 30 acres, bought of Jonas Holmes and Nathaniel Hubbard. I hereby bequeath to my son George and my son John all my wearing apparell of every sort, each a half part. It is my will that my wife Rebeckah shall have the remainder of all my land to use and improve during her natural life or widowhood (excepting one piece bott of David Smith on ye east side of the Great River in Hartford, about 6 1-2 acres, which I give to my three sons, Nathaniel, John and Benjamin Stilman, to them and their heirs). And after her decease or marriage, ye lands aforesd. to be to my 3 sons also. I appoint my wife Rebeckah and my sons Nathaniel Stilman and John Stilman executors.

Witness: *John Austin,*   GEORGE STILMAN, LS.
Mary Austin, Abigail Hooker.

Court Record, Page 208—18 December, 1728: Will now exhibited by Rebeckah Stilman, Nathaniel Stilman and John Stilman, executors named in the will. Proven. Invt. exhibited.

Invt. in Vol. XII, Page 201.

Stocking, John, Middletown. Invt. £632-04-00. Taken 29 March, 1726-7, by Capt. William Savage, Capt. John Warner and Joseph Whitmore.

Court Record, Page 109—7 December, 1725: Adms. granted to Daniel Stocking, brother of sd. decd., and Samuel Stow.

Page 153—2 May, 1727: The Adms. exhibit now an account of their Adms. Accepted.

Agreement on File: We whose names are underwritten, being the heirs of John Stocking, late of Middletown decd., have agreed upon a distribution of the estate: First, to the heirs of George Stocking of Middletown, to Daniel Stocking, to Bethiah Stow, to Lydia Ranney, to each of them their single parts of sd. estate. Signed and sealed July, 1727.

THOMAS X STOW, LS.	GEORGE STOCKING, LS.
BETHIA X STOW, LS.	JOHN CHURCHILL, LS.
DANIEL STOCKING, LS.	ELIZABETH X STOCKING, LS.
LYDIA RANNEY, LS.	BETHIA X STOCKING ALIAS CHURCHILL.
STEPHEN STOCKING, LS.	SAMUEL HALL, LS., GUARDIAN TO
SAMUEL STOCKING, LS.	NATHANIEL STOCKING.

Page 158—3 July, 1727: Agreement acknowledged in Court and accepted.

Page 268-276.

Stoddard, Bethiah, Wethersfield. April the 28th, 1725: We, the subscribers, being desired by Samuel Smith and Joseph Smith, of Glastonbury, to apprise the estate of their sister, Bethiah Stoddard, of Wethersfield, late deceased, have according to the best of oure judgments apprised the sd. estate at £24-02-02:

> Beriah Stoddard,
> John Wells,
> Joseph Dickinson.

The verbill will of Bethia Stoddard, deliuered to us the subscribers as witness the 19th of April, 1725, as followeth: I giue to my cousin Doratha Smith, daughter to my brother Benjamin Smith, of Glastonbury, one brass kettle holding about foure pailfulls, and three puter platters, and two iron kittles, and one porridg pot, and one warming pan, and 1 little brass skillett, and one pr. of cards, and a siluer bodkin. These to be deliuered after my deceas.

> ISAAC DEMING,
> LYDIA X DEMING.

Court Record, Page 82—4 May, 1725: A nuncupative will of Bethiah Stoddard, late of Wethersfield decd., was now exhibited. The same being proved, is allowed by this Court, and ordered to be kept upon file. And grant letters of Adms. to Joseph Smith, Jun.

Page 103—4 October, 1725: Joseph Smith, Adms. on the estate of Bethiah Stoddard, late of Wethersfield, late decd., exhibited an account of his Adms.: Paid in debts and charges, £4; which account the Court accepts. The inventory, £24-02-02; subtracting £4, there remains £20-02-02. Order to be distributed to the brothers and sisters of sd. decd. in equal parts: To Samuel Smith, Joseph Smith, Benjamin Smith and Beriah Fox, to each of them, £4-00-05; and to the heirs of Esther Strickland, £4-00-05; which is their equal portion of sd. estate. And appoint Samuel Smith, Jr., Ebenezer Fox and Joseph Fox, distributors.

Page 228.

Invt. in Vol. XII, Page 169.

Stoddard, Joshua, Wethersfield. Invt. £124-05-00. Taken 1st March, 1725-6, by Daniel Rose and James Butler. Will dated 29 September, 1703.

I, Joshua Stoddard, being sick and weak yet of sound memory, considering the shortness and uncertainty of my life here in this world, and desireing to settle and dispose of my estate, do make this my last will and testament: I give unto my loving wife Bethiah Stoddard all my homestead and all my land in Wethersfield meadow during her natural life, and after her decease to return to my brothers John Stoddard and Nathaniel Stoddard, equally to be divided between them. And if my wife shall survive my brothers, or any one of them, then the half of the sd. land I give to the children of my brother John, and the other half to the children of my brother Nathaniel Stoddard. I give unto my sd. wife all my household goods whatsoever, to be hers forever, except 1 frying pan and 1 iron pot which was mine before marriage, which I give to my brothers John Stoddard and Nathaniel Stoddard, that is to say, after my wife's death. Likewise, I give unto my wife 1 cowe and a hefer, 1 mare and colt, to be hers forever, and all my bees. It is my further will and pleasure to constitute and appoint my well-beloved wife Bethiah Stoddard to be the whole and sole executrix of this my last will and testament.

Witness: *Thomas Tousey,*   JOSHUA STODDARD, LS.
John Curtice, Ephraim Whaples.

The abovesd. will not proved, but disallowed in Court.

Page 100—7 September, 1725: Letters of Adms. was granted unto John Stoddard.

Court Record, Page 121—1st March, 1725-6: Invt. now exhibited in lands. Order to dist. to brothers and sisters, vizt., to heirs of John Stoddard decd., to the heirs of Nathaniel Stoddard decd., to the heirs of Elizabeth Wright decd., to the heirs of Mary Wright decd. By James Butler, Joseph Goodrich and Eleazer Goodrich.

Page 133—2 August, 1726: Report of dist. exhibited by John Stoddard.

Page 120-1.

Stoddard, Samuel, Wethersfield. Inventory taken 12 April, 1725, by James Butler and Joseph Goodrich.

Court Record, Page 79—12 April, 1725: Adms. to John Stoddard, brother of sd. deceased. Exhibit of inventory.

Page 134—2 August, 1726: An agreement among the brothers and sisters was now exhibited under their hands and seals. Accepted.

Record on File, dated 16 May, 1725: We the subscribers joyntly and severally have agreed to distribute among ourselves the estate of Samuel Stoddard, which is done to our good satisfaction, as doth and will appear by affixing our hands and seals.

JOHN STODDARD, LS.
JONATHAN STODDARD, LS.
DAVID STODDARD, LS.
ELIZABETH STODDARD, LS.
MARY WARNER, LS.

At a Court of Probate held at Hartford, 2 August, 1726: Then the within-named John Stoddard, Jonathan Stoddard, David Stoddard, Elizabeth Stoddard, and the said David Stoddard as attourney to the within named Mary Warner, appeared before this Court and acknowledged the within instrument to be their free act and deed.

Test: Hez: Wyllys, Clerk.

Recorded in Vol. XII, Page 221-2-3.

Stow, Nathaniel, Middletown. Invt. £1057-18-01. Taken 12 June, 1728, by John Collins, Israhiah Wetmore and Joseph Rockwell.

Court Record, Page 195—3 July, 1728: This Court grants Adms. on the estate of Nathaniel Stow, late of Middletown decd., unto Sarah Stow and Nathaniel Stow, widow and son of the sd. deceased, who gave bond jointly and severally.

Page 219—3 June, 1729: This Court appoint Nathaniel Stow of Middletown to be guardian unto Sumner Stow, a minor, 16 years of age. Recog., £200.

Page 13 (Vol. XI) 3 March, 1730: The Adms. exhibited an account of their Adms., which this Court accepts.

Page 97—12 September, 1733: Jabez Stow, a minor, chose Samuel Ward of Middletown to be his guardian. Recog., £50.

Page 39 (Vol. XII) 3 February, 1735-6: Sarah Ward, who was formerly wife of Nathaniel Stow, late decd., made choice of William Rockwell of Middletown to be guardian to her son James Stow, age 9 years.

Page 40—9 February, 1735-6: Seth Wetmore to be guardian to Ebenezer Stow, age 11 years. And Sarah Stow, age 16 years, chose William Rockwell to be her guardian.

Strickland, Joseph, Glastonbury. Court Record, Page 137—1st November, 1726: Adms. granted to Naomi Strickland and David Hubbard, who with Richard Smith, recognized in £150.

Page 166—3 October, 1727: The Adms. exhibit an account of their Adms. Accepted.

Page 201—1st October, 1728: The Adms. exhibit a further account of their Adms. Also accepted by the Court.

Page 27 (Vol. XIII) 10 April, 1738: Joseph Strickland, age 16 years, John, age 14 years, both sons of Joseph Strickland deceased, chose their father-in-law Thomas Loveland of Glastonbury to be their guardian. Recog., £200.

Recorded in Vol. XII, Page 101-2-3.

Strong, Return, Lt., Windsor. Invt. £392-04-00. Taken May, 1726, by Thomas Fyler, John Stoughton and Alexander Allyn.

10 April, 1719: I, Return Strong of Windsor, do make this my last will and testament: To my son Samuel Strong I give and bequeath and to his heirs and assigns forever, all my land with the priviledges and the appurtenances thereof, lying on the south side of the Little River, which was formerly Mr. Warham's, which I bought of Mr. Stoddard. I give to my son Samuel 4 1-2 acres of my lott in the Great Meadow, which was Mr. Warham's. I give to my son Benjamin Strong my house and homestead lying on the north side of the Little River, and the lott that lyeth in the Great Meadow near the Ferry, being about 8 acres, and 6 acres in the lower lott next the Little River in the Great Meadow. I give to my 6 daughters, Sarah, Abigail, Elizabeth, Dameras, Hannah and Margaret, £60 apiece with what they have received already. I give to my grandson, John Warham Strong, 5 shillings. I appoint my son Samuel Strong sole executor.

Witness: *Thomas Fyler,*   RETURN STRONG, LS.
Stephen Fyler, Ebenezer Fitch.

Court Record, Page 128—5 May, 1726: Will now exhibited by Samuel Strong, executor named in the will. Proven. Exhibit of inventory.

Taylor, Ebenezer. Court Record, Page 185—21st April, 1726: Ebenezer .... a minor, ..., before this Court........ choice of Samuel Bigelow to be h.............., which this Court allows. The sd. Samuel Bigelow rec. in £50.

Page 248.

Taylor, Jonathan, Hartford. 20 July, 1725: Then an invt. taken of the estate of Jonathan Taylor, a transient person, late of Cituate decd.:

	£	s	d
To one coat of plain cloth,	2-10-00		
To two vests and two old pr. britches, att	0-05-00		

	£	s	d
To 3 shirts, all,	0	13	00
One muslin cap and two muslin stocks,	0	09	00
One silk muslin neck cloth,	0	03	00
3 pr. old stockings and one pr. of garters,	0	04	06
A two-foot rule,	0	02	06
A felt hatt,	0	03	06

4-10-06

The above articles was apprised by us the subscribers.

Richard Seamore,
Samuel Green,
Thos. Clapp.

Recorded in Vol. XII, Page 9.

Talcott, Benjamin, Glastonbury. Invt. £2563-15-08. Taken 27
November, 1727, by Nathaniel Talcott and Thomas Welles. Will dated
13 October, 1727.

I, Benjamin Talcott of Glastonbury, do make this my last will and
testament: I give to my wife the sum of 4 score pounds out of my moveable estate at the inventory price, or in money if my executor shall think
best, excepting what my sd. wife brought with her, which my mind and
will is that she have it back again at inventory price as part of the 4 score
pounds (what may be found left of it), and the use of the parlour in the
house I now dwell, and a convenient part of the cellar underneath it, and
the garrett room that is over it, and the use of my ovens, and the use of
such a part of my gardings as may be necessary for her own comfort, and
the use of 1-3 part of my orchard on the west side of the highway on the
lott I now dwell, with the use of 1-3 part of all the rest of my land on
that side of sd. highway down to the Great River. It is to be understood
that my sd. wife is to have the use of the sd. house and land no longer
than she remains my widow. I give to my son Benjamin all my right
of land in the Town of Bolton, and 124 acres of land in the Town of Hebron which I bought of Joseph and John Phelps of sd. Hebron, with
what I have already given to my sd. son, as may appear by my book of
accounts. I give to my son John all the rest of my land in the Town of
Hebron, particularly that tract of land in sd. Hebron lying west of Jacob
Root's land, containing 300 acres; and that 50 acres of land in sd. Hebron
I bought of Asahell Owen, lying northward of Richard Curtice's; and
one yoke of steers coming 4 years old; and £10 out of my moveable estate besides what I have already given, as appears by my book of account,
and £15 money, to be paid by my son Elizer at or before he my sd. son
Elizer arrive to the age of 21 years. I give to my son Samuel the 1-2
of the lott of land (I now dwell upon), on the south side, and 153 acres
of lands lying within the bounds of Glastonbury, beyond Blacklidge's
River, adjoining to Hebron bounds, and the 1-2 of my undivided land in
sd. Glastonbury, and my smith's shop and all my smithery tools (ex-

cepting any I shall give to my sd. son John), and my longest gunn, and 1-2 of my present team and team tackling, as collars, haims, chains, cart and wheels, plows and harrows. I give to my son Elizer the other half of my lott of land I now dwell upon, on the north side, with the buildings thereon (excepting the smith shop) ; and 60 acres of land lying in Glastonbury, eastward of and adjoining to lands of the heirs of the Reverd. Mr. Stevens decd., at a place called the Ash Swamp; and 96 acres of land in sd. Glastonbury, lying eastward of the Great or Bare Hill, adjoining southwardly to land of Samuel Loveland ; and the other half of all my undivided land in sd. Glastonbury, and my newest gunn, and the other half of my team and team tackling as above mentioned, he my sd. son Elizer paying to my sd. son John the sum of £15 money as above mentioned. And further, my mind and will is, that all the wollen cloth (and one piece of linen of about 40 yards that is now about to weave) which my wife has made or shall make this present year be disposed of to my wife and my children unmarried, as my wife thought to do in my lifetime. I give to my daughter Sarah £100 in or as money, with what I have already given her. I give to my daughter Hananh £100 and a decent suit of clothes or £10 money. I give to my daughter Mehetabell £100 and a decent suit of clothes or £10 money when she shall arrive at the age of 18 years or her day of marriage, which shall happen first. I appoint my son Jonathan Hale and Benjamin Talcott to be my executors.

Witness: *Samuel Smith, Jr.,*   BENJAMIN TALCOTT, LS.
Nathaniel Talcott, Thomas Welles.

Court Record, Page 169—5 December, 1727: Will exhibited by Jonathan Hall and Benjamin Talcott, executors. Proven. And this Court appoint Benjamin Talcott of Glastonbury to be guardian unto Mehetabell Talcott of Glastonbury, a minor, 15 years of age. Recog., £100.

Page 299-300.

Terrie, John. Died 25 May, 1725. Invt. £352-15-08. Taken 8 June, 1725, by James Cornish, Sen., John Case, Jr., and James Hilyard.

Court Record, Page 90—6 July, 1725: Adms. granted to Mary Terrie, widow.

Page 159—4 July, 1727: This Court appoint Mary Terrie of Simsbury to be guardian to her children, viz., ... Terrie, about 12 years of age, Stephen 10 years, ...at 7, Mary 4, Elizabeth ....provided bond be given as the law directs. Recog., £300.

Page 55 (Vol. XI) 2 November, 1731: John Terry of Simsbury, 16 years of age, son of John Terry, chose Samuel Wadsworth to be his guardian.

Page 62—7 March, 1731-2: Mary Fowler alias Terry, Adms., was summoned 20th January, 1731-2, to render an account of her Adms. She now appeared and rendered an account:

	£	s	d
Paid in debts and charges,	52	09	07
The moveable estate amounting to the sum of,	91	12	02
Subtracting,	52	09	06
There remains to be distributed,	39	02	07

Samuel Wadsworth, of Farmington, guardian to John Terry, son of John Terry, moves this Court for a dist. of sd. estate. This Court appoint Lt. Samuel Griswold, James Cornish, Jr., and John Humphries, Jr., distributors.

Page 105—5 February, 1733-4: John Terry, by Samuel Wadsworth his guardian, cited Mary Terry alias Fowler and John Fowler her husband, as per writ on file, to render account of her guardianship to sd. minor. The case was decided against Wadsworth with costs.

Page 44 (Vol. XII) 3 April, 1736: Solomon Terry, age 16 years, son of John Terry, with his mother Fowler's consent, chose Timothy Stanly to be his guardian.

Page 2 (Vol. XIII) 1st March, 1736-7: Elizabeth Terry, 12 years of age, with the consent of her mother Mary Terry alias Fowler, former guardian, chose Amos Phelps to be her guardian. Recog., £150. Cert: *John Humphrey, J. P.* Mary Terry, age 14 years, chose her brother John Terry to be her guardian. Recog., £150.

Page 65-96.

Terry, Samuel, Symsbury. Inventory taken 24 February, 1724-5, by James Cornish, Sen., James Hillyer and Samuel Humphries. Will dated 6th February, 1724-5.

I, Samuel Terrey of Simsbury, do make this my last will and testament: Imprimis. After my funeral charges and all my other debts be paid, I give unto my brother John's eldest son John Terry, Jr., my home lot with my house and barn that now stands upon it, to him and his heirs forever. Also I give unto sd. John Terry, Jr., Stephen Terry, Jr., and Solomon Terry, my brother John's three sons, all my meadow and woodlands, to be equally divided amongst them. I give to my brother John's two daughters, vizt., Mary and Elizabeth, £8 to each of them. I give to my cousin Elizabeth Holcomb, alias Goff, £10. I give to my sister Sarah's daughter, Elizabeth Hill, £8. I give to my brother John my gunn, team, tackling, plow, cart and plow irons. Also all my other estate not yet disposed of. And appoint him my executor.

Witness: *Samuel Higley,* SAMUEL X TERRY, LS.
Nathaniel Alford, Joseph Alderman.

Court Record, Page 71—2 March, 1724-5: Will now exhibited by John Terry, named executor in sd. will. Proven. Invt. exhibited.

Page 90—6 July, 1725: This Court grants Adms. on the estate of Samuel Terrey, late of Simsbury decd., unto Mary Terrey, widow of John Terrey, late decd., who was executor of the last will of Samuel

Terrey, with his last will annexed. Exhibit of an inventory of what estate of sd. Samuel Terry rested in the hands of her late husband John Terry as executor aforesd., £68-07-00.

Dist. on File, 11 March, 1732: To the sons of John Terry deceased, viz., to John, to Stephen, to Solomon Terry. By John Humphreys and James Cornish, Jr.

Recorded in Vol. XII, Page 39-40.

Thomasson (Thomlinson), Henry, Colchester. Invt. £400-00-00 plus. Taken by Joseph Wright and John Skinner.

Court Record, Page 152—2 May, 1727: This Court grant Adms. unto Elizabeth Thomlinson, widow and relict, who recog. with Benjamin Quitafield joyntly and severally in £200.

Page 218-269-70-71-2-4-5-6.

Thrall, Timothy, Windsor. Invt. £5025-09-03. (Paper money.) Taken by John Thrall, Samuel Strong and John Stoughton. Will dated 28 January, 1723-4.

I, Timothy Thrall of Windsor, do make this my last will and testament: I give to my wife Sarah Thrall £500 in money to be to her forever. Also the use of half my house, orchard and homested during her widowhood; also to keep two cows summer and winter, with pasture, and may cut grass where she may choose in any of my grass land for sd. cows. I give to my two sons William and Timothy Thrall, after all debts and legacies are paid, the rest of my estate, to be divided equally between them. My son William may have the use and improvement of Timothy's portion until he come of age, provided my son William shall well and truly pay and deliver unto his brother Timothy Thrall his part at the age of 21 years with the interest and improvement of ye sum of £500 money. I give to my daughter Sarah £500 in current money. I give to my daughter Abigail Thrall £500 in money, to be paid at the age of 21 years or previous marriage. I also will that Margaret, my Indian girl, shall have her liberty and freedom allowed her, provided she faithfully serve my wife for the space of 13 years from this, or, in case of her prior decease, to serve the remainder of the time with my son William. I appoint my wife and son William to be overseers and guardians over and for my children; also to be executors.

Witness: *Samuel Mather,*   TIMOTHY THRALL, LS.
Samuel Strong, John Stoughton.

Codicil: We the subscribers being at the house of Captain Timothy Thrall of Windsor sometime in his last sickness, we heard the sd. Thrall declare that his son William Thrall should have all the interest he had in or at the iron works at Suffield and the oare and coal that he had pro-

cured. He also said he would give all those things to William, and I would not have it put in my inventory. Dated 4th May, 1725.
Witness: *Samuel Mather,*
John Stoughton, Samuel Strong.

Court Record, Page 39—3 March, 1723-4: Will proven.

Invt. in Vol. XII, Page 194.

Toobe, John, Middletown. Invt. £1713-17-09. Taken 4 and 13th November, 1728, by Ebenezer Prout, George Philips and James Brown. The abovesd. inventory includes goods in Boston in the hands of Nicholas Davis, with small debts due from 100 persons, afterward collected, £133-02-05.

Page 200.

A list of debtors to the estate of John Toobee, late of Middletown:

John Dewolph,
Joseph Rockwell Jun.
Ebenezer Hubbard,
John Taylor,
Simon, Indian,
John Andrews,
David Johnson,
Mercy Miller,
Daniel Stocking,
John Smith, Durham,
Samuel Baker,
Ebenezer Arnold,
Anna Cornwell,
Ephraim Adkins,
Daniel Hubbard,
Isaac Lane,
Thomas Stow,
John Arnold,
Richard Beach,
Dible Comer,
Gideon Leete,
Casehog, Indian,
Mary Delle,
William Seward,
Samuel Starr,
Martha Miller,
Benjamin Penfield,
John Sivadle,
Benedict Arnold,

John Dible,
Robert Coe,
Thomas Hurlbut,
Peter Samhues,
Edward Adams, Importer,
Edward Foster,
Jonathan Roberts,
Samuel Peck,
Samuel Roberts,
Giles Southmaid,
William Ward, Cooper,
Thomas Strong,
Thomas Cooper,
Edward Hamlin,
Ruth Bowe,
Deborah Lewcas,
Samuel Roberts,
Daniel Clark,
John Prout,
Nathaniel Hurlbut,
Jacob Cornwell, Importer,
Moses Bidwell,
Abraham Dolittle,
Bethia Stow,
John Roberts,
Deborah Ward,
James Tappin,
Joseph Druss,
Thomas Ward,

Jacob White,
William Lewcas,
Samuel Allen,
William Markham,
William Ward, Newfield,
William Hamlin,
Mary Butler,
Samuel Miller,
Benjamin Cornwell,
Solomon Adkins,
Thomas Roster,
Nathaniel Stow,
Thomas Barns,
Daniel Ranney,
Doc: Ebenezer Cooper,
Mary Horton,
Nathaniel Stow. Jun.,
James Stanclift,
Jonathan Burr,

Samuel Galpin,
John Leete,
Joseph Starr, Jun:
Gideon Lewcas,
Jonathan Collins,
William Whitmore,
Seth Wetmore,
Thomas Alverd,
Matthew Beckwith,
Benjamin Armstrong,
Obadiah Allen,
David Hurlbut,
Thomas Porter,
Nathaniel Roberts,
Thomas Stephens,
Christian Savidge,
Jonah Strickland,
Abner Newton.

Court Record, Page 204—4 November, 1728: Adms. granted to Sarah Toobe, widow of sd. decd.

Page 221—12 November, 1728: This Court having granted Adms. on the estate of Mr. John Toobe, late of Middletown decd., unto Sarah Toobe, widow and relict of the sd. decd., and the sd. Sarah Toobe, Jeremiah Osgood and Thomas Foster of Middletown personally appeared in Hartford before sd. Court and acknowledged themselves to stand jointly and severally bound to the sd. Joseph Talcott, Esq., Judge of the Probates, or his successors, in a recog. of £2000 current money, that the sd. Sarah Toobe, Adms. on the estate of John Toobe aforesd., shall faithfully administer on the goods, credits and chattells of the sd. John Toobe, and that she shall make a true and perfect inventory of the goods, chattells and credits of the sd. decd., and the same exhibit into this Court within 1 month. And that she the sd. Adms. shall pay the debts and gather in the debts due to sd. estate within 18 months, and fully administer on the sd. estate as the law directs, and account with this Court thereon on or before the 12th day of May in the year of our Lord 1730.

Page 19 (Vol. XI) 5 May, 1730: The case continued. Sarah Marks appears in Court and offered an addition to the inventory of £133-03-03.

Page 20—28 May, 1730: Thomas Marks, husband of Sarah Marks, and Mrs. Sarah Marks, Adms. on the estate of John Toobee, appeared before this Court of Probates, and not having perfected the inventory as they were required, with consent of the parties this case is continued until the first week of June next.

Page 23—5 June, 1730: Thomas Marks and Sarah Marks, formerly Sarah Toobee, relict of John Toobee, were ordered to procure better sureties, which as yet they have not procured, and pray for longer time, which was granted.

Page 24—30 June, 1730: Sarah Marks, Adms. on the estate of John Toobee, appeared before this Court and pleaded that by reason of one Broughton's running away with a sloop from New London and carrying with him the goods of her husband Thomas Marks, that sd. Sarah and Thomas Marks, being strangers in this place, could not procure sufficient sureties for the faithfull discharging of the trust of Adms. on the estate of her former husband John Toobe, but prays still for longer time that they may, when recovered their goods, also in hope of recovering their credit, and so may be able to get sureties sufficient.

Page 26—4 August, 1730: In Court a note of Mr. John Austin, which showed that Mr. Ozias Goodwin, Mr. Joseph Pitkin and himself were willing that Thomas and Sarah Marks should remain Adms. until October next.

Page 38—1st May, 1730-1: Anthony Toobe, a minor, 15 years of age, chose Capt. Giles Hall to be his guardian. Recog., £100.

Page 58—17 December, 1731: Thomas and Sarah Marks exhibit account, £1699-07-06. The Court allows the same, they not having fully perfected their Adms. The Court now grants them until the first Tuesday of June next.

Page 83—22 February, 1732-3: Ozias Pitkin, Esq., attorney to Edward Bromfield of Boston, now exhibited an execution against Thomas and Sarah Marks, Adms. on the estate of John Toobe, whereby it appeared that the sd. Pitkin, attorney, has received of the Adms. the sum of £185-16-06, which execution is lodged and filed in this Court.

Page 92—5 June, 1733: Additional accompt of Adms. on the estate of John Toobe as per receipt from Thomas Wallace, William Randall, Hannah Deming and Robert Stevenson, all which amounts to the sum of £47-00-00, which account is accepted and placed on file.

Page 5 (Vol. XII) 4 June, 1734: Thomas Marks, with the assistance of Jabez Hamlin, is ordered to sell land in Middletown to the value of £742-08-08.

Page 7—17 July, 1734: Report of sale of land: Sold to Giles Hall, the highest bidder, for £672-10-00.

Invt. in Vol. XII, Page 149.

Treadway, James, Colchester. Invt. £708-07-00. Taken 18 June, 1728, by Nathaniel Otis, Noah Welles and Isaac Jones.

Court Record, Page 213—4 March, 1728-9: Adms. granted to James Treadway, son of the decd.

Invt. in Vol. XII, Page 87.

Treat, Matthias, Hartford (East). Invt. £141-19-02. Taken 26 October, 1726, by John Benjamin and Charles Buckland.

Court Record, Page 148—7 March, 1726-7: This Court grant Adms. unto Hannah Treat, widow, and the sd. Hannah Treat and Abraham

Warren of Wethersfield acknowledged themselves joyntly and severally bound in a recog. of £100.

Recorded in Vol. XII, Page 22-3-4.

Tudor, Samuel, Windsor. Died 6 July, 1727. Inventory taken by Hezekiah Porter, Henry Woolcott and John Bissell. Will dated 13 June, 1727.

I, Samuel Tudor of Windsor, do make and ordain this my last will and testament: Item. I give unto my son Samuel 12 rods in breadth on the north side of the lott I live on, from the Great River to the country road, and from the country road my will is yt he shall have 14 rods in breadth eastward to the end of 3 miles, on the north side of sd. lott, with the buildings and appurtenances thereof. Item. I give unto my daughter Abigail Tudor 1-2 of the remaining part of the lott I now live on, from the river to the end of the 3 miles, after Samuel's part as abovesd. is taken out of sd. lott. Item. I give unto my daughter Mary Kilbourn, besides what I have already given her, the sum of £50. Item. I give unto my daughter Sarah Morsse £50 besides what I have already given her. Item. I give unto my daughter Margaret Tudor the other half of my lott I live on, together with my daughter Abigail, vizt., 1-2 thereof after Samuel's part aforesd. is taken out, to be divided between Abigail and Margaret. Item. I give unto my daughter Elizabeth Marshall, besides what I have already given her, £50. My will also is that all my outland, common right and divisions, layd out and not layd out, in Windsor, as also a piece of meadow land which descendeth to me of my brother Owen's estate, of about 2 3-4 acres, and all my moveable, of what kind and sort soever, after my debts and the legacies to Mary, Sary and Elizabeth be paid, shall be equally divided between my sons Samuel and my daughters Abigail and Margaret. My will also is that my son Samuel shall be brought up at college out of my estate till he shall come regularly out. I appoint my son Samuel Tudor sole executor.

Witness: *Nathaniel Porter,*   SAMUEL TUDOR, LS.
John Bissell, John Loomis.

Court Record, Page 161—August, 1727: Will now exhibited by Samuel Tudor, executor named in the will. Proven. Exhibit of inventory.

Invt. in Vol. XII, Page 229.

Turner, Mary, Hartford. Invt. £229-05-08. Taken 29 April, 1728, by Thomas Hopkins and Jonathan Steele.

Court Record, Page 192—3 May, 1728: Adms. granted to John Skinner, Jr.

Page 211.

Viet, John, Symsbury. He died 18 November, 1723. Inventory taken 31 December, 1723, by Thomas Holcomb, Ephraim Griffin and Samuel Griswold.

Court Record, Page 34—3 January, 1723-4: Adms. to Katharine Viett, widow, and Andrew Henning. Invt. exhibited. This Court order to be sett out to the widow for her support, £8-18-08 of the estate of John Viett, Sen.

Page 54—1st September, 1724: The Adms. reports estate insolvent and asks to be discharged, and that commissioners be appointed on the estate.

Page 310.

Waddams, Elizabeth, Wethersfield. Invt. £63-15-00. (Item, 127 acres of land.) Taken 6 July, 1725, by Joseph Churchill and Nathaniel Stilman.

Court Record, Page 90—6 July, 1725: Adms. granted to Thomas Stedman on the estate of Elizabeth Waddams, alias Sage, decd.

Page 96—3 August, 1725: Whereas, Elizabeth Waddams, late of Wethersfield, died seized of 120 acres of land lying in Middletown valued at £63-15-00, Thomas Stedman, Adms., now moves this Court that it may be dist. Order to dist. to Mary Stedman, sister of sd. decd. By James Butler, Joseph Goodrich and Daniel Rose.

Wadsworth, Ruth. Court Record, Page 56—6 October, 1724: This Court appoint John Palmer, Jr., of Windsor, to be guardian unto Ruth Wadsworth of Hebron, a minor, 14 years of age. Recog., £40.

Page 124-5.

Wadsworth, Thomas, Hartford. Will dated 11 August, 1725: I, Thomas Wadsworth of Hartford, do make this my last will and testament: I give to my daughter Sarah Burr, for the love and respect I bear to her, 10 acres of land lying westward of Brick Hill Bridge, formerly belonging to Edward Cadwell, west and south upon common highway, north upon John Barnard, east upon Thomas Cadwell, which I give to her forever. To my daughter Elizabeth Wadsworth, 6 acres of land lying upon the hill by Nathaniel and Thomas Andrews' lands where they now dwell, butting southwardly upon their lands, westwardly upon my own land, northwardly upon the highway. And also I give her, for her comfortable subsistence, one dwelling room in my house in part with her brother John Wadsworth, which is the southerly lower room, which I give to her only during her natural life, and 1 square rod of ground in my

garden for her free use and improvement during her life. I give to my grandson Thomas Wadsworth 10 shillings. I give to my son John Wadsworth, for the love and respect I bear to him, all my estate besides what I have above mentioned, all lands and moveables, bills, bonds and notes, book debts or whatsoever estate I am now seized of in my own right, or whatsoever shall after my death be added to this estate which I am not now in the actual possession of in my own right. All which I give to him and to his heirs and assigns forever after my decease, he paying all my just debts. I make my son John Wadsworth to be executor.
Witness: *Timothy Woodbridge,*   THOMAS WADSWORTH, LS.
William Goodrich, James Church.

Codicil, dated 22 November, 1725: As an addition to what I have already given to my daughter Elizabeth, I give her one milch cow, with two of the swine that are now fatting, and also five bushels of indian corne, and also 40 shillings for 5 years next following my decease, if her present infirmity should continue with her.
Witness: *T. Woodbridge,*   THOMAS WADSWORTH, LS.
       Gared Spencer.

Court Record, Page 129—5 May, 1726: The last will and testament of Mr. Thomas Wadsworth was now exhibited by John Wadsworth, executor. Proven.
Page 99 (Vol. XV) 2 May, 1749: Elizabeth Wadsworth, one of the heirs to the estate of Mr. Thomas Wadsworth, late of Hartford decd., now moves to this Court that distributors may be appointed to set out to her 3 acres of land given her by the last will and testament of the sd. deceased in a piece of land in Hartford on the east side of the Great River. Whereupon this Court appoint Joseph Talcott and Capt. Jonathan Hale of Hartford to set out to sd. Elizabeth 3 acres of land according to the will, and make return of their doings to this Court.

Page 201-2.

Wale, John, Hartford. Inventory taken 30 November, 1723, by Disbrow Spencer and Hezekiah Goodwin.
Court Record, Page 31—1st October, 1723: This Court grant letters of Adms. on the estate of John Wale, late of Hartford decd., unto John Tyley and Thomas Collett.
Page 35—3 January, 1723-4: Invt. exhibited.

Invt. from File. Recorded on Page 156 (Vol. XII).

Ward, Andrew, Middletown, son of John Ward. Invt. £143-00-00. Taken 24 March, 1728-9, by Samuel Gipson and Joseph Rockwell.

Invt. on File. Recorded on Page 4 (Vol. XI).

Ward, Andrew, Middletown. Invt. £223-03-00. Taken 1st September, 1729, by John Collins and Joseph Rockwell.

Court Record, Page 214—4 March, 1728-9: Adms. granted unto William Ward, brother of the deceased.

Page 2 (Vol. XI) 2nd August, 1729: William and Esther Ward exhibited in this Court an invt. of the estate of Andrew Ward. Accepted.

See File: September 1st, 1729: Then wee the subscribers, being acquainted with the dificulty William Ward hath been at, and also the charge he and his brother Samll. Ward hath been at with theire brother Andrew Ward decd. in his destraction, being desired to give oure judgments of the charge, wee give it as followeth: He returned from Boston to Middletown in May, 1698, and continued dumb and very dificult to manage for the space of three years, which we can't judge less than worth £150-00-00. And five years in distraction at £250. The last 20 years, when he remained very dificult for the most part, we cant judge less than £30 a yeare, is £600. Total, £1000. We the subscribers hereunto being desired to give oure judgment pr us, Joseph Rockwell and John Collins, concerning the above writen, do conseed with the same as to the first eight years, and as to the last 20 years we judge it cant be less than £20 a yeare. October 7th, 1729.

As witness our hands:
Israhiah Wetmore,
John Bacon.

The estate of Andrew Ward is indebted unto Wm. Ward, Adms. on the estate of Andrew Ward, late of Middletown decd.:

	£	s	d
To journey to Hartford to take Adms.,		00-10-00	
The return of the inventory and Court fees,		1-00-00	
The aboue accompts of Adms. allowed in Court, 7th October, 1729,		1-10-00	
		801-10-00	

Examined: Pr. *Jos: Talcott, Jr., Clerk.*

Upon the 21st January, 1730-1, William Ward, Adms. on the estate of Andrew Ward, was summoned before the Probate Court with Mrs. Elizabeth Ward, widow of Samuel Ward, now decd., concerning a debt due to them from the estate of their brother Andrew Ward decd., for a settlement by the Court, the estate not being sufficient to pay the debts.
Seth Wetmore, Constable. Fees, 4 shillings.

Ward, James. Court Record, Page 60—1st December, 1724: Adms. granted to James Ward, son of James Ward decd.

Recorded in Vol. XII, Page 204-5.

Ward, Thomas, Middletown. Will dated 3 May, 1728: I, Thomas Ward, Sen., of Middletown, do make this my last will and testament: I give to Elizabeth my wife the one equal half of my now dwelling house and cellaring, which parts she shall choose; also the 1-2 of my homestead, 1-2 of my barn, 1-2 of the cellar under it, 1-2 of my lott called Bow Lott, and also the whole of that land which I bought of Daniel Harris, Jr., and also my negro man called Peter, for her improvement for comfort of life so long as she shall live and continue my widow, and no longer. I give to my wife 1 equal half of a pair of oxen and of one horse kind, with one equal half of my cart, plows, harrows, sleds, with all iron and wooden utensils, and also one-half of my cider mill and presses, with my cider tub and empty casks. And yt remains at her decease or marriage shall return to my son James Ward. And whereas, I have in this my will given my wife Elizabeth considerable estate so long as she shall continue my widow, and that if she marry it will fail her, it is my will that if my wife should by the providence of God be joined in marriage to another man, that then my sd. son James Ward shall pay to her £50 in or as money within one year after such marriage. I give unto my son Thomas Ward, besides what I have given him already, 7 acres of my Hornet Bay meadow. Also I give unto my sd. son Thomas his two sons Thomas and Tappin the whole of my right in the lottment of land which was my hond. father William Ward's decd., which lyeth in the West Division lotts, of which my son William hath a part, and my part lying on the southern side, this I give unto my above named grandsons equally to be divided between them. I give to my son Thomas one equal third part of my wearing apparel, to be equally divided between him and his brothers William and James. I give to my son William Ward, besides what I have given him, the whole remainder part of my Hornet Bay land besides what I have given to my son Thomas. And also I give unto my sd. son William my lottment of land on the east side of the Great River in the last division. I give to my son William one equal third part of my wearing apparrell. I give unto my son James Ward, besides what I have given him before, the one equal half part of my dwelling house and barn and cellering, and the one-half of my homested and 1-2 of my bow lott so called, both plowing and mowing and orcharding. These I give to my son James to enjoy and improve with my wife equally (with her half so long as she shall continue my widow, and at her decease or marriage shall be the proper propriety of my abovesd. son James Ward). So that I do hereby invest my sd. son James Ward in the possession and reversion rights of the whole of my now dwelling house, barn, cellering, homested, bow lott, Harris lott and negro man called Peter. I also give to my son James Ward my Hubbard lott and my Crowel lott so called, he paying to my two daughters, his sisters, Phebe, now the wife of Daniel Hall, and Mary, now the wife of Benedict Alverd, £50 to each of them in or as current money. I also give to my son James my gunn and sword and amunition. I appoint my beloved wife and my son James Ward executors.

Witness: *William Ward,*   THOMAS WARD, LS.
John Ward, Joseph Rockwell.

Court Record, Page 194—3 July, 1728: The last will and testament of Capt. Thomas Ward, late of Middletown decd., was now exhibited. Proven.

Recorded in Vol. XII, Page 172-3-4.

Warner, Andrew, Middletown. Invt. £624-12-10. Taken 29 April, 1726, by John Collins, Joseph Rockwell and Robert Warner. Will dated 6 April, 1726.

I, Andrew Warner of Middletown, do make this my last will and testament: I give to my loving sister Hannah Warner the use of all my dwelling house and barn and all my home lott, and the meadow I bought of Thomas Stow, and the land we call Addams lott, and my Indian Hill lott, the use of the whole of these till my nephew Andrew Warner, who dwells with me, shall come of age, and then to resign 1-2 of the barn and house and 1-2 of all the above specified land to him, and to keep the use of the other half during her natural life. Also I give to her, after my just debts and funeral charges are paid, and the legacies after mentioned to the church, and that to John Barnes, the use of all my household stuff, money, stock, husbandry utensils and moveables of all kinds, during her natural life, then to be equally divided among my brethren and my sisters. I give to my cousin Andrew Warner, who now lives with me, my house and barn and all my house lotts, and the meadow I bought of Thomas Stow, and the land we call Addams lott by Sergt. Stow's, and my lott at Indian Hill, all the above-mentioned I give to him and his heirs forever, to have the possession and use of, with 1-2 when he shall arrive at the age of 21 years, and the other half at the decease of his Aunt Hannah. To my brothers John and Joseph, and my sisters Mary and Rebeckah, I give all my other land, excepting what was given to John Barnes, to be equally divided among them. And also, what shall be left of my household stuff and stock at my sister Hannah's decease to be equally divided among them and their heirs. I give to the church in this place £10 to be delivered to the pastor and deacons, to be laid out in a piece of plate for the sd. church's use. To John Barnes, all my whealwright tools of what name soever. Also I appoint my sister Hannah, with my brothers John and Joseph, my executors. I desire the Rev. Mr. Russell and Deacon Rockwell to be overseers to this my will.

Witness: *William Russell,*   ANDREW WARNER, LS.
Joseph Rockwell, Robert Warner.

An addition to what is written on the other side this paper, and explanation: My will is that if my cousin Andrew Warner should die without issue, then what I have given him shall be equally divided between my brothers and sisters and their heirs. I give to John Barnes (besides the tools mentioned on the other side) 10 acres of land out of my mountain lott, to him and his heirs forever.

Witness: *William Russell,*   ANDREW WARNER, LS.
Joseph Rockwell, Robert Warner.

Court Record, Page 128—5 May, 1726: Will now exhibited by John and Hannah Warner, executors named in the will. Exhibit of Invt.

Page 158—6 June, 1727: Some real estate in Middletown not yet disposed of: Adms. on this estate to John Warner, son of sd. deceased.

Page 164—5 September, 1727: Some additional invt. exhibited.

Recorded in Vol. XII, Page 63-4-5-6-7-8-9.

Warner, Capt. William, Wethersfield. Died 16 October, 1726. Invt. £2111-10-09. Taken 23 and 24 day of November, 1726, by Edward Bulkeley, John Rennolds and Jonathan Robbins.

I, William Warner of Wethersfield, do make this my last will and testament: I give to my beloved wife Elizabeth, of my estate, both real and personal, one-third part while she remains my widow, and no longer. I give to my eldest son John Warner my house, barn and homelott, containing 10 acres, with the trees, fence and other buildings thereon growing and standing, sd. homelott being butted and bounded on the Beaver Dam or brook east, on the highway leading to Middletown west, on land which I bought of Joseph Rily north, and on land of Joseph Grimes south; and also 4 acres on the west side of the aforesd. highway, butting and bounding east on sd. highway, west partly on comon and partly on land of William Blin, north on land herein given to my son Jonathan, and south on land of Joshua Robbins; also I give to my son John Warner 2 acres of my land I had of my brother Daniel Warner, lying in the Great Meadow, which was Porter's land, butted and bounded east on a highway, west on the Great Plain, north on Eliz: Warner, and south on land of John Coleman. Also 2 acres in the Great Swamp, butted and bounded east on the Great River, west on a highway, north on land of Daniel Warner, and south on land of William Stilman. Also 4 acres in the Great Meadow in a place called the Nook, butted and bounded on a highway west and south, and on the Beaver Brook east and north. And also all my right and title in a 22-acre lott lying in Fairfull Swamp, which land joins to the aforesd. homelott. Also 2 acres of land at a place called the Westfield Hill, butted and bounded east and north on a highway, south on land of Jacob Griswold, and west on land herein given to my son John Warner. I give to my son Jonathan Warner these pieces of land: 6 acres which I bought of Joseph Rily, also 6 acres at a place called Hangdog, also 2 acres in the Great Meadow, and 1 1-2 acre in Mile Meadow, also 3 acres of land in the Dry Swamp, also 3 1-2 acres in the Wet Swamp, also 2 acres of land in the South Field, and 2 acres of land at a place called the Westfield Hill. I give to my son William Warner several pieces of land: 6 acres of land at a place called Hangdog, 2 acres of land in Beaver Meadow. Adjoining proprietors: Capt. John Chester, heirs of Samuel Wollcott decd., Eliphalet Dickinson, Ebenezer Belding, Jacob Williams, Capt. Robbins, heirs of Israel Crane, Isaac Rily, Noadiah Dickinson, Jacob Griswold, Samuel Benton and Nathaniel Boreman. My will is that my children which I had by my first wife have all that land which came to me by her, lying in that tier of lotts next to Farmingtown line, that it be equally divided amongst them. I give to my 3 daughters, vizt., to Mary, Hannah and Abigail Warner, to each of them £80 paid to them out of my moveable estate. What my daughter Mary hath already had, and an £8 right in the 52-acre lott which I bought of Elijah Crane, I give to my sd. daughter Mary and to her son Elisha Dunham, to be a part of ye sd. £80. I appoint my son John Warner and my brother Joshua Robbins executors. I do desire my brother Thomas Welles and my brother Daniel Warner and Mr. Richard Robbins to see this my will executed.

Witness: *Edward Bulkeley,*   WILLIAM WARNER, LS.
Jonathan Bull, Jonathan Belding, Jr.

See agreement as per File: Articles of agreement indented, concluded and fully agreed upon by and between Eliz: Warner, widdow and relict of Capt. Willm. Warner, late of Wethersfield, in the County of Hartford, in ye Colony of Connecticut, in New England, decd., of ye one party, and ye children and heirs of ye sd. Capt. Wm. Warner, viz., John Warner, Jonathan Warner, Solomon Dunham with Mary his wife, Abigail Warner, Hannah Warner and Willm. Warner on the other party, witnesseth: that whereas, upon ye death of ye sd. Capt. Warner sundry matters of difference did arise respecting ye estate of ye decd., and also with respect to the estate of ye sd. Eliz. Warner which was hers when she married ye sd. Capt. Warner: Now, for a showing and final issue of ye sd. matter of difference, and that ye last will and testament of ye said Capt. Warner should not be controverted by any of the parties aforesd., they have agreed as followeth: viz: First, they have agreed that ye whole of ye estate (yt is now in being) of her first husband, and yt she had at ye time of her marriage with ye sd. Capt. Warner, shall be returned to her again, with those bills and bonds now out for money wch belong to her first husband's estate, and she hath hereby full power to use and improve as her own, notwithstanding ye claims and demands of any person or persons claiming from, by or under ye heirs of ye said Capt. Warner. It is further agreed that John and Jonathan Warner shall have those parcels of lands given them by sd. will, Elizabeth Warner to have the improvement of all lands given to William Warner until he comes to the age of 21 years (to William 3 acres of land in Blackledge's Swamp, bounding on Nathaniel Boardman and John Warner). Also that Elizabeth Warner shall have paid out to her in moveable estate of Capt. Warner the sum of £100, she resigning up all her right in ye moveable estate to ye daughters of ye decd. And the sd. Elizabeth Warner, widow, together with ye children and heirs of ye sd. Capt. Warner, do hereby oblige themselves not to controvert ye sd. will of ye decd., but do hereby desire that it may be confirmed as his last will and testament. In testimony whereof we have hereunto set our hands and seals this 6th day of December, 1725.

ELIZABETH X WARNER, LS.	ABIGAIL X WARNER, LS.
JOHN WARNER FOR HIMSELF, LS.	HANNAH X WARNER, LS.
AND AS GRD. TO JONATHAN WARNER, LS.	ELIZABETH X WARNER, LS.
SOLOMON DUNHAM, LS.	IN BEHALF OF HER
MARY DUNHAM, LS.	SON WILLIAM WARNER, LS.

Court Record, Page 141—6 December, 1726: Adms. to John Warner, son of sd. deceased, with will annexed, to report in 12 months.

An agreement for the settlement of the estate now exhibited by the widow and heirs, vizt., Elizabeth Warner, Widow, John Warner for himself and as guardian to Jonathan Warner, Solomon Dunham and Mary Dunham, Abigail Warner and Hannah Warner, and the sd. Elizabeth Warner in behalf of her son William Warner, all of whom appeared in Court and acknowledged this to be their free act and deed.

Jonathan Warner, a minor, 14 years of age, chose his brother John Warner of Wethersfield to be his guardian. Recog., £200.

Page 142—6 December, 1726: This Court appoint Mrs. Elizabeth Warner to be guardian unto her son William Warner, a minor, 9 years of age. Recog., £200.

Page 195—3 July, 1728: John Warner, Adms. with the will annexed, being summoned to answer the complaint of Elizabeth Warner that the sd. William Warner was her guardian and did not in his lifetime account to her for the estate of hers he had in his custody in the time of her minority, and the sd. John Warner refuses, he also now appeared and declared that he is ready to account with her according to the dist. Whereupon this Court allow the sd. John Warner till 1st Tuesday of August next to make up an account with the sd. Elizabeth Warner for that estate and then produce her discharge for the same, or else to account before this Court.

Page 215—4 March, 1728-9: John Warner exhibits now an account of his Adms. on sd. estate. Allowed. £0-13-09 allowed to Solomon Dunham against John Warner for attendance at Court on two citations of sd. Adms. to render the above sd. account.

Will and Invt. in Vol. XII, Page 120-1-2-3.

Waters, Bevel, Hartford. Invt. £1483-16-00 (realty). Taken 13 March, 1729, by Thomas Hosmer, Samuel Webster and John Whiting. Will dated 1st February, 1720-1.

I, Bevel Waters of Hartford, do make and ordain this my last will and testament: I give to my eldest daughter, Sarah Benton, wife of Joseph Benton, £100 in money. I give to my 2nd daughter, Mary Seymour, wife of Thomas Seymour, £100 in money. I give to my 3rd daughter, Hannah Merrells, wife of Willterton Merrells, £100 in money. I give to my grandson Joseph Waters, besides what I have already given him, 5 acres of meadow land more or less, lying and being in Hartford South Meadow, bounded on the land belonging to heirs of Capt. Joseph Whiting decd., west, on land sometime belonging to Capt. Watts decd. north, on land of the heirs of Jno. Merrells decd. south, on lands of the heirs of Thomas Bunce decd., to be to him the sd. Joseph Waters, his heirs and assigns forever, he or they always rendering and paying the rate arising from sd. land towards the support of the ministry to the maintenance of the minister of the South Church in Hartford, of which Church the Reverd. Mr.

Thomas Buckingham is at present pastor. I give and bequeath to my grandson Samuel Waters all the rest of my houseing and lands, wheresoever lying or being, to be to him the sd. Samuel Waters and the eldest male heir of his body lawfully begotten, and so to divolve to the eldest male heir (lawfully begotten) in a right line, descending from sd. Samuel Waters from generation to generation forever. And for want of such male heir I then give and bequeath all those houseing and lands now bequeathed to my sd. grandson Samuel as followeth: viz., to the right lawfull heir descending to my son Thomas Waters decd., 2 shares or a double portion, and the remainder to be divided equally in proportion to my three daughters, Sarah, Mary and Hannah, to be to them and their heirs forever; always provided that the rate arising from sd. land for the support of the ministry shall be paid to the maintenance of ye minister of the South Church in Hartford, of which church the Reverend Mr. Thomas Buckingham is now pastor. My will is that the legacies given my three daughters shall be paid by my executors out of my moveable estate, reserving the long table, two other tables, wainscut foarm, leather chair, iron back and best featherbed and furniture to remain in the house for my grandson Samuel Waters. And what may be needfull to repair the buildings at my decease also to be reserved in moveable estate; and if there be wanting of sd. moveable estate (reserving what is before mentioned for my grandson Samuel and repairing the buildings) to paying sd. three daughters their legacies and my just debts, then sd. legacies shall be made up in meadow land which lies in Wethersfield (belonging to me) to the value to my sd. daughters at £12 as money pr. acre. My will is, also, and I do desire, that my executor will take care, after my decease, that the buildings be kept in good repair until my grandson Samuel Waters shall arrive to the age of 21 years, and for that end to reserve so much loose estate as will answer the design. My will is, likewise, that when the legacies to my daughters and my just debts are paid, and things before mentioned to be reserved in the house are so reserved, and so much money or loose estate left in my executor's hands as will repair the buildings, that if there shall be any moveable estate left (always provided my executors be well paid), I give sd. moveable estate so remaining to the three daughters of my son Thomas Waters, equally to be divided between them, and their heirs and assigns forever. And I do hereby appoint Mr. Nathaniel Stanly and John Skinner, both of Hartford, to be executors, and my grandson Samuel Waters also as executor with them.

Witness: *John Austin,*   BEVILL X WATERS, LS.
Mary Austin, Alice Howard.

This codicil hereafter should have been entered at the end of the will, but through mistake was not, but is here recorded:

Memorandum: Upon further consideration concerning the devises made in my foregoing will, I see cause to add this codicil as follows: That is to say, I give and bequeath 1 piece or percell of land more to my grandson Joseph Waters, son to Tho. deceased, lying and being in Hartford aforesd., containing 4 acres, joining to land belonging to Jonathan Bigelow at the lower end of the South Meadow, to be to him and his heirs forever. Also, that in case my grandson Samuel Waters die before he arrive to the age of 21 years, then my will is that the land and other estate before given to him shall descend and be 2-3 thereof to the children of my son Thomas decd., to them and their heirs forever, and the other 1-3 of sd. land and other estate to be divided equally amongst my three daughters, to be to them and their heirs forever. Also, my will is, that if any part of the legacies given to my daughters, that is to say, any part of the £100 I have given them before in this my will, shall be paid in meadow land in Wethersfield, that it shall be valued at the rate of £20 per acre.

Date 30 April, 1722.
Witness: *John Austin,*   BEVELL X WATERS, LS.
Josiah Hart, Edward Allyn.

Court Record, Page 216—1st April, 1729: Will proven.

Recorded in Vol. XII, Page 1-2.

Watson, Caleb, Hartford. Invt. £300 plus. Taken 2 July, 1726, by Thomas Hosmer, Richard Seamore and Ichabod Welles. Will dated 27 January, 1721-2.

I, Caleb Watson of Hartford, do make this my last will and testament: I give to Mary my wife all my lands and tenements, with the buildings and other appurtenances, to have and to hold for ye term of her natural life. Likewise, all my estate and possessions which I hold by lease, either for term of life or for years, to hold according to ye tenure of such lease or leases. Also ye use of all my goods and chattells, intending hereby all my moveable estate, effects and things, whether within doors or without, whether in action or in possession, in what specie, name or denomination soever, nothing excepted, to injoy, possess and improve ye sd. goods and chattells during ye term of her natural life, she paying all my just debts, funeral charges, and a legacy of £5 which I will to Dorcas Warner, daughter of my eldest sister, Dorcas Addams of Ipswich. I bequeath to my loving kinsman, Mr. Samuel Mihall, after my wife's decease, all my land, tenements, goods, chattells and estate of every kind and denomination, to hold and use for his benefit during his natural life. I will yt whatsoever lands I have already passed to him by deeds shall be and remain to him, his heirs and assigns in fee simple. I bequeath my loving kinswoman, Sarah Mihill, wife of sd. Samuel Mihill, excepting what lands I have passed away by deed to ye sd. Samuel Mihill, all my lands, tenements, hereditamts., goods, chattells, estate, utensils, effects and things of all sorts, after ye decease of ye sd. Samuel, to have and to hold to ye sd. Sarah, her heirs and assigns forever in fee simple, she paying £15 in legacy which I Will as follows, vizt., to my loving kinswomen Anne Hosmer and Patience Bulkeley £5 apiece out of ye sd. chattells or in money, at her election, and to ye heirs of my kinswoman Elizabeth Hitchcock £5. I constitute my wife Mary sole executrix.

Witness: *Peter Pratt,*   CALEB WATSON, LS.
Sarah Cook, Mehetabell Pratt.

Court Record, Page 133—5 July, 1726: Will now exhibited by Mary Watson, executrix named in the will. Proven.

2 August, 1726: Will now exhibited by Samuel Mihill, now appointed Adms. with the will annexed. And Mary Watson exhibited an inventory.

Page 34-5-6.

Watson, John, Jr., Hartford. Inventory taken 25 December, 1724, by Abram Merrells and John Webster.

Court Record, Page 64—5 January, 1724-5: Adms. to Sarah Watson, widow, and Caleb Watson, brother of sd. decd. Exhibit of Invt.

Page 85—4 May, 1725: The moveable estate not being sufficient to pay the debts, this Court now set out some of the moveables to the value of £17-19-06 to the widow for her necessary support and subsistence.

Page 92—6 July, 1725: Act of General Assembly, granting liberty to Sarah Watson and Caleb Watson, Adms. on the estate of John Watson, Jr., decd., to make sale of land for the payment of debts, £90-10-05.

Page 135—5 September, 1726: In pursuance of the act of the General Assembly in May last, this Court do direct the Adms. on the estate of John Watson, Jr., to sell at vandue so much of the lands as may provide the sum of £45 and incident charges to answer the debt due from sd. estate.

Page 137—1st November, 1726: Caleb Watson to be guardian to John Watson, age 12 years, Margaret 11, Abigail 10, and Sarah Watson 7 years of age. Recog., £200. Also Jonathan Steele to be guardian to Mary Watson, 15 years of age, Elizabeth 8, and Deborah 4 years of age. Recog., £200.

Page 3 (Vol. XI) 18 April, 1734: Sarah Watson and Caleb Watson, Adms., are ordered to sell 16 acres of land in the West Division to the highest bidder, which was Cyprian Watson, a brother of the decd.

Page 390 (Vol. XII, Probate Side) 7 June, 1736: A dist. of the estate of John Watson, Jun., is as followeth:

	£ s d	
To Mary Webster,	53-09-00	Ls., the wife of William Webster.
To Margaret Watson,	53-09-00	Ls.
To Abigail Watson,	53-09-00	Lamrock Flowers, guardian, Ls.
To Elizabeth Watson,	53-09-00	Lamrock Flowers, guardian, Ls.
To Sarah Watson,	53-09-00	William Webster, guardian, Ls.
To Deborah Watson	......	William Webster, guardian, Ls.

Page 48—6 July, 1736: An agreement was exhibited, and acknowledged by the heirs to be their free act and deed.

Page 316-17.

Watson, John, Sen., Hartford. Invt. £1106-16-10. Taken by John
Seamore and Thomas Seymore.

Court Record, Page 91—6 July, 1725: Adms. to Sarah Watson,
widow, and Cyprian Watson and Caleb Watson.

Page 198—6 July, 1728: Order to sell such real estate as may be
best vendable, to pay £88-07-11 of debts.

Page 63 (Probate Side, Vol. XI) : A dist. of the estate of Mr. John
Watson, Sen., as followeth: To Sarah Watson, relict of John Watson,
her thirds; to John Watson, Jr. heirs, their part of his father's estate,
which is £68-02-00; to Thomas Watson, to Cyprian Watson, to Caleb
Watson, to each of them, £68-02-00; to Anne Flowers, wife of Lamrock
Flowers, £134; to Sarah Watson, £134.

<table>
<tr><td>Signed: David Ensign,</td><td>John Whiting,</td></tr>
<tr><td>Daniel Webster,</td><td>William Bacor.</td></tr>
<tr><td>John Camp,</td><td></td></tr>
</table>

Whereas, John Watson, heir to John Watson, Jr., late of Hartford
decd., Thomas Watson, Cyprian Watson, Caleb Watson, Lamrock Flowers and Ann his wife, and Sarah Watson did enter into a certain covenant
under hands and seals bearing date June 19th, 1730, to stand to and abide
by the dist. made by the above named distributors, sd. dist. have perfected
sd. covenant and agreement to our mutual satisfaction.

<table>
<tr><td>Caleb Watson, ls.</td><td>Zachariah Seymour, ls.</td></tr>
<tr><td>Anne Flowers, ls.</td><td>Cyprian Watson, ls.</td></tr>
<tr><td>Sarah Watson, ls.</td><td>Lamrock Flowers, ls.</td></tr>
<tr><td>John Watson, ls.</td><td></td></tr>
</table>

It appeareth that Mr. John Watson had a right in the land commonly
called the Western Grant, and also in the land called the Five Miles Lotts
on the east side of the Great River in Hartford, which is not considered in
this dist. before named: Wherefore we, the subscribers, agree to dist. the
above-named as followeth: viz.: To the heirs of John Watson, Jr., a
double portion or 2 shares; to Thomas Watson, 1-7 part; to Cyprian, 1-7
part; to Caleb Watson, 1-7 part; to Anne Flowers, 1-7 part; to Sarah
Watson, 1-7 part.

Court Record, Page 25—7 July, 1730: Agreement signed and sealed
for a dist. of sd. estate, under a bond of £2000 to abide the decision of
the distributors.

See the Agreement on File: 2 July, 1730: To Sarah Watson, the
widow of John Watson, Sen., decd.; to John Watson, to Thomas, to
Cyprian, to Caleb, to Anna Watson (wife of Lamrock Flowers), to Sarah
Watson. By John Camp, Jno. Whiting and William Baker. Zachariah
Seymour, attorney for Cyprian Watson. All signed and sealed as above.

Another paper mentions Thomas Watson of Jamaico, in the Provence
of New York, while the other mentions him in Hartford.

Page 48 (Vol. XII) 6 July, 1736: Agreement exhibited in Court and
acknowledged by the heirs to be their free act and deed. Accepted.

Page 28 (Vol. XIV) 2 August, 1743: Sarah Watson, the relict of John Watson, of Hartford, decd., by her attorney, Lamrock Flowers, of sd. Hartford, showed to this Court, by an agreement under the hands and seals of the heirs to the estate of sd. decd., that although by sd. agreement the relict was to have her thirds of the house of the sd. deceased, but in sd. agreement it is not said which part of the house the widow is to have for her thirds, this Court therefore order and appoint Capt. Daniel Webster, David Ensign and Jonathan Sedgewick of Hartford to set out and ascertain which third part of the dwelling house sd. widow shall have for her thirds.

Page 42—April, 1744: A return of the widow's dowry of the estate of John Watson to Sarah Watson, widow and relict, under the hands of Capt. Daniel Webster, David Ensign and Jonathan Sedgewick of Hartford.

Invt. in Vol. XII, Page 85.

Watson, Sarah, Widow, Hartford. Invt. £16-07-02. Taken 6 December, 1726, by Samuel Sedgewick and Stephen Sedgewick.

Court Record, Page 137—1st November, 1726: Adms. granted to Caleb Watson and Jonathan Steele. Recog., £100.

Recorded in Vol. XII, Page 100-101.

Webster, Jacob, Hartford. Invt. £593-08-05. Taken 8 June, 1727, by Samuel Catlin and James Ensign.

Court Record, Page 164—5 September, 1727: Adms. to Elizabeth Webster, widow.

Page 165—3 October, 1727: Invt. now exhibited.

Page 179—5 March, 1727-8: Capt. Cyprian Nichols to be guardian to his grandchildren, Elizabeth age 7 years, Jacob 5 years, and Hezekiah 18 months, children of Jacob Webster decd.

Page 3 (Vol. XI) 7 October, 1729: Elizabeth Webster, Adms., exhibits an account of her Adms. And this Court order that the moveables be set out to the widow, there not being enough to pay the debts.

Page 6 (Vol. XIII) 3 May, 1737: The children of Jacob Webster, by Cyprian Nichols their guardian, moves this Court that the dower belonging to the widow Elizabeth Webster, alias Powell, be set out to her, and that the remainder of lands may be improved for the heirs. This Court appoint James Ensign, Thomas Richards and Samuel Catlin to set out the widow's dower.

Page 72—2 September, 1740: Benjamin Osborn, of Litchfield, in right of his wife Elizabeth Webster, daughter of Jacob Webster, moves this Court for a dist. of the moveable estate, of which Elizabeth Webster, widow and Adms., exhibited an account, which is accepted. Order to dist. to the heirs:

	£ s d
To the widow,	32-16-00
To Jacob Webster, eldest son,	28-01-01½
To Hezekiah and Elizabeth Webster, alias Osborn, to each,	14-00-07
The distributors were allowed,	1-08-00

And appoint Capt. Joseph Cooke, James Ensign and Deacon Thomas Richard, distributors.

Page 266-7.

Webster, Robert, Jr., Hartford. Inventory taken 7 April, 1725, by John Brace and John Seymour.

Court Record, Page 74—2 March, 1724-5: Adms. granted to Lois Webster, widow of sd. decd.

Page 154—2 May, 1727: Lois Webster, Adms., exhibits an account of her Adms. Accepted.

Page 252-3.

Webster, Stephen, Hartford. Invt. £240-09-00. Taken 2 July, 1724, by Jonathan Steele and Samuel Catlin.

Court Record, Page 53—4 August, 1724: Adms. granted to Mrs. Mary Webster, widow of sd. decd.

Page 16 (Vol. XI) 7 April, 1730: Mary Webster, Adms., exhibits an account of her Adms., which this Court accepts, orders recorded and kept on file.

Page 17—7 April, 1730: This Court appoint Mary Webster to be guardian to her three children, viz., Isaac 11 years, Mary 9 years, and Timothy 5 years. Recog., £50.

Page 10 (Vol. XII) 19 September, 1734: Isaac Webster, 17 years of age, chose Ebenezer Merrells to be his guardian.

Page 57 (Vol. XIII) 4 December, 1739: Timothy Webster, age 17 years, son of Stephen Webster, chose his father-in-law Ebenezer Merrells to be his guardian. Recog., £200.

Page 316 (Probate Side): An agreement made by Ebenezer Merrill and Mary, his wife, with the heirs of Stephen Webster, late of Hartford decd., for the full settlement of sd. estate among the surviving heirs, viz., to Mary the relict, in moveable estate, £19-19-09; to Isaac Webster, £266-00-00; to Timothy Webster, £133-00-00; and to Mary Webster, the sum of £133. This agreement on this paper was made by us the subscribers whose names are underwritten, on the 25 day of December, 1739.

EBENEZER MERRILL, LS.   MARY X WEBSTER, LS.
MARY X MERRILL, LS.   EBENEZER MERRILL, GUARDIAN
ISAAC WEBSTER, LS.   FOR TIMOTHY WEBSTER, LS.

Page 69—1st July, 1740: Agreement exhibited in Court, and acknowledged by the heirs to be their free act and deed. Accepted.

Test: Joseph Talcott, Clerk.

Page 176-7-8.

Welles, Eleazer, Capt., Hartford. Inventory taken 29 May, 1723, by Joseph Allyn of Wethersfield and Jonah Gross of Hartford. Part of the inventory as followeth:

	£	s	d
1 quadrant, 1 Forestaff, 2 scales and nocturnall,	1	00	00
A parcell of whetstones, 2s; 7 bottles, 3s; 3 casks of rum 9t., viz.: 1 terce, 76 gallons, markd (Wells); 1 ditto, 70 1-2, T. E. D. W.; small ditto, 28, T. W.; gall. rum, 174 1-2, at 3s-6 pr.,	30	10	09
Three casks of molasses, vizt. 1 qt. 110 gall.; one ditto, 98 gall.; one ditto, 89; molasses, 288 gall., at 2s-2 pr.,	26	08	00
Two casks of sugar, one qt. neat, 1-1-18 1-2, at 65s pr. Ct.,	4	12	½
One ditto neat, 2-1-1, at 53s pct.,	5	19	06
Item. His sloop and appurtenances, as sails, anchor, buckett, cannoe, hatchell, porridge pott, &c., prized at	45	00	00
Item. A quantity of salt, vizt., 20 Bush at 4s pr.,	4	00	00

Joseph Allyn, Jonah Gross, Apprisers under oath.

Court Record, Page 20—4 June, 1723: This Court grant Adms. on the estate of Eleazer Welles, mariner, late of Middletown decd., unto Thomas Welles of Deerfield, brother of sd. decd.

Page 29—27 September, 1723: Thomas Welles, Adms., exhibited an account of his Adms., whereby it appears that the sd. estate is indebted in the whole the sum of £328-14-00. The sd. estate being indebted more than the inventory, this Court order the Clerk to make a rule of averidge upon sd. estate unto the creditors thereof, viz., the sum of £115-09-04 to be paid in whole, and the sum of £213-04-08 to be paid in proportion.

Welles, Joseph. Court Record, Page 97—1st August, 1725: This Court grant Adms. unto Ebenezer Welles, brother of sd. decd., and he took letters of Adms. this day.

Page 268 (Probate Side, Vol. XI): Know all men by these presents: That we, Jonathan Welles, Ebenezer Welles and Anne Welles, of Hartford, being the only heirs to the estate of our brother Joseph Welles, of sd. Hartford decd., do make this agreement for ourselves and heirs: We agree that Jonathan Welles shall have a brown mare; and Anne Welles shall have 40 shillings in money and a chest which she has now in keeping; and Ebenezer Welles shall have all the residue of the estate. And we do agree with each other that this shall be a full settlement of our deceased brother's estate.

JONATHAN WELLES, LS.
EBENEZER WELLES, LS.
ANNE WELLES, LS.

Witness: *Joseph Talcott,*
Joseph Talcott, Jr.

The foregoing agreement was acknowledged in Court, 3 April, 1733.

Invt. in Vol. XII, Page 151-2.

Wetmore, Israhiah,Middletown.   Invt. £884-15-05.   Taken November, 1728, by Joseph Rockwell, George Phillips and Solomon Adkins.

Court Record, Page 205—12 November, 1728: The last will and testament of Israhiah Wetmore, Jr., late of Middletown decd., was exhibited in Court by Sarah Wetmore, executrix.   Will proven.   (This will cannot be found.)

Page 56 (Vol. XIV) 5 March, 1744-5: Israhiah Wetmore, a minor, age 17 years, son of Israhiah Wetmore, chose Seth Wetmore of Middletown to be his guardian.   Recog., £1000.

Page 64—25 September, 1745: Booth Wetmore, a minor, 16 years of age, son of Israhiah Wetmore, Jr., chose his uncle Seth Wetmore to be his guardian.   Recog., £500.

Page 215-16.

Wetmore, John, late of Middletown, decd.   Invt. £239-13-08.   Taken 20 February, 1723-4, by William Savage, Andrew Warner and John Collins.

See Agreement on File: These may certifie the honble. Court of Probates in Hartford: That we, Ebbenezer Wetmore and Elizabeth Elton, the only brother and sister of John Wetmore, deceased, he the sayd Ebbenezer for himself, and Elizabeth the wife of Richard Elton with the consent of her husband Richard Elton, have agreed as followeth, viz., that the sayd Ebbenezer do pay to the sayd Richard Elton and his wife Elizabeth the sum of £94 mony, £80 being on accott. of their brother's estate, and £14 for her third of the revertion of her mother's estate, which makes in the whole the sum aboue of £94, all which being payd or seuered to be payd, is a finall issue between them respecting her part of the estate of our brother John Wetmore deceased, and of the revertion of our mother's estate, also deceased.   As witness our hands and seals this 2nd day of March, Anno. Domini 1723-4.

> EBENEZER WETMORE, LS.
> RICHARD ELTON, LS.
> ELIZABETH X ELTON, LS.

Witness: *John Hamlin,*
        John Collins.

Court Record, Page 39—3 March, 1723-4: An agreement for the settlement or settleing the estate of John Wetmore, late of Middletown decd., under the hands and seals of the heirs, was now exhibited, and they acknowledged the same before this Court to be their voluntary act and deed.   This Court grant letters of Adms. on the estate of John Wetmore, late of Middletown decd., unto Ebenezer Wetmore, brother of sd. decd.

Page 19 (Vol. XI) 5 May, 1730: Adms. account exhibited and accepted.

Page 68-9.

Wheeler, John, Hartford. Invt. £111-06-07. Taken 21 January, 1724-5, by James Ensign and Daniel Merrells.

Court Record, Page 65—20 January, 1724-5: Adms. granted to Sarah Wheeler, widow, and Benjamin Denton of Farmington, a brother of the widow.

Page 51 (Vol. XII) 5 October, 1736: The Adms. exhibit an account of their Adms., which this Court accepts.

Page 63 (Vol. XIII) 3 April, 1740: Joseph Wheeler, a minor, 16 years of age, chose his mother Sarah Wheeler to be his guardian.

Page 50 (Vol. XIV) 4 December, 1744: Sarah Wheeler, Adms., exhibited a further account of debts due from sd. estate of £2-19-01, which account is allowed.

Page 63—3 September, 1745: Sarah Wheeler, the widow, now moves that a dist. on sd. estate might be granted. The Court order as followeth:

	£ s d
To the widow, her thirds,	10-06-00
To Joseph Wheeler, only son, his double part,	13-06-00
To Mary Wheeler, daughter of sd. deceased,	6-13-08

And appoint Capt. Joseph Cook and Ebenezer Webster, both of Hartford, distributors.

Page 83 (Vol. XV) 28 December, 1748: Sarah Wheeler, the widow, now moves to this Court that her right of dowry in the real estate may be set out to her. Whereupon this Court appoint and impower Ebenezer Webster and Joseph Holcomb of Hartford to set out to sd. widow 1-3 part of the buildings and lands of the sd. decd. to her by bounds.

Page 88—28 January, 1748-9: A return of the setting out of the dowry was now exhibited in Court, accepted, and ordered to be kept on file.

Invt. in Vol. XII, Page 192.

Wheeler, Samuel, Haddam. Invt. £35-10-00. Taken 5 January, 1725-6, by James Brainard and Jonathan Arnold.

Court Record, Page 122—1st March, 1725-6: Adms. granted unto Hannah Wheeler, widow, and the sd. widow and Jonathan Arnold of sd. Haddam recog. in £100.

Page 42 (Vol. XIII) 1739: Moses Wheeler, a minor, 16 years old, chose his mother Hannah Way to be his guardian. Also, this Court appoint her guardian to her son John Wheeler, a minor, 14 years. Recog., £500. Cert: *Hezekiah Brainard, J. P.*

Recorded in Vol. XII, Page 70-1-2-3.

White, Capt. Daniel, Windsor. Invt. £917-11-07 plus. Taken 27 June, 1726, and 30 August, 1726, by Thomas Fyler, Samuel Strong and

Alexander Allyn. Also, land in Hebron, taken by Timothy Olcott and Samuel Brown. Will dated 9 June, 1726.

I, Daniel White of Windsor, give to my wife Elizabeth White my plate or silver utensils, 1 silver tankard, 2 silver cups, and all my silver spoons, to her the sd. Elizabeth and to her heirs forever. Also, my will and pleasure is that my beloved wife shall have her dowry as the law allows to widows out of my estate over and above and besides the plate above bequeathed to her. I give to my son Daniel White my dwelling house in Hatfield, in ye Province of Massachusets Bay, and an acre of land on which the house now stands. I give to my son Daniel 9 acres of land lying in Hatfield, adjoining to the houselott above mentioned; also three acres of land lying in Hatfield the south meadow, known by the name of the 3-acre lott, in the middle division; also I give the 1-2 of that tract of land lying in Hatfield commonly called the Mill Swamp, in the lowermost Mill Swamp; also I give to my son Daniel White the 1-2 of all my improved lands lying in the Township of Hatfield. Item. I give and bequeath to my son Thomas White my clock; also I give and remit to him all that he the sd. Thomas oweth or is indebted to me. Item. I give and bequeath to my son Joel White my whole right of land in the Township of Bolton, and also my house and the lott it standeth on in the Town of Bolton, to him and his heirs forever. Item. I give to my 3 sons, Elisha, Simon and Seth White, all my lands lying in the Township of Hebron, to be equally divided to them and their heirs forever when they shall come to the age of 21 years. I give to my son Oliver White 10 acres of meadow land lying in Hatfield; also the 1-2 of the Mill Swamp land so called; also the 1-2 of my improved land lying in the Township of Hatfield, forever. I give to my daughter Sarah Griswold £20 money besides what I have given her before. I give my two daughters, Lucy and Elizabeth White, £50 to each of them in current money. My will is that all my personal and moveable estate should be sold towards paying of my just debts. And I will also that my house and all my lands lying in Windsor, and also all my land not herein mentioned and disposed lying in the Township of Hatfield, shall be sold by my executors at their discretion towards the payment of my just debts. My will is that my executors shall give and deliver £3 in money out of my estate to the Rev. Mr. Jonathan Marsh of Windsor. And after my decease all the remainder of my estate shall be equally divided among all my children. I appoint my son Daniel White and Thomas White to be executors.

Witness: *Samuel Hayden,*   DANIEL WHITE, LS.
Jeremiah Bissell, John Elsworth.

Court Record, Page 132—5 July, 1726: Will now exhibited by Daniel White and Thomas White, executors named in sd. will. Proven.

Page 132—5 July, 1726: Capt. Daniel White in his last will did appoint his sons Daniel and Thomas White not only executors but guardians to his children that are minors, to Seth, age 13 years, to Lucy 11, to Elizabeth 9, and Oliver, 6 years of age, sd. Daniel and Thomas White to be guardians to the children, appointed by the Court.

Page 135—5 August, 1726: Invt. now exhibited and accepted. Dist. now exhibited and accepted.

Page 255.

White, Joseph, Middletown. Invt. £886-03-01. Taken 8 April, 1725, by William Savage, Hugh White and Samuel Stow. Will dated 26 February, 1724-5.

I, Joseph White of Middletown, doe make this my last will and testament: I give to my wife Mary White the use and improvement of my homested and lands, excepting 50 acres; also, cattle, sheep and swine until my son Ebenezer come of age, and then the 1-2 during her widowhood. My son Ebenezer, when he comes of age, shall have the other half during his mother's widowhood, and after her decease or marriage the other half to be to him and to his heirs forever. I give to my four daughters £100 apiece with what they have already had. I give to the Rev. Mr. Joseph Smith, oure pastore, 30 shillings.

Witness: *John White,*
Jacob White, Hugh White.
                    JOSEPH WHITE, LS.

Court Record, Page 82—4 May, 1725: Will now exhibited. No executor named in the will. Adms. to Mary White, widow, with will annexed. Invt. exhibited.

Page 128—5 May, 1726: Adms. account of payment of debts.

Page 27 (Vol. XI) 1st September, 1730: The widow Mary White, Adms., deceased before finishing her Adms. This Court appoint Ebenezer White, son of the decd., Adms. on the unsettled estate.

Page 267-8.

Wilcocks, Ephraim, Middletown. Died 4th January, 1712-13. Invt. £210-13-04. Taken 29 April, 1725, by Samuel Hall and Ebenezer Smith.

Court Record, Page 83—4 May, 1725: Adms. to Janna Wilcocks, son of sd. deceased. Exhibit of inventory.

Page 91—6 July, 1725: This Court appoint Janna Wilcox to be guardian unto Ephraim Wilcox, 14 years, and John Wilcox, 13 years of age. Recog., £200.

Page 102—4 October, 1725: Janna Wilcocks, Adms. on the estate of Ephraim Wilcocks, late of Middletown decd., exhibited an account of Adms., £4-18-00; moveable part, £64-06-00, 1-3 part whereof was taken by the widow; subtracting £4-18-00, there remains £37-19-04. The real estate was prised at £210-15-00. There remains of real and personal estate £248-14-04 to be distributed. Order: To Janna Wilcocks, eldest son, £63-03-06, which is his double portion of sd. estate; to Ephraim, John, Thankfull, Mary and Jane Wilcocks and Esther Ranney, the rest of the children of sd. deceased, to each of them, £31-01-01, which is their single portion of sd. estate. And appoint Samuel Hall, Ebenezer Smith and Thomas Hale, distributors.

Recorded in Vol. XII, Page 157-8-9.

Wilcocks, Samuel, Middletown. Inventory taken 27 February, 1727, by John Sage, John Wilcox and John Warner. Will dated 10 July, 1727.

I, Samuel Wilcocks of Middletown, husbandman, do make and ordain this my last will and testament: I give to Hannah my wife the use of my improved land, with my dwelling house and barn, and the use of my part of the barn that stands on my brother John Wilcock's land near John Kirbey's, during her widowhood. After my eldest son comes of age, I give to my wife the 1-2 of my dwelling house, and 1-2 of my seller, and 1-2 of my barn, 1-2 of my land at home, 1-2 of my pasture at Wolphpit Hill so called, 1-2 of my land within fence from the Ledge to the river, westward of the barn, and all my land at a place called Goose Delight. I give to my son Daniel, when he comes of age, and then the rest of the stock and land in this second part of the will is my wife's during her natural life. And after my wife's decease, the house and land to be divided between my two sons, and the stock of household goods I have given to my wife shall be divided among my three daughters as part of their portion after their mother's decease. I give to my three daughters £80 to each; to Hannah £80, to Rachel £80, and to Elizabeth £80, to be paid to them out of my stock and household goods so far as my stock and household goods will do, and what they fall short of £80 to each of my daughters shall be made up to them by my two sons Daniel and Josiah. I give to my two sons Daniel and Josiah all my land that I have not given to my wife in this my will during her natural life, to be equally divided between my two sons. I make my wife and brother John Wilcocks executors.

Signed, sealed, published, announced and declared in the presence of us:

Thomas Savage, William Savage,
   John Warner.

Court Record, Page 178—5 March, 1727-8: Will proven.

Page 3 (Vol. XIII) 22 March, 1737: Daniel Wilcox, son of the deceased, showing to this Court by his father's will that divers parcells of land of real estate were willed to him when he should come to the age of 21 years, viz., 1-2 of what was willed to the widow his mother Hannah Wilcocks alias Lewis, and also 1-2 of all those lands that the deceased hath not given to his sd. wife for her use during her natural life, and declaring that his sd. mother hath hitherto refused or neglected to divide sd. land to him, though often requested, and that his brother Josiah, being a minor and not capable of coming to a division with him, he the sd. Daniel moved that distributors may be appointed in both sd. parts to distribute to him his part of sd. houseing and lands according to the will. This Court appoint Jabez Hamlin, Thomas Johnson and Samuel Shepherd to distribute and set out to the sd. Daniel Wilcocks that part given to him, viz., that 1-2 part of the house as given to the sd. widow until he the sd. Daniel should come of age, giving notice first to sd. Hannah Lewis and her husband Malachi Lewis of the time they shall proceed on sd. service. This Court do also appoint the sd. Jabez Hamlin, Esq., Thomas Johnson and

Samuel Shephard and John Wilcocks, guardians to Josiah Wilcocks, to distribute 1-2 of the land of sd. deceased, not given to the sd. widow to the sd. Daniel Wilcocks, and the other half thereof unto the sd. Josiah Wilcocks, minor, and that they set it out by meets and bounds. Josiah Wilcox, age 19 years, and Rachel, age 15 years, children of Samuel Wilcox, chose Deacon John Wilcox to be their guardian. Recog., £300.

Page 253.

Wilcox, Samuel, Middletown. Invt. £971-13-06. Taken 17 April, 1725, by William Savage, Francis Wilcock and Samuel Gipson.

Court Record, Page 81—4 May, 1725: This Court grant letters of Adms. on the estate of Samuel Wilcox, late of Middletown decd., unto Esther Wilcox, widow, and Francis Wilcox, brother of sd. decd., and they gave bond and took letters of Adms.

Page 71 (Vol. XI) 6 June, 1732: Jeremiah Wilcox of Middletown chose his mother Esther Wilcox to be his guardian; and this Court do allow the sd. Esther to be guardian to Esther Wilcox, age 8 years, and Elisha Wilcock, age 11 years.

Agreement on File:

Wilcox, Sarah. An agreement for the settlement of the real and personal estate of Sarah Wilcocks, our honoured mother, dated this 1st February, 1724-5, was divided amongst the heirs: To Israel Wilcock, eldest son, to John, to Samuel, to Thomas Wilcocks, to Sarah Riley, and to Jonathan Riley. In confirmation whereof we have set to our hands and seals.

Witness: *John Warner,*
   Thomas Tilletson.

ISRAEL WILCOCK, LS.
JOHN WILCOCK, LS.
SAMUEL WILCOCK, LS.
THOMAS WILCOCK, LS.
SARAH RILEY, LS.
JONATHAN RILEY, LS.

Court Record, Page 67—2 February, 1724-5: Agreement exhibited, and acknowledged by the heirs to be their free act and deed. Accepted by the Court.

Wilcocks, Silence (alias Warner), Middletown, deceased. Court Record, Page 83—4 May, 1725: Adms. granted to Janna Wilcocks, her son.

Recorded in Vol. XII, Page 34-5-6.

Wilcox, Thomas, Middletown. Invt. £387-16-01. Taken 1st March, 1726-7, by John Wilcox, Samuel Stow and John Sage. Will dated 16 January, 1726-7.

I give to my wife Anne Wilcock the improvement of my dwelling house and of all my improveable lands until my sone come of age, and after my sone come of age I give the 1-2 of my house, well, cellar and home lott during her natural life. And my will is yt my wife shall have the whole of my stock and the whole of my moveable estate during her widowhood; if she marry again, but 1-2 of it. I give to my son Thomas Wilcock the 1-2 of my dwelling house, cellar, well and homested when he comes to the age of 21 years, and after his mother's decease I give him the whole of it. And further, my house and the whole of my homelott yt my house stands on, all the above mentioned land and house on the west side of the Great River, I give to my son Thomas and to his heirs forever. Also, I give to my son Jonathan Wilcock all my lands in the Northwest Quarter yt lyeth between Brother Israel's lott and the Common, and my will is that all my lands above mentioned I give to Jonathan Wilcock and to his heirs forever. I give to my two daughters, Martha Wilcock and Hannah Wilcock, £50 apiece. And my will is yt ye remainder of my lands in the Northwest Quarter (not willed away to Jonathan), and Siding Hill lott, and Plain lott, and Goose's Delight land, and my Bogg Meadow lott, to be equally divided between my two sons Thomas and Jonathan Wilcock, to them and their heirs forever.

Witness: *William Savage,*   THOMAS WILCOCK, LS.
John Wilcock, Joseph Whitmore.

Court Record, Page 146—7 March, 1726-7: Will now exhibited. No executor named in the will. Adms. to Anna Wilcox, widow, with the will annexed.

Page 211-212—4 February, 1728-9: Anna Wilcox, alias Coleman, Adms. with the will annexed upon the estate of Thomas Wilcox late of Middletown decd., exhibited an accompt of Adms., £37-18-02, which account is allowed, and order that Mr. John Warner, Samuel Stow and Samuel Gipson of Middletown, after deducting £37-18-02 out of the moveable estate in the inventory, distribute the estate of the sd. deceased to the widow and heirs of sd. deceased according to his last will and testament. This Court appoint Israel Wilcox of Middletown to be guardian unto Jonathan Wilcox, 6 years of age, and Hannah Wilcox, 4 years of age. Recog., £100.

Page 46 (Vol. XIII) 3 April, 1737: Jonathan Wilcocks, age 17 years, chose his uncle John Wilcocks of Middletown to be his guardian.

Page 6 (Vol. XIV) 4 May, 1742: Thomas Wilcoks, eldest son of the decd., being arrived to the age of 21 years, showing to this Court by one paragraph in the will of the sd. decd. that the sd. decd. hath given to him the sd. Thomas Wilcocks and Jonathan Wilcocks several pieces of land to be equally divided between them the sd. Thomas and Jonathan Wilcocks, viz., what he hath not willed away in the Northwest Quarter, Siding Hill lott, Plain lott, Goose's Delight and Bogg Meadow and Fur Neck, and hath not in sd. will appointed who should distribute and divide sd. lands between them the sd. Thomas and Jonathan, and desired this Court to appoint suitable persons to make divisions of the aforesd. lands according to sd. will: Whereupon this Court appoint Lt. Joseph Ranny, Joseph Frary and Joseph Savage, of Middletown, distributors.

Page 13—7 December, 1742: A return of the setting out several pieces of land according to the will of Thomas Wilcocks, by order of this Court, to Thomas and Jonathan Wilcocks, heirs to the estate of the sd. decd., under the hands of Joseph Savage and Joseph Frary, distributors. Accepted by the Court, and ordered to be kept on file.

Willard, Symon, Wethersfield. Court Record, Page 147—8 March, 1726-7: Adms. granted to Josiah Willard, eldest son, who gave bond with John Williams of £700. Exhibit of an inventory of sd. estate.

Page 29 (Vol. XI, Probate Side): An agreement, dated 6 March, 1729, made between the heirs and legatees to the estate of Symon Willard, late of Newington decd., for a settlement of sd. estate. Signed and sealed by the heirs.

JOSIAH WILLARD, JONATHAN GRISWOLD,
JOHN WILLARD, MARY GRISWOLD, HIS WIFE,
HANNAH WILLARD, EPHRAIM WILLIARD.
DANIEL WILLARD,

Page 147—7 March, 1726-7: Daniel Willard, a minor, 16 years of age, chose his brother Josiah Willard to be his guardian.

Page 197—6 June, 1728: The Adms. exhibit an account of their Adms., which this Court accepts. And also exhibit an addition to the inventory.

Page 9 (Vol. XI) 6 January, 1729-30: Agreement exhibited and accepted.

Invt. in Vol. XII, Page 141.

Williams, Henry, Haddam (East). Died 23 October, 1728. Invt. £239-07-10. Taken 3 January, 1728, by Joshua Brainard, Isaac Spencer and Daniel Cone.

Court Record, Page 212—5 February, 1728-9: Adms. granted to Elizabeth Williams, widow of sd. deceased.

Page 5 (Vol. XI) 21 November, 1729: Elizabeth, the widow, exhibits now an account of her Adms. Accepted. Order to dist. the estate, viz.: Unto Elizabeth Williams, 1-3 part of sd. estate in lands during life, and 1-3 part of the personal estate to be her own forever; the rest to be dist. to the children of sd. deceased, viz., to Mary and Sarah Williams, their equal proportion of the rest of the estate. And appoint Joshua Brainard, Mr. Timothy Fuller and Thomas Cone, of East Haddam, distributors. This Court appoint Elizabeth Williams to be guardian to two of her children, viz., Mary and Sarah Williams, the eldest age 12 years, the other about 2 years.

Page 5 (Vol. XII) 4 June, 1734: Joseph Grover and Elizabeth his wife, Adms., exhibit an account of sundry things that were burnt with sd. Williams's house, and moveables amounting to the sum of £54-04-06, which were almost spoiled. Account accepted.

Page 213-14.

Williams, John, Hartford. Died 15 September, 1723. Inventory taken 2 December, 1723, by Samuel Burnham and Gabriel Williams.

Court Record, Page 36—3 January, 1723-4: Adms. to Sarah Williams, widow, and Jacob Williams, a brother of sd. deceased. Exhibit of inventory.

Page 77—6 April, 1725: Jacob Williams, Adms. on the estate of John Williams, late of Hartford decd., exhibited account of Adms. Paid in debts and charges, £65-18-11; the inventory, £270-04-06; subtracting £65-18-11, there remains £236-04-06, including £66-00-00 to be dist. Order: to Sarah Williams, the widow, £32-01-10 with dower; to Samuel Williams, eldest son, £95-05-06, which is his double portion of sd. estate; to Abraham, Isaac and Sarah Williams, the rest of the children, to each of them, £47-18-09, which is their single portion of sd. estate. And appoint Gabriel Williams, Samuel Burnham and Joseph Williams, distributors. This Court appoint Sarah Williams of Hartford, widow, to be guardian to her children, viz., Isaac Williams, 4 years, and Sarah Williams, 3 years of age. Recog., £100. This Court also appoint Jacob Williams to be guardian unto Samuel Williams, 8 years of age, and Abraham, 6 years of age, sons of John Williams, late of Hartford decd. Recog., £100.

Page 14.

Williams, John, Haddam. He died 28 November, 1722. Inventory taken by Daniel Brainard and Timothy Fuller.

Court Record, Page 7—5 March, 1722-3: Adms. to Elizabeth Williams, the widow.

Page 45—7 April, 1724: Elizabeth Williams, Adms., exhibits account of Adms. Allowed.

Page 46: Order to dist. to Elizabeth Williams, widow, and to Elizabeth, only child. By Thomas Gates, Thomas Robinson and Robert Chapman.

Page 211.

Williams, Joseph, Hartford. Died 19 September, 1723. Invt. £67-15-00 in real estate. Taken 6 January, 1723-4, by Samuel Burnham and Abram Williams.

Court Record, Page 36—8 January, 1723-4: Adms. to Jacob Williams, a brother of sd deceased. Exhibit now of an inventory.

Page 85—11 May, 1725: Exhibit now debts due from the estate.

Page 93—6 July, 1725: Jacob Williams, Adms., allowed to sell land in Hartford to pay debts.

Page 106—5 October, 1725: Adms. account exhibits £72-15-00 debts due to the estate. Dist. was ordered before this was received. This Court now order it carried into the dist., proportional to the widow and heirs.

Wilson, Elizabeth,* widow of Phineas Wilson, Hartford. The identity of this woman having been questioned, and conflicting claims having been made in regard thereto, the compiler of this work has spared no pains in order to make it as clear as possible, with the following result :—

By the will of John Warren of Boston, Mass. (a cardmaker), dated 10 July, 1677, and probated 31 July, 1677 [see Suffolk County, Mass., Probate Book 6, page 191], he gives all his personal estate to his wife *Elizabeth* to bring up "my son *Nathaniel* and *Abigail.*" He also mentions "my other children," also "son Joshua" and "son Thomas." The witnesses to this will were John Comer and John ffernside. This, according to the research which has been made, is the first mention of the Elizabeth Wilson named above, when she appears (1677) as *Elizabeth Warren, widow of John Warren.* It seems evident by a comparison of dates that at this time she was at least 40 years of age.

This *Elizabeth Warren, widow,* next appears (1681) as one of the principal parties to a marriage contract, the other being Samuel Sendall, a limeburner, of Boston. By this contract (ante-nuptial) Samuel Sendall quitclaims to *Elizabeth Warren, widow,* all his right, title and interest in any property at that time in her possession as John Warren's widow, an inventory of which accompanies the contract ; and as a further inducement to effect the marriage, Samuel Sendall gives to *Elizabeth Warren, widow,* certain real estate in Condit Street, Boston, the same being mentioned in later deeds and agreements. The "feoffees in trust" to this agreement or contract were John Danson, a pastry cook, and Edward Drinker, a potter. The date is 29 September, 1681.—[Suffolk County Land Records, Book 12, pages 1, 2, 3.

She next appears (1685) as the widow of Samuel Sendall (limeburner) of Boston, and also as a party to a "triparte" indenture made 11 July, 1685, between John Hayward (public notary), of the first part; *Elizabeth Sendall, widow of Samuel Sendall* (limeburner), of the second part ; and John Comer (pewterer) and Edward Drinker (potter), of the third part, all of Boston; which indenture is simply another ante-nuptial

---

*The facts here given in relation to this woman were extracted from the original records in Boston, Mass., and furnished the compiler through the kindness and courtesy of Mr. James Allen Kibbe of Warehouse Point, Conn., and Mr. Alanson H. Reed of Wellesley Hills, Mass.—[*C. W. M.*

contract between *Elizabeth Sendall, widow,* and John Hayward, public notary (with John Comer and Edward Drinker as witnesses), which secures to her the property already given her by her former husbands, John Warren and Samuel Sendall.—[Suffolk County Land Records, Book 13, page 354.

It may be interesting to note right here that this John Hayward (public notary) testifies in a deposition made 28 November, 1672 (he being then 33 years old), as to instructions given him to make a certain deed, etc. This is mentioned because an ante-nuptial agreement or contract apparently existed between John Warren and his wife Elizabeth, as he mentions it in his will (1677). If so, it may be that the above mentioned deposition refers to that agreement, as its date (1672) would be about the time that John Warren and Elizabeth his wife were married. And if this agreement could be found anywhere upon record, it might disclose the identity of her maiden name, which is believed to have been Danson, and *might* also prove that she was *Elizabeth Crossthwayt, widow,* when she married John Warren, about 1672. Thus it is possible that this woman Elizabeth Danson had during her life five husbands, as follows:

Elizabeth Danson,
$$\begin{cases} \ldots\ldots\ldots \textit{Crossthwayt,} \\ \textit{John Warren, cardmaker,} \\ \textit{Samuel Sendall, limeburner,} \\ \textit{John Hayward, public notary,} \\ \textit{Phineas Wilson, merchant.} \end{cases}$$

Of the first husband mentioned here we are not sure, but of the four others, in the order mentioned, there is no doubt.

We next meet with her (1687) as the widow of John Hayward, public notary, who, in his will (dated 15 February, 1687-8) ratifies and confirms " that covenant which I made with my now wife, or feoffees in trust in her behalfe, before marriage, relating to her house and lands in Condit street, in said Boston. Also, I doe hereby confirme unto my said wife the warehouse and land wch : I purchased for her of Gyles Dyer, adjoyning to her said lands, wch : I caused to be made over to feoffees in trust for her use. All of which is in lieue of her right of dower or thirds in or to my estate." She was also appointed executrix of his will.—[Suffolk County Probate Records, Vol. 10, pp. 224-226.

At last she appears (in 1692) as the widow of Phineas Wilson, who, in his will (dated 6 May, 1691) gives "to Elizabeth, my well-beloved wife, my new dwelling house scituate in Hartford." Also, "to my only son (by a former wife, daughter of Nathaniel Sanford, of Hartford) Nathaniel Wilson, lands in Hartford, formerly the estate of his grandfather, Mr. Nathaniel Sanford decd." Also, unto "my wife's daughter, *Abigail Warren,* ten pounds in money." Here we have in this Abigail Warren, mentioned by Phineas Wilson as "my wife's daughter," added and sufficient proof that Mrs. Elizabeth Wilson was originally the wife of John Warren, and, if so, then necessarily the wife successively of Samuel Sendall and John Hayward.—[Suffolk County Probate Records, Vol. 13, pp. 37, 106; Vol. 15, p. 120.

This Abigail Warren, daughter of Mrs. Elizabeth Wilson by a former husband (John Warren of Boston) was married about 1691 to Richard Lord of Hartford, who died in January or February, 1711-12 (see pages 254 and 255 of this book), and after Mr. Lord's death she became the wife of the Rev. Timothy Woodbridge.

The next we hear from Mrs. Elizabeth Wilson (1717) is through a Probate Court Record entry at Hartford, Vol. IX, Page 32, wherein she, "being indisposed in body and not able to go from home" (she was at this time probably about 80 years old), desires that a Court of Probate might be held at her house, in Hartford, which was accordingly granted. And at this session of the Hartford Probate Court, held in her own house, 8 May, 1717, Mrs. Elizabeth Wilson, now widow of Phineas Wilson, renders an additional account to the Court on the estate of her *former husband*, Mr. John "Howard" of Boston, Pub: Notary (a sale of £100 worth of lands in Dunstable, Mass., and disbursements of £68-13-00 on account of his estate), she being his executrix. A record of this meeting is also to be found in Probate Book 19, pp. 332-333, Suffolk County Probate Records (Boston), to which Samuel Sewell, Esq., Judge of Probate at that time, added: "Mrs. Elizabeth Hayward (now Wilson), the executrix, being unable to travel by reason of her great age and infirmity, and having seen the vouchers, I allow the foregoing account," etc. A record of this meeting also appears on page 405 of this volume, under *"Howard," John*, which is as it is recorded in Hartford, but nevertheless should have been Hayward.

Finally, on the 5th of January, 1724-5, and when she could not have been far from 87 years old, she makes her own will, signing it as Elizabeth Wilson, and then lived some three years longer, as her death occurred in July, 1727, and her will was probated in August of the same year, thus making her age at death about 90 years.

The account of this person is really very interesting, and shows her to have been a woman of great business ability; and, when taken in connection with the account of Nathaniel Wilson, son of Phineas Wilson (see page 140 of this volume), proves not only that truth is stranger than fiction, but also how easy it is to be mistaken.

WILL OF MRS. ELIZABETH WILSON.

Recorded in Vol. XII, Hartford Probate Records, pages 28 to 34.

Inventory, £7154-04-02. Taken 26 July, 1727, by Hez: Wyllys and John Austin. Will dated 5 January, 1724-5.

I, Elizabeth Wilson, do make this my last will and testament: I give to my son, Rev. Mr. Timothy Woodbridge, the sum of £50. I give to my grandson, Elisha Lord, £200. I give to my grandsons, Richard Lord, Epaphras Lord, Ichabod Lord and Theodore Woodbridge, to each of them the sum of £200. I give to my three granddaughters, Jerusha Whiting, Mary Pitkin and Elizabeth Lord, to each of them £100. I give unto each of my granddaughters 1-4 part of my household stuff, to be equally divided between them. I give unto each of my son Woodbridge's children a gold ring. I give unto the Rev. Mr. Thomas Buckingham, of Hartford, the sum of £10. I give to Joanna Stone of Boston £10, and to my daughter Warren of Boston £10, and to her son Thomas Warren £10. I give to my daughter King £10, and to Wilson Rowlandson £10, and to Elizabeth Hunlock ye sum of £3, and to Sarah Battis £3. I give to my daughter Mary Bird of Hingham £10, and to my daughter Sarah Gardner £10, and to my daughter Lydia Davis of Long Island £10, and to my granddaughter Mary Jesse ye sum of £5. I give to the poor widows in Hartford £40, which I leave at the discretion of my executrix to distribute. And all the rest and residue of my estate, after my just debts, funeral expenses and legacies given as aforesd. are satisfied, I give and bequeath unto my dutiful daughter Abigail Woodbridge, to be to her and her heirs forever, with the limitation and condition only yt such in my real estate as shall remain undisposed of by will or otherwise by my sd. daughter after the time of her death shall be and remain unto my 5 grandsons, Elisha Lord, Richard Lord, Epaphras Lord, Ichabod Lord and Theodore Woodbridge, in such proportion and in such manner as followeth: that is to say, unto Elisha Lord, Richard Lord and Theodore Woodbridge, to each of them so much as upon a just apprisement will make them an estate equal to what I have already given by deed to either of my grandsons Epaphras Lord or Ichabod Lord, and what remains over and above such adjustment and equality shall be equally divided between my sd. 5 grandsons, and the legacies given to my sd. 5 grandsons shall be to them and their heirs forever. Only it is my will that if Theodore Woodbridge shall die without issue, such lands as are given to him by this testament and are by him undisposed of, shall be equally divided between the other sons of my daughter Woodbridge, and belong to them and their heirs forever. But if my daughter Woodbridge shall die before me, then it is my will that the real estate given to her shall be and remain to my five grandsons, her children, as followeth: To Elisha Lord, Richard Lord and Theodore Woodbridge, to each of them so much as upon a just valuation will make them an estate equal to the lands I have given in ye Nip Mugg country to either Epaphras or Ichabod Lord, and what remains over and above such an equality to be equally divided between my sd. grandsons, Elisha Lord, Richard Lord, Epaphras Lord, Ichabod Lord and Theodore Woodbridge. My will is yt my estate be inventoried and apprised as it may be worth in bills of public credit, and that the lands I have before given to my grandsons Epaphras and Ichabod Lord at Sutton be also apprised in order to a true judgement. I appoint my daughter Abigail Woodbridge executrix, and substitute my grandson Elisha Lord to be executor in his mother's place in case she decease before she hath fully administered.

Witness: *Roger Woolcott,*   ELIZABETH WILSON, LS.
Ephraim Minor, Nathaniel Goodwin.

Court Record, Page 161—August, 1727: Will now exhibited by Abigail Woodbridge, executrix named in the will. Proven.

Page 191—3 May, 1728: Inventory exhibited and accepted.

WILL OF PHINEAS WILSON:

The will of Phineas Wilson, merchant, of Hartford and Boston, may be found on record in Suffolk County Probate Records, Vol. 13, page 37; and in Hartford Probate Records, Vol. V, page 139; also on page 522, Vol. I, of this work. See also page 358, Vol. I, of this work, a petition of Phineas Wilson to the Court of Probate at Hartford in behalf of his son Nathaniel Wilson, that the latter might be awarded his legal share (in right of his mother deceased) in the estate of his maternal grandfather, Nathaniel Sandford, whose daughter was the first wife of Phineas Wilson.

WILL AND INVENTORY OF JOHN HAYWARD:

The will and inventory of John Hayward, public notary, of Boston, Mass., whose widow married Phineas Wilson, is as follows:

Suffolk County Probate Records, Vol. 10, pp. 224-226.

Will:

In the name of God, amen. The eight day of July, Anno Dom. One Thousand Six Hundred Eighty and Seaven. I, John Hayward, of Boston, in New England, notary, make and ordain this my last will and testament:

First. My soule into the hands of Almighty God my Creator, and my body to the earth to be buryed (intirely and without mangling for the sattisfaction of the curiosities of any person whatsoever) and in such desent manner (yett without any millitary or expensive ceremonies whatsoever) as to my executrix shall be thought meete.

Item. I do hereby ratifie and confirm that covenant which I made with my now wife, or feoffees in trust in her behalfe, before marriage, relateing to her house and lands in Condit Streete, in said Boston. Alsoe I doe hereby confirme unto my said wife the warehouse and land wch: I purchased for her of Gyles Dyer, adjoyning to her said lands, wch: I caused to be made over to feoffees in trust for her use. All of which is in leiue of her right of dower or thirds in or to my estate.

Item. I give to my daughter Abigaell ten pounds.

Item. I give to my father and mother-in-law Danson twenty shilds a peece to buy them rings.

Item. I give the full remainder of my estate, reale and personall, unto my two sonns, Samll and John, to be equally divided betweene them.

Item. John shall be mainteyned out of my entire estate and therewith educated untill he attaine the age of sixteene yeares.

To my two sisters, namely, Hannah and Sarah.

Item. I doe hereby nominate and appoint my wife Elizabeth Hayward executrix, and my very loveing friends, Mr. Edward Wyllys, of Boston, and Mr. Benjamin Browne, of Salem, merchants, to be overseers and guardians to my children til they come of age.

JOHN HAYWARD. [SEAL.]

The Witnesses: *Thomas Smith,*   Made oath to the signing of the
         Benjamin Bullivant,   will, the 15th ffebruary, 1687.
         Thomas Creese.   Before me,

ANDROSS.

Inventory:

An inventory of the estate of John Hayward of Boston, public notary, late decd., taken this 23 day of February, Anno Dom. 1687-8, as followeth, vizt.: [A list of personal property] ; land at Dunstable containing about 540 acres in severall parcells, as per deeds and platts are mentioned. Item. A parcell of land in Boston.

Elizabeth *Howard,* executrix of the last will and testament of John *Howard,* late of Boston decd., exhibited the within inventory and made oath, etc.

Sworne the 14th ffebruary, 1688-9, before me,

J. DUDLEY.

Wilson, Stebbin. Court Record, Page 53—4 August, 1724: Stebbin Wilson of Hartford, a minor, 16 years of age, chose Richard Seymour of Hartford to be his guardian. Recog., £100.

Winchell, Hannah, Windsor. Court Record, Page 109—7 December, 1725: Adms. to John Winchell, son of sd. decd.

Page 113—4 January, 1725-6: Invt. exhibited by John Winchell, Adms.

Invt. in Vol. XII, Page 192.

Winchell, Sarah, Widow. Invt. £18-12-06. Taken 8 December, 1725, by Nathaniel Gillett, 2nd, and John Allyn.

Court Record, Page 113—4 January, 1725-6: Invt. exhibited by John Winchell, Adms. Ordered recorded.

Recorded in Vol. XII, Page 135-6.

Winchell, Stephen, Simsbury. Invt. £884-05-04. Taken 5th April, 1726, by Joseph Barnard, Nathaniel Pinney and Nathaniel Pinney, Jr.

I, Stephen Winchell of Simsbury, do make this my last will and testament: I give to my wife Abigail the 1-3 part of my moveable estate, to her and her dispose forever, with the improvement of 1-3 part of my lands during her natural life. I give to my five sons, viz., Stephen Winchell, Thomas Winchell, Caleb Winchell, Robert Winchell and Martin Winchell, all my estate, both real and personal, to be divided amongst them in equal shares, excepting £5 in moveables at inventory price, which I give to my daughter Dorothy with what I have already given her. And I do by these present make and ordain my two eldest sons, Stephen Winchell and Thomas Winchell, the executors to this my last will and testament.

Witness: *John Owen,*   STEPHEN WINCHELL, LS.
Henry Millington, Samuell Higley.

Court Record, Page 113—4 January, 1725-6: The last will and testament of Stephen Winchell was exhibited by Stephen and Thomas Winchell, executors. Proven.

Page 127—5 April, 1726: Martin Winchell, a minor, 18 years of age, chose Stephen Winchell of Simsbury to be his guardian. Recog., £100.

Recorded in Vol. XII, Page 25-26.

Woodruff, John, Kensington.   Invt. £425-00-00.   Taken 1st June, 1727, by Thomas Curtice and Joseph Smith.

I, John Woodruff of Kensington, in the County of Hartford and Colony of Connecticut, do make this my last will and testament: I give to my wife the bed which was hers before we were married, and all the furniture now belonging to it; also the iron pot and iron kettle, and tramel, tongs and peal, two pewter platters and one pewter bason, and a chest of draws, all which she had before marriage and brought with her. And also I give her one black cow, four years old, forever. Also, I give her the improvement of 1-2 of my dwelling house and of my barn, and the improvement of 4 acres of land extending eastward from the west side of my orchard, and of 4 acres plough land westward of my barn, so long she lives a widow. To my four sons, John, Joseph, Simmons and Elijah, I give all my real estate in houseing and lands (not only lands divided, but also all my right and interest in undivided, common or sequestered lands), to be equally divided among them, excepting that my two eldest sons, John and Joseph, shall have my dwelling house and barn above their equal parts with the rest of my three eldest sons, paying to their sisters their legacies, in all amounting to £104, which my will is to have payd as followeth, viz.:

	£	s	d
By my son John,	38	16	08
By my son Joseph,	38	16	08
By my son Simmons,	26	06	08

To each of my two elder daughters, Elizabeth and Mary, I give 40 shillings a piece in current money of sd. Colony, to be paid to them within the space of 6 years after my decease. To each of my five younger daughters, viz., Susannah, Margaret, Abigail, Ann and Sarah, I give £20 apiece. My will is that all my sons (except Simmons, whom I would have speedily put to a trade) shall continue in their mother's service till they come of age. I give all the rest of my estate to my wife (to pay my debts with), whom I hereby appoint my sole executrix.

Witness: *William Burnham,*   JOHN WOODRUFF, LS.
Joseph Root, Henry Kirkam.

Court Record, Page 161—August, 1727: Will exhibited by Mary Woodruff, executrix. Proven.

Wolcott, Mrs. Abiah, Windsor. Court Record, Page 25—8 July, 1723: Will now exhibited by Mr. Ebenezer Fitch and Mrs. Abiah Chauncy, executors, who render an account of debts. This Court appoint Samuel Strong, Daniel Bissell and Thomas Fyler to dist. the estate to the legatees according to the will.

Page 142—6 December, 1726: Distributors now report. Accepted.

Dist. File, 8 July, 1723: 1-2 of the estate to Mrs. Abiah Woolcott Chauncy, and the other half to Robert Chauncy, to Ichabod Wolcott Chauncy, and to Abiah Chauncy. By Daniel Bissell, Thomas Fyler and Samuel Strong. (See Henry Woolcott.)

Page 6.

Wolcott, Benjamin, Windsor. An addition to the invt., £9-04-00. Taken 21 August, 1723, by Henry Wolcott, James Enno and Timothy Loomis.

	£	s	d
Imp. To a rapier, 18s; Sea Bed and my Colony Rug, to it, 40s; old book of Mr. Bolton's Works, 4s; a book called Virgill's Poetry, 6s,		3-08-00	
To a book titled "The Joy of Faith," 2s; kirbine pistol, 12s; blue broadcloth, cut out for a coat and part lost, 30s; great brass kettle, 70s; old chest, 2s,		5-16-00	
		£9-04-00	

Henry Wolcott, James Enno and Timothy Loomis, apprisers.

Page 65 (Vol. XI) 11th April, 1732: John Wolcott, Adms., was summoned to appear before this Court to make up his account of Adms., and prayed for longer time, which was granted.

Page 70—6 June, 1732: Hannah Wolcott, wife of Henry Wolcott, Charles Wolcott and William Wolcott, all of Windsor, were summoned to appear before this Court as per writ bearing date 3rd June, 1732, to render an account of the estate of Benjamin Wolcott, late of Windsor, or of Great Britain, deceased, and to be interrogated according to sd. will. Hannah Wolcott and William Wolcott appeared and answered all questions under oath as were put to them by the Court, which questions are in the files of this Court. And it not appearing that sd. Hannah Wolcott and Henry Wolcott, William Wolcott or either of them had concealed any part of the estate of the sd. Benjamin Wolcot decd.: Whereupon this Court orders John Wolcott, the Adms. to sd. estate, to pay the cost of prosecution, which is allowed to be £0-15-06.

Invt. in Vol. XII, Page 169.

Wolcott, Christopher, Windsor. Invt. £40-01-07. Taken 15 May, 1728, by Joshua Loomis and Moses Loomis, Jr.

Court Record, Page 189—2 April, 1728: Adms. granted unto James Wolcott, brother of the deceased.

Page 217—1st April, 1729: James Wolcott, Adms., exhibited an account of his Adms., and reports the estate insolvent. This Court appoint James Wolcott and John Loomis commissioners.

Recorded in Vol. XII, Page 76.

Wolcott, George, Wethersfield. Invt. £890-13-11. Taken 7 September, 1726, by Josiah Churchill, Samuel Curtice and Samuel Butler.

Ye 21st day of February, in ye beginning of ye year 1725, I, George Wolcott of Wethersfield, in the County of Hartford, being aged but of common health and of perfect mind and memory, do make this my last will and testament: I give to Elizabeth my wife, whome I ordain and constitute my executrix joyntly with my son Joshua hereafter named, one bed and common furniture to the same belonging, and of other household goods to the value of 50 shillings and 4d; use of the 1-2 of my dwelling house, and 2-3 of my homelott, orchard and gardens, all which to remain to the use, benefit and behoof of her my sd. wife during the time of her natural life or widowhood. I give unto my eldest son George Wolcott 100 acres of land lying within the bounds of the Township of Hebron, in the County aforesd., as may more amply appear by a deed of gift under my hand and seal, to be his whole portion out of my estate, together with what other things he has already received. I give unto my son Joshua, whome I likewise constitute executor with his mother, and at her decease to be my sole executor, all and singular my lands lying within ye bounds of Wethersfield, at my wife's decease; and during her natural life or widowhood, the 1-2 part of my dwelling house and half. my barn, and the use of 1-3 of my home lott, 1-3 of my orchard and 1-3 of my gardens during the natural life or widowhood of his mother as aforesd. And my will is that my son Joshua, whome I have appointed executor, be under the direction, guidance and instruction of my good friends, Mr. Joshua Robbins and Mr. Thomas Wright. I give unto my other two sons, namely, Daniel and Josiah, all my lands in Hebron aforesd. to be equally divided to them both, whether purchased of Mr. Elay or my brother Samuel Curtice or otherways, or coming by rights; and also 1 young horse or mare worth 3 or £4, to each of them my sons, to be divided to them when they shall come of age.

I give unto my sd. wife and son Joshua, executors, all my other household goods and all other my personal estate, in consideration of and for the obliging of these my executors in the faithfull discharge of their care in providing for my children which are yet under age until they arrive to lawfull age. And the executors are hereby willed and required to pay out of the estate which I have commited to them the following gifts: To my daughter Elizabeth, the sum of £45 as money; to my daughter Deborah, the wife of John Taylor, £14 as money to make up her portion with what she received at her marriage; to my other three daughters, namely, Eunice, Anna and Sarah, to each of them £40 money or equivalent thereto. Further, my will is, that all the household goods which I have given to my wife during her natural life shall at her death be equally divided to my daughters.

Witness: *Samuel Curtice,*   GEORGE WOLCOTT, LS.
Joseph Woodhouse, Josiah Churchill.

Court Record, Page 133—2 August, 1726: Will now exhibited by Elizabeth Woolcott and Joshua Woolcott, executors named in the will. Proven.

Page 136—4 October, 1726: Invt. now exhibited and allowed.

Page 138—1st November, 1726: (Broken page)—Woolcott, a minor, 16 years old, chose his mother Elizabeth Woolcott to be his guardian.

Page 137.

Wyard, John, Farmington. Died 20 April, 1725. Invt. (1 item is 1205 acres of land, £300). Taken by Timothy Porter, Isaac Cowles and Samuel Stanly.

Court Record, Page 80—12 April, 1725: Adms. to Phebe Wyard, widow of sd. deceased.

Page 84—4 May, 1725: Invt. now exhibited by Phebe Wyard and Thomas Hurlbut, Adms. Accepted.

Page 94—14 July, 1725: Adms. report estate insolvent, and moves that commissioners may be appointed to examine claims. This Court appoint John Austin and John Cadwell of Hartford, and Josiah Goodrich of Wethersfield, and order to be set out the widow's thirds of moveables, £41-19-06, and 1-3 of the real estate by meets and bounds for improvement during life, by John Hart, Timothy Porter and Isaac Cowles.

Page 130—5 May, 1726: Adms. now report the estate insolvent. Nathaniel Stanly, John Austin and John Curtice appointed Commissioners.

Page 141—6 December, 1726: John Wyard, late of Wethersfield: Order to sell land to pay debts.

Recorded in Vol. XII, Page 215. Invt. on Page 233.

Yeomans, John, Tolland. Invt. £647-06-02. Taken 10 March, 1728-9, by Joseph Hatch, Timothy Hatch and Jonathan Delano. Will dated 28 June, 1725.

I, John Yeomans of Tolland, in the County of Hartford and Colony of Connecticut, in New England, do make and ordain this my last will and Testament: I give to Millicent my wife the 1-3 of all that upland and meadow I shall hereafter give to my two sons, Elisha Yeomans and Elijah Yeomans, during my wife's natural life. I give to my sd. wife the 1-3 of all my moveable estate; also, the lower room of ye west end of my dwelling house and half the cellar under the same, during her widow-hood. I give to my son Elisha Yeomans, whome I ordain with my wife sole executor, also part of my homestead with all the houseing on sd. part hereafter expressed, excepting what I have given to my sd. wife, and that to return to my sd. son Elisha at the end of my sd. wife's widowhood. I give to my son Elisha Yeomans 1-2 of my Entervail meadow, joining to Willimantic River, together with 1-2 of the upland that lies within the fence that incloses above sd. meadow. I give to my son Elisha Yeomans the remaining part of my personal estate. I give to my son Elijah Yeomans the 1-2 of my Entervail meadow, and upland within the fence that incloses it. I give to my son Elijah the remaining part of my sd. homestead. I give to my son Eleazer Yeomans all my land lying south-ward of the land that I have given to my two sons as is before mentioned, that is to say, Elisha and Elijah, and sd. land now given to my sd. son Ebenezer bounds north on Nath. Beary and easterly on Willimantick River. I give to my son Thomas Yeomans a certain piece of land north of my dwelling house and north of the road that leads from Williman-tick River along by my homestead; sd. land bounds east on Capt. Jo-seph Hatche's land, and bounds north on John Dady's and Timothy Hatche's land, sd. land bounds west on sd. Thomas Yeomans's own land, south on the abovesd. road. I give to my son John Yeomans, with what he has already, 10 shillings. I give to my daughter, Sarah Knap, £20 in money. I give to my daughter, Elizabeth Yeomans, £40 in money. I give to my daughter Millicent, £40 in money. I give to my daughter Mary Yeomans, £30 in money. I give to my daughter Mabel Yeomans, £30 in money.

Witness: *Willm. Easton (Eaton?)*,   JOHN X YEOMANS, LS.
Timothy Hatch, Jonathan Delano.

Page 28 (Vol. XI) 1st September, 1730: Whereas, the debts due from the estate of John Yeomans, late of Tolland decd., doe altogether or well nigh amount to as much as the moveable part of his estate, and the widow, Millicent Yeomans, moving to this Court that there might be set out to her use so much of the utensils of housekeeping during her widow-hood as is necessary, this Court do now set out to the sd. widow, of the moveable estate of her late husband, John Yeomans, for her use during life or widowhood, the sum of £27-04-06. A list of the debts appears on file.

Court Record, Page 16—27 December, 1734: An account of Adms. on the estate of John Yeomans, late of Tolland deceased, was now ex-hibited in Court by Elisha Yeomans, one of the sons of the sd. deceased, which account is by this Court accepted and ordered to be kept upon file.

Page 56 (Vol. XIV) 5 March, 1744-5: John Yeomans, a minor, 17 years of age, son of John Yeomans, chose Nathaniel Olcott of Hartford to be his guardian. Recog., £200.

INDEXES.

INDEX TO ESTATES.

Abby, John, Windham, 1700. Will.......................... 3
Ackley, Nathaniel, Haddam, 1709-10. Will.................. 144
Ackley, Thomas, Haddam, 1703-4.......................... 3
Addams, Benjamin, Wethersfield, 1725...................... 456
Addams, Daniel, Simsbury, 1713. Will..................... 144
Addams, Daniel, Jr., Simsbury, 1712-13. Will.............. 145
Addams, John, Wethersfield, 1721.......................... 348
Adjett, John, Hartford, 1712.............................. 146
Adjett, Samuel, Hartford, 1712............................ 147
Adkins, Elizabeth, Middletown, widow of Josiah, 1700........... 4
Adkins, Josiah, Hartford, 1713............................ 147
Adkins, Josiah, Middletown, 1724......................... 456
Adkins, Thomas, Hartford, 1709.........................5, 148
Alderman, William, Simsbury, 1717........................ 348
Alford, Elizabeth, Windsor, 1727......................... 457
Alford, Jeremiah, Windsor, 1709.......................... 5
Allin, Alexander, Windsor, 1708. Will..................... 7
Allyn, Benjamin, Windsor, 1712........................... 148
Allyn, John, Middletown, 1724............................ 457
Allyn, John, Windsor, 1707. Will......................... 9
Allyn, Joshua, Sen., Windham, 1699....................... 11
Allyn, Obadiah, Middletown, 1712. Will................... 148
Allyn, Obadiah, Jr., Middletown, 1702.................... 11
Allyn, Samuel, Coventry, 1717............................ 348
Allyn, Thomas, Windsor, 1709............................ 149
Alsopp, Thomas, Simsbury, 1724-5......................... 458
Alverd, Jane, Windsor, 1715.............................. 150
Alverd, Josias, Simsbury, 1722........................... 349
Andrews, Ann, Hartford, 1707-8........................... 12
Andrews, Benjamin, Wethersfield, 1719..................... 349
Andrews, Edward, 1707-8................................. 11
Andrews, Edward, Jr., Hartford, 1707-8.................... 12
Andrews, Elizabeth, Hartford, 1716-17. Will............... 350
Andrews, Joseph, Sen., Wethersfield, 1706. Will............ 12
Andrews, Samuel, Hartford, 1711-12. Will................. 150
Andrews, Solomon and Elizabeth his wife, Hartford, 1716-17...... 350
Andrews, Solomon, Hartford, 1712. Will................... 151
Andrews, William, Wethersfield, 1722...................... 351
Andrus, Benjamin, Sen., Farmington, 1727. Will............ 458
Andrus, Benjamin, Farmington, 1727-8. Will............... 458
Arnold, Henry, Hartford, 1724. Will...................... 459

Arnold, Henry, Jr., 1725.. 460
Arnold, Jonathan, Haddam, 1728-9. Will..................... 461
Arnold, Jonathan, Hartford, 1719........................... 351
Arnold, Josiah, Haddam, 1711-12. Will...................... 151
Arnold, Mary, Haddam, 1714. Will............................ 352
Ashley, Jonathan, Sen., Hartford, 1704-5. Will.............. 14
Atwood, Edward, Middletown, 1717-18........................ 352
Ayrault, Nicholas (physician), Wethersfield, 1705-6. Will....... 14

Bacon, Andrew, Middletown, 1723............................ 462
Bacon, Nathaniel, Sen., Middletown, 1705-6. Will.............. 15
Baker, Bazey, Middletown, 1723............................. 462
Baker, Samuel, Windham, 1715............................... 152
Baker, Timothy, Wethersfield, 1709......................... 152
Baker, Timothy, Wethersfield, 1709......................... 16
Barber, Abigail, Simsbury, 1727............................ 463
Barber, John, Simsbury, 1711-12. Will...................... 153
Barber, Mindwell, Windsor, 1712-13......................... 153
Barber, Samuel, Windsor, 1722-3............................ 463
Barber, Samuel, Sen., Windsor, 1709. Will.................. 17
Barber, Thomas, Jr., Simsbury, 1714........................ 155
Barber, Thomas, Sen., Simsbury, 1713....................... 154
Barber, William, Windsor, 1704............................. 18
Barbour, Samuel, Simsbury, 1725. Will...................... 464
Barnard, Thomas, Simsbury, 1724. Will...................... 464
Barnes, William, East Haddam, 1715-16...................... 352
Bartlett, John, Windsor, 1728-9............................ 465
Bartlett, Samuel, Hartford, 1711........................... 155
Bate, James, Haddam, 1718.................................. 353
Bates, John, Haddam, 1718-19............................... 353
Beckwith, Nathaniel, Haddam, 1717.......................... 354
Belding, John, Wethersfield, 1713-14....................... 155
Belding, John, Wethersfield, 1725.......................... 465
Belding, Joseph, Wethersfield, 1724-5...................... 465
Benjamin, Caleb, Hartford, 1710............................ 18
Benton, Andrew, Hartford, 1703-4........................... 19
Benton, Edward, Glastonbury, 1713.......................... 156
Berry, Nathaniel, Mansfield, 1718.......................... 354
Bidwell, Deacon Daniel, Hartford, 1719. Will............... 355
Bidwell, James, Hartford, 1718............................. 356
Bidwell, Jonathan, Hartford, 1712. Will.................... 156
Bidwell, Samuel, Middletown, 1727.......................... 466
Bidwell, Samuel, Sen., Middletown, 1715. Will.............. 356
Bidwell, Sarah, Hartford, 1708-9........................... 19
Bidwell, Thomas, Hartford, 1716-17......................... 357
Bigelow, John, Hartford, 1721.............................. 357
Bigelow, Jonathan, Sen., Hartford, 1710-11. Will........... 156
Birchard, Samuel, Coventry, 1713........................... 157

Bird, Thomas, Farmington, 1725. Will...................... 466
Bissell, Deliverance (widow of Nathaniel), Windsor, 1718........ 358
Bissell, Ephraim, Tolland, 1718............................. 358
Bissell, Hezekiah, Windsor, 1709........................... 21
Bissell, Joseph, Windsor, 1713............................. 157
Bissell, Josias, Windsor, 1724............................. 467
Bissell, Mary, Simsbury, 1718.............................. 359
Bissell, Nathaniel, Windsor, 1713-14. Will.................. 157
Bissell, Samuel, Windsor, 1720............................. 359
Bissell, Samuel, Sen., Windsor, 1700. Will.................. 21
Blackleach, Mrs. Elizabeth, 1708. Will..................... 22
Blackleach, John, Jr., Farmington, 1700-1.................. 25
Blackleach, John, Sen., Wethersfield, 1703. Will........... 24
Blake, John, Middletown, 1724............................. 468
Blinn, Peter, Wethersfield, 1724-5........................ 468
Boardman, Daniel, Wethersfield, 1725. Will................ 469
Boardman, Isaac, Jr., Wethersfield, 1719.................. 470
Boardman, Isaac, Sen., Wethersfield, 1719................. 359
Boardman, Israel, Wethersfield, 1725..................... 470
Boardman, Samuel, Wethersfield, 1720. Will............... 360
Boarn (Bourn), John, Middletown, 1707.................... 25
Boarne, Joseph, Middletown, 1714......................... 159
Boarne, Nathaniel, Middletown, 1712-13................... 160
Boarne, Thomas, Middletown, 1711-12...................... 160
Booth, Symon, Hartford, 1702-3. Will..................... 26
Boreman, Lieut. Jonathan, Wethersfield, 1712. Will........ 158
Boreman, Nathaniel, Wethersfield, 1712-13. Will........... 159
Bow, Edward, Middletown, 1725............................ 471
Bowen, Josiah, Wethersfield, 1717........................ 361
Bowers, Ebenezer, (minor), 1726.......................... 471
Bowman, Nathaniel, (innholder), 1706-7. Will............. 27
Brace, Mrs. Elizabeth, Hartford, 1724.................... 471
Brainard, Daniel, Haddam, 1715........................... 160
Brainard, Sergt. Daniel, Haddam, 1728.................... 471
Brainard, Hezekiah, Haddam, 1727. Will................... 472
Brooks, John, Simsbury, 1682............................. 27
Brooks, Susannah, Wethersfield, 1721. Will............... 361
Brounson, Jacob, Farmington, 1710........................ 162
Brounson, Jacob, Sen., Farmington, 1708. Will............ 28
Brounson, Moses, Farmington, 1712........................ 163
Brounson, Sarah, (widow), Farmington, 1711-12............ 163
Brown, John, Middletown, 1719. Will...................... 362
Brown, John, Sen., Windsor, 1728-9. Will................. 473
Brown, Peter, Windsor, 1722. Will........................ 363
Brown, Peter, Windsor, 1724-5............................ 474
Brown, Thomas, Colchester, 1717. Will.................... 364
Browne, Eleanor, Middletown, 1713. Will.................. 161
Browne, Nathaniel, Sen., Middletown, 1712................ 162

Brunson, Samuel, Farmington, 1724-5........................ 475
Buck, Daniel, Wethersfield, 1726............................ 475
Buck, David, Jr., Wethersfield, 1726........................ 475
Buck, Ezekiel, Wethersfield, 1712-13. Will.................. 163
Buck, Samuel, Wethersfield, 1709........................... 164
Buckland, Elizabeth, Hartford, 1712........................ 164
Buckland, Nicholas, Windsor, 1728. Will.................... 476
Buckland, William, Hartford, 1724. Will.................... 476
Buel, Peter, Simsbury, 1728-9. Will........................ 477
Buell, Ephraim, Simsbury, 1719............................. 364
Bulkeley, Gershom, Wethersfield, 1713. Will................ 165
Bulkeley, Peter, Wethersfield, 1702........................ 28
Bull, John, Hartford, 1705................................. 29
Bull, Major Jonathan, Hartford, 1702....................... 30
Bull, Jonathan, Jr., Hartford, 1714........................ 167
Bull, Joseph, Hartford, 1712............................... 167
Bull, Deacon Thomas, Farmington, 1708. Will................ 31
Bunce, Jonathan, Hartford, 1717............................ 365
Bunce, Thomas, Hartford, 1712. Will........................ 168
Bunce, Thomas, Jr., Hartford, 1712......................... 169
Burd, James, Farmington, 1708.............................. 32
Burd, James, Farmington, 1709.............................. 32
Burd, Joseph, Farmington, 1708. Will....................... 33
Burd, Nathaniel, Farmington, 1703-4. Will.................. 34
Burd, Thomas, Farmington, 1706-7. Will..................... 35
Burge, John, Windsor, 1718................................. 365
Burge, Joseph, Windsor, 1705-6............................. 35
Burnham, John, Hartford, 1721. Will........................ 365
Burnham, Samuel, Sen., Hartford, 1728. Will................ 478
Burnham, Thomas, Jr., Hartford, 1726. Will................. 479
Burnham, Thomas, Sen., Hartford, 1726. Will................ 478
Burrell, Charles, (minor), 1728............................ 480
Butler, Charles, Wethersfield, 1711........................ 170
Butler, Samuel, Wethersfield, 1711-12. Will................ 171
Butler, Samuel, Hartford, 1712............................. 170
Butler, Thomas, Hartford, 1725. Will....................... 480
Butler, William, Wethersfield, 1714........................ 171
Buttolph, David, Simsbury, 1717............................ 366

Cadwell, Edward, Hartford, 1719. Will...................... 367
Cadwell, Matthew, Hartford, 1719........................... 368
Cadwell, Matthew, Hartford, 1723........................... 481
Cadwell, Samuel, Hartford, 1725. Will...................... 481
Cakebread, Isaac, Hartford, 1709........................... 35
Camp, John, Sen., Hartford, 1710-11. Will.................. 172
Camp, Joseph, Wethersfield, 1712-13........................ 172
Camp, Mary, Hartford, 1727. Will........................... 481
Carpenter, David, Hartford, 1722........................... 482

Carrington, Ebenezer, Waterbury, 1711........................ 173
Case, Bartholomew, Simsbury, 1725........................... 482
Case, John, Hartford, 1724-5................................. 483
Case, John, Sen., Simsbury, 1703-4. Will.................... 36
Case, Richard, Hartford, 1724-5. Will....................... 484
Case, Samuel, Simsbury, 1725. Will.......................... 484
Case, William, Simsbury, 1700............................... 38
Chapman, Edward, Windsor, 1724.............................. 485
Chapman, Hannah, Windsor, 1718.............................. 369
Chapman, Henry, Windsor, 1713............................... 173
Chapman, Capt. John, Haddam, 1712........................... 173
Chauncey, Rev. Charles, Clerk of Stratford, 1710............ 174
Cheeny, William, Middletown, 1705. Will.................... 39
Chester, John, Wethersfield, 1711-12. Will................. 174
Chester, Stephen, Wethersfield, 1705........................ 40
Chester, Thomas, Wethersfield, 1712-13...................... 176
Chubb, Stephen, (minor), 1724............................... 486
Church, Samuel, Hartford, 1718.............................. 369
Churchill, Nathaniel, Wethersfield, 1715-16................. 370
Clark, Daniel, Hartford, 1724-5............................. 487
Clark, Daniel, Middletown, 1724-5. Will.................... 486
Clark, George, Milford, 1688. Will......................... 41
Clark, John, Sen., Farmington, 1712-13. Will............... 179
Clark, John, Jr., Farmington, 1709.......................... 178
Clark, Joseph, Windsor, 1718................................ 370
Clark, Josiah, Hartford, 1712............................... 179
Clark, William, Sen., Wethersfield, 1711-12. Will.......... 179
Clarke, Capt. Daniel, Windsor, 1710. Will.................. 177
Clarke, John, Windsor, 1715................................. 370
Clarke, Thomas (tanner), Hartford, 1703..................... 42
Clarke, William, Wethersfield, 1708......................... 43
Coal, Nathaniel, Hartford, 1713............................. 180
Coale, Ichabod, Middletown, 1711............................ 180
Coale, Nathaniel, Sen., Hartford, 1708. Will............... 43
Cockshott, Elizabeth, (widow), Haddam, 1699-1700............ 44
Cole, John, Jr., Farmington, 1708........................... 44
Cole, Samuel, Farmington, 1718.............................. 371
Cole, Samuel, Wethersfield, 1718............................ 371
Coleman, Noah, Colchester, 1711............................. 181
Colfax, Jonathan, Wethersfield, 1711-12..................... 181
Colt, Abraham, Glastonbury, 1717............................ 372
Colt, Joseph, Windsor, 1720-21.............................. 373
Cone, Deacon Daniel, East Haddam, 1725...................... 487
Cone, Jared, Haddam, 1718................................... 373
Cook, Nathaniel, Windsor, 1688.............................. 45
Cook, Thomas, Windsor, 1724-5. Will........................ 489
Cooke, Aaron, (son of Noah Cooke), Hartford, 1720. Will..... 374
Cooke, Capt. Aaron, Hartford, 1725. Will................... 488

Cooke, Benjamin, (minor), 1727-8.......................... 489
Cooke, John, Middletown, 1704-5. Will...................... 45
Cooke, John, Windsor, 1712................................. 182
Cooke, Nathaniel, Windsor, 1725........................... 489
Cornish, James, Wethersfield, 1711. Will................... 183
Cornwall, David, Middletown, 1725......................... 490
Cornwall, Jacob, Sen., (mariner), Middletown, 1708......... 47
Cornwall, John, Sen., Middletown, 1707. Will.............. 47
Cornwall, Jonathan, Middletown, 1705-6.................... 48
Cornwall, Samuel, Sen., Middletown, 1728-9. Will.......... 491
Cornwall, Thomas, Middletown, 1702....................... 48
Cornwall, William, Middletown, 1704...................... 50
Cornwell, Sergt. William, Middletown, 1726. Will.......... 492
Coult, Jonathan, (cordwainer), Windsor, 1711............. 182
Cowles, Caleb, Kensington, 1725-6........................ 493
Cowles, Nathaniel, Jr., Farmington, 1724-5............... 493
Crane, Abraham, Wethersfield, 1713....................... 183
Crane, Isaac, Wethersfield, 1712-13. Will................ 184
Crane, Israel, Wethersfield, 1707........................ 50
Crane, Jacob, Wethersfield, 1718-19...................... 374
Crane, Joseph, Wethersfield, 1707........................ 51
Crippin, Thomas, Sen., Haddam, 1709. Will................ 185
Cross, John, Windsor, 1721............................... 374
Cross, Capt. Samuel, Windsor, 1707. Will................. 53
Crow, John, Hartford, 1714............................... 185
Crowfoot, Joseph, Wethersfield, 1722..................... 375
Curtis, John, Wethersfield, 1714-15...................... 375
Curtis, John, Jr., Wethersfield, 1712. Will.............. 186
Curtiss, Samuel, Wethersfield, 1688...................... 54

Dart, Mary, New London, 1727. Will....................... 494
Davis, Jemima, Hartford, 1706............................ 55
Day, Jonathan, Windsor, 1721............................. 375
Day, Thomas, Colchester, 1728-9.......................... 494
Day, Thomas, Hartford, 1724-5............................ 493
Deming, Ebenezer, Wethersfield, 1705..................... 187
Deming, Elizabeth, Wethersfield, 1714. Will.............. 187
Deming, John, Sen., Wethersfield, 1705. Will............. 55
Deming, Jonathan, Wethersfield, 1727..................... 496
Deming, Lemuell, 1724-5. Will............................ 496
Deming, Samuel, Wethersfield, 1709....................... 188
Denison, Mary, Wethersfield, 1721........................ 376
Deverieux, Jonathan, Hartford, 1726-7.................... 497
Dewey, Daniel, Farmington, 1717.......................... 376
De Wholph, Joseph, Middletown, 1720...................... 376
Dibble, Benjamin, Simsbury, 1712......................... 189
Dibble, George, Windsor, 1709............................ 56
Dibble, Thomas, Sen., Windsor, 1700. Will................ 56

Dickinson, Obadiah, Jr., Wethersfield, 1700...................... 57
Dickinson, Thomas, Glastonbury, 1717......................... 377
Dickinson, Thomas, Hartford, 1723-4. Will.................... 497
Dickinson, Thomas, Wethersfield, 1712-13..................... 189
Diggins, Thomas, Windsor, 1720.............................. 377
Dimock, Timothy, Ashford, 1718.............................. 377
Dodd, Edward, Hartford, 1728................................ 498
Doolittle, Samuel, Middletown, 1714. Will................... 190
Drake, Job, Sen., Windsor, 1711............................. 191
Drake, Job, Jr., Windsor, 1712. Will........................ 192
Drake, John, Simsbury, 1724-5............................... 498
Drake, Jonathan, Windsor, 1716.............................. 378
Drake, Symon, Windsor, 1712................................. 192
Duce, Abda, alias Ginnings (a mulatto), Hartford, 1708-9......... 58
Dunham, Thomas (yeoman), Mansfield, 1717-18................ 378
Dyxx, John, Hartford, 1722. Will............................ 379
Dyxx, John, Wethersfield, 1711-12........................... 193
Dyxx, Sarah, Wethersfield, 1709. Will....................... 58

Easton, John, Hartford, 1726................................ 498
Easton, John, Sen., Hartford, 1718.......................... 380
Easton, Jonathan, Hartford, 1724............................ 499
Easton, Joseph, Sen., Hartford, 1711-12. Will............... 193
Edwards, David, Wethersfield, 1723-4........................ 501
Edwards, John, Wethersfield, 1716........................... 381
Edwards, Joseph, Wethersfield, 1725......................... 501
Edwards, Richard, Hartford, 1718. Will...................... 382
Edwards, Thomas, Wethersfield, 1712......................... 194
Eliot, Mrs. Elizabeth, Windsor, 1702. Will.................. 59
Eliot, John, Esq. Windsor, 1719............................. 382
Elmer, John, Windsor, 1722.................................. 383
Elmer, Mary, daughter of Edward Elmer, 1712-13.............. 195
Elmor, Edward, Windsor, 1725................................ 502
Elmore, John, Windsor, 1711-12.............................. 194
Elmore, John, Jr., Windsor, 1722............................ 383
Elsworth, Lieut. John, Windsor, 1720........................ 383
Elsworth, Josiah, Windsor, 1706. Will....................... 59
Elsworth, Josiah, Windsor, 1718. Will....................... 384
Elsworth, Martha, Windsor, 1721............................. 384
Enno, Abigail, Windsor, 1728. Will.......................... 502
Enno. James, Sen., Windsor, 1714. Will...................... 195
Ensign, David, Hartford, 1728-9............................. 503
Ensign, Jonathan, Hartford, 1724............................ 504

Field, John, Coventry, 1718. Will........................... 385
Filley, Mary (widow), Windsor, 1708-9....................... 61
Filley, Samuel, Windsor, 1711-12. Will...................... 196
Filley, William, Windsor, 1707. Will........................ 61

Fitch, Ebenezer, Windsor, 1724............................... 505
Fitch, Capt. Joseph, Windsor, 1727........................... 508
Fitch, Martha, single woman, Wethersfield, 1713............... 197
Fitch, Thomas, Wethersfield, 1704............................ 62
Flowers, Lamrock, Hartford, 1716. Will...................... 385
Foote, Nathaniel, Wethersfield, 1715......................... 197
Forbes, John, Hartford, 1713................................. 198
Foster, Ann, Windsor, 1721.................................. 386
Fowdrie, James, Horseneck, 1727.............................. 508
Fox, Beriah, Glastonbury, 1727.............................. 508
Fox, Richard, Glastonbury, 1709. Will....................... 62
Francis, John, Sen., Wethersfield, 1711-12................... 198
Francis, Robert, Wethersfield, 1711-12...................... 199
Frank, (a free negro), Farmington, 1725..................... 508
Fuller, John, Haddam, 1725-6. Will.......................... 509
Fuller, Samuel, Mansfield, 1716. Will....................... 386
Fuller, Thomas, Windham, 1718. Will......................... 386
Fyler, John, Windsor, 1723.................................. 510
Fyler, Samuel, Hebron, 1710................................. 199
Fyler, Zerubbabell, Windsor, 1714-15........................ 200

Gains, Samuel, Glastonbury, 1700............................ 63
Gardner, Benjamin, Wethersfield, 1713-14.................... 201
Gates, George, East Haddam, 1724............................ 511
Gates, Joseph, Haddam, 1711-12.............................. 201
Gaylord, Elea:or, Windsor, 1714-15.......................... 202
Gaylord, John, Windsor, 1722................................ 387
Gaylord, Nathaniel, Windsor, 1720........................... 388
Gaylord, Samuel, Middletown, 1729........................... 512
Gibbs, Jacob, Windsor, 1711-12.............................. 202
Gibbs, Samuel, Windsor, 1719-20. Will....................... 388
Giffie, Caleb, Haddam, 1725 (minor)......................... 517
Gilbert, Benjamin, Wethersfield, 1711-12.................... 203
Gilbert, Eleazer, Middletown, 1728-9 (minor)................ 512
Gilbert, George, Middletown, 1717-18........................ 389
Gilbert, John, Middletown, 1727............................. 512
Gilbert, Josiah, Wethersfield, 1704-5. Will................. 63
Gilbert, Mary (widow), Hartford, 1700. Will................. 64
Gilbert, Mary, Middletown, 1729............................. 513
Gilbert, Thomas (glazier), Hartford, 1705-6................. 66
Gill, John, Jr., Middletown, 1713. Will..................... 205
Gill, John, Sen., Middletown, 1712.......................... 204
Gillett, Cornelius, Sen., Windsor, 1711. Will............... 205
Gillett, William, Simsbury, 1718-19......................... 389
Goff, Jacob, Wethersfield, 1723............................. 513
Goff, Philip, Middletown, 1727.............................. 513
Goffe, Aaron, Wethersfield, 1711-12......................... 206
Goffe, Moses, Wethersfield, 1712. Will...................... 206

Goodrich, Ephraim, Wethersfield, 1728.................... 513
Goodwin, Lois, Hartford, 1711-12, minor................. 208
Goodwin, Nathaniel, Sen., Hartford, 1713-14. Will........ 207
Goodwin, Samuel, Hartford, 1711-12...................... 208
Goring, William, Simsbury, 1715. Will................... 390
Goslin, Henry, Glastonbury, 1724........................ 514
Graham, Benjamin, Hartford, 1724-5. Will............... 514
Graham, John, Jr., Hartford, 1720....................... 515
Grant, Noah, Tolland, 1727.............................. 515
Grant, Rachell (spinster), Hartford, 1704-5. Will........ 66
Grant, Samuel (carpenter), Windsor, 1710................ 208
Grant, Samuel, Windsor, 1718............................ 391
Grant, Thomas, Windsor, 1726............................ 517
Grave, John, Hartford, 1702. Will....................... 67
Graves, Martha (widow), Wethersfield, 1701.............. 68
Graves, Thomas, Hartford, 1713-14. Will................. 209
Gridley, Samuel, Farmington, 1712....................... 209
Gridley, Samuel, Jr., Farmington, 1714.................. 210
Griffee, John, Haddam, 1697-8........................... 69
Griffin, Ephraim, Simsbury, 1725........................ 517
Griffin, Mindwell, Simsbury, 1725, (minor).............. 517
Griffin, Nathaniel, Simsbury, 1712-13................... 211
Griffin, Ruth, Simsbury, 1719. Will..................... 391
Griffin, Thomas, Simsbury, 1719......................... 391
Griswold, Edward, Windsor, 1715-16...................... 211
Griswold, George, Sen., Windsor, 1704................... 70
Griswold, Joseph, Windsor, 1716. Will................... 392
Griswold, Joseph, Windsor, 1725......................... 517
Gross, Isaac, Windham, 1716............................. 393

Hail, John, Windsor, 1708-9............................. 72
Hale, Mary, Glastonbury, 1715........................... 211
Hale, Phebe, Wethersfield, 1712......................... 213
Hale, Samuel, Sen., Glastonbury, 1712. Will............. 213
Hale, Thomas, Sen., Glastonbury, 1723-4. Will........... 518
Hall, Daniel, Windsor, 1723-4 (minor)................... 519
Hall, Elizabeth, Sen., Middletown, 1711-12. Will........ 214
Hall, Hannah, Middletown, 1719-20....................... 393
Hall, Capt. John, Middletown, 1711-12. Will............. 215
Hall, John, Jr., mariner, son of Capt. John Hall of Middletown,
    1711-12... 216
Hall, Deacon Joseph, Mansfield, 1716.................... 394
Hamlin, John, Jr., Middletown, 1718..................... 394
Hampton, William, New York, 1715. Will.................. 394
Hancox, William, Farmington (Kensington), 1721.......... 396
Hand, Esther, Guilford, 1715............................ 216
Handerson, Martha, Hartford, 1711-12. Will.............. 217
Harris, Capt. Daniel, Middletown, 1701. Will............ 72

Harris, Daniel, Wethersfield, 1724 (minor).................... 519
Harris, Ephraim, Hartford, 1712-13.......................... 218
Harris, Mary, (single woman), Middletown, daughter of Thomas
    Harris, 1712-13... 218
Harris, Thomas, 1700.. 74
Harris, Walter, Wethersfield, 1715-16......................... 396
Harris, William, Middletown, 1719........................... 396
Hart, John, Hartford, 1724 (minor).......................... 520
Hart, Capt. John, Farmington, 1714-15....................... 218
Hart, Thomas, Sen., Farmington, 1726. Will.................. 520
Hart, Sergt. Thomas, Farmington, 1728. Will................. 522
Hawley, Jehial, Middletown, 1727............................. 523
Hayden, Daniel, Windsor, 1713............................... 219
Hayden, William, Windsor, 1713.............................. 219
Hayes, Elizabeth, Farmington, 1703........................... 74
Hayes, George, Sen., Simsbury, 1725. Will.................... 523
Hayes, Luke, Farmington 1713. Will.......................... 220
Haynes, John, Esq., Hartford, 1713-14........................ 221
Haynes, Joseph, Hartford, 1716-17........................... 398
Haynes, Miss Mabell, Hartford, 1713-14...................... 221
Haynes, Mrs. Mary, Hartford, 1726-7......................... 524
Haynes, Mrs. Sarah (widow), Hartford, 1705. Will............ 75
Hayward, John, public notary, Boston, 1687. Will............. 623
Hemsted, Joshua, New London, 1706. Will.................... 76
Henning, Andrew, Simsbury, 1724-5. Will.................... 524
Hibbard, Robert, Sen., Windham, 1710........................ 222
Hide, Timothy, Hartford, 1710. Will......................... 222
Higby, John, Middletown, 1688............................... 77
Higginson, William, Farmington, 1720........................ 399
Higley, Capt. John, Simsbury, 1714. Will.................... 223
Higley, Jonathan, Simsbury, 1716. Will...................... 398
Higley, Jonathan, Simsbury, 1722-3.......................... 525
Higley, Joseph, Simsbury, 1715. Will........................ 224
Hill, Eleazer, Windsor, 1725. Will.......................... 525
Hill, Lieut. Jonathan, Hartford, 1727. Will................. 526
Hill, Thomas, Jr., Hartford, 1706-7......................... 78
Hill, Thomas, Sen., (joiner), Hartford, 1704. Will........... 77
Hillier, James, Simsbury, 1720.............................. 399
Hills, Benjamin, Hartford, 1728. Will....................... 526
Hills, Benjamin, Jr., tailor, Hartford, 1712................ 225
Hills, Ebenezer, doctor, Hartford, 1711. Will............... 225
Hills, Joseph, Sen., Glastonbury, 1713. Will................ 225
Hills, Samuel, Glastonbury, 1727............................ 527
Hilyer, Mary, (widow), Simsbury, 1725. Will................ 525
Hinsdale, Barnabas, Hartford, 1724-5. Will................. 527
Hitchcock, Samuel, Waterbury, 1713.......................... 226
Hobart, Rev. Jeremiah, Haddam, 1715. Will.................. 400
Hodge, James, Wethersfield, 1712-13......................... 227

Holcomb, Benajah, Jr., Windsor, 1716........................ 400
Holcomb, Ensign Joshua, 1728. Will........................ 528
Holcomb, Samuel, Windsor, 1722............................ 401
Holiberd, Joseph, (minor), 1726............................ 530
Hollister, Lazarus, Wethersfield, 1709........................ 79
Hollister, Jacob, Middletown, (Bristol, Eng.) 1722. Will......... 402
Hollister, Jerusha (single woman), daughter of Capt. Stephen
    Hollister, Wethersfield, 1710............................ 230
Hollister, John, Jr., Wethersfield, 1711. Will................. 229
Hollister, John, Sen., Glastonbury, 1712. Will,............... 227
Hollister, Jonathan (mariner), Wethersfield, 1712............. 230
Hollister, Jonathan, Wethersfield............................ 530
Hollister, Capt. Stephen, Wethersfield, 1710.................. 228
Hollister, Lt. Thomas, Wethersfield, 1701.................... 80
Holman, Samuel, Windsor, 1728-9. Will...................... 530
Holmes, John, (minor) Hartford, 1723-4..................... 531
Holton, Mrs. Sarah (widow), Hartford, 1711-12. Will.......... 231
Holton, William, Hartford, 1711-12. Will.................... 232
Holyoke, Thomas, 1703-4, (minor).......................... 81
Hooker, Nathaniel, Hartford, 1711-12........................ 232
Hooker, Thomas (doctor), Hartford, 1720. Will............... 402
Hopewell, Sarah (Indian woman), Wethersfield, 1704........... 81
Hopkins, Ebenezer, Hartford, 1711.......................... 234
Hopkins, Consider, Hartford, 1726-7......................... 531
Hopkins, Stephen, Hartford, 1703........................... 81
Hopson, John, Colchester, 1714............................. 233
Hoskins, Anthony, Sen., Windsor, 1706-7. Will............... 81
Hossington, John, 1728-9................................... 532
House, John, Glastonbury, 1711-12.......................... 236
House, William, Glastonbury, 1703-4........................ 83
Howard, Benjamin, Windsor, 1711........................... 236
Howard, Henry, Hartford, 1708-9. Will...................... 84
Howard (Hayward), John, Boston, 1717. Will................. 405
Howard, John, Wethersfield, 1720-1......................... 404
Howard, Samuel, Hartford, 1716. Will....................... 405
Hubbard, Daniel, Middletown, 1704. Will.................... 85
Hubbard, John, Middletown, 1726-7......................... 532
Hubbard, Jonathan, Bolton (Hanover), 1720.................. 406
Humphrev, Capt. Samuel, Simsbury, 1725.................... 533
Humphrey, Thomas, Simsbury, 1714......................... 237
Humphries, Nathaniel, Hartford, 1711....................... 237
Hungerford, Thomas, East Haddam, 1713-14. Will............ 238
Hunn, George, Wethersfield, 1712-13........................ 239
Hunn, Nathaniel, Sen., Farmington, 1712. Will............... 230
Hunnewell, Elizabeth, Middletown, 1712..................... 236
Hunt, Joseph, Stafford, 1728............................... 534

Jennings, Joseph, (a mulatto), 1718-19....................... 406

Johnson, Isaac, Middletown, 1720. Will...................... 406
Johnson, Mrs. Mary, (widow), Coventry, 1712................. 240
Johnson, Nathaniel, Middletown, 1704-5...................... 85
Johnson, William, Coventry, 1710........................... 240
Jones, Caleb, Hebron, 1711-12.............................. 240
Judd, John, Waterbury 1717-18.............................. 407
Judd, John, (son of William Judd), Farmington, 1710.......... 241
Judd, Jonathan, Middletown, 1725........................... 534
Judd, Rachel, Farmington, 1703. Will........................ 86
Judd, Rachel, Farmington, 1717............................. 407
Judd, Samuel, Farmington, 1727-8........................... 534
Judd, Thomas, Farmington, 1724. Will....................... 535
Judd, Lt. Thomas, Waterbury, 1702-3........................ 86
Judd, Deacon Thomas, Farmington, (Northampton, Mass.), 1714.. 241

Keats, Richard, Hartford, 1711-12........................... 242
Kellogg, Abram, Hartford, 1718. Will........................ 408
Kellogg, John, Hartford, 1725.............................. 536
Kellogg, Samuel, Colchester, 1708.......................... 87
Kellogg, Deacon Samuel, Hartford, 1717..................... 409
Kellogg, Sarah, Hartford, 1718-19.......................... 410
Kelsey, Elizabeth, Windsor, 1725-6......................... 536
Kelsey, Stephen, Hartford, 1710............................ 243
Kelsey, Thomas, Windsor, 1715............................. 243
Kennard, John, Haddam, 1709............................... 244
Kilbourn, Abraham, Wethersfield, 1713...................... 245
Kilbourn, David, Glastonbury, 1713......................... 245
Kilbourn, Ebenezer, Wethersfield, 1711-12.................. 246
Kilbourn, John, Glastonbury, 1711. Will.................... 247
Kilbourn, Sergt. John, Sen., Wethersfield, 1703. Will....... 88
Kilbourn, Sarah, Farmington, 1724.......................... 537
Kilbourn, Thomas, Hartford, 1712........................... 248
Kilbourn, Thomas, Jr., Hartford, 1712...................... 249
Kimberly, Eleazer, Glastonbury, 1708-9. Will............... 89
King, Edward, Windsor, 1702............................... 90
King, Sarah, late wife of Capt. John King of Northampton,
    1705-6............................ 90
King, Thomas, Hartford, 1711-12............................ 250
Kirby, Joseph, Middletown, 1711-12. Will................... 244
Knight, George, Hartford, 1699............................ 90

Lane, Isaac, Sen., Middletown, 1711........................ 250
Lane, John, Middletown, 1716............................... 410
Lattimer, Jonathan, Wethersfield, 1711-12.................. 251
Lattimer, Luther, Wethersfield, 1722-3..................... 537
Lawrence, Capt. John, 1727-8............................... 538
Lee, John, Farmington, 1723. Will.......................... 538
Lefeavor, Philip, Windsor, 1705............................ 90

Lewis, John, Simsbury, 1713-14........................... 252
Lewis, Joseph, Simsbury, 1706........................... 90
Lewis, Sergt. Samuel, Farmington 539
Loomis, Benjamin, Windsor, 1725. Will.................... 540
Loomis, Ebenezer, Windsor, 1709......................... 253
Loomis, Isaac, Windsor, 1704............................ 91
Loomis, Jonathan (blacksmith), Windsor, 1707............. 91
Loomis, Stephen, Windsor, 1711.......................... 253
Loomis, Timothy, Windsor, 1710.......................... 254
Long, Jerusha, Hartford, 1722-3.......................... 539
Long, Thomas, Sen., Windsor, 1711-12.................... 252
Lord, Elisha, Hartford, 1725. Will....................... 540
Lord, Richard Hartford 1711-12........................... 254
Loveman Children (minors), 1725......................... 541
Lucas, John, Middletown, 1704........................... 92

Macky, John, Wethersfield, 1712.......................... 256
Mansfield, John and Sarah, Windsor, 1727. Will.......... 541
Manure, Philip, Windsor, 1711........................... 256
Mark William, Middletown, 1728.......................... 542
Markham, Deacon Daniel, Middletown, 1711-12. Will....... 257
Marsh, John, Hartford, 1727. Will....................... 543
Marshall, Benjamin, Hartford, 1696...................... 92
Marshall, Joel, Hartford, 1721-22. Will................. 411
Marshall, Thomas, (seaman), Hartford, 1700. Will........ 92
Mason, Ann, Wethersfield, 1711. Will.................... 257
Mather, Rev. Samuel, Windsor, 1728...................... 544
Mather, William, (minor), Wethersfield, 1726............ 544
Matson, John, Simsbury, 1728. Will..................... 544
Meakins, John, Sen., Hartford, 1706. Will.............. 93
Meakins, Joseph, Hartford, 1724-5....................... 545
Meakins, Thomas, Hartford, 1723......................... 546
Mentor, Robert, Colchester, 1720........................ 411
Mercer, Mary, Hartford, 1710. Will..................... 258
Merrells, Jacob, Hartford, 1725......................... 546
Merrells, John, Sen., Hartford, 1712.................... 258
Merrells, Nathaniel, Hartford, 1725..................... 546
Miller, Joseph, Middletown, 1717-18..................... 411
Miller, Thomas, Middletown, 1727-8...................... 548
Miller, Thomas, East Haddam, 1728. Will................ 546
Miller, William, (tanner), Glastonbury, 1705............ 94
Miller, William, Glastonbury, 1723...................... 548
Mills, Dorcas, Windsor, 1720. Will..................... 411
Mills, Peter, Sen., (tailor), Windsor, 1710............. 260
Mitchell William, Windsor, 1725. Will.................. 548
Modsley, Capt. Joseph, Glastonbury, 1719. Will......... 412
Moore, Andrew, Windsor, 1719............................ 413

Moore, Dorothy, (late wife of Deacon Isaac Moore), Farmington, 1706. Will 96
Moore, Edward, Windsor, 1725 549
Moore, John, Sen., Windsor, 1718. Will 413
Moore, Joseph, Windsor, 1714 260
Morgan, Benjamin, Middletown, 1723 550
Morgan, Thomas, Hartford, 1725. Will 550
Morley, Thomas, Sen., Glastonbury, 1711-12. Will 261
Morton, Mary, Windsor, 1719-20. Will 415
Morton, Thomas, Windsor, 1708 96
Morton, Thomas, Simsbury, 1725-6 551
Morton, William, Sen., Windsor, 1711-12 261
Morton, William, Jr., Windsor, 1711-12 262
Moses, John, Simsbury, 1715. Will 262
Mudge, Micah, Hebron, 1724-5. Will 551
Mygatt, Joseph, Hartford, 1724 552

Newbery, Benjamin, Windsor, 1709. Will 264
Newbery, Capt. Benjamin, Windsor, 1710. Will 263
Newbery, Benjamin, Windsor, 1718-19 416
Newell, Thomas, Farmington, 1723-24 553
North, John, Farmington, 1709-10 265
North, Samuel, Farmington, 1706. Will 97
North, Thomas (son of Samuel North) 1707-8 98
North, Thomas, Farmington, 1712 265
North, Thomas, Kensington, 1724-25 553
Norton, John, Farmington, 1725 554
Norton, Thomas, Simsbury, 1725 555
Norton, Thomas, Sen., Farmington, 1729. Will 554
Nott, John, Sen., Wethersfield, 1710 266

Olcott, George, Hartford, 1710-11 267
Olcott, John, Hartford, 1712 267
Olcott, Samuel, Hartford, 1704. Will 98
Olcott, Thomas, Jr., Hartford, 1712-13. Will 268
Olmsted, Joseph, Sen., Hartford, 1726. Will 555
Olmsted, Nicholas (son of Joseph Olmsted), Hartford, 1717 416
Olmsted, Samuel, East Haddam, 1726 557
Onepenny, Sarah, (Indian), Hartford, 1713. Will 269
Onepenny, Sarah, (Indian), Hartford, 1728. Will 557
Osborne, Sergt. John, Windsor, 1706. Will 99
Owen, Daniel, (mariner), Windsor, 1712-13 270
Owen, Isaac, 1709-10 270
Owen, Josiah, Windsor, 1722. Will 417
Owen, Obadiah, Windsor, 1728-29 558

Palmer, Stephen, Windsor, 1720 418
Palmer, Timothy, Windsor, 1713 270

Pampenum, (Indian woman), Haddam, 1703-4. Will............ 100
Pantry, John, Jr., Hartford, 1713............................. 270
Parsons, Samuel, Simsbury, 1708. Will...................... 101
Peck, Paul, Hartford, 1724-25............................... 558
Persivall, James, Haddam, 1728. Will....................... 559
Person, John, Farmington, 1725. Will...................... 559
Pettebone, Benjamin, Simsbury, 1706...................... 101
Pettebone, John, Sen., Simsbury, 1713. Will................. 271
Phelps, Capt. Abraham, Windsor, 1728....................... 560
Phelps, Joseph, Windsor, 1716. Will......................... 418
Phelps, Timothy, Hartford, 1712. Will 271
Phelps, Capt. Timothy, Windsor, 1719. Will................. 420
Phelps, William, Windsor, 1711-12........................... 272
Pinney, Isaac, Windsor, 1709............................... 272
Pinney, Isaac, Jr., Windsor, 1717........................... 420
Pinney, Josiah, Windsor, 1728. Will........................ 560
Pinney, Sarah, Windsor, 1715. Will......................... 421
Pitkin, George, Hartford, 1702.............................. 102
Pitkin, John, Hartford, 1706. Will........................... 103
Pitkin, William, Sen., Hartford, 1723. Will.................. 561
Porter, Daniel, (minor), Windsor, 1724...................... 561
Porter, James, Windsor, 1727............................... 562
Porter, John, Windsor, 1724................................ 562
Porter, Nathaniel, Lebanon, 1710........................... 273
Porter, Nehemiah, Farmington, 1722. Will.................. 421
Porter, Deacon Thomas, Farmington, 1711. Will............. 273
Porter, Thomas, Farmington, 1718-19. Will.................. 422
Porter, Thomas, Farmington, 1727........................... 562
Porter, William, Haddam, 1713.............................. 274
Powell, Thomas, (minor), Wethersfield, 1713................. 275
Pratt, Daniel, Hartford, 1703-4............................. 103
Pratt, Esther, Hartford, 1702. Will.......................... 104
Prior, Humphrey, Windsor, 1719............................ 423
Purple, Edward, Haddam, 1719-20. Will..................... 423

Quittafield, Clement, Colchester, 1724.......................562

Ranney, George, Middletown, 1725.......................... 562
Ranney, Thomas, Middletown, 1727. Will................... 563
Ranny, Hannah, (single woman), Middletown, 1713............ 275
Ranny, Thomas, Middletown, 1713. Will.................... 275
Read, Arthur, Hartford, (Hatfield, Mass.), 1711.............. 276
Read, Jacob, Simsbury, 1709................................ 276
Reignolds, Samuel, Coventry, 1720......................... 424
Reynolds, Jonathan, Wethersfield, 1704..................... 105
Richards, Benjamin, Waterbury, 1714....................... 277
Richards, Obadiah, Waterbury, 1702........................ 106
Richards, Thomas, Boston, 1714. Will...................... 424

Richardson, Hannah, widow of Israel Richardson, Waterbury,
   1713...... 278
Richardson, Israel, Waterbury, 1712.......................... 278
Richardson, John, Waterbury, 1712............................ 278
Richardson, Lemuel, East Haddam, 1713. Will................. 279
Richardson, Nathaniel, Waterbury, 1712....................... 280
Richardson, Thomas, Waterbury, 1712........................ 280
Robbins, John, Wethersfield, 1712............................ 280
Robbinson, John, Hartford, 1719. Will........................ 427
Roberts, John, Middletown, 1721............................. 427
Roberts, John, Jr., Simsbury, 1724............................ 564
Roberts, Samuel, Jr., Middletown, 1724....................... 564
Roberts, William, Jr., Hartford, 1726......................... 564
Robinson, Ensign Thomas, Haddam, 1725...................... 565
Rockwell, Matthew, Windsor, 1725 (minor).................... 565
Rockwell, Samuel, Windsor, 1711. Will...................... 281
Rockwell, Samuel, Windsor, 1725............................ 565
Rockwell, Samuel, Jr., Windsor, 1725......................... 565
Rollo, Alexander, Middletown, 1709........................... 106
Root, Caleb, Farmington, 1712................................ 281
Root, John, Farmington, 1709-10.............................. 282
Root, Stephen, Sen., Farmington, 1716-17. Will.............. 428
Root, Timothy, Farmington, 1713............................. 283
Rowlandson, Joseph, Wethersfield, 1712-13.................... 283
Rowley, Moses, Sen., Haddam, 1705. Will.................... 107
Rowley, Shubael, Colchester, 1714............................ 283
Rowley, Thomas, Colchester, 1719............................ 428
Rowley, Thomas, Sen., (cordwainer), Windsor, 1708............. 107
Rudd, Jonathan, Windham, 1712............................... 284
Rue, John, Hartford, 1717.................................... 429
Ruggles, Abigail, (minor), Farmington, 1716.................. 429
Russell, Daniel, Charlestown, Mass........................... 108
Russell, Mrs. Mary, Middletown, 1725........................ 566
Russell, Rev. Noadiah, Middletown, 1713...................... 284
Russell, Rev. Noadiah, Middletown, 1725...................... 566
Ryley, Sergt. Jonathan, Sen., Wethersfield, 1711-12............. 285
Ryley, Joseph, Wethersfield, 1706............................ 108

Sadd, Hepzibah, (widow), Hartford, 1711-12. Will............. 286
Sage, David, Jr., Middletown, 1712-13........................ 286
Sage, David, Sen., Middletown, 1703. Will................... 109
Sage, Jonathan, Middletown, 1713............................ 287
Sage, Marcy, Middletown, 1711-12........................... 287
Sage, Timothy, Middletown, 1725............................ 566
Sampson, (negro), Farmington, 1704.......................... 110
Sandford, Lieut. Zachariah, Hartford, 1713-14. Will........... 287
Sanford, Robert, Hartford, 1728-9. Will..................... 567
Savage, Capt. John, Middletown, 1724. Will................. 567

Savage, Capt. William, Middletown, 1726-7. Will.............. 569
Saxton, Richard, Simsbury, 1714........................... 293
Scofell, Edward, Haddam, 1703........................... |111
Scott, Joseph, Farmington, 1708........................... 111
Scovell, James, Middletown, 1711-12. Will.................... 289
Scovell, John, Middletown, 1712-13......................... 290
Scovell, William, Haddam, 1712........................... 290
Seamore, Hannah, widow of Richard Seamore, Farmington, 1712.. 291
Seamore, John, Sen., Hartford, 1713. Will.................... 290
Seamore, Richard, Farmington, 1710........................ 292
Seamore, Zachariah, Wethersfield, 1702. Will................. 111
Sedgwick, Samuel, Jr., Hartford, 1724...................... 570
Selden, Joseph, East Haddam, 1729. Will.................... 571
Sexton, John, Simsbury, 1718. Will........................ 429
Seymour, Jonathan, Farmington, 1725....................... 570
Shaler, Thomas, Haddam, 1714............................ 293
Shaylor, Sergt. Timothy, Haddam, 1727..................... 572
Shepherd, Edward, Middletown, 1711-12..................... 294
Shepherd, Edward, Middletown, 1721....................... 430
Shepherd, Sergt. John (cooper), Hartford, 1707............... 112
Sherman, Theophalus, Wethersfield, 1711-12. Will............. 295
Shipman, William, Hebron, 1725........................... 572
Shippason, Nathaniel, Hebron, 1718........................ 430
Shirley, Robert, Hartford, 1711. Will....................... 295
Silsbe, Jonathan, Windham, 1714.......................... 296
Skinner, Deacon Joseph, Windsor, 1724. Will................. 572
Skinner, Richard, Hartford, 1716.......................... 431
Slate, Daniel, Windsor, 1725-6 (minor)...................... 573
Slater, Henry, Wethersfield, 1727-8........................ 573
Slater, Deacon John, Simsbury, 1717. Will................... 431
Slater, John, Sen., Simsbury, 1713. Will.................... 296
Slater, Thomas, Simsbury, 1700........................... 113
Smead, Richard, Hartford, 1704........................... 114
Smith, Arthur, Hartford, 1712-13. Will..................... 296
Smith, Elisha, Windham, 1714............................ 297
Smith, Esther, Farmington, 1725.......................... 574
Smith, George, Hebron, 1725. Will........................ 574
Smith, John (mariner), Haddam, 1712....................... 297
Smith, Jonathan, Sen., Farmington, 1721. Will............... 431
Smith, Sergt. Jonathan, Wethersfield, 1728-9................. 574
Smith, Joseph, Glastonbury, 1725. Will..................... 575
Smith, Joseph, Hartford, 1711-12.......................... 298
Smith, Joseph, Sen., Farmington, 1718...................... 433
Smith, Lydia (widow), Hartford, 1711-12.................... 298
Smith, Nathaniel, Hartford, 1711-12....................... 298
Smith, Philip, Hartford, 1724-5........................... 576
Smith, Philip, Jr.. Hartford, 1712......................... 299
Smith, Rebeckah, Wethersfield, 1725. Will................... 577

Smith, Samuel, Farmington, 1724-5. Will..................... 577
Smith, Samuel, Hartford, 1707............................... 114
Smith, Thomas, Haddam, 1709................................ 299
Smith, William, Farmington, 1718........................... 434
Soper, Mary, 1720.. 434
Southmayd, Giles, Middletown, 1728......................... 578
Southmayd, John, Waterbury, 1705-6......................... 115
Southmayd, William (mariner), Middletown, 1702............. 115
Sparks, John, Windsor, 1710................................ 299
Spencer, Jared, Sen., Hartford, 1712. Will................ 300
Spencer, Jonathan, Haddam, 1714............................ 300
Spencer, Joseph, Haddam, 1714-15........................... 301
Spencer, Obadiah, Sen., Hartford, 1712. Will.............. 302
Spencer, Samuel, Haddam, 1705-6............................ 116
Spencer, Timothy, Haddam, 1704............................. 117
Spencer, William, East Haddam, 1712-13..................... 302
Stanclift, James, Middletown, 1712......................... 303
Stanly, Caleb, Hartford, 1718. Will....................... 434
Stanly, Caleb, Jr., Hartford, 1711-12...................... 303
Stanly, Capt. John, Farmington, 1706. Will................ 117
Stanly, Nathaniel, Hartford, 1712. Will................... 304
Stanly, Thomas, Farmington, 1713........................... 305
Starr, Jehoshaphat, Newport, R. I., 1717................... 435
Stedman, Robert, Windsor, 1721............................. 436
Stedman, Simmons, Wethersfield, 1709....................... 118
Steele, Ebenezer, Farmington, 1722. Will.................. 436
Steele, Elizabeth, 1723.................................... 578
Steele, Lieut. James, Hartford, 1712. Will................ 305
Steele, Capt. James, Wethersfield, 1713.................... 306
Steele, Mercy, Hartford, 1720.............................. 438
Steele, Samuel, Jr., (blacksmith), Hartford, 1709-10....... 307
Steele, Samuel, Sen., Hartford, 1709-10.................... 307
Steele, William, Hartford, 1712-13......................... 307
Stephens, Thomas, Middletown, 1714. Will.................. 308
Stevens, Rev. Timothy, Glastonbury, 1726. Will............ 579
Stiles, John, Windsor, 1728. Will......................... 580
Stiles, Samuel, Windsor, 1712-13........................... 308
Stilman, George, Wethersfield, 1728-9. Will............... 581
Stocking, George, Middletown, 1713-14...................... 308
Stocking, John, Middletown, 1713........................... 309
Stocking, John, Middletown, 1726-7......................... 582
Stoddar, Nathaniel, Wethersfield, 1704-5................... 119
Stoddard, Bethiah, Wethersfield, 1725...................... 583
Stoddard, Joshua, Wethersfield, 1725-6. Will.............. 584
Stoddard, Nathaniel, Wethersfield, 1717.................... 438
Stoddard, Samuel, Wethersfield, 1725....................... 584
Stodder, John, Sen., Wethersfield, 1703. Will............. 119
Storrs, Samuel, Sen., Mansfield, 1719. Will............... 438

Stoughton, John 1701... 120
Stoughton, John, Windsor, 1712............................... 309
Stoughton, Samuel, Windsor, 1711-12......................... 310
Stow, John, Jr., Middletown, 1722............................ 439
Stow, Nathaniel, Middletown, 1728........................... 585
Stow, Sergt. Nathaniel, Middletown, 1704-5.................. 120
Stow, Rev. Samuel, Middletown, 1704. Will.................. 120
Stow, Samuel (son of John Stow, flax dresser), Middle wn,
    1708-9... 122
Stratton, William, Windsor 1709-10.......................... 123
Strickland, John, Jr., Glastonbury, 1711-12................. 310
Strickland, Joseph, Glastonbury, 1726....................... 585
Strickland, Joseph, Simsbury, 1702-3........................ 123
Strickland, Joseph, Simsbury, 1714.......................... 310
Strong, Return, Jr., (tanner), Windsor, 1708............... 123
Strong, Lt. Return, Windsor, 1726. Will.................... 586
Styles, Robert, Hebron, 1721................................ 439
Sumner, William, Middletown, 1703.......................... 124

Talcott, Benjamin, Glastonbury, 1727. Will................. 587
Taphannah, Richard, (Indian), Glastonbury, 1709-10......... 310
Tappin, James, Sen., Middletown, 1712. Will................ 310
Taylor, Ebenezer, 1726 (minor)............................. 586
Taylor, Jonathan, Hartford, 1725........................... 586
Taylor, Samuel, Wethersfield, 1711-12. Will................ 311
Taylor, Stephen, Colchester, 1718-19....................... 440
Taylor, Stephen, Jr., Windsor, 1709........................ 311
Taylor, Stephen, Sen., Windsor, 1707....................... 125
Terrie, John, Simsbury, 1725............................... 588
Terry, Samuel, Simsbury, 1724-5. Will..................... 589
Thomasson, (Thomlinson), Henry, Colchester, 1727.......... 590
Thompson, John, Farmington, 1711-12........................ 312
Thompson, Thomas, Sen., Farmington, 1705-6................. 126
Thornton, Samuel, Hartford, 1714........................... 313
Thornton, Thomas, Hartford, 1703. Will.................... 127
Thrall, Samuel, Windsor, 1709.............................. 313
Thrall, Timothy, Windsor, 1723-4. Will.................... 590
Toobe, John, Middletown, 1728.............................. 591
Towsey, Thomas, Wethersfield, 1712. Will.................. 313
Treadway, James, Colchester, 1728.......................... 593
Treat, James, Sen., Wethersfield, 1708-9. Will............ 127
Treat, Matthias, Hartford, (East), 1726.................... 593
Treat, Richard, Wethersfield, 1713. Will.................. 314
Treat, Thomas, Glastonbury, 1712-13. Will................. 314
Trill, Thomas, Hartford, 1700.............................. 129
Tryon, William, Wethersfield, 1711-12...................... 316
Tudor, Owen, Windsor, 1717................................. 440
Tudor, Samuel, Windsor, 1727. Will........................ 594

Tuller, Samuel, Simsbury, 1719-20.......................... 441
Turner, Edward, Middletown, 1717. Will.................... 441
Turner, Ephraim, Hartford, 1705-6......................... 129
Turner, Mary, Hartford, 1728.............................. 594
Tyler, Isaac, Haddam, 1718-19............................. 442

Ventrus, Mary, Farmington, 1718-19........................ 442
Ventrus, Moses, Farmington, 1721. Will.................... 443
Ventrus, William, Haddam, 1701. Will...................... 129
Vibbard, John, Hartford, 1714-15.......................... 317
Viet, John, Simsbury, 1723................................ 595

Waddams, Elizabeth, Wethersfield, 1725.................... 595
Waddams, John, Wethersfield, 1718......................... 443
Wadsworth, Deacon John, Farmington, 1718. Will........... 444
Wadsworth, Ruth, Hebron, 1724 (minor)..................... 595
Wadsworth, Sarah, Farmington, 1718. Will.................. 445
Wadsworth, Thomas, Hartford, 1726. Will................... 595
Wadsworth, Thomas, Jr., Hartford, 1717.................... 446
Wait, William (Indian), Hartford, 1711.................... 317
Waldo, John, Windham, 1700. Will.......................... 130
Wale, John, Hartford, 1723................................ 596
Ward, Andrew, Middletown, 1728-9.......................... 596
Ward, Andrew, Middletown, 1729............................ 597
Ward, Lieut. James, Middletown, 1711-12................... 317
Ward, James, 1724... 597
Ward, Samuel, Middletown, 1715............................ 446
Ward, Thomas, Middletown, 1728. Will...................... 598
Warner, Andrew, Middletown, 1726. Will.................... 599
Warner, Daniel, Waterbury, 1713........................... 317
Warner, Hannah, Wethersfield, 1714. Will.................. 318
Warner, John, Middletown, 1700............................ 131
Warner, John, (son of Robert Warner), Middletown, 1712.... 319
Warner, John, Wethersfield, 1714.......................... 319
Warner, John, Sen., Waterbury, 1706-7. Will............... 131
Warner, Seth, Middletown, 1713-14......................... 319
Warner, Thomas, Waterbury, 1714........................... 320
Warner, William, Wethersfield, 1714. Will................. 320
Warner, Capt. William, Wethersfield, 1726. Will........... 600
Warren, John, Hartford, 1722.............................. 447
Waters, Bevel, Hartford, 1729. Will....................... 602
Waters, Joseph, Middletown, 1710.......................... 447
Waters, Thomas, Hartford, 1718-19......................... 448
Watson, Caleb, Hartford, 1726. Will....................... 604
Watson, John, Jr., Hartford, 1724-25...................... 605
Watson, John, Sen., Hartford, 1725........................ 606
Watson, Samuel, Windsor, 1711............................. 322
Watson, Sarah (widow), Hartford, 1726..................... 607

Way, Mrs. Mary (widow), Hartford, 1701.................... 132
Webb, Orange (minor), Wethersfield, 1713-14................ 322
Webster, Jacob, Hartford, 1727............................. 607
Webster, John, Hartford, 1694............................. 132
Webster, Mrs. Susannah (widow of Robert Webster), Hartford,
    1705........................ 133
Webster, Robert, Jr., Hartford, 1724-5...................... 608
Webster, Stephen, Hartford, 1724.......................... 608
Webster, William, Hartford, 1722.......................... 448
Welles, Capt. Eleazer, Hartford, 1723...................... 609
Welles, Joseph, Hartford, 1725............................ 609
Welles, Noah, Colchester, 1714............................ 323
Welles, Capt. Robert, Wethersfield, 1714. Will.............. 323
Welles, Capt. Thomas, Wethersfield, 1711-12................ 325
Welles, Thomas, Haddam, 1711-12.......................... 324
Welton, Stephen, Waterbury, 1713......................... 326
Welton, Thomas, Waterbury, 1717.......................... 448
Westover, Hannah (widow), Simsbury, 1714. Will........... 326
Westover, Jonah, Simsbury, 1714.......................... 327
Westover, Jonah, Sen., Simsbury, 1708-09. Will............. 135
Wetmore, ffrancis, Middletown, 1700....................... 135
Wetmore, Israhiah, Middletown, 1728....................... 610
Wetmore, John, Middletown, 1723-24....................... 610
Wetmore, Joseph, Middletown, 1717........................ 449
Wetmore, Nathaniel, Middletown, 1708-9................... 136
Wetmore, Thomas, Middletown, 1711-12.................... 327
Whaples, Ephraim, Wethersfield, 1713. Will................ 327
Whaples, Joseph, Hartford, 1717........................... 449
Whaples, Thomas, Sen., Hartford, 1713. Will............... 328
Wheeler, John, Hartford, 1724-25.......................... 611
Wheeler, Samuel, Hartford, 1712.......................... 329
Wheeler, Samuel, Haddam, 1725-26......................... 611
White, Daniel, Windsor, 1711.............................. 329
White, Capt. Daniel, Windsor, 1726. Will.................. 611
White, Elizabeth, (widow) Hartford, 1716.................. 449
White, Ensign Jacob, Hartford, 1701....................... 137
White, Joseph, Middletown, 1725. Will.................... 613
White, Capt. Nathaniel, Middletown, 1711. Will........... 329
Whiting, John, Hartford, 1715............................. 330
Whiting, Joseph, Hartford, 1717-18........................ 450
Wilcocks, Ephraim, Middletown, 1712-13................... 613
Wilcocks, Samuel, Middletown, 1727. Will................. 614
Wilcocks, Silence (alias Warner), Middletown, 1725.......... 615
Wilcox, Samuel, Middletown, 1714......................... 451
Wilcox, Samuel, Middletown, 1725......................... 615
Wilcox, Sarah, 1724-25.................................... 615
Wilcox, Thomas, Middletown, 1726-27. Will................ 616
Willard, Symon, Wethersfield, 1726-27..................... 617

Willcocks, Ephraim, Middletown, 1713...........................330
Willcoxson, Margaret, Simsbury, 1714....................... 451
Willcoxson, Samuel, Simsbury, 1712-13....................... 331
Willcoxson, Samuel, Jr., Simsbury, 1713...................... 331
Willes, Joshua, Windsor, 1721-2............................ 452
Williams, Abraham, Wethersfield, 1711-12.................... 332
Williams, Elias, (minor) 1717.............................. 452
Williams, Esther, Windsor, 1692-3.......................... 452
Williams, Francis, Simsbury, 1705.......................... 138
Williams, Henry, East Haddam, 1728........................ 617
Williams, Jacob, Wethersfield, 1712......................... 332
Williams, Job, Windsor, 1712. Will........................ 333
Williams, John, Haddam, 1722.............................. 618
Williams, John, Hartford, 1723............................. 618
Williams, John (minor), Windsor, 1713...................... 336
Williams, John, Sen., Hartford, 1712-13..................... 335
Williams, Jonas, Hartford, 1714............................ 335
Williams, Joseph, Hartford, 1723........................... 618
Williams, Dr. Richard, 1701-2.............................. 139
Williams, Thomas, Sen., Wethersfield, 1692-3. Will............ 139
Williamson, Alexander, Hartford, 1716...................... 453
Willis, John, Windsor, 1706................................ 139
Wilson, Elizabeth, widow of Phineas Wilson, Hartford, 1727...... 619
　　　Will of... 621
Wilson, John, Hartford, 1712............................... 336
Wilson, Nathaniel, Hartford, 1703.......................... 140
Wilson, Stebbin, Hartford, 1708............................ 142
Wilson, Stebbin (minor), Hartford, 1724..................... 624
Winchell, Hannah (widow), Windsor, 1725.................... 624
Winchell, Sarah (widow), 1725.............................. 624
Winchell, Stephen, Simsbury, 1725-26. Will.................. 624
Wolcott, Mrs. Abiah, Windsor, 1717. Will................... 453
Wolcott, Mrs. Abiah, Windsor, 1723......................... 626
Wolcott, Abigail, Wethersfield, 1714........................ 336
Wolcott, Benjamin, Windsor, 1723.......................... 626
Wolcott, Christopher, Windsor, 1728........................ 626
Wolcott, George, Wethersfield, 1726. Will................... 627
Wolcott, Henry, Windsor, 1707............................. 143
Wolcott, Henry, Windsor, 1710............................. 337
Wolcott, John, Sen., Windsor, 1711-12...................... 338
Wolcott, Josiah, Wethersfield, 1712. Will................... 339
Wolcott, Capt. Samuel, Windsor, 1712....................... 339
Wood, Obadiah, Hartford, 1712. Will....................... 340
Woodbridge, Mrs. Abigail, Simsbury, 1715................... 454
Woodbridge, Rev. Dudley, Simsbury, 1710................... 341
Woodbridge, Rev. John, Springfield, Mass., 1718. Will......... 454
Woodbridge, Rev. John, Wethersfield, 1696.................. 341
Woodford, Joseph, Sen., Farmington, 1710. Will.............. 342

Woodruff, John, Farmington, 1707-8........................... 143
Woodruff, John, Kensington, 1727. Will...................... 625
Woodruff, Jonathan, Farmington, 1712........................343
Woodruff, Joseph, Farmington, 1712.......................... 343
Wright, John, Wethersfield, 1713-14......................... 343
Wright, Jonas, Middletown, 1709. Will...................... 143
Wright, Joseph, Wethersfield, 1714-15. Will................ 344
Wright, Thomas, Wethersfield, 1711. Will................... 345
Wyard, John, Farmington, 1725.............................. 628
Wyer, Abigail, Hartford, 1718.............................. 455

Yeomans, John, Tolland, 1728-29. Will...................... 628

INDEX TO NAMES.

A

Abbey, Hannah, 469.
  John, 3.
  Jonathan, 387.
Abby, Hannah, 3.
  John, 3.
  Richard, 393.
Achett, see Adjett, Atchett.
Achett, John, 84.
  Samuel, 84.
Ackley, Ann, 4.
  Anne, 144.
  Hannah, 3, 4, 144.
  James, 144, 302.
  Job, 4, 144.
  John, 4, 144.
  Nathaniel, 4, 144, 565.
  Samuel, 144, 423, 471, 472.
  Thomas, 3, 4, 144.
Adams, Edward, 591.
Addams, Abigail, 456.
  Abraham, 145, 146.
  Amasa, 456.
  Benjamin, 145, 349, 361, 366, 367, 391,
    421, 429, 431, 456, 564.
  Ephraim, 145.
  Daniel, 144, 145, 146.
  Dorcas, 604.
  Elizabeth, 190, 348.
  Hannah, 145, 146.
  James, 145, 146.
  Jeremiah, 76.
  John, 348.
  Joseph, 145.
  Martha, 367.
  Mary, 145, 421.
  Mr., 599.
  Samuel, 145, 327.
  Thanks, 145, 146.
  Thomas, 145.
Addington, Isaac, 93, 426, 427.
  Mr., 93.
Adjett, see Achett, Atchett.
Adjett, John, 146, 147.
  Samuel, 147.
Adkins, Abigail, 4, 5, 456.
  Benjamin, 4, 5, 16, 180, 308, 456.
  Elizabeth, 4, 5, 456.
  Ephraim, 4, 5, 327, 512, 591.
  Joanna, 147, 154.

Adkins, John, 456, 457.
  Joseph, 456, 457.
  Josiah, 4, 5, 147, 456, 457.
  Mary, 456.
  Sarah, 4, 5, 296.
  Solomon, 4, 5, 16, 160, 410, 449, 456,
    512, 592, 610.
  Thomas, 5, 148.
Alcock, see Olcock, Olcot, Olcott.
Alcock, Philip, 15, 27, 54.
Alderman, Elizabeth, 526.
  John, 525, 526.
  Joseph, 526, 589.
  Thomas, 348.
  William, 348, 458, 525.
Alexander, Ebenezer, 348, 349.
  George, 196, 197.
Alford, see Alvard, Alverd, Alvord.
Alford, Benedict, 457.
  Benjamin, 425, 579.
  Daniel, 425.
  Elizabeth, 457.
  Isabell, 82.
  Jane, 5, 82.
  Jeremiah, 5, 45, 61, 82.
  Joanna, 425.
  Josiah, 529.
  Mr., 529.
  Nathaniel, 589.
Allen, see Allin, Alling, Allyn.
Allen, Alexander, 56, 517.
  Obadiah, 592.
  Samuel, 592.
  Thomas, 191, 308, 457.
  William, 297.
Allin, see Allen, Alling, Allyn.
Allin, Alexander, 7, 8, 56, 505.
  Elizabeth, 7, 8, 552.
  Fitz John, 8.
  John, 8, 530, 544.
  Mary, 8.
  Noah, 552.
  Obadiah, 148.
  Robert, 8.
  Rust, 552.
  Ruth, 552.
  Thomas, 148, 149.
  William, 8.
Alling, Thomas, 11.

Allyn, see Allen, Allin, Alling.
Allyn, Alexander, 9, 82, 382, 548, 586, 612.
 Ann, 457.
 Anna, 148.
 Anne, 10, 148.
 Benjamin, 9, 10, 148, 149.
 Bridgett, 26.
 Caleb, 501.
 Dorcas, 11.
 Edward, 78, 81, 156, 217, 231, 232, 250, 305, 306, 381, 604.
 Elizabeth, 9, 337, 340, 453.
 George, 387.
 Gideon, 11.
 Henry, 415, 420, 453, 457, 474, 475, 562, 572.
 Joanna, 149.
 Johanna, 149.
 Johannah, 149.
 John, 9, 10, 11, 55, 148, 149, 231, 389, 457, 476, 485, 517, 624.
 Joseph, 609.
 Joshua, 11.
 Josiah, 573.
 Josias, 9.
 Mary, 148, 457.
 Matthew, 6, 8, 9, 10, 21, 22, 71, 72, 81, 139, 148, 149, 177, 178, 197, 263, 264, 333, 337, 338, 339, 340, 413, 420, 421, 474, 572, 573.
 Mercy, 348, 349.
 Mr., 451.
 Obadiah, 11, 121, 148, 149.
 Peletiah, 60, 561, 580.
 Rachel, 217, 579.
 Samuel, 9, 10, 148, 149, 348, 349, 375, 489, 490.
 Thomas, 9, 10, 11, 149, 180, 191, 410, 449, 457.
Alsopp, Thomas, 458.
Alvard, see Alford, Alverd, Alvord.
Alvard, Benedict, 5.
 Elizabeth, 5.
 Jane, 5, 6.
 Jeremiah, 5.
 Job, 5.
 Johanna, 5.
Alverd, see Alford, Alvard, Alvord.
Alverd, Benedict, 6, 7, 150, 457, 598.
 Dorothy, 349.
 Ebenezer, 33.
 Elizabeth, 6, 7, 33, 150, 457.
 Hannah, 326, 349.
 Jane, 6, 150.
 Jeremiah, 6, 7, 150, 457.
 Joanna, 6, 7, 150.
 Job, 6, 7, 150, 457.
 Josiah, 485.

Alverd, Josias, 349.
 Mary, 598.
 Thomas, 592.
Alvord, see Alford, Alvard, Alverd.
Alvord, Dorothy, 349.
 Elizabeth, 349.
 Hannah, 349.
 Jane, 192.
 Jeremiah, 457.
 Josiah, 349.
 Mary, 425.
 Nathaniel, 349.
 Sarah, 425.
Anderson, John, 195, 383, 479.
 Mary, 479.
Andrew (negro), 254.
Andrews, see Andros, Andross, Andrus, Andruss.
Andrews, Ann, 11, 12, 13, 14.
 Benjamin, 13, 136, 349, 351, 458, 467, 559.
 Caleb, 13, 351.
 Daniel, 13, 33, 44, 45, 97, 106, 110, 163, 167, 178, 179, 210, 218, 273, 305, 315, 538.
 David, 227.
 Dorcas, 136.
 Edward, 11, 12.
 Eliza, 350.
 Elizabeth, 150, 151, 349, 350, 458.
 Ephraim, 13, 351.
 James, 459.
 Jemima, 349.
 John, 150, 151, 320, 548, 559, 591.
 Joseph, 12, 13, 14, 186, 349, 351.
 Martha, 320.
 Mary, 151.
 Nathaniel, 150, 515, 595.
 Phineas, 349.
 Rebeckah, 12, 13, 349.
 Samuel, 150, 151, 193, 458.
 Sarah, 11, 53, 537.
 Solomon, 12, 151, 350, 351.
 Thomas, 150, 169, 595.
 Timothy, 349.
 William, 13, 351.
Andros, Elizabeth, 316.
Andross, Daniel, 167.
 Edmund, 623.
 Samuel, 301.
Andrus, see Andrews, Andross, Andruss.
Andrus, Benjamin, 458, 459.
 Daniel, 458.
 Elizabeth, 458.
 Gideon, 458.
 James, 459.
 Johannah, 458.
 John, 458.

Andrus, Jonathan, 458.
 Joseph, 351.
 Samuel, 458.
 Sarah, 459.
 Stephen, 459.
 Thomas, 515.
Andruss, John, 361.
Arcoss, John, 425.
Armstrong, Benjamin, 592.
Arnold, Abigail, 461.
 Benedict, 591.
 David, 152.
 Ebenezer, 591.
 Elizabeth, 459, 460, 461.
 Esther, 461.
 Henry, 459, 460, 461.
 Huldah, 461.
 Irene, 152.
 James, 152.
 John, 11, 109, 354, 355, 423, 459, 460, 461, 591.
 Jonathan, 351, 352, 382, 427, 442, 461, 611.
 Joseph, 101, 129, 152, 160, 275, 290, 293, 294, 298, 352, 353, 354, 400, 423, 442, 461, 472, 572.
 Josiah, 44, 111, 151, 152, 352, 461.

Arnold, Mary, 152, 352, 460, 461.
 Samuel, 185, 461.
 Sarah, 351, 460.
Ashley, Jonathan, 14, 150.
 Joseph, 14, 306, 498.
 Mary, 306.
 Rebeckah, 14.
 Samuel, 14.
 Sarah, 14, 579.
Ashmun, John, 396.
Atchett, see Achett, Adjett.
Atchett, John, 146.
Attkison, Mr., 582.
Atwood, Andrew, 158.
 Bathshua, 251.
 Edward, 352.
 Josiah, 251.
 Thomas, 352.
Austin, John, 232, 351, 357, 365, 382, 394, 396, 403, 451, 505, 506, 507, 515, 549, 567, 582, 593, 603, 604, 621, 628.
 Mary, 232, 233, 582, 603.
Avery, Hannah, 165.
Ayrault, Marian, 15.
 Nicholas, 14, 15.
 Peeter, 14.

B

Backus, Joseph, 510.
Bacon, Abigail, 16, 462.
 Andrew, 11, 15, 16, 25, 136, 461, 462.
 Ann, 410, 462.
 Beriah, 15, 16.
 Bethia, 252.
 Daniel, 462.
 Esther, 462.
 Hannah, 15, 16.
 John, 15, 16, 25, 26, 40, 47, 216, 256, 284, 308, 319, 327, 362, 377, 394, 439, 440, 446, 447, 462, 597.
 Joseph, 462.
 Josiah, 462.
 Lydia, 16.
 Mary, 16.
 Mehetabell, 462.
 Mr., 25.
 Nathaniel, 11, 15, 16, 410, 456, 457, 462.
 Thomas, 15, 138, 139.
Bacor, William, 551, 606.
Bailey, see Bayley.
Bailey, Elizabeth, 353, 354.
Baker, Abigail, 152.
 Basey, 20, 462.
 Hannah, 462, 463.
 Jeremiah, 462.

Baker, Joseph, 45, 46.
 Nathaniel, 462, 463.
 Samuel, 45, 46, 152, 591.
 Sarah, 45, 79, 297, 411.
 Susannah, 462, 463.
 Thankful, 462.
 Timothy, 16, 17, 27, 152, 462.
 William, 16, 17, 297, 411, 462, 463, 606.
Baldwin, Timothy, 42.
Bancroft, Anna, 333.
 Hannah, 158.
 Joanna, 10, 149.
 Nathaniel, 334.
 Samuel, 10, 149, 253, 416, 508.
Barber, see Barbor, Barbour.
Barber, Abigail, 155, 463.
 Benjamin, 18, 154.
 David, 17, 154.
 Easter, 18.
 Elizabeth, 18, 154.
 Esther, 363.
 Ezekiel, 463.
 Isaac, 153.
 John, 17, 18, 153, 154.
 Joseph, 17, 18, 153, 154, 463.
 Marcy, 153.
 Martha, 463.

Barber, Mary, 18, 153, 154, 197, 478.
  Mercy, 153.
  Mindwell, 18, 153.
  Mr., 398.
  Ruth, 17, 18, 154.
  Samuel, 17, 18, 72, 154, 463.
  Sarah, 18, 154.
  Thomas, 123, 154, 155.
  William, 17, 18, 153, 154.
Barbor, Joseph, 474.
Barbour, see Barber.
Barbour, Abigail, 463.
  Jane, 457.
  John, 418, 457, 464, 475, 529.
  Jonathan, 388, 464.
  Joseph, 473.
  Mercy, 464.
  Mr., 363, 473.
  Rachell, 388.
  Samuel, 464.
  Sarah, 464.
  Thomas, 463, 464.
Barker, Lydia, 258.
Barn, see Barnes, Barns.
Barn, Shamgar, 143.
Barnard, Abigail, 333.
  John, 131, 208, 313, 488, 595.
  Joseph, 71, 84, 85, 189, 190, 211, 243,
    244, 267, 301, 334, 369, 392, 393,
    401, 405, 417, 418, 517, 518, 624.
  Samuel, 189, 250.
  Thomas, 464.
Barnes, See Barn, Barns.
Barnes, Abigail, 352, 353.
  Benjamin, 278, 280.
  Elizabeth, 121, 122, 379, 380.
  Eunice, 352, 353.
  Hannah, 494.
  Jacob, 442, 443.
  John, 599.
  Mabel, 396.
  Mary, 311, 352, 353.
  Matthew, 501.
  Maybee, 121.
  Samuel, 121, 352, 353.
  Thomas, 352, 353, 494.
  William, 352, 353.
Barnett, see Burnett.
Barnett, Robert, 580.
Barns, see Barn, Barnes.
Barns, Elizabeth, 121, 122.
  Thomas, 592.
Barrett, Jonathan, 449.
  Robert, 542.
Barrit, Jonathan, 449.
Bartlett, Elizabeth, 524, 572.
  John, 404, 465.
  Robert, 465.

Bartlett, Samuel, 155.
  Sarah, 404.
Bassett, Nathaniel, 393.
  Robert, 96.
Bate, Elizabeth, 353, 354.
  James, 353.
  John, 354, 423, 487.
  Jonathan, 353, 354.
  Solomon, 354, 423.
Bates, Elizabeth, 257.
  Hannah, 353.
  James, 4, 511.
  John, 53, 353, 354, 488.
  Jonathan, 53, 354.
  Samuel, 53.
  Sarah, 375.
Battis, Sarah, 622.
Baxter, Elizabeth, 176.
  Mary, 176.
  Thomas, 176.
Bayley, see Bailey.
Bayley, Mr., 404.
  Susannah, 404.
Beach, see Beech.
Beach, Abill, 511.
  Margaret, 312.
  Richard, 591.
Beaman, Samuel, 123.
Beamon, see Bemond.
Beamon, Samuel, 333.
Beary, Nathaniel, 629.
Beckley, Ann, 55.
  Martha, 554.
Beckly, Mrs., 55.
Beckwith, Jerusha, 354.
  Job, 354.
  Joseph, 354.
  Matthew, 592.
  Nathaniel, 354.
  Patience, 354.
  Sarah, 354.
Beech, see Beach.
Beech, Richard, 353.
Beecher, Elizabeth, 559.
Belcher, Andrew, 65, 66.
  Sarah, 64, 65, 66.
Belden, see Belding.
Belden, Ebenezer, 50.
  Jonathan, 41, 63, 108, 109, 127.
  Joseph, 58, 81, 193, 251, 316.
  Mary, 94.
Belding, see Belden.
Belding, Amos, 466.
  Benjamin, 156, 197.
  Dorothy, 155, 156.
  Ebenezer, 183, 184, 321, 376, 465, 600.
  Elizabeth, 112.
  Esther, 466.

Belding, Ezra, 155, 156.
  Gideon, 206.
  Hannah, 156.
  Henry, 112.
  James, 181.
  John, 155, 156, 203, 204, 361, 465.
  Jonathan, 50, 51, 52, 88, 129, 155, 156,
    174, 175, 184, 190, 203, 246, 247, 267,
    280, 286, 307, 314, 317, 321, 325, 345,
    346, 347, 362, 376, 443, 465, 466, 601.
  Joseph, 50, 183, 189, 190, 217, 246, 251,
    360, 465, 466, 470.
  Josiah, 155, 156, 164, 181, 465, 470, 482,
    536.
  Kezia, 203.
  Lydia, 156.
  Marah, 465.
  Margaret, 468.
  Mary, 345, 465, 466.
  Samuel, 185.
  Sarah, 465, 466.
  Silas, 345, 466.
  Stephen, 155, 156.
  Thomas, 466.
  Timothy, 465.
Bemond, see Beamon.
Bemond, Samuel, 391.
Benjamin, Caleb, 18, 225.
  John, 18, 19, 576, 577, 593.
  Mary, 576.
  Sarah, 23.
Benton, Andrew, 19.
  Ebenezer, 19, 43, 44.
  Edward, 156.
  John, 19.
  Joseph, 19, 355, 358, 602.
  Mary, 19, 156.
  Samuel, 19, 132, 140, 141, 142, 157, 168,
    172, 328, 469, 470, 515, 600.
  Sarah, 49, 602, 603.
Berry, Abigail, 355.
  Elizabeth, 354, 355.
  Nathaniel, 354, 355.
  Sarah, 355.
Bevin, John, 143, 303.
Bevins, John, 83.
Bidwell, Abigail, 357.
  Ann, 466.
  Daniel, 93, 94, 103, 164, 198, 355, 356,
    466.
  David, 20.
  Dorothy, 355, 356.
  Elizabeth, 120.
  Hannah, 355, 356, 357.
  James, 19, 20, 21, 356.
  John, 19, 20, 94, 356, 483.
  Jonathan, 20, 156.
  Lydia, 355, 356.

Bidwell, Martha, 156.
  Mary, 355, 356, 357, 466.
  Moses, 357, 591.
  Mr., 168.
  Nathaniel, 315, 316, 356.
  Prudence, 357.
  Ruth, 356.
  Samuel, 73, 74, 92, 120, 124, 257, 356,
    357, 466.
  Sarah, 19, 20, 466.
  Thankful, 73, 74, 357.
  Thomas, 19, 20, 21, 156, 242, 357.
  William, 355, 356, 484.
Bigelow, Abigail, 156.
  Daniel, 156, 157, 356.
  John, 156, 357, 358, 377.
  Jonathan, 19, 44, 156, 157, 340, 603.
  Joseph, 156, 157, 358, 558.
  Mary, 98, 156, 157.
  Mr., 358.
  Rebeckah, 113, 357.
  Samuel, 156, 157, 586.
  Sarah, 156.
  Violet, 156, 157.
Bill, Sarah, 425.
Bingham, Abell, 284.
  Jonathan, 297.
  Mr., 3.
  Thomas, 387.
Birchard, Mr., 496.
  Samuel, 157, 240.
Bird, see Burd.
Bird, Dorcas, 554.
  Esther, 559.
  Hannah, 312, 322.
  James, 32, 467.
  John, 467.
  Jonathan, 467.
  Joseph, 33, 34, 35, 467.
  Lydia, 467.
  Mary, 34, 467, 622.
  Mindwell, 35, 559.
  Mr., 432.
  Mrs., 432.
  Rebeckah, 467.
  Samuel, 34, 35, 559, 578.
  Sarah, 352, 467.
  Thomas, 32, 33, 35, 110, 432, 433, 434,
    466, 467, 537.
Birge, see Burge.
Birge, Mary, 359.
Bissell, Abell, 358.
  Abigail, 21, 22, 158.
  Ann, 21, 158.
  Benjamin, 358, 511.
  Benoni, 157, 474.
  Daniel, 21, 35, 174, 219, 220, 270, 310,
    359, 382, 383, 388, 453, 467, 505, 560,
    565, 580, 626.

Bissell, David, 157, 158, 359, 375, 383, 384, 387, 436, 465, 479.
    Deborah, 21.
    Deliverance, 358.
    Dorothy, 21, 158.
    Elizabeth, 21, 158, 359.
    Ephraim, 126, 312, 358, 359.
    Hannah, 21, 359.
    Hezekiah, 21.
    Isaac, 100, 358, 489.
    Jacob, 22.
    Jeremiah, 21, 359, 612.
    Joanna, 126.
    John, 18, 22, 72, 154, 157, 182, 183, 196, 253, 254, 270, 334, 406, 414, 418, 419, 440, 594.
    Jonathan, 158, 420.
    Joseph, 157, 223.
    Joshua, 22.
    Josiah, 21, 220, 270, 359, 389.
    Josias, 467.
    Mary, 21, 22, 158, 359.
    Mindwell, 158.
    Miriam, 220, 389, 467, 468.
    Mr., 196, 529.
    Nathaniel, 157, 158, 358.
    Samuel, 21, 22, 359.
    Stephen, 358.
    Thomas, 208, 358.
Blackleach, Betty, 23.
    Elizabeth, 22, 23, 24.
    John, 24, 25, 132, 138.
    John, Mrs., 24.
    Mary, 23.
    Mr., 161, 193, 344.
Blackledge, Mr., 601.
Blackley, Grace, 443.
Blackman, Abigail, 96.
    Dorothy, 96.
    Ebenezer, 96.
    Elizabeth, 96.
    John, 96.
    Joseph, 96.
    Rebeckah, 96.
    Samuel, 96.
Blake, Elizabeth, 468.
    Freelove, 468.
    John, 427, 468.
    Jonathan, 468, 491.
    Joseph, 468.
    Stephen, 468.
Blakeley, Eleanor, 251.
    Samuel, 251.
Blin, see Blinn, Blyn, Blynn.
Blin, James, 468.
    Jonathan, 444.
    Mary, 444.

Blin, William, 600.
Blinn, see Blin, Blyn, Blynn.
Blinn, Daniel, 468.
    Deliverance, 468.
    George, 468.
    Jonathan, 468.
    Peter, 43, 287, 468.
    William, 468.
Bliss, John, 574.
Blyn, see Blin, Blinn, Blynn.
Blyn, Peter, 25.
Blynn, see Blin, Blinn, Blyn.
Blynn, Deliverance, 577.
    Elizabeth, 582.
    George, 582.
    Mary, 468, 582.
    Mollie, 577.
    Rebeckah, 577.
    William, 266, 582.
Boardman, see Bordman, Boreman, Borman, Bowman.
Boardman, Abiah, 360.
    Benjamin, 469.
    Charles, 469.
    Daniel, 62, 105, 193, 197, 469.
    David, 360, 361.
    Edward, 470.
    Elisha, 470.
    Elizabeth, 470.
    Ephraim, 470.
    Hannah, 469.
    Isaac, 359, 360, 470.
    Israel, 469, 470.
    Jonathan, 206, 285, 360.
    Joseph, 183, 184, 360, 361.
    Joshua, 469.
    Josiah, 470.
    Martha, 469.
    Mary, 64.
    Moses, 466.
    Nathaniel, 601.
    Olive, 470.
    Rebeckah, 470.
    Richard, 469, 475, 476, 501.
    Samuel, 360, 361.
    Sarah, 360.
    Silence, 49, 490.
    Thomas, 231, 360.
    Timothy, 469.
Boarn, see Bourn.
Boarn, Ann, 26.
    Frances, 26.
    Hannah, 25, 26.
    John, 25, 26.
    Joseph, 26.
    Nathaniel, 26.
    Thomas, 26.
Boarne, Joseph, 159, 160.

Boarne, Nathaniel, 160.
    Thomas, 160.
Bodwitha, Joseph, 455.
Bogue, see Booge.
Bogue, John, 354, 511.
Bolton, Mr., 626.
Boltwood, Mary, 554.
    Solomon, 271.
Booge, see Bogue.
Booge, John, 69, 70, 299, 511, 571.
Booth, Elizabeth, 26.
    John, 96.
    Pheebe, 26.
    Robert, 26, 570.
    Sarah, 26.
    Simon, 64.
    Symon, 26.
    William, 26.
    Zachariah, 26.
Bordman, see Boardman, Boreman, Borman, Bowman.
Bordman, Daniel, 63.
Boreman, Daniel, 139, 159, 319.
    Elizabeth, 159.
    Isaac, 80, 323.
    Jonathan, 68, 80, 81, 88, 111, 158, 159, 295, 332.
    Mercy, 158.
    Nathaniel, 159, 344, 600.
    Richard, 328.
    Samuel, 89, 128.
Borland, John, 8, 9.
Borman, see Boardman, Bordman, Boreman, Bowman.
Borman, Daniel, 163.
    Richard, 163.
Bostick, John 506.
Bostwick, John, 469, 505.
Bourn, see Boarn, Boarne, Bourne.
Bourn, Hannah, 26.
    John, 25, 26.
Bourne, Elizabeth, 159.
Bow, Anna, 471.
    Ann, 471.
    Edward, 471.
    Martha, 471.
    Mary, 441, 471.
    Samuel, 441.
Bowe, Ruth, 591.
Bowen, Josiah, 361.
Bowers, Ebenezer, 471.
Bowman, see Boardman, Bordman, Boreman, Borman.
Bowman, Nathaniel, 27, 54.
    Brace, Elizabeth, 471.
    Henry, 67, 298, 471.
    John, 350, 608.
    Stephen, 296.

Bracy, John, 350, 351.
    Stephen, 380.
Bradford, Joseph, 231, 232.
Bradley, Abraham, 320.
Brainard, see Braynard.
Brainard, Caleb, 160, 472, 473.
    Daniel, 107, 129, 144, 160, 161, 201, 238, 300, 302, 324, 443, 471, 472, 473, 487, 560, 565, 618.
    David, 473.
    Dorothy, 472.
    Elijah, 160, 275, 473.
    Elizabeth, 356, 473.
    Hannah, 160, 471, 472.
    Hezekiah, 125, 160, 161, 274, 275, 298, 354, 393, 472, 473, 495, 611.
    Israel, 473.
    James, 160, 400, 423, 611.
    John, 473.
    Joshua, 107, 144, 160, 488, 494, 495, 557, 617.
    Martha, 473.
    Mehetabell, 494, 495.
    Nehemiah, 472, 473.
    Noadiah, 472.
    Susannah, 472.
    William, 151, 160, 461.
Brainwood, Susanna, 130.
Braynard, see Brainard.
Braynard, Caleb, 161.
    Elijah, 161, 274.
    Hezekiah, 161, 274.
    James, 117, 161, 353.
    Joshua, 161, 352, 373.
    Sarah, 356.
    William, 161.
Brewer, Beriah, 514.
    Hezekiah, 514.
    Joseph, 514.
Bridgman, Dorothy, 375.
Brocket, John, 175.
Bromfield, Edward, 593.
Bronson, see Brounson, Brownson, Brunson.
Bronson, John, 280.
    Rachel, 164.
Brooks, John, 27, 28.
    Lydia, 27, 362.
    Marcy, 27.
    Mary, 27.
    Mercy, 362.
    Samuel, 28, 167, 316, 362.
    Sarah, 167.
    Susannah, 27, 361, 362.
    Thomas, 117, 152, 297, 298.
Broughton, Mr., 593.
Brounson, see Bronson, Brownson, Brunson.

Brounson, Dorothy, 163.
    Ebenezer, 163.
    Grace, 163.
    Isaac, 28.
    Jacob, 28, 162.
    John, 163, 321.
    Lydia, 132.
    Mary, 28.
    Moses, 163.
    Roger, 28, 162.
    Samuel, 28, 132, 162.
    Sarah, 163.
    William, 118, 163.
Brown, Abigail, 362, 363.
    Ann, 362, 363, 474.
    Cornelius, 195, 363.
    Daniel, 364, 474.
    Dinah, 363.
    Hannah, 364.
    Isaac, 474.
    James, 16, 17, 244, 582, 591.
    John, 17, 362, 363, 473, 474.
    Jonathan, 17, 363, 364, 418.
    Kezia, 364.
    Mary, 363, 364, 474.
    Mindwell, 363.
    Nathaniel, 15, 40.
    Peter, 363, 364, 473, 474, 475.
    Rachel, 474.
    Samuel, 363, 364, 612.
    Sarah, 364, 474.
    Thomas, 364.
Browne, Benjamin, 623.
    Cornelius, 197.
    Eleanor, 161, 162.
    Martha, 162.
    Mary, 154, 161, 162.
    Nathaniel, 161, 162.
    Peter, 154.
    Sarah, 161.
Brownson, see Bronson, Brounson, Brunson.
Brownson, Elijah, 433,
    John, 581.
Brunson, see Bronson, Brounson, Brownson.
Brunson, Elijah, 432, 475.
    Isaac, 162, 475.
    Israel, 278.
    John, 278, 280, 443.
    Mercy, 432, 475.
    Moses, 443.
    Ruth, 475.
    Samuel, 432, 475.
    Sarah, 443.
    Thomas, 475.
    William, 443.
Buck, Abigail, 164.

Buck, Comfort, 164.
    Daniel, 475.
    David, 266, 448, 475, 476.
    Elizabeth, 164, 475.
    Enock, 163, 164.
    Eunice, 475, 476.
    Ezekiel, 163, 164.
    Hannah, 164, 475.
    Henry, 324.
    Isaac, 164.
    Jonathan, 163, 164.
    Josiah, 476.
    Mabel, 27.
    Martha, 164.
    Mr., 476.
    Peletiah, 164.
    Rachell, 163.
    Samuel, 27, 54, 164, 361.
    Sarah, 163, 164.
    Stephen, 164.
    Thomas, 214, 329.
Buckingham, Joseph, 508.
    Mr., 17, 42, 168.
    Sarah, 403, 404.
    Stephen, 403.
    Thomas, 13, 425, 435, 603, 622.
Buckland, Ann, 477.
    Charles, 164, 379, 380, 447, 476, 477, 483,
        484, 545, 593.
    Elizabeth, 164, 477.
    John, 477.
    Jonathan, 477.
    Nicholas, 476.
    William, 164, 165, 476, 477.
Buel, Peter, 296, 341, 477.
Buell, Abigail, 477.
    Ephraim, 153, 364, 477.
    Esther, 478.
    Hannah, 478.
    John, 469.
    Jonathan, 477.
    Martha, 478, 516.
    Mary, 153, 365, 477, 478.
    Mindwell, 153.
    Miriam, 478.
    Mr., 273.
    Peter, 123, 341, 477, 478, 516.
    Samuel, 153, 273, 477.
    Sarah, 478.
    William, 477, 478.
Bulkeley, Charles, 29, 165.
    Dorothe, 165, 166.
    Edward, 52, 79, 127, 129, 162, 165, 166,
        167, 185, 203, 280, 285, 314, 319,
        320, 323, 332, 360, 374, 376, 403, 443,
        600, 601.
    G., 167.
    Gershom, 29, 165, 167.

Bulkeley, Grace, 165, 166.
   John, 166, 167, 361.
   Margaret, 165.
   Mr. 52, 139, 167.
   Patience, 604.
   Peter, 28, 29, 64, 165.
   Rachel, 29.
Bulkley, Mr., 213.
Bull, Abigail, 30.
   Caleb, 36, 167, 168, 170, 381, 438, 496.
   Daniel, 168.
   David, 31, 167, 521.
   Ebenezer, 30.
   Elizabeth, 170, 287.
   Esther, 29.
   Ezekiel, 109, 287.
   Hannah, 167, 168.
   John, 29, 31, 167.
   Jonathan, 30, 31, 64, 93, 137, 138, 167, 382, 455, 601.
   Joseph, 30, 73, 167, 168, 234, 286.
   Mary, 31, 168.
   Moses, 30.
   Mr., 168.
   Mrs., 109.
   Nehemiah, 29, 31.
   Ruth, 30.
   Samuel, 30, 31, 167.
   Sarah, 30, 31, 101, 167.
   Susannah, 167.
   Sybell, 30.
   Thomas, 29, 31, 118, 131.
Bullivant, Benjamin, 623.
Bunce, Abigail, 169, 288, 365.
   Abijah, 289.
   Elizabeth, 169, 170.
   John, 112, 169, 223, 231, 235, 267, 329, 449, 450, 514.
   Jonathan, 169, 242, 288, 289, 329, 365, 449, 450.
   Joseph, 169, 288, 289, 450.
   Sarah, 169, 288, 289, 365.
   Susannah, 169, 170, 288, 365.
   Thomas, 30, 93, 127, 168, 169, 214, 344, 367, 449, 450, 500, 575, 602.
   Zachariah, 289, 365.
Burd, see Bird.
Burd, Elizabeth, 32.
   Esther, 342.
   James, 32, 467.
   Joseph, 33, 34.
   Mary, 33, 34, 342.
   Mehetabell, 32, 33.
   Mindwell, 467.
   Nathaniel, 34.
   Ruth, 33, 34.
   Samuel, 34, 467.
   Sarah, 34, 342.

Burd, Thomas, 32, 33, 34, 35, 265, 407, 467.
Burge, see Birge.
Burge, Abigail, 365.
   John, 35, 365.
   Joseph, 35, 270.
   Mr., 99.
Burnett, see Barnett.
Burnett, Mr., 402.
Burnham, Amy, 366.
   Caleb, 366.
   Charles, 478, 479.
   Daniel, 478.
   Elizabeth, 366, 479.
   Esther, 479.
   Hannah, 336, 337.
   Jabez, 335, 366, 478.
   John, 5, 148, 262, 365, 366, 478, 479.
   Jonathan, 247, 266, 267, 286, 366, 478, 496.
   Joseph, 478.
   Josiah, 479.
   Mary, 366, 478.
   Naomy, 479.
   Nathaniel, 51, 246, 247, 267, 362, 376, 577.
   Rachell, 366.
   Rebeckah, 478.
   Richard, 68, 103, 255.
   Samuel, 5, 96, 148, 182, 208, 261, 262, 299, 309, 335, 365, 366, 478, 479, 618.
   Sarah, 366.
   Thomas, 415, 478, 479.
   Timothy, 478.
   William, 43, 91, 336, 337, 344, 345, 359, 360, 375, 421, 478, 625.
Burr, John, 529.
   Jonathan, 43, 592.
   Sarah, 595.
   Thomas, 43.
Burrell, Charles, 480.
   Jonathan, 480.
Burton, Samuel, 490.
   Sarah, 490.
Bushnell, Mary, 539.
Butler, Abigail, 113, 480.
   Abraham, 171.
   Bathsheba, 170.
   Charles, 170.
   Daniel, 171, 480.
   Deborah, 480.
   Elisha, 480.
   Elizabeth, 171, 480, 481.
   Esther, 52.
   George, 171.
   Hannah, 171.
   Isaac, 480.
   James, 164, 171, 181, 187, 199, 361, 438, 465, 584, 595.

Butler, John, 496, 501.
  Jonathan, 234, 358, 480, 488, 498, 499, 500, 558.
  Joseph, 94, 95, 356, 386, 471, 548.
  Marcey, 171.
  Mary, 95, 170, 171, 381, 537, 548, 592.
  Mr., 95.
  Mrs., 95.
  Nathaniel, 175.
  Samuel, 27, 40, 89, 170, 171, 344, 573, 627.
  Sarah, 171.

Butler, Sibel, 480.
  Susannah, 170.
  Thomas, 64, 171, 480.
  Vilot, 480.
  William, 25, 171.
Buttolph, David, 145, 366, 367.
  Hannah, 367.
  John, 529.
  Jonathan, 366, 367, 529.
  Mary, 366, 367.
  Temperance, 367.
Byington, Jane, 327.

C

Cadwell, Abell, 368, 369.
  Abigail, 368, 369.
  Ann, 368, 369.
  Daniel, 368, 369.
  Dorothy, 250.
  Edward, 193, 367, 368, 370, 435, 481, 500, 501, 508, 557, 595.
  Elias, 368, 369.
  Elizabeth, 367, 368.
  Esther, 481.
  Hannah, 480.
  John, 250, 368, 369, 496, 628.
  Joseph, 481.
  Mary, 481.
  Matthew, 368, 369, 481.
  Morgan, 550.
  Mr., 169, 207, 385, 485.
  Rachel, 368.
  Ruth, 501.
  Samuel, 218, 267, 481.
  Thankfull, 218.
  Thomas, 349, 595.
  William, 367, 368, 481, 500.
Cakebread, Hepzibah, 36.
  Isaac, 35.
  Margaret, 36.
Caldwell, Hannah, 582.
  James, 582.
  John, 582.
Calkin, John, 273.
Camp, Abigail, 172.
  Amos, 351.
  Ann, 351.
  Hannah, 172, 481.
  John, 172, 328, 349, 351, 481, 482, 606.
  Joseph, 172, 186.
  Lydia, 172.
  Mary, 481, 482.
  Sarah, 172.
Cande, Zacheus, 47.
Candee, Sarah, 251.
  Zacheus, 180, 251, 441.

Carey, see Cary.
Carey, Joseph, 222.
Carpenter, Benjamin, 240.
  David, 482.
Carrier, Andrew, 283.
Carrington, Clark, 399.
  Ebenezer, 173.
  Sarah, 399.
Carter, Elizabeth, 537.
  Jonathan, 537.
  Joshua, 67, 328.
Cary, see Carey.
Cary, Joseph, 284, 296, 297, 393, 394.
Case, Abigail, 36, 37, 482, 483, 485.
  Abraham, 482.
  Abram, 483.
  Alpheus, 483, 484.
  Amos, 482, 483.
  Arriam, 485.
  Azariacom, 485.
  Barthelme, 38.
  Bartholomew, 36, 37.
  Benjamin, 478, 485.
  Daniel, 367.
  Elizabeth, 36, 38, 39, 313, 417, 483, 484, 485.
  Eunice, 485.
  Hannah, 485.
  Irena, 485.
  Isaac, 482, 483.
  James, 38, 39, 485, 517, 528.
  John, 36, 37, 38, 113, 135, 145, 223, 224, 252, 293, 327, 398, 429, 451, 464, 483, 484, 517, 524, 526, 545, 561, 588.
  Jonah, 485.
  Joseph, 36, 37, 38, 39, 91, 144, 146, 154, 155, 196, 237, 238, 263, 271, 277, 327, 331, 332, 367, 392, 441, 463, 464, 477, 482, 483, 484, 485, 498, 503, 528, 533.
  Joshua, 38, 39.
  Lucy, 483.

Case, Marcey, 485.
  Mary, 36, 37, 38, 39, 327, 482, 483, 485.
  Mindwell, 38, 39.
  Mrs., 91.
  Nathaniel, 485.
  Orpheus, 483.
  Peletiah, 485.
  Penelope, 367.
  Phineas, 483.
  Rachel, 38, 39.
  Richard, 36, 37, 38, 94, 224, 277, 326, 484, 525.
  Samuel, 36, 37, 38, 135, 313, 327, 331, 348, 484, 485.
  Sarah, 36, 37, 38, 460, 482, 483, 484.
  Thomas, 482, 483.
  Timothy, 483, 484.
  William, 36, 37, 38, 39, 366.
Casehog (Indian), 591.
Catlin, Benjamin, 408, 409, 411.
  Elizabeth, 554.
  John, 67, 92, 93, 113, 129, 193, 367.
  Joseph, 269.
  Margaret, 408, 409, 410.
  Samuel, 411, 448, 504, 527, 528, 579, 607, 608.
Catling, Samuel, 578.
Center, Jonathan, 257.
  Martha, 257.
Chalker, Stephen, 173, 174.
Chamberlain, Benjamin, 404.
  Joseph, 283, 364, 382.
  Sarah, 404.
Chamberlin, Joseph, 234.
Chaplin, Benjamin, 387.
Chapman, Anne, 173.
  David, 173.
  Edward, 485.
  Elizabeth, 173.
  Hannah, 173, 302, 369, 472.
  Henry, 173.
  Jabez, 173, 174, 279, 302, 471, 472, 546, 547.
  John, 69, 70, 107, 116, 117, 173, 174.
  Jonathan, 472.
  Joseph, 117, 173, 174, 300, 301.
  Lydia, 64, 65, 173, 174, 279.
  Mehetabell, 173.
  Mr., 64, 571.
  Robert, 565, 618.
  Samuel, 173, 174, 302.
  Sarah, 117, 173.
  Symon, 9, 53, 173, 236, 369, 375, 382, 495, 549.
  William, 76.
Chatterton, Eliza, 320.
  Samuel, 320.
Chauncey, Abiah, 174, 338, 340, 453.

Chauncey, Abiah Wolcott, 453.
  Charles, 174, 337, 339.
  Ichabod Wolcott, 174, 338, 340, 453.
  Israel, 96.
  Robert, 174, 338, 340, 453.
  Sarah, 337, 338, 340.
Chauncy, Abiah, 453, 626.
  Ichabod Wolcott, 453.
  Robert, 626.
Chauntrell, Mary, 92, 93.
Cheeney, William, 39, 40.
Chester, Eunice, 175.
  Hannah, 175, 176.
  Jemima, 164, 177, 314.
  John, 24, 40, 41, 43, 128, 132, 174, 175, 176, 344, 600.
  Mahetabell, 175.
  Mary, 175, 176, 177.
  Penelope, 175.
  Prudence, 175.
  Sarah, 175.
  Stephen, 40, 41, 175, 323, 324, 344.
  Thomas, 79, 175, 176, 177, 228, 324.
Chiles, Experience, 511.
Chitester, Eunice, 570.
  William, 570.
Chubb, Stephen, 486.
Church, Caleb, 498.
  Ebenezer, 369.
  Elizabeth, 369, 557.
  Esther, 369.
  James, 369, 484, 493, 496, 562, 596.
  John, 302, 497, 546, 547, 571, 572.
  Joseph, 577.
  Mary, 478.
  Samuel, 207, 369.
  Sarah, 369.
Churchill, Benjamin, 24, 52, 80, 164, 201, 246, 247, 266, 317, 341, 342, 359, 365, 370, 375, 404.
  Bethia, 583.
  Daniel, 370.
  Elizabeth, 314.
  John, 370, 583.
  Joseph, 252, 324, 348, 403, 595.
  Josiah, 112, 164, 179, 180, 183, 200, 201, 239, 314, 325, 365, 370, 448, 577, 627, 628.
  Marcy, 370.
  Martha, 469.
  Mary, 345, 370.
  Nathaniel, 172, 344, 370.
  Samuel, 501.
  Sarah, 188, 189.
Clapp, Thomas, 558, 587.
Clark, Aaron, 487.
  Abigail, 486.
  Ambrose, 39, 40.

Clark, Anne, 43.
    Cheeny, 39, 40.
    Cheney, 491.
    Daniel, 43, 46, 486, 487, 569, 591.
    David, 60, 384.
    Elisha, 486.
    Elizabeth, 179, 374, 486, 487.
    Eunice, 40.
    Francis, 486, 487.
    George, 41, 42.
    Hannah, 87, 88.
    Isaac, 487.
    John, 32, 36, 39, 40, 42, 110, 126, 131,
        178, 179, 298.
    Joseph, 42, 43, 349, 370, 486, 487.
    Josiah, 179, 222.
    Marcy, 179.
    Martha, 178, 486.
    Mary, 42, 101, 178, 487.
    Matthew, 178, 179, 554.
    Moses, 46.
    Nathaniel, 87.
    Rebecca, 178.
    Samuel, 17, 41, 42, 370, 426.
    Sarah, 41, 42.
    Susannah, 179, 180.
    Thomas, 41, 42, 43, 178, 180.
    William, 179, 180, 273, 326, 361, 561.
Clarke, Aaron, 487.
    Benoni, 370.
    Daniel, 22, 43, 61, 177, 178, 370, 487.
    Elizabeth, 43, 177, 370.
    Hannah, 104, 487.
    John, 109, 152, 177, 178, 179, 370.
    Johnny, 177.
    Jonas, 178.
    Josiah, 82, 101.
    Margaret, 43.
    Martha, 22, 177.
    Mary, 177, 178, 370, 371, 487.
    Matthew, 179.
    Mr., 192.
    Samuel, 177.
    Sarah, 177, 178.
    Solomon, 370.
    Susannah, 180.
    Thomas, 42, 238, 326.
    William, 43.
Clements, John, 142.
Cleveland, Benjamin, 496.
Coal, see Cole.
Coal, Elizabeth, 180.
    Nathaniel, 180.
Coale, Ichabod, 43, 67, 180.
    John, 44.
    Mary, 43, 45.
    Matthew, 45.
    Mehetabell, 44, 45.

Coale, Nathaniel, 43, 44, 126.
    Ruth, 45.
    Sarah, 45.
    Stephen, 45.
Cockshott, Elizabeth, 44.
Coe, Joseph, 353, 488.
    Robert, 591.
Coit, Daniel, 404.
    John, 397.
    Joseph, 397.
    Martha, 397, 398.
    Mehetabell, 404.
    Solomon, 397, 398.
Cole, see Coal.
Cole, Abigail, 285.
    Elizabeth, 180, 181.
    John, 44, 180, 181, 260.
    Joseph, 285, 332, 372.
    Lydia, 180, 181, 372.
    Mary, 371, 432.
    Mr., 447.
    Nathaniel, 180.
    Rachel, 180.
    Samuel, 371, 432, 433.
    Sarah, 180.
    Thomas, 229, 372.
    Timothy, 341.
Colefax, see Colfax.
Colefax, Elizabeth, 181.
    Hannah, 181.
    John, 181.
    Jonathan, 43, 181.
    Mary, 181.
    Sarah, 181.
Coleman, Anna, 616.
    Ebenezer, 411, 440.
    Hannah, 181, 182.
    Joseph, 182.
    John, 182, 183, 226, 324, 600.
    Noah, 181, 182.
Coles, see Cowles, Coules.
Coles, Henry, 121.
Colfax, see Colefax.
Colfax, Jonathan, 181, 255.
    Sarah, 181.
Colle, Mr., 340.
Collens, John, 447.
Collet, Thomas, 402.
Collett, Thomas, 402, 596.
Collins, John, 39, 122, 161, 162, 216, 308,
      319, 327, 358, 376, 377, 394, 439,
      440, 446, 447, 461, 462, 512, 513,
      566, 570, 578, 585, 597, 599, 610.
    Jonathan, 592.
    Mr., 121.
Collyer, see Colyer.
Collyer, Joseph, 487.
Colt, see Coult.

Colt, Abraham, 372, 373.
    Benjamin, 147.
    Isaac, 372.
    Jabez, 261, 365.
    Joanna, 147.
    Joseph, 373.
    Mary, 261, 262, 372.
    Ruth, 373.
    Susannah, 372.
Colton, Benjamin, 209, 386, 408.
Colyer, see Collyer.
Colyer, Abell, 551.
    Joseph, 26.
    Rachell, 551.
Comer, Dible, 591.
    John, 619, 620.
Cone, Caleb, 461.
    Daniel, 201, 238, 352, 353, 373, 472,
        487, 488, 560, 617.
    Ebenezer, 373, 471.
    Elizabeth, 373.
    Garred, 373.
    George, 488.
    Gerrard, 300.
    Hannah, 373.
    Jared, 373, 488.
    Joseph, 488.
    Mary, 487, 488, 511.
    Ruth, 373, 374.
    Sarah, 557.
    Stephen, 373.
    Thomas, 373, 557, 565, 617.
Coney, Benjamin, 96.
Conner, John, 357.
Cook, see Cooke.
Cook, Aaron, 99, 255.
    Hannah, 73.
    John, 45, 46, 73, 420, 489, 490, 496, 497.
    Joseph, 68, 408, 611.
    Josiah, 45, 46.
    Lydia, 46, 362.
    Moses, 451.
    Mr., 550.
    Nathaniel, 45, 46, 562.
    Robert, 402.
    Sarah, 182, 605.
    Thomas, 17, 489, 490.
    Westwood, 175.
Cooke, see Cook.
Cooke, Aaron, 19, 22, 30, 81, 84, 90, 98, 103,
        104, 115, 116, 141, 142, 168, 208,
        242, 243, 254, 267, 268, 271, 304,
        338, 339, 374, 409, 450, 488, 489, 493.
    Abigail, 46.
    Anna, 489.
    Annah, 488.
    Benjamin, 489.
    Daniel, 45.

Cooke, Ebenezer, 45.
    Eliakim, 374.
    Hannah, 45, 46.
    John, 45, 47, 145, 182, 183, 488, 489,
        498.
    Joseph, 329, 374, 608.
    Josiah, 6, 47, 150, 182.
    Lydia, 46, 47, 489.
    Martha, 488.
    Mary, 45, 488.
    Moses, 488, 489.
    Mr., 90.
    Nathaniel, 46, 61, 386, 489.
    Noah, 374.
    Richard, 489.
    Robert, 402.
    Sarah, 45, 46, 182, 374.
    Theophilus, 182, 183.
Cooley, Jemima, 370.
    Mary, 370.
    Samuel, 501.
Cooly, Joseph, 71.
    Mary, 71.
Cooper, Desire, 566.
    Ebenezer, 592.
    Thomas, 566, 591.
Corbee, see Corby.
Corbee, Mary, 185.
Corbett, Mary, 447.
Corby, William, 294.
Corning, Mr., 233.
Cornish, Dammary, 183.
    Hannah, 238.
    James, 36, 37, 101, 123, 154, 155, 183,
        223, 237, 238, 263, 310, 331, 399,
        588, 589, 590.
    Joseph, 502, 533, 534, 551.
    Mr., 359.
Cornwall, Abraham, 49.
    Benjamin, 47, 48, 191, 462.
    Daniel, 47.
    David, 49, 490, 491, 550.
    Ebenezer, 491.
    Elizabeth, 47, 491.
    Esther, 513.
    Hannah, 48.
    Hester, 50.
    Isaac, 47.
    Jacob, 47, 48.
    Jemima, 50, 491.
    John, 11, 47, 48, 85, 122.
    Jonathan, 48, 49.
    Joseph, 47, 48, 462.
    Lois, 50, 491.
    Martha, 47, 48.
    Mary, 47, 490, 513.
    Nathaniel, 47.
    Paul, 48.

Cornwall, Rebeckah, 491.
  Samuel, 39, 48, 50, 435, 436, 491.
  Silence, 49.
  Stephen, 49, 490.
  Thankful, 48.
  Thomas, 48, 49.
  Timothy, 47.
  Waite, 47.
  William, 47, 50, 287, 308, 309, 486, 491.
Cornwell, Ann, 492.
  Anna, 591.
  Benjamin, 592.
  Jacob, 591.
  Joseph, 462.
  Samuel, 492.
  Thomas, 492.
  William, 492, 562.
Cotton, Mary, 120.
  Samuel, 120.
Couch, Thomas, 213.
Coules, see Coles, Cowles.
Coules, Isaac, 482.
Coult, see Colt.
Coult, Abraham, 372.
  Benjamin, 299.
  Esther, 415.
  Isaac, 372.
  Jabez, 299, 300.
  Jonathan, 182.
  Joseph, 182.
  Mary, 416.
Courtney, H., 395.
Cowles, see Coles, Coules.
Cowles, Abigail, 493.
  Ann, 371.
  Caleb, 493.
  Elizabeth, 434.
  Hannah, 102, 103, 493.
  Hester, 493.
  Hezekiah, 493.
  John, 493.
  Joseph, 304, 483, 500.
  Mary, 459, 493.
  Nathaniel, 423, 493.
  Samuel, 74, 371, 422, 423, 493.
  Sarah, 445, 493.
  Susannah, 371.
  Thomas, 443.
  Timothy, 102, 114, 147, 164, 165, 198,
    225, 249, 299, 304, 335, 340, 350,
    355, 356, 380, 416, 417, 447, 476,
    483, 484, 526, 545, 555, 561, 576,
    577.
  William, 335.
Crafts, Moses, 361.
Crafts, Moses, 15, 16, 152, 188, 195, 361.
Crane, Abraham, 58, 183, 184, 193.
  Benjamin, 51, 52.

Crane, Benoni, 183, 184.
  Elijah, 295, 601.
  Elizabeth, 50, 51.
  Esther, 52, 185.
  Hannah, 50, 183, 184.
  Isaac, 52, 184, 185.
  Israel, 50, 51, 600.
  Jacob, 230, 374, 530.
  John, 183, 184.
  Jonathan, 3, 11, 130, 131, 222, 296, 297,
    374.
  Joseph, 51, 52, 53, 184, 233.
  Lucy, 183.
  Lydia, 50, 345, 346.
  Martha, 50, 51.
  Mary, 183, 222, 295.
  Sarah, 51, 52, 88.
Creese, Thomas, 623.
Crippen, Mary, 107.
  Thomas, 107.
Crippin, Experience, 185.
  Frances, 185.
  Jabez, 185.
  Mercy, 185.
  Thomas, 185, 283.
Crofoot, see Crowfoot.
Crofoot, Joseph, 581.
Crow, Hannah, 185, 186.
  John, 185, 186.
  Nathaniel, 185, 186.
  Ruth, 580.
Crowel, Mr., 598.
Crowfoot, see Crofoot.
Crowfoot, Joseph, 375.
  Margaret, 375.
Cross, Elizabeth, 53.
  John, 8, 53, 374.
  Mary, 8, 375.
  Nathaniel, 53, 375.
  Samuel, 18, 53, 56, 123.
Crossthwayt, Elizabeth, 620.
Cuffe (negro), 254.
Culver, Ephraim, 222.
  Martha, 222.
  Sarah, 540.
Curtice, see Curtis, Curtiss.
Curtice, John, 375, 584, 628.
  Jonathan, 53, 170, 231, 375, 574.
  Joseph, 96, 455.
  Lydia, 375.
  Richard, 587.
  Samuel, 361, 439, 573, 627, 628.
  Susannah, 361.
  Thomas, 375, 376, 396, 553, 554, 625.
  William, 375.
Curtis, see Curtice, Curtiss.
Curtis, Elizabeth, 186, 187, 344, 345.
  Hannah, 186, 187.

Curtis, Isaac, 324.
    John, 12, 40, 62, 89, 105, 119, 186, 187,
       198, 228, 257, 266, 285, 313, 314, 344,
       375, 513.
    Jonathan, 285, 360.
    Josiah, 186.
    Lydia, 375.
    Mrs., 54.
    Ruth, 54.

Curtis, Samuel, 54, 181, 240.
    Sarah, 54.
    Thomas, 239, 292, 375, 475.
Curtiss, see Curtice, Curtis.
Curtiss, Enos, 471.
    Ruth, 54.
    Samuel, 54, 247.
    Sarah, 54.
Cutlar, John, 98.

D

Dady, John, 629.
Danson, Elizabeth, 620.
    John, 619.
    Mr., 223.
    Mrs., 623.
Darrow, Christopher, 482.
    Elizabeth, 92.
Dart, Mary, 494, 495.
    Richard, 494.
    Roger, 495.
Davenport, William, 539, 540.
Davis, Comfort, 49, 492.
    Isaac, 420, 421.
    Jemima, 55.
    Lydia, 622.
    Nicholas, 591.
    William, 425.
Day, Ebenezer, 233.
    Hannah, 143, 493.
    John, 64, 494, 543.
    Jonathan, 375.
    Mehetabell, 494.
    Nathaniel, 494.
    Thomas, 143, 181, 234, 336, 376, 493,
      494.
Debill, see Dibble.
Debill, Jane, 511.
Delano, Jonathan, 359, 515, 628, 629.
Delle, Mary, 591.
DeMedina, Isaac, 505.
Deming, Abigail, 187, 496, 510, 511.
    Ann, 187.
    Benjamin, 159, 496.
    Charles, 51, 496, 511.
    David, 55, 188, 189, 215, 276.
    Ebenezer, 55, 128, 187, 188, 229, 325.
    Elizabeth, 56, 187.
    Ephraim, 188.
    Hannah, 593.
    Hezekiah, 16, 152, 172, 180, 239.
    Honour, 188, 189.
    Isaac, 583.
    John, 55, 68, 164, 188, 189, 323, 328,
      344, 351, 475, 501.

Deming, Jonathan, 16, 17, 55, 118, 152, 159,
      187, 200, 285, 333, 376, 496, 510, 511.
    Joseph, 128.
    Josiah, 188, 361.
    Lemuell, 496.
    Lydia, 583.
    Mary, 187.
    Rebeckah, 128.
    Samuel, 55, 56, 188, 189.
    Sarah, 187, 188.
    Susannah, 497.
    Thomas, 185, 496.
    William, 188, 189.
Denison, Mary, 376.
Denslow, Benjamin, 485.
    Palidence, 57.
    Patience, 389.
Denton, Benjamin, 611.
Deverieux, Jonathan, 497.
Devotion, Ebenezer, 78.
Dewey, Daniel, 376.
    Jedediah, 334.
    Josiah, 561.
    Katharine, 376.
DeWholph, Azuba, 376, 377.
    Elizabeth, 376, 377.
    Joseph, 376.
    John, 591.
Dibble, see Debill.
Dibble, Abraham, 56.
    Abram, 56.
    Benjamin, 189.
    Ebenezer, 428.
    George, 56.
    Jane, 510.
    Josiah, 56.
    Mr., 389.
    Samuel, 56, 333.
    Thomas, 56, 57.
    Wakefield, 56, 200, 510.
Dibel, Abraham, 545.
    Wakefield, 510.
Dible, John, 591.
Dibol, Wakefield, 510.

Dick (negro), 192.
Dickeson, see Dickson, Diggeson.
Dickeson, Daniel, 576.
Dickinson, Azariah, 117.
    Charles, 64.
    Daniel, 57, 58, 186, 249, 427, 498, 526, 545.
    Deborah, 377.
    Ebenezer, 190, 203, 444, 456, 555.
    Elihu, 189, 190, 497.
    Eliphalet, 57, 58, 162, 295, 600.
    Elizabeth, 497.
    Esther, 497.
    Hannah, 117, 189, 190, 494, 498.
    Hepsibah, 389.
    Jemima, 498.
    Joseph, 377, 583.
    Lois, 498.
    Mary, 377.
    Mehetabell, 450, 497, 498.
    Moses, 497.
    Nathaniel, 189, 494.
    Noadiah, 184, 247, 600.
    Obadiah, 57.
    Phebe, 377.
    Rebeckah, 28.
    Sarah, 498.
    Susannah, 444, 498.
    Thomas, 14, 64, 189, 190, 213, 298, 299, 310, 377, 497, 498.
Dickson, see Dickeson, Diggeson.
Dickson, Hepzibah, 57.
Diego (negro), 191, 254, 367, 368.
Diggeson, Daniel, 576.
    Noadiah, 523.
Diggins, Jeremiah, 377.
    Thomas, 377.
Dike, Abigail, 379.
    Deborah, 379.
    Isaac, 379.
    Jemimah, 379.
    John, 379, 380.
    Margaret, 379.
    Rachell, 379.
    Sarah, 379.
Dimmock, Shuball, 131.
    Shubael, 438.
Dimock, Abigail, 378.
    Shubael, 11, 378, 394.
    Timothy, 377.
Disbrow, Mr., 94.
Dix, see Dixx, Dyx, Dyxx.
Dix, John, 380, 444.
    Susannah, 23.
Dixx, see Dix, Dyx, Dyxx.
Dixx, Leonard, 189.
Dodd, Edward, 425, 498.
    Lydia, 498.

Dolittle, Abraham, 591.
Doolittle, Abigail, 191.
    Abraham, 191.
    Esther, 191.
    Hannah, 191.
    Jonathan, 190, 191.
    Joseph, 191.
    Martha, 191.
    Mary, 191.
    Nathaniel, 191.
    Rachel, 180.
    Samuel, 47, 190, 191.
    Thankfull, 191.
Douglas, Mary, 240.
    Robert, 76, 77.
Downing, Jonathan, 450.
Drake, Ann, 261, 262, 416.
    Benjamin, 378.
    Elizabeth, 178, 191, 192, 386, 453.
    Enoch, 72, 363.
    Esther, 378.
    Eunice, 378.
    Hannah, 193, 478.
    Jacob, 10, 191, 192, 244, 254, 489, 562.
    Job, 5, 17, 35, 56, 61, 125, 149, 157, 158, 178, 191, 192, 196, 208, 272, 281, 309, 311, 378, 414, 415, 452, 453, 565.
    John, 322, 498.
    Jonathan, 378.
    Joseph, 261, 309.
    Martha, 414, 415.
    Mary, 322, 498.
    Mr., 99.
    Nathaniel, 7, 414, 415, 418, 452, 549.
    Sarah, 309.
    Symon, 192.
Driggs, Elizabeth, 159.
    Joseph, 159.
Drinker, Edward, 619, 620.
Druss, Joseph, 591.
Drusus (Indian), 288.
Duce, Abda (a mulatto), 58.
    Joseph, 58.
    Lydia, 58.
Dudley, Daniel, 495.
    Elizabeth, 78, 495.
    J., 98, 624.
    Joseph, 426, 495.
    Mary, 78.
    Paul, 426.
    William, 495.
Dunham, Benjamin, 378, 379.
    Ebenezer, 378, 379.
    Elisha, 378, 379, 601.
    John, 378, 379, 534.
    Jonathan, 302, 573.
    Marcy, 378, 379.
    Marshy, 378.

Dunham, Mary, 302, 379, 601, 602.
  Nathaniel, 233, 430.
  Solomon, 601, 602.
  Thomas, 378, 379.
Durin, Ned, 303.
Durke, John, 387.
  Sarah, 387.
  Thomas, 386.
Durrant, John, 324, 360.
Dutton, Joseph, 547.
  Mr., 547.
  Samuel, 547.
Dyer, Gyles, 620, 623.

Dyx, see Dix, Dixx, Dyxx.
Dyx, Samuel, 58.
Dyxx, Abigail, 380.
  Abraham, 380.
  Deborah, 380.
  Isaac, 380.
  Jemima, 380.
  John, 58, 193, 206, 379, 380, 444.
  Leonard, 193, 360.
  Rachell, 380.
  Samuel, 287.
  Sarah, 58, 380, 444.

E

Eaglestone, see Eglestone.
Eaglestone, Esther, 412.
East, Joseph, 524.
Easton, Abigail, 381.
  Elizabeth, 194, 499, 500.
  James, 170, 193.
  John, 380, 381, 498, 499.
  Jonathan, 169, 193, 194, 368, 429, 499, 500, 501.
  Joseph, 101, 113, 167, 193, 194, 484, 496.
  Lemuel, 500.
  Mr., 368.
  Prudence, 477.
  Samuel, 500.
  Sarah, 498, 499.
  Thankfull, 194.
  Thomas, 500, 501.
  William, 629.
Eaton, William, 629.
Edgecomb, Elizabeth, 77.
  John 77.
Edwards, Abigail, 382.
  Ann, 382.
  Churchill, 501.
  D., 42.
  Daniel, 382, 404.
  David, 501.
  Edward, 501.
  Elizabeth, 382.
  Hannah, 382.
  John, 127, 187, 381, 382, 487, 546.
  Jonathan, 404, 501.
  Joseph, 501.
  Josias, 501.
  Lucy, 381, 382.
  Mabell, 382.
  Mary, 382, 501.
  Nathaniel, 501.
  Ray, 404.
  Richard, 58, 64, 65, 66, 141, 142, 165, 169, 179, 240, 300, 334, 336, 357, 382.

Edwards, Samuel, 382, 496, 499.
  Sarah, 404.
  Thomas, 194.
  Timothy, 382, 502.
  William, 64.
Eells, Samuel, 42.
Eely, see Elay, Ely.
Eely, William, 130.
Eglestone, see Eaglestone.
Eglestone, Benjamin, 56.
  Dorcas, 412.
  Ebenezer, 441.
  Grace, 82, 172.
  Martha, 370.
  Mary, 441.
  Sarah, 260, 261.
  Thomas, 59.
Elay, see Eely, Ely.
Elay, Mr., 627.
Elgar, Thomas, 519.
Elger, Rachel, 244.
  Thomas, 244.
Eliot, Ann, 383.
  Elizabeth, 59.
  John, 53, 56, 57, 59, 124, 200, 242, 264, 338, 382, 383, 389.
  Mary, 200, 338, 383.
  Mrs., 383.
Eliott, John, 59.
Elliot, John, 56, 242.
Elmer, Edward, 195.
  John, 383.
  Joseph, 501.
  Mary, 195.
  Samuel, 373.
  Thomas, 383.
  William, 383.
Elmor, John, 147.
  Joseph, 147, 194.
  Samuel, 377.
Elmore, Amos, 502.

Elmore, Ann, 502.
  Caleb, 502.
  Edward, 502.
  Hezekiah, 502.
  John, 194, 195, 383.
  Rebeckah, 502.
  Samuel, 508.
  Thomas, 195.
  William, 195.
Elsworth, Abigail, 60.
  Ann, 384.
  Anna, 384.
  Daniel, 384.
  Elizabeth, 60.
  Esther, 384.
  Job, 240, 359, 565.
  John, 157, 240, 365, 383, 384, 391, 420,
    612.
  Jonathan, 21, 53, 60, 100, 173, 200, 202,
    220, 308, 310, 313, 374, 383, 384,
    388, 417, 467, 510, 548, 580.
  Joseph, 59, 60, 384.
  Josiah, 59, 60, 384.
  Martha, 60, 384.
  Mary, 60.
  Samuel, 59, 60, 384.
  Sarah, 359.
  Thomas, 100.
Elton, Elizabeth, 610.
  Mr., 248.
  Richard, 610.
Ely, see Eely, Elay.
Ely, Samuel, 455.

Emmons, Jonathan, 510.
  Ruth, 374.
  Samuel, 374, 510, 557.
Endsworth, Tixwell, 480.
Enno, Abigail, 196, 363, 502, 503.
  Anne, 196.
  David, 196, 430.
  James, 6, 7, 22, 61, 72, 91, 149, 150,
    154, 157, 183, 195, 196, 236, 243,
    244, 254, 263, 339, 375, 418, 419,
    452, 453, 476, 489, 490, 502, 525, 549,
    626.
  John, 17, 195.
  Mary, 196.
  Samuel, 195, 196, 502.
  Sarah, 206.
  Susannah, 196.
  Suzanna, 502.
  William, 195.
Ensign, David, 462, 463, 503, 504, 539, 540,
    551, 606, 607.
  Hannah, 113.
  James, 19, 170, 218, 234, 235, 290, 367,
    448, 463, 499, 504, 578, 579, 607,
    608, 611.
  Jonathan, 504.
  Phebe, 504.
  Thomas, 307, 429, 504.
Euerts, Hannah, 406.
  James, 406.
Euit, Hannah, 406.
  Jeams, 406.
Evans, Samuel, 352.

F

Fairweather, Mr., 505, 506.
Farnsworth, Joseph, 267, 268, 414, 513, 515.
  Marah, 267.
  Mary, 268.
  Samuel, 82, 196.
Farren, Nathaniel, 127.
Fenton, Ann, 355.
Ferriss, Zachariah, 469.
ffernside, John, 619.
Field, John, 385.
  Mary, 385.
Filer, see Fyler.
Filer, Experience, 510.
  Samuel, 511.
  Stephen, 510.
  Thomas, 510.
Filler, Zerubbabell, 510.
Filley, Elizabeth, 61.
  John, 196, 197.
  Jonathan, 196, 197.
  Josiah, 196, 197.

Filley, Mary, 61.
  Samuel, 61, 196, 197.
  William, 61, 196, 197.
Fisk, John, 471.
  Phineas, 423.
Fiske, Joh:, 461.
  Phineas, 461.
Fitch, Alice, 505, 506, 507, 508.
  Bridget, 389, 505, 552.
  Ebenezer, 202, 224, 273, 359, 369, 374,
    375, 382, 389, 420, 453, 490, 505, 506,
    507, 508, 510, 552, 586, 626.
  Eleazer, 505, 507, 508.
  Elijah, 505, 506, 507, 508.
  James, 14, 505, 506, 507, 508.
  John, 11, 130, 131, 297, 505, 506, 507,
    508.
  Joseph, 182, 194, 252, 508.
  Martha, 62, 197.
  Medinah, 505, 506, 507, 508.
  Mr., 435.

Fitch, Samuel, 62, 159.
   Sarah, 62, 159, 197.
   Thomas, 62.
Flower, Francis, 496.
   Lamrock, 386.
Flowers, Ann, 386, 606.
   Elizabeth, 386.
   Francis, 386.
   Joseph, 386.
   Lamrock, 385, 386, 605, 606, 607.
   Lydia, 386.
   Mary, 386.
Foot, Nathaniel, 175, 323, 324, 494.
Foote, Daniel, 260.
   Margaret, 197, 198.
   Nathaniel, 57, 81, 93, 182, 197, 364, 562.
   Sarah, 323.
Forbes, David, 11, 12, 151, 198, 239, 350, 351.
   James, 198.
   John, 198, 477.
   Joseph, 198.
   Lucy, 184.
   Lydia, 198.
   Mary, 198, 527.
   Samuel, 198.
   Sarah, 12.
Forward, Deborah, 413.
   Samuel, 202.
Foster, Ann, 26, 78, 386.
   Bartholomew, 13.
   David, 160.
   Edward, 78, 79, 397, 591.
   Elizabeth, 398.
   Thomas, 215, 311, 402, 406, 592.
Fowdrie, James, 508.
Fowler, John, 589.
   Mary, 588, 589.
Fox, Abraham, 63, 236.
   Beriah, 62, 63, 508, 584.
   Ebenezer, 62, 63, 460, 508, 575, 584.
   Elizabeth, 205, 460, 541.
   John, 62.
   Joseph, 63, 514, 584.
   Richard, 62, 63, 236, 575.
Francis, Abigail, 199.
   Daniel, 199.
   Elizabeth, 405.
   Hannah, 199.
   James, 180, 199, 501.
   John, 198, 230, 361, 438.

Francis, Joseph, 199.
   Marcy, 199.
   Mary, 198, 199.
   Prudence, 199.
   Robert, 199.
   Sarah, 199.
   Sybbarance, 199.
   Thomas, 199.
Frank (negro), 508.
Frarey, Samuel, 332.
Frary, Joseph, 16, 491, 492, 617.
   Mr., 563.
   Samuel, 275, 276.
   Sarah, 360.
French, Thomas, 46.
Frisbie, Ebenezer, 352.
Fuller, Benjamin, 509.
   Daniel, 377.
   Edward, 509.
   Elizabeth, 386, 509.
   John, 4, 107, 185, 301, 387, 509, 510.
   Jonathan, 387.
   Joseph, 387, 509.
   Martha, 387.
   Mary, 488.
   Mehetabell, 107.
   Mehetable, 509.
   Mr., 561.
   Samuel, 386, 509.
   Shubael, 509.
   Stephen, 387.
   Thankful, 509.
   Thomas, 386, 387, 509, 510.
   Timothy, 4, 373, 559, 565, 617, 618.
   William, 387.
Fulshom, Rachel, 355.
Fyler, see Filer.
Fyler, Abigail, 199.
   Ann, 199.
   Bethesda, 8.
   Elizabeth, 200, 510.
   Experience, 200, 510.
   John, 423, 510, 511.
   Samuel, 199, 419, 420, 510, 511.
   Silas, 511.
   Stephen, 200, 510, 511, 549, 586.
   Thomas, 8, 9, 53, 199, 200, 411, 453, 510,
     511, 586, 611, 626.
   Zerubbabell, 8, 200, 510, 511.

G

Gailer, see Gaylor, Gaylord.
Gailer, Naomey, 479.
Gains, Anna, 350.
   Daniel, 389.

Gains, Hannah, 63.
   John, 49, 205, 287, 309, 490, 491.
   Samuel, 63, 293, 575, 592.
Gardner, Benjamin, 17, 201.

Gardner, Margaret, 201.
  Martha, 201.
  Moses, 201.
  Mr., 196.
  Peter, 201.
  Samuel, 82.
  Sarah, 201, 622.
Garret, Sarah, 441.
Gary, Mehetabell, 439.
Gates, Daniel, 511, 559.
  Dorothy, 488.
  Elizabeth, 201, 202.
  George, 511.
  Hannah, 160, 161.
  Jacob, 201, 202.
  Jeremiah, 559.
  John, 201.
  Jonathan, 201, 202.
  Joseph, 201, 202.
  Patience, 201, 202.
  Samuel, 201, 202, 511.
  Sarah, 201, 202, 488.
  Susannah, 201.
  Thomas, 70, 160, 161, 201, 301, 302, 324, 353, 373, 511, 618.
Gaylor, see Gailer, Gaylord.
Gaylor, Eleazer, 173, 202.
  John, 388.
  Nathaniel, 219.
Gaylord, see Gailer, Gaylor.
Gaylord, Abigail, 388.
  Alexander, 387, 388.
  Ann, 387, 388.
  Charles, 387, 388.
  Eleazer, 8, 35, 53, 202, 337, 512.
  Elizabeth, 202, 388, 512.
  Ensign, 505, 506.
  Esther, 388.
  Hannah, 202, 387, 388.
  Hezekiah, 388.
  John, 353, 387, 388, 561.
  Joseph, 388.
  Josiah, 388.
  Margaret, 512.
  Martha, 202.
  Mary, 574.
  Millicent, 512.
  Mr., 392.
  Nathaniel, 53, 56, 219, 308, 322, 388.
  Rachell, 388.
  Ruth, 388.
  Samuel, 202, 512.
  Sarah, 118, 202.
  William, 515, 531.
Gibbs, Abigail, 202, 203.
  Benjamin, 389, 411.
  Easter, 202, 203.
  Ebenezer, 202, 203.

Gibbs, Eliza, 57.
  Elizabeth, 202, 203.
  Experience, 57.
  Henry, 100.
  Jacob, 100, 202, 203, 313, 333, 470, 476, 485.
  John, 202, 203.
  Mary, 202, 203.
  Mirriam, 57.
  Samuel, 8, 56, 57, 388, 389.
Gibbins, William, 14.
Gibbon, William, 66.
Giddings, Jasper, 501.
Giffie, Caleb, 517.
  Thomas, 517.
Gilbert, Abigail, 389.
  Amy, 63.
  Benjamin, 40, 63, 64, 81, 108, 139, 203, 204.
  Caleb, 56.
  Dorothy, 121.
  Ebenezer, 10, 64, 65, 66, 119, 121, 243, 292, 570.
  Eleazer, 512.
  George, 389.
  Hannah, 203, 204.
  J., 181, 495.
  John, 512, 514, 581.
  Jonathan, 582.
  Joseph, 66, 207, 302, 368, 369, 464, 498, 504, 524.
  Josiah, 63, 64.
  Mary, 64, 65, 66, 109, 203, 204, 397, 398, 513.
  Moses, 63.
  Mr., 292.
  Mrs., 120, 121.
  Nathaniel, 512.
  Samuel, 64, 323, 440.
  Sarah, 122.
  Theodore, 501.
  Thomas, 64, 65, 66, 103.
Giles, Samuel, 404.
Gill, Ebenezer, 204, 205.
  John, 15, 143, 204, 205.
  Joshua, 204, 205.
  Judith, 204, 205.
  Mr., 121.
  Richard, 204, 205.
Gillett, Abigail, 205.
  Abner, 399.
  Benjamin, 351.
  Cornelius, 45, 46, 205, 206.
  Daniel, 205.
  Hannah, 370.
  Hester, 205.
  Joanna, 205.
  John, 17.

Gillett, Jonathan, 22, 363, 502.
    Joseph, 393, 546, 550.
    Josiah, 196.
    Mary, 205, 389, 399, 429.
    Miriam, 56, 57.
    Nathan, 530.
    Nathaniel, 333, 363, 485, 624.
    Priscilla, 46, 205.
    Rebeckah, 351.
    Sarah, 205, 317, 393.
    William, 37, 389, 429, 430.
Gillum, Jeames, 574.
Gilman, Elizabeth, 479.
    Solomon, 248, 249.
Gilsman, Richard, 262, 366.
Ginnings, Abda (a mulatto), 58.
Gipson, John, 567.
    Roger, 563, 564.
    Samuel, 190, 191, 244, 286, 289, 290, 486, 563, 567, 596, 615, 616.
    Thomas, 144.
Goff, Elizabeth, 231, 589.
    Ephraim, 513.
    Jacob, 256, 513.
    Mercy, 58.
    Philip, 105, 112, 187, 200, 230, 256, 295, 381, 513.
    Samuel, 229, 231.
Goffe, Aaron, 206.
    Benjamin, 206.
    David, 206.
    Ephraim, 206.
    Gershom, 206.
    Hannah, 206.
    Jacob, 206.
    Jerusha, 206.
    Mary, 191.
    Moses, 58, 206.
    Philip, 206, 513.
    Samuel, 206.
    Solomon, 191, 206.
Goodman, Richard, 99.
Goodrich, Abigail, 345, 346, 347.
    Allen, 346, 553.
    Allyn, 554.
    Benjamin, 247.
    David, 28, 51, 52, 54, 80, 164, 188, 201, 245, 246, 313, 317, 324, 342, 344, 345, 346, 347, 468, 514, 581.
    Ebenezer, 511.
    Eleazer, 347, 584.
    Elizabeth, 345.
    Elizer, 239, 267, 345, 346.
    Ephraim, 52, 112, 170, 185, 190, 231, 323, 325, 332, 333, 375, 513, 514.
    Grace, 109.
    Hannah, 165.
    Jacob, 245, 267.

Goodrich, Jerusha, 325.
    John, 62, 105, 227, 245, 345.
    Jonathan, 360.
    Joseph, 513, 514, 584, 595.
    Josiah, 345, 346, 515, 628.
    Mr., 52, 550.
    Prudence, 345.
    Richard, 315, 316, 466.
    Susannah, 513.
    Thomas, 315.
    William, 27, 51, 198, 230, 245, 325, 361, 513, 537, 596.
Goodwin, ———, 304.
    Eleazer, 500, 501.
    Elizabeth, 104, 113, 207, 208.
    Eunice, 208, 274.
    Hannah, 500, 501, 550.
    Hezekiah, 543, 596.
    Isaac, 551.
    John, 18, 207, 208, 299, 340.
    Lois, 208, 274.
    Mary, 208.
    Mehetabell, 551.
    Nathaniel, 170, 179, 207, 208, 235, 243, 269, 270, 274, 300, 304, 368, 369, 370, 480, 481, 485, 487, 493, 498, 499, 546, 567, 622.
    Ozias, 207, 208, 593.
    Samuel, 207, 208.
    Sarah, 381, 551.
    Thomas, 381.
    William, 94, 142, 450.
Gordon, James, 402.
Goring, Sarah, 390.
    William, 390.
Goron, Sarah, 390.
    William, 390.
Goslin, Bethiah, 514.
    Elizabeth, 514.
    Henry, 514.
    Mary, 514.
    Thomas, 514.
    Timothy, 514.
    William, 514.
Gove, Bethiah, 355.
Graham, Benjamin, 19, 58, 66, 90, 114, 133, 134, 156, 172, 250, 330, 357, 514, 515.
    Christopher, 468, 577.
    Hannah, 515.
    Hezekiah, 52.
    Isaac, 515.
    John, 515.
    Joseph, 159, 230, 231, 256, 285, 343.
    Mary, 514, 515.
    Samuel, 515.
    Sarah, 133, 447, 514.
Grant, Abigail, 8, 208.
    Adoniram, 516.

Grant, David, 208.
  Ebenezer, 208.
  Elizabeth, 573.
  Ephraim, 208, 516.
  Grace, 208, 209.
  Jehiel, 517.
  John, 8, 485, 573.
  Josiah, 182.
  Martha, 516.
  Mary Olmsted, 557.
  Matthew, 97, 158, 182, 208, 209, 240, 281,
    391, 420, 471, 479.
  Noah, 208, 515, 516.
  Rachell, 66, 67.
  Samuel, 46, 208, 391.
  Sarah, 8, 182, 183, 421.
  Solomon, 516.
  Tahan, 82.
  Thomas, 8, 421, 465, 517, 565.
Grave, Elizabeth, 67, 134.
  George, 55.
  John, 67, 68, 134.
  Mabel, 134.
  Mehetabell, 67.
  Sarah, 67, 68.
  Susannah, 67, 134.
Graves, Deliverance, 209, 550.
  Elizabeth, 209.
  Jemima, 361.
  John, 137, 138, 286.
  Joseph, 354.
  Lydia, 286.
  Martha, 68.
  Mary, 286.
  Mr., 321.
  Mrs., 138.
  Nathaniel, 68.
  Sarah, 209.
  Thomas, 209.
Green, Samuel, 435, 436, 543, 587.
Greenfield, Hannah, 436.
Greenwood, Samuel, 426.
Gridley, Daniel, 209, 210.
  Elizabeth, 178.
  Esther, 210.
  Hannah, 539.
  Hezekiah, 209, 210.
  James, 210, 493.
  John, 210.
  Joseph, 209, 210.
  Mary, 209, 210, 273.
  Mr., 445.
  Nathaniel, 209, 210.
  Ruth, 210, 211.
  Samuel, 209, 210, 219, 482.
  Sarah, 210.
  Thomas, 178, 210, 574.
Griffee, John, 69, 70.

Griffee, Mehetabell, 69, 70.
  Thomas, 69, 70.
Griffin, Alyce, 517.
  Anna, 517.
  Benoni, 392.
  Elizabeth, 391, 517.
  Ephraim, 517, 533, 595.
  John, 391, 392.
  Mary, 391.
  Mindwell, 517.
  Nathaniel, 211, 392.
  Ruth, 391.
  Sheba, 517.
  Silence, 517.
  Stephen, 391, 392.
  Thomas, 211, 391, 392.
Grimes, Benjamin, 250.
  Henry, 112.
  John, 205, 206.
  Joseph, 158, 184, 206, 230, 332, 333, 343,
    496, 513, 530, 600.
Griswold, Abell, 518.
  Abigail, 71, 388.
  Benjamin, 71.
  Daniel, 70, 71, 72, 392.
  Deborah, 518.
  Edward, 71, 123, 211, 333, 334.
  Elizabeth, 388.
  Francis, 392, 393.
  George, 70, 71, 72, 393, 518.
  Jacob, 155, 323, 465, 469, 470, 536, 600.
  John, 71, 313, 388, 417, 418.
  Jonah, 518.
  Jonathan, 617.
  Joseph, 70, 392, 393, 421, 517, 518.
  Lois, 517, 518.
  Mary, 71, 199, 203, 344, 345, 392, 393,
    617.
  Matthew, 370, 392, 419, 518.
  Michael, 119, 181, 183, 203, 204, 246,
    306, 307.
  Mr., 71.
  Nathaniel, 421.
  Pellatiah, 393.
  Roger, 518.
  Samuel, 199, 223, 388, 391, 392, 517,
    523, 524, 525, 529, 544, 588, 595.
  Sarah, 612.
  Shubael, 518.
  Thomas, 71, 191, 211, 272, 313, 333, 370,
    392, 400, 401, 417.
Gross, Isaac, 393.
  Jonah, 464, 609.
Grover, Elizabeth, 618.
  Joseph, 618.
Gunn, John, 334.
  Mary, 333.

H

Hadlock, Elizabeth, 217.
James, 294.
Hager (negro), 254.
Haies, see Hayes, Hays.
Haies, George, 544.
Hail, see Hale.
Hail, John, 72.
Haines, see Haynes.
Haines, John, 64.
Hale, see Hail.
Hale, Benezer, 213.
Benjamin, 211, 212, 213, 214.
David, 211, 212, 213, 214.
Ebenezer, 54, 225, 337.
Eunice, 519.
John, 72, 225.
Jonathan, 211, 212, 213, 214, 236, 372, 412, 580, 588, 596.
Mary, 83, 194, 211, 212, 213, 214, 518, 519.
Naomi, 88, 519.
Phebe, 213.
Ruth, 54, 212, 519.
Samuel, 63, 89, 194, 211, 212, 213, 214, 225, 227, 248, 377, 519.
Thomas, 63, 83, 84, 156, 194, 213, 225, 227, 246, 247, 261, 372, 377, 518, 519, 613.
Timothy, 518, 519.
Hall, Benjamin, 394.
Daniel, 49, 215, 393, 468, 512, 519, 598.
Elisha, 394.
Elizabeth, 214, 215.
Frances, 216.
Francis, 96.
Gershom, 394.
Giles, 49, 215, 389, 402, 490, 566, 593.
Hannah, 124, 393.
Jacob, 215.
John, 15, 48, 49, 74, 77, 85, 120, 131, 135, 136, 214, 215, 216, 250, 394, 473.
Jonathan, 215, 588.
Joseph, 11, 394.
Mary, 96, 216, 257, 394.
Nathaniel, 394.
Phebe, 598.
Richard, 215.
Samuel, 85, 110, 160, 162, 204, 205, 214, 215, 218, 287, 303, 308, 309, 330, 411, 490, 534, 566, 570, 583, 613.
Thomas, 214, 562.
William, 394.
Haly, see Hely.
Haly, Elizabeth, 250.
Hames, John, 402.

Hamlin, Edward, 591.
Elizabeth, 394.
Giles, 121, 216, 250, 394.
Jabez, 566, 593, 614.
John, 16, 39, 40, 47, 48, 72, 109, 110, 115, 116, 121, 124, 131, 135, 136, 215, 216, 256, 257, 285, 303, 308, 330, 352, 356, 394, 457, 492, 610.
Mr., 116.
William, 566, 581, 582, 592.
Hammond, Mary, 573.
Hampton, Anne, 394, 395.
William, 394, 395.
Hancox, Daniel, 396.
John, 396.
Rachel, 396.
Thomas, 396.
William, 396.
Hand, Benjamin, 39.
Esther, 216, 217.
Janna, 216, 217.
Joseph, 216.
Richard, 222.
Sarah, 344, 345.
Handerson, see Hannison.
Handerson, James, 67, 68, 101, 217, 218, 235.
Martha, 217, 218.
Mehetabell, 68.
Sarah, 217, 218.
Hanmer, Francis, 189.
Hanna (negro), 254.
Hannah (negro), 166.
Hannah (Indian woman), 269.
Hannison, see Handerson.
Hannison, James, 67, 68.
Harbert, Benjamin, 24.
Christian, 24.
Harbord, Benjamin, 24.
Jane, 24.
Harris, Abraham, 520.
Daniel, 45, 50, 72, 73, 74, 218, 357, 519, 598.
Elizabeth, 24, 25, 28.
Ephraim, 218.
John, 73, 74, 86, 218, 223, 236, 407, 427.
Mary, 74, 80, 218, 235, 236, 396.
Mr., 45, 397, 398, 486.
Samuel, 218.
Sarah, 73, 291.
Tabithy, 74.
Thomas, 73, 74, 218, 266, 519, 520.
Walter, 80, 290, 396, 581.
William, 39, 73, 85, 162, 218, 236, 356, 396, 397, 407, 411, 427, 446.
Hart, Abigail, 404.

Hart, Ebenezer, 520.
  Elizabeth, 522, 523.
  Esther, 210.
  Hannah, 437.
  Hezekiah, 421, 520, 521.
  Howkins, 520, 521.
  Isaac, 219, 421, 422, 532, 570.
  Jeams, 522.
  John, 28, 106, 110, 112, 132, 162, 179, 218, 219, 220, 241, 273, 274, 281, 282, 312, 342, 371, 399, 408, 422, 428, 431, 434, 437, 442, 443, 493, 498, 520, 521, 522, 538, 554, 628.
  Joseph, 34, 522.
  Josiah, 29, 167, 458, 521, 538, 604.
  Mary, 34, 218, 219, 404.
  Matthew, 218, 219.
  Mr., 521.
  Nathaniel, 218, 219, 404.
  Ruth, 520.
  Samuel, 219, 404, 522, 523.
  Sarah, 219.
  Stephen, 162, 522.
  Thomas, 36, 162, 221, 292, 312, 396, 421, 422, 493, 520, 521, 522, 523.
  William, 521, 522, 523.
Haskins, see Hoskins.
Haskins, John, 197.
Hasseltine, see Hazeltine.
Hasseltine, John, 498.
Hatch, Joseph, 628, 629.
  Timothy, 628, 629.
Haward, see Hayward, Howard, Howd.
Haward, Samuel, 165.
Hawley, Benjamin, 523.
  Hannah, 523.
  Hope, 523.
  Jehial, 523.
  Joseph, 33, 34, 35, 126, 242, 283, 312, 375, 434, 436.
  Samuel Stow, 523.
Hayden, see Heyden.
Hayden, Daniel, 21, 219, 270.
  Ebenezer, 219, 467.
  Elizabeth, 389.
  Hannah, 219.
  Miriam, 219, 220.
  Samuel, 219, 272, 417, 612.
  William, 219.
Haydon, see Heydon.
Haydon, Samuel, 401, 530.
Hayes, see Haies, Hays.
Hayes, Abigail, 399, 523, 524.
  Benjamin, 523, 524.
  Daniel, 523, 524.
  Doritha, 524.
  Elizabeth, 74, 75.
  George, 523, 524, 545.

Hayes, Jane, 545.
  Johanna, 524.
  Luke, 74, 75, 118, 220, 221.
  Mary, 524.
  Maudlin, 220, 221.
  Samuel, 524.
  Sarah, 524.
  Thankfull, 524.
  William, 524.
Haynes, see Haines.
Haynes, John, 75, 76, 104, 132, 150, 221, 258, 304, 336, 524.
  Joseph, 75, 76, 398.
  Mabell, 75, 221.
  Mary, 75, 76, 221, 398, 524.
  Mr., 221.
  Sarah, 75.
Hays, see Haies, Hayes.
Hays, Samuel, 545.
Hayward, see Haward, Howard, Howd.
Hayward, Elizabeth, 621, 623.
  Hannah, 623.
  John, 619, 620, 623, 624.
  Samuel, 623.
  Sarah, 623.
Hazeltine, see Hasseltine.
Hazeltine, John, 526.
Heacox, Mercy, 343, 344.
Hebard, see Hebbard, Hibbard, **Hobart,** Hubbard.
Hebard, Robert, 3, 222.
Hebbard, see Hebard, Hibbard, **Hubbard,** Hobart.
Hebbard, Abigail, 222.
  Hannah, 222.
  Sarah, 222.
Hely, see Haly.
Hely, Marcy, 38.
Hemsted, Elizabeth, 76, 77.
  Hannah, 76.
  Josiah, 76, 77.
  Lucy, 77.
  Mary, 76.
  Patience, 77.
  Phebe, 77.
  Robert, 76.
Hendee, Richard, 222.
Henning, Andrew, 524, 595.
Hewitt, Sarah, 554.
Heyden, see Hayden.
Heyden, Elizabeth, 220.
  Mary, 220.
  Mr., 322.
Heydon, see Haydon.
Heydon, Daniel, 99, 322, 338.
  Ebenezer, 220.
  Elizabeth, 220.
  Mary, 220.

Heydon, Miriam, 220.
Hibbard, see Hebard, Hebbard, Hobart, Hubbard.
Hibbard, Abigail, 222.
   Ebenezer, 222.
   Hannah, 222.
   Joseph, 222.
   Mary, 222.
   Nathaniel, 222.
   Robert, 222.
   Sarah, 222.
Hickcock, Thomas, 318.
   William, 318.
Hickcocks, Thomas, 407.
   William, 326, 407.
Hickcox, William, 226, 280, 326.
Hickock, Mr., 106.
Hickox, Thomas, 407.
   William, 407.
Hide, Timothy, 222, 223, 267.
Higbee, Edward, 457.
Higby, Edward, 77.
   John, 77.
   Rebeckah, 77.
Higginson, Elizabeth, 399.
   Margaret, 399.
   Mary, 399.
   Sarah, 399.
   William, 399.
Higley, Abigail, 223.
   Ann, 154, 391, 398, 399, 525.
   Anna, 223.
   Anne, 398.
   Brewster, 223, 224, 225, 398, 399.
   David, 398.
   Elizabeth, 223.
   Isaac, 223, 224, 398.
   John, 22, 28, 135, 145, 223, 224, 225, 271, 276, 293, 346, 398, 399, 523, 524, 525, 544.
   Jonathan, 153, 154, 155, 211, 223, 293, 391, 398, 399, 525.
   Joseph, 223, 224, 225.
   Josiah, 223, 398.
   Katharine, 223.
   Mary, 391.
   Mercy, 398, 525.
   Mindwell, 223.
   Nathaniel, 223, 398, 510, 511.
   Samuel, 223, 224, 391, 398, 399, 430, 589, 624.
   Sarah, 223, 224.
   Susannah, 223.
Hill, see Hills.
Hill, Ann, 78.
   Benoni, 226.
   Charles, 76, 77.
   Dorothy, 526, 527.

Hill, Ebenezer, 473.
   Eleazer, 6, 107, 108, 370, 390, 525.
   Elizabeth, 226, 317, 525, 589.
   Henry, 226.
   Isaac, 473.
   John, 77, 380.
   Jonathan, 18, 114, 186, 249, 372, 526.
   Joseph, 226, 248.
   Luke, 473.
   Margaret, 380.
   Mary, 77.
   Samuel, 248.
   Sarah, 78, 525, 589.
   Susannah, 78, 79.
   Thankful, 120, 527.
   Thomas, 77, 78, 79.
Hillier, see Hillyer, Hilyer.
Hillier, James, 238, 359, 399, 400, 482, 483.
   Jane, 359.
   Mary, 348, 399, 400.
Hillior, James, 503.
Hilliyer, Andrew, 17.
Hills, see Hill.
Hills, Abigail, 526.
   Benjamin, 225, 460, 526.
   David, 372, 373, 527.
   Dorothy, 225.
   Ebenezer, 144, 225.
   Eleazer, 548.
   Elizabeth, 447.
   John, 379.
   Jonathan, 10, 19, 225, 248, 250, 372, 484, 526, 527, 556.
   Joseph, 211, 225, 226, 527, 581.
   Rebeckah, 556.
   Samuel, 526, 527.
   Susannah, 78, 79, 526.
Hillyard, Mary, 90.
Hillyer, see Hillier, Hilyer.
Hillyer, James, 463, 524, 533, 534, 589.
   Mary, 533.
Hilyard, James, 588.
Hilyer, see Hillier, Hillyer.
Hilyer, James, 502, 525, 533.
   Jeams, 528.
   Mary, 525, 526.
Hinks, John, 259.
Hinsdale, see Hynsdale.
Hinsdale, Amos, 527, 528.
   Barnabas, 527, 528.
   Daniel, 527, 528.
   Elizabeth, 527, 528.
   Isaac, 179.
   Jacob, 527, 528.
   John, 527, 528.
   Martha, 527, 528.
   Mary, 527, 528.
   Sarah, 527, 528.

Hinsdall, Jacob, 558.
Hinsdell, Sarah, 137, 138.
Hitchcock, Ebenezer, 226.
    Elizabeth, 226, 605.
    Gideon, 226.
    Hannah, 226.
    John, 226, 227, 321.
    Luke, 321.
    Samuel, 226, 227.
    Sarah, 226.
    Silence, 226.
    Thomas, 226.
Hixley, Lydia, 524.
Hixson, Sarah, 137, 138.
Hobart, see Hebard, Hebbard, Hibbard,
    Hubbard.
Hobart, Elizabeth, 400.
    Jeremiah, 400.
Hodge, James, 227.
Hoit, see Hoite, Hoyte.
Hoit, Abigail, 45.
    Daniel, 45.
    David, 46.
    Jonathan, 511.
    Mary, 53.
    Mr., 53.
Hoite, see Hoit, Hoyte.
Hoite, David, 46.
Holcomb, Ann, 401.
    Benajah, 21, 22, 36, 59, 70, 123, 195, 219,
        272, 333, 400, 401, 421.
    Benjamin, 21, 464.
    Caleb, 529.
    David, 529.
    Elener, 529.
    Elizabeth, 517, 589.
    Experience, 529.
    Hannah, 529.
    Joel, 529.
    Jonathan, 332, 389, 399, 545.
    Joseph, 392, 401, 611.
    Joshua, 135, 349, 364, 366, 391, 392, 517,
        524, 528, 529.
    Martha, 401.
    Mary, 389, 392, 529.
    Matthew, 529.
    Mehetabell, 367.
    Mercy, 529.
    Miriam, 529.
    Nathaniel, 39, 123, 135, 243, 327, 341,
        364, 389, 399, 477, 555.
    Parnell, 401.
    Pernall, 401.
    Phineas, 529.
    Samuel, 199, 393, 400, 401.
    Thankful, 529.
    Thomas, 38, 153, 189, 211, 223, 224, 293,
        327, 331, 364, 391, 392, 398, 517, 524,
        525, 551, 555, 595.

Holiberd, Joseph, 530.
Holliberd, Joseph, 530.
Hollister, Abigail, 81.
    Abijah, 80.
    Daniel, 229.
    David, 227, 541.
    Dorothy, 226.
    Elizabeth, 79, 80, 105, 227, 228, 229, 230,
        231, 402.
    Ephraim, 227.
    Eunice, 229.
    Gershom, 229, 292.
    Jacob, 230, 231, 402.
    Jerusha, 230.
    John, 79, 80, 167, 175, 227, 229, 315, 316,
        323, 581.
    Jonathan, 79, 80, 228, 229, 230, 231, 311,
        324, 530.
    Joseph, 80, 185, 225, 227, 228.
    Lazarus, 79, 80, 227.
    Martha, 95.
    Mary, 230, 231.
    Nathaniel, 228.
    Samuel, 228.
    Sarah, 79, 227.
    Stephen, 79, 105, 213, 228, 229, 230, 231,
        324.
    Thomas, 79, 80, 128, 229, 230, 377.
Hollybush, Sarah, 242.
Holman, Abigail, 530.
    Ebenezer, 530, 531.
    Katharine, 530.
    Katherine, 549.
    Mr., 530.
    Samuel, 530, 531, 549.
Holmes, John, 354, 531, 571.
    Jonas, 582.
    Richard, 490.
Holton, Mr., 232.
    Sarah, 231.
    William, 231.
Holyoke, Thomas, 81.
Honeywell, see Hunewell, Hunnewell.
Honeywell, Elizabeth, 218.
    John, 236.
Honneywell, John, 237.
Hooker, Abigail, 118, 233, 404, 582.
    Alice, 233, 403.
    Benjamin, 464.
    Daniel, 141, 165, 195, 402, 403, 404, 406.
    Hannah, 404.
    Hezekiah, 399, 532.
    James, 403, 404.
    John, 31, 32, 34, 118, 126, 220, 221, 233,
        403, 404, 432, 437, 467, 522, 538, 555,
        559, 578.
    Joseph, 404, 555.
    Mary, 232, 233, 304, 403, 404, 567.
    Nathaniel, 12, 19, 140, 157, 232, 233, 317,
        346, 404.

Hooker, Roger, 404.
 Samuel, 31, 74, 115, 403, 404, 422, 429, 445, 446.
 Sarah, 233.
 Thomas, 150, 214, 258, 402, 403, 404, 459, 567.
 William, 404.
Hopewell, Sarah (Indian woman), 81.
Hopkins, Anna, 235.
 Asa, 531, 532.
 Consider, 322, 531, 532.
 Dorcas, 235, 236.
 Ebenezer, 35, 43, 78, 81, 234.
 Elias, 531, 532.
 Elizabeth, 476, 531, 532.
 Hannah, 81, 235, 236, 286.
 Hezekiah, 234.
 Isaac, 234.
 John, 106, 226, 278, 280, 326, 531, 532.
 Jonathan, 234, 552.
 Joseph, 81, 101, 180, 217, 234, 235.
 Mary, 234, 235.
 Rachel, 81.
 Robert, 476.
 Ruth, 235, 236.
 Sarah, 81, 234.
 Stephen, 81, 86, 87, 234.
 Thomas, 81, 86, 87, 235, 236, 594.
Hopson, Elizabeth, 233, 234.
 John, 233, 234.
 Mary, 233.
Horsford, see Hosford.
Horsford, Mr., 200.
 Nathaniel, 333, 334, 388.
 Timothy, 17, 333.
Horton, Benony, 471.
 Mary, 592.
Hosford, see Horsford.
Hosford, Nathaniel, 200, 203, 336.
Hoskins, see Haskins.
Hoskins, Anthony, 81, 82, 83, 192.
 John, 82, 83.
 Joseph, 82, 529.
 Mary, 82, 296.
 Robert, 82, 223.
 Thomas, 82, 489.
Hosmer, Anne, 604.
 Stephen, 238, 571.
 Thomas, 43, 146, 147, 179, 180, 222, 237, 258, 270, 291, 295, 299, 305, 307, 313, 329, 357, 405, 408, 431, 449, 450, 558, 602, 604.
Hosmore, Thomas, 269.
Hossington, Elisha, 532.
 Elizabeth, 532.
 John, 532.
House, Anne, 83.
 Daniel, 545.

House, Eunice, 236.
 John, 62, 63, 83, 84, 236.
 Joseph, 83, 84, 236.
 Sarah, 236.
 Silence, 236.
 William, 83, 84.
Howard, see Haward, Hayward, Howd.
Howard, Abigail, 405.
 Alice, 233, 603.
 Benjamin, 236.
 Elizabeth, 624.
 Henry, 84, 85.
 John, 84, 85, 146, 147, 171, 325, 361, 404, 405, 621, 624.
 Jonathan, 405.
 Lydia, 84, 405.
 Margaret, 404, 405.
 Mary, 84, 236, 405.
 Ruth, 405.
 Samuel, 30, 36, 55, 84, 127, 146, 147, 168, 242, 328, 405, 406.
 Sarah, 84, 85, 405.
 Susannah, 405, 406, 450.
 William, 201, 405.
Howd, see Haward, Hayward, Howard.
Howd, John, 446.
Howkins, Anthony, 521.
 Mr., 521.
Hoyte, see Hoit, Hoite.
Hoyte, Joshua, 375.
Hubbard, see Hebard, Hebbard, Hibbard, Hobart.
Hubbard, Bathsheba, 440.
 Daniel, 85, 591.
 David, 585.
 Ebenezer, 190, 591.
 Elizabeth, 440.
 George, 292, 532, 570.
 Hannah, 406.
 Jeremiah, 400.
 John, 89, 108, 194, 246, 247, 406, 518, 532.
 Jonathan, 406.
 Joseph, 16.
 Mabell, 108.
 Margaret, 85.
 Martha, 559.
 Mary, 85, 89, 95, 532.
 Mehetabell, 85.
 Mr., 276, 598.
 Nathaniel, 582.
 Rachel, 406.
 Richard, 48, 85.
 Robert, 393, 446.
 Samuel, 101, 206, 559.
 Sarah, 85.
Hubbart, Hannah, 406.
 John, 406.
Hubburd, Jeremiah, 400.

Hull, John, 134.
Humphrey, Abigail, 244.
  Bathsheba, 533, 534.
  Hannah, 237, 238.
  Hekiah, 533.
  Hepzibah, 533.
  Hezekiah, 533.
  John, 399, 431, 482, 533, 589.
  Jonathan, 273, 369, 429, 526.
  Martha, 238.
  Mary, 263, 533.
  Michael, 517, 533.
  Mr., 429.
  Samuel, 38, 113, 144, 196, 238, 262, 277, 331, 458, 526, 533, 534.
  Sarah, 503.
  Thomas, 237, 238, 263.
Humphreys, John, 359, 502, 590.
  Joseph, 244.
  Mary, 359.
  Samuel, 101, 359.
  Sarah, 502.
Humphries, Agnes, 237.
  John, 36, 38, 263, 331, 332, 391, 441, 463, 482, 483, 484, 589.
  Nathaniel, 237.
  Samuel, 91, 263, 485, 589.
Humphry, Samuel, 502.
Hunewell, see Honeywell, Hunnewell.
Hunewell, Bridget, 237.
  John, 237.
Hungerford, Deborah, 117.
  Elizabeth, 238.
  Esther, 144, 238.
  Green, 238, 301.
  John, 117, 238, 244, 300, 301.

Hungerford, Mary, 238.
  Sarah, 238.
  Susannah, 238.
  Thomas, 69, 238.
Hunlock, Elizabeth, 622.
Hunn, George, 239.
  Joseph, 239.
  Martha, 239.
  Nathaniel, 225, 239.
  Samuel, 13, 239, 247, 351, 455.
  Sarah, 380.
Hunnewell, Elizabeth, 236.
  John, 237.
Hunt, Anna, 534.
  Joseph, 534.
  Nathaniel, 534.
  Obadiah, 402.
Huntington, Jedediah, 508.
  John, 152.
  Mary, 178.
  Samuel, 178,
  Thomas, 130, 354, 355, 378, 394, 438.
Hurlbut, David, 244, 496, 592.
  Ebenezer, 173, 303, 534.
  Joseph, 62, 328.
  Mary, 468.
  Mrs., 55.
  Nathaniel, 591.
  Sibbell, 62.
  Thomas, 255, 314, 546, 591, 628.
Hurlbutt, David, 357.
  Stephen, 15.
Huxley, Experience, 389.
Hynsdale, see Hinsdale.
Hynsdale, Isaac, 449.

I

Ingersoll, Thomas, 412.
Ingram, Samuel, 353, 354, 423, 572.

Ishmail (negro), 42.

J

Jacob (negro), 186.
Jagger, Hannah, 375.
Jaggers, Jonathan, 53.
Janes, John, 386, 531.
  Mary, 86.
  Rachel, 86.
Jarrell, James, 288.
Jegcome, John, 550.
Jennings, Joseph, 406.
Jesse, David, 140, 141.
  Mary, 140, 141, 142, 258, 622.
  Mrs., 23.

Johnson, Daniel, 73, 407.
  David, 591.
  Elizabeth, 407.
  Isaac, 73, 74, 237, 356, 406, 407, 492.
  Jonathan, 407.
  Joseph, 45, 86, 407, 427.
  Mary, 73, 86, 240, 287, 406, 407.
  Mrs., 109.
  Nathaniel, 85, 86, 407.
  Samuel, 109, 287.
  Thomas, 614.
  William, 240.

Jones, Caleb, 178, 240.
  Hezekiah, 240.
  Isaac, 593.
  Rachel, 178.
  Rachell, 240.
  Sarah, 258, 450.
  Sylvanus, 240.
  William, 42.
Judd, Abigail, 534, 536.
  Anna, 535.
  Anthony, 475.
  Benjamin, 118, 119, 241, 407.
  Daniel, 32, 33, 34, 86, 241, 407, 433, 434,
    458, 466, 509, 534, 535, 539, 554, 555,
    559.
  Ebenezer, 407, 535, 536.
  Elizabeth, 86, 242, 536.
  Eunice, 241, 312, 408.
  Hannah, 20, 21, 407, 534.
  Joanna, 536.

Judd, John, 33, 35, 86, 87, 226, 241, 242, **277,**
    317, 318, 320, 407, 534.
  Jonathan, 310, 534.
  Joseph, 21, 33, 86, 434, 522, 535, **536,**
    574.
  Mary, 242, 428, 536.
  Philip, 242.
  Rachel, 86, 241, 407, 536.
  Rhoda, 241, 408.
  Ruth, 242.
  Samuel, 86, 241, 242, 307, 406, 407, **436,**
    437, 438, 508, 534, 538, 578.
  Sarah, 535.
  Thomas, 86, 87, 106, 131, 225, **227, 241,**
    242, 278, 280, 317, 318, 320, 407, **408,**
    409, 410, 424, 534, 535, 536.
  William, 86, 241, 242, 279, 407, 408, **424,**
    449, 475, 534, 535, 537.
Judson, Mary, 440.

K

Kady, Sarah, 90.
Keats, Richard, 242.
Keeney, Eunice, 236.
  Joseph, 225.
Keeny, Hannah, 226.
  Joseph, 19.
Kellog, Benjamin, 410.
  Daniel, 410.
  Isaac, 410.
  Jacob, 410.
  John, 410.
  Joseph, 410.
Kellogg, Abraham, 408, **409.**
  Abram, 408.
  Benjamin, 408, 409.
  Daniel, 408, 409.
  Eunice, 87, 88.
  Hannah, 87.
  Isaac, 408, 409, 501, 503, 551.
  Jacob, 408, 409.
  John, 408, 409, 410, 536, 539.
  Jonathan, 364.
  Joseph, 87, 88, 408, 409.
  Martin, 475.
  Miriam, 408, 409.
  Mrs., 408.
  Nathaniel, 87, 494.
  Samuel, 19, 21, 29, 44, 87, 88, **127, 232,**
    259, 260, 298, 329, 408, **409,** 410.
  Sarah, 408, 409, 410, 536, 546.
Kelsey, Abigail, 243.
  Charles, 243, 370.
  Daniel, 243.
  Dorothy, 163.

Kelsey, Elizabeth, 243, 244, 536.
  Hannah, 243, 244.
  James, 243.
  John, 14, 243.
  Mabel, 243, 244.
  Mark, 243, 244.
  Rachel, 243.
  Rebeckah, 243, 244.
  Ruth, 243, 244.
  Stephen, 243.
  Thomas, 243, 244, 536.
  William, 243, 515.
Kelsy, Mary, 164.
Kendall, Joshua, 377.
  Samuel, 257.
Kennard, John, 244.
Ker, William, 395.
Kerby, see Kirby.
Kerby, John, 245.
  Joseph, 244, 245.
  Susannah, 245.
Kibbe, Hannah, 243.
  James Allen, 619.
Kilbourn, Abraham, 51, 88, 171, 245, **246,**
    248, 316, 537.
  Abram, 412.
  Benjamin, 248.
  Daniel, 246, 247.
  David, 245, 248.
  Dorothy, 249.
  Ebenezer, 29, 88, 89, 128, 162, 245, **246,**
    247, 248, 360, 537.
  Eleazer, 246, 247.
  Elizabeth, 248, 519.

Kilbourn, George, 43, 88, 112, 119, 162, 171,
    176, 177, 179, 183, 199, 201, 245, 246,
    247, 325, 345, 537, 581.
  Grace, 246, 247.
  Hannah, 249.
  John, 88, 89, 185, 194, 245, 246, 247,
    248, 527.
  Jonathan, 246, 248.
  Joseph, 52, 88, 183, 360, 469, 537.
  Josiah, 246.
  Mabell, 249.
  Margaret, 246.
  Mary, 88, 594.
  Samuel, 245.
  Sarah, 88, 245, 246, 537.
  Susannah, 226, 249, 250.
  Thomas, 88, 225, 248, 249, 250.
Kilburn, Abraham, 181.
Kimberly, Abigail, 62.
  Abraham, 62.
  Eleazer, 89, 213, 321.
  Elizabeth, 89.
  Joseph, 62.
  Ruth, 89, 194, 213.
  Samuel, 213, 519.
  Thomas, 89, 95, 153, 184, 192, 194, 204,
    213, 214, 225, 226, 227, 229, 255,
    284, 303, 332, 368, 377, 396, 519, 527,
    548, 549.

King, Abigail, 250.
  Edward, 90.
  Hezekiah, 386.
  John, 90.
  Joseph, 142, 361.
  Mary, 134, 142, 250, 302.
  Mr., 340.
  Mrs., 622.
  Robert, 250.
  Sarah, 90.
  Thomas, 77, 90, 134, 250.
Kirby, see Kerby.
Kirby, John, 244, 245, 486, 614.
  Joseph, 244, 330, 486.
  Mary, 244.
  Mr., 73.
Kircum, Thomas, 227.
Kirkam, Henry, 625.
Kirkum, John, 464.
Kitchum, Sarah, 53.
Knap, Sarah, 629.
Knight, George, 90.
  John, 496.
  Sarah, 90.
Knott, William, 361.

L

Lamb, Rebecca, 32, 33.
  Samuel, 32, 33.
Lamson, Ebenezer, 545.
  Mary, 545.
Lancton, see Langton, Lankton.
Lancton, John, 74.
  Joseph, 74, 446.
  Samuel, 74, 75.
Landue, Peter, 538.
Lane, Ann, 410.
  Elizabeth, 251.
  Isaac, 191, 250, 251, 410, 591.
  John, 48, 250, 251, 410.
Langton, see Lancton, Lankton.
Langton, Elizabeth, 538.
  Joseph, 74, 75, 220.
Lankton, see Lancton, Langton.
Lankton, Samuel, 523.
Larrabee, Mr., 3.
Lattemore, Abigail, 251.
  Ann, 251, 252.
  Charles, 251, 252.
  David, 251, 252.
  John, 396.
  Jonathan, 251, 252.
  Mr., 551.

Lattimer, Abigail, 251.
  Bezaleel, 256.
  John, 127, 129, 132, 246.
  Jonathan, 231, 251.
  Luther, 537.
  Mary, 231.
  Wickham, 537.
Lattimere, John, 320.
Lattimore, Bezaleel, 176.
  Elizabeth, 537.
  John, 176, 247.
  Luther, 537.
  Sybill, 176.
Law, Jonathan, 42.
  Samuel, 277.
  Sarah, 42.
Lawrence, John, 538.
  Mary Ann, 538.
Laws, Jonathan, 42.
  Sarah, 41, 42.
Layns, William, 117.
Leaming, Jeremiah, 442.
Leazer (negro), 254.
Lee, David, 240.
  Elizabeth, 538.
  Hezekiah, 538.

Lee, Isaac, 119.
　John, 44, 241, 242, 538.
　Jonathan, 475, 538.
　Lydia, 481.
　Mary, 482.
　Ruth, 538.
　Samuel, 538.
　Stephen, 32, 119, 239.
　Thomas, 498.
Leet, Abigail, 368.
Leete, Abigail, 368, 369.
　Caleb, 368.
　Gideon, 591.
　John, 592.
Lefeavor, Philip, 90.
Leffingwell, Hannah, 190.
　Mary, 284.
Leonard, Sarah, 51, 52.
Lester, Daniel, 482.
　John, 482.
　Mary, 323.
Lewcas, see Lucas.
Lewcas, Deborah, 591.
　Gideon, 592.
　William, 592.
Lewis, Abigail, 252, 375.
　Edmund, 505, 506.
　Elizabeth, 216, 377, 553.
　Ezekiel, 98.
　Gershom, 436, 437.
　Hannah, 614.
　Isaac, 539, 559.
　John, 91, 252, 539.
　Joseph, 90, 91, 226, 278, 317, 318, 423.
　Josiah, 539.
　Malachi, 614.
　Mary, 450, 539.
　Nathan, 539.
　Nathaniel, 554, 559.
　Nehemiah, 539.
　Samuel, 29, 216, 371, 539.
Liman, Abigail, 412.
Long, Jerusha, 539.
　Joseph, 539.
　Samuel, 252.
　Sarah, 252.
　Thomas, 252.
　William, 539, 540.
Loomis, Abigail, 196, 253.
　Amos, 254.
　Ann, 10, 540.
　Anne, 254.
　Benjamin, 241, 457, 508, 540.
　Charles, 364.
　Daniel, 6, 91, 107, 108, 150, 154, 253,
　　254, 260, 263, 337, 338, 370, 440,
　　453, 489, 525.
　Ebenezer, 253.
　Elizabeth, 154, 244.
　Esther, 253.

Loomis, Hannah, 254.
　Ichabod, 254.
　Isaac, 91.
　Israel, 253, 254.
　James, 253.
　Jemima, 253.
　Joanna, 7, 57, 457.
　Joannah, 389.
　Job, 243, 244, 260, 261, 489.
　John, 594, 627.
　Jonathan, 91.
　Joseph, 502.
　Joshua, 626.
　Josiah, 243, 536, 564.
　Mary, 253, 254, 281.
　Moses, 389, 626.
　Nathaniel, 59, 87, 90, 91, 149, 253, 260,
　　322, 338, 383, 440.
　Noah, 262, 496.
　Odiah, 254.
　Rebeckah, 254.
　Samuel, 87, 181, 233, 322, 323, 562.
　Sarah, 91, 253, 254, 416.
　Stephen, 91, 253, 254, 519.
　Timothy, 6, 7, 10, 18, 91, 107, 150, 244,
　　253, 254, 260, 261, 263, 272, 370, 401,
　　413, 418, 457, 476, 489, 525, 549,
　　561, 562, 626.
　Uriah, 254.
Lord, Abigail, 254.
　Elisha, 255, 272, 540, 541, 621, 622.
　Elizabeth, 255, 540, 621.
　Epaphras, 255, 540, 621, 622.
　Hannah, 4.
　Ichabod, 255, 540, 621, 622.
　Jerusha, 255.
　John, 4.
　John Haynes, 524, 540, 541.
　Mary, 255, 524, 540, 541.
　Mary Jones, 240.
　Richard, 67, 75, 103, 254, 255, 360, 367,
　　472, 540, 621, 622.
Loveland, Samuel, 310, 588.
　Thomas, 586.
Loveman, Benjamin, 541.
　Children, 541.
　Elisha, 541.
　Elizabeth, 541.
　Joseph, 541.
　Mary, 541.
　Sarah, 541.
　Thomas, 541.
Lucas, see Lewcas.
Lucas, Daniel, 92.
　Easter, 92.
　John, 92.
　Mary, 92.
　Mr., 39.
　Thankful, 92.
Lynn, John, 575.

M

Macky, Anna, 256.
 Daniel, 256.
 Elizabeth, 256.
 John, 256.
 Mary, 256, 291.
 Samuel, 256.
Mahametups (Indian), 100.
Maken, John, 102, 483.
Maltbie, John, 412.
Mansfield, John, 419, 420, 541, 542.
 Sarah, 541, 542.
Manure, Philip, 256.
Margaret (Indian girl), 590.
Mark, Jonathan, 542.
 Joseph, 542.
 Mary, 542.
 Sarah, 542.
 William, 542, 543.
Markham, Daniel, 256, 257, 397.
 Edith, 257.
 James, 257.
 Martha, 257.
 Patience, 257, 397, 398.
 William, 592.
Marks, Sarah, 592, 593.
 Thomas, 592, 593.
Marsh, Ann, 544.
 Elizabeth, 102, 103.
 Hannah, 544.
 Hepzibah, 544.
 John, 102, 104, 133, 207, 287, 303, 356,
  368, 434, 435, 543, 544.
 Jonathan, 8, 382, 450, 451, 543, 544, 612.
 Joseph, 543.
 Nathaniel, 102, 171, 272, 487, 497, 543,
  544, 564.
 Sarah, 544.
Marshall, Benjamin, 92.
 Eliakim, 36, 124, 423, 510.
 Elizabeth, 92, 411, 594.
 Joel, 411.
 Mary, 92, 93, 411.
 Mr., 36.
 Samuel, 411.
 Sarah, 411.
 Thomas, 17, 18, 92, 93, 108, 153, 192,
  256, 270, 463, 511, 572.
Marshfield, Josiah, 66, 231.
 Rachell, 64, 65.
Maskpooh (Indian), 100.
Mason, Ann, 257, 258.
 John, 76.
 Jonathan, 181, 258, 379.
 Samuel, 101.
 Susannah, 379, 380.
Masshoot, Robin (Indian), 81.

Mather, Asrahiah, 544.
 Atherton, 8, 21, 403.
 Azariah, 412.
 Cotton, 425.
 Elizabeth, 309.
 Hannah, 476.
 Increase, 425.
 John, 412, 544.
 Joseph, 309, 544.
 Mr., 8, 392.
 Nathaniel, 427, 544.
 Rebeckah, 59.
 Samuel, 7, 8, 9, 57, 59, 60, 100, 383, 384,
  389, 453, 476, 544, 590, 591.
 William, 59, 458, 544.
Matson, Edward, 545.
 Elizabeth, 545.
 Esther, 545.
 John, 189, 544, 545.
 Joshua, 545.
 Mary, 545.
Maudsley, see Modsley.
Maudsley, Abner, 580.
 Isaac, 413.
 Joseph, 413.
May, Anne, 582.
 Hezekiah, 184, 513.
 Samuel, 582.
Meacham, Joseph, 385.
Meakin, John, 484.
Meakings, John, 484.
Meakins, Abigail, 545, 546.
 Hannah, 94, 545, 546.
 John, 93, 94, 103, 450, 483, 545, 546,
  576, 577.
 Joseph, 93, 94, 545, 546.
 Mary, 94, 450, 545.
 Mr., 484.
 Rebeckah, 94, 545, 546.
 Samuel, 93, 94, 545.
 Sarah, 545, 546.
 Thomas, 382, 449, 450, 546.
Meekin, John, 484.
Meekins, John, 335.
 Thomas, 301, 449.
Megs, Return, 394.
Mengo (negro), 73.
Mentor, Robert, 411.
Mercer, Mary, 258.
Merrells, Abell, 259, 260, 546.
 Abigail, 133, 134, 546.
 Abraham, 259, 260, 408, 409.
 Abram, 29, 410, 546, 570, 605.
 Daniel, 35, 78, 167, 233, 234, 250, 259,
  260, 299, 374, 380, 408, 409, 458,
  498, 546, 611.

Merrells, Ebenezer, 608.
  Hannah, 602, 603.
  Isaac, 259, 260, 535, 536, 546.
  Jacob, 259, 535, 546.
  John, 77, 258, 259, 260, 408, 409, 410,
    546, 602.
  Moses, 458.
  Nathaniel, 258, 259, 260, 500, 546.
  Noah, 536.
  Sarah, 259, 260, 374.
  Susannah, 286.
  Wilterton, 259, 260, 515, 546, 602.
Merrill, Ebenezer, 608.
  Mary, 608.
Merriman, Hannah, 264.
Merrold, Mehetabell, 381.
Merrow, Henry, 427, 428.
Merwin, Daniel, 488.
Messenger, Daniel, 454, 552.
  Elizabeth, 532.
  Mr., 82.
  Nathan, 82.
  Nehemiah, 532.
Messinger, Lydia, 515.
Michell, see Mitchell.
Michell, John, 193.
Mihall, Samuel, 604.
Mihill, Samuel, 604, 605.
  Sarah, 604.
Miles, Richard, 194.
Miller, Abigail, 441.
  Elijah, 411.
  Elizabeth, 441, 547.
  Hannah, 547, 548.
  Jared, 411.
  John, 94, 95, 547, 548.
  Jonathan, 94, 95.
  Joseph, 411.
  Martha, 94, 95, 591.
  Mary, 94, 548.
  Matthew, 547, 548.
  Mercy, 591.
  Nathaniel, 411.
  Rebeckah, 411, 546, 547, 548.
  Samuel, 357, 592.
  Sarah, 94, 95.
  Stephen, 548.
  Susannah, 249, 250.
  Tabitha, 411.
  Thomas, 287, 441, 546, 547, 548.
  William, 94, 95, 249, 250, 548, 580.
Millington, Henry, 624.
Mills, Dorcas, 411, 412.
  Hannah, 146.
  John, 359.
  Joseph, 146.
  Peter, 254, 260, 508.
  Sarah, 271.

Mills, Simon, 82, 359.
Minor, Ephraim, 622.
Mitchell, see Michell.
Mitchell, Thomas, 549.
  William, 548, 549.
Mitchelson, William, 490.
Mix, Stephen, 158, 176.
Modsley, see Maudsley.
Modsley, Abigail, 412, 413.
  Abner, 412.
  David, 412.
  Hannah, 412.
  Isaac, 412.
  Job, 412.
  Joseph, 412.
  Mary, 412.
  Rachell, 412.
  Sarah, 412.
  Thankful, 412.
Mold, Hugh, 569.
Molford, Sarey, 479.
Montague, Richard, 468.
Montgomery, Genett, 549.
Moody, Eliezer, 93.
  Mrs., 55.
Moore, Abell, 76.
  Abijah, 564.
  Amos, 413.
  Andrew, 71, 413.
  Anna, 258.
  Benjamin, 413.
  Deborah, 71, 261.
  Dorothy, 96.
  Edward, 414, 549.
  Hannah, 540.
  Isaac, 96.
  John, 6, 8, 9, 17, 18, 21, 22, 61, 81, 90,
    91, 99, 123, 124, 148, 154, 174, 177,
    178, 183, 192, 196, 202, 206, 254,
    263, 264, 337, 390, 413, 414, 415.
  Jonathan, 413.
  Joseph, 260, 261, 414.
  Josiah, 260, 261, 414.
  Lydia, 260, 261.
  Martha, 413, 414, 415.
  Martin, 286.
  Mary, 390, 413, 549.
  Mr., 338.
  Nathaniel, 413.
  Phebe, 260, 261.
  Samuel, 5, 9, 53, 81, 82, 149, 205, 322,
    378, 413, 414.
  Sarah, 260, 261, 413, 421.
  Thomas, 7, 18, 71, 91, 150, 153, 178, 192,
    223, 224, 243, 254, 256, 264, 322, 337,
    338, 414, 415, 418, 419, 420, 452,
    453, 457, 502, 562.
  William, 413.

Morecock, Nicholas, 175.
Morgan, Benjamin, 550.
  Hannah, 32, 33.
  Joseph, 550.
  Leah, 550.
  Lydia, 32, 33.
  Mrs., 55.
  Nathaniel, 32, 33.
  Peletiah, 32, 33.
  Rachel, 550.
  Thomas, 209, 550, 551.
Morie, Elizabeth, 180.
Morley, Abel, 261.
  Martha, 261.
  Mary, 261.
  Thomas, 261.
Morly, Thomas, 63.
Morrison, Abraham, 51, 52, 232.
Morriss, Abraham, 159.
  Abram, 159, 170, 343, 565.
Morsse, Sarah, 594.
Morton, Elizabeth, 450.
  Hannah, 97, 208, 416, 551.
  Jane, 335.
  John, 261, 262, 335, 366, 415, 416, 479.
  Mary, 261, 415, 416.
  Rachel, 551.
  Samuel, 261, 262, 415.

Morton, Sarah, 261, 262.
  Thomas, 96, 97, 261, 262, 416, 551.
  William, 261, 262, 551, 561.
Moseley, Consider, 412.
  Joseph, 412.
Moses, Caleb, 263.
  Deborah, 262, 263.
  Elizabeth, 276, 277.
  John, 113, 262, 263, 399, 485.
  Joshua, 263, 464.
  Martha, 263.
  Mary, 263.
  Thomas, 263.
  Timothy, 485.
  William, 262, 263, 276, 277.
Moulton, Robert, 386.
Mudge, Ebenezer, 430, 551.
  Mary, 551, 552.
  Micah, 551, 552.
  Moses, 552.
  Susannah, 552.
Munnumquask (Indian), 81.
Mygatt, Elizabeth, 552, 553.
  Jacob, 499, 552, 553.
  Joseph, 90, 132, 156, 250, 380, 552, 553.
  Mary, 553.
  Sarah, 134, 552, 553.
  Zebulon, 552, 553.

N

Nannicos, Pauhakehun (Indian), 100.
  Takamisk (Indian), 100.
Nash, Moses, 481.
Neal, Edward, 399.
  Margaret, 399.
  Noah, 176.
Neuill, see Newell.
Neuill, Sarah, 575.
Newbery, Abigail, 264.
  Benjamin, 9, 61, 82, 263, 264, 265, 416.
  Hannah, 61, 264.
  Joseph, 91, 253, 265.
  Mary, 264.
  Roger, 264, 420.
  Ruth, 264, 416, 562.
  Sarah, 91.
Newell, see Neuill.
Newell, Elizabeth, 553.
  Esther, 553.
  Joseph, 553.
  Mary, 521, 538.
  Nathan, 538.
  Samuel, 126, 167, 265, 266, 342, 371, 521, 553.
  Sarah, 553.
  Simeon, 553.

Newell, Thomas, 553.
Newton, Abner, 592.
  Isaac, 422.
Niccols, Comfort, 295.
  Cyprian, 151.
  Richard, 295.
Nicholls, Ciprian, 254, 298.
  Cyprian, 255, 321.
  Thankfull, 551, 552.
Nichols, Ciprian, 14, 129, 167.
  Cyprian, 12, 133, 180, 295, 350, 449, 607.
  Mabel, 469.
Nickcolls, Cyprian, 43.
Nickolls, Ciprian, 138.
  Cyprian, 218, 267, 329.
Nickols, Ciprian, 25, 132, 231.
  Cyprian, 137.
Nickolss, Mabel, 469.
Nicols, Ciprian, 81.
Noble, Stephen, 507.
Nobles, David, 505, 506.
  Stephen, 505, 506.
North, Anna, 131.
  Daniel, 97, 98.
  Ebenezer, 265, 266.
  Elizabeth, 432.

North, Hannah, 265, 266, 342, 554.
    Isaac, 553, 554.
    James, 554.
    Jane, 265.
    John, 97, 131, 265, 421, 432, 433.
    Joseph, 110, 265, 266, 554.
    Josiah, 97, 98.
    Lydia, 265, 266.
    Martha, 553, 554.
    Mary, 131, 265, 266, 291.
    Nathaniel, 265, 266, 464.
    Rebeckah, 265, 266.
    Samuel, 97, 98.
    Sarah, 265, 266, 554.
    Thomas, 97, 98, 265, 266, 434, 553, 554.
Northam, Isaac, 570.
    Jonathan, 233, 234.
    Samuel, 197, 233, 382.
Northaway, Hannah, 97.
Northway, Hannah, 23.

Olcock, Philip, 248.
Olcot, Abigail, 268.
Olcott, see Alcott.
Olcott, Abigail, 267, 268.
    Elizabeth, 98, 268.
    George, 99, 267.
    Hannah, 268, 269.
    John, 23, 24, 25, 222, 223, 267, 268.
    Jonathan, 269.
    Joseph, 269.
    Josiah, 499.
    Mary, 23, 24, 25, 267, 268.
    Mr., 94.
    Nathaniel, 499, 629.
    Rachel, 267, 268.
    Samuel, 14, 90, 98, 99, 269.
    Sarah, 267.
    Thomas, 99, 103, 146, 147, 157, 222, 223,
        267, 268, 269, 271, 340, 341, 367.
    Timothy, 406, 612.
Ollcot, Rachel, 268.
Olmstead, Joseph, 249.
Olmsted, Abigail, 416, 417.
    Ann, 133, 134.
    Isaac, 416, 417.
    James, 556, 557.
    John, 557.
    Joseph, 93, 102, 103, 114, 165, 186, 198,
        261, 262, 273, 335, 355, 416, 555,
        556, 557, 561.
    Mary, 416, 417, 556, 557.
    Mr., 561.
    Nathaniel, 416, 417.
    Nehemiah, 417, 556, 557.
    Nicholas, 416, 417, 556, 557.

Northway, George, 313.
Norton, Elizabeth, 555.
    Hannah, 404, 554.
    John, 97, 117, 493, 554, 555.
    Reuben, 404.
    Ruth, 554.
    Samuel, 182, 555.
    Thomas, 219, 554, 555.
Nott, Abraham, 266.
    Ann, 266.
    Gershom, 266.
    John, 266, 267, 324, 345.
    Jonathan, 266.
    Nathaniel, 266, 581.
    Patience, 266, 267, 448.
    Thankful, 266.
    William, 230, 266, 311.
Noyes, James, 279.
    John, 279.
    Moses, 428.

O

Olmsted, Richard, 556, 557.
    Samuel, 301, 472, 510, 557.
    Stephen, 416, 417.
    Thomas, 133.
Onepenny, Sarah (Indian woman), 81, 269,
    557, 558.
Orton, Thomas, 32, 33, 35.
Orvice, Miriam, 217.
Orvis, Roger, 559.
Osborn, Benjamin, 607.
    Elizabeth, 608.
Osbourn, Isaac, 100.
    Jacob, 100.
    John, 100.
    Martha, 100.
Osbourne, Abigail, 99.
    Elizabeth, 99, 100.
    John, 99, 100.
    Martha, 99, 100.
    Mary, 99.
    Mindwell, 99.
    Samuel, 100.
Osgood, Jeremiah, 592.
Otis, Nathaniel, 593.
Owaneco (Indian), 76, 177.
Owen, Asabell, 587.
    Daniel, 270.
    Elizabeth, 417.
    Isaac, 270.
    Jedediah, 558.
    John, 82, 270, 417, 624.
    Josiah, 123, 417, 418.
    Obadiah, 401, 417, 558.
    Samuel, 558.
    Sarah, 417.

P

Paine, Job, 92.
Palmer, Benjamin, 304.
  Daniel, 399, 400.
  Elizabeth, 399, 400.
  John, 6, 7, 195, 205, 270, 334, 363, 418, 419, 420, 463, 473, 486, 502, 552, 562, 595.
  Jonah 222.
  Samuel, 199, 234.
  Sarah, 418, 552.
  Stephen, 418.
  Timothy, 418.
Pampenum (Indian woman), 100, 101.
Pantry, Abigail, 271.
  John, 270, 271.
  Mary, 270.
Parker, Samuel, 349, 385, 539, 540.
  Sarah, 351.
Parsivall, see Persivall.
Parsivall, James, 144.
Parsivell, Mary, 513.
Parsons, see Persons.
Parsons, John, 299, 300.
  Samuel, 64, 101, 353.
  William, 173.
Partridge, Mr., 367.
  Samuel, 138, 276, 455.
Partrigg, Samuel, 137.
Patterson, James, 79, 80, 163, 171, 179, 188, 195, 201, 227, 245, 266, 349, 375.
Peck, Elijah, 404.
  Jeremiah, 279.
  Jeremy, 280.
  John, 558, 559.
  Joseph, 359.
  Mary, 404.
  Nathaniel, 180.
  Paul, 558, 559.
  Ruth, 559.
  Samuel, 101, 206, 559, 591.
  Sarah, 180.
Peese, Elizabeth, 26.
Pendall, John, 411.
Penfield, Ann, 49, 490.
  Benjamin, 591.
  John, 490, 491, 492.
Pengilly, John, 501.
Perkins, see Pirkins.
Perkins, John, 98.
  Mr., 88.
Perrie, Bridget, 505.
  John, 505.
Perry, Bridget, 505, 508.
  John, 505, 506.
  Joseph, 508.
  William, 548.
Perse, Isaac, 100.

Persivall, see Parsivall.
Persivall, James, 559, 560.
  John, 559, 560.
  Joseph, 560.
  Mary, 559, 560.
Person, John, 559.
Persons, see Parsons.
Persons, Hezekiah, 542.
  William, 559.
Peter (negro), 598.
Pettebone, Anne, 271.
  Benjamin, 101, 102.
  Elizabeth, 313.
  Henry, 271.
  James, 502.
  John, 22, 36, 91, 102, 135, 146, 271, 277, 331, 391, 431, 441, 562.
  Joseph, 146, 271, 331.
  Mary, 562.
  Rebeckah, 271.
  Samuel, 38, 90, 145, 146, 237, 271, 262, 313, 331, 348, 441, 451, 498, 517, 526, 533, 562.
  Sarah, 271.
  Stephen, 271.
  Thanks, 146.
Pettibone, Damaris, 238.
  Deborah, 502, 503.
  Hepsibah, 533.
  Isaac, 533, 534.
  John, 310, 502.
  Mary, 502, 503.
  Stephen, 502.
Pettus, Sir John, 166.
Phebe (negro woman), 324.
Phelps, Abell, 418.
  Abiall, 333.
  Abigail, 393, 418, 419.
  Abraham, 59, 272, 273, 322, 560.
  Abram, 420.
  Amos, 589.
  Ann, 419.
  Charles, 272.
  Cornelius, 419, 474, 541, 542.
  Daniel, 272, 418, 476.
  David, 417.
  Edward, 418.
  Elizabeth, 272.
  Ephraim, 53.
  Hannah, 272, 419.
  Ichabod, 418.
  Israel, 241.
  John, 272, 333, 418, 587.
  Jonathan, 418, 419, 420.
  Joseph, 154, 182, 189, 196, 199, 205, 206, 256, 271, 277, 359, 417, 418, 419, 421, 439, 458, 464, 473, 485, 572, 587.

Phelps, Josiah, 393, 413.
    Martha, 419.
    Mary, 417, 418, 419.
    Mindwell, 476.
    Mr., 474, 529.
    Nathaniel, 195, 199, 419, 420, 430, 439,
        552, 572.
    Phebe, 272.
    Rachel, 240, 413, 417.
    Ruth, 154.
    Samuel, 196, 334, 363, 364, 418, 419.
    Sarah, 36, 104, 272, 418, 419, 541.
    Thomas, 417.
    Timothy, 70, 82, 103, 199, 267, 271, 272,
        419, 420, 496.
    William, 18, 82, 154, 192, 199, 224, 272,
        363, 401, 413, 418, 419, 420, 463,
        474, 517, 518, 573.
Phillips, George, 122, 216, 330, 402, 591, 610.
    Hope, 122.
    Mr., 500.
    Samuel, 42.
Pickett, James, 53.
    Mary, 375.
Pierpont, Abigail, 75, 221.
    James, 75, 121, 221, 404.
    Mary, 403, 404.
    Mr., 75, 122.
Pinney, Abigail, 420.
    Ann, 420.
    Daniel, 273.
    Hannah, 273.
    Humphrey, 560.
    Isaac, 272, 273, 420, 421.
    Josiah, 560, 561.
    Nathaniel, 123, 272, 401, 413, 517, 518,
        624.
    Noah, 273.
    Oliver, 420, 421.
    Prudence, 420.
    Samuel, 560, 561.
    Sarah, 272, 273, 421.
Pirkins, see Perkins.
Pirkins, Ralph, 93.
Pitkin, Caleb, 335, 500, 527.
    Daniel, 340.
    Dorothy, 527.
    Elizabeth, 379, 380, 435, 561.
    George, 102, 103.
    Jerusha, 561.
    John, 10, 102, 103, 129, 561.
    Jonathan, 484.
    Joseph, 272, 304, 416, 447, 483, 484, 561,
        576, 593.
    Mary, 527, 540, 621.
    Nathaniel, 102, 103, 198, 261, 262, 335,
        561.

Pitkin, Ozias, 102, 103, 355, 356, 416, 447,
        479, 481, 526, 561, 555, 556, 593.
    Roger, 12, 93, 94, 102, 103, 114, 165, 185,
        186, 198, 261, 273, 340, 350, 355, 356,
        435, 556.
    Thankfull, 527.
    Thomas, 406, 561.
    William, 25, 102, 103, 177, 294, 304,
        366, 379, 380, 417, 435, 455, 478, 500,
        546, 556, 561.
Pixley, Abigail, 178.
    Joseph, 178.
Platt, Richard, 42.
Poisson, see Poyson.
Poisson, James, 258, 263.
Pomeroy, see Pumry.
Pomeroy, Hannah, 292.
    Jonathan, 292.
    Joseph, 292.
Pond, Moses, 442.
Poole, Sarah, 52.
Porter, Abial, 275.
    Abiall, 274.
    Abigail, 421, 422, 423.
    Alexander, 192.
    Amos, 275.
    Ann, 421, 562.
    Benjamin, 422.
    Catharine, 562.
    Daniel, 326, 367, 422, 536, 561.
    David, 551.
    Elizabeth, 423.
    Esther, 190, 299.
    Ezekiel, 422.
    Hannah, 235, 339, 421, 559.
    Hezekiah, 114, 225, 249, 273, 299, 562,
        594.
    James, 264, 416, 562.
    Joanna, 434.
    John, 28, 34, 167, 191, 192, 209, 210, 220,
        235, 386, 399, 421, 422, 444, 445,
        539, 559, 562.
    Jonathan, 421, 422.
    Joseph, 523.
    Katharine, 192.
    Lois, 273.
    Lydia, 562.
    Martha, 275, 421, 422.
    Mary, 191, 192, 275, 434.
    Mr., 274, 422, 600.
    Nathaniel, 273, 422, 574, 594.
    Nehemiah, 421, 422.
    Rachel, 422.
    Rebekah, 342.
    Richard, 145, 448.
    Robert, 422, 423.
    Samuel, 179, 209, 274, 421, 422, 437.
    Sarah, 274, 275, 440, 561, 562.

Porter, Susannah, 30, 31.
  Thomas, 28, 31, 132, 241, 273, 274, 421, 422, 423, 424, 521, 562, 592.
  Timothy, 45, 208, 273, 274, 422, 442, 443, 444, 493, 521, 562, 577, 628.
  William, 155, 274, 275, 422, 555.
Post, Mary, 574.
  Stephen, 240, 552.
Powell, Elizabeth, 607.
  John, 550.
  Thomas, 275.
  William, 275.
Poyson, see Poisson.
Poyson, James, 538.
Pratt, Daniel, 103, 104.
  Elisha, 104.
  Elizabeth, 103, 104.
  Esther, 104.
  Hannah, 554, 567.
  John, 98, 267, 268, 271, 272, 300, 481, 544.

Pratt, Jonathan, 183, 286, 469, 501.
  Joseph, 543.
  Mehetabell, 605.
  Peter, 106, 351, 605.
  Rebeckah, 104.
Prentis, Mr., 175.
Prior, Humphrey, 423.
Prout, Ebenezer, 155, 167, 206, 591.
  John, 591.
Pryar, Mr., 99.
Pryor, Daniel, 159.
Pumry, see Pomeroy.
Pumry, Joseph, 293.
Purple, Edward, 44, 144, 423, 424.
  Hannah, 52, 185, 423.
  John, 423.
  Richard, 423.
Pynchon, John, 455.
  Mr., 175.

Q

Quitafield, Benjamin, 590.
Quittafield, Benjamin, 562.
  Clement, 562.
  Elizabeth, 562.

Quittafield, John, 562.
  Priscilla, 562.
  Richard, 562.

R

Randall, Mary, 370, 371.
  William, 593.
Ranney, Abigail, 276.
  Anne, 563, 564.
  Daniel, 592.
  Ebenezer, 276, 563.
  Esther, 613.
  George, 562, 563.
  Hannah, 276.
  John, 276, 486.
  Joseph, 276, 563, 564, 570.
  Lydia, 583.
  Margaret, 276, 563, 564.
  Mary, 562.
  Mr., 582.
  Nathaniel, 563, 564.
  Rebeckah, 563, 564.
  Thomas, 276, 563, 564.
  Willet, 563, 564.
  Willett, 276.
Ranny, Abigail, 275.
  Ebenezer, 131, 275.
  Hannah, 275, 441.
  John, 244, 275, 441.
  Joseph, 275, 617.

Ranny, Margaret, 275.
  Mary, 275.
  Thomas, 275, 290, 356.
Ray, James, 354.
Read, Arthur, 276.
  Elizabeth, 276, 277.
  Jacob, 37, 276, 277, 402.
  John, 75, 214, 221, 402, 453.
  Lydia, 277.
Reed, Alanson H., 619.
  John, 3.
Reeve, see Reve.
Reeve, Robert, 147.
Reignolds, see Reynolds, Rennolds.
Reignolds, Anne, 105.
  John, 361.
  Samuel, 424.
  Susannah, 424.
Remington, Elizabeth, 494, 495.
  Joseph, 495.
  Thomas, 72.
Rennolds, see Reignolds, Reynolds.
Rennolds, Hannah, 58.
  John, 206, 424, 600.
  Jonathan, 424.

Rennolds, Samuel, 424.
    Susannah, 424.
Reve, see Reeve.
Reve, Robert, 175.
Rew, see Rue.
Rew, John, 245, 283.
    Margaret, 283.
Reynolds, see Reignolds, Rennolds.
Reynolds, Anna, 105.
    Anne, 229.
    Elizabeth, 105.
    John, 105.
    Jonathan, 105.
    Keziah, 105.
Richard (negro), 521.
    Thomas, 112, 608.
Richards, Benjamin, 106, 277.
    Easter, 278.
    Elizabeth, 106, 278.
    Esther, 106.
    Hannah, 106, 278.
    Joanna, 424, 425, 426, 536.
    John, 46, 106, 278, 326, 392, 449.
    Mary, 106, 278, 425.
    Mr., 81.
    Obadiah, 106, 278.
    Rachel, 106, 278.
    Samuel, 114, 134, 410.
    Sarah, 106, 278.
    Susannah, 424.
    Thomas, 58, 66, 67, 68, 90, 106, 114, 172,
        235, 278, 290, 296, 297, 320, 327,
        336, 374, 411, 424, 426, 448, 504, 607.
Richardson, Amos, 534.
    Ebenezer, 280, 320.
    Elizabeth, 278, 279.
    Hannah, 278.
    Israel, 278, 280.
    Joanna, 280.
    John, 278, 279, 280.
    Jonathan, 64.
    Joseph, 278.
    Lemuel, 173, 174, 279.
    Margaret, 320.
    Mary, 278, 279.
    Mehetabell, 279.
    Mr., 64.
    Nathaniel, 280.
    Rebeckah, 280.
    Ruth, 279, 280.
    Samuel, 279.
    Sarah, 279, 280.
    Stephen, 279.
    Thomas, 279, 280.
Righley, see Riley, Rily, Ryley, Ryly.
Righley, James, 52.
    Joseph, 52.
Riley, David, 286.

Riley, Isaac, 537.
    Jacob, 286.
    John, 285.
    Jonathan, 286, 476, 615.
    Lydia, 63.
    Sarah, 285, 615.
    Stephen, 286.
Rily, Isaac, 600.
    Joseph, 600.
Ripley, Joshua, 3, 131, 222.
    Mr., 393.
Risley, see Wrisley.
Risley, John, 460.
    Mary, 460.
    Nathaniel, 526.
Robbins, Abigail, 321, 362.
    John, 145, 280, 321, 360.
    Jonathan, 600.
    Joshua, 24, 50, 51, 105, 129, 155, 156,
        163, 174, 175, 177, 183, 230, 256,
        281, 285, 295, 314, 316, 318, 319, 321,
        323, 361, 362, 376, 465, 468, 469, 600,
        601, 627.
    Lucy, 336, 337, 362.
    Martha, 186, 187.
    Mr., 256, 466, 600.
    Richard, 281, 362, 374, 376, 601.
    Samuel, 252, 281, 336, 337, 362, 376, 470.
    Sarah, 20.
    Thomas, 362.
Robbinson, see Robinson.
Robbinson, Thomas, 487.
Robe, Andrew, 36, 153, 189, 252, 263, 296,
    349, 389, 390, 429, 451, 464, 477,
    478, 484, 498.
    Sarah, 154.
Robee, Andrew, 529.
Roberts, Benjamin, 531.
    Daniel, 427.
    David, 427.
    Deborah, 263.
    Ebenezer, 427.
    Eunice, 564.
    Frances, 564.
    James, 233.
    John, 293, 348, 427, 430, 564, 591.
    Jonathan, 427, 591.
    Joseph, 565.
    Mary, 427.
    Nathaniel, 427, 592.
    Samuel, 564, 591.
    Sarah, 427.
    Thomas, 402.
    William, 185, 198, 427, 564, 565.
Robertson, Thomas, 302.
Robin (negro), 254.
Robinson, see Robbinson.
Robinson, Elizabeth, 144.

Robinson, John, 427, 428.
   Lydia, 565.
   Mary, 565.
   Mrs., 122.
   Thomas, 3, 144, 185, 324, 428, 565, 618.
Rockwell, Ann, 573.
   Elizabeth, 565.
   John, 237, 281.
   Joseph, 11, 26, 30, 39, 40, 47, 49, 106,
     110, 116, 120, 122, 136, 148, 149, 161,
     162, 180, 191, 195, 215, 216, 237, 251,
     256, 257, 281, 285, 287, 294, 308, 309,
     310, 311, 317, 319, 356, 358, 362, 363,
     376, 377, 383, 393, 394, 397, 406, 410,
     441, 446, 447, 449, 456, 461, 462, 491,
     502, 512, 513, 523, 542, 564, 565, 566,
     578, 585, 591, 596, 597, 598, 599, 610.
   Josiah, 281.
   Mary, 281.
   Matthew, 565.
   Mr., 124, 599.
   Samuel, 56, 96, 97, 209, 281, 309, 359,
     365, 375, 378, 383, 387, 391, 420, 436,
     452, 565.
   William, 512, 566, 585.
Rogers, James, 530.
Rolland, John, 30.
Rollo, Alexander, 4, 15, 40, 45, 47, 48, 73,
     85, 106, 109, 120, 149.
   Hannah, 107.
   William, 107, 574.
Root, Caleb, 281, 282.
   Elizabeth, 282.
   Hannah, 409, 428.
   Jacob, 439, 495, 574, 587.
   John, 239, 282, 396, 412, 428.
   Jonathan, 283, 428.
   Joseph, 220, 233, 242, 282, 343, 409, 428,
     625.
   Margaret, 283, 291.
   Mary, 282.
   Mr., 239.
   Samuel, 282.
   Sarah, 178, 428, 446.
   Solomon, 516.
   Stephen, 283, 428.
   Thankfull, 282.
   Thomas, 178, 282, 304, 348, 349, 386,
     516.
   Timothy, 283, 428.
Roote, Jacob, 495.
Rose, Daniel, 251, 584, 595.
   John, 251, 252, 361, 404, 405, 470.
Ross, Benjamin, 316.
Roster, Thomas, 592.
Rowell, Mary, 108.
   Thomas, 119.
   Violet, 119.

Rowlandson, Joseph, 140, 283.
   Wilson, 283, 622.
Rowley, Abigail, 108, 488.
   Deborah, 108.
   Elizabeth, 108, 283.
   Elnathan, 283.
   Grace, 108.
   Hannah, 144.
   Isaac, 283.
   Jabez, 283.
   Katharine, 185, 283.
   Martha, 108.
   Mary, 107, 108, 283, 429.
   Matthew, 107, 283.
   Moses, 107, 283, 301.
   Samuel, 185.
   Shubael, 283.
   Thomas, 107, 108, 283, 428.
Royce, Samuel, 256.
Rudd, Abigail, 284.
   Jonathan, 284.
   Nathaniel, 284.
Rue, see Rew.
Rue, Hezekiah, 429.
   John, 429, 555.
Ruggles, Abigail, 429.
Russell, Daniel, 108, 285, 566.
   Desire, 566.
   Hannah, 285, 566.
   John, 50, 68, 167, 184, 285, 321, 443,
     446, 468, 566, 582.
   Mabell, 285.
   Mary, 285, 566.
   Mehetabell, 566.
   Mr., 161, 257, 599.
   Noadiah, 16, 48, 121, 149, 215, 257, 284,
     330, 566.
   Prudence, 41.
   Thomas, 40, 41.
   William, 215, 285, 303, 308, 363, 407,
     491, 566, 599.
Rust, Hannah, 386.
   Nathaniel, 240, 304, 424.
Ryley, see Righley, Riley, Rily, Ryly.
Ryley, Eunice, 476.
   Isaac, 203, 285, 360, 465.
   John, 109.
   Jonathan, 285, 286, 360, 476.
   Joseph, 108.
Ryly, see Righley, Riley, Rily, Ryley.
Ryly, David, 285.
   Isaac, 109, 159.
   Jacob, 285.
   John, 203.
   Jonathan, 80, 81, 108, 109, 285.
   Joseph, 109, 285.
   Mehetabell, 285.
   Sarah, 285.
   Stephen, 285.

S

Sachem, Joshua (Indian), 14, 84, 102.
Sacket, Jonathan, 510.
Sackett, Deborah, 197.
    Jonathan, 511.
Sadd, Hepzibah, 232, 286.
    John, 25.
    Mrs., 232.
    Thomas, 286, 387.
Sage, Amos, 567.
    Amy, 287.
    David, 109, 110, 131, 286, 287, 567.
    Elizabeth, 287, 595.
    John, 109, 275, 287, 290, 475, 566, 567,
      614, 616.
    Jonathan, 109, 110, 287.
    Marcy, 287.
    Margaret, 215, 567.
    Mary, 109, 287.
    Mercy, 109.
    Solomon, 567.
    Timothy, 109, 110, 276, 287, 486, 566,
      567.
Saltonstall, Mrs., 425.
Samhues, Peter, 591.
Sampson (negro), 110, 257.
Sanders, Mr., 27.
Sandford, Abigail, 288, 289.
    Mary, 104.
    Mr., 90.
    Nathaniel, 623.
    Robert, 98, 102, 104, 131, 170, 208, 235,
      255, 365, 480, 481, 482, 488, 498, 499,
      540, 567.
    Thomas, 567.
    Zachariah, 25, 55, 56, 140, 287, 288, 289.
Sanford, Nathaniel, 620.
    Zachary, 90.
Sanger, Richard, 402.
Sauidg, (Savage), Nathaniel, 562.
Savage, see Savidge.
Savage, Christian, 569.
    Easter, 276.
    Elizabeth, 568, 569.
    Esther, 275.
    Hannah, 218, 569.
    John, 275, 276, 294, 567, 568, 569.
    Joseph, 569, 570, 617.
    Marcey, 568.
    Martha, 569.
    Mary, 275, 276, 568.
    Nathaniel, 204, 214, 275, 276, 308, 466.
    Rachel, 568.
    Sarah, 568, 569.
    Thomas, 276, 568, 569, 614.
    William, 287, 289, 294, 396, 397, 398,
      430, 451, 486, 567, 568, 569, 570, 582,
      610, 613, 614, 615, 616.

Savidge, see Savage.
Savidge, Christian, 592.
Saxton, see Sexton.
Saxton, Hannah, 293.
    John, 17, 38.
    Lucy, 293.
    Mary, 293.
    Richard, 293.
Saymour, see Seamore, Seamour, Seymore.
Saymore, Richard, 237.
Scipio (Indian), 269, 270.
    Two Shoes (Indian), 558.
Scofell, see Scovell, Scovill.
Scofell, Edward, 110, 111.
    Hannah, 111.
    William, 110, 111.
Scott, George, 326.
    Joseph, 111.
    Robert, 474.
    Samuel, 111.
Scovell, see Scofell, Scovill.
Scovell, Edward, 111.
    Hannah, 290.
    James, 289, 290.
    John, 278, 279, 280, 290, 424, 448, 475.
    Martha, 290.
    Mary, 290.
    Susannah, 111.
    William, 44, 290.
Scovill, see Scofell, Scovell.
Scovill, William, 130.
Seamore, see Saymore, Seamour, Seymour.
Seamore, Abigail, 112.
    Ebenezer, 292.
    Eliakim, 570.
    Elizabeth, 134.
    Eunice, 570.
    Hannah, 291, 292.
    Jerusha, 570.
    John, 111, 112, 134, 290, 291, 606.
    Jonathan, 292, 570.
    Lois, 570.
    Martha, 570.
    Mary, 112, 143, 290, 291.
    Mercy, 292.
    Mr., 535.
    Richard, 111, 143, 291, 292, 336, 357,
      587, 604.
    Ruth, 112.
    Samuel, 292, 293.
    Thomas, 35, 44, 111, 132, 156, 250, 269,
      270, 291, 292, 298, 330, 498.
    Zachariah, 111, 112, 283, 291, 481.
Seamour, see Saymore, Seamore, Seymour.
Seamour, Ebenezer, 228, 229.
Searles, James, 541.
    Mary, 541.

Sears, Sarah, 109.
Sedgewick, Jonathan, 463, 607.
    Samuel, 209, 235, 298, 385, 386, 438, 531,
      546, 607.
    Stephen, 607.
Sedgwick, Daniel, 570.
    Jerusha, 570.
    Mary, 570.
    Ruth, 559, 570.
    Samuel, 307, 551, 570.
    Thankful, 570.
Seemook (Indian), 100.
Selden, Ann, 571, 572.
    Elizabeth, 571, 572.
    Hannah, 571, 572.
    Hepsibah, 571, 572.
    Joseph, 173, 174, 279, 571.
    Rebeckah, 571, 572.
Sendall, Elizabeth, 619, 620.
    Samuel, 619, 620.
Sergeant, Hopestill, 258.
Seward, William, 591.
Sewell, Samuel, 621.
Sexton, see Saxton.
Sexton, Abigail, 250.
    George, 151, 367, 369.
    Gershom, 150.
    Hannah, 293, 429.
    John, 38, 429, 430, 525.
    Lucy, 293.
    Mary, 293.
    Richard, 429.
Seymor, Jonathan, 552.
Seymore, Thomas, 606.
Seymour, see Saymore, Seamore, Seamour.
Seymour, Ebenezer, 105.
    Hannah, 556.
    John, 374, 409, 608.
    Jonathan, 570.
    Mary, 602, 603.
    Mr., 293.
    Richard, 329, 546, 624.
    Ruth, 554.
    Samuel, 554.
    Thomas, 30, 190, 233, 235, 271, 455, 497,
      527, 528, 546, 602.
    William, 501.
    Zachariah, 556, 606.
Shailor, Timothy, 110.
Shaler, Abell, 293, 294.
    Thomas, 293, 294.
    Timothy, 293, 294.
Shalor, Abell, 294.
    Thomas, 294.
    Timothy, 294.
Sharpe, William, 395.
Shaw, John, 340, 341.
    Mary, 340.
Shayler, Joshua, 572.

Shayler, Martha, 572.
    Sarah, 572.
    Timothy, 572.
Shaylor, Abel, 406.
    Joseph, 572.
    Sarah, 511.
    Thomas, 111, 290, 572.
    Timothy, 111, 290, 572.
Shelding, Epaphras, 511.
    Hannah, 530.
    John, 243, 480, 481, 487.
    Remembrance, 476.
Sheldon, Elizabeth, 104.
    John, 104, 171, 243, 244, 269, 338, 339,
      431, 480, 497, 498, 499, 567.
    Remembrance, 476.
    Thomas, 75, 325.
Shepard, Samuel, 615.
Shephard, John, 258.
Shepherd, Edward, 294, 295, 430.
    John, 81, 112, 113, 193, 235, 259, 286,
      294, 295, 367, 430, 579.
    Martha, 112, 113.
    Samuel, 113, 157, 294, 295, 306, 430, 614.
    Thomas, 112, 113, 531.
    Violet, 113.
Sherman, Mary, 295.
    Samuel, 96.
    Theophalus, 295.
Shipman, Samuel, 572.
    William, 572.
Shippason, Elizabeth, 430, 431.
    Joanna, 430, 431.
    John, 430, 431.
    Jonathan, 430, 431.
    Mary, 430, 431.
    Mercy, 430, 431.
    Nathaniel, 430, 431.
Shirley, Robert, 295, 296.
    Sarah, 295.
Shurley, Robert, 58.
    Sarah, 68.
Sibbelle (negro), 254.
Silsbe, Jonathan, 296.
Simon (Indian), 591.
Sivadle, John, 591.
Skene, Alexander, 395.
Skinner, Benjamin, 199, 430.
    Elizabeth, 556.
    Isaac, 573.
    John, 104, 142, 150, 156, 170, 207, 221,
      234, 258, 270, 272, 287, 296, 303, 304,
      369, 382, 431, 435, 481, 487, 499,
      524, 527, 528, 540, 543, 562, 573,
      590, 594, 603.
    Joseph, 36, 46, 168, 169, 201, 264,
      309, 328, 357, 420, 421, 449, 455, 456,
      499, 556, 572, 573.
    Mary, 573.

Skinner, Mr., 535.
   Rachel, 104, 258.
   Richard, 201, 295, 296, 431, 573.
   Sarah, 196, 208.
   Thomas, 104, 233.
Slate, Daniel, 573.
   Samuel, 573.
Slater, Abiah, 296.
   Elias, 37, 296, 390.
   Elizabeth, 39, 296, 431, 573.
   Henry, 573.
   John, 36, 37, 38, 39, 114, 135, 144, 145,
     146, 153, 154, 155, 223, 243, 271, 296,
     327, 331, 341, 390, 398, 431.
   Marah, 431.
   Rebekah, 431.
   Reuben, 431.
   Samuel, 296, 573.
   Sarah, 390.
   Thomas, 113.
Slaughter, John, 276.
Smead, Richard, 114.
Smith, Aaron, 576.
   Abigail, 281, 299, 432, 296, 297.
   Benjamin, 111, 151, 251, 290, 293, 400,
     442, 464, 575, 581, 582, 583, 584.
   Benoni, 114, 577.
   Daniel, 274, 368, 432, 433, 496.
   David, 249, 250, 299, 576.
   Dinah, 575.
   Doratha, 583.
   Dorothy, 473, 575.
   Easter, 297, 299.
   Ebenezer, 35, 204, 205, 251, 303, 351,
     432, 433, 466, 490, 576, 613.
   Edward, 35.
   Elisha, 297.
   Elizabeth, 91, 297, 298, 362, 574.
   Ephraim, 34.
   Esther, 297, 298, 299, 434, 574.
   Experience, 434.
   Francis, 194, 534.
   George, 574.
   Gershom, 83, 95, 310, 372, 377, 508, 514,
     519, 548.
   Gideon, 299.
   Hannah, 249, 250, 251, 297, 404, 574,
     575, 576, 577.
   Helena, 434.
   Hepzibah, 36.
   James, 352, 574, 578.
   Jane, 440.
   Jeduthan, 575.
   Jemima, 464, 465.
   Jerusha, 299, 534.
   Joanna, 433.
   Jobanah, 433.
   Jobanna, 434, 550, 551.

Smith, John, 130, 152, 238, 244, 273, 297, 298,
     301, 337, 404, 578, 591.
   Jonathan, 52, 62, 94, 134, 158, 170, 282,
     287, 314, 332, 344, 431, 432, 433, 442,
     443, 542, 574.
   Joseph, 62, 63, 83, 84, 94, 119, 152, 156,
     236, 298, 299, 432, 433, 434, 486, 533,
     534, 554, 569, 575, 583, 584, 613,
     625.
   Lucy, 298, 534.
   Lydia, 298.
   Manoah, 575.
   Marcy, 114.
   Margaret, 574.
   Martha, 297, 577.
   Martin, 475, 581.
   Mary, 35, 114, 240, 248, 297, 497, 574,
     576, 577.
   Matthew, 299.
   Mehetabell, 114, 404.
   Mehetable, 577.
   Mercy, 434, 577.
   Mrs., 433.
   Nathaniel, 298, 299, 574.
   Nehemiah, 576.
   Noah, 432, 433.
   Phebe, 297.
   Philip, 115, 299, 351, 379, 380, 427, 428,
     576.
   Rebeckah, 114, 434, 576, 577.
   Richard, 213, 225, 502, 575, 585.
   Ruth, 434, 577, 578.
   Samuel, 62, 94, 114, 115, 167, 206, 213,
     248, 261, 266, 310, 311, 314, 421, 422,
     432, 472, 484, 575, 576, 577, 578, 579,
     580, 583, 584, 588.
   Sarah, 83, 297, 298, 431, 432, 497.
   Seth, 297.
   Simon, 151, 275, 297, 298, 352, 400, 570,
     572.
   Stephen, 578.
   Steven, 577.
   Susannah, 299, 434.
   Symon, 353.
   Thankfull, 298, 434.
   Thomas, 299, 535, 577, 623.
   Timothy, 114, 577.
   William, 35, 298, 432, 433, 434, 574, 577,
     578.
Snow, Mr., 232, 404.
Southmaid, Giles, 402, 591.
   John, 115, 116.
   William, 115.
Southmayd, Allyn, 116.
   Anne, 116.
   Giles, 116, 578.
   John, 115, 116, 225.
   Joseph, 116, 512.

Southmayd, Margaret, 115, 116.
  Millicent, 116.
  Mr., 48.
  William, 115, 116, 512.
Soper, Abigail, 434.
  Dorcas, 434.
  John, 434.
  Mary, 412, 434.
  Peletiah, 434.
  Return, 434.
  Sarah, 434.
Spalding, Mary, 120.
Sparks, Anne, 300.
  Dorothy, 299, 300.
  Esther, 299.
  John, 299, 300.
  Martha, 299.
  Noah, 300.
  Ruth, 300.
  Thomas, 300.
Spencer, Alexander, 4, 174, 302.
  Ann, 4.
  Caleb, 498.
  Deborah, 117.
  Disbrow, 26, 301, 302, 484, 596.
  Ebenezer, 302.
  Elizabeth, 300, 495.
  Gared, 596.
  Garrard, 150, 151.
  Gerrard, 26, 78, 160.
  Hannah, 117, 300, 301.
  Isaac, 116, 117, 354, 488, 511, 557, 617.
  Jared, 300, 472, 473, 515.
  Jerusha, 473.
  John, 70, 116, 117, 301, 302, 464, 500, 501,
    546, 547.
  Jonathan, 117, 300, 301.
  Joseph, 301, 449.
  Mary, 26, 300.
  Miriam, 116, 117.
  Mr., 353, 482.
  Nathaniel, 129, 160, 353.
  Obadiah, 78, 190, 243, 244, 269, 301, 302,
    482.
  Ruth, 117.
  Samuel, 37, 64, 69, 75, 76, 116, 117, 301,
    302, 565.
  Sarah, 94, 117, 279, 300, 302, 303, 484.
  Thankful, 500, 501.
  Thomas, 294, 301, 302, 427, 546.
  Timothy, 44, 117, 300, 301.
  William, 107, 116, 144, 174, 185, 244,
    299, 302, 324, 472.
Stanclift, James, 303, 592.
  Mary, 303.
  William, 303.
Standidge, Thomas, 55.
  Unis, 55.

Standish, Thomas, 171, 344.
Standly, Caleb, 64, 65, 92, 101.
  Lydia, 65.
  Timothy, 106.
Stanly, Abigail, 289, 302, 304, 435, 450.
  Ann, 305, 435.
  Anna, 305.
  Anne, 305.
  Caleb, 1, 19, 23, 54, 65, 66, 75, 101, 102,
    104, 132, 134, 138, 214, 274, 289, 302,
    303, 304, 346, 434, 435, 561.
  Isaac, 118.
  John, 29, 31, 111, 112, 117, 118, 131, 220,
    265, 266, 280, 296, 297, 342.
  Jonathan, 304, 435.
  Lydia, 65, 435.
  Martha, 578.
  Nathaniel, 36, 69, 84, 128, 232, 234, 255,
    268, 304, 305, 313, 341, 351, 356, 357,
    365, 367, 368, 369, 434, 450, 451, 524,
    553, 603, 628.
  Ruth, 435.
  Samuel, 628.
  Sarah, 118, 304, 578.
  Thomas, 118, 178, 305, 406.
  Timothy, 106, 118, 225, 277, 304, 434,
    435, 522, 589.
  William, 304, 435.
Starr, Comfort, 72.
  Jehosaphat, 435.
  Joseph, 237, 435, 491, 578, 592.
  Mr., 582.
  Samuel, 591.
Stebbin, Mahumah, 231.
Stebbins, Mehumahne, 232.
Stedman, Abigail, 151.
  John, 22, 25, 57, 66, 92, 119, 140, 199,
    240, 275, 341, 456, 457, 559, 566.
  Joseph, 312, 358.
  Mary, 456, 595.
  Mr., 82.
  Thomas, 118, 119, 287, 455, 595.
  Robert, 436.
  Samuel, 119.
  Simmons, 118.
Steele, Abiall, 307.
  Ann, 306.
  Anna, 306.
  Anne, 212, 283, 306.
  Daniel, 307, 438.
  David, 306, 307, 437, 438.
  Ebenezer, 118, 219, 241, 282, 283, 312,
    343, 436, 437, 579.
  Eliphalet, 307, 438.
  Elizabeth, 305, 578.
  Hannah, 306.

Steele, James, 21, 44, 78, 79, 81, 112, 113, 128, 159, 162, 169, 176, 189, 208, 214, 228, 246, 251, 267, 280, 283, 285, 286, 305, 306, 307, 316, 317, 332, 437.
John, 34, 67, 549.
Jonathan, 305, 306, 411, 515, 578, 579, 594, 605, 607, 608.
Joseph, 306.
Marcy, 307.
Mary, 305, 307, 436, 437.
Mercy, 438.
Mr., 106, 432.
Prudence, 306.
Samuel, 306, 307.
Sarah, 219, 305, 306, 436, 437.
Stephen, 305, 306, 579.
Thomas, 307, 385, 386, 438, 471, 504, 549.
William, 307, 438.
Stephens, Benjamin, 553.
Elizabeth, 553.
Hannah, 308.
Jane, 308.
Sarah, 308.
Thomas, 308, 592.
Stetson, see Studson.
Stetson, Desire, 379.
Samuel, 379, 394.
Stevens, Benjamin, 579, 580.
Joseph, 579, 580.
Mr., 588.
Samuel, 579.
Thomas, 48, 523.
Timothy, 167, 212, 575, 579, 580.
Stevenson, Robert, 593.
Stiles, see Styles.
Stiles, Elizabeth, 580, 581.
Esther, 404.
Henry, 60.
Isaac, 404.
John, 580, 581.
Jonathan, 60, 517, 530, 544, 560, 581.
Martha, 308.
Samuel, 308, 580.
Stilman, Benjamin, 581, 582.
George, 80, 114, 167, 197, 306, 307, 325, 581, 582.
John, 581, 582.
Lydia, 582.
Nathaniel, 465, 513, 577, 581, 582, 595.
Rebeckah, 581, 582.
William, 600.
Stocking, Bethiah, 308, 583.
Daniel, 244, 308, 309, 330, 577, 583, 591.
Elizabeth, 308, 583.
George, 308, 309, 583.
John, 309, 582, 583.
Nathaniel, 308, 309, 583.

Stocking, Samuel, 308, 583.
Stephen, 308, 583.
Stoddar, see Stoddard, Stodder.
Stoddar, John, 239.
Nathaniel, 118, 119.
Stoddard, see Stoddar, Stodder.
Stoddard, Beriah, 583.
Bethiah, 583, 584.
David, 585.
Elizabeth, 425, 585.
John, 584, 585.
Jonathan, 585.
Joshua, 438, 584.
Keziah, 105.
Mr., 586.
Nathaniel, 92, 186, 438, 584.
Sampson, 425.
Samuel, 584, 585.
Thomas, 438.
Stodder, see Stoddar, Stoddard.
Stodder, David, 119.
Elizabeth, 119.
John, 119.
Jonathan, 119.
Mary, 119.
Nathaniel, 12, 119, 313.
Samuel, 119.
Sarah, 481, 482.
Thomas, 119.
Stone, Joanna, 622.
Mr., 22, 150.
Samuel, 36.
Sarah, 113.
Storrs, Anna, 438.
Cordial, 439.
Elizabeth, 438.
Esther, 438, 439.
Lydia, 438, 439.
Samuel, 11, 438, 439.
Sarah, 438.
Thomas, 355, 378, 438, 439.
Stoughton, Anne, 309.
Daniel, 501.
Dorothy, 59, 310.
Elizabeth, 59, 309.
Hannah, 309.
Israel, 10, 59, 60, 202, 203, 219, 273, 308, 310, 340, 388, 560, 561, 580.
Joanna, 10.
John 8, 59, 90, 120, 281, 309, 310, 485, 548, 549, 586, 590, 591.
Mary, 59, 309.
Nathaniel, 309.
Rachel, 309.
Rebeckah, 309.
Samuel, 59, 310.
Sarah, 309.

Stoughton, Thomas, 59, 97, 125, 194, 209, 252, 309, 452.
   William, 59, 93, 120, 309, 310.
Stow, Bathsheba, 439, 440.
   Bethiah, 583, 591.
   Ebenezer, 440, 585.
   Hope, 121.
   Ichabod, 121.
   Jabez, 585.
   James, 585.
   Jeremiah, 440.
   John, 109, 120, 121, 122, 439, 440.
   Martha, 440.
   Mr., 356.
   Nathaniel, 4, 5, 11, 77, 120, 124, 136, 393, 439, 440, 585, 592.
   Samuel, 120, 121, 122, 123, 583, 613, 616.
   Sarah, 393, 585.
   Solomon, 439, 440.
   Sumner, 585.
   Thomas, 120, 161, 244, 290, 329, 330, 356, 441, 451, 583, 591, 599.
Stowe, Nathaniel, 121, 148.
   Samuel, 295, 568, 569.
Stratton, Abigail, 123, 413.
   Serajah, 123.
   William, 123.
Strickland, Benjamin, 582.
   Edward, 123, 529.
   Elizabeth, 123, 310.
   Esther, 584.
   Hannah, 123.
   John, 310, 586.
   Jonah, 592.
   Joseph, 123, 310, 331, 585, 586.
   Mary, 123.
   Naomi, 585.
   Samuel, 123, 310.
   William, 310.
Strong, Abigail, 586.
   Asahel, 404.
   Benjamin, 586.

Strong, Dameras, 586.
   Daniel, 476, 549.
   Elizabeth, 124, 586.
   Esther, 231, 232.
   Hannah, 231, 232, 586.
   Israel, 521.
   Jemima, 439.
   John, 96, 281, 479, 530, 560.
   John Warham, 124, 586.
   Joseph, 439.
   Margaret, 521, 586.
   Martha, 476.
   Mary, 231, 232, 560.
   Newell, 404.
   Return, 53, 123, 124, 199, 236, 263, 337, 338, 339, 586.
   Ruth, 404, 439.
   Samuel, 7, 124, 199, 202, 223, 224, 338, 369, 374, 389, 423, 453, 476, 485, 505, 506, 510, 530, 549, 586, 590, 591, 611, 626.
   Sarah, 86, 404, 586.
   Thomas, 591.
Stubbins, Daniel, 76.
   John, 76.
Studson, see Stetson.
Studson, Desiah, 378, 379.
   Samuel, 378, 379.
Styles, see Stiles.
Styles, Amos, 439.
   Hepzibah, 439.
   Job, 439.
   Nathaniel, 439.
   Robert, 439.
   Ruth, 439.
Sumner, Abigail, 356.
   Daniel, 124, 125, 393.
   Hannah, 124, 486.
   Hezekiah, 124, 125, 393, 441, 466.
   Sarah, 124, 125, 393.
   William, 72, 115, 124, 125, 135, 393.

T

Taintor, Michael, 22, 59, 181, 182, 233, 234.
Talcot, Benjamin, 63.
   Elizur, 175.
   Joseph, 496.
Talcott, Benjamin, 211, 212, 213, 214, 236, 247, 412, 514, 575, 580, 587, 588.
   Elizer, 587, 588.
   Eunice, 382.
   Hannah, 588.
   J., 484.
   John, 406, 488, 588.

Talcott, Joseph, 14, 25, 30, 66, 84, 99, 133, 188, 199, 221, 257, 268, 302, 304, 316, 379, 382, 383, 385, 405, 415, 433, 456, 480, 482, 487, 507, 508, 544, 592, 596, 597, 608, 609.
   Mehetabell, 588.
   Mr., 38, 90.
   Nathaniel, 227, 518, 579, 587, 588.
   Samuel, 55, 139, 189, 544, 587.
   Sarah, 133, 134, 188, 588.
   William, 562.

Taphannah, Richard (Indian), 310.
Tappan, James, 393.
Tappin, Anna, 311.
   Anne, 311.
   James, 310, 311, 441, 591.
   Mary, 311.
Taylor, Abigail, 544, 580.
   Ebenezer, 586.
   Hezekiah, 574.
   Joanna, 125, 126, 312.
   John, 229, 311, 591, 627.
   Jonathan, 586.
   Mercy, 440.
   Mr., 248.
   Nathaniel, 358.
   (negro), 31.
   Patience, 440.
   Samuel, 311.
   Sarah, 126, 137, 138, 311.
   Sary, 125.
   Stephen, 125, 126, 311, 312, 440.
   William, 125, 126, 209, 312.
Terrey, John, 589.
   Mary, 589.
   Samuel, 589, 590.
Terrie, Elizabeth, 588.
   John, 588.
   Mary, 588.
   Stephen, 588.
Terry, Elizabeth, 589.
   John, 588, 589, 590.
   Mary, 588, 589.
   Mr., 529.
   Samuel, 184, 589, 590.
   Solomon, 589, 590.
   Stephen, 589, 590.
Thatcher, Thomas, 386.
Thomas, Richard, 242.
   Sarah, 242.
   Steven, 395.
Thomasson (Thomlinson), Henry, 590.
Thomlinson, Elizabeth, 590.
   Henry, 590.
Thompson, Anne, 126.
   Daniel, 126, 127.
   Ezekiel, 312.
   Hezekiah, 312.
   James, 312.
   John, 126, 312, 436.
   Mary, 126.
   Mercy, 126.
   Mrs., 312.
   Nathaniel, 312.
   Samuel, 126, 523.
   Solomon, 312.
   Thomas, 126, 437, 493.
Thornton, Hannah, 127.
   Mr., 450.

Thornton, Samuel, 127, 146, 147, 168, 313, 336.
   Susannah, 313.
   Thomas, 127.
Thrall, Abigail, 590.
   Elizabeth, 313.
   John, 313, 476, 590.
   Samuel, 313.
   Sarah, 590.
   Thomas, 389.
   Timothy, 7, 10, 21, 148, 191, 202, 203, 205, 334, 339, 590.
   William, 10, 383, 590, 591.
Tilden, Isaac, 552.
Tilletson, Thomas, 615.
Tillotson, Joseph, 168.
   Moriss, 439.
   Morriss, 439.
Tillottson, Hannah, 515.
Tinker, John, 71.
   Mr., 71.
Toobe, Anthony, 593.
   John, 591, 592, 593.
   Sarah, 592.
Toobee, John, 591, 592, 593.
   Sarah, 592.
Tooley, Sarah, 185.
Tothill, see Tuthill.
Tothill, Jeremiah, 30.
Tousey, Thomas, 584.
Towsey, Thomas, 313, 314.
Tozar, Richard, 411.
Tracy, Joseph, 490.
   Mr., 496.
Treadway, James, 283, 364, 593.
Treat, Catherine, 166.
   Charles, 315, 316.
   Dorothe, 166, 167.
   Dorotheus, 315, 316.
   Dorothy, 315, 316.
   Hannah, 593.
   Isaac, 315, 316.
   James, 81, 127, 128, 129, 132, 175, 176, 177, 184, 314, 325, 396.
   Joseph, 128, 314, 360.
   Katharine, 314.
   Mabel, 128, 314.
   Mary, 184.
   Matthias, 12, 151, 593.
   Mr., 42.
   Rebecca, 314.
   Rebeckah, 128.
   Richard, 128, 129, 166, 314, 315, 316.
   Salmon, 128, 314.
   Samuel, 127, 128, 129, 325.
   Sarah, 11.
   Thomas, 166, 167, 213, 229, 314, 315, 316.
Trill, Ann, 129.

Trill, Thomas, 129.
Trowbridge, Benjamin, 3, 4.
   Hannah, 3, 4.
   Thankful, 121.
   William, 121.
Trumble, Ammy, 56.
   Ann, 478.
   Mr., 478.
Trumbull, Ammy, 56.
Tryon, Abell, 317.
   Abiall, 316, 317.
   David, 184, 316, 317, 444.
   Hannah, 444.
   Joseph, 225, 316, 317, 581.
   Mabell, 317.
   Thomas, 317, 581.
   William, 316.
   Zybah, 317.
Tucker, Ephraim, 350.
Tudor, Abigail, 594.
   Margaret, 594.
   Owen, 440, 594.
   Samuel, 253, 440, 594.
Tullar, Samuel, 331.
Tuller, Elizabeth, 36, 38, 90, 91.
   Isaac, 441.
   John, 90, 276, 277.
   Joseph, 441.

Tuller, Samuel, 441.
   Sarah, 441.
   William, 183, 256.
Tully, William, 298.
Turner, Abigail, 441, 442.
   Edward, 441, 442.
   Ephraim, 129, 140.
   Eunice, 427.
   Jerusha, 572.
   John, 259, 260, 441, 442.
   Mary, 129, 594.
   Mercy, 441.
   Richard, 311, 441.
   Stephen, 441.
   Susannah, 546.
Tuthill, see Tothill.
Tuthill, Jonathan, 427.
Tyler, Abigail, 442.
   Abraham, 442.
   Abram, 442.
   Ann, 442.
   Hannah, 442.
   Isaac, 442.
   Israel, 442.
   John, 402.
   Watchfull, 442.
Tyley, John, 402, 596.
   Samuel, 426.

U

Uncas (Indian Sachem), 76.

Upson, Stephen, 86, 106, 241.

V

Veit, Katharine, 524.
Ventrus, Elizabeth, 130.
   John, 110, 130.
   Mary, 442, 443.
   Mehetabell, 443.
   Moses, 130, 293, 442, 443.
   Samuel, 443.
   Sarah, 275.
   William, 129, 130.

Vibbard, James, 317.
   John, 317.
   Mary, 317.
Viet, John, 595.
Viett, John, 595.
   Katharine, 525, 595.
Vincent, Elizabeth, 58.
Voar, Lydia, 46.
Vore, Richard, 46.
Vryling, Mrs., 425.

W

Waddams, Abigail, 443, 444.
   Charity, 377.
   Daniel, 443, 444.
   Elizabeth, 595.
   John, 443, 444.
   Noah, 444.

Wadsworth, Abigail, 481, 482.
   Daniel, 445.
   Elizabeth, 118, 268, 445, 595, 596.
   Hezekiah, 445, 446.
   Ichabod, 382.
   James, 115, 116, 125, 393, 445, 446, **473**.

Wadsworth, John, 97, 115, 126, 132, 163, 167,
		178, 179, 209, 210, 218, 220, 241, 242,
		281, 408, 428, 444, 445, 446, 595, 596.
	Joseph, 14, 22, 26, 45, 66, 71, 81, 84, 129,
		151, 155, 169, 243, 268, 329, 367,
		386, 405, 406, 448, 535, 564.
	Lydia, 445.
	Mary, 24, 210, 268, 444.
	Mr., 459.
	Nathaniel, 111, 445, 446, 520.
	Ruth, 445, 595.
	Samuel, 117, 220, 280, 445, 446, 588, 589.
	Sarah, 445, 446, 450.
	Thomas, 31, 268, 312, 445, 446, 538, 577,
		595, 596.
	William, 283, 371, 434, 445, 446, 493,
		498.
Wait, William (Indian), 317.
Waldo, Abigail, 131.
	Edward, 131.
	John, 130, 131.
	Katharine, 131.
	Rebeckah, 130, 131.
	Ruth, 131.
	Sarah, 131.
Wale, John, 596.
Walker, Anna, 258.
	Jacob, 96.
	John, 25.
	Nathaniel, 402.
	Rebeckah, 258.
	Samuel, 58, 258.
Wallace, see Wollis.
Wallace, Thomas, 593.
Wampeawask (Indian woman), 100.
Ward, Abigail, 447.
	Andrew, 513, 596, 597.
	Anna, 311.
	Deborah, 591.
	Elizabeth, 317, 436, 597, 598.
	Esther, 597.
	Frances, 216.
	James, 10, 30, 143, 317, 447, 490, 597,
		598.
	John, 397, 596, 598.
	Mary, 513.
	Samuel, 446, 490, 585, 597.
	Sarah, 10, 585.
	Tappin, 598.
	Thomas, 4, 5, 26, 45, 85, 106, 120, 135,
		136, 162, 216, 218, 250, 251, 427,
		436, 441, 591, 598, 599.
	William, 16, 45, 50, 74, 124, 143, 216,
		218, 237, 310, 393, 396, 397, 398, 406,
		513, 564, 578, 591, 592, 597, 598.
Warham, John, 485.
	Mr., 586.
Warner, Abigail, 318, 601, 602.

Warner, Abraham, 318.
	Andrew, 121, 599, 610.
	Ann, 447.
	Benjamin, 320.
	Daniel, 317, 318, 319, 321, 360, 600, 601.
	Dorcas, 604.
	Ebenezer, 132, 318.
	Elizabeth, 131, 275, 276, 319, 399, 600,
		601, 602.
	Ephraim, 131, 279, 318, 320.
	Hannah, 131, 318, 320, 599, 600, 601,
		602.
	Joanna, 280, 318.
	Johanna, 317, 318.
	John, 131, 132, 190, 244, 275, 279, 286,
		287, 290, 318, 319, 321, 329, 430,
		446, 451, 563, 564, 566, 567, 568, 569,
		582, 599, 600, 601, 602, 614, 615, 616.
	Jonathan, 131, 275, 276, 357, 600, 601,
		602.
	Joseph, 205, 599.
	Mary, 131, 265, 318, 319, 361, 447, 585,
		599, 601.
	Mr., 344.
	Rebeckah, 280, 599.
	Robert, 16, 132, 319, 362, 446, 523, 599.
	Ruth, 318, 319.
	Samuel, 122, 317, 318, 319, 320, 399.
	Sarah, 318.
	Seth, 120, 317, 319.
	Silence, 615.
	Thomas, 131, 320.
	William, 105, 108, 109, 139, 159, 256,
		318, 320, 321, 344, 374, 468, 600,
		601, 602.
Warren, Abigail, 619, 620, 621, 623.
	Abraham, 594.
	Elizabeth, 619, 620.
	Hannah, 447.
	John, 447, 619, 620, 621.
	Joshua, 619.
	Mary, 12, 151, 447.
	Mrs., 622.
	Nathaniel, 619.
	Thomas, 299, 447, 450, 451, 619, 622.
	William, 12, 151, 350, 351, 561.
Warriner, Rebecca, 333.
Waters, Bevel, 602.
	Bevell, 604.
	Bevil, 93.
	Bevill, 603.
	Jabez, 106.
	Joseph, 447, 448, 602, 603.
	Samuel, 430, 448, 603, 604.
	Sarah, 106.
	Thomas, 448, 603, 604.
Watson, Abigail, 605.
	Anna, 606.

Watson, Caleb, 222, 223, 604, 605, 606, 607.
  Cyprian, 306, 503, 605, 606.
  Deborah, 605.
  Ebenezer, 322.
  Elizabeth, 306, 605.
  Jaddadih, 387.
  Jedediah, 322.
  John, 306, 307, 322, 605, 606, 607.
  Margaret, 605.
  Mary, 222, 223, 579, 604, 605.
  Mr., 267.
  Nathaniel, 322.
  Samuel, 322.
  Sarah, 306, 605, 606, 607.
  Thomas, 606.
Watts, Mr., 602.
Wawquashat (Indian), 100.
Way, Ebenezer, 14, 132.
  Eleazer, 94, 132
  Hannah, 611.
  Lydia, 132.
  Mary, 132.
Webb, Hannah, 53.
  Henry, 322.
  John, 353.
  Orange, 322.
  Samuel, 222, 297.
Webster, Abiah, 438.
  Abiall, 438.
  Abigail, 134.
  Ann, 134.
  Cyprian, 448.
  Daniel, 133, 134, 408, 409, 504, 606, 607.
  Ebenezer, 133, 134, 611.
  Elizabeth, 607, 608.
  Hannah, 462, 463.
  Hezekiah, 607, 608.
  Isaac, 608.
  Jacob, 133, 134, 607, 608.
  John, 132, 133, 134, 438, 504, 539, 550, 605.
  Jonathan, 44, 92, 133, 134, 336.
  Joseph, 133, 134, 462, 463, 503.
  Lois, 608.
  Mary, 366, 605, 608.
  Miriam, 374, 408.
  Moses, 448.
  Robert, 67, 133, 134, 181, 291, 608.
  Samuel, 133, 134, 374, 448, 498, 602.
  Sarah, 133, 134, 181, 448.
  Stephen, 608.
  Susannah, 133, 134, 448.
  Timothy, 608.
  William, 134, 172, 327, 328, 448, 605.
Welch, Paul, 505, 506, 507.
Welles, see Wells, Willes, Wills.
Welles, Anne, 609.
  Ebenezer, 609.

Welles, Eleazer, 609.
  Elizabeth, 132, 324, 325.
  Ephraim, 323.
  Esther, 384.
  Gideon, 323, 324.
  Hannah, 323.
  Ichabod, 55, 132, 291, 325, 350, 604.
  James, 290, 400, 471.
  Jerusha, 128, 325.
  John, 54, 139, 313, 323, 325.
  Jonathan, 251, 323, 481, 609.
  Joseph, 213, 323, 324, 609.
  Martha, 324, 561.
  Mary, 79, 186, 187, 323, 324.
  Mr., 575.
  Noah, 322, 323, 593.
  Robert, 23, 68, 111, 187, 228, 229, 266, 321, 323, 324, 336, 337, 344.
  Ruth, 212, 350.
  Samuel, 171, 189, 211, 213, 225, 248, 300, 323, 480, 481, 484, 487, 497, 575.
  Sarah, 132, 336, 337.
  Thomas, 25, 128, 226, 228, 230, 258, 316, 318, 323, 324, 325, 372, 412, 447, 514, 546, 573, 580, 587, 588, 601, 609.
  Wait, 247, 325.
  William, 128, 325.
Wellock, Ralph, 297.
Wells, see Welles, Willes, Wills.
Wells, Ebenezer, 531.
  Elizabeth, 79.
  Gideon, 267, 324.
  Hannah, 321.
  Ichabod, 180.
  James, 111, 117, 152, 293, 294, 297, 298, 352.
  John, 583.
  Rebeckah, 352.
  Robert, 28, 176, 314, 346.
  Samuel, 10, 43.
  Thomas, 25, 95, 228, 236, 541. 548.
Welton, see Wilton.
Welton, Abigail, 326.
  Eunice, 326.
  George, 326, 449.
  Hannah, 349, 449.
  Joanna, 326.
  Josiah, 449.
  Mary, 326.
  Richard, 326, 448, 449.
  Sarah, 164.
  Stephen, 326.
  Thomas, 326, 448.
West, Francis, 359.
Westland, Robert, 101.
Westover, Abegall, 38.
  Abigail, 327.
  Hannah, 135, 326, 327.

Westover, Jane, 135.
    Johanna, 135.
    Johannah, 327.
    John, 327.
    Jonah, 135, 145, 326, 327.
    Jonas, 39.
    Jonathan, 135, 224, 293, 326, 327, 349,
        464, 480, 485, 523, 525, 545, 555.
    Margaret, 135.
    Mary, 135.
    Nathaniel, 327.
Wetmore, see Whetmore, Whitmore.
Wetmore, Abigail, 135, 136.
    Ann, 449.
    Benajah, 457.
    Benjamin, 121.
    Beriah, 121, 136, 180.
    Booth, 610.
    Dorcas, 11, 136.
    Ebenezer, 610.
    Edith, 135, 136.
    Elizabeth, 135, 136.
    Esther, 136.
    Francis, 135, 136, 397.
    Hannah, 135, 136.
    Ichabod, 121.
    Isabell, 135, 136.
    Israhiah, 4, 5, 15, 40, 72, 120, 121, 122,
        161, 162, 190, 191, 284, 310, 327,
        358, 396, 397, 398, 410, 456, 461,
        462, 557, 564, 566, 585, 597, 610.
    John, 15, 135, 136, 610.
    Joseph, 4, 135, 136, 148, 449.
    Lydia, 449.
    Margaret, 121, 122.
    Martha, 135, 136.
    Nathaniel, 136, 449.
    Rachel, 121, 122.
    Sarah, 610.
    Seth, 512, 585, 592, 597, 610.
    Thomas, 327.
    William, 135, 136.
Whaples, Abigail, 328, 449.
    Elizabeth, 328, 449.
    Ephraim, 13, 327, 328, 584.
    Hannah, 328.
    Joseph, 328, 449.
    Mary, 328, 449.
    Mindwell, 328.
    Nathan, 328, 449.
    Rebeckah, 328.
    Thomas, 140, 328.
Wheeler, Ann, 67.
    Elizabeth, 329.
    Hannah, 611.
    Isaac, 329.
    Jemima, 455.
    John, 329, 611.

Wheeler, Joseph, 611.
    Mary, 329, 611.
    Moses, 329, 611.
    Mr., 67.
    Rachel, 67, 329.
    Samuel, 67, 329, 611.
    Sarah, 67, 611.
Whetmore, see Wetmore, Whitmore.
Whetmore, Hannah, 398.
    John, 136.
White, Ann, 359.
    Anthony, 395.
    Daniel, 7, 99, 137, 138, 329, 330, 384,
        611, 612.
    Deborah, 113.
    Ebenezer, 613.
    Elisha, 329, 612.
    Elizabeth, 137, 138, 329, 330, 449, 450,
        612.
    Hugh, 567, 613.
    Jacob, 137, 138, 295, 329, 330, 568, 592,
        613.
    Joel, 329, 612.
    John, 137, 138, 328, 329, 330, 436, 450,
        613.
    Joseph, 329, 330, 466, 486, 487, 562, 613.
    Lucy, 612.
    Martha, 329.
    Mary, 329, 330, 450, 613.
    Nathaniel, 16, 47, 109, 115, 116, 131,
        135, 137, 138, 276, 329, 330, 528.
    Oliver, 612.
    Sarah, 137, 138, 329, 330, 450, 528.
    Seth, 612.
    Simeon, 329.
    Simon, 612.
    Thomas, 612.
Whiting, Anna, 450.
    Anne, 450.
    Dorcas, 40.
    Jerusha, 255, 540, 621.
    John, 181, 236, 255, 330, 450, 451, 488,
        489, 602, 606.
    Joseph, 93, 115, 313, 330, 367, 450, 451,
        602.
    Mary, 269.
    Mr., 140, 141, 269, 270.
    Samuel, 40, 169, 175.
    William, 30, 62, 66, 67, 71, 115, 116, 133,
        134, 139, 140, 141, 168, 221, 254, 269,
        304, 339, 357, 450, 481.
Whitman, Elnathan, 451.
    Samuel, 31, 220, 437, 459, 467, 538.
Whitmore, see Wetmore, Whetmore.
Whitmore, Francis, 77, 136, 159, 160, 471.
    Hannah, 397.
    Joseph, 446, 486, 582, 616.
    William, 136, 427, 468, 486, 491, 592.

Whittlesey, Eliphalet, 328.
 Jabez, 323, 328, 349, 370, 475, 476, 501.
Wiard, see Wyard, Wyott.
Wiard, Thomas, 576.
Wiat, see Wyatt, Wyott.
Wiat, John, 130.
 Mr., 130.
Wiatt, Mr., 130.
Wickham, Thomas, 23, 24, 40, 54, 261, 325,
  361, 403.
 William, 89, 225, 372, 377, 508, 519.
Wilcock, Anne, 616.
 Elisha, 615.
 Francis, 451, 615.
 Hannah, 616.
 Israel, 615, 616.
 John, 615, 616.
 Jonathan, 616.
 Martha, 616.
 Samuel, 244, 451, 615.
 Thomas, 615, 616.
Wilcocks, Daniel, 614, 615.
 Elizabeth, 614.
 Ephraim, 613.
 Hannah, 614.
 Jane, 613.
 Janna, 613, 615.
 John, 613, 614, 615, 616.
 Jonathan, 616.
 Josiah, 614, 615.
 Mary, 613.
 Rachel, 614, 615.
 Samuel, 614, 615.
 Sarah, 615.
 Silence, 615.
 Thankfull, 613.
 Thomas, 615, 616, 617.
Wilcockson, Mr., 36.
 Samuel, 271, 276.
Wilcox, Anna, 616.
 Daniel, 614.
 Ephraim, 613.
 Esther, 615.
 Hannah, 616.
 Israel, 616.
 Janna, 613.
 Jeremiah, 615.
 John, 613, 614, 615, 616.
 Jonathan, 616.
 Josiah, 615.
 Mr., 277.
 Samuel, 91, 451, 615.
 Sarah, 615.
 Thanks, 146.
 Thomas, 616.
 William, 146.
Wilcoxson, Azariah, 430.

Wilcoxson, Margaret, 331.
 Samuel, 90, 331.
Wilkins, Richard, 93.
Willard, see Williard.
Willard, Daniel, 617.
 Elizabeth, 510, 511.
 Hannah, 617.
 John, 617.
 Josiah, 63, 510, 617.
 Mary, 63.
 Mr., 63, 476.
 Samuel, 582.
 Sarah, 582.
 Symon, 63, 617.
Willcock, Francis, 290.
 John, 216, 356.
 Samuel, 287.
Willcocks, Ephraim, 330.
 Samuel, 330.
 Silence, 331.
Willcockson, Mr., 145.
Willcox, Ebenezer, 551.
Willcoxson, Ephraim, 332.
 John, 332.
 Joseph, 331, 332, 451, 452.
 Margaret, 331, 451.
 Mindwell, 331, 332.
 Samuel, 331, 332.
 William, 331.
Willee, see Willey, Wylley, Willy.
Willee, Abell, 238.
 John, 238, 244.
Willes, Abigail, 452.
 Hannah, 452.
 Henry, 452.
 Jacob, 452.
 Joshua, 281, 322, 358, 452.
 Susannah, 452.
Willey, see Willee, Wylley, Willy.
Willey, Abel, 572.
 Abram, 571.
 John, 354.
William III., King, 138.
William, John, 618.
Williams, Abiah, 332.
 Abigail, 40, 332, 479.
 Abraham, 139, 332, 335, 618.
 Abram, 618.
 Amos, 80.
 Anne, 333, 336.
 Charles, 565.
 Daniel, 333.
 David, 333, 468.
 Deborah, 452.
 Ebenezer, 101.
 Eleazer, 439.

Williams, Elias, 452.
  Elisha, 177, 231.
  Elizabeth, 237, 335, 487, 617, 618.
  Ephraim, 501.
  Esther, 333, 334, 452, 453.
  Eunice, 177, 332, 336, 360.
  Francis, 138, 139.
  Gabriel, 415, 416, 478, 618.
  Hannah, 139.
  Henry, 300, 301, 617.
  Isaac, 452, 453, 618.
  Jacob, 53, 139, 332, 333, 335, 344, 574, 600, 618, 619.
  Jane, 335.
  John, 40, 80, 98, 139, 299, 333, 334, 335, 336, 389, 452, 453, 564, 617, 618.
  Jonah, 336, 478, 479.
  Jonas, 147, 335, 336.
  Joseph, 335, 618.
  Lydia, 336.
  Mary, 139, 333, 336, 355, 439, 565, 617, 618.
  Mehetabell, 488.
  Nathaniel, 333, 334, 336.
  Rebeckah, 139, 332.
  Richard, 139.
  Samuel, 170, 187, 206, 230, 237, 333, 381, 530, 618.
  Sarah, 80, 98, 99, 280, 333, 617, 618.
  Silence, 332.
  Stephen, 286, 333.
  Thomas, 139.
  Timothy, 336, 526.
  William, 147, 335, 415, 416.
Williamson, Alexander, 453.
  Caleb, 454.
  Ebenezer, 250, 510.
Williard, see Willard.
Williard, Ephraim, 617.
Willis, see Wyllys.
Willis, Henry, 139.
  Hezekiah, 43, 44, 75, 108, 127, 129.
  Jacob, 140.
  John, 139.
  Joshua, 139, 140.
  Mr., 55.
  Samuel, 75, 108.
Wills, see Welles, Wells, Willes.
Wills, Henry, 452.
  Joshua, 322.
  Lampson, 452.
  Samuel, 452.
Willy, see Willee, Willey, Wylley.
Willy, John, 69.
Wilson, Elizabeth, 141, 405, 619, 620, 621, 622.
  John, 127, 143, 336.
  Mr., 392.
  Mrs., 75, 82, 217.

Wilson, Nathaniel, 140, 141, 142, 620, 621, 623.
  Noah, 511.
  Phineas, 142, 619, 620, 621, 623.
  Samuel, 391, 552.
  Stebbin, 142, 143, 624.
  Susannah, 140.
Wilton, see Welton.
Wilton, George, 422.
Winchell, Abigail, 421, 624.
  Caleb, 624.
  Dorothy, 624.
  Hannah, 624.
  Hezekiah, 523.
  John, 624.
  Martin, 624, 625.
  Nathaniel, 282, 376, 422.
  Robert, 624.
  Sarah, 413, 624.
  Stephen, 624, 625.
  Thomas, 624, 625.
Witchfield, John, 82.
Wolcott, Abiah, 265, 337, 338, 453, 626.
  Abigail, 336, 337.
  Anna, 628.
  Benjamin, 338, 626.
  Charles, 338, 339, 626.
  Christopher, 626.
  Daniel, 627.
  Deborah, 627.
  Elizabeth, 192, 336, 337, 627, 628.
  Eunice, 628.
  George, 54, 183, 324, 627, 628.
  Hannah, 265, 338, 339, 626.
  Henry, 8, 10, 82, 90, 143, 149, 177, 253, 337, 338, 373, 416, 440, 453, 502, 594, 626.
  Ichabod, 626.
  James, 627.
  John, 123, 338, 339, 626.
  Joshua, 627, 628.
  Josiah, 213, 321, 339, 627.
  Judith, 336, 337, 339.
  Lucy, 339.
  Mary, 337.
  Mr., 7, 192, 453.
  Rachel, 165.
  Roger, 8, 9, 125, 158, 178, 191, 192, 253, 261, 262, 264, 311, 340, 383, 452, 502, 622.
  Samuel, 35, 53, 82, 174, 175, 192, 229, 247, 336, 337, 339, 340, 465, 600.
  Sarah, 191, 192, 340, 628.
  Simon, 175, 177, 440.
  Thomas, 10.
  William, 125, 253, 265, 340, 377, 378, 421, 436, 626.
Wollis, see Wallace.
Wollis, Elizabeth, 549.

Wood, Abigail, 340.
 John, 262, 340, 478.
 Margaret, 340.
 Martha, 340, 341.
 Mary, 340.
 Obadiah, 340, 341, 477.
 Samuel, 340.
Woodbridge, Abigail, 255, 342, 454, 541, 622.
 Benjamin, 454.
 Dorothy, 341.
 Dudley, 135, 271, 341, 342.
 Ephraim, 342.
 Jemima, 454, 455.
 John, 341, 342, 454, 455.
 Joseph, 454, 455.
 Mercy, 342.
 Mr., 145.
 Samuel, 103, 165, 355, 477, 556.
 T., 87, 596.
 Theodore, 540, 621, 622.
 Timothy, 99, 108, 145, 169, 194, 208, 255,
  271, 296, 341, 431, 454, 458, 464, 472,
  541, 596, 621, 622.
Woodford, Abigail, 342.
 Elizabeth, 342.
 Joseph, 342.
 Lydia, 434.
 Susannah, 342.
Woodhouse, Dorothy, 164.
 Joseph, 573, 628.
Woodruff, Abigail, 625.
 Ann, 625.
 Daniel, 86, 422.
 Elijah, 625.
 Elizabeth, 126, 143, 375, 625.
 Hannah, 178, 343.
 John, 119, 143, 282, 625.
 Jonathan, 343.
 Joseph, 34, 178, 282, 343, 529, 578, 625.
 Josiah, 343.
 Margaret, 625.
 Mary, 126, 143, 625.
 Matthew, 554.
 Nathaniel, 554.
 Rebecca, 178, 179.
 Samuel, 126, 178, 278, 282, 343, 349,
  535, 577.
 Sarah, 343, 625.
 Simmons, 625.
 Susannah, 625.
Worthington, William, 440, 450.
 Williams, 334.

Yale, Thomas, 175.
Yeomans, Ebenezer, 629.
 Eleazer, 629.
 Elijah, 628, 629.
 Elisha, 628, 629.
 Elizabeth, 335, 629.
 John, 534, 628, 629.

Wright, Benjamin, 332, 343, 344, 574.
 Daniel, 143, 575.
 David, 155, 314, 469.
 Elizabeth, 584.
 Esther, 374.
 Eunice, 143.
 James, 143.
 John, 51, 158, 184, 333, 343, 344.
 Jonas, 143.
 Jonathan, 344.
 Joseph, 87, 88, 197, 344, 345, 562, 581,
  590.
 Marcy, 343.
 Mary, 158, 217, 584.
 Mercy, 159, 343, 344.
 Mrs., 55.
 Nathaniel, 344.
 Olive, 143.
 Prudence, 188.
 Samuel, 28, 80, 197, 251, 252, 306, 344.
 Thomas, 51, 143, 159, 186, 187, 188, 201,
  239, 303, 324, 343, 344, 345, 346, 405,
  438, 627.
 Timothy, 231.
Wrisly, see Risley.
Wrisly, Nathaniel, 527.
Wroe, see Rew, Rue.
Wroe, Joshua, 395.
Wyard, see Wiard, Wiat, Wiatt, Wyott.
Wyard, John, 628.
 Martha, 576.
 Phebe, 628.
 Thomas, 239.
Wyatt, see Wiat, Wiatt, Wyott.
Wyatt, Israel, 87, 88, 233.
 John, 323.
Wyer, Abigail, 455.
 John, 55.
 Sarah, 55.
Wylley, see Willee, Willey, Willy.
Wylley, Abell, 571.
 Isaac, 547.
Wyllys, see Willis.
Wyllys, Edward, 623.
 Elizabeth, 312, 472.
 Hezekiah, 21, 38, 87, 151, 167, 168, 169,
  181, 221, 234, 242, 259, 267, 268, 291,
  295, 296, 305, 307, 312, 363, 372, 405,
  435, 524, 544, 585, 621.
 Mr., 210, 269, 432, 460.
Wyott, see Wiat, Wiatt, Wiard, Wyard,
  Wyatt, Wyer.
Wyott, John, 25.

Y

Yeomans, Jonathan, 512.
 Mabel, 629.
 Mary, 629.
 Millicent, 628, 629.
 Thomas, 629.
Youngs, Joseph, 574.

ERRATA.

VOLUME I.

Page 33—Sixteenth line from foot of page—For Elizabeth *Standly,* read Elizabeth *Loomis.*

Page 97—Eighth line—For *Commisin,* read *Tommisin* (Thomasine).

Page 125—Sixteenth line—For *Cophall* in England, read *Coxhall.*

Page 149—Estate of Thomas Selden—Third line—For 1665, read 1655, twice.

Page 210—First line—For John *Howkins,* read John *Judd;* and insert *Judd* after name *Mary.*

Page 244—Estate of John Tinker—Fourth line—For 1665, read 1655.

Page 246—Estate of William Wadsworth—Sixteenth line—For *Ferris* read *Terry.*

Page 253—Seventh line from bottom—After Thomas Hosmer, omit the word *and.*

Page 386—Dist. File, 1701—For William *Boardman,* read William *Burnham.*

Page 393—Children of Nicholas Ackley—For Mary X *Beppin,* read *Crippin.*

Page 447—Estate of Samuel Gaylord—Fourth line—For Samuel *Griswold,* read Samuel *Gaylord.*

Page 475—Seventeenth line—"Page 67—5 April, 1703-4"—This Court Record belongs under Estate of Benjamin Judd on opposite page (474).

Page 489—Witness to will of Mary Moses—For *George* Drake, Jr., read *Job* Drake, Jr.

Page 490—Twelfth line—For *Henry* Wolcott, read *John* Wolcott.

Page 491—Estate of Thomas Newell—In signatures to "Agreement," omit *Richard Newell.* In "Account" following, for Hannah *Smith,* read Hannah *North.*

Page 515—Estate of Ensign William Ward, Sen., Middletown—Fourth line—After Thomas Ward, insert William Ward, John Ward, Phebe Hall, Sarah Hand.

Page 533—Children of Samuel Abby—*Eleazer* as recorded in Vol. VI with the inventory, but *Elizabeth* in the distributors' report. The name is not written out in full upon the original inventory, but reads *Elez.*

Page 537—Children of Richard Beckley—For Thomas *Hoskins,* read
  Hopkins.
Page 543—Twenty-ninth line—For 4 May, 1707, read 7 July, 1707.
Page 564—Estate of Rev. Samuel Hooker, Sen., Farmington—Fourth
  line—For 1695, read 1698.
Page 606—(Index to Estates)—For Beckley, *Samuel,* read *Nathaniel.*
  (See page 536.)

VOLUME II.

Page 172—Sixth line—For *Lydia,* read *Mary.*
Page 192—Tenth line—For *Samuel* Wolcott, read *Sarah* Wolcott.
Page 450—Seventh line—For *Mary* White, read *Sarah* White.